Oxford Paperback French Dictionary

Third Edition

FRENCH–ENGLISH
ENGLISH–FRENCH

OXFORD
UNIVERSITY PRESS

OXFORD

UNIVERSITY PRESS

Great Clarendon Street, Oxford OX2 6DP

Oxford University Press is a department of the University of Oxford.
It furthers the University's objective of excellence in research, scholarship,
and education by publishing worldwide in

Oxford New York

Auckland Bangkok Buenos Aires Cape Town Chennai
Dar es Salaam Delhi Hong Kong Istanbul Karachi Kolkata
Kuala Lumpur Madrid Melbourne Mexico City Mumbai Nairobi
São Paulo Shanghai Taipei Tokyo Toronto

Oxford is a registered trade mark of Oxford University Press
in the UK and in certain other countries

Published in the United States
by Oxford University Press Inc., New York

© Oxford University Press 1986, 1993, 2002

First published 1986
Second edition published 1993
Third edition published 2002

British Library Cataloguing in Publication Data

Data available

Library of Congress Cataloging in Publication Data

Data available

ISBN 0–19–860516–1

10 9 8 7 6 5 4 3

Typeset by Tradespools
Printed in Great Britain by
Clays Ltd, Bungay, Suffolk

Contents

Introduction   iv

The pronunciation of French   v

Abbreviations   vi

French-English   **1–249**

English-French   **251–464**

French verb tables   465–73

List of contributors

First Edition

Editor:

Michael Janes

Second Edition

Editors:

Michael Janes
Dora Latiri-Carpenter
Edwin Carpenter

Third Edition

Editors:

Marianne Chalmers
Rosalind Combley
Catherine Roux
Laura Wedgeworth

Proprietary terms

Introduction

Enhanced coverage

The wordlist has been comprehensively revised to reflect recent additions to both languages and to cover such topics as **computing** and the **Internet**.

A further new feature of the dictionary is the special status given to more complex grammatical words which provide the basic structure of both languages. These *function words* are given a special layout to make them instantly accessible and offer clearly presented translation options and examples, with **short usage notes** to warn of possible pitfalls.

Coverage of verbs has been significantly extended so that all **French verbs** in the text are cross-referenced to the appropriate section of the expanded verb tables. Examples of the three main French verb groups, as well as *avoir* and *être*, are conjugated in the most commonly used tenses.

Easy reference

The dictionary layout has been designed to be **clear**, streamlined, and easy to consult. The wordlist has been fully **alphabetized**, with all English compounds and French hyphenated compounds in their correct alphabetical positions. **Bullet points** separate each new part of speech within an entry, making it easy to scan. Nuances of sense or usage are pinpointed by semantic indicators (in condensed type in round brackets) or by typical collocates (*in italics in round brackets*) with which the word frequently occurs, quickly guiding the user to the appropriate translation. Extra help is given in the form of **symbols** to mark the register of language unambiguously. An exclamation mark ⟦!⟧ indicates colloquial language and a cross ⟦✖⟧ indicates slang.

The pronunciation of French

Vowels

a	*as in*	patte	/pat/	ɑ	*as in*	pâte	/pɑt/
ɑ̃		clan	/klɑ̃/	e		dé	/de/
ɛ		belle	/bɛl/	ɛ̃		lin	/lɛ̃/
ə		demain	/dəmɛ̃/	i		gris	/gʀi/
o		gros	/gʀo/	ɔ		corps	/kɔʀ/
ɔ̃		long	/lɔ̃/	œ		leur	/lœʀ/
œ̃		brun	/bʀœ̃/	ø		deux	/dø/
u		fou	/fu/	y		pur	/pyʀ/

Semi-Vowels

j	*as in*	fille	/fij/
ɥ		huit	/ɥit/
w		oui	/wi/

Consonants

Aspiration of 'h'
Where it is impossible to make a liaison this is indicated by /'/ immediately after the slash e.g. *haine* /'ɛn/.

b	*as in*	bal	/bal/	ŋ	*as in*	camping	/kɑ̃piŋ/
d		dent	/dɑ̃/	p		porte	/pɔʀt/
f		foire	/fwaʀ/	ʀ		rire	/ʀiʀ/
g		gomme	/gɔm/	s		sang	/sɑ̃/
k		clé	/kle/	ʃ		chien	/ʃjɛ̃/
l		lien	/ljɛ̃/	t		train	/tʀɛ̃/
m		mer	/mɛʀ/	v		voile	/vwal/
n		nage	/naʒ/	z		zèbre	/zɛbʀ/
ɲ		gnon	/ɲɔ̃/	ʒ		jeune	/ʒœn/

Abbreviations

adjective	*adj*	adjectif
abbreviation	*abbr, abrév*	abréviation
adverb	*adv*	adverbe
anatomy	*Anat*	anatomie
archeology	*Archeol, Archéol*	archéologie
architecture	*Archit*	architecture
motoring	*Auto*	automobile
auxiliary	*aux*	auxiliaire
aviation	*Aviat*	aviation
botany	*Bot*	botanique
commerce	*Comm*	commerce
computing	*Comput*	informatique
conjunction	*conj*	conjonction
cookery	*Culin*	culinaire
determiner	*det, dét*	déterminant
electricity	*Electr, Électr*	électricité
figurative	*fig*	sens figuré
geography	*Geog, Géog*	géographie
geology	*Geol, Géol*	géologie
grammar	*Gram*	grammaire
humorous	*hum*	humoristique
interjection	*interj*	interjection
invariable	*inv*	invariable
law	*Jur*	droit
linguistics	*Ling*	linguistique
literal	*lit*	littéral
phrase	*loc*	locution
medicine	*Med, Méd*	médecine
military	*Mil*	armée
music	*Mus*	musique
noun	*n*	nom
nautical	*Naut*	nautisme
feminine noun	*nf*	nom féminin
masculine noun	*nm*	nom masculin
masculine and feminine noun	*nm,f* or *nmf* or *nm/f*	nom masculin et féminin
computing	*Ordinat*	informatique

pejorative	*pej, péj*	péjoratif
philosophy	*Phil*	philosophie
photography	*Photo*	photographie
plural	*pl*	pluriel
politics	*Pol*	politique
possessive	*poss*	possessif
past participle	*pp*	participe passé
prefix	*pref, préf*	préfixe
preposition	*prep, prép*	préposition
present participle	*pres p*	participe présent
pronoun	*pron*	pronom
psychology	*Psych*	psychologie
past	*pt*	prétérit
something	*qch*	quelque chose
somebody	*qn*	quelqu'un
railway	*Rail*	chemin de fer
relative pronoun	*rel pron, pron rel*	pronom relatif
religion	*Relig*	religion
somebody	*sb*	quelqu'un
school	*School, Scol*	scolaire
sport	*Sport*	sport
something	*sth*	quelque chose
technology	*Tech*	technologie
theatre	*Theat, Théât*	théâtre
television	*TV*	télévision
university	*Univ*	université
American English	*US*	anglais américain
auxiliary verb	*v aux*	verbe auxiliaire
intransitive verb	*vi*	verbe intransitif
reflexive verb	*vpr*	verbe pronominal
transitive verb	*vt*	verbe transitif
transitive and intransitive verb	*vt/i*	verbe transitif et intransitif
translation equivalent	≈	équivalent approximatif
trademark	®	marque déposée
colloquial	🛈	familier
slang	✖	argot

a /a/ ⇒AVOIR [5].

à /a/ *préposition*

à+le = au
à+les = aux

····➤ (avec verbe de mouvement) to.

····➤ (pour indiquer où l'on se trouve) ~ **la maison** at home; ~ **Nice** in Nice.

····➤ (âge, date, heure) ~ **l'âge de…** at the age of…; **au XIXe siècle** in the 19th century; ~ **deux heures** at two o'clock.

····➤ (description) with; **aux yeux verts** with green eyes.

····➤ (appartenance) ~ **qui est ce stylo?** whose pen is this?; **c'est** ~ **vous?** is this yours?

····➤ (avec nombre) ~ **90 km/h** at 90 km per hour; ~ **10 minutes d'ici** 10 minutes from here; **des tomates** ~ **3 francs le kilo** tomatoes at 3 francs a kilo; **un timbre** ~ **3 francs** a 3-franc stamp; **nous avons fait le travail** ~ **deux** two of us did the work; **mener 5** ~ **4** to lead 5 (to) 4.

····➤ (avec être) **c'est** ~ **moi** it's my turn; **je suis** ~ **vous tout de suite** I'll be with you in a minute; **c'est** ~ **toi de décider** it's up to you to decide.

····➤ (hypothèse) ~ **ce qu'il paraît** apparently; ~ **t'entendre** to hear you talk.

····➤ (exclamatif) ~ **ta santé!** cheers!; ~ **demain/bientôt!** see you tomorrow/soon!

····➤ (moyen) ~ **la main** by hand; ~ **vélo** by bike; ~ **pied** on foot; **chauffage au gaz** gas heating.

abaissement /abɛsmã/ *nm* (de taux, de prix) cut; (de seuil) lowering.

abaisser /abese/ [1] *vt* lower; (*levier*) pull *ou* push down; (fig) humiliate. □ **s'**~ *vpr* go down, drop; (fig) demean oneself; **s'**~ **à** to stoop to.

abandon /abãdɔ̃/ *nm* abandonment; (de personne) desertion; (de course) withdrawal; (naturel) abandon; **à l'**~ in a state of neglect.

abandonner /abãdɔne/ [1] *vt* abandon; (*épouse, cause*) desert; (renoncer à) give up, abandon; (céder) give (à to); (*course*) withdraw from; (Ordinat) abort. □ **s'**~ **à** *vpr* give oneself up to.

abasourdir /abazurdir/ [2] *vt* stun.

abat-jour /abaʒur/ *nm inv* lampshade.

abats /aba/ *nmpl* offal.

abattement /abatmã/ *nm* dejection; (faiblesse) exhaustion; (Comm) reduction; ~ **fiscal** tax allowance.

abattre /abatr/ [11] *vt* knock down; (*arbre*) cut down; (*animal*) slaughter; (*avion*) shoot down; (affaiblir) weaken; (démoraliser) demoralize; **ne pas se laisser** ~ not let things get one down. □ **s'**~ *vpr* come down, fall (down).

abbaye /abei/ *nf* abbey.

abbé /abe/ *nm* priest; (supérieur d'une abbaye) abbot.

abcès /apsɛ/ *nm* abscess.

abdiquer /abdike/ [1] *vt/i* abdicate.

abdomen /abdɔmɛn/ *nm* abdomen.

abdominal (*pl* **-aux**) /abdɔminal/ *adj* abdominal. **abdominaux** *nmpl* (Sport) stomach exercises.

abeille /abɛj/ *nf* bee.

aberrant, ~**e** /abɛrã, -t/ *adj* absurd.

abêtir /abetir/ [2] *vt* turn into a moron.

abîme /abim/ *nm* abyss.

abîmer /abime/ [1] *vt* damage, spoil. □ **s'**~ *vpr* get damaged *ou* spoilt.

ablation /ablasjɔ̃/ *nf* removal.

aboiement /abwamã/ *nm* bark, barking; ~**s** barking.

abolir /abɔlir/ [2] *vt* abolish.

abondance /abɔ̃dãs/ *nf* abundance; (prospérité) affluence. **abondant**, ~**e** *adj* abundant, plentiful.

a

abonder /abɔ̃de/ [1] *vi* abound (**en** in); ~ **dans le sens de qn** agree wholeheartedly with sb.

abonné, ~**e** /abɔne/ *nm,f* (lecteur) subscriber; (voyageur, spectateur) season-ticket holder.

abonnement /abɔnmɑ̃/ *nm* (à un journal) subscription; (de bus, Théât) season-ticket; (au gaz) standing charge.

abonner (**s'**) /(s)abɔne/ [1] *vpr* subscribe (**à** to).

abord /abɔR/ *nm* access; ~**s** surroundings; **d'**~ first.

abordable /abɔRdabl/ *adj* (*prix*) affordable; (*personne*) approachable; (*texte*) accessible.

aborder /abɔRde/ [1] *vt* approach; (*lieu*) reach; (*problème*) tackle. ● *vi* reach land.

aborigène /abɔRiʒɛn/ *nm* aborigine.

aboutir /abutiR/ [2] *vi* succeed, achieve a result; ~ **à** end (up) in, lead to; **n'**~ **à rien** come to nothing.

aboutissement /abutismɑ̃/ *nm* outcome; (de carrière, d'évolution) culmination.

aboyer /abwaje/ [31] *vi* bark.

abrégé /abReʒe/ *nm* summary.

abréger /abReʒe/ [14] [40] *vt* (*texte*) shorten, abridge; (*mot*) abbreviate, shorten; (*visite*) cut short.

abreuver /abRœve/ [1] *vt* water; (fig) overwhelm (**de** with). □ **s'**~ *vpr* drink.

abréviation /abRevjasjɔ̃/ *nf* abbreviation.

abri /abRi/ *nm* shelter; **à l'**~ under cover; (en lieu sûr) safe; **à l'**~ **de** sheltered from; **se mettre à l'**~ take shelter.

abricot /abRiko/ *nm* apricot.

abriter /abRite/ [1] *vt* shelter; (recevoir) house. □ **s'**~ *vpr* (take) shelter.

abrupt, ~**e** /abRypt/ *adj* steep, sheer; (fig) abrupt.

abruti, ~**e** /abRyti/ *nm,f* 🔲 idiot.

absence /apsɑ̃s/ *nf* absence; **il a des** ~**s** sometimes his mind goes blank.

absent, ~**e** /apsɑ̃, -t/ *adj* (*personne*) absent, away; (*chose*) missing; **il est**

toujours ~ he's still away; **d'un air** ~ absently. ● *nm,f* absentee.

absenter (**s'**) /(s)apsɑ̃te/ [1] *vpr* go ou be away; (sortir) go out, leave.

absolu, ~**e** /apsɔly/ *adj* absolute.

absorbant, ~**e** /apsɔRbɑ̃, -t/ *adj* (*travail*) absorbing; (*matière*) absorbent.

absorber /apsɔRbe/ [1] *vt* absorb; **être absorbé par qch** be engrossed in sth.

abstenir (**s'**) /(s)apstəniR/ [58] *vpr* abstain; **s'**~ **de** refrain from.

abstrait, ~**e** /apstRɛ, -t/ *a & nm* abstract.

absurde /apsyRd/ *adj* absurd.

abus /aby/ *nm* abuse, misuse; (injustice) abuse; ~ **de confiance** breach of trust.

abuser /abyze/ [1] *vt* deceive. ● *vi* go too far; ~ **de** abuse, misuse; (profiter de) take advantage of; (*alcool*) overindulge in. □ **s'**~ *vpr* be mistaken.

abusif, **-ive** /abyzif, -v/ *adj* excessive; (impropre) wrong; (injuste) unfair.

académie /akademi/ *nf* academy; (circonscription) local education authority.

acajou /akaʒu/ *nm* mahogany.

accablant, ~**e** /akablɑ̃, -t/ *adj* (*chaleur*) oppressive; (*fait, témoignage*) damning.

accabler /akable/ [1] *vt* overwhelm; ~ **d'impôts** burden with taxes; ~ **d'injures** heap insults upon.

accéder /aksede/ [14] *vi* ~ **à** (*lieu*) reach; (*pouvoir, trône*) accede to; (*requête*) grant; (Ordinat) access; ~ **à la propriété** become a homeowner.

accélérateur /akseleRatœR/ *nm* accelerator.

accélérer /akseleRe/ [14] *vt/i* accelerate. □ **s'**~ *vpr* speed up.

accent /aksɑ̃/ *nm* accent; (sur une syllabe) stress, accent; **mettre l'**~ **sur** stress; ~ **aigu/grave/circonflexe** acute/grave/circumflex accent.

accentuer /aksɑ̃tɥe/ [1] *vt* (*lettre, syllabe*) accent; (fig) emphasize, accentuate. □ **s'**~ *vpr* become more pronounced, increase.

accepter /aksɛpte/ [1] vt accept; ~ de faire agree to do.

accès /aksɛ/ nm access; (porte) entrance; (de fièvre) bout; (de colère) fit; (d'enthousiasme) burst; (Ordinat) access; **les ~ de** (voies) the approaches to; **facile d'~** easy to get to.

accessoire /akseswaʀ/ adj secondary, incidental. ● nm accessory; (Théât) prop.

accident /aksidã/ nm accident; ~ de train/d'avion train/plane crash; par ~ by accident. **accidenté**, ~e adj (personne) injured (in an accident); (voiture) damaged; (terrain) uneven, hilly. **accidentel**, ~le adj accidental.

acclamer /aklame/ [1] vt cheer, acclaim.

accommoder /akɔmɔde/ [1] vt adapt (à to); (cuisiner) prepare; (assaisonner) flavour. □ s'~ de vpr make the best of.

accompagnateur, -trice /akɔ̃paɲatœʀ, -tʀis/ nm, f (Mus) accompanist; (guide) guide; ~ d'enfants accompanying adult.

accompagner /akɔ̃paɲe/ [1] vt accompany. □ s'~ de vpr be accompanied by.

accomplir /akɔ̃pliʀ/ [2] vt carry out, fulfil. □ s'~ vpr take place, happen; (vœu) be fulfilled.

accord /akɔʀ/ nm agreement; (harmonie) harmony; (Mus) chord; être d'~ agree (pour to); se mettre d'~ come to an agreement, agree; d'~! all right!, OK!

accorder /akɔʀde/ [1] vt grant; (couleurs) match; (Mus) tune; (attribuer) (valeur, importance) assign. □ s'~ vpr (se mettre d'accord) agree; (s'octroyer) allow oneself; s'~ avec (s'entendre avec) get on with.

accotement /akɔtmã/ nm verge; ~ non stabilisé soft verge.

accouchement /akuʃmã/ nm childbirth; (travail) labour.

accoucher /akuʃe/ [1] vi give birth (de to); (être en travail) be in labour. ● vt deliver. **accoucheur** nm médecin ~ obstetrician.

accoudoir /akudwaʀ/ nm arm-rest.

accoupler /akuple/ [1] vt (Tech) couple. □ s'~ vpr mate.

accourir /akuʀiʀ/ [20] vi run up.

accoutumance /akutymãs/ nf familiarization; (Méd) addiction.

accoutumer /akutyme/ [1] vt accustom. □ s'~ vpr get accustomed.

accro /akʀo/ nmf Ⓘ (drogué) addict; (amateur) fan.

accroc /akʀo/ nm tear, rip; (fig) hitch.

accrochage /akʀɔʃaʒ/ nm hanging; hooking; (Auto) collision; (dispute) clash; (Mil) encounter.

accrocher /akʀɔʃe/ [1] vt (suspendre) hang up; (attacher) hook, hitch; (déchirer) catch; (heurter) hit; (attirer) attract. □ s'~ vpr cling, hang on (à to); (se disputer) clash.

accroissement /akʀwasmã/ nm increase (de in).

accroître /akʀwatʀ/ [24] vt increase. □ s'~ vpr increase.

accroupir (s') /(s)akʀupiʀ/ [2] vpr squat.

accru, ~e /akʀy/ adj increased, greater.

accueil /akœj/ nm reception, welcome.

accueillant, ~e /akœjã, -t/ adj friendly, welcoming.

accueillir /akœjiʀ/ [25] vt receive, welcome; (film, livre) receive; (prendre en charge) (réfugiés, patients) take care of, cater for.

accumuler /akymyle/ [1] vt (énergie) store up; (capital) accumulate. □ s'~ vpr (neige, ordures) pile up; (dettes) accrue.

accusation /akyzasjɔ̃/ nf accusation; (Jur) charge; l'~ (magistrat) the prosecution.

accusé, ~e /akyze/ adj marked. ● nm, f defendant, accused.

accuser /akyze/ [1] vt accuse (de of); (blâmer) blame (de for); (Jur) charge (de with); (fig) emphasize; ~ réception de acknowledge receipt of.

acharné, ~e /aʃaʀne/ adj relentless, ferocious. **acharnement** nm (énergie) furious energy; (ténacité) determination.

acharner (s') /(s)aʃaʀne/ [1] vpr persevere; s'~ sur set upon;

a

(poursuivre) hound; **s'~ à faire** (s'évertuer) try desperately; (s'obstiner) keep on doing.

achat /aʃa/ *nm* purchase; ~s shopping; **faire l'~ de** buy; **faire des** ~s do some shopping.

acheminer /aʃ(ə)mine/ [1] *vt* dispatch, convey; (*courrier*) handle. □ **s'~ vers** *vpr* head for.

acheter /aʃ(ə)te/ [6] *vt* buy; ~ **qch à qn** (pour lui) buy sth for sb; (chez lui) buy sth from sb. **acheteur, -euse** *nm,f* buyer; (client de magasin) shopper.

achèvement /aʃɛvmɑ̃/ *nm* completion.

achever /aʃ(ə)ve/ [6] *vt* finish (off). □ **s'~** *vpr* end.

acide /asid/ *adj* acid, sharp. ● *nm* acid.

acier /asje/ *nm* steel.

acné /akne/ *nf* acne.

acompte /akɔ̃t/ *nm* deposit, part-payment.

à-côté (*pl* ~s) /akote/ *nm* side issue; ~s (argent) extras.

acoustique /akustik/ *nf* acoustics (+ *sg*). ● *adj* acoustic.

acquéreur /akerœr/ *nm* purchaser, buyer.

acquérir /akerir/ [7] *vt* acquire, gain; (*biens*) purchase, acquire.

acquis, ~e /aki, -z/ *adj* acquired; (*fait*) established; **tenir qch pour ~** take sth for granted. ● *nm* experience. **acquisition** *nf* acquisition; purchase.

acquitter /akite/ [1] *vt* acquit; (*dette*) settle. □ **s'~ de** *vpr* (*promesse*) fulfil; (*devoir*) discharge.

âcre /akr/ *adj* acrid.

acrobatie /akrɔbasi/ *nf* acrobatics (+ *pl*); ~ **aérienne** aerobatics (+ *pl*).

acte /akt/ *nm* act, action, deed; (Théât) act; (Jur) deed; ~ **de naissance/mariage** birth/marriage certificate; ~s (compte rendu) proceedings; **prendre ~ de** note.

acteur /aktœr/ *nm* actor.

actif, -ive /aktif, -v/ *adj* active; (*population*) working. ● *nm* (Comm) assets; **avoir à son ~** have to one's credit *ou* name.

action /aksjɔ̃/ *nf* action; (Comm) share; (Jur) action; (effet) effect; (initiative) initiative. **actionnaire** *nmf* shareholder.

activer /aktive/ [1] *vt* speed up; (*feu*) boost. □ **s'~** *vpr* hurry up; (s'affairer) be very busy.

activité /aktivite/ *nf* activity; **en ~** (*volcan*) active; (*fonctionnaire*) working; (*usine*) in operation.

actrice /aktris/ *nf* actress.

actualité /aktɥalite/ *nf* topicality; **l'~** current affairs; **les ~s** news; **d'~** topical.

actuel, ~le /aktɥɛl/ *adj* current, present; (d'actualité) topical. **actuellement** *adv* currently, at the present time.

acupuncture /akypɔ̃ktyr/ *nf* acupuncture.

adaptateur /adaptatœr/ *nm* (Électr) adapter.

adapter /adapte/ [1] *vt* adapt; (fixer) fit. □ **s'~** *vpr* adapt (oneself); (Tech) fit.

additif /aditif/ *nm* (note) rider; (substance) additive.

addition /adisjɔ̃/ *nf* addition; (au café) bill; (US) check. **additionner** [1] *vt* add; (totaliser) add (up).

adepte /adɛpt/ *nmf* follower; (d'activité) enthusiast.

adéquat, ~e /adekwa, -t/ *adj* suitable; (suffisant) adequate.

adhérent, ~e /aderɑ̃, -t/ *nm,f* member.

adhérer /adere/ [14] *vi* adhere, stick (à to); ~ **à** (*club*) be a member of; (s'inscrire à) join.

adhésif, -ive /adezif, -v/ *adj* adhesive; **ruban ~** sticky tape.

adhésion /adezjɔ̃/ *nf* membership; (soutien) support.

adieu (*pl* ~**x**) /adjø/ *interj* & *nm* goodbye, farewell.

adjectif /adʒɛktif/ *nm* adjective.

adjoint, ~e /adʒwɛ̃, -t/ *nm,f* assistant; ~ **au maire** deputy mayor. ● *adj* assistant.

adjuger /adʒyʒe/ [40] *vt* award; (aux enchères) auction. □ **s'~** *vpr* take (for oneself).

admettre /admɛtʀ/ [42] *vt* let in, admit; (tolérer) allow; (reconnaître) admit, acknowledge; (*candidat*) pass.

administrateur, -trice /administratœʀ, -tʀis/ *nm, f* administrator, director; (Jur) trustee; ~ **de site Internet** Webmaster.

administratif, -ive /administratif, -v/ *adj* administrative; (*document*) official. **administration** *nf* administration; (gestion) management; **l'A~** Civil Service.

administrer /administʀe/ [1] *vt* run, manage; (*justice, biens, antidote*) administer.

admirateur, -trice /admiʀatœʀ, -tʀis/ *nm, f* admirer.

admiration /admiʀasjɔ̃/ *nf* admiration.

admirer /admiʀe/ [1] *vt* admire.

admission /admisjɔ̃/ *nf* admission.

ADN *abrév m* (**acide désoxyribonucléique**) DNA.

adolescence /adɔlesɑ̃s/ *nf* adolescence. **adolescent, ~e** *nm, f* adolescent, teenager.

adopter /adɔpte/ [1] *vt* adopt. **adoptif, -ive** *adj* (*enfant*) adopted; (*parents*) adoptive.

adorer /adɔʀe/ [1] *vt* love; (plus fort) adore; (Relig) worship, adore.

adosser /adose/ [1] *vt* lean (**à, contre** against). □ **s'~** *vpr* lean back (**à, contre** against).

adoucir /adusiʀ/ [2] *vt* soften; (*boisson*) sweeten; (*chagrin*) ease. □ **s'~** *vpr* soften; (*chagrin*) ease; (*temps*) become milder. **adoucissant** *nm* (fabric) softener.

adresse /adʀɛs/ *nf* address; (habileté) skill; ~ **électronique** e-mail address.

adresser /adʀese/ [1] *vt* send; (écrire l'adresse sur) address; (*remarque*) address; ~ **la parole à** speak to. □ **s'~ à** *vpr* address; (aller voir) (*personne*) go and ask *ou* see; (*bureau*) enquire at; (viser, intéresser) be directed at.

adroit, ~e /adʀwa, -t/ *adj* skilful, clever.

adulte /adylt/ *nmf* adult. ● *adj* adult; (*plante, animal*) fully-grown.

adultère /adyltɛʀ/ *adj* adulterous. ● *nm* adultery.

adverbe /advɛʀb/ *nm* adverb.

adversaire /advɛʀsɛʀ/ *nmf* opponent, adversary.

aérer /aeʀe/ [1] *vt* air; (*texte*) space out. □ **s'~** *vpr* get some air.

aérien, ~ne /aeʀjɛ̃, -jɛn/ *adj* air; (*photo*) aerial; (*câble*) overhead.

aérobic /aeʀɔbik/ *nm* aerobics (+ sg).

aérogare /aeʀɔgaʀ/ *nf* air terminal.

aéroglisseur /aeʀɔglisœʀ/ *nm* hovercraft.

aérogramme /aeʀɔgʀam/ *nm* airmail letter; (US) aerogram.

aéronautique /aeʀɔnotik/ *adj* aeronautical. ● *nf* aeronautics (+ sg).

aéroport /aeʀɔpɔʀ/ *nm* airport.

aérospatial, ~e (*mpl* **-iaux**) /aeʀɔspasjal, -jo/ *adj* aerospace.

affaiblir /afebliʀ/ [2] *vt* weaken. □ **s'~** *vpr* get weaker.

affaire /afɛʀ/ *nf* affair, matter; (Jur) case; (histoire, aventure) affair; (occasion) bargain; (entreprise) business; (transaction) deal; (question, problème) matter; ~**s** (Comm) business; (Pol) affairs; (problèmes personnels) business; (effets personnels) things; **c'est mon** ~ that's my business; **avoir** ~ **à** deal with; **ça fera l'**~ that will do the job; **ça fera leur** ~ that's just what they need; **tirer qn d'**~ help sb out of a tight spot; **se tirer d'**~ get out of trouble.

affairé, ~e /afeʀe/ *adj* busy.

affaisser (s') /(s)afese/ [1] *vpr* (*terrain, route*) sink, subside; (*poutre*) sag; (*personne*) collapse.

affamé, ~e /afame/ *adj* starving.

affectation /afɛktasjɔ̃/ *nf* (nomination) (à une fonction) appointment; (dans un lieu) posting; (de matériel, d'argent) allocation; (comportement) affectation.

affecter /afɛkte/ [1] *vt* (feindre) affect; (toucher, affliger) affect; (destiner) assign; (nommer) appoint, post.

affectif, -ive /afɛktif, -v/ *adj* emotional.

affection /afɛksjɔ̃/ *nf* affection; (maladie) complaint.

affectueux, -euse /afɛktɥ̞ø, -z/ *adj* affectionate.

a

affichage /afiʃaʒ/ nm billposting; (électronique) display.

affiche /afiʃ/ nf (public) notice; (publicité) poster; (Théât) bill; **être à l'~** (film) be showing; (pièce) be on.

afficher /afiʃe/ [1] vt (annonce) put up; (événement) announce; (sentiment) display; (Ordinat) display.

affirmatif, **-ive** /afiʀmatif, -v/ adj affirmative. **affirmation** nf assertion.

affirmer /afiʀme/ [1] vt assert; (soutenir) maintain.

affligé, **~e** /afliʒe/ adj distressed; **~ de** afflicted with.

affluer /aflye/ [1] vi flood in; (sang) rush.

affolant, **~e** /afɔlɑ̃, -t/ adj alarming.

affoler /afɔle/ [1] vt throw into a panic. □ **s'~** vpr panic.

affranchir /afʀɑ̃ʃiʀ/ [2] vt stamp; (à la machine) frank; (esclave) emancipate; (fig) free. **affranchissement** nm (tarif) postage.

affreux, **-euse** /afʀø, -z/ adj (laid) hideous; (mauvais) awful.

affrontement /afʀɔ̃tmɑ̃/ nm confrontation.

affronter /afʀɔ̃te/ [1] vt confront. □ **s'~** vpr confront each other.

affûter /afyte/ [1] vt sharpen.

afin /afɛ̃/ prép & conj **~ de faire** in order to do; **~ que** so that.

africain, **~e** /afʀikɛ̃, -ɛn/ adj African. **A~**, **~e** nm, f African.

Afrique /afʀik/ nf Africa; **~ du Sud** South Africa.

agacer /agase/ [10] vt irritate, annoy.

âge /aʒ/ nm age; (vieillesse) (old) age; **quel ~ avez-vous?** how old are you?; **~ adulte** adulthood; **~ mûr** maturity; **d'un certain ~** middle-aged.

âgé, **~e** /aʒe/ adj elderly; **~ de cinq ans** five years old.

agence /aʒɑ̃s/ nf agency, bureau, office; (succursale) branch; **~ d'interim** employment agency; **~ de voyages** travel agency; **~ publicitaire** advertising agency.

agenda /aʒɛ̃da/ nm diary; **~ électronique** electronic organizer.

agent /aʒɑ̃/ nm agent; (fonctionnaire) official; **~ (de police)** policeman; **~ de change** stockbroker; **~ commercial** sales representative.

agglomération /aglɔmeʀasjɔ̃/ nf town, built-up area.

aggraver /agʀave/ [1] vt aggravate, make worse. □ **s'~** vpr get worse.

agile /aʒil/ adj agile, nimble.

agir /aʒiʀ/ [2] vi act; (se comporter) behave; (avoir un effet) work, take effect. □ **s'~ de** vpr (être nécessaire) **il s'agit de faire** we/you etc. must do; (être question de) **il s'agit de faire** it is a matter of doing; **dans ce livre il s'agit de** this book is about; **dont il s'agit** in question; **il s'agit de ton fils** it's about your son; **de quoi s'agit-il?** what is it about?

agitation /aʒitasjɔ̃/ nf bustle; (trouble) agitation; (malaise social) unrest.

agité, **~e** /aʒite/ adj restless, fidgety; (troublé) agitated; (mer) rough.

agiter /aʒite/ [1] vt (bras, mouchoir) wave; (liquide, boîte) shake; (troubler) agitate; (discuter) debate. □ **s'~** vpr bustle about; (enfant) fidget; (foule, pensées) stir.

agneau (pl **~x**) /aɲo/ nm lamb.

agrafe /agʀaf/ nf hook; (pour papiers) staple. **agrafeuse** nf stapler.

agrandir /agʀɑ̃diʀ/ [2] vt enlarge; (maison) extend. □ **s'~** vpr expand, grow. **agrandissement** nm extension; (de photo) enlargement.

agréable /agʀeabl/ adj pleasant.

agréé, **~e** /agʀee/ adj (agence) authorized; (nourrice, médecin) registered; (matériel) approved.

agréer /agʀee/ [15] vt accept; **~ à** please; **veuillez ~, Monsieur, mes salutations distinguées** (personne non nommée) yours faithfully; (personne nommée) yours sincerely.

agrégation /agʀegasjɔ̃/ nf highest examination for recruitment of teachers. **agrégé**, **~e** nm, f teacher (who has passed the agrégation).

agrément /agʀemɑ̃/ nm charm; (plaisir) pleasure; (accord) assent.

agresser /agʀese/ [1] vt attack; (pour voler) mug.

agressif, -ive /agʀesif, -v/ adj aggressive. **agression** nf attack; (pour voler) mugging; (Mil) aggression.

agricole /agʀikɔl/ adj agricultural; (ouvrier, produit) farm. **agriculteur** nm farmer. **agriculture** nf agriculture, farming.

agripper /agʀipe/ [1] vt grab. □ s'~ vpr cling (à to).

agroalimentaire /agʀɔalimɑ̃tɛʀ/ nm food industry.

agrumes /agʀym/ nmpl citrus fruit(s).

ai /e/ ⇒avoir [5].

aide /ɛd/ nf help, assistance; (en argent) aid; à l'~ de with the help of; venir en ~ à help; ~ à domicile home help; ~ familiale mother's help; ~ sociale social security; (US) welfare. ● nmf assistant. **aide-mémoire** nm inv handbook of key facts.

aider /ede/ [1] vt/i help, assist; (subventionner) aid, give aid to; ~ à faire help to do. □ s' ~ de vpr use.

aïeul, ~e /ajœl/ nm,f grandparent.

aigle /ɛgl/ nm eagle.

aigre /ɛgʀ/ adj sour, sharp; (fig) sharp.

aigrir /egʀiʀ/ [2] vt embitter. □ s'~ vpr turn sour; (personne) become embittered.

aigu, ~ë /egy/ adj (douleur, problème) acute; (objet) sharp; (voix) shrill; (Mus) high(pitched); (accent) acute.

aiguille /egɥij/ nf needle; (de montre) hand; (de balance) pointer; ~ à tricoter knitting needle.

aiguilleur /egɥijœʀ/ nm pointsman; ~ du ciel air traffic controller.

aiguiser /eg(ɥ)ize/ [1] vt sharpen; (fig) stimulate.

ail (pl ~s ou aulx) /aj, o/ nm garlic.

aile /ɛl/ nf wing.

ailier /elje/ nm winger; (US) end.

aille /aj/ ⇒ALLER [8].

ailleurs /ajœʀ/ adv elsewhere, somewhere else; d'~ besides, moreover; nulle part ~ nowhere else; par ~ moreover, furthermore; partout ~ everywhere else.

aimable /ɛmabl/ adj kind.

aimant /ɛmɑ̃/ nm magnet.

aimer /eme/ [1] vt like; (d'amour) love; j'aimerais faire I'd like to do; ~ bien quite like; ~ mieux ou autant prefer.

aîné, ~e /ene/ adj eldest; (de deux) elder. ● nm,f eldest (child); (premier de deux) elder (child); ~s elders; il est mon ~ he is older than me ou my senior.

ainsi /ɛ̃si/ adv like this, thus; (donc) so; et ~ de suite and so on; pour ~ dire so to speak, as it were; ~ que as well as; (comme) as.

air /ɛʀ/ nm air; (mine) look, air; (mélodie) tune; ~ conditionné air-conditioning; avoir l'~ look, appear; avoir l'~ de look like; avoir l'~ de faire appear to be doing; en l'~ (up) in the air; (promesses) empty; prendre l'~ get some fresh air.

aire /ɛʀ/ nf area; ~ d'atterrissage landing-strip; ~ de pique-nique picnic area; ~ de repos rest area; ~ de services (motorway) services.

aisance /ɛzɑ̃s/ nf ease; (richesse) affluence.

aise /ɛz/ nf joy; à l'~ (sur un siège) comfortable; (pas gêné) at ease; (fortuné) comfortably off; mal à l'~ uncomfortable; ill at ease; aimer ses ~s like one's creature comforts; mettre qn à l'~ put sb at ease; se mettre à l'~ make oneself comfortable.

aisé, ~e /eze/ adj easy; (fortuné) well-off.

aisselle /ɛsɛl/ nf armpit.

ait /ɛ/ ⇒AVOIR [5].

ajourner /aʒuʀne/ [1] vt postpone; (débat, procès) adjourn.

ajout /aʒu/ nm addition.

ajouter /aʒute/ [1] vt add (à to); ~ foi à lend credence to. □ s'~ vpr be added.

ajuster /aʒyste/ [1] vt adjust; (cible) aim at; (adapter) fit; ~ son coup adjust one's aim.

alarme /alaʀm/ nf alarm; donner l'~ raise the alarm.

alarmer /alaʀme/ [1] vt alarm. □ s'~ vpr become alarmed (de at).

Albanie /albani/ *nf* Albania.

alcool /alkɔl/ *nm* alcohol; (eau de vie) brandy; ~ **à brûler** methylated spirit. **alcoolique** *a* & *nmf* alcoholic. **alcoolisé**, ~**e** *adj* (boisson) alcoholic. **alcoolisme** *nm* alcoholism.

alcootest /alkɔtɛst/ *nm* breath test; (appareil) Breathalyser®.

aléa /alea/ *nm* hazard. **aléatoire** *adj* unpredictable, uncertain; (Ordinat) random.

alentours /alɑ̃tuʀ/ *nmpl* surroundings; **aux** ~ **de** (de lieu) around; (de chiffre, date) about, around.

alerte /alɛʀt/ *adj* (personne) alert; (vif) lively. ● *nf* alert; ~ **à la bombe** bomb scare. **alerter** [1] *vt* alert.

algèbre /alʒɛbʀ/ *nf* algebra.

Algérie /alʒeʀi/ *nf* Algeria.

algue /alg/ *nf* seaweed; **les** ~**s** (Bot) algae.

aliéné, ~**e** /aljene/ *nm,f* insane person.

aliéner /aljene/ [14] *vt* alienate; (céder) give up. □ **s'**~ *vpr* alienate.

aligner /aliɲe/ [1] *vt* (objets) line up, make lines of; (chiffres) string together; ~ **sur** bring into line with. □ **s'**~ *vpr* line up; **s'**~ **sur** align oneself on.

aliment /alimɑ̃/ *nm* food.

alimentaire /alimɑ̃tɛʀ/ *adj* (industrie) food; (habitudes) dietary; **produits** ~**s** foodstuffs.

alimentation /alimɑ̃tasjɔ̃/ *nf* feeding, supply(ing); (régime) diet; (aliments) food; **magasin d'**~ grocery shop *ou* store.

alimenter /alimɑ̃te/ [1] *vt* feed; (fournir) supply; (fig) sustain. □ **s'**~ *vpr* eat.

allaiter /alete/ [1] *vt* (bébé) breast-feed; (US) nurse; (animal) suckle.

allée /ale/ *nf* path, lane; (menant à une maison) drive(way); (dans un cinéma, magasin) aisle; (rue) road; ~**s et venues** comings and goings.

allégé, ~**e** /aleʒe/ *adj* diet; (beurre, yaourt) low-fat.

alléger /aleʒe/ [14] [40] *vt* make lighter; (fardeau, chargement) lighten; (fig) (souffrance) alleviate.

allégresse /alegʀɛs/ *nf* gaiety, joy.

alléguer /alege/ [14] *vt* (exemple) invoke; (prétexter) allege.

Allemagne /alman/ *nf* Germany.

allemand, ~**e** /almɑ̃, -d/ *adj* German. ● *nm* (Ling) German. **A**~, ~**e** *nm,f* German.

----

aller /ale/ [8]

● *verbe auxiliaire*

····➤ **je vais l'appeler** I'm going to call him; **j'allais partir** I was about to leave; **va savoir!** who knows?; ~ **en s'améliorant** be improving.

● *verbe intransitif*

····➤ (se déplacer) go; **allons-y!** let's go!; **allez!** come on!

····➤ (se porter) **comment allez-vous?**, **comment ça va?** how are you?; **ça va (bien)** I'm fine; **qu'est-ce qui ne va pas?** what's the matter?; **ça ne va pas la tête?** 🖪 are you mad? 🖪.

····➤ (mettre en valeur) ~ **à qn** suit sb; **ça te va bien** it really suits you.

····➤ (convenir) **ça va ma coiffure?** is my hair OK?; **ça ne va pas du tout** that's no good at all.

□ **s'en aller** *verbe pronominal*

····➤ go; **va-t'en!** go away!; **ça ne s'en va pas** (tache) it won't come out.

● *nom masculin*

····➤ outward journey; ~ (**simple**) single (ticket); (US) one-way (ticket); ~ **retour** return (ticket); (US) round trip (ticket); **à l'**~ on the way out.

----

allergie /alɛʀʒi/ *nf* allergy. **allergique** *adj* allergic (**à** to).

alliance /aljɑ̃s/ *nf* alliance; (bague) wedding-ring; (mariage) marriage.

allier /alje/ [45] *vt* combine; (Pol) ally. □ **s'**~ *vpr* combine; (Pol) form an alliance; (famille) become related (**à** to).

allô /alo/ *interj* hallo, hello.

allocation /alɔkasjɔ̃/ *nf* allowance; ~ **chômage** unemployment benefit; ~**s familiales** family allowance.

allonger /alɔ̃ʒe/ [40] *vt* lengthen; (bras, jambe) stretch (out); (coucher) lay down. □ **s'**~ *vpr* get longer;

(s'étendre) lie down; (s'étirer) stretch (oneself) out.

allouer /alwe/ [1] vt allocate; (prêt) grant.

allumer /alyme/ [1] vt (bougie, gaz) light; (lampe, appareil) turn on; (pièce) switch the light(s) on in; (fig) arouse. □ **s'~** vpr (lumière, appareil) come on.

allumette /alymɛt/ nf match.

allure /alyʀ/ nf speed, pace; (démarche) walk; (apparence) appearance; **à toute ~** at full speed; **avoir de l'~** have style; **avoir des ~s de** look like; **avoir une drôle d'~** be funny-looking.

allusion /alyzjɔ̃/ nf allusion (à to); (implicite) hint (à at); **faire ~ à** allude to; hint at.

alors /alɔʀ/ adv (à ce moment-là) then; (de ce fait) so; (dans ce cas-là) then; **ça ~!** well!; **et ~?** so what? ● conj **~ que** (pendant que) while; (tandis que) when, whereas.

alouette /alwɛt/ nf lark.

alourdir /aluʀdiʀ/ [2] vt weigh down; (rendre plus important) increase.

aloyau (pl **~x**) /alwajo/ nm sirloin.

Alpes /alp/ nfpl **les ~** the Alps.

alphabet /alfabɛ/ nm alphabet. **alphabétique** adj alphabetical.

alphabétiser /alfabetize/ [1] vt teach to read and write.

alpinist /alpinist/ nmf mountaineer.

altérer /alteʀe/ [14] vt (fait, texte) distort; (abîmer) spoil; (donner soif à) make thirsty. □ **s'~** vpr deteriorate.

alternance /altɛʀnɑ̃s/ nf alternation; **en ~** alternately.

altitude /altityd/ nf altitude, height.

amabilité /amabilite/ nf kindness.

amaigrir /amegʀiʀ/ [2] vt make thin(ner).

amande /amɑ̃d/ nf almond; (d'un fruit à noyau) kernel.

amant /amɑ̃/ nm lover.

amarre /amaʀ/ nf (mooring) rope; **~s** moorings.

amas /ama/ nm heap, pile.

amasser /amase/ [1] vt amass, gather; (empiler) pile up. □ **s'~** vpr pile up; (gens) gather.

amateur /amatœʀ/ nm amateur; **~ de** lover of; **d'~** amateur; (péj) amateurish,

ambassade /ɑ̃basad/ nf embassy. **ambassadeur, -drice** nm,f ambassador.

ambiance /ɑ̃bjɑ̃s/ nf atmosphere. **ambiant, ~e** adj surrounding.

ambigu, ~ë /ɑ̃bigy/ adj ambiguous.

ambitieux, -ieuse /ɑ̃bisjø, -z/ adj ambitious. **ambition** nf ambition.

ambulance /ɑ̃bylɑ̃s/ nf ambulance.

ambulant, ~e /ɑ̃bylɑ̃, -t/ adj itinerant, travelling.

âme /am/ nf soul; **~ sœur** soul mate.

amélioration /ameljɔʀasjɔ̃/ nf improvement.

améliorer /ameljɔʀe/ [1] vt improve. □ **s'~** vpr improve.

aménagement /amenaʒmɑ̃/ nm (de magasin) fitting out; (de grenier) conversion; (de territoire) development; (de cuisine) equipping.

aménager /amenaʒe/ [40] vt (magasin) fit out; (transformer) convert; (territoire) develop; (cuisine) equip.

amende /amɑ̃d/ nf fine; **faire ~ honorable** make amends.

amener /am(ə)ne/ [6] vt bring; (causer) bring about; **~ qn à faire** cause sb to do. □ **s'~** vpr 🔲 turn up.

amer, -ère /amɛʀ/ adj bitter.

américain, ~e /ameʀikɛ̃, -ɛn/ adj American. **A~, ~e** nm,f American.

Amérique /ameʀik/ nf America; **~ centrale/latine** Central/Latin America; **~ du Nord/Sud** North/ South America.

amertume /amɛʀtym/ nf bitterness.

ami, ~e /ami/ nm,f friend; (amateur) lover; **un ~ des bêtes** an animal lover. ● adj friendly.

amiable /amjabl/ adj amicable; **à l'~** (divorcer) by mutual consent; (se séparer) on friendly terms; (séparation) amicable.

amical, ~e (mpl **-aux**) /amikal, -o/ adj friendly.

amiral (pl **-aux**) /amiʀal, -o/ nm admiral.

amitié /amitje/ *nf* friendship; **∼s** (en fin de lettre) kind regards; **prendre qn en ∼** take a liking to sb.

amnistie /amnisti/ *nf* amnesty.

amoindrir /amwɛ̃dRiR/ [2] *vt* reduce.

amont: **en ∼** /ɑ̃namɔ̃/ *loc* upstream.

amorcer /amɔRse/ [10] *vt* start; (*hameçon*) bait; (*pompe*) prime; (*arme à feu*) arm.

amortir /amɔRtiR/ [2] *vt* (*choc*) cushion; (*bruit*) deaden; (*dette*) pay off; **∼ un achat** make a purchase pay for itself.

amortisseur /amɔRtisœR/ *nm* shock absorber.

amour /amuR/ *nm* love; **pour l'∼ de** for the sake of.

amoureux, -euse /amuRø, -z/ *adj* (*personne*) in love; (*relation, regard*) loving; (*vie*) love; **∼ de qn** in love with sb. ● *nm, f* lover.

amour-propre /amuRpRɔpR/ *nm* self-esteem.

amphithéâtre /ɑ̃fiteatR/ *nm* amphitheatre; (d'université) lecture hall.

ampleur /ɑ̃plœR/ *nf* extent, size; (de vêtement) fullness; **prendre de l'∼** spread, grow.

amplifier /ɑ̃plifje/ [45] *vt* amplify; (fig) expand, develop. □ **s'∼** *vpr* (*son*) grow; (*scandale*) intensify.

ampoule /ɑ̃pul/ *nf* (électrique) bulb; (sur la peau) blister; (Méd) phial, ampoule.

amusant, ∼e /amyzɑ̃, -t/ *adj* (*blague*) funny; (*soirée*) enjoyable, entertaining.

amuse-gueule /amyzgœl/ *nm inv* cocktail snack.

amusement /amyzmɑ̃/ *nm* amusement; (passe-temps) entertainment.

amuser /amyze/ [1] *vt* amuse; (détourner l'attention de) distract. □ **s'∼** *vpr* enjoy oneself; (jouer) play.

amygdale /amidal/ *nf* tonsil.

an /ɑ̃/ *nm* year; **avoir dix ∼s** be ten years old; **un garçon de deux ∼s** a two-year-old boy; **à soixante ∼s** at the age of sixty; **les moins de dix-huit ∼s** under eighteens.

analogie /analɔʒi/ *nf* analogy.

analogue /analɔg/ *adj* similar, analogous (**à** to).

analphabète /analfabɛt/ *a & nmf* illiterate.

analyse /analiz/ *nf* analysis; (Méd) test. **analyser** [1] *vt* analyse; (Méd) test.

ananas /anana(s)/ *nm* pineapple.

anarchie /anaRʃi/ *nf* anarchy.

anatomie /anatɔmi/ *nf* anatomy.

ancêtre /ɑ̃sɛtR/ *nm* ancestor.

anchois /ɑ̃ʃwa/ *nm* anchovy.

ancien, ∼ne /ɑ̃sjɛ̃, -jɛn/ *adj* old; (de jadis) ancient; (*meuble*) antique; (précédent) former, ex-, old; (dans une fonction) senior; **∼ combattant** veteran. ● *nm, f* senior; (par l'âge) elder. **anciennement** *adv* formerly. **ancienneté** *nf* age, seniority.

ancre /ɑ̃kR/ *nf* anchor; **jeter/lever l'∼** cast/weigh anchor.

andouille /ɑ̃duj/ *nf* sausage (*filled with chitterlings*); (idiot 🄸) fool; **faire l'∼** fool around.

âne /ɑn/ *nm* donkey, ass; (imbécile 🄸) dimwit 🄸.

anéantir /aneɑ̃tiR/ [2] *vt* destroy; (exterminer) annihilate; (accabler) overwhelm.

anémie /anemi/ *nf* anaemia.

ânerie /ɑnRi/ *nf* stupid remark.

anesthésie /anɛstezi/ *nf* (opération) anaesthetic.

ange /ɑ̃ʒ/ *nm* angel; **aux ∼s** in seventh heaven.

angine /ɑ̃ʒin/ *nf* throat infection.

anglais, ∼e /ɑ̃glɛ, -z/ *adj* English. ● *nm* (Ling) English. **A∼, ∼e** *nm, f* Englishman, Englishwoman.

angle /ɑ̃gl/ *nm* angle; (coin) corner.

Angleterre /ɑ̃glətɛR/ *nf* England.

anglophone /ɑ̃glɔfɔn/ *adj* English-speaking. ● *nmf* English speaker.

angoissant, ∼e /ɑ̃gwasɑ̃, -t/ *adj* alarming; (effrayant) harrowing.

angoisse /ɑ̃gwas/ *nf* anxiety. **angoissé, ∼e** *adj* anxious. **angoisser** [1] *vi* worry.

animal (*pl* **-aux**) /animal, -o/ *nm* animal; **∼ familier, ∼ de compagnie** pet. ● *adj* (*mpl* **-aux**) animal.

animateur, -trice /animatœʀ,
-tʀis/ *nm,f* organizer, leader; (TV)
host, hostess.

animation /animasjɔ̃/ *nf* liveliness;
(affairement) activity; (au cinéma)
animation; (activité dirigée) organized
activity.

animé, ∼e /anime/ *adj* lively;
(affairé) busy; (être) animate.

animer /anime/ [1] *vt* liven up;
(débat, atelier) lead; (spectacle) host;
(pousser) drive; (encourager) spur on.
□ **s'∼** *vpr* liven up.

anis /ani(s)/ *nm* (Culin) aniseed; (Bot)
anise.

anneau (pl ∼**x**) /ano/ *nm* ring; (de
chaîne) link.

année /ane/ *nf* year; ∼ **bissextile**
leap year; ∼ **civile** calendar year.

annexe /anɛks/ *adj* (document)
attached; (question) related;
(bâtiment) adjoining. ● *nf* (bâtiment)
annexe; (US) annex; (document)
appendix; (électronique) attachment.
annexer [1] *vt* annex; (document)
attach.

anniversaire /anivɛʀsɛʀ/ *nm*
birthday; (d'un événement)
anniversary. ● *adj* anniversary.

annonce /anɔ̃s/ *nf* announcement;
(publicitaire) advertisement; (indice)
sign.

annoncer /anɔ̃se/ [10] *vt* announce;
(prédire) forecast; (être l'indice de)
herald. □ **s'∼** *vpr* (crise, tempête) be
brewing; **s'∼ bien/mal** look good/
bad. **annonceur** *nm* advertiser.

annuaire /anɥɛʀ/ *nm* year-book; ∼
(téléphonique) (telephone) directory.

annuel, ∼le /anɥɛl/ *adj* annual,
yearly.

annulation /anylasjɔ̃/ *nf*
cancellation; (de sanction, loi) repeal;
(de mesure) abolition.

annuler /anyle/ [1] *vt* cancel;
(contrat) nullify; (jugement) quash;
(loi) repeal. □ **s'∼** *vpr* cancel each
other out.

anodin, ∼e /anɔdɛ̃, -in/ *adj*
insignificant; (sans risques) harmless,
safe.

anonymat /anɔnima/ *nm*
anonymity; **garder l'∼** remain

anonymous. **anonyme** *adj*
anonymous.

anorexie /anɔʀɛksi/ *nf* anorexia.

anormal, ∼e (mpl -**aux**) /anɔʀmal,
-o/ *adj* abnormal.

anse /ɑ̃s/ *nf* handle; (baie) cove.

Antarctique /ɑ̃taʀktik/ *nm*
Antarctic.

antenne /ɑ̃tɛn/ *nf* aerial; (US)
antenna; (d'insecte) antenna;
(succursale) agency; (Mil) outpost; **à l'∼**
on the air; ∼ **chirurgicale** mobile
emergency unit; ∼ **parabolique**
satellite dish.

antérieur, ∼e /ɑ̃teʀjœʀ/ *adj*
previous, earlier; (placé devant) front;
∼ **à** prior to.

antiaérien, ∼ne /ɑ̃tiaeʀjɛ̃, -ɛn/ *adj*
anti-aircraft; **abri** ∼ air-raid shelter.

antiatomique /ɑ̃tiatɔmik/ *adj* **abri**
∼ nuclear fall-out shelter.

antibiotique /ɑ̃tibjɔtik/ *nm*
antibiotic.

anticipation /ɑ̃tisipasjɔ̃/ *nf* **d'∼**
(livre, film) science fiction; **par** ∼ in
advance.

anticiper /ɑ̃tisipe/ [1] *vt* ∼ (**sur**)
anticipate; (effectuer à l'avance) bring
forward.

anticorps /ɑ̃tikɔʀ/ *nm* antibody.

antidater /ɑ̃tidate/ [1] *vt* backdate,
antedate.

antigel /ɑ̃tiʒɛl/ *nm* antifreeze.

Antilles /ɑ̃tij/ *nfpl* **les** ∼ the West
Indies.

antipathique /ɑ̃tipatik/ *adj*
unpleasant.

antiquaire /ɑ̃tikɛʀ/ *nmf* antique
dealer.

antiquité /ɑ̃tikite/ *nf* (objet) antique;
l'A∼ antiquity.

antisémite /ɑ̃tisemit/ *adj* anti-
Semitic.

antiseptique /ɑ̃tisɛptik/ *a & nm*
antiseptic.

antivol /ɑ̃tivɔl/ *nm* anti-theft device;
(Auto) steering lock.

anxiété /ɑ̃ksjete/ *nf* anxiety.

anxieux, -ieuse /ɑ̃ksjø, -z/ *adj*
anxious. ● *nm,f* worrier.

août /u(t)/ *nm* August.

apaiser /apeze/ [1] *vt* calm down;
(colère, militant) appease; (douleur)

soothe; (*faim*) satisfy. □ **s'~** *vpr* (*tempête*) die down.

apathie /apati/ *nf* apathy.
apathique *adj* apathetic.

apercevoir /apɛʀsəvwaʀ/ [52] *vt* see. □ **s'~ de** *vpr* notice; **s'~ que** notice *ou* realize that.

aperçu /apɛʀsy/ *nm* (échantillon) glimpse, taste; (intuition) insight.

apéritif /apeʀitif/ *nm* aperitif, drink.

aphte /aft/ *nm* mouth ulcer.

apitoyer /apitwaje/ [31] *vt* move (to pity). □ **s'~** *vpr* **s'~ sur** (**le sort de**) **qn** feel sorry for sb.

aplanir /aplaniʀ/ [2] *vt* level; (fig) iron out.

aplatir /aplatiʀ/ [2] *vt* flatten (out). □ **s'~** *vpr* (s'immobiliser) flatten oneself.

aplomb /aplɔ̃/ *nm* balance; (fig) self-confidence; **d'~** (en équilibre) steady; **je ne suis pas bien d'~** 🎯 I don't feel very well.

apogée /apɔʒe/ *nm* peak.

apologie /apɔlɔʒi/ *nf* panegyric.

apostrophe /apɔstʀɔf/ *nf* apostrophe; (remarque) remark.

apothéose /apɔteoz/ *nf* high point; (d'événement) grand finale.

apparaître /apaʀɛtʀ/ [18] *vi* appear; **il apparaît que** it appears that.

appareil /apaʀɛj/ *nm* device; (électrique) appliance; (Anat) system; (téléphone) phone; (avion) plane; (Culin) mixture; (système administratif) apparatus; **~** (**dentaire**) brace; (dentier) dentures; **~** (**photo**) camera; **c'est Gabriel à l'~** it's Gabriel on the phone; **~ auditif** hearing aid; **~ électroménager** household electrical appliance.

appareiller /apaʀeje/ [1] *vi* (navire) cast off, put to sea.

apparemment /apaʀamɑ̃/ *adv* apparently.

apparence /apaʀɑ̃s/ *nf* appearance; **en ~** outwardly; (apparemment) apparently.

apparent, **~e** /apaʀɑ̃, -t/ *adj* apparent; (visible) conspicuous.

apparenté, **~e** /apaʀɑ̃te/ *adj* related; (semblable) similar.

apparition /apaʀisjɔ̃/ *nf* appearance; (spectre) apparition.

appartement /apaʀtəmɑ̃/ *nm* flat; (US) apartment.

appartenir /apaʀtəniʀ/ [58] *vi* belong (à to); **il lui appartient de** it is up to him to.

appât /apɑ/ *nm* bait; (fig) lure.

appauvrir /apovʀiʀ/ [2] *vt* impoverish. □ **s'~** *vpr* become impoverished.

appel /apɛl/ *nm* call; (Jur) appeal; (supplique) appeal, plea; (Mil) call-up; (US) draft; **faire ~** appeal; **faire ~ à** (recourir à) call on; (invoquer) appeal to; (évoquer) call up; (exiger) call for; **faire l'~** (Scol) call the register; (Mil) take a roll-call; **~ d'offres** (Comm) invitation to tender; **faire un ~ de phares** flash one's headlights.

appeler /aple/ [38] *vt* call; (téléphoner) phone, call; (nécessiter) call for; **en ~ à** appeal to; **appelé à** (destiné) destined for. □ **s'~** *vpr* be called; **il s'appelle Tim** his name is Tim *ou* he is called Tim.

appellation /apelasjɔ̃/ *nf* name, designation.

appendice /apɛ̃dis/ *nm* appendix.
appendicite *nf* appendicitis.

appesantir /apəzɑ̃tiʀ/ [2] *vt* weigh down. □ **s'~** *vpr* grow heavier; **s'~ sur** dwell upon.

appétissant, **~e** /apetisɑ̃, -t/ *adj* appetizing.

appétit /apeti/ *nm* appetite; **bon ~!** enjoy your meal!

applaudir /aplodiʀ/ [2] *vt/i* applaud.
applaudissements *nmpl* applause.

application /aplikasjɔ̃/ *nf* (soin) care; (de loi) (respect) application; (mise en œuvre) implementation; (Ordinat) application program.

appliqué, **~e** /aplike/ *adj* (travail) painstaking; (sciences) applied; (élève) hard-working.

appliquer /aplike/ [1] *vt* apply; (loi) enforce. □ **s'~** *vpr* apply oneself (à to), take great care (à faire to do); **s'~ à** (concerner) apply to.

appoint /apwɛ̃/ *nm* support; **d'~** extra; **faire l'~** give the correct money.

apport /apɔʀ/ *nm* contribution.

apporter /apɔʀte/ [1] *vt* bring; (*aide, précision*) give; (*causer*) bring about.

appréciation /apʀesjasjɔ̃/ *nf* estimate, evaluation; (de monnaie) appreciation; (*jugement*) assessment.

apprécier /apʀesje/ [45] *vt* appreciate; (évaluer) assess; (*objet*) value, appraise.

appréhender /apʀeɑ̃de/ [1] *vt* dread, fear; (arrêter) apprehend.

apprendre /apʀɑ̃dʀ/ [50] *vt* learn; (être informé de) hear, learn; (de façon indirecte) hear of; ~ qch à qn teach sb sth; (informer) tell sb sth; ~ à faire learn to do; ~ à qn à faire teach sb to do; ~ que learn that; (être informé) hear that.

apprenti, ~e /apʀɑ̃ti/ *nm,f* apprentice. **apprentissage** *nm* apprenticeship; (d'un sujet) learning.

apprêter /apʀete/ [1] *vt* prepare; (*bois*) prime; (*mur*) size. □ s'~ à *vpr* prepare to.

apprivoiser /apʀivwaze/ [1] *vt* tame.

approbation /apʀɔbasjɔ̃/ *nf* approval.

approchant, ~e /apʀɔʃɑ̃, -t/ *adj* close, similar.

approcher /apʀɔʃe/ [1] *vt* (*objet*) move near(er) (de to); (*personne*) approach; ~ de get nearer ou closer to. ● *vi* approach. □ s'~ de *vpr* approach, move near(er) to.

approfondir /apʀɔfɔ̃diʀ/ [2] *vt* deepen; (fig) (*sujet*) go into sth in depth; (*connaissances*) improve.

approprié, ~e /apʀɔpʀije/ *adj* appropriate.

approprier (s') /(s)apʀɔpʀije/ [45] *vpr* appropriate.

approuver /apʀuve/ [1] *vt* approve; (trouver louable) approve of; (soutenir) agree with.

approvisionner /apʀɔvizjɔne/ [1] *vt* supply (en with); (*compte en banque*) pay money into. □ s'~ *vpr* stock up.

approximatif, -ive /apʀɔksimatif, -v/ *adj* approximate.

appui /apɥi/ *nm* support; (de fenêtre) sill; (pour objet) rest; à l'~ de in support of; prendre ~ sur lean on.

appui-tête (*pl* **appuis-tête**) /apɥitɛt/ *nm* headrest.

appuyer /apɥije/ [31] *vt* lean, rest; (presser) press; (soutenir) support, back. ● *vi* ~ sur press (on); (fig) stress. □ s'~ sur *vpr* lean on; (compter sur) rely on.

après /apʀɛ/ *prép* after; (au-delà de) after, beyond; ~ avoir fait after doing; ~ tout after all; ~ coup after the event; d'~ (selon) according to; (en imitant) from; (adapté de) based on. ● *adv* after(wards); (plus tard) later; le bus d'~ the next bus. ● *conj* ~ qu'il est parti after he left. **après-demain** *adv* the day after tomorrow. **après-guerre** (*pl* ~s) *nm ou f* postwar period. **après-midi** *nm ou f inv* afternoon. **après-rasage** (*pl* ~s) *nm* aftershave. **après-ski** *nm inv* moonboot. **après-vente** *a inv* after-sales.

a priori /apʀijɔʀi/ *adv* (à première vue) offhand, on the face of it; (sans réfléchir) out of hand. ● *nm* preconception.

à-propos /apʀopo/ *nm* timing, timeliness; (fig) presence of mind.

apte /apt/ *adj* capable (à of); (ayant les qualités requises) suitable (à for); (en état) fit (à for).

aptitude /aptityd/ *nf* aptitude, ability.

aquarelle /akwaʀɛl/ *nf* water-colour.

aquatique /akwatik/ *adj* aquatic; (Sport) water.

arabe /aʀab/ *adj* Arab; (Ling) Arabic; (désert) Arabian. ● *nm* (Ling) Arabic. **A~** *nmf* Arab.

Arabie /aʀabi/ *nf* ~ Saoudite Saudi Arabia.

arachide /aʀaʃid/ *nf* groundnut; huile d'~ groundnut oil.

araignée /aʀeɲe/ *nf* spider.

arbitraire /aʀbitʀɛʀ/ *adj* arbitrary.

arbitre /aʀbitʀ/ *nm* referee; (au cricket, tennis) umpire; (expert) arbiter; (Jur) arbitrator. **arbitrer** [1] *vt* (*match*) referee, umpire; (Jur) arbitrate in.

arbre /aʀbʀ/ *nm* tree; (Tech) shaft.

arbuste /aʀbyst/ *nm* shrub.

arc /aʀk/ nm (arme) bow; (courbe) curve; (voûte) arch; ~ **de cercle** arc of a circle.

arc-en-ciel (pl **arcs-en-ciel**) /aʀkɑ̃sjɛl/ nm rainbow.

arche /aʀʃ/ nf arch; ~ **de Noé** Noah's ark.

archéologie /aʀkeɔlɔʒi/ nf archaeology.

archevêque /aʀʃəvɛk/ nm archbishop.

architecte /aʀʃitɛkt/ nmf architect. **architecture** nf architecture.

Arctique /aʀktik/ nm Arctic.

ardent, **~e** /aʀdɑ̃, -t/ adj burning; (passionné) ardent; (foi) fervent. **ardeur** nf ardour; (chaleur) heat.

ardoise /aʀdwaz/ nf slate; ~ **électronique** notepad computer.

arène /aʀɛn/ nf arena; **~s** amphitheatre; (pour corridas) bullring.

arête /aʀɛt/ nf (de poisson) bone; (bord) ridge.

argent /aʀʒɑ̃/ nm money; (métal) silver; ~ **comptant** cash; **prendre pour ~ comptant** take at face value; ~ **de poche** pocket money.

argenté, **~e** /aʀʒɑ̃te/ adj silver(y); (métal) (silver-)plated.

argenterie /aʀʒɑ̃tʀi/ nf silverware.

Argentine /aʀʒɑ̃tin/ nf Argentina.

argile /aʀʒil/ nf clay.

argot /aʀgo/ nm slang.

argument /aʀgymɑ̃/ nm argument; ~ **de vente** selling point. **argumenter** [1] vi argue.

aristocratie /aʀistɔkʀasi/ nf aristocracy.

arithmétique /aʀitmetik/ nf arithmetic. ● adj arithmetical.

armature /aʀmatyʀ/ nf framework; (de tente) frame.

arme /aʀm/ nf arm, weapon; ~ **à feu** firearm; **~s** (blason) coat of arms.

armée /aʀme/ nf army; ~ **de l'air** Air Force; ~ **de terre** Army.

armer /aʀme/ [1] vt arm; (fusil) cock; (navire) equip; (renforcer) reinforce; (Photo) wind on; ~ **de** (garnir de) fit with. □ **s'~ de** vpr arm oneself with.

armoire /aʀmwaʀ/ nf cupboard; (penderie) wardrobe; (US) closet; ~ **à pharmacie** medicine cabinet.

armure /aʀmyʀ/ nf armour.

arnaque /aʀnak/ nf 🔲 swindling; **c'est de l'~** it's a swindle ou con 🔲.

aromate /aʀɔmat/ nm herb, spice.

aromatisé, **~e** /aʀɔmatize/ adj flavoured.

arôme /aʀom/ nm aroma; (additif) flavouring.

arpenter /aʀpɑ̃te/ [1] vt pace up and down; (terrain) survey.

arqué, **~e** /aʀke/ adj arched; (jambes) bandy.

arrache-pied: d'~ /daʀaʃpje/ loc relentlessly.

arracher /aʀaʃe/ [1] vt pull out ou off; (plante) pull ou dig up; (cheveux, page) tear ou pull out; (par une explosion) blow off; ~ **à** (enlever à) snatch from; (fig) force ou wrest from. □ **s'~ qch** vpr fight over sth.

arranger /aʀɑ̃ʒe/ [40] vt arrange, fix up; (réparer) put right; (régler) sort out; (convenir à) suit. □ **s'~** vpr (se mettre d'accord) come to an arrangement; (se débrouiller) manage (**pour** to).

arrestation /aʀɛstasjɔ̃/ nf arrest.

arrêt /aʀɛ/ nm stopping; (de combats) cessation; (de production) halt; (lieu) stop; (pause) pause; (Jur) ruling; **aux ~s** (Mil) under arrest; **à l'~** (véhicule) stationary; (machine) idle; **faire un ~** (make a) stop; **sans ~** (sans escale) nonstop; (sans interruption) constantly; ~ **maladie** sick leave; ~ **de travail** (grève) stoppage; (Méd) sick leave.

arrêté /aʀete/ nm order; ~ **municipal** bylaw.

arrêter /aʀete/ [1] vt stop; (date) fix; (appareil) turn off; (renoncer à) give up; (appréhender) arrest. ● vi stop. □ **s'~** vpr stop; **s'~ de faire** stop doing.

arrhes /aʀ/ nfpl deposit; **verser des ~** pay a deposit.

arrière /aʀjɛʀ/ a inv back, rear. ● nm back, rear; (football) back; **à l'~** in ou at the back; **en ~** behind; (marcher, tomber) backwards; **en ~ de** behind. **arrière-boutique** (pl **~s**) nf back room (of the shop). **arrière-garde** (pl **~s**) nf

rearguard. **arrière-goût** (*pl* ∼s)
nm after-taste. **arrière-grand-
mère** (*pl* **arrière-grands-mères**)
nf great-grandmother. **arrière-
grand-père** (*pl* **arrière-grands-
pères**) *nm* great-grandfather.
arrière-pays *nm inv* backcountry.
arrière-pensée (*pl* ∼s) *nf* ulterior
motive. **arrière-plan** *nm* (*pl* ∼s)
background.

arrimer /aʀime/ [1] *vt* secure;
(*cargaison*) stow.

arrivage /aʀivaʒ/ *nm* consignment.

arrivée /aʀive/ *nf* arrival; (Sport)
finish.

arriver /aʀive/ [1] *vi* (*aux être*)
arrive, come; (*réussir*) succeed; (se
produire) happen; ∼ **à** (atteindre) reach;
∼ **à faire** manage to do; **je n'arrive
pas à faire** I can't do; **en** ∼ **à faire** get
to the stage of doing; **il arrive que** it
happens that; **il lui arrive de faire** he
(sometimes) does.

arriviste /aʀivist/ *nmf* go-getter,
self-seeker.

arrondir /aʀɔ̃diʀ/ [2] *vt* (make)
round; (*somme*) round off. □ **s'**∼ *vpr*
become round(ed).

arrondissement /aʀɔ̃dismɑ̃/ *nm*
district.

arroser /aʀoze/ [1] *vt* water; (*repas*)
wash down (with a drink); (*rôti*)
baste; (*victoire*) drink to. **arrosoir**
nm watering-can.

art /aʀ/ *nm* art; (don) knack (**de faire**
of doing); ∼**s et métiers** arts and
crafts; ∼**s ménagers** home
economics (+ *sg*).

artère /aʀtɛʀ/ *nf* artery; (**grande**) ∼
main road.

arthrite /aʀtʀit/ *nf* arthritis.

arthrose /aʀtʀoz/ *nf* osteoarthritis.

artichaut /aʀtiʃo/ *nm* artichoke.

article /aʀtikl/ *nm* article; (Comm)
item, article; **à l'**∼ **de la mort** at
death's door; ∼ **de fond** feature
(article); ∼**s de voyage** travel goods.

articulation /aʀtikylasjɔ̃/ *nf*
articulation; (Anat) joint.

articuler /aʀtikyle/ [1] *vt* articulate;
(structurer) structure; (assembler)
connect (**sur** to).

artificiel, ∼le /aʀtifisjɛl/ *adj*
artificial.

artisan /aʀtizɑ̃/ *nm* artisan,
craftsman; **l'**∼ **de** (fig) the architect
of.

artisanal, ∼e (*mpl* ∼**aux**)
/aʀtizanal/ *adj* craft; (*méthode*)
traditional; (amateur) home-made; **de
fabrication** ∼**e** hand-made, hand-
crafted.

artiste /aʀtist/ *nmf* artist.
artistique *adj* artistic.

as[1] /a/ ⇒AVOIR [5].

as[2] /ɑs/ *nm* ace.

ascenseur /asɑ̃sœʀ/ *nm* lift; (US)
elevator.

ascension /asɑ̃sjɔ̃/ *nf* ascent; **l'A**∼
Ascension.

aseptiser /asɛptize/ [1] *vt* disinfect;
(stériliser) sterilize; **aseptisé** (péj)
sanitized.

asiatique /azjatik/ *adj* Asian. **A**∼
nmf Asian.

Asie /azi/ *nf* Asia.

asile /azil/ *nm* refuge; (Pol) asylum;
(pour malades, vieillards) home; ∼ **de
nuit** night shelter.

aspect /aspɛ/ *nm* appearance;
(facettes) aspect; (perspective) side; **à
l'**∼ **de** at the sight of.

asperge /aspɛʀʒ/ *nf* asparagus.

asperger /aspɛʀʒe/ [40] *vt* spray.

asphyxier /asfiksje/ [45] *vt*
(*personne*) asphyxiate; (*entreprise,
réseau*) paralyse. □ **s'**∼ *vpr*
suffocate; gas oneself; (*entreprise,
réseau*) become paralysed.

aspirateur /aspiratœʀ/ *nm*
vacuum cleaner.

aspirer /aspiʀe/ [1] *vt* inhale;
(*liquide*) suck up. ● *vi* ∼ **à** aspire to.

aspirine® /aspiʀin/ *nf* aspirin.

assainir /aseniʀ/ [2] *vt* clean up.

assaisonnement /asɛzɔnmɑ̃/ *nm*
seasoning.

assassin /asasɛ̃/ *nm* murderer; (Pol)
assassin. **assassiner** [1] *vt* murder;
(Pol) assassinate.

assaut /aso/ *nm* assault, onslaught;
donner l'∼ **à**, **prendre d'**∼ storm.

assemblage /asɑ̃blaʒ/ *nm*
assembly; (combinaison) collection;
(Tech) joint.

assemblée /asɑ̃ble/ *nf* meeting;
(gens réunis) gathering; (Pol) assembly.

a

assembler /asãble/ [1] *vt* assemble, put together; (réunir) gather. □ **s'~** *vpr* gather, assemble.

asseoir /aswaR/ [9] *vt* sit (down), seat; (*bébé, malade*) sit up; (affermir) establish; (baser) base. □ **s'~** *vpr* sit (down).

assermenté, **~e** /asɛRmãte/ *adj* sworn.

assez /ase/ *adv* (suffisamment) enough; (plutôt) quite, fairly; **~ grand/rapide** big/fast enough (**pour** to); **~ de** enough; **j'en ai ~ (de)** I've had enough (of).

assidu, **~e** /asidy/ *adj* (zélé) assiduous; (régulier) regular; **~ auprès de** attentive to. **assiduité** *nf* assiduousness, regularity.

assiéger /asjeʒe/ [14] [40] *vt* besiege.

assiette /asjɛt/ *nf* plate; (équilibre) seat; **~ anglaise** assorted cold meats; **~ creuse/plate** soup-/dinner-plate; **ne pas être dans son ~** feel out of sorts.

assigner /asiɲe/ [1] *vt* assign; (*limite*) fix.

assimilation /asimilasjõ/ *nf* assimilation; (comparaison) likening, comparison.

assimiler /asimile/ [1] *vt* **~ à** liken to; (classer) class as. □ **s'~** *vpr* assimilate; (être comparable) be comparable (**à** to).

assis, **~e** /asi, -z/ *adj* sitting (down), seated. ● →ASSEOIR [9].

assise /asiz/ *nf* (base) foundation; **~s** (tribunal) assizes; (congrès) conference, congress.

assistance /asistãs/ *nf* audience; (aide) assistance; **l'A~** (**publique**) welfare services.

assistant, **~e** /asistã, -t/ *nm,f* assistant; (Scol) foreign language assistant; **~s** (spectateurs) members of the audience; **~e sociale** social worker.

assister /asiste/ [1] *vt* assist; **~ à** attend, be (present) at; (*accident*) witness; **assisté par ordinateur** computer-assisted.

association /asɔsjasjõ/ *nf* association.

associé, **~e** /asɔsje/ *nm,f* partner, associate. ● *adj* associate.

associer /asɔsje/ [45] *vt* associate; (mêler) combine (**à** with); **~ qn à** (*projet*) involve sb in; (*bénéfices*) give sb a share of. □ **s'~** *vpr* (*sociétés, personnes*) become associated, join forces (**à** with); (s'harmoniser) combine (**à** with); **s'~ à** (*joie, opinion de qn*) share; (*projet*) take part in.

assommer /asɔme/ [1] *vt* knock out; (*animal*) stun; (fig) overwhelm; (ennuyer [1]) bore.

Assomption /asõpsjõ/ *nf* Assumption.

assortiment /asɔRtimã/ *nm* assortment.

assortir /asɔRtiR/ [2] *vt* match (**à** with, to); **~ de** accompany with. □ **s'~** *vpr* match; **s'~ à qch** match sth.

assoupir (s') /(s)asupiR/ [2] *vpr* doze off; (s'apaiser) subside.

assouplir /asupliR/ [2] *vt* make supple; (fig) make flexible.

assourdir /asuRdiR/ [2] *vt* (*personne*) deafen; (*bruit*) muffle.

assouvir /asuviR/ [2] *vt* satisfy.

assujettir /asyʒetiR/ [2] *vt* subjugate, subdue; **~ à** subject to.

assumer /asyme/ [1] *vt* assume; (*coût*) meet; (accepter) come to terms with, accept.

assurance /asyRãs/ *nf* (self-) assurance; (garantie) assurance; (contrat) insurance; **~s sociales** social insurance; **~ automobile/maladie** car/health insurance.

assuré, **~e** /asyRe/ *adj* certain, assured; (sûr de soi) confident, assured. ● *nm,f* insured party.

assurer /asyRe/ [1] *vt* ensure; (fournir) provide; (exécuter) carry out; (Comm) insure; (stabiliser) steady; (*frontières*) make secure; **~ à qn que** assure sb that; **~ qn de** assure sb of; **~ la gestion/défense de** manage/defend. □ **s'~** *vpr* take out insurance; **s'~ de/que** make sure of/ that; **s'~ qch** (se procurer) secure sth. **assureur** *nm* insurer.

astérisque /asteRisk/ *nm* asterisk.

asthmatique /asmatik/ *a & nmf* asthmatic.

asthme /asm/ *nm* asthma.

asticot /astiko/ *nm* maggot.

astreindre /astʀɛ̃dʀ/ [22] *vt* ~ qn à qch force sth on sb; ~ qn à faire force sb to do.

astrologie /astʀɔlɔʒi/ *nf* astrology. **astrologue** *nmf* astrologer.

astronaute /astʀɔnot/ *nmf* astronaut.

astronomie /astʀɔnɔmi/ *nf* astronomy.

astuce /astys/ *nf* smartness; (truc) trick; (plaisanterie) wisecrack.

astucieux, -ieuse /astysjø, -z/ *adj* smart, clever.

atelier /atəlje/ *nm* (local) workshop; (de peintre) studio; (séance de travail) workshop.

athée /ate/ *nmf* atheist. ● *adj* atheistic.

athlète /atlɛt/ *nmf* athlete. **athlétisme** *nm* athletics.

Atlantique /atlɑ̃tik/ *nm* Atlantic (Ocean).

atmosphère /atmɔsfɛʀ/ *nf* atmosphere.

atomique /atɔmik/ *adj* atomic; (énergie, centrale) nuclear.

atomiseur /atɔmizœʀ/ *nm* spray.

atout /atu/ *nm* trump (card); (avantage) asset.

atroce /atʀɔs/ *adj* atrocious.

attabler (s') /(s)atable/ [1] *vpr* sit down at table.

attachant, ~e /ataʃɑ̃, -t/ *adj* charming.

attache /ataʃ/ *nf* (agrafe) fastener; (lien) tie.

attaché, ~e /ataʃe/ *adj* être ~ à (aimer) be attached to. ● *nm,f* (Pol) attaché.

attacher /ataʃe/ [1] *vt* tie (up); (ceinture, robe) fasten; (bicyclette) lock; ~ à (attribuer à) attach to. ● *vi* (Culin) stick. □ **s'~** *vpr* fasten, do up; **s'~ à** (se lier à) become attached to; (se consacrer à) apply oneself to.

attaquant, ~e /atakɑ̃, -t/ *nm,f* attacker; (au football) striker; (au football américain) forward.

attaque /atak/ *nf* attack; ~ (cérébrale) stroke; **il va en faire une**

~ he'll have a fit; ~ **à main armée** armed attack.

attaquer /atake/ [1] *vt* attack; (banque) raid. ● *vi* attack. □ **s'~ à** *vpr* attack; (problème, sujet) tackle.

attardé, ~e /ataʀde/ *adj* backward; (idées) outdated; (en retard) late.

attarder (s') /(s)ataʀde/ [1] *vpr* linger.

atteindre /atɛ̃dʀ/ [22] *vt* reach; (blesser) hit; (affecter) affect.

atteint, ~e /atɛ̃, -t/ *adj* ~ **de** suffering from.

atteinte /atɛ̃t/ *nf* attack (à on); **porter ~ à** attack; (droit) infringe.

atteler /atle/ [38] *vt* (cheval) harness; (remorque) couple. □ **s'~ à** *vpr* get down to.

attelle /atɛl/ *nf* splint.

attenant, ~e /atnɑ̃, -t/ *adj* ~ **(à)** adjoining.

attendant: **en ~** /ɑ̃natɑ̃dɑ̃/ *loc* meanwhile.

attendre /atɑ̃dʀ/ [3] *vt* wait for; (bébé) expect; (être le sort de) await; (escompter) expect; ~ **que qn fasse** wait for sb to do. ● *vi* wait; (au téléphone) hold. □ **s'~ à** *vpr* expect.

attendrir /atɑ̃dʀiʀ/ [2] *vt* move (to pity). □ **s'~** *vpr* be moved to pity.

attendu¹ /atɑ̃dy/ *prép* given, considering; ~ **que** considering that.

attendu², ~e /atɑ̃dy/ *adj* (escompté) expected; (espéré) long-awaited.

attentat /atɑ̃ta/ *nm* assassination attempt; ~ **(à la bombe)** (bomb) attack.

attente /atɑ̃t/ *nf* wait(ing); (espoir) expectations (+ pl).

attenter /atɑ̃te/ [1] *vi* ~ **à** make an attempt on; (fig) violate.

attentif, -ive /atɑ̃tif, -v/ *adj* attentive; (scrupuleux) careful; ~ **à** mindful of; (soucieux) careful of.

attention /atɑ̃sjɔ̃/ *nf* attention; (soin) care; ~ **(à)!** watch out (for)!; **faire ~ à** (écouter) pay attention to; (prendre garde à) watch out for; (prendre soin de) take care of; **faire ~ à faire** be careful to do. **attentionné, ~e** *adj* considerate.

attentisme /atɑ̃tism/ *nm* wait-and-see policy.

atténuer /atenɥe/ [1] *vt* (*violence*) reduce; (*critique*) tone down; (*douleur*) ease; (*faute*) mitigate. □ **s'~** *vpr* subside.

atterrir /ateʀiʀ/ [2] *vi* land. **atterrissage** *nm* landing.

attestation /atɛstasjɔ̃/ *nf* certificate.

attester /atɛste/ [1] *vt* testify to; ~ **que** testify that.

attirant, **~e** /atiʀɑ̃, -t/ *adj* attractive.

attirer /atiʀe/ [1] *vt* draw, attract; (*causer*) bring. □ **s'~** *vpr* bring upon oneself; (*amis*) win.

attiser /atize/ [1] *vt* (*feu*) poke; (*sentiment*) stir up.

attitré, **~e** /atitʀe/ *adj* accredited; (*habituel*) usual, regular.

attitude /atityd/ *nf* attitude; (*maintien*) bearing.

attraction /atʀaksjɔ̃/ *nf* attraction.

attrait /atʀɛ/ *nm* attraction.

attraper /atʀape/ [1] *vt* catch; (*corde, main*) catch hold of; (*habitude, accent*) pick up; (*maladie*) catch; **se faire ~** 🔢 get told off.

attrayant, **~e** /atʀɛjɑ̃, -t/ *adj* attractive.

attribuer /atʀibɥe/ [1] *vt* allocate; (*prix*) award; (imputer) attribute. □ **s'~** *vpr* claim (for oneself). **attribution** *nf* awarding, allocation.

attrouper (**s'**) /(s)atʀupe/ [1] *vpr* gather.

au /o/ ⇨À.

aubaine /obɛn/ *nf* godsend, opportunity.

aube /ob/ *nf* dawn, daybreak.

auberge /obɛʀʒ/ *nf* inn; ~ **de jeunesse** youth hostel.

aubergine /obɛʀʒin/ *nf* aubergine; (US) eggplant.

aucun, **~e** /okœ̃, okyn/ *adj* (dans une phrase négative) no, not any; (positif) any. ● *pron* (dans une phrase négative) none, not any; (positif) any; ~ **des deux** neither of the two; **d'~s** some. **aucunement** *adv* not at all, in no way.

audace /odas/ *nf* daring; (impudence) audacity.

audacieux, **-ieuse** /odasjø, -z/ *adj* daring.

au-delà /od(ə)la/ *adv* beyond. ● *prép* ~ **de** beyond.

au-dessous /od(ə)su/ *adv* below. ● *prép* ~ **de** below; (couvert par) under.

au-dessus /od(ə)sy/ *adv* above. ● *prép* ~ **de** above.

au-devant /od(ə)vɑ̃/ *prép* aller ~ **de qn** go to meet sb; **aller ~ des désirs de qn** anticipate sb's wishes.

audience /odjɑ̃s/ *nf* audience; (d'un tribunal) hearing; (succès, attention) success.

audimat® /odimat/ *nm* l'~ the TV ratings.

audiovisuel, **~le** /odjɔvizɥɛl/ *adj* audio-visual.

auditeur, **-trice** /oditœʀ, -tʀis/ *nm,f* listener.

audition /odisjɔ̃/ *nf* hearing; (Théât, Mus) audition.

auditoire /oditwaʀ/ *nm* audience.

augmentation /ogmɑ̃tasjɔ̃/ *nf* increase; ~ **(de salaire)** (pay) rise; (US) raise.

augmenter /ogmɑ̃te/ [1] *vt/i* increase; (*employé*) give a pay rise *ou* raise to.

augure /ogyʀ/ *nm* (devin) oracle; **être de bon/mauvais ~** be a good/bad sign.

aujourd'hui /oʒuʀdɥi/ *adv* today.

auparavant /opaʀavɑ̃/ *adv* (avant) before; (précédemment) previously; (en premier lieu) beforehand.

auprès /opʀɛ/ *prép* ~ **de** (à côté de) beside, next to; (comparé à) compared with; **s'excuser/se plaindre ~ de** apologize/complain to.

auquel /okɛl/ ⇨LEQUEL.

aura, **aurait** /ɔʀa, ɔʀɛ/ ⇨AVOIR [5].

aurore /ɔʀɔʀ/ *nf* dawn.

aussi /osi/ *adv* (également) too, also, as well; (dans une comparaison) as; (si, tellement) so; ~ **bien que** as well as. ● *conj* (donc) so, consequently.

aussitôt /osito/ *adv* immediately; ~ **que** as soon as, the moment; ~ **arrivé** as soon as he arrived.

austère /ostɛʀ/ *adj* austere.

Australie /ɔstʀali/ *nf* Australia.

australien, **∼ne** /ɔstʁaljɛ̃, -ɛn/ *adj* Australian. **A∼**, **∼ne** *nm, f* Australian.

autant /otɑ̃/ *adv* (*travailler, manger*) as much (**que** as); **∼** (**de**) (quantité) as much (**que** as); (nombre) as many (**que** as); (tant) so much, so many; **∼ faire** one had better do; **d'∼ plus que** all the more than; **en faire ∼** do the same; **pour ∼** for all that.

autel /otɛl/ *nm* altar.

auteur /otœʁ/ *nm* author; **l'∼ du crime** the perpetrator of the crime.

authentifier /otɑ̃tifje/ [45] *vt* authenticate.

authentique /otɑ̃tik/ *adj* authentic.

auto /oto/ *nf* car; **∼ tamponneuse** dodgem, bumper car.

autobus /otɔbys/ *nm* bus.

autocar /otɔkaʁ/ *nm* coach.

autochtone /otɔktɔn/ *nmf* native.

autocollant, **∼e** /otɔkɔlɑ̃, -t/ *adj* self-adhesive. ● *nm* sticker.

autodidacte /otɔdidakt/ *nmf* self-taught person.

auto-école (*pl* **∼s**) /otɔekɔl/ *nf* driving school.

automate /otɔmat/ *nm* automaton, robot.

automatique /otɔmatik/ *adj* automatic.

automatisation /otɔmatizasjɔ̃/ *nf* automation.

automne /otɔn/ *nm* autumn; (US) fall.

automobile /otɔmɔbil/ *adj* motor, car; (US) automobile. ● *nf* (motor) car; **l'∼** the motor industry; (Sport) motoring. **automobiliste** *nmf* motorist.

autonome /otɔnɔm/ *adj* autonomous; (Ordinat) stand-alone.

autoradio /otɔʁadjo/ *nm* car radio.

autorisation /otɔʁizasjɔ̃/ *nf* permission, authorization; (permis) permit.

autorisé, **∼e** /otɔʁize/ *adj* (*opinions*) authoritative; (approuvé) authorized.

autoriser /otɔʁize/ [1] *vt* authorize, permit; (rendre possible) allow (of);

(donner un droit) **∼ qn à faire** entitle sb to do.

autoritaire /otɔʁitɛʁ/ *adj* authoritarian.

autorité /otɔʁite/ *nf* authority; **faire ∼** be authoritative.

autoroute /otɔʁut/ *nf* motorway; (US) highway; **∼ de l'information** (Ordinat) information superhighway.

auto-stop /otɔstɔp/ *nm* hitch-hiking; **faire de l'∼** hitch-hike; **prendre qn en ∼** give a lift to sb.

autour /otuʁ/ *adv* around; **tout ∼** all around. ● *prép* **∼ de** around.

autre /otʁ/ *adj* other; **un ∼ jour/livre** another day/book; **∼ chose/part** something/somewhere else; **quelqu'un/rien d'∼** somebody/ nothing else; **quoi d'∼?** what else?; **d'∼ part** on the other hand; (de plus) moreover, besides; **vous ∼s Anglais** you English. ● *pron* **un ∼**, **une ∼** another (one); **l'∼** the other (one); **les ∼s** the others; (autrui) others; **d'∼s** (some) others; **l'un l'∼** each other; **l'un et l'∼** both of them; **d'un jour à l'∼** (bientôt) any day now; **entre ∼s** among other things.

autrefois /otʁəfwa/ *adv* in the past; (précédemment) formerly.

autrement /otʁəmɑ̃/ *adv* differently; (sinon) otherwise; (plus 🗓) far more; **∼ dit** in other words.

Autriche /otʁiʃ/ *nf* Austria.

autrichien, **∼ne** /otʁiʃjɛ̃, -jɛn/ *adj* Austrian. **A∼**, **∼ne** *nm, f* Austrian.

autruche /otʁyʃ/ *nf* ostrich.

autrui /otʁɥi/ *pron* others, other people.

aux /o/ ⇨ À.

auxiliaire /oksiljɛʁ/ *adj* auxiliary. ● *nmf* (assistant) auxiliary. ● *nm* (Gram) auxiliary.

auxquels, **-quelles** /okɛl/ ⇨LEQUEL.

aval: **en ∼** /ɑ̃naval/ *loc* downstream.

avaler /avale/ [1] *vt* swallow.

avance /avɑ̃s/ *nf* advance; (sur un concurrent) lead; **∼** (**de fonds**) advance; **à l'∼** in advance; **d'∼** already; **en ∼** early; (*montre*) fast; **en ∼** (**sur**) (menant) ahead (of).

avancement /avɑ̃smɑ̃/ *nm* promotion.

avancé, **~e** /avɑ̃se/ *adj* advanced.

avancer /avɑ̃se/ [10] *vi* move forward, advance; (*travail*) make progress; (*montre*) be fast; (faire saillie) jut out. ● *vt* move forward; (dans le temps) bring forward; (*argent*) advance; (*montre*) put forward. □ **s'~** *vpr* move forward, advance; (se hasarder) commit oneself.

avant /avɑ̃/ *nm* front; (Sport) forward. ● *a inv* front. ● *prép* before; **~ de faire** before doing; **en ~ de** in front of; **~ peu** shortly; **~ tout** above all. ● *adv* (dans le temps) before, beforehand; (d'abord) first; **en ~** (dans l'espace) forward(s); (dans le temps) ahead; **le bus d'~** the previous bus. ● *conj* **~ que** before; **~ qu'il (ne) fasse** before he does.

avantage /avɑ̃taʒ/ *nm* advantage; (Comm) benefit.

avantager /avɑ̃taʒe/ [40] *vt* favour; (embellir) show off to advantage.

avantageux, **-euse** /avɑ̃taʒø, -z/ *adj* advantageous, favourable; (*prix*) attractive.

avant-bras /avɑ̃bʀa/ *nm inv* forearm.

avant-centre (*pl* **avants-centres**) /avɑ̃sɑ̃tʀ/ *nm* centre forward.

avant-coureur (*pl* **~s**) /avɑ̃kuʀœʀ/ *adj* precursory, foreshadowing.

avant-dernier, **-ière** (*pl* **~s**) /avɑ̃dɛʀnje, -jɛʀ/ *a & nm,f* last but one.

avant-goût (*pl* **~s**) /avɑ̃gu/ *nm* foretaste.

avant-hier /avɑ̃tjɛʀ/ *adv* the day before yesterday.

avant-poste (*pl* **~s**) /avɑ̃pɔst/ *nm* outpost.

avant-première (*pl* **~s**) /avɑ̃pʀəmjɛʀ/ *nf* preview.

avant-propos /avɑ̃pʀɔpo/ *nm inv* foreword.

avare /avaʀ/ *adj* miserly; **~ de** sparing with. ● *nmf* miser.

avarié, **~e** /avaʀje/ *adj* (*aliment*) spoiled.

avatar /avataʀ/ *nm* misfortune.

avec /avɛk/ *prép* with. ● *adv* 🆃 with it *ou* them.

avènement /avɛnmɑ̃/ *nm* advent; (d'un roi) accession.

avenir /avniʀ/ *nm* future; **à l'~** in future; **d'~** with (future) prospects.

aventure /avɑ̃tyʀ/ *nf* adventure; (sentimentale) affair. **aventureux**, **-euse** *adj* adventurous; (hasardeux) risky.

avérer (**s'**) /(s)aveʀe/ [14] *vpr* prove (to be).

averse /avɛʀs/ *nf* shower.

avertir /avɛʀtiʀ/ [2] *vt* inform; (mettre en garde, menacer) warn. **avertissement** *nm* warning.

avertisseur /avɛʀtisœʀ/ *nm* alarm; (Auto) horn; **~ d'incendie** fire-alarm; **~ lumineux** warning light.

aveu (*pl* **~x**) /avø/ *nm* confession; **de l'~ de** by the admission of.

aveugle /avœgl/ *adj* blind. ● *nmf* blind man, blind woman.

aviateur, **-trice** /avjatœʀ, -tʀis/ *nm,f* aviator.

aviation /avjasjɔ̃/ *nf* flying; (industrie) aviation; (Mil) air force.

avide /avid/ *adj* greedy (**de** for); (anxieux) eager (**de** for); **~ de faire** eager to do.

avion /avjɔ̃/ *nm* plane, aeroplane, aircraft; (US) airplane; **~ à réaction** jet.

aviron /aviʀɔ̃/ *nm* oar; **l'~** (Sport) rowing.

avis /avi/ *nm* opinion; (conseil) advice; (renseignement) notification; (Comm) advice; **à mon ~** in my opinion; **changer d'~** change one's mind; **être d'~ que** be of the opinion that; **~ au lecteur** foreword.

avisé, **~e** /avize/ *adj* sensible; **être bien/mal ~ de** be well-/ill-advised to.

aviser /avize/ [1] *vt* advise, notify. ● *vi* decide what to do. □ **s'~ de** *vpr* suddenly realize; **s'~ de faire** take it into one's head to do.

avocat, **~e** /avɔka, -t/ *nm,f* barrister; (US) attorney; (fig) advocate; **~ de la défense** counsel for the defence. ● *nm* (fruit) avocado (pear).

avoine /avwan/ *nf* oats (+ *pl*).

avoir /avwaʀ/ [5]

● *verbe auxiliaire*

····➤ have; **il nous a appelés hier** he called us yesterday.

● *verbe transitif*

····➤ (possession) have (got).

····➤ (obtenir) get; (au téléphone) get through to.

····➤ (duper) 🔲 have; **on m'a eu!** I've been had!

····➤ ~ **chaud/faim** be hot/hungry.

····➤ ~ **dix ans** be ten years old.

● **avoir à** *verbe + préposition*

····➤ to have to; **j'ai beaucoup à faire** I have a lot to do; **tu n'as qu'à leur écrire** all you have to do is write to them.

● **en avoir pour** *verbe + préposition*

····➤ **j'en ai pour une minute** I will only be a minute; **j'en ai eu pour 100 francs** it cost me 100 francs.

● **il y a** *verbe impersonnel*

····➤ there is; (pluriel) there are; **qu'est-ce qu'il y a?** what's the matter?; **il est venu il y a cinq ans** he came here five years ago; **il y a au moins 5 km jusqu'à la gare** it's at least 5 km to the station.

● *nom masculin*

····➤ (dans un magasin) credit note.

····➤ (biens) asset (+ *pl*).

avortement /avɔʀtəmɑ̃/ *nm* (Méd) abortion.

avorter /avɔʀte/ [1] *vi* (*projet*) abort; (**se faire**) ~ have an abortion.

avoué, ~**e** /avwe/ *adj* avowed. ● *nm* solicitor; (US) attorney.

avouer /avwe/ [1] *vt* (*amour, ignorance*) confess; (*crime*) confess to, admit. ● *vi* confess.

avril /avʀil/ *nm* April.

axe /aks/ *nm* axis; (essieu) axle; (d'une politique) main line(s), basis; ~ (routier) main road.

ayant /ɛjɑ̃/ ⇒AVOIR [5].

azote /azɔt/ *nm* nitrogen.

azur /azyʀ/ *nm* sky-blue.

Bb

baba /baba/ *nm* ~ (**au rhum**) (rum) baba; **en rester** ~ 🔲 be flabbergasted.

babillard /babijaʀ/ *nm* ~ **électronique** (Internet) bulletin board system, BBS.

babines /babin/ *nfpl* **se lécher les** ~ lick one's chops.

babiole /babjɔl/ *nf* trinket.

bâbord /babɔʀ/ *nm* port (side).

baby-foot /babifut/ *nm inv* table football.

bac /bak/ *nm* (Scol) ⇒BACCALAURÉAT; (bateau) ferry; (récipient) tub; (plus petit) tray.

baccalauréat /bakalɔʀea/ *nm* school leaving certificate.

bâche /baʃ/ *nf* tarpaulin.

bachelier, -ière /baʃəlje, -jɛʀ/ *nm,f* holder of the *baccalauréat*.

bachoter /baʃote/ [1] *vi* cram (for an exam).

bâcler /bakle/ [1] *vt* botch (up).

bactérie /bakteʀi/ *nf* bacterium; ~**s** bacteria.

badaud, ~**e** /bado, -d/ *nm,f* onlooker.

badigeonner /badiʒɔne/ [1] *vt* whitewash; (barbouiller) daub.

badiner /badine/ [1] *vi* banter.

baffe /baf/ *nf* 🔲 slap.

baffle /bafl/ *nm* speaker.

bafouiller /bafuje/ [1] *vt/i* stammer.

bagage /bagaʒ/ *nm* bag; (connaissances) knowledge; ~**s** luggage; ~ **à main** hand luggage.

bagarre /bagaʀ/ *nf* fight.

bagatelle /bagatɛl/ *nf* trifle; (somme) trifling amount.

bagnard /baɲaʀ/ *nm* convict.

bagnole /baɲɔl/ *nf* 🔲 car.

bague /bag/ *nf* (bijou) ring.

baguette /bagɛt/ *nf* stick; (de chef d'orchestre) baton; (chinoise) chopstick; (pain) baguette; ～ **magique** magic wand; ～ **de tambour** drumstick.

baie /bɛ/ *nf* (Géog) bay; (fruit) berry; ～ (vitrée) picture window; (Ordinat) bay.

baignade /bɛɲad/ *nf* swimming.

baigner /beɲe/ [1] *vt* bathe; (*enfant*) bath. ● *vi* ～ **dans l'huile** swim in grease. □ **se** ～ *vpr* have a swim. **baigneur, -euse** *nm, f* swimmer.

baignoire /beɲwaʀ/ *nf* bath(tub).

bail (*pl* **baux**) /baj, bo/ *nm* lease.

bâiller /baje/ [1] *vi* yawn; (être ouvert) gape.

bailleur /bajœʀ/ *nm* ～ **de fonds** (Comm) sleeping partner.

bain /bɛ̃/ *nm* bath; (baignade) swim; **prendre un** ～ **de soleil** sunbathe; ～ **de bouche** mouthwash; **être dans le** ～ (fig) be in the swing of things; **se remettre dans le** ～ get back into the swing of things; **prendre un** ～ **de foule** mingle with the crowd.

bain-marie (*pl* **bains-marie**) /bɛ̃maʀi/ *nm* double boiler.

baiser /beze/ [1] *vt* (*main*) kiss; ⊠ screw ⊠. ● *nm* kiss.

baisse /bɛs/ *nf* fall, drop; **être en** ～ be going down.

baisser /bese/ [1] *vt* lower; (*radio, lampe*) turn down. ● *vi* (*niveau*) go down, fall; (*santé, forces*) fail. □ **se** ～ *vpr* bend down.

bal (*pl* ～**s**) /bal/ *nm* dance; (habillé) ball; (lieu) dance-hall; ～ **costumé** fancy-dress ball.

balade /balad/ *nf* stroll; (en auto) drive.

balader /balade/ [1] *vt* take for a stroll. □ **se** ～ *vpr* (à pied) (go for a) stroll; (en voiture) go for a drive; (voyager) travel.

baladeur /baladœʀ/ *nm* personal stereo.

balafre /balafʀ/ *nf* gash; (cicatrice) scar.

balai /balɛ/ *nm* broom.

balance /balɑ̃s/ *nf* scales (+ *pl*); **la B**～ Libra.

balancer /balɑ̃se/ [10] *vt* swing; (doucement) sway; (lancer ⊞) chuck ⊞; (se débarrasser de ⊞) chuck out ⊞.

● *vi* sway. □ **se** ～ *vpr* swing; sway; **s'en** ～ ⊞ not to give a damn ⊞.

balancier /balɑ̃sje/ *nm* (d'horloge) pendulum; (d'équilibriste) pole.

balançoire /balɑ̃swaʀ/ *nf* swing.

balayage /baleja3/ *nm* sweeping; (cheveux) highlights.

balayer /baleje/ [31] *vt* sweep (up); (*vent*) sweep away; (se débarrasser de) sweep aside.

balbutiement /balbysimɑ̃/ *nm* stammering; **les** ～**s** (fig) the first steps.

balcon /balkɔ̃/ *nm* balcony; (Théât) dress circle.

baleine /balɛn/ *nf* whale.

balise /baliz/ *nf* beacon; (bouée) buoy; (Auto) (road) sign. **baliser** [1] *vt* mark out (with beacons); (*route*) signpost; (*sentier*) mark out.

balivernes /balivɛʀn/ *nfpl* nonsense.

ballant, ～e /balɑ̃, -t/ *adj* dangling.

balle /bal/ *nf* (projectile) bullet; (Sport) ball; (paquet) bale.

ballerine /balʀin/ *nf* (danseuse) ballerina; (chaussure) ballet pump.

ballet /balɛ/ *nm* ballet.

ballon /balɔ̃/ *nm* (Sport) ball; ～ (de baudruche) balloon; ～ **de football** football.

ballonné, ～e /balɔne/ *adj* bloated.

balnéaire /balneɛʀ/ *adj* seaside.

balourd, ～e /baluʀ, -d/ *nm, f* oaf. ● *adj* uncouth.

balustrade /balystʀad/ *nf* railing.

ban /bɑ̃/ *nm* round of applause; ～**s** (de mariage) banns; **mettre au** ～ **de** cast out from.

banal, ～e (*mpl* ～**s**) /banal/ *adj* commonplace, banal.

banane /banan/ *nf* banana.

banc /bɑ̃/ *nm* bench; (de poissons) shoal; ～ **des accusés** dock; ～ **d'essai** (test) testing ground.

bancaire /bɑ̃kɛʀ/ *adj* (*secteur*) banking; (*chèque*) bank.

bancal, ～e (*mpl* ～**s**) /bɑ̃kal/ *adj* wobbly; (*solution*) shaky.

bande /bɑ̃d/ *nf* (groupe) gang; (de papier) strip; (rayure) stripe; (de film) reel; (pansement) bandage; ～ **dessinée**

comic strip; ∼ **(magnétique)** tape; ∼ **sonore** sound-track.

bande-annonce (*pl* **bandes-annonces**) /bɑ̃danɔ̃s/ *nf* trailer.

bandeau (*pl* ∼**x**) /bɑ̃do/ *nm* headband; (sur les yeux) blindfold.

bander /bɑ̃de/ [1] *vt* bandage; (*arc*) bend; (*muscle*) tense; ∼ **les yeux à** blindfold.

banderole /bɑ̃dʀɔl/ *nf* banner.

bandit /bɑ̃di/ *nm* bandit. **banditisme** *nm* crime.

bandoulière: **en** ∼ /ɑ̃bɑ̃duljɛʀ/ *loc* across one's shoulder.

banlieue /bɑ̃ljø/ *nf* suburbs; **de** ∼ suburban. **banlieusard**, ∼**e** *nm,f* (suburban) commuter.

bannir /baniʀ/ [2] *vt* banish.

banque /bɑ̃k/ *nf* bank; (activité) banking; ∼ **de données** databank.

banqueroute /bɑ̃kʀut/ *nf* bankruptcy.

banquet /bɑ̃kɛ/ *nm* banquet.

banquette /bɑ̃kɛt/ *nf* seat.

banquier, -ière /bɑ̃kje, -jɛʀ/ *nm,f* banker.

baptême /batɛm/ *nm* baptism, christening. **baptiser** [1] *vt* baptize, christen; (nommer) call.

bar /baʀ/ *nm* (lieu) bar.

baragouiner /baʀagwine/ [1] *vt/i* gabble; (*langue*) speak a few words of.

baraque /baʀak/ *nf* hut, shed; (maison 🄵) house.

baratin /baʀatɛ̃/ *nm* 🄵 sweet *ou* smooth talk.

barbare /baʀbaʀ/ *adj* barbaric. ● *nmf* barbarian.

barbe /baʀb/ *nf* beard; ∼ **à papa** candy-floss; (US) cotton candy; **quelle** ∼**!** 🄵 what a drag! 🄵.

barbelé /baʀbəle/ *adj* **fil** ∼ barbed wire.

barber /baʀbe/ [1] *vt* 🄵 bore.

barboter /baʀbɔte/ [1] *vi* (dans l'eau) paddle, splash. ● *vt* (voler 🄵) pinch.

barbouiller /baʀbuje/ [1] *vt* (souiller) smear (de with); **tu es tout barbouillé** your face is all dirty; **être barbouillé** feel queasy.

barbu, ∼**e** /baʀby/ *adj* bearded.

barème /baʀɛm/ *nm* list, table; (échelle) scale.

baril /baʀil/ *nm* barrel; (de poudre) keg.

bariolé, ∼**e** /baʀjɔle/ *adj* multicoloured.

baromètre /baʀɔmɛtʀ/ *nm* barometer.

baron, ∼**ne** /baʀɔ̃, -ɔn/ *nm,f* baron, baroness.

barque /baʀk/ *nf* (small) boat.

barrage /baʀaʒ/ *nm* dam; (sur route) roadblock.

barre /baʀ/ *nf* bar; (trait) line, stroke; (Naut) helm; ∼ **de boutons** (Ordinat) toolbar.

barreau (*pl* ∼**x**) /baʀo/ *nm* bar; (d'échelle) rung; **le** ∼ (Jur) the bar.

barrer /baʀe/ [1] *vt* block; (*porte*) bar; (rayer) cross out; (Naut) steer. □ **se** ∼ *vpr* 🄵 leave.

barrette /baʀɛt/ *nf* (hair) slide.

barrière /baʀjɛʀ/ *nf* (porte) gate; (clôture) fence; (obstacle) barrier.

bar-tabac (*pl* **bars-tabac**) /baʀtaba/ *nm* café (*selling stamps and cigarettes*).

bas, basse /bɑ, bɑs/ *adj* (*niveau, table*) low; (*action*) base; **au** ∼ **mot** at the lowest estimate; **en** ∼ **âge** young; ∼ **morceaux** (viande) cheap cuts. ● *nm* bottom; (chaussette) stocking; ∼ **de laine** (fig) nest-egg. ● *adv* low; **en** ∼ down below; (dans une maison) downstairs; **en** ∼ **de la page** at the bottom of the page; **plus** ∼ further *ou* lower down; **mettre** ∼ give birth (to). **bas de casse** *nm inv* lower case. **bas-côté** (*pl* ∼**s**) *nm* (de route) verge; (US) shoulder.

bascule /baskyl/ *nf* (balance) scales (+ *pl*); **cheval/fauteuil à** ∼ rocking-horse/-chair.

basculer /baskyle/ [1] *vi* topple over; (benne) tip up.

base /bɑz/ *nf* base; (fondement) basis; (Pol) rank and file; **de** ∼ basic. **base de données** *nf* data-base.

baser /bɑze/ [1] *vt* base. □ **se** ∼ **sur** *vpr* go by.

bas-fonds /bɑfɔ̃/ *nmpl* (eau) shallows; (fig) dregs.

basilic /bazilik/ *nm* basil.

basilique /bazilik/ *nf* basilica.

basque /bask/ *adj* Basque. **B∼** *nmf* Basque.

basse /bɑs/ ⇒BAS.

basse-cour (*pl* **basses-cours**) /baskuʀ/ *nf* farmyard.

bassesse /bases/ *nf* baseness; (*action*) base act.

bassin /basɛ̃/ *nm* (pièce d'eau) pond; (de piscine) pool; (Géog) basin; (Anat) pelvis; (plat) bowl; ∼ **houiller** coalfield.

bassine /basin/ *nf* bowl.

basson /basɔ̃/ *nm* bassoon.

bas-ventre (*pl* ∼**s**) /bavɑ̃tʀ/ *nm* lower abdomen.

bat /ba/ ⇒BATTRE [11].

bataille /batɑj/ *nf* battle; (fig) fight.

bâtard, ∼e /bɑtaʀ, -d/ *adj* (solution) hybrid. ● *nm, f* bastard.

bateau (*pl* ∼**x**) /bato/ *nm* boat; ∼ **pneumatique** rubber dinghy. **bateau-mouche** (*pl* **bateaux-mouches**) *nm* sightseeing boat.

bâti, ∼e /bɑti/ *adj* **bien** ∼ well-built.

bâtiment /bɑtimɑ̃/ *nm* building; (industrie) building trade; (navire) vessel.

bâtir /bɑtiʀ/ [2] *vt* build.

bâton /bɑtɔ̃/ *nm* stick; **conversation à** ∼**s rompus** rambling conversation; ∼ **de rouge** lipstick.

battant /batɑ̃/ *nm* (vantail) flap; **porte à deux** ∼**s** double door.

battement /batmɑ̃/ *nm* (de cœur) beat(ing); (temps) interval; (Mus) beat.

batterie /batʀi/ *nf* (Mil, Électr) battery; (Mus) drums; ∼ **de cuisine** pots and pans.

batteur /batœʀ/ *nm* (Mus) drummer; (Culin) whisk.

battre /batʀ/ [11] *vt/i* beat; (cartes) shuffle; (Culin) whisk; (l'emporter sur) beat; ∼ **des ailes** flap its wings; ∼ **des mains** clap; ∼ **des paupières** blink; ∼ **en retraite** beat a retreat; ∼ **la semelle** stamp one's feet; ∼ **son plein** be in full swing. □ **se** ∼ *vpr* fight.

baume /bom/ *nm* balm.

bavard, ∼e /bavaʀ, -d/ *adj* talkative. ● *nm, f* chatterbox.

bavardage /bavaʀdaʒ/ *nm* chatter, gossip. **bavarder** [1] *vi* chat; (jacasser) chatter, gossip.

bave /bav/ *nf* dribble, slobber; (de limace) slime. **baver** [1] *vi* dribble, slobber. **baveux, -euse** *adj* dribbling; (omelette) runny.

bavoir /bavwaʀ/ *nm* bib.

bavure /bavyʀ/ *nf* smudge; (erreur) blunder; ∼ **policière** police blunder.

bazar /bazaʀ/ *nm* bazaar; (objets 🔢) clutter.

BCBG *abrév mf* (**bon chic bon genre**). posh.

BD *abrév f* (**bande dessinée**) comic strip.

béant, ∼e /beɑ̃, -t/ *adj* gaping.

béat, ∼e /bea, -t/ *adj* (hum) blissful; ∼ **d'admiration** wide-eyed with admiration.

beau (**bel** *before vowel or mute h*), **belle** (*mpl* ∼**x**) /bo, bɛl/ *adj* beautiful; (femme) beautiful; (homme) handsome; (temps) fine, nice. ● *nm* beauty. ● *adv* **il fait** ∼ the weather is nice; **au** ∼ **milieu** right in the middle; **bel et bien** well and truly; **de plus belle** more than ever; **faire le** ∼ sit up and beg; **on a** ∼ **essayer/insister** however much one tries/insists.

beaucoup /boku/ *adv* a lot, very much; ∼ **de** (nombre) many; (quantité) a lot of; **pas** ∼ (**de**) not many; (quantité) not much; ∼ **plus/mieux** much more/better; ∼ **trop** far too much; **de** ∼ by far.

beau-fils (*pl* **beaux-fils**) /bofis/ *nm* (remariage) stepson.

beau-frère (*pl* **beaux-frères**) /bofʀeʀ/ *nm* brother-in-law.

beau-père (*pl* **beaux-pères**) /bopeʀ/ *nm* father-in-law; (remariage) stepfather.

beauté /bote/ *nf* beauty; **finir en** ∼ end magnificently.

beaux-arts /bozaʀ/ *nmpl* fine arts.

beaux-parents /bopaʀɑ̃/ *nmpl* parents-in-law.

bébé /bebe/ *nm* baby. **bébé-éprouvette** (*pl* **bébés-éprouvette**) *nm* test-tube baby.

bec /bɛk/ *nm* beak; (de théière) spout; (de casserole) lip; (bouche 🔲) mouth; ∼ de gaz gas street-lamp.

bécane /bekan/ *nf* 🔲 bike.

bêche /bɛʃ/ *nf* spade.

bégayer /begeje/ [31] *vt/i* stammer.

bègue /bɛg/ *nmf* stammerer. ● *adj* être ∼ stammer.

bégueule /begœl/ *adj* prudish.

beige /bɛʒ/ *a* & *nm* beige.

beignet /bɛɲɛ/ *nm* fritter.

bel /bɛl/ ⇒BEAU.

bêler /bele/ [1] *vi* bleat.

belette /bəlɛt/ *nf* weasel.

belge /bɛlʒ/ *adj* Belgian. **B**∼ *nmf* Belgian.

Belgique /bɛlʒik/ *nf* Belgium.

bélier /belje/ *nm* ram; le B∼ Aries.

belle /bɛl/ ⇒BEAU.

belle-fille (*pl* **belles-filles**) /bɛlfij/ *nf* daughter-in-law; (remariage) stepdaughter.

belle-mère (*pl* **belles-mères**) /bɛlmɛR/ *nf* mother-in-law; (remariage) stepmother.

belle-sœur (*pl* **belles-sœurs**) /bɛlsœR/ *nf* sister-in-law.

belliqueux, **-euse** /belikø, -z/ *adj* warlike.

bémol /bemɔl/ *nm* (Mus) flat.

bénédiction /benediksjɔ̃/ *nf* blessing.

bénéfice /benefis/ *nm* (gain) profit; (avantage) benefit.

bénéficiaire /benefisjɛR/ *nmf* beneficiary.

bénéficier /benefisje/ [45] *vi* ∼ de benefit from; (jouir de) enjoy, have.

bénéfique /benefik/ *adj* beneficial.

Bénélux /benelyks/ *nm* Benelux.

bénévole /benevɔl/ *adj* voluntary.

bénin, **-igne** /benɛ̃, -iɲ/ *adj* minor; (tumeur) benign.

bénir /beniR/ [2] *vt* bless. **bénit**, ∼**e** *adj* (eau) holy; (pain) consecrated.

benjamin, ∼**e** /bɛ̃ʒamɛ̃, -in/ *nm,f* youngest child.

benne /bɛn/ *nf* (de grue) scoop; ∼ à ordures (camion) waste disposal truck; (conteneur) skip; ∼ (**basculante**) dump truck.

béquille /bekij/ *nf* crutch; (de moto) stand.

berceau (*pl* ∼**x**) /bɛRso/ *nm* (de bébé, civilisation) cradle.

bercer /bɛRse/ [10] *vt* (balancer) rock; (apaiser) lull; (leurrer) delude.

béret /beRɛ/ *nm* beret.

berge /bɛRʒ/ *nf* (bord) bank.

berger, **-ère** /bɛRʒe, -ɛR/ *nm,f* shepherd, shepherdess.

berne: **en** ∼ /ɑ̃bɛRn/ *loc* at half-mast.

berner /bɛRne/ [1] *vt* fool.

besogne /bəzɔɲ/ *nf* task, job.

besoin /bəzwɛ̃/ *nm* need; **avoir** ∼ **de** need; **au** ∼ if need be; **dans le** ∼ in need.

bestiole /bɛstjɔl/ *nf* 🔲 bug.

bétail /betaj/ *nm* livestock.

bête /bɛt/ *adj* stupid. ● *nf* animal; ∼ **noire** pet hate; ∼ **sauvage** wild beast; **chercher la petite** ∼ be overfussy.

bêtise /betiz/ *nf* stupidity; (action) stupid thing.

béton /betɔ̃/ *nm* concrete; ∼ **armé** reinforced concrete; **en** ∼ (*mur*) concrete; (*argument* 🔲) watertight. **bétonnière** *nf* concrete mixer.

betterave /bɛtRav/ *nf* beet; ∼ **rouge** beetroot.

beugler /bøgle/ [1] *vi* bellow; (*radio*) blare out.

beur /bœR/ *nmf* & *a* 🔲 second-generation North African living in France.

beurre /bœR/ *nm* butter. **beurré**, ∼**e** *adj* buttered; 🔲 drunk. **beurrier** *nm* butter-dish.

bévue /bevy/ *nf* blunder.

biais /bjɛ/ *nm* (moyen) way; **par le** ∼ **de** by means of; **de** ∼, **en** ∼ at an angle; **regarder qn de** ∼ look sideways at sb.

bibelot /biblo/ *nm* ornament.

biberon /bibRɔ̃/ *nm* (feeding) bottle; **nourrir au** ∼ bottle-feed.

bible /bibl/ *nf* bible; **la B**∼ the Bible.

bibliographie /biblijɔgRafi/ *nf* bibliography.

bibliothécaire /biblijɔtekɛR/ *nmf* librarian.

bibliothèque /biblijɔtɛk/ *nf* library; (meuble) bookcase.

bic® /bik/ *nm* biro®.

bicarbonate /bikaʀbɔnat/ *nm* ~ (de soude) bicarbonate (of soda).

biceps /bisɛps/ *nm* biceps.

biche /biʃ/ *nf* doe; **ma** ~ darling.

bichonner /biʃɔne/ [1] *vt* pamper.

bicyclette /bisiklɛt/ *nf* bicycle.

bide /bid/ *nm* (ventre 𝕀) paunch; (échec 𝕀) flop.

bidet /bidɛ/ *nm* bidet.

bidon /bidɔ̃/ *nm* can; (plus grand) drum; (ventre 𝕀) belly; **c'est du** ~ 𝕀 it's a load of hogwash 𝕀. ● *a inv* 𝕀 phoney.

bidonville /bidɔ̃vil/ *nf* shanty town.

bidule /bidyl/ *nm* 𝕀 thing.

Biélorussie /bjelɔʀysi/ *nf* Byelorussia.

bien /bjɛ̃/ *adv* well; (très) quite, very; ~ **des** (nombre) many; **tu as** ~ **de la chance** you are very lucky; **j'aimerais** ~ I would like to; **ce n'est pas** ~ **de** it is not nice to; ~ **sûr** of course. ● *nm* good; (patrimoine) possession; ~**s de consommation** consumer goods. ● *a inv* good; (passable) all right; (en forme) well; (à l'aise) comfortable; (beau) attractive; (respectable) nice, respectable. ● *conj* ~ **que** (al-) though; ~ **que ce soit** although it is. **bien-aimé**, ~**e** *a & nm,f* beloved. **bien-être** *nm* well-being.

bienfaisance /bjɛ̃fəzɑ̃s/ *nf* charity; **fête de** ~ charity event.

bienfaisant, ~**e** *adj* beneficial.

bienfait /bjɛ̃fɛ/ *nm* (kind) favour; (avantage) beneficial effect. **bienfaiteur, -trice** *nm,f* benefactor.

bien-pensant, ~**e** /bjɛ̃pɑ̃sɑ̃, -t/ *adj* right-thinking.

bienséance /bjɛ̃seɑ̃s/ *nf* propriety.

bientôt /bjɛ̃to/ *adv* soon; **à** ~ see you soon.

bienveillance /bjɛ̃vɛjɑ̃s/ *nf* kind-(li)ness.

bienvenu, ~**e** /bjɛ̃vny/ *adj* welcome. ● *nm,f* **être le** ~, **être la** ~**e** be welcome.

bienvenue /bjɛ̃vny/ *nf* welcome; **souhaiter la** ~ **à** welcome.

bière /bjɛʀ/ *nf* beer; (cercueil) coffin; ~ **blonde** lager; ~ **brune** ≈ stout; ~ **pression** draught beer.

bifteck /biftɛk/ *nm* steak.

bifurquer /bifyʀke/ [1] *vi* branch off, fork.

bigarré, ~**e** /bigaʀe/ *adj* motley.

bigoudi /bigudi/ *nm* curler.

bijou (*pl* ~**x**) /biʒu/ *nm* jewel; ~**x en or** gold jewellery. **bijouterie** *nf* (boutique) jewellery shop; (Comm) jewellery. **bijoutier, -ière** *nm,f* jeweller.

bilan /bilɑ̃/ *nm* outcome; (d'une catastrophe) (casualty) toll; (Comm) balance sheet; **faire le** ~ **de** assess; ~ **de santé** check-up.

bile /bil/ *nf* bile; **se faire de la** ~ 𝕀 worry.

bilingue /bilɛ̃g/ *adj* bilingual.

billard /bijaʀ/ *nm* billiards (+ *pl*); (table) billiard-table.

bille /bij/ *nf* (d'enfant) marble; (de billard) billiard-ball.

billet /bijɛ/ *nm* ticket; (lettre) note; (article) column; ~ **(de banque)** (bank) note; ~ **de 50 francs** 50-franc note.

billetterie /bijɛtʀi/ *nf* cash dispenser.

billion /biljɔ̃/ *nm* billion; (US) trillion.

bimensuel, ~**e** /bimɑ̃sɥɛl/ *adj* fortnightly, bimonthly. ● *nm* fortnightly magazine.

binette /binɛt/ *nf* hoe; (visage) face; (Internet) smiley.

biochimie /bjɔʃimi/ *nf* biochemistry.

biodégradable /bjɔdegʀadabl/ *adj* biodegradable.

biographie /bjɔgʀafi/ *nf* biography.

biologie /bjɔlɔʒi/ *nf* biology. **biologique** *adj* biological; (*produit*) organic.

bis /bis/ *nm & interj* encore.

biscornu, ~**e** /biskɔʀny/ *adj* crooked; (bizarre) cranky 𝕀.

biscotte /biskɔt/ *nf* continental toast.

biscuit /biskɥi/ *nm* biscuit; (US) cookie; ~ **salé** cracker; ~ **de Savoie** sponge-cake.

bise /biz/ *nf* 𝕀 kiss; (vent) north wind.

bison /bizɔ̃/ *nm* buffalo.

bisou /bizu/ *nm* 𝕀 kiss.

bistro(t) /bistʀo/ *nm* 🔲 café, bar.

bit /bit/ *nm* (Ordinat) bit.

bitume /bitym/ *nm* asphalt.

bizarre /bizaʀ/ *adj* odd, strange. **bizzarrerie** *nf* peculiarity.

blafard, ~e /blafaʀ, -d/ *adj* pale.

blague /blag/ *nf* 🔲 joke; **sans** ~! no kidding! 🔲.

blaguer /blage/ [1] 🔲 *vi* joke.

blaireau (*pl* ~x) /blɛʀo/ *nm* shaving-brush; (animal) badger.

blâmer /blame/ [1] *vt* criticize.

blanc, **blanche** /blɑ̃, blɑ̃ʃ/ *adj* white; (*papier, page*) blank. ● *nm* white; (espace) blank; ~ **d'œuf** egg white; ~ **de poireau** white part of the leek; ~ (**de poulet**) chicken breast; **le** ~ (linge) whites; **laisser en** ~ leave blank. **B**~, **Blanche** *nm,f* white man, white woman. **blanche** *nf* (Mus) minim.

blanchiment /blɑ̃ʃimɑ̃/ *nm* (d'argent) laundering.

blanchir /blɑ̃ʃiʀ/ [2] *vt* whiten; (*personne*: fig) clear; (*argent*) launder; (Culin) blanch; ~ (**à la chaux**) whitewash. ● *vi* turn white.

blanchisserie /blɑ̃ʃisʀi/ *nf* laundry.

blason /blazɔ̃/ *nm* coat of arms.

blasphème /blasfɛm/ *nm* blasphemy.

blé /ble/ *nm* wheat.

blême /blɛm/ *adj* pallid.

blessant, ~e /blesɑ̃, -t/ *adj* hurtful.

blessé, ~e /blese/ *nm,f* casualty, injured person.

blesser /blese/ [1] *vt* injure, hurt; (par balle) wound; (offenser) hurt. □ **se** ~ *vpr* injure *ou* hurt oneself. **blessure** *nf* wound.

bleu, ~e /blø/ *adj* blue; (Culin) very rare; ~ **marine/turquoise** navy blue/turquoise; **avoir une peur** ~e be scared stiff. ● *nm* blue; (contusion) bruise; ~ (**de travail**) overalls (+ *pl*).

bleuet /bløɛ/ *nm* cornflower.

blindé, ~e /blɛ̃de/ *adj* armoured; (fig) immune (**contre** to); **porte** ~e security car. ● *nm* armoured car, tank.

blinder /blɛ̃de/ [1] *vt* armour; (fig) harden.

bloc /blɔk/ *nm* block; (de papier) pad; **serrer à** ~ tighten hard; **en** ~ (matériau) in a block; (nier) outright.

blocage /blɔkaʒ/ *nm* (des prix) freeze, freezing; (des roues) locking; (Psych) block.

bloc-notes (*pl* **blocs-notes**) /blɔknɔt/ *nm* note-pad.

blocus /blɔkys/ *nm* blockade.

blond, ~e /blɔ̃, -d/ *adj* fair, blond. ● *nm,f* fair-haired man, fair-haired woman.

bloquer /blɔke/ [1] *vt* block; (*porte, machine*) jam; (*roues*) lock; (*prix, crédits*) freeze. □ **se** ~ *vpr* jam; (*roues*) lock; (*freins*) jam; (*ordinateur*) crash; **bloqué par la neige** snowbound.

blottir (**se**) /(sə)blɔtiʀ/ [2] *vpr* snuggle, huddle (**contre** against).

blouse /bluz/ *nf* overall. **blouse blanche** *nf* white coat.

blouson /bluzɔ̃/ *nm* jacket, blouson.

bluffer /blœfe/ [1] *vt/i* bluff.

bobine /bɔbin/ *nf* (de fil, film) reel; (Électr) coil.

bobo /bobo/ *nm* 🔲 sore, cut; **avoir** ~ have a pain.

bocal (*pl* **-aux**) /bɔkal, -o/ *nm* jar.

bœuf (*pl* ~s) /bœf, bø/ *nm* bullock; (US) steer; (viande) beef; ~s oxen.

bogue /bɔg/ *nm* (Ordinat) bug.

bohème /bɔɛm/ *a & nmf* bohemian.

boire /bwaʀ/ [12] *vt/i* (*personne, plante*) drink; (*argile*) soak up; ~ **un coup** 🔲 have a drink.

bois /bwa/ ⇒BOIRE [12]. ● *nm* (matériau, forêt) wood; **de** ~, **en** ~ wooden. ● *nmpl* (de cerf) antlers.

boiseries /bwazʀi/ *nfpl* panelling.

boisson /bwasɔ̃/ *nf* drink.

boit /bwa/ ⇒BOIRE [12].

boîte /bwat/ *nf* box; (de conserves) tin, can; (entreprise 🔲) firm; **en** ~ tinned, canned; ~ **à gants** glove compartment; ~ **aux lettres** letter-box; ~ **aux lettres électronique**, **blé mailbox**; ~ **de nuit** night-club; ~ **postale** post-office box; ~ **de vitesses** gear box.

boiter /bwate/ [1] *vi* limp. **boiteux, -euse** *adj* lame; (*raisonnement*) shaky.

boîtier /bwatje/ *nm* case.

bol /bɔl/ *nm* bowl; ~ **d'air** a breath of fresh air; **avoir du** ~ 🔢 be lucky.

bolide /bɔlid/ *nm* racing car.

Bolivie /bɔlivi/ *nf* Bolivia.

bombardement /bɔ̃baʀdəmɑ̃/ *nm* bombing; shelling.

bombarder /bɔ̃baʀde/ [1] *vt* bomb; (par obus) shell; ~ **qn de** (fig) bombard sb with. **bombardier** *nm* (Aviat) bomber.

bombe /bɔ̃b/ *nf* bomb; (atomiseur) spray, aerosol.

bombé, ~**e** /bɔ̃be/ *adj* rounded; (route) cambered.

bon, bonne /bɔ̃, bɔn/ *adj* good; (qui convient) right; ~ **à/pour** (approprié) fit to/for; **bonne année** happy New Year; ~ **anniversaire** happy birthday; ~ **appétit/voyage** enjoy your meal/trip; **bonne chance/nuit** good luck/night; ~ **sens** common sense; **bonne femme** (péj) woman; **de bonne heure** early; **à quoi** ~**?** what's the point? ● *adv* **sentir** ~ smell nice; **tenir** ~ stand firm; **il fait** ~ the weather is mild. ● *interj* right, well. ● *nm* (billet) voucher, coupon; ~ **de commande** order form; **pour de** ~ for good. **bonne** *nf* (domestique) maid.

bonbon /bɔ̃bɔ̃/ *nm* sweet; (US) candy.

bonbonne /bɔ̃bɔn/ *nf* demijohn; (de gaz) cylinder.

bond /bɔ̃/ *nm* leap; **faire un** ~ (de surprise) jump.

bonde /bɔ̃d/ *nf* plug; (trou) plughole.

bondé, ~**e** /bɔ̃de/ *adj* packed.

bondir /bɔ̃diʀ/ [2] *vi* leap; (de surprise) jump.

bonheur /bɔnœʀ/ *nm* happiness; (chance) (good) luck; **au petit** ~ haphazardly; **par** ~ luckily.

bonhomme (*pl* **bonshommes**) /bɔnɔm, bɔ̃zɔm/ *nm* fellow; ~ **de neige** snowman. ● *a inv* goodhearted.

bonifier (se) /(sə)bɔnifje/ [45] *vpr* improve.

bonjour /bɔ̃ʒuʀ/ *nm & interj* hallo, hello, good morning *ou* afternoon.

bon marché /bɔ̃maʀʃe/ *a inv* cheap. ● *adv* cheap(ly).

bonne /bɔn/ ⇒BON.

bonne-maman (*pl* **bonnes-mamans**) /bɔnmamɑ̃/ *nf* 🔢 granny.

bonnement /bɔnmɑ̃/ *adv* **tout** ~ quite simply.

bonnet /bɔnɛ/ *nm* hat; (de soutien-gorge) cup; ~ **de bain** swimming cap. **bonneterie** *nf* hosiery.

bonsoir /bɔ̃swaʀ/ *nm* good evening; (en se couchant) good night.

bonté /bɔ̃te/ *nf* kindness.

bonus /bɔnys/ *nm* (Auto) no-claims bonus.

boots /buts/ *nmpl* ankle boots.

bord /bɔʀ/ *nm* edge; (rive) bank; **à** ~ **(de)** on board; **au** ~ **de la mer** at the seaside; **au** ~ **des larmes** on the verge of tears; ~ **de la route** roadside.

bordeaux /bɔʀdo/ *a inv* maroon. ● *nm inv* Bordeaux.

bordel /bɔʀdɛl/ *nm* brothel; (désordre 🔢) shambles.

border /bɔʀde/ [1] *vt* line, border; (tissu) edge; (personne, lit) tuck in.

bordereau (*pl* ~**x**) /bɔʀdəʀo/ *nm* (document) slip.

bordure /bɔʀdyʀ/ *nf* border; **en** ~ **de** on the edge of.

borgne /bɔʀɲ/ *adj* one-eyed.

borne /bɔʀn/ *nf* boundary marker; (pour barrer le passage) bollard; ~ **(kilométrique)** ≈ milestone; ~**s** limits.

borné, ~**e** /bɔʀne/ *adj* (esprit) narrow; (personne) narrow-minded.

borner (se) /(sə)bɔʀne/ [1] *vpr* confine oneself (à to).

bosniaque /bɔsnjak/ *adj* Bosnian. **B**~ *nmf* Bosnian.

Bosnie /bɔsni/ *nf* Bosnia.

bosse /bɔs/ *nf* bump; (de chameau) hump; **avoir la** ~ **de** 🔢 have a gift for; **avoir roulé sa** ~ have been around. **bosselé**, ~**e** *adj* dented; (terrain) bumpy.

bosser /bɔse/ [1] *vi* 🔢 work (hard).

bossu, ~**e** /bɔsy/ *adj* hunchbacked. ● *nm,f* hunchback.

botanique /bɔtanik/ *nf* botany. ● *adj* botanical.

botte /bɔt/ *nf* boot; (de fleurs, légumes) bunch; (de paille) bundle, bale; ~**s de caoutchouc** wellingtons.

botter /bɔte/ [1] *vt* 🅵 **ça me botte** I like the idea.

bottin® /bɔtɛ̃/ *nm* phone book.

bouc /buk/ *nm* (billy-)goat; (barbe) goatee; **~ émissaire** scapegoat.

boucan /bukɑ̃/ *nm* 🅵 din.

bouche /buʃ/ *nf* mouth; (lèvres) lips; **~ bée** open-mouthed; **~ d'égout** manhole; **~ d'incendie** (fire) hydrant; **~ de métro** entrance to the underground *ou* subway (US). **bouche-à-bouche** *nm inv* mouth-to-mouth resuscitation. **bouche-à-oreille** *nm inv* word of mouth.

bouché, **~e** /buʃe/ *adj* (*profession, avenir*) oversubscribed; (stupide: péj) stupid.

bouchée /buʃe/ *nf* mouthful.

boucher[1] /buʃe/ [1] *vt* block; (*bouteille*) cork. □ **se ~** *vpr* get blocked; **se ~ le nez** hold one's nose.

boucher[2], **-ère** /buʃe, -ɛʀ/ *nm,f* butcher. **boucherie** *nf* butcher's (shop); (carnage) butchery.

bouchon /buʃɔ̃/ *nm* stopper; (en liège) cork; (de stylo, tube) cap; (de pêcheur) float; (embouteillage) traffic jam; **~ de cérumen** plug of earwax.

boucle /bukl/ *nf* (de ceinture) buckle; (de cheveux) curl; (forme) loop; **~ d'oreille** earring. **bouclé**, **~e** *adj* (*cheveux*) curly.

boucler /bukle/ [1] *vt* fasten; (enfermer 🅵) shut up; (encercler) seal off; (*budget*) balance; (terminer) finish off. ● *vi* curl.

bouclier /buklije/ *nm* shield.

bouddhiste /budist/ *a & nmf* Buddhist.

bouder /bude/ [1] *vi* sulk. ● *vt* stay away from.

boudin /budɛ̃/ *nm* black pudding.

boue /bu/ *nf* mud.

bouée /bwe/ *nf* buoy; **~ de sauvetage** lifebuoy.

boueux, **-euse** /buø, -z/ *adj* muddy.

bouffe /buf/ *nf* 🅵 food, grub.

bouffée /bufe/ *nf* puff, whiff; (d'orgueil) fit; **~ de chaleur** (Méd) hot flush.

bouffi, **~e** /bufi/ *adj* bloated.

bouffon, **~ne** /bufɔ̃, -ɔn/ *adj* farcical. ● *nm* buffoon.

bougeoir /buʒwaʀ/ *nm* candlestick.

bougeotte /buʒɔt/ *nf* **avoir la ~** 🅵 have the fidgets.

bouger /buʒe/ [40] *vt/i* move. □ **se ~** *vpr* 🅵 move.

bougie /buʒi/ *nf* candle; (Auto) spark(ing)-plug.

bouillant, **~e** /bujɑ̃, -t/ *adj* boiling; (très chaud) boiling hot.

bouillie /buji/ *nf* (pour bébé) baby cereal; (péj) mush; **en ~** crushed, mushy.

bouillir /bujiʀ/ [13] *vi* boil; (fig) seethe; **faire ~** boil.

bouilloire /bujwaʀ/ *nf* kettle.

bouillon /bujɔ̃/ *nm* (de cuisson) stock; (potage) broth.

bouillonner /bujɔne/ [1] *vi* bubble.

bouillotte /bujɔt/ *nf* hot-water bottle.

boulanger, **-ère** /bulɑ̃ʒe, -ɛʀ/ *nm,f* baker. **boulangerie** *nf* bakery. **boulangerie-pâtisserie** *nf* bakery (*selling cakes and pastries*).

boule /bul/ *nf* ball; **~s** (jeu) boules; **jouer aux ~s** play boules; **une ~ dans la gorge** a lump in one's throat; **~ de neige** snowball.

bouleau (*pl* **~x**) /bulo/ *nm* (silver) birch.

boulet /bulɛ/ *nm* (de forçat) ball and chain; **~ (de canon)** cannonball; **~ de charbon** coal nut.

boulette /bulɛt/ *nf* (de pain, papier) pellet; (bévue) blunder; **~ de viande** meat ball.

boulevard /bulvaʀ/ *nm* boulevard.

bouleversant, **~e** /bulvɛʀsɑ̃, -t/ *adj* deeply moving. **bouleversement** *nm* upheaval. **bouleverser** [1] *vt* turn upside down; (*pays, plans*) disrupt; (émouvoir) upset.

boulimie /bulimi/ *nf* bulimia.

boulon /bulɔ̃/ *nm* bolt.

boulot, **~te** /bulo, -ɔt/ *adj* (rond 🅵) dumpy. ● *nm* (travail 🅵) work.

boum /bum/ *nm & interj* bang. ● *nf* (fête 🅵) party.

bouquet /bukɛ/ *nm* (de fleurs) bunch, bouquet; (d'arbres) clump; **c'est le ~!** 🅵 that's the last straw!

bouquin /bukɛ̃/ nm ⊞ book.
bouquiner [1] vt/i ⊞ read.
bouquiniste nmf second-hand
bookseller.

bourbier /buʀbje/ nm mire; (fig)
tangle.

bourde /buʀd/ nf blunder.

bourdon /buʀdɔ̃/ nm bumble-bee.
bourdonnement nm buzzing.

bourg /buʀ/ nm (market) town
(centre), village centre.

bourgeois, **~e** /buʀʒwa, -z/ a &
nm,f middle-class (person); (péj)
bourgeois. **bourgeoisie** nf middle
class(es).

bourgeon /buʀʒɔ̃/ nm bud.

bourgogne /buʀgɔɲ/ nm
Burgundy.

bourlinguer /buʀlɛ̃ge/ [1] vi ⊞
travel about.

bourrage /buʀaʒ/ nm ~ de crâne
brainwashing.

bourratif, **-ive** /buʀatif, -v/ adj
stodgy.

bourreau (pl ~x) /buʀo/ nm
executioner; ~ de travail (fig)
workaholic.

bourrelet /buʀlɛ/ nm weather-strip,
draught excluder; (de chair) roll of fat.

bourrer /buʀe/ [1] vt cram (de with);
(pipe) fill; ~ de (nourriture) stuff
with; ~ de coups thrash; ~ le crâne
à qn brainwash sb.

bourrique /buʀik/ nf donkey; ⊞
pig-headed person.

bourru, **~e** /buʀy/ adj gruff.

bourse /buʀs/ nf purse; (subvention)
grant; la B~ the Stock Exchange.

boursier, **-ière** /buʀsje, -jɛʀ/ adj
(valeurs) Stock Exchange. ● nm,f
grant holder.

boursoufler /buʀsufle/ [1] vt (visage) cause to swell; (peinture) blister.

bousculade /buskylad/ nf crush;
(précipitation) rush. **bousculer** [1] vt
(pousser) jostle; (presser) rush;
(renverser) knock over.

bousiller /buzije/ [1] vt ⊞ wreck.

boussole /busɔl/ nf compass.

bout /bu/ nm end; (de langue, bâton)
piece; (morceau) bit; à ~ exhausted; à
~ de souffle out of breath; à ~
portant point-blank; au ~ de (après)

after; venir à ~ de (finir) manage to
finish; d'un ~ à l'autre throughout;
au ~ du compte in the end; ~ filtre
filter-tip.

bouteille /butɛj/ nf bottle; ~
d'oxygène oxygen cylinder.

boutique /butik/ nf shop; (de mode)
boutique.

bouton /butɔ̃/ nm button; (sur la
peau) spot, pimple; (pousse) bud; (de
porte, radio) knob; ~ de manchette
cuff-link. **boutonner** [1] vt button
(up). **boutonnière** nf buttonhole.
bouton-pression (pl boutons-
pression) nm press-stud; (US) snap.

bouture /butyʀ/ nf cutting.

bovin, **~e** /bɔvɛ̃, -in/ adj bovine.
bovins nmpl cattle (pl).

box (pl ~ ou **boxes**) /bɔks/ nm
lock-up garage; (de dortoir) cubicle;
(d'écurie) (loose) box; (Jur) dock.

boxe /bɔks/ nf boxing.

boyau (pl ~x) /bwajo/ nm gut;
(corde) catgut; (galerie) gallery; (de
bicyclette) tyre; (US) tire.

boycotter /bɔjkɔte/ [1] vt boycott.

BP abrév f (**boîte postale**) PO Box.

bracelet /bʀaslɛ/ nm bracelet; (de
montre) watchstrap.

braconnier /bʀakɔnje/ nm
poacher.

brader /bʀade/ [1] vt sell off.
braderie nf clearance sale.

braguette /bʀagɛt/ nf fly.

braille /bʀaj/ nm & a Braille.

brailler /bʀaje/ [1] vt/i bawl.

braise /bʀez/ nf embers (+ pl).

braiser /bʀeze/ [1] vt (Culin) braise.

brancard /bʀɑ̃kaʀ/ nm stretcher;
(de charrette) shaft.

branche /bʀɑ̃ʃ/ nf branch.

branché, **~e** /bʀɑ̃ʃe/ adj ⊞ trendy.

branchement /bʀɑ̃ʃmɑ̃/ nm
connection. **brancher** [1] vt (prise)
plug in; (à un réseau) connect.

brandir /bʀɑ̃diʀ/ [2] vt brandish.

branler /bʀɑ̃le/ [1] vi be shaky.

braquer /bʀake/ [1] vt (arme) aim;
(regard) fix; (roue) turn; (banque: ⊞)
hold up; ~ qn contre turn sb
against. ● vi (Auto) turn (the wheel).
□ **se** ~ vpr dig one's heels in.

bras /bʀɑ/ nm arm; (de rivière) branch; (Tech) arm; ∼ **dessus** ∼ **dessous** arm in arm; ∼ **droit** (fig) right hand man; ∼ **de mer** sound; **en** ∼ **de chemise** in one's shirtsleeves. ● nmpl (fig) labour, hands.

brasier /bʀɑzje/ nm blaze.

brassard /bʀasaʀ/ nm armband.

brasse /bʀas/ nf breast-stroke; ∼ **papillon** butterfly (stroke).

brasser /bʀase/ [1] vt mix; (bière) brew; (affaires) handle a lot of. **brasserie** nf brewery; (café) brasserie.

brave /bʀav/ adj (bon) good; (valeureux) brave. **braver** [1] vt defy.

bravo /bʀavo/ interj bravo. ● nm cheer.

bravoure /bʀavuʀ/ nf bravery.

break /bʀɛk/ nm estate car; (US) station-wagon.

brebis /bʀəbi/ nf ewe.

brèche /bʀɛʃ/ nf gap, breach; **être sur la** ∼ be on the go.

bredouille /bʀəduj/ adj empty-handed.

bredouiller /bʀəduje/ [1] vt/i mumble.

bref, **brève** /bʀɛf, -v/ adj short, brief. ● adv in short; **en** ∼ in short.

Brésil /bʀezil/ nm Brazil.

Bretagne /bʀətaɲ/ nf Brittany.

bretelle /bʀətɛl/ nf (de sac, maillot) strap; (d'autoroute) access road; ∼s (pour pantalon) braces; (US) suspenders.

breton, ∼**ne** /bʀətɔ̃, -ɔn/ a & nm (Ling) Breton. **B**∼, ∼**ne** nm, f Breton.

breuvage /bʀœvaʒ/ nm beverage.

brève /bʀɛv/ ⇒BREF.

brevet /bʀəvɛ/ nm ∼ **(d'invention)** patent; (diplôme) diploma.

breveté, ∼**e** /bʀəvte/ adj patented.

bribes /bʀib/ nfpl scraps.

bricolage /bʀikɔlaʒ/ nm do-it-yourself (jobs).

bricole /bʀikɔl/ nf trifle.

bricoler /bʀikɔle/ [1] vi do DIY; (US) fix things, tinker with.

bricoleur, **-euse** /bʀikɔlœʀ, -øz/ nm, f handyman, handywoman.

bride /bʀid/ nf bridle.

bridé, ∼**e** /bʀide/ adj **yeux** ∼**s** slanting eyes.

brider /bʀide/ [1] vt (cheval) bridle; (fig) keep in check.

brièvement /bʀijɛvmɑ̃/ adv briefly.

brigade /bʀigad/ nf (de police) squad; (Mil) brigade; (fig) team. **brigadier** nm (de gendarmerie) sergeant.

brigand /bʀigɑ̃/ nm robber.

brillant, ∼**e** /bʀijɑ̃, -t/ adj (couleur) bright; (luisant) shiny; (remarquable) brilliant. ● nm (éclat) shine; (diamant) diamond.

briller /bʀije/ [1] vi shine.

brimade /bʀimad/ nf vexation. **brimer** [1] vt bully, harass; **se sentir brimé** feel put down.

brin /bʀɛ̃/ nm (de muguet) sprig; (d'herbe) blade; (de paille) wisp; **un** ∼ **de** (un peu) a bit of.

brindille /bʀɛ̃dij/ nf twig.

brioche /bʀijɔʃ/ nf brioche, sweet bun; (ventre 🔲) paunch.

brique /bʀik/ nf brick.

briquet /bʀikɛ/ nm (cigarette-) lighter.

brise /bʀiz/ nf breeze.

briser /bʀize/ [1] vt break. □ **se** ∼ vpr break.

britannique /bʀitanik/ adj British. **B**∼ nmf Briton; **les B**∼**s** the British.

brocante /bʀɔkɑ̃t/ nf bric-à-brac trade; (marché) flea market.

broche /bʀɔʃ/ nf brooch; (Culin) spit; **à la** ∼ spit-roasted.

broché, ∼**e** /bʀɔʃe/ adj paperback.

brochet /bʀɔʃɛ/ nm pike.

brochette /bʀɔʃɛt/ nf skewer.

brochure /bʀɔʃyʀ/ nf brochure, booklet.

broder /bʀɔde/ [1] vt/i embroider. **broderie** nf embroidery.

broncher /bʀɔ̃ʃe/ [1] vi **sans** ∼ without turning a hair.

bronchite /bʀɔ̃ʃit/ nf bronchitis.

bronze /bʀɔ̃z/ nm bronze.

bronzé, ∼**e** /bʀɔ̃ze/ adj (sun-)tanned.

bronzer /bʀɔ̃ze/ [1] vi (personne) get a (sun-)tan.

brosse /bʀɔs/ *nf* brush; ~ **à dents** toothbrush; ~ **à habits** clothes brush; **en** ~ (*coiffure*) in a crew cut.

brosser /bʀɔse/ [1] *vt* brush; (*fig*) paint. □ **se** ~ *vpr* **se** ~ **les dents/les cheveux** brush one's teeth/hair.

brouette /bʀuɛt/ *nf* wheelbarrow.

brouhaha /bʀuaa/ *nm* hubbub.

brouillard /bʀujaʀ/ *nm* fog.

brouille /bʀuj/ *nf* quarrel.

brouiller /bʀuje/ [1] *vt* (*vue*) blur; (*œufs*) scramble; (*amis*) set at odds; ~ **les pistes** cloud the issue. □ **se** ~ *vpr* (*ciel*) cloud over; (*amis*) fall out.

brouillon, ~ne /bʀujɔ̃, -ɔn/ *adj* untidy. ● *nm* (rough) draft.

brousse /bʀus/ *nf* **la** ~ the bush.

brouter /bʀute/ [1] *vt/i* graze.

broyer /bʀwaje/ [31] *vt* crush; (*moudre*) grind.

bru /bʀy/ *nf* daughter-in-law.

bruine /bʀɥin/ *nf* drizzle.

bruissement /bʀɥismɑ̃/ *nm* rustling.

bruit /bʀɥi/ *nm* noise; ~ **de couloir** (*fig*) rumour.

bruitage /bʀɥitaʒ/ *nm* sound effects.

brûlant, ~e /bʀylɑ̃, -t/ *adj* burning (hot); (*sujet*) red-hot; (*passion*) fiery.

brûlé /bʀyle/ *nm* burning; **ça sent le** ~ I can smell something burning. ● ⇒BRÛLER [1].

brûler /bʀyle/ [1] *vt/i* burn; (*essence*) use (up); (*cierge*) light (à to); ~ **un feu** (**rouge**) jump the lights; ~ **d'envie de faire** be longing to do. □ **se** ~ *vpr* burn oneself.

brûlure /bʀylyʀ/ *nf* burn; ~**s d'estomac** heartburn.

brume /bʀym/ *nf* mist. **brumeux, -euse** *adj* misty; (*esprit*) hazy.

brun, ~e /bʀœ̃, -yn/ *adj* brown, dark. ● *nm* brown. ● *nm,f* dark-haired person. **brunir** [2] *vi* turn brown; (*bronzer*) get a tan.

brushing /bʀœʃiŋ/ *nm* blow-dry.

brusque /bʀysk/ *adj* (*personne*) abrupt; (*geste*) violent; (*soudain*) sudden.

brusquer /bʀyske/ [1] *vt* be abrupt with; (*précipiter*) rush.

brut, ~e /bʀyt/ *adj* (*diamant*) rough; (*champagne*) dry; (*pétrole*) crude; (Comm) gross.

brutal, ~e (*mpl* **-aux**) /bʀytal, -o/ *adj* brutal. **brutalité** *nf* brutality.

brute /bʀyt/ *nf* brute.

Bruxelles /bʀysɛl/ *npr* Brussels.

bruyant, ~e /bʀɥijɑ̃, -t/ *adj* noisy.

bruyère /bʀyjɛʀ/ *nf* heather.

bu /by/ ⇒BOIRE [12].

bûche /byʃ/ *nf* log; ~ **de Noël** Christmas log; **ramasser une** ~ ⊡ fall.

bûcher /byʃe/ [1] *vt/i* ⊡ slog away (at) ⊡. ● *nm* (supplice) stake.

bûcheron /byʃʀɔ̃/ *nm* lumberjack.

budget /bydʒɛ/ *nm* budget. **budgétaire** *adj* budgetary.

buée /bɥe/ *nf* condensation.

buffet /byfɛ/ *nm* sideboard; (table garnie) buffet.

buffle /byfl/ *nm* buffalo.

buisson /bɥisɔ̃/ *nm* bush.

buissonnière /bɥisɔnjɛʀ/ *af* **faire l'école** ~ play truant.

bulbe /bylb/ *nm* bulb.

bulgare /bylgaʀ/ *a & nm* Bulgarian. **B~** *nmf* Bulgarian.

Bulgarie /bylgaʀi/ *nf* Bulgaria.

bulldozer /byldozɛʀ/ *nm* bulldozer.

bulle /byl/ *nf* bubble.

bulletin /byltɛ̃/ *nm* bulletin, report; (Scol) report; ~ **d'information** news bulletin; ~ **météorologique** weather report; ~ (**de vote**) ballot-paper; ~ **de salaire** pay-slip.

buraliste /byʀalist/ *nmf* tobacconist.

bureau (*pl* ~**x**) /byʀo/ *nm* office; (meuble) desk; (comité) board; ~ **d'études** design office; ~ **de poste** post office; ~ **de tabac** tobacconist's (shop); ~ **de vote** polling station.

bureaucrate /byʀokʀat/ *nmf* bureaucrat. **bureaucratie** *nf* bureaucracy. **bureaucratique** *adj* bureaucratic.

bureautique /byʀotik/ *nf* office automation.

burlesque /byʀlɛsk/ *a* (*histoire*) ludicrous; (*film*) farcical.

bus /bys/ *nm* bus.

buste /byst/ *nm* bust.

but /by(t)/ *nm* target; (dessein) aim, goal; (football) goal; **avoir pour ~ de** aim to; **de ~ en blanc** point-blank; **dans le ~ de** with the intention of; **aller droit au ~** go straight to the point.

butane /bytan/ *nm* butane, Calor gas®.

buté,**~e** /byte/ *adj* obstinate.

buter /byte/ [1] *vi* ~ **contre** knock against; (*problème*) come up against. ● *vt* antagonize. □ **se ~** *vpr* (s'entêter) become obstinate.

buteur /bytœʀ/ *nm* (au football) striker.

butin /bytɛ̃/ *nm* booty, loot.

butte /byt/ *nf* mound; **en ~ à** exposed to.

buvard /byvaʀ/ *nm* blotting-paper.

buvette /byvɛt/ *nf* (refreshment) bar.

buveur, -euse /byvœʀ, -øz/ *nm, f* drinker.

....

Cc

....

c' /s/ ⇒CE.

....

ça /sa/

● *pronom démonstratif*

····▸ (sujet) it; that; ~ **flotte** it floats; ~ **suffit!** that's enough!; ~ **y est!** that's it!; ~ **sent le brûlé** there's a smell of burning; ~ **va?** how are things?

····▸ (objet) (proche) this; (plus éloigné) that; **c'est** ~ that's right.

····▸ (dans expressions) **où** ~? where?; **quand** ~? when?; **et avec** ~? anything else?

....

çà /sa/ *adv* ~ **et là** here and there.

cabane /kaban/ *nf* hut; (à outils) shed.

cabaret /kabaʀɛ/ *nm* cabaret.

cabillaud /kabijo/ *nm* cod.

cabine /kabin/ *nf* (à la piscine) cubicle; (de bateau) cabin; (de camion) cab; (d'ascenseur) cage; ~ **d'essayage** fitting room; ~ **de pilotage** cockpit; ~ **de plage** beach hut; ~ **(téléphonique)** phone booth, phone box.

cabinet /kabinɛ/ *nm* (de médecin) surgery; (US) office; (d'avocat) office; (clientèle) practice; (cabinet collectif) firm; (Pol) Cabinet; (pièce) room; **~s** (toilettes) toilet; (US) bathroom; ~ **de toilette** bathroom.

câble /kɑbl/ *nm* cable; (corde) rope; (TV) cable TV. **câbler** *vt* [1] cable; (TV) install cable television in.

cabosser /kabose/ [1] *vt* dent.

cabotage /kabotaʒ/ *nm* coastal navigation.

cabrer (se) /(sə)kabʀe/ [1] *vpr* (*cheval*) rear; **se ~ contre** rebel against.

cabriole /kabʀijɔl/ *nf* **faire des ~s** caper about.

cacahuète /kakawɛt/ *nf* peanut.

cacao /kakao/ *nm* cocoa.

cachalot /kaʃalo/ *nm* sperm whale.

cache /kaʃ/ *nm* mask. ● *nf* hiding place; ~ **d'armes** arms cache.

cache-cache /kaʃkaʃ/ *nm inv* hide-and-seek.

cache-nez /kaʃne/ *nm inv* scarf.

cacher /kaʃe/ [1] *vt* hide, conceal (à from). □ **se ~** *vpr* hide; (se trouver caché) be hidden.

cachet /kaʃɛ/ *nm* (de cire) seal; (à l'encre) stamp; (de la poste) postmark; (comprimé) tablet; (d'artiste) fee; (chic) style, cachet.

cachette /kaʃɛt/ *nf* hiding-place; **en ~** in secret.

cachot /kaʃo/ *nm* dungeon.

cachottier, -ière /kaʃotje, -jɛʀ/ *adj* secretive.

cacophonie /kakɔfɔni/ *nf* cacophony.

cactus /kaktys/ *nm* cactus.

cadavérique /kadaveʀik/ *adj* (*teint*) deathly pale.

cadavre /kadavʀ/ *nm* corpse; (de victime) body.

caddie /kadi/ *nm* (de supermarché)® trolley; (au golf) caddie.

cadeau (*pl* ∼**x**) /kado/ *nm* present, gift; **faire un** ∼ **à qn** give sb a present.

cadenas /kadna/ *nm* padlock.

cadence /kadɑ̃s/ *nf* rhythm, cadence; (*de travail*) rate; **en** ∼ in time; (*marcher*) in step.

cadet, ∼**te** /kadɛ, -t/ *adj* youngest; (*entre deux*) younger. ● *nm, f* youngest (child); younger (child).

cadran /kadrɑ̃/ *nm* dial; ∼ **solaire** sundial.

cadre /kadR/ *nm* frame; (*lieu*) setting; (*milieu*) surroundings; (*limites*) scope; (*contexte*) framework; **dans le** ∼ **de** (à l'occasion de) on the occasion of; (*dans le contexte de*) in the framework of. ● *nm* (*personne*) executive; **les** ∼**s** the managerial staff.

cadrer /kadRe/ [1] *vi* ∼ **avec** tally with. ● *vt* (*photo*) centre.

cafard /kafaR/ *nm* (insecte) cockroach; **avoir le** ∼ 🄸 be down in the dumps.

café /kafe/ *nm* coffee; (bar) café; ∼ **crème** espresso with milk; ∼ **en grains** coffee beans; ∼ **au lait** white coffee.

cafetière /kaftjɛR/ *nf* coffee-pot; ∼ **électrique** coffee machine.

cage /kaʒ/ *nf* cage; ∼ **d'ascenseur** lift shaft; ∼ **d'escalier** stairwell; ∼ **thoracique** rib cage.

cageot /kaʒo/ *nm* crate.

cagibi /kaʒibi/ *nm* storage room.

cagneux, -**euse** /kaɲø, -z/ *adj* **avoir les genoux** ∼ be knock-kneed.

cagnotte /kaɲɔt/ *nf* kitty.

cagoule /kagul/ *nf* hood; (passe-montagne) balaclava.

cahier /kaje/ *nm* notebook; (Scol) exercise book; ∼ **de textes** homework notebook; ∼ **des charges** (Tech) specifications (+ *pl*).

cahot /kao/ *nm* bump, jolt. **cahoteux**, -**euse** *adj* bumpy.

caïd /kaid/ *nm* 🄸 big shot.

caille /kɑj/ *nf* quail.

cailler /kɑje/ [1] *vi* curdle; **ça caille** 🄸 it's freezing. □ **se** ∼ *vpr* (*sang*) clot; (*lait*) curdle. **caillot** *nm* (blood) clot.

caillou (*pl* ∼**x**) /kaju/ *nm* stone; (galet) pebble.

caisse /kɛs/ *nf* crate, case; (tiroir, machine) till; (guichet) cash desk; (au supermarché) check-out; (bureau) office; (Mus) drum; ∼ **enregistreuse** cash register; ∼ **d'épargne** savings bank; ∼ **de retraite** pension fund. **caissier**, -**ière** *nm, f* cashier.

cajoler /kaʒɔle/ [1] *vt* coax.

calcaire /kalkɛR/ *adj* (*sol*) chalky; (*eau*) hard.

calciné, ∼**e** /kalsine/ *adj* charred.

calcul /kalkyl/ *nm* calculation; (Scol) arithmetic; (différentiel) calculus; ∼ **biliaire** gallstone.

calculatrice /kalkylatRis/ *nf* calculator. **calculer** [1] *vt* calculate. **calculette** *nf* (pocket) calculator.

cale /kal/ *nf* wedge; (pour roue) chock; (de navire) hold; ∼ **sèche** dry dock.

calé, ∼**e** /kale/ *adj* 🄸 clever.

caleçon /kalsɔ̃/ *nm* boxer shorts (+ *pl*); underpants (+ *pl*); (de femme) leggings.

calembour /kalɑ̃buR/ *nm* pun.

calendrier /kalɑ̃dRije/ *nm* calendar; (fig) schedule, timetable.

calepin /kalpɛ̃/ *nm* notebook.

caler /kale/ [1] *vt* wedge. ● *vi* stall; (abandonner 🄸) give up.

calfeutrer /kalføtRe/ [1] *vt* (*fissure*) stop up; (*porte*) draught proof.

calibre /kalibR/ *nm* calibre; (d'un œuf, fruit) grade.

calice /kalis/ *nm* (Relig) chalice; (Bot) calyx.

califourchon: **à** ∼ /akalifuRʃɔ̃/ *loc* astride.

câlin, ∼**e** /kɑlɛ̃, -in/ *adj* (*regard, ton*) affectionate; (*personne*) cuddly.

calmant /kalmɑ̃/ *nm* sedative.

calme /kalm/ *adj* calm. ● *nm* peace; calm; (maîtrise de soi) composure; **du** ∼**!** calm down!

calmer /kalme/ [1] *vt* (*personne*) calm down; (*situation*) defuse; (*douleur*) ease; (*soif*) quench. □ **se** ∼ *vpr* (*personne, situation*) calm down; (*agitation, tempête*) die down; (*douleur*) ease.

calomnie /kalɔmni/ *nf* (*orale*) slander; (écrite) libel. **calomnier** [45]

vt slander; libel. **calomnieux,
-ieuse** *adj* slanderous; libellous.

calorie /kalɔri/ *nf* calorie.

calque /kalk/ *nm* tracing; **(papier)** ~
tracing paper; (fig) exact copy.

calquer /kalke/ [1] *vt* trace; (fig)
copy; ~ **qch sur** model sth on.

calvaire /kalvɛʀ/ *nm* (croix) Calvary;
(fig) suffering.

calvitie /kalvisi/ *nf* baldness.

camarade /kamaʀad/ *nmf* friend;
(Pol) comrade; ~ **de jeu** playmate.
camaraderie *nf* friendship.

cambouis /kɑ̃bwi/ *nm* dirty oil.

cambrer /kɑ̃bʀe/ [1] *vt* arch. □ **se**
~ *vpr* arch one's back.

cambriolage /kɑ̃bʀijɔlaʒ/ *nm*
burglary. **cambrioler** [1] *vt* burgle.
cambrioleur, -euse *nm,f* burglar.

camelot /kamlo/ *nm* Ⓘ street
vendor.

camelote /kamlɔt/ *nf* Ⓘ junk.

caméra /kameʀa/ *nf* (cinéma,
télévision) camera.

caméscope® /kameskɔp/ *nm*
camcorder.

camion /kamjõ/ *nm* lorry, truck.
camion-citerne (*pl* **camions-
citernes**) *nm* tanker.
camionnage *nm* haulage.
camionnette *nf* van.
camionneur *nm* lorry *ou* truck
driver; (entrepreneur) haulage
contractor.

camisole /kamizɔl/ *nf* ~ **(de force)**
straitjacket.

camoufler /kamufle/ [1] *vt*
camouflage.

camp /kɑ̃/ *nm* camp; (Sport, Pol) side.

campagnard, ~e /kɑ̃paɲaʀ, -d/
adj country. ● *nm,f* countryman,
countrywoman.

campagne /kɑ̃paɲ/ *nf* country;
countryside; (Mil, Pol) campaign.

campement /kɑ̃pmɑ̃/ *nm* camp,
encampment.

camper /kɑ̃pe/ [1] *vi* camp. ● *vt*
(esquisser) sketch. □ **se** ~ *vpr* plant
oneself. **campeur, -euse** *nm,f*
camper.

camping /kɑ̃piŋ/ *nm* camping; **faire
du** ~ go camping; **(terrain de)** ~
campsite. **camping-car** (*pl* ~**s**) *nm*

camper-van; (US) motorhome.
camping-gaz® *nm inv* (réchaud)
camping stove.

Canada /kanada/ *nm* Canada.

canadien, ~ne /kanadjɛ̃, -ɛn/ *adj*
Canadian. **C~, ~ne** *nm,f* Canadian.
canadienne *nf* (veste) fur-lined
jacket; (tente) ridge tent.

canaille /kanɑj/ *nf* rogue.

canal (*pl* -**aux**) /kanal, -o/ *nm*
(artificiel) canal; (bras de mer) channel;
(Tech, TV) channel; (moyen) channel;
par le ~ **de** through. **canalisation**
nf (tuyaux) mains (+ *pl*). **canaliser**
[1] *vt* (eau) canalize; (fig) channel.

canapé /kanape/ *nm* sofa.

canard /kanaʀ/ *nm* duck; (journal Ⓘ)
rag.

canari /kanaʀi/ *nm* canary.

cancans /kɑ̃kɑ̃/ *nmpl* Ⓘ gossip.

cancer /kɑ̃sɛʀ/ *nm* cancer; **le C~**
Cancer. **cancéreux, -euse** *adj*
cancerous. **cancérigène** *adj*
carcinogenic.

cancre /kɑ̃kʀ/ *nm* dunce.

candeur /kɑ̃dœʀ/ *nf* ingenuousness.

candidat, ~e /kɑ̃dida, -t/ *nm,f* (à
un examen, Pol) candidate; (à un poste)
applicant, candidate (à for).

candidature /kɑ̃didatyʀ/ *nf*
application; (Pol) candidacy; **poser sa**
~ **à un poste** apply for a job.

candide /kɑ̃did/ *adj* ingenuous.

cane /kan/ *nf* (female) duck.
caneton *nm* duckling.

canette /kanɛt/ *nf* (bouteille) bottle;
(boîte) can.

canevas /kanva/ *nm* canvas;
(ouvrage) tapestry; (plan) framework,
outline.

caniche /kaniʃ/ *nm* poodle.

canicule /kanikyl/ *nf* scorching
heat; (vague de chaleur) heatwave.

canif /kanif/ *nm* penknife.

canine /kanin/ *nf* canine (tooth).

caniveau (*pl* ~**x**) /kanivo/ *nm*
gutter.

cannabis /kanabis/ *nm* cannabis.

canne /kan/ *nf* (walking) stick; ~ **à
pêche** fishing rod; ~ **à sucre** sugar
cane.

cannelle /kanɛl/ *nf* cinnamon.

cannibale /kanibal/ a & nmf cannibal.

canoë /kanɔe/ nm canoe; (Sport) canoeing.

canon /kanɔ̃/ nm (big) gun; (ancien) cannon; (d'une arme) barrel; (principe, règle) canon.

canot /kano/ nm dinghy, (small) boat; ∼ de sauvetage lifeboat; ∼ pneumatique rubber dinghy. **canotier** nm boater.

cantatrice /kɑ̃tatris/ nf opera singer.

cantine /kɑ̃tin/ nf canteen.

cantique /kɑ̃tik/ nm hymn.

cantonner /kɑ̃tɔne/ [1] vt (Mil) billet. □ se ∼ dans vpr confine oneself to.

cantonnier /kɑ̃tɔnje/ nm road mender.

canular /kanylaʀ/ nm hoax.

caoutchouc /kautʃu/ nm rubber; (élastique) rubber band; ∼ mousse foam rubber.

cap /kap/ nm cape, headland; (direction) course; (obstacle) hurdle; franchir le ∼ de la cinquantaine pass the fifty mark; mettre le ∼ sur steer a course for.

capable /kapabl/ adj capable (de of); ∼ de faire able to do, capable of doing.

capacité /kapasite/ nf ability; (contenance, potentiel) capacity.

cape /kap/ nf cape; rire sous ∼ laugh up one's sleeve.

capillaire /kapileʀ/ adj (lotion, soins) hair; (vaisseau) ∼ capillary.

capitaine /kapitɛn/ nm captain.

capital, ∼e (mpl -aux) /kapital, -o/ adj key, crucial, fundamental; (peine, lettre) capital. ● nm (pl -aux) (Comm) capital; (fig) stock; capitaux (Comm) capital. **capitale** nf (ville, lettre) capital.

capitalisme /kapitalism/ nm capitalism.

capitonné, ∼e /kapitɔne/ adj padded.

capituler /kapityle/ [1] vi capitulate.

caporal (pl -aux) /kapɔral, -o/ nm corporal.

capot /kapo/ nm (Auto) bonnet; (US) hood.

capote /kapɔt/ nf (Auto) hood; (US) top; (préservatif 🚹) condom.

capoter /kapɔte/ [1] vi overturn; (fig) collapse.

câpre /kɑpʀ/ nf (Culin) caper.

caprice /kapʀis/ nm whim; (colère) tantrum; faire un ∼ throw a tantrum. **capricieux, -ieuse** adj capricious; (appareil) temperamental.

Capricorne /kapʀikɔʀn/ nm le ∼ Capricorn.

capsule /kapsyl/ nf capsule; (de bouteille) cap.

capter /kapte/ [1] vt (eau) collect; (émission) get; (signal) pick up; (fig) win, capture.

captif, -ive /kaptif, -v/ a & nm,f captive.

captiver /kaptive/ [1] vt captivate.

capturer /kaptyʀe/ [1] vt capture.

capuche /kapyʃ/ nf hood. **capuchon** nm hood; (de stylo) cap.

car /kaʀ/ conj because, for. ● nm coach; (US) bus.

carabine /kaʀabin/ nf rifle.

caractère /kaʀaktɛʀ/ nm (lettre) character; (nature) nature; ∼s d'imprimerie block letters; avoir bon/mauvais ∼ be good-natured/bad-tempered; avoir du ∼ have character.

caractériel, ∼le /kaʀakteʀjɛl/ adj (trait) character; (enfant) disturbed.

caractériser /kaʀakteʀize/ [1] vt characterize. □ se ∼ par vpr be characterized by. **caractéristique** a & nf characteristic.

carafe /kaʀaf/ nf carafe.

Caraïbes /kaʀaib/ nfpl les ∼ the Caribbean.

carambolage /kaʀɑ̃bɔlaʒ/ nm pile-up.

caramel /kaʀamɛl/ nm caramel; (bonbon) toffee.

carapace /kaʀapas/ nf shell.

caravane /kaʀavan/ nf (Auto) caravan; (US) trailer; (convoi) caravan.

carbone /kaʀbɔn/ nm carbon; (**papier**) ∼ carbon (paper).
carboniser [1] vt burn (to ashes).

carburant /kaʀbyʀɑ̃/ nm (motor) fuel.

carburateur /kaʀbyʀatœʀ/ nm carburettor; (US) carburetor.

carcan /kaʀkɑ̃/ nm constraints (+ pl).

carcasse /kaʀkas/ nf (squelette) carcass; (armature) frame; (de voiture) shell.

cardiaque /kaʀdjak/ adj heart. ● nmf heart patient.

cardinal, ∼e (mpl -aux) /kaʀdinal, -o/ a & nm cardinal.

Carême /kaʀɛm/ nm le ∼ Lent.

carence /kaʀɑ̃s/ nf shortcomings (+ pl); inadequacy; (Méd) deficiency; (absence) lack.

caresse /kaʀɛs/ nf caress; (à un animal) stroke. **caresser** [1] vt caress, stroke; (espoir) cherish.

cargaison /kaʀgɛzɔ̃/ nf cargo.

cargo /kaʀgo/ nm cargo boat.

caricature /kaʀikatyʀ/ nf caricature.

carie /kaʀi/ nf (trou) cavity; **la** ∼ (dentaire) tooth decay.

carillon /kaʀijɔ̃/ nm chimes (+ pl); (horloge) chiming clock.

caritatif, -ive /kaʀitatif, -v/ adj **association caritative** charity.

carnage /kaʀnaʒ/ nm carnage.

carnassier, -ière /kaʀnasje, -jɛʀ/ adj carnivorous.

carnaval (pl ∼s) /kaʀnaval/ nm carnival.

carnet /kaʀnɛ/ nm notebook; (de tickets, timbres) book; ∼ **d'adresses** address book; ∼ **de chèques** chequebook.

carotte /kaʀɔt/ nf carrot.

carpe /kaʀp/ nf carp.

carré, ∼e /kaʀe/ adj (forme, mesure) square; (fig) straightforward; **un mètre** ∼ one square metre. ● nm square; (de terrain) patch.

carreau (pl ∼x) /kaʀo/ nm (window) pane; (dessin) check; (aux cartes) diamonds (+ pl); **à** ∼**x** (tissu) check(ed); (papier) squared.

carrefour /kaʀfuʀ/ nm crossroads (+ sg).

carrelage /kaʀlaʒ/ nm tiling; (sol) tiles.

carrément /kaʀemɑ̃/ adv (complètement) completely; (stupide, dangereux) downright; (dire) straight out; **elle a** ∼ **démissionné** she went straight ahead and resigned.

carrière /kaʀjɛʀ/ nf career; (terrain) quarry.

carrossable /kaʀɔsabl/ adj suitable for vehicles.

carrosse /kaʀɔs/ nm (horse-drawn) coach.

carrosserie /kaʀɔsʀi/ nf (Auto) body(work).

carrure /kaʀyʀ/ nf shoulders; (fig) necessary qualities, calibre.

cartable /kaʀtabl/ nm satchel.

carte /kaʀt/ nf card; (Géog) map; (Naut) chart; (au restaurant) menu; ∼**s** (jeu) cards; **à la** ∼ (manger) à la carte; (horaire) personalized; **donner** ∼ **blanche à** give a free hand to; ∼ **de crédit** credit card; ∼ **grise** (car) registration document; ∼ **d'identité** identity card; ∼ **magnétique** swipe card; ∼ **de paiement** debit card; ∼ **postale** postcard; ∼ **à puce** smart card; ∼ **de séjour** resident's permit; ∼ **des vins** wine list; ∼ **de visite** (business) card.

cartilage /kaʀtilaʒ/ nm cartilage.

carton /kaʀtɔ̃/ nm cardboard; (boîte) (cardboard) box; ∼ **à dessin** portfolio; **faire un** ∼ 🔲 do well.

cartonné, ∼e /kaʀtɔne/ adj **livre** ∼ hardback.

cartouche /kaʀtuʃ/ nf cartridge; (de cigarettes) carton. **cartouchière** nf cartridge-belt.

cas /kɑ/ nm case; **au** ∼ **où** in case; ∼ **urgent** emergency; **en aucun** ∼ on no account; **en** ∼ **de** in the event of, in case of; **en tout** ∼ in any case; (du moins) at least; **faire** ∼ **de** set great store by; ∼ **de conscience** moral dilemma.

casanier, -ière /kazanje, -jɛʀ/ adj home-loving.

cascade /kaskad/ nf waterfall; (au cinéma) stunt; (fig) spate, series (+ sg).

cascadeur, -euse /kaskadœʀ, -øz/ *nm, f* stuntman, stuntwoman.

case /kaz/ *nf* hut; (de damier) square; (compartiment) pigeon-hole; (sur un formulaire) box.

caser /kaze/ [1] *vt* 🔲 (mettre) put; (loger) put up; (dans un travail) find a job for; (marier: péj) marry off.

caserne /kazɛʀn/ *nf* barracks; ~ **de sapeurs-pompiers** fire station.

casier /kazje/ *nm* pigeon-hole, compartment; (à bouteilles, chaussures) rack; ~ **judiciaire** criminal record.

casque /kask/ *nm* (de motard) crash helmet; (de cycliste) cycle helmet; (chez le coiffeur) (hair-)drier; ~ **(à écouteurs)** headphones; ~ **anti-bruit** ear defenders; ~ **de protection** safety helmet.

casquette /kaskɛt/ *nf* cap.

cassant, ~e /kasã, -t/ *adj* brittle; (brusque) curt.

cassation /kasasjɔ̃/ *nf* **cour de** ~ appeal court.

casse /kas/ *nf* (objets) breakages; (lieu) breaker's yard; **mettre à la** ~ scrap.

casse-cou /kasku/ *nmf inv* daredevil.

casse-croûte /kaskʀut/ *nm inv* snack.

casse-noix /kasnwa/ *nm inv* nutcrackers (+ *pl*).

casse-pieds /kaspje/ *nmf inv* 🔲 pain (in the neck) 🔲.

casser /kase/ [1] *vt* break; (annuler) annul; ~ **les pieds à qn** 🔲 annoy sb. ● *vi* break. ☐ **se** ~ *vpr* break; (partir 🔲) be off 🔲.

casserole /kasʀɔl/ *nf* saucepan.

casse-tête /kastɛt/ *nm inv* (problème) headache; (jeu) brain teaser.

cassette /kasɛt/ *nf* casket; (de magnétophone) cassette, tape; (de vidéo) video tape; ~ **audionumérique** digital audio tape.

cassis /kasi(s)/ *nm inv* blackcurrant.

cassure /kasyʀ/ *nf* break.

castor /kastɔʀ/ *nm* beaver.

castration /kastʀasjɔ̃/ *nf* castration.

catalogue /katalɔg/ *nm* catalogue.

catalyseur /katalizœʀ/ *nm* catalyst; (Auto) catalytic convertor.

catastrophe /katastʀɔf/ *nf* disaster, catastrophe.

catastrophique *adj* catastrophic.

catch /katʃ/ *nm* (all-in) wrestling.

catéchisme /kateʃism/ *nm* catechism.

catégorie /kategɔʀi/ *nf* category.

catégorique *adj* categorical.

cathédrale /katedʀal/ *nf* cathedral.

catholique /katɔlik/ *adj* Catholic; **pas très** ~ a bit fishy.

catimini: **en** ~ /ɑ̃katimini/ *loc* on the sly.

cauchemar /koʃmaʀ/ *nm* nightmare.

cause /koz/ *nf* cause; (raison) reason; (Jur) case; **à** ~ **de** because of; **en** ~ (en jeu, concerné) involved; **pour** ~ **de** on account of; **mettre en** ~ implicate; **remettre en** ~ call into question.

causer /koze/ [1] *vt* cause; (discuter de 🔲) ~ **travail** talk shop; ~ **de** talk about. ● *vi* chat. **causerie** *nf* talk.

causette /kozɛt/ *nf* **faire la** ~ have a chat.

caution /kosjɔ̃/ *nf* surety; (Jur) bail; (appui) backing; (garantie) deposit; **libéré sous** ~ released on bail.

cautionner [1] *vt* guarantee; (soutenir) back.

cavalcade /kavalkad/ *nf* stampede, rush.

cavalier, -ière /kavalje, -jɛʀ/ *adj* offhand; **allée cavalière** bridle path. ● *nm, f* rider; (pour danser) partner. ● *nm* (aux échecs) knight.

cave /kav/ *nf* cellar. ● *adj* sunken.

caveau (*pl* ~**x**) /kavo/ *nm* vault.

caverne /kavɛʀn/ *nf* cave.

CCP *abrév m* (**compte chèque postal**) post office account.

CD *abrév m* (**compact disc**) CD.

CD-ROM *abrév m inv* (**compact disc read only memory**) CD-ROM.

....

ce, c', cet, cette (*pl* **ces**) /sə,s, sɛt, se/

c' before e. **cet** before vowel or mute h.

● **ce, cet, cette** (pl **ces**) adjectif démonstratif
····▸ this; (plus éloigné) that; **ces** these; (plus éloigné) those; **cette nuit** (passée) last night; (à venir) tonight.

● **ce, c'** pronom démonstratif
····▸ **c'est** it's ou it is; **c'est un policier** he's a policeman; ∼ **sont eux qui l'ont fait** THEY did it; **qui est-∼?** who is it?
····▸ **ce que/qui** what; ∼ **que je ne comprends pas** what I don't understand; **elle est venue, ∼ qui est étonnant** she came, which is surprising; ∼ **que tu as de la chance!** how lucky you are!; **tout ∼ que je sais** all I know; **tout ∼ qu'elle trouve/peut** everything she finds/can.

··

CE abrév f (**Communauté européenne**) EC.
ceci /səsi/ pron this.
cécité /sesite/ nf blindness.
céder /sede/ [14] vt give up; ∼ **le passage** give way; (vendre) sell. ● vi (se rompre) give way; (se soumettre) give in.
cédérom /sederɔm/ nm CD-ROM.
cédille /sedij/ nf cedilla.
cèdre /sɛdʀ/ nm cedar.
CEI abrév f (**Communauté des États indépendants**) CIS.
ceinture /sɛ̃tyʀ/ nf belt; (taille) waist; ∼ **de sauvetage** lifebelt; ∼ **de sécurité** seatbelt.
cela /səla/ pron that, it; (pour désigner) that; ∼ **va de soi** it is obvious; ∼ **dit/fait** having said/done that.
célèbre /selɛbʀ/ adj famous.
célébrer [14] vt celebrate.
célébrité nf fame; (personne) celebrity.
céleri /sɛlʀi/ nm (en branches) celery.
céleri-rave (pl **céleris-raves**) nm celeriac.
célibat /seliba/ nm celibacy; (état) single status.
célibataire /selibatɛʀ/ adj single.
● nm bachelor. ● nf single woman.

celle, celles /sɛl/ ⇒CELUI.
cellier /selje/ nm wine cellar.
cellulaire /selylɛʀ/ adj cell; **emprisonnement** ∼ solitary confinement; **fourgon** ou **voiture** ∼ prison van; **téléphone** ∼ cellular phone.
cellule /selyl/ nf cell.
celui, celle (pl **ceux, celles**) /səlɥi, sɛl, sø/ pron the one; ∼ **de mon ami** my friend's; ∼**-ci** this (one); ∼**-là** that (one); **ceux-ci** these (ones); **ceux-là** those (ones).
cendre /sɑ̃dʀ/ nf ash.
cendrier /sɑ̃dʀije/ nm ashtray.
censé, ∼e /sɑ̃se/ adj **être** ∼ **faire** be supposed to do.
censeur /sɑ̃sœʀ/ nm censor; (Scol) administrator in charge of discipline.
censure /sɑ̃syʀ/ nf censorship.
censurer [1] vt censor; (critiquer) censure.
cent /sɑ̃/ a & nm (a) hundred; ∼ **un** a hundred and one; **20 pour** ∼ 20 per cent.
centaine /sɑ̃tɛn/ nf hundred; **une** ∼ (**de**) (about) a hundred.
centenaire /sɑ̃tnɛʀ/ nm (anniversaire) centenary.
centième /sɑ̃tjɛm/ a & nmf hundredth.
centimètre /sɑ̃timɛtʀ/ nm centimetre; (ruban) tape-measure.
central, ∼e (mpl **-aux**) /sɑ̃tʀal, -o/ adj central. ● nm (pl **-aux**) ∼ (**téléphonique**) (telephone) exchange.
centrale nf power-station.
centre /sɑ̃tʀ/ nm centre; ∼ **commercial** shopping centre; (US) mall; ∼ **de formation** training centre; ∼ **hospitalier** hospital. **centrer** [1] vt centre. **centre-ville** (pl **centres-villes**) nm town centre.
centuple /sɑ̃typl/ nm **le** ∼ **de** a hundred times; **au** ∼ a hundredfold.
cep /sɛp/ nm vine stock.
cépage /sepaʒ/ nm grape variety.
cèpe /sɛp/ nm cep.
cependant /səpɑ̃dɑ̃/ adv however.
céramique /seramik/ nf ceramic; (art) ceramics (+ sg).

C

cercle /sɛʀkl/ *nm* circle; (cerceau) hoop; (association) society, club; ～ **vicieux** vicious circle.

cercueil /sɛʀkœj/ *nm* coffin.

céréale /seʀeal/ *nf* cereal; ～**s** (Culin) (breakfast) cereal.

cérébral, ～**e** (*mpl* **-aux**) /seʀebʀal, -o/ *adj* cerebral; (*travail*) intellectual.

cérémonie /seʀemɔni/ *nf* ceremony; **sans** ～**s** (*repas*) informal; (*recevoir*) informally.

cerf /sɛʀ/ *nm* stag.

cerfeuil /sɛʀfœj/ *nm* chervil.

cerf-volant (*pl* **cerfs-volants**) /sɛʀvɔlɑ̃/ *nm* kite.

cerise /s(ə)ʀiz/ *nf* cherry. **cerisier** *nm* cherry tree.

cerne /sɛʀn/ *nm* ring.

cerner /sɛʀne/ [1] *vt* surround;. (*question*) define; **avoir les yeux cernés** have rings under one's eyes.

certain, ～**e** /sɛʀtɛ̃, -ɛn/ *adj* certain; (*sûr*) certain, sure (**de** of; **que** that); **d'un** ～ **âge** no longer young; **un** ～ **temps** some time. **certainement** *adv* (probablement) most probably; (avec certitude) certainly. **certains**, **-es** *pron* some people.

certes /sɛʀt/ *adv* (sans doute) admittedly; (bien sûr) of course.

certificat /sɛʀtifika/ *nm* certificate.

certifier /sɛʀtifje/ [45] *vt* certify; ～ **qch à qn** assure sb of sth; **copie certifiée conforme** certified true copy.

certitude /sɛʀtityd/ *nf* certainty.

cerveau (*pl* ～**x**) /sɛʀvo/ *nm* brain.

cervelle /sɛʀvɛl/ *nf* (Anat) brain; (Culin) brains.

ces /se/ ⇒CE.

césarienne /sezaʀjɛn/ *nf* Caesarean (section).

cesse /sɛs/ *nf* **n'avoir de** ～ **que** have no rest until; **sans** ～ constantly, incessantly.

cesser /sese/ [1] *vt* stop; ～ **de faire** stop doing. ● *vi* cease; **faire** ～ put an end to.

cessez-le-feu /seselfø/ *nm inv* ceasefire.

cession /sɛsjɔ̃/ *nf* transfer.

c'est-à-dire /sɛtadiʀ/ *conj* that is (to say).

cet, **cette** /sɛt/ ⇒CE.

ceux /sø/ ⇒CELUI.

chacun, ～**e** /ʃakœ̃, -yn/ *pron* each (one), every one; (tout le monde) everyone; ～ **d'entre nous** each (one) of us.

chagrin /ʃagʀɛ̃/ *nm* sorrow; **avoir du** ～ be sad.

chahut /ʃay/ *nm* row, din.

chahuter /ʃayte/ [1] *vi* make a row. ● *vt* (*enseignant*) be rowdy with; (*orateur*) heckle.

chaîne /ʃɛn/ *nf* chain; (de télévision) channel; ～ (**d'assemblage**) assembly line; ～**s** (Auto) snow chains; ～ **de montagnes** mountain range; ～ **de montage/fabrication** assembly/production line; ～ **hi-fi** hi-fi system; ～ **laser** CD player; **en** ～ (*accidents*) multiple; (*réaction*) chain. **chaînette** *nf* (small) chain. **chaînon** *nm* link.

chair /ʃɛʀ/ *nf* flesh; **bien en** ～ plump; **en** ～ **et en os** in the flesh; ～ **à saucisses** sausage meat; **la** ～ **de poule** goose pimples. ● *a inv* (couleur) ～ flesh-coloured.

chaire /ʃɛʀ/ *nf* (d'église) pulpit; (Univ) chair.

chaise /ʃɛz/ *nf* chair; ～ **longue** deckchair.

châle /ʃal/ *nm* shawl.

chaleur /ʃalœʀ/ *nf* heat; (moins intense) warmth; (d'un accueil, d'une couleur) warmth. **chaleureux**, **-euse** *adj* warm.

chalumeau (*pl* ～**x**) /ʃalymo/ *nm* blowtorch.

chalutier /ʃalytje/ *nm* trawler.

chamailler (**se**) /(sə)ʃamɑje/ [1] *vpr* squabble.

chambre /ʃɑ̃bʀ/ *nf* (bed)room; (Pol, Jur) chamber; **faire** ～ **à part** sleep in separate rooms; ～ **à air** inner tube; ～ **d'amis** spare *ou* guest room; ～ **de commerce** (**et d'industrie**) Chamber of Commerce; ～ **à coucher** bedroom; ～ **à un lit/deux lits** single/twin room; ～ **pour deux personnes** double room; ～ **forte** strong-room; ～ **d'hôte** bed and breakfast, B and B.

chambrer [1] *vt* (*vin*) bring to room temperature.

chameau (*pl* ~**x**) /ʃamo/ *nm* camel.

chamois /ʃamwa/ *nm* chamois.

champ /ʃɑ̃/ *nm* field; ~ **de bataille** battlefield; ~ **de courses** racecourse; ~ **de tir** firing range.

champêtre /ʃɑ̃pɛtʀ/ *adj* rural.

champignon /ʃɑ̃piɲɔ̃/ *nm* mushroom; (moisissure) fungus; ~ **de Paris** button mushroom.

champion, ~**ne** /ʃɑ̃pjɔ̃, -ɔn/ *nm,f* champion. **championnat** *nm* championship.

chance /ʃɑ̃s/ *nf* (good) luck; (possibilité) chance; **avoir de la** ~ be lucky; **quelle** ~! what luck!

chanceler /ʃɑ̃sle/ [38] *vi* stagger; (fig) falter, waver.

chancelier /ʃɑ̃səlje/ *nm* chancellor.

chanceux, -**euse** /ʃɑ̃sø, -z/ *adj* lucky.

chandail /ʃɑ̃daj/ *nm* sweater.

chandelier /ʃɑ̃dəlje/ *nm* candlestick.

chandelle /ʃɑ̃dɛl/ *nf* candle; **dîner aux** ~**s** candlelight dinner.

change /ʃɑ̃ʒ/ *nm* (foreign) exchange; (taux) exchange rate.

changement /ʃɑ̃ʒmɑ̃/ *nm* change; ~ **de vitesse** (dispositif) gears.

changer /ʃɑ̃ʒe/ [40] *vt* change; ~ **qch de place** move sth; (échanger) change (**pour**, **contre** for); ~ **de nom/ voiture** change one's name/car; ~ **de place/train** change places/trains; ~ **de direction** change direction; ~ **d'avis** *ou* **d'idée** change one's mind; ~ **de vitesse** change gear. □ **se** ~ *vpr* change, get changed.

chanson /ʃɑ̃sɔ̃/ *nf* song.

chant /ʃɑ̃/ *nm* singing; (chanson) song; (Relig) hymn.

chantage /ʃɑ̃taʒ/ *nm* blackmail.

chanter /ʃɑ̃te/ [1] *vt* sing; **si cela vous chante** 🄸 if you feel like it. ● *vi* sing; **faire** ~ (délit) blackmail.

chanteur, -**euse** *nm,f* singer.

chantier /ʃɑ̃tje/ *nm* building site; ~ **naval** shipyard; **mettre en** ~ get under way, start.

chaos /kao/ *nm* chaos.

chaparder /ʃapaʀde/ [1] *vt* 🄸 pinch 🄸, filch.

chapeau (*pl* ~**x**) /ʃapo/ *nm* hat; ~! well done!

chapelet /ʃaplɛ/ *nm* rosary; (fig) string.

chapelle /ʃapɛl/ *nf* chapel.

chapelure /ʃaplyʀ/ *nf* (Culin) breadcrumbs.

chaperonner /ʃapʀɔ̃ne/ [1] *vt* chaperone.

chapiteau (*pl* ~**x**) /ʃapito/ *nm* marquee; (de cirque) big top; (de colonne) capital.

chapitre /ʃapitʀ/ *nm* chapter; (fig) subject.

chaque /ʃak/ *adj* every, each.

char /ʃaʀ/ *nm* (Mil) tank; (de carnaval) float; (charrette) cart; (dans l'antiquité) chariot.

charabia /ʃaʀabja/ *nm* 🄸 gibberish.

charade /ʃaʀad/ *nf* riddle.

charbon /ʃaʀbɔ̃/ *nm* coal; ~ **de bois** charcoal.

charcuterie /ʃaʀkytʀi/ *nf* pork butcher's shop; (aliments) (cooked) pork meats. **charcutier**, -**ière** *nm,f* pork butcher.

chardon /ʃaʀdɔ̃/ *nm* thistle.

charge /ʃaʀʒ/ *nf* load, burden; (Mil, Électr, Jur) charge; (responsabilité) responsibility; **avoir qn à** ~ be responsible for; ~**s** expenses; (de locataire) service charges; **être à la** ~ **de** (*personne*) be the responsibility of; (*frais*) be payable by; ~**s sociales** social security contributions; **prendre en** ~ take charge of.

chargé, ~**e** /ʃaʀʒe/ *adj* (*véhicule*) loaded; (*journée, emploi du temps*) busy; (*langue*) coated. ● *nm,f* ~ **de mission** head of mission; ~ **d'affaires** chargé d'affaires, ~ **de cours** lecturer.

chargement /ʃaʀʒəmɑ̃/ *nm* loading; (objets) load.

charger /ʃaʀʒe/ [40] *vt* load; (Ordinat, Photo) load; (attaquer) charge; (*batterie*) charge; ~ **qn de** (*fardeau*) weigh sb down with; (*tâche*) entrust sb with; ~ **qn de faire** make sb responsible for doing. ● *vi* (attaquer) charge. □ **se ~ de** *vpr* take charge *ou* care of.

chariot /ʃaʀjo/ *nm* (à roulettes) trolley; (US) cart; (charrette) cart.

charitable /ʃaʀitabl/ *adj* charitable.

charité /ʃaʀite/ *nf* charity; **faire la ~ à** give (money) to.

charlatan /ʃaʀlatɑ̃/ *nm* charlatan.

charmant, ~e /ʃaʀmɑ̃, -t/ *adj* charming.

charme /ʃaʀm/ *nm* charm; (qui envoûte) spell. **charmer** [1] *vt* charm. **charmeur, -euse** *nm,f* charmer.

charnel, ~le /ʃaʀnɛl/ *adj* carnal.

charnière /ʃaʀnjɛʀ/ *nf* hinge; **à la ~ de** at the meeting point between.

charnu, ~e /ʃaʀny/ *adj* plump, fleshy.

charpente /ʃaʀpɑ̃t/ *nf* framework; (carrure) build.

charpentier /ʃaʀpɑ̃tje/ *nm* carpenter.

charpie /ʃaʀpi/ *nf* **en ~** in shreds.

charrette /ʃaʀɛt/ *nf* cart.

charrue /ʃaʀy/ *nf* plough.

chasse /ʃas/ *nf* hunting; (au fusil) shooting; (poursuite) chase; (recherche) hunt(ing); **~ (d'eau)** (toilet) flush; **~ sous-marine** harpoon fishing.

chasse-neige /ʃasnɛʒ/ *nm inv* snowplough.

chasser /ʃase/ [1] *vt* hunt; (au fusil) shoot; (faire partir) chase away; (odeur, employé) get rid of. ● *vi* go hunting; (au fusil) go shooting.

chasseur, -euse /ʃasœʀ, -øz/ *nm,f* hunter. ● *nm* bellboy; (US) bellhop; (avion) fighter plane.

châssis /ʃasi/ *nm* frame; (Auto) chassis.

chasteté /ʃastəte/ *nf* chastity.

chat /ʃa/ *nm* cat; (mâle) tomcat.

châtaigne /ʃatɛɲ/ *nf* chestnut. **châtaignier** *nm* chestnut tree. **châtain** *a inv* chestnut (brown).

château (*pl* **~x**) /ʃato/ *nm* castle; (manoir) manor; **~ d'eau** water tower; **~ fort** fortified castle.

châtiment /ʃatimɑ̃/ *nm* punishment.

chaton /ʃatɔ̃/ *nm* (chat) kitten.

chatouillement /ʃatujmɑ̃/ *nm* tickling. **chatouiller** [1] *vt* tickle. **chatouilleux, -euse** *adj* ticklish; (susceptible) touchy.

châtrer /ʃatʀe/ [1] *vt* castrate; (chat) neuter.

chatte /ʃat/ *nf* female cat.

chaud, ~e /ʃo, -d/ *adj* warm; (brûlant) hot; (vif: fig) warm. ● *nm* heat; **au ~** in the warm(th); **avoir ~** be warm; be hot; **il fait ~** it is warm; it is hot; **pour te tenir ~** to keep you warm. **chaudement** *adv* warmly; (disputé) hotly.

chaudière /ʃodjɛʀ/ *nf* boiler.

chaudron /ʃodʀɔ̃/ *nm* cauldron.

chauffage /ʃofaʒ/ *nm* heating; **~ central** central heating.

chauffard /ʃofaʀ/ *nm* (péj) reckless driver.

chauffer /ʃofe/ [1] *vt/i* heat (up); (moteur, appareil) overheat. □ **se ~** *vpr* warm oneself (up).

chauffeur /ʃofœʀ/ *nm* driver; (aux gages de qn) chauffeur.

chaume /ʃom/ *nm* (de toit) thatch.

chaussée /ʃose/ *nf* road(way).

chausse-pied (*pl* **~s**) /ʃospje/ *nm* shoehorn.

chausser /ʃose/ [1] *vt* (chaussures) put on; (enfant) put shoes on (to). ● *vi* **~ bien** (aller) fit well; **~ du 35** take a size 35 shoe. □ **se ~** *vpr* put one's shoes on.

chaussette /ʃosɛt/ *nf* sock.

chausson /ʃosɔ̃/ *nm* slipper; (de bébé) bootee; **~ de danse** ballet shoe; **~ aux pommes** apple turnover.

chaussure /ʃosyʀ/ *nf* shoe; **~ de ski** ski boot; **~ de marche** hiking boot.

chauve /ʃov/ *adj* bald.

chauve-souris (*pl* **chauves-souris**) /ʃovsuʀi/ *nf* bat.

chauvin, ~e /ʃovɛ̃, -in/ *adj* chauvinistic. ● *nm,f* chauvinist.

chavirer /ʃaviʀe/ [1] *vt* (bateau) capsize; (objets) tip over.

chef /ʃɛf/ *nm* leader, head; (supérieur) boss, superior; (Culin) chef; (de tribu) chief; **architecte en ~** chief *ou* head architect; **~ d'accusation** (Jur) charge; **~ d'équipe** foreman; (Sport) captain; ∼ **d'État** head of State; ∼ **de famille** head of the family; ∼ **de file** (Pol) leader; ∼ **de gare** stationmaster; ∼ **d'orchestre** conductor; ∼ **de service** department head; ∼ **de train** guard; (US) conductor.

chef-d'œuvre (*pl* **chefs-d'œuvre**) /ʃɛdœvʀ/ *nm* masterpiece.

chef-lieu (*pl* **chefs-lieux**) /ʃɛfljø/ *nm* county town, administrative centre.

chemin /ʃəmɛ̃/ *nm* road; (étroit) lane; (de terre) track; (pour piétons) path; (passage) way; (direction, trajet) way; **avoir du** ∼ **à faire** have a long way to go; ∼ **de fer** railway; **par** ∼ **de fer** by rail; ∼ **de halage** towpath; ∼ **vicinal** country lane.

cheminée /ʃəmine/ *nf* chimney; (intérieure) fireplace; (encadrement) mantelpiece; (de bateau) funnel.

cheminot /ʃəmino/ *nm* railwayman; (US) railroad man.

chemise /ʃəmiz/ *nf* shirt; (dossier) folder; (de livre) jacket; ∼ **de nuit** nightdress. **chemisette** *nf* short-sleeved shirt. **chemisier** *nm* blouse.

chêne /ʃɛn/ *nm* oak.

chenil /ʃəni(l)/ *nm* (pension) kennels (+ *sg*).

chenille /ʃənij/ *nf* caterpillar; **véhicule à** ∼**s** tracked vehicle.

cheptel /ʃɛptɛl/ *nm* livestock.

chèque /ʃɛk/ *nm* cheque; ∼ **sans provision** bad cheque; ∼ **de voyage** traveller's cheque. **chéquier** *nm* chequebook.

cher, chère /ʃɛʀ/ *adj* (coûteux) dear, expensive; (aimé) dear; (dans la correspondance) dear. ● *adv* (coûter, payer) a lot (of money); (en importance) dearly. ● *nm,f* **mon** ∼, **ma chère** my dear.

chercher /ʃɛʀʃe/ [1] *vt* look for; (aide, paix, gloire) seek; **aller** ∼ go and get *ou* fetch, go for; ∼ **à faire** attempt to do; ∼ **la petite bête** be finicky.

chercheur, -euse /ʃɛʀʃœʀ, -øz/ *nm,f* research worker.

chèrement /ʃɛʀmɑ̃/ *adv* dearly.

chéri, ∼e /ʃeʀi/ *adj* beloved. ● *nm,f* darling.

chérir /ʃeʀiʀ/ [2] *vt* cherish.

chétif, -ive /ʃetif, -v/ *adj* puny.

cheval (*pl* **-aux**) /ʃəval, -o/ *nm* horse; **à** ∼ on horseback; **à** ∼ **sur** astride, straddling; **faire du** ∼ ride, go horse-riding.

chevalerie /ʃəvalʀi/ *nf* chivalry.

chevalet /ʃəvalɛ/ *nm* easel; (de menuisier) trestle.

chevalier /ʃəvalje/ *nm* knight.

chevalière /ʃəvaljɛʀ/ *nf* signet ring.

cheval-vapeur (*pl* **chevaux-vapeur**) /ʃəvalvapœʀ/ *nm* horsepower.

chevaucher /ʃəvoʃe/ [1] *vt* sit astride. □ **se** ∼ *vpr* overlap.

chevelu, ∼e /ʃəvly/ *adj* (péj) long-haired; (Bot) hairy.

chevelure /ʃəvlyʀ/ *nf* hair.

chevet /ʃəvɛ/ *nm* **au** ∼ **de** at the bedside of; **livre de** ∼ bedside book.

cheveu (*pl* ∼**x**) /ʃəvø/ *nm* (poil) hair; ∼**x** (chevelure) hair; **avoir les** ∼**x longs** have long hair.

cheville /ʃəvij/ *nf* ankle; (fiche) peg, pin; (pour mur) (wall) plug.

chèvre /ʃɛvʀ/ *nf* goat.

chevreuil /ʃəvʀœj/ *nm* roe (deer); (Culin) venison.

chevron /ʃəvʀɔ̃/ *nm* (poutre) rafter; **à** ∼**s** herringbone.

chez /ʃe/ *prép* (au domicile de) at the house of; (parmi) among; (dans le caractère ou l'œuvre de) in; **aller** ∼ **qn** go to sb's house; ∼ **le boucher** at *ou* to the butcher's; ∼ **soi** at home; **rentrer** ∼ **soi** go home. **chez-soi** *nm inv* home.

chic /ʃik/ *a inv* smart; (gentil) kind. ● *nm* style; **avoir le** ∼ **pour** have a knack for; ∼ **(alors)!** great!

chicane /ʃikan/ *nf* double bend; **chercher** ∼ **à qn** pick a quarrel with sb.

chiche /ʃiʃ/ *adj* mean (de with); ∼ **que je le fais!** 🇬🇧 I bet I can do it.

chichis /ʃiʃi/ *nmpl* 🇬🇧 fuss.

chicorée /ʃikɔʀe/ *nf* (frisée) endive; (à café) chicory.

chien /ʃjɛ̃/ *nm* dog; ∼ **d'aveugle** guide dog; ∼ **de garde** watch-dog. **chienne** *nf* dog, bitch.

chiffon /ʃifɔ̃/ nm rag; (pour nettoyer) duster; ~ **humide** damp cloth.
chiffonner [1] vt crumple; (préoccuper 🖪) bother.

chiffre /ʃifʀ/ nm figure; (numéro) number; (code) code; ~**s arabes/ romains** Arabic/Roman numerals; ~**s (statistiques)** statistics; ~ **d'affaires** turnover.

chiffrer /ʃifʀe/ [1] vt put a figure on, assess; (texte) encode. □ **se** ~ **à** vpr come to.

chignon /ʃiɲɔ̃/ nm bun, chignon.

Chili /ʃili/ nm Chile.

chimère /ʃimɛʀ/ nf fantasy.

chimie /ʃimi/ nf chemistry.
chimique adj chemical. **chimiste** nmf chemist.

chimpanzé /ʃɛ̃pɑ̃ze/ nm chimpanzee.

Chine /ʃin/ nf China.

chinois, ~**e** /ʃinwa, -z/ adj Chinese. ● nm (Ling) Chinese. **C**~, ~**e** nm,f Chinese.

chiot /ʃjo/ nm pup(py).

chipoter /ʃipɔte/ [1] vi (manger) pick at one's food; (discuter) quibble.

chips /ʃips/ nf inv crisp; (US) chip.

chirurgie /ʃiʀyʀʒi/ nf surgery; ~ **esthétique** plastic surgery. **chirurgien** nm surgeon.

chlore /klɔʀ/ nm chlorine.

choc /ʃɔk/ nm (heurt) impact, shock; (émotion) shock; (collision) crash; (affrontement) clash; (Méd) shock; **sous le** ~ in shock.

chocolat /ʃɔkɔla/ nm chocolate; (à boire) drinking chocolate; ~ **au lait** milk chocolate; ~ **chaud** hot chocolate; ~ **noir** plain ou dark chocolate.

chœur /kœʀ/ nm (antique) chorus; (chanteurs, nef) choir; **en** ~ in chorus.

choisir /ʃwaziʀ/ [2] vt choose, select.

choix /ʃwa/ nm choice, selection; **fromage ou dessert au** ~ a choice of cheese or dessert; **de** ~ choice; **de premier** ~ top quality.

chômage /ʃomaʒ/ nm unemployment; **au** ~, **en** ~ unemployed; **mettre en** ~ **technique** lay off.

chômeur, -**euse** /ʃomœʀ, -øz/ nm,f unemployed person; **les** ~**s** the unemployed.

choquer /ʃɔke/ [1] vt shock; (commotionner) shake.

choral, ~**e** (mpl ~**s**) /kɔʀal/ adj choral. **chorale** nf choir, choral society.

chorégraphie /kɔʀegʀafi/ nf choreography.

choriste /kɔʀist/ nmf (à l'église) chorister; (à l'opéra) member of the chorus ou choir.

chose /ʃoz/ nf thing; (très) **peu de** ~ nothing much; **pas grand** ~ not much.

chou (pl ~**x**) /ʃu/ nm cabbage; ~ (à **la crème**) cream puff; ~ **de Bruxelles** Brussels sprout; **mon petit** ~ 🖪 my dear.

chouchou, ~**te** /ʃuʃu, -t/ nm,f (de professeur) pet; (du public) darling.

choucroute /ʃukʀut/ nf sauerkraut.

chouette /ʃwɛt/ nf owl. ● adj 🖪 super.

chou-fleur (pl **choux-fleurs**) /ʃuflœʀ/ nm cauliflower.

choyer /ʃwaje/ [31] vt pamper.

chrétien, ~**ne** /kʀetjɛ̃, -jɛn/ a & nm,f Christian.

Christ /kʀist/ nm **le** ~ Christ.

chrome /kʀom/ nm chromium, chrome.

chromosome /kʀomozom/ nm chromosome.

chronique /kʀonik/ adj chronic. ● nf (rubrique) column; (nouvelles) news; (annales) chronicle.

chronologique /kʀonɔlɔʒik/ adj chronological.

chronomètre /kʀonɔmɛtʀ/ nm stopwatch. **chronométrer** [14] vt time.

chrysanthème /kʀizɑ̃tɛm/ nm chrysanthemum.

chuchoter /ʃyʃɔte/ [1] vt/i whisper.

chut /ʃyt/ interj shh, hush.

chute /ʃyt/ nf fall; (déchet) offcut; ~ (**d'eau**) waterfall; ~ **de pluie** rainfall; ~ **des cheveux** hair loss; ~ **des ventes** drop in sales; ~ **de 5%** 5% drop. **chuter** [1] vi fall.

Chypre /ʃipʀ/ nf Cyprus.

ci /si/ adv here; ~-**gît** here lies; **cet homme**-~ this man; **ces maisons**-~ these houses.

ci-après /siapʀɛ/ adv below.

cible /sibl/ nf target.

ciboulette /sibulɛt/ nf (Culin) chives (+ pl).

cicatrice /sikatʀis/ nf scar.

cicatriser /sikatʀize/ [1] vt heal. □ **se** ~ vpr heal.

ci-dessous /sidəsu/ adv below.

ci-dessus /sidəsy/ adv above.

cidre /sidʀ/ nm cider.

ciel (pl **cieux**, **ciels**) /sjɛl, sjø/ nm sky; (Relig) heaven; **cieux** (Relig) heaven.

cierge /sjɛʀʒ/ nm (church) candle.

cigale /sigal/ nf cicada.

cigare /sigaʀ/ nm cigar.

cigarette /sigaʀɛt/ nf cigarette.

cigogne /sigɔɲ/ nf stork.

ci-joint /siʒwɛ̃/ adv enclosed.

cil /sil/ nm eyelash.

cime /sim/ nf peak, tip.

ciment /simɑ̃/ nm cement.

cimetière /simtjɛʀ/ nm cemetery, graveyard; ~ **de voitures** breaker's yard.

cinéaste /sineast/ nmf film-maker.

cinéma /sinema/ nm cinema; (US) movie theater. **cinémathèque** nf film archive; (salle) film theatre. **cinématographique** adj cinema.

cinéphile /sinefil/ nmf film lover.

cinglant, ~**e** /sɛ̃glɑ̃, -t/ adj (vent) biting; (remarque) scathing.

cinglé, ~**e** /sɛ̃gle/ adj 🔢 crazy.

cinq /sɛ̃k/ a & nm five.

cinquante /sɛ̃kɑ̃t/ a & nm fifty.

cinquième /sɛ̃kjɛm/ a & nmf fifth.

cintre /sɛ̃tʀ/ nm coat-hanger; (Archit) curve.

cirage /siʀaʒ/ nm polish.

circoncision /siʀkɔ̃sizjɔ̃/ nf circumcision.

circonflexe /siʀkɔ̃flɛks/ adj circumflex.

circonscription /siʀkɔ̃skʀipsjɔ̃/ nf district; ~ **électorale** constituency; (US) district; (de conseiller, maire) ward.

circonscrire /siʀkɔ̃skʀiʀ/ [30] vt (incendie, épidémie) contain; (sujet) define.

circonspect, ~**e** /siʀkɔ̃spɛkt/ adj circumspect.

circonstance /siʀkɔ̃stɑ̃s/ nf circumstance; (situation) situation; (occasion) occasion; ~**s atténuantes** mitigating circumstances.

circuit /siʀkɥi/ nm circuit; (trajet) tour, trip.

circulaire /siʀkylɛʀ/ a & nf circular.

circulation /siʀkylasjɔ̃/ nf circulation; (de véhicules) traffic.

circuler /siʀkyle/ [1] vi (se répandre, être distribué) circulate; (aller d'un lieu à un autre) get around; (en voiture) travel; (piéton) walk; (être en service) (bus, train) run; **faire** ~ (badauds) move on; (rumeur) spread.

cire /siʀ/ nf wax.

ciré /siʀe/ nm oilskin.

cirer /siʀe/ [1] vt polish.

cirque /siʀk/ nm circus; (arène) amphitheatre; (désordre: fig) chaos; **faire le** ~ 🔢 make a racket 🔢.

ciseau (pl ~**x**) /sizo/ nm chisel; ~**x** scissors.

ciseler /sizle/ [6] vt chisel.

citadelle /sitadɛl/ nf citadel.

citadin, ~**e** /sitadɛ̃, -in/ nm,f city-dweller. ● adj city.

citation /sitasjɔ̃/ nf quotation; (Jur) summons.

cité /site/ nf city; (logements) housing estate; ~ **universitaire** (university) halls of residence.

citer /site/ [1] vt quote, cite; (Jur) summon.

citerne /sitɛʀn/ nf tank.

citoyen, ~**ne** /sitwajɛ̃, -ɛn/ nm,f citizen.

citron /sitʀɔ̃/ nm lemon; ~ **vert** lime. **citronnade** nf lemon squash, (still) lemonade.

citrouille /sitʀuj/ nf pumpkin.

civet /sivɛ/ nm stew; ~ **de lièvre** jugged hare.

civière /sivjɛʀ/ nf stretcher.

civil, ~**e** /sivil/ adj civil; (non militaire) civilian; (poli) civil. ● nm civilian;

dans le ∼ in civilian life; **en** ∼ in plain clothes.

civilisation /sivilizasjɔ̃/ *nf* civilization.

civiliser /sivilize/ [1] *vt* civilize. □ **se** ∼ *vpr* become civilized.

civique /sivik/ *adj* civic.

clair, ∼**e** /klɛʀ/ *adj* clear; (éclairé) light, bright; (*couleur*) light; **le plus** ∼ **de** most of. ● *adv* clearly; **il faisait** ∼ it was already light. ● *nm* ∼ **de lune** moonlight; **tirer une histoire au** ∼ get to the bottom of things. **clairement** *adv* clearly.

clairière /klɛʀjɛʀ/ *nf* clearing.

clairsemé, ∼**e** /klɛʀsəme/ *adj* sparse.

clamer /klame/ [1] *vt* proclaim.

clameur /klamœʀ/ *nf* clamour.

clan /klɑ̃/ *nm* clan.

clandestin, ∼**e** /klɑ̃dɛstɛ̃, -in/ *adj* secret; (*journal*) underground; (*immigration, travail*) illegal; **passager** ∼ stowaway.

clapier /klapje/ *nm* (rabbit) hutch.

clapoter /klapɔte/ [1] *vi* lap.

claquage /klakaʒ/ *nm* strained muscle; **se faire un** ∼ pull a muscle.

claque /klak/ *nf* slap; **en avoir sa** ∼ **(de)** 🄸 be fed up (with) 🄸.

claquer /klake/ [1] *vi* bang; (*porte*) slam, bang; (*fouet*) crack; (se casser 🄸) conk out; (mourir 🄸) snuff it 🄸; ∼ **des doigts** snap one's fingers; ∼ **des mains** clap one's hands; **il claque des dents** his teeth are chattering. ● *vt* (*porte*) slam, bang; (dépenser 🄸) blow; (fatiguer 🄸) tire out.

claquettes /klakɛt/ *nfpl* tap dancing.

clarifier /klaʀifje/ [45] *vt* clarify.

clarinette /klaʀinɛt/ *nf* clarinet.

clarté /klaʀte/ *nf* light, brightness; (netteté) clarity.

classe /klas/ *nf* class; (salle: Scol) classroom; (cours) class, lesson; **aller en** ∼ go to school; **faire la** ∼ teach; ∼ **ouvrière/moyenne** working/middle class.

classement /klasmɑ̃/ *nm* classification; (d'élèves) grading; (de documents) filing; (rang) place, grade; (de coureur) placing.

classer /klase/ [1] *vt* classify; (par mérite) grade; (*papiers*) file; (Jur) (*affaire*) close. □ **se** ∼ *vpr* rank.

classeur /klasœʀ/ *nm* (meuble) filing cabinet; (chemise) file; (à anneaux) ring binder.

classification /klasifikasjɔ̃/ *nf* classification.

classique /klasik/ *adj* classical; (de qualité) classic; (habituel) classic, standard. ● *nm* classic; (auteur) classical author.

clavecin /klavsɛ̃/ *nm* harpsichord.

clavicule /klavikyl/ *nf* collarbone.

clavier /klavje/ *nm* keyboard; ∼ **numérique** keypad.

clé, **clef** /kle/ *nf* key; (outil) spanner; (Mus) clef; ∼ **anglaise** (monkey-) wrench; ∼ **de contact** ignition key; ∼ **à molette** adjustable spanner; ∼ **de voûte** keystone; **prix** ∼**s en main** (de voiture) on-the-road price. ● *a inv* key.

clémence /klemɑ̃s/ *nf* (de climat) mildness; (indulgence) leniency.

clergé /klɛʀʒe/ *nm* clergy.

clérical, ∼**e** (*mpl* -**aux**) /kleʀikal, -o/ *adj* clerical.

cliché /kliʃe/ *nm* cliché; (Photo) negative.

client, ∼**e** /klijɑ̃, -t/ *nm, f* customer; (d'un avocat) client; (d'un médecin) patient; (d'hôtel) guest; (de taxi) passenger.

clientèle /klijɑ̃tɛl/ *nf* customers, clientele; (d'un avocat) clients, practice; (d'un médecin) patients, practice; (soutien) custom.

cligner /kliɲe/ [1] *vi* ∼ **des yeux** blink; ∼ **de l'œil** wink.

clignotant /kliɲɔtɑ̃/ *nm* (Auto) indicator, turn.

clignoter /kliɲɔte/ [1] *vi* blink; (*lumière*) flicker; (comme signal) flash.

climat /klima/ *nm* climate.

climatisation /klimatizasjɔ̃/ *nf* air-conditioning.

clin d'œil /klɛ̃dœj/ *nm* wink; **en un** ∼ in a flash.

clinique /klinik/ *adj* clinical. ● *nf* (private) clinic.

clinquant, ∼**e** /klɛ̃kɑ̃, -t/ *adj* showy.

clip /klip/ *nm* video.

cliquer /klike/ [1] *vi* (Ordinat) click (**sur** on).

cliqueter /klikte/ [38] *vi* (*couverts*) clink; (*clés, monnaie*) jingle; (*ferraille*) rattle. **cliquetis** *nm* clink (ing), jingle, rattle.

clivage /klivaʒ/ *nm* divide.

clochard, **~e** /klɔʃaʀ, -d/ *nm,f* tramp.

cloche /klɔʃ/ *nf* bell; (imbécile 🗉) idiot; **~ à fromage** cheese-cover.

cloche-pied: **à ~** /aklɔʃpje/ *loc* **sauter à ~** hop on one leg.

clocher /klɔʃe/ *nm* bell-tower; (pointu) steeple; **de ~** parochial.

cloison /klwazɔ̃/ *nf* partition; (fig) barrier.

cloître /klwatʀ/ *nm* cloister. **cloîtrer (se)** [1] *vpr* shut oneself away.

cloque /klɔk/ *nf* blister.

clos, **~e** /klo, -z/ *adj* closed.

clôture /klotyʀ/ *nf* fence; (fermeture) closure; (de magasin, bureau) closing; (de débat, liste) close; (en Bourse) close of trading. **clôturer** [1] *vt* enclose, fence in; (*festival, séance*) close.

clou /klu/ *nm* nail; (furoncle) boil; (de spectacle) star attraction; **les ~s** (passage) pedestrian crossing; (US) crosswalk.

clouer /klue/ [1] *vt* nail down; (fig) pin down; **être cloué au lit** be confined to one's bed; **~ le bec à qn** shut sb up.

clouté, **~e** /klute/ *adj* studded; **passage ~** pedestrian crossing; (US) crosswalk.

coaliser (se) /(sə)kɔalize/ [1] *vpr* join forces.

coalition /kɔalisjɔ̃/ *nf* coalition.

cobaye /kɔbaj/ *nm* guinea-pig.

cocaïne /kɔkain/ *nf* cocaine.

cocasse /kɔkas/ *adj* comical.

coccinelle /kɔksinɛl/ *nf* ladybird; (US) ladybug.

cocher /kɔʃe/ [1] *vt* tick (off), check. ● *nm* coachman.

cochon, **~ne** /kɔʃɔ̃, -ɔn/ *nm,f* (personne 🗉) pig. ● *adj* 🗉 filthy. ● *nm* pig. **cochonnerie** *nf* (saleté 🗉) filth; (marchandise 🗉) rubbish, junk.

cocon /kɔkɔ̃/ *nm* cocoon.

cocorico /kɔkɔʀikɔ/ *nm* cock-a-doodle-doo.

cocotier /kɔkɔtje/ *nm* coconut palm.

cocotte /kɔkɔt/ *nf* (marmite) casserole; **~ minute®** pressure-cooker; **ma ~** 🗉 my dear.

cocu, **~e** /kɔky/ *nm,f* 🗉 deceived husband, deceived wife.

code /kɔd/ *nm* code; **~s** dipped headlights; **se mettre en ~s** dip one's headlights; **~ (à) barres** bar code; **~ confidentiel (d'identification)** PIN number; **~ postal** post code; (US) zip code; **~ de la route** Highway Code. **coder** [1] *vt* code, encode.

coéquipier, **-ière** /kɔekipje, -jɛʀ/ *nm,f* team mate.

cœur /kœʀ/ *nm* heart; (aux cartes) hearts (+ *pl*); **~ d'artichaut** artichoke heart; **~ de palmier** palm heart; **à ~ ouvert** (*opération*) open-heart; (*parler*) freely; **avoir bon ~** be kind-hearted; **de bon ~** willingly; (*rire*) heartily; **par ~** by heart; **avoir mal au ~** feel sick *ou* nauseous; **je veux en avoir le ~ net** I want to be clear in my own mind (about it).

coffre /kɔfʀ/ *nm* chest; (pour argent) safe; (Auto) boot; (US) trunk. **coffre-fort** (*pl* **coffres-forts**) *nm* safe.

coffret /kɔfʀɛ/ *nm* casket, box; (de livres, cassettes) boxed set.

cogner /kɔɲe/ [1] *vt/i* knock. □ **se ~** *vpr* knock oneself; **se ~ la tête** bump one's head.

cohabiter /kɔabite/ [1] *vi* live together.

cohérent, **~e** /kɔeʀɑ̃, -t/ *adj* coherent; (homogène) consistent.

cohue /kɔy/ *nf* crowd.

coi, **~te** /kwa, -t/ *adj* silent.

coiffe /kwaf/ *nf* headgear.

coiffer /kwafe/ [1] *vt* do the hair of; (*chapeau*) put on; (surmonter) cap; **~ qn d'un chapeau** put a hat on sb; **coiffé de** wearing; **être bien/mal coiffé** have tidy/untidy hair. □ **se ~** *vpr* do one's hair.

coiffeur, **-euse** /kwafœʀ, -øz/ *nm,f* hairdresser. **coiffeuse** *nf* dressing-table.

coiffure /kwafyʀ/ nf hairstyle; (métier) hairdressing; (chapeau) hat.

coin /kwɛ̃/ nm corner; (endroit) spot; (cale) wedge; **au ~ du feu** by the fireside; **dans le ~** locally; **du ~** local.

coincer /kwɛse/ [10] vt jam; (caler) wedge; (attraper 🆃) catch. □ **se ~** vpr get jammed.

coïncidence /kɔɛsidɑ̃s/ nf coincidence.

coing /kwɛ̃/ nm quince.

coït /kɔit/ nm intercourse.

col /kɔl/ nm collar; (de bouteille) neck; (de montagne) pass; **~ blanc** white-collar worker; **~ roulé** polo-neck; (US) turtle-neck; **~ de l'utérus** cervix; **se casser le ~ du fémur** break one's hip.

colère /kɔlɛʀ/ nf anger; (accès) fit of anger; **en ~** angry; **se mettre en ~** lose one's temper; **faire une ~** throw a tantrum.

coléreux, -euse /kɔleʀø, -z/ adj quick-tempered.

colin /kɔlɛ̃/ nm (merlu) hake; (lieu noir) coley.

colique /kɔlik/ nf diarrhoea; (Méd) colic.

colis /kɔli/ nm parcel.

collaborateur, -trice /kɔlabɔʀatœʀ, -tʀis/ nm,f collaborator; (journaliste) contributor; (collègue) colleague.

collaboration /kɔlabɔʀasjɔ̃/ nf collaboration (à on); (à ouvrage, projet) contribution (à to).

collaborer /kɔlabɔʀe/ [1] vi collaborate (à on); **~ à** (journal) contribute to.

collant, ~e /kɔlɑ̃, -t/ adj (moulant) skin-tight; (poisseux) sticky. ● nm (bas) tights; (US) panty hose.

colle /kɔl/ nf glue; (en pâte) paste; (problème 🆃) poser; (Scol 🆃) detention.

collecter /kɔlɛkte/ [1] vt collect.

collectif, -ive /kɔlɛktif, -v/ adj collective; (billet, voyage) group.

collection /kɔlɛksjɔ̃/ nf collection; (ouvrages) series (+ sg); (du même auteur) set. **collectionner** [1] vt collect. **collectionneur, -euse** nm,f collector.

collectivité /kɔlɛktivite/ nf community; **~ locale** local authority.

collège /kɔlɛ3/ nm secondary school (up to age 15); (US) junior high school; (assemblée) college. **collégien, ~ne** nm,f schoolboy, schoolgirl.

collègue /kɔlɛg/ nmf colleague.

coller /kɔle/ [1] vt stick; (avec colle liquide) glue; (affiche) stick up; (mettre 🆃) stick; (par une question 🆃) stump; (Scol 🆃) **se faire ~** get a detention; **je me suis fait ~ en maths** I failed ou flunked maths. ● vi stick (à to); (être collant) be sticky; **~ à** (convenir à) fit, correspond to.

collet /kɔlɛ/ nm (piège) snare; **~ monté** prim and proper; **mettre la main au ~ de qn** collar sb.

collier /kɔlje/ nm necklace; (de chien) collar.

colline /kɔlin/ nf hill.

collision /kɔlizjɔ̃/ nf (choc) collision; (lutte) clash; **entrer en ~ (avec)** collide (with).

collyre /kɔliʀ/ nm eye drops (+ pl).

colmater /kɔlmate/ [1] vt plug, seal.

colombe /kɔlɔ̃b/ nf dove.

Colombie /kɔlɔ̃bi/ nf Colombia.

colon /kɔlɔ̃/ nm settler.

colonel /kɔlɔnɛl/ nm colonel.

colonie /kɔlɔni/ nf colony; **~ de vacances** children's holiday camp.

colonne /kɔlɔn/ nf column; **~ vertébrale** spine; **en ~ par deux** in double file.

colorant /kɔlɔʀɑ̃/ nm colouring.

colorier /kɔlɔʀje/ [45] vt colour (in).

colosse /kɔlɔs/ nm giant.

colza /kɔlza/ nm rape(-seed).

coma /kɔma/ nm coma; **dans le ~** in a coma.

combat /kɔ̃ba/ nm fight; (Sport) match; **~s** fighting. **combatif, -ive** adj eager to fight; (esprit) fighting.

combattre /kɔ̃batʀ/ [11] vt/i fight.

combien /kɔ̃bjɛ̃/ adv **~ (de)** (quantité) how much; (nombre) how many; (temps) how long; **~ il a changé!** (comme) how he has changed!; **~ y a-t-il d'ici à …?** how far is it to …?; **on est le ~ aujourd'hui?** what's the date today?

combinaison /kɔ̃binɛzɔ̃/ *nf*
combination; (de femme) slip; (bleu de
travail) boiler suit; (US) overalls; ~
d'aviateur flying-suit; ~ de plongée
wetsuit.

combine /kɔ̃bin/ *nf* trick; (fraude)
fiddle; (intrigue) scheme.

combiné /kɔ̃bine/ *nm* (de téléphone)
receiver, handset.

combiner /kɔ̃bine/ [1] *vt* (réunir)
combine; (calculer) devise; ~ de faire
plan to do.

comble /kɔ̃bl/ *adj* packed. ● *nm*
height; ~s (mansarde) attic, loft; c'est
le ~! that's the (absolute) limit!

combler /kɔ̃ble/ [1] *vt* fill; (perte,
déficit) make good; (désir) fulfil; ~ qn
de cadeaux lavish gifts on sb.

combustible /kɔ̃bystibl/ *nm* fuel.

comédie /kɔmedi/ *nf* comedy;
(histoire 🗓) fuss; ~ musicale musical;
jouer la ~ put on an act.
comédien, ~ne *nm, f* actor,
actress.

comestible /kɔmɛstibl/ *adj* edible.

comète /kɔmɛt/ *nf* comet.

comique /kɔmik/ *adj* comical,
funny; (genre) comic. ● *nm* (acteur)
comic; (comédie) comedy; (côté drôle)
comical aspect.

commandant /kɔmɑ̃dɑ̃/ *nm*
commander; (dans l'armée de terre)
major; ~ (de bord) captain; ~ en
chef Commander-in-Chief.

commande /kɔmɑ̃d/ *nf* (Comm)
order; (Tech) control; ~s (d'avion)
controls.

commandement /kɔmɑ̃dmɑ̃/ *nm*
command; (Relig) commandment.

commander /kɔmɑ̃de/ [1] *vt*
command; (acheter) order; (étude,
œuvre d'art) commission; ~ à
(maîtriser) control; ~ à qn de
command sb to. ● *vi* be in command.

comme /kɔm/ *adv* ~ c'est bon! it's
so good!; ~ il est mignon! isn't he
sweet! ● *conj* (dans une comparaison) as;
(dans une équivalence, illustration) like; (en
tant que) as; (puisque) as, since; (au
moment où) as; vif ~ l'éclair as quick
as a flash; travailler ~ sage-femme
work as a midwife; ~ ci ~ ça so-so;
~ il faut properly; ~ pour faire as if
to do; jolie ~ tout as pretty as

anything; qu'est-ce qu'il y a ~
légumes? what is there in the way
of vegetables?

commencer /kɔmɑ̃se/ [10] *vt/i*
begin, start; ~ à faire begin *ou* start
to do.

comment /kɔmɑ̃/ *adv* how; ~?
(répétition) pardon?; (surprise) what?; ~
est-il? what is he like?; le ~ et le
pourquoi the whys and wherefores.

commentaire /kɔmɑ̃tɛr/ *nm*
comment; (d'un texte, événement)
commentary. **commentateur**,
-trice *nm, f* commentator.

commenter /kɔmɑ̃te/ [1] *vt*
comment on; (film, visite) provide a
commentary for; (radio, TV)
commentate.

commérages /kɔmeraʒ/ *nmpl*
gossip.

commerçant, ~e /kɔmɛrsɑ̃, -t/
adj (rue) shopping; (personne)
business-minded. ● *nm, f*
shopkeeper.

commerce /kɔmɛrs/ *nm* trade,
commerce; (magasin) business; faire
du ~ be in business.

commercial, ~e (*mpl* -iaux)
/kɔmɛrsjal, -jo/ *adj* commercial.
commercialiser [1] *vt* market.

commettre /kɔmɛtr/ [42] *vt*
commit.

commis /kɔmi/ *nm* (de magasin)
assistant; (de bureau) clerk.

commissaire /kɔmisɛr/ *nm*
commissioner; (Sport) steward; ~ (de
police) (police) superintendent.
commissaire-priseur (*pl* **com-
missaires-priseurs**) *nm* auctioneer.

commissariat /kɔmisarja/ *nm* ~
(de police) police station.

commission /kɔmisjɔ̃/ *nf*
commission; (course) errand;
(message) message; ~s shopping.

commode /kɔmɔd/ *adj* handy,
convenient; (facile) easy; il n'est pas
~ he's a difficult customer. ● *nf*
chest (of drawers). **commodité** *nf*
convenience.

commotion /kɔmosjɔ̃/ *nf* ~
(cérébrale) concussion.

commun, ~e /kɔmœ̃, -yn/ *adj*
common; (effort, action) joint; (frais,

pièce) shared; **en ~** jointly; **avoir** *ou* **mettre en ~** share; **le ~ des mortels** ordinary mortals. **communal, ~e** (*mpl* **-aux**) *adj* of the commune, local.

communauté /kɔmynote/ *nf* community; **~ de biens** joint ownership.

commune /kɔmyn/ *nf* (circonscription, collectivité) commune.

communicatif, -ive /kɔmynikatif, -v/ *adj* (*personne*) talkative; (*gaieté*) infectious.

communication /kɔmynikasjɔ̃/ *nf* communication; (téléphonique) call; **~s** (relations) communications (+ *pl*); **voies** *ou* **moyens de ~** communications (+ *pl*).

communier /kɔmynje/ [45] *vi* (Relig) receive communion; (fig) commune.

communiqué /kɔmynike/ *nm* statement; (de presse) communiqué.

communiquer /kɔmynike/ [1] *vt* pass on, communicate; (*date, décision*) announce. ● *vi* communicate. □ **se ~ à** *vpr* spread to.

communiste /kɔmynist/ *a & nmf* communist.

commutateur /kɔmytatœʀ/ *nm* (Électr) switch.

compagne /kɔ̃paɲ/ *nf* companion.

compagnie /kɔ̃paɲi/ *nf* company; **tenir ~ à** keep company; **en ~ de** together with; **~ aérienne** airline.

compagnon /kɔ̃paɲɔ̃/ *nm* companion.

comparable /kɔ̃paʀabl/ *adj* comparable (à to). **comparaison** *nf* comparison; (littéraire) simile.

comparaître /kɔ̃paʀɛtʀ/ [18] *vi* (Jur) appear (**devant** before).

comparatif, -ive /kɔ̃paʀatif, -v/ *a & nm* comparative.

comparer /kɔ̃paʀe/ [1] *vt* compare (à with). □ **se ~** *vpr* compare oneself; (être comparable) be comparable.

compartiment /kɔ̃paʀtimã/ *nm* compartment.

comparution /kɔ̃paʀysjɔ̃/ *nf* (Jur) appearance.

compas /kɔ̃pa/ *nm* (pair of) compasses; (boussole) compass.

compassion /kɔ̃pasjɔ̃/ *nf* compassion.

compatible /kɔ̃patibl/ *adj* compatible.

compatir /kɔ̃patiʀ/ [2] *vi* sympathize; **~ à** share in.

compatriote /kɔ̃patʀijɔt/ *nmf* compatriot.

compensation /kɔ̃pãsasjɔ̃/ *nf* compensation. **compenser** [1] *vt* compensate for, make up for.

compère /kɔ̃pɛʀ/ *nm* accomplice.

compétence /kɔ̃petãs/ *nf* competence; (fonction) domain, sphere; **entrer dans les ~s de qn** be in sb's domain. **compétent, ~e** *adj* competent.

compétition /kɔ̃petisjɔ̃/ *nf* competition; (sportive) event; **de ~** competitive.

complaire (se) /(sə)kɔ̃plɛʀ/ [47] *vpr* **se ~ dans** delight in.

complaisance /kɔ̃plɛzãs/ *nf* kindness; (indulgence) indulgence.

complément /kɔ̃plemã/ *nm* supplement; (Gram) complement; **~ (d'objet)** (Gram) object; **~ d'information** further information. **complémentaire** *adj* complementary; (*renseignements*) supplementary.

complet, -ète /kɔ̃plɛ, -t/ *adj* complete; (*train, hôtel*) full. ● *nm* suit.

compléter /kɔ̃plete/ [14] *vt* complete; (agrémenter) complement. □ **se ~** *vpr* complement each other.

complexe /kɔ̃plɛks/ *adj* complex. ● *nm* (sentiment, bâtiments) complex.

complexé, ~e /kɔ̃plekse/ *adj* **être ~** have a lot of hang-ups.

complice /kɔ̃plis/ *nm* accomplice.

compliment /kɔ̃plimã/ *nm* compliment; **~s** (félicitations) compliments, congratulations.

compliquer /kɔ̃plike/ [1] *vt* complicate. □ **se ~** *vpr* become complicated.

complot /kɔ̃plo/ *nm* plot.

comportement /kɔ̃pɔʀtəmã/ *nm* behaviour; (de joueur, voiture) performance.

comporter /kɔ̃pɔʀte/ [1] vt (être composé de) comprise; (inclure) include; (risque) entail. □ se ~ vpr behave; (joueur, voiture) perform.

composant /kɔ̃pozɑ̃/ nm component.

composé, ~e /kɔ̃poze/ adj composite; (salade) mixed; (guindé) affected. ● nm compound.

composer /kɔ̃poze/ [1] vt make up, compose; (chanson, visage) compose; (numéro) dial; (page) typeset. ● vi (transiger) compromise. □ se ~ de vpr be made up ou composed of.

compositeur, -trice nm,f (Mus) composer.

composter /kɔ̃pɔste/ [1] vt (billet) punch.

compote /kɔ̃pɔt/ nf stewed fruit; ~ de pommes stewed apples.

compréhensible /kɔ̃pʀeɑ̃sibl/ adj understandable; (intelligible) comprehensible.

compréhensif, -ive /kɔ̃pʀeɑ̃sif, -v/ adj understanding.

compréhension /kɔ̃pʀeɑ̃sjɔ̃/ nf understanding, comprehension.

comprendre /kɔ̃pʀɑ̃dʀ/ [50] vt understand; (comporter) comprise, be made up of. □ se ~ vpr (personnes) understand each other; **ça se comprend** that is understandable.

compresse /kɔ̃pʀɛs/ nf compress.

comprimé /kɔ̃pʀime/ nm tablet.

comprimer /kɔ̃pʀime/ [1] vt compress; (réduire) reduce.

compris, ~e /kɔ̃pʀi, -z/ adj included; (d'accord) agreed; ~ entre (contained) between; **service (non) ~** service (not) included; **tout ~** (all) inclusive; **y ~** including.

compromettre /kɔ̃pʀɔmɛtʀ/ [42] vt compromise. **compromis** nm compromise.

comptabilité /kɔ̃tabilite/ nf accountancy; (comptes) accounts; (service) accounts department.

comptable /kɔ̃tabl/ adj accounting. ● nmf accountant.

comptant /kɔ̃tɑ̃/ adv (payer) (in) cash; (acheter) for cash.

compte /kɔ̃t/ nm count; (facture, comptabilité) account; (nombre exact) right number; ~ **bancaire**, ~ **en** banque bank account; **prendre en** ~, **tenir** ~ **de qch** take sth into account; **se rendre** ~ **de** realize; **demander/rendre des** ~s ask for/ give an explanation; **à bon** ~ cheaply; **s'en tirer à bon** ~ get off lightly; **travailler à son** ~ be self-employed; **faire le** ~ **de** count; **pour le** ~ **de** on behalf of; **sur le** ~ **de** about; **au bout du** ~ all things considered; ~ **à rebours** countdown.

compte-gouttes /kɔ̃tgut/ nm inv (Méd) dropper; **au** ~ (fig) in dribs and drabs.

compter /kɔ̃te/ [1] vt count; (prévoir) allow, reckon on; (facturer) charge for; (avoir) have; (classer) consider; ~ **faire** intend to do. ● vi (calculer, importer) count; ~ **avec** reckon with; ~ **parmi** (figurer) be considered among; ~ **sur** rely on, count on.

compte(-)rendu /kɔ̃tʀɑ̃dy/ nm report; (de film, livre) review.

compteur /kɔ̃tœʀ/ nm meter; ~ **de vitesse** speedometer.

comptine /kɔ̃tin/ nf nursery rhyme.

comptoir /kɔ̃twaʀ/ nm counter; (de café) bar.

comte /kɔ̃t/ nm count.

comté /kɔ̃te/ nm county.

comtesse /kɔ̃tɛs/ nf countess.

con, ~ne /kɔ̃, kɔn/ adj ⚠ bloody stupid ⚠. ● nm,f ⚠ bloody fool ⚠.

concentrer /kɔ̃sɑ̃tʀe/ [1] vt concentrate. □ se ~ vpr be concentrated.

concept /kɔ̃sɛpt/ nm concept.

concerner /kɔ̃sɛʀne/ [1] vt concern; **en ce qui me concerne** as far as I am concerned.

concert /kɔ̃sɛʀ/ nm concert; **de** ~ in unison.

concerter /kɔ̃sɛʀte/ [1] vt organize, prepare. □ se ~ vpr confer.

concession /kɔ̃sesjɔ̃/ nf concession; (terrain) plot.

concevoir /kɔ̃svwaʀ/ [52] vt (imaginer, engendrer) conceive; (comprendre) understand; (élaborer) design.

concierge /kɔ̃sjɛʀʒ/ nmf caretaker.

concilier /kɔ̃silje/ [45] vt reconcile. □ se ~ vpr (s'attirer) win (over).

concis, ~e /kɔ̃si, -z/ adj concise.

conclure /kɔ̃klyʀ/ [16] *vt* conclude; ~ à conclude in favour of. ● *vi* ~ en faveur de/contre find in favour of/against. **conclusion** *nf* conclusion.

concombre /kɔ̃kɔ̃bʀ/ *nm* cucumber.

concordance /kɔ̃kɔʀdɑ̃s/ *nf* agreement.

concourir /kɔ̃kuʀiʀ/ [20] *vi* compete. ● *vt* ~ à contribute towards.

concours /kɔ̃kuʀ/ *nm* competition; (examen) competitive examination; (aide) help; (de circonstances) combination.

concret, -ète /kɔ̃kʀɛ, -t/ *adj* concrete.

concrétiser /kɔ̃kʀetize/ [1] *vt* give concrete form to. □ se ~ *vpr* materialize.

conçu, ~e /kɔ̃sy/ *adj* bien/mal ~ well/badly designed.

concubinage /kɔ̃kybinaʒ/ *nm* cohabitation; vivre en ~ live together, cohabit.

concurrence /kɔ̃kyʀɑ̃s/ *nf* competition; faire ~ à compete with; jusqu'à ~ de up to a limit of.

concurrencer /kɔ̃kyʀɑ̃se/ [10] *vt* compete with.

concurrent, ~e /kɔ̃kyʀɑ̃, -t/ *nm,f* competitor; (Scol) candidate. ● *adj* rival.

condamnation /kɔ̃danasjɔ̃/ *nf* condemnation; (peine) sentence; ~ centralisée des portières central locking. **condamné, ~e** *nm,f* condemned man, condemned woman. **condamner** [1] *vt* (censurer, obliger) condemn; (Jur) sentence; (*porte*) block up.

condition /kɔ̃disjɔ̃/ *nf* condition; ~s (prix) terms; à ~ de *ou* que provided (that); sans ~ unconditional(ly); sous ~ conditionally.

conditionnel, ~le /kɔ̃disjɔnɛl/ *adj* conditional. ● *nm* conditional (tense).

conditionnement /kɔ̃disjɔnmɑ̃/ *nm* conditioning; (emballage) packaging.

condoléances /kɔ̃dɔleɑ̃s/ *nfpl* condolences.

conducteur, -trice /kɔ̃dyktœʀ, -tʀis/ *nm,f* driver.

conduire /kɔ̃dɥiʀ/ [17] *vt* take (à to); (guider) lead; (Auto) drive; (*affaire*) conduct; ~ à (faire aboutir) lead to. ● *vi* drive. □ se ~ *vpr* behave.

conduit /kɔ̃dɥi/ *nm* duct.

conduite /kɔ̃dɥit/ *nf* conduct, behaviour; (Auto) driving; (tuyau) pipe; voiture avec ~ à droite right-hand drive car.

confection /kɔ̃fɛksjɔ̃/ *nf* making; de ~ ready-made; la ~ the clothing industry.

conférence /kɔ̃feʀɑ̃s/ *nf* conference; (exposé) lecture; ~ au sommet summit meeting. **conférencier, -ière** *nm,f* lecturer.

confesser /kɔ̃fese/ [1] *vt* confess. □ se ~ *vpr* go to confession.

confiance /kɔ̃fjɑ̃s/ *nf* trust; avoir ~ en trust.

confiant, ~e /kɔ̃fjɑ̃, -t/ *adj* (assuré) confident; (sans défiance) trusting.

confidence /kɔ̃fidɑ̃s/ *nf* confidence.

confidentiel, ~le /kɔ̃fidɑ̃sjɛl/ *adj* confidential.

confier /kɔ̃fje/ [45] *vt* ~ à qn entrust sb with; ~ un secret à qn tell sb a secret. □ se ~ à *vpr* confide in.

confiner /kɔ̃fine/ [1] *vt* confine; ~ à border on. □ se ~ *vpr* confine oneself (à, dans to).

confirmation /kɔ̃fiʀmasjɔ̃/ *nf* confirmation. **confirmer** [1] *vt* confirm.

confiserie /kɔ̃fizʀi/ *nf* sweet shop; ~s confectionery.

confisquer /kɔ̃fiske/ [1] *vt* confiscate.

confit, ~e /kɔ̃fi, -t/ *adj* candied; (*fruits*) crystallized. ● *nm* ~ de canard confit of duck.

confiture /kɔ̃fityʀ/ *nf* jam.

conflit /kɔ̃fli/ *nm* conflict.

confondre /kɔ̃fɔ̃dʀ/ [3] *vt* confuse, mix up; (étonner) confound. □ se ~ *vpr* merge; se ~ en excuses apologize profusely.

conforme /kɔ̃fɔʀm/ *adj* être ~ à comply with; (être en accord) be in keeping with.

conformer /kɔ̃fɔʀme/ [1] *vt* adapt.
□ **se ~ à** *vpr* conform to.

conformité /kɔ̃fɔʀmite/ *nf*
compliance, conformity; **agir en ~
avec** act in accordance with.

confort /kɔ̃fɔʀ/ *nm* comfort; **tout ~**
with all mod cons. **confortable** *adj*
comfortable.

confrère /kɔ̃fʀɛʀ/ *nm* colleague.

confronter /kɔ̃fʀɔ̃te/ [1] *vt*
confront; (*textes*) compare. □ **se ~ à**
vpr be confronted with.

confus, **~e** /kɔ̃fy, -z/ *adj* confused;
(gêné) embarrassed.

congé /kɔ̃ʒe/ *nm* holiday; (arrêt
momentané) time off, leave; (avis de
départ) notice; **en ~** on holiday *ou*
leave; **~ de maladie/maternité** sick/
maternity leave; **jour de ~** day off;
prendre ~ de take one's leave of.

congédier /kɔ̃ʒedje/ [45] *vt* dismiss.

congélateur /kɔ̃ʒelatœʀ/ *nm*
freezer.

congeler /kɔ̃ʒle/ [6] *vt* freeze.

congère /kɔ̃ʒɛʀ/ *nf* snowdrift.

congrès /kɔ̃gʀɛ/ *nm* conference;
(Pol) congress.

conjoint, **~e** /kɔ̃ʒwɛ̃, -t/ *nm,f*
spouse. ● *adj* joint.

conjonctivite /kɔ̃ʒɔ̃ktivit/ *nf*
conjunctivitis.

conjoncture /kɔ̃ʒɔ̃ktyʀ/ *nf*
situation; (économique) economic
climate.

conjugaison /kɔ̃ʒygɛzɔ̃/ *nf*
conjugation.

conjugal, **~e** (*mpl* **-aux**) /kɔ̃ʒygal,
-o/ *adj* conjugal, married.

conjuguer /kɔ̃ʒyge/ [1] *vt* (Gram)
conjugate; (*efforts*) combine. □ **se ~**
vpr (Gram) be conjugated; (*facteurs*)
be combined.

conjurer /kɔ̃ʒyʀe/ [1] *vt* (éviter)
avert; (implorer) beg.

connaissance /kɔnɛsɑ̃s/ *nf*
knowledge; (personne) acquaintance;
~s (science) knowledge; **faire la ~ de**
meet; (apprécier une personne) get to
know; **perdre/reprendre ~** lose/
regain consciousness; **sans ~**
unconscious.

connaisseur /kɔnɛsœʀ/ *nm*
expert, connoisseur.

connaître /kɔnɛtʀ/ [18] *vt* know;
(*difficultés, faim, succès*) experience;
faire ~ make known. □ **se ~** *vpr* (se
rencontrer) meet; **s'y ~ en** know (all)
about.

connecter /kɔnɛkte/ [1] *vt* connect;
être/ne pas être connecté be on-/
off-line. □ **se ~ à** *vpr* (Ordinat) log on
to.

connerie /kɔnʀi/ *nf* ⊠ **faire une ~**
do something stupid; **dire des ~s**
talk rubbish.

connu, **~e** /kɔny/ *adj* well-known.

conquérant, **~e** /kɔ̃keʀɑ̃, -t/ *nm,f*
conqueror.

conquête /kɔ̃kɛt/ *nf* conquest.

consacrer /kɔ̃sakʀe/ [1] *vt* devote;
(Relig) consecrate; (sanctionner)
sanction. □ **se ~ à** *vpr* devote
oneself to.

conscience /kɔ̃sjɑ̃s/ *nf* conscience;
(perception) awareness; (de collectivité)
consciousness; **avoir/prendre ~ de**
be/become aware of; **perdre/
reprendre ~** lose/regain
consciousness; **avoir bonne/mauvaise
~** have a clear/guilty conscience.

conscient, **~e** /kɔ̃sjɑ̃, -t/ *adj*
conscious; **~ de** aware *ou* conscious
of.

conseil /kɔ̃sɛj/ *nm* (piece of) advice;
(assemblée) council, committee;
(séance) meeting; (personne)
consultant; **~ d'administration** board
of directors; **~ en gestion**
management consultant; **~ des
ministres** Cabinet; **~ municipal** town
council.

conseiller[1] /kɔ̃seje/ [1] *vt* advise; **~
à qn de** advise sb to; **~ qch à qn**
recommend sth to sb.

conseiller[2], **-ère** /kɔ̃seje, -jɛʀ/
nm,f adviser, counsellor; **~
municipal** town councillor; **~
d'orientation** careers adviser.

consentement /kɔ̃sɑ̃tmɑ̃/ *nm*
consent.

conséquence /kɔ̃sekɑ̃s/ *nf*
consequence; **en ~** (comme il convient)
accordingly; **en ~** (de quoi) as a
result of which.

conséquent, **~e** /kɔ̃sekɑ̃, -t/ *adj*
consistent, logical; (important)

substantial; **par** ~ consequently, therefore.

conservateur, **-trice** /kɔ̃sɛʀvatœʀ, -tʀis/ adj conservative. ● nm,f (Pol) conservative; (de musée) curator. ● nm preservative.

conservation /kɔ̃sɛʀvasjɔ̃/ nf preservation; (d'espèce, patrimoine) conservation.

conservatoire /kɔ̃sɛʀvatwaʀ/ nm academy.

conserve /kɔ̃sɛʀv/ nf tinned ou canned food; **en** ~ tinned, canned; **boîte de** ~ tin, can.

conserver /kɔ̃sɛʀve/ [1] vt keep; (en bon état) preserve; (Culin) preserve. □ **se** ~ vpr (Culin) keep.

considérer /kɔ̃sidere/ [14] vt consider; (respecter) esteem; ~ **comme** consider to be.

consigne /kɔ̃siɲ/ nf (de gare) left-luggage office; (US) baggage checkroom; (somme) deposit; (ordres) orders; ~ **automatique** left-luggage lockers; (US) baggage lockers.

consistance /kɔ̃sistɑ̃s/ nf consistency; (fig) substance, weight. **consistant**, **~e** adj solid; (épais) thick.

consister /kɔ̃siste/ [1] vi ~ **en/dans** consist of/in; ~ **à faire** consist in doing.

consoler /kɔ̃sɔle/ [1] vt console. □ **se** ~ vpr find consolation; **se** ~ **de qch** get over sth.

consolider /kɔ̃sɔlide/ [1] vt strengthen; (fig) consolidate.

consommateur, **-trice** /kɔ̃sɔmatœʀ, -tʀis/ nm,f (Comm) consumer; (dans un café) customer.

consommation /kɔ̃sɔmasjɔ̃/ nf consumption; (accomplissement) consummation; (boisson) drink; **de** ~ (Comm) consumer.

consommer /kɔ̃sɔme/ [1] vt consume, use; (manger) eat; (boire) drink; (mariage) consummate. □ **se** ~ vpr (être mangé) be eaten; (être utilisé) be used.

consonne /kɔ̃sɔn/ nf consonant.

constat /kɔ̃sta/ nm (official) report; ~ (**à l'**)**amiable** accident report drawn up by those involved.

constatation /kɔ̃statasjɔ̃/ nf observation, statement of fact. **constater** [1] vt note, notice; (certifier) certify.

consternation /kɔ̃stɛʀnasjɔ̃/ nf dismay.

constipé, **~e** /kɔ̃stipe/ adj constipated; (fig) uptight.

constituer /kɔ̃stitɥe/ [1] vt (composer) make up, constitute; (organiser) form; (être) constitute; **constitué de** made up of. □ **se** ~ vpr **se** ~ **prisonnier** give oneself up.

constitution /kɔ̃stitysjɔ̃/ nf formation, setting up; (Pol, Méd) constitution.

constructeur /kɔ̃stʀyktœʀ/ nm manufacturer, builder.

construction /kɔ̃stʀyksjɔ̃/ nf building; (structure, secteur) construction; (fabrication) manufacture.

construire /kɔ̃stʀɥiʀ/ [17] vt build; (système, phrase) construct.

consulat /kɔ̃syla/ nm consulate.

consultation /kɔ̃syltasjɔ̃/ nf consultation; (réception: Méd) surgery; (US) office; **heures de** ~ surgery ou office (US) hours.

consulter /kɔ̃sylte/ [1] vt consult. ● vi (médecin) hold surgery, see patients. □ **se** ~ vpr consult together.

contact /kɔ̃takt/ nm contact; (toucher) touch; **au** ~ **de** on contact with; (personne) by contact with, by seeing; **mettre/couper le** ~ (Auto) switch on/off the ignition; **prendre** ~ **avec** get in touch with. **contacter** [1] vt contact.

contagieux, **-ieuse** /kɔ̃taʒjø, -z/ adj contagious.

conte /kɔ̃t/ nm tale; ~ **de fées** fairy tale.

contempler /kɔ̃tɑ̃ple/ [1] vt contemplate.

contemporain, **~e** /kɔ̃tɑ̃pɔʀɛ̃, -ɛn/ a & nm,f contemporary.

contenance /kɔ̃t(ə)nɑ̃s/ nf (volume) capacity; (allure) bearing; **perdre** ~ lose one's composure.

contenir /kɔ̃t(ə)niʀ/ [58] vt contain; (avoir une capacité de) hold. □ **se** ~ vpr contain oneself.

content, ∼e /kɔ̃tɑ̃, -t/ *adj* pleased, happy (de with); ∼ de faire pleased *ou* happy to do.

contenter /kɔ̃tɑ̃te/ [1] *vt* satisfy. □ **se** ∼ **de** *vpr* content oneself with.

contenu /kɔ̃t(ə)ny/ *nm* (de récipient) contents (+ *pl*); (de texte) content.

conter /kɔ̃te/ [1] *vt* tell, relate.

contestation /kɔ̃tɛstasjɔ̃/ *nf* dispute; (opposition) protest.

contester /kɔ̃tɛste/ [1] *vt* question, dispute; (s'opposer) protest against. ● *vi* protest.

conteur, -euse /kɔ̃tœʀ, -øz/ *nm,f* storyteller.

contigu, ∼ë /kɔ̃tigy/ *adj* adjacent (à to).

continent /kɔ̃tinɑ̃/ *nm* continent.

continu, ∼e /kɔ̃tiny/ *adj* continuous.

continuer /kɔ̃tinɥe/ [1] *vt* continue. ● *vi* continue, go on; ∼ à *ou* de faire carry on *ou* go on *ou* continue doing.

contorsionner (se) /(sə)kɔ̃tɔʀsjɔne/ [1] *vpr* wriggle.

contour /kɔ̃tuʀ/ *nm* outline, contour; ∼s (d'une route) twists and turns, bends.

contourner /kɔ̃tuʀne/ [1] *vt* go round, by-pass; (difficulté) get round.

contraceptif, -ive /kɔ̃tʀasɛptif, -v/ *adj* contraceptive. ● *nm* contraceptive. **contraception** *nf* contraception.

contracter /kɔ̃tʀakte/ [1] *vt* (maladie) contract; (dette) incur; (muscle) tense; (assurance) take out. □ **se** ∼ *vpr* contract.

contractuel, ∼le /kɔ̃tʀaktɥɛl/ *nm,f* (agent) traffic warden.

contradictoire /kɔ̃tʀadiktwaʀ/ *adj* contradictory; (débat) open.

contraignant, ∼e /kɔ̃tʀɛɲɑ̃, -t/ *adj* restricting.

contraindre /kɔ̃tʀɛ̃dʀ/ [22] *vt* force, compel (à faire to do).

contrainte /kɔ̃tʀɛ̃t/ *nf* constraint.

contraire /kɔ̃tʀɛʀ/ *adj* opposite; ∼ à contrary to. ● *nm* opposite; au ∼ on the contrary; au ∼ de unlike.

contrarier /kɔ̃tʀaʀje/ [45] *vt* annoy; (projet, volonté) frustrate; (chagriner) upset.

contraste /kɔ̃tʀast/ *nm* contrast.

contrat /kɔ̃tʀa/ *nm* contract.

contravention /kɔ̃tʀavɑ̃sjɔ̃/ *nf* (parking) ticket; en ∼ in breach (à of).

contre /kɔ̃tʀ(ə)/ *prép* against; (en échange de) for; par ∼ on the other hand; tout ∼ close by. **contre-attaque** (*pl* ∼s) *nf* counter-attack. **contre-attaquer** [1] *vt* counter-attack. **contre-balancer** [10] *vt* counterbalance.

contrebande /kɔ̃tʀəbɑ̃d/ *nf* contraband; faire la ∼ de smuggle.

contrebas: en ∼ /ɑ̃kɔ̃tʀəba/ *loc* below.

contrebasse /kɔ̃tʀəbas/ *nf* double bass.

contrecœur: à ∼ /akɔ̃tʀəkœʀ/ *loc* reluctantly.

contrecoup /kɔ̃tʀəku/ *nm* effects, repercussions.

contredire /kɔ̃tʀədiʀ/ [37] *vt* contradict. □ **se** ∼ *vpr* contradict oneself.

contrée /kɔ̃tʀe/ *nf* region; (pays) land.

contrefaçon /kɔ̃tʀəfasɔ̃/ *nf* (objet imité, action) forgery.

contre-indiqué, ∼e /kɔ̃tʀɛ̃dike/ *adj* (Méd) contra-indicated; (déconseillé) not recommended.

contre-jour: à ∼ /akɔ̃tʀəʒuʀ/ *loc* against the light.

contrepartie /kɔ̃tʀəpaʀti/ *nf* compensation; en ∼ in exchange, in return.

contreplaqué /kɔ̃tʀəplake/ *nm* plywood.

contresens /kɔ̃tʀəsɑ̃s/ *nm* misinterpretation; (absurdité) nonsense; à ∼ the wrong way.

contretemps /kɔ̃tʀətɑ̃/ *nm* hitch; à ∼ (fig) at the wrong time.

contribuable /kɔ̃tʀibɥabl/ *nmf* taxpayer.

contribuer /kɔ̃tʀibɥe/ [1] *vt* contribute (à to, towards).

contrôle /kɔ̃tʀol/ *nm* (maîtrise) control; (vérification) check; (des prix) control; (poinçon) hallmark; (Scol) test; ∼ continu continuous assessment; ∼ des changes exchange control; ∼ des naissances birth control; ∼ de soi-même self-control; ∼ **technique** (des véhicules) MOT (test).

contrôler /kɔ̃tʀole/ [1] *vt* (vérifier) check; (surveiller, maîtriser) control. □ **se** ∼ *vpr* control oneself.

contrôleur, -euse /kɔ̃tʀolœʀ, -øz/ *nm,f* inspector.

convaincre /kɔ̃vɛ̃kʀ/ [59] *vt* convince; ∼ **qn de faire** persuade sb to do.

convalescence /kɔ̃valesɑ̃s/ *nf* convalescence; **être en** ∼ be convalescing.

convenable /kɔ̃vnabl/ *adj* (correct) decent, proper; (approprié) suitable; (acceptable) reasonable, acceptable.

convenance /kɔ̃vnɑ̃s/ *nf* **à ma** ∼ to my satisfaction; **les** ∼**s** convention.

convenir /kɔ̃vniʀ/ [58] *vt/i* be suitable; ∼ **à** suit; ∼ **que** admit that; ∼ **de qch** (avouer) admit sth; (s'accorder sur) agree on sth; ∼ **de faire** agree to do; **il convient de** it is advisable to; (selon les bienséances) it would be right to.

convention /kɔ̃vɑ̃sjɔ̃/ *nf* agreement, convention; (clause) article, clause; ∼**s** (convenances) convention; **de** ∼ conventional; ∼ **collective** industrial agreement.

convenu, -e /kɔ̃vny/ *adj* agreed.

conversation /kɔ̃vɛʀsasjɔ̃/ *nf* conversation.

convertir /kɔ̃vɛʀtiʀ/ [2] *vt* convert (à to; en into). □ **se** ∼ *vpr* be converted, convert.

conviction /kɔ̃viksjɔ̃/ *nf* conviction; **avoir la** ∼ **que** be convinced that.

convivial, ∼e (*mpl* **-iaux**) /kɔ̃vivjal, -jo/ *adj* convivial; (Ordinat) user-friendly.

convocation /kɔ̃vɔkasjɔ̃/ *nf* (Jur) summons; (d'une assemblée) convening; (document) notification to attend.

convoi /kɔ̃vwa/ *nm* convoy; (train) train; ∼ **(funèbre)** funeral procession.

convoquer /kɔ̃vɔke/ [1] *vt* (*assemblée*) convene; (*personne*) summon; **être convoqué pour un entretien** be called for interview.

coopération /kɔɔpeʀasjɔ̃/ *nf* cooperation; (Mil) civilian national service abroad.

coordination /kɔɔʀdinasjɔ̃/ *nf* coordination. **coordonnées** *nfpl* coordinates; (adresse) address and telephone number.

copain /kɔpɛ̃/ *nm* friend; (petit ami) boyfriend.

copie /kɔpi/ *nf* copy; (Scol) paper; ∼ **d'examen** exam paper *ou* script; ∼ **de sauvegarde** back-up copy.

copier /kɔpje/ [45] *vt/i* copy; ∼ **sur** (Scol) copy *ou* crib from.

copieux, -ieuse /kɔpjø, -z/ *adj* copious.

copine /kɔpin/ *nf* friend; (petite amie) girlfriend.

coq /kɔk/ *nm* cockerel.

coque /kɔk/ *nf* shell; (de bateau) hull.

coquelicot /kɔkliko/ *nm* poppy.

coqueluche /kɔklyʃ/ *nf* whooping cough.

coquet, -te /kɔkɛ, -t/ *adj* flirtatious; (élégant) pretty; (somme 𝟭) tidy.

coquetier /kɔktje/ *nm* eggcup.

coquillage /kɔkijaʒ/ *nm* shellfish; (coquille) shell.

coquille /kɔkij/ *nf* shell; (faute) misprint; ∼ **Saint-Jacques** scallop.

coquin, -e /kɔkɛ̃, -in/ *adj* mischievous. ● *nm,f* rascal.

cor /kɔʀ/ *nm* (Mus) horn; (au pied) corn.

corail (*pl* **-aux**) /kɔʀaj, -o/ *nm* coral.

corbeau (*pl* **-x**) /kɔʀbo/ *nm* (oiseau) crow.

corbeille /kɔʀbɛj/ *nf* basket; ∼ **à papier** waste-paper basket.

corbillard /kɔʀbijaʀ/ *nm* hearse.

cordage /kɔʀdaʒ/ *nm* rope; ∼**s** (Naut) rigging.

corde /kɔʀd/ *nf* rope; (d'arc, de violon) string; ∼ **à linge** washing line; ∼ **à sauter** skipping-rope; ∼ **raide** tightrope; ∼**s vocales** vocal cords.

cordon /kɔʀdɔ̃/ *nm* string, cord; ∼ **de police** police cordon.

cordonnier /kɔʀdɔnje/ *nm* cobbler.

Corée /kɔʀe/ *nf* Korea.

coriace /kɔʀjas/ *adj* tough.

corne /kɔʀn/ *nf* horn.

corneille /kɔʀnɛj/ nf crow.

cornemuse /kɔʀnəmyz/ nf bagpipes (+ pl).

corner /kɔʀne/ [1] vt (page) turn down the corner of; **page cornée** dog-eared page. ● vi (Auto) hoot, honk.

cornet /kɔʀnɛ/ nm (paper) cone; (crème glacée) cornet, cone.

corniche /kɔʀniʃ/ nf cornice; (route) cliff road.

cornichon /kɔʀniʃɔ̃/ nm gherkin.

corporel, ~**le** /kɔʀpɔʀɛl/ adj bodily; (châtiment) corporal.

corps /kɔʀ/ nm body; (Mil) corps; **combat** ~ **à** ~ hand-to-hand combat; ~ **électoral** electorate; ~ **enseignant** teaching profession.

correct, ~**e** /kɔʀɛkt/ adj proper, correct; (exact) correct.

correcteur, **-trice** /kɔʀɛktœʀ, -tʀis/ nm, f (d'épreuves) proofreader; (Scol) examiner; ~ **liquide** correction fluid; ~ **d'orthographe** spell-checker.

correction /kɔʀɛksjɔ̃/ nf correction; (d'examen) marking, grading; (punition) beating.

correspondance /kɔʀɛspɔ̃dɑ̃s/ nf correspondence; (de train, d'autobus) connection; **vente par** ~ mail order; **faire des études par** ~ do a correspondence course.

correspondant, ~**e** /kɔʀɛspɔ̃dɑ̃, -t/ adj corresponding. ● nm, f correspondent; penfriend; (au téléphone) **votre** ~ the person you are calling.

correspondre /kɔʀɛspɔ̃dʀ/ [3] vi (s'accorder, écrire) correspond; (chambres) communicate. ● v + prép ~ **à** (être approprié à) match, suit; (équivaloir à) correspond to. □ **se** ~ vpr correspond.

corrida /kɔʀida/ nf bullfight.

corriger /kɔʀiʒe/ [40] vt correct; (devoir) mark, grade, correct; (punir) beat; (guérir) cure.

corsage /kɔʀsaʒ/ nm bodice; (chemisier) blouse.

corsaire /kɔʀsɛʀ/ nm pirate.

Corse /kɔʀs/ nf Corsica. ● nmf Corsican. **corse** adj Corsican.

corsé, ~**e** /kɔʀse/ adj (vin) full-bodied; (café) strong; (scabreux) racy; (problème) tough.

cortège /kɔʀtɛʒ/ nm procession; ~ **funèbre** funeral procession.

corvée /kɔʀve/ nf chore.

cosmonaute /kɔsmɔnot/ nmf cosmonaut.

cosmopolite /kɔsmɔpɔlit/ adj cosmopolitan.

cosse /kɔs/ nf (de pois) pod.

cossu, ~**e** /kɔsy/ adj (gens) well-to-do; (demeure) opulent.

costaud, ~**e** /kɔsto, -d/ 🄸 adj strong. ● nm strong man.

costume /kɔstym/ nm suit; (Théât) costume.

cote /kɔt/ nf (classification) mark; (en Bourse) quotation; (de cheval) odds (de on); (de candidat, acteur) rating; ~ **d'alerte** danger level; **avoir la** ~ be popular.

côte /kot/ nf (littoral) coast; (pente) hill; (Anat) rib; (Culin) chop; ~ **à** ~ side by side; **la C**~ **d'Azur** the (French) Riviera.

côté /kote/ nm side; (direction) way; **à** ~ nearby; **voisin d'à** ~ next-door neighbour; **à** ~ **de** next to; (comparé à) compared to; **à** ~ **de la cible** wide of the target; **aux** ~**s de** by the side of; **de** ~ (regarder) sideways; (sauter) to one side; **mettre de** ~ put aside; **de ce** ~ this way; **de chaque** ~ on each side; **de tous les** ~**s** on every side; (partout) everywhere; **du** ~ **de** (vers) towards; (dans les environs de) near.

côtelette /kotlɛt/ nf chop.

coter /kote/ [1] vt (Comm) quote; **coté en Bourse** listed on the Stock Exchange; **très coté** highly rated.

cotiser /kotize/ [1] vi pay one's contributions (**à** to); (à un club) pay one's subscription. □ **se** ~ vpr club together.

coton /kotɔ̃/ nm cotton; ~ **hydrophile** cotton wool.

cou /ku/ nm neck.

couchant /kuʃɑ̃/ nm sunset.

couche /kuʃ/ nf layer; (de peinture) coat; (de bébé) nappy; (US) diaper; ~**s** (Méd) childbirth; ~**s sociales** social strata.

coucher /kuʃe/ [1] vt put to bed; (loger) put up; (étendre) lay down; ∼ **(par écrit)** set down. ● vi sleep. □ **se** ∼ vpr go to bed; (s'étendre) lie down; (soleil) set. ● nm ∼ **(de soleil)** sunset; **au** ∼ **du soleil** at sunset.

couchette /kuʃɛt/ nf (de train) couchette; (Naut) berth.

coude /kud/ nm elbow; (de rivière, chemin) bend; ∼ **à** ∼ side by side.

cou-de-pied (pl **cous-de-pied**) /kudpje/ nm instep.

coudre /kudʀ/ [19] vt/i sew.

couette /kwɛt/ nf duvet, continental quilt.

couler /kule/ [1] vi flow, run; (fromage, nez) run; (fuir) leak; (bateau) sink; (entreprise) go under; **faire** ∼ **un bain** run a bath. ● vt (bateau) sink; (sculpture, métal) cast. □ **se** ∼ vpr slip (**dans** into).

couleur /kulœʀ/ nf colour; (peinture) paint; (aux cartes) suit; ∼s (teint) colour; **de** ∼ (homme, femme) coloured; **en** ∼s (télévision, film) colour.

couleuvre /kulœvʀ/ nf grass snake.

coulisse /kulis/ nf (de tiroir) runner; **à** ∼ (porte, fenêtre) sliding; ∼s (Théât) wings; **dans les** ∼s (fig) behind the scenes.

couloir /kulwaʀ/ nm corridor; (Sport) lane; ∼ **de bus** bus lane.

coup /ku/ nm blow; (choc) knock; (Sport) stroke; (de crayon, chance, cloche) stroke; (de fusil, pistolet) shot; (fois) time; (aux échecs) move; **donner un** ∼ **de pied/poing à** kick/punch; **à** ∼ **sûr** definitely; **après** ∼ after the event; **boire un** ∼ 🔟 have a drink; ∼ **sur** ∼ in rapid succession; **du** ∼ as a result; **d'un seul** ∼ in one go; **du premier** ∼ first go; **sale** ∼ dirty trick; **sous le** ∼ **de la fatigue/colère** out of tiredness/anger; **sur le** ∼ instantly; **tenir le** ∼ hold out; **manquer son** ∼ 🔟 blow it 🔟; ∼ **de chiffon** wipe (with a rag); ∼ **de coude** nudge; ∼ **de couteau** stab; ∼ **d'envoi** kick-off; ∼ **d'État** (Pol) coup; ∼ **de feu** shot; ∼ **de fil** 🔟 phone call; ∼ **de filet** haul; (fig) police raid; ∼ **de foudre** love at first sight; ∼ **franc** free kick; ∼ **de frein** sudden braking;

∼ **de grâce** coup de grâce; ∼ **de main** helping hand; ∼ **d'œil** glance; ∼ **de pied** kick; ∼ **de poing** punch; ∼ **de soleil** sunburn; ∼ **de sonnette** ring (on a bell); ∼ **de téléphone** (tele-)phone call; ∼ **de tête** wild impulse; ∼ **de théâtre** dramatic event; ∼ **de tonnerre** thunderclap; ∼ **de vent** gust of wind.

coupable /kupabl/ adj guilty. ● nmf culprit.

coupe /kup/ nf cup; (de champagne) goblet; (à fruits) dish; (de vêtement) cut; (dessin) section; ∼ **de cheveux** haircut.

couper /kupe/ [1] vt cut; (arbre) cut down; (arrêter) cut off; (voyage) break up; (appétit) take away; (vin) water down; ∼ **par** take a short cut via; ∼ **la parole à qn** cut sb short. ● vi cut. □ **se** ∼ vpr cut oneself; **se** ∼ **le doigt** cut one's finger; (routes) intersect; **se** ∼ **de** cut oneself off from.

couple /kupl/ nm couple; (d'animaux) pair.

coupure /kupyʀ/ nf cut; (billet de banque) note; (de presse) cutting; (pause, rupture) break; ∼ **(de courant)** power cut.

cour /kuʀ/ nf (court)yard; (du roi) court; (tribunal) court; ∼ **(de récréation)** playground; ∼ **martiale** court-martial; **faire la** ∼ **à** court.

courageux, -euse /kuʀaʒø, -z/ adj courageous.

couramment /kuʀamã/ adv frequently; (parler) fluently.

courant, ∼e /kuʀã, -t/ adj standard, ordinary; (en cours) current. ● nm current; (de mode, d'idées) trend; ∼ **d'air** draught; **dans le** ∼ **de** in the course of; **être/mettre au** ∼ **de** know/tell about; (à jour) be/bring up to date on.

courbature /kuʀbatyʀ/ nf ache; **avoir des** ∼s be stiff, ache.

courber /kuʀbe/ [1] vt bend.

coureur, -euse /kuʀœʀ, -øz/ nm,f (Sport) runner; ∼ **automobile** racing driver; ∼ **cycliste** racing cyclist. ● nm womanizer.

courgette /kuʀʒɛt/ nf courgette; (US) zucchini.

courir /kuʀiʀ/ [20] *vi* run; (se hâter) rush; (*nouvelles*) go round; ∼ après qn/qch chase after sb/sth. ● *vt* (*risque*) run; (*danger*) face; (*épreuve sportive*) run *ou* compete in; (*fréquenter*) do the rounds of; (*filles*) chase (after).

couronne /kuʀɔn/ *nf* crown; (de fleurs) wreath.

couronnement /kuʀɔnmɑ̃/ *nm* coronation, crowning; (fig) crowning achievement.

courrier /kuʀje/ *nm* post, mail; (à écrire) letters; ∼ du cœur problem page; ∼ électronique e-mail.

cours /kuʀ/ *nm* (leçon) class; (série de leçons) course; (prix) price; (cote) (de valeur, denrée) price; (de devises) exchange rate; (déroulement, d'une rivière) course; (allée) avenue; au ∼ de in the course of; avoir ∼ (*monnaie*) be legal tender; (fig) be current; (Scol) have a lesson; ∼ d'eau river, stream; ∼ du soir evening class; ∼ particulier private lesson; ∼ magistral (Univ) lecture; en ∼ current; (*travail*) in progress; en ∼ de route along the way.

course /kuʀs/ *nf* running; (épreuve de vitesse) race; (activité) racing; (entre rivaux: fig) race; (de projectile) flight; (voyage) journey; (commission) errand; ∼s (achats) shopping; (de chevaux) races; faire la ∼ avec qn race sb.

coursier, -ière /kuʀsje, -jɛʀ/ *nm,f* messenger.

court, ∼e /kuʀ, -t/ *adj* short. ● *adv* short; à ∼ de short of; pris de ∼ caught unawares. ● *nm* ∼ (de tennis) (tennis) court.

courtier, -ière /kuʀtje, -jɛʀ/ *nm,f* broker.

courtiser /kuʀtize/ [1] *vt* woo, court.

courtois, ∼e /kuʀtwa, -z/ *adj* courteous. **courtoisie** *nf* courtesy.

cousin, ∼e /kuzɛ̃, -in/ *nm,f* cousin; ∼ germain first cousin.

coussin /kusɛ̃/ *nm* cushion.

coût /ku/ *nm* cost; le ∼ de la vie the cost of living.

couteau (*pl* ∼x) /kuto/ *nm* knife; ∼ à cran d'arrêt flick knife.

coûter /kute/ [1] *vt/i* cost; **coûte que coûte** at all costs; **au prix coûtant** at cost (price).

coutume /kutym/ *nf* custom.

couture /kutyʀ/ *nf* sewing; (métier) dressmaking; (points) seam. **couturier** *nm* fashion designer. **couturière** *nf* dressmaker.

couvée /kuve/ *nf* brood.

couvent /kuvɑ̃/ *nm* convent.

couver /kuve/ [1] *vt* (*œufs*) hatch; (*personne*) overprotect, pamper; (*maladie*) be coming down with, be sickening for. ● *vi* (*feu*) smoulder; (*mal*) be brewing.

couvercle /kuvɛʀkl/ *nm* (de marmite, boîte) lid; (qui se visse) screwtop.

couvert, ∼e /kuvɛʀ, -t/ *adj* covered (de with); (habillé) covered up; (*ciel*) overcast. ● *nm* (à table) place setting; (prix) cover charge; ∼s (couteaux etc.) cutlery; mettre le ∼ lay the table; (abri) cover; à ∼ (Mil) under cover; à ∼ de (fig) safe from.

couverture /kuvɛʀtyʀ/ *nf* cover; (de lit) blanket; (toit) roofing; (dans la presse) coverage; ∼ chauffante electric blanket.

couvre-feu (*pl* ∼x) /kuvʀəfø/ *nm* curfew.

couvre-lit (*pl* ∼s) /kuvʀəli/ *nm* bedspread.

couvrir /kuvʀiʀ/ [21] *vt* cover. □ se ∼ *vpr* (s'habiller) wrap up; (se coiffer) put one's hat on; (*ciel*) become overcast.

covoiturage /kɔvwatyʀaʒ/ *nm* car sharing.

cracher /kʀaʃe/ [1] *vi* spit; (radio) crackle. ● *vt* spit (out); (*fumée*) belch out.

crachin /kʀaʃɛ̃/ *nm* drizzle.

craie /kʀɛ/ *nf* chalk.

craindre /kʀɛ̃dʀ/ [22] *vt* be afraid of, fear; (être sensible à) be easily damaged by.

crainte /kʀɛ̃t/ *nf* fear (pour for); de ∼ de/que for fear of/that. **craintif, -ive** *adj* timid.

crampon /kʀɑ̃pɔ̃/ *nm* (de chaussure) stud.

cramponner (se) /(sə)kʀɑ̃pɔne/ [1] *vpr* se ∼ à cling to.

cran /kʀɑ̃/ *nm* (entaille) notch; (trou) hole; (courage 🔟) guts 🔟, courage; ~ **de sûreté** safety catch.

crâne /kʀɑn/ *nm* skull.

crapaud /kʀapo/ *nm* toad.

craquer /kʀake/ [1] *vi* crack, snap; (*plancher*) creak; (*couture*) split; (fig) (*personne*) break down; (céder) give in. ● *vt* (*allumette*) strike; (*vêtement*) split.

crasse /kʀas/ *nf* grime.

cravache /kʀavaʃ/ *nf* (horse)whip.

cravate /kʀavat/ *nf* tie.

crayon /kʀɛjɔ̃/ *nm* pencil; ~ **de couleur** coloured pencil; ~ **à bille** ballpoint pen; ~ **optique** light pen.

créateur, -trice /kʀeatœʀ, -tʀis/ *adj* creative. ● *nm, f* creator, designer.

crèche /kʀɛʃ/ *nf* day nursery, crèche; (Relig) crib.

crédit /kʀedi/ *nm* credit; (somme allouée) funds; **à** ~ on credit; **faire** ~ give credit (à to).

créer /kʀee/ [15] *vt* create; (*produit*) design; (*société*) set up.

crémaillère /kʀemajɛʀ/ *nf* **pendre la** ~ have a house-warming party.

crème /kʀɛm/ *a inv* cream. ● *nm* (café) ~ espresso with milk. ● *nf* cream; (dessert) cream dessert; ~ **anglaise** egg custard; ~ **fouettée** whipped cream; ~ **pâtissière** confectioner's custard. **crémerie** *nf* dairy. **crémeux, -euse** *adj* creamy. **crémier, -ière** *nm, f* dairyman, dairywoman.

créneau (*pl* ~**x**) /kʀeno/ *nm* (trou, moment) slot, window; (dans le marché) gap; **faire un** ~ parallel-park.

crêpe /kʀɛp/ *nf* (galette) pancake. ● *nm* (tissu) crêpe; (matière) crêpe (rubber).

crépitement /kʀepitmɑ̃/ *nm* crackling; (d'huile) sizzling.

crépuscule /kʀepyskyl/ *nm* twilight, dusk.

cresson /kʀəsɔ̃/ *nm* (water)cress.

crête /kʀɛt/ *nf* crest; (de coq) comb.

crétin, ~e /kʀetɛ̃, -in/ *nm, f* 🔟 moron 🔟.

creuser /kʀøze/ [1] *vt* dig; (évider) hollow out; (fig) go into in depth.

□ **se** ~ *vpr* (écart) widen; **se** ~ (**la cervelle**) 🔟 rack one's brains.

creux, -euse /kʀø, -z/ *adj* hollow; (*heures*) off-peak. ● *nm* hollow; (de l'estomac) pit; **dans le** ~ **de la main** in the palm of the hand.

crevaison /kʀəvɛzɔ̃/ *nf* puncture.

crevasse /kʀəvas/ *nf* crack; (de glacier) crevasse; (de la peau) chap.

crevé, ~e /kʀəve/ *adj* 🔟 worn out.

crever /kʀəve/ [1] *vt* burst; (*pneu*) puncture, burst; (exténuer 🔟) exhaust; (œil) put out. ● *vi* (pneu, sac) burst; (mourir 🔟) die.

crevette /kʀəvɛt/ *nf* ~ **grise** shrimp; ~ **rose** prawn.

cri /kʀi/ *nm* cry; (de douleur) scream, cry; **pousser un** ~ cry out, scream.

criard, ~e /kʀijaʀ, -d/ *adj* (couleur) garish; (voix) shrill.

crier /kʀije/ [45] *vi* (fort) shout, cry (out); (de douleur) scream; (grincer) creak. ● *vt* (ordre) shout (out).

crime /kʀim/ *nm* crime; (meurtre) murder.

criminel, ~le /kʀiminɛl/ *adj* criminal. ● *nm, f* criminal; (assassin) murderer.

crinière /kʀinjɛʀ/ *nf* mane.

crise /kʀiz/ *nf* crisis; (Méd) attack; (de colère) fit; ~ **cardiaque** heart attack; ~ **de foie** bilious attack; ~ **de nerfs** hysterics (+ *pl*).

crisper /kʀispe/ [1] *vt* tense; (énerver 🔟) irritate. □ **se** ~ *vpr* tense; (mains) clench.

critère /kʀitɛʀ/ *nm* criterion.

critique /kʀitik/ *adj* critical. ● *nf* criticism; (article) review; (commentateur) critic; **la** ~ (personnes) the critics. **critiquer** [1] *vt* criticize.

Croate /kʀɔat/ *adj* Croatian. **C~** *nmf* Croatian.

Croatie /kʀɔasi/ *nf* Croatia.

croche /kʀɔʃ/ *nf* quaver.

croche-pied (*pl* ~**s**) /kʀɔʃpje/ *nm* 🔟 **faire un** ~ **à** trip up.

crochet /kʀɔʃɛ/ *nm* hook; (détour) detour; (signe) square bracket; (tricot) crochet; **faire au** ~ crochet.

crochu, ~e /kʀɔʃy/ *adj* hooked.

crocodile /kʀɔkɔdil/ *nm* crocodile.

croire /kʀwaʀ/ [23] *vt* believe (à, en in); (estimer) think, believe (**que** that). ● *vi* believe.

croisade /kʀwazad/ *nf* crusade.

croisement /kʀwazmɑ̃/ *nm* crossing; (fait de passer à côté de) passing; (carrefour) crossroads.

croiser /kʀwaze/ [1] *vi* (*bateau*) cruise. ● *vt* cross; (*passant, véhicule*) pass; ~ **les bras** fold one's arms; ~ **les jambes** cross one's legs; (*animaux*) crossbreed. □ **se** ~ *vpr* (*véhicules, piétons*) pass each other; (*lignes*) cross. **croisière** *nf* cruise.

croissance /kʀwasɑ̃s/ *nf* growth.

croissant, ~**e** /kʀwasɑ̃, -t/ *adj* growing. ● *nm* crescent; (pâtisserie) croissant.

croix /kʀwa/ *nf* cross; ~ **gammée** swastika; **C~-Rouge** Red Cross.

croquant, ~**e** /kʀɔkɑ̃, -t/ *adj* crunchy.

croque-monsieur /kʀɔkməsjø/ *nm inv* toasted ham and cheese sandwich.

croque-mort (*pl* ~**s**) /kʀɔkmɔʀ/ *nm* 🔲 undertaker.

croquer /kʀɔke/ [1] *vt* crunch; (dessiner) sketch; **chocolat à** ~ plain chocolate. ● *vi* be crunchy.

croquis /kʀɔki/ *nm* sketch.

crotte /kʀɔt/ *nf* dropping.

crotté, ~**e** /kʀɔte/ *adj* muddy.

crottin /kʀɔtɛ̃/ *nm* (horse) dropping.

croupir /kʀupiʀ/ [2] *vi* stagnate.

croustillant, ~**e** /kʀustijɑ̃, -t/ *adj* crispy; (*pain*) crusty; (fig) spicy.

croûte /kʀut/ *nf* crust; (de fromage) rind; (de plaie) scab; **en** ~ (Culin) in pastry.

croûton /kʀutɔ̃/ *nm* (bout de pain) crust; (avec potage) croûton.

CRS *abrév m* (**Compagnie républicaine de sécurité**) French riot police; **un** ~ *a member of the French riot police.*

cru¹ /kʀy/ ⇒CROIRE [23].

cru², ~**e** /kʀy/ *adj* raw; (*lumière*) harsh; (*propos*) crude. ● *nm* vineyard; (vin) vintage wine.

crû /kʀy/ ⇒CROÎTRE [24].

cruauté /kʀyote/ *nf* cruelty.

cruche /kʀyʃ/ *nf* jug, pitcher.

crucial, ~**e** (*mpl* -**iaux**) /kʀysjal, -jo/ *adj* crucial.

crudité /kʀydite/ *nf* (de langage) crudeness; ~**s** (Culin) raw vegetables.

crue /kʀy/ *nf* rise in water level; **en** ~ in spate.

crustacé /kʀystase/ *nm* shellfish.

cube /kyb/ *nm* cube. ● *adj* (*mètre*) cubic.

cueillir /kœjiʀ/ [25] *vt* pick, gather; (*personne* 🔲) pick up.

cuiller, cuillère /kɥijɛʀ/ *nf* spoon; ~ **à soupe** soup spoon; (mesure) tablespoonful.

cuir /kɥiʀ/ *nm* leather; ~ **chevelu** scalp.

cuire /kɥiʀ/ [17] *vt* cook; ~ (**au four**) bake. ● *vi* cook; **faire** ~ cook.

cuisine /kɥizin/ *nf* kitchen; (art) cookery, cooking; (aliments) food; **faire la** ~ cook.

cuisiner /kɥizine/ [1] *vt* cook; (interroger 🔲) grill. ● *vi* cook.

cuisinier, -ière /kɥizinje, -jɛʀ/ *nm, f* cook. **cuisinière** *nf* (appareil) cooker, stove.

cuisse /kɥis/ *nf* thigh; (de poulet) thigh; (de grenouille) leg.

cuisson /kɥisɔ̃/ *nf* cooking.

cuit, ~**e** /kɥi, -t/ *adj* cooked; **bien** ~ well done *ou* cooked; **trop** ~ overdone.

cuivre /kɥivʀ/ *nm* copper; ~ (**jaune**) brass; ~**s** (Mus) brass.

cul /ky/ *nm* (derrière 🔀) backside, bottom, arse 🔀.

culbuter /kylbyte/ [1] *vi* (*personne*) tumble; (*objet*) topple (over). ● *vt* knock over.

culminer /kylmine/ [1] *vi* reach its highest point *ou* peak.

culot /kylo/ *nm* (audace 🔲) nerve, cheek; (Tech) base.

culotte /kylɔt/ *nf* (de femme) pants (+ *pl*), knickers (+ *pl*); (US) panties (+ *pl*); ~ **de cheval** riding breeches; **en** ~ **courte** in short trousers.

culpabilité /kylpabilite/ *nf* guilt.

culte /kylt/ *nm* cult, worship; (religion) religion; (office protestant) service.

cultivateur, -trice /kyltivatœʀ, -tʀis/ *nm, f* farmer.

cultiver /kyltive/ [1] *vt* cultivate; (*plantes*) grow.

culture /kyltyʀ/ *nf* cultivation; (de plantes) growing; (agriculture) farming; (éducation) culture; (connaissances) knowledge; ~s (terrains) lands under cultivation; ~ **physique** physical training.

culturel, ~**le** /kyltyʀɛl/ *adj* cultural.

cumuler /kymyle/ [1] *vt* accumulate; (*fonctions*) hold concurrently.

cure /kyʀ/ *nf* (course of) treatment.

curé /kyʀe/ *nm* (parish) priest.

cure-dent (*pl* ~**s**) /kyʀdɑ̃/ *nm* toothpick.

curer /kyʀe/ [1] *vt* clean. □ **se** ~ *vpr* **se** ~ **les dents/ongles** clean one's teeth/nails.

curieux, **-ieuse** /kyʀjø, -z/ *adj* curious. ● *nm,f* (badaud) onlooker.

curiosité /kyʀjozite/ *nf* curiosity; (objet) curio; (spectacle) unusual sight.

curriculum vitae /kyʀikylɔm vite/ *nm inv* curriculum vitae; (US) résumé.

curseur /kyʀsœʀ/ *nm* cursor.

cutané, ~**e** /kytane/ *adj* skin.

cuve /kyv/ *nf* vat; (à mazout, eau) tank.

cuvée /kyve/ *nf* (de vin) vintage.

cuvette /kyvɛt/ *nf* bowl; (de lavabo) (wash)basin; (des cabinets) pan, bowl.

CV *abrév m* (**curriculum vitae**) CV.

cyberbranché, ~**e** /sibɛʀbʀɑ̃ʃe/ *adj* cyberwired.

cybercafé /sibɛʀkafe/ *nm* cybercafe.

cyberespace /sibɛʀsɛpas/ *nm* cyberspace.

cybernaute /sibɛʀnot/ *nmf* Netsurfer.

cybernétique /sibɛʀnetik/ *nf* cybernetics (+ *pl*).

cyclisme /siklism/ *nm* cycling.

cycliste /siklist/ *nmf* cyclist. ● *nm* cycling shorts. ● *adj* cycle.

cyclone /siklon/ *nm* cyclone.

cygne /siɲ/ *nm* swan.

cynique /sinik/ *adj* cynical. ● *nm* cynic.

Dd

d'/d/ ⇒DE.

d'abord /dabɔʀ/ *adv* first; (au début) at first.

dactylo /daktilo/ *nf* typist. **dactylographier** [45] *vt* type.

dada /dada/ *nm* hobby-horse.

daim /dɛ̃/ *nm* (fallow) deer; (cuir) suede.

dallage /dalaʒ/ *nm* paving. **dalle** *nf* slab.

daltonien, ~**ne** /daltɔnjɛ̃, -ɛn/ *adj* colour-blind.

dame /dam/ *nf* lady; (cartes, échecs) queen; ~**s** (jeu) draughts; (US) checkers.

damier /damje/ *nm* draught-board; (US) checker-board; **à** ~ chequered.

damner /dane/ [1] *vt* damn.

dandiner (se) /(sə)dɑ̃dine/ [1] *vpr* waddle.

Danemark /danmaʀk/ *nm* Denmark.

danger /dɑ̃ʒe/ *nm* danger; **en** ~ in danger; **mettre en** ~ endanger.

dangereux, **-euse** /dɑ̃ʒ(ə)ʀø, -z/ *adj* dangerous.

danois, ~**e** /danwa, -z/ *adj* Danish. ● *nm* (Ling) Danish. **D**~, ~**e** *nm,f* Dane.

dans /dɑ̃/ *prép* in; (mouvement) into; (à l'intérieur de) inside, in; **être** ~ **un avion** be on a plane; ~ **dix jours** in ten days' time; **boire** ~ **un verre** drink out of a glass; ~ **les 10 francs** about 10 francs.

danse /dɑ̃s/ *nf* dance; (art) dancing.

danser /dɑ̃se/ [1] *vt/i* dance. **danseur**, **-euse** *nm,f* dancer.

darne /daʀn/ *nf* steak (of fish).

date /dat/ *nf* date; ~ **limite** deadline; ~ **limite de vente** sell-by date; ~ **de péremption** use-by date.

dater /date/ [1] *vt/i* date; **à ~ de** as
from.

datte /dat/ *nf* (fruit) date.

daube /dob/ *nf* casserole.

dauphin /dofɛ̃/ *nm* (animal) dolphin.

davantage /davɑ̃taʒ/ *adv* more;
(plus longtemps) longer; **~ de** more; **je
n'en sais pas ~** that's as much as I
know.

---

de, d' /də, d/

d' before vowel or mute h.

● *préposition*

····➤ of; **le livre ~ mon ami** my friend's
book; **un pont ~ fer** an iron bridge.

····➤ (provenance) from.

····➤ (temporel) from; **~ 8 heures à 10
heures** from 8 till 10.

····➤ (mesure, manière) **dix mètres ~ haut**
ten metres high; **pleurer ~ rage** cry
with rage.

····➤ (agent) by; **un livre ~ Marcel Aymé**
a book by Marcel Aymé.

● **de, de l', de la, du,** (*pl* **des**)
déterminant

····➤ some; **du pain** (some) bread; **des
fleurs** (some) flowers; **je ne bois
jamais ~ vin** I never drink wine.

de + le = du
de + les = des

---

dé /de/ *nm* (à jouer) dice; (à coudre)
thimble; **~s** (jeu) dice.

débâcle /debakl/ *nf* (Géog) breaking
up; (Mil) rout.

déballer /debale/ [1] *vt* unpack;
(révéler) spill out.

débarbouiller /debaʀbuje/ *vt* wash
the face of. □ **se ~** *vpr* wash one's
face.

débarcadère /debaʀkadɛʀ/ *nm*
landing-stage.

débardeur /debaʀdœʀ/ *nm*
(vêtement) tank top.

débarquement /debaʀkəmɑ̃/ *nm*
disembarkation. **débarquer** [1] *vt/i*
disembark, land; (arriver 🆃) turn up.

débarras /debaʀa/ *nm* junk room;
bon ~! good riddance!

débarrasser /debaʀase/ [1] *vt*
clear (**de** of); **~ qn de** relieve sb of;
(*défaut, ennemi*) rid sb of. □ **se ~
de** *vpr* get rid of.

débat /deba/ *nm* debate.

débattre /debatʀ/ [11] *vt* debate.
● *vi* **~ de** discuss. □ **se ~** *vpr*
struggle (to get free).

débauche /deboʃ/ *nf* debauchery;
(fig) profusion.

débaucher /deboʃe/ [1] *vt* (licencier)
lay off; (distraire) tempt away.

débile /debil/ *adj* weak; 🆃 stupid.
● *nmf* moron 🆃.

débit /debi/ *nm* (rate of) flow;
(élocution) delivery; (de compte) debit;
~ de tabac tobacconist's shop; **~ de
boissons** bar.

débiter /debite/ [1] *vt* (compte) debit;
(fournir) produce; (vendre) sell; (dire: péj)
spout; (couper) cut up.

débiteur, -trice /debitœʀ, -tʀis/
nm, f debtor. ● *adj* (compte) in debit.

déblayer /debleje/ [31] *vt* clear.

déblocage /deblɔkaʒ/ *nm* (de prix)
deregulating. **débloquer** [1] *vt*
(prix, salaires) unfreeze.

déboiser /debwaze/ [1] *vt* clear (of
trees).

déboîter /debwate/ [1] *vi* (véhicule)
pull out. ● *vt* (membre) dislocate.

débordement /debɔʀdəmɑ̃/ *nm* (de
joie) excess.

déborder /debɔʀde/ [1] *vi* overflow.
● *vt* (dépasser) extend beyond; **~ de**
(*joie etc.*) be brimming over with.

débouché /debuʃe/ *nm* opening;
(carrière) prospect; (Comm) outlet;
(sortie) end, exit.

déboucher /debuʃe/ [1] *vt*
(bouteille) uncork; (évier) unblock.
● *vi* come out (**de** from); **~ sur** (rue)
lead into.

débourser /debuʀse/ [1] *vt* pay out.

debout /dəbu/ *adv* standing; (levé,
éveillé) up; **être ~, se tenir ~** be
standing, stand; **se mettre ~** stand
up.

déboutonner /debutɔne/ [1] *vt*
unbutton. □ **se ~** *vpr* unbutton
oneself; (vêtement) come undone.

débrancher /debʀɑ̃ʃe/ [1] *vt* (prise)
unplug; (système) disconnect.

d

débrayer /debʀeje/ [31] *vi* (Auto) declutch; (faire grève) stop work.

débris /debʀi/ *nmpl* fragments; (détritus) rubbish (+ *sg*); debris.

débrouillard, ∼**e** /debʀujaʀ, -d/ *adj* ① resourceful.

débrouiller /debʀuje/ [1] *vt* disentangle; (*problème*) solve. □ **se** ∼ *vpr* manage.

début /deby/ *nm* beginning; **faire ses** ∼**s** (en public) make one's début; **à mes** ∼**s** when I started out.

débutant, ∼**e** *nm,f* beginner.

débuter [1] *vi* begin; (dans un métier etc.) start out.

déca /deka/ *nm* ① decaf.

deçà: **en** ∼ /ãdəsa/ *loc* this side.
● *prép* **en** ∼ **de** this side of.

décacheter /dekaʃte/ [6] *vt* open.

décade /dekad/ *nf* ten days; (décennie) decade.

décadent, ∼**e** /dekadã, -t/ *adj* decadent.

décalage /dekalaʒ/ *nm* (écart) gap; ∼ **horaire** time difference. **décaler** [1] *vt* shift.

décalquer /dekalke/ [1] *vt* trace.

décamper /dekãpe/ [1] *vi* clear off.

décanter /dekãte/ *vt* allow to settle. □ **se** ∼ *vpr* settle.

décapant /dekapã/ *nm* chemical agent; (pour peinture) paint stripper.
● *adj* (*humour*) caustic.

décapotable /dekapɔtabl/ *adj* convertible.

décapsuleur /dekapsylœʀ/ *nm* bottle-opener.

décédé, ∼**e** /desede/ *adj* deceased. **décéder** [14] *vi* die.

déceler /desle/ [6] *vt* detect; (démontrer) reveal.

décembre /desãbʀ/ *nm* December.

décemment /desamã/ *adv* decently. **décence** *nf* decency.

décent, ∼**e** *adj* decent.

décennie /deseni/ *nf* decade.

décentralisation /desãtʀalizasjɔ̃/ *nf* decentralization. **décentraliser** [1] *vt* decentralize.

déception /desɛpsjɔ̃/ *nf* disappointment.

décerner /desɛʀne/ [1] *vt* award.

décès /desɛ/ *nm* death.

décevant, ∼**e** /des(ə)vã, -t/ *adj* disappointing. **décevoir** [52] *vt* disappoint.

déchaîner /deʃene/ [1] *vt* (*enthousiasme*) rouse. □ **se** ∼ *vpr* go wild.

décharge /deʃaʀʒ/ *nf* (de fusil) discharge; ∼ **électrique** electric shock; ∼ **publique** municipal dump.

décharger /deʃaʀʒe/ [40] *vt* unload; ∼ **qn de** relieve sb from. □ **se** ∼ *vpr* (*batterie, pile*) go flat.

déchausser (**se**) /(sə)deʃose/ [1] *vpr* take off one's shoes; (*dent*) work loose.

dèche /dɛʃ/ *nf* ① **dans la** ∼ broke.

déchéance /deʃeãs/ *nf* decay.

déchet /deʃɛ/ *nm* (reste) scrap; (perte) waste; ∼**s** (ordures) refuse.

déchiffrer /deʃifʀe/ [1] *vt* decipher.

déchiqueter /deʃikte/ [38] *vt* tear to shreds.

déchirement /deʃiʀmã/ *nm* heartbreak; (conflit) split.

déchirer /deʃiʀe/ [1] *vt* (par accident) tear; (lacérer) tear up; (arracher) tear off *ou* out; (diviser) tear apart. □ **se** ∼ *vpr* tear. **déchirure** *nf* tear.

décibel /desibɛl/ *nm* decibel.

décidément /desidemã/ *adv* really.

décider /deside/ [1] *vt* decide on; (persuader) persuade; ∼ **que/de** decide that/to; ∼ **de qch** decide on sth. □ **se** ∼ *vpr* make up one's mind (**à** to).

décimal, ∼**e** (*mpl* ∼**aux**) /desimal, -o/ *a & nf* decimal.

décisif, -**ive** /desizif, -v/ *adj* decisive.

décision /desizjɔ̃/ *nf* decision.

déclaration /deklaʀasjɔ̃/ *nf* declaration; (commentaire politique) statement; ∼ **d'impôts** tax return.

déclarer /deklaʀe/ [1] *vt* declare; (*naissance*) register; **déclaré coupable** found guilty; ∼ **forfait** (Sport) withdraw. □ **se** ∼ *vpr* (*feu*) break out.

déclencher /deklãʃe/ [1] *vt* (Tech) set off; (*conflit*) spark off; (*avalanche*) start; (*rire*) provoke. □ **se** ∼ *vpr* (Tech) go off. **déclencheur** *nm* (Photo) shutter release.

déclic /deklik/ *nm* click.

déclin /deklɛ̃/ *nm* decline.

déclinaison /deklinɛzɔ̃/ *nf* (Ling) declension.

décliner /dekline/ [1] *vt* (*refuser*) decline; (*dire*) state; (Ling) decline.

décocher /dekɔʃe/ [1] *vt* (*coup*) fling; (*regard*) shoot.

décollage /dekɔlaʒ/ *nm* take-off.

décoller /dekɔle/ [1] *vt* unstick. ● *vi* (*avion*) take off. □ **se ∼** *vpr* come off.

décolleté, **∼e** /dekɔlte/ *adj* low-cut. ● *nm* low neckline.

décolorer /dekɔlɔʀe/ [1] *vt* fade; (*cheveux*) bleach. □ **se ∼** *vpr* fade.

décombres /dekɔ̃bʀ/ *nmpl* rubble.

décommander /dekɔmɑ̃de/ [1] *vt* cancel.

décomposer /dekɔ̃poze/ [1] *vt* break up; (*substance*) decompose. □ **se ∼** *vpr* (*pourrir*) decompose.

décompte /dekɔ̃t/ *nm* deduction; (*détail*) breakdown.

décongeler /dekɔ̃ʒle/ [6] *vt* thaw.

déconseillé, **∼e** /dekɔ̃sɛje/ *adj* not recommended, inadvisable.

déconseiller /dekɔ̃sɛje/ [1] *vt* **∼ qch à qn** advise sb against sth.

décontracté, **∼e** /dekɔ̃tʀakte/ *adj* relaxed.

déconvenue /dekɔ̃vny/ *nf* disappointment.

décor /dekɔʀ/ *nm* (*paysage*) scenery; (*de cinéma, théâtre*) set; (*cadre*) setting; (*de maison*) décor.

décoratif, **-ive** /dekɔʀatif, -v/ *adj* decorative.

décorateur, **-trice** /dekɔʀatœʀ, -tʀis/ *nm,f* (*de cinéma*) set designer. **décoration** *nf* decoration. **décorer** [1] *vt* decorate.

décortiquer /dekɔʀtike/ [1] *vt* shell; (fig) dissect.

découdre (**se**) /(sə)dekudʀ/ [19] *vpr* come unstitched.

découler /dekule/ [1] *vi* **∼ de** follow from.

découper /dekupe/ [1] *vt* cut up; (*viande*) carve; (*détacher*) cut out.

découragement /dekuʀaʒmɑ̃/ *nm* discouragement.

décourager /dekuʀaʒe/ [40] *vt* discourage. □ **se ∼** *vpr* become discouraged.

décousu, **∼e** /dekuzy/ *adj* (*vêtement*) which has come unstitched; (*idées*) disjointed.

découvert, **∼e** /dekuvɛʀ, -t/ *adj* (*tête*) bare; (*terrain*) open. ● *nm* (*de compte*) overdraft; **à ∼** exposed; (fig) openly.

découverte /dekuvɛʀt/ *nf* discovery; **à la ∼ de** in search of.

découvrir /dekuvʀiʀ/ [21] *vt* discover; (*voir*) see; (*montrer*) reveal. □ **se ∼** *vpr* (se décoiffer) take one's hat off; (*ciel*) clear.

décrasser /dekʀase/ [1] *vt* clean.

décrépit, **∼e** /dekʀepi, -t/ *adj* decrepit. **décrépitude** *nf* decay.

décret /dekʀɛ/ *nm* decree. **décréter** [14] *vt* order; (*dire*) declare.

décrié, **∼e** /dekʀije/ *adj* criticized.

décrire /dekʀiʀ/ [30] *vt* describe.

décroché, **∼e** /dekʀɔʃe/ *adj* (*téléphone*) off the hook.

décrocher /dekʀɔʃe/ [1] *vt* unhook; (*obtenir* 🔲) get. ● *vi* (*abandonner* 🔲) give up; **∼** (**le téléphone**) pick up the phone.

décroître /dekʀwatʀ/ [24] *vi* decrease.

déçu, **∼e** /desy/ *adj* disappointed.

décupler /dekyple/ [1] *vt/i* increase tenfold.

dédaigner /dedeɲe/ [1] *vt* scorn.

dédain /dedɛ̃/ *nm* scorn.

dédale /dedal/ *nm* maze.

dedans /dədɑ̃/ *adv & nm* inside; **en ∼** on the inside.

dédicacer /dedikase/ [10] *vt* dedicate; (*signer*) sign.

dédier /dedje/ [45] *vt* dedicate.

dédommagement /dedɔmaʒmɑ̃/ *nm* compensation. **dédommager** [40] *vt* compensate (**de** for).

déduction /dedyksjɔ̃/ *nf* deduction; **∼ d'impôts** tax deduction.

déduire /deduiʀ/ [17] *vt* deduct; (*conclure*) deduce.

déesse /deɛs/ *nf* goddess.

défaillance /defajɑ̃s/ *nf* (*panne*) failure; (*évanouissement*) blackout.

défaillant, ~e adj (système) faulty; (personne) faint.

défaire /defɛʀ/ [33] vt undo; (valise) unpack; (démonter) take down. □ se ~ vpr come undone; se ~ de rid oneself of.

défait, ~e /defɛ, -t/ adj (cheveux) ruffled; (visage) haggard; (nœud) undone. **défaite** nf defeat.

défaitiste /defetist/ a & nmf defeatist.

défalquer /defalke/ [1] vt (somme) deduct.

défaut /defo/ nm fault, defect; (d'un verre, diamant, etc.) flaw; (pénurie) shortage; à ~ de for lack of; pris en ~ caught out; faire ~ (argent etc.) be lacking; par ~ (Jur) in one's absence; ~ de paiement non-payment.

défavorable /defavɔʀabl/ adj unfavourable.

défavoriser /defavɔʀize/ [1] vt discriminate against.

défectueux, -euse /defɛktɥø, -z/ adj faulty, defective.

défendre /defɑ̃dʀ/ [3] vt defend; (interdire) forbid; ~ à qn de forbid sb to. □ se ~ vpr defend oneself; (se protéger) protect oneself; (se débrouiller) manage; se ~ de (refuser) refrain from.

défense /defɑ̃s/ nf defence; ~ de fumer no smoking; (d'éléphant) tusk. **défenseur** nm defender. **défensif, -ive** adj defensive.

déferler /defɛʀle/ [1] vi (vagues) break; (violence) erupt.

défi /defi/ nm challenge; (provocation) defiance; mettre au ~ challenge.

déficience /defisjɑ̃s/ nf deficiency. **déficient**, ~e adj deficient.

déficit /defisit/ nm deficit. **déficitaire** adj in deficit.

défier /defje/ [45] vt challenge; (braver) defy.

défilé /defile/ nm procession; (Mil) parade; (fig) (continual) stream; (Géog) gorge; ~ de mode fashion parade.

défiler /defile/ [1] vi march; (visiteurs) stream; (images) flash by; (chiffres, minutes) add up. □ se ~ vpr 🗆 sneak off.

défini, ~e /defini/ adj (Ling) definite.

définir /definiʀ/ [2] vt define.

définitif, -ive /definitif, -v/ adj final, definitive; en définitive in the end.

définition /definisjɔ̃/ nf definition; (de mots croisés) clue.

définitivement /definitivmɑ̃/ adv definitively, permanently.

déflagration /deflagʀasjɔ̃/ nf explosion.

déflation /deflasjɔ̃/ nf deflation. **déflationniste** adj deflationary.

défoncé, ~e /defɔ̃se/ adj (terrain) full of potholes; (siège) broken; (drogué: 🗆) high.

défoncer /defɔ̃se/ [10] vt (porte) break down; (mâchoire) break. □ se ~ vpr 🗉 to give one's all.

déformation /defɔʀmasjɔ̃/ nf distortion. **déformer** [1] vt put out of shape; (faits, pensée) distort.

défouler (se) /(sə)defule/ [1] vpr let off steam.

défrayer /defʀeje/ [31] vt (payer) pay the expenses of; ~ la chronique be the talk of the town.

défricher /defʀiʃe/ [1] vt clear.

défroisser /defʀwase/ [1] vt smooth out.

défunt, ~e /defœ̃, -t/ adj (mort) late. ● nm, f deceased.

dégagé, ~e /degaʒe/ adj (ciel) clear; (front) bare; d'un ton ~ casually.

dégagement /degaʒmɑ̃/ nm clearing; (football) clearance.

dégager /degaʒe/ [40] vt (exhaler) give off; (désencombrer) clear; (faire ressortir) bring out; (ballon) clear. □ se ~ vpr free oneself; (ciel, rue) clear; (odeur) emanate.

dégarnir (se) /(sə)degaʀniʀ/ [2] vpr clear, empty; (personne) be going bald.

dégâts /dega/ nmpl damage (+ sg).

dégel /deʒɛl/ nm thaw. **dégeler** [6] vi thaw (out).

dégénéré, ~e /deʒeneʀe/ a & nm,f degenerate.

dégivrer /deʒivʀe/ [1] vt (Auto) de-ice; (réfrigérateur) defrost.

déglinguer /deglɛ̃ge/ 🗉 [1] vt bust. □ se ~ vpr break down.

dégonflé, ~e /degõfle/ *adj* (*pneu*)
flat; (*lâche* 🇹) yellow 🇹.

dégonfler /degõfle/ [1] *vt* deflate.
● *vi* (*blessure*) go down. □ **se** ~ *vpr*
🇹 chicken out.

dégouliner /deguline/ [1] *vi* trickle.

dégourdi, ~e /deguʀdi/ *adj* smart.

dégourdir /deguʀdiʀ/ [2] *vt*
(*membre, liquide*) warm up. □ **se** ~
vpr se ~ **les jambes** stretch one's
legs.

dégoût /degu/ *nm* disgust.

dégoûtant, ~e /degutã, -t/ *adj*
disgusting.

dégoûter /degute/ [1] *vt* disgust; ~
qn de qch put sb off sth.

dégradant, ~e /degʀadã, -t/ *adj*
degrading.

dégradation /degʀadasjõ/ *nf*
damage; **commettre des** ~s cause
damage.

dégrader /degʀade/ [1] *vt* (*abîmer*)
damage. □ **se** ~ *vpr* (*se détériorer*)
deteriorate.

dégrafer /degʀafe/ [1] *vt* unhook.

degré /dəgʀe/ *nm* degree; (*d'escalier*)
step.

dégressif, -ive /degʀesif, -v/ *adj*
graded; **tarif** ~ tapering charge.

dégrèvement /degʀɛvmã/ *nm* ~
fiscal *ou* **d'impôts** tax reduction.

dégringolade /degʀɛ̃gɔlad/ *nf*
tumble.

dégrossir /degʀosiʀ/ [2] *vt* (*bois*)
trim; (*projet*) rough out.

déguerpir /degɛʀpiʀ/ [2] *vi* clear
off.

dégueulasse /degœlas/ *adj* 🗵
disgusting, lousy.

dégueuler /degœle/ [1] *vt* 🗵 throw
up.

déguisement /degizmã/ *nm* (*de
carnaval*) fancy dress; (*pour duper*)
disguise.

déguiser /degize/ [1] *vt* dress up;
(*pour duper*) disguise. □ **se** ~ *vpr* (*au
carnaval etc.*) dress up; (*pour duper*)
disguise oneself.

déguster /degyste/ [1] *vt* taste,
sample; (*savourer*) enjoy.

dehors /dəoʀ/ *adv* **en** ~ **de** outside;
(*hormis*) apart from; **jeter/mettre** ~

throw/put out. ● *nm* outside. ● *nmpl*
(*aspect de qn*) exterior.

déjà /deʒa/ *adv* already; (*avant*)
before, already.

déjeuner /deʒœne/ [1] *vi* have
lunch; (*le matin*) have breakfast. ● *nm*
lunch; **petit** ~ breakfast.

delà /dəla/ *adv & prép* **au** ~ (**de**), **par**
~ beyond.

délai /delɛ/ *nm* time-limit; (*attente*)
wait; (*sursis*) extension (of time); **sans**
~ immediately; **dans un** ~ **de 2
jours** within 2 days; **finir dans les** ~s
finish within the deadline; **dans les
plus brefs** ~s as soon as possible.

délaisser /delese/ [1] *vt* (*négliger*)
neglect.

délassement /delasmã/ *nm*
relaxation.

délation /delasjõ/ *nf* informing.

délavé, ~e /delave/ *adj* faded.

délayer /deleje/ [31] *vt* mix (with
liquid); (*idée*) drag out.

délecter (se) /(sə)delɛkte/ [1] *vpr*
se ~ **de** delight in.

délégué, ~e /delege/ *nm, f* delegate.

délibéré, ~e /delibeʀe/ *adj*
deliberate; (*résolu*) determined.

délicat, ~e /delika, -t/ *adj* delicate;
(*plein de tact*) tactful. **délicatesse** *nf*
delicacy; (*tact*) tact. **délicatesses**
nfpl (kind) attentions.

délice /delis/ *nm* delight.
délicieux, -ieuse *adj* (*au goût*)
delicious; (*charmant*) delightful.

délier /delje/ [45] *vt* untie; (*délivrer*)
free. □ **se** ~ *vpr* come untied.

délimiter /delimite/ [1] *vt*
determine, demarcate.

délinquance /delɛ̃kãs/ *nf*
delinquency. **délinquant**, ~e *a &
nm, f* delinquent.

délirant, ~e /deliʀã, -t/ *adj*
delirious; (*frénétique*) frenzied; 🇹
wild.

délire /deliʀ/ *nm* delirium; (*fig*)
frenzy. **délirer** [1] *vi* be delirious
(**de** with); 🇹 be off one's rocker 🇹.

délit /deli/ *nm* offence.

délivrance /delivʀãs/ *nf* release;
(*soulagement*) relief; (*remise*) issue.
délivrer [1] *vt* free, release; (*pays*)
liberate; (*remettre*) issue.

déloyal, ~e (*mpl* **-aux**) /delwajal, -jo/ *adj* disloyal; (*procédé*) unfair.

deltaplane /dɛltaplan/ *nm* hang-glider.

déluge /delyʒ/ *nm* downpour; le D~ the Flood.

démagogie /demagɔʒi/ *nm* demagogy. **démagogue** *nmf* demagogue.

demain /dəmɛ̃/ *adv* tomorrow.

demande /dəmɑ̃d/ *nf* request; ~ d'emploi job application; ~ en mariage marriage proposal.

demander /dəmɑ̃de/ [1] *vt* ask for; (*chemin, heure*) ask; (*nécessiter*) require; ~ que/si ask that/if; ~ qch à qn ask sb sth; ~ à qn de ask sb to; ~ en mariage propose to. □ se ~ *vpr* se ~ si/où wonder if/where.

demandeur, -euse /dəmɑ̃dœr, -øz/ *nm,f* ~ d'emploi job seeker; ~ d'asile asylum-seeker.

démangeaison /demɑ̃ʒezɔ̃/ *nf* itch(ing).

démanteler /demɑ̃tle/ [6] *vt* break up.

démaquillant /demakijɑ̃/ *nm* make-up remover. **démaquiller (se)** [1] *vpr* remove one's make-up.

démarchage /demarʃaʒ/ *nm* door-to-door selling.

démarche /demàrʃ/ *nf* walk, gait; (*procédé*) step.

démarcheur, -euse /demarʃœr, -øz/ *nm,f* (door-to-door) canvasser.

démarrage /demaraʒ/ *nm* start.

démarrer /demare/ [1] *vi* (*moteur*) start (up); (*partir*) move off; (fig) get moving. ● *vt* 🗓 get moving.

démarreur /demarœr/ *nm* starter.

démêlant /demelɑ̃/ *nm* conditioner. **démêler** [1] *vt* disentangle.

déménagement /demenaʒmɑ̃/ *nm* move; (*transport*) removal.

déménager /demenaʒe/ [40] *vi* move (house). ● *vt* (*meubles*) remove.

déménageur /demenaʒœr/ *nm* removal man.

démence /demɑ̃s/ *nf* insanity.

démener (se) /(sə)demne/ [6] *vpr* move about wildly; (fig) put oneself out.

dément, ~e /demɑ̃, -t/ *adj* insane. ● *nm,f* lunatic.

démenti /demɑ̃ti/ *nm* denial.

démentir /demɑ̃tir/ [46] *vt* deny; (*contredire*) refute; ~ que deny that.

démerder (se) /(sə)demɛrde/ [1] *vpr* 🗵 manage.

démettre /demɛtr/ [42] *vt* (*poignet etc.*) dislocate; ~ qn de relieve sb of. □ se ~ *vpr* resign (de from).

demeure /dəmœr/ *nf* residence; mettre en ~ de order to.

demeurer /dəmœre/ [1] *vi* live; (*rester*) remain.

demi, ~e /dəmi/ *adj* half(-). ● *nm,f* half. ● *nm* (*bière*) (half-pint) glass of beer; (football) half-back. ● *adv* à ~ half; (*ouvrir, fermer*) half-way; à la ~e at half past; une heure et ~e an hour and a half; (à l'horloge) half past one; une ~-journée/-livre half a day/pound. **demi-cercle** (*pl* ~s) *nm* semicircle. **demi-finale** (*pl* ~s) *nf* semifinal. **demi-frère** (*pl* ~s) *nm* half-brother, stepbrother. **demi-heure** (*pl* ~s) *nf* half-hour, half an hour. **demi-litre** (*pl* ~s) *nm* half a litre. **demi-mesure** (*pl* ~s) *nf* half-measure. **à demi-mot** *adv* without having to express every word. **demi-pension** *nf* half-board. **demi-queue** *nm* boudoir grand piano. **demi-sel** *a inv* slightly salted. **demi-sœur** (*pl* ~s) *nf* half-sister, stepsister.

démission /demisjɔ̃/ *nf* resignation.

demi-tarif (*pl* ~s) /dəmitarif/ *nm* half-fare.

demi-tour (*pl* ~s) /dəmitur/ *nm* about turn; (Auto) U-turn; faire ~ turn back.

démocrate /demɔkrat/ *nmf* democrat. ● *adj* democratic. **démocratie** *nf* democracy.

démodé, ~e /demɔde/ *adj* old-fashioned.

demoiselle /dəmwazɛl/ *nf* young lady; (*célibataire*) single lady; ~ d'honneur bridesmaid.

démolir /demɔlir/ [2] *vt* demolish.

démon /demɔ̃/ *nm* demon; le D~ the Devil. **démoniaque** *adj* fiendish.

démonstration /demɔ̃strasjɔ̃/ nf demonstration; (de force) show.

démonter /demɔ̃te/ [1] vt take apart, dismantle; (installation) take down; (fig) disconcert. □ **se** ∼ vpr come apart.

démontrer /demɔ̃tre/ [1] vt demonstrate; (indiquer) show.

démoraliser /demɔralize/ [1] vt demoralize.

démuni, ∼**e** /demyni/ adj impoverished; ∼ **de** without.

démunir /demyniʀ/ [2] vt ∼ **de** deprive of. □ **se** ∼ **de** vpr part with.

dénaturer /denatyʀe/ [1] vt (faits) distort.

dénigrement /denigʀəmɑ̃/ nm denigration.

dénivellation /denivɛlasjɔ̃/ nf (pente) slope.

dénombrer /denɔ̃bʀe/ [1] vt count.

dénomination /denɔminasjɔ̃/ nf designation.

dénommé, ∼**e** /denɔme/ nm,f le ∼ X the said X.

dénoncer /denɔ̃se/ [10] vt denounce. □ **se** ∼ vpr give oneself up. **dénonciateur, -trice** nm,f informer.

dénouement /denumɑ̃/ nm outcome; (Théât) dénouement.

dénouer /denwe/ [1] vt undo. □ **se** ∼ vpr (nœud) come undone.

dénoyauter /denwajote/ [1] vt stone.

denrée /dɑ̃ʀe/ nf ∼ **alimentaire** foodstuff.

dense /dɑ̃s/ adj dense. **densité** nf density.

dent /dɑ̃/ nf tooth; **faire ses** ∼**s** teethe; ∼ **de lait** milk tooth; ∼ **de sagesse** wisdom tooth; (de roue) cog. **dentaire** adj dental.

denté, ∼**e** /dɑ̃te/ adj (roue) toothed.

dentelé, ∼**e** /dɑ̃tle/ adj jagged.

dentelle /dɑ̃tɛl/ nf lace.

dentier /dɑ̃tje/ nm dentures (+ pl), false teeth (+ pl).

dentifrice /dɑ̃tifʀis/ nm toothpaste.

dentiste /dɑ̃tist/ nmf dentist.

dentition /dɑ̃tisjɔ̃/ nf teeth, dentition.

dénudé, ∼**e** /denyde/ adj bare.

dénué, ∼**e** /denɥe/ adj ∼ **de** devoid of.

dénuement /denymɑ̃/ nm destitution.

déodorant /deɔdɔʀɑ̃/ nm deodorant.

dépannage /depanaʒ/ nm repair; (Ordinat) troubleshooting. **dépanner** [1] vt repair; (fig) help out. **dépanneuse** nf breakdown lorry.

dépareillé, ∼**e** /depaʀeje/ adj odd, not matching.

départ /depaʀ/ nm departure; (Sport) start; **au** ∼ **de Nice** from Nice; **au** ∼ (d'abord) at first.

département /depaʀtəmɑ̃/ nm department.

dépassé, ∼**e** /depase/ adj outdated.

dépasser /depase/ [1] vt go past, pass; (véhicule) overtake; (excéder) exceed; (rival) surpass; **ça me dépasse** 🄸 it's beyond me. ● vi stick out.

dépaysement /depeizmɑ̃/ nm change of scenery; (désagréable) disorientation.

dépêche /depɛʃ/ nf dispatch.

dépêcher /depɛʃe/ [1] vt dispatch. □ **se** ∼ vpr hurry (up).

dépendance /depɑ̃dɑ̃s/ nf dependence; (à une drogue) dependency; (bâtiment) outbuilding.

dépendre /depɑ̃dʀ/ [3] vt take down. ● vi depend (de on); ∼ **de** (appartenir à) belong to.

dépens /depɑ̃/ nmpl **aux** ∼ **de** at the expense of.

dépense /depɑ̃s/ nf expense; expenditure.

dépenser /depɑ̃se/ [1] vt/i spend; (énergie etc.) use up. □ **se** ∼ vpr get some exercise.

dépérir /depeʀiʀ/ [2] vi wither.

dépêtrer (se) /(sə)depetʀe/ [1] vpr get oneself out (de of).

dépeupler /depœple/ [1] vt depopulate. □ **se** ∼ vpr become depopulated.

déphasé, ∼**e** /defaze/ adj 🄸 out of step.

dépilatoire /depilatwaʀ/ a & nm depilatory.

dépistage /depistaʒ/ *nm* screening. **dépister** [1] *vt* detect; (*criminel*) track down.

dépit /depi/ *nm* resentment; **par ~** out of pique; **en ~ de** despite; **en ~ du bon sens** in a very illogical way. **dépité, ~e** *adj* vexed.

déplacé, ~e /deplase/ *adj* (*remarque*) uncalled for.

déplacement /deplasmɑ̃/ *nm* (voyage) trip.

déplacer /deplase/ [10] *vt* move. □ **se ~** *vpr* move; (voyager) travel.

déplaire /deplɛʀ/ [47] *vi* **~ à** (irriter) displease; **ça me déplaît** I don't like it.

déplaisant, ~e /deplɛzɑ̃, -t/ *adj* unpleasant, disagreeable.

dépliant /deplijɑ̃/ *nm* leaflet.

déplier /deplije/ [45] *vt* unfold.

déploiement /deplwamɑ̃/ *nm* (démonstration) display; (militaire) deployment.

déplorable /deploʀabl/ *adj* deplorable. **déplorer** [1] *vt* (trouver regrettable) deplore; (*mort*) lament.

déployer /deplwaje/ [31] *vt* (*ailes, carte*) spread; (*courage*) display; (*armée*) deploy.

déportation /depɔʀtasjɔ̃/ *nf* (en 1940) internment in a concentration camp.

déposer /depoze/ [1] *vt* put down; (laisser) leave; (*passager*) drop; (*argent*) deposit; (*plainte*) lodge; (*armes*) lay down. ● *vi* (Jur) testify. □ **se ~** *vpr* settle.

dépositaire /depozitɛʀ/ *nmf* (Comm) agent.

déposition /depozisjɔ̃/ *nf* (Jur) statement.

dépôt /depo/ *nm* (entrepôt) warehouse; (d'autobus) depot; (particules) deposit; (garantie) deposit; **laisser en ~** give for safe keeping; **~ légal** formal deposit of a publication with an institution.

dépouille /depuj/ *nf* skin, hide; **~ (mortelle)** mortal remains.

dépouiller /depuje/ [1] *vt* (*courrier*) open; (*scrutin*) count; (écorcher) skin; **~ qn de** strip sb of.

dépourvu, ~e /depuʀvy/ *adj* **~ de** devoid of; **prendre au ~** catch unawares.

déprécier /depʀesje/ [45] *vt* depreciate. □ **se ~** *vpr* depreciate.

déprédations /depʀedasjɔ̃/ *nfpl* damage (+ *sg*).

dépression /depʀesjɔ̃/ *nf* depression; **~ nerveuse** nervous breakdown.

déprimer /depʀime/ [1] *vt* depress.

depuis /dəpɥi/

● *préposition*

····▸ (point de départ) since; **~ quand attendez-vous?** how long have you been waiting?

····▸ (durée) for; **~ toujours** always; **~ peu** recently.

● *adverbe*

····▸ since; **il a eu une attaque le mois dernier, ~ nous sommes inquiets** he had a stroke last month and we've been worried ever since.

● **depuis que** *conjonction*

····▸ since, ever since; **Sophie a beaucoup changé depuis que Camille est née** Sophie has changed a lot since Camille was born.

député /depyte/ *nm* ≈ Member of Parliament.

déraciné, -e /deʀasine/ *nm,f* rootless person.

déraillement /deʀajmɑ̃/ *nm* derailment.

dérailler /deʀaje/ [1] *vi* be derailed; (fig 🔢) be talking nonsense; **faire ~** derail. **dérailleur** *nm* (de vélo) derailleur.

déraisonnable /deʀɛzɔnabl/ *adj* unreasonable.

dérangement /deʀɑ̃ʒmɑ̃/ *nm* bother; (désordre) disorder, upset; **en ~** out of order; **les ~s** the fault reporting service.

déranger /deʀɑ̃ʒe/ [40] *vt* (gêner) bother, disturb; (dérégler) upset, disrupt. □ **se ~** *vpr* (aller) go; (fig) put oneself out; **ça te dérangerait de...?** would you mind...?

dérapage /deʀapaʒ/ *nm* skid.
déraper [1] *vi* skid; (fig) (*prix*) get out of control.

déréglé, **~e** /deʀegle/ *adj* (*vie*) dissolute; (*estomac*) upset; (*mécanisme*) (that is) not running properly.

dérégler /deʀegle/ [14] *vt* make go wrong. □ **se ~** *vpr* go wrong.

dérision /deʀizjɔ̃/ *nf* mockery; **tourner en ~** ridicule.

dérive /deʀiv/ *nf* **aller à la ~** drift.

dérivé /deʀive/ *nm* by-product.

dériver /deʀive/ [1] *vi* (*bateau*) drift; **~ de** stem from.

dermatologie /dɛʀmatɔlɔʒi/ *nf* dermatology.

dernier, **-ière** /dɛʀnje, -jɛʀ/ *adj* last; (*nouvelles, mode*) latest; (*étage*) top. ● *nm,f* last (one); **ce ~** the latter; **le ~ de mes soucis** the least of my worries.

dernièrement /dɛʀnjɛʀmɑ̃/ *adv* recently.

dérober /deʀɔbe/ [1] *vt* steal. □ **se ~** *vpr* slip away; **se ~ à** (*obligation*) shy away from.

dérogation /deʀɔgasjɔ̃/ *nf* special authorization.

déroger /deʀɔʒe/ [40] *vi* **~ à** depart from.

déroulement /deʀulmɑ̃/ *nm* (d'une action) development.

dérouler /deʀule/ [1] *vt* (*fil etc.*) unwind. □ **se ~** *vpr* unwind; (avoir lieu) take place; (*récit, paysage*) unfold.

déroute /deʀut/ *nf* (Mil) rout.

dérouter /deʀute/ [1] *vt* disconcert.

derrière /dɛʀjɛʀ/ *prép & adv* behind. ● *nm* back, rear; (postérieur 🆒) behind 🆒; **de ~** (*fenêtre*) back, rear; (*pattes*) hind.

des /de/ ⇨**DE**.

dès /dɛ/ *prép* (right) from; **~ lors** from then on; **~ que** as soon as.

désabusé, **~e** /dezabyze/ *adj* disillusioned.

désaccord /dezakɔʀ/ *nm* disagreement.

désaffecté, **~e** /dezafɛkte/ *adj* disused.

désagréable /dezagʀeabl/ *adj* unpleasant.

désagrément /dezagʀemɑ̃/ *nm* annoyance, inconvenience.

désaltérer (**se**) /(sə)dezaltere/ [14] *vpr* quench one's thirst.

désamorcer /dezamɔʀse/ [10] *vt* (*situation, obus*) defuse.

désapprobation /dezapʀɔbasjɔ̃/ *nf* disapproval. **désapprouver** [1] *vt* disapprove of.

désarçonner /dezaʀsɔne/ [1] *vt* throw.

désarmement /dezaʀməmɑ̃/ *nm* (Pol) disarmament.

désarroi /dezaʀwa/ *nm* distress.

désastre /dezastʀ/ *nm* disaster. **désastreux**, **-euse** *adj* disastrous.

désavantage /dezavɑ̃taʒ/ *nm* disadvantage. **désavantager** [40] *vt* put at a disadvantage.

désaveu (*pl* **~x**) /dezavø/ *nm* denial. **désavouer** [1] *vt* deny.

descendance /desɑ̃dɑ̃s/ *nf* descent; (enfants) descendants (+ *pl*). **descendant**, **~e** *nm,f* descendant.

descendre /desɑ̃dʀ/ [3] *vi* (aux **être**) go down; (venir) come down; (*passager*) get off *ou* out; (*nuit*) fall; **~ à pied** walk down; **~ par l'ascenseur** take the lift down; **~ de** (être issu de) be descended from; **~ à l'hôtel** go to a hotel; **~ dans la rue** (Pol) take to the streets. ● *vt* (aux **avoir**) (*escalier etc.*) go *ou* come down; (*objet*) take down; (abattre 🆒) shoot down.

descente /desɑ̃t/ *nf* descent; (à ski) downhill; (raid) raid; **dans la ~** going downhill; **~ de lit** bedside rug.

descriptif, **-ive** /dɛskʀiptif, -v/ *adj* descriptive. **description** *nf* description.

désemparé, **~e** /dezɑ̃paʀe/ *adj* distraught.

désendettement /dezɑ̃dɛtmɑ̃/ *nm* reduction of the debt.

déséquilibré, **~e** /dezekilibʀe/ *adj* unbalanced; 🆒 crazy. ● *nm,f* lunatic. **déséquilibrer** [1] *vt* throw off balance.

désert, **~e** /dezɛʀ, -t/ *adj* deserted. ● *nm* desert.

déserter /dezɛʀte/ [1] *vt/i* desert.
déserteur *nm* deserter.

désertique /dezɛʀtik/ *adj* desert.

désespérant, **~e** /dezɛspeʀɑ̃, -t/
adj utterly disheartening.

désespéré, **~e** /dezɛspeʀe/ *adj* in
despair; (*état, cas*) hopeless; (*effort*)
desperate.

désespérer /dezɛspeʀe/ [14] *vt*
drive to despair. ● *vi* despair, lose
hope; **~ de** despair of. □ **se ~** *vpr*
despair.

désespoir /dezɛspwaʀ/ *nm* despair;
en ~ de cause as a last resort.

déshabillé, **~e** /dezabije/ *adj*
undressed. ● *nm* négligee.

déshabiller /dezabije/ [1] *vt*
undress. □ **se ~** *vpr* get undressed.

désherbant /dezɛʀbɑ̃/ *nm* weed-
killer.

déshérité, **~e** /dezeʀite/ *adj*
(*région*) deprived; (*personne*) the
underprivileged.

déshériter /dezeʀite/ [1] *vt*
disinherit.

déshonneur /dezɔnœʀ/ *nm*
disgrace.

déshonorer /dezɔnɔʀe/ [1] *vt*
dishonour.

déshydrater /dezidʀate/ [1] *vt*
dehydrate. □ **se ~** *vpr* get
dehydrated.

désigner /dezine/ [1] *vt* (montrer)
point to *ou* out; (élire) appoint;
(signifier) designate.

désillusion /dezilyzjɔ̃/ *nf*
disillusionment.

désinence /dezinɑ̃s/ *nf* (Gram)
ending.

désinfectant /dezɛ̃fɛktɑ̃/ *nm*
disinfectant. **désinfecter** [1] *vt*
disinfect.

désintéressé, **~e** /dezɛ̃teʀese/
adj (*personne, acte*) selfless.

désintéresser (se) /(sə)dezɛ̃te-
ʀese/ [1] *vpr* se **~ de** lose interest in.

désintoxiquer /dezɛ̃tɔksike/ [1] *vt*
detoxify; **se faire ~** to undergo
detoxification.

désinvolte /dezɛ̃vɔlt/ *adj* casual.
désinvolture *nf* casualness.

désir /deziʀ/ *nm* wish, desire;
(convoitise) desire.

désirer /deziʀe/ [1] *vt* want;
(sexuellement) desire; **vous désirez?**
what would you like?

désireux, **-euse** /deziʀø, -z/ *adj* **~**
de faire anxious to do.

désistement /dezistəmɑ̃/ *nm*
withdrawal.

désobéir /dezɔbeiʀ/ [2] *vi* **~ (à)**
disobey. **désobéissant**, **~e** *adj*
disobedient.

désobligeant, **~e** /dezɔbliʒɑ̃, -t/
adj disagreeable, unkind.

désodorisant /dezɔdɔʀizɑ̃/ *nm* air
freshener.

désodoriser /dezɔdɔʀize/ [1] *vt*
freshen up.

désœuvré, **~e** /dezœvʀe/ *adj* at a
loose end. **désœuvrement** *nm* lack
of anything to do.

désolation /dezɔlasjɔ̃/ *nf* distress.

désolé, **~e** /dezɔle/ *adj* (au regret)
sorry; (région) desolate.

désoler /dezɔle/ [1] *vt* distress. □ **se**
~ *vpr* be upset (**de qch** about sth).

désopilant, **~e** /dezɔpilɑ̃, -t/ *adj*
hilarious.

désordonné, **~e** /dezɔʀdɔne/ *adj*
untidy; (mouvements) uncoordinated.

désordre /dezɔʀdʀ/ *nm* untidiness;
(Pol) disorder; **en ~** untidy.

désorganiser /dezɔʀganize/ [1] *vt*
disorganize.

désorienter /dezɔʀjɑ̃te/ [1] *vt*
disorient.

désormais /dezɔʀmɛ/ *adv* from
now on.

desquels, **desquelles** /dekɛl/
⇒LEQUEL.

dessécher /deseʃe/ [1] *vt* dry out.
□ **se ~** *vpr* dry out, become dry;
(plante) wither.

dessein /desɛ̃/ *nm* intention; **à ~**
intentionally.

desserrer /deseʀe/ [1] *vt* loosen; **il**
n'a pas desserré les dents he never
once opened his mouth. □ **se ~** *vpr*
come loose.

dessert /desɛʀ/ *nm* dessert; **en ~**
for dessert.

desservir /desɛʀviʀ/ [46] *vt/i*
(débarrasser) clear away; (autobus)
serve.

dessin /desɛ̃/ nm drawing; (motif) design; (discipline) art; (contour) outline; **professeur de ~** art teacher; **~ animé** (cinéma) cartoon; **~ humoristique** cartoon.

dessinateur, -trice /desinatœR, -tRis/ nm, f artist; (industriel) draughtsman.

dessiner /desine/ [1] vt/i draw; (fig) outline. □ **se ~** vpr appear, take shape.

dessoûler /desule/ [1] vt/i sober up.

dessous /dəsu/ adv underneath. ● nm underside, underneath. ● nmpl underwear; **les ~ d'une histoire** what is behind a story; **du ~** bottom; (voisins) downstairs; **en ~, par-~** underneath. **dessous-de-plat** nm inv (heat-resistant) table-mat. **dessous-de-table** nm inv backhander. **dessous-de-verre** nm inv coaster.

dessus /dəsy/ adv on top (of it), on it. ● nm top; **du ~** top; (voisins) upstairs; **avoir le ~** get the upper hand. **dessus-de-lit** nm inv bedspread.

destabiliser /destabilize/ [1] vt destabilize, unsettle.

destin /dɛstɛ̃/ nm (sort) fate; (avenir) destiny.

destinataire /dɛstinatɛR/ nmf addressee.

destination /dɛstinasjɔ̃/ nf destination; (fonction) purpose; **vol à ~ de** flight to.

destinée /dɛstine/ nf destiny.

destiner /dɛstine/ [1] vt **~ à** intend for; (vouer) destine for; **le commentaire m'est destiné** this comment is aimed at me; **être destiné à faire** be intended to do; (obligé) be destined to do. □ **se ~ à** vpr (carrière) intend to take up.

destituer /dɛstitɥe/ [1] vt discharge.

destructeur, -trice /dɛstRyktœR, -tRis/ adj destructive. **destruction** nf destruction.

désuet, -ète /dezɥɛ, -t/ adj outdated.

détachant /detaʃɑ̃/ nm stain remover.

détacher /detaʃe/ [1] vt untie; (ôter) remove, detach; (déléguer) second. □ **se ~** vpr come off, break away; (nœud etc.) come undone; (ressortir) stand out.

détail /detaj/ nm detail; (de compte) breakdown; (Comm) retail; **au ~** (vendre etc.) retail; **de ~** (prix etc.) retail; **en ~** in detail; **entrer dans les ~s** go into detail.

détaillant, ~e /detajɑ̃, -t/ nm, f retailer.

détaillé, ~e /detaje/ adj detailed.

détailler /detaje/ [1] vt (rapport) detail; **~ ce que qn fait** scrutinize what sb does.

détaler /detale/ [1] vi 🆄 bolt.

détartrant /detaRtRɑ̃/ nm descaler.

détecter /detɛkte/ [1] vt detect. **détecteur** nm detector.

détective /detɛktiv/ nm detective.

déteindre /detɛ̃dR/ [22] vi (dans l'eau) run (**sur** on to); (au soleil) fade; **~ sur** (fig) rub off on.

détendre /detɑ̃dR/ [3] vt slacken; (ressort) release; (personne) relax. □ **se ~** vpr (ressort) slacken; (personne) relax. **détendu, ~e** adj (calme) relaxed.

détenir /det(ə)niR/ [58] vt hold; (secret, fortune) possess.

détente /detɑ̃t/ nf relaxation; (Pol) détente; (saut) spring; (gâchette) trigger; **être lent à la ~** 🆄 be slow on the uptake.

détenteur, -trice /detɑ̃tœR, -tRis/ nm, f holder.

détention /detɑ̃sjɔ̃/ nf detention; **~ provisoire** custody.

détenu, ~e /detny/ nm, f prisoner.

détergent /detɛRʒɑ̃/ nm detergent.

détérioration /deteRjɔRasjɔ̃/ nf deterioration; (dégât) damage.

détériorer /deteRjɔRe/ [1] vt damage. □ **se ~** vpr deteriorate.

détermination /detɛRminasjɔ̃/ nf determination. **déterminé, ~e** adj (résolu) determined; (précis) definite. **déterminer** [1] vt determine.

déterrer /detere/ [1] vt dig up.

détestable /detɛstabl/ adj (caractère, temps) foul.

détester /detɛste/ [1] *vt* hate. □ **se**
~ *vpr* hate each other.

détonation /detɔnasjɔ̃/ *nf*
explosion, detonation.

détour /detuʀ/ *nm* (crochet) detour;
(fig) roundabout means; (virage) bend.

détournement /detuʀnəmɑ̃/ *nm*
hijack(ing); (de fonds) embezzlement.

détourner /detuʀne/ [1] *vt*
(attention) divert; (tête, yeux) turn
away; (avion) hijack; (argent)
embezzle. □ **se** ~ **de** *vpr* stray
from.

détraquer /detʀake/ [1] *vt* make go
wrong; (estomac) upset. □ **se** ~ *vpr*
(machine) go wrong.

détresse /detʀɛs/ *nf* distress; **dans
la** ~, **en** ~ in distress.

détritus /detʀity(s)/ *nmpl* rubbish
(+ *sg*).

détroit /detʀwa/ *nm* strait.

détromper /detʀɔ̃pe/ [1] *vt* set
straight. □ **se** ~ *vpr* **détrompe-toi!**
you'd better think again!

détruire /detʀɥiʀ/ [17] *vt* destroy.

dette /dɛt/ *nf* debt.

deuil /dœj/ *nm* (période) mourning;
(décès) bereavement; **porter le** ~ be
in mourning; **faire son** ~ **de qch**
give sth up as lost.

deux /dø/ *a & nm* two; ~ **fois** twice;
tous (les) ~ both. **deuxième** *a &
nmf* second. **deux-pièces** *nm inv*
(maillot de bain) two-piece; (logement)
two-room flat. **deux-points** *nm inv*
(Gram) colon. **deux-roues** *nm inv*
two-wheeled vehicle.

dévaliser /devalize/ [1] *vt* rob,
clean out.

dévalorisant, ~**e** /devalɔʀizɑ̃,.-t/
adj demeaning.

dévaloriser /devalɔʀize/ [1] *vt*
(monnaie) devalue. □ **se** ~ *vpr*
(personne) put oneself down.

dévaluation /devalɥasjɔ̃/ *nf*
devaluation.

dévaluer /devalɥe/ [1] *vt* devalue.
□ **se** ~ *vpr* devalue.

devancer /dəvɑ̃se/ [10] *vt* be *ou* go
ahead of; (arriver) arrive ahead of;
(prévenir) anticipate.

devant /d(ə)vɑ̃/ *prép* in front of;
(distance) ahead of; (avec mouvement)
past; (en présence de) in front of; (face

à) in the face of; **avoir du temps** ~
soi have plenty of time. ● *adv* in
front; (à distance) ahead; **de** ~ front.
● *nm* front; **prendre les** ~**s** take the
initiative.

devanture /dəvɑ̃tyʀ/ *nf* shop front;
(vitrine) shop window.

développement /devlɔpmɑ̃/ *nm*
development; (de photos) developing.

développer /devlɔpe/ [1] *vt*
develop. □ **se** ~ *vpr* (corps, talent)
develop; (entreprise) grow, expand.

devenir /dəvniʀ/ [58] *vi* (aux être)
become; **qu'est-il devenu?** what has
become of him?

dévergondé, ~**e** /devɛʀgɔ̃de/ *a &
nm,f* shameless (person).

déverser /devɛʀse/ [1] *vt* (liquide)
pour; (ordures, pétrole) dump. □ **se**
~ *vpr* (rivière) flow; (égout, foule)
pour.

dévêtir /devetiʀ/ [61] *vt* undress.
□ **se** ~ *vpr* get undressed.

déviation /devjasjɔ̃/ *nf* diversion.

dévier /devje/ [45] *vt* divert; (coup)
deflect. ● *vi* (ballon, balle) veer;
(personne) deviate.

devin /dəvɛ̃/ *nm* soothsayer.

deviner /dəvine/ [1] *vt* guess;
(apercevoir) distinguish.

devinette /dəvinɛt/ *nf* riddle.

devis /dəvi/ *nm* estimate, quote.

dévisager /devizaʒe/ [40] *vt* stare
at.

devise /dəviz/ *nf* motto; ~**s** (monnaie)
(foreign) currency.

dévisser /devise/ [1] *vt* unscrew.

dévitaliser /devitalize/ [1] *vt* (dent)
carry out root canal treatment on.

dévoiler /devwale/ [1] *vt* reveal.

....

devoir /dəvwaʀ/ [26]

● *verbe auxiliaire*

····▸ ~ **faire** (obligation, hypothèse) must
do; (nécessité) have got to do; **je dois
dire que...** I have to say that...; **il a
dû partir** (nécessité) he had to leave;
(hypothèse) he must have left.

····▸ (prévision) **je devais lui dire** I was to
tell her; **elle doit rentrer bientôt** she's
due back soon.

····▸ (conseil) **tu devrais** you should.

● *verbe transitif*

····▸ (*argent, excuses*) owe; **combien je vous dois?** (en achetant) how much is it?

□ **se devoir** *verbe pronominal*

····▸ **je me dois de le faire** it's my duty to do it.

● *nom masculin*

····▸ duty; **faire son ~** do one's duty.

····▸ (Scol) **~** (**surveillé**) test; **les ~s** homework (+ *sg*); **faire ses ~s** do one's homework.

dévorer /devɔʀe/ [1] *vt* devour.

dévot, **~e** /devo, -ɔt/ *adj* devout.

dévoué, **~e** /devwe/ *adj* devoted. **dévouement** *nm* devotion.

dévouer (**se**) /(sə)devwe/ [1] *vpr* devote oneself (**à** to); (se sacrifier) sacrifice oneself.

dextérité /dɛksteʀite/ *nf* skill.

diabète /djabɛt/ *nm* diabetes. **diabétique** *a* & *nmf* diabetic.

diable /djɑbl/ *nm* devil.

diagnostic /djagnɔstik/ *nm* diagnosis. **diagnostiquer** [1] *vt* diagnose.

diagonal, **~e** (*mpl* **-aux**) /djagɔnal, -o/ *adj* diagonal. **diagonale** *nf* diagonal; **en ~e** diagonally.

diagramme /djagʀam/ *nm* diagram; (graphique) graph.

dialecte /djalɛkt/ *nm* dialect.

dialogue /djalɔg/ *nm* dialogue. **dialoguer** [1] *vi* have talks, enter into a dialogue.

diamant /djamɑ̃/ *nm* diamond.

diamètre /djamɛtʀ/ *nm* diameter.

diapositive /djapozitiv/ *nf* slide.

diarrhée /djaʀe/ *nf* diarrhoea.

dictateur /diktatœʀ/ *nm* dictator.

dicter /dikte/ [1] *vt* dictate. **dictée** *nf* dictation.

dictionnaire /diksjɔnɛʀ/ *nm* dictionary.

dicton /diktɔ̃/ *nm* saying.

dièse /djɛz/ *nm* (Mus) sharp.

diesel /djezɛl/ *nm* & *a inv* diesel.

diète /djɛt/ *nf* restricted diet.

diététicien, **~ne** /djetetisjɛ̃, -ɛn/ *nm,f* dietician.

diététique /djetetik/ *nf* dietetics.

● *adj* **produit** *ou* **aliment ~** dietary product; **magasin ~** health food shop *ou* store.

dieu (*pl* **~x**) /djø/ *nm* god; **D~** God.

diffamation /difamasjɔ̃/ *nf* slander; (par écrit) libel. **diffamer** [1] *vt* slander; (par écrit) libel.

différé: **en ~** /ɑ̃difeʀe/ *loc* (*émission*) pre-recorded.

différemment /difeʀamɑ̃/ *adv* differently.

différence /difeʀɑ̃s/ *nf* difference; **à la ~ de** unlike.

différencier /difeʀɑ̃sje/ [45] *vt* differentiate. □ **se ~** *vpr* differentiate oneself; **se ~ de** (différer de) differ from.

différend /difeʀɑ̃/ *nm* difference (of opinion).

différent, **~e** /difeʀɑ̃, -t/ *adj* different (**de** from).

différer /difeʀe/ [14] *vt* postpone. ● *vi* differ (**de** from).

difficile /difisil/ *adj* difficult; (exigeant) fussy. **difficilement** *adv* with difficulty.

difficulté /difikylte/ *nf* difficulty; **faire des ~s** raise objections.

diffus, **~e** /dify, -z/ *adj* diffuse.

diffuser /difyze/ [1] *vt* (*émission*) broadcast; (*nouvelle*) spread; (*lumière, chaleur*) diffuse; (Comm) distribute. **diffusion** *nf* broadcasting; diffusion; distribution.

digérer /diʒeʀe/ [14] *vt* digest; (endurer ⚇) stomach. **digeste** *adj* digestible.

digestif, **-ive** /diʒɛstif, -v/ *adj* digestive. ● *nm* after-dinner liqueur.

digital, **~e** (*mpl* **-aux**) /diʒital, -o/ *adj* digital.

digne /diɲ/ *adj* (noble) dignified; (approprié) worthy; **~ de** worthy of; **~ de foi** trustworthy.

digue /dig/ *nf* dyke; (US) dike.

dilater /dilate/ [1] *vt* dilate. □ **se ~** *vpr* dilate; (*estomac*) distend.

dilemme /dilɛm/ *nm* dilemma.

dilettante /diletɑ̃t/ *nmf* amateur.

diluant /dilɥɑ̃/ *nm* thinner.

diluer /dilɥe/ [1] *vt* dilute.

dimanche /dimɑ̃ʃ/ *nm* Sunday.

dimension /dimɑ̃sjɔ̃/ *nf* (taille) size; (mesure) dimension; (aspect) dimension.

diminuer /diminɥe/ [1] *vt* reduce, decrease; (plaisir, courage) dampen; (dénigrer) diminish. ● *vi* (se réduire) decrease; (faiblir) (bruit, flamme) die down; (ardeur) cool. **diminutif** *nm* diminutive; (surnom) pet name. **diminution** *nf* decrease (de in); (réduction) reduction; (affaiblissement) diminishing.

dinde /dɛ̃d/ *nf* turkey.

dîner /dine/ [1] *vi* have dinner. ● *nm* dinner.

dingue /dɛ̃g/ *adj* 🔲 crazy.

dinosaure /dinozɔʀ/ *nm* dinosaur.

diphtongue /diftɔ̃g/ *nf* diphthong.

diplomate /diplɔmat/ *nmf* diplomat. ● *adj* diplomatic. **diplomatique** *adj* diplomatic.

diplôme /diplom/ *nm* certificate, diploma; (Univ) degree. **diplômé, ~e** *adj* qualified.

dire /diʀ/ [27] *vt* say; (secret, vérité, heure) tell; (penser) think; ~ que say that; ~ à qn que tell sb that; ~ à qn de tell sb to; ça me dit de faire I feel like doing; on dirait que it would seem that, it seems that; **dis/dites donc!** hey! □ **se ~** *vpr* (mot) be said; (penser) tell oneself; (se prétendre) claim to be. ● *nm* au ~ de, selon les ~s de according to.

direct, ~e /diʀɛkt/ *adj* direct. ● *nm* (train) express train; **en ~** (émission) live.

directeur, -trice /diʀɛktœʀ, -tʀis/ *nm,f* director; (chef de service) manager, manageress; (de journal) editor; (d'école) headteacher; (US) principal; ~ **de banque** bank manager; ~ **commercial** sales manager; ~ **des ressources humaines** human resources manager.

direction /diʀɛksjɔ̃/ *nf* (sens) direction; (de société) management; (Auto) steering; **en ~ de** (going) to.

dirigeant, ~e /diʀiʒɑ̃, -t/ *nm,f* (Pol) leader; (Comm) manager. ● *adj* (classe) ruling.

diriger /diʀiʒe/ [40] *vt* (service, école, parti, pays) run; (entreprise, usine) manage; (travaux) supervise; (véhicule) steer; (orchestre) conduct; (braquer) aim; (tourner) turn. □ **se ~** *vpr* (s'orienter) find one's way; **se ~ vers** head for, make for.

▸ **dis** /di/ ⇒DIRE [27].

discernement /disɛʀnəmɑ̃/ *nm* discernment.

disciplinaire *adj* disciplinary. **discipline** *nf* discipline.

discontinu, ~e /diskɔ̃tiny/ *adj* intermittent.

discordant, ~e /diskɔʀdɑ̃, -t/ *adj* discordant.

discothèque /diskɔtɛk/ *nf* record library; (boîte de nuit) disco(thèque).

discours /diskuʀ/ *nm* speech; (propos) views.

discret, -ète /diskʀɛ, -t/ *adj* discreet.

discrétion /diskʀesjɔ̃/ *nf* discretion; **à ~** (vin) unlimited; (manger, boire) as much as one desires.

discrimination /diskʀiminasjɔ̃/ *nf* discrimination. **discriminatoire** *adj* discriminatory.

disculper /diskylpe/ [1] *vt* exonerate. □ **se ~** *vpr* vindicate oneself.

discussion /diskysjɔ̃/ *nf* discussion; (querelle) argument.

discutable /diskytabl/ *adj* debatable; (critiquable) questionable.

discuter /diskyte/ [1] *vt* discuss; (contester) question. ● *vi* (parler) talk; (répliquer) argue; ~ **de** discuss.

disette /dizɛt/ *nf* food shortage.

disgrâce /disgʀɑs/ *nf* disgrace.

disgracieux, -ieuse /disgʀasjø, -z/ *adj* ugly, unsightly.

disjoindre /disʒwɛ̃dʀ/ [22] *vt* take apart. □ **se ~** *vpr* come apart.

disloquer /dislɔke/ [1] *vt* (membre) dislocate; (machine) break (apart). □ **se ~** *vpr* (parti, cortège) break up; (meuble) come apart.

disparaître /dispaʀɛtʀ/ [18] *vi* disappear; (mourir) die; **faire ~** get rid of. **disparition** *nf* disappearance; (mort) death.

disparate /dispaʀat/ *adj* ill-assorted.

disparu, ~e /dispaʀy/ *adj* missing.
● *nm, f* missing person; (mort) dead person.

dispensaire /dispɑ̃sɛʀ/ *nm* clinic.

dispense /dispɑ̃s/ *nf* exemption.

dispenser /dispɑ̃se/ [1] *vt* exempt (de from). □ **se** ~ **de** *vpr* avoid.

disperser /dispɛʀse/ [1] *vt* (éparpiller) scatter; (répartir) disperse. □ **se** ~ *vpr* disperse.

disponibilité /dispɔnibilite/ *nf* availability. **disponible** *adj* available.

dispos, ~e /dispo, -z/ *adj* **frais et** ~ fresh and alert.

disposé, ~e /dispoze/ *adj* **bien/mal** ~ in a good/bad mood; ~ **à** prepared to; ~ **envers** disposed towards.

disposer /dispoze/ [1] *vt* arrange; ~ **à** (engager à) incline to. ● *vi* ~ **de** have at one's disposal. □ **se** ~ **à** *vpr* prepare to.

dispositif /dispozitif/ *nm* device; (ensemble de mesures) operation.

disposition /dispozisjɔ̃/ *nf* arrangement, layout; (tendance) tendency; ~**s** (humeur) mood; (préparatifs) arrangements; (mesures) measures; (aptitude) aptitude; **mettre à la** ~ **de** place *ou* put at the disposal of.

disproportionné, ~e /dispʀo-pɔʀsjɔne/ *adj* disproportionate; ~ **à** out of proportion with.

dispute /dispyt/ *nf* quarrel.

disputer /dispyte/ [1] *vt* (match) play; (course) run in; (prix) fight for; (gronder [I]) tell off. □ **se** ~ *vpr* quarrel; (se battre pour) fight over; (match) be played.

disquaire /diskɛʀ/ *nmf* record dealer.

disque /disk/ *nm* (Mus) record; (Sport) discus; (cercle) disc, disk; (Ordinat) disk; ~ **compact** compact disc; ~ **dur** hard disk; ~ **optique compact** CD-ROM; ~ **souple** floppy disk.

disquette /diskɛt/ *nf* floppy disk, diskette; ~ **de sauvegarde** back-up disk.

disséminer /disemine/ [1] *vt* spread, scatter.

dissertation /disɛʀtasjɔ̃/ *nf* essay, paper.

disserter /disɛʀte/ [1] *vi* ~ **sur** speak about; (par écrit) write about.

dissident, ~e /disidɑ̃, -t/ *a & nm, f* dissident.

dissimulation /disimylasjɔ̃/ *nf* concealment; (fig) deceit.

dissimuler /disimyle/ [1] *vt* conceal (à from). □ **se** ~ *vpr* conceal oneself.

dissipé, ~e /disipe/ *adj* (élève) unruly.

dissiper /disipe/ [1] *vt* (fumée, crainte) dispel; (fortune) squander; (personne) distract. □ **se** ~ *vpr* disappear; (élève) grow restless.

dissolvant /disɔlvɑ̃/ *nm* solvent; (pour ongles) nail polish remover.

dissoudre /disudʀ/ [53] *vt* dissolve. □ **se** ~ *vpr* dissolve.

dissuader /disɥade/ [1] *vt* dissuade (de from).

dissuasion /disɥazjɔ̃/ *nf* dissuasion; **force de** ~ deterrent force.

distance /distɑ̃s/ *nf* distance; (écart) gap; **à** ~ at *ou* from a distance.

distancer /distɑ̃se/ [10] *vt* outdistance.

distendre /distɑ̃dʀ/ [3] *vt* (estomac) distend; (corde) stretch.

distinct, ~e /distɛ̃(kt), -ɛ̃kt/ *adj* distinct.

distinctif, **-ive** /distɛ̃ktif, -v/ *adj* (trait) distinctive; (signe, caractère) distinguishing.

distinction /distɛ̃ksjɔ̃/ *nf* distinction; (récompense) honour.

distinguer /distɛ̃ge/ [1] *vt* distinguish.

distraction /distʀaksjɔ̃/ *nf* absent-mindedness; (passe-temps) entertainment, leisure; (détente) recreation.

distraire /distʀɛʀ/ [29] *vt* amuse; (rendre inattentif) distract; ~ **qn de qch** take sb's mind off sth. □ **se** ~ *vpr* amuse oneself.

distrait, ~e /distʀɛ, -t/ *adj* absent-minded; (élève) inattentive.

distrayant, ~e /distʀɛjɑ̃, -t/ *adj* entertaining.

distribuer /distribɥe/ [1] *vt* hand out, distribute; (*répartir*) distribute; (*tâches, rôles*) allocate; (*cartes*) deal; (*courrier*) deliver.

distributeur /distribytœʀ/ *nm* (Auto, Comm) distributor; ∼ (**automatique**) vending-machine; ∼ **de billets** (**de banque**) cash dispenser. **distribution** *nf* distribution; (*du courrier*) delivery; (*acteurs*) cast; (*secteur*) retailing.

district /distʀikt/ *nm* district.

dit[1], **dites** /di, dit/ ⇒DIRE [27].

dit[2], ∼**e** /di, dit/ *adj* (*décidé*) agreed; (*surnommé*) known as.

diurne /djyʀn/ *adj* diurnal; (*activité*) daytime.

divagations /divagasjɔ̃/ *nfpl* ravings.

divergence /divɛʀʒɑ̃s/ *nf* divergence. **divergent**, ∼**e** *adj* divergent. **diverger** [40] *vi* diverge.

divers, ∼**e** /divɛʀ, -s/ *adj* (*varié*) diverse; (*différent*) various; (*frais*) miscellaneous; **dépenses** ∼**es** sundries. **diversifier** [45] *vt* diversify.

diversité /divɛʀsite/ *nf* diversity, variety.

divertir /divɛʀtiʀ/ [2] *vt* amuse, entertain. □ **se** ∼ *vpr* amuse oneself; (*passer du bon temps*) enjoy oneself. **divertissement** *nm* amusement, entertainment.

dividende /dividɑ̃d/ *nm* dividend.

divin, ∼**e** /divɛ̃, -in/ *adj* divine. **divinité** *nf* divinity.

diviser /divize/ [1] *vt* divide. □ **se** ∼ *vpr* become divided; **se** ∼ **par sept** be divisible by seven. **division** *nf* division.

divorce /divɔʀs/ *nm* divorce.

divorcé, ∼**e** /divɔʀse/ *adj* divorced. ● *nm, f* divorcee.

divorcer /divɔʀse/ [10] *vi* ∼ (**d'avec**) divorce.

dix /dis/ (/di/ *before consonant,* /diz/ *before vowel*) *a & nm* ten.

dix-huit /dizɥit/ *a & nm* eighteen.

dixième /dizjɛm/ *a & nmf* tenth.

dix-neuf /diznœf/ *a & nm* nineteen.

dix-sept /disɛt/ *a & nm* seventeen.

docile /dɔsil/ *adj* docile.

docteur /dɔktœʀ/ *nm* doctor.

doctorat /dɔktɔʀa/ *nm* doctorate, PhD.

document /dɔkymɑ̃/ *nm* document. **documentaire** *a & nm* documentary.

documentaliste /dɔkymɑ̃talist/ *nmf* information officer; (Scol) librarian.

documentation /dɔkymɑ̃tasjɔ̃/ *nf* information, literature; **centre de** ∼ resource centre.

documenté, ∼**e** /dɔkymɑ̃te/ *adj* well-documented.

documenter /dɔkymɑ̃te/ [1] *vt* provide with information. □ **se** ∼ *vpr* collect information.

dodo /dodo/ *nm* **faire** ∼ (*langage enfantin*) sleep.

dodu, ∼**e** /dɔdy/ *adj* plump.

dogmatique /dɔgmatik/ *adj* dogmatic. **dogme** *nm* dogma.

doigt /dwa/ *nm* finger; **un** ∼ **de** a drop of; **montrer qch du** ∼ point at sth; **à deux** ∼**s de** a hair's breadth away from; ∼ **de pied** toe. **doigté** *nm* (Mus) fingering, touch; (*diplomatie*) tact.

dois, **doit** /dwa/ ⇒DEVOIR [26].

doléances /dɔleɑ̃s/ *nfpl* grievances.

dollar /dɔlaʀ/ *nm* dollar.

domaine /dɔmɛn/ *nm* estate, domain; (*fig*) domain, field.

domestique /dɔmɛstik/ *adj* domestic. ● *nmf* servant. **domestiquer** [1] *vt* domesticate.

domicile /dɔmisil/ *nm* home; **à** ∼ at home; (*livrer*) to the home.

domicilié, ∼**e** /dɔmisilje/ *adj* resident; **être** ∼ **à Paris** live *ou* be resident in Paris.

dominant, ∼**e** /dɔminɑ̃, -t/ *adj* dominant. **dominante** *nf* dominant feature.

dominer /dɔmine/ [1] *vt* dominate; (*surplomber*) tower over, dominate; (*sujet*) master; (*peur*) overcome. ● *vi* dominate; (*équipe*) be in the lead; (*prévaloir*) stand out.

domino /dɔmino/ *nm* domino.

dommage /dɔmaʒ/ *nm* (*tort*) harm; ∼(**s**) (*dégâts*) damage; **c'est** ∼ it's a pity *ou* shame; **quel** ∼ what a pity *ou* shame. **dommages-intérêts** *nmpl* (Jur) damages.

dompter /dɔ̃te/ [1] *vt* tame. **dompteur, -euse** *nm,f* tamer.

DOM-TOM /dɔmtɔm/ *abrév mpl* (**départements et territoires d'outre-mer**) French overseas departments and territories.

don /dɔ̃/ *nm* (cadeau, aptitude) gift. **donateur, -trice** *nm,f* donor. **donation** *nf* donation.

donc /dɔ̃k/ *conj* so, then; (par conséquent) so, therefore; **quoi** ∼? what did you say?; **tiens** ∼! fancy that!

donjon /dɔ̃ʒɔ̃/ *nm* (tour) keep.

donné, ∼e /dɔne/ *adj* (fixé) given; (pas cher 🔢) dirt cheap; **étant** ∼ **que** given that.

donnée /dɔne/ *nf* (élément d'information) fact; ∼**s** data.

donner /dɔne/ [1] *vt* give; (vieilles affaires) give away; (distribuer) give out; (fruits, résultats) produce; (film) show; (pièce) put on; **ça donne soif/ faim** it makes one thirsty/hungry; ∼ **qch à réparer** take sth to be repaired; ∼ **lieu à** give rise to. ● *vi* ∼ **sur** look out on to; ∼ **dans** tend towards. □ **se** ∼ **à** *vpr* devote oneself to; **se** ∼ **du mal** go to a lot of trouble (**pour faire** to do).

dont /dɔ̃/

● *pronom*

····▸ (personne) **la fille** ∼ **je te parlais** the girl I was telling you about; **l'homme** ∼ **la fille a dit…** the man whose daughter said…

····▸ (chose) which, **l'affaire** ∼ **il parle** the matter which he is referring to; **la manière** ∼ **elle parle** the way she speaks; **ce** ∼ **il parle** what he's talking about.

····▸ (provenance) from which.

····▸ (parmi lesquels) **deux personnes** ∼ **toi** two people, one of whom is you; **plusieurs thèmes** ∼ **l'identité et le racisme** several topics including identity and racism.

dopage /dɔpaʒ/ *nm* (de cheval) doping; (d'athlète) illegal drug-use.

doper /dɔpe/ [1] *vt* dope. □ **se** ∼ *vpr* take drugs.

doré, ∼e /dɔʀe/ *adj* (couleur d'or) golden; (qui rappelle de l'or) gold; (avec de l'or) gilt; **la jeunesse** ∼**e** gilded youth.

dorénavant /dɔʀenavɑ̃/ *adv* henceforth.

dorer /dɔʀe/ [1] *vt* gild; (Culin) brown.

dormir /dɔʀmiʀ/ [46] *vi* sleep; (être endormi) be asleep; ∼ **debout** be asleep on one's feet; **une histoire à** ∼ **debout** a cock-and-bull story.

dortoir /dɔʀtwaʀ/ *nm* dormitory.

dorure /dɔʀyʀ/ *nf* gilding.

dos /do/ *nm* back; (de livre) spine; **à** ∼ **de** riding on; **au** ∼ **de** (chèque) on the back of; **de** ∼ from behind; ∼ **crawlé** backstroke.

dosage /dozaʒ/ *nm* (mélange) mixture; (quantité) amount, proportions. **dose** *nf* dose. **doser** [1] *vt* measure out; (contrôler) use in a controlled way.

dossier /dɔsje/ *nm* (documents) file; (Jur) case; (de chaise) back; (TV, presse) special feature.

dot /dɔt/ *nf* dowry.

douane /dwan/ *nf* customs.

douanier, -ière /dwanje, -jɛʀ/ *adj* customs. ● *nm* customs officer.

double /dubl/ *a & adv* double. ● *nm* (copie) duplicate; (sosie) double; **le** ∼ (**de**) twice as much *ou* as many (as); **le** ∼ **messieurs** the men's doubles.

doubler /duble/ [1] *vt* double; (dépasser) overtake; (vêtement) line; (film) dub; (classe) repeat; (cap) round. ● *vi* double.

doublure /dublyʀ/ *nf* (étoffe) lining; (acteur) understudy.

douce /dus/ ⇒DOUX.

doucement /dusmɑ̃/ *adv* gently; (sans bruit) quietly; (lentement) slowly.

douceur /dusœʀ/ *nf* (mollesse) softness; (de climat) mildness; (de personne) gentleness; (friandise) sweet; (US) candy; **en** ∼ smoothly.

douche /duʃ/ *nf* shower.

d

doucher /duʃe/ [1] *vt* give a shower to. □ **se** ~ *vpr* have *ou* take a shower.

doudoune /dudun/ *nf* 🅸 down jacket.

doué, ~**e** /dwe/ *adj* gifted; ~ **de** endowed with.

douille /duj/ *nf* (Électr) socket.

douillet, ~**te** /dujɛ, -t/ *adj* cosy, comfortable; (*personne*: péj) soft.

douleur /dulœʀ/ *nf* pain; (chagrin) sorrow, grief. **douloureux**, -**euse** *adj* painful.

doute /dut/ *nm* doubt; **sans** ~ no doubt; **sans aucun** ~ without doubt.

douter /dute/ [1] *vt* ~ **de** doubt; ~ **que** doubt that. ● *vi* doubt. □ **se** ~ **de** *vpr* suspect; **je m'en doutais** I thought so.

douteux, -**euse** /dutø, -z/ *adj* dubious, doubtful.

Douvres /duvʀ/ *npr* Dover.

doux, **douce** /du, dus/ *adj* (moelleux) soft; (sucré) sweet; (clément, pas fort) mild; (pas brusque, bienveillant) gentle.

douzaine /duzɛn/ *nf* about twelve; (douze) dozen; **une** ~ **d'œufs** a dozen eggs.

douze /duz/ *a* & *nm* twelve. **douzième** *a* & *nmf* twelfth.

doyen, ~**ne** /dwajɛ̃, -ɛn/ *nm,f* dean; (en âge) most senior person.

dragée /dʀaʒe/ *nf* sugared almond.

draguer /dʀage/ [1] *vt* (*rivière*) dredge; (*filles* 🅸) chat up, try to pick up.

drainer /dʀene/ [1] *vt* drain.

dramatique /dʀamatik/ *adj* dramatic; (tragique) tragic. ● *nf* (television) drama.

dramatiser /dʀamatize/ [1] *vt* dramatize.

dramaturge /dʀamatyʀʒ/ *nmf* dramatist.

drame /dʀam/ *nm* (genre) drama; (pièce) play; (événement tragique) tragedy.

drap /dʀa/ *nm* sheet; (tissu) (woollen) cloth.

drapeau (*pl* ~**x**) /dʀapo/ *nm* flag.

drap-housse (*pl* **draps-housses**) /dʀaus/ *nm* fitted sheet.

dressage /dʀɛsaʒ/ *nm* training; (compétition équestre) dressage.

dresser /dʀese/ [1] *vt* put up, erect; (*tête*) raise; (*animal*) train; (*liste, plan*) draw up; ~ **l'oreille** prick up one's ears. □ **se** ~ *vpr* (*bâtiment*) stand; (*personne*) draw oneself up. **dresseur**, -**euse** *nm,f* trainer.

dribbler /dʀible/ [1] *vi* (Sport) dribble.

drive /dʀajv/ *nm* (Ordinat) drive.

drogue /dʀɔg/ *nf* drug; **la** ~ drugs.

drogué, ~**e** /dʀɔge/ *nm,f* drug addict.

droguer /dʀɔge/ [1] *vt* (*malade*) drug heavily; (*victime*) drug. □ **se** ~ *vpr* take drugs.

droguerie /dʀɔgʀi/ *nf* hardware shop. **droguiste** *nmf* owner of a hardware shop.

droit, ~**e** /dʀwa, -t/ *adj* (contraire de gauche) right; (non courbe) straight; (loyal) upright; **angle** ~ right angle. ● *adv* straight. ● *nm* right; ~(**s**) (taxe) duty; **le** ~ (Jur) law; **avoir** ~ **à** be entitled to; **avoir le** ~ **de** be allowed to; **être dans son** ~ be in the right; ~ **d'auteur** copyright; ~ **d'inscription** registration fee; ~**s d'auteur** royalties.

droite /dʀwat/ *nf* (contraire de gauche) right; **à** ~ on the right; (direction) (to the) right; **la** ~ the right (side); (Pol) the right (wing); (ligne) straight line. **droitier**, -**ière** *adj* right-handed.

drôle /dʀol/ *adj* (amusant) funny; (bizarre) funny, odd. **drôlement** *adv* funnily; (très 🅸) really.

dru, ~**e** /dʀy/ *adj* thick; **tomber** ~ fall thick and fast.

drugstore /dʀœgstɔʀ/ *nm* drugstore.

du /dy/ ⇒DE.

dû, **due** /dy/ *adj* due. ● *nm* due; (argent) dues; ~ **à** due to. ● ⇒DEVOIR [26].

duc, **duchesse** /dyk, dyʃɛs/ *nm,f* duke, duchess.

duo /dɥo/ *nm* (Mus) duet; (fig) duo.

dupe /dyp/ *nf* dupe.

duplex /dyplɛks/ *nm* split-level apartment; (US) duplex; (émission) link-up.

duplicata /dyplikata/ *nm inv* duplicate.

duquel /dykɛl/ ⇒LEQUEL.

dur, ~**e** /dyʀ/ *adj* hard; (sévère) harsh, hard; (*viande*) tough; (*col, brosse*) stiff; ~ **d'oreille** hard of hearing. ● *adv* hard. ● *nm, f* tough nut 🄸; (Pol) hardliner.

durable /dyʀabl/ *adj* lasting.

durant /dyʀɑ̃/ *prép* (au cours de) during; (avec mesure de temps) for; ~ **des heures** for hours; **des heures** ~ for hours and hours.

durcir /dyʀsiʀ/ [2] *vt* harden. ● *vi* (*terre*) harden; (*ciment*) set; (*pain*) go hard. □ **se** ~ *vpr* harden.

durée /dyʀe/ *nf* length; (période) duration; **de courte** ~ short-lived; **pile longue** ~ long-life battery.

durer /dyʀe/ [1] *vi* last.

dureté /dyʀte/ *nf* hardness; (sévérité) harshness.

duvet /dyvɛ/ *nm* down; (sac) sleeping-bag.

dynamique /dinamik/ *adj* dynamic.

dynamite /dinamit/ *nf* dynamite.

dynamo /dinamo/ *nf* dynamo.

Ee

---

eau (*pl* ~**x**) /o/ *nf* water; ~ **courante** running water; ~ **de mer** seawater; ~ **de source** spring water; ~ **douce/ salée** fresh/salt water; ~ **de pluie** rainwater; ~ **potable** drinking water; ~ **de Javel** bleach; ~ **minérale** mineral water; ~ **gazeuse** sparkling water; ~ **plate** still water; ~ **de toilette** eau de toilette; ~**x usées** dirty water; ~**x et forêts** forestry commission (+ *sg*); **tomber à l'**~ (fig) fall through; **prendre l'**~ take in water. **eau-de-vie** (*pl* **eaux-de-vie**) *nf* brandy.

ébahi, ~**e** /ebai/ *adj* dumbfounded.

ébauche /eboʃ/ *nf* (dessin) sketch; (fig) attempt.

ébéniste /ebenist/ *nm* cabinet-maker.

éblouir /ebluiʀ/ [2] *vt* dazzle.

éboueur /ebwœʀ/ *nm* dustman.

ébouillanter /ebujɑ̃te/ [1] *vt* scald.

éboulement /ebulmɑ̃/ *nm* landslide.

ébouriffé, ~**e** /eburife/ *adj* dishevelled.

ébrécher /ebʀeʃe/ [14] *vt* chip.

ébruiter /ebʀɥite/ [1] *vt* spread about. □ **s'**~ *vpr* get out.

ébullition /ebylisjɔ̃/ *nf* boiling; **en** ~ boiling.

écaille /ekaj/ *nf* (de poisson) scale; (de peinture, roc) flake; (matière) tortoiseshell.

écarlate /ekaʀlat/ *adj* scarlet.

écarquiller /ekaʀkije/ [1] *vt* ~ **les yeux** open one's eyes wide.

écart /ekaʀ/ *nm* gap; (de prix) difference; (embardée) swerve; ~ **de conduite** lapse in behaviour; **être à l'**~ be isolated; **se tenir à l'**~ **de** stand apart from; (fig) keep out of the way of.

écarté, ~**e** /ekaʀte/ *adj* (*lieu*) remote; **les jambes** ~**es** (with) legs apart; **les bras** ~**s** with one's arms out.

écarter /ekaʀte/ [1] *vt* (séparer) move apart; (*membres*) spread; (*branches*) part; (éliminer) dismiss; ~ **qch de** move sth away from; ~ **qn de** keep sb away from. □ **s'**~ *vpr* (s'éloigner) move away; (quitter son chemin) move aside; **s'**~ **de** stray from.

ecchymose /ekimoz/ *nf* bruise.

écervelé, ~**e** /esɛʀvəle/ *adj* scatterbrained. ● *nm, f* scatterbrain.

échafaudage /eʃafodaʒ/ *nm* scaffolding; (amas) heap.

échalote /eʃalɔt/ *nf* shallot.

échancré, ~**e** /eʃɑ̃kʀe/ *adj* low-cut.

échange /eʃɑ̃ʒ/ *nm* exchange; **en** ~ (**de**) in exchange (for). **échanger** [40] *vt* exchange (**contre** for).

échangeur /eʃɑ̃ʒœʀ/ *nm* (Auto) interchange.

échantillon /eʃɑ̃tijɔ̃/ *nm* sample.

échappatoire /eʃapatwaʀ/ *nf* way out.

échappement /eʃapmã/ *nm* exhaust.

échapper /eʃape/ [1] *vi* ~ à escape; (en fuyant) escape (from); ~ des mains de slip out of the hands of; **ça m'a échappé** (fig) it just slipped out; **l'~ belle** have a narrow *ou* lucky escape. □ **s'~** *vpr* escape.

écharde /eʃaʀd/ *nf* splinter.

écharpe /eʃaʀp/ *nf* scarf; (de maire) sash; **en ~** (*bras*) in a sling.

échasse /eʃas/ *nf* stilt.

échauffement /eʃofmã/ *nm* (Sport) warm-up.

échauffer /eʃofe/ [1] *vt* heat; (fig) excite. □ **s'~** *vpr* warm up.

échéance /eʃeãs/ *nf* due date (for payment); (délai) deadline; (obligation) (financial) commitment.

échéant: le cas ~ /ləkazeʃeã/ *loc* if need be.

échec /eʃɛk/ *nm* failure; ~**s** (jeu) chess; ~ **et mat** checkmate; **tenir en ~** hold in check.

échelle /eʃɛl/ *nf* ladder; (dimension) scale.

échelon /eʃlɔ̃/ *nm* rung; (hiérarchique) grade; (niveau) level.

échevelé, ~**e** /eʃəvle/ *adj* dishevelled.

écho /eko/ *nm* echo; ~**s** (dans la presse) gossip.

échographie /ekɔgʀafi/ *nf* (ultrasound) scan.

échouer /eʃwe/ [1] *vi* (bateau) run aground; (ne pas réussir) fail; ~ **à un examen** fail an exam. ● *vt* (bateau) ground. □ **s'~** *vpr* run aground.

échu, ~**e** /eʃy/ *adj* (délai) expired.

éclabousser /eklabuse/ [1] *vt* splash.

éclair /eklɛʀ/ *nm* (flash of) lightning; (fig) flash; (gâteau) éclair. ● *a inv* (visite) brief.

éclairage /eklɛʀaʒ/ *nm* lighting.

éclaircie /eklɛʀsi/ *nf* sunny interval.

éclaircir /eklɛʀsiʀ/ [2] *vt* lighten; (mystère) clear up. □ **s'~** *vpr* (ciel) clear; (mystère) become clearer. **éclaircissement** *nm* clarification.

éclairer /ekleʀe/ [1] *vt* light (up); (personne) (fig) enlighten; (situation) throw light on. ● *vi* give light. □ **s'~** *vpr* become clearer; **s'~ à la bougie** use candle-light.

éclaireur, -**euse** /eklɛʀœʀ, -øz/ *nm,f* (boy) scout, (girl) guide. ● *nm* (Mil) scout.

éclat /ekla/ *nm* fragment; (de lumière) brightness; (splendeur) brilliance; ~ **de rire** burst of laughter.

éclatant, ~**e** /eklatã, -t/ *adj* brilliant; (soleil) dazzling.

éclater /eklate/ [1] *vi* burst; (exploser) go off; (verre) shatter; (guerre) break out; (groupe) split up; ~ **de rire** burst out laughing.

éclipse /eklips/ *nf* eclipse.

éclosion /eklozjɔ̃/ *nf* hatching, opening.

écluse /eklyz/ *nf* (de canal) lock.

écœurant, ~**e** /ekœʀã, -t/ *adj* (gâteau) sickly; (fig) disgusting. **écœurer** [1] *vt* sicken.

école /ekɔl/ *nf* school; ~ **maternelle**/**primaire**/**secondaire** nursery/primary/secondary school; ~ **normale** teachers' training college. **écolier**, -**ière** *nm,f* schoolboy, schoolgirl.

écologie /ekɔlɔʒi/ *nf* ecology. **écologique** *adj* ecological, green. **écologiste** *nmf* (chercheur) ecologist; (dans l'âme) environmentalist; (Pol) Green.

économie /ekɔnɔmi/ *nf* economy; (discipline) economics; ~**s** (argent) savings; **une ~ de** (gain) a saving of. **économique** *adj* (Pol) economic; (bon marché) economical.

économiser /ekɔnɔmize/ [1] *vt/i* save.

écorce /ekɔʀs/ *nf* bark; (de fruit) peel.

écorcher /ekɔʀʃe/ [1] *vt* (genou) graze; (animal) skin. □ **s'~** *vpr* graze oneself. **écorchure** *nf* graze.

écossais, ~**e** /ekɔsɛ, -z/ *adj* Scottish. **É~**, ~**e** *nm,f* Scot.

Écosse /ekɔs/ *nf* Scotland.

écoulement /ekulmã/ *nm* flow.

écouler /ekule/ [1] *vt* dispose of, sell. □ **s'~** *vpr* (liquide) flow; (temps) pass.

écourter /ekuʀte/ [1] *vt* shorten.

écoute /ekut/ *nf* listening; **à l'~ (de)** listening in (to); **heures de grande ~** prime time; **~s téléphoniques** phone tapping.

écouter /ekute/ [1] *vt* listen to. ● *vi* listen; **~ aux portes** eavesdrop. **écouteur** *nm* earphones (+ *pl*); (de téléphone) receiver.

écran /ekrɑ̃/ *nm* screen; **~ total** sun-block.

écraser /ekrɑze/ [1] *vt* crush; (*piéton*) run over; (*cigarette*) stub out. □ **s'~** *vpr* crash (**contre** into).

écrémé, **~e** /ekreme/ *adj* skimmed; **demi-~** semi-skimmed.

écrevisse /ekrəvis/ *nf* crayfish.

écrier (s') /(s)ekrije/ [45] *vpr* exclaim.

écrin /ekrɛ̃/ *nm* case.

écrire /ekrir/ [30] *vt/i* write; (orthographier) spell. □ **s'~** *vpr* (*mot*) be spelt.

écrit /ekri/ *nm* document; (examen) written paper; **par ~** in writing.

écriteau (*pl* **~x**) /ekrito/ *nm* notice.

écriture /ekrityr/ *nf* writing; **~s** (Comm) accounts.

écrivain /ekrivɛ̃/ *nm* writer.

écrou /ekru/ *nm* (Tech) nut.

écrouler (s') /(s)ekrule/ [1] *vpr* collapse.

écru, **~e** /ekry/ *adj* (*couleur*) natural; (*tissu*) raw.

écueil /ekœj/ *nm* reef; (fig) danger.

éculé, **~e** /ekyle/ *adj* (*soulier*) worn at the heel; (fig) well-worn.

écume /ekym/ *nf* foam; (Culin) scum.

écumer /ekyme/ [1] *vt* skim. ● *vi* foam.

écureuil /ekyrœj/ *nm* squirrel.

écurie /ekyri/ *nf* stable.

écuyer, -ère /ekɥije, -jɛr/ *nm,f* (horse) rider.

eczéma /ɛgzema/ *nm* eczema.

EDF *abrév f* (**Électricité de France**) *French electricity board.*

édifice /edifis/ *nm* building.

édifier /edifje/ [45] *vt* construct; (porter à la vertu) edify.

Édimbourg /edɛ̃bur/ *npr* Edinburgh.

édit /edi/ *nm* edict.

éditer /edite/ [1] *vt* publish; (annoter) edit. **éditeur, -trice** *nm,f* publisher; (réviseur) editor.

édition /edisjɔ̃/ *nf* (activité) publishing; (livre, disque) edition.

éditique /editik/ *nf* electronic publishing.

éditorial, **~e** (*pl* **-iaux**) /editɔrjal, -jo/ *a & nm* editorial.

édredon /edrədɔ̃/ *nm* eiderdown.

éducateur, -trice /edykatœr, -tris/ *nm,f* youth worker.

éducatif, -ive /edykatif, -v/ *adj* educational.

éducation /edykasjɔ̃/ *nf* (façon d'élever) upbringing; (enseignement) education; (manières) manners; **~ physique** physical education.

éduquer /edyke/ [1] *vt* (élever) bring up; (former) educate.

effacé, **~e** /efase/ *adj* (modeste) unassuming.

effacer /efase/ [10] *vt* (gommer) rub out; (à l'écran) delete; (*souvenir*) erase. □ **s'~** *vpr* fade; (s'écarter) step aside.

effarer /efare/ [1] *vt* alarm; **être effaré** be astounded.

effaroucher /efaruʃe/ [1] *vt* scare away.

effectif, -ive /efɛktif, -v/ *adj* effective. ● *nm* (d'école) number of pupils; **~s** numbers. **effectivement** *adv* effectively; (en effet) indeed.

effectuer /efɛktɥe/ [1] *vt* carry out, make.

efféminé, **~e** /efemine/ *adj* effeminate.

effervescent, **~e** /efɛrvesɑ̃, -t/ *adj* **comprimé ~** effervescent tablet.

effet /efɛ/ *nm* effect; (impression) impression; **~s** (habits) clothes, things; **sous l'~ d'une drogue** under the influence of drugs; **en ~** indeed; **faire de l'~** have an effect, be effective; **faire bon/mauvais ~** make a good/bad impression; **ça fait un drôle d'~** it feels strange.

efficace /efikas/ *adj* effective; (*personne*) efficient. **efficacité** *nf* effectiveness; (de personne) efficiency.

effleurer /eflœre/ [1] *vt* touch lightly; (*sujet*) touch on; **ça ne m'a**

pas effleuré it did not cross my mind.

effondrement /efɔ̃drəmɑ̃/ nm collapse. **effondrer (s')** [1] vpr collapse.

efforcer (s') /(s)efɔrse/ [10] vpr try (hard) (**de** to).

effort /efɔr/ nm effort.

effraction /efraksjɔ̃/ nf **entrer par** ∼ break in.

effrayant, ∼e /efrejɑ̃, -t/ adj frightening; (fig) frightful.

effrayer /efreje/ [31] vt frighten; (décourager) put off. □ **s'**∼ vpr be frightened.

effréné, ∼e /efrene/ adj wild.

effriter (s') /(s)efrite/ [1] vpr crumble.

effroi /efrwa/ nm dread.

effronté, ∼e /efrɔ̃te/ adj cheeky. ● nm,f cheeky boy, cheeky girl.

effroyable /efrwajabl/ adj dreadful.

égal, ∼e (mpl **-aux**) /egal, -o/ adj equal; (surface, vitesse) even. ● nm,f equal; **ça m'est/lui est** ∼ it is all the same to me/him; **sans** ∼ matchless; **d'**∼ **à** ∼ between equals. **également** adv equally; (aussi) as well. **égaler** [1] vt equal.

égaliser /egalize/ [1] vt/i (Sport) equalize; (niveler) level out; (cheveux) trim.

égalitaire /egaliter/ adj egalitarian.

égalité /egalite/ nf equality; (de surface) evenness; **être à** ∼ be level.

égard /egar/ nm consideration; ∼s respect (+ sg); **par** ∼ **pour** out of consideration for; **à cet** ∼ in this respect; **à l'**∼ **de** with regard to; (envers) towards.

égarer /egare/ [1] vt mislay; (tromper) lead astray. □ **s'**∼ vpr get lost; (se tromper) go astray.

égayer /egeje/ [31] vt (personne) cheer up; (pièce) brighten up.

église /egliz/ nf church.

égoïsme /egɔism/ nm selfishness, egoism.

égoïste /egɔist/ adj selfish. ● nmf egoist.

égorger /egɔrʒe/ [40] vt slit the throat of.

égout /egu/ nm sewer.

égoutter /egute/ [1] vt drain. □ **s'**∼ vpr (vaisselle) drain; (lessive) drip dry. **égouttoir** nm draining-board.

égratigner /egratiɲe/ [1] vt scratch. **égratignure** nf scratch.

Égypte /eʒipt/ nf Egypt.

éjecter /eʒɛkte/ [1] vt eject.

élaboration /elabɔrasjɔ̃/ nf elaboration. **élaborer** [1] vt elaborate.

élan /elɑ̃/ nm (animal) moose; (Sport) run-up; (vitesse) momentum; (fig) surge.

élancé, ∼e /elɑ̃se/ adj slender.

élancement /elɑ̃smɑ̃/ nm twinge.

élancer (s') /(s)elɑ̃se/ [10] vpr leap forward, dash; (arbre, édifice) soar.

élargir /elarʒir/ [2] vt (route) widen; (connaissances) broaden. □ **s'**∼ vpr (famille) expand; (route) widen; (écart) increase; (vêtement) stretch.

élastique /elastik/ adj elastic. ● nm elastic band; (tissu) elastic.

électeur, -trice /elɛktœr, -tris/ nm,f voter. **élection** nf election. **électoral, ∼e** (mpl **-aux**) adj (réunion) election. **électorat** nm electorate, voters (+ pl).

électricien, ∼ne /elɛktrisjɛ̃, ɛn/ nm,f electrician. **électricité** nf electricity.

électrifier /elɛktrifje/ [45] vt electrify.

électrique /elɛktrik/ adj electric; (installation) electrical.

électrocuter /elɛktrɔkyte/ [1] vt electrocute.

électroménager /elɛktrɔmenaʒe/ nm l'∼ household appliances (+ pl).

électron /elɛktrɔ̃/ nm electron. **électronicien, ∼ne** nm,f electronics engineer.

électronique /elɛktrɔnik/ adj electronic. ● nf electronics.

élégance /elegɑ̃s/ nf elegance. **élégant, ∼e** adj elegant.

élément /elemɑ̃/ nm element; (meuble) unit. **élémentaire** adj elementary.

éléphant /elefɑ̃/ nm elephant.

élevage /ɛlvaʒ/ *nm* (stock-)
breeding.

élévation /elevasjɔ̃/ *nf* rise; (hausse)
rise; (plan) elevation; ~ **de terrain**
rise in the ground.

élève /elɛv/ *nmf* pupil.

élevé, **~e** /ɛlve/ *adj* high; (noble)
elevated; **bien** ~ well-mannered.

élever /ɛlve/ [6] *vt* (lever) raise;
(*enfants*) bring up, raise; (*animal*)
breed. □ **s'~** *vpr* rise; (dans le ciel)
soar up; **s'~ à** amount to. **éleveur**,
-euse *nm,f* (stock-)breeder.

éligible /eliʒibl/ *adj* eligible.

élimination /eliminasjɔ̃/ *nf*
elimination.

éliminatoire /eliminatwaʀ/ *adj*
qualifying. ● *nf* (Sport) heat.

éliminer /elimine/ [1] *vt* eliminate.

élire /eliʀ/ [39] *vt* elect.

elle /ɛl/ *pron* she; (complément) her;
(chose) it. **elle-même** *pron* herself;
itself. **elles** *pron* they; (complément)
them. **elles-mêmes** *pron*
themselves.

élocution /elɔkysjɔ̃/ *nf* diction.

éloge /elɔʒ/ *nm* praise; **faire l'~ de**
praise; **~s** praise (+ *sg*).

éloigné, **~e** /elwaɲe/ *adj* distant; ~
de far away from; **parent** ~ distant
relative.

éloigner /elwaɲe/ [1] *vt* take away
ou remove (**de** from); (*danger*) ward
off; (*visite*) put off. □ **s'~** *vpr* go *ou*
move away (**de** from); (affectivement)
become estranged (**de** from).

élongation /elɔ̃gasjɔ̃/ *nf* strained
muscle.

éloquent, **~e** /elɔkɑ̃, -t/ *adj*
eloquent.

élu, **~e** /ely/ *adj* elected. ● *nm,f* (Pol)
elected representative.

élucider /elyside/ [1] *vt* elucidate.

éluder /elyde/ [1] *vt* evade.

émacié, **~e** /emasje/ *adj*
emaciated.

émail (*pl* **-aux**) /emaj, -o/ *nm*
enamel.

émanciper /emɑ̃sipe/ [1] *vt*
emancipate. □ **s'~** *vpr* become
emancipated.

émaner /emane/ [1] *vi* emanate.

emballage /ɑ̃balaʒ/ *nm* (dur)
packaging; (souple) wrapping.

emballer /ɑ̃bale/ [1] *vt* pack; (en
papier) wrap; **ça ne m'emballe pas** 🄸
I'm not really taken by it. □ **s'~** *vpr*
(*moteur*) race; (*cheval*) bolt;
(*personne*) get carried away; (*prices*)
shoot up.

embarcadère /ɑ̃baʀkadɛʀ/ *nm*
landing-stage.

embarcation /ɑ̃baʀkasjɔ̃/ *nf* boat.

embardée /ɑ̃baʀde/ *nf* swerve.

embarquement /ɑ̃baʀkəmɑ̃/ *nm*
(de passagers) boarding; (de fret)
loading.

embarquer /ɑ̃baʀke/ [1] *vt* take on
board; (*frêt*) load; (emporter 🄸) cart
off. ● *vi* board. □ **s'~** *vpr* board; **s'~
dans** embark upon.

embarras /ɑ̃baʀa/ *nm* (gêne)
embarrassment; (difficulté) difficulty.

embarrasser /ɑ̃baʀase/ [1] *vt*
(encombrer) clutter (up); (fig)
embarrass. □ **s'~ de** *vpr* burden
oneself with.

embauche /ɑ̃boʃ/ *nf* hiring.
embaucher [1] *vt* hire, take on.

embaumer /ɑ̃bome/ [1] *vt* (*pièce*)
fill; (*cadavre*) embalm. ● *vi* be
fragrant.

embellir /ɑ̃beliʀ/ [2] *vt* make more
attractive; (*récit*) embellish.

embêtant, **~e** /ɑ̃bətɑ̃, -t/ *adj* 🄸
annoying.

embêter /ɑ̃bete/ [1] *vt* bother.
□ **s'~** *vpr* be bored.

emblée: **d'~** /dɑ̃ble/ *loc* right away.

emblème /ɑ̃blɛm/ *nm* emblem.

emboîter /ɑ̃bwate/ [1] *vt* fit
together; ~ **le pas à qn** (imiter) follow
suit. □ **s'~** *vpr* fit together; (**s'**)~
dans fit into.

embonpoint /ɑ̃bɔ̃pwɛ̃/ *nm*
stoutness.

embouchure /ɑ̃buʃyʀ/ *nf* (de fleuve)
mouth; (Mus) mouthpiece.

embourber (**s'**) /(s)ɑ̃buʀbe/ [1] *vpr*
get stuck in the mud; (fig) get bogged
down.

embouteillage /ɑ̃butɛjaʒ/ *nm*
traffic jam.

emboutir /ɑ̃butiʀ/ [2] *vt* (Auto) crash
into.

embraser (s') /(s)ɑ̃bRɑze/ [1] *vpr* catch fire.

embrasser /ɑ̃bRɑse/ [1] *vt* kiss; (adopter, contenir) embrace. □ **s'**~ *vpr* kiss.

embrayage /ɑ̃bRɛjaʒ/ *nm* clutch. **embrayer** [31] *vi* engage the clutch.

embrouiller /ɑ̃bRuje/ [1] *vt* confuse; (*fils*) tangle. □ **s'**~ *vpr* become confused.

embryon /ɑ̃bRijɔ̃/ *nm* embryo.

embûches /ɑ̃byʃ/ *nfpl* traps.

embuer (s') /(s)ɑ̃bɥe/ [1] *vpr* mist up.

embuscade /ɑ̃byskad/ *nf* ambush.

émeraude /ɛmRod/ *nf* emerald.

émerger /emɛRʒe/ [40] *vi* emerge; (fig) stand out.

émeri /ɛmRi/ *nm* emery.

émerveillement /emɛRvɛjmɑ̃/ *nm* amazement, wonder.

émerveiller /emɛRveje/ [1] *vt* fill with wonder. □ **s'**~ *vpr* marvel at.

émetteur /emɛtœR/ *nm* transmitter.

émettre /emɛtR/ [42] *vt* (*son*) produce; (*message*) send out; (*timbre, billet*) issue; (*opinion*) express.

émeute /emøt/ *nf* riot.

émietter /emjete/ [1] *vt* crumble. □ **s'**~ *vpr* crumble.

émigrant, ~**e** /emigRɑ̃, -t/ *nm,f* emigrant. **émigration** *nf* emigration. **émigrer** [1] *vi* emigrate.

émincer /emɛ̃se/ [10] *vt* cut into thin slices.

éminent, ~**e**/eminɑ̃, -t/ *adj* eminent.

émissaire /emisɛR/ *nm* emissary.

émission /emisjɔ̃/ *nf* (programme) programme; (de chaleur, gaz) emission; (de timbre) issue.

emmagasiner /ɑ̃magazine/ [1] *vt* store.

emmanchure /ɑ̃mɑ̃ʃyR/ *nf* armhole.

emmêler /ɑ̃mele/ [1] *vt* tangle. □ **s'**~ *vpr* get mixed up.

emménager /ɑ̃menaʒe/ [40] *vi* move in; ~ **dans** move into.

emmener /ɑ̃mne/ [6] *vt* take; (comme prisonnier) take away.

emmerder /ɑ̃mɛRde/ [1] ▣ *vt* ~ **qn** get on sb's nerves. □ **s'**~ *vpr* be bored.

emmitoufler /ɑ̃mitufle/ [1] *vt* wrap up warmly. □ **s'**~ *vpr* wrap oneself up warmly.

émoi /emwa/ *nm* turmoil; (plaisir) excitement.

émotif, -ive /emɔtif, -v/ *adj* emotional. **émotion** *nf* emotion; (peur) fright. **émotionnel**, ~**le** *adj* emotional.

émousser /emuse/ [1] *vt* blunt.

émouvant, ~**e** /emuvɑ̃, -t/ *adj* moving.

empailler /ɑ̃paje/ [1] *vt* stuff.

empaqueter /ɑ̃pakte/ [38] *vt* package.

emparer (s') /(s)ɑ̃paRe/ [1] *vpr* **s'**~ **de** get hold of.

empêchement /ɑ̃pɛʃmɑ̃/ *nm* **avoir un** ~ to be held up.

empêcher /ɑ̃peʃe/ [1] *vt* prevent; ~ **de faire** prevent *ou* stop (from) doing; (il) **n'empêche que** still. □ **s'**~ *vpr* **il ne peut pas s'en** ~ he cannot help it.

empereur /ɑ̃pRœR/ *nm* emperor.

empester /ɑ̃pɛste/ [1] *vt* stink out; (*essence*) stink of. ● *vi* stink.

empêtrer (s') /(s)ɑ̃petRe/ [1] *vpr* become entangled.

empiéter /ɑ̃pjete/ [14] *vi* ~ **sur** encroach upon.

empiffrer (s') /(s)ɑ̃pifRe/ [1] *vpr* ▣ stuff oneself.

empiler /ɑ̃pile/ [1] *vt* pile up. □ **s'**~ *vpr* pile up.

empire /ɑ̃piR/ *nm* empire.

emplacement /ɑ̃plasmɑ̃/ *nm* site.

emplâtre /ɑ̃plɑtR/ *nm* (Méd) plaster.

emploi /ɑ̃plwa/ *nm* (travail) job; (embauche) employment; (utilisation) use; **un** ~ **de chauffeur** a job as a driver; ~ **du temps** timetable. **employé**, ~**e** *nm,f* employee.

employer /ɑ̃plwaje/ [31] *vt* (*personne*) employ; (utiliser) use. □ **s'**~ *vpr* be used; **s'**~ **à** devote oneself to. **employeur, -euse** *nm,f* employer.

empoigner /ɑ̃pwaɲe/ [1] *vt* grab. □ **s'**~ *vpr* come to blows.

empoisonnement /ɑ̃pwazɔnmɑ̃/ *nm* poisoning.

empoisonner /ɑ̃pwazɔne/ [1] *vt* poison; (embêter 🔟) annoy. □ **s'∼** *vpr* to poison oneself.

emporter /ɑ̃pɔʀte/ [1] *vt* take (away); (entraîner) sweep away; (arracher) tear off. □ **s'∼** *vpr* lose one's temper; **l'∼** get the upper hand (sur *de*); **plat à ∼** take-away.

empoté, **∼e** /ɑ̃pɔte/ *adj* clumsy.

empreinte /ɑ̃pʀɛ̃t/ *nf* mark; **∼ (digitale)** fingerprint; **∼ de pas** footprint.

empressé, **∼e** /ɑ̃pʀese/ *adj* eager, attentive.

empresser (s') /(s)ɑ̃pʀese/ [1] *vpr* **s'∼ de** hasten to; **s'∼ auprès de** be attentive to.

emprise /ɑ̃pʀiz/ *nf* influence.

emprisonnement /ɑ̃pʀizɔnmɑ̃/ *nm* imprisonment. **emprisonner** [1] *vt* imprison.

emprunt /ɑ̃pʀœ̃/ *nm* loan; **faire un ∼** take out a loan.

emprunté, **∼e** /ɑ̃pʀœ̃te/ *adj* awkward.

emprunter /ɑ̃pʀœ̃te/ [1] *vt* borrow (à from); (*route*) take; (fig) assume. **emprunteur**, **-euse** *nm,f* borrower.

ému, **∼e** /emy/ *adj* moved; (intimidé) nervous.

émule /emyl/ *nmf* imitator.

∙∙∙∙∙∙∙∙∙∙∙∙∙∙∙∙∙∙∙∙∙∙∙∙∙∙∙∙∙∙∙∙∙∙∙∙∙∙

en /ɑ̃/

➡ Pour les expressions comme **en principe**, **en train de**, **s'en aller**, etc. ⇒**principe**, **train**, **aller**, etc.

● *préposition*

∙∙∙➤ (lieu) in.

∙∙∙➤ (avec mouvement) to.

∙∙∙➤ (temps) in.

∙∙∙➤ (manière, état) in; **∼ faisant** by *ou* while doing; **je t'appelle ∼ rentrant** I will call you when I get back.

∙∙∙➤ (en qualité de) as.

∙∙∙➤ (transport) by.

∙∙∙➤ (composition) made of; **table ∼ bois** wooden table.

● *pronom*

∙∙∙➤ **∼ avoir/vouloir** have/want some; **ne pas ∼ avoir/vouloir** not have/want any; **j'∼ ai deux** I've got two; **prends-∼ plusieurs** take several; **il m'∼ reste un** I have one left; **j'∼ suis content** I am pleased with him/her/it/them; **je m'∼ souviens** I remember it.

∙∙∙➤ **∼ êtes-vous sûr?** are you sure?

∙∙∙∙∙∙∙∙∙∙∙∙∙∙∙∙∙∙∙∙∙∙∙∙∙∙∙∙∙∙∙∙∙∙∙∙∙∙

encadrement /ɑ̃kadʀəmɑ̃/ *nm* framing; (de porte) frame. **encadrer** [1] *vt* frame; (entourer d'un trait) circle; (superviser) supervise.

encaisser /ɑ̃kese/ [1] *vt* (*argent*) collect; (*chèque*) cash; (*coups* 🔟) take.

encart /ɑ̃kaʀ/ *nm* **∼ publicitaire** (advertising) insert.

en-cas /ɑ̃kɑ/ *nm* (stand-by) snack.

encastré, **∼e** /ɑ̃kastʀe/ *adj* built-in.

encaustique /ɑ̃kɔstik/ *nf* wax polish.

enceinte /ɑ̃sɛ̃t/ *af* pregnant; **∼ de 3 mois** 3 months pregnant. ● *nf* enclosure; **∼ (acoustique)** speaker.

encens /ɑ̃sɑ̃/ *nm* incense.

encercler /ɑ̃sɛʀkle/ [1] *vt* surround.

enchaînement /ɑ̃ʃɛnmɑ̃/ *nm* (suite) chain; (d'idées) sequence.

enchaîner /ɑ̃ʃene/ [1] *vt* chain (up); (*phrases*) link (up). ● *vi* continue. □ **s'∼** *vpr* follow on.

enchanté, **∼e** /ɑ̃ʃɑ̃te/ *adj* (ravi) delighted. **enchanter** [1] *vt* delight; (ensorceler) enchant.

enchère /ɑ̃ʃɛʀ/ *nf* bid; **mettre** *ou* **vendre aux ∼s** sell by auction.

enchevêtrer /ɑ̃ʃəvetʀe/ [1] *vt* tangle. □ **s'∼** *vpr* become tangled.

enclave /ɑ̃klav/ *nf* enclave.

enclencher /ɑ̃klɑ̃ʃe/ [1] *vt* engage.

enclin, **∼e** /ɑ̃klɛ̃, -in/ *adj* **∼ à** inclined to.

enclos /ɑ̃klo/ *nm* enclosure.

enclume /ɑ̃klym/ *nf* anvil.

encoche /ɑ̃kɔʃ/ *nf* notch.

encolure /ɑ̃kɔlyʀ/ *nf* neck.

encombrant, **∼e** /ɑ̃kɔ̃bʀɑ̃, -t/ *adj* cumbersome.

encombre /ɑ̃kɔ̃bʀ/ *nm* **sans ∼** without any problems.

encombrement /ãkɔ̃brəmã/ *nm* (Auto) traffic congestion; (volume) bulk.

encombrer /ãkɔ̃bre/ [1] *vt* clutter (up); (obstruer) obstruct. □ **s'~ de** *vpr* burden oneself with.

encontre: à l'~ de /alãkɔ̃trədə/ *loc* against.

encore /ãkɔr/ *adv* (toujours) still; (de nouveau) again; (de plus) more; (aussi) also; ~ **plus grand** even larger; ~ **un café** another coffee; **pas** ~ not yet; **si** ~ if only; **et puis quoi** ~? ☐ what next?

encouragement /ãkuraʒmã/ *nm* encouragement. **encourager** [40] *vt* encourage.

encourir /ãkurir/ [20] *vt* incur.

encrasser /ãkrase/ [1] *vt* clog up (with dirt).

encre /ãkr/ *nf* ink. **encrier** *nm* ink-well.

encyclopédie /ãsiklɔpedi/ *nf* encyclopaedia.

endettement /ãdɛtmã/ *nm* debt.

endetter /ãdete/ [1] *vt* put into debt. ☐ **s'~** *vpr* get into debt.

endiguer /ãdige/ [1] *vt* dam; (fig) curb.

endimanché, ~**e** /ãdimãʃe/ *adj* in one's Sunday best.

endive /ãdiv/ *nf* chicory.

endoctriner /ãdɔktrine/ [1] *vt* indoctrinate.

endommager /ãdɔmaʒe/ [40] *vt* damage.

endormi, ~**e** /ãdɔrmi/ *adj* asleep; (apathique) sleepy.

endormir /ãdɔrmir/ [46] *vt* send to sleep; (médicalement) put to sleep; (duper) dupe (**avec** with). ☐ **s'~** *vpr* fall asleep.

endosser /ãdɔse/ [1] *vt* (vêtement) put on; (assumer) take on; (Comm) endorse.

endroit /ãdrwa/ *nm* place; (de tissu) right side; **à l'~** the right way round; **par** ~**s** in places.

enduire /ãdɥir/ [17] *vt* coat. **enduit** *nm* coating.

endurance /ãdyrãs/ *nf* endurance. **endurant**, ~**e** *adj* tough.

endurcir /ãdyrsir/ [2] *vt* strengthen. ☐ **s'~** *vpr* become hard (ened).

endurer /ãdyre/ [1] *vt* endure.

énergétique /enɛrʒetik/ *adj* energy; (food) high-calorie. **énergie** *nf* energy; (Tech) power. **énergique** *adj* energetic.

énervant, ~**e** /enɛrvã, -t/ *adj* irritating, annoying.

énerver /enɛrve/ [1] *vt* irritate. ☐ **s'~** *vpr* get worked up.

enfance /ãfãs/ *nf* childhood; **la petite** ~ infancy.

enfant /ãfã/ *nmf* child. **enfantillage** *nm* childishness. **enfantin**, ~**e** *adj* simple, easy; (puéril) childish; (jeu, langage) children's.

enfer /ãfɛr/ *nm* (Relig) Hell; (fig) hell.

enfermer /ãfɛrme/ [1] *vt* shut up. ☐ **s'~** *vpr* shut oneself up.

enfiler /ãfile/ [1] *vt* (aiguille) thread; (vêtement) slip on; (rue) take.

enfin /ãfɛ̃/ *adv* (de soulagement) at last; (en dernier lieu) finally; (résignation, conclusion) well; ~ **presque** well nearly.

enflammé, ~**e** /ãflame/ *adj* (Méd) inflamed; (discours) fiery; (lettre) passionate.

enflammer /ãflame/ [1] *vt* set fire to. ☐ **s'~** *vpr* catch fire.

enfler /ãfle/ [1] *vt* (histoire) exaggerate. ● *vi* (partie du corps) swell (up); (mer) swell; (rumeur, colère) spread. ☐ **s'~** *vpr* (colère) mount; (rumeur) grow.

enfoncer /ãfɔ̃se/ [10] *vt* (épingle) push *ou* drive in; (chapeau) push down; (porte) break down. ● *vi* sink. ☐ **s'~** *vpr* sink (**dans** into).

enfouir /ãfwir/ [2] *vt* bury.

enfourcher /ãfurʃe/ [1] *vt* mount.

enfreindre /ãfrɛ̃dr/ [22] *vt* infringe, break.

enfuir (s') /(s)ãfɥir/ [35] *vpr* run away.

enfumé, ~**e** /ãfyme/ *adj* filled with smoke.

engagé, ~**e** /ãgaʒe/ *adj* committed.

engagement /ɑ̃gaʒmɑ̃/ *nm* (promesse) promise; (Pol, Comm) commitment.

engager /ɑ̃gaʒe/ [40] *vt* (lier) bind, commit; (embaucher) take on; (commencer) start; (introduire) insert; (investir) invest. □ s'~ *vpr* (promettre) commit oneself; (commencer) start; (soldat) enlist; (concurrent) enter; s'~ à faire undertake to do; s'~ dans (voie) enter.

engelure /ɑ̃ʒlyʀ/ *nf* chilblain.

engendrer /ɑ̃ʒɑ̃dʀe/ [1] *vt* (causer) generate.

engin /ɑ̃ʒɛ̃/ *nm* device; (véhicule) vehicle; (missile) missile.

engloutir /ɑ̃glutiʀ/ [2] *vt* swallow (up).

engouement /ɑ̃gumɑ̃/ *nm* passion.

engouffrer /ɑ̃gufʀe/ [1] *vt* 🖪 gobble up. □ s'~ dans *vpr* rush in.

engourdir /ɑ̃guʀdiʀ/ [2] *vt* numb. □ s'~ *vpr* go numb.

engrais /ɑ̃gʀɛ/ *nm* manure; (chimique) fertilizer.

engrenage /ɑ̃gʀənaʒ/ *nm* gears (+ *pl*); (fig) spiral.

engueuler /ɑ̃gœle/ [1] 🖾 *vt* shout at. □ s'~ *vpr* have a row.

enhardir (s') /(s)ɑ̃aʀdiʀ/ [2] *vpr* become bolder.

énième /ɛnjɛm/ *adj* umpteenth.

énigmatique /enigmatik/ *adj* enigmatic. **énigme** *nf* enigma; (devinette) riddle.

enivrer /ɑ̃nivʀe/ [1] *vt* intoxicate. □ s'~ *vpr* get intoxicated.

enjambée /ɑ̃ʒɑ̃be/ *nf* stride. **enjamber** [1] *vt* step over; (pont) span.

enjeu (*pl* ~x) /ɑ̃ʒø/ *nm* stake.

enjoué, ~e /ɑ̃ʒwe/ *adj* cheerful.

enlacer /ɑ̃lase/ [10] *vt* entwine.

enlèvement /ɑ̃lɛvmɑ̃/ *nm* (de colis) removal; (d'ordures) collection; (rapt) kidnapping.

enlever /ɑ̃lve/ [6] *vt* remove (à from); (vêtement) take off; (tache, organe) take out, remove; (kidnapper) kidnap; (gagner) win.

enliser (s') /(s)ɑ̃lize/ [1] *vpr* get bogged down.

enneigé, ~e /ɑ̃neʒe/ *adj* snow-covered.

ennemi, ~e /ɛnmi/ *a & nm* enemy; ~ de (fig) hostile to.

ennui /ɑ̃nɥi/ *nm* problem; (tracas) boredom; **s'attirer des ~s** run into trouble.

ennuyer /ɑ̃nɥije/ [31] *vt* bore; (irriter) annoy; (préoccuper) worry; **si cela ne t'ennuie pas** if you don't mind. □ s'~ *vpr* get bored.

ennuyeux, **-euse** /ɑ̃nɥijø, -z/ *adj* boring; (fâcheux) annoying.

énoncé /enɔ̃se/ *nm* wording, text; (Gram) utterance.

énoncer /enɔ̃se/ [10] *vt* express, state.

enorgueillir (s') /(s)ɑ̃nɔʀgœjiʀ/ [2] *vpr* **s'~ de** pride oneself on.

énorme /enɔʀm/ *adj* enormous.

enquête /ɑ̃kɛt/ *nf* (Jur) investigation, inquiry; (sondage) survey; **mener l'~** lead the inquiry. **enquêter** [1] *vi* ~ (sur) investigate. **enquêteur**, **-euse** *nm,f* investigator.

enquiquinant, ~e /ɑ̃kikinɑ̃, -t/ *adj* 🖪 irritating.

enraciné, ~e /ɑ̃ʀasine/ *adj* deep-rooted.

enragé, ~e /ɑ̃ʀaʒe/ *adj* furious; (chien) rabid; (fig) fanatical.

enrager /ɑ̃ʀaʒe/ [40] *vi* be furious; **faire ~ qn** annoy sb.

enregistrement /ɑ̃ʀ(ə)ʒistʀəmɑ̃/ *nm* recording; (des bagages) check-in. **enregistrer** [1] *vt* (Mus, TV) record; (mémoriser) take in; (bagages) check in.

enrhumer (s') /(s)ɑ̃ʀyme/ [1] *vpr* catch a cold.

enrichir /ɑ̃ʀiʃiʀ/ [2] *vt* enrich. □ s'~ *vpr* grow rich(er). **enrichissant**, ~e *adj* (expérience) rewarding.

enrober /ɑ̃ʀɔbe/ [1] *vt* coat (de with).

enrôler /ɑ̃ʀole/ [1] *vt* recruit. □ s'~ *vpr* enlist, enrol.

enroué, ~e /ɑ̃ʀwe/ *adj* hoarse.

enrouler /ɑ̃ʀule/ [1] *vt* wind, wrap. □ s'~ *vpr* wind; **s'~ dans une couverture** roll oneself up in a blanket.

ensanglanté, ~e /ɑ̃sɑ̃glɑ̃te/ *adj* bloodstained.

enseignant, ~e /ɑ̃sɛɲɑ̃, -t/ *nm, f* teacher. ● *adj* teaching.

enseigne /ɑ̃sɛɲ/ *nf* sign.

enseignement /ɑ̃sɛɲəmɑ̃/ *nm* (profession) teaching; (instruction) education.

enseigner /ɑ̃seɲe/ [1] *vt/i* teach; ~ qch à qn teach sb sth.

ensemble /ɑ̃sɑ̃bl/ *adv* together. ● *nm* group; (Mus) ensemble; (vêtements) outfit; (cohésion) unity; (maths) set; **dans l'~** on the whole; **d'~** (idée) general; **l'~ de** (totalité) all of, the whole of.

ensevelir /ɑ̃səvliʀ/ [2] *vt* bury.

ensoleillé, ~e /ɑ̃sɔleje/ *adj* sunny.

ensorceler /ɑ̃sɔʀsəle/ [38] *vt* bewitch.

ensuite /ɑ̃sɥit/ *adv* next, then; (plus tard) later.

ensuivre (s') /(s)ɑ̃sɥivʀ/ [57] *vpr* follow; **et tout ce qui s'ensuit** and all the rest of it.

entaille /ɑ̃tɑj/ *nf* cut; (profonde) gash; (encoche) notch.

entamer /ɑ̃tame/ [1] *vt* start; (inciser) cut into; (ébranler) shake.

entasser /ɑ̃tase/ [1] *vt* (livres) pile; (argent) hoard; (personnes) cram (**dans** into). □ **s'~** *vpr* (objets) pile up (**dans** into); (personnes) squeeze (**dans** into).

entendement /ɑ̃tɑ̃dmɑ̃/ *nm* understanding; **ça dépasse l'~** it's beyond belief.

entendre /ɑ̃tɑ̃dʀ/ [3] *vt* hear; (comprendre) understand; (vouloir dire) mean; ~ **parler de** hear of; ~ **dire que** hear that. □ **s'~** *vpr* (être d'accord) agree; **s'~ (bien)** get on (**avec** with); **cela s'entend** of course.

entendu, ~e /ɑ̃tɑ̃dy/ *adj* (convenu) agreed; (sourire, air) knowing; **bien ~** of course; **(c'est) ~!** all right!

entente /ɑ̃tɑ̃t/ *nf* understanding; **bonne ~** good relationship.

enterrement /ɑ̃tɛʀmɑ̃/ *nm* funeral.

enterrer /ɑ̃teʀe/ [1] *vt* bury.

en-tête /ɑ̃tɛt/ *nm* heading; **à ~** headed.

entêté, ~e /ɑ̃tete/ *adj* stubborn.

entêtement *nm* stubbornness.

entêter (s') [1] *vpr* persist (**à**, **dans** in).

enthousiasme /ɑ̃tuzjasm/ *nm* enthusiasm. **enthousiasmer** [1] *vt* fill with enthusiasm. **enthousiaste** *adj* enthusiastic.

enticher (s') /(s)ɑ̃tiʃe/ [1] *vpr* **s'~ de** become infatuated with.

entier, **-ière** /ɑ̃tje, -jɛʀ/ *adj* whole; (absolu) absolute; (entêté) unyielding. ● *nm* whole; **en ~** entirely.

entonnoir /ɑ̃tɔnwaʀ/ *nm* funnel; (trou) crater.

entorse /ɑ̃tɔʀs/ *nf* sprain; (fig) ~ **à** (loi) infringement of.

entortiller /ɑ̃tɔʀtije/ [1] *vt* wind, wrap (**autour** around); (duper 🄘) get round.

entourage /ɑ̃tuʀaʒ/ *nm* circle of family and friends; (bordure) surround.

entouré, ~e /ɑ̃tuʀe/ *adj* (personne) supported.

entourer /ɑ̃tuʀe/ [1] *vt* surround (**de** with); (réconforter) rally round; ~ **qch de mystère** shroud sth in mystery.

entracte /ɑ̃tʀakt/ *nm* interval.

entraide /ɑ̃tʀɛd/ *nf* mutual aid. **entraider (s')** [1] *vpr* help each other.

entrain /ɑ̃tʀɛ̃/ *nm* zest, spirit.

entraînement /ɑ̃tʀɛnmɑ̃/ *nm* (Sport) training.

entraîner /ɑ̃tʀene/ [1] *vt* (emporter) carry away; (provoquer) lead to; (Sport) train; (actionner) drive. □ **s'~** *vpr* train. **entraîneur** *nm* trainer.

entrave /ɑ̃tʀav/ *nf* hindrance. **entraver** [1] *vt* hinder.

entre /ɑ̃tʀ(ə)/ *prép* between; (parmi) among(st); ~ **autres** among other things; **l'un d'~ nous/eux** one of us/them.

entrebâillé, ~e /ɑ̃tʀəbaje/ *adj* ajar, half-open.

entrechoquer (s') /(s)ɑ̃tʀəʃɔke/ [1] *vpr* knock against each other.

entrecôte /ɑ̃tʀəkot/ *nf* rib steak.

entrecouper /ɑ̃tʀəkupe/ [1] *vt* ~ **de** intersperse with.

entrecroiser (s') /(s)ɑ̃trəkrwaze/ [1] *vpr* (routes) intertwine.

entrée /ɑ̃tre/ *nf* entrance; (vestibule) hall; (accès) admission, entry; (billet) ticket; (Culin) starter; (Ordinat) **tapez sur E~** press Enter; **'~ interdite'** 'no entry'.

entrejambes /ɑ̃trəʒɑ̃b/ *nm* crotch.

entremets /ɑ̃trəmɛ/ *nm* dessert.

entremise /ɑ̃trəmiz/ *nf* intervention; **par l'~ de** through.

entreposer /ɑ̃trəpoze/ [1] *vt* store.

entrepôt /ɑ̃trəpo/ *nm* warehouse.

entreprenant, ~e /ɑ̃trəprənɑ̃, -t/ *adj* (actif) enterprising; (séducteur) forward.

entreprendre /ɑ̃trəprɑ̃dr/ [50] *vt* start on, undertake; (*personne*) buttonhole; **~ de faire** undertake to do.

entrepreneur /ɑ̃trəprənœr/ *nm* (de bâtiment) contractor; (chef d'entreprise) firm manager.

entreprise /ɑ̃trəpriz/ *nf* (projet) undertaking; (société) firm, business, company.

entrer /ɑ̃tre/ [1] *vi* (*aux être*) go in, enter; (venir) come in, enter; **~ dans** go *ou* come into, enter; (*club*) join; **~ en collision** collide (**avec** with); **faire ~** (*personne*) show in; **laisser ~** let in; **~ en guerre** go to war. ● *vt* (*données*) enter.

entre-temps /ɑ̃trətɑ̃/ *adv* meanwhile.

entretenir /ɑ̃trət(ə)nir/ [58] *vt* (*appareil*) maintain; (*vêtement*) look after; (alimenter) (*feu*) keep going; (*amitié*) keep alive; **~ qn de** converse with sb about. □ **s'~** *vpr* speak (**de** about; **avec** to). **entretien** *nm* maintenance; (discussion) talk; (pour un emploi) interview.

entrevoir /ɑ̃trəvwar/ [63] *vt* make out; (brièvement) glimpse.

entrevue /ɑ̃trəvy/ *nf* meeting.

entrouvert, ~e /ɑ̃truvɛr, -t/ *adj* ajar, half-open.

énumération /enymerasjɔ̃/ *nf* enumeration. **énumérer** [14] *vt* enumerate.

envahir /ɑ̃vair/ [2] *vt* invade, overrun; (*douleur, peur*) overcome.

enveloppe /ɑ̃vlɔp/ *nf* envelope; (emballage) wrapping; **~ budgétaire** budget. **envelopper** [1] *vt* wrap (up); (fig) envelop.

envergure /ɑ̃vɛrgyr/ *nf* wingspan; (importance) scope; (qualité) calibre.

envers /ɑ̃vɛr/ *prép* toward(s), to. ● *nm* (de tissu) wrong side; **à l'~** (*tableau*) upside down; (devant derrière) back to front; (*chaussette*) inside out.

envie /ɑ̃vi/ *nf* urge; (jalousie) envy; **avoir ~ de qch** feel like sth; **avoir ~ de faire** want to do; (moins urgent) feel like doing; **faire ~ à qn** make sb envious.

envier /ɑ̃vje/ [45] *vt* envy. **envieux, -ieuse** *adj* envious.

environ /ɑ̃virɔ̃/ *adv* about.

environnant, ~e /ɑ̃virɔnɑ̃, -t/ *adj* surrounding.

environnement /ɑ̃virɔnmɑ̃/ *nm* environment.

environs /ɑ̃virɔ̃/ *nmpl* vicinity; **aux ~ de** (*lieu*) in the vicinity of; (*heure*) round about.

envisager /ɑ̃vizaʒe/ [40] *vt* consider; (imaginer) envisage; **~ de faire** consider doing.

envoi /ɑ̃vwa/ *nm* dispatch; (paquet) consignment; **faire un ~** send; **coup d'~** (Sport) kick-off.

envoler (s') /(s)ɑ̃vɔle/ [1] *vpr* fly away; (*avion*) take off; (*papiers*) blow away.

envoyé, ~e /ɑ̃vwaje/ *nm,f* envoy; **~ spécial** special correspondent.

envoyer /ɑ̃vwaje/ [32] *vt* send; (lancer) throw; **~ promener qn** Ⅰ send sb packing Ⅰ.

épais, ~se /epɛ, -s/ *adj* thick. **épaisseur** *nf* thickness.

épaissir /epesir/ [2] *vt/i* thicken. □ **s'~** *vpr* thicken; (*mystère*) deepen.

épanoui, ~e /epanwi/ *adj* (*personne*) beaming, radiant.

épanouir (s') /(s)epanwir/ [2] *vpr* (*fleur*) open out; (*visage*) beam; (*personne*) blossom. **épanouissement** *nm* (éclat) blossoming, full bloom.

épargne /eparɲ/ *nf* savings.

épargner /eparɲe/ [1] *vt/i* save; (ne pas tuer) spare; **~ qch à qn** spare sb sth.

éparpiller /epaʀpije/ [1] *vt* scatter.
□ **s'∼** *vpr* scatter; (*fig*) dissipate one's efforts.

épars, **∼e** /epaʀ, -s/ *adj* scattered.

épatant, **∼e** /epatɑ̃, -t/ *adj* 🆋 amazing.

épaule /epol/ *nf* shoulder.

épave /epav/ *nf* wreck.

épée /epe/ *nf* sword.

épeler /ɛple/ [6] *vt* spell.

éperdu, **∼e** /epɛʀdy/ *adj* wild, frantic.

éperon /epʀɔ̃/ *nm* spur.

éphémère /efemɛʀ/ *adj* ephemeral.

épi /epi/ *nm* (de blé) ear; (mèche) tuft of hair; **∼ de maïs** corn cob.

épice /epis/ *nf* spice. **épicé**, **∼e** *adj* spicy.

épicerie /episʀi/ *nf* grocery shop; (produits) groceries. **épicier**, **-ière** *nm,f* grocer.

épidémie /epidemi/ *nf* epidemic.

épiderme /epidɛʀm/ *nm* skin.

épier /epje/ [45] *vt* spy on.

épilepsie /epilɛpsi/ *nf* epilepsy. **épileptique** *a* & *nmf* epileptic.

épiler /epile/ [1] *vt* remove unwanted hair from; (sourcils) pluck.

épilogue /epilɔg/ *nm* epilogue; (fig) outcome.

épinard /epinaʀ/ *nm* **∼s** spinach (+ *sg*).

épine /epin/ *nf* thorn, prickle; (d'animal) prickle, spine; **∼ dorsale** backbone. **épineux**, **-euse** *adj* thorny.

épingle /epɛ̃gl/ *nf* pin; **∼ de nourrice**, **∼ de sûreté** safety-pin.

épisode /epizɔd/ *nm* episode; **à ∼s** serialized.

épitaphe /epitaf/ *nf* epitaph.

épluche-légumes /eplyʃlegym/ *nm inv* (potato) peeler.

éplucher /eplyʃe/ [1] *vt* peel; (examiner: fig) scrutinize.

épluchure /eplyʃyʀ/ *nf* **∼s** peelings.

éponge /epɔ̃ʒ/ *nf* sponge. **éponger** [40] *vt* (liquide) mop up; (surface, front) mop; (fig) (dettes) wipe out.

épopée /epɔpe/ *nf* epic.

époque /epɔk/ *nf* time, period; **à l'∼** at the time; **d'∼** period.

épouse /epuz/ *nf* wife.

épouser /epuze/ [1] *vt* marry; (forme, idée) adopt.

épousseter /epuste/ [38] *vt* dust.

épouvantable /epuvɑ̃tabl/ *adj* appalling.

épouvantail /epuvɑ̃taj/ *nm* scarecrow.

épouvante /epuvɑ̃t/ *nf* terror. **épouvanter** [1] *vt* terrify.

époux /epu/ *nm* husband; **les ∼** the married couple.

éprendre (**s'**) /(s)epʀɑ̃dʀ/ [50] *vpr* **s'∼ de** fall in love with.

épreuve /epʀœv/ *nf* test; (Sport) event; (malheur) ordeal; (Photo, d'imprimerie) proof; **mettre à l'∼** put to the test.

éprouver /epʀuve/ [1] *vt* (ressentir) experience; (affliger) distress; (tester) test.

éprouvette /epʀuvɛt/ *nf* test-tube.

EPS *abrév f* (**éducation physique et sportive**) PE.

épuisé, **∼e** /epɥize/ *adj* exhausted; (livre) out of print. **épuisement** *nm* exhaustion.

épuiser /epɥize/ [1] *vt* (fatiguer, user) exhaust. □ **s'∼** *vpr* become exhausted.

épuration /epyʀasjɔ̃/ *nf* purification; (Pol) purge. **épurer** [1] *vt* purify; (Pol) purge.

équateur /ekwatœʀ/ *nm* equator.

équilibre /ekilibʀ/ *nm* balance; **être** *ou* **se tenir en ∼** (personne) balance; (objet) be balanced. **équilibré**, **∼e** *adj* well-balanced.

équilibrer /ekilibʀe/ [1] *vt* balance. □ **s'∼** *vpr* balance each other.

équilibriste /ekilibʀist/ *nmf* acrobat.

équipage /ekipaʒ/ *nm* crew.

équipe /ekip/ *nf* team; **∼ de nuit/ jour** night/day shift.

équipé, **∼e** /ekipe/ *adj* equipped; **cuisine ∼e** fitted kitchen.

équipement /ekipmɑ̃/ *nm* equipment; **∼s** (installations) amenities, facilities.

équiper /ekipe/ [1] *vt* equip (**de** with). □ **s'∼** *vpr* equip oneself.

équipier, -ière /ekipje, -jɛʀ/ *nm, f* team member.

équitable /ekitabl/ *adj* fair.

équitation /ekitasjɔ̃/ *nf* (horse-) riding.

équivalence /ekivalɑ̃s/ *nf* equivalence. **équivalent, ~e** *adj* equivalent.

équivaloir /ekivalwaʀ/ [60] *vi* ~ à be equivalent to.

équivoque /ekivɔk/ *adj* equivocal; (louche) questionable. ● *nf* ambiguity.

érable /eʀabl/ *nm* maple.

érafler /eʀafle/ [1] *vt* scratch. **éraflure** *nf* scratch.

éraillé, ~e /eʀaje/ *adj* (voix) raucous.

ère /ɛʀ/ *nf* era.

éreintant, ~e /eʀɛ̃tɑ̃, -t/ *adj* exhausting. **éreinter (s')** [1] *vpr* wear oneself out.

ériger /eʀiʒe/ [40] *vt* erect. □ **s'~ en** *vpr* set (oneself) up as.

éroder /eʀɔde/ [1] *vt* erode. **érosion** *nf* erosion.

errer /eʀe/ [1] *vi* wander.

erreur /eʀœʀ/ *nf* mistake, error; **dans l'~** mistaken; **par ~** by mistake; **~ judiciaire** miscarriage of justice.

erroné, ~e /eʀɔne/ *adj* erroneous.

érudit, ~e /eʀydi, -t/ *adj* scholarly. ● *nm, f* scholar.

éruption /eʀypsjɔ̃/ *nf* eruption; (Méd) rash.

es /ɛ/ ⇒ÊTRE [4].

escabeau (*pl* ~**x**) /ɛskabo/ *nm* step-ladder.

escadron /ɛskadʀɔ̃/ *nm* (Mil) company.

escalade /ɛskalad/ *nf* climbing; (Pol, Comm) escalation. **escalader** [1] *vt* climb.

escale /ɛskal/ *nf* (d'avion) stopover; (port) port of call; **faire ~ à** (avion, passager) stop over at; (navire, passager) put in at.

escalier /ɛskalje/ *nm* stairs (+ *pl*); **~ mécanique** *ou* **roulant** escalator.

escalope /ɛskalɔp/ *nf* escalope.

escargot /ɛskaʀgo/ *nm* snail.

escarpé, ~e /ɛskaʀpe/ *adj* steep.

escarpin /ɛskaʀpɛ̃/ *nm* court shoe; (US) pump.

escient: **à bon ~** /abɔnesjɑ̃/ *loc* wisely.

esclandre /ɛsklɑ̃dʀ/ *nm* scene.

esclavage /ɛsklavaʒ/ *nm* slavery. **esclave** *nmf* slave.

escompte /ɛskɔ̃t/ *nm* discount. **escompter** [1] *vt* expect; (Comm) discount.

escorte /ɛskɔʀt/ *nf* escort.

escrime /ɛskʀim/ *nf* fencing.

escroc /ɛskʀo/ *nm* swindler.

escroquer /ɛskʀɔke/ [1] *vt* swindle; **~ qch à qn** swindle sb out of sth. **escroquerie** *nf* swindle.

espace /ɛspas/ *nm* space; **~s verts** gardens and parks.

espacer /ɛspase/ [10] *vt* space out. □ **s'~** *vpr* become less frequent.

espadrille /ɛspadʀij/ *nf* rope sandal.

Espagne /ɛspaɲ/ *nf* Spain.

espagnol, ~e /ɛspaɲɔl/ *adj* Spanish. ● *nm* (Ling) Spanish. **E~, ~e** *nm, f* Spaniard.

espèce /ɛspɛs/ *nf* kind, sort; (race) species; **en ~s** (argent) in cash; **~ d'idiot!** 🔢 you idiot! 🔢.

espérance /ɛspeʀɑ̃s/ *nf* hope.

espérer /ɛspeʀe/ [14] *vt* hope for; **~ faire/que** hope to do/that. ● *vi* hope.

espiègle /ɛspjɛgl/ *adj* mischievous.

espion, ~ne /ɛspjɔ̃, -ɔn/ *nm, f* spy. **espionnage** *nm* espionage, spying. **espionner** [1] *vt* spy (on).

espoir /ɛspwaʀ/ *nm* hope; **reprendre ~** feel hopeful again.

esprit /ɛspʀi/ *nm* (intellect) mind; (humour) wit; (fantôme) spirit; (ambiance) atmosphere; **perdre l'~** lose one's mind; **reprendre ses ~s** come to; **faire de l'~** try to be witty.

esquimau, ~de (*mpl* ~**x**) /ɛskimo, -d/ *nm, f* Eskimo.

esquinter /ɛskɛ̃te/ [1] *vt* 🔢 ruin.

esquisse /ɛskis/ *nf* sketch; (fig) outline.

esquiver /ɛskive/ [1] *vt* dodge. □ **s'~** *vpr* slip away.

essai /esɛ/ *nm* (épreuve) test, trial; (tentative) try; (article) essay; (au rugby) try; ~s (Auto) qualifying round (+ *sg*); **à l'~** on trial.

essaim /esɛ̃/ *nm* swarm.

essayage /esɛjaʒ/ *nm* fitting; **salon d'~** fitting room.

essayer /eseje/ [31] *vt/i* try; (*vêtement*) try (on); (*voiture*) try (out); **~ de faire** try to do.

essence /esɑ̃s/ *nf* (*carburant*) petrol; (*nature, extrait*) essence; **~ sans plomb** unleaded petrol.

essentiel, **~le** /esɑ̃sjɛl/ *adj* essential. ● *nm* **l'~** the main thing; (*quantité*) the main part.

essieu (*pl* ~**x**) /esjø/ *nm* axle.

essor /esɔʀ/ *nm* expansion; **prendre son ~** expand.

essorage /esɔʀaʒ/ *nm* spin-drying. **essorer** [1] *vt* (*linge*) spin-dry; (en tordant) wring.

essoreuse /esɔʀøz/ *nf* spin-drier; **~ à salade** salad spinner.

essoufflé, **~e** /esufle/ *adj* out of breath.

essuie-glace /esɥiglas/ *nm inv* windscreen wiper.

essuie-mains /esɥimɛ̃/ *nm inv* hand-towel.

essuie-tout /esɥitu/ *nm inv* kitchen paper.

essuyer /esɥije/ [31] *vt* wipe; (subir) suffer. ◻ **s'~** *vpr* dry *ou* wipe oneself.

est¹ /ɛ/ ⇒ÊTRE [4].

est² /ɛst/ *nm* east. ● *a inv* east; (*partie*) eastern; (*direction*) easterly.

estampe /ɛstɑ̃p/ *nf* print.

esthète /ɛstɛt/ *nmf* aesthete.

esthéticienne /ɛstetisjɛn/ *nf* beautician.

esthétique /ɛstetik/ *adj* aesthetic.

estimation /ɛstimasjɔ̃/ *nf* (de coûts) estimate; (valeur) valuation.

estime /ɛstim/ *nf* esteem.

estimer /ɛstime/ [1] *vt* (*tableau*) value; (calculer) estimate; (respecter) esteem; (considérer) consider (**que** that).

estival, **~e** (*mpl* **-aux**) /ɛstival, -o/ *adj* summer. **estivant**, **~e** *nm,f* summer visitor.

estomac /ɛstɔma/ *nm* stomach.

estomaqué, **~e** /ɛstɔmake/ *adj* ◻ stunned.

Estonie /ɛstɔni/ *nf* Estonia.

estrade /ɛstʀad/ *nf* platform.

estragon /ɛstʀagɔ̃/ *nm* tarragon.

estropié, **~e** /ɛstʀɔpje/ *nm,f* cripple. ● *adj* crippled.

estuaire /ɛstɥɛʀ/ *nm* estuary.

et /e/ *conj* and; **~ moi?** what about me?; **~ alors?** so what?

étable /etabl/ *nf* cow-shed.

établi, **~e** /etabli/ *adj* established; **un fait bien ~** a well-established fact. ● *nm* work-bench.

établir /etabliʀ/ [2] *vt* establish; (*liste, facture*) draw up; (*personne, camp, record*) set up. ◻ **s'~** *vpr* (*personne*) settle; **s'~ à son compte** set up on one's own.

établissement /etablismɑ̃/ *nm* (entreprise) organization; (institution) establishment; **~ scolaire** school.

étage /etaʒ/ *nm* floor, storey; (de fusée) stage; **à l'~** upstairs; **au premier ~** on the first floor.

étagère /etaʒɛʀ/ *nf* shelf; (meuble) shelving unit.

étain /etɛ̃/ *nm* pewter.

étais, **était** /etɛ/ ⇒ÊTRE [4].

étalage /etalaʒ/ *nm* display; (vitrine) shop-window; **faire ~ de** flaunt. **étalagiste** *nmf* window-dresser.

étaler /etale/ [1] *vt* spread; (*journal*) spread (out); (*pâte*) roll out; (exposer) display; (*richesse*) flaunt. ◻ **s'~** *vpr* (prendre de la place) spread out; (tomber ◻) fall flat; **s'~ sur** (*paiement*) be spread over.

étalon /etalɔ̃/ *nm* (cheval) stallion; (modèle) standard.

étanche /etɑ̃ʃ/ *adj* watertight; (*montre*) waterproof.

étancher /etɑ̃ʃe/ [1] *vt* (*soif*) quench.

étang /etɑ̃/ *nm* pond.

étant /etɑ̃/ ⇒ÊTRE [4].

étape /etap/ *nf* stage; (lieu d'arrêt) stopover; (fig) stage.

état /eta/ *nm* state; (liste) statement; (métier) profession; **en bon/mauvais ~** in good/bad condition; **en ~ de** in a position to; **en ~ de marche** in working order; **faire ~ de** (citer) mention; **être dans tous ses ~s** be in a state; **~ civil** civil status; **~ des lieux** inventory of fixtures. **État** *nm* State.

état-major (*pl* **états-majors**) /etamaʒɔʀ/ *nm* (officiers) staff (+ *pl*).

États-Unis /etazyni/ *nmpl* **~** (d'Amérique) United States (of America).

étau (*pl* **~x**) /eto/ *nm* vice.

étayer /eteje/ [31] *vt* prop up.

été¹ /ete/ ⇒ÊTRE [4].

été² /ete/ *nm* summer.

éteindre /etɛ̃dʀ/ [22] *vt* (*feu*) put out; (*lumière, radio*) turn off. □ **s'~** *vpr* (*feu, lumière*) go out; (*appareil*) go off; (*mourir*) die. **éteint, ~e** *adj* (*feu*) out; (*volcan*) extinct.

étendard /etɑ̃daʀ/ *nm* standard.

étendre /etɑ̃dʀ/ [3] *vt* (*nappe*) spread (out); (*bras, jambes*) stretch (out); (*linge*) hang out; (*agrandir*) extend. □ **s'~** *vpr* (s'allonger) lie down; (se propager) spread; (*plaine*) stretch; **s'~ sur** (*sujet*) dwell on.

étendu, ~e /etɑ̃dy/ *adj* extensive. **étendue** *nf* area; (d'eau) stretch; (importance) extent.

éternel, ~le /etɛʀnɛl/ *adj* (*vie*) eternal; (fig) endless.

éterniser (s') /(s)etɛʀnize/ [1] *vpr* (durer) drag on.

éternité /etɛʀnite/ *nf* eternity.

éternuement /etɛʀnymɑ̃/ *nm* sneeze. **éternuer** [1] *vi* sneeze.

êtes /ɛt/ ⇒ÊTRE [4].

éthique /etik/ *adj* ethical. ● *nf* ethics (+ *sg*).

ethnie /ɛtni/ *nf* ethnic group. **ethnique** *adj* ethnic.

étincelant, ~e /etɛ̃slɑ̃, -t/ *adj* sparkling. **étinceler** [38] *vi* sparkle. **étincelle** *nf* spark.

étiqueter /etikte/ [38] *vt* label. **étiquette** *nf* label; (protocole) etiquette.

étirer /etiʀe/ [1] *vt* stretch. □ **s'~** *vpr* stretch.

étoffe /etɔf/ *nf* fabric.

étoffer /etɔfe/ [1] *vt* expand. □ **s'~** *vpr* fill out.

étoile /etwal/ *nf* star; **à la belle ~** in the open; **~ filante** shooting star; **~ de mer** starfish.

étonnant, ~e /etɔnɑ̃, -t/ *adj* (curieux) surprising; (formidable) amazing. **étonnement** *nm* surprise; (plus fort) amazement.

étonner /etɔne/ [1] *vt* amaze. □ **s'~** *vpr* be amazed (de at).

étouffant, ~e /etufɑ̃, -t/ *adj* stifling.

étouffer /etufe/ [1] *vt/i* suffocate; (*sentiment, révolte*) stifle; (*feu*) smother; (*bruit*) muffle; **on étouffe** it is stifling. □ **s'~** *vpr* suffocate; (en mangeant) choke.

étourderie /etuʀdəʀi/ *nf* thoughtlessness; (acte) careless mistake.

étourdi, ~e /etuʀdi/ *adj* absent-minded. ● *nm,f* scatterbrain.

étourdir /etuʀdiʀ/ [2] *vt* stun; (fatiguer) make sb's head spin. **étourdissant, ~e** *adj* stunning.

étourneau (*pl* **~x**) /etuʀno/ *nm* starling.

étrange /etʀɑ̃ʒ/ *adj* strange.

étranger, -ère /etʀɑ̃ʒe, -ɛʀ/ *adj* (inconnu) strange, unfamiliar; (d'un autre pays) foreign. ● *nm,f* foreigner; (inconnu) stranger; **à l'~** abroad; **de l'~** from abroad.

étrangler /etʀɑ̃gle/ [1] *vt* strangle; (*col*) throttle. □ **s'~** *vpr* choke.

être /ɛtʀ/ [4]

● *verbe auxiliaire*

····▸ (du passé) have; **elle est partie; venue hier** she left/came yesterday.

····▸ (de la voix passive) be.

● *verbe intransitif* (*aux avoir*)

····▸ be; **~ médecin** be a doctor; **je suis à vous** I'm all yours; **j'en suis à me demander si…** I'm beginning to wonder whether…; **qu'en est-il de…?** what's the news about…?

····▸ (appartenance) be, belong to.

····▸ (heure, date) be; **nous sommes le 3 mars** it's March 3.

····▸ (aller) be; **je n'y ai jamais été** I've never been; **il a été le voir** he went to see him.

····▶ c'est it is *or* it's; **c'est moi qui l'ai fait** I did it; **est-ce que tu veux du thé?** do you want some tea?

● *nom masculin*

····▶ being; ∼ **humain** human being.

····▶ (*personne*) person; **un** ∼ **cher** a loved one.

étreindre /etʀɛ̃dʀ/ [22] *vt* embrace. **étreinte** *nf* embrace.

étrennes /etʀɛn/ *nfpl* (New Year's) gift (+ *sg*); (*argent*) money.

étrier /etʀije/ *nm* stirrup.

étriqué, ∼**e** /etʀike/ *adj* tight.

étroit, ∼**e** /etʀwa, -t/ *adj* narrow; (*vêtement*) tight; (*liens, surveillance*) close; **à l'**∼ cramped. **étroitement** *adv* closely. **étroitesse** *nf* narrowness.

étude /etyd/ *nf* study; (*enquête*) survey; (*bureau*) office; (**salle d'**)∼ (Scol) prep room; **à l'**∼ under consideration; **faire des** ∼**s** (**de**) study; **il n'a pas fait d'**∼**s** he didn't go to university; ∼ **de marché** market research.

étudiant, ∼**e** /etydjɑ̃, -t/ *nm,f* student.

étudier /etydje/ [45] *vt/i* study.

étui /etɥi/ *nm* case.

étuve /etyv/ *nf* steam room.

eu, ∼**e** /y/ ➡AVOIR [5].

euro /øʀo/ *nm* euro.

Europe /øʀɔp/ *nf* Europe.

européen, ∼**ne** /øʀɔpeɛ̃, -eɛn/ *adj* European. **E**∼, ∼**ne** *nm,f* European.

euthanasie /øtanazi/ *nf* euthanasia.

eux /ø/ *pron* they; (*complément*) them. **eux-mêmes** *pron* themselves.

évacuation /evakɥasjɔ̃/ *nf* evacuation; (*d'eaux usées*) discharge. **évacuer** [1] *vt* evacuate.

évadé, ∼**e** /evade/ *adj* escaped. ● *nm,f* escaped prisoner. **évader** (**s'**) [1] *vpr* escape.

évaluation /evalɥasjɔ̃/ *nf* assessment. **évaluer** [1] *vt* assess.

évangile /evɑ̃ʒil/ *nm* gospel; **l'É**∼ the Gospel.

évanouir (**s'**) /(s)evanwiʀ/ [2] *vpr* faint; (*disparaître*) vanish.

évaporation /evapɔʀasjɔ̃/ *nf* evaporation. **évaporer** (**s'**) [1] *vpr* evaporate.

évasif, **-ive** /evazif, -v/ *adj* evasive.

évasion /evazjɔ̃/ *nf* escape.

éveil /evɛj/ *nm* awakening; **en** ∼ alert.

éveillé, ∼**e** /eveje/ *adj* awake; (*intelligent*) alert.

éveiller /eveje/ [1] *vt* awake(n); (*susciter*) arouse. □ **s'**∼ *vpr* awake.

événement /evɛnmɑ̃/ *nm* event.

éventail /evɑ̃taj/ *nm* fan; (*gamme*) range.

éventrer /evɑ̃tʀe/ [1] *vt* (*sac*) rip open.

éventualité /evɑ̃tɥalite/ *nf* possibility; **dans cette** ∼ in that event.

éventuel, ∼**le** /evɑ̃tɥɛl/ *adj* possible. **éventuellement** *adv* possibly.

évêque /evɛk/ *nm* bishop.

évertuer (**s'**) /(s)evɛʀtɥe/ [1] *vpr* **s'**∼ **à** struggle hard to.

éviction /eviksjɔ̃/ *nf* eviction.

évidemment /evidamɑ̃/ *adv* obviously; (*bien sûr*) of course.

évidence /evidɑ̃s/ *nf* obviousness; (*fait*) obvious fact; **être en** ∼ be conspicuous; **mettre en** ∼ (*fait*) highlight. **évident**, ∼**e** *adj* obvious, evident.

évier /evje/ *nm* sink.

évincer /evɛ̃se/ [10] *vt* oust.

éviter /evite/ [1] *vt* avoid (**de faire** doing); ∼ **qch à qn** (*dérangement*) save sb sth.

évocateur, **-trice** /evɔkatœʀ, -tʀis/ *adj* evocative. **évocation** *nf* evocation.

évolué, ∼**e** /evɔlɥe/ *adj* highly developed.

évoluer /evɔlɥe/ [1] *vi* evolve; (*situation*) develop; (*se déplacer*) glide. **évolution** *nf* evolution; (*d'une situation*) development.

évoquer /evɔke/ [1] *vt* call to mind, evoke.

exacerber /ɛgzasɛʀbe/ [1] *vt* exacerbate.

exact, ∼**e** /ɛgza(kt), -akt/ *adj* (*précis*) exact, accurate; (*juste*) correct;

(*personne*) punctual. **exactement** *adv* exactly. **exactitude** *nf* exactness; punctuality.

ex æquo /ɛgzeko/ *adv* être ~ tie (avec qn with sb).

exagération /ɛgzaʒeRasjõ/ *nf* exaggeration. **exagéré**, ~e *adj* excessive.

exagérer /ɛgzaʒeRe/ [14] *vt/i* exaggerate; (abuser) go too far.

exalté, ~e /ɛgzalte/ *nm,f* fanatic. **exalter** [1] *vt* excite; (glorifier) exalt.

examen /ɛgzamɛ̃/ *nm* examination; (Scol) exam. **examinateur, -trice** *nm,f* examiner. **examiner** [1] *vt* examine.

exaspération /ɛgzaspeRasjõ/ *nf* exasperation. **exaspérer** [14] *vt* exasperate.

exaucer /ɛgzose/ [10] *vt* grant; (*personne*) grant the wish(es) of.

excédent /ɛksedɑ̃/ *nm* surplus; ~ de bagages excess luggage; ~ de la balance commerciale trade surplus. **excédentaire** *adj* excess, surplus.

excéder /ɛksede/ [14] *vt* (dépasser) exceed; (agacer) irritate.

excellence /ɛksɛlɑ̃s/ *nf* excellence. **excellent**, ~e *adj* excellent. **exceller** [1] *vi* excel (dans in).

excentricité /ɛksɑ̃tRisite/ *nf* eccentricity. **excentrique** *a & nmf* eccentric.

excepté, ~e /ɛksɛpte/ *a & prép* except.

excepter /ɛksɛpte/ [1] *vt* except.

exception /ɛksɛpsjõ/ *nf* exception; à l'~ de except for; d'~ exceptional; faire ~ be an exception. **exceptionnel**, ~le *adj* exceptional. **exceptionnellement** *adv* exceptionally.

excès /ɛksɛ/ *nm* excess; ~ de vitesse speeding.

excessif, -ive /ɛksesif, -v/ *adj* excessive.

excitant, ~e /ɛksitɑ̃, -t/ *adj* stimulating; (palpitant) exciting. ● *nm* stimulant.

exciter /ɛksite/ [1] *vt* excite; (irriter) get excited. □ **s'**~ *vpr* get excited.

exclamer (s') /(s)ɛksklame/ [1] *vpr* exclaim.

exclure /ɛksklyR/ [16] *vt* exclude; (expulser) expel; (empêcher) preclude.

exclusif, -ive /ɛksklyzif, -v/ *adj* exclusive.

exclusion /ɛksklyzjõ/ *nf* exclusion.

exclusivité /ɛksklyzivite/ *nf* (Comm) exclusive rights (+ *pl*); projeter en ~ show exclusively.

excursion /ɛkskyRsjõ/ *nf* excursion; (à pied) hike.

excuse /ɛkskyz/ *nf* excuse; ~s apology (+ *sg*); faire des ~s apologize.

excuser /ɛkskyze/ [1] *vt* excuse; excusez-moi excuse me. □ **s'**~ *vpr* apologize (de for).

exécrable /ɛgzekRabl/ *adj* dreadful. **exécrer** [14] *vt* loathe.

exécuter /ɛgzekyte/ [1] *vt* carry out, execute; (Mus) perform; (tuer) execute.

exécutif, -ive /ɛgzekytif, -v/ *a & nm* (Pol) executive.

exécution /ɛgzekysjõ/ *nf* execution; (Mus) performance.

exemplaire /ɛgzɑ̃plɛR/ *adj* exemplary. ● *nm* copy.

exemple /ɛgzɑ̃pl/ *nm* example; par ~ for example; donner l'~ set an example.

exempt, ~e /ɛgzɑ̃, -t/ *adj* ~ de exempt (de from).

exempter /ɛgzɑ̃te/ [1] *vt* exempt (de from). **exemption** *nf* exemption.

exercer /ɛgzɛRse/ [10] *vt* exercise; (*influence, contrôle*) exert; (former) train, exercise; ~ un métier have a job; ~ le métier de... work as a... □ **s'**~ *vpr* practise.

exercice /ɛgzɛRsis/ *nm* exercise; (de métier) practice; en ~ in office; (*médecin*) in practice.

exhaler /ɛgzale/ [1] *vt* emit.

exhaustif, -ive /ɛgzostif, -v/ *adj* exhaustive.

exhiber /ɛgzibe/ [1] *vt* exhibit.

exhorter /ɛgzɔRte/ [1] *vt* exhort (à to).

exigeant, ~e /ɛgziʒɑ̃, -t/ *adj* demanding; être ~ avec qn demand a lot of sb. **exigence** *nf* demand. **exiger** [40] *vt* demand.

exigu, ~ë /ɛgzigy/ *adj* tiny.

exil /ɛgzil/ *nm* exile. **exilé**, ∼**e** *nm,f* exile.

exiler /ɛgzile/ [1] *vt* exile. □ **s'**∼ *vpr* go into exile.

existence /ɛgzistɑ̃s/ *nf* existence. **exister** [1] *vi* exist.

exode /ɛgzɔd/ *nm* exodus.

exonérer /ɛgzɔneʀe/ [14] *vt* exempt (**de** from).

exorbitant, ∼**e** /ɛgzɔʀbitɑ̃, -t/ *adj* exorbitant.

exorciser /ɛgzɔʀsize/ [1] *vt* exorcize.

exotique /ɛgzɔtik/ *adj* exotic.

expansé, ∼**e** /ɛkspɑ̃se/ *adj* (Tech) expanded.

expansif, **-ive** /ɛkspɑ̃sif, -v/ *adj* expansive. **expansion** *nf* expansion.

expatrié, ∼**e** /ɛkspatʀije/ *nm,f* expatriate.

expectative /ɛkspɛktativ/ *nf* **être dans l'**∼ wait and see.

expédient /ɛkspedjɑ̃/ *nm* expedient; **vivre d'**∼**s** live by one's wits; **user d'**∼**s** resort to expedients.

expédier /ɛkspedje/ [45] *vt* send, dispatch; (*tâche* 🖬) polish off. **expéditeur**, **-trice** *nm,f* sender.

expéditif, **-ive** /ɛkspeditif, -v/ *adj* quick.

expédition /ɛkspedisjɔ̃/ *nf* (envoi) dispatching; (voyage) expedition.

expérience /ɛkspeʀjɑ̃s/ *nf* experience; (scientifique) experiment.

expérimental, ∼**e** (*mpl* **-aux**) /ɛkspeʀimɑ̃tal, o/ *adj* experimental. **expérimentation** *nf* experimentation. **expérimenté**, ∼**e** *adj* experienced. **expérimenter** [1] *vt* test, experiment with.

expert, ∼**e** /ɛkspɛʀ, -t/ *adj* expert. ● *nm* expert; (d'assurances) adjuster. **expert-comptable** (*pl* **experts-comptables**) *nm* accountant.

expertise /ɛkspɛʀtiz/ *nf* valuation; (de dégâts) assessment. **expertiser** [1] *vt* value; (*dégâts*) assess.

expier /ɛkspje/ [45] *vt* atone for.

expiration /ɛkspiʀasjɔ̃/ *nf* expiry.

expirer /ɛkspiʀe/ [1] *vi* breathe out; (finir, mourir) expire.

explicatif, **-ive** /ɛksplikatif, -v/ *adj* explanatory.

explication /ɛksplikasjɔ̃/ *nf* explanation; (fig) discussion; ∼ **de texte** (Scol) literary commentary.

explicite /ɛksplisit/ *adj* explicit.

expliquer /ɛksplike/ [1] *vt* explain. □ **s'**∼ *vpr* explain oneself; (discuter) discuss things; (être explicable) be understandable.

exploit /ɛksplwa/ *nm* exploit.

exploitant, ∼**e** /ɛksplwatɑ̃, -t/ *nm,f* ∼ (**agricole**) farmer.

exploitation /ɛksplwatasjɔ̃/ *nf* exploitation; (d'entreprise) running; (ferme) farm.

exploiter /ɛksplwate/ [1] *vt* exploit; (*ferme*) run; (*mine*) work.

explorateur, **-trice** /ɛksplɔʀatœʀ, -tʀis/ *nm,f* explorer. **exploration** *nf* exploration. **explorer** [1] *vt* explore.

exploser /ɛksploze/ [1] *vi* explode; **faire** ∼ explode; (*bâtiment*) blow up.

explosif, **-ive** /ɛksplozif, -v/ *a & nm* explosive. **explosion** *nf* explosion.

exportateur, **-trice** /ɛkspɔʀtatœʀ, -tʀis/ *nm,f* exporter. ● *adj* exporting. **exportation** *nf* export. **exporter** [1] *vt* export.

exposant, ∼**e** /ɛkspozɑ̃, -t/ *nm,f* exhibitor.

exposé, ∼**e** /ɛkspoze/ *nm* talk (**sur** on); (d'une action) account; **faire l'**∼ **de la situation** give an account of the situation. ● *adj* ∼ **au nord** facing north.

exposer /ɛkspoze/ [1] *vt* display, show; (expliquer) explain; (soumettre, mettre en danger) expose (**à** to); (*vie*) endanger. □ **s'**∼ **à** *vpr* expose oneself to.

exposition /ɛkspozisjɔ̃/ *nf* (d'art) exhibition; (de faits) exposition; (géographique) aspect.

exprès[1] /ɛkspʀɛ/ *adv* specially; (délibérément) on purpose.

exprès[2], **-esse** /ɛkspʀɛs/ *adj* express.

express /ɛkspʀɛs/ *a & nm inv* (café) ∼ espresso; (train) ∼ fast train.

expressif, **-ive** /ɛkspʀɛsif, -v/ *adj* expressive. **expression** *nf* expression.

exprimer /ɛkspʀime/ [1] *vt* express.
□ **s'~** *vpr* express oneself.

expulser /ɛkspylse/ [1] *vt* expel;
(*locataire*) evict; (*joueur*) send off.

expulsion *nf* (d'élève) expulsion; (de
locataire) eviction; (d'immigré)
deportation.

exquis, ~e /ɛkski, -z/ *adj* exquisite.

extase /ɛkstɑz/ *nf* ecstasy.

extasier (**s'**) /(s)ɛkstɑzje/ [45] *vpr*
s'~ sur be ecstatic about.

extensible /ɛkstɑ̃sibl/ *adj* (*tissu*)
stretch.

extension /ɛkstɑ̃sjɔ̃/ *nf* extension;
(expansion) expansion.

exténuer /ɛkstenɥe/ [1] *vt* exhaust.

extérieur, ~e /ɛksteʀjœʀ/ *adj*
outside; (*signe, gaieté*) outward;
(*politique*) foreign. ● *nm* outside,
exterior; (de personne) exterior; **à l'~**
(de) outside. **extérioriser** [1] *vt*
show, externalize.

extermination /ɛkstɛʀminasjɔ̃/ *nf*
extermination. **exterminer** [1] *vt*
exterminate.

externe /ɛkstɛʀn/ *adj* external.
● *nmf* (Scol) day pupil.

extincteur /ɛkstɛ̃ktœʀ/ *nm* fire
extinguisher.

extinction /ɛkstɛ̃ksjɔ̃/ *nf*
extinction; **avoir une ~ de voix** have
lost one's voice.

extorquer /ɛkstɔʀke/ [1] *vt* extort.

extra /ɛkstʀa/ *a inv* first-rate. ● *nm
inv* (repas) (special) treat.

extraction /ɛkstʀaksjɔ̃/ *nf*
extraction.

extrader /ɛkstʀade/ [1] *vt* extradite.

extraire /ɛkstʀɛʀ/ [29] *vt* extract.
extrait *nm* extract.

extraordinaire /ɛkstʀaɔʀdinɛʀ/
adj extraordinary.

extravagance /ɛkstʀavagɑ̃s/ *nf*
extravagance. **extravagant, ~e**
adj extravagant.

extraverti, ~e /ɛkstʀavɛʀti/ *nm, f*
extrovert.

extrême /ɛkstʀɛm/ *a & nm*
extreme. **extrêmement** *adv*
extremely.

Extrême-Orient /ɛkstʀɛmɔʀjɑ̃/
nm Far East.

extrémiste /ɛkstʀemist/ *nmf*
extremist.

extrémité /ɛkstʀemite/ *nf* end;
(mains, pieds) extremity.

exubérance /ɛgzybeʀɑ̃s/ *nf*
exuberance. **exubérant, ~e** *adj*
exuberant.

Ff

F *abrév f* (**franc, francs**) franc,
francs.

fabricant, ~e /fabʀikɑ̃, -t/ *nm, f*
manufacturer. **fabrication** *nf*
making; manufacture.

fabrique /fabʀik/ *nf* factory.
fabriquer [1] *vt* make;
(industriellement) manufacture; (fig)
make up.

fabuler /fabyle/ [1] *vi* fantasize.

fabuleux, -euse /fabylø, -z/ *adj*
fabulous.

fac /fak/ *nf* 🄵 university.

façade /fasad/ *nf* front; (fig) façade.

face /fas/ *nf* face; (d'un objet) side; **en
~ (de), d'en ~** opposite; **en ~ de** (fig)
faced with; **~ à** facing; (fig) faced
with; **faire ~ à** face. **face-à-face**
nm inv (débat) one-to-one debate.

fâcher /faʃe/ [1] *vt* anger; **fâché**
angry; (désolé) sorry. □ **se ~** *vpr* get
angry; (se brouiller) fall out.

facile /fasil/ *adj* easy; (*caractère*)
easygoing.

facilité /fasilite/ *nf* easiness;
(aisance) ease; (aptitude) ability; **~s**
(possibilités) facilities, opportunities;
~s d'importation import
opportunities; **~s de paiement** easy
terms.

faciliter /fasilite/ [1] *vt* facilitate,
make easier.

façon /fasɔ̃/ *nf* way; (de vêtement) cut;
de cette ~ in this way; **de ~ à** so as
to; **de toute ~** anyway; **~s** (chichis)
fuss; **faire des ~s** stand on
ceremony; **sans ~s** (repas) informal;

(*personne*) unpretentious. **façonner**
[1] *vt* shape; (faire) make.

fac-similé (*pl* ~s) /faksimile/ *nm*
facsimile.

facteur, -trice /faktœR, -tRis/ *nm, f*
postman, postwoman. ● *nm* (élément)
factor.

facture /faktyR/ *nf* bill; (Comm)
invoice; ~ **détaillée** itemized bill.
facturer [1] *vt* invoice. **facturette**
nf credit card slip.

facultatif, -ive /fakyltatif, -v/ *adj*
optional.

faculté /fakylte/ *nf* faculty;
(possibilité) power; (Univ) faculty.

fade /fad/ *adj* insipid.

faible /fɛbl/ *adj* weak; (*espoir,
quantité, écart*) slight; (*revenu,
intensité*) low; ~ **d'esprit** feeble-
minded. ● *nm* (personne) weakling;
(penchant) weakness. **faiblesse** *nf*
weakness. **faiblir** [2] *vi* weaken.

faïence /fajãs/ *nf* earthenware.

faillir /fajiR/ [2] *vi* **j'ai failli acheter** I
almost bought.

faillite /fajit/ *nf* bankruptcy; (fig)
collapse.

faim /fɛ̃/ *nf* hunger; **avoir** ~ be
hungry; **rester sur sa** ~ (fig) be left
wanting more.

fainéant, ~e /feneã, -t/ *adj* idle.
● *nm, f* idler.

....

faire /fɛR/ [33]

⇒ Pour les expressions comme
**faire attention, faire la
cuisine**, etc. ⇒**attention,
cuisine**, etc.

● *verbe transitif*

····▸ (préparer, créer) make; ~ **une tarte/
une erreur** make a tart/a mistake.

····▸ (se livrer à une activité) do; ~ **du droit**
do law; ~ **du foot/du violon** play
football/the violin; **qu'est-ce qu'elle
fait?** (dans la vie) what does she do?;
(en ce moment précis) what is she
doing?

····▸ (dans les calculs, mesures, etc.) **10 et
10 font 20** 10 and 10 make 20; **ça fait**
25 francs that's 25 francs; ~ **60 kilos**
weigh 60 kilos; **il fait 1,75 m** he's 1.75
m tall.

····▸ (dans les expressions de temps) **ça fait
une heure que j'attends** I have been
waiting for an hour.

····▸ (imiter) ~ **le clown** act the clown;
faire le malade pretend to be ill.

····▸ (parcourir) ~ **10 km** do *ou* cover 10
km; ~ **les musées** go round the
museums.

····▸ (entraîner, causer) **ça ne fait rien** it
doesn't matter; **l'accident a fait 8
morts** 8 people died in the accident.

····▸ (dire) say; **'excusez-moi', fit-elle**
'excuse me', she said.

● *verbe auxiliaire*

····▸ (**faire** + infinitif + qn) make; ~
pleurer qn make sb cry.

····▸ (**faire** + infinitif + qch) have, get; ~
réparer sa voiture have *ou* get one's
car mended.

····▸ (**ne faire que** + infinitif)
(continuellement) **ne** ~ **que pleurer** do
nothing but cry; (seulement) **je ne fais
qu'obéir** I'm only following orders.

● *verbe intransitif*

····▸ (agir) do, act; ~ **vite** act quickly;
fais comme tu veux do as you please;
fais comme chez toi make yourself at
home.

····▸ (paraître) look; ~ **joli** look pretty;
ça fait cher it's expensive.

····▸ (en parlant du temps) **il fait chaud/
gris** it's hot/overcast.

□ **se faire** *verbe pronominal*

····▸ (obtenir, confectionner) make; **se** ~
des amis make friends; **se** ~ **un thé**
make (oneself) a cup of tea.

····▸ (**se faire** + infinitif) **se** ~ **gronder** be
scolded; **se** ~ **couper les cheveux**
have one's hair cut.

····▸ (devenir) **il se fait tard** it's getting
late.

····▸ (être d'usage) **ça ne se fait pas** it's
not the done thing.

····▸ (emploi impersonnel) **comment se
fait-il que tu sois ici?** how come
you're here?

····▸ □ **se faire à** get used to; **je ne
m'y fais pas** I can't get used to it.

····▸ □ **s'en faire** worry; **ne t'en fais
pas** don't worry.

! Lorsque **faire** remplace un verbe plus précis, on traduira ■ quelquefois par ce dernier: **faire une visite** *pay a visit*, **faire un nid** *build a nest*.

faire-part /fɛʀpaʀ/ *nm inv* announcement.

fais /fɛ/ ⇒FAIRE [33].

faisan /fəzɑ̃/ *nm* pheasant.

faisceau (*pl* ~x) /fɛso/ *nm* (rayon) beam; (fagot) bundle.

fait, ~e /fɛ, fɛt/ *adj* done; (*fromage*) ripe; ~ **pour** made for; **tout** ~ ready made; **c'est bien** ~ **pour toi** it serves you right. ● *nm* fact; (événement) event; **au** ~ (**de**) informed (of); **de ce** ~ therefore; **du** ~ **de** on account of; ~ **divers** (trivial) news item; ~ **nouveau** new development; **prendre qn sur le** ~ catch sb in the act. ● ⇒FAIRE [33].

faîte /fɛt/ *nm* top; (fig) peak.

faites /fɛt/ ⇒FAIRE [33].

falaise /falɛz/ *nf* cliff.

falloir /falwaʀ/ [34] *vi* il faut qch/qn we/you *etc.* need sth/so; **il lui faut du pain** he needs bread; **il faut rester** we/you *etc.* have to *ou* must stay; **il faut que j'y aille** I have to *ou* must go; **il faudrait que tu partes** you should leave; **il aurait fallu le faire** we/you *etc.* should have done it; **comme il faut** (*manger, se tenir*) properly; (*personne*) respectable, proper. □ **s'en** ~ *vpr* **il s'en est fallu de peu qu'il ne gagne** he nearly won; **il s'en faut de beaucoup que je sois** I am far from being.

falsifier /falsifje/ [45] *vt* falsify; (*signature, monnaie*) forge.

famé, ~e /fame/ *adj* **mal** ~ disreputable, seedy.

fameux, -**euse** /famø, -z/ *adj* famous; (excellent Ⅰ) first-rate.

familial, ~e (*mpl* -**iaux**) /familjal, -jo/ *adj* family.

familiale /familjal/ *nf* estate car; (US) station wagon.

familiariser /familjaʀize/ [1] *vt* familiarize (**avec** with). □ **se** ~ *vpr* familiarize oneself.

familier, -**ière** /familje, -jɛʀ/ *adj* familiar; (amical) informal.

famille /famij/ *nf* family; **en** ~ with one's family.

famine /famin/ *nf* famine.

fanatique /fanatik/ *adj* fanatical. ● *nmf* fanatic.

fanfare /fɑ̃faʀ/ *nf* brass band; (musique) fanfare.

fantaisie /fɑ̃tezi/ *nf* imagination, fantasy; (caprice) whim; (**de**) ~ (*boutons etc.*) fancy. **fantaisiste** *adj* unorthodox; (*personne*) eccentric.

fantasme /fɑ̃tasm/ *nm* fantasy.

fantastique /fɑ̃tastik/ *adj* fantastic.

fantôme /fɑ̃tom/ *nm* ghost; **cabinet(-)~** (Pol) shadow cabinet.

faon /fɑ̃/ *nm* fawn.

FAQ *abrév f* (**Foire aux questions**) (Internet) FAQ, Frequently Asked Questions.

farce /faʀs/ *nf* (practical) joke; (Théât) farce; (hachis) stuffing.

farcir /faʀsiʀ/ [2] *vt* stuff.

fard /faʀ/ *nm* make-up; ~ **à paupières** eye-shadow; **piquer un** ~ blush.

fardeau (*pl* ~x) /faʀdo/ *nm* burden.

farfelu, ~e /faʀfəly/ *a & nm,f* eccentric.

farine /faʀin/ *nf* flour. **farineux**, -**euse** *adj* floury. **farineux** *nmpl* starchy food.

farouche /faʀuʃ/ *adj* shy; (peu sociable) unsociable; (violent) fierce.

fascicule /fasikyl/ *nm* (brochure) booklet; (partie d'un ouvrage) fascicule.

fasciner /fasine/ [1] *vt* fascinate.

fascisme /faʃism/ *nm* fascism.

fasse /fas/ ⇒FAIRE [33].

fast-food /fastfud/ *nm* fast-food place.

fastidieux, -**ieuse** /fastidjø, -z/ *adj* tedious.

fatal, ~e (*mpl* ~s) /fatal/ *adj* inevitable; (mortel) fatal. **fatalité** *nf* (destin) fate.

fatigant, ~e /fatigɑ̃, -t/ *adj* tiring; (ennuyeux) tiresome.

fatigue /fatig/ *nf* fatigue, tiredness.

fatigué, ~e /fatige/ *adj* tired.

fatiguer /fatige/ [1] vt tire; (*yeux, moteur*) strain. ● vi (*moteur*) labour. □ se ~ vpr get tired, tire (**de** of).

faubourg /fobuʀ/ nm suburb.

faucher /foʃe/ [1] vt (*herbe*) mow; (voler 🛈) pinch; ~ **qn** (*véhicule, tir*) mow sb down.

faucon /fokɔ̃/ nm falcon, hawk.

faudra, faudrait /fodʀa, fodʀɛ/ ⇒FALLOIR [34].

faufiler (se) /(sə)fofile/ [1] vpr edge one's way, squeeze.

faune /fon/ nf wildlife, fauna.

faussaire /fosɛʀ/ nmf forger.

fausse /fos/ ⇒FAUX².

fausser /fose/ [1] vt buckle; (fig) distort; ~ **compagnie à qn** give sb the slip.

faut /fo/ ⇒FALLOIR [34].

faute /fot/ nf mistake; (responsabilité) fault; (délit) offence; (péché) sin; **en ~** at fault; ~ **de** for want of; ~ **de quoi** failing which; **sans ~** without fail; ~ **de frappe** typing error; ~ **de goût** bad taste; ~ **professionnelle** professional misconduct.

fauteuil /fotœj/ nm armchair; (de président) chair; (Théât) seat; ~ **roulant** wheelchair.

fautif, -ive /fotif, -v/ adj guilty; (faux) faulty. ● nm,f guilty party.

fauve /fov/ adj (couleur) fawn, tawny. ● nm wild cat.

faux¹ /fo/ nf scythe.

faux², fausse /fo, fos/ adj false; (falsifié) fake, forged; (numéro, calcul) wrong; (voix) out of tune; **c'est ~!** that is wrong!; ~ **témoignage** perjury; **faire ~ bond à qn** stand sb up; **fausse couche** miscarriage; ~ **frais** incidental expenses. ● adv (chanter) out of tune. ● nm forgery.

faux-filet (pl ~s) nm sirloin.

faveur /favœʀ/ nf favour; **de ~** (régime) preferential; **en ~ de** in favour of.

favorable /favɔʀabl/ adj favourable.

favori, ~te /favɔʀi, -t/ a & nm,f favourite. **favoriser** [1] vt favour.

fax /faks/ nm fax. **faxer** [1] vt fax.

fébrile /febʀil/ adj feverish.

fécond, ~e /fekɔ̃, -d/ adj fertile. **féconder** [1] vt fertilize. **fécondité** nf fertility.

fédéral, ~e (mpl **-aux**) /federal, -o/ adj federal. **fédération** nf federation.

fée /fe/ nf fairy. **féerie** nf magical spectacle. **féerique** adj magical.

feindre /fɛ̃dʀ/ [22] vt feign; ~ **de** pretend to.

fêler /fele/ [1] vt crack. □ se ~ vpr crack.

félicitations /felisitasjɔ̃/ nfpl congratulations (**pour** on). **féliciter** [1] vt congratulate (**de** on).

félin, ~e /felɛ̃, -in/ a & nm feline.

femelle /fəmɛl/ a & nf female.

féminin, ~e /feminɛ̃, -in/ adj feminine; (sexe) female; (mode, équipe) women's. ● nm feminine. **féministe** nmf feminist.

femme /fam/ nf woman; (épouse) wife; ~ **au foyer** housewife; ~ **de chambre** chambermaid; ~ **de ménage** cleaning lady.

fémur /femyʀ/ nm thigh-bone.

fendre /fɑ̃dʀ/ [3] vt (couper) split; (fissurer) crack. □ se ~ vpr crack.

fenêtre /fənɛtʀ/ nf window.

fenouil /fənuj/ nm fennel.

fente /fɑ̃t/ nf (ouverture) slit, slot; (fissure) crack.

féodal, ~e (mpl **-aux**) /feodal, -o/ adj feudal.

fer /fɛʀ/ nm iron; ~ (**à repasser**) iron; ~ **à cheval** horseshoe; ~ **de lance** spearhead; ~ **forgé** wrought iron.

fera, ferait /fəʀa, fəʀɛ/ ⇒FAIRE [33].

férié, ~e /feʀje/ adj **jour ~** public holiday.

ferme /fɛʀm/ nf farm; (maison) farm (house). ● adj firm. ● adv (travailler) hard.

fermé, ~e /fɛʀme/ adj closed; (gaz, radio) off.

fermenter /fɛʀmɑ̃te/ [1] vi ferment.

fermer /fɛʀme/ [1] vt/i close, shut; (cesser d'exploiter) close ou shut down; (gaz, robinet) turn off. □ se ~ vpr close, shut.

fermeté /fɛʀməte/ nf firmness.

fermeture /fɛʀmətyʀ/ nf closing; (dispositif) catch; ~ **annuelle** annual closure; ~ **éclair**® zip(-fastener); (US) zipper.

fermier, -ière /fɛʀmje, -jɛʀ/ *adj* farm. ● *nm* farmer. **fermière** *nf* farmer's wife.

féroce /feʀɔs/ *adj* ferocious.

ferraille /feʀaj/ *nf* scrap-iron.

ferrer /feʀe/ [1] *vt* (*cheval*) shoe.

ferroviaire /feʀɔvjɛʀ/ *adj* rail(way).

ferry /feʀi/ *nm* ferry.

fertile /fɛʀtil/ *adj* fertile; ~ **en** (fig) rich in. **fertiliser** [1] *vt* fertilize. **fertilité** *nf* fertility.

fervent, ~e /fɛʀvã, -t/ *adj* fervent. ● *nm, f* enthusiast (**de** of).

fesse /fɛs/ *nf* buttock. **fessée** *nf* spanking, smack.

festin /fɛstɛ̃/ *nm* feast.

festival (*pl* ~s) /fɛstival/ *nm* festival.

fêtard, ~e /fɛtaʀ, -d/ *nm, f* Ⓘ party animal.

fête /fɛt/ *nf* holiday; (religieuse) feast; (du nom) name-day; (réception) party; (en famille) celebration; (foire) fair; (folklorique) festival; ~ **des Mères** Mother's Day; ~ **foraine** fun-fair; **faire la** ~ live it up; **les** ~s **(de fin d'année)** the Christmas season. **fêter** [1] *vt* celebrate; (*personne*) give a celebration for.

fétiche /fetiʃ/ *nm* fetish; (fig) mascot.

feu¹ (*pl* ~x) /fø/ *nm* fire; (lumière) light; (de réchaud) burner; **à** ~ **doux/vif** on a low/high heat; ~ **rouge/vert/orange** red/green/amber light; **aux** ~x, **tournez à droite** turn right at the traffic lights; **avez-vous du** ~? (pour cigarette) have you got a light?; **au** ~! fire!; **mettre le** ~ **à** set fire to; **prendre** ~ catch fire; **jouer avec le** ~ play with fire; **ne pas faire long** ~ not last; ~ **d'artifice** firework display; ~ **de joie** bonfire; ~ **de position** sidelight.

feu² /fø/ *a inv* (mort) late.

feuillage /fœjaʒ/ *nm* foliage.

feuille /fœj/ *nf* leaf; (de papier) sheet; (formulaire) form; ~ **d'impôts** tax return; ~ **de paie** payslip.

feuilleté, ~e /fœjte/ *adj* **pâte** ~**e** puff pastry. ● *nm* savoury pasty.

feuilleter /fœjte/ [1] *vt* leaf through.

feuilleton /fœjtɔ̃/ *nm* (à suivre) serial; (histoire complète) series.

feutre /føtʀ/ *nm* felt; (chapeau) felt hat; (crayon) felt-tip (pen).

fève /fɛv/ *nf* broad bean.

février /fevʀije/ *nm* February.

fiable /fjabl/ *adj* reliable.

fiançailles /fjãsaj/ *nfpl* engagement.

fiancé, ~e /fjãse/ *adj* engaged. ● *nm* fiancé. **fiancée** *nf* fiancée. **fiancer (se)** [10] *vpr* become engaged (**avec** to).

fibre /fibʀ/ *nf* fibre; ~ **de verre** fibreglass.

ficeler /fisle/ [38] *vt* tie up.

ficelle /fisɛl/ *nf* string.

fiche /fiʃ/ *nf* (index) card; (formulaire) form, slip; (Électr) plug.

ficher¹ /fiʃe/ [1] *vt* (enfoncer) drive (**dans** into).

ficher² /fiʃe/ [1] Ⓘ *vt* (faire) do; (donner) give; (mettre) put; ~ **le camp** clear off. □ **se** ~ *vpr* make fun of; **il s'en fiche** he couldn't care less.

fichier /fiʃje/ *nm* file.

fichu, ~e /fiʃy/ *adj* Ⓘ (mauvais) rotten; (raté) done for; **mal** ~ terrible.

fictif, -ive /fiktif, -v/ *adj* fictitious. **fiction** *nf* fiction.

fidèle /fidɛl/ *adj* faithful. ● *nmf* (client) regular; (Relig) believer; ~s (à l'église) congregation. **fidélité** *nf* fidelity.

fier¹, fière /fjɛʀ/ *adj* proud (**de** of).

fier² (se) /(sə)fje/ [45] *vpr* **se** ~ **à** trust.

fierté /fjɛʀte/ *nf* pride.

fièvre /fjɛvʀ/ *nf* fever; **avoir de la** ~ have a temperature. **fiévreux, -euse** *adj* feverish.

figer /fiʒe/ [40] *vi* (graisse) congeal; (sang) clot; **figé sur place** frozen to the spot. □ **se** ~ *vpr* (personne, sourire) freeze; (graisse) congeal; (sang) clot.

figue /fig/ *nf* fig.

figurant, ~e /figyʀã, -t/ *nm, f* (au cinéma) extra.

figure /figyʀ/ *nf* face; (forme, personnage) figure; (illustration) picture.

figuré, ~e /figyʀe/ *adj* (sens) figurative.

figurer /figyʀe/ [1] *vi* appear. ● *vt* represent. □ **se** ~ *vpr* imagine.

fil /fil/ *nm* thread; (métallique, électrique) wire; (de couteau) edge; (à coudre) cotton; **au** ~ **de** with the passing of; **au** ~ **de l'eau** with the current; ~ **de fer** wire; **au bout du** ~ 🔲 on the phone.

file /fil/ *nf* line; (voie: Auto) lane; ~ **(d'attente)** queue; (US) line; **en** ~ **indienne** in single file.

filer /file/ [1] *vt* spin; (suivre) shadow; ~ **qch à qn** 🔲 slip sb sth. ● *vi* (*bas*) ladder, run; (*liquide*) run; (aller vite 🔲) speed along, fly by; (partir 🔲) dash off; (disparaître 🔲) ~ **entre les mains** slip through one's fingers; ~ **doux** do as one's told; ~ **à l'anglaise** take French leave.

filet /filɛ/ *nm* net; (d'eau) trickle; (de viande) fillet; ~ **(à bagages)** (luggage) rack; ~ **à provisions** string bag (*for shopping*).

filiale /filjal/ *nf* subsidiary (company).

filière /filjɛʀ/ *nf* (official) channels; (de trafiquants) network; **passer par** *ou* **suivre la** ~ (*employé*) work one's way up.

fille /fij/ *nf* girl; (opposé à fils) daughter. **fillette** *nf* little girl.

filleul /fijœl/ *nm* godson.

filleule /fijœl/ *nf* god-daughter.

film /film/ *nm* film; ~ **d'épouvante/ muet/parlant** horror/silent/talking film; ~ **dramatique** drama. **filmer** [1] *vt* film.

filon /filɔ̃/ *nm* (Géol) seam; (travail lucratif 🔲) money spinner; **avoir trouvé le bon** ~ be onto a good thing.

fils /fis/ *nm* son.

filtre /filtʀ/ *nm* filter. **filtrer** [1] *vt/i* filter; (*personne*) screen.

fin¹ /fɛ̃/ *nf* end; **à la** ~ finally; **en** ~ **de compte** all things considered; ~ **de semaine** weekend; **mettre** ~ **à** put an end to; **prendre** ~ come to an end.

fin², ~**e** /fɛ̃, in/ *adj* fine; (*tranche, couche*) thin; (*taille*) slim; (*plat*) exquisite; (*esprit, vue*) sharp; ~**es herbes** mixed herbs. ● *adv* (*couper*) finely.

final, ~**e** (*mpl* **-aux**) /final, -o/ *adj* final.

finale /final/ *nm* (Mus) finale. ● *nf* (Sport) final; (Gram) final syllable. **finalement** *adv* finally; (somme toute) after all. **finaliste** *nmf* finalist.

finance /finɑ̃s/ *nf* finance. **financer** [10] *vt* finance.

financier, -ière /finɑ̃sje, -jɛʀ/ *adj* financial. ● *nm* financier.

finesse /finɛs/ *nf* fineness; (de taille) slimness; (acuité) sharpness; ~**s** (de langue) niceties.

finir /finiʀ/ [2] *vt/i* finish, end; (arrêter) stop; (manger) finish (up); **en** ~ **avec** have done with; ~ **par faire** end up doing; **ça va mal** ~ it will turn out badly.

finlandais, ~**e** /fɛ̃lɑ̃dɛ, -z/ *adj* Finnish. **F**~, ~**e** *nm,f* Finn.

Finlande /fɛ̃lɑ̃d/ *nf* Finland.

finnois, ~**e** /finwa/ *adj* Finnish. ● *nm* (Ling) Finnish.

firme /fiʀm/ *nf* firm.

fisc /fisk/ *nm* tax authorities. **fiscal**, ~**e** (*mpl* **-aux**) *adj* tax, fiscal. **fiscalité** *nf* tax system.

fissure /fisyʀ/ *nf* crack.

fixe /fiks/ *adj* fixed; (stable) steady; **à heure** ~ at a set time; **menu à prix** ~ set menu. ● *nm* basic pay.

fixer /fikse/ [1] *vt* fix; ~ **(du regard)** stare at; **être fixé** (*personne*) have made up one's mind. □ **se** ~ *vpr* (s'attacher) be attached; (s'installer) settle down.

flacon /flakɔ̃/ *nm* bottle.

flagrant, ~**e** /flagʀɑ̃, -t/ *adj* flagrant, blatant; **en** ~ **délit** in the act.

flair /flɛʀ/ *nm* (sense of) smell; (fig) intuition.

flamand, ~**e** /flamɑ̃, -d/ *adj* Flemish. ● *nm* (Ling) Flemish. **F**~, ~**e** *nm,f* Fleming.

flamant /flamɑ̃/ *nm* flamingo.

flambeau (*pl* ~**x**) /flɑ̃bo/ *nm* torch.

flambée /flɑ̃be/ *nf* blaze; (fig) explosion.

flamber /flɑ̃be/ [1] *vi* blaze; (*prix*) shoot up. ● *vt* (*aiguille*) sterilize; (*volaille*) singe.

flamme /flam/ *nf* flame; (fig) ardour; **en ~s** ablaze.

flan /flã/ *nm* custard tart.

flanc /flã/ *nm* side; (d'animal, d'armée) flank.

flâner /flɑne/ [1] *vi* stroll. **flânerie** *nf* stroll.

flanquer /flɑ̃ke/ [1] *vt* flank; (jeter 🔢) chuck; (donner 🔢) give; **~ à la porte** kick out.

flaque /flak/ *nf* (d'eau) puddle; (de sang) pool.

flash (*pl* **~es**) /flaʃ/ *nm* (Photo) flash; (information) news flash; **~ publicitaire** commercial.

flatter /flate/ [1] *vt* flatter. □ **se ~ de** *vpr* pride oneself on.

flatteur, -euse /flatœʀ, -øz/ *adj* flattering. ● *nm,f* flatterer.

fléau (*pl* **~x**) /fleo/ *nm* (désastre) scourge; (personne) pest.

flèche /flɛʃ/ *nf* arrow; (de clocher) spire; **monter en ~** spiral; **partir en ~** shoot off.

flécher /fleʃe/ [14] *vt* mark *ou* signpost (with arrows). **fléchette** *nf* dart.

fléchir /fleʃiʀ/ [2] *vt* bend; (*personne*) move, sway. ● *vi* (faiblir) weaken; (*prix*) fall; (*poutre*) sag, bend.

flemme /flɛm/ *nf* 🔢 laziness; **j'ai la ~ de faire** I can't be bothered doing.

flétrir (se) /(sə)fletʀiʀ/ [2] *vpr* (*plante*) wither; (*fruit*) shrivel; (*beauté*) fade.

fleur /flœʀ/ *nf* flower; **à ~ de terre/ d'eau** just above the ground/water; **à ~s** flowery; **~ de l'âge** prime of life; **en ~s** in flower.

fleurir /flœʀiʀ/ [2] *vi* flower; (*arbre*) blossom; (fig) flourish. ● *vt* decorate with flowers. **fleuriste** *nmf* florist.

fleuve /flœv/ *nm* river.

flic /flik/ *nm* 🔢 cop.

flipper /flipœʀ/ *nm* pinball (machine).

flirter /flœʀte/ [1] *vi* flirt.

flocon /flɔkɔ̃/ *nm* flake.

flore /flɔʀ/ *nf* flora.

florissant, ~e /flɔʀisã, -t/ *adj* flourishing.

flot /flo/ *nm* flood, stream; **être à ~** be afloat; **les ~s** the waves.

flottant, ~e /flɔtã, -t/ *adj* (*vêtement*) loose; (indécis) indecisive.

flotte /flɔt/ *nf* fleet; (pluie 🔢) rain; (eau 🔢) water.

flottement /flɔtmã/ *nm* (incertitude) indecision.

flotter /flɔte/ [1] *vi* float; (*drapeau*) flutter; (*nuage, parfum, pensées*) drift; (pleuvoir 🔢) rain. **flotteur** *nm* float.

flou, ~e /flu/ *adj* out of focus; (fig) vague.

fluctuer /flyktɥe/ [1] *vi* fluctuate.

fluet, ~te /flyɛ, -t/ *adj* thin.

fluide /flɥid/ *a* & *nm* fluid.

fluor /flyɔʀ/ *nm* (pour les dents) fluoride.

fluorescent, ~e /flyɔʀesã, -t/ *adj* fluorescent.

flûte /flyt/ *nf* flute; (verre) champagne glass.

fluvial, ~e (*mpl* **-iaux**) /flyvjal, -jo/ *adj* river.

flux /fly/ *nm* flow; **~ et reflux** ebb and flow.

FM *abrév f* (**frequency modulation**) FM.

fœtus /fetys/ *nm* foetus.

foi /fwa/ *nf* faith; **être de bonne/ mauvaise ~** be acting in good/bad faith; **ma ~!** well (indeed)!

foie /fwa/ *nm* liver.

foin /fwɛ̃/ *nm* hay.

foire /fwaʀ/ *nf* fair; **faire la ~** 🔢 live it up.

fois /fwa/ *nf* time; **une ~** once; **deux ~** twice; **à la ~** at the same time; **des ~** (parfois) sometimes; **une ~ pour toutes** once and for all.

fol /fɔl/ ⇒**FOU**.

folie /fɔli/ *nf* madness; (bêtise) foolish thing, folly; **faire une ~, faire des ~s** be extravagant.

folklore /fɔlklɔʀ/ *nm* folklore. **folklorique** *adj* folk; 🔢 eccentric.

folle /fɔl/ ⇒**FOU**.

foncé, ~e /fɔ̃se/ *adj* dark.

foncer /fɔ̃se/ [10] *vt* darken. ● *vi* (s'assombrir) darken; (aller vite 🔢) dash along; **~ sur** 🔢 charge at.

foncier, -ière /fɔ̃sje, -jɛʀ/ *adj* fundamental; (Comm) real estate.

fonction /fɔ̃ksjɔ̃/ *nf* function; (emploi) position; ~s (obligations) duties; **en ~ de** according to; ~ **publique** civil service; **voiture de ~** company car. **fonctionnaire** *nmf* civil servant. **fonctionnement** *nm* working.

fonctionner /fɔ̃ksjɔne/ [1] *vi* work; **faire ~** work.

fond /fɔ̃/ *nm* bottom; (de salle, magasin, etc.) back; (essentiel) basis; (contenu) content; (plan) background; (Sport) long-distance running; **à ~** thoroughly; **au ~** basically; **de ~** (bruit) background; **de ~ en comble** from top to bottom; **au** *ou* **dans le ~** really; ~ **de teint** foundation, make-up base.

fondamental, ~**e** (*mpl* -**aux**) /fɔ̃damɑ̃tal, -o/ *adj* fundamental.

fondateur, -**trice** /fɔ̃datœʀ, -tʀis/ *nm,f* founder. **fondation** *nf* foundation.

fonder /fɔ̃de/ [1] *vt* found; (baser) base (**sur** on); (bien) **fondé** well-founded. □ **se ~ sur** *vpr* be guided by, be based on.

fonderie /fɔ̃dʀi/ *nf* foundry.

fondre /fɔ̃dʀ/ [3] *vt/i* melt; (dans l'eau) dissolve; (mélanger) merge; **faire ~** melt; dissolve; ~ **en larmes** burst into tears; ~ **sur** swoop on. □ **se ~** *vpr* merge.

fonds /fɔ̃/ *nm* fund; ~ **de commerce** business. ● *nmpl* (capitaux) funds.

fondu, ~**e** /fɔ̃dy/ *adj* melted; (métal) molten.

font /fɔ̃/ ⇒FAIRE [33].

fontaine /fɔ̃tɛn/ *nf* fountain; (source) spring.

fonte /fɔ̃t/ *nf* melting; (fer) cast iron; ~ **des neiges** thaw.

foot /fut/ *nm* 🔲 football.

football /futbol/ *nm* football.

footing /futiŋ/ *nm* jogging.

forain /fɔʀɛ̃/ *nm* fairground entertainer; **marchand ~** stall-holder.

forçat /fɔʀsa/ *nm* convict.

force /fɔʀs/ *nf* force; (physique) strength; (hydraulique etc.) power; ~**s** (physiques) strength; **à ~ de** by sheer force of; **de ~, par la ~** by force; ~ **de dissuasion** deterrent; ~ **de frappe** strike force, deterrent; ~ **de l'âge** prime of life; ~**s de l'ordre** police (force); ~**s de marché** market forces.

forcé, ~**e** /fɔʀse/ *adj* forced; (inévitable) inevitable; **c'est ~ qu'il fasse** 🔲 he's bound to do. **forcément** *adv* necessarily; (évidemment) obviously.

forcené, ~**e** /fɔʀsəne/ *adj* frenzied. ● *nm,f* maniac.

forcer /fɔʀse/ [10] *vt* force (**à faire** to do); (voix) strain; ~ **la dose** 🔲 overdo it. ● *vi* force; (exagérer) overdo it. □ **se ~** *vpr* force oneself.

forer /fɔʀe/ [1] *vt* drill.

forestier, -**ière** /fɔʀɛstje, -jɛʀ/ *adj* forest. ● *nm,f* forestry worker.

forêt /fɔʀɛ/ *nf* forest.

forfait /fɔʀfɛ/ *nm* (Comm) (prix fixe) fixed price; (offre promotionnelle) package. **forfaitaire** *adj* (prix) fixed.

forger /fɔʀʒe/ [40] *vt* forge; (inventer) make up.

forgeron /fɔʀʒəʀɔ̃/ *nm* blacksmith.

formaliser (se) /(sə)fɔʀmalize/ [1] *vpr* take offence (**de** at).

formalité /fɔʀmalite/ *nf* formality.

format /fɔʀma/ *nm* format. **formater** [1] *vt* (Ordinat) format.

formation /fɔʀmasjɔ̃/ *nf* formation; (professionnelle) training; (culture) education; ~ **permanente** *ou* **continue** continuing education.

forme /fɔʀm/ *nf* form; (contour) shape, form; ~**s** (de femme) figure; **être en ~** be in good shape, be on form; **en ~ de** in the shape of; **en bonne et due** ~ in due form.

formel, ~**le** /fɔʀmɛl/ *adj* formal; (catégorique) positive.

former /fɔʀme/ [1] *vt* form; (instruire) train. □ **se ~** *vpr* form.

formidable /fɔʀmidabl/ *adj* fantastic.

formulaire /fɔʀmylɛʀ/ *nm* form.

formule /fɔʀmyl/ *nf* formula; (expression) expression; (feuille) form; ~ **de politesse** polite phrase, letter ending. **formuler** [1] *vt* formulate.

fort, ~**e** /fɔʀ, -t/ *adj* strong; (grand) big; (pluie) heavy; (bruit) loud; (pente) steep; (élève) clever; **au plus ~ de** at the height of; **c'est une ~e tête** she/he's headstrong. ● *adv* (*frapper*) hard; (*parler*) loud; (très) very; (beaucoup) very much. ● *nm* (atout) strong point; (Mil) fort.

fortifiant /fɔʀtifjɑ̃/ *nm* tonic. **fortifier** [45] *vt* fortify.

fortune /fɔʀtyn/ *nf* fortune; de ∼ (improvisé) makeshift; faire ∼ make one's fortune.

forum /fɔʀɔm/ *nm* forum; ∼ de discussion (Internet) newsgroup.

fosse /fos/ *nf* pit; (tombe) grave; ∼ d'orchestre orchestra pit; ∼ septique septic tank.

fossé /fose/ *nm* ditch; (fig) gulf.

fossette /fosɛt/ *nf* dimple.

fossile /fosil/ *nm* fossil.

fou (**fol** *before vowel or mute h*), **folle** /fu, fɔl/ *adj* mad; (*course, regard*) wild; (énorme 🔢) tremendous; ∼ de crazy about; le ∼ rire the giggles. ● *nm* madman; (bouffon) jester. **folle** *nf* madwoman.

foudre /fudʀ/ *nf* lightning.

foudroyant, ∼e /fudʀwajɑ̃, -t/ *adj* (*mort, maladie*) violent.

foudroyer /fudʀwaje/ [31] *vt* (*orage*) strike; (*maladie etc.*) strike down; ∼ qn du regard look daggers at sb.

fouet /fwɛ/ *nm* whip; (Culin) whisk.

fougère /fuʒɛʀ/ *nf* fern.

fougue /fug/ *nf* ardour. **fougueux**, **-euse** *adj* ardent.

fouille /fuj/ *nf* search; (Archéol) excavation.

fouiller /fuje/ [1] *vt/i* search; (creuser) dig; ∼ dans (tiroir) rummage through.

fouillis /fuji/ *nm* jumble.

foulard /fulaʀ/ *nm* scarf.

foule /ful/ *nf* crowd; une ∼ de (fig) a mass of.

foulée /fule/ *nf* stride; il l'a fait dans la ∼ he did it while he was at *ou* about it.

fouler /fule/ [1] *vt* (*raisin*) press; (*sol*) set foot on; ∼ qch aux pieds trample sth underfoot; (fig) ride roughshod over sth. ▢ se ∼ *vpr* se ∼ le poignet/le pied sprain one's wrist/foot; ne pas se ∼ 🔢 not strain oneself.

four /fuʀ/ *nm* oven; (de potier) kiln; (Théât) flop; ∼ à micro-ondes

microwave oven; ∼ crématoire crematorium.

fourbe /fuʀb/ *adj* deceitful.

fourche /fuʀʃ/ *nf* fork; (à foin) pitchfork. **fourchette** *nf* fork; (Comm) bracket, range.

fourgon /fuʀgɔ̃/ *nm* van; (wagon) wagon; ∼ mortuaire hearse.

fourmi /fuʀmi/ *nf* ant; avoir des ∼s have pins and needles.

fourmiller /fuʀmije/ [1] *vi* swarm (de with).

fourneau (*pl* ∼x) /fuʀno/ *nm* stove.

fourni, ∼e /fuʀni/ *adj* (épais) thick.

fournir /fuʀniʀ/ [2] *vt* supply, provide; (*client*) supply; (*effort*) put in; ∼ à qn supply sb with. ▢ se ∼ chez *vpr* shop at.

fournisseur /fuʀnisœʀ/ *nm* supplier; ∼ d'accès à l'Internet Internet service provider.

fourniture /fuʀnityʀ/ *nf* supply.

fourrage /fuʀaʒ/ *nm* fodder.

fourré, ∼e /fuʀe/ *adj* (*vêtement*) fur-lined; (*gâteau etc.*) filled (*with jam, cream, etc.*). ● *nm* thicket.

fourre-tout /fuʀtu/ *nm inv* (sac) holdall.

fourreur /fuʀœʀ/ *nm* furrier.

fourrière /fuʀjɛʀ/ *nf* (lieu) pound.

fourrure /fuʀyʀ/ *nf* fur.

foutre /futʀ/ [3] *vt* 🔀 = **ficher²** [1].

foutu, ∼e /futy/ *adj* 🔀 = **fichu**.

foyer /fwaje/ *nm* home; (âtre) hearth; (club) club; (d'étudiants) hostel; (Théât) foyer; (Photo) focus; (centre) centre.

fracas /fʀaka/ *nm* din; (de train) roar; (d'objet qui tombe) crash. **fracassant**, ∼e *adj* (bruyant) deafening; (violent) shattering.

fraction /fʀaksjɔ̃/ *nf* fraction.

fracture /fʀaktyʀ/ *nf* fracture; ∼ du poignet fractured wrist.

fragile /fʀaʒil/ *adj* fragile; (*peau*) sensitive; (*cœur*) weak. **fragilité** *nf* fragility.

fragment /fʀagmɑ̃/ *nm* bit, fragment. **fragmenter** [1] *vt* split, fragment.

fraîchement /fʀɛʃmɑ̃/ *adv* (récemment) freshly; (avec froideur) coolly. **fraîcheur** *nf* coolness;

(nouveauté) freshness. **fraîchir** [2] *vi* freshen, become colder.

frais¹, fraîche /fʀɛ, -ʃ/ *adj* fresh; (*temps, accueil*) cool; (*peinture*) wet; ∼ **et dispos** fresh; **il fait** ∼ it is cool. ● *adv* (*récemment*) newly, freshly. ● *nm* **mettre au** ∼ put in a cool place; **prendre le** ∼ get some fresh air.

frais² /fʀɛ/ *nmpl* expenses; (droits) fees; **aux** ∼ **de** at the expense of; **faire des** ∼ spend a lot of money; ∼ **généraux** (Comm) overheads, running expenses; ∼ **de scolarité** school fees.

fraise /fʀɛz/ *nf* strawberry. **fraisier** *nm* strawberry plant; (gâteau) strawberry gateau.

framboise /fʀɑ̃bwaz/ *nf* raspberry. **framboisier** *nm* raspberry bush.

franc, franche /fʀɑ̃, -ʃ/ *adj* frank; (*regard*) frank, candid; (*cassure*) clean; (net) clear; (libre) free; (véritable) downright. ● *nm* franc.

français, ∼e /fʀɑ̃sɛ, -z/ *adj* French. ● *nm* (Ling) French. **F∼, ∼e** *nm,f* Frenchman, Frenchwoman.

France /fʀɑ̃s/ *nf* France.

franchement /fʀɑ̃ʃmɑ̃/ *adv* frankly; (nettement) clearly; (tout à fait) really.

franchir /fʀɑ̃ʃiʀ/ [2] *vt* (obstacle) get over; (distance) cover; (limite) exceed; (traverser) cross.

franchise /fʀɑ̃ʃiz/ *nf* (qualité) frankness; (Comm) franchise; (exemption) exemption; ∼ **douanière** exemption from duties.

franc-maçon (*pl* **francs-maçons**) /fʀɑ̃masɔ̃/ *nm* Freemason. **franc-maçonnerie** *nf* Freemasonry.

franco /fʀɑ̃ko/ *adv* postage paid.

francophone /fʀɑ̃kɔfɔn/ *adj* French-speaking. ● *nmf* French speaker.

franc-parler /fʀɑ̃paʀle/ *nm inv* outspokenness.

frange /fʀɑ̃ʒ/ *nf* fringe.

frappe /fʀap/ *nf* (de texte) typing.

frappé, ∼e /fʀape/ *adj* chilled.

frapper /fʀape/ [1] *vt/i* strike; (battre) hit, strike; (monnaie) mint; (à la porte) knock, bang; **frappé de panique** panic-stricken.

fraternel, ∼le /fʀatɛʀnɛl/ *adj* brotherly. **fraternité** *nf* brotherhood.

fraude /fʀod/ *nf* fraud; (à un examen) cheating; **passer qch en** ∼ smuggle sth in. **frauder** [1] *vt/i* cheat. **frauduleux, -euse** *adj* fraudulent.

frayer /fʀeje/ [31] *vt* open up. □ **se** ∼ *vpr* **se** ∼ **un passage** force one's way (à travers, dans through).

frayeur /fʀɛjœʀ/ *nf* fright.

fredonner /fʀədɔne/ [1] *vt* hum.

free-lance /fʀilɑ̃s/ *a & nmf* freelance.

freezer /fʀizœʀ/ *nm* freezer.

frein /fʀɛ̃/ *nm* brake; **mettre un** ∼ **à** curb; ∼ **à main** hand brake.

freiner /fʀene/ [1] *vt* slow down; (modérer, enrayer) curb. ● *vi* (Auto) brake.

frêle /fʀɛl/ *adj* frail.

frelon /fʀəlɔ̃/ *nm* hornet.

frémir /fʀemiʀ/ [2] *vi* shudder, shake; (feuille, eau) quiver.

frêne /fʀɛn/ *nm* ash.

frénésie /fʀenezi/ *nf* frenzy. **frénétique** *adj* frenzied.

fréquemment /fʀekamɑ̃/ *adv* frequently. **fréquence** *nf* frequency. **fréquent, ∼e** *adj* frequent. **fréquentation** *nf* frequenting.

fréquentations /fʀekɑ̃tasjɔ̃/ *nfpl* acquaintances; **avoir de mauvaises** ∼ keep bad company.

fréquenter /fʀekɑ̃te/ [1] *vt* frequent; (école) attend; (personne) see.

frère /fʀɛʀ/ *nm* brother.

fret /fʀɛt/ *nm* freight.

friand, ∼e /fʀijɑ̃, -d/ *adj* ∼ **de** very fond of.

friandise /fʀijɑ̃diz/ *nf* sweet; (US) candy; (gâteau) cake.

fric /fʀik/ *nm* 🔲 money.

friction /fʀiksjɔ̃/ *nf* friction; (massage) rub-down.

frigidaire® /fʀiʒidɛʀ/ *nm* refrigerator.

frigo /fʀigo/ *nm* 🔲 fridge. **frigorifique** *adj* (vitrine etc.) refrigerated.

frileux, -euse /fʀilø, -z/ *adj* sensitive to cold.

frime /fʀim/ nf 🗆 c'est de la ~ it's all pretence; **pour la** ~ for show.

frimousse /fʀimus/ nf face.

fringale /fʀɛ̃gal/ nf 🗆 ravenous appetite.

fringant, **~e** /fʀɛ̃gɑ̃, -t/ adj dashing.

fringues /fʀɛ̃g/ nfpl 🗆 gear.

friper /fʀipe/ [1] vt crumple, crease. 🗆 **se** ~ vpr crumple, crease.

fripon, **~ne** /fʀipɔ̃, -ɔn/ nm, f rascal. ● adj mischievous.

fripouille /fʀipuj/ nf rogue.

frire /fʀiʀ/ [56] vt/i fry; **faire** ~ fry.

frise /fʀiz/ nf frieze.

friser /fʀize/ [1] vt/i (cheveux) curl; (personne) curl the hair of; **frisé** curly.

frisson /fʀisɔ̃/ nm (de froid) shiver; (de peur) shudder. **frissonner** [1] vi shiver; shudder.

frit, **~e** /fʀi, -t/ adj fried.

frite /fʀit/ nf chip; **avoir la** ~ 🗆 feel good.

friteuse /fʀitøz/ nf chip pan; (électrique) (deep) fryer.

friture /fʀityʀ/ nf fried fish; (huile) (frying) oil ou fat.

frivole /fʀivɔl/ adj frivolous.

froid, **~e** /fʀwa, -d/ a & nm cold; **avoir/prendre** ~ be/catch cold; **il fait** ~ it is cold. **froidement** adv coldly; (calculer) coolly. **froideur** nf coldness.

froisser /fʀwase/ [1] vt crumple; (fig) offend. 🗆 **se** ~ vpr crumple; (fig) take offence; **se** ~ **un muscle** strain a muscle.

frôler /fʀole/ [1] vt brush against, skim; (fig) come close to.

fromage /fʀɔmaʒ/ nm cheese.

fromager, **-ère** /fʀɔmaʒe, -ɛʀ/ adj cheese. ● nm, f (fabricant) cheese-maker; (marchand) cheesemonger.

froment /fʀɔmɑ̃/ nm wheat.

froncer /fʀɔ̃se/ [10] vt gather; ~ **les sourcils** frown.

front /fʀɔ̃/ nm forehead; (Mil, Pol) front; **de** ~ at the same time; (de face) head-on; (côte à côte) abreast; **faire** ~ à face up to. **frontal**, **~e** (mpl **-aux**) adj frontal; (Ordinat) front-end.

frontalier, **-ière** /fʀɔ̃talje, -jɛʀ/ adj border; **travailleur** ~ commuter from across the border.

frontière /fʀɔ̃tjɛʀ/ nf border, frontier.

frottement /fʀɔtmɑ̃/ nm rubbing; (Tech) friction. **frotter** [1] vt/i rub; (allumette) strike.

frottis /fʀɔti/ nm ~ **vaginal cervical** smear.

frousse /fʀus/ nf 🗆 fear; **avoir la** ~ 🗆 be scared.

fructifier /fʀyktifje/ [45] vi **faire** ~ put to work.

fructueux, **-euse** /fʀyktɥø, -z/ adj fruitful.

frugal, **~e** (mpl **-aux**) /fʀygal, -o/ adj frugal.

fruit /fʀɥi/ nm fruit; **des** ~s (some) fruit; ~s **de mer** seafood. **fruité**, **~e** adj fruity.

frustrant, **~e** /fʀystʀɑ̃, -t / adj frustrating. **frustrer** [1] vt frustrate.

fuel /fjul/ nm fuel oil.

fugitif, **-ive** /fyʒitif, -v/ adj (passager) fleeting. ● nm, f fugitive.

fugue /fyg/ nf (Mus) fugue; **faire une** ~ run away.

fuir /fɥiʀ/ [35] vi flee, run away; (eau, robinet, etc.) leak. ● vt (quitter) flee; (éviter) shun.

fuite /fɥit/ nf flight; (de liquide, d'une nouvelle) leak; **en** ~ on the run; **mettre en** ~ put to flight; **prendre la** ~ take flight.

fulgurant, **~e** /fylgyʀɑ̃, -t/ adj (vitesse) lightning.

fumé, **~e** /fyme/ adj (poisson, verre) smoked.

fumée /fyme/ nf smoke; (vapeur) steam.

fumer /fyme/ [1] vt/i smoke.

fumeur, **-euse** /fymœʀ, -øz/ nm, f smoker; **zone non-~s** no smoking area.

fumier /fymje/ nm manure.

funambule /fynɑ̃byl/ nmf tightrope walker.

funèbre /fynɛbʀ/ adj funeral; (fig) gloomy.

funérailles /fyneʀaj/ nfpl funeral.

funéraire /fyneʀɛʀ/ adj funeral.

funeste /fynɛst/ adj fatal.

f

fur: au ~ et à mesure /ofyʀea-məzyʀ/ *loc* as one goes along, progressively; **au ~ et à mesure que** as.

furet /fyʀɛ/ *nm* ferret.

fureur /fyʀœʀ/ *nf* fury; (passion) passion; **avec ~** furiously; passionately; **mettre en ~** infuriate; **faire ~** be all the rage.

furieux, -ieuse /fyʀjø, -z/ *adj* furious.

furoncle /fyʀɔ̃kl/ *nm* boil.

furtif, -ive /fyʀtif, -v/ *adj* furtive.

fuseau (*pl* ~**x**) /fyzo/ *nm* ski trousers; (pour filer) spindle; **~ horaire** time zone.

fusée /fyze/ *nf* rocket.

fusible /fyzibl/ *nm* fuse.

fusil /fyzi/ *nm* rifle, gun; (de chasse) shotgun; **~ mitrailleur** machine-gun.

fusion /fyzjɔ̃/ *nf* fusion; (Comm) merger. **fusionner** [1] *vt/i* merge.

fut /fy/ ⇒ÊTRE [5].

fût /fy/ *nm* (tonneau) barrel; (d'arbre) trunk.

futé, ~e /fyte/ *adj* cunning.

futile /fytil/ *adj* futile.

futur, ~e /fytyʀ/ *adj* future; **~e femme-/maman** wife-/mother-to-be. ● *nm* future.

fuyant, ~e /fɥijɑ̃, -t/ *adj* (*front, ligne*) receding; (*personne*) evasive.

fuyard, ~e /fɥijaʀ, -d/ *nm,f* runaway.

Gg

gabardine /gabaʀdin/ *nf* raincoat.

gabarit /gabaʀi/ *nm* size; (patron) template; (fig) calibre.

gâcher /gɑʃe/ [1] *vt* (gâter) spoil; (gaspiller) waste.

gâchette /gɑʃɛt/ *nf* trigger.

gâchis /gɑʃi/ *nm* waste.

gaffe /gaf/ *nf* 🔲 blunder; **faire ~** be careful (à of).

gage /gaʒ/ *nm* security; (de bonne foi) pledge; (de jeu) forfeit; **~s** (salaire)

wages; **en ~ de** as a token of; **mettre en ~** pawn; **tueur à ~s** hired killer.

gageure /gaʒyʀ/ *nf* challenge.

gagnant, ~e /gaɲɑ̃, -t/ *adj* winning. ● *nm,f* winner.

gagne-pain /gaɲpɛ̃/ *nm inv* job.

gagner /gaɲe/ [1] *vt* (*match, prix*) win; (*argent, pain*) earn; (*terrain*) gain; (*temps*) save; (atteindre) reach; (convaincre) win over; **~ sa vie** earn one's living. ● *vi* win; (fig) gain.

gai, ~e /ge/ *adj* cheerful; (ivre) merry. **gaiement** *adv* cheerfully. **gaieté** *nf* cheerfulness.

gain /gɛ̃/ *nm* (salaire) earnings; (avantage) gain; (économie) saving; **~s** (Comm) profits; (au jeu) winnings.

gaine /gɛn/ *nf* (corset) girdle; (étui) sheath.

galant, ~e /galɑ̃, -t/ *adj* courteous; (amoureux) romantic.

galaxie /galaksi/ *nf* galaxy.

gale /gal/ *nf* (de chat etc.) mange.

galère /galɛʀ/ *nf* (navire) galley; **c'est la ~!** 🔲 what an ordeal!

galérer /galeʀe/ [14] *vi* 🔲 (peiner) have a hard time.

galerie /galʀi/ *nf* gallery; (Théât) circle; (de voiture) roof-rack; **~ marchande** shopping arcade.

galet /galɛ/ *nm* pebble.

galette /galɛt/ *nf* flat cake; **~ des Rois** Twelfth Night cake.

Galles /gal/ *nfpl* **le pays de ~** Wales.

gallois, ~e /galwa, -z/ *adj* Welsh. ● *nm* (Ling) Welsh. **G~, ~e** *nm,f* Welshman, Welshwoman.

galon /galɔ̃/ *nm* braid; (Mil) stripe; **prendre du ~** be promoted.

galop /galo/ *nm* canter; **aller au ~** canter; **grand ~** gallop; **~ d'essai** trial run. **galoper** [1] *vi* (*cheval*) canter; (au grand galop) gallop; (*personne*) run.

galopin /galɔpɛ̃/ *nm* 🔲 rascal.

gambader /gɑ̃bade/ [1] *vi* leap about.

gamelle /gamɛl/ *nf* (de soldat) mess kit; (d'ouvrier) lunch-box.

gamin, ~e /gamɛ̃, -in/ *adj* childish; (*air*) youthful. ● *nm,f* 🔲 kid.

gamme /gam/ *nf* (Mus) scale; (série) range; **haut de ~** up-market, top of the range; **bas de ~** down-market, bottom of the range.

gang /gɑ̃g/ *nm* 🔢 gang.

ganglion /gɑ̃glijɔ̃/ *nm* ganglion.

gangster /gɑ̃gstɛʀ/ *nm* gangster; (escroc) crook.

gant /gɑ̃/ *nm* glove; **~ de ménage** rubber glove; **~ de toilette** face-flannel, face-cloth.

garage /gaʀaʒ/ *nm* garage. **garagiste** *nmf* garage owner; (employé) car mechanic.

garant, **~e** /gaʀɑ̃, -t/ *nm,f* guarantor. ● *adj* **se porter ~ de** vouch for.

garanti, **~e** /gaʀɑ̃ti/ *adj* guaranteed.

garantie /gaʀɑ̃ti/ *nf* guarantee; **~s** (de police d'assurance) cover. **garantir** [2] *vt* guarantee; (protéger) protect (**de** from).

garçon /gaʀsɔ̃/ *nm* boy; (jeune homme) young man; (célibataire) bachelor; **~ (de café)** waiter; **~ d'honneur** best man. **garçonnière** *nf* bachelor flat.

garde¹ /gaʀd/ *nf* guard; (d'enfants, de bagages) care; (service) guard (duty); (infirmière) nurse; **de ~** on duty; **~ à vue** (police) custody; **mettre en ~** warn; **prendre ~** be careful (**à** of); (droit de) **~** custody (**de** of).

garde² /gaʀd/ *nm* guard; (de propriété, parc) warden; **~ champêtre** village policeman; **~ du corps** bodyguard.

garde-à-vous /gaʀdavu/ *nm inv* (Mil) **se mettre au ~** stand to attention.

garde-chasse (*pl* **~s**) /gaʀdəʃas/ *nm* gamekeeper.

garde-manger /gaʀdmɑ̃ʒe/ *nm inv* meat safe; (placard) larder.

garder /gaʀde/ [1] *vt* (conserver, maintenir) keep; (vêtement) keep on; (surveiller) look after; (défendre) guard; **~ le lit** stay in bed. □ **se ~** *vpr* (denrée) keep; **se ~ de faire** be careful not to do.

garderie /gaʀdəʀi/ *nf* day nursery.

garde-robe (*pl* **~s**) /gaʀdəʀɔb/ *nf* wardrobe.

gardien, **~ne** /gaʀdjɛ̃, -ɛn/ *nm,f* (de locaux) security guard; (de prison, réserve) warden; (d'immeuble) caretaker; (de musée) attendant; (de zoo) keeper; (de traditions) guardian; **~ de but** goalkeeper; **~ de la paix** policeman; **~ de nuit** night watchman; **gardienne d'enfants** childminder.

gare /gaʀ/ *nf* (Rail) station; **~ routière** coach station; (US) bus station. ● *interj* **(à toi)** watch out!

garer /gaʀe/ [1] *vt* park. □ **se ~** *vpr* park; (s'écarter) move out of the way.

gargouille /gaʀguj/ *nf* water-spout; (sculptée) gargoyle. **gargouiller** [1] *vi* gurgle; (stomach) rumble.

garni, **~e** /gaʀni/ *adj* (plat) served with vegetables; **bien ~** (rempli) well-filled.

garnir /gaʀniʀ/ [2] *vt* (remplir) fill; (décorer) decorate; (couvrir) cover; (doubler) line; (Culin) garnish. **garniture** *nf* (légumes) vegetables; (ornement) trimming; (de voiture) trim.

gars /gɑ/ *nm* 🔢 lad; (adulte) guy, bloke.

gas-oil /gazwal/ *nm* diesel (oil).

gaspillage /gaspijaʒ/ *nm* waste. **gaspiller** [1] *vt* waste.

gastrique /gastʀik/ *adj* gastric.

gastronome /gastʀɔnɔm/ *nmf* gourmet.

gâteau (*pl* **~x**) /gɑto/ *nm* cake; **~ sec** biscuit; (US) cookie; **un papa ~** a doting dad.

gâter /gɑte/ [1] *vt* spoil. □ **se ~** *vpr* (viande) go bad; (dent) rot; (temps) get worse.

gâterie /gɑtʀi/ *nf* little treat.

gâteux, **-euse** /gɑtø, -z/ *adj* senile.

gauche /goʃ/ *adj* left; (maladroit) awkward. ● *nf* left; **à ~** on the left; (direction) (to the) left; **la ~** the left (side); (Pol) the left (wing).

gaucher, **-ère** /goʃe, -ɛʀ/ *adj* left-handed.

gaufre /gofʀ/ *nf* waffle. **gaufrette** *nf* wafer.

gaulois, **~e** /golwa, -z/ *adj* Gallic; (fig) bawdy. **G~**, **~e** *nm,f* Gaul.

gaver /gave/ [1] *vt* force-feed; (fig) cram. □ **se ~ de** *vpr* gorge oneself with; (fig) devour.

gaz /gɑz/ nm inv gas; ~ d'échappement exhaust fumes; ~ lacrymogène tear-gas.

gaze /gɑz/ nf gauze.

gazer /gɑze/ [1] vi 🔟 ça gaze? how's things?

gazette /gazɛt/ nf newspaper.

gazeux, -euse /gazø, -z/ adj (boisson) fizzy; (eau) sparkling.

gazoduc /gazɔdyk/ nm gas pipeline.

gazon /gɑzɔ̃/ nm lawn, grass.

gazouiller /gazuje/ [1] vi (oiseau) chirp; (bébé) babble.

GDF abrév m (**Gaz de France**) French gas board.

géant, ~e /ʒeɑ̃, -t/ adj giant. ● nm giant. **géante** nf giantess.

geindre /ʒɛ̃dʀ/ [22] vi groan, moan.

gel /ʒɛl/ nm frost; (produit) gel; (Comm) freeze; ~ coiffant hair gel.

gelée /ʒ(ə)le/ nf frost; (Culin) jelly; ~ blanche hoarfrost.

geler /ʒəle/ [6] vt/i freeze; **on gèle** (on a froid) it's freezing; **il** ou **ça gèle** (il fait froid) it's freezing.

gélule /ʒelyl/ nf (Méd) capsule.

Gémeaux /ʒemo/ nmpl Gemini.

gémir /ʒemiʀ/ [2] vi groan.

gênant, ~e /ʒenɑ̃, -t/ adj embarrassing; (irritant) annoying; (incommode) cumbersome.

gencive /ʒɑ̃siv/ nf gum.

gendarme /ʒɑ̃daʀm/ nm policeman, gendarme. **gendarmerie** nf police force; (local) police station.

gendre /ʒɑ̃dʀ/ nm son-in-law.

gène /ʒɛn/ nm gene.

gêne /ʒɛn/ nf discomfort; (confusion) embarrassment; (dérangement) trouble, inconvenience; (pauvreté) poverty.

gêné, ~e /ʒene/ adj embarrassed; (désargenté) short of money.

généalogie /ʒenealɔʒi/ nf genealogy.

gêner /ʒene/ [1] vt bother, disturb; (troubler) embarrass; (entraver) block; (faire mal) hurt.

général, ~e (mpl -**aux**) /ʒeneʀal, -o/ adj general; **en** ~ in general. ● nm (pl -**aux**) general.

généralement /ʒeneʀalmɑ̃/ adv generally.

généraliser /ʒeneʀalize/ [1] vt make general. ● vi generalize. □ **se** ~ vpr become widespread ou general.

généraliste /ʒeneʀalist/ nmf general practitioner, GP.

généralité /ʒeneʀalite/ nf general point.

génération /ʒeneʀasjɔ̃/ nf generation.

généreux, ~euse /ʒeneʀø, -z/ adj generous.

générique /ʒeneʀik/ nm (au cinéma) credits. ● adj generic.

générosité /ʒeneʀozite/ nf generosity.

génétique /ʒenetik/ adj genetic. ● nf genetics.

Genève /ʒənɛv/ npr Geneva.

génial, ~e (mpl -**iaux**) /ʒenjal, -jo/ adj brilliant; (fantastique 🔟) fantastic.

génie /ʒeni/ nm genius; ~ **civil** civil engineering.

génital, ~e (mpl -**aux**) /ʒenital, -o/ adj genital.

génocide /ʒenɔsid/ nm genocide.

génoise /ʒenwaz/ nf sponge (cake).

génothèque /ʒenɔtɛk/ nf gene bank.

genou (pl ~**x**) /ʒənu/ nm knee; **être à** ~**x** be kneeling.

genre /ʒɑ̃ʀ/ nm sort, kind; (Gram) gender; (allure) **avoir bon/mauvais** ~ to look nice/disreputable; (comportement) **c'est bien son** ~ it's just like him/her; ~ **de vie** life-style.

gens /ʒɑ̃/ nmpl people.

gentil, ~le /ʒɑ̃ti, -j/ adj kind, nice; (sage) good. **gentillesse** nf kindness. **gentiment** adv kindly.

géographie /ʒeɔgʀafi/ nf geography.

geôlier, -ière /ʒolje, -jɛʀ/ nm,f gaoler, jailer.

géologie /ʒeɔlɔʒi/ nf geology.

géomètre /ʒeɔmɛtʀ/ nm surveyor.

géométrie /ʒeɔmetʀi/ nf geometry. **géométrique** adj geometric.

gérance /ʒeʀɑ̃s/ nf management.

gérant, ~e /ʒeʀɑ̃, -t/ nm,f manager, manageress; ~ **d'immeuble** landlord's agent.

gerbe /ʒɛʀb/ nf (de fleurs) bunch, bouquet; (d'eau) spray; (de blé) sheaf.

gercer /ʒɛʀse/ [10] vt chap; **avoir les lèvres gercées** have chapped lips. ● vi become chapped. **gerçure** nf crack, chap.

gérer /ʒeʀe/ [14] vt manage, run; (traiter: fig) (crise, situation) handle.

germe /ʒɛʀm/ nm germ; ~s **de soja** bean sprouts.

germer /ʒɛʀme/ [1] vi germinate.

gestation /ʒɛstasjõ/ nf gestation.

geste /ʒɛst/ nm gesture.

gesticuler /ʒɛstikyle/ [1] vi gesticulate.

gestion /ʒɛstjõ/ nf management. **gestionnaire** nmf administrator.

ghetto /geto/ nm ghetto.

gibier /ʒibje/ nm (animaux) game.

giboulée /ʒibule/ nf shower.

gicler /ʒikle/ [1] vi squirt; **faire ~** squirt.

gifle /ʒifl/ nf slap in the face. **gifler** [1] vt slap.

gigantesque /ʒigãtɛsk/ adj gigantic.

gigot /ʒigo/ nm leg (of lamb).

gigoter /ʒigɔte/ [1] vi wriggle; (nerveusement) fidget.

gilet /ʒilɛ/ nm waistcoat; (cardigan) cardigan; ~ **de sauvetage** life-jacket.

gingembre /ʒɛ̃ʒãbʀ/ nm ginger.

girafe /ʒiʀaf/ nf giraffe.

giratoire /ʒiʀatwaʀ/ adj **sens ~** roundabout.

girofle /ʒiʀɔfl/ nm **clou de ~** clove.

girouette /ʒiʀwɛt/ nf weathercock, weathervane.

gisement /ʒizmã/ nm deposit.

gitan, ~e /ʒitã, -an/ nm,f gypsy.

gîte /ʒit/ nm (maison) home; (abri) shelter; ~ **rural** holiday cottage.

givre /ʒivʀ/ nm frost; (sur pare-brise) ice.

givré, ~e /ʒivʀe/ adj 🅸 crazy.

glace /glas/ nf ice; (crème) ice-cream; (vitre) window; (miroir) mirror; (verre) glass.

glacé, ~e /glase/ adj (vent, accueil) icy; (hands) frozen; (gâteau) iced.

glacer /glase/ [10] vt freeze; (gâteau, boisson) chill; (pétrifier) chill. □ **se ~** vpr freeze.

glacier /glasje/ nm (Géog) glacier; (vendeur) ice-cream seller. **glacière** nf coolbox. **glaçon** nm ice-cube.

glaïeul /glajœl/ nm gladiolus.

glaise /glɛz/ nf clay.

gland /glã/ nm acorn; (ornement) tassel.

glande /glãd/ nf gland.

glander /glãde/ [1] vi 🅸 laze around.

glaner /glane/ [1] vt glean.

glauque /glok/ adj (fig) murky; (street) squalid.

glissade /glisad/ nf (jeu) slide; (dérapage) skid.

glissant, ~e /glisã, -t/ adj slippery.

glissement /glismã/ nm sliding; gliding; (fig) shift; ~ **de terrain** landslide.

glisser /glise/ [1] vi slide; (être glissant) be slippery; (sur l'eau) glide; (déraper) slip; (véhicule) skid. ● vt (objet) slip (dans into); (remarque) slip in. □ **se ~** vpr slip (dans into).

glissière /glisjɛʀ/ nf slide; **porte à ~** sliding door; ~ **de sécurité** (Auto) crash-barrier; **fermeture à ~** zip.

global, ~e (mpl **-aux**) /glɔbal, -o/ adj (entier, général) overall. **globalement** adv as a whole.

globe /glɔb/ nm globe; ~ **oculaire** eyeball; ~ **terrestre** globe.

globule /glɔbyl/ nm (du sang) corpuscle.

gloire /glwaʀ/ nf glory, fame. **glorieux, -ieuse** adj glorious. **glorifier** [45] vt glorify.

glose /gloz/ nf gloss.

glossaire /glɔsɛʀ/ nm glossary.

gloussement /glusmã/ nm chuckle; (de poule) cluck.

glouton, ~ne /glutõ, -ɔn/ adj gluttonous. ● nm,f glutton.

gluant, ~e /glyã, -t/ adj sticky.

glucose /glykoz/ nm glucose.

glycérine /gliseʀin/ nf glycerin(e).

GO abrév fpl (**grandes ondes**) long wave.

goal /gol/ nm 🅸 goalkeeper.

gobelet /gɔblɛ/ nm cup; (en verre) tumbler.

g

gober /gɔbe/ [1] *vt* swallow (whole); **je ne peux pas le ~** 🔟 I can't stand him.

goéland /gɔelɑ̃/ *nm* (sea)gull.

gogo: **à ~** /agɔgo/ *loc* 🔟 galore, in abundance.

goinfre /gwɛ̃fʀ/ *nm* (glouton 🔟) pig. **goinfrer (se)** [1] *vpr* 🔟 stuff oneself (de with).

golf /gɔlf/ *nm* golf; (terrain) golf course.

golfe /gɔlf/ *nm* gulf.

gomme /gɔm/ *nf* rubber; (US) eraser; (résine) gum. **gommer** [1] *vt* rub out.

gond /gɔ̃/ *nm* hinge; **sortir de ses ~s** 🔟 go mad.

gondoler (se) /(sə)gɔ̃dɔle/ [1] *vpr* (bois) warp; (métal) buckle.

gonflé, **~e** /gɔ̃fle/ *adj* swollen; **il est ~** 🔟 he's got a nerve.

gonflement /gɔ̃fləmɑ̃/ *nm* swelling.

gonfler /gɔ̃fle/ [1] *vt* (ballon, pneu) pump up, blow up; (augmenter) increase; (exagérer) inflate. ● *vi* swell.

gorge /gɔʀʒ/ *nf* throat; (poitrine) breast; (vallée) gorge.

gorgée /gɔʀʒe/ *nf* sip, gulp.

gorger /gɔʀʒe/ [40] *vt* fill (de with); **gorgé de** full of. □ **se ~** *vpr* gorge oneself (de with).

gorille /gɔʀij/ *nm* gorilla; (garde 🔟) bodyguard.

gosier /gozje/ *nm* throat.

gosse /gɔs/ *nmf* 🔟 kid.

gothique /gɔtik/ *adj* Gothic.

goudron /gudʀɔ̃/ *nm* tar. **goudronner** [1] *vt* tarmac.

gouffre /gufʀ/ *nm* abyss, gulf.

goujat /guʒa/ *nm* lout, boor.

goulot /gulo/ *nm* neck; **boire au ~** drink from the bottle.

goulu, **~e** /guly/ *adj* gluttonous. ● *nm, f* glutton.

gourde /guʀd/ *nf* (à eau) flask; (idiot 🔟) fool.

gourer (se) /(sə)guʀe/ [1] *vpr* 🔟 make a mistake.

gourmand, **~e** /guʀmɑ̃, -d/ *adj* greedy. ● *nm, f* glutton.

gourmandise /guʀmɑ̃diz/ *nf* greed; **~s** sweets.

gourmet /guʀmɛ/ *nm* gourmet.

gourmette /guʀmɛt/ *nf* chain bracelet.

gousse /gus/ *nf* **~ d'ail** clove of garlic.

goût /gu/ *nm* taste; (gré) liking; **prendre ~ à** develop a taste for; **avoir bon ~** (aliment) taste nice; (personne) have good taste; **donner du ~ à** give flavour.

goûter /gute/ [1] *vt* taste; (apprécier) enjoy; **~ à** *ou* **de** taste. ● *vi* have tea. ● *nm* tea, snack.

goutte /gut/ *nf* drop; (Méd) gout. **goutte-à-goutte** *nm inv* drip. **goutter** [1] *vi* drip.

gouttière /gutjɛʀ/ *nf* gutter.

gouvernail /guvɛʀnaj/ *nm* rudder; (barre) helm.

gouvernement /guvɛʀnəmɑ̃/ *nm* government.

gouverner /guvɛʀne/ [1] *vt/i* govern; (dominer) control. **gouverneur** *nm* governor.

grâce /gʀɑs/ *nf* (charme) grace; (faveur) favour; (volonté) grace; (Jur) pardon; (Relig) grace; **~ à** thanks to; **rendre ~(s) à** give thanks to.

gracier /gʀasje/ [45] *vt* pardon.

gracieusement /gʀasjøzmɑ̃/ *adv* gracefully; (gratuitement) free (of charge).

gracieux, **-ieuse** /gʀasjø, -z/ *adj* graceful.

grade /gʀad/ *nm* rank; **monter en ~** be promoted.

gradin /gʀadɛ̃/ *nm* tier, step; **en ~s** terraced; **les ~s** terraces.

gradué, **~e** /gʀadɥe/ *adj* graded, graduated; **verre ~** measuring jug.

graffiti /gʀafiti/ *nmpl* graffiti.

grain /gʀɛ̃/ *nm* grain; (Naut) squall; **~ de beauté** beauty spot; **~ de café** coffee bean; **~ de poivre** pepper corn; **~ de raisin** grape.

graine /gʀɛn/ *nf* seed.

graisse /gʀɛs/ *nf* fat; (lubrifiant) grease. **graisser** [1] *vt* grease. **graisseux**, **-euse** *adj* greasy.

grammaire /gʀam(m)ɛʀ/ *nf* grammar.

gramme /gʀam/ *nm* gram.

grand, **~e** /gʀɑ̃, -d/ *adj* big, large; (haut) tall; (intense, fort) great; (brillant) great; (principal) main; (plus âgé) big, elder; (adulte) grown-up; **au ~ air** in the open air; **au ~ jour** in broad daylight; (fig) in the open; **en ~e partie** largely; **~e banlieue** outer suburbs; **~ ensemble** housing estate; **~es lignes** (Rail) main lines; **~ magasin** department store; **~e personne** grown-up; **~ public** general public; **~e surface** hypermarket; **~es vacances** summer holidays. ● *adv* (*ouvrir*) wide; **~ ouvert** wide open; **voir ~** think big. ● *nm, f* (adulte) grown-up; (enfant) big boy, big girl; (Scol) senior.

Grande-Bretagne /gʀɑ̃dbʀətaɲ/ *nf* Great Britain.

grand-chose /gʀɑ̃ʃoz/ *pron* **pas ~** not much, not a lot.

grandeur /gʀɑ̃dœʀ/ *nf* greatness; (dimension) size; **folie des ~s** delusions of grandeur.

grandir /gʀɑ̃diʀ/ [2] *vi* grow; (bruit) grow louder. ● *vt* (talons) make taller; (loupe) magnify.

grand-mère (*pl* **grands-mères**) /gʀɑ̃mɛʀ/ *nf* grandmother.

grand-père (*pl* **grands-pères**) /gʀɑ̃pɛʀ/ *nm* grandfather.

grands-parents /gʀɑ̃paʀɑ̃/ *nmpl* grandparents.

grange /gʀɑ̃ʒ/ *nf* barn.

granulé /gʀanyle/ *nm* granule.

graphique /gʀafik/ *adj* graphic; (Ordinat) graphics; **informatique ~** computer graphics. ● *nm* graph.

graphologie /gʀafɔlɔʒi/ *nf* graphology.

grappe /gʀap/ *nf* cluster; **~ de raisin** bunch of grapes.

gras, **~se** /gʀɑ, -s/ *adj* (gros) fat; (aliment) fatty; (surface, peau, cheveux) greasy; (épais) thick; (caractères) bold; **faire la ~se matinée** sleep late. ● *nm* (Culin) fat.

gratifiant, **~e** /gʀatifjɑ̃, -t/ *adj* gratifying; (travail) rewarding.

gratifier /gʀatifje/ [45] *vt* favour, reward (**de** with).

gratin /gʀatɛ̃/ *nm* gratin (baked dish with cheese topping); (élite 🅸) upper crust.

gratis /gʀatis/ *adv* free.

gratitude /gʀatityd/ *nf* gratitude.

gratte-ciel /gʀatsjɛl/ *nm inv* skyscraper.

gratter /gʀate/ [1] *vt/i* scratch; (avec un outil) scrape; **ça me gratte** 🅸 it itches. □ **se ~** *vpr* scratch oneself; **se ~ la tête** scratch one's head.

gratuiciel /gʀatɥisjɛl/ *nm* (Internet) freeware.

gratuit, **~e** /gʀatɥi, -t/ *adj* free; (acte) gratuitous. **gratuitement** *adv* free (of charge).

grave /gʀav/ *adj* (maladie, accident, problème) serious; (solennel) grave; (voix) deep; (accent) grave. **gravement** *adv* seriously; gravely.

graver /gʀave/ [1] *vt* engrave; (sur bois) carve.

gravier /gʀavje/ *nm* **du ~** gravel.

gravité /gʀavite/ *nf* gravity.

graviter /gʀavite/ [1] *vi* revolve.

gravure /gʀavyʀ/ *nf* engraving; (de tableau, photo) print, plate.

gré /gʀe/ *nm* (volonté) will; (goût) taste; **à son ~** (agir) as one likes; **de bon ~** willingly; **bon ~ mal ~** like it or not; **je vous en saurais ~** I'd be grateful for that.

grec, **~que** /gʀɛk/ *adj* Greek. ● *nm* (Ling) Greek. **G~**, **~que** *nm, f* Greek.

Grèce *nf* /gʀɛs/ Greece.

greffe /gʀɛf/ *nf* graft; (d'organe) transplant. **greffer** [1] *vt* graft; transplant.

greffier, **-ière** /gʀɛfje, -jɛʀ/ *nm, f* clerk of the court.

grêle /gʀɛl/ *adj* (maigre) spindly; (voix) shrill. ● *nf* hail.

grêler /gʀele/ [1] *vi* hail; **il grêle** it's hailing. **grêlon** *nm* hailstone.

grelot /gʀəlo/ *nm* (little) bell.

grelotter /gʀəlɔte/ [1] *vi* shiver.

grenade /gʀənad/ *nf* (fruit) pomegranate; (explosif) grenade.

grenat /gʀəna/ *a inv* dark red.

grenier /gʀənje/ *nm* attic; (pour grain) loft.

grenouille /gʀənuj/ *nf* frog.

grès /gʀɛ/ *nm* sandstone; (poterie) stoneware.

grésiller /gʀezije/ [1] *vi* sizzle; (radio) crackle.

grève /gʀɛv/ *nf* (rivage) shore; (cessation de travail) strike; **faire ~**, **être**

en ~ be on strike; **se mettre en ~** go on strike. **gréviste** *nmf* striker.

gribouiller /gʀibuje/ [1] *vt/i* scribble.

grief /gʀijɛf/ *nm* grievance.

grièvement /gʀijɛvmɑ̃/ *adv* seriously.

griffe /gʀif/ *nf* claw; (de couturier) label; **coup de ~** scratch.

griffé, ~e /gʀife/ *adj* (vêtement, article) designer.

griffer /gʀife/ [1] *vt* scratch, claw.

grignoter /gʀiɲɔte/ [1] *vt/i* nibble.

gril /gʀil/ *nm* (de cuisinière) grill; (plaque) grill pan.

grillade /gʀijad/ *nf* (viande) grill.

grillage /gʀijaʒ/ *nm* wire netting.

grille /gʀij/ *nf* railings; (portail) (metal) gate; (de fenêtre) bars; (de cheminée) grate; (fig) grid. **grille-pain** *nm inv* toaster.

griller /gʀije/ [1] *vt* (pain) toast; (viande) grill; (ampoule) blow; (feu rouge) go through; (appareil) burn out. ● *vi* (ampoule) blow; (Culin) **faire ~** (viande) grill; (pain) toast.

grillon /gʀijɔ̃/ *nm* cricket.

grimace /gʀimas/ *nf* (funny) face; (de douleur, dégoût) grimace; **faire des ~s** make faces; **faire la ~** pull a face, grimace.

grimper /gʀɛ̃pe/ [1] *vt* climb. ● *vi* climb; **~ sur** *ou* **dans un arbre** climb a tree.

grincement /gʀɛ̃smɑ̃/ *nm* creak (ing).

grincer /gʀɛ̃se/ [10] *vi* creak; **~ des dents** grind one's teeth.

grincheux, -euse /gʀɛ̃ʃø, -z/ *adj* grumpy.

grippe /gʀip/ *nf* influenza, flu.

grippé, ~e /gʀipe/ *adj* **être ~** have (the) flu; (mécanisme) be seized up *ou* jammed.

gris, ~e /gʀi, -z/ *adj* grey; (saoul) tipsy.

grivois, ~e /gʀivwa, -z/ *adj* bawdy.

grog /gʀɔg/ *nm* hot toddy.

grogner /gʀɔɲe/ [1] *vi* (animal) growl; (personne) grumble.

grognon /gʀɔɲɔ̃/ *am* grumpy.

groin /gʀwɛ̃/ *nm* snout.

gronder /gʀɔ̃de/ [1] *vi* (tonnerre, volcan) rumble; (chien) growl; (conflit) be brewing. ● *vt* scold.

groom /gʀum/ *nm* bellboy.

gros, ~se /gʀo, -s/ *adj* big, large; (gras) fat; (important) big; (épais) thick; (lourd) heavy; (buveur, fumeur) heavy; **~ bonnet** Ⓕ bigwig; **~ lot** jackpot; **~ mot** swear word; **~ plan** close-up; **~se caisse** bass drum; **~ titre** headline. ● *nm, f* fat man, fat woman. ● *adv* (écrire) big; (risquer, gagner) a lot. ● *nm* **le ~ de** the bulk of; **de ~** (Comm) wholesale; **en ~** roughly; (Comm) wholesale.

groseille /gʀozɛj/ *nf* redcurrant; **~ à maquereau** gooseberry.

grossesse /gʀosɛs/ *nf* pregnancy.

grosseur /gʀosœʀ/ *nf* (volume) size; (enflure) lump.

grossier, -ière /gʀosje, -jɛʀ/ *adj* (sans finesse) coarse, rough; (rudimentaire) crude; (vulgaire) coarse; (impoli) rude; (erreur) gross. **grossièrement** *adv* (sommairement) roughly; (vulgairement) coarsely. **grossièreté** *nf* coarseness; crudeness; rudeness; (mot) rude word.

grossir /gʀosiʀ/ [2] *vt* (faire augmenter) increase, boost; (agrandir) enlarge; (exagérer) exaggerate; **~ les rangs** *ou* **la foule** swell the ranks. ● *vi* (personne) put on weight; (augmenter) grow.

grossiste /gʀosist/ *nmf* wholesaler.

grosso modo /gʀosomodo/ *adv* roughly.

grotesque /gʀɔtɛsk/ *adj* grotesque; (ridicule) ludicrous.

grotte /gʀɔt/ *nf* cave; grotto.

grouiller /gʀuje/ [1] *vi* swarm; **~ de** be swarming with.

groupe /gʀup/ *nm* group; (Mus) group, band; **~ électrogène** generating set; **~ scolaire** school; **~ de travail** working party.

groupement /gʀupmɑ̃/ *nm* grouping.

grouper /gʀupe/ [1] *vt* put together. □ **se ~** *vpr* group (together).

grue /gʀy/ *nf* (machine, oiseau) crane.

gruyère /gʀyjɛʀ/ *nm* gruyère (cheese).

gué /ge/ *nm* ford; **passer** *ou* **traverser à** ∼ ford.

guenon /gənõ/ *nf* female monkey.

guépard /gepaʀ/ *nm* cheetah.

guêpe /gɛp/ *nf* wasp.

guère /gɛʀ/ *adv* **ne** ∼ hardly; **il n'y a** ∼ **d'espoir** there is no hope; **elle n'a** ∼ **dormi** she didn't sleep much, she hardly slept.

guérilla /geʀija/ *nf* guerrilla warfare; (groupe) guerillas.

guérir /geʀiʀ/ [2] *vt* (*personne, maladie, mal*) cure (**de** of); (*plaie, membre*) heal. ● *vi* get better; (*blessure*) heal; ∼ **de** recover from. **guérison** *nf* curing; healing; (de personne) recovery.

guerre /gɛʀ/ *nf* war; **en** ∼ at war; **faire la** ∼ wage war (**à** against); ∼ **civile** civil war; ∼ **mondiale** world war.

guerrier, -ière /gɛʀje, -jɛʀ/ *adj* warlike. ● *nm, f* warrior.

guet /gɛ/ *nm* watch; **faire le** ∼ be on the watch. **guet-apens** (*pl* **guets-apens**) *nm* ambush.

guetter /gete/ [1] *vt* watch; (attendre) watch out for.

gueule /gœl/ *nf* mouth; (figure 🔲) face; **ta** ∼! 🔳 shut up!; ∼ **de bois** 🔲 hangover.

gueuleton /gœltõ/ *nm* 🔲 blow-out, slap-up meal.

gui /gi/ *nm* mistletoe.

guichet /giʃɛ/ *nm* window, counter; (de gare) ticket-office; (Théât) box-office; **jouer à** ∼**s fermés** (*pièce*) be sold out; ∼ **automatique** cash dispenser.

guide /gid/ *nm* guide. ● *nf* (fille scout) girl guide.

guider /gide/ [1] *vt* guide.

guidon /gidõ/ *nm* handlebars.

guignol /giɲɔl/ *nm* puppet; (personne) clown; (spectacle) puppet-show.

guillemets /gijmɛ/ *nmpl* quotation marks, inverted commas; **entre** ∼ in inverted commas.

guillotine /gijɔtin/ *nf* guillotine.

guimauve /gimov/ *nf* marshmallow; **c'est de la** ∼ 🔲 it's slushy *ou* schmaltzy 🔲.

guindé, ∼**e** /gɛ̃de/ *adj* stiff, formal; (*style*) stilted.

guirlande /giʀlɑ̃d/ *nf* garland; tinsel.

guitare /gitaʀ/ *nf* guitar.

gym /ʒim/ *nf* gymnastics; (Scol) physical education, PE.

gymnase /ʒimnaz/ *nm* gym-(nasium). **gymnastique** *nf* gymnastics.

gynécologie /ʒinekɔlɔʒi/ *nf* gynaecology.

Hh

habile /abil/ *adj* skilful, clever.

habillé, ∼**e** /abije/ *adj* (*vêtement*) smart; (*soirée*) formal.

habillement /abijmɑ̃/ *nm* clothing.

habiller /abije/ [1] *vt* dress (**de** in); (équiper) clothe; (recouvrir) cover (**de** with). □ **s'**∼ *vpr* get dressed; (élégamment) dress up.

habit /abi/ *nm* (de personnage) outfit; (de cérémonie) tails; ∼**s** clothes.

habitant, ∼**e** /abitɑ̃, -t/ *nm, f* (de maison, quartier) resident; (de pays) inhabitant.

habitat /abita/ *nm* (mode de peuplement) settlement; (conditions) housing.

habitation /abitasjõ/ *nf* (logement) house.

habité, ∼**e** /abite/ *adj* (*terre*) inhabited.

habiter /abite/ [1] *vi* live. ● *vt* live in.

habitude /abityd/ *nf* habit; **avoir l'**∼ **de** be used to; **d'**∼ usually; **comme d'**∼ as usual.

habitué, ∼**e** /abitɥe/ *nm, f* (client) regular.

habituel, ∼**le** /abitɥɛl/ *adj* usual. **habituellement** *adv* usually.

habituer /abitɥe/ [1] *vt* ∼ **qn à** get sb used to. □ **s'**∼ **à** *vpr* get used to.

hache /'aʃ/ *nf* axe.

haché, ~e /'aʃe/ adj (viande) minced; (phrases) jerky.

hacher /'aʃe/ [1] vt mince; (au couteau) chop.

hachis /'aʃi/ nm minced meat; (US) ground meat; **~ Parmentier** ≈ shepherd's pie.

hachisch /'aʃiʃ/ nm hashish.

hachoir /'aʃwaʀ/ nm (appareil) mincer; (couteau) chopper; (planche) chopping board.

haie /'ɛ/ nf hedge; (de personnes) line; **course de ~s** hurdle race.

haillon /'ajɔ̃/ nm rag.

haine /'ɛn/ nf hatred.

haïr /'aiʀ/ [36] vt hate.

hâlé /'ɑle/ adj (sun-)tanned.

haleine /alɛn/ nf breath; **travail de longue ~** long job.

haleter /'alte/ [6] vi pant.

hall /'ol/ nm hall; (de gare) concourse.

halle /'al/ nf market hall; **~s** covered market.

halte /'alt/ nf stop; **faire ~** stop. ● interj stop; (Mil) halt.

haltère /altɛʀ/ nm dumbbell; **faire des ~s** to do weightlifting.

hameau (pl **~x**) /'amo/ nm hamlet.

hameçon /amsɔ̃/ nm hook.

hanche /'ɑ̃ʃ/ nf hip.

handicap /'ɑ̃dikap/ nm handicap. **handicapé, ~e** a & nm,f disabled (person).

hangar /'ɑ̃gaʀ/ nm shed; (pour avions) hangar.

hanter /'ɑ̃te/ [1] vt haunt.

hantise /'ɑ̃tiz/ nf dread; **avoir la ~ de** dread.

haras /'aʀɑ/ nm stud-farm.

harasser /'aʀase/ [1] vt exhaust.

harcèlement /'aʀsɛlmɑ̃/ nm **~ sexuel** sexual harassment.

harceler /'aʀsəle/ [6] vt harass.

hardi, ~e /'aʀdi/ adj bold.

hareng /'aʀɑ̃/ nm herring.

hargne /'aʀɲ/ nf (aggressive) bad temper.

haricot /'aʀiko/ nm bean; **~ vert** French bean; (US) green bean.

harmonie /aʀmɔni/ nf harmony. **harmonieux, -ieuse** adj harmonious.

harmoniser /aʀmɔnize/ [1] vt harmonize. □ **s'~** vpr harmonize.

harnacher /'aʀnaʃe/ [1] vt harness.

harnais /'aʀnɛ/ nm harness.

harpe /'aʀp/ nf harp.

harpon /'aʀpɔ̃/ nm harpoon.

hasard /'azaʀ/ nm chance; (coïncidence) coincidence; **les ~s de** the fortunes of; **au ~** (choisir etc.) at random; (flâner) aimlessly. **hasardeux, -euse** adj risky.

hasarder /'azaʀde/ [1] vt risk; (remarque) venture.

hâte /'ɑt/ nf haste; **à la ~, en ~** hurriedly; **avoir ~ de** look forward to.

hâter /'ɑte/ [1] vt hasten. □ **se ~** vpr hurry (**de** to).

hâtif, -ive /'ɑtif, -v/ adj hasty; (précoce) early.

hausse /'os/ nf rise (**de** in); **~ des prix** price rise; **en ~** rising.

hausser /'ose/ [1] vt raise; (épaules) shrug.

haut, ~e /'o, 'ot/ adj high; (de taille) tall; **à voix ~e** aloud; **~ en couleur** colourful; **plus ~** higher up; (dans un texte) above; **en ~ lieu** in high places. ● adv high; **tout ~** out loud. ● nm top; **des ~s et des bas** ups and downs; **en ~** (regarder) up; (à l'étage) upstairs; **en ~ (de)** at the top (of).

hautbois /'obwa/ nm oboe.

haut-de-forme /'odfɔʀm/ (pl **hauts-de-forme**) nm top hat.

hauteur /'otœʀ/ nf height; (colline) hill; (arrogance) haughtiness; **être à la ~** be up to it; **à la ~ de** (ville) near; **être à la ~ de la situation** be equal to the situation.

haut-le-cœur /'olkœʀ/ nm inv nausea.

haut-parleur (pl **~s**) /'opaʀlœʀ/ nm loudspeaker.

havre /'avʀ/ nm haven (**de** of).

hayon /'ajɔ̃/ nm (Auto) hatchback.

hebdomadaire /ɛbdɔmadɛʀ/ a & nm weekly.

hébergement /ebɛʀʒəmɑ̃/ nm accommodation.

héberger /ebɛʀʒe/ [40] vt (ami) put up; (réfugiés) take in.

hébreu (*pl ~x*) /ebʀø/ *am* Hebrew. ● *nm* (Ling) Hebrew; **c'est de l'~!** it's all Greek to me!

Hébreu (*pl ~x*) /ebʀø/ *nm* Hebrew; **les ~x** the Hebrews.

hécatombe /ekatɔ̃b/ *nf* slaughter.

hectare /ɛktaʀ/ *nm* hectare (= 10,000 square metres).

hélas /'elɑs/ *interj* alas. ● *adv* sadly.

hélice /elis/ *nf* propeller.

hélicoptère /elikɔptɛʀ/ *nm* helicopter.

helvétique /ɛlvetik/ *adj* Swiss.

hématome /ematom/ *nm* bruise.

hémorragie /emɔʀaʒi/ *nf* haemorrhage.

hémorroïdes /emɔʀɔid/ *nfpl* piles, haemorrhoids.

hennir /'eniʀ/ [2] *vi* neigh.

hépatite /epatit/ *nf* hepatitis.

herbe /ɛʀb/ *nf* grass; (Méd, Culin) herb; **en ~** in the blade; (fig) budding.

héréditaire /eʀeditɛʀ/ *adj* hereditary.

hérédité /eʀedite/ *nf* heredity.

hérisser /'eʀise/ [1] *vt* bristle; **~ qn** (fig) ruffle sb. □ **se ~** *vpr* bristle.

hérisson /'eʀisɔ̃/ *nm* hedgehog.

héritage /eʀitaʒ/ *nm* inheritance; (spirituel) heritage.

hériter /eʀite/ [1] *vt/i* inherit (**de** from); **~ de qch** inherit sth.

héritier, -ière *nm, f* heir, heiress.

hermétique /ɛʀmetik/ *adj* airtight; (fig) unfathomable.

hernie /'ɛʀni/ *nf* hernia.

héroïne /eʀɔin/ *nf* (femme) heroine; (drogue) heroin.

héroïque /eʀɔik/ *adj* heroic.

héros /'eʀo/ *nm* hero.

hésiter /ezite/ [1] *vi* hesitate (**à** to); **j'hésite** I'm not sure.

hétérogène /eteʀɔʒɛn/ *adj* heterogeneous.

hétérosexuel, ~le /eteʀɔseksɥɛl/ *nm/f & a* heterosexual.

hêtre /'ɛtʀ/ *nm* beech.

heure /œʀ/ *nf* time; (soixante minutes) hour; **quelle ~ est-il?** what time is it?; **il est dix ~s** it is ten o'clock; **à l'~** (*venir, être*) on time; **d'~ en ~** by the hour; **toutes les deux ~s** every two hours; **~ de pointe** rush-hour; **~ de cours** (Scol) period; **~ indue** ungodly hour; **~s creuses** off-peak periods; **~s supplémentaires** overtime.

heureusement /œʀøzmɑ̃/ *adv* fortunately, luckily.

heureux, -euse /œʀø, -z/ *adj* happy; (chanceux) lucky, fortunate.

heurt /'œʀ/ *nm* collision; (conflit) clash; **sans ~** smoothly.

heurter /'œʀte/ [1] *vt* (cogner) hit; (*mur*) bump into, hit; (choquer) offend. □ **se ~ à** *vpr* bump into, hit; (fig) come up against.

hexagone /ɛgzagon/ *nm* hexagon; **l'~** France.

hiberner /ibɛʀne/ [1] *vi* hibernate.

hibou (*pl ~x*) /'ibu/ *nm* owl.

hier /jɛʀ/ *adv* yesterday; **~ soir** last night, yesterday evening.

hiérarchie /'jeʀaʀʃi/ *nf* hierarchy.

hilare /ilaʀ/ *adj* (visage) merry; **être ~** be laughing.

hindou, ~e /ɛ̃du/ *a & nm, f* Hindu. **H~, ~e** *nm, f* Hindu.

hippique /ipik/ *adj* equestrian; **le concours ~** showjumping.

hippodrome /ipɔdʀom/ *nm* racecourse.

hippopotame /ipɔpɔtam/ *nm* hippopotamus.

hirondelle /iʀɔ̃dɛl/ *nf* swallow.

hisser /'ise/ [1] *vt* hoist, haul. □ **se ~** *vpr* heave oneself up.

histoire /istwaʀ/ *nf* (récit) story; (étude) history; (affaire) business; **~(s)** (chichis) fuss; (ennuis) trouble.

historique *adj* historical.

hiver /ivɛʀ/ *nm* winter. **hivernal, ~e** (*mpl -aux*) *adj* winter; (glacial) wintry.

H.L.M. *abbrév m ou f* (**habitation à loyer modéré**) block of council flats; (US) low-rent apartment building.

hocher /'ɔʃe/ [1] *vt* **~ la tête** (pour dire oui) nod; (pour dire non) shake one's head.

hochet /'ɔʃɛ/ *nm* rattle.

hockey /'ɔkɛ/ *nm* hockey; **~ sur glace** ice hockey.

hollandais, ~e /'ɔlɑ̃dɛ, -z/ adj Dutch. ● nm (Ling) Dutch. **H**~, ~**e** nm,f Dutchman, Dutchwoman.

Hollande /'ɔlɑ̃d/ nf Holland.

homard /'ɔmar/ nm lobster.

homéopathie /ɔmeɔpati/ nf homoeopathy.

homicide /ɔmisid/ nm homicide; ~ **involontaire** manslaughter.

hommage /ɔmaʒ/ nm tribute; ~**s** (salutations) respects; **rendre** ~ **à** pay tribute to.

homme /ɔm/ nm man; (espèce) man (kind); ~ **d'affaires** businessman; ~ **de la rue** man in the street; ~ **d'État** statesman; ~ **politique** politician.

homogène /ɔmɔʒɛn/ adj homogeneous.

homonyme /ɔmɔnim/ nm (personne) namesake.

homosexualité /ɔmɔsɛksɥalite/ nf homosexuality.

homosexuel, ~**le** /ɔmɔsɛksɥɛl/ a & nm,f homosexual.

Hongrie /'ɔ̃gri/ nf Hungary.

hongrois, ~**e** /'ɔ̃grwa, -z/ adj Hungarian. ● nm (Ling) Hungarian. **H**~, ~**e** nm,f Hungarian.

honnête /ɔnɛt/ adj honest; (juste) fair. **honnêteté** nf honesty.

honneur /ɔnœr/ nm honour; (mérite) credit; **d'**~ (invité, place) of honour; **en l'**~ **de** in honour of; **en quel** ~? 🛈 why?; **faire** ~ **à** (équipe, famille) bring credit to.

honorable /ɔnɔrabl/ adj honourable; (convenable) respectable.

honoraire /ɔnɔrɛr/ adj honorary. **honoraires** nmpl fees.

honorer /ɔnɔre/ [1] vt honour; (faire honneur à) do credit to.

honte /'ɔ̃t/ nf shame; **avoir** ~ be ashamed (de of); **faire** ~ **à** make ashamed. **honteux**, -**euse** adj (personne) ashamed (de of); (action) shameful.

hôpital (pl -**aux**) /ɔpital, -o/ nm hospital.

hoquet /'ɔkɛ/ nm **le** ~ (the) hiccups.

horaire /ɔrɛr/ adj hourly. ● nm timetable; ~**s libres** flexitime.

horizon /ɔrizɔ̃/ nm horizon; (Fig) outlook.

horizontal, ~**e** (mpl -**aux**) /ɔrizɔ̃tal, -o/ adj horizontal.

horloge /ɔrlɔʒ/ nf clock.

hormis /'ɔrmi/ prép save.

hormonal, ~**e** (mpl -**aux**) /ɔrmɔnal, -o/ adj hormonal, hormone.

hormone /ɔrmon/ nf hormone.

horreur /ɔrœr/ nf horror; **avoir** ~ **de** hate.

horrible /ɔribl/ adj horrible.

horrifier /ɔrifje/ [45] vt horrify.

hors /'ɔr/ prép ~ **de** outside, (avec mouvement) out of; ~ **d'atteinte** out of reach; ~ **d'haleine** out of breath; ~ **de prix** extremely expensive; ~ **pair** outstanding; ~ **de soi** beside oneself. **hors-bord** nm inv speedboat. **hors-d'œuvre** nm inv hors-d'œuvre. **hors-jeu** a inv offside. **hors-la-loi** nm inv outlaw. **hors-piste** nm off-piste skiing. **hors-taxe** a inv duty-free.

horticulteur, -**trice** /ɔrtikyltœr, -tris/ nm,f horticulturist.

hospice /ɔspis/ nm home.

hospitalier, -**ière** /ɔspitalje, -jɛr/ adj hospitable; (Méd) hospital. **hospitaliser** [1] vt take to hospital. **hospitalité** nf hospitality.

hostile /ɔstil/ adj hostile. **hostilité** nf hostility.

hôte /ot/ nm (maître) host; (invité) guest.

hôtel /otɛl/ nm hotel; ~ (**particulier**) (private) mansion; ~ **de ville** town hall.

hôtelier, -**ière** /otəlje, -jɛr/ adj hotel. ● nm,f hotel keeper. **hôtellerie** nf hotel business.

hôtesse /otɛs/ nf hostess; ~ **de l'air** stewardess.

hotte /'ɔt/ nf basket; ~ **aspirante** extractor (hood), (US) ventilator.

houblon /'ublɔ̃/ nm **le** ~ hops.

houille /'uj/ nf coal; ~ **blanche** hydroelectric power.

houle /'ul/ nf swell. **houleux**, -**euse** adj (mer) rough; (débat) stormy.

housse /'us/ nf cover; ~ **de siège** seat cover.

houx /'u/ nm holly.

huées /ˈɥe/ *nfpl* boos. **huer** [1] *vt* boo.

huile /ɥil/ *nf* oil; (personne 🖪) bigwig. **huiler** [1] *vt* oil. **huileux, -euse** *adj* oily.

huis /ˈɥi/ *nm* **à ~ clos** in camera.

huissier /ɥisje/ *nm* (Jur) bailiff; (portier) usher.

huit /ˈɥi(t)/ *adj* eight; **~ jours** a week; **lundi en ~** a week on Monday. ● *nm* eight. **huitième** *a* & *nmf* eighth.

huître /ɥitʀ/ *nf* oyster.

humain, ~e /ymɛ̃, -ɛn/ *adj* human; (compatissant) humane. **humanitaire** *adj* humanitarian. **humanité** *nf* humanity.

humble /œbl/ *adj* humble.

humeur /ymœʀ/ *nf* mood; (tempérament) temper; **de bonne/ mauvaise ~** in a good/bad mood.

humide /ymid/ *adj* damp; (*chaleur, climat*) humid; (*lèvres, yeux*) moist. **humidité** *nf* humidity.

humilier /ymilje/ [45] *vt* humiliate.

humoristique /ymɔʀistik/ *adj* humorous.

humour /ymuʀ/ *nm* humour; **avoir de l'~** have a sense of humour.

hurlement /ˈyʀləmã/ *nm* howl(ing). **hurler** [1] *vt/i* howl.

hutte /ˈyt/ *nf* hut.

hydratant, ~e /idʀatã, -t/ *adj* (*lotion*) moisturizing.

hydravion /idʀavjɔ̃/ *nm* seaplane.

hydroélectrique /idʀɔelɛktʀik/ *adj* hydroelectric.

hydrogène /idʀɔʒɛn/ *nm* hydrogen.

hygiène /iʒjɛn/ *nf* hygiene. **hygiénique** *adj* hygienic.

hymne /imn/ *nm* hymn; **~ national** national anthem.

hyperlien /ipɛʀljɛ̃/ *nm* (Internet) hyperlink.

hypermarché /ipɛʀmaʀʃe/ *nm* (supermarché) hypermarket.

hypertension /ipɛʀtãsjɔ̃/ *nf* high blood-pressure.

hypertexte /ipɛʀtɛkst/ *nm* (Internet) hypertext.

hypnotiser /ipnɔtize/ [1] *vt* hypnotize.

hypocrisie /ipɔkʀizi/ *nf* hypocrisy.

hypocrite /ipɔkʀit/ *adj* hypocritical. ● *nmf* hypocrite.

hypothèque /ipɔtɛk/ *nf* mortgage.

hypothèse /ipɔtɛz/ *nf* hypothesis.

hystérie /isteʀi/ *nf* hysteria.

I i

ici /isi/ *adv* (dans l'espace) here; (dans le temps) now; **d'~ demain** by tomorrow; **d'~ là** in the meantime; **d'~ peu** shortly; **~ même** in this very place; **jusqu'~** until now; (dans le passé) until then.

idéal, ~e (*mpl* **-aux**) /ideal, -o/ *a* & *nm* ideal. **idéaliser** [1] *vt* idealize.

idée /ide/ *nf* idea; (esprit) mind; **avoir dans l'~ de faire** plan to do; **il ne me viendrait jamais à l'~ de faire** it would never occur to me to do; **~ fixe** obsession; **~ reçue** conventional opinion.

identification /idãtifikasjɔ̃/ *nf* identification. **identifier** [45] *vt*, **s'identifier** *vpr* identify (à with).

identique /idãtik/ *adj* identical.

identité /idãtite/ *nf* identity.

idéologie /ideɔlɔʒi/ *nf* ideology.

idiome /idjɔm/ *nm* idiom.

idiot, ~e /idjo, -ɔt/ *adj* idiotic. ● *nm, f* idiot. **idiotie** *nf* idiocy; (acte, parole) idiotic thing.

idole /idɔl/ *nf* idol.

if /if/ *nm* yew.

ignare /iɲaʀ/ *adj* ignorant. ● *nmf* ignoramus.

ignoble /iɲɔbl/ *adj* vile.

ignorance /iɲɔʀãs/ *nf* ignorance.

ignorant, ~e /iɲɔʀã, -t/ *adj* ignorant. ● *nm, f* ignoramus.

ignorer /iɲɔʀe/ [1] *vt* not know; **je l'ignore** I don't know; (*personne*) ignore.

il /il/ *pron* (personne, animal familier) he; (chose, animal) it; (impersonnel) it; **~ est vrai que** it is true that; **~ neige/pleut** it is snowing/raining; **~ y a** there is; (pluriel) there are; (temps) ago; (durée) for; ~ y a 2 ans 2 years ago; ~ y a plus d'une heure que j'attends I've been waiting for over an hour.

île /il/ *nf* island; ~ **déserte** desert island; ~s **anglo-normandes** Channel Islands; ~s **Britanniques** British Isles.

illégal, ~e (*mpl* ~**aux**) /ilegal, -o/ *adj* illegal.

illégitime /ileʒitim/ *adj* illegitimate.

illettré, ~e /iletʀe/ *a* & *nm,f* illiterate.

illicite /ilisit/ *adj* illicit; (Jur) unlawful.

illimité, ~e /ilimite/ *adj* unlimited.

illisible /ilizibl/ *adj* illegible; (*livre*) unreadable.

illogique /iloʒik/ *adj* illogical.

illuminé, ~e /ilymine/ *adj* lit up; (*monument*) floodlit.

illusion /ilyzjɔ̃/ *nf* illusion; **se faire des** ~s delude oneself. **illusoire** *adj* illusory.

illustre /ilystʀ/ *adj* illustrious.

illustré, ~e /ilystʀe/ *adj* illustrated. ● *nm* comic.

illustrer /ilystʀe/ [1] *vt* illustrate. □ **s'**~ *vpr* become famous.

îlot /ilo/ *nm* islet; (de maisons) block.

ils /il/ *pron* they.

image /imaʒ/ *nf* picture; (métaphore) image; (reflet) reflection. **imagé**, ~e *adj* full of imagery.

imaginaire /imaʒinɛʀ/ *adj* imaginary. **imaginatif**, -ive *adj* imaginative. **imagination** *nf* imagination.

imaginer /imaʒine/ [1] *vt* imagine; (inventer) think up. □ **s'**~ *vpr* (se représenter) imagine (**que** that); (croire) think (**que** that).

imbécile /ɛ̃besil/ *adj* idiotic. ● *nmf* idiot.

imbiber /ɛ̃bibe/ [1] *vt* soak (de with). □ **s'**~ *vpr* become soaked (**de** with).

imbriqué, ~e /ɛ̃bʀike/ *adj* (lié) interlinked, interlocking; (tuiles) overlapping.

imbu, ~e /ɛ̃by/ *adj* ~ **de** full of.

imitateur, -trice /imitatœʀ, -tʀis/ *nm,f* imitator; (comédien) impersonator. **imiter** [1] *vt* imitate;

(*personnage*) impersonate; (*signature*) forge; (faire comme) do the same as.

immatriculation /imatʀikylasjɔ̃/ *nf* registration.

immatriculer /imatʀikyle/ [1] *vt* register; **se faire** ~ register; **faire** ~ **une voiture** have a car registered.

immédiat, ~e /imedja, -t/ *adj* immediate. ● *nm* **dans l'**~ for the time being.

immense /imɑ̃s/ *adj* huge, immense.

immerger /imɛʀʒe/ [40] *vt* immerse. □ **s'**~ *vpr* immerse oneself (**dans** in).

immeuble /imœbl/ *nm* block of flats, building; ~ **de bureaux** office building *ou* block.

immigrant, ~e /imigʀɑ̃, -t/ *a* & *nm,f* immigrant. **immigration** *nf* immigration. **immigré**, ~e *a* & *nm,f* immigrant. **immigrer** [1] *vi* immigrate.

imminent, ~e /iminɑ̃, -t/ *adj* imminent.

immobile /imɔbil/ *adj* still, motionless.

immobilier, -ière /imɔbilje, -jɛʀ/ *adj* property; **agence immobilière** estate agent's office; (US) real estate office; **agent** ~ estate agent; (US) real estate agent. ● *nm* **l'**~ property; (US) real estate.

immobiliser /imɔbilize/ [1] *vt* immobilize; (stopper) stop. □ **s'**~ *vpr* stop.

immonde /imɔ̃d/ *adj* filthy.

immoral, ~e (*mpl* -**aux**) /imɔʀal, -o/ *adj* immoral.

immortel, ~le /imɔʀtɛl/ *adj* immortal.

immuable /imɥabl/ *adj* unchanging.

immuniser /imynize/ [1] *vt* immunize; **immunisé contre** (à l'abri de) immune to. **immunité** *nf* immunity.

impact /ɛ̃pakt/ *nm* impact.

impair, ~e /ɛ̃pɛʀ/ *adj* (numéro) odd. ● *nm* blunder, faux pas.

imparfait, ~e /ɛ̃paʀfɛ, -t/ *a* & *nm* imperfect.

impasse /ɛ̃pas/ *nf* (rue) dead end; (situation) deadlock.

impatient, ~e /ɛ̃pasjɑ̃, -t/ *adj* impatient.

impatienter /ɛ̃pasjɑ̃te/ [1] *vt* annoy. □ **s'**~ *vpr* get impatient (**contre qn** with sb).

impayé, ~e /ɛ̃peje/ *adj* unpaid.

impeccable /ɛ̃pekabl/ *adj* (propre) impeccable, spotless; (soigné) perfect.

impensable /ɛ̃pɑ̃sabl/ *adj* unthinkable.

impératif, -ive /ɛ̃peratif, -v/ *adj* imperative. ● *nm* (Gram) imperative; (contrainte) imperative; ~s (exigences) requirements, demands (**de** of).

impératrice /ɛ̃peratris/ *nf* empress.

impérial, ~e (*mpl* **-iaux**) /ɛ̃perjal, -jo/ *adj* imperial.

impérieux, -ieuse /ɛ̃perjø, -z/ *adj* imperious; (pressant) pressing.

imperméable /ɛ̃pɛrmeabl/ *adj* impervious (**à** to); (*manteau, tissu*) waterproof. ● *nm* raincoat.

impersonnel, ~le /ɛ̃pɛrsɔnɛl/ *adj* impersonal.

impertinent, ~e /ɛ̃pɛrtinɑ̃, -t/ *adj* impertinent.

imperturbable /ɛ̃pɛrtyrbabl/ *adj* unshakeable, unruffled.

impétueux, -euse /ɛ̃petɥø, -z/ *adj* impetuous.

impitoyable /ɛ̃pitwajabl/ *adj* merciless.

implant /ɛ̃plɑ̃/ *nm* implant.

implanter /ɛ̃plɑ̃te/ [1] *vt* establish, set up. □ **s'**~ *vpr* become established.

implication /ɛ̃plikasjɔ̃/ *nf* (conséquence) implication; (participation) involvement.

impliquer /ɛ̃plike/ [1] *vt* (mêler) implicate (**dans** in); (signifier) imply, mean (**que** that); (nécessiter) involve (**de faire** doing).

implorer /ɛ̃plɔre/ [1] *vt* implore, beg for.

impoli, ~e /ɛ̃pɔli/ *adj* impolite, rude.

importance /ɛ̃pɔrtɑ̃s/ *nf* importance; (taille) size; (ampleur) extent; **sans** ~ unimportant.

important, ~e /ɛ̃pɔrtɑ̃, -t/ *adj* important; (en quantité) considerable,

sizeable, big; (*air*) self-important. ● *nm* l'~ the important thing.

importateur, -trice /ɛ̃pɔrtatœr, -tris/ *nm, f* importer. ● *adj* importing. **importation** *nf* import.

importer /ɛ̃pɔrte/ [1] *vt* (Comm) import. ● *vi* matter, be important (**à** to); **il importe que** it is important that; **n'importe, peu importe** it does not matter; **n'importe comment** anyhow; **n'importe où** anywhere; **n'importe qui** anybody; **n'importe quoi** anything.

importun, ~e /ɛ̃pɔrtœ̃, -yn/ *adj* troublesome. ● *nm, f* nuisance.

imposer /ɛ̃poze/ [1] *vt* impose (**à** on); (taxer) tax; **en** ~ **à qn** impress sb. □ **s'**~ *vpr* (action) be essential; (se faire reconnaître) stand out; (s'astreindre à) **s'**~ **de faire** force oneself to do.

imposition /ɛ̃pozisjɔ̃/ *nf* taxation; ~ **des mains** laying-on of hands.

impossible /ɛ̃posibl/ *adj* impossible. ● *nm* **faire l'**~ do one's utmost.

impôt /ɛ̃po/ *nm* tax; ~s (contributions) tax(ation), taxes; ~ **sur le revenu** income tax.

impotent, ~e /ɛ̃pɔtɑ̃, -t/ *adj* disabled.

imprécis, ~e /ɛ̃presi, -z/ *adj* imprecise.

imprégner /ɛ̃preɲe/ [14] *vt* fill (**de** with); (imbiber) impregnate (**de** with). □ **s'**~ **de** *vpr* (fig) immerse oneself in.

impression /ɛ̃presjɔ̃/ *nf* impression; (de livre) printing. **impressionnant** *adj* impressive; (choquant) disturbing. **impressionner** [1] *vt* impress; (choquer) disturb.

imprévisible /ɛ̃previzibl/ *adj* unpredictable.

imprévu, ~e /ɛ̃prevy/ *adj* unexpected. ● *nm* unexpected incident; **sauf** ~ unless anything unexpected happens.

imprimante /ɛ̃primɑ̃t/ *nf* (Ordinat) printer; ~ **à jet d'encre** ink-jet printer; ~ **(à) laser** laser printer.

imprimé, ~e /ɛ̃prime/ *adj* printed. ● *nm* printed form.

imprimer /ɛ̃pʀime/ [1] *vt* print; (marquer) imprint. **imprimerie** *nf* (art) printing; (lieu) printing works. **imprimeur** *nm* printer.

improbable /ɛ̃pʀɔbabl/ *adj* unlikely, improbable.

impropre /ɛ̃pʀɔpʀ/ *adj* incorrect; ~ à unfit for.

improviste: à l'~ /alɛ̃pʀɔvist/ *loc* unexpectedly.

imprudence /ɛ̃pʀydɑ̃s/ *nf* carelessness; (acte) careless action.

imprudent, ~e /ɛ̃pʀydɑ̃, -t/ *adj* careless; il est ~ de it is unwise to.

impudent, ~e /ɛ̃pydɑ̃, -t/ *adj* impudent.

impuissant, ~e /ɛ̃pɥisɑ̃, -t/ *adj* helpless; (Méd) impotent; ~ à faire powerless to do.

impulsif, **-ive** /ɛ̃pylsif, -v/ *adj* impulsive. **impulsion** *nf* (poussée, influence) impetus; (instinct, mouvement) impulse.

impur, ~e /ɛ̃pyʀ/ *adj* impure.

imputer /ɛ̃pyte/ [1] *vt* ~ à attribute to, impute to.

inabordable /inabɔʀdabl/ *adj* (prix) prohibitive.

inacceptable /inaksɛptabl/ *adj* unacceptable.

inactif, **-ive** /inaktif, -v/ *adj* inactive.

inadapté, ~e /inadapte/ *adj* maladjusted. ● *nm, f* (Psych) maladjusted person.

inadmissible /inadmisibl/ *adj* unacceptable.

inadvertance /inadvɛʀtɑ̃s/ *nf* par ~ by mistake.

inanimé, ~e /inanime/ *adj* (évanoui) unconscious; (mort) lifeless; (matière) inanimate.

inaperçu, ~e /inapɛʀsy/ *adj* unnoticed.

inapte /inapt/ *adj* unsuited (à to); ~ à faire incapable of doing; ~ au service militaire unfit for military service.

inattendu, ~e /inatɑ̃dy/ *adj* unexpected.

inaugurer /inogyʀe/ [1] *vt* inaugurate.

incapable /ɛ̃kapabl/ *adj* incapable (de qch of sth); ~ de faire unable to do, incapable of doing. ● *nmf* incompetent.

incapacité /ɛ̃kapasite/ *nf* inability, incapacity; être dans l'~ de faire be unable to do.

incarcérer /ɛ̃kaʀseʀe/ [14] *vt* imprison, incarcerate.

incarnation /ɛ̃kaʀnasjɔ̃/ *nf* embodiment, incarnation. **incarné**, ~e *adj* (ongle) ingrowing.

incassable /ɛ̃kɑsabl/ *adj* unbreakable.

incendiaire /ɛ̃sɑ̃djɛʀ/ *adj* incendiary; (propos) inflammatory. ● *nmf* arsonist.

incendie /ɛ̃sɑ̃di/ *nm* fire; ~ criminel arson. **incendier** [45] *vt* set fire to.

incertain, ~e /ɛ̃sɛʀtɛ̃, -ɛn/ *adj* uncertain; (contour) vague; (temps) unsettled. **incertitude** *nf* uncertainty.

inceste /ɛ̃sɛst/ *nm* incest.

incidence /ɛ̃sidɑ̃s/ *nf* effect.

incident /ɛ̃sidɑ̃/ *nm* incident; ~ technique technical hitch.

incinérer /ɛ̃sineʀe/ [14] *vt* incinerate; (mort) cremate.

inciser /ɛ̃size/ [1] *vt* make an incision in; (abcès) lance. **incisif**, **-ive** *adj* incisive. **incision** *nf* incision; (d'abcès) lancing.

incitation /ɛ̃sitasjɔ̃/ *nf* (Jur) incitement (à to); (encouragement) incentive. **inciter** [1] *vt* incite (à to); (encourager) encourage.

inclinaison /ɛ̃klinɛzɔ̃/ *nf* incline; (de la tête) tilt.

inclination /ɛ̃klinasjɔ̃/ *nf* (penchant) inclination; (geste) (du buste) bow; (de la tête) nod.

incliner /ɛ̃kline/ [1] *vt* tilt, lean; (courber) bend; (inciter) encourage (à to); ~ la tête (approuver) nod; (révérence) bow. ● *vi* ~ à be inclined to. □ s'~ *vpr* lean forward; (se courber) bow down (devant before); (céder) give in, yield (devant to); (chemin) slope.

inclure /ɛ̃klyʀ/ [16] *vt* include; (enfermer) enclose; jusqu'au lundi inclus up to and including Monday.

incohérence /ɛ̃kɔeRɑ̃s/ *nf*
incoherence; (contradiction)
discrepancy. **incohérent**, ~**e** *adj*
incoherent, inconsistent.

incolore /ɛ̃kɔlɔR/ *adj* colourless;
(*verre*) clear.

incommoder /ɛ̃kɔmɔde/ [1] *vt*
inconvenience, bother.

incompatible /ɛ̃kɔ̃patibl/ *adj*
incompatible.

incompétent, ~**e** /ɛ̃kɔ̃petɑ̃, -t/ *adj*
incompetent.

incomplet, -ète /ɛ̃kɔ̃plɛ, -t/ *adj*
incomplete.

incompréhension /ɛ̃kɔ̃pReɑ̃sjɔ̃/
nf lack of understanding.

incompris, ~**e** /ɛ̃kɔ̃pRi, -z/ *adj*
misunderstood.

inconcevable /ɛ̃kɔ̃svabl/ *adj*
inconceivable.

incongru, ~**e** /ɛ̃kɔ̃gRy/ *adj*
unseemly.

inconnu, ~**e** /ɛ̃kɔny/ *adj* unknown
(à to). ● *nm,f* stranger. ● *nm* **l'**~ the
unknown.

inconscience /ɛ̃kɔ̃sjɑ̃s/ *nf*
unconsciousness; (folie) madness.

inconscient, ~**e** /ɛ̃kɔ̃sjɑ̃, -t/ *adj*
unconscious (de of); (fou) mad. ● *nm*
(Psych) subconscious.

incontestable /ɛ̃kɔ̃tɛstabl/ *adj*
indisputable.

incontrôlable /ɛ̃kɔ̃tRolabl/ *adj*
unverifiable; (non maîtrisé)
uncontrollable.

inconvenant, ~**e** /ɛ̃kɔ̃vnɑ̃, -t/ *adj*
improper.

inconvénient /ɛ̃kɔ̃venjɑ̃/ *nm*
disadvantage, drawback; (objection)
objection.

incorporer /ɛ̃kɔRpɔRe/ [1] *vt*
incorporate; (Culin) blend (à into);
(Mil) enlist.

incorrect, ~**e** /ɛ̃kɔRɛkt/ *adj* (faux)
incorrect; (malséant) improper; (impoli)
impolite; (déloyal) unfair.

incrédule /ɛ̃kRedyl/ *adj*
incredulous.

incriminer /ɛ̃kRimine/ [1] *vt*
(*personne*) incriminate; (*conduite,
action*) attack.

incroyable /ɛ̃kRwajabl/ *adj*
incredible.

incruster /ɛ̃kRyste/ [1] *vt* inlay (**de**
with).

incubateur /ɛ̃kybatœR/ *nm*
incubator.

inculpation /ɛ̃kylpasjɔ̃/ *nf* charge
(**de, pour** of). **inculpé**, ~**e** *nm,f*
accused. **inculper** [1] *vt* charge (**de**
with).

inculquer /ɛ̃kylke/ [1] *vt* instil (**à**
into).

inculte /ɛ̃kylt/ *adj* uncultivated;
(*personne*) uneducated.

incurver /ɛ̃kyRve/ [1] *vt* curve,
bend. □ **s'**~ *vpr* curve, bend.

Inde /ɛ̃d/ *nf* India.

indécent, ~**e** /ɛ̃desɑ̃, -t/ *adj*
indecent.

indécis, ~**e** /ɛ̃desi, -z/ *adj* (de nature)
indecisive; (temporairement) undecided.

indéfini, ~**e** /ɛ̃defini/ *adj* (Gram)
indefinite; (vague) undefined; (sans
limites) indeterminate.

indemne /ɛ̃dɛmn/ *adj* unharmed.

indemniser /ɛ̃dɛmnize/ [1] *vt*
compensate (**de** for).

indemnité /ɛ̃dɛmnite/ *nf*
indemnity, compensation; (allocation)
allowance; ~**s de licenciement**
redundancy payment.

indépendance /ɛ̃depɑ̃dɑ̃s/ *nf*
independence. **indépendant**, ~**e**
adj independent.

indéterminé, ~**e** /ɛ̃detɛRmine/ *adj*
unspecified.

index /ɛ̃dɛks/ *nm* forefinger; (liste)
index.

indicateur, -trice /ɛ̃dikatœR, -tRis/
nm,f (police) informer. ● *nm* (livre)
guide; (Tech) indicator.

indicatif, -ve /ɛ̃dikatif, -v/ *adj*
indicative (**de** of). ● *nm* (à la radio)
signature tune; (téléphonique) dialling
code; (Gram) indicative.

indication /ɛ̃dikasjɔ̃/ *nf* indication;
(renseignement) information; (directive)
instruction.

indice /ɛ̃dis/ *nm* sign; (dans une
enquête) clue; (des prix) index; (évaluation) rating; ~ **d'écoute** audience
ratings.

indifférence /ɛ̃difeRɑ̃s/ *nf*
indifference.

indifférent, **∼e** /ɛ̃difeʀɑ̃, -t/ *adj*
indifferent (**à** to); **ça m'est ∼** it
makes no difference to me.

indigène /ɛ̃diʒɛn/ *a & nmf* native,
indigenous; (**du pays**) local. ●*nmf*
native.

indigent, **∼e** /ɛ̃diʒɑ̃, -t/ *adj*
destitute.

indigeste /ɛ̃diʒɛst/ *adj* indigestible.
indigestion *nf* indigestion.

indigne /ɛ̃diɲ/ *adj* unworthy (**de** of);
(*acte*) vile. **indigner** (**s'**) [1] *vpr*
become indignant (**de** at).

indiqué, **∼e** /ɛ̃dike/ *adj* (*heure*)
appointed; (*opportun*) appropriate;
(*conseillé*) recommended.

indiquer /ɛ̃dike/ [1] *vt* (*montrer*)
show, indicate; (*renseigner sur*) point
out, tell; (*déterminer*) give, state,
appoint; **∼ du doigt** point to *ou* out
ou at.

indirect, **∼e** /ɛ̃diʀɛkt/ *adj* indirect.

indiscipliné, **∼e** /ɛ̃disipline/ *adj*
unruly.

indiscret, **-ète** /ɛ̃diskʀɛ, -t/ *adj*
(*personne*) inquisitive; (*question*)
indiscreet.

indiscutable /ɛ̃diskytabl/ *adj*
unquestionable.

indispensable /ɛ̃dispɑ̃sabl/ *adj*
indispensable; **il est ∼ qu'il vienne** it
is essential that he comes.

individu /ɛ̃dividy/ *nm* individual.

individuel, **∼le** /ɛ̃dividɥɛl/ *adj*
(*pour une personne*) individual; (*qui
concerne l'individu*) personal; **chambre
∼le** single room; **maison ∼le**
detached house.

indolore /ɛ̃dɔlɔʀ/ *adj* painless.

Indonésie /ɛ̃dɔnezi/ *nf* Indonesia.

indu, **∼e** /ɛ̃dy/ *adj* **à une heure ∼e** at
some ungodly hour.

induire /ɛ̃dɥiʀ/ [17] *vt* infer (**de**
from); (*inciter*) induce (**à faire** to do);
∼ en erreur mislead.

indulgence /ɛ̃dylʒɑ̃s/ *nf*
indulgence; (*de jury*) leniency.
indulgent, **∼e** *adj* indulgent;
(*clément*) lenient.

industrialisé, **∼e** /ɛ̃dystʀijalize/
adj industrialized.

industrie /ɛ̃dystʀi/ *nf* industry.

industriel, **∼le** /ɛ̃dystʀijɛl/ *adj*
industrial. ●*nm* industrialist.

inédit, **∼e** /inedi, -t/ *adj*
unpublished; (*fig*) original.

inefficace /inefikas/ *adj* (*remède,
mesure*) ineffective; (*appareil,
système*) inefficient.

inégal, **∼e** (*mpl* **-aux**) /inegal, -o/
adj unequal; (*irrégulier*) uneven.
inégalable *adj* matchless.
inégalité *nf* (*injustice*) inequality;
(*irrégularité*) unevenness; (*disproportion*)
disparity.

inéluctable /inelyktabl/ *adj*
inescapable.

inepte /inɛpt/ *adj* inept, absurd.

inerte /inɛʀt/ *adj* inert; (*immobile*)
lifeless; (*sans énergie*) apathetic.
inertie *nf* inertia; (*fig*) apathy.

inespéré, **∼e** /inɛspeʀe/ *adj*
unhoped for.

inestimable /inɛstimabl/ *adj*
priceless; (*aide*) invaluable.

inexact, **∼e** /inɛgza(kt), -kt/ *adj*
(*imprécis*) inaccurate; (*incorrect*)
incorrect.

in extremis /inɛkstʀemis/ *adv* (*par
nécessité*) as a last resort; (*au dernier
moment*) at the last minute. ●*adj*
last-minute.

infaillible /ɛ̃fajibl/ *adj* infallible.

infâme /ɛ̃fɑm/ *adj* vile.

infantile /ɛ̃fɑ̃til/ *adj* (*puéril*) infantile;
(*maladie*) childhood; (*mortalité*)
infant.

infarctus /ɛ̃faʀktys/ *nm* coronary,
heart attack.

infatigable /ɛ̃fatigabl/ *adj* tireless.

infect, **∼e** /ɛ̃fɛkt/ *adj* revolting.

infecter /ɛ̃fɛkte/ [1] *vt* infect. □ **s'∼**
vpr become infected. **infectieux**,
-ieuse *adj* infectious. **infection** *nf*
infection.

inférieur, **∼e** /ɛ̃feʀjœʀ/ *adj* (*plus
bas*) lower; (*moins bon*) inferior (**à** to);
∼ à (*plus petit que*) smaller than; (*plus
bas que*) lower than. ●*nm,f* inferior.
infériorité *nf* inferiority.

infernal, **∼e** (*mpl* **-aux**) /ɛ̃fɛʀnal,
-o/ *adj* infernal.

infester /ɛ̃fɛste/ [1] *vt* infest.

infidèle /ɛ̃fidɛl/ *adj* unfaithful (à to). **infidélité** *nf* unfaithfulness; (acte) infidelity.

infiltrer (s') /sɛ̃filtre/ [1] *vpr* s'~ (dans) (*personnes, idées*) infiltrate; (*liquide*) seep through.

infime /ɛ̃fim/ *adj* tiny, minute.

infini, ~e /ɛ̃fini/ *adj* infinite. ● *nm* infinity; à l'~ endlessly.

infinité /ɛ̃finite/ *nf* l'~ infinity; une ~ de an endless number of.

infinitif /ɛ̃finitif/ *nm* infinitive.

infirme /ɛ̃firm/ *adj* disabled. ● *nmf* disabled person. **infirmerie** *nf* sickbay, infirmary. **infirmier** *nm* (male) nurse. **infirmière** *nf* nurse. **infirmité** *nf* disability.

inflammable /ɛ̃flamabl/ *adj* inflammable.

inflation /ɛ̃flasjɔ̃/ *nf* inflation.

infliger /ɛ̃fliʒe/ [40] *vt* inflict; (*sanction*) impose.

influence /ɛ̃flyɑ̃s/ *nf* influence. **influencer** [10] *vt* influence. **influent, ~e** *adj* influential.

influer /ɛ̃flye/ [1] *vi* ~ sur influence.

informateur, -trice /ɛ̃fɔrmatœr, -tris/ *nm, f* informant; (pour la police) informer.

informaticien, ~ne /ɛ̃fɔrmatisjɛ̃, -ɛn/ *nm, f* computer scientist.

information /ɛ̃fɔrmasjɔ̃/ *nf* information; (Jur) inquiry; une ~ (some) information; (nouvelle) (some) news; les ~s the news.

informatique /ɛ̃fɔrmatik/ *nf* computer science; (techniques) information technology. **informatiser** [1] *vt* computerize.

informer /ɛ̃fɔrme/ [1] *vt* inform (de about, of). □ s'~ *vpr* enquire (de about).

inforoute /ɛ̃fɔrut/ *nf* (Ordinat) information highway.

infortune /ɛ̃fɔrtyn/ *nf* misfortune.

infraction /ɛ̃fraksjɔ̃/ *nf* offence; ~ à (*loi, règlement*) breach of.

infrastructure /ɛ̃frastryktyr/ *nf* infrastructure; (équipements) facilities.

infructueux, -euse /ɛ̃fryktɥø, -z/ *adj* fruitless.

infuser /ɛ̃fyze/ [1] *vt/i* infuse, brew. **infusion** *nf* herbal tea, infusion.

ingénier (s') /(s)ɛ̃ʒenje/ [45] *vpr* s'~ à strive to.

ingénieur /ɛ̃ʒenjœr/ *nm* engineer.

ingénieux, -ieuse /ɛ̃ʒenjø, -z/ *adj* ingenious. **ingéniosité** *nf* ingenuity.

ingénu, ~e /ɛ̃ʒeny/ *adj* naïve.

ingérence /ɛ̃ʒerɑ̃s/ *nf* interference.

ingérer (s') /sɛ̃ʒere/ [14] *vpr* s'~ dans interfere in.

ingrat, ~e /ɛ̃gra, -t/ *adj* (*personne*) ungrateful; (*travail*) unrewarding, thankless; (*visage*) unattractive.

ingrédient /ɛ̃gredjɑ̃/ *nm* ingredient.

ingurgiter /ɛ̃gyrʒite/ [1] *vt* swallow.

inhabité, ~e /inabite/ *adj* uninhabited.

inhabituel, ~le /inabitɥɛl/ *adj* unusual.

inhumain, ~e /inymɛ̃, -ɛn/ *adj* inhuman.

inhumation /inymasjɔ̃/ *nf* burial.

initial, ~e (*mpl* **-iaux**) /inisjal, -jo/ *adj* initial. **initiale** *nf* initial.

initialisation /inisjalizasjɔ̃/ *nf* (Ordinat) formatting. **initialiser** [1] *vt* format.

initiation /inisjasjɔ̃/ *nf* initiation; (formation) introduction (à to); cours d'~ introductory course.

initiative /inisjativ/ *nf* initiative.

initier /inisje/ [45] *vt* initiate (à into); (faire découvrir) introduce (à to). □ s'~ *vpr* s'~ à qch learn sth.

injecter /ɛ̃ʒɛkte/ [1] *vt* inject; injecté de sang bloodshot. **injection** *nf* injection.

injure /ɛ̃ʒyr/ *nf* insult. **injurier** [45] *vt* insult. **injurieux, -ieuse** *adj* insulting.

injuste /ɛ̃ʒyst/ *adj* unjust, unfair. **injustice** *nf* injustice.

inné, ~e /inne/ *adj* innate, inborn.

innocence /inɔsɑ̃s/ *nf* innocence. **innocent, ~e** *a & nm, f* innocent. **innocenter** [1] *vt* clear, prove innocent.

innombrable /inɔ̃brabl/ *adj* countless.

innovateur, -trice /inɔvatœr, -tris/ *nm, f* innovator. **innovation**

nf innovation. **innover** [1] *vi* innovate.

inodore /inɔdɔʀ/ *adj* odourless.

inoffensif, -ive /inɔfɑ̃sif, -v/ *adj* harmless.

inondation /inɔ̃dasjɔ̃/ *nf* flood; (action) flooding.

inonder /inɔ̃de/ [1] *vt* flood; (mouiller) soak; (envahir) inundate (**de** with); **inondé de soleil** bathed in sunlight.

inopiné, ~e /inɔpine/ *adj* unexpected; (*mort*) sudden.

inopportun, ~e /inɔpɔʀtœ̃, -yn/ *adj* inopportune, ill-timed.

inoubliable /inublijabl/ *adj* unforgettable.

inouï, ~e /inwi/ *adj* incredible; (*événement*) unprecedented.

inox® /inɔks/ *nm* stainless steel.

inoxydable /inɔksidabl/ *adj* **acier ~** stainless steel.

inqualifiable /ɛ̃kalifjabl/ *adj* unspeakable.

inquiet, -iète /ɛ̃kjɛ, -t/ *adj* worried. **inquiétant, ~e** *adj* worrying.

inquiéter /ɛ̃kjete/ [14] *vt* worry. □ **s'~** *vpr* worry (**de** about). **inquiétude** *nf* anxiety, worry.

insaisissable /ɛ̃sezisabl/ *adj* (*personne*) elusive; (*nuance*) indefinable.

insalubre /ɛ̃salybʀ/ *adj* unhealthy.

insatisfaisant, ~e /ɛ̃satisfəzɑ̃, -t/ *adj* unsatisfactory. **insatisfait, ~e** *adj* (mécontent) dissatisfied; (frustré) unfulfilled.

inscription /ɛ̃skʀipsjɔ̃/ *nf* inscription; (immatriculation) enrolment.

inscrire /ɛ̃skʀiʀ/ [30] *vt* write (down); (graver, tracer) inscribe; (*personne*) enrol; (sur une liste) put down. □ **s'~** *vpr* put one's name down; **s'~ à** (école) enrol at; (club, parti) join; (examen) enter for.

insecte /ɛ̃sɛkt/ *nm* insect.

insécurité /ɛ̃sekyʀite/ *nf* insecurity.

insensé, ~e /ɛ̃sɑ̃se/ *adj* mad.

insensibilité /ɛ̃sɑ̃sibilite/ *nf* insensitivity. **insensible** *adj* insensitive (**à** to); (graduel) imperceptible.

insérer /ɛ̃seʀe/ [14] *vt* insert. □ **s'~** *vpr* be inserted; **s'~ dans** be part of.

insigne /ɛ̃siɲ/ *nm* badge; **~s** (d'une fonction) insignia.

insignifiant, ~e /ɛ̃siɲifjɑ̃, -t/ *adj* insignificant.

insinuation /ɛ̃sinɥasjɔ̃/ *nf* insinuation.

insinuer /ɛ̃sinɥe/ [1] *vt* insinuate. □ **s'~** *vpr* (socialement) ingratiate oneself (**auprès de qn** with sb); **s'~ dans** (se glisser) slip into; (idée, nuance) creep into.

insipide /ɛ̃sipid/ *adj* insipid.

insistance /ɛ̃sistɑ̃s/ *nf* insistence. **insistant, ~e** *adj* insistent.

insister /ɛ̃siste/ [1] *vi* insist (**pour faire** on doing); **~ sur** stress.

insolation /ɛ̃sɔlasjɔ̃/ *nf* (Méd) sunstroke.

insolent, ~e /ɛ̃sɔlɑ̃, -t/ *adj* insolent.

insolite /ɛ̃sɔlit/ *adj* unusual.

insolvable /ɛ̃sɔlvabl/ *adj* insolvent.

insomnie /ɛ̃sɔmni/ *nf* insomnia.

insonoriser /ɛ̃sɔnɔʀize/ [1] *vt* soundproof.

insouciance /ɛ̃susjɑ̃s/ *nf* lack of concern. **insouciant, ~e** *adj* carefree.

insoutenable /ɛ̃sutnabl/ *adj* unbearable; (argument) untenable.

inspecter /ɛ̃spɛkte/ [1] *vt* inspect. **inspecteur, -trice** *nm, f* inspector. **inspection** *nf* inspection.

inspiration /ɛ̃spiʀasjɔ̃/ *nf* inspiration; (respiration) breath.

inspirer /ɛ̃spiʀe/ [1] *vt* inspire; **~ la méfiance à qn** inspire distrust in sb. ● *vi* breathe in. □ **s'~ de** *vpr* be inspired by.

instabilité /ɛ̃stabilite/ *nf* instability; unsteadiness. **instable** *adj* unstable; (temps) unsettled.

installation /ɛ̃stalasjɔ̃/ *nf* installation; (de local) fitting out; (de locataire) settling in. **installations** *nfpl* facilities.

installer /ɛ̃stale/ [1] *vt* install; (meuble) put in; (étagère) put up; (gaz, téléphone) connect; (équiper) fit out. □ **s'~** *vpr* settle (down); (emménager) settle in; **s'~ comme** set oneself up as.

instance /ɛ̃stɑ̃s/ nf authority; (prière) entreaty; **avec ~** with insistence; **en ~** pending; **en ~ de** in the course of, on the point of.

instant /ɛ̃stɑ̃/ nm moment, instant; **à l'~** this instant.

instantané, ~e /ɛ̃stɑ̃tane/ adj instantaneous; (café) instant.

instar: à l'~ de /alɛstaʀdə/ loc like.

instaurer /ɛ̃stoʀe/ [1] vt institute.

instigateur, -trice /ɛ̃stigatœʀ, -tʀis/ nm,f instigator.

instinct /ɛ̃stɛ̃/ nm instinct; **d'~** instinctively. **instinctif, -ive** adj instinctive.

instituer /ɛ̃stitɥe/ [1] vt establish.

institut /ɛ̃stity/ nm institute; **~ de beauté** beauty parlour.

instituteur, -trice /ɛ̃stitytœʀ, -tʀis/ nm,f primary-school teacher.

institution /ɛ̃stitysjɔ̃/ nf institution; (école) private school.

instructif, -ive /ɛ̃stʀyktif, -v/ adj instructive.

instruction /ɛ̃stʀyksjɔ̃/ nf (formation) education; (Mil) training; (document) directive; **~s** (ordres, mode d'emploi) instructions; (Ordinat) (énoncé) instruction; (pas de séquence) statement.

instruire /ɛ̃stʀɥiʀ/ [17] vt teach, educate; **~ de** inform of. □ **s'~** vpr learn, educate oneself; **s'~ de** enquire about. **instruit, ~e** adj educated.

instrument /ɛ̃stʀymɑ̃/ nm instrument; (outil) tool; (moyen: fig) instrument; **~ de gestion** management tool; **~s de bord** (Aviat) controls.

insu: à l'~ de /alɛ̃sydə/ loc without the knowledge of.

insuffisance /ɛ̃syfizɑ̃s/ nf (pénurie) shortage; (médiocrité) inadequacy. **insuffisant, ~e** adj inadequate; (en nombre) insufficient.

insulaire /ɛ̃sylɛʀ/ adj island. ● nmf islander.

insuline /ɛ̃sylin/ nf insulin.

insulte /ɛ̃sylt/ nf insult. **insulter** [1] vt insult.

insupportable /ɛ̃sypɔʀtabl/ adj unbearable.

insurger (s') /(s)ɛ̃syʀʒe/ [40] vpr rebel.

intact, ~e /ɛ̃takt/ adj intact.

intangible /ɛ̃tɑ̃ʒibl/ adj intangible; (principe) inviolable.

intarissable /ɛ̃taʀisabl/ adj inexhaustible.

intégral, ~e (mpl **-aux**) /ɛ̃tegʀal, -o/ adj complete; (texte, édition) unabridged; (paiement) full, in full. **intégralement** adv in full. **intégralité** nf whole.

intègre /ɛ̃tɛgʀ/ adj upright.

intégrer /ɛ̃tegʀe/ [14] vt integrate. □ **s'~** vpr (personne) integrate; (maison) fit in.

intégriste /ɛ̃tegʀist/ nmf fundamentalist.

intégrité /ɛ̃tegʀite/ nf integrity.

intellect /ɛ̃telɛkt/ nm intellect. **intellectuel, ~le** a & nm,f intellectual.

intelligence /ɛ̃teliʒɑ̃s/ nf intelligence; (compréhension) understanding; (complicité) agreement; **agir d'~ avec qn** act in agreement with sb. **intelligent, ~e** adj intelligent.

intempéries /ɛ̃tɑ̃peʀi/ nfpl severe weather.

intempestif, -ive /ɛ̃tɑ̃pɛstif, -v/ adj untimely.

intenable /ɛ̃tnabl/ adj unbearable; (enfant) impossible.

intendance /ɛ̃tɑ̃dɑ̃s/ nf (Scol) bursar's office.

intendant, ~e /ɛ̃tɑ̃dɑ̃, -t/ nm (Mil) quartermaster. ● nm,f (Scol) bursar.

intense /ɛ̃tɑ̃s/ adj intense; (circulation) heavy. **intensif, -ive** adj intensive. **intensité** nf intensity.

intenter /ɛ̃tɑ̃te/ [1] vt **~ un procès ou une action** institute proceedings (**à, contre** against).

intention /ɛ̃tɑ̃sjɔ̃/ nf intention (**de faire** of doing); **à l'~ de qn** for sb. **intentionnel, ~le** adj intentional.

interactif, -ive /ɛ̃teʀaktif, -v/ adj (TV, vidéo) interactive.

interaction /ɛ̃teʀaksjɔ̃/ nf interaction.

intercaler /ɛ̃teʀkale/ [1] vt insert.

intercéder /ɛ̃tɛʀsede/ [14] *vi*
intercede (**en faveur de** on behalf of).

intercepter /ɛ̃tɛʀsɛpte/ [1] *vt*
intercept.

interdiction /ɛ̃tɛʀdiksjɔ̃/ *nf* ban; ∼
de fumer no smoking.

interdire /ɛ̃tɛʀdiʀ/ [37] *vt* forbid;
(officiellement) ban, prohibit; ∼ **à qn de
faire** forbid sb to do.

interdit, ∼**e** /ɛ̃tɛʀdi, -t/ *adj*
prohibited, forbidden; (étonné)
dumbfounded.

intéressant, ∼**e** /ɛ̃teʀɛsɑ̃, -t/ *adj*
interesting; (avantageux) attractive.

intéressé, ∼**e** /ɛ̃teʀese/ *adj* (en
cause) concerned; (pour profiter) self-
interested. ● *nm, f* person concerned.

intéresser /ɛ̃teʀese/ [1] *vt* interest;
(concerner) concern. □ **s'**∼ **à** *vpr* be
interested in.

intérêt /ɛ̃teʀɛ/ *nm* interest; (égoïsme)
self-interest; ∼(**s**) (Comm) interest;
vous avez ∼ **à** it is in your interest
to.

interface /ɛ̃tɛʀfas/ *nf* (Ordinat)
interface.

intérieur, ∼**e** /ɛ̃teʀjœʀ/ *adj* inner,
inside; (*mur, escalier*) internal; (*vol,
politique*) domestic; (*vie, calme*)
inner. ● *nm* interior; (de boîte, tiroir)
inside; **à l'**∼ (**de**) inside; (fig) within.
intérieurement *adv* inwardly.

intérim /ɛ̃teʀim/ *nm* interim;
assurer l'∼ deputize (**de** for); **par** ∼
on an interim basis; **président par** ∼
acting president; **faire de l'**∼ temp.

intérimaire /ɛ̃teʀimɛʀ/ *adj*
temporary, interim. ● *nmf* (secrétaire)
temp; (médecin) locum.

interjection /ɛ̃tɛʀʒɛksjɔ̃/ *nf*
interjection.

interlocuteur, **-trice**
/ɛ̃tɛʀlɔkytœʀ, -tʀis/ *nm, f* **son** ∼ the
person one is speaking to.

interloqué, ∼**e** /ɛ̃tɛʀlɔke/ *adj* **être**
∼ be taken aback.

intermède /ɛ̃tɛʀmɛd/ *nm* interlude.

intermédiaire /ɛ̃tɛʀmedjɛʀ/ *adj*
intermediate. ● *nmf* intermediary.
● *nm* **sans** ∼ without an
intermediary, direct; **par l'**∼ **de**
through.

interminable /ɛ̃tɛʀminabl/ *adj*
endless.

intermittence /ɛ̃tɛʀmitɑ̃s/ *nf* **par**
∼ intermittently.

internat /ɛ̃tɛʀna/ *nm* boarding-
school.

international, ∼**e** (*mpl* **-aux**)
/ɛ̃tɛʀnasjɔnal, -o/ *adj* international.

internaute /ɛ̃tɛʀnot/ *nmf* (Ordinat)
Netsurfer, Internet user.

interne /ɛ̃tɛʀn/ *adj* internal; (*cours,
formation*) in-house. ● *nmf* (Scol)
boarder; (Méd) house officer; (US)
intern.

internement /ɛ̃tɛʀnəmɑ̃/ *nm* (Pol)
internment. **interner** [1] *vt* (Pol)
intern; (Méd) commit.

Internet /ɛ̃tɛʀnɛt/ *nm* Internet.

interpellation /ɛ̃tɛʀpelasjɔ̃/ *nf*
(Pol) questioning. **interpeller** [1] *vt*
shout to; (apostropher) shout at;
(interroger) question.

interphone /ɛ̃tɛʀfɔn/ *nm* intercom;
(d'immeuble) entry phone.

interposer (**s'**) /(s)ɛ̃tɛʀpoze/ [1] *vpr*
intervene.

interprétariat /ɛ̃tɛʀpʀetaʀja/ *nm*
interpreting. **interprétation** *nf*
interpretation; (d'artiste) performance.
interprète *nmf* interpreter; (artiste)
performer. **interpréter** [14] *vt*
interpret; (jouer) play; (chanter) sing.

interrogateur, **-trice** /ɛ̃tɛʀɔgatœʀ,
-tʀis/ *adj* questioning. **interrogatif**,
-ive *adj* interrogative.
interrogation *nf* question; (action)
questioning; (épreuve) test.
interrogatoire *nm* interrogation.
interroger [40] *vt* question; (élève)
test.

interrompre /ɛ̃tɛʀɔ̃pʀ/ [3] *vt* break
off, interrupt; (*personne*) interrupt.
□ **s'**∼ *vpr* break off. **interrupteur**
nm switch. **interruption** *nf*
interruption; (arrêt) break.

interurbain, ∼**e** /ɛ̃tɛʀyʀbɛ̃, -ɛn/ *adj*
long-distance, trunk.

intervalle /ɛ̃tɛʀval/ *nm* space;
(temps) interval; **dans l'**∼ in the
meantime.

intervenir /ɛ̃tɛʀvəniʀ/ [58] *vi* (agir)
intervene (**auprès de qn** with sb);
(survenir) occur, take place; (Méd)
operate. **intervention** *nf*
intervention; (Méd) operation.

intervertir /ɛ̃tɛʀvɛʀtiʀ/ [2] *vt*
invert; (*rôles*) reverse.

interview /ɛ̃tɛʀvju/ *nf* interview.
interviewer [1] *vt* interview.

intestin /ɛ̃tɛstɛ̃/ *nm* intestine.

intime /ɛ̃tim/ *adj* intimate; (*fête, vie*)
private; (*dîner*) quiet. ● *nmf* intimate
friend.

intimider /ɛ̃timide/ [1] *vt*
intimidate.

intimité /ɛ̃timite/ *nf* intimacy; (*vie
privée*) privacy.

intituler /ɛ̃tityle/ [1] *vt* call, entitle.
□ **s'~** *vpr* be called *ou* entitled.

intolérable /ɛ̃tɔleʀabl/ *adj*
intolerable. **intolérance** *nf*
intolerance. **intolérant, ~e** *adj*
intolerant.

intonation /ɛ̃tɔnasjɔ̃/ *nf* intonation.

intox /ɛ̃tɔks/ *nf* 🄸 brainwashing.

intoxication /ɛ̃tɔksikasjɔ̃/ *nf*
poisoning; (fig) brainwashing; **~
alimentaire** food poisoning.
intoxiquer [1] *vt* poison; (fig)
brainwash.

intraitable /ɛ̃tʀɛtabl/ *adj* inflexible.

Intranet /ɛ̃tʀanɛt/ *nm* (Ordinat)
Intranet.

intransigeant, ~e /ɛ̃tʀɑ̃ziʒɑ̃, -t/
adj intransigent.

intransitif, -ive /ɛ̃tʀɑ̃zitif, -v/ *adj*
intransitive.

intraveineux, -euse /ɛ̃tʀavɛnø, -z/
adj intravenous.

intrépide /ɛ̃tʀepid/ *adj* fearless.

intrigue /ɛ̃tʀig/ *nf* intrigue; (scénario)
plot.

intrinsèque /ɛ̃tʀɛ̃sɛk/ *adj* intrinsic.

introduction /ɛ̃tʀɔdyksjɔ̃/ *nf*
introduction; (insertion) insertion.

introduire /ɛ̃tʀɔdɥiʀ/ [17] *vt*
introduce, bring in; (insérer) put in,
insert; **~ qn** show sb in. □ **s'~** *vpr*
get in; **s'~ dans** get into, enter.

introuvable /ɛ̃tʀuvabl/ *adj* that
cannot be found.

introverti, ~e /ɛ̃tʀɔvɛʀti/ *nm,f*
introvert. ● *adj* introverted.

intrus, ~e /ɛ̃tʀy, -z/ *nm,f* intruder.
intrusion *nf* intrusion.

intuitif, -ive /ɛ̃tɥitif, -iv/ *adj*
intuitive. **intuition** *nf* intuition.

inusable /inyzabl/ *adj* hard-
wearing.

inusité, ~e /inyzite/ *adj* little used.

inutile /inytil/ *adj* useless; (vain)
needless. **inutilement** *adv*
needlessly. **inutilisable** *adj*
unusable.

invalide /ɛ̃valid/ *a* & *nmf* disabled
(person).

invariable /ɛ̃vaʀjabl/ *adj*
invariable.

invasion /ɛ̃vazjɔ̃/ *nf* invasion.

invectiver /ɛ̃vɛktive/ [1] *vt* abuse.

inventaire /ɛ̃vɑ̃tɛʀ/ *nm* inventory;
(Comm) stocklist; **faire l'~** draw up
an inventory; (Comm) do a stocktake.

inventer /ɛ̃vɑ̃te/ [1] *vt* invent.
inventeur, -trice *nm,f* inventor.
inventif, -ive *adj* inventive.
invention *nf* invention.

inverse /ɛ̃vɛʀs/ *adj* opposite; (ordre)
reverse; **en sens ~** in *ou* from the
opposite direction. ● *nm* reverse;
c'est l'~ it's the other way round.
inversement *adv* conversely.
inverser [1] *vt* reverse, invert.

investir /ɛ̃vɛstiʀ/ [2] *vt* invest.
investissement *nm* investment.

investiture /ɛ̃vɛstityʀ/ *nf* (de
candidat) nomination; (de président)
investiture.

invétéré, ~e /ɛ̃vetere/ *adj*
inveterate; (menteur) compulsive;
(enraciné) deep-rooted.

invisible /ɛ̃vizibl/ *adj* invisible.

invitation /ɛ̃vitasjɔ̃/ *nf* invitation.
invité, ~e *nm,f* guest. **inviter** [1]
vt invite (**à** to).

involontaire /ɛ̃vɔlɔ̃tɛʀ/ *adj*
involuntary; (témoin, héros)
unwitting.

invoquer /ɛ̃vɔke/ [1] *vt* call upon,
invoke.

invraisemblable /ɛ̃vʀɛsɑ̃blabl/
adj improbable, unlikely; (incroyable)
incredible. **invraisemblance** *nf*
improbability.

iode /jɔd/ *nm* iodine.

ira, irait /iʀa, iʀɛ/ ⇒ALLER [8].

Irak /iʀak/ *nm* Iraq.

Iran /iʀɑ̃/ *nm* Iran.

iris /iʀis/ *nm* iris.

irlandais, ~e /iʀlɑ̃dɛ, -z/ *adj* Irish. **I~**, ~e *nm,f* Irishman, Irishwoman.

Irlande /iʀlɑ̃d/ *nf* Ireland.

ironie /iʀɔni/ *nf* irony. **ironique** *adj* ironic.

irrationnel, ~le /iʀasjɔnɛl/ *adj* irrational.

irréalisable /iʀealizabl/ *adj* (*idée, rêve*) unachievable; (*projet*) unworkable.

irrécupérable /iʀekypeʀabl/ *adj* irretrievable; (*capital*) irrecoverable.

irréel, ~le /iʀeɛl/ *adj* unreal.

irréfléchi, ~e /iʀefleʃi/ *adj* thoughtless.

irrégulier, **-ière** /iʀegylje, -jɛʀ/ *adj* irregular.

irrémédiable /iʀemedjabl/ *adj* irreparable.

irremplaçable /iʀɑ̃plasabl/ *adj* irreplaceable.

irréparable /iʀepaʀabl/ *adj* (*objet*) beyond repair; (*tort, dégâts*) irreparable.

irréprochable /iʀepʀɔʃabl/ *adj* flawless.

irrésistible /iʀezistibl/ *adj* irresistible; (*drôle*) hilarious.

irrésolu, ~e /iʀezɔly/ *adj* indecisive; (*problème*) unsolved.

irrespirable /iʀɛspiʀabl/ *adj* stifling.

irresponsable /iʀɛspɔ̃sabl/ *adj* irresponsible.

irrigation /iʀigasjɔ̃/ *nf* irrigation. **irriguer** [1] *vt* irrigate.

irritable /iʀitabl/ *adj* irritable.

irriter /iʀite/ [1] *vt* irritate. □ **s'~** *vpr* get annoyed (**de** at).

irruption /iʀypsjɔ̃/ *nf* **faire** ~ **dans** burst into.

Islam /islam/ *nm* Islam. **islamique** *adj* Islamic.

islandais, ~e /islɑ̃dɛ, -z/ *adj* Icelandic. ● *nm* (Ling) Icelandic. **I~**, ~e *nm,f* Icelander.

Islande /islɑ̃d/ *nf* Iceland.

isolant /izɔlɑ̃/ *nm* insulating material. **isolation** *nf* insulation.

isolé, ~e /izɔle/ *adj* isolated. **isolement** *nm* isolation.

isoler /izɔle/ [1] *vt* isolate; (Électr) insulate. □ **s'~** *vpr* isolate oneself.

isoloir /izɔlwaʀ/ *nm* polling booth.

Isorel® /izɔʀɛl/ *nm* hardboard.

Israël /isʀaɛl/ *nm* Israel. **israélien**, ~ne *adj* Israeli.

israélite /isʀaelit/ *adj* Jewish. ● *nmf* Jew.

issu, ~e /isy/ *adj* **être** ~ **de** (*personne*) come from; (résulter de) result *ou* stem from.

issue /isy/ *nf* (sortie) exit; (résultat) outcome; (fig) solution; **à l'~** **de** at the conclusion of; ~ **de secours** emergency exit; **rue** *ou* **voie sans** ~ dead end.

Italie /itali/ *nf* Italy.

italien, ~ne /italjɛ̃, -ɛn/ *adj* Italian. ● *nm* (Ling) Italian. **I~**, ~ne *nm,f* Italian.

italique /italik/ *nm* italics.

itinéraire /itineʀɛʀ/ *nm* itinerary, route.

I.U.T. *abrév m* (**Institut universitaire de technologie**) university institute of technology.

I.V.G. *abrév f* (**interruption volontaire de grossesse**) abortion.

ivoire /ivwaʀ/ *nm* ivory.

ivre /ivʀ/ *adj* drunk. **ivresse** *nf* drunkenness; (fig) exhilaration. **ivrogne** *nmf* drunk(ard).

Jj

j' /ʒ/ ⇒JE.

jacinthe /ʒasɛ̃t/ *nf* hyacinth.

jadis /ʒadis/ *adv* long ago.

jaillir /ʒajiʀ/ [2] *vi* (*liquide*) spurt (out); (*lumière*) stream out; (apparaître) burst forth, spring out.

jalonner /ʒalɔne/ [1] *vt* mark (out).

jalousie /ʒaluzi/ *nf* jealousy; (store) (venetian) blind. **jaloux**, **-ouse** *adj* jealous.

jamais /ʒamɛ/ *adv* ever; **ne** ~ never; **il ne boit** ~ he never drinks; **à** ~ for ever; **si** ~ if ever.

jambe /ʒɑ̃b/ *nf* leg.

jambon /ʒɑ̃bɔ̃/ *nm* ham.
 jambonneau (*pl* ∼**x**) *nm* knuckle of ham.

janvier /ʒɑ̃vje/ *nm* January.

Japon /ʒapɔ̃/ *nm* Japan.

japonais, ∼**e** /japɔnɛ, -z/ *adj* Japanese. ● *nm* (Ling) Japanese. **J**∼, ∼**e** *nm,f* Japanese.

japper /ʒape/ [1] *vi* yap.

jaquette /ʒakɛt/ *nf* (de livre, femme) jacket; (d'homme) morning coat.

jardin /ʒaʀdɛ̃/ *nm* garden; ∼ **d'enfants** nursery (school); ∼ **public** public park. **jardinage** *nm* gardening. **jardiner** [1] *vi* do some gardening, garden. **jardinier, -ière** *nm, f* gardener.

jardinière /ʒaʀdinjɛʀ/ *nf* (meuble) plant-stand; ∼ **de légumes** mixed vegetables.

jarretelle /ʒaʀtɛl/ *nf* suspender; (US) garter.

jarretière /ʒaʀtjɛʀ/ *nf* garter.

jatte /ʒat/ *nf* bowl.

jauge /ʒoʒ/ *nf* capacity; (de navire) tonnage; (compteur) gauge; ∼ **d'huile** dipstick.

jaune /ʒon/ *a & nm* yellow; (péj) scab; ∼ **d'œuf** (egg) yolk; **rire** ∼ give a forced laugh. **jaunir** [2] *vt/i* turn yellow. **jaunisse** *nf* jaundice.

javelot /ʒavlo/ *nm* javelin.

jazz /dʒaz/ *nm* jazz.

J.C. *abrév m* (**Jésus-Christ**) 500 avant/après ∼ 500 B.C./A.D.

je, j' /ʒə, ʒ/ *pron* I.

jean /dʒin/ *nm* jeans; **un** ∼ a pair of jeans.

jet¹ /ʒɛ/ *nm* throw; (de liquide, vapeur) jet; ∼ **d'eau** fountain.

jet² /dʒɛt/ *nm* (avion) jet.

jetable /ʒətabl/ *adj* disposable.

jetée /ʒəte/ *nf* pier.

jeter /ʒəte/ [38] *vt* throw; (au rebut) throw away; (regard, ancre, lumière) cast; (cri) utter; (bases) lay; ∼ **un coup d'œil** have *ou* take a look (**à** at). □ **se** ∼ *vpr* **se** ∼ **contre** crash *ou* bash into; **se** ∼ **dans** (fleuve) flow into; **se** ∼ **sur** (se ruer sur) rush at.

jeton /ʒətɔ̃/ *nm* token; (pour compter) counter; (au casino) chip.

jeu (*pl* ∼**x**) /ʒø/ *nm* game; (amusement) play; (au casino) gambling; (Théât) acting; (série) set; (de lumière, ressort) play; **en** ∼ (honneur) at stake; (forces) at work; ∼ **de cartes** (paquet) pack of cards; ∼ **d'échecs** (boîte) chess set; ∼ **de mots** pun; ∼ **télévisé** television quiz; ∼**x de grattage** scratch cards.

jeudi /ʒødi/ *nm* Thursday.

jeun: à ∼ /aʒœ̃/ *loc* on an empty stomach.

jeune /ʒœn/ *adj* young; ∼ **fille** girl; ∼**s mariés** newlyweds. ● *nmf* young person; **les** ∼**s** young people.

jeûne /ʒøn/ *nm* fast.

jeunesse /ʒœnɛs/ *nf* youth; (apparence) youthfulness; **la** ∼ (jeunes) the young.

joaillerie /ʒɔajʀi/ *nf* jewellery; (magasin) jeweller's shop.

joie /ʒwa/ *nf* joy.

joindre /ʒwɛ̃dʀ/ [22] *vt* join (**à** to); (mains, pieds) put together; (efforts) combine; (contacter) contact; (dans une enveloppe) enclose. □ **se** ∼ **à** *vpr* join.

joint, ∼**e** /ʒwɛ̃, -t/ *adj* (efforts) joint; (pieds) together. ● *nm* joint; (de robinet) washer.

joli, ∼**e** /ʒɔli/ *adj* pretty, nice; (somme, profit) nice; **c'est du** ∼! (ironique) charming! **c'est bien** ∼ **mais** that is all very well but.

joncher /ʒɔ̃ʃe/ [1] *vt* litter, be strewn over; **jonché de** littered with.

jonction /ʒɔ̃ksjɔ̃/ *nf* junction.

jongleur, -euse /ʒɔ̃glœʀ, øz/ *nm, f* juggler.

jonquille /ʒɔ̃kij/ *nf* daffodil.

joue /ʒu/ *nf* cheek.

jouer /ʒwe/ [1] *vt/i* play; (Théât) act; (au casino) gamble; (fonctionner) work; (film, pièce) put on; (cheval) back; (être important) count; ∼ **à** (jeu, Sport) play; ∼ **de** (Mus) play; ∼ **la comédie** put on an act; **bien joué!** well done!

jouet /ʒwɛ/ *nm* toy; (personne: fig) plaything; (victime) victim.

joueur, -euse /ʒwœʀ, -øz/ *nm, f* player; gambler.

joufflu, ∼**e** /ʒufly/ *adj* chubby-cheeked; (visage) chubby.

jouir /ʒwiʀ/ [2] *vi* (sexe) come; ∼ **de** (droit, avantage) enjoy; (bien, *concession*) enjoy the use of.

jouissance *nf* pleasure; (usage) use (de qch of sth).

joujou (*pl* ~**x**) /ʒuʒu/ *nm* 🆃 toy.

jour /ʒuʀ/ *nm* day; (opposé à nuit) day (time); (lumière) daylight; (aspect) light; (ouverture) gap; **de nos** ~**s** nowadays; **du** ~ **au lendemain** overnight; **il fait** ~ it is (day)light; ~ **chômé** *ou* **férié** public holiday; ~ **de fête** holiday; ~ **ouvrable**, ~ **de travail** working day; **mettre à** ~ update; **mettre au** ~ uncover; **au grand** ~ in the open; **donner le** ~ give birth; **voir le** ~ be born; **vivre au** ~ **le jour** live from day to day.

journal (*pl* **-aux**) /ʒuʀnal, -o/ *nm* (news)paper; (spécialisé) journal; (intime) diary; (à la radio) news; ~ **de bord** log-book.

journalier, -ière /ʒuʀnalje, -jɛʀ/ *adj* daily.

journalisme /ʒuʀnalism/ *nm* journalism. **journaliste** *nmf* journalist.

journée /ʒuʀne/ *nf* day.

jovial, ~**e** (*mpl* **-iaux**) /ʒɔvjal, -jo/ *adj* jovial.

joyau (*pl* ~**x**) /ʒwajo/ *nm* gem.

joyeux, -euse /ʒwajø, -z/ *a* merry, joyful; ~ **anniversaire** happy birthday.

jubiler /ʒybile/ [1] *vi* be jubilant.

jucher /ʒyʃe/ [1] *vt* perch. □ **se** ~ *vpr* perch.

judaïsme /ʒydaism/ *nm* Judaism.

judiciaire /ʒydisjɛʀ/ *adj* judicial.

judicieux, -ieuse /ʒydisjø, -z/ *adj* judicious.

judo /ʒydo/ *nm* judo.

juge /ʒyʒ/ *nm* judge; (arbitre) referee; ~ **de paix** Justice of the Peace; ~ **de touche** linesman.

jugé: au ~ /oʒyʒe/ *loc* by guesswork.

jugement /ʒyʒmɑ̃/ *nm* judgement; (criminel) sentence.

juger /ʒyʒe/ [40] *vt/i* judge; (estimer) consider (**que** that); ~ **de** judge.

juguler /ʒygyle/ [1] *vt* stamp out; curb.

juif, -ive /ʒɥif, -v/ *adj* Jewish. ● *nm,f* Jew.

juillet /ʒɥijɛ/ *nm* July.

juin /ʒɥɛ̃/ *nm* June.

jumeau, -elle (*mpl* ~**x**) /ʒymo, -ɛl/ *a & nm,f* twin. **jumeler** [38] *vt* (villes) twin.

jumelles /ʒymɛl/ *nfpl* binoculars.

jument /ʒymɑ̃/ *nf* mare.

junior /ʒynjɔʀ/ *a & nmf* junior.

jupe /ʒyp/ *nf* skirt.

jupon /ʒypɔ̃/ *nm* slip, petticoat.

juré, ~e /ʒyʀe/ *nm,f* juror. ● *adj* sworn.

jurer /ʒyʀe/ [1] *vt* swear (**que** that). ● *vi* (pester) swear; (contraster) clash (**avec** with).

juridiction /ʒyʀidiksjɔ̃/ *nf* jurisdiction; (tribunal) court of law.

juridique /ʒyʀidik/ *adj* legal.

juriste /ʒyʀist/ *nmf* legal expert.

juron /ʒyʀɔ̃/ *nm* swear-word.

jury /ʒyʀi/ *nm* (Jur) jury; (examinateurs) panel of judges.

jus /ʒy/ *nm* juice; (de viande) gravy; ~ **de fruit** fruit juice.

jusque /ʒysk(ə)/ *prép* **jusqu'à** (up) to, as far as; (temps) until, till; (limite) up to; (y compris) even; **jusqu'à ce que** until; **jusqu'à présent** until now; **jusqu'en** until; **jusqu'où?** how far?; ~ **dans**, ~ **sur** as far as.

juste /ʒyst/ *adj* fair, just; (légitime) just; (correct, exact) right; (vrai) true; (vêtement) tight; (quantité) on the short side; **le** ~ **milieu** the happy medium. ● *adv* rightly, correctly; (chanter) in tune; (seulement, exactement) just; (un peu) ~ (calculer, mesurer) a bit fine *ou* close; **au** ~ exactly; **c'était** ~ (presque raté) it was a close thing. **justement** *adv* (précisément) precisely; (à l'instant) just; (avec justesse) correctly; (légitimement) justifiably.

justesse /ʒystɛs/ *nf* accuracy; **de** ~ just, narrowly.

justice /ʒystis/ *nf* justice; (autorités) law; (tribunal) court.

justifier /ʒystifje/ [45] *vt* justify. ● *vi* ~ **de** prove. □ **se** ~ *vpr* justify oneself.

juteux, -euse /ʒytø, -z/ *adj* juicy.

juvénile /ʒyvenil/ *adj* youthful; (*délinquance, mortalité*) juvenile.

Kk

kaki /kaki/ *a inv & nm* khaki.
kangourou /kɑ̃guʀu/ *nm* kangaroo.
karaté /kaʀate/ *nm* karate.
kart /kaʀt/ *nm* go-cart.
kascher /kaʃɛʀ/ *a inv* kosher.
kayak /kajak/ *nm* kayak.
képi /kepi/ *nm* kepi.
kermesse /kɛʀmɛs/ *nf* fête.
kidnapper /kidnape/ [1] *vt* kidnap.
kilo /kilo/ *nm* kilo.
kilogramme /kiloɡʀam/ *nm* kilogram.
kilométrage /kilometʀaʒ/ *nm* ≈ mileage. **kilomètre** *nm* kilometre.
kinésithérapeute /kineziteʀapøt/ *nmf* physiotherapist. **kinésithérapie** *nf* physiotherapy.
kiosque /kjɔsk/ *nm* kiosk; ~ à musique bandstand.
kit /kit/ *nm* kit.
kiwi /kiwi/ *nm* kiwi.
klaxon® /klaksɔn/ *nm* (Auto) horn. **klaxonner** [1] *vi* sound one's horn.
Ko *abrév m* (**kilo-octet**) (Ordinat) KB.
KO *abrév m* (**knock-out**) KO 🔲.
K-way® /kawɛ/ *nm inv* windcheater.
kyste /kist/ *nm* cyst.

Ll

l', la /l, la/ ⇒LE.

là /la/

● *adverbe*

····▸ (dans ce lieu) there; (ici) here; (chez soi) in; **c'est ~ que** this is where; ~

où where; **par ~** (dans cette direction) this way; (dans cette zone) around there; **de ~** hence.

····▸ (à ce moment) then; **c'est ~ que** that's when.

····▸ **cet homme-~** that man; **ces maisons-~** those houses.

● *interjection*

····▸ **~!** **c'est fini** there (now), it's all over!

là-bas /labɑ/ *adv* there; (à l'endroit que l'on indique) over there.
label /labɛl/ *nm* seal, label.
laboratoire /labɔʀatwaʀ/ *nm* laboratory.
laborieux, -ieuse /labɔʀjø, -z/ *adj* laborious; (*personne*) industrious; **classes laborieuses** working classes.
labour /labuʀ/ *nm* ploughing; (US) plowing. **labourer** [1] *vt* plough; (US) plow; (*déchirer*) rip at.
labyrinthe /labiʀɛ̃t/ *nm* maze, labyrinth.
lac /lak/ *nm* lake.
lacer /lase/ [10] *vt* lace up.
lacet /lasɛ/ *nm* (de chaussure) (shoe-)lace; (de route) sharp bend.
lâche /lɑʃ/ *adj* cowardly; (détendu) loose; (sans rigueur) lax. ● *nmf* coward.
lâcher /lɑʃe/ [1] *vt* let go of; (laisser tomber) drop; (abandonner) give up; (laisser) leave; (libérer) release; (*flèche, balle*) fire; (*juron, phrase*) come out with; (desserrer) loosen; ~ **prise** let go. ● *vi* give way.
lâcheté /lɑʃte/ *nf* cowardice.
lacrymogène /lakʀimɔʒɛn/ *adj* **gaz ~** tear gas.
lacune /lakyn/ *nf* gap.
là-dedans /lad(ə)dɑ̃/ *adv* (près) in here; (plus loin) in there.
là-dessous /lad(ə)su/ *adv* (près) under here; (plus loin) under there.
là-dessus /lad(ə)sy/ *adv* (sur une surface) on here; (plus loin) on there; (sur ce) with that; (quelque temps après) after that; **qu'avez-vous à dire ~?** what have you got to say about it?
ladite /ladit/ ⇒LEDIT.
lagune /lagyn/ *nf* lagoon.

là-haut /lao/ *adv* (en hauteur) up here; (plus loin) up there; (à l'étage) upstairs.

laïc /laik/ *nm* layman.

laid, ~**e** /lɛ, lɛd/ *adj* ugly; (*action*) vile. **laideur** *nf* ugliness.

lainage /lɛnaʒ/ *nm* woollen garment.

laine /lɛn/ *nf* wool; **de** ~ woollen.

laïque /laik/ *adj* (*état, loi*) secular; (*habit, personne*) lay; (*école*) nondenominational. ● *nmf* layman, laywoman.

laisse /lɛs/ *nf* lead, leash; **tenir en** ~ keep on a lead.

laisser /lese/ [1] *vt* (déposer) leave, drop off; (confier) leave (**à qn** with sb); (abandonner) leave; (rendre) ~ **qn perplexe/froid** leave sb puzzled/cold; ~ **qch à qn** (céder, prêter) let sb have sth; (donner) (*choix, temps*) give sb sth. □ **se** ~ *vpr* **se** ~ **persuader/insulter** let oneself be persuaded/insulted; **elle ne se laisse pas faire** she won't be pushed around; **laisse-toi faire** leave it to me/him/her *etc.*; **se** ~ **aller** let oneself go. ● *v aux* ~ **qn/qch faire** let sb/sth do; **laisse-moi faire** (ne m'aide pas) let me do it; (je m'en occupe) leave it to me; **laisse faire!** so what! **laisser-aller** *nm inv* carelessness; (dans la tenue) scruffiness. **laissez-passer** *nm inv* pass.

lait /lɛ/ *nm* milk; ~ **longue conservation** long-life *ou* UHT milk; **frère/sœur de** ~ foster-brother/-sister. **laitage** *nm* milk product. **laiterie** *nf* dairy. **laiteux, -euse** *adj* milky.

laitier, -ière /letje, -jɛʀ/ *adj* dairy. ● *nm,f* (livreur) milkman, milkwoman.

laiton /lɛtɔ̃/ *nm* brass.

laitue /lety/ *nf* lettuce.

lama /lama/ *nm* llama.

lambeau (*pl* ~**x**) /lɑ̃bo/ *nm* shred; **en** ~**x** in shreds.

lame /lam/ *nf* blade; (lamelle) strip; (vague) wave; ~ **de fond** ground swell; ~ **de rasoir** razor blade.

lamentable /lamɑ̃tabl/ *adj* deplorable. **lamenter (se)** [1] *vpr* moan (**sur** about, over).

lampadaire /lɑ̃padɛʀ/ *nm* standard lamp; (de rue) street lamp.

lampe /lɑ̃p/ *nf* lamp; (ampoule) bulb; (de radio) valve; ~ **(de poche)** torch; (US) flashlight; ~ **à souder** blowlamp; ~ **de chevet** bedside lamp; ~ **solaire**, ~ **à bronzer** sunlamp.

lance /lɑ̃s/ *nf* spear; (de tournoi) lance; (tuyau) hose; ~ **d'incendie** fire hose.

lancement /lɑ̃smɑ̃/ *nm* throwing; (de navire, de missile, mise sur le marché) launch.

lance-missiles /lɑ̃smisil/ *nm inv* missile launcher.

lance-pierres /lɑ̃spjɛʀ/ *nm inv* catapult.

lancer /lɑ̃se/ [10] *vt* throw; (avec force) hurl; (*navire, idée, artiste*) launch; (émettre) give out; (*regard*) cast; (*moteur*) start. □ **se** ~ *vpr* (Sport) gain momentum; (se précipiter) rush; **se** ~ **dans** (*explication*) launch into; (*passe-temps*) take up. ● *nm* throw; (action) throwing.

lancinant, ~**e** /lɑ̃sinɑ̃, -t/ *adj* (*douleur*) shooting; (*problème*) nagging.

landau /lɑ̃do/ *nm* pram; (US) baby carriage.

lande /lɑ̃d/ *nf* heath, moor.

langage /lɑ̃gaʒ/ *nm* language; ~ **machine/de programmation** machine/programming language.

langouste /lɑ̃gust/ *nf* spiny lobster. **langoustine** *nf* Dublin Bay prawn.

langue /lɑ̃g/ *nf* (Anat) tongue; (Ling) language; **il m'a tiré la** ~ he stuck his tongue out at me; **de** ~ **anglaise** (*personne*) English-speaking; (*journal*) English-language; ~ **maternelle** mother tongue; ~ **vivante** modern language.

lanière /lanjɛʀ/ *nf* strap.

lanterne /lɑ̃tɛʀn/ *nf* lantern; (électrique) lamp; (de voiture) sidelight.

lapin /lapɛ̃/ *nm* rabbit; **poser un** ~ **à qn** 🄴 stand sb up; **le coup du** ~ rabbit punch; (en voiture) whiplash injury.

lapsus /lapsys/ *nm* slip (of the tongue).

laque /lak/ *nf* lacquer; (pour cheveux) hairspray; (peinture) gloss paint.

laquelle /lakɛl/ ⇒LEQUEL.

lard /laʀ/ *nm* streaky bacon.

large /laʀʒ/ *adj* wide, broad; (grand) large; (généreux) generous; **avoir les idées ~s** be broad-minded; **~ d'esprit** broad-minded. ● *adv* (*calculer, mesurer*) on the generous side; **voir ~** think big. ● *nm* **faire 10 cm de ~** be 10 cm wide; **le ~** (mer) the open sea; **au ~ de** (Naut) off. **largement** *adv* widely; (*ouvrir*) wide; (amplement) amply; (généreusement) generously; (au moins) easily.

largesse /laʀʒɛs/ *nf* generous gift.

largeur /laʀʒœʀ/ *nf* width, breadth; **~ d'esprit** broad-mindedness.

larguer /laʀge/ [1] *vt* drop; **~ les amarres** cast off.

larme /laʀm/ *nf* tear; (goutte 🅣) drop; **en ~s** in tears.

larmoyant, ~e /laʀmwajɑ̃, -t/ *adj* full of tears. **larmoyer** [31] *vi* (*yeux*) water; (pleurnicher) whine.

larynx /laʀɛ̃ks/ *nm* larynx.

las, ~se /lɑ, lɑs/ *adj* weary.

lasagnes /lazaɲ/ *nfpl* lasagna.

laser /lazɛʀ/ *nm* laser.

lasser /lɑse/ [1] *vt* weary. □ **se ~** *vpr* grow tired, get weary (**de** of).

latéral, ~e (*mpl* **-aux**) /lateʀal, -o/ *adj* lateral.

latin, ~e /latɛ̃, -in/ *adj* Latin. ● *nm* (Ling) Latin.

latte /lat/ *nf* lath; (de plancher) board; (de siège) slat; (de mur, plafond) lath.

lauréat, ~e /lɔʀea, -t/ *adj* prize-winning. ● *nm, f* prize-winner.

laurier /lɔʀje/ *nm* (Bot) laurel; (Culin) bay-leaves.

lavable /lavabl/ *adj* washable.

lavabo /lavabo/ *nm* wash-basin; **~s** toilet(s).

lavage /lavaʒ/ *nm* washing; **~ de cerveau** brainwashing.

lavande /lavɑ̃d/ *nf* lavender.

lave /lav/ *nf* lava.

lave-glace (*pl* **~s**) /lavglas/ *nm* windscreen washer.

lave-linge /lavlɛ̃ʒ/ *nm inv* washing machine.

laver /lave/ [1] *vt* wash; **~ qn de** (fig) clear sb of. □ **se ~** *vpr* wash (oneself); **se ~ les mains** wash one's hands.

laverie /lavʀi/ *nf* **~ (automatique)** launderette; (US) laundromat.

lave-vaisselle /lavvɛsɛl/ *nm inv* dishwasher.

laxatif, -ive /laksatif, -v/ *a & nm* laxative.

layette /lɛjɛt/ *nf* baby clothes.

⋯⋯⋯⋯⋯⋯⋯⋯⋯⋯⋯⋯⋯⋯⋯⋯⋯⋯⋯⋯⋯

le, la, l' (*pl* **les**) /lə, la, l, le/
   l' before vowel or mute h.

●*déterminant*

⋯⋯► the.

⋯⋯► (notion générale) **aimer la musique** like music; **l'amour** love.

⋯⋯► (possession) **avoir les yeux verts** have green eyes; **il s'est cassé la jambe** he broke his leg.

⋯⋯► (prix) **10 francs ~ kilo** 10 francs a kilo.

⋯⋯► (temps) **~ lundi** on Mondays; **tous les mardis** every Tuesday.

⋯⋯► (avec nom propre) **les Dury** the Durys; **la reine Margot** Queen Margot; **la Belgique** Belgium.

⋯⋯► (avec adjectif) the; **je veux la rouge** I want the red one; **les riches** the rich.

●*pronom*

⋯⋯► (homme) him; (femme) her; (chose, animal) it; (au pluriel) them.

⋯⋯► (remplaçant une phrase) **je te l'avais bien dit** I told you so; **je ~ croyais aussi** I thought so too.

⋯⋯⋯⋯⋯⋯⋯⋯⋯⋯⋯⋯⋯⋯⋯⋯⋯⋯⋯⋯⋯

lécher /leʃe/ [14] *vt* lick; (*flamme*) lick; (*mer*) lap.

lèche-vitrines /lɛʃvitʀin/ *nm inv* **faire du ~** go window-shopping.

leçon /ləsɔ̃/ *nf* lesson; **faire la ~ à** lecture; **~ particulière** private lesson; **~s de conduite** driving lessons.

lecteur, -trice /lɛktœʀ, -tʀis/ *nm, f* reader; (Univ) foreign language assistant; **~ de cassettes** cassette player; **~ de disquettes** (disk) drive; **~ laser** CD player; **~ optique** optical scanner.

lecture /lɛktyʀ/ *nf* reading.

ledit, **ladite** (*pl* **lesdit(e)s**) / lədi, ladit, ledi(t)/ *adj* the aforementioned.

légal, ∼e (*mpl* **-aux**) /legal, -o/ *adj* legal. **légaliser** [1] *vt* legalize. **légalité** *nf* legality; (loi) law.

légendaire /leʒɑ̃dɛʀ/ *adj* legendary. **légende** *nf* (histoire, inscription) legend; (de carte) key; (d'illustration) caption.

léger, **-ère** /leʒe, -ɛʀ/ *adj* light; (*bruit, faute, maladie*) slight; (café, argument) weak; (imprudent) thoughtless; (frivole) fickle; **à la légère** thoughtlessly. **légèrement** *adv* lightly; (agir) thoughtlessly; (un peu) slightly. **légèreté** *nf* lightness; thoughtlessness.

légion /leʒjɔ̃/ *nf* legion.

législatif, **-ive** /leʒislatif, -v/ *adj* legislative; **élections législatives** general election.

legislature /leʒislatyʀ/ *nf* term of office.

légitime /leʒitim/ *adj* (Jur) legitimate; (fig) rightful; **agir en état de** ∼ **défense** act in self-defence. **légitimité** *nf* legitimacy.

legs /lɛg/ *nm* legacy; (d'effets personnels) bequest.

léguer /lege/ [14] *vt* bequeath.

légume /legym/ *nm* vegetable.

lendemain /lɑ̃dmɛ̃/ *nm* **le** ∼ the next day; (fig) the future; **le** ∼ **de** the day after; **le** ∼ **matin/soir** the next morning/evening; **du jour au** ∼ from one day to the next.

lent, ∼e /lɑ̃, -t/ *adj* slow. **lentement** *adv* slowly. **lenteur** *nf* slowness.

lentille /lɑ̃tij/ *nf* (Culin) lentil; (verre) lens; ∼s **de contact** contact lenses.

léopard /leɔpaʀ/ *nm* leopard.

lèpre /lɛpʀ/ *nf* leprosy.

....

lequel, **laquelle** (*pl* **les-quel(le)s**), **auquel** (*pl* **auxquel(le)s**), **duquel** (*pl* **desquel(le)s**) /ləkɛl, lakɛl, lekɛl, ɔkɛl, dykɛl, dekɛl/

à + lequel	= auquel,
à + lesquel(le)s	= auxquel(le)s;
de + lequel	= duquel,

de + lesquel(le)s = desquel(le)s

●*pronom*

····▸ (relatif) (personne) who; (complément indirect) whom; (autres cas) which; **l'ami auquel tu as écrit** the friend to whom you wrote; **les voisins chez lesquels Sophie est allée** the neighbours whose house Sophie went to.

····▸ (interrogatif) which; ∼ **tu veux?** which one do you want?

●*adjectif*

····▸ **auquel cas** in which case.

....

les /le/ ⇒LE.

lesbienne /lɛsbjɛn/ *nf* lesbian.

léser /leze/ [14] *vt* wrong.

lésiner /lezine/ [1] *vi* **ne pas** ∼ **sur** not stint on.

lesquels, **lesquelles** /lekɛl/ ⇒LEQUEL.

lessive /lesiv/ *nf* (poudre) washing-powder; (liquide) washing liquid; (linge, action) washing.

leste /lɛst/ *adj* agile, nimble; (grivois) coarse.

Lettonie /letɔni/ *nf* Latvia.

lettre /lɛtʀ/ *nf* letter; **à la** ∼, **au pied de la** ∼ literally; **en toutes** ∼s in full; **les** ∼s (Univ) (the) arts.

leucémie /løsemi/ *nf* leukaemia.

....

leur (*pl* ∼s) /lœʀ/

●*pronom personnel invariable*

····▸ them; **donne-le** ∼ give it to them; **je** ∼ **fais confiance** I trust them.

●*adjectif possessif*

····▸ their; ∼s **enfants** their children; **à** ∼ **arrivée** when they arrived.

●**le leur**, **la leur**, (*pl* **les leurs**) *pronom possessif*

····▸ theirs; **chacun le** ∼ one each; **je suis des** ∼s I am one of them.

....

levain /ləvɛ̃/ *nm* leaven.

levé, ∼e /ləve/ *adj* (debout) up.

levée /ləve/ *nf* (de peine, de sanctions) lifting; (de courrier) collection; (de troupes, d'impôts) levying.

lever /ləve/ [6] *vt* lift (up), raise; (*interdiction*) lift; (*séance*) close; (*armée, impôts*) levy. ● *vi* (*pâte*) rise. □ **se ~** *vpr* get up; (*soleil, rideau*) rise; (*jour*) break. ● *nm* au **~** on getting up; **~ du jour** daybreak; **~ de rideau** (Théât) curtain (up); **~ du soleil** sunrise.

levier /ləvje/ *nm* lever; **~ de changement de vitesse** gear lever.

lèvre /lɛvʀ/ *nf* lip.

lévrier /levʀije/ *nm* greyhound.

levure /ləvyʀ/ *nf* yeast; **~ chimique** baking powder.

lexique /lɛksik/ *nm* vocabulary; (*glossaire*) lexicon.

lézard /lezaʀ/ *nm* lizard.

lézarde /lezaʀd/ *nf* crack.

liaison /ljɛzɔ̃/ *nf* connection; (transport, Ordinat) link; (contact) contact; (Gram, Mil) liaison; (*amoureuse*) affair; **être en ~ avec** be in contact with; **assurer la ~ entre** liaise between.

liane /ljan/ *nf* creeper.

Liban /libã/ *nm* Lebanon.

libeller /libele/ [1] *vt* (*chèque*) write; (contrat) draw up; **libellé à l'ordre de** made out to.

libellule /libelyl/ *nf* dragonfly.

libéral, ~e (*mpl* **-aux**) /libeʀal, -o/ *adj* liberal; **les professions ~es** the professions.

libérateur, -trice /libeʀatœʀ, -tʀis/ *adj* liberating. ● *nm,f* liberator.

libération *nf* release; (de pays) liberation.

libérer /libeʀe/ [14] *vt* (*personne*) free, release; (*pays*) liberate, free; (*bureau, lieux*) vacate; (*gaz*) release. □ **se ~** *vpr* free oneself.

liberté /libɛʀte/ *nf* freedom, liberty; (loisir) free time; **être/mettre en ~** be/set free; **~ conditionnelle** parole; **~ provisoire** provisional release (*pending trial*); **~ surveillée** probation; **~s publiques** civil liberties.

Libertel /libɛʀtɛl/ *nm* (Internet) Freenet.

libraire /libʀɛʀ/ *nmf* bookseller. **librairie** *nf* bookshop.

libre /libʀ/ *adj* free; (*place, pièce*) vacant, free; (*passage*) clear; (*école*) private (*usually religious*); **~ de qch/ de faire** free from sth/to do. **libre-échange** *nm* free trade. **libre-service** (*pl* **libres-services**) *nm* (magasin) self-service shop; (restaurant) self-service restaurant.

licence /lisɑ̃s/ *nf* licence; (Univ) degree.

licencié, ~e /lisɑ̃sje/ *nm,f* graduate; **~ ès lettres/sciences** Bachelor of Arts/Science.

licenciements /lisɑ̃simɑ̃/ *nm* redundancy; (pour faute) dismissal. **licencier** [45] *vt* make redundant; (pour faute) dismiss.

licorne /likɔʀn/ *nf* unicorn.

liège /liɛʒ/ *nm* cork.

lien /ljɛ̃/ *nm* (rapport) link; (attache) bond, tie; (corde) rope; **~s affectifs/de parenté** emotional/family ties.

lier /lje/ [45] *vt* tie (up), bind; (relier) link; (engager, unir) bind; **~ conversation** strike up a conversation; **ils sont très liés** they are very close. □ **se ~ avec** *vpr* make friends with.

lierre /ljɛʀ/ *nm* ivy.

lieu (*pl* **~x**) /ljø/ *nm* place; **~x** (locaux) premises; (d'un accident) scene; **sur les ~x** at the scene; **au ~ de** instead of; **avoir ~** take place; **donner ~ à** give rise to; **tenir ~ de** serve as; **s'il y a ~** if necessary; **en premier ~** firstly; **en dernier ~** lastly; **~ commun** commonplace; **~ de rencontre** meeting place.

lièvre /ljɛvʀ/ *nm* hare.

lifting /liftiŋ/ *nm* face-lift.

ligne /liɲ/ *nf* line; (trajet) route; (de métro, train) line; (formes) lines; (de femme) figure; **en ~** (joueurs) lined up; (au téléphone) on the phone; (Ordinat) on line; **~ spécialisée** (Internet) dedicated line.

ligoter /ligɔte/ [1] *vt* tie up.

ligue /lig/ *nf* league. **liguer (se)** [1] *vpr* join forces (**contre** against).

lilas /lila/ *nm & a inv* lilac.

limace /limas/ *nf* slug.

limande /limɑ̃d/ *nf* (poisson) dab.

lime /lim/ *nf* file; **~ à ongles** nail file.

limitation /limitasjɔ̃/ *nf* limitation; **~ de vitesse** speed limit.

limite /limit/ nf limit; (de jardin, champ) boundary; **à la ~ de** (fig) verging on, bordering on; **à la ~** if it comes to it, at a pinch; **dans une certaine ~** up to a point; **dans la ~ du possible** as far as possible. ● adj (vitesse, âge) maximum; **cas ~** borderline case; **date ~** deadline; **date ~ de vente** sell-by date.

limiter /limite/ [1] vt limit; (délimiter) form the border of. □ **se ~** vpr limit oneself (**à** to).

limonade /limɔnad/ nf lemonade.

limpide /lɛ̃pid/ adj limpid, clear.

lin /lɛ̃/ nm (tissu) linen.

linge /lɛ̃ʒ/ nm linen; (lessive) washing; (torchon) cloth; **~ (de corps)** underwear. **lingerie** nf underwear. **lingette** nf wipe.

lingot /lɛ̃go/ nm ingot.

linguistique /lɛ̃gɥistik/ adj linguistic. ● nf linguistics.

lion /ljɔ̃/ nm lion; **le L~** Leo. **lionceau** (pl ~x) nm lion cub. **lionne** nf lioness.

liquidation /likidasjɔ̃/ nf liquidation; (vente) (clearance) sale; **entrer en ~** go into liquidation.

liquide /likid/ adj liquid. ● nm (argent) **~** ready money; **payer en ~** pay cash; **~ de frein** brake fluid.

liquider /likide/ [1] vt liquidate; (vendre) sell.

lire /liʀ/ [39] vt/i read. ● nf lira.

lis¹ /li/ ⇒LIRE[39].

lis² /lis/ nm (fleur) lily.

lisible /lizibl/ adj legible; (roman) readable.

lisière /lizjɛʀ/ nf edge.

lisse /lis/ adj smooth.

liste /list/ nf list; **~ d'attente** waiting list; **~ électorale** register of voters; **être sur (la) ~ rouge** be ex-directory.

listing /listiŋ/ nm printout.

lit /li/ nm bed; **se mettre au ~** get into bed; **~ de camp** camp-bed; **~ d'enfant** cot; **~ d'une personne** single bed; **~ de deux personnes, grand ~** double bed.

literie /litʀi/ nf bedding.

litière /litjɛʀ/ nf litter.

litige /litiʒ/ nm dispute.

litre /litʀ/ nm litre.

littéraire /liteʀɛʀ/ adj literary; (études, formation) arts.

littéral, ~e (mpl -aux) /liteʀal, -o/ adj literal.

littérature /liteʀatyʀ/ nf literature.

littoral (pl -aux) /litɔʀal, -o/ nm coast.

Lituanie /litɥani/ nf Lithuania.

livide /livid/ adj deathly pale.

livraison /livʀɛzɔ̃/ nf delivery.

livre /livʀ/ nf (monnaie, poids) pound. ● nm book; **~ de bord** log-book; **~ de compte** books; **~ de poche** paperback.

livrer /livʀe/ [1] vt (Comm) deliver; (abandonner) give over (**à** to); (remettre) (coupable, document) hand over (**à** to); **livré à soi-même** left to oneself. □ **se ~** vpr (se rendre) give oneself up (**à** to); **se ~ à** (boisson, actes) indulge in; (ami) confide in.

livret /livʀɛ/ nm book; (Mus) libretto; **~ de caisse d'épargne** savings book; **~ scolaire** school report (book).

livreur, -euse /livʀœʀ, -øz/ nm, f delivery man, delivery woman.

local¹, ~e (mpl -aux) /lɔkal, -o/ adj local.

local² (pl -aux) /lɔkal, -o/ nm premises; **locaux** premises.

localement /lɔkalmɑ̃/ adv locally.

localiser /lɔkalize/ [1] vt (repérer) locate; (circonscrire) localize.

locataire /lɔkatɛʀ/ nmf tenant; (de chambre) lodger.

location /lɔkasjɔ̃/ nf (de maison) renting; (de voiture, de matériel) hire, rental; (de place) booking, reservation; (par propriétaire) renting out; hiring out; **en ~** (voiture) on hire, rented; (habiter) in rented accommodation.

locomotive /lɔkɔmɔtiv/ nf engine, locomotive.

locution /lɔkysjɔ̃/ nf phrase.

loge /lɔʒ/ nf (de concierge, de franc-maçons) lodge; (d'acteur) dressing-room; (de spectateur) box.

logement /lɔʒmɑ̃/ nm accommodation; (appartement) flat; (habitat) housing.

loger /lɔʒe/ [40] vt (réfugié, famille) house; (ami) put up; (client)

accommodate. ● *vi* live. □ **se** ~ *vpr*
live; **trouver à se** ~ find
accommodation; **se** ~ **dans** (*balle*)
lodge itself in.

logiciel /lɔʒisjɛl/ *nm* software; ~
contributif shareware; ~
d'application application software; ~
de groupe groupware; ~ **de jeux**
games software; ~ **de navigation**
browser; ~ **public** freeware.

logique /lɔʒik/ *adj* logical. ● *nf*
logic.

logis /lɔʒi/ *nm* dwelling.

logistique /lɔʒistik/ *nf* logistics.

loi /lwa/ *nf* law.

loin /lwɛ̃/ *adv* far (away); **au** ~ far
away; **de** ~ from far away; (de
beaucoup) by far; ~ **de là** far from it;
plus ~ further; **il revient de** ~ (fig)
he had a close shave.

lointain, ~**e** /lwɛ̃tɛ̃, -ɛn/ *adj* distant.
● *nm* distance; **dans le** ~ in the
distance.

loir /lwaʀ/ *nm* dormouse.

loisir /lwaziʀ/ *nm* (spare) time; ~**s**
(temps libre) leisure, spare time;
(distractions) leisure activities; **à** ~ at
one's leisure; **avoir le** ~ **de faire**
have time to do.

londonien, ~**ne** /lɔ̃dɔnjɛ̃, -ɛn/ *adj*
London. **L**~, ~**e** *nm,f* Londoner.

Londres /lɔ̃dʀ/ *npr* London.

long, **longue** /lɔ̃, lɔ̃g/ *adj* long; **à** ~
terme long-term; **être** ~ **à faire** be a
long time doing. ● *nm* **de** ~ (mesure)
long; **de** ~ **en large** back and forth;
(tout) **le** ~ **de** (all) along. ● *adv* **en**
dire ~ **sur qn/qch** say a lot about sb/
sth; **en savoir plus** ~ **sur** know more
about.

longer /lɔ̃ʒe/ [40] *vt* go along; (limiter)
border.

longitude /lɔ̃ʒityd/ *nf* longitude.

longtemps /lɔ̃tɑ̃/ *adv* a long time;
avant ~ before long; **trop** ~ too long;
ça prendra ~ it will take a long
time; **prendre plus** ~ **que prévu** take
longer than anticipated.

longuement /lɔ̃gmɑ̃/ *adv*
(longtemps) for a long time; (en détail)
at length.

longueur /lɔ̃gœʀ/ *nf* length; ~**s** (de
texte) over-long parts; **à** ~ **de journée**

all day long; **en** ~ lengthwise; ~
d'onde wavelength.

lopin /lɔpɛ̃/ *nm* ~ **de terre** patch of
land.

loque /lɔk/ *nf* ~**s** rags; ~ (**humaine**)
(human) wreck.

loquet /lɔkɛ/ *nm* latch.

lors de /lɔʀdə/ *prép* (au moment de) at
the time of; (pendant) during.

lorsque /lɔʀsk(ə)/ *conj* when.

losange /lɔzɑ̃ʒ/ *nm* diamond.

lot /lo/ *nm* (portion) share; (aux
enchères) lot; (Ordinat) batch; (destin)
lot; **gagner le gros** ~ hit the jackpot.

loterie /lɔtʀi/ *nf* lottery.

lotion /losjɔ̃/ *nf* lotion.

lotissement /lɔtismɑ̃/ *nm* (à
construire) building plot; (construit)
(housing) development.

louable /luabl/ *adj* praiseworthy.
louange *nf* praise.

louche /luʃ/ *adj* shady, dubious.
● *nf* ladle.

loucher /luʃe/ [1] *vi* squint.

louer /lwe/ [1] *vt* (approuver) praise
(**de** for); (prendre en location) (*maison*)
rent; (*voiture, matériel*) hire, rent;
(*place*) book, reserve; (donner en
location) (*maison*) rent out; (*matériel*)
rent out, hire out; **à** ~ to let, for rent
(US).

loufoque /lufɔk/ *adj* 🄘 crazy.

loup /lu/ *nm* wolf.

loupe /lup/ *nf* magnifying glass.

louper /lupe/ [1] *vt* 🄘 miss; (*examen*)
flunk 🄘.

lourd, ~**e** /luʀ, -d/ *adj* heavy; (*faute*)
serious; ~ **de dangers** fraught with
danger; **il fait** ~ it's close *ou* muggy.

loutre /lutʀ/ *nf* otter.

louveteau (*pl* ~**x**) /luvto/ *nm* wolf
cub; (scout) Cub (Scout).

loyal, ~**e** (*mpl* **-aux**) /lwajal, -o/ *adj*
loyal, faithful; (honnête) fair. **loyauté**
nf loyalty; fairness.

loyer /lwaje/ *nm* rent.

lu /ly/ ⇒LIRE [39].

lubrifiant /lybʀifjɑ̃/ *nm* lubricant.

lucide /lysid/ *adj* lucid. **lucidité** *nf*
lucidity.

lucratif, **-ive** /lykʀatif, -v/ *adj*
lucrative; **à but non** ~ non-profit-
making.

ludiciel /lydisjɛl/ *nm* (Ordinat) games software.

lueur /lɥœʀ/ *nf* (faint) light, glimmer; (fig) glimmer, gleam.

luge /lyʒ/ *nf* toboggan.

lugubre /lygybʀ/ *adj* gloomy.

lui /lɥi/

● *pronom*

····▸ (masculin) (sujet) he; ∼, **il est à l'étranger** he's abroad; **c'est ∼!** it's him!; (objet) him; (animal) it; **c'est à ∼** it's his; **elle conduit mieux que ∼** she's a better driver than he is.

····▸ (féminin) her; **je ∼ ai annoncé** I told her.

····▸ (masculin/féminin) **donne-le-∼** give it to him/her.

lui-même /lɥimɛm/ *pron* himself; (animal) itself.

luire /lɥiʀ/ [17] *vi* shine; (reflet humide) glisten; (reflet chaud, faible) glow.

lumière /lymjɛʀ/ *nf* light; ∼**s** (connaissances) knowledge; **faire (toute) la ∼ sur une affaire** clear a matter up.

luminaire /lyminɛʀ/ *nm* lamp.

lumineux, -euse /lyminø, -z/ *adj* luminous; (éclairé) illuminated; (*rayon*) of light; (radieux) radiant; **source lumineuse** light source.

lunaire /lynɛʀ/ *adj* lunar.

lunatique /lynatik/ *adj* temperamental.

lunch /lœnʃ/ *nm* buffet lunch.

lundi /lœdi/ *nm* Monday.

lune /lyn/ *nf* moon; ∼ **de miel** honeymoon.

lunettes /lynɛt/ *nfpl* glasses; (de protection) goggles; ∼ **de ski/natation** ski/swimming goggles; ∼ **noires** dark glasses; ∼ **de soleil** sun-glasses.

lustre /lystʀ/ *nm* (éclat) lustre; (objet) chandelier.

lutin /lytɛ̃/ *nm* goblin.

lutte /lyt/ *nf* fight, struggle; (Sport) wrestling. **lutter** [1] *vi* fight, struggle; (Sport) wrestle. **lutteur, -euse** *nm, f* fighter; (Sport) wrestler.

luxe /lyks/ *nm* luxury; **de ∼** luxury; (*produit*) de luxe.

Luxembourg /lyksɑ̃buʀ/ *nm* Luxemburg.

luxer (se) /(sə)lykse/ [1] *vpr* **se ∼ le genou** dislocate one's knee.

luxueux, -euse /lyksɥø, -z/ *adj* luxurious.

lycée /lise/ *nm* (secondary) school. **lycéen, ∼ne** *nm, f* pupil (at secondary school).

lyophilisé, ∼e /ljɔfilize/ *adj* freeze-dried.

lyrique /liʀik/ *adj* (*poésie*) lyric; (passionné) lyrical; **artiste/théâtre ∼** opera singer/house.

lys /lis/ *nm* lily.

Mm

m' /m/ ⇒ME.

ma /ma/ ⇒MON.

macabre /makabʀ/ *adj* macabre.

macadam /makadam/ *nm* Tarmac®.

macaron /makaʀɔ̃/ *nm* (gâteau) macaroon; (insigne) badge.

macédoine /masedwan/ *nf* mixed diced vegetables; ∼ **de fruits** fruit salad.

macérer /maseʀe/ [14] *vt/i* soak; (dans du vinaigre) pickle.

mâcher /mɑʃe/ [1] *vt* chew; **ne pas ∼ ses mots** not mince one's words.

machin /maʃɛ̃/ *nm* (chose) thing; (dont on ne trouve pas le nom) whatsit .

machinal, ∼e (*mpl* **-aux**) /maʃinal, -o/ *adj* automatic. **machinalement** *adv* mechanically, automatically.

machination /maʃinasjɔ̃/ *nf* plot; **des ∼s** machinations.

machine /maʃin/ *nf* machine; (d'un train, navire) engine; ∼ **à écrire** typewriter; ∼ **à laver/coudre** washing-/sewing-machine; ∼ **à sous** fruit machine; (US) slot-machine. **machine-outil** (*pl* **machines-**

outils) *nf* machine tool.
machinerie *nf* machinery.

machiniste /maʃinist/ *nm* (Théât) stage-hand; (conducteur) driver.

mâchoire /mɑʃwaʀ/ *nf* jaw.

mâchonner /mɑʃɔne/ [1] *vt* chew.

maçon /masɔ̃/ *nm* (entrepreneur) builder; (poseur de briques) bricklayer; (qui construit en pierre) mason.
maçonnerie *nf* (briques) brickwork; (pierres) stonework, masonry; (travaux) building.

madame (*pl* **mesdames**) /madam, medam/ *nf* (à une inconnue) (dans une lettre) **M∼** Dear Madam; **bonjour, ∼** good morning; **mesdames et messieurs** ladies and gentlemen; (à une femme dont on connaît le nom) (dans une lettre) **Chère M∼** Dear Mrs *ou* Ms X; **bonjour, ∼** good morning Mrs *ou* Ms X; **oui M∼ le Ministre** yes Minister; (formule de respect) **oui M∼** yes madam.

mademoiselle (*pl* **mesdemoiselles**) /madmwazɛl, medmwazɛl/ *nf* (à une inconnue) (dans une lettre) **M∼** Dear Madam; **bonjour, ∼** good morning; **entrez mesdemoiselles** come in (ladies); (à une jeune fille dont on connaît le nom) (dans une lettre) **Chère M∼** Dear Ms *ou* Miss X; **bonjour, ∼** good morning Miss *ou* Ms X.

magasin /magazɛ̃/ *nm* shop, store; (entrepôt) warehouse; (d'une arme) magazine; **en ∼** in stock.

magazine /magazin/ *nm* magazine; (émission) programme.

Maghreb /magʀɛb/ *nm* North Africa.

magicien, ∼ne /maʒisjɛ̃, -ɛn/ *nm,f* magician.

magie /maʒi/ *nf* magic. **magique** *adj* magic; (mystérieux) magical.

magistral, ∼e (*mpl* **-aux**) /maʒistʀal, -o/ *adj* masterly; (grand: hum) tremendous; **cours ∼** lecture.

magistrat /maʒistʀa/ *nm* magistrate.

magistrature /maʒistʀatyʀ/ *nf* judiciary; (fonction) public office.

magner (se) /(sə)maɲe/ [1] *vpr* ✦ get a move on.

magnétique /maɲetik/ *adj* magnetic. **magnétiser** [1] *vt* magnetize. **magnétisme** *nm* magnetism.

magnétophone /maɲetɔfɔn/ *nm* tape recorder; (à cassettes) cassette recorder.

magnétoscope /maɲetɔskɔp/ *nm* video recorder.

magnificence /maɲifisɑ̃s/ *nf* magnificence. **magnifique** *adj* magnificent.

magot /mago/ *nm* ⚀ hoard (of money).

magouille /maguj/ *nf* ⚀ scheming, skulduggery.

magret /magʀɛ/ *nm* ∼ **de canard** duck breast.

mai /mɛ/ *nm* May.

maigre /mɛgʀ/ *adj* thin; (viande) lean; (yaourt) low-fat; (fig) poor, meagre; **faire ∼** abstain from meat.
maigreur *nf* thinness; leanness; (fig) meagreness.

maigrir /megʀiʀ/ [2] *vi* get thin(ner); (en suivant un régime) slim. ● *vt* make thin(ner).

maille /maj/ *nf* stitch; (de filet) mesh; **∼ qui file** ladder, run; **avoir ∼ à partir avec qn** have a brush with sb.

maillet /majɛ/ *nm* mallet.

maillon /majɔ̃/ *nm* link.

maillot /majo/ *nm* (Sport) shirt, jersey; **∼ (de corps)** vest; (US) undershirt; **∼ (de bain)** (swimming) costume.

main /mɛ̃/ *nf* hand; **donner la ∼ à qn** hold sb's hand; **se donner la ∼** hold hands; **en ∼s propres** in person; **en bonnes ∼s** in good hands; **∼ courante** handrail; **se faire la ∼** get the hang of it; **perdre la ∼** lose one's touch; **sous la ∼** to hand; **vol à ∼ armée** armed robbery; **fait (à la) ∼** handmade; **haut les ∼s!** hands up!
main-d'œuvre (*pl* **mains-d'œuvre**) *nf* labour; (ouvriers) labour force.

main-forte /mɛ̃fɔʀt/ *nf inv* **prêter ∼ à qn** come to sb's aid.

maint, ∼e /mɛ̃, mɛ̃t/ *adj* many a (+ *sg*); **∼s** many; **à ∼es reprises** many times.

maintenant /mɛt(ə)nɑ̃/ adv now; (de nos jours) nowadays; (l'époque actuelle) today.

maintenir /mɛt(ə)niʀ/ [58] vt keep, maintain; (soutenir) support, hold up; (affirmer) maintain; (decision) stand by. □ se ~ vpr (tendance) persist; (prix, malade) remain stable.

maintien /mɛtjɛ̃/ nm (attitude) bearing; (conservation) maintenance.

maire /mɛʀ/ nm mayor.

mairie /meʀi/ nf town hall; (administration) town council.

mais /mɛ/ conj but; ~ oui of course; ~ non of course not.

maïs /mais/ nm maize, corn; (Culin) sweetcorn.

maison /mɛzɔ̃/ nf house; (foyer) home; (immeuble) building; ~ (de commerce) firm; à la ~ at home; rentrer ou aller à la ~ go home; ~ des jeunes (et de la culture) youth club; ~ de repos rest home; ~ de convalescence convalescent home; ~ de retraite old people's home; ~ mère parent company. ● a inv (Culin) home-made.

maître, -esse /mɛtʀ, -ɛs/ adj (qui contrôle) être ~ de soi be one's own master; ~ de la situation in control of the situation; (principal) (idée, qualité) key, main. ● nm, f (Scol) teacher; (d'animal) owner, master. ● nm (expert, guide) master; (dirigeant) leader; ~ de conférences senior lecturer; ~ d'hôtel head waiter; (domestique) butler. **maître-assistant, ~e** (pl **maîtres-assistants**) nm, f lecturer. **maître-chanteur** (pl **maîtres-chanteurs**) nm blackmailer. **maître-nageur** (pl **maîtres-nageurs**) nm swimming instructor. **maîtresse** nf (amante) mistress.

maîtrise /mɛtʀiz/ nf mastery; (contrôle) control; (Mil) supremacy; (Univ) master's degree; ~ (de soi) self-control.

maîtriser /mɛtʀize/ [1] vt (sujet, technique) master; (incendie, sentiment, personne) control. □ se ~ vpr have self-control.

maïzena® /maizena/ nf cornflour.

majesté /maʒɛste/ nf majesty.

majestueux, -euse /maʒɛstɥø, z/ adj majestic.

majeur, ~e /maʒœʀ/ adj major, main; (Jur) of age; en ~e partie mostly; la ~e partie de most of. ● nm middle finger.

majoration /maʒɔʀasjɔ̃/ nf increase (de in). **majorer** [1] vt increase.

majoritaire /maʒɔʀitɛʀ/ adj majority; être ~ be in the majority. **majorité** nf majority; en ~ chiefly.

Majorque /majɔʀk/ nf Majorca.

majuscule /maʒyskyl/ adj capital. ● nf capital letter.

mal[1] /mal/ adv badly; (incorrectement) wrong(ly); **aller ~** (personne) be unwell; (affaires) go badly; ~ **entendre/comprendre** not hear/understand properly; ~ **en point** in a bad state; **pas ~** quite a lot. ● a inv bad, wrong; **c'est ~ de** it is wrong ou bad to; **ce n'est pas ~** 🔟 it's not bad; **Nick n'est pas ~** 🔟 Nick is not bad-looking.

mal[2] (pl **maux**) /mal, mo/ nm evil; (douleur) pain, ache; (maladie) disease; (effort) trouble; (dommage) harm; (malheur) misfortune; **avoir ~ à la tête/à la gorge** have a headache/a sore throat; **avoir le ~ de mer/du pays** be seasick/homesick; **faire ~** hurt; **se faire ~** hurt oneself; **j'ai ~** it hurts; **faire du ~ à** hurt, harm; **se donner du ~ pour faire qch** go to a lot of trouble to do sth.

malade /malad/ adj sick, ill; (bras, œil) bad; (plante, poumons, côlon) diseased; **tomber ~** fall ill; (fou 🔟) mad. ● nmf sick person; (d'un médecin) patient; ~ **mental** mentally ill person.

maladie /maladi/ nf illness, disease; (manie 🔟) mania.

maladif, -ive /maladif, -v/ adj sickly; (jalousie, peur) pathological.

maladresse /maladʀɛs/ nf clumsiness; (erreur) blunder.

maladroit, ~e /maladʀwa, -t/ adj clumsy; (sans tact) tactless.

malaise /malɛz/ nm feeling of faintness; (gêne) uneasiness; (état de crise) unrest.

malaisé, ~e /maleze/ adj difficult.

Malaisie /malɛzi/ *nf* Malaysia.

malaria /malaʀja/ *nf* malaria.

malaxer /malakse/ [1] *vt* (pétrir) knead; (mêler) mix.

malchance /malʃɑ̃s/ *nf* misfortune. **malchanceux, -euse** *adj* unlucky.

mâle /mɑl/ *adj* male; (viril) manly. ● *nm* male.

malédiction /malediksjɔ̃/ *nf* curse.

maléfice /malefis/ *nm* evil spell. **maléfique** *adj* evil.

malentendant, ~e /malɑ̃tɑ̃dɑ̃, -t/ *adj* hard of hearing.

malentendu /malɑ̃tɑ̃dy/ *nm* misunderstanding.

malfaçon /malfasɔ̃/ *nf* defect.

malfaisant, ~e /malfəzɑ̃, -t/ *adj* harmful; (*personne*) evil.

malfaiteur /malfɛtœʀ/ *nm* criminal.

malformation /malfɔʀmasjɔ̃/ *nf* malformation.

malgré /malgʀe/ *prép* in spite of, despite; ~ **tout** nevertheless.

malheur /malœʀ/ *nm* misfortune; (accident) accident; **par ~** unfortunately; **faire un ~** 🆃 be a big hit; **porter ~** be *ou* bring bad luck.

malheureusement /malœʀøzmɑ̃/ *adv* unfortunately.

malheureux, -euse /malœʀø, -z/ *adj* unhappy; (regrettable) unfortunate; (sans succès) unlucky; (insignifiant) paltry, pathetic. ● *nm,f* (poor) wretch.

malhonnête /malɔnɛt/ *adj* dishonest. **malhonnêteté** *nf* dishonesty.

malice /malis/ *nf* mischief; **sans ~** harmless; **avec ~** mischievously. **malicieux, -ieuse** *adj* mischievous.

malignité /maliɲite/ *nf* malignancy. **malin, -igne** *adj* clever, smart; (méchant) malicious; (*tumeur*) malignant; (difficile 🆃) difficult.

malingre /malɛ̃gʀ/ *adj* puny.

malle /mal/ *nf* (valise) trunk; (Auto) boot; (US) trunk.

mallette /malɛt/ *nf* (small) suitcase; (pour le bureau) briefcase.

malmener /malmøne/ [6] *vt* manhandle; (fig) give a rough ride to.

malnutrition /malnytʀisjɔ̃/ *nf* malnutrition.

malodorant, ~e /malɔdɔʀɑ̃, -t/ *adj* smelly, foul-smelling.

malpoli, ~e /malpɔli/ *adj* rude, impolite.

malpropre /malpʀɔpʀ/ *adj* dirty.

malsain, ~e /malsɛ̃, -ɛn/ *adj* unhealthy.

malt /malt/ *nm* malt.

Malte /malt/ *nf* Malta.

maltraiter /maltʀete/ [1] *vt* ill-treat.

malveillance /malvɛjɑ̃s/ *nf* malice. **malveillant, ~e** *adj* malicious.

maman /mamɑ̃/ *nf* mum(my), mother; (US) mom(my).

mamelle /mamɛl/ *nf* teat.

mamelon /mamlɔ̃/ *nm* (Anat) nipple; (colline) hillock.

mamie /mami/ *nf* 🆃 granny.

mammifère /mamifɛʀ/ *nm* mammal.

manche /mɑ̃ʃ/ *nf* sleeve; (Sport, Pol) round. ● *nm* (d'un instrument) handle; **~ à balai** broomstick; (Aviat) joystick. **M~** *nf* **la M~** the Channel; **le tunnel sous la M~** the Channel tunnel.

manchette /mɑ̃ʃɛt/ *nf* cuff; (de journal) headline.

manchot, ~te /mɑ̃ʃo, -ɔt/ *nm,f* one-armed person; (sans bras) armless person. ● *nm* (oiseau) penguin.

mandarine /mɑ̃daʀin/ *nf* tangerine, mandarin (orange).

mandat /mɑ̃da/ *nm* (postal) money order; (Pol) mandate; (procuration) proxy; (de police) warrant; **~ d'arrêt** arrest warrant.

mandataire /mɑ̃datɛʀ/ *nm* representative; (Jur) proxy.

manège /manɛʒ/ *nm* riding school; (à la foire) merry-go-round; (manœuvre) trick, ploy.

manette /manɛt/ *nf* lever; (de jeu) joystick.

mangeable /mɑ̃ʒabl/ *adj* edible.

mangeoire /mɑ̃ʒwaʀ/ *nf* trough; (pour oiseaux) feeder.

manger /mɑ̃ʒe/ [40] *vt* eat; (*fortune*) go through; (*profits*) eat away at;

(*économies*) use up; (*ronger*) eat into.
● *vi* eat; **donner à ~ à** feed. ● *nm* food.

mangue /mɑ̃g/ *nf* mango.

maniable /manjabl/ *adj* easy to handle.

maniaque /manjak/ *adj* fussy.
● *nmf* fusspot; (*fou*) maniac; (*fanatique*) fanatic; **un ~ de l'ordre** a stickler for tidiness.

manie /mani/ *nf* habit; (*marotte*) obsession.

maniement /manimɑ̃/ *nm* handling. **manier** [45] *vt* handle.

manière /manjɛʀ/ *nf* way, manner; **~s** (*politesse*) manners; (*chichis*) fuss; **à la ~ de** in the style of; **de ~ à** so as to; **de toute ~** anyway, in any case.

maniéré, ~e /manjeʀe/ *adj* affected.

manif /manif/ *nf* 🇫 demo.

manifestant, ~e /manifɛstɑ̃, -t/ *nm,f* demonstrator.

manifestation /manifɛstasjɔ̃/ *nf* expression, manifestation; (*de maladie, phénomène*) appearance; (Pol) demonstration; (*événement*) event; **~ culturelle** cultural event.

manifeste /manifɛst/ *adj* obvious.
● *nm* manifesto.

manifester /manifɛste/ [1] *vt* show, manifest; (*désir, crainte*) express.
● *vi* (Pol) demonstrate. □ **se ~** *vpr* (*sentiment*) show itself; (*apparaître*) appear; (*répondre à un appel*) come forward.

manigance /manigɑ̃s/ *nf* little plot. **manigancer** [10] *vt* plot.

manipulation /manipylasjɔ̃/ *nf* handling; (*péj*) manipulation.

manivelle /manivɛl/ *nf* handle, crank.

mannequin /mankɛ̃/ *nm* (*personne*) model; (*statue*) dummy.

manœuvrer /manœvʀe/ [1] *vt* manoeuvre; (*machine*) operate. ● *vi* manoeuvre.

manoir /manwaʀ/ *nm* manor.

manque /mɑ̃k/ *nm* lack (**de** of); (*lacune*) gap; **~ à gagner** loss of earnings; **en (état de) ~** having withdrawal symptoms.

manqué, ~e /mɑ̃ke/ *adj* (*écrivain*) failed; **garçon ~** tomboy.

manquement /mɑ̃kmɑ̃/ *nm* **~ à** breach of.

manquer /mɑ̃ke/ [1] *vt* miss; (*gâcher*) spoil; **~ à** (*devoir*) fail in; **~ de** be short of, lack; **il/ça lui manque** he misses him/it; **~ (de) faire** (*faillir*) nearly do; **ne manquez pas de** be sure to; **~ à sa parole** break one's word. ● *vi* be short *ou* lacking; (*être absent*) be absent; (*en moins, disparu*) be missing; **il me manque 20 francs** I'm 20 francs short.

mansarde /mɑ̃saʀd/ *nf* attic (room).

manteau (*pl* **~x**) /mɑ̃to/ *nm* coat.

manucure /manykyʀ/ *nmf* manicurist. ● *nf* (*soins*) manicure.

manuel, ~le /manɥɛl/ *adj* manual.
● *nm* (*livre*) manual; (Scol) textbook.

manufacture /manyfaktyʀ/ *nf* factory; (*fabrication*) manufacture. **manufacturer** [1] *vt* manufacture.

manuscrit, ~e /manyskʀi, -t/ *adj* handwritten. ● *nm* manuscript.

mappemonde /mapmɔ̃d/ *nf* world map; (*sphère*) globe.

maquereau (*pl* **~x**) /makʀo/ *nm* (*poisson*) mackerel; 🇫 pimp.

maquette /makɛt/ *nf* (*scale*) model; **~ (de mise en page)** paste-up.

maquillage /makijaʒ/ *nm* make-up.

maquiller /makije/ [1] *vt* make up; (*truquer*) doctor, fake. □ **se ~** *vpr* make (oneself) up.

maquis /maki/ *nm* (*paysage*) scrub; (Mil) Maquis, underground.

maraîcher, -ère /maʀeʃe, -ɛʀ/ *nm,f* market gardener; (US) truck farmer.

marais /maʀɛ/ *nm* marsh.

marasme /maʀasm/ *nm* slump, stagnation; **dans le ~** in the doldrums.

marbre /maʀbʀ/ *nm* marble.

marc /maʀ/ *nm* (*eau-de-vie*) marc; **~ de café** coffee grounds.

marchand, ~e /maʀʃɑ̃, -d/ *adj* (*valeur*) market. ● *nm,f* trader; (*de charbon, vins*) merchant; **~ de couleurs** ironmonger; (US) hardware merchant; **~ de journaux** newsagent; **~ de légumes** greengrocer; **~ de poissons** fishmonger.

marchander /maʁʃɑ̃de/ [1] *vt* haggle over. ● *vi* haggle.

marchandise /maʁʃɑ̃diz/ *nf* goods.

marche /maʁʃ/ *nf* (démarche, trajet) walk; (rythme) pace; (Mil, Mus, Pol) march; (d'escalier) step; (Sport) walking; (de machine) operation, working; (de véhicule) running; **en ~** (*train*) moving; (*moteur, machine*) running; **faire ~ arrière** (*véhicule*) reverse; **mettre en ~** start (up); **se mettre en ~** start moving.

marché /maʁʃe/ *nm* market; (contrat) deal; **faire son ~** do one's shopping; **~ aux puces** flea market; **~ noir** black market.

marchepied /maʁʃəpje/ *nm* (de train, camion) step.

marcher /maʁʃe/ [1] *vi* walk; (poser le pied) tread (**sur** on); (aller) go; (fonctionner) work, run; (prospérer) go well; (*film, livre*) do well; (consentir 🔲) agree; **faire ~ qn** 🔲 pull sb's leg.

mardi /maʁdi/ *nm* Tuesday; **M~ gras** Shrove Tuesday.

mare /maʁ/ *nf* (étang) pond; (flaque) pool.

marécage /maʁekaʒ/ *nm* marsh; (sous les tropiques) swamp.

maréchal (*pl* **-aux**) /maʁeʃal, -o/ *nm* field marshal.

maréchal-ferrant (*pl* **-aux-ferrants** /maʁeʃalfeʁɑ̃/ *nm* blacksmith.

marée /maʁe/ *nf* tide; (poissons) fresh fish; **~ haute/basse** high/low tide; **~ noire** oil slick.

marelle /maʁɛl/ *nf* hopscotch.

margarine /maʁɡaʁin/ *nf* margarine.

marge /maʁʒ/ *nf* margin; **en ~ de** (à l'écart de) on the fringe(s) of; **~ bénéficiaire** profit margin.

marginal, **~e** (*mpl* **-aux**) /maʁʒinal, -o/ *adj* marginal. ● *nm,f* drop-out.

marguerite /maʁɡəʁit/ *nf* daisy; (qui imprime) daisy-wheel.

mari /maʁi/ *nm* husband.

mariage /maʁjaʒ/ *nm* marriage; (cérémonie) wedding.

marié, **~e** /maʁje/ *adj* married. ● *nm,f* (bride)groom, bride; **les ~s** the bride and groom.

marier /maʁje/ [45] *vt* marry. □ **se ~** *vpr* get married, marry; **se ~ avec** marry, get married to.

marin, **~e** /maʁɛ̃, -in/ *adj* sea. ● *nm* sailor.

marine /maʁin/ *nf* navy; **~ marchande** merchant navy. ● *a inv* navy (blue).

marionnette /maʁjɔnɛt/ *nf* puppet; (à fils) marionette.

maritalement /maʁitalmɑ̃/ *adv* (*vivre*) as husband and wife.

maritime /maʁitim/ *adj* maritime, coastal; (*agent, compagnie*) shipping.

marmaille /maʁmaj/ *nf* 🔲 brats.

marmelade /maʁməlad/ *nf* stewed fruit; **~ d'oranges** (orange) marmalade.

marmite /maʁmit/ *nf* (cooking-)pot.

marmonner /maʁmɔne/ [1] *vt* mumble.

marmot /maʁmo/ *nm* 🔲 kid.

Maroc /maʁɔk/ *nm* Morocco.

maroquinerie /maʁɔkinʁi/ *nf* (magasin) leather goods shop.

marquant, **~e** /maʁkɑ̃, -t/ *adj* (remarquable) outstanding; (qu'on n'oublie pas) memorable.

marque /maʁk/ *nf* mark; (de produits) brand, make; (décompte) score; **à vos ~s!** (Sport) on your marks!; **de ~** (Comm) brand name; (fig) important; **~ de fabrique** trademark; **~ déposée** registered trademark.

marquer /maʁke/ [1] *vt* mark; (indiquer) show, say; (écrire) note down; (*point, but*) score; (*joueur*) mark; (influencer) leave its mark on; (exprimer) (*volonté, sentiment*) show. ● *vi* (laisser une trace) leave a mark; (*événement*) stand out; (Sport) score.

marquis, **~e** /maʁki, -z/ *nm,f* marquis, marchioness.

marraine /maʁɛn/ *nf* godmother.

marrant, **~e** /maʁɑ̃, -t/ *adj* 🔲 funny.

marre /maʁ/ *adv* **en avoir ~** 🔲 be fed up (**de** with).

marrer (se) /(sə)maʁe/ [1] *vpr* 🔲 laugh, have a (good) laugh.

marron /maʁɔ̃/ *nm* chestnut; (couleur) brown; (coup 🔲) thump; **~ d'Inde** horse chestnut. ● *a inv* brown.

mars /maRs/ nm March.

marteau (pl ∼x) /maRto/ nm hammer; ∼ **(de porte)** (door) knocker; ∼ **piqueur** ou **pneumatique** pneumatic drill; **être** ∼ 🄸 be mad.

marteler /maRtəle/ [6] vt hammer; (poings, talons) pound; (scander) rap out.

martial, ∼e (mpl -iaux) /maRsjal, -jo/ adj military; (art) martial.

martien, ∼ne /maRsjɛ̃, -ɛn/ a & nm, f Martian.

martyr, ∼e /maRtiR/ nm, f martyr. ● adj martyred; (enfant) battered.

martyre /maRtiR/ nm (Relig) martyrdom; (fig) agony, suffering.

martyriser /maRtiRize/ [1] vt (Relig) martyr; (torturer) torture; (enfant) batter.

marxisme /maRksism/ nm Marxism. **marxiste** a & nmf Marxist.

masculin, ∼e /maskylɛ̃, -in/ adj masculine; (sexe) male; (mode, équipe) men's. ● nm masculine.

masochisme /mazoʃism/ nm masochism.

masochiste /mazoʃist/ nmf masochist. ● adj masochistic.

masque /mask/ nm mask; ∼ **de beauté** face pack. **masquer** [1] vt (cacher) hide, conceal (à from); (lumière) block (off).

massacre /masakR/ nm massacre. **massacrer** [1] vt massacre; (abîmer 🄸) ruin.

massage /masaʒ/ nm massage.

masse /mas/ nf (volume) mass; (gros morceau) lump, mass; (outil) sledge-hammer; **en** ∼ (vendre) in bulk; (venir) in force; **produire en** ∼ mass-produce; **la** ∼ (foule) the masses; **une** ∼ **de** 🄸 masses of; **la** ∼ **de** the majority of.

masser /mase/ [1] vt (assembler) assemble; (pétrir) massage. □ **se** ∼ vpr (gens, foule) mass.

massif, **-ive** /masif, -v/ adj massive; (or, argent) solid. ● nm (de fleurs) clump; (parterre) bed; (Géog) massif. **massivement** adv (en masse) in large numbers.

massue /masy/ nf club, bludgeon.

mastic /mastik/ nm putty; (pour trous) filler.

mastiquer /mastike/ [1] vt (mâcher) chew.

mat /mat/ adj (couleur) matt; (bruit) dull; (teint) olive; **être** ∼ (aux échecs) be in checkmate.

mât /mɑ/ nm mast; (pylône) pole; ∼ **de drapeau** flagpole.

match /matʃ/ nm match; (US) game; **faire** ∼ **nul** tie, draw; ∼ **aller** first leg; ∼ **retour** return match.

matelas /matla/ nm mattress; ∼ **pneumatique** air bed.

matelassé, ∼e /matlase/ adj padded; (tissu) quilted.

matelot /matlo/ nm sailor.

mater /mate/ [1] vt (révolte) put down; (personne) bring into line.

matérialiser (se) /(sə)materjalize/ [1] vpr materialize.

matérialiste /materjalist/ adj materialistic. ● nmf materialist.

matériau (pl ∼x) /materjo/ nm material.

matériel, ∼le /materjɛl/ adj material. ● nm equipment, materials; ∼ **informatique** hardware.

maternel, ∼le /matɛRnɛl/ adj maternal; (comme d'une mère) motherly. **maternelle** nf nursery school.

maternité /matɛRnite/ nf maternity hospital; (état de mère) motherhood; **de** ∼ maternity.

mathématicien, ∼ne /matematisjɛ̃, -ɛn/ nm, f mathematician.

mathématique /matematik/ adj mathematical. **mathématiques** nfpl mathematics (+ sg).

maths /mat/ nfpl 🄸 maths (+ sg).

matière /matjɛR/ nf matter; (produit) material; (sujet) subject; **en** ∼ **de** as regards; ∼ **plastique** plastic; ∼**s grasses** fat content; ∼**s premières** raw materials.

matin /matɛ̃/ nm morning; **de bon** ∼ early in the morning.

matinal, ∼e (mpl -aux) /matinal, -o/ adj morning; (de bonne heure) early; **être** ∼ be up early; (d'habitude) be an early riser.

matinée /matine/ *nf* morning; (spectacle) matinée.

matou /matu/ *nm* tomcat.

matraque /matʀak/ *nf* (de police) truncheon; (US) billy (club). **matraquer** [1] *vt* club, beat; (*produit, chanson*) plug.

matrimonial, ∼e (*mpl* -iaux) /matʀimɔnjal, -jo/ *adj* matrimonial; **agence** ∼e marriage bureau.

maturité /matyʀite/ *nf* maturity.

maudire /modiʀ/ [41] *vt* curse.

maudit, ∼e /modi, -t/ *adj* 🅣 blasted, damned.

maugréer /mogʀee/ [15] *vi* grumble.

mausolée /mozɔle/ *nm* mausoleum.

maussade /mosad/ *adj* gloomy.

mauvais, ∼e /mɔvɛ, -z/ *adj* bad; (erroné) wrong; (malveillant) evil; (désagréable) nasty, bad; (*mer*) rough; **le** ∼ **moment** the wrong time; ∼e **herbe** weed; ∼e **langue** gossip; ∼e **passe** tight spot; ∼ **traitements** ill-treatment. ● *adv* (*sentir*) bad; **il fait** ∼ the weather is bad. ● *nm* **le bon et le** ∼ the good and the bad.

mauve /mov/ *a & nm* mauve.

mauviette /movjɛt/ *nf* weakling, wimp.

maux /mo/ ⇒ MAL².

maximal, ∼e (*mpl* -aux) /maksimal, -o/ *adj* maximum.

maxime /maksim/ *nf* maxim.

maximum /maksimɔm/ *adj* maximum. ● *nm* maximum; **au** ∼ as much as possible; (tout au plus) at most; **faire le** ∼ do one's utmost.

mazout /mazut/ *nm* (fuel) oil.

me, m' /mə, m/ *pron* me; (indirect) (to) me; (réfléchi) myself.

méandre /meɑ̃dʀ/ *nm* meander.

mec /mɛk/ *nm* 🅣 bloke, guy.

mécanicien, ∼ne /mekanisjɛ̃, -jɛn/ *nm, f* mechanic. ● *nm* train driver.

mécanique /mekanik/ *adj* mechanical; (*jouet*) clockwork; **problème** ∼ engine trouble. ● *nf* mechanics (+ *sg*); (mécanisme) mechanism. **mécaniser** [1] *vt* mechanize.

mécanisme /mekanism/ *nm* mechanism.

méchamment /meʃamɑ̃/ *adv* spitefully. **méchanceté** *nf* nastiness; (action) wicked action.

méchant, ∼e /meʃɑ̃, -t/ *adj* (cruel) wicked; (désagréable, grave) nasty; (*enfant*) naughty; (*chien*) vicious; (sensationnel 🅣) terrific. ● *nm, f* (enfant) naughty child.

mèche /mɛʃ/ *nf* (de cheveux) lock; (de bougie) wick; (d'explosif) fuse; (outil) drill bit; **de** ∼ **avec** in league with.

méconnaissable /mekɔnɛsabl/ *adj* unrecognizable.

méconnaître /mekɔnɛtʀ/ [18] *vt* misunderstand, misread; (mésestimer) underestimate.

méconnu, ∼e /mekɔny/ *adj* unrecognized; (*artiste*) neglected.

mécontent, ∼e /mekɔ̃tɑ̃, -t/ *adj* dissatisfied (**de** with); (irrité) annoyed (**de** at, with). **mécontentement** *nm* dissatisfaction; annoyance. **mécontenter** [1] *vt* dissatisfy; (irriter) annoy.

médaille /medaj/ *nf* medal; (insigne) badge; (bijou) medallion. **médaillé**, ∼e *nm, f* medallist.

médaillon /medajɔ̃/ *nm* medallion; (bijou) locket.

médecin /mɛdsɛ̃/ *nm* doctor.

médecine /mɛdsin/ *nf* medicine.

média /medja/ *nm* medium; **les** ∼s the media.

médiateur, -trice /medjatœʀ, -tʀis/ *nm, f* mediator.

médiatique /medjatik/ *adj* (événement, personnalité) media.

médical, ∼e (*mpl* -aux) /medikal, -o/ *adj* medical.

médicament /medikamɑ̃/ *nm* medicine, drug.

médico-légal, ∼e (*mpl* -aux) /medikɔlegal, -o/ *adj* forensic.

médiéval, ∼e (*mpl* -aux) /medjeval, -o/ *adj* medieval.

médiocre /medjɔkʀ/ *adj* mediocre, poor. **médiocrité** *nf* mediocrity.

médire /mediʀ/ [37] *vi* ∼ **de** speak ill of, malign.

médisance /medizɑ̃s/ *nf* ∼(s) malicious gossip.

méditer /medite/ [1] *vi* meditate (**sur** on). ● *vt* contemplate; (*paroles, conseils*) mull over; ~ **de** plan to.

Méditerranée /mediteʀane/ *nf* **la** ~ the Mediterranean.

méditerranéen, ~ne /mediteʀaneɛ̃, -ɛn/ *adj* Mediterranean.

médium /medjɔm/ *nm* (personne) medium.

méduse /medyz/ *nf* jellyfish.

meeting /mitiŋ/ *nm* meeting.

méfait /mefɛ/ *nm* misdeed; **les ~s de** (conséquences) the ravages of.

méfiance /mefjɑ̃s/ *nf* suspicion, distrust. **méfiant, ~e** *adj* suspicious, distrustful.

méfier (se) /(sə)mefje/ [45] *vpr* be wary *ou* careful; **se ~ de** distrust, be wary of.

mégaoctet /megaɔkte/ *nm* (Ordinat) megabyte.

mégère /meʒɛʀ/ *nf* (femme) shrew.

mégot /mego/ *nm* cigarette end.

meilleur, ~e /mɛjœʀ/ *adj* (comparatif) better (**que** than); (superlatif) best; **le ~ livre** the best book; **mon ~ ami** my best friend; ~ **marché** cheaper. ● *nm, f* **le ~, la ~e** the best (one). ● *adv* (*sentir*) better; **il fait ~** the weather is better.

mél /mel/ *nm* e-mail; **envoyer un ~** send an e-mail.

mélancolie /melɑ̃kɔli/ *nf* melancholy.

mélange /melɑ̃ʒ/ *nm* mixture, blend.

mélanger /melɑ̃ʒe/ [40] *vt* mix; (*thés, parfums*) blend. □ **se ~** *vpr* mix; (*thés, parfums*) blend; (*idées*) get mixed up.

mélasse /melas/ *nf* black treacle; (US) molasses.

mêlée /mele/ *nf* free for all; (au rugby) scrum.

mêler /mele/ [1] *vt* mix (**à** with); (*qualités*) combine; (embrouiller) mix up; ~ **qn à** (impliquer dans) involve sb in. □ **se ~** *vpr* mix; combine; **se ~ à** (se joindre à) mingle with; (participer à) join in; **se ~ de** meddle in; **mêle-toi de ce qui te regarde** mind your own business.

méli-mélo (*pl* **mélis-mélos**) /melimelo/ *nm* jumble.

mélo /melo/ 🄸 *nm* melodrama. ● *a inv* slushy, schmaltzy 🄸.

mélodie /melɔdi/ *nf* melody. **mélodieux, -ieuse** *adj* melodious. **mélodique** *adj* melodic.

mélodramatique /melɔdʀamatik/ *adj* melodramatic. **mélodrame** *nm* melodrama.

mélomane /melɔman/ *nmf* music lover.

melon /məlɔ̃/ *nm* melon; (chapeau) ~ **bowler** (hat).

membrane /mɑ̃bʀan/ *nf* membrane.

membre /mɑ̃bʀ/ *nm* (Anat) limb; (adhérent) member.

même /mɛm/ *adj* same; **ce livre ~** this very book; **la bonté ~** kindness itself; **en ~ temps** at the same time. ● *pron* **le ~, la ~** the same (one). ● *adv* even; **à ~** (sur) directly on; **à ~ de** in a position to; **de ~** (aussi) too; (de la même façon) likewise; **de ~ que** just as; **~si** even if.

mémé /meme/ *nf* 🄸 granny.

mémo /memo/ *nm* note, memo.

mémoire /memwaʀ/ *nm* (rapport) memorandum; (Univ) dissertation; **~s** (souvenirs écrits) memoirs. ● *nf* memory; **à la ~ de** to the memory of; **de ~** from memory; **~ morte/vive** (Ordinat) ROM/RAM.

mémorable /memɔʀabl/ *adj* memorable.

menace /mənas/ *nf* threat. **menacer** [10] *vt* threaten (**de faire** to do).

ménage /menaʒ/ *nm* (couple) couple; (travail) housework; (famille) household; **se mettre en ~** set up house.

ménagement /menaʒmɑ̃/ *nm* **avec ~s** gently; **sans ~s** (*dire*) bluntly; (*jeter, pousser*) roughly.

ménager¹, -ère /menaʒe, -ɛʀ/ *adj* household, domestic; **travaux ~s** housework.

ménager² /menaʒe/ [40] *vt* be gentle with, handle carefully; (utiliser) be careful with; (organiser) prepare (carefully); **ne pas ~ ses efforts** spare no effort.

m

ménagère /menaʒɛʀ/ nf housewife.

ménagerie /menaʒʀi/ nf menagerie.

mendiant, ∼e /mɑ̃djɑ̃, -t/ nm, f beggar.

mendier /mɑ̃dje/ [45] vt beg for. ● vi beg.

mener /məne/ [6] vt lead; (entreprise, pays) run; (étude, enquête) carry out; (politique) pursue; ∼ à (accompagner à) take to; (faire aboutir) lead to; ∼ à bien see through. ● vi lead.

méningite /menɛ̃ʒit/ nf meningitis.

menotte /mənɔt/ nf 🔲 hand; ∼s handcuffs.

mensonge /mɑ̃sɔ̃ʒ/ nm lie; (action) lying. **mensonger, -ère** adj untrue, false.

mensualité /mɑ̃sɥalite/ nf monthly payment.

mensuel, ∼le /mɑ̃sɥɛl/ adj monthly. ● nm monthly (magazine). **mensuellement** adv monthly.

mensurations /mɑ̃syʀasjɔ̃/ nfpl measurements.

mental, ∼e (mpl -aux) /mɑ̃tal, -o/ adj mental; **malade** ∼ mentally ill person; **handicapé** ∼ mentally handicapped person.

mentalité /mɑ̃talite/ nf mentality.

menteur, -euse /mɑ̃tœʀ, -øz/ nm, f liar. ● adj untruthful.

menthe /mɑ̃t/ nf mint.

mention /mɑ̃sjɔ̃/ nf mention; (annotation) note; (Scol) grade; **rayer la** ∼ **inutile** delete as appropriate. **mentionner** [1] vt mention.

mentir /mɑ̃tiʀ/ [46] vi lie.

menton /mɑ̃tɔ̃/ nm chin.

menu, ∼e /məny/ adj (petit) tiny; (fin) fine; (insignifiant) minor. ● adv (couper) fine. ● nm (carte) menu; (repas) meal; (Ordinat) menu; ∼ **déroulant** pull-down menu.

menuiserie /mənɥizʀi/ nf carpentry, joinery. **menuisier** nm carpenter, joiner.

méprendre (se) /(sə)mepʀɑ̃dʀ/ [50] vpr **se** ∼ **sur** be mistaken about.

mépris /mepʀi/ nm contempt, scorn (de for); **au** ∼ **de** regardless of.

méprisable /mepʀizabl/ adj contemptible, despicable.

méprise /mepʀiz/ nf mistake.

méprisant, ∼e /mepʀizɑ̃, -t/ adj scornful. **mépriser** [1] vt scorn, despise.

mer /mɛʀ/ nf sea; (marée) tide; **en pleine** ∼ out at sea.

mercenaire /mɛʀsənɛʀ/ nm & a mercenary.

mercerie /mɛʀs(ə)ʀi/ nf haberdashery; (US) notions store. **mercier, -ière** nm, f haberdasher; (US) notions seller.

merci /mɛʀsi/ interj thank you, thanks (de, pour for); ∼ **beaucoup**, ∼ **bien** thank you very much. ● nm thank you. ● nf mercy.

mercredi /mɛʀkʀədi/ nm Wednesday; ∼ **des Cendres** Ash Wednesday.

merde /mɛʀd/ nf 🔲 shit 🔲.

mère /mɛʀ/ nf mother; ∼ **de famille** mother.

méridional, ∼e (mpl -aux) /meʀidjɔnal, -o/ adj southern. ● nm, f Southerner.

mérite /meʀit/ nm merit; **avoir du** ∼ **à faire** deserve credit for doing.

mériter /meʀite/ [1] vt deserve; ∼ **d'être lu** be worth reading.

méritoire /meʀitwaʀ/ adj commendable.

merlan /mɛʀlɑ̃/ nm whiting.

merle /mɛʀl/ nm blackbird.

merveille /mɛʀvɛj/ nf wonder, marvel; **à** ∼ wonderfully; **faire des** ∼s work wonders.

merveilleux, -euse /mɛʀvɛjø, -z/ adj wonderful, marvellous.

mes /me/ ⇒MON.

mésange /mezɑ̃ʒ/ nf tit(mouse).

mésaventure /mezavɑ̃tyʀ/ nf misadventure; **par** ∼ by some misfortune.

mesdames /medam/ ⇒MADAME.

mesdemoiselles /medmwazɛl/ ⇒MADEMOISELLE.

mésentente /mezɑ̃tɑ̃t/ nf disagreement.

mesquin, ∼e /mɛskɛ̃, -in/ adj mean-minded, petty; (chiche) mean. **mesquinerie** nf meanness.

mess /mɛs/ nm (Mil) mess.

m

message /mesaʒ/ *nm* message; **un ~ électronique** an e-mail.

messager, -ère /mesaʒe, -ɛʀ/ *nm,f* messenger. ● *nm* **~ de poche** pager.

messagerie /mesaʒʀi/ *nf* (transports) freight forwarding; (télécommunications) messaging; **~ électronique** electronic mail; **~ vocale** voice mail.

messe /mɛs/ *nf* (Relig) mass.

messieurs /mesjø/ ⇒MONSIEUR.

mesure /məzyʀ/ *nf* measurement; (quantité, unité) measure; (disposition) measure, step; (cadence) time; **en ~** in time; (modération) moderation; **à ~ que** as; **dans la ~ où** in so far as; **dans une certaine ~** to some extent; **en ~ de** in a position to; **sans ~** to excess; **(fait) sur ~** made-to-measure.

mesuré, ~e /məzyʀe/ *adj* measured; (atttitude) moderate.

mesurer /məzyʀe/ [1] *vt* measure; (juger) assess; (argent, temps) ration. ● *vi* **~ 15 mètres de long** be 15 metres long. □ **se ~ avec** *vpr* pit oneself against.

met /mɛ/ ⇒METTRE [42].

métal (*pl* **-aux**) /metal, -o/ *nm* metal. **métallique** *adj* (objet) metal; (éclat) metallic.

métallurgie /metalyʀʒi/ *nf* (industrie) metalworking industry.

métamorphoser /metamɔʀfoze/ [1] *vt* transform. □ **se ~** *vpr* be transformed; **se ~ en** metamorphose into.

métaphore /metafɔʀ/ *nf* metaphor.

météo /meteo/ *nf* (bulletin) weather forecast.

météore /meteɔʀ/ *nm* meteor.

météorologie /meteɔʀɔlɔʒi/ *nf* meteorology.

météorologique /meteɔʀɔlɔʒik/ *adj* meteorological; **conditions ~s** weather conditions.

méthode /metɔd/ *nf* method; (ouvrage) course, manual. **méthodique** *adj* methodical.

méticuleux, -euse /metikylø, -z/ *adj* meticulous.

métier /metje/ *nm* job; (manuel) trade; (intellectuel) profession; (expérience) experience, skill; **~ (à tisser)** loom; **remettre qch sur le ~** rework sth.

métis, ~se /metis/ *adj* mixed race. ● *nm,f* person of mixed race.

métrage /metʀaʒ/ *nm* length; **court ~** short (film); **long ~** feature-length film.

mètre /mɛtʀ/ *nm* metre; (règle) rule; **~ ruban** tape-measure.

métreur, -euse /metʀœʀ, -øz/ *nm,f* quantity surveyor.

métrique /metʀik/ *adj* metric.

métro /metʀo/ *nm* underground; (US) subway.

métropole /metʀɔpɔl/ *nf* metropolis; (pays) mother country. **métropolitain, ~e** *adj* metropolitan.

mets /mɛ/ *nm* dish. ● ⇒METTRE [42].

mettable /metabl/ *adj* wearable.

metteur /metœʀ/ *nm* **~ en scène** director.

mettre /mɛtʀ/ [42] *vt* put; (radio, chauffage) put *ou* switch on; (réveil) set; (installer) put in; (revêtir) put on; (porter habituellement) (vêtement, lunettes) wear; (prendre) take; (investir, dépenser) put; (écrire) write, say; **elle a mis deux heures** it took her two hours; **~ la table** lay the table; **~ en question** question; **~ en valeur** highlight; (terrain) develop; **mettons que** let's suppose that. ● *vi* **~ bas** (animal) give birth. □ **se ~** *vpr* (vêtement, maquillage) put on; (se placer) (objet) go; (personne) (debout) stand; (assis) sit; (couché) lie; **se ~ en short** put shorts on; **se ~ debout** stand up; **se ~ au lit** go to bed; **se ~ à table** sit down at table; **se ~ en ligne** line up; **se ~ du sable dans les yeux** get sand in one's eyes; **se ~ au chinois/ tennis** take up Chinese/tennis; **se ~ au travail** set to work; **se ~ à faire** start to do.

meuble /mœbl/ *nm* piece of furniture; **~s** furniture.

meublé /møble/ *nm* furnished flat.

meubler /møble/ [1] *vt* furnish; (fig) fill. □ **se ~** *vpr* buy furniture.

meugler /møgle/ [1] *vi* moo.

meule /møl/ *nf* millstone; **~ de foin** haystack.

meunier, -ière /mønje, -jɛʀ/ *nm,f* miller.

meurs, meurt /mœʀ/ ⇒MOURIR [43].

meurtre /mœʀtʀ/ *nm* murder.

meurtrier, -ière /mœʀtʀije, -jɛʀ/ *adj* deadly. ● *nm,f* murderer, murderess.

meurtrir /mœʀtʀiʀ/ [2] *vt* bruise.

meute /møt/ *nf* pack of hounds.

Mexique /mɛksik/ *nm* Mexico.

mi- /mi/ *préf* mid-, half-; **à mi-chemin** half-way; **à mi-pente** half-way up the hill; **à la mi-juin** in mid-June.

miauler /mjole/ [1] *vi* miaow.

micro /mikʀo/ *nm* microphone, mike; (Ordinat) micro.

microbe /mikʀɔb/ *nm* germ.

microfilm /mikʀɔfilm/ *nm* microfilm.

micro-onde /mikʀɔɔd/ *nf* microwave; **un four à ~s** microwave (oven). **micro-ondes** *nm inv* microwave (oven).

micro-ordinateur (*pl* ~s) /mikʀɔɔʀdinatœʀ/ *nm* personal computer.

microphone /mikʀɔfɔn/ *nm* microphone.

microprocesseur /mikʀɔpʀɔsɛsœʀ/ *nm* microprocessor.

microscope /mikʀɔskɔp/ *nm* microscope.

midi /midi/ *nm* twelve o'clock, midday, noon; (déjeuner) lunch-time; (sud) south. **Midi** *nm* **le M~** the South of France.

mie /mi/ *nf* soft part (of the loaf); **un pain de ~** a sandwich loaf.

miel /mjɛl/ *nm* honey.

mielleux, -euse /mjɛlø, -z/ *adj* unctuous.

mien, ~ne /mjɛ̃, -ɛn/ *pron* **le ~, la ~ne, les ~(ne)s** mine.

miette /mjɛt/ *nf* crumb; (fig) scrap; **en ~s** in pieces.

mieux /mjø/ *a inv* better (**que** than); **le** *ou* **la** *ou* **les ~** (the) best. ● *nm* best; (progrès) improvement; **faire de son ~** do one's best; **le ~ serait de** the best thing would be to. ● *adv* better; **le** *ou* **la** *ou* **les ~** (de deux) the better; (de plusieurs) the best; **elle va**

~ she is better; **j'aime ~ rester** I'd rather stay; **il vaudrait ~ partir** it would be best to leave; **tu ferais ~ de faire** you would be best to do.

mièvre /mjɛvʀ/ *adj* insipid.

mignon, ~ne /miɲɔ̃, -ɔn/ *adj* cute; (gentil) kind.

migraine /migʀɛn/ *nf* headache; (plus fort) migraine.

migration /migʀasjɔ̃/ *nf* migration.

mijoter /miʒɔte/ [1] *vt/i* simmer; (tramer ⚅) cook up.

mil /mil/ *nm* a thousand.

milice /milis/ *nf* militia.

milieu (*pl* ~x) /miljø/ *nm* middle; (environnement) environment; (appartenance sociale) background; (groupe) circle; (voie) middle way; (criminel) underworld; **au ~ de** in the middle of; **en plein** *ou* **au beau ~ de** right in the middle (of).

militaire /militɛʀ/ *adj* military. ● *nm* soldier, serviceman.

militant, ~e /militɑ̃, -t/ *nm,f* militant.

militer /milite/ [1] *vi* be a militant; **~ pour** militate in favour of.

mille[1] /mil/ *a & nm inv* a thousand; **deux ~** two thousand; **mettre dans le ~** (fig) hit the nail on the head.

mille[2] /mil/ *nm* **~ (marin)** (nautical) mile.

millénaire /milenɛʀ/ *nm* millennium. ● *adj* a thousand years old.

mille-pattes /milpat/ *nm inv* centipede.

millésime /milezim/ *nm* date; (de vin) vintage.

millet /mijɛ/ *nm* millet.

milliard /miljaʀ/ *nm* thousand million, billion. **milliardaire** *nmf* multimillionaire.

millième /miljɛm/ *a & nmf* thousandth.

millier /milje/ *nm* thousand; **un ~ (de)** about a thousand.

millimètre /milimɛtʀ/ *nm* millimetre.

million /miljɔ̃/ *nm* million; **deux ~s (de)** two million. **millionnaire** *nmf* millionaire.

mime /mim/ *nmf* mime-artist. ● *nm* (art) mime. **mimer** [1] *vt* mime; (imiter) mimic.

mimique /mimik/ *nf* expressions and gestures.

minable /minabl/ *adj* Ⓣ (logement) shabby; (médiocre) pathetic, crummy.

minauder /minode/ [1] *vi* simper.

mince /mɛ̃s/ *adj* thin; (svelte) slim; (faible) (espoir, majorité) slim. ● *interj* Ⓣ blast Ⓣ, darn it Ⓣ. **minceur** *nf* thinness; slimness.

mincir /mɛ̃siʀ/ [2] *vi* get slimmer; ça te mincit it makes you look slimmer.

mine /min/ *nf* expression; (allure) appearance; **avoir bonne** ~ look well; **faire** ~ **de** make as if to; (exploitation, explosif) mine; (de crayon) lead; ~ **de charbon** coal-mine.

miner /mine/ [1] *vt* (saper) undermine; (garnir d'explosifs) mine.

minerai /minʀɛ/ *nm* ore.

minéral, ~**e** (*mpl* -**aux**) /mineʀal, -o/ *adj* mineral. ● *nm* (*pl* -**aux**) mineral.

minéralogique /mineʀalɔʒik/ *adj* **plaque** ~ numberplate; (US) license plate.

minet, ~**te** /minɛ, -t/ *nm,f* (chat Ⓣ) pussy(cat).

mineur, ~**e** /minœʀ/ *adj* minor; (Jur) under age. ● *nm,f* (Jur) minor. ● *nm* (ouvrier) miner.

miniature /minjatyʀ/ *nf & a* miniature.

minier, -**ière** /minje, -jɛʀ/ *adj* mining.

minimal, ~**e** (*mpl* -**aux**) /minimal,o/ *adj* minimal, minimum.

minime /minim/ *adj* minimal, minor. ● *nmf* (Sport) junior.

minimum /minimɔm/ *adj* minimum. ● *nm* minimum; **au** ~ (pour le moins) at the very least; **en faire un** ~ do as little as possible.

ministère /ministɛʀ/ *nm* ministry; (gouvernement) government; ~ **public** public prosecutor's office. **ministériel**, ~**le** *adj* ministerial, government.

ministre /ministʀ/ *nm* minister; (au Royaume-Uni) Secretary of State; (US) Secretary.

Minitel® /minitɛl/ *nm* Minitel (telephone videotext system).

minorer /minɔʀe/ [1] *vt* reduce.

minoritaire /minɔʀitɛʀ/ *adj* minority; **être** ~ be in the minority. **minorité** *nf* minority.

minuit /minɥi/ *nm* midnight.

minuscule /minyskyl/ *adj* minute. ● *nf* (lettre) ~ lower case.

minute /minyt/ *nf* minute; '**talons** ~' 'heels repaired while you wait'.

minuterie /minytʀi/ *nf* time-switch.

minutie /minysi/ *nf* meticulousness. **minutieux**, -**ieuse** /minysjø, -z/ *adj* meticulous.

mioche /mjɔʃ/ *nm,f* Ⓣ kid.

mirabelle /miʀabɛl/ *nf* (mirabelle) plum.

miracle /miʀakl/ *nm* miracle; **par** ~ miraculously.

miraculeux, -**euse** /miʀakylø, -z/ *adj* miraculous.

mirage /miʀaʒ/ *nm* mirage.

mire /miʀ/ *nf* (fig) centre of attraction; (TV) test card.

mirobolant, ~**e** /miʀɔbɔlɑ̃, -t/ *adj* Ⓣ marvellous.

miroir /miʀwaʀ/ *nm* mirror.

miroiter /miʀwate/ [1] *vi* shimmer, sparkle.

mis, ~**e** /mi, miz/ *adj* **bien** ~ well-dressed. ● ⇒**METTRE** [42].

mise /miz/ *nf* (argent) stake; (tenue) attire; ~ **à feu** blast-off; ~ **au point** adjustment; (fig) clarification; ~ **de fonds** capital outlay; ~ **en garde** warning; ~ **en plis** set; ~ **en scène** direction.

miser /mize/ [1] *vt* (argent) bet, stake (**sur** on). ● *vi* ~ **sur** (parier) place a bet on; (compter sur) bank on.

misérable /mizeʀabl/ *adj* miserable, wretched; (indigent) destitute; (minable) seedy, squalid.

misère /mizɛʀ/ *nf* destitution; (malheur) trouble, woe. **miséreux**, -**euse** *nm,f* destitute person.

miséricorde /mizeʀikɔʀd/ *nf* mercy.

missel /misɛl/ *nm* missal.

missile /misil/ *nm* missile.

mission /misjɔ̃/ *nm* mission. **missionnaire** *nmf* missionary.

missive /misiv/ *nf* missive.

mistral /mistʀal/ *nm* (vent) mistral.

mitaine /mitɛn/ *nf* fingerless mitt.

mite /mit/ *nf* (clothes-)moth.

mi-temps /mitɑ̃/ *nf inv* (arrêt) half-time; (période) half. ● *nm inv* part-time work; **à ~** part-time.

miteux, **-euse** /mitø, -z/ *adj* shabby.

mitigé, **~e** /mitiʒe/ *adj* (modéré) lukewarm; (succès) qualified.

mitonner /mitɔne/ [1] *vt* cook slowly with care; (fig) cook up.

mitoyen, **~ne** /mitwajɛ̃, -ɛn/ *adj* **mur ~** party wall.

mitrailler /mitʀaje/ [1] *vt* machine-gun; (fig) bombard.

mitraillette /mitʀajɛt/ *nf* submachine gun. **mitrailleuse** *nf* machine gun.

mi-voix: à ~ /amivwa/ *loc* in a low voice.

mixeur /miksœʀ/ *nm* liquidizer, blender; (batteur) mixer.

mixte /mikst/ *adj* mixed; (commission) joint; (école) coeducational; (peau) combination.

mobile /mɔbil/ *adj* mobile; (pièce) moving; (feuillet) loose. ● *nm* (art) mobile; (raison) motive.

mobilier /mɔbilje/ *nm* furniture.

mobilisation /mɔbilizasjɔ̃/ *nf* mobilization. **mobiliser** [1] *vt* mobilize.

mobilité /mɔbilite/ *nf* mobility.

mobylette® /mɔbilɛt/ *nf* moped.

moche /mɔʃ/ *adj* Ⓘ (laid) ugly; (mauvais) lousy.

modalités /mɔdalite/ *nfpl* (conditions) terms; (façon de fonctionner) practical details.

mode /mɔd/ *nf* fashion; (coutume) custom; **à la ~** fashionable. ● *nm* method, mode; (genre) way; **~ d'emploi** directions (for use).

modèle /mɔdɛl/ *adj* model. ● *nm* model; (exemple) example; (Comm) (type) model; (taille) size; (style) style; **~ familial** family size; **~ réduit** (small-scale) model.

modeler /mɔdle/ [6] *vt* model (sur on). □ **se ~ sur** *vpr* model oneself on.

modem /mɔdɛm/ *nm* modem.

modérateur, **-trice** /mɔdeʀatœʀ, -tʀis/ *adj* moderating. **modération** *nf* moderation.

modéré, **~e** /mɔdeʀe/ *a & nm, f* moderate.

modérer /mɔdeʀe/ [14] *vt* (propos) moderate; (désirs, sentiments) curb. □ **se ~** *vpr* restrain oneself.

moderne /mɔdɛʀn/ *adj* modern. **moderniser** [1] *vt* modernize.

modeste /mɔdɛst/ *adj* modest. **modestie** *nf* modesty.

modification /mɔdifikasjɔ̃/ *nf* modification.

modifier /mɔdifje/ [45] *vt* change, modify. □ **se ~** *vpr* change, alter.

modique /mɔdik/ *adj* modest.

modiste /mɔdist/ *nf* milliner.

moduler /mɔdyle/ [1] *vt* modulate; (adapter) adjust.

moelle /mwal/ *nf* marrow; **~ épinière** spinal cord; **~ osseuse** bone marrow.

moelleux, **-euse** /mwalø, -z/ *adj* soft; (onctueux) smooth.

mœurs /mœʀ(s)/ *nfpl* (morale) morals; (usages) customs; (manières) habits, ways.

moi /mwa/ *pron* me; (indirect) (to) me; (sujet) I. ● *nm* self.

moignon /mwaɲɔ̃/ *nm* stump.

moi-même /mwamɛm/ *pron* myself.

moindre /mwɛ̃dʀ/ *adj* (moins grand) lesser; **le ou la ~**, **les ~s** the slightest, the least.

moine /mwan/ *nm* monk.

moineau (*pl* **~x**) /mwano/ *nm* sparrow.

moins /mwɛ̃/ *prép* minus; (pour dire l'heure) to; **une heure ~ dix** ten to one. ● *adv* less (que than); **le ou la ou les ~** the least; **le ~** the least/lowest; **~ de** (avec un nom non dénombrable) less (que than); **~ de dix francs** less than ten francs; **~ de livres** fewer books; **au ~**, **du ~** at least; **à ~ que** unless; **de ~** less; **de ~ en ~** less and less; **en ~** less; (manquant) missing.

mois /mwa/ *nm* month.

moisi, ~e /mwazi/ *adj* mouldy.
● *nm* mould; de ~ (*odeur*) musty.
moisir [2] *vi* go mouldy.
moisissure *nf* mould.

moisson /mwasɔ̃/ *nf* harvest.

moissonner /mwasɔne/ [1] *vt* harvest, reap. **moissonneur**, **-euse** *nm,f* harvester.

moite /mwat/ *adj* sticky, clammy.

moitié /mwatje/ *nf* half; (milieu) halfway mark; **s'arrêter à la** ~ stop halfway through; **à** ~ **vide** half empty; **à** ~ **prix** (at) half-price; **la** ~ **de** half (of). **moitié-moitié** *adv* half-and-half.

mol /mɔl/ ⇒MOU.

molaire /mɔlɛR/ *nf* molar.

molécule /mɔlekyl/ *nf* molecule.

molester /mɔlɛste/ [1] *vt* manhandle, rough up.

molle /mɔl/ ⇒MOU.

mollement /mɔlmɑ̃/ *adv* softly; (faiblement) feebly. **mollesse** *nf* softness; (faiblesse) feebleness; (apathie) listlessness.

mollet /mɔlɛ/ *nm* (de jambe) calf.

mollir /mɔliR/ [2] *vi* soften; (céder) yield.

môme /mom/ *nmf* 🔲 kid.

moment /mɔmɑ̃/ *nm* moment; (période) time; (**petit**) ~ short while; **au** ~ **où** when; **par** ~s now and then; **du** ~ **où** *ou* **que** (pourvu que) as long as, provided that; (puisque) since; **en ce** ~ at the moment.

momentané, ~e /mɔmɑ̃tane/ *adj* momentary. **momentanément** *adv* momentarily; (en ce moment) at present.

momie /mɔmi/ *nf* mummy.

mon, **ma** (**mon** *before vowel or mute h*) (*pl* **mes**) /mɔ̃, ma, mɔ̃, me/ *adj* my.

Monaco /mɔnako/ *npr* Monaco.

monarchie /mɔnaRʃi/ *nf* monarchy.

monarque /mɔnaRk/ *nm* monarch.

monastère /mɔnastɛR/ *nm* monastery.

monceau (*pl* ~**x**) /mɔ̃so/ *nm* heap, pile.

mondain, ~e /mɔ̃dɛ̃, -ɛn/ *adj* society, social.

monde /mɔ̃d/ *nm* world; **du** ~ (a lot of) people; (quelqu'un) somebody; **le** (**grand**) ~ (high) society; **se faire** (**tout**) **un** ~ **de qch** make a great deal of fuss about sth; **pas le moins du** ~ not in the least.

mondial, ~e (*mpl* **-iaux**) /mɔ̃djal, -jo/ *adj* world; (influence) worldwide. **mondialement** *adv* the world over.

monétaire /mɔnetɛR/ *adj* monetary.

moniteur, **-trice** /mɔnitœR, -tRis/ *nm,f* instructor; (de colonie de vacances) group leader; (US) (camp) counselor.

monnaie /mɔnɛ/ *nf* currency; (pièce) coin; (appoint) change; **faire la** ~ **de** get change for; **faire de la** ~ **à qn** give sb change; **menue** *ou* **petite** ~ small change.

monnayer /mɔneje/ [31] *vt* convert into cash.

mono /mɔno/ *a inv* mono.

monologue /mɔnɔlɔg/ *nm* monologue.

monopole /mɔnɔpɔl/ *nm* monopoly. **monopoliser** [1] *vt* monopolize.

monospace /mɔnɔspas/ *nm* (Auto) people carrier.

monotone /mɔnɔtɔn/ *adj* monotonous. **monotonie** *nf* monotony.

Monseigneur (*pl* **Messeigneurs**) /mɔ̃sɛɲœR/ *nm* (à un duc, archevêque) Your Grace; (à un prince) Your Highness.

monsieur (*pl* **messieurs**) /məsjø, mesjø/ *nm* (à un inconnu) (dans une lettre) **M**~ Dear Sir; (dans une lettre) **Cher M**~ Dear Sir; **bonjour**, ~ good morning; **mesdames et messieurs** ladies and gentlemen; (à un homme dont on connaît le nom) (dans une lettre) **Cher M**~ Dear Mr X; **bonjour**, ~ good morning Mr X; **M**~ **le curé** Father X; **oui M**~ **le ministre** yes Minister; (homme) man; (formule de respect) sir.

monstre /mɔ̃stR/ *nm* monster. ● *adj* 🔲 colossal.

monstrueux, **-euse** /mɔ̃stRyø, -z/ *adj* monstrous. **monstruosité** *nf* monstrosity.

mont /mɔ̃/ nm mountain; le ~ Everest Mount Everest; **être toujours par ~s et par vaux** be always on the move.

montage /mɔ̃taʒ/ nm (assemblage) assembly; (au cinéma) editing.

montagne /mɔ̃taɲ/ nf mountain; (région) mountains; **~s russes** roller-coaster. **montagneux, -euse** adj mountainous.

montant, ~e /mɔ̃tã, -t/ adj rising; (col) high; (chemin) uphill. ● nm amount; (pièce de bois) upright.

mont-de-piété (pl monts-de-piété) /mɔ̃dpjete/ nm pawnshop.

monte-charge /mɔ̃tʃaʀʒ/ nm inv goods lift.

montée /mɔ̃te/ nf ascent, climb; (de prix) rise; (de coûts, risques) increase; (côte) hill.

monter /mɔ̃te/ [1] vt (aux. avoir) take up; (à l'étage) take upstairs; (escalier, rue, pente) go up; (assembler) assemble; (tente, échafaudage) put up; (col, manche) set in; (organiser) (pièce) stage; (société) set up; (attaque, garde) mount. ● vi (aux. être) go ou come up; (à l'étage) go ou come upstairs; (avion) climb; (route) go uphill, climb; (augmenter) rise; (marée) come up; ~ **sur** (trottoir, toit) get up on; (cheval, bicyclette) get on; ~ **à l'échelle/l'arbre** climb the ladder/tree; ~ **dans** (voiture) get in; (train, bus, avion) get on; ~ **à bord** climb on board; ~ (**à cheval**) ride; ~ **à bicyclette/moto** ride a bike/motorbike.

monteur, -euse /mɔ̃tœʀ, -øz/ nm,f (Tech) fitter; (au cinéma) editor.

montre /mɔ̃tʀ/ nf watch; **faire ~ de** show.

montrer /mɔ̃tʀe/ [1] vt show (à to); ~ **du doigt** point to. □ **se ~** vpr show oneself; (être) be; (s'avérer) prove to be.

monture /mɔ̃tyʀ/ nf (cheval) mount; (de lunettes) frames (+ pl); (de bijou) setting.

monument /mɔnymã/ nm monument; ~ **aux morts** war memorial. **monumental** (mpl -aux) adj monumental.

moquer (se) /(sə)mɔke/ [1] vpr se ~ **de** make fun of; **je m'en moque** 🔲 I couldn't care less. **moquerie** nf mockery. **moqueur, -euse** adj mocking.

moquette /mɔkɛt/ nf fitted carpet; (US) wall-to-wall carpeting.

moral, ~e (mpl -aux) /mɔʀal, -o/ adj moral. ● nm (pl -aux) morale; **ne pas avoir le ~** feel down; **avoir le ~** be in good spirits; **ça m'a remonté le ~** it gave me a boost.

morale /mɔʀal/ nf moral code; (mœurs) morals; (de fable) moral; **faire la ~ à** lecture. **moralité** nf (de personne) morals (+ pl); (d'action, œuvre) morality; (de fable) moral.

moralisateur, -trice /mɔʀalizatœʀ, -tʀis/ adj moralizing.

morbide /mɔʀbid/ adj morbid.

morceau (pl ~x) /mɔʀso/ nm piece, bit; (de sucre) lump; (de viande) cut; (passage) passage; **manger un ~** 🔲 have a bite to eat; **mettre en ~x** smash ou tear to bits.

morceler /mɔʀsəle/ [6] vt divide up.

mordant, ~e /mɔʀdã, -t/ adj scathing; (froid) biting. ● nm vigour, energy.

mordiller /mɔʀdije/ [1] vt nibble at.

mordre /mɔʀdʀ/ [3] vi bite (dans into); ~ **sur** (ligne) go over; (territoire) encroach on; ~ **à l'hameçon** bite. ● vt bite.

mordu, ~e /mɔʀdy/ 🔲 nm,f fan. ● adj smitten; ~ **de** crazy about.

morfondre (se) /(sə)mɔʀfɔ̃dʀ/ [3] vpr wait anxiously; (languir) mope.

morgue /mɔʀg/ nf morgue, mortuary; (attitude) arrogance.

moribond, ~e /mɔʀibɔ̃, -d/ adj dying.

morne /mɔʀn/ adj dull.

morphine /mɔʀfin/ nf morphine.

mors /mɔʀ/ nm (de cheval) bit.

morse /mɔʀs/ nm (animal) walrus; (code) Morse code.

morsure /mɔʀsyʀ/ nf bite.

mort¹ /mɔʀ/ nf death.

mort², ~e /mɔʀ, -t/ adj dead; ~ **de fatigue** dead tired. ● nm,f dead man, dead woman; **les ~s** the dead.

m

mortalité /mɔʀtalite/ nf mortality; (taux de) ~ death rate.

mortel, **~le** /mɔʀtɛl/ adj mortal; (accident) fatal; (poison, silence) deadly. ● nm, f mortal.
mortellement adv mortally.

mortifié, **~e** /mɔʀtifje/ adj mortified.

mort-né, **~e** /mɔʀne/ adj stillborn.

mortuaire /mɔʀtɥɛʀ/ adj (cérémonie) funeral.

morue /mɔʀy/ nf cod.

mosaïque /mozaik/ nf mosaic.

mosquée /mɔske/ nf mosque.

mot /mo/ nm word; (lettre, message) note; ~ d'ordre watchword; ~ de passe password; ~s croisés crossword (puzzle).

motard /mɔtaʀ/ nm biker; (policier) police motorcyclist.

moteur, **-trice** /mɔtœʀ, -tʀis/ adj (Méd) motor; (force) driving; à 4 roues motrices 4-wheel drive. ● nm engine, motor; barque à ~ motor launch; ~ de recherche (Internet) search engine.

motif /mɔtif/ nm (raisons) grounds (+ pl); (cause) reason; (Jur) motive; (dessin) pattern.

motion /mosjɔ̃/ nf motion.

motivation /mɔtivasjɔ̃/ nf motivation. **motiver** [1] vt motivate.

moto /mɔto/ nf motor cycle.
motocycliste nmf motorcyclist.

motorisé, **~e** /mɔtɔʀize/ adj motorized.

motrice /mɔtʀis/ ⇒MOTEUR.

motte /mɔt/ nf lump; (de beurre) slab; (de terre) clod; ~ de gazon turf.

mou (**mol** before vowel or mute h), **molle** /mu, mɔl/ adj soft; (ventre) flabby; (sans conviction) feeble; (apathique) sluggish, listless. ● nm slack; avoir du ~ be slack.

mouchard, **~e** /muʃaʀ, -d/ nm,f informer; (Scol) sneak.

mouche /muʃ/ nf fly; (de cible) bull's eye.

moucher (se) /(sə)muʃe/ [1] vpr blow one's nose.

moucheron /muʃʀɔ̃/ nm midge.

moucheté, **~e** /muʃte/ adj speckled.

mouchoir /muʃwaʀ/ nm handkerchief, hanky; ~ en papier tissue.

moue /mu/ nf pout; faire la ~ pout.

mouette /mwɛt/ nf (sea)gull.

moufle /mufl/ nf (gant) mitten.

mouillé, **~e** /muje/ adj wet.

mouiller /muje/ [1] vt wet, make wet; ~ l'ancre drop anchor. □ se ~ vpr get (oneself) wet.

moulage /mulaʒ/ nm cast.

moule /mul/ nf (coquillage) mussel. ● nm mould; ~ à gâteau cake tin; ~ à tarte flan dish. **mouler** [1] vt mould; (statue) cast.

moulin /mulɛ̃/ nm mill; ~ à café coffee grinder; ~ à poivre pepper mill; ~ à vent windmill.

moulinet /mulinɛ/ nm (de canne à pêche) reel; faire des ~s avec qch twirl sth around.

moulinette® /mulinɛt/ nf vegetable mill.

moulu, **~e** /muly/ adj ground; (fatigué 🔢) worn out.

moulure /mulyʀ/ nf moulding.

mourant, **~e** /muʀɑ̃, -t/ adj dying. ● nm, f dying person.

mourir /muʀiʀ/ [43] vi (aux. être) die; ~ d'envie de be dying to; ~ de faim be starving; ~ d'ennui be dead bored.

mousquetaire /muskətɛʀ/ nm musketeer.

mousse /mus/ nf moss; (écume) froth, foam; (de savon) lather; (dessert) mousse; ~ à raser shaving foam. ● nm ship's boy.

mousseline /muslin/ nf muslin; (de soie) chiffon.

mousser /muse/ [1] vi froth, foam; (savon) lather.

mousseux, **-euse** /musø, -z/ adj frothy. ● nm sparkling wine.

mousson /musɔ̃/ nf monsoon.

moustache /mustaʃ/ nf moustache; ~s (d'animal) whiskers.

moustique /mustik/ nm mosquito.

moutarde /mutaʀd/ nf mustard.

mouton /mutɔ̃/ nm sheep; (peau) sheepskin; (viande) mutton.

mouvant, ~e /muvɑ̃, -t/ *adj* changing; (*terrain*) shifting, unstable.

mouvement /muvmɑ̃/ *nm* movement; (*agitation*) bustle; (en gymnastique) exercise; (*impulsion*) impulse; (*tendance*) tend, tendency; **en** ~ in motion.

mouvementé, ~e /muvmɑ̃te/ *adj* eventful.

moyen, ~ne /mwajɛ̃, -ɛn/ *adj* average; (*médiocre*) poor; **de taille moyenne** medium-sized. ● *nm* means, way; ~s means; (*dons*) ability; **au** ~ **de** by means of; **il n'y a pas** ~ **de** it is not possible to. **Moyen Âge** *nm* Middle Ages (+ *pl*).

moyennant /mwajɛnɑ̃/ *prép* (pour) for; (grâce à) with.

moyenne /mwajɛn/ *nf* average; (Scol) pass-mark; **en** ~ on average; ~ **d'âge** average age. **moyennement** *adv* moderately.

Moyen-Orient /mwajɛnɔʀjɑ̃/ *nm* Middle East.

moyeu (*pl* ~**x**) /mwajø/ *nm* hub.

mû, **mue** /my/ *adj* driven (**par** by).

mucoviscidose /mykɔvisidoz/ *nf* cystic fibrosis.

mue /my/ *nf* moulting; (de voix) breaking of the voice.

muer /mɥe/ [1] *vi* moult; (*voix*) break. □ **se** ~ **en** *vpr* change into.

muet, ~**te** /mɥɛ, -t/ *adj* (Méd) dumb; (fig) speechless (**de** with); (silencieux) silent. ● *nm,f* mute.

mufle /myfl/ *nm* nose, muzzle; (personne I) boor, lout.

mugir /myʒiʀ/ [2] *vi* (*vache*) moo; (*bœuf*) bellow; (fig) howl.

muguet /mygɛ/ *nm* lily of the valley.

mule /myl/ *nf* (female) mule; (pantoufle) mule.

mulet /mylɛ/ *nm* (male) mule.

multicolore /myltikɔlɔʀ/ *adj* multicoloured.

multimédia /myltimedja/ *a & nm* multimedia.

multinational, ~e (*mpl* -**aux**) /myltinasjɔnal, -o/ *adj* multinational. **multinationale** *nf* multinational (company).

multiple /myltipl/ *nm* multiple. ● *adj* numerous, many; (naissances) multiple.

multiplication /myltiplikasjɔ̃/ *nf* multiplication.

multiplicité /myltiplisite/ *nf* multiplicity.

multiplier /myltiplije/ [45] *vt* multiply; (*risques*) increase. □ **se** ~ *vpr* multiply; (*accidents*) be on the increase; (*difficultés*) increase.

multitude /myltityd/ *nf* multitude, mass.

municipal, ~e (*mpl* -**aux**) /mynisipal, -o/ *adj* municipal; **conseil** ~ town council. **municipalité** *nf* (ville) municipality; (conseil) town council.

munir /myniʀ/ [2] *vt* ~ **de** provide with. □ **se** ~ **de** *vpr* (apporter) bring; (emporter) take.

munitions /mynisjɔ̃/ *nfpl* ammunition.

mur /myʀ/ *nm* wall; ~ **du son** sound barrier.

mûr, ~e /myʀ/ *adj* ripe; (personne) mature.

muraille /myʀaj/ *nf* (high) wall.

mural, ~e (*mpl* -**aux**) /myʀal, -o/ *adj* wall; **peinture** ~e mural.

mûre /myʀ/ *nf* blackberry.

mûrir /myʀiʀ/ [2] *vi* ripen; (abcès) come to a head; (personne, projet) mature. ● *vt* (fruit) ripen; (personne) mature.

murmure /myʀmyʀ/ *nm* murmur.

musc /mysk/ *nm* musk.

muscade /myskad/ *nf* noix ~ nutmeg.

muscle /myskl/ *nm* muscle. **musclé**, ~e *adj* muscular. **musculaire** *adj* muscular.

musculation /myskylasjɔ̃/ *nf* bodybuilding.

musculature /myskylatyʀ/ *nf* muscles (+ *pl*).

museau (*pl* ~**x**) /myzo/ *nm* muzzle; (de porc) snout.

musée /myze/ *nm* museum; (de peinture) art gallery.

muselière /myzəljɛʀ/ *nf* muzzle.

musette /myzɛt/ *nf* haversack.

m

muséum /myzeɔm/ nm natural history museum.

musical, ~e (mpl -aux) /myzikal, -o/ adj musical.

musicien, ~ne /myzisjɛ̃, -ɛn/ adj musical. ● nm, f musician.

musique /myzik/ nf music; (orchestre) band.

musulman, ~e /myzylmɑ̃, -an/ a & nm,f Muslim.

mutation /mytasjɔ̃/ nf change; (biologique) mutation; (d'un employé) transfer.

muter /myte/ [1] vt transfer. ● vi mutate.

mutilation /mytilasjɔ̃/ nf mutilation. **mutiler** [1] vt mutilate. **mutilé**, ~e nm, f disabled person.

mutin, ~e /mytɛ̃, -in/ adj mischievous. ● nm mutineer; (prisonnier) rioter.

mutinerie /mytinʀi/ nf mutiny; (de prisonniers) riot.

mutisme /mytism/ nm silence.

mutuel, ~le /mytɥɛl/ adj mutual. **mutuelle** nf mutual insurance company. **mutuellement** adv mutually; (l'un l'autre) each other.

myope /mjɔp/ adj short-sighted. **myopie** nf short-sightedness.

myosotis /mjozɔtis/ nm forget-me-not.

myrtille /miʀtij/ nf bilberry, blueberry.

mystère /mistɛʀ/ nm mystery.

mystérieux, -ieuse /misteʀjø, -z/ adj mysterious.

mystification /mistifikasjɔ̃/ nf hoax.

mysticisme /mistisism/ nm mysticism.

mystique /mistik/ adj mystic(al). ● nmf mystic. ● nf mystique.

mythe /mit/ nm myth. **mythique** adj mythical.

mythologie /mitɔlɔʒi/ nf mythology.

n' /n/ ⇒NE.

nacre /nakʀ/ nf mother-of-pearl.

nage /naʒ/ nf swimming; (manière) stroke; **traverser à la** ~ swim across; **en** ~ sweating.

nageoire /naʒwaʀ/ nf fin; (de mammifère) flipper.

nager /naʒe/ [40] vt/i swim. **nageur**, -euse nm, f swimmer.

naguère /nagɛʀ/ adv (autrefois) formerly.

naïf, -ive /naif, -v/ adj naïve.

nain, ~e /nɛ̃, nɛn/ nm,f & a dwarf.

naissance /nɛsɑ̃s/ nf birth; **donner** ~ **à** give birth to; (fig) give rise to.

naître /nɛtʀ/ [44] vi be born; (résulter) arise (**de** from); **faire** ~ (susciter) give rise to.

naïveté /naivte/ nf naïvety.

nappe /nap/ nf tablecloth; (de pétrole, gaz) layer; ~ **phréatique** ground water.

napperon /napʀɔ̃/ nm (cloth) tablemat.

narco-dollars /naʀkodɔlaʀ/ nmpl drug money.

narcotique /naʀkɔtik/ a & nm narcotic. **narco(-)trafiquant**, ~e (pl ~s) nm,f drug trafficker.

narguer /naʀge/ [1] vt taunt; (autorité) flout.

narine /naʀin/ nf nostril.

nasal, ~e (mpl -aux) /nazal, -o/ adj nasal.

naseau (pl ~x) /nazo/ nm nostril.

natal, ~e (mpl ~s) /natal/ adj native.

natalité /natalite/ nf birth rate.

natation /natasjɔ̃/ nf swimming.

natif, -ive /natif, -v/ adj native.

nation /nasjɔ̃/ nf nation.

national, ~e (mpl -aux) /nasjɔnal, -o/ adj national. **nationale** nf A road; (US) highway. **nationaliser** [1] *vt* nationalize.

nationalité /nasjɔnalite/ *nf* nationality.

natte /nat/ *nf* (de cheveux) plait; (US) braid; (tapis de paille) mat.

nature /natyʀ/ *nf* nature; ~ **morte** still life; **de** ~ **à** likely to; **payer en** ~ pay in kind. ● *a inv* plain; (*yaourt*) natural; (*thé*) black.

naturel, ~**le** /natyʀɛl/ *adj* natural. ● *nm* nature; (simplicité) naturalness; (Culin) **au** ~ plain; (*thon*) in brine.

naturellement *adv* naturally; (bien sûr) of course.

naufrage /nofʀaʒ/ *nm* shipwreck; **faire** ~ be shipwrecked; (*bateau*) be wrecked.

nauséabond, ~**e** /nozeabɔ̃, -d/ *adj* nauseating.

nausée /noze/ *nf* nausea.

nautique /notik/ *adj* nautical; **sports** ~**s** water sports.

naval, ~**e** (*mpl* ~**s**) /naval/ *adj* naval; **chantier** ~ shipyard.

navet /navɛ/ *nm* turnip; (film: péj) flop; (US) turkey.

navette /navɛt/ *nf* shuttle (service); **faire la** ~ shuttle back and forth.

navigateur, **-trice** /navigatœʀ, -tʀis/ *nm,f* sailor; (qui guide) navigator; (Internet) browser. **navigation** *nf* navigation; (trafic) shipping; (Internet) browsing.

naviguer /navige/ [1] *vi* sail; (piloter) navigate; (Internet) browse; ~ **dans l'Internet** surf the Internet.

navire /naviʀ/ *nm* ship.

navré, ~**e** /navʀe/ *adj* sorry (de to).

---

ne, **n'** /nə, n/

n' before vowel or mute h.

● *adverbe*

····➤ **je n'ai que 10 francs** I've only got 10 francs.

····➤ **tu n'avais qu'à le dire!** you only had to say so!

····➤ **je crains qu'il** ~ **parte** I am afraid he will leave.

! ■ Pour les expressions comme ne... guère, ne... jamais, ne... pas, ne... plus, etc. ⇒**guère**, **jamais**, **pas**, **plus**, etc.

---

né, ~**e** /ne/ *adj* born; ~**e Martin** née Martin; (dans composés) **dernier-**~ last-born. ● ⇒NAÎTRE [44].

néanmoins /neɑ̃mwɛ̃/ *adv* nevertheless.

néant /neɑ̃/ *nm* nothingness; **réduire à** ~ (*effet, efforts*) negate, nullify; (*espoir*) dash; 'revenus: ~' 'income: nil'.

nécessaire /nesesɛʀ/ *adj* necessary. ● *nm* (sac) bag; (trousse) kit; **le** ~ (l'indispensable) the necessities *ou* essentials; **faire le** ~ do what is necessary.

nécessité /nesesite/ *nf* necessity; **de première** ~ vital.

nécessiter /nesesite/ [1] *vt* necessitate.

néerlandais, ~**e** /neɛʀlɑ̃dɛ, -z/ *adj* Dutch. ● *nm* (Ling) Dutch. **N**~, ~**e** *nm,f* Dutchman, Dutchwoman.

néfaste /nefast/ *adj* harmful (à to).

négatif, **-ive** /negatif, -v/ *a & nm* negative.

négligé, ~**e** /negliʒe/ *adj* (*travail*) careless; (*tenue*) scruffy. ● *nm* (tenue) negligee.

négligent, ~**e** /negliʒɑ̃, -t/ *adj* careless, negligent.

négliger /negliʒe/ [40] *vt* neglect; (ne pas tenir compte de) ignore, disregard; ~ **de faire** fail to do. □ **se** ~ *vpr* neglect oneself.

négoce /negɔs/ *nm* business, trade. **négociant**, ~**e** *nm,f* merchant.

négociation /negɔsjasjɔ̃/ *nf* negotiation. **négocier** [45] *vt/i* negotiate.

nègre /nɛgʀ/ *adj* (*musique, art*) Negro. ● *nm* (écrivain) ghost writer.

neige /nɛʒ/ *nf* snow. **neiger** [40] *vi* snow.

nénuphar /nenyfaʀ/ *nm* waterlily.

nerf /nɛʀ/ *nm* nerve; (vigueur) stamina; **être sur les** ~**s** be on edge.

nerveux, **-euse** /nɛʀvø, -z/ *adj* nervous; (irritable) nervy; (*centre, cellule*) nerve; (*voiture*) responsive.

n

nervosité *nf* nervousness; (irritabilité) touchiness.

net, **~te** /nɛt/ *adj* (clair, distinct) clear; (propre) clean; (notable) marked; (soigné) neat; (*prix, poids*) net. ● *adv* (*s'arrêter*) dead; (*refuser*) flatly; (*parler*) plainly; (*se casser*) cleanly; (*tuer*) outright. **nettement** *adv* (*expliquer*) clearly; (*augmenter, se détériorer*) markedly; (indiscutablement) distinctly, decidedly. **netteté** *nf* clearness.

nettoyage /nɛtwajaʒ/ *nm* cleaning; **~ à sec** dry-cleaning; **produit de ~** cleaner.

nettoyer /nɛtwaje/ [31] *vt* clean.

neuf¹ /nœf/ (/nœv/ *before vowels and mute h*) *a inv* & *nm* nine.

neuf², **-euve** /nœf, -v/ *adj* new; **tout ~** brand new. ● *nm* new; **remettre à ~** brighten up; **du ~** a new development; **quoi de ~?** what's new?

neutre /nøtʀ/ *adj* neutral; (Gram) neuter. ● *nm* (Gram) neuter.

neutron /nøtʀɔ̃/ *nm* neutron.

neuve /nœv/ ⇒NEUF².

neuvième /nœvjɛm/ *a* & *nm, f* ninth.

neveu (*pl* **~x**) /nəvø/ *nm* nephew.

névrose /nevʀoz/ *nf* neurosis. **névrosé**, **~e** *a* & *nm,f* neurotic.

nez /ne/ *nm* nose; **~ à ~** face to face; **~ retroussé** turned-up nose; **avoir du ~** have flair.

ni /ni/ *conj* neither, nor; **~ grand ~ petit** neither big nor small; **~ l'un ~ l'autre ne fument** neither (one nor the other) smokes; **sortir sans manteau ~ chapeau** go without a coat or hat; **elle n'a dit ~ oui ~ non** she didn't say either yes or no.

niais, **~e** /njɛ, -z/ *adj* silly.

niche /niʃ/ *nf* (de chien) kennel; (cavité) niche.

nicher /niʃe/ [1] *vi* nest. □ **se ~** *vpr* nest; (se cacher) hide.

nicotine /nikɔtin/ *nf* nicotine.

nid /ni/ *nm* nest; **faire un ~** build a nest. **nid-de-poule** (*pl* **nids-de-poule**) *nm* pot-hole.

nièce /njɛs/ *nf* niece.

nier /nje/ [45] *vt* deny.

nigaud, **~e** /nigo, -d/ *nm,f* silly idiot.

nippon, **~ne** /nipɔ̃, -ɔn/ *adj* Japanese. **N~**, **~ne** *nm,f* Japanese.

niveau (*pl* **~x**) /nivo/ *nm* level; (compétence) standard; (étage) storey; (US) story; **au ~** up to standard; **mettre à ~** (Ordinat) upgrade; **~ à bulle** (d'air) spirit-level; **~ de vie** standard of living.

niveler /nivle/ [6] *vt* level.

noble /nɔbl/ *adj* noble. ● *nm,f* nobleman, noblewoman. **noblesse** *nf* nobility.

noce /nɔs/ *nf* (fête 🎎) party; (invités) wedding guests; **~s** wedding; **faire la ~** 🎎 live it up, party.

nocif, **-ive** /nɔsif, -v/ *adj* harmful.

noctambule /nɔktɑ̃byl/ *nmf* late-night reveller.

nocturne /nɔktyʀn/ *adj* nocturnal. ● *nm* (Mus) nocturne. ● *nf* (Sport) evening fixture; (de magasin) late-night opening.

Noël /nɔɛl/ *nm* Christmas.

nœud /nø/ *nm* (Naut) knot; (pour lier) knot; (pour orner) bow; **~s** (fig) ties; **~ coulant** slipknot, noose; **~ papillon** bow-tie.

noir, **~e** /nwaʀ/ *adj* black; (obscur, sombre) dark; (triste) gloomy. ● *nm* black; (obscurité) dark; **travail au ~** moonlighting. ● *nm,f* (personne) Black.

noircir /nwaʀsiʀ/ [2] *vt* blacken; **~ la situation** paint a black picture of the situation. ● *vi* (banane) go black; (*mur*) get dirty; (*métal*) tarnish. □ **se ~** *vpr* (ciel) darken.

noire /nwaʀ/ *nf* (Mus) crotchet.

noisette /nwazɛt/ *nf* hazelnut; (de beurre) knob.

noix /nwa/ *nf* nut; (du noyer) walnut; (de beurre) knob; **~ de cajou** cashew nut; **~ de coco** coconut; **à la ~** 🎎 useless.

nom /nɔ̃/ *nm* name; (Gram) noun; **au ~ de** on behalf of; **~ et prénom** full name; **~ déposé** registered trademark; **~ de famille** surname; **~ de jeune fille** maiden name; **~ de plume** pen name; **~ propre** proper noun.

nomade /nɔmad/ *adj* nomadic.
● *nmf* nomad.

nombre /nɔ̃bʀ/ *nm* number; **au ~ de** (parmi) among; (l'un de) one of; **en (grand) ~** in large numbers; **sans ~** countless.

nombreux, -euse /nɔ̃bʀø, -z/ *adj* (en grand nombre) many, numerous; (important) large; **de ~ enfants** many children; **nous étions très ~** there were a great many of us.

nombril /nɔ̃bʀil/ *nm* navel.

nomination /nɔminasjɔ̃/ *nf* appointment.

nommer /nɔme/ [1] *vt* name; (élire) (à un poste) appoint; (à un lieu) post. □ **se ~** *vpr* (s'appeler) be called.

non /nɔ̃/ *adv* no; (pas) not; **~ (pas) que** not that; **il vient, ~?** he is coming, isn't he?; **moi ~ plus** neither am/do/can/*etc.* I. ● *nm inv* no.

non- /nɔ̃/ *préf* non-; **~-fumeur** non-smoker.

nonante /nɔnɑ̃t/ *a & nm* ninety.

non-sens /nɔ̃sɑ̃s/ *nm inv* absurdity.

nord /nɔʀ/ *a inv* (façade, côte) north; (frontière, zone) northern. ● *nm* north; **le ~ de l'Europe** northern Europe; **vent de ~** northerly (wind); **aller vers le ~** go north; **le Nord** the North; **du Nord** northern. **nord-est** *nm* north-east.

nordique /nɔʀdik/ *adj* Scandinavian.

nord-ouest /nɔʀwɛst/ *nm* north-west.

normal, ~e (*mpl* **-aux**) /nɔʀmal, -o/ *adj* normal. **normale** *nf* normality; (norme) norm; (moyenne) average.

normand, ~e /nɔʀmɑ̃, -d/ *adj* Norman. **N~, ~e** *nm, f* Norman.

Normandie /nɔʀmɑ̃di/ *nf* Normandy.

norme /nɔʀm/ *nf* norm; (de production) standard; **~s de sécurité** safety standards.

Norvège /nɔʀvɛʒ/ *nf* Norway.

norvégien, ~ne /nɔʀveʒjɛ̃, -ɛn/ *adj* Norwegian. **N~, ~ne** *nm, f* Norwegian.

nos /no/ ⇒NOTRE.

nostalgie /nɔstalʒi/ *nf* nostalgia; **avoir la ~ de son pays** be homesick. **nostalgique** *adj* nostalgic.

notaire /nɔtɛʀ/ *nm* notary public.

notamment /nɔtamɑ̃/ *adv* notably.

note /nɔt/ *nf* (remarque) note; (chiffrée) mark, grade; (facture) bill; (Mus) note; **~ (de service)** memorandum; **prendre ~ de** take note of.

noter /nɔte/ [1] *vt* note, notice; (écrire) note (down); (devoir) mark; (US) grade; **bien/mal noté** (employé) highly/poorly rated.

notice /nɔtis/ *nf* note; (mode d'emploi) instructions, directions.

notifier /nɔtifje/ [45] *vt* notify (à to).

notion /nosjɔ̃/ *nf* notion; **avoir des ~s de** have a basic knowledge of.

notoire /nɔtwaʀ/ *adj* well-known; (criminel) notorious.

notre (*pl* **nos**) /nɔtʀ, no/ *adj* our.

nôtre /notʀ/ *pron* **le** *ou* **la ~, les ~s** ours.

nouer /nwe/ [1] *vt* tie, knot; (relations) strike up.

nouille /nuj/ *nf* (Culin) noodle; **des ~s** noodles, pasta; (idiot 🅸) idiot.

nounours /nunuʀs/ *nm* 🅸 teddy bear.

nourri, ~e /nuʀi/ *adj* **être logé ~** have bed and board; **~ au sein** breastfed.

nourrice /nuʀis/ *nf* childminder.

nourrir /nuʀiʀ/ [2] *vt* feed; (espoir, crainte) harbour; (projet) nurture; (passion) fuel. ● *vi* be nourishing. □ **se ~** *vpr* eat; **se ~ de** feed on. **nourrissant, ~e** *adj* nourishing.

nourrisson /nuʀisɔ̃/ *nm* infant.

nourriture /nuʀityʀ/ *nf* food.

nous /nu/ *pron* (sujet) we; (complément) us; (indirect) (to) us; (réfléchi) ourselves; (l'un l'autre) each other; **la voiture est à ~** the car is ours. **nous-mêmes** *pron* ourselves.

nouveau (**nouvel** *before vowel or mute h*), **nouvelle** (*mpl* **~x**) /nuvo, nuvɛl/ *adj* new; **nouvel an** new year; **~x mariés** newly-weds; **~ venu, nouvelle venue** newcomer. ● *nm, f* (élève) new boy, new girl. ● *nm* **du ~** (fait nouveau) a new development; **de ~, à ~** again. **nouveau-né** (*pl* **~s**) *nm* newborn baby.

n

nouveauté /nuvote/ *nf* novelty; (chose) new thing; (livre) new publication; (disque) new release.

nouvelle /nuvɛl/ *nf* (piece of) news; (récit) short story; ~s news.

Nouvelle-Zélande /nuvɛlzelãd/ *nf* New Zealand.

novembre /nɔvãbʀ/ *nm* November.

noyade /nwajad/ *nf* drowning.

noyau (*pl* ~x) /nwajo/ *nm* (de fruit) stone; (US) pit; (de cellule) nucleus; (groupe) group; (centre: fig) core.

noyer /nwaje/ [31] *vt* drown; (inonder) flood. □ **se** ~ *vpr* drown; (volontairement) drown oneself; **se** ~ **dans un verre d'eau** make a mountain out of a molehill. ● *nm* walnut-tree.

nu, **~e** /ny/ *adj* (corps, personne) naked; (mains, mur, fil) bare; **à l'œil** ~ to the naked eye. ● *nm* nude; **mettre à** ~ expose.

nuage /nyaʒ/ *nm* cloud.

nuance /nyãs/ *nf* shade; (de sens) nuance; (différence) difference. **nuancer** [10] *vt* (opinion) qualify.

nucléaire /nykleeʀ/ *adj* nuclear. ● *nm* **le** ~ nuclear energy.

nudisme /nydism/ *nm* nudism.

nudité /nydite/ *nf* nudity; (de lieu) bareness.

nuée /nɥe/ *nf* swarm, host.

nues /ny/ *nfpl* **tomber des** ~ be amazed; **porter qn aux** ~ praise sb to the skies.

nuire /nɥiʀ/ [17] *vi* ~ **à** harm.

nuisible /nɥizibl/ *adj* harmful (**à** to).

nuit /nɥi/ *nf* night; **cette** ~ tonight; (hier) last night; **il fait** ~ it is dark; ~ **blanche** sleepless night; **la** ~, **de** ~ at night; ~ **de noces** wedding night.

nul, **~le** /nyl/ *adj* (aucun) no; (zéro) nil; (qui ne vaut rien) useless; (non valable) null; (contrat) void; (testament) invalid; **match** ~ draw; ~ **en sciences** no good at science; **nulle part** nowhere; ~ **autre** no one else. ● *pron* no one. **nullement** *adv* not at all. **nullité** *nf* uselessness; (personne) nonentity.

numérique /nymeʀik/ *adj* numerical; (montre, horloge) digital.

numéro /nymeʀo/ *nm* number; (de journal) issue; (spectacle) act; ~ **de téléphone** telephone number; ~ **vert** freephone number. **numéroter** [1] *vt* number.

nuque /nyk/ *nf* nape (of the neck).

nurse /nœʀs/ *nf* nanny.

nutritif, **-ive** /nytʀitif, -v/ *adj* nutritious; (valeur) nutritional.

Oo

oasis /ɔazis/ *nf* oasis.

obéir /ɔbeiʀ/ [2] *vt* ~ **à** obey. ● *vi* obey. **obéissance** *nf* obedience. **obéissant**, **~e** *adj* obedient.

obèse /ɔbɛz/ *adj* obese.

objecter /ɔbʒɛkte/ [1] *vt* object.

objectif, **-ive** /ɔbʒɛktif, -v/ *adj* objective. ● *nm* objective; (Photo) lens.

objection /ɔbʒɛksjõ/ *nf* objection; **soulever des** ~s raise objections.

objet /ɔbʒɛ/ *nm* (chose) object; (sujet) subject; (but) purpose, object; **être** *ou* **faire l'**~ **de** be the subject of; ~ **d'art** objet d'art; ~s **trouvés** lost property; (US) lost and found.

obligation /ɔbligasjõ/ *nf* obligation; (Comm) bond; **être dans l'**~ **de** be under obligation to.

obligatoire /ɔbligatwaʀ/ *adj* compulsory. **obligatoirement** *adv* (par règlement) of necessity; (inévitablement) inevitably.

obligeance /ɔbliʒãs/ *nf* **avoir l'**~ **de faire** be kind enough to do.

obliger /ɔbliʒe/ [40] *vt* compel, force (**à faire** to do); (aider) oblige; **être obligé de** have to (**de** for).

oblique /ɔblik/ *adj* oblique; **regard** ~ sidelong glance; **en** ~ at an angle.

oblitérer /ɔblitere/ [14] *vt* (timbre) cancel.

obnubilé, **~e** /ɔbnybile/ *adj* obsessed.

obscène /ɔpsɛn/ *adj* obscene.

obscur, ∼e /ɔpskyR/ adj dark; (confus, humble) obscure; (vague) vague.

obscurcir /ɔpskyRsiR/ [2] vt make dark; (fig) obscure. □ **s'**∼ vpr (ciel) darken.

obscurité /ɔpskyRite/ nf dark-(ness); (de passage, situation) obscurity.

obsédant, ∼e /ɔpsedɑ̃, -t/ adj (problème) nagging; (musique, souvenir) haunting.

obsédé, ∼e /ɔpsede/ nm,f ∼ (sexuel) sex maniac; ∼ du ski/jazz ski/jazz freak.

obséder /ɔpsede/ [14] vt obsess.

obsèques /ɔpsɛk/ nfpl funeral.

observateur, **-trice** /ɔpsɛR-vatœR, -tRis/ adj observant. ● nm,f observer.

observation /ɔpsɛRvasjɔ̃/ nf observation; (remarque) remark, comment; (reproche) criticism; (obéissance) observance; **en** ∼ under observation.

observer /ɔpsɛRve/ [1] vt (regarder) observe; (surveiller) watch, observe; (remarquer) notice, observe; **faire** ∼ **qch** point sth out (à to).

obsession /ɔpsesjɔ̃/ nf obsession.

obstacle /ɔpstakl/ nm obstacle; (pour cheval) fence, jump; (pour athlète) hurdle; **faire** ∼ **à** stand in the way of, obstruct.

obstétrique /ɔpstetRik/ nf obstetrics (+ sg).

obstiné, ∼e /ɔpstine/ adj stubborn, obstinate.

obstiner (**s'**) /(s)ɔpstine/ [1] vpr persist (à in).

obstruction /ɔpstRyksjɔ̃/ nf obstruction; (de conduit) blockage.

obstruer /ɔpstRye/ [1] vt obstruct, block.

obtenir /ɔptəniR/ [58] vt get, obtain. **obtention** nf obtaining.

obus /ɔby/ nm shell.

occasion /ɔkazjɔ̃/ nf opportunity; (de faire of doing); (circonstance) occasion; (achat) bargain; (article non neuf) second-hand buy; **à l'**∼ sometimes; **d'**∼ second-hand. **occasionnel**, ∼le adj occasional.

occasionner /ɔkazjɔne/ [1] vt cause.

occident /ɔksidɑ̃/ nm (direction) west; **l'O**∼ the West.

occidental, ∼e (mpl **-aux**) /ɔksidɑ̃tal, -o/ adj western. **O**∼, ∼e (mpl **-aux**) nm,f westerner.

occulte /ɔkylt/ adj occult.

occupant, ∼e /ɔkypɑ̃, -t/ nm,f occupant. ● nm (Mil) forces of occupation.

occupation /ɔkypasjɔ̃/ nf occupation.

occupé, ∼e /ɔkype/ adj busy; (place, pays) occupied; (téléphone) engaged, busy; (toilettes) engaged.

occuper /ɔkype/ [1] vt occupy; (poste) hold; (espace, temps) take up. □ **s'**∼ vpr (s'affairer) keep busy (à faire doing); **s'**∼ **de** (personne, problème) take care of; (bureau, firme) be in charge of; (se mêler) **occupe-toi de tes affaires** mind your own business.

occurrence: **en l'**∼ /ɑ̃lɔkyRɑ̃s/ loc in this case.

océan /ɔseɑ̃/ nm ocean.

Océanie /ɔseani/ nf Oceania.

ocre /ɔkR/ a inv ochre.

octante /ɔktɑ̃t/ adj eighty.

octet /ɔktɛ/ nm byte.

octobre /ɔktɔbR/ nm October.

octogone /ɔktɔgɔn/ nm octagon.

octroyer /ɔktRwaje/ [31] vt grant.

oculaire /ɔkylɛR/ adj témoin ∼ eye-witness; **troubles** ∼s eye trouble.

oculiste /ɔkylist/ nmf ophthalmologist.

odeur /ɔdœR/ nf smell.

odieux, **-ieuse** /ɔdjø, -z/ adj odious.

odorant, ∼e /ɔdɔRɑ̃, -t/ adj sweet-smelling.

odorat /ɔdɔRa/ nm sense of smell.

œil (pl **yeux**) /œj, jø/ nm eye; **à l'**∼ 🔢 for free; **à mes yeux** in my view; **faire de l'**∼ **à** make eyes at; **faire les gros yeux à** glare at; **ouvrir l'**∼ keep one's eyes open; ∼ **poché** black eye; **fermer les yeux** shut one's eyes; (fig) turn a blind eye.

œillères /œjɛR/ nfpl blinkers.

œillet /œjɛ/ nm (plante) carnation; (trou) eyelet.

œuf (*pl* ∼s) /œf, ø/ *nm* egg; ∼ à la coque/dur/sur le plat boiled/hard-boiled/fried egg.

œuvre /œvʀ/ *nf* (ouvrage, travail) work; ∼ d'art work of art; ∼ (de bienfaisance) charity; être à l'∼ be at work; mettre en ∼ (*réforme, moyens*) implement; mise en ∼ implementation. ● *nm* (ensemble spécifié) l'∼ sculpté de X the sculptures of X; l'∼ entier de Beethoven the complete works of Beethoven.

œuvrer /œvʀe/ [1] *vi* work.

off /ɔf/ *a inv* voix ∼ voice-over.

offense /ɔfɑ̃s/ *nf* insult.

offenser /ɔfɑ̃se/ [1] *vt* offend. □ s'∼ *vpr* take offence (de at).

offensive /ɔfɑ̃siv/ *nf* offensive.

offert, ∼e /ɔfɛʀ, -t/ ⇒OFFRIR [21].

office /ɔfis/ *nm* office; (Relig) service; (de cuisine) pantry; faire ∼ de act as; d'∼ without consultation, automatically; ∼ du tourisme tourist information office.

officiel, ∼le /ɔfisjɛl/ *adj* official. ● *nm* official.

officier /ɔfisje/ [45] *vi* (Relig) officiate. ● *nm* officer.

officieux, -ieuse /ɔfisjø, -z/ *adj* unofficial.

offre /ɔfʀ/ *nf* offer; (aux enchères) bid; l'∼ et la demande supply and demand; '∼s d'emploi' 'situations vacant'.

offrir /ɔfʀiʀ/ [21] *vt* offer (de faire to do); (*cadeau*) give; (acheter) buy; ∼ à boire à (chez soi) give a drink to; (au café) buy a drink for. □ s'∼ *vpr* (se proposer) offer oneself (comme as); (*solution*) present itself; (s'acheter) treat oneself to.

ogive /ɔʒiv/ *nf* ∼ nucléaire nuclear warhead.

oie /wa/ *nf* goose.

oignon /ɔɲɔ̃/ *nm* (légume) onion; (de fleur) bulb.

oiseau (*pl* ∼x) /wazo/ *nm* bird.

oisif, -ive /wazif, -v/ *adj* idle.

olive /ɔliv/ *nf & a inv* olive. **olivier** *nm* olive tree.

olympique /ɔlɛ̃pik/ *adj* Olympic.

ombrage /ɔ̃bʀaʒ/ *nm* shade; prendre ∼ de take offence at. **ombragé, ∼e** *adj* shady. **ombrageux, -euse** *adj* easily offended.

ombre /ɔ̃bʀ/ *nf* (pénombre) shade; (contour) shadow; (soupçon: fig) hint, shadow; dans l'∼ (*agir, rester*) behind the scenes; faire de l'∼ à qn be in sb's light.

ombrelle /ɔ̃bʀɛl/ *nf* parasol.

omelette /ɔmlɛt/ *nf* omelette.

omettre /ɔmɛtʀ/ [42] *vt* omit, leave out.

omnibus /ɔmnibys/ *nm* stopping *ou* local train.

omoplate /ɔmɔplat/ *nf* shoulder blade.

on /ɔ̃/ *pron* (tu, vous) you; (nous) we; (ils, elles) they; (les gens) people, they; (quelqu'un) someone; (indéterminé) one, you; ∼ dit people say, they say, it is said; ∼ m'a demandé mon avis I was asked for my opinion.

oncle /ɔ̃kl/ *nm* uncle.

onctueux, -euse /ɔ̃ktɥø, -z/ *adj* smooth.

onde /ɔ̃d/ *nf* wave; ∼s courtes/longues short/long wave; sur les ∼s on the air.

on-dit /ɔ̃di/ *nm inv* les ∼ hearsay.

onduler /ɔ̃dyle/ [1] *vi* undulate; (*cheveux*) be wavy.

onéreux, -euse /ɔneʀø, -z/ *adj* costly.

ongle /ɔ̃gl/ *nm* (finger)nail; ∼ de pied toenail; se faire les ∼s do one's nails.

ont /ɔ̃/ ⇒AVOIR [5].

ONU *abrév f* (**Organisation des Nations unies**) UN.

onze /ɔ̃z/ *a & nm* eleven. **onzième** *a & nmf* eleventh.

OPA *abrév f* (**offre publique d'achat**) takeover bid.

opéra /ɔpeʀa/ *nm* opera; (édifice) opera house. **opéra-comique** (*pl* **opéras-comiques**) *nm* light opera.

opérateur, -trice /ɔpeʀatœʀ, -tʀis/ *nm, f* operator; ∼ (de prise de vue) cameraman.

opération /ɔpeʀasjɔ̃/ *nf* operation; (Comm) deal; (calcul) calculation.

opératoire /ɔpeʀatwaʀ/ *adj* (Méd) surgical; bloc ∼ operating suite.

opérer /ɔpeʀe/ [14] vt (personne) operate on; (exécuter) carry out, make; ~ qn d'une tumeur operate on sb to remove a tumour; **se faire** ~ have surgery ou an operation. ● vi (Méd) operate; (faire effet) work. □ **s'**~ vpr (se produire) occur.

opiniâtre /ɔpinjɑtʀ/ adj tenacious.

opinion /ɔpinjɔ̃/ nf opinion.

opportuniste /ɔpɔʀtynist/ nmf opportunist.

opposant, ~**e** /ɔpozɑ̃, -t/ nm, f opponent.

opposé, ~**e** /ɔpoze/ adj (sens, angle, avis) opposite; (factions) opposing; (intérêts) conflicting; **être** ~ **à** be opposed to. ● nm opposite; **à l'**~ **de** (contrairement à) contrary to, unlike.

opposer /ɔpoze/ [1] vt (objets) place opposite each other; (personnes) match, oppose; (contraster) contrast; (résistance, argument) put up. □ **s'**~ vpr (personnes) confront each other; (styles) contrast; **s'**~ **à** oppose.

opposition /ɔpozisjɔ̃/ nf opposition; **par** ~ **à** in contrast with; **entrer en** ~ **avec** come into conflict with; **faire** ~ **à un chèque** stop a cheque.

oppressant, ~**e** /ɔpʀesɑ̃, -t/ adj oppressive.

opprimer /ɔpʀime/ [1] vt oppress.

opter /ɔpte/ [1] vi ~ **pour** opt for.

opticien, ~**ne** /ɔptisjɛ̃, -ɛn/ nm, f optician.

optimisme /ɔptimism/ nm optimism.

optimiste /ɔptimist/ nmf optimist. ● adj optimistic.

option /ɔpsjɔ̃/ nf option.

optique /ɔptik/ adj (verre) optical. ● nf (science) optics (+ sg); (perspective) perspective.

or[1] /ɔʀ/ nm gold; **d'**~ golden; **en** ~ gold; (occasion) golden.

or[2] /ɔʀ/ conj now, well; (indiquant une opposition) and yet.

orage /ɔʀaʒ/ nm (thunder)storm. **orageux**, -**euse** adj stormy.

oral, ~**e** (mpl -**aux**) /ɔʀal, -o/ adj oral. ● nm (pl -**aux**) oral.

orange /ɔʀɑ̃ʒ/ a inv orange; (Aut) (feu) amber; (US) yellow. ● nf orange. **orangeade** nf orangeade. **oranger** nm orange tree.

orateur, -**trice** /ɔʀatœʀ, -tʀis/ nm, f speaker.

orbite /ɔʀbit/ nf orbit; (d'œil) socket.

orchestre /ɔʀkɛstʀ/ nm orchestra; (de jazz) band; (parterre) stalls.

ordinaire /ɔʀdinɛʀ/ adj ordinary; (habituel) usual; (qualité) standard; (médiocre) very average. ● nm **l'**~ the ordinary; (nourriture) the standard fare; **d'**~, **à l'**~ usually. **ordinairement** adv usually.

ordinateur /ɔʀdinatœʀ/ nm computer; ~ **personnel/de bureau** personal/desktop computer; ~ **portable** laptop (computer); ~ **hôte** (Internet) host.

ordonnance /ɔʀdɔnɑ̃s/ nf (ordre, décret) order; (de médecin) prescription.

ordonné, ~**e** /ɔʀdɔne/ adj tidy.

ordonner /ɔʀdɔne/ [1] vt order (**à qn de** sb to); (agencer) arrange; (Méd) prescribe; (prêtre) ordain.

ordre /ɔʀdʀ/ nm order; (propreté) tidiness; **aux** ~**s de qn** at sb's disposal; **avoir de l'**~ be tidy; **en** ~ tidy, in order; **de premier** ~ first-rate; **d'**~ **officiel** of an official nature; **l'**~ **du jour** (programme) agenda; **mettre de l'**~ **dans** tidy up; **jusqu'à nouvel** ~ until further notice; **un** ~ **de grandeur** an approximate idea.

ordure /ɔʀdyʀ/ nf filth; ~**s** (détritus) rubbish; (US) garbage; ~**s ménagères** household refuse.

oreille /ɔʀɛj/ nf ear.

oreiller /ɔʀeje/ nm pillow.

oreillons /ɔʀɛjɔ̃/ nmpl mumps.

orfèvre /ɔʀfɛvʀ/ nm goldsmith.

organe /ɔʀgan/ nm organ.

organigramme /ɔʀganigʀam/ nm organization chart; (Ordinat) flowchart.

organique /ɔʀganik/ adj organic.

organisateur, -**trice** /ɔʀganizatœʀ, -tʀis/ nm, f organizer.

organisation /ɔʀganizasjɔ̃/ nf organization.

organiser /ɔʀganize/ [1] vt organize. □ **s'**~ vpr organize oneself, get organized.

organisme /ɔʀganism/ nm body, organism.

orge /ɔʀʒ/ *nf* barley.

orgelet /ɔʀʒəlɛ/ *nm* sty.

orgue /ɔʀg/ *nm* organ; ~ de Barbarie barrel-organ. **orgues** *nfpl* organ.

orgueil /ɔʀgœj/ *nm* pride. **orgueilleux, -euse** *adj* proud.

orient /ɔʀjã/ *nm* (direction) east; l'O~ the Orient.

oriental, ~e (*mpl* **-aux**) /ɔʀjãtal, -o/ *adj* eastern; (de l'Orient) oriental. **O~, ~e** (*mpl* **-aux**) *nm, f* Asian.

orientation /ɔʀjãtasjõ/ *nf* direction; (tendance politique) leanings (+ *pl*); (de maison) aspect; (Sport) orienteering; ~ **professionnelle** careers advice; ~ **scolaire** curriculum counselling.

orienter /ɔʀjãte/ [1] *vt* position; (*personne*) direct. □ **s'**~ *vpr* (se repérer) find one's bearings; **s'**~ **vers** turn towards.

origan /ɔʀigã/ *nm* oregano.

originaire /ɔʀiʒinɛʀ/ *adj* être ~ de be a native of.

original, ~e (*mpl* **-aux**) /ɔʀiʒinal, -o/ *adj* original; (curieux) eccentric. ● *nm* (œuvre) original. ● *nm, f* eccentric. **originalité** *nf* originality; eccentricity.

origine /ɔʀiʒin/ *nf* origin; à l'~ originally; d'~ (*pièce, pneu*) original; être d'~ **noble** come from a noble background.

originel, ~le /ɔʀiʒinɛl/ *adj* original.

orme /ɔʀm/ *nm* elm.

ornement /ɔʀnəmã/ *nm* ornament.

orner /ɔʀne/ [1] *vt* decorate.

orphelin, ~e /ɔʀfəlɛ̃, -in/ *nm, f* orphan. ● *adj* orphaned. **orphelinat** *nm* orphanage.

orteil /ɔʀtɛj/ *nm* toe.

orthodoxe /ɔʀtɔdɔks/ *adj* orthodox.

orthographe /ɔʀtɔgraf/ *nf* spelling.

ortie /ɔʀti/ *nf* nettle.

os /ɔs, o/ *nm inv* bone.

OS *abrév m* ⇒OUVRIER SPÉCIALISÉ.

osciller /ɔsile/ [1] *vi* sway; (Tech) oscillate; (hésiter) waver; (fluctuer) fluctuate.

osé, ~e /oze/ *adj* daring.

oseille /ozɛj/ *nf* (plante) sorrel.

oser /oze/ [1] *vi* dare.

osier /ozje/ *nm* wicker.

ossature /ɔsatyʀ/ *nf* skeleton, frame.

ossements /ɔsmã/ *nmpl* bones, remains.

osseux, -euse /ɔsø, -z/ *adj* bony; (Méd) bone.

otage /ɔtaʒ/ *nm* hostage.

OTAN /ɔtã/ *abrév f* (**Organisation du traité de l'Atlantique Nord**) NATO.

otarie /ɔtaʀi/ *nf* eared seal.

ôter /ote/ [1] *vt* remove (**à qn** from sb); (déduire) take away.

otite /ɔtit/ *nf* ear infection.

ou /u/ *conj* or; ~ **bien** or else; ~ (**bien**)... ~ (**bien**)... either... or...; **vous** ~ **moi** either you or me.

où /u/ *pron* where; (dans lequel) in which; (sur lequel) on which; (auquel) at which; **d'**~ from which; (pour cette raison) hence; **par** ~ through which; ~ **qu'il soit** wherever he may be; **juste au moment** ~ just as; **le jour** ~ the day when. ● *adv* where; **d'**~? where from?

ouate /wat/ *nf* cotton wool; (US) absorbent cotton.

oubli /ubli/ *nm* forgetfulness; (trou de mémoire) lapse of memory; (négligence) oversight; **tomber dans l'**~ sink into oblivion.

oublier /ublije/ [45] *vt* forget; (omettre) leave out, forget. □ **s'**~ *vpr* (*chose*) be forgotten.

ouest /wɛst/ *a inv* (*façade, côte*) west; (*frontière, zone*) western. ● *nm* west; l'~ de l'Europe western Europe; **vent d'**~ westerly (wind); **aller vers l'**~ go west; l'O~ the West; **de l'O**~ western.

oui /wi/ *adv & nm inv* yes.

ouï-dire: **par** ~ /paʀwidiʀ/ *loc* by hearsay.

ouïe /wi/ *nf* hearing; (de poisson) gill.

ouragan /uʀagã/ *nm* hurricane.

ourlet /uʀlɛ/ *nm* hem.

ours /uʀs/ *nm* bear; ~ **blanc** polar bear; ~ **en peluche** teddy bear.

outil /uti/ *nm* tool. **outillage** *nm* tools (+ *pl*). **outiller** [1] *vt* equip.

outrage /utʀaʒ/ *nm* (grave) insult.

outrance /utʀɑ̃s/ *nf* à ∼ excessively. **outrancier, -ière** *adj* extreme.

outre /utʀ/ *prép* besides. ● *adv* **passer** ∼ pay no heed; ∼ **mesure** unduly; **en** ∼ in addition. **outre-mer** *adv* overseas.

outrepasser /utʀəpase/ [1] *vt* exceed.

outrer /utʀe/ [1] *vt* exaggerate; (*indigner*) incense.

ouvert, ∼e /uvɛʀ, -t/ *adj* open; (*gaz, radio*) on. ●⇒OUVRIR [21].

ouverture /uvɛʀtyʀ/ *nf* opening; (Mus) overture; (Photo) aperture; ∼**s** (*offres*) overtures; ∼ **d'esprit** open-mindedness.

ouvrable /uvʀabl/ *adj* jour ∼ working day; **aux heures** ∼**s** during business hours.

ouvrage /uvʀaʒ/ *nm* (*travail, livre*) work; (*couture*) (piece of) needlework.

ouvre-boîtes /uvʀəbwat/ *nm inv* tin-opener.

ouvre-bouteilles /uvʀəbutɛj/ *nm inv* bottle-opener.

ouvreur, -euse /uvʀœʀ, -øz/ *nm,f* usherette.

ouvrier, -ière /uvʀije, -jɛʀ/ *nm,f* worker; ∼ **qualifié/spécialisé** skilled/unskilled worker. ● *adj* working-class; (*conflit*) industrial; **syndicat** ∼ trade union.

ouvrir /uvʀiʀ/ [21] *vt* open (up); (*gaz, robinet*) turn *ou* switch on. ● *vi* open (up). □ **s'**∼ *vpr* open (up); **s'**∼ **à qn** open one's heart to sb.

ovaire /ɔvɛʀ/ *nm* ovary.

ovale /ɔval/ *a & nm* oval.

ovni /ɔvni/ *abrév m* (**objet volant non-identifié**) UFO.

ovule /ɔvyl/ *nm* (à féconder) ovum; (*gynécologique*) pessary.

oxygène /ɔksiʒɛn/ *nm* oxygen.

oxygéner (s') /(s)ɔksiʒene/ [14] *vpr* get some fresh air.

ozone /ozon/ *nf* ozone; **la couche d'**∼ the ozone layer.

Pp

pacifique /pasifik/ *adj* peaceful; (*personne*) peaceable; (Géog) Pacific. **P**∼ *nm* **le P**∼ the Pacific (Ocean).

pacotille /pakɔtij/ *nf* junk, rubbish.

pagaie /pagɛ/ *nf* paddle.

pagaille /pagaj/ *nf* 🔲 mess, shambles (+ *sg*).

page /paʒ/ *nf* page; **mise en** ∼ layout; **tourner la** ∼ turn over a new leaf; **être à la** ∼ be up to date; ∼ **d'accueil** (Internet) home page.

paie /pɛ/ *nf* pay.

paiement /pɛmɑ̃/ *nm* payment.

païen, ∼ne /pajɛ̃, -ɛn/ *a & nm,f* pagan.

paillasson /pajasɔ̃/ *nm* doormat.

paille /pɑj/ *nf* straw. ● *adj* (*cheveux*) straw-coloured; **jaune** ∼ straw yellow.

paillette /pajɛt/ *nf* (sur robe) sequin; (de savon) flake; **robe à** ∼**s** sequined dress.

pain /pɛ̃/ *nm* bread; (miche) loaf (of bread); (de savon, cire) bar; ∼ **d'épices** gingerbread; ∼ **grillé** toast.

pair, ∼e /pɛʀ/ *adj* (*nombre*) even. ● *nm* (personne) peer; **aller de** ∼ go together (**avec** with); **au** ∼ (*jeune fille*) au pair. **paire** *nf* pair.

paisible /pezibl/ *adj* peaceful.

paître /pɛtʀ/ [44] *vi* graze.

paix /pɛ/ *nf* peace; **fiche-moi la** ∼! 🔲 leave me alone!

Pakistan /pakistɑ̃/ *nm* Pakistan.

palace /palas/ *nm* luxury hotel.

palais /palɛ/ *nm* palace; (Anat) palate; ∼ **de Justice** law courts; ∼ **des sports** sports stadium.

pâle /pɑl/ *adj* pale.

Palestine /palɛstin/ *nf* Palestine.

palier /palje/ *nm* (d'escalier) landing; (étape) stage.

pâlir /pɑliʀ/ [2] *vt/i* (turn) pale.

o
p

palissade /palisad/ nf fence.

pallier /palje/ [45] vt compensate for.

palmarès /palmaʀɛs/ nm list of prize-winners.

palme /palm/ nf palm leaf; (de nageur) flipper. **palmé**, ~**e** adj (patte) webbed.

palmier /palmje/ nm palm (tree).

palper /palpe/ [1] vt feel.

palpiter /palpite/ [1] vi (battre) pound; (frémir) quiver.

paludisme /palydism/ nm malaria.

pamplemousse /pɑ̃pləmus/ nm grapefruit.

panaché, ~**e** /panaʃe/ adj (bariolé, mélangé) motley; glace ~**e** mixed-flavour ice cream. ● nm shandy.

pancarte /pɑ̃kaʀt/ nf sign; (de manifestant) placard.

pané, ~**e** /pane/ adj breaded.

panier /panje/ nm basket; (de basket-ball) basket; **mettre au** ~ 🔁 throw out; ~ **à salade** salad shaker; (fourgon 🔁) police van.

panique /panik/ nf panic. **paniquer** [1] vi panic.

panne /pan/ nf breakdown; **être en** ~ have broken down; **être en** ~ **sèche** have run out of petrol; ~ **d'électricité** ou **de courant** power failure.

panneau (pl ~**x**) /pano/ nm sign; (publicitaire) hoarding; (de porte) panel; ~ **(d'affichage)** notice board; ~ **(de signalisation)** road sign.

panoplie /panɔpli/ nf (jouet) outfit; (gamme) range.

pansement /pɑ̃smɑ̃/ nm dressing; ~ **adhésif** plaster. **panser** [1] vt (plaie) dress; (personne) dress the wound(s) of; (cheval) groom.

pantalon /pɑ̃talɔ̃/ nm trousers (+ pl).

panthère /pɑ̃tɛʀ/ nf panther.

pantin /pɑ̃tɛ̃/ nm puppet.

pantomime /pɑ̃tɔmim/ nf mime; (spectacle) mime show.

pantoufle /pɑ̃tufl/ nf slipper.

paon /pɑ̃/ nm peacock.

papa /papa/ nm dad(dy).

pape /pap/ nm pope.

paperasse /papʀas/ nf (péj) bumf.

papeterie /papɛtʀi/ nf (magasin) stationer's shop.

papier /papje/ nm paper; (formulaire) form; ~**s (d'identité)** (identity) papers; ~ **absorbant** kitchen paper; ~ **aluminium** tin foil; ~ **buvard** blotting paper; ~ **cadeau** wrapping paper; ~ **calque** tracing paper; ~ **carbone** carbon-paper; ~ **collant** adhesive tape; ~ **hygiénique** toilet paper; ~ **journal** newspaper; ~ **à lettres** writing paper; ~ **mâché** papier mâché; ~ **peint** wallpaper; ~ **de verre** sandpaper.

papillon /papijɔ̃/ nm butterfly; (contravention 🔁) parking-ticket; ~ **de nuit** moth.

papoter /papɔte/ [1] vi 🔁 chatter.

paquebot /pakbo/ nm liner.

pâquerette /pɑkʀɛt/ nf daisy.

Pâques /pɑk/ nfpl & nm Easter.

paquet /pakɛ/ nm packet; (de cartes) pack; (colis) parcel; **un** ~ **de** (beaucoup 🔁) a mass of.

par /paʀ/ prép by; (à travers) through; (motif) out of, from; (provenance) from; **commencer/finir** ~ **qch** begin/end with sth; **commencer/finir** ~ **faire** begin by/end up (by) doing; ~ **an/ mois** a ou per year/month; ~ **jour** a day; ~ **personne** each, per person; ~ **avion** (lettre) (by) airmail; ~**-ci**, ~**-là** here and there; ~ **contre** on the other hand; ~ **ici/là** this/that way.

parachute /paʀaʃyt/ nm parachute. **parachutiste** nmf parachutist; (Mil) paratrooper.

parader /paʀade/ [1] vi show off.

paradis /paʀadi/ nm (Relig) heaven; (lieu idéal) paradise; ~ **fiscal** tax haven.

paradoxal, ~**e** (mpl **-aux**) /paʀadɔksal, -o/ adj paradoxical.

paraffine /paʀafin/ nf paraffin wax.

parages /paʀaʒ/ nmpl **dans les** ~ around.

paragraphe /paʀagʀaf/ nm paragraph.

paraître /paʀɛtʀ/ [18] vi (se montrer) appear; (sembler) seem, appear; (ouvrage) be published, come out; **faire** ~ (ouvrage) bring out; **il paraît qu'ils...** apparently they...; **oui, il paraît** so I hear.

parallèle /paʀalɛl/ *adj* parallel; (illégal) unofficial. ● *nm* parallel; **faire le** ~ make a connection. ● *nf* parallel (line).

paralyser /paʀalize/ [1] *vt* paralyse. **paralysie** *nf* paralysis.

parapente /paʀapɑ̃t/ *nm* paraglider; (activité) paragliding.

parapher /paʀafe/ [1] *vi* initial; (signer) sign.

parapluie /paʀaplɥi/ *nm* umbrella.

parasite /paʀazit/ *nm* parasite; ~**s** (radio) interference (+ *sg*).

parasol /paʀasɔl/ *nm* sunshade.

paratonnerre /paʀatɔnɛʀ/ *nm* lightning conductor *ou* rod.

paravent /paʀavɑ̃/ *nm* screen.

parc /paʀk/ *nm* park; (de bétail) pen; (de bébé) play-pen; (entrepôt) depot; ~ **relais** park and ride; ~ **de stationnement** car park.

parce que /paʀsk(ə)/ *conj* because.

parchemin /paʀʃəmɛ̃/ *nm* parchment.

parcmètre /paʀkmɛtʀ/ *nm* parking meter.

parcourir /paʀkuʀiʀ/ [20] *vt* travel *ou* go through; (distance) travel; (des yeux) glance at *ou* over.

parcours /paʀkuʀ/ *nm* route; (voyage) journey.

par-delà /paʀdəla/ *prép* beyond.

par-derrière /paʀdɛʀjɛʀ/ *adv* (attaquer) from behind; (critiquer) behind sb's back.

par-dessous /paʀdəsu/ *prép & adv* under(neath).

pardessus /paʀdəsy/ *nm* overcoat.

par-dessus /paʀdəsy/ *prép & adv* over; **bord** overboard; ~ **le marché** 🔢 into the bargain; ~ **tout** above all.

par-devant /paʀdəvɑ̃/ *adv* (passer) by the front.

pardon /paʀdɔ̃/ *nm* forgiveness; (je **vous demande**) ~! (I am) sorry!; (pour demander qch) excuse me.

pardonner /paʀdɔne/ [1] *vt* forgive; ~ **qch à qn** forgive sb for sth.

pare-brise /paʀbʀiz/ *nm inv* windscreen.

pare-chocs /paʀʃɔk/ *nm inv* bumper.

pareil, ~**le** /paʀɛj/ *adj* similar (à to); (tel) such (a); **c'est** ~ it's the same; **ce n'est pas** ~ it's not the same thing. ● *nm, f* equal. ● *adv* 🔢 the same.

parent, ~**e** /paʀɑ̃, -t/ *adj* related (de to). ● *nm, f* relative, relation; ~**s** (père et mère) parents; ~ **isolé** single parent; **réunion de** ~**s d'élèves** parents' evening.

parenté /paʀɑ̃te/ *nf* relationship.

parenthèse /paʀɑ̃tɛz/ *nf* bracket, parenthesis; (fig) digression.

parer /paʀe/ [1] *vt* (esquiver) parry; (orner) adorn. ● *vi* ~ **à** deal with; ~ **au plus pressé** tackle the most urgent things first.

paresse /paʀɛs/ *nf* laziness.

paresseux, **-euse** /paʀɛsø, -z/ *adj* lazy. ● *nm, f* lazy person.

parfait, ~**e** /paʀfɛ, -t/ *adj* perfect. **parfaitement** *adv* perfectly; (bien sûr) absolutely.

parfois /paʀfwa/ *adv* sometimes.

parfum /paʀfœ̃/ *nm* (senteur) scent; (substance) perfume, scent; (goût) flavour. **parfumé**, ~**e** *adj* fragrant; (savon) scented; (thé) flavoured.

parfumer /paʀfyme/ [1] *vt* (embaumer) scent; (gâteau) flavour. □ **se** ~ *vpr* put on one's perfume. **parfumerie** *nf* (produits) perfumes; (boutique) perfume shop.

pari /paʀi/ *nm* bet.

Paris /paʀi/ *npr* Paris.

parisien, ~**ne** /paʀizjɛ̃, -ɛn/ *adj* Parisian; (banlieue) Paris. **P**~, ~**ne** *nm, f* Parisian.

parking /paʀkiŋ/ *nm* car park.

parlement /paʀləmɑ̃/ *nm* parliament.

parlementaire /paʀləmɑ̃tɛʀ/ *adj* parliamentary. ● *nmf* Member of Parliament.

parlementer /paʀləmɑ̃te/ [1] *vi* negotiate.

parler /paʀle/ [1] *vi* talk (à to); ~ **de** talk about; **tu parles d'un avantage!** call that a benefit!; **de quoi ça parle?** what is it about? ● *vt* (langue) speak; (politique, affaires) talk. □ **se** ~ *vpr* (personnes) talk (to each other); (langue) be spoken. ● *nm* speech; (dialecte) dialect.

p

parmi /paʀmi/ *prép* among(st).

paroi /paʀwa/ *nf* wall; ~ **rocheuse** rock face.

paroisse /paʀwas/ *nf* parish.

parole /paʀɔl/ *nf* (mot, promesse) word; (langage) speech; **demander la** ~ ask to speak; **prendre la** ~ (begin to) speak; **tenir** ~ keep one's word; **croire qn sur** ~ take sb's word for it.

parquet /paʀkɛ/ *nm* (parquet) floor; **lame de** ~ floorboard; **le** ~ (Jur) prosecution.

parrain /paʀɛ̃/ *nm* godfather; (fig) sponsor.

parsemer /paʀsəme/ [6] *vt* strew (de with).

part /paʀ/ *nf* share, part; **à** ~ (de côté) aside; (séparément) separate; (excepté) apart from; **d'une** ~ on the one hand; **d'autre** ~ on the other hand; (de plus) moreover; **de la** ~ **de** from; **de toutes** ~s from all sides; **de** ~ **et d'autre** on both sides; **faire** ~ **à qn** inform sb (**de** of); **faire la** ~ **des choses** make allowances; **prendre** ~ **à** take part in; (*joie, douleur*) share; **pour ma** ~ as for me.

partage /paʀtaʒ/ *nm* (division) dividing; (répartition) sharing out; **recevoir qch en** ~ be left sth in a will.

partager /paʀtaʒe/ [40] *vt* divide; (distribuer) share out; (avoir en commun) share. □ **se** ~ **qch** *vpr* share sth.

partenaire /paʀtənɛʀ/ *nmf* partner.

parterre /paʀtɛʀ/ *nm* flower-bed; (Théât) stalls.

parti /paʀti/ *nm* (Pol) party; (décision) decision; (en mariage) match; ~ **pris** bias; **prendre** ~ get involved; **prendre** ~ **pour qn** side with sb; **j'en ai pris mon** ~ I've come to terms with that.

partial, ~**e** (*mpl* **-iaux**) /paʀsjal, -jo/ *adj* biased.

participe /paʀtisip/ *nm* (Gram) participle.

participant, ~**e** /paʀtisipɑ̃, -t/ *nm,f* participant (**à** in).

participation /paʀtisipasjɔ̃/ *nf* participation; (financière) contribution; (d'un artiste) appearance.

participer /paʀtisipe/ [1] *vi* ~ **à** take part in, participate in; (*profits, frais*) share.

particule /paʀtikyl/ *nf* particle.

particulier, **-ière** /paʀtikylje, -jɛʀ/ *adj* (spécifique) particular; (bizarre) unusual; (privé) private; **rien de** ~ nothing special. ● *nm* private individual; **en** ~ in particular, particularly. **particulièrement** *adv* particularly.

partie /paʀti/ *nf* part; (cartes, Sport) game; (Jur) party; **une** ~ **de pêche** a fishing trip; **en** ~ partly, in part; **en grande** ~ largely; **faire** ~ **de** be part of; (adhérer à) be a member of; **faire** ~ **intégrante de** be an integral part of.

partiel, ~**le** /paʀsjɛl/ *adj* partial. ● *nm* (Univ) exam based on a module.

partir /paʀtiʀ/ [46] *vi* (*aux être*) go; (quitter un lieu) leave, go; (*tache*) come out; (*bouton*) come off; (*coup de feu*) go off; (commencer) start; ~ **pour le Brésil** leave for Brazil; ~ **du principe que** work on the assumption that; **à** ~ **de** from; **à** ~ **de maintenant** from now on.

partisan, ~**e** /paʀtizɑ̃, -an/ *nm,f* supporter. ● *nm* (Mil) partisan; **être** ~ **de** be in favour of.

partition /paʀtisjɔ̃/ *nf* (Mus) score.

partout /paʀtu/ *adv* everywhere; ~ **où** wherever.

paru /paʀy/ ⇒**PARAÎTRE** [18].

parure /paʀyʀ/ *nf* finery; (bijoux) set of jewels; (de draps) set.

parution /paʀysjɔ̃/ *nf* publication.

parvenir /paʀvəniʀ/ [58] *vi* (*aux être*) ~ **à** reach; ~ **à faire** manage to do; **faire** ~ send.

parvenu, ~**e** /paʀvəny/ *nm,f* upstart.

....

pas¹ /pɑ/

> Pour les expressions comme **pas encore**, **pas mal**, etc. ⇒**encore**, **mal**, etc.

● *adverbe*

····▸ not; **ne** ~ not; **je ne sais** ~ I don't know; **je ne pense** ~ I don't think so; **il a aimé, moi** ~ he liked it, I didn't; ~ **cher/poli** cheap/impolite.

····▶ ~ **du tout** not at all; ~ **de chance!** tough luck!

····▶ **on a bien ri,** ~ **vrai?** 🔲 we had a good laugh, didn't we?

> ❗ In spoken colloquial French **ne… pas** is often shortened to **pas**. You will often hear **j'ai pas compris** instead of **je n'ai pas compris** (*I didn't understand*). Note that this would not be correct in written French.

pas² /pɑ/ *nm* step; (bruit) footstep; (trace) footprint; (vitesse) pace; **à deux** ~ **(de)** a step away (from); **marcher au** ~ march; **rouler au** ~ move very slowly; **à** ~ **de loup** stealthily; **faire les cent** ~ walk up and down; **faire le premier** ~ make the first move; ~ **de porte** doorstep; ~ **de vis** (Tech) thread.

passage /pɑsaʒ/ *nm* (traversée) crossing; (visite) visit; (chemin) way, passage; (d'une œuvre) passage; **de** ~ (*voyageur*) visiting; (*amant*) casual; **la tempête a tout emporté sur son** ~ the storm swept everything away; ~ **clouté** pedestrian crossing; ~ **interdit** (panneau) no thoroughfare; ~ **à niveau** level crossing; ~ **souterrain** subway.

passager, -ère /pɑsaʒe, -ɛʀ/ *adj* temporary. ● *nm,f* passenger; ~ **clandestin** stowaway.

passant, ~**e** /pɑsɑ̃, -t/ *adj* (*rue*) busy. ● *nm,f* passer-by. ● *nm* (anneau) loop.

passe /pɑs/ *nf* pass; **bonne/mauvaise** ~ good/bad patch; **en** ~ **de** on the road to.

passé, ~**e** /pɑse/ *adj* (révolu) past; (dernier) last; (fané) faded; ~ **de mode** out of fashion. ● *nm* past. ● *prép* after.

passe-partout /pɑspaʀtu/ *nm inv* master-key. ● *a inv* for all occasions.

passeport /pɑspɔʀ/ *nm* passport.

passer /pɑse/ [1] *vi* (aux être ou avoir) go past, pass; (aller) go; (venir) come; (temps, douleur) pass; (film) be on; (couleur) fade; **laisser** ~ let through; (occasion) miss; ~ **devant** (à pied) walk past; (en voiture) drive past;

~ **par** go through; **où est-il passé?** where did he get to?; ~ **outre** take no notice; **passons!** let's forget about it!; **passons aux choses sérieuses** let's turn to serious matters; ~ **dans la classe supérieure** go up a year; ~ **pour un idiot** look a fool. ● *vt* (*aux avoir*) (franchir) pass, cross; (donner) pass, hand; (temps) spend; (enfiler) slip on; (*vidéo, disque*) put on; (*examen*) take, sit; (*commande*) place; (faire) ~ **le temps** while away the time; ~ **l'aspirateur** hoover; ~ **un coup de fil à qn** give sb a ring; **je vous passe Mme X** (par le standard) I'll put you through to Mrs X; (en donnant l'appareil) I'll pass you over to Mrs X; ~ **qch en fraude** smuggle sth. ▢ **se** ~ *vpr* happen, take place; (s'écouler) go by; **se** ~ **de** go *ou* do without.

passerelle /pɑsʀɛl/ *nf* footbridge; (de navire) gangway; (d'avion) (passenger) footbridge; (Internet) gateway.

passe-temps /pɑstɑ̃/ *nm inv* pastime.

passif, -ive /pasif, -v/ *adj* passive. ● *nm* (Comm) liabilities.

passion /pɑsjɔ̃/ *nf* passion. **passionnant,** ~**e** *adj* fascinating.

passionné, ~**e** /pɑsjɔne/ *adj* passionate; **être** ~ **de** have a passion for.

passionner /pɑsjɔne/ [1] *vt* fascinate. ▢ **se** ~ **pour** *vpr* have a passion for.

passoire /pɑswaʀ/ *nf* (à thé) strainer; (à légumes) colander.

pastèque /pastɛk/ *nf* watermelon.

pasteur /pastœʀ/ *nm* (Relig) minister.

pastille /pastij/ *nf* (médicament) pastille, lozenge.

patate /patat/ *nf* 🔲 spud; ~ **(douce)** sweet potato.

patauger /patoʒe/ [40] *vi* splash about.

pâte /pɑt/ *nf* paste; (à gâteau) dough; (à tarte) pastry; (à frire) batter; ~**s (alimentaires)** pasta (+ *sg*); ~ **à modeler** Plasticine®; ~ **d'amandes** marzipan.

pâté /pɑte/ *nm* (Culin) pâté; (d'encre) blot; (de sable) sandpie; ~ **en croûte**

p

≈ pie; ~ **de maisons** block (of houses).

pâtée /pɑte/ *nf* feed, mash.

patente /patɑ̃t/ *nf* trade licence.

paternel, ~le /patɛʀnɛl/ *adj* paternal. **paternité** *nf* paternity.

pathétique /patetik/ *adj* moving.

patience /pasjɑ̃s/ *nf* patience. **patient, ~e** *a* & *nm,f* patient. **patienter** [1] *vi* wait.

patin /patɛ̃/ *nm* skate; ~ **à roulettes** roller-skate.

patinage /patinaʒ/ *nm* skating. **patiner** [1] *vi* skate; (*roue*) spin. **patinoire** *nf* ice rink.

pâtisserie /pɑtisʀi/ *nf* cake shop; (*gâteau*) pastry; (*secteur*) cake making. **pâtissier, -ière** *nm,f* confectioner, pastry-cook.

patrie /patʀi/ *nf* homeland.

patrimoine /patʀimwan/ *nm* heritage.

patriote /patʀijɔt/ *adj* patriotic. ● *nmf* patriot.

patron, ~ne /patʀɔ̃, -ɔn/ *nm,f* employer, boss; (*propriétaire*) owner, boss; (*saint*) patron saint. ● *nm* (couture) pattern. **patronal, ~e** (*mpl* -aux) *adj* employers'. **patronat** *nm* employers (+ *pl*).

patrouille /patʀuj/ *nf* patrol.

patte /pat/ *nf* leg; (*pied*) foot; (*de chat*) paw; ~s (*favoris*) sideburns; **marcher à quatre ~s** walk on all fours; (*bébé*) crawl; ~s **de derrière** hind legs.

paume /pom/ *nf* (*de main*) palm.

paumé, ~e /pome/ *nm,f* 🔢 misfit.

paupière /popjɛʀ/ *nf* eyelid.

pause /poz/ *nf* pause; (*halte*) break.

pauvre /povʀ/ *adj* poor. ● *nmf* poor man, poor woman. **pauvreté** *nf* poverty.

pavé /pave/ *nm* cobblestone.

pavillon /pavijɔ̃/ *nm* (*maison*) house; (*drapeau*) flag.

payant, ~e /pɛjɑ̃, -t/ *adj* (*hôte*) paying; **c'est ~** you have to pay to get in.

payer /peje/ [31] *vt/i* pay; (*service, travail*) pay for; ~ **qch à qn** buy sb sth; **faire ~ qn** charge sb; **il me le paiera!** he'll pay for this. ☐ **se ~** *vpr*

se ~ qch buy oneself sth; **se ~ la tête de** make fun of.

pays /pei/ *nm* country; (*région*) region; **du ~** local.

paysage /peizaʒ/ *nm* landscape.

paysan, ~ne /peizɑ̃, -an/ *nm,f* farmer, country person; (*péj*) peasant. ● *adj* (*agricole*) farming; (*rural*) country.

Pays-Bas /peibɑ/ *nmpl* **les ~** the Netherlands.

PCV *abrév m* (**paiement contre vérification**) **téléphoner en ~** reverse the charges.

PDG *abrév m* (**président-directeur général**) chairman and managing director.

péage /peaʒ/ *nm* toll; (*lieu*) tollgate.

peau (*pl* ~**x**) /po/ *nf* skin; (*cuir*) hide; ~ **de chamois** shammy (leather); ~ **de mouton** sheepskin; **être bien/mal dans sa ~** be/not be at ease with oneself.

pêche /pɛʃ/ *nf* (*fruit*) peach; (*activité*) fishing; (*poissons*) catch; ~ **à la ligne** angling.

péché /peʃe/ *nm* sin.

pêcher /peʃe/ *vt* (*poisson*) catch; (*dénicher* 🔢) dig up. ● *vi* fish. **pêcheur** *nm* fisherman; (*à la ligne*) angler.

pécuniaire /pekynjɛʀ/ *adj* financial.

pédagogie /pedagɔʒi/ *nf* education.

pédale /pedal/ *nf* pedal.

pédalo® /pedalo/ *nm* pedal boat.

pédant, ~e /pedɑ̃, -t/ *adj* pedantic.

pédestre /pedɛstʀ/ *adj* **faire de la randonnée ~** go walking *ou* hiking.

pédiatre /pedjatʀ/ *nmf* paediatrician.

pédicure /pedikyʀ/ *nmf* chiropodist.

peigne /pɛɲ/ *nm* comb.

peigner /peɲe/ [1] *vt* comb; (*personne*) comb the hair of. ☐ **se ~** *vpr* comb one's hair.

peignoir /pɛɲwaʀ/ *nm* dressing-gown.

peindre /pɛ̃dʀ/ [22] *vt* paint.

peine /pɛn/ *nf* sadness, sorrow; (*effort, difficulté*) trouble; (*Jur*) sentence; **avoir de la ~** feel sad; **faire de la ~ à**

hurt; **ce n'est pas la ~ de sonner** you don't need to ring the bell; **j'ai de la ~ à le croire** I find it hard to believe; **se donner** ou **prendre la ~ de faire** go to the trouble of doing; **~ de mort** death penalty. ● adv **à ~** hardly.

peiner /pene/ [1] vi struggle. ● vt sadden.

peintre /pɛ̃tʀ/ nm painter; **~ en bâtiment** house painter.

peinture /pɛ̃tyʀ/ nf painting; (matière) paint; **~ à l'huile** oil painting.

péjoratif, -ive /peʒɔʀatif, -v/ adj pejorative.

pelage /pəlaʒ/ nm coat, fur.

pêle-mêle /pɛlmɛl/ adv in a jumble.

peler /pəle/ [6] vt/i peel.

pèlerinage /pɛlʀinaʒ/ nm pilgrimage.

pelle /pɛl/ nf shovel; (d'enfant) spade.

pellicule /pelikyl/ nf film; **~s** (cheveux) dandruff.

pelote /pələt/ nf (of wool) ball.

peloton /p(ə)lətɔ̃/ nm platoon; (Sport) pack; **~ d'exécution** firing squad.

pelotonner (se) /(sə)plətɔne/ [1] vpr curl up.

pelouse /p(ə)luz/ nf lawn.

peluche /p(ə)lyʃ/ nf (matière) plush; (jouet) cuddly toy; **en ~** (lapin, chien) fluffy.

pénal, ~e (mpl **-aux**) /penal, -o/ adj penal. **pénaliser** [1] vt penalize. **pénalité** nf penalty.

penchant /pɑ̃ʃɑ̃/ nm inclination; (goût) liking (**pour** for).

pencher /pɑ̃ʃe/ [1] vt tilt; **~ pour** favour. ● vi lean (over), tilt. □ **se ~** vpr lean (forward); **se ~ sur** (problème) examine.

pendaison /pɑ̃dɛzɔ̃/ nf hanging.

pendant¹ /pɑ̃dɑ̃/ prép (au cours de) during; (durée) for; **~ que** while.

pendant², ~e /pɑ̃dɑ̃, -t/ adj hanging; **jambes ~es** with one's legs dangling. ● nm (contrepartie) matching piece (**de** to); **~ d'oreille** drop ear-ring.

pendentif /pɑ̃dɑ̃tif/ nm pendant.

penderie /pɑ̃dʀi/ nf wardrobe.

pendre /pɑ̃dʀ/ [3] vt/i hang. □ **se ~** vpr hang (**à** from); (se tuer) hang oneself.

pendule /pɑ̃dyl/ nf clock. ● nm pendulum.

pénétrer /penetʀe/ [14] vi **~ (dans)** enter; **faire ~ une crème** rub a cream in. ● vt penetrate.

pénible /penibl/ adj (travail) hard; (nouvelle) painful; (enfant) tiresome.

péniche /peniʃ/ nf barge.

pénitence /penitɑ̃s/ nf (Relig) penance; (punition) punishment; **faire ~** repent.

pénitentiaire /penitɑ̃sjɛʀ/ adj (établissement) penal.

pénombre /penɔ̃bʀ/ nf half-light.

pensée /pɑ̃se/ nf (idée) thought; (fleur) pansy.

penser /pɑ̃se/ [1] vt/i think; **~ à** (réfléchir à) think about; (se souvenir de, prévoir) think of; **~ faire** think of doing; **faire ~ à** remind one of.

pensif, -ive /pɑ̃sif, -v/ adj pensive.

pension /pɑ̃sjɔ̃/ nf (Scol) boarding school; (repas, somme) board; (allocation) pension; **~ (de famille)** guest house; **~ alimentaire** (Jur) alimony. **pensionnaire** nmf (Scol) boarder; (d'hôtel) guest. **pensionnat** nm boarding school.

pente /pɑ̃t/ nf slope; **en ~** sloping.

Pentecôte /pɑ̃tkot/ nf **la ~** Whitsun.

pénurie /penyʀi/ nf shortage.

pépin /pepɛ̃/ nm (graine) pip; (ennui 🔢) hitch.

pépinière /pepinjɛʀ/ nf (tree) nursery.

perçant, ~e /pɛʀsɑ̃, -t/ adj (cri) shrill; (regard) piercing.

perce-neige /pɛʀsənɛʒ/ nm or f inv snowdrop.

percepteur /pɛʀsɛptœʀ/ nm tax inspector.

percer /pɛʀse/ [10] vt pierce; (avec perceuse) drill; (mystère) penetrate. ● vi break through; (dent) come through. **perceuse** nf drill.

percevoir /pɛʀsəvwaʀ/ [52] vt perceive; (impôt) collect.

perche /pɛʀʃ/ nf (bâton) pole.

p

percher (se) /(sə)pɛRʃe/ [1] *vpr* perch.

percolateur /pɛRkɔlatœR/ *nm* coffee machine.

percuter /pɛRkyte/ [1] *vt* (*véhicule*) crash into.

perdant, **~e** /pɛRdɑ̃, -t/ *adj* losing. ● *nm, f* loser.

perdre /pɛRdR/ [3] *vt/i* lose; (*gaspiller*) waste; **~ ses poils** (*chat*) moult. □ **se ~** *vpr* get lost; (*rester inutilisé*) go to waste.

perdrix /pɛRdRi/ *nf* partridge.

perdu, **~e** /pɛRdy/ *adj* lost; (*endroit*) isolated; (*balle*) stray; **c'est du temps ~** it's a waste of time.

père /pɛR/ *nm* father; **~ de famille** father, family man; **~ spirituel** father figure; **le ~ Noël** Santa Claus.

perfection /pɛRfɛksjɔ̃/ *nf* perfection.

perfectionner /pɛRfɛksjɔne/ [1] *vt* (*technique*) perfect; (*art*) refine. □ **se ~** *vpr* improve; **se ~ en anglais** improve one's English.

perforer /pɛRfɔRe/ [1] *vt* perforate; (*billet, bande*) punch.

performance /pɛRfɔRmɑ̃s/ *nf* performance.

perfusion /pɛRfyzjɔ̃/ *nf* drip; **sous ~** on a drip.

péridurale /peRidyRal/ *nf* epidural.

péril /peRil/ *nm* peril; **à tes risques et ~s** at your own risk.

périlleux, **-euse** /peRijø, -z/ *adj* perilous.

périmé, **~e** /peRime/ *adj* (*produit*) past its use-by date; (*désuet*) outdated.

période /peRjɔd/ *nf* period.

périodique /peRjɔdik/ *adj* period-ic(al). ● *nm* (*journal*) periodical.

péripétie /peRipesi/ *nf* (unexpected) event, adventure.

périphérique /peRifeRik/ *adj* peripheral. ● *nm* (**boulevard**) **~** ring road.

périple /peRipl/ *nm* journey.

périr /peRiR/ [2] *vi* perish, die.

perle /pɛRl/ *nf* (d'huître) pearl; (de verre) bead.

permanence /pɛRmanɑ̃s/ *nf* permanence; (Scol) study room; **de ~**

on duty; **en ~** permanently; **assurer une ~** keep the office open.

permanent, **~e** /pɛRmanɑ̃, -t/ *adj* permanent; (*constant*) constant; **formation ~e** continuous education. **permanente** *nf* (coiffure) perm.

permettre /pɛRmɛtR/ [42] *vt* allow; **~ à qn de** allow sb to. □ **se ~** *vpr* (*achat*) afford; **se ~ de faire** take the liberty of doing.

permis, **~e** /pɛRmi, -z/ *adj* allowed. ● *nm* licence, permit; **~ (de conduire)** driving licence.

permission /pɛRmisjɔ̃/ *nf* permission; **en ~** (Mil) on leave.

Pérou /peRu/ *nm* Peru.

perpendiculaire /pɛRpɑ̃dikylɛR/ *a* & *nf* perpendicular.

perpétuité /pɛRpetɥite/ *nf* **à ~** for life.

perplexe /pɛRplɛks/ *adj* perplexed.

perquisition /pɛRkizisjɔ̃/ *nf* (police) search.

perron /pɛRɔ̃/ *nm* (front) steps.

perroquet /pɛRɔkɛ/ *nm* parrot.

perruche /peRyʃ/ *nf* budgerigar.

perruque /peRyk/ *nf* wig.

persécuter /pɛRsekyte/ [1] *vt* persecute.

persévérance /pɛRseveRɑ̃s/ *nf* perseverance. **persévérer** [14] *vi* persevere.

persienne /pɛRsjɛn/ *nf* (outside) shutter.

persil /pɛRsi/ *nm* parsley.

persistance /pɛRsistɑ̃s/ *nf* persistence. **persistant**, **~e** *adj* persistent; (*feuillage*) evergreen.

persister /pɛRsiste/ [1] *vi* persist (**à faire** in doing).

personnage /pɛRsɔnaʒ/ *nm* character; (personne célèbre) personality.

personnalité /pɛRsɔnalite/ *nf* personality.

personne /pɛRsɔn/ *nf* person; **~s** people. ● *pron* nobody, no-one; **je n'ai vu ~** I didn't see anybody.

personnel, **~le** /pɛRsɔnɛl/ *adj* personal; (*égoïste*) selfish. ● *nm* staff.

perspective /pɛRspɛktiv/ *nf* (art, point de vue) perspective; (vue) view; (éventualité) prospect.

perspicace /pɛʀspikas/ adj
shrewd. **perspicacité** nf
shrewdness.

persuader /pɛʀsɥade/ [1] vt
persuade (**de faire** to do).

persuasif, -ive /pɛʀsɥazif, -v/ adj
persuasive.

perte /pɛʀt/ nf loss; (ruine) ruin; **à ~
de vue** as far as the eye can see; **~
de** (temps, argent) waste of; **~ sèche**
total loss; **~s** (Méd) discharge.

pertinent, ~e /pɛʀtinɑ̃, -t/ adj
pertinent.

perturbateur, -trice /pɛʀtyʀ-
batœʀ, -tʀis/ nm,f disruptive
element. **perturbation** nf
disruption. **perturber** [1] vt disrupt;
(personne) perturb.

pervers, ~e /pɛʀvɛʀ, -s/ adj
(dépravé) perverted; (méchant) wicked.

pervertir /pɛʀvɛʀtiʀ/ [2] vt pervert.

pesant, ~e /pəzɑ̃, -t/ adj heavy.

pesanteur /pəzɑ̃tœʀ/ nf heaviness;
la ~ (force) gravity.

pesée /pəze/ nf weighing; (effort)
pressure.

pèse-personne (pl **~s**) /pɛzpɛʀ-
sɔn/ nm (bathroom) scales.

peser /pəze/ [6] vt/i weigh; **~ sur**
bear upon.

pessimiste /pesimist/ adj
pessimistic. ● nmf pessimist.

peste /pɛst/ nf plague; (personne 🔲)
pest.

pet /pɛ/ nm 🔲 fart 🔲.

pétale /petal/ nm petal.

pétard /petaʀ/ nm banger.

péter /pete/ [14] vi 🔲 fart 🔲, go
bang; (casser) snap.

pétillant, ~e /petijɑ̃, -t/ adj
(boisson) sparkling; (personne)
bubbly.

pétiller /petije/ [1] vi (feu) crackle;
(champagne, yeux) sparkle; **~
d'intelligence** sparkle with
intelligence.

petit, ~e /p(ə)ti, -t/ adj small; (avec
nuance affective) little; (jeune) young,
small; (défaut) minor; (mesquin) petty;
en ~ in miniature; **~ à ~** little by
little; **un ~ peu** a little bit; **~ ami**
boyfriend; **~e amie** girlfriend; **~es
annonces** small ads; **~e cuillère**

teaspoon; **~ déjeuner** breakfast; **~
pois** garden pea. ● nm,f little child;
(Scol) junior; **~s** (de chat) kittens; (de
chien) pups. **petite-fille** (pl
petites-filles) nf granddaughter.
petit-fils (pl **petits-fils**) nm
grandson.

pétition /petisjɔ̃/ nf petition.

petits-enfants /pətizɑ̃fɑ̃/ nmpl
grandchildren.

pétrin /petʀɛ̃/ nm **dans le ~** 🔲 in a
fix 🔲.

pétrir /petʀiʀ/ [2] vt knead.

pétrole /petʀɔl/ nm oil; **~ brut**
crude oil.

pétrolier, -ière /petʀɔlje, -jɛʀ/ adj
oil. ● nm (navire) oil-tanker.

peu /pø/ adv **~ (de)** (quantité) little,
not much; (nombre) few, not many; **~
intéressant** not very interesting; **il
mange ~** he doesn't eat very much.
● pron few. ● nm little; **un ~ (de)** a
little; **à ~ près** more or less; **~**
only just; **~ à ~** gradually; **~ après/
avant** shortly after/before; **~ de
chose** not much; **~ nombreux** few;
~ souvent seldom; **pour ~ que** if.

peuple /pœpl/ nm people. **peupler**
[1] vt populate.

peuplier /pøplije/ nm poplar.

peur /pœʀ/ nf fear; **avoir ~** be afraid
(**de** of); **de ~ de** for fear of; **faire ~ à**
frighten. **peureux, -euse** adj
fearful.

peut /pø/ ⇒POUVOIR [49].

peut-être /pøtɛtʀ/ adv perhaps,
maybe; **~ qu'il viendra** he might
come.

peux /pø/ ⇒POUVOIR [49].

phare /faʀ/ nm (tour) lighthouse; (de
véhicule) headlight; **~ antibrouillard**
fog lamp.

pharmacie /faʀmasi/ nf (magasin)
chemist's (shop), pharmacy; (science)
pharmacy; (armoire) medicine cabinet.
pharmacien, ~ne nm,f chemist,
pharmacist.

phénomène /fenɔmɛn/ nm
phenomenon; (personne 🔲) eccentric.

philosophe /filɔzɔf/ nmf
philosopher. ● adj philosophical.
philosophie nf philosophy.
philosophique adj philosophical.

phobie /fɔbi/ nf phobia.

p

phonétique /fɔnetik/ *adj* phonetic.
● *nf* phonetics.

phoque /fɔk/ *nm* (animal) seal.

photo /foto/ *nf* photo; (art)
photography; **prendre en** ~ take a
photo of; ~ **d'identité** passport
photograph.

photocopie /fɔtɔkɔpi/ *nf*
photocopy. **photocopier** [45] *vt*
photocopy.

photographe /fɔtɔgraf/ *nmf*
photographer. **photographie** *nf*
photograph; (art) photography.
photographier [45] *vt* take a photo
of.

phrase /fraz/ *nf* sentence.

physicien, ~**ne** /fizisjɛ̃, -ɛn/ *nm, f*
physicist.

physique /fizik/ *adj* physical. ● *nm*
physique; **au** ~ physically. ● *nf*
physics (+ *sg*).

piano /pjano/ *nm* piano.

pianoter /pjanɔte/ [1] *vi* tinkle; ~
sur (*ordinateur*) tap at.

PIB *abrév m* (**produit intérieur
brut**) GDP.

pic /pik/ *nm* (outil) pickaxe; (sommet)
peak; (oiseau) woodpecker; **à** ~
(*falaise*) sheer; (*couler*) straight to
the bottom; **tomber à** ~ 🆃 come just
at the right time.

pichet /piʃɛ/ *nm* jug.

picorer /pikɔre/ [1] *vt/i* peck.

picotement /pikɔtmɑ̃/ *nm*
tingling. **picoter** [1] *vt* sting; (*yeux*)
sting.

pie /pi/ *nf* magpie.

pièce /pjɛs/ *nf* (d'habitation) room; (de
monnaie) coin; (Théât) play; (pour
raccommoder) patch; (écrit) document;
(morceau) piece; ~ (**de théâtre**) play;
dix francs (**la**) ~ ten francs each; ~
détachée part; ~ **d'identité** identity
paper; ~**s jointes** enclosures; (courrier
électronique) attachments; ~**s
justificatives** written proof; ~
montée tiered cake; ~ **de rechange**
spare part; **un deux-**~**s** a two-room
flat.

pied /pje/ *nm* foot; (de meuble) leg; (de
lampe) base; (de verre) stem; (d'appareil
photo) stand; **être** ~**s nus** be bare-
foot; **à** ~ on foot; **au** ~ **de la lettre**
literally; **avoir** ~ be able to touch the
bottom; **jouer au tennis comme un** ~
🆃 be hopeless at tennis; **mettre sur**
~ set up; **sur un** ~ **d'égalité** on an
equal footing; **mettre les** ~**s dans le
plat** 🆃 put one's foot in it; **c'est le** ~
🆃 it's great. **pied-bot** (*pl* **pieds-
bots**) *nm* club-foot.

piédestal /pjedɛstal/ *nm* pedestal.

piège /pjɛʒ/ *nm* trap.

piéger /pjeʒe/ [14] [40] *vt* trap; **lettre/
voiture piégée** letter/car bomb.

pierre /pjɛʀ/ *nf* stone; ~ **précieuse**
precious stone; ~ **tombale**
tombstone.

piétiner /pjetine/ [1] *vi* (avancer
lentement) shuffle along; (fig) make no
headway; ~ **d'impatience** hop up and
down with impatience. ● *vt* trample
(on).

piéton /pjetɔ̃/ *nm* pedestrian.

pieu (*pl* ~**x**) /pjø/ *nm* post, stake.

pieuvre /pjœvʀ/ *nf* octopus.

pieux, -ieuse /pjø, -z/ *adj* pious.

pigeon /piʒɔ̃/ *nm* pigeon.

piger /piʒe/ [40] *vt/i* 🆃 understand,
get (it).

pile /pil/ *nf* (tas) pile; (Électr) battery;
~ **ou face?** heads or tails? ● *adv*
(*s'arrêter* 🆃) dead; **à dix heures** ~ 🆃
at ten on the dot.

pilier /pilje/ *nm* pillar.

pillage /pijaʒ/ *nm* looting. **pillard,
~e** *nm, f* looter. **piller** [1] *vt* loot.

pilote /pilɔt/ *nm* (Aviat, Naut) pilot;
(Auto) driver. ● *adj* pilot. **piloter** [1]
vt (Aviat, Naut) pilot; (Auto) drive; (fig)
guide.

pilule /pilyl/ *nf* pill; **la** ~ the pill.

piment /pimɑ̃/ *nm* hot pepper; (fig)
spice. **pimenté, ~e** *adj* spicy.

pin /pɛ̃/ *nm* pine.

pinard /pinaʀ/ *nm* 🆃 plonk 🆃,
cheap wine.

pince /pɛ̃s/ *nf* (outil) pliers (+ *pl*);
(levier) crowbar; (de crabe) pincer; (à
sucre) tongs (+ *pl*); ~ **à épiler**
tweezers (+ *pl*); ~ **à linge** clothes
peg.

pinceau (*pl* ~**x**) /pɛ̃so/ *nm*
paintbrush.

pincée /pɛ̃se/ *nf* pinch (**de** of).

pincer /pɛ̃se/ [10] *vt* pinch; (attraper 🔲) catch. □ **se ~** *vpr* catch oneself; **se ~ le doigt** catch one's finger.

pince-sans-rire /pɛ̃ssɑ̃ʀiʀ/ *nmf inv* **c'est un ~** he has a deadpan sense of humour.

pingouin /pɛ̃gwɛ̃/ *nm* penguin.

pingre /pɛ̃gʀ/ *adj* stingy.

pintade /pɛ̃tad/ *nf* guinea fowl.

piocher /pjɔʃe/ [1] *vt/i* dig; (étudier 🔲) study hard, slog away (at).

pion /pjɔ̃/ *nm* (de jeu) counter; (aux échecs) pawn; (Scol 🔲) supervisor.

pipe /pip/ *nf* pipe; **fumer la ~** smoke a pipe.

piquant, ~e /pikɑ̃, -t/ *adj* (*barbe*) prickly; (*goût*) pungent; (*remarque*) cutting. ● *nm* prickle.

pique /pik/ *nm* (aux cartes) spades.

pique-nique (*pl* ~**s**) /piknik/ *nm* picnic.

piquer /pike/ [1] *vt* (*épine*) prick; (*épice*) burn, sting; (*abeille, ortie*) sting; (*serpent, moustique*) bite; (enfoncer) stick; (coudre) (machine-) stitch; (*curiosité*) excite; (voler 🔲) pinch. ● *vi* (*avion*) dive; (*goût*) be hot. □ **se ~** *vpr* prick oneself.

piquet /pikɛ/ *nm* stake; (de tente) peg; (de parasol) pole; ~ **de grève** (strike) picket.

piqûre /pikyʀ/ *nf* prick; (d'abeille) sting; (de serpent) bite; (point) stitch; (Méd) injection, jab; **faire une ~ à qn** give sb an injection.

pirate /piʀat/ *nm* pirate; ~ **informatique** computer hacker; ~ **de l'air** hijacker.

pire /piʀ/ *adj* worse (**que** than); **les ~s mensonges** the most wicked lies. ● *nm* **le ~** the worst; **au ~** at worst.

pis /pi/ *nm* (de vache) udder. ● *a inv & adv* worse; **aller de mal en ~** go from bad to worse.

piscine /pisin/ *nf* swimming-pool; ~ **couverte** indoor swimming-pool.

pissenlit /pisɑ̃li/ *nm* dandelion.

pistache /pistaʃ/ *nf* pistachio.

piste /pist/ *nf* track; (de personne, d'animal) track, trail; (Aviat) runway; (de cirque) ring; (de ski) slope; (de danse) floor; (Sport) racetrack; ~ **cyclable** cycle lane.

pistolet /pistɔlɛ/ *nm* gun, pistol; (de peintre) spray-gun.

piteux, -euse /pitø, -z/ *adj* pitiful.

pitié /pitje/ *nf* pity; **il me fait ~** I feel sorry for him.

piton /pitɔ̃/ *nm* (à crochet) hook; (sommet pointu) peak.

pitoyable /pitwajabl/ *adj* pitiful.

pitre /pitʀ/ *nm* clown; **faire le ~** clown around.

pittoresque /pitɔʀɛsk/ *adj* picturesque.

pivot /pivo/ *nm* pivot. **pivoter** [1] *vi* revolve; (*personne*) swing round.

placard /plakaʀ/ *nm* cupboard; (affiche) poster. **placarder** [1] *vt* (*affiche*) post up; (*mur*) cover with posters.

place /plas/ *nf* place; (espace libre) room, space; (siège) seat, place; (prix d'un trajet) fare; (esplanade) square; (emploi) position; (de parking) space; **à la ~ de** instead of; **en ~, à sa ~** in its place; **faire ~ à** give way to; **sur ~** on the spot; **remettre qn à sa ~** put sb in his place; **ça prend de la ~** it takes up a lot of room; **se mettre à la ~ de qn** put oneself in sb's shoes *ou* place.

placement /plasmɑ̃/ *nm* (d'argent) investment.

placer /plase/ [10] *vt* place; (*invité, spectateur*) seat; (*argent*) invest. □ **se ~** *vpr* (*personne*) take up a position.

plafond /plafɔ̃/ *nm* ceiling.

plage /plaʒ/ *nf* beach; ~ **horaire** time slot.

plagiat /plaʒja/ *nm* plagiarism.

plaider /plede/ [1] *vt/i* plead. **plaidoirie** *nf* (defence) speech. **plaidoyer** *nm* plea.

plaie /plɛ/ *nf* wound; (personne 🔲) nuisance.

plaignant, ~e /plɛɲɑ̃, -t/ *nm,f* plaintiff.

plaindre /plɛ̃dʀ/ [22] *vt* pity. □ **se ~** *vpr* complain (**de** about); **se ~ de** (souffrir de) complain of.

plaine /plɛn/ *nf* plain.

plainte /plɛ̃t/ *nf* complaint; (gémissement) groan. **plaintif, -ive** *adj* plaintive.

p

plaire /plɛʀ/ [47] vi ~ à please; ça lui plaît he likes it; elle lui plaît he likes her; ça me plaît de faire I like ou enjoy doing; s'il vous plaît please. □ se ~ vpr il se plaît ici he likes it here.

plaisance /plɛzɑ̃s/ nf la (navigation de) ~ boating.

plaisant, ~e /plɛzɑ̃, -t/ adj pleasant; (drôle) amusing.

plaisanter /plɛzɑ̃te/ [1] vi joke. **plaisanterie** nf joke. **plaisantin** nm joker.

plaisir /plɛziʀ/ nm pleasure; faire ~ à please; pour le ~ for fun ou pleasure.

plan /plɑ̃/ nm plan; (de ville) map; (de livre) outline; ~ d'eau artificial lake; premier ~ foreground.

planche /plɑ̃ʃ/ nf board, plank; (gravure) plate; ~ à repasser ironing-board; ~ à voile windsurfing board; (Sport) windsurfing.

plancher /plɑ̃ʃe/ nm floor.

planer /plane/ [1] vi glide; ~ sur (mystère, danger) hang over.

planète /planɛt/ nf planet.

planeur /planœʀ/ nm (avion) glider.

planifier /planifje/ [45] vt plan.

plant /plɑ̃/ nm seedling; (de légumes) patch.

plante /plɑ̃t/ nf plant; ~ d'appartement houseplant; ~ des pieds sole (of the foot).

planter /plɑ̃te/ [1] vt (plante) plant; (enfoncer) drive in; (tente) put up; rester planté Ⓣ stand still, remain standing.

plaque /plak/ nf plate; (de marbre) slab; (insigne) badge; ~ chauffante hotplate; ~ commémorative plaque; ~ minéralogique numberplate; ~ de verglas patch of ice.

plaquer /plake/ [1] vt (bois) veneer; (aplatir) flatten; (rugby) tackle; (abandonner Ⓣ) ditch Ⓣ; tout ~ chuck it all.

plastique /plastik/ a & nm plastic; en ~ plastic.

plastiquer /plastike/ [1] vt blow up.

plat, ~e /pla, -t/ adj flat. ● nm (Culin) dish; (partie de repas) course; (de la main) flat. ● à plat adv (poser) flat;

(batterie, pneu) flat; à ~ ventre flat on one's face.

platane /platan/ nm plane tree.

plateau (pl ~x) /plato/ nm tray; (de cinéma) set; (de balance) pan; (Géog) plateau; ~ de fromages cheeseboard; ~ de fruits de mer seafood platter.

plate-bande (pl **plates-bandes**) nf flower-bed.

platine /platin/ nm platinum. ● nf (tourne-disque) turntable; ~ laser compact disc player.

plâtre /plɑtʀ/ nm plaster; (Méd) (plaster) cast.

plein, ~e /plɛ̃, -ɛn/ adj full (de of); (total) complete. ● nm faire le ~ (d'essence) fill up (the tank); à ~ fully; à ~ temps full-time; en ~ air in the open air; en ~ milieu/visage right in the middle/the face; en ~e nuit in the middle of the night. ● adv avoir des idées ~ la tête be full of ideas. **pleinement** adv fully.

pleurer /plœʀe/ [1] vi cry, weep (sur over); (yeux) water. ● vt mourn.

pleurnicher /plœʀniʃe/ [1] vi Ⓣ snivel.

pleurs /plœʀ/ nmpl tears; en ~ in tears.

pleuvoir /pløvwaʀ/ [48] vi rain; (fig) rain ou shower down; il pleut it is raining; il pleut à verse ou des cordes it is pouring.

pli /pli/ nm fold; (de jupe) pleat; (de pantalon) crease; (lettre) letter; (habitude) habit; (faux) ~ crease.

pliant, ~e /plijɑ̃, -t/ adj folding. ● nm folding stool, camp-stool.

plier /plije/ [45] vt fold; (courber) bend; (soumettre) submit (à to). ● vi bend. □ se ~ vpr fold; se ~ à submit to.

plinthe /plɛ̃t/ nf skirting-board.

plissé, ~e /plise/ adj (jupe) pleated.

plisser /plise/ [1] vt crease; (yeux) screw up.

plomb /plɔ̃/ nm lead; (fusible) fuse; ~s (de chasse) lead shot; de ou en ~ lead. **plombage** nm filling.

plomberie /plɔ̃bʀi/ nf plumbing. **plombier** nm plumber.

plongée /plɔ̃ʒe/ nf diving; en ~ (sous-marin) submerged.

plongeoir /plɔ̃ʒwaʀ/ nm diving-board.

plonger /plɔ̃ʒe/ [40] *vi* dive; (*route*) plunge. ● *vt* plunge. □ **se** ~ *vpr* plunge into; **se** ~ **dans** (fig) (*lecture*) bury oneself in. **plongeur, -euse** *nm, f* diver; (de restaurant) dishwasher.

plu /ply/ ⇒PLAIRE [47], PLEUVOIR [48].

pluie /plɥi/ *nf* rain; (averse) shower; ~ **battante/diluvienne** driving/ torrential rain.

plume /plym/ *nf* feather; (pointe) nib.

plumeau (*pl* ~**x**) /plymo/ *nm* feather duster.

plumier /plymje/ *nm* pencil box.

plupart: **la** ~ /laplypaʀ/ *loc* **la** ~ **des** (*gens, cas*) most; **la** ~ **du temps** most of the time; **pour la** ~ for the most part.

pluriel, ~**le** /plyʀjɛl/ *a & nm* plural.

----

plus /ply, plys, plyz/

●*adverbe de comparaison*

••••➤ more (que than); ~ **âgé/tard** older/later; ~ **beau** more beautiful; ~ **j'y pense…** the more I think about it…; **deux fois** ~ twice as much; **deux fois** ~ **cher** twice as expensive.

••••➤ **le** ~ the most; **le** ~ **grand** the biggest; (de deux) the bigger.

••••➤ ~ **de** (*pain*) more; (*dix jours*) more than; **il est** ~ **de 8 heures** it is after 8 o'clock.

••••➤ **de** ~ more (que than); (en outre) moreover; **les enfants de** ~ **de 10 ans** children over 10 years old; **de** ~ **en** ~ more and more.

••••➤ **en** ~ on top of that; **c'est en** ~ it's extra; **en** ~ **de** in addition to.

••••➤ ~ **ou moins** more or less.

••••➤ **au** ~ **tard** at the latest.

●*adverbe de négation*

••••➤ **ne** ~ (*temps*) no longer, not any more; **je n'y vais** ~ I don't go there any longer *ou* any more.

••••➤ **ne** ~ **de** (quantité) no more; **il n'y a** ~ **de pain** there is no more bread.

••••➤ ~ **que deux jours!** only two days left!

●*préposition & nom masculin*

••••➤ (maths) plus.

----

plusieurs /plyzjœʀ/ *a & pron* several.

plus-value (*pl* ~**s**) /plyvaly/ *nf* (bénéfice) profit.

plutôt /plyto/ *adv* rather (que than).

pluvieux, -ieuse /plyvjø, -z/ *adj* rainy.

PME *abrév f* (**petites et moyennes entreprises**) SME.

PNB *abrév m* (**produit national brut**) GNP.

pneu (*pl* ~**s**) /pnø/ *nm* tyre. **pneumatique** *adj* inflatable.

poche /pɔʃ/ *nf* pocket; (sac) bag; ~**s** (sous les yeux) bags.

pocher /pɔʃe/ [1] *vt* (œuf) poach.

pochette /pɔʃɛt/ *nf* (de documents) folder; (sac) bag, pouch; (d'allumettes) book; (de disque) sleeve; (mouchoir) pocket handkerchief.

poêle /pwal/ *nf* ~ (**à frire**) frying-pan. ● *nm* stove.

poème /pɔɛm/ *nm* poem. **poésie** *nf* poetry; (poème) poem. **poète** *nm* poet. **poétique** *adj* poetic.

poids /pwa/ *nm* weight; ~ **coq/ lourd/plume** bantam weight/ heavyweight/featherweight; ~ **lourd** (camion) lorry, juggernaut; (US) truck.

poignard /pwaɲaʀ/ *nm* dagger. **poignarder** [1] *vt* stab.

poigne /pwaɲ/ *nf* **avoir de la** ~ have a strong grip.

poignée /pwaɲe/ *nf* (de porte) handle; (quantité) handful; ~ **de main** handshake.

poignet /pwaɲɛ/ *nm* wrist; (de chemise) cuff.

poil /pwal/ *nm* hair; (pelage) fur; (de brosse) bristle; ~**s** (de tapis) pile; **à** ~ 🄸 naked; ~ **à gratter** itching powder. **poilu**, ~**e** *adj* hairy.

poinçon /pwɛ̃sɔ̃/ *nm* awl; (marque) hallmark. **poinçonner** [1] *vt* (*billet*) punch.

poing /pwɛ̃/ *nm* fist.

point /pwɛ̃/ *nm* (endroit, Sport) point; (marque visible) spot, dot; (de couture) stitch; (pour évaluer) mark; **enlever un** ~ **par faute** take a mark off for each mistake; **à** ~ (Culin) medium; (*arriver*) at the right time; **faire le** ~ take stock; **mettre au** ~ (*photo*) focus; (*technique*) develop; **mettre les**

p

choses au ~ get things clear;
**Camille n'est pas encore au ~ pour
ses examens** Camille is not ready
for her exams; **sur le ~ de** about to;
au ~ que to the extent that; **~ (final)**
full stop, period; **deux ~s** colon; **~
d'interrogation/d'exclamation**
question/exclamation mark; **~s de
suspension** suspension points; **~
virgule** semicolon; **~ culminant** peak;
~ du jour daybreak; **~ mort** (Auto)
neutral; **~ de repère** landmark; **~ de
suture** (Méd) stitch; **~ de vente** point
of sale; **~ de vue** point of view.
● *adv* (ne) ~ not.

pointe /pwɛ̃t/ *nf* point, tip; (clou)
tack; (de grille) spike; (fig) touch (**de**
of); **de ~** (*industrie*) high-tech; **en ~**
pointed; **heure de ~** peak hour; **sur
la ~ des pieds** on tiptoe.

pointer /pwɛ̃te/ [1] *vt* (cocher) tick
off; (diriger) point, aim. ● *vi* (*employé*)
(en arrivant) clock in; (en sortant) clock
out. □ **se ~** *vpr* Ⅰ turn up.

pointillé /pwɛ̃tije/ *nm* dotted line.

pointilleux, -euse /pwɛ̃tijø, -z/ *adj*
fastidious, particular.

pointu, ~e /pwɛ̃ty/ *adj* pointed;
(aiguisé) sharp.

pointure /pwɛ̃tyʀ/ *nf* size.

poire /pwaʀ/ *nf* pear.

poireau (*pl* ~**x**) /pwaʀo/ *nm* leek.

poirier /pwaʀje/ *nm* pear tree.

pois /pwa/ *nm* pea; (motif) dot; **robe à
~** polka dot dress.

poison /pwazɔ̃/ *nm* poison.

poisseux, -euse /pwasø, -z/ *adj*
sticky.

poisson /pwasɔ̃/ *nm* fish; **~ rouge**
goldfish; **~ d'avril** April fool; **les
P~s** Pisces. **poissonnerie** *nf* fish
shop. **poissonnier, -ière** *nm,f*
fishmonger.

poitrine /pwatʀin/ *nf* chest; (seins)
bosom.

poivre /pwavʀ/ *nm* pepper. **poivré,
~e** *adj* peppery. **poivrière** *nf*
pepper-pot.

poivron /pwavʀɔ̃/ *nm* sweet pepper.

polaire /pɔlɛʀ/ *adj* polar. ● *nf*
(veste) fleece.

pôle /pol/ *nm* pole.

polémique /pɔlemik/ *nf* debate.
● *adj* controversial.

poli, ~e /pɔli/ *adj* (*personne*) polite.

police /pɔlis/ *nf* (force) police (+ *pl*);
(discipline) (law and) order; (d'assurance) policy.

policier, -ière /pɔlisje, -jɛʀ/ *adj*
police; (*roman*) detective. ● *nm*
policeman.

polir /pɔliʀ/ [2] *vt* polish.

politesse /pɔlitɛs/ *nf* politeness;
(parole) polite remark.

politicien, ~ne /pɔlitisjɛ̃, -ɛn/ *nm,f*
(péj) politician.

politique /pɔlitik/ *adj* political;
homme ~ politician. ● *nf* politics;
(ligne de conduite) policy.

pollen /pɔlɛn/ *nm* pollen.

polluant, ~e /pɔlɥɑ̃, -t/ *adj*
polluting. ● *nm* pollutant.

polluer /pɔlɥe/ [1] *vt* pollute.

pollution *nf* pollution.

polo /pɔlo/ *nm* (Sport) polo; (vêtement)
polo shirt.

Pologne /pɔlɔɲ/ *nf* Poland.

polonais, ~e /pɔlɔnɛ, -z/ *adj*
Polish. ● *nm* (Ling) Polish. **P~, ~e**
nm,f Pole.

poltron, ~ne /pɔltʀɔ̃, -ɔn/ *adj*
cowardly. ● *nm,f* coward.

polygame /pɔligam/ *nmf* polyg-
amist.

polyvalent, ~e /pɔlivalɑ̃, -t/ *adj*
varied; (*personne*) versatile.

pommade /pɔmad/ *nf* ointment.

pomme /pɔm/ *nf* apple; (d'arrosoir)
rose; **~ d'Adam** Adam's apple; **~ de
pin** pine cone; **~ de terre** potato; **~s
frites** chips; (US) French fries;
tomber dans les ~s Ⅰ pass out.

pommette /pɔmɛt/ *nf* cheekbone.

pommier /pɔmje/ *nm* apple tree.

pompe /pɔ̃p/ *nf* pump; (splendeur)
pomp; **~ à incendie** fire-engine; **~s
funèbres** undertaker's (+ *sg*).

pomper /pɔ̃pe/ [1] *vt* pump; (copier
Ⅰ) copy, crib; **~ l'air à qn** Ⅰ get on
sb's nerves.

pompier /pɔ̃pje/ *nm* fireman.

pomponner (se) /(sə)pɔ̃pɔne/ [1]
vpr get dolled up.

poncer /pɔ̃se/ [10] *vt* sand.

ponctuation /pɔ̃ktɥasjɔ̃/ *nf*
punctuation.

ponctuel, ~le /pɔ̃ktɥɛl/ *adj*
punctual.

pondre /pɔ̃dʀ/ [3] *vt/i* lay.

poney /pɔnɛ/ *nm* pony.

pont /pɔ̃/ *nm* bridge; (de navire) deck;
(de graissage) ramp; **faire le ~** get an
extended weekend; **~ aérien** airlift.
pont-levis (*pl* **ponts-levis**) *nm*
drawbridge.

populaire /pɔpylɛʀ/ *adj* popular;
(*expression*) colloquial; (*quartier,
origine*) working-class. **popularité**
nf popularity.

population /pɔpylasjɔ̃/ *nf*
population.

porc /pɔʀ/ *nm* pig; (viande) pork.

porcelaine /pɔʀsəlɛn/ *nf* china,
porcelain.

porc-épic (*pl* **porcs-épics**)
/pɔʀkepik/ *nm* porcupine.

porcherie /pɔʀʃəʀi/ *nf* pigsty.

pornographie /pɔʀnɔɡʀafi/ *nf*
pornography.

port /pɔʀ/ *nm* port, harbour; **à bon ~**
safely; **~ maritime** seaport; (transport)
carriage; (d'armes) carrying; (de barbe)
wearing.

portable /pɔʀtabl/ *nm* (Ordinat)
laptop (computer); (telephone) mobile
(phone).

portail /pɔʀtaj/ *nm* gate.

portatif, -ive /pɔʀtatif, -v/ *adj*
portable.

porte /pɔʀt/ *nf* door; (passage)
doorway; (de jardin, d'embarquement)
gate; **mettre à la ~** throw out; **~
d'entrée** front door.

porté, ~e /pɔʀte/ *adj* **~ à** inclined
to; **~ sur** keen on.

porte-avions /pɔʀtavjɔ̃/ *nm inv*
aircraft carrier.

porte-bagages /pɔʀtbaɡaʒ/ *nm
inv* (de vélo) carrier.

porte-bonheur /pɔʀtbɔnœʀ/ *nm
inv* lucky charm.

porte-clefs /pɔʀtəkle/ *nm inv* key
ring.

porte-documents /pɔʀtdɔkymɑ̃/
nm inv briefcase.

portée /pɔʀte/ *nf* (d'une arme) range;
(de voûte) span; (d'animaux) litter;
(impact) significance; (Mus) stave; **à ~
de (la) main** within (arm's) reach;

hors de **~ (de)** out of reach (of); **à la
~ de qn** at sb's level.

porte-fenêtre (*pl* **portes-
fenêtres**) /pɔʀtfənɛtʀ/ *nf* French
window.

portefeuille /pɔʀtəfœj/ *nm* wallet;
(de ministre) portfolio.

porte-jarretelles /pɔʀtʒaʀtɛl/ *nm
inv* suspender belt.

portemanteau (*pl* **~x**) /pɔʀt-
mɑ̃to/ *nm* coat *ou* hat stand.

porte-monnaie /pɔʀtmɔnɛ/ *nm
inv* purse.

porte-parole /pɔʀtpaʀɔl/ *nm inv*
spokesperson.

porter /pɔʀte/ [1] *vt* carry; (vêtement,
bague) wear; (fruits, responsabilité,
nom) bear; (coup) strike; (amener)
bring; (inscrire) enter. ● *vi* (bruit)
carry; (coup) hit home; **~ sur** rest
on; (concerner) be about. □ **se ~** *vpr*
bien se ~ be *ou* feel well; **se ~
candidat** stand as a candidate.

porteur, -euse /pɔʀtœʀ, -øz/ *nm,f*
(de nouvelles) bearer; (Méd) carrier.
● *nm* (Rail) porter.

portier /pɔʀtje/ *nm* doorman.

portière /pɔʀtjɛʀ/ *nf* door.

porto /pɔʀto/ *nm* port (wine).

portrait /pɔʀtʀɛ/ *nm* portrait.
portrait-robot (*pl* **portraits-
robots**) *nm* identikit®, photofit®.

portuaire /pɔʀtɥɛʀ/ *adj* port.

portugais, ~e /pɔʀtyɡɛ, -z/ *adj*
Portuguese. ● *nm* (Ling) Portuguese.
P~, ~e *nm,f* Portuguese.

Portugal /pɔʀtyɡal/ *nm* Portugal.

pose /poz/ *nf* installation; (attitude)
pose; (Photo) exposure.

posé, ~e /poze/ *adj* calm, serious.

poser /poze/ [1] *vt* put (down);
(installer) install, put in; (fondations)
lay; (question) ask; (problème) pose;
~ sa candidature apply (à for). ● *vi*
(modèle) pose. □ **se ~** *vpr* (avion,
oiseau) land; (regard) fall; (se
présenter) arise.

positif, -ive /pozitif, -v/ *adj* positive.

position /pozisjɔ̃/ *nf* position;
prendre ~ take a stand.

posologie /pozɔlɔʒi/ *nf* dosage.

p

posséder /pɔsede/ [14] *vt* (*propriété*) own, possess; (*diplôme*) have.

possessif, -ive /pɔsesif, -v/ *adj* possessive.

possession /pɔsesjɔ̃/ *nf* possession; **prendre ~ de** take possession of.

possibilité /pɔsibilite/ *nf* possibility.

possible /pɔsibl/ *adj* possible; **dès que ~** as soon as possible; **le plus tard ~** as late as possible. ● *nm* **le ~** what is possible; **faire son ~** do one's utmost.

postal, ~e (*mpl* **-aux**) /pɔstal, -o/ *adj* postal.

poste /pɔst/ *nf* (service) post; (bureau) post office; **~ aérienne** airmail; **mettre à la ~** post; **~ restante** poste restante. ● *nm* (lieu, emploi) post; (de radio, télévision) set; (téléphone) extension (number); **~ d'essence** petrol station; **~ d'incendie** fire point; **~ de pilotage** cockpit; **~ de police** police station; **~ de secours** first-aid post.

poster[1] /pɔste/ [1] *vt* (*lettre, personne*) post.

poster[2] /pɔstɛʁ/ *nm* poster.

postérieur, ~e /pɔsteʁjœʁ/ *adj* later; (*partie*) back; **~ à** after. ● *nm* Ⓘ posterior.

posthume /pɔstym/ *adj* posthumous.

postiche /pɔstiʃ/ *adj* false.

postier, -ière /pɔstje, -jɛʁ/ *nm, f* postal worker.

post-scriptum /pɔstskʁiptɔm/ *nm inv* postscript.

postuler /pɔstyle/ [1] *vt/i* apply (à for); (*principe*) postulate.

pot /po/ *nm* pot; (en plastique) carton; (en verre) jar; (chance Ⓘ) luck; (boisson Ⓘ) drink; **~ catalytique** catalytic converter; **~ d'échappement** exhaust pipe.

potable /pɔtabl/ *adj* **eau ~** drinking water.

potage /pɔtaʒ/ *nm* soup.

potager, -ère /pɔtaʒe, -ɛʁ/ *adj* vegetable. ● *nm* vegetable garden.

pot-au-feu /pɔtofø/ *nm inv* (plat) stew.

pot-de-vin (*pl* **pots-de-vin**) /podvɛ̃/ *nm* bribe.

poteau (*pl* **~x**) /pɔto/ *nm* post; (télégraphique) pole; **~ indicateur** signpost.

potelé, ~e /pɔtle/ *adj* plump.

potentiel, ~le /pɔtɑ̃sjɛl/ *a & nm* potential.

poterie /pɔtʁi/ *nf* pottery; (objet) piece of pottery. **potier** *nm* potter.

potins /pɔtɛ̃/ *nmpl* gossip (+ *sg*).

potiron /pɔtiʁɔ̃/ *nm* pumpkin.

pou (*pl* **~x**) /pu/ *nm* louse.

poubelle /pubɛl/ *nf* dustbin.

pouce /pus/ *nm* thumb; (de pied) big toe; (mesure) inch.

poudre /pudʁ/ *nf* powder; **~ (à canon)** gunpowder; **en ~** (*lait*) powdered; (*chocolat*) drinking.

poudrier /pudʁije/ *nm* (powder) compact.

pouf /puf/ *nm* pouffe.

poulailler /pulaje/ *nm* hen house.

poulain /pulɛ̃/ *nm* foal; (protégé) protégé.

poule /pul/ *nf* hen; (Culin) fowl; (femme Ⓧ) tart.

poulet /pulɛ/ *nm* chicken.

pouliche /puliʃ/ *nf* filly.

poulie /puli/ *nf* pulley.

pouls /pu/ *nm* pulse.

poumon /pumɔ̃/ *nm* lung.

poupe /pup/ *nf* stern.

poupée /pupe/ *nf* doll.

pour /puʁ/ *prép* for; (envers) to; (à la place de) on behalf of; (comme) as; **~ cela** for that reason; **~ cent** per cent; **~ de bon** for good; **~ faire** (in order) to do; **~ que** so that; **~ moi** (à mon avis) as for me; **trop poli ~** too polite to; **~ ce qui est de** as for; **être ~** be in favour. ● *nm inv* **le ~ et le contre** the pros and cons.

pourboire /puʁbwaʁ/ *nm* tip.

pourcentage /puʁsɑ̃taʒ/ *nm* percentage.

pourparlers /puʁpaʁle/ *nmpl* talks.

pourpre /puʁpʁ/ *a & nm* crimson; (violet) purple.

pourquoi /puʁkwa/ *conj & adv* why. ● *nm inv* **le ~ et le comment** the why and the wherefore.

pourra, pourrait /puʀa, puʀɛ/
⇒POUVOIR [49].

pourri, ~e /puʀi/ *adj* rotten.
pourrir [2] *vt/i* rot. **pourriture** *nf*
rot.

poursuite /puʀsɥit/ *nf* pursuit (de
of); **~s** (Jur) legal action (+ *sg*).

poursuivre /puʀsɥivʀ/ [57] *vt*
pursue; (continuer) continue (with); **~**
(en justice) take to court; (droit civil)
sue. ● *vi* continue. □ **se ~** *vpr*
continue.

pourtant /puʀtɑ̃/ *adv* yet.

pourvoir /puʀvwaʀ/ [63] *vi* **~ à**
provide for; **pourvu de** supplied
with.

pourvu que /puʀvyk(ə)/ *conj*
(condition) provided (that); (souhait) let
us hope (that).

pousse /pus/ *nf* growth; (bourgeon)
shoot.

poussé, ~e /puse/ *adj* (*études*)
advanced; (*enquête*) thorough.

poussée /puse/ *nf* pressure; (coup)
push; (de prix) upsurge; (Méd) attack.

pousser /puse/ [1] *vt* push; (cri) let
out; (soupir) heave; (continuer)
continue; (exhorter) urge (à to); (forcer)
drive (à to). ● *vi* push; (grandir) grow;
faire ~ (*cheveux*) let grow; (*plante*)
grow. □ **se ~** *vpr* move over *ou* up;
pousse-toi! move over!

poussette /pusɛt/ *nf* pushchair.

poussière /pusjɛʀ/ *nf* dust.
poussiéreux, -euse *adj* dusty.

poussin /pusɛ̃/ *nm* chick.

poutre /putʀ/ *nf* beam; (en métal)
girder.

pouvoir /puvwaʀ/ [49] *v aux*
(possibilité) can, be able; (permission,
éventualité) may, can; **il peut/pouvait/
pourrait venir** he can/could/might
come; **je n'ai pas pu** I couldn't; **j'ai pu
faire** (réussi à) I managed to do; **je
n'en peux plus** I am exhausted; **il se
peut que** it may be that. ● *nm*
power; (gouvernement) government; **au
~** in power; **~s publics** authorities.

prairie /pʀeʀi/ *nf* meadow.

praticien, ~ne /pʀatisjɛ̃, -ɛn/ *nm,f*
practitioner.

pratiquant, ~e /pʀatikɑ̃, -t/ *adj*
practising. ● *nm,f* churchgoer.

pratique /pʀatik/ *adj* practical. ● *nf*
practice; (expérience) experience; **la ~
du golf/du cheval** golfing/riding.
pratiquement *adv* (en pratique) in
practice; (presque) practically.

pratiquer /pʀatike/ [1] *vt/i* practise;
(Sport) play; (faire) make.

pré /pʀe/ *nm* meadow.

préalable /pʀealabl/ *adj*
preliminary, prior. ● *nm*
precondition; **au ~** first.

préambule /pʀeɑ̃byl/ *nm* preamble.

préavis /pʀeavi/ *nm* notice.

précaire /pʀekɛʀ/ *adj* precarious.
précarité *nf* (d'emploi) insecurity.

précaution /pʀekosjɔ̃/ *nf* (mesure)
precaution; (prudence) caution.

précédent, ~e /pʀesedɑ̃, -t/ *adj*
previous. ● *nm* precedent.

précéder /pʀesede/ [14] *vt/i*
precede.

précepteur, -trice /pʀesɛptœʀ,
-tʀis/ *nm, f* (private) tutor.

prêcher /pʀeʃe/ [1] *vt/i* preach.

précieux, -ieuse /pʀesjø, -z/ *adj*
precious.

précipitamment /pʀesipitamɑ̃/
adv hastily. **précipitation** *nf* haste.

précipiter /pʀesipite/ [1] *vt* throw,
precipitate; (hâter) hasten. □ **se ~**
vpr (se dépêcher) rush (sur at, on to);
(se jeter) throw oneself; (s'accélérer)
speed up.

précis, ~e /pʀesi, -z/ *adj* precise,
specific; (*mécanisme*) accurate; **dix
heures ~es** ten o'clock sharp. ● *nm*
summary.

préciser /pʀesize/ [1] *vt* specify;
précisez votre pensée could you be
more specific. □ **se ~** *vpr* become
clear(er). **précision** *nf* precision;
(détail) detail.

précoce /pʀekɔs/ *adj* (enfant)
precocious.

préconiser /pʀekɔnize/ [1] *vt*
advocate.

précurseur /pʀekyʀsœʀ/ *nm*
forerunner.

prédicateur /pʀedikatœʀ/ *nm*
preacher.

prédilection /pʀedilɛksjɔ̃/ *nf*
preference.

prédire /pʀediʀ/ [37] *vt* predict.

p

prédominer /pʀedɔmine/ [1] *vi* predominate.

préface /pʀefas/ *nf* preface.

préfecture /pʀefɛktyʀ/ *nf* prefecture; ~ **de police** police headquarters.

préféré, ~**e** /pʀefeʀe/ *a* & *nm,f* favourite.

préférence /pʀefeʀɑ̃s/ *nf* preference; **de** ~ preferably.

préférentiel, ~**le** /pʀefeʀɑ̃sjɛl/ *adj* preferential.

préférer /pʀefeʀe/ [14] *vt* prefer (**à** to); ~ **faire** prefer to do; **je ne préfère pas** I'd rather not; **j'aurais préféré ne pas savoir** I wish I hadn't found out.

préfet /pʀefɛ/ *nm* prefect; ~ **de police** prefect *ou* chief of police.

préfixe /pʀefiks/ *nm* prefix.

préhistorique /pʀeistɔʀik/ *adj* prehistoric.

préjudice /pʀeʒydis/ *nm* harm, prejudice; **porter** ~ **à** harm.

préjugé /pʀeʒyʒe/ *nm* prejudice; **être plein de** ~**s** be very prejudiced.

prélasser (se) /(sə)pʀelɑse/ [1] *vpr* loll (about).

prélèvement /pʀelɛvmɑ̃/ *nm* deduction; (de sang) sample. **prélever** [6] *vt* deduct (**sur** from); (*sang*) take.

préliminaire /pʀeliminɛʀ/ *a* & *nm* preliminary; ~**s** (sexuels) foreplay.

prématuré, ~**e** /pʀematyʀe/ *adj* premature. ● *nm* premature baby.

premier, -**ière** /pʀəmje, -jɛʀ/ *adj* first; (*rang*) front, first; (*enfance*) early; (*nécessité, souci*) prime; (*qualité*) top, prime; **de** ~ **ordre** first-rate; ~ **ministre** Prime Minister. ● *nm,f* first (one). ● *nm* (date) first; (étage) first floor; **en** ~ first. **première** *nf* (Rail) first class; (exploit jamais vu) first; (cinéma, Théât) première; (Aut) (vitesse) first (gear). **premièrement** *adv* firstly.

prémunir /pʀemyniʀ/ [2] *vt* protect (**contre** against).

prenant, ~**e** /pʀənɑ̃, -t/ *adj* (*activité*) engrossing; (*enfant*) demanding.

prénatal, ~**e** (*mpl* ~**s**) /pʀenatal/ *adj* antenatal.

prendre /pʀɑ̃dʀ/ [50] *vt* take; (attraper) catch, get; (acheter) get; (*repas*) have; (engager, adopter) take on; (*poids*) put on; (chercher) pick up; **qu'est-ce qui te prend?** what's the matter with you? ● *vi* (*liquide*) set; (*feu*) catch; (*vaccin*) take. □ **se** ~ *vpr* **se** ~ **pour** think one is; **s'en** ~ **à** attack; (rendre responsable) blame; **s'y** ~ set about (it).

preneur, -**euse** /pʀənœʀ, -øz/ *nm,f* buyer; **être** ~ be willing to buy; **trouver** ~ find a buyer.

prénom /pʀenɔ̃/ *nm* first name.

prénommer /pʀenɔme/ [1] *vt* call. □ **se** ~ *vpr* be called.

préoccupation /pʀeɔkypasjɔ̃/ *nf* (souci) worry; (idée fixe) preoccupation.

préoccuper /pʀeɔkype/ [1] *vt* worry; (absorber) preoccupy. □ **se** ~ **de** *vpr* think about.

préparation /pʀepaʀasjɔ̃/ *nf* preparation. **préparatoire** *adj* preparatory.

préparer /pʀepaʀe/ [1] *vt* prepare; (*repas, café*) make; **plats préparés** ready-cooked meals. □ **se** ~ *vpr* prepare oneself (**à** for); (s'apprêter) get ready; (être proche) be brewing.

préposé, ~**e** /pʀepoze/ *nm,f* employee; (des postes) postman, postwoman.

préposition /pʀepozisjɔ̃/ *nf* preposition.

préretraite /pʀeʀətʀɛt/ *nf* early retirement.

près /pʀɛ/ *adv* near, close; ~ **de** near (to), close to; (presque) nearly; **à cela** ~ except that; **de** ~ closely.

présage /pʀezaʒ/ *nm* omen.

presbyte /pʀɛsbit/ *adj* long-sighted, far-sighted.

prescrire /pʀɛskʀiʀ/ [30] *vt* prescribe.

préséance /pʀeseɑ̃s/ *nf* precedence.

présence /pʀezɑ̃s/ *nf* presence; (Scol) attendance.

présent, ~**e** /pʀezɑ̃, -t/ *adj* present. ● *nm* (temps, cadeau) present; **à** ~ now.

présentateur, -**trice** /pʀezɑ̃tatœʀ, -tʀis/ *nm,f* presenter.

présentation /pʀezɑ̃tasjɔ̃/ nf (de personne) introduction; (exposé) presentation.

présenter /pʀezɑ̃te/ [1] vt present; (personne) introduce (à to); (montrer) show. ● vi ~ **bien** have a pleasing appearance. □ **se** ~ vpr introduce oneself (à to); (aller) go; (apparaître) appear; (candidat) come forward; (occasion) arise; **se** ~ **à** (examen) sit for; (élection) stand for; **se** ~ **bien** look good.

préservatif /pʀezɛʀvatif/ nm condom.

préserver /pʀezɛʀve/ [1] vt protect.

présidence /pʀezidɑ̃s/ nf (d'État) presidency; (de société) chairmanship.

président, ~**e** /pʀezidɑ̃, -t/ nm,f president; (de société, comité) chairman, chairwoman; ~-**directeur général** managing director.

présidentiel, ~**le** /pʀezidɑ̃sjɛl/ adj presidential.

présider /pʀezide/ [1] vt preside.

présomptueux, -**euse** /pʀezɔ̃ptɥø, -z/ adj presumptuous.

presque /pʀɛsk(ə)/ adv almost, nearly; ~ **jamais** hardly ever; ~ **rien** hardly anything; ~ **pas (de)** hardly any.

presqu'île /pʀɛskil/ nf peninsula.

pressant, ~**e** /pʀesɑ̃, -t/ adj pressing, urgent.

presse /pʀɛs/ nf (journaux, appareil) press.

pressentiment /pʀesɑ̃timɑ̃/ nm premonition. **pressentir** [46] vt have a premonition of.

pressé, ~**e** /pʀese/ adj in a hurry; (orange, citron) freshly squeezed.

presser /pʀese/ [1] vt squeeze, press; (appuyer sur, harceler) press; (hâter) hasten; (inciter) urge (de to). ● vi (temps) press; (affaire) be pressing. □ **se** ~ vpr (se hâter) hurry; (se grouper) crowd.

pressing /pʀesiŋ/ nm (teinturerie) dry-cleaner's.

pression /pʀesjɔ̃/ nf pressure; (bouton) press-stud.

prestance /pʀɛstɑ̃s/ nf (imposing) presence.

prestation /pʀɛstasjɔ̃/ nf allowance; (d'artiste) performance.

prestidigitation /pʀɛstidiʒitasjɔ̃/ nf conjuring.

prestige /pʀɛstiʒ/ nm prestige. **prestigieux**, -**ieuse** adj prestigious.

présumer /pʀezyme/ [1] vt presume; ~ **que** assume that; ~ **de** overrate.

prêt, ~**e** /pʀɛ, -t/ adj ready (à qch for sth, à faire to do). ● nm loan. **prêt-à-porter** nm inv ready-to-wear clothes.

prétendre /pʀetɑ̃dʀ/ [3] vt claim (que that); (vouloir) intend; **on le prétend riche** he is said to be very rich. **prétendu**, ~**e** adj so-called. **prétendument** adv supposedly, allegedly.

prétentieux, -**ieuse** /pʀetɑ̃sjø, -z/ adj pretentious.

prêter /pʀete/ [1] vt lend (à to); (attribuer) attribute; ~ **son aide à qn** give sb some help; ~ **attention** pay attention; ~ **serment** take an oath. ● vi ~ **à** lead to.

prêteur, -**euse** /pʀetœʀ, -øz/ nm,f (money-)lender; ~ **sur gages** pawnbroker.

prétexte /pʀetɛkst/ nm pretext, excuse.

prêtre /pʀɛtʀ/ nm priest.

preuve /pʀœv/ nf proof; **des** ~**s** evidence (+ sg); **faire** ~ **de** show; **faire ses** ~**s** prove oneself.

prévaloir /pʀevalwaʀ/ [60] vi prevail.

prévenant, ~**e** /pʀevnɑ̃, -t/ adj thoughtful.

prévenir /pʀevniʀ/ [58] vt (menacer) warn; (informer) tell; (médecin) call; (éviter, anticiper) prevent.

préventif, -**ive** /pʀevɑ̃tif, -v/ adj preventive.

prévention /pʀevɑ̃sjɔ̃/ nf prevention; **faire de la** ~ take preventive action; ~ **routière** road safety.

prévenu, ~**e** /pʀevny/ nm,f defendant.

prévisible /pʀevizibl/ adj predictable. **prévision** nf prediction; (météorologique) forecast.

prévoir /pʀevwaʀ/ [63] vt foresee; (temps) forecast; (organiser) plan (for),

provide for; (envisager) allow (for);
prévu pour (*jouet*) designed for;
comme prévu as planned.

prévoyance /pʀevwajɑ̃s/ *nf*
foresight. **prévoyant**, **~e** *adj* far-
sighted.

prier /pʀije/ [45] *vi* pray. ● *vt* pray
to; (demander à) ask (**de** to); **je vous en
prie** please; (il n'y a pas de quoi) don't
mention it.

prière /pʀijɛʀ/ *nf* prayer; (demande)
request; **~ de** (vous êtes prié de) will
you please.

primaire /pʀimɛʀ/ *adj* primary.

prime /pʀim/ *nf* free gift; (d'employé)
bonus; (subvention) subsidy; (d'assurance) premium.

primé, **~e** /pʀime/ *adj* prize-
winning.

primeurs /pʀimœʀ/ *nfpl* early fruit
and vegetables.

primevère /pʀimvɛʀ/ *nf* primrose.

primitif, **-ive** /pʀimitif, -v/ *adj*
primitive; (d'origine) original. ● *nm,f*
primitive.

primordial, **~e** (*mpl* **-iaux**)
/pʀimɔʀdjal, -jo/ *adj* essential.

prince /pʀɛ̃s/ *nm* prince.
princesse *nf* princess. **princier**,
-ière *adj* princely.

principal, **~e** (*mpl* **-aux**) /pʀɛ̃sipal,
-o/ *adj* main, principal. ● *nm*
headmaster; (chose) main thing.

principe /pʀɛ̃sip/ *nm* principle; **en
~** in theory; (d'habitude) as a rule.

printanier, **-ière** /pʀɛ̃tanje, -jɛʀ/
adj spring(-like).

printemps /pʀɛ̃tɑ̃/ *nm* spring.

prioritaire /pʀijɔʀitɛʀ/ *adj* priority;
être ~ have priority. **priorité** *nf*
priority; (Auto) right of way.

pris, **~e** /pʀi, -z/ *adj* (*place*) taken;
(*personne, journée*) busy; (*nez*)
stuffed up; **~ de** (*peur, fièvre*)
stricken with; **~ de panique** panic-
stricken. ● ⇒PRENDRE [50].

prise /pʀiz/ *nf* hold, grip; (animal
attrapé) catch; (Mil) capture; **~ (de
courant)** (mâle) plug; (femelle) socket;
~ multiple multiplug adapter; **avoir
~ sur qn** have a hold over sb; **aux
~s avec** to grips with; **~ de
conscience** awareness; **~ de contact**

first contact, initial meeting; **~ de
position** stand; **~ de sang** blood test.

prisé, **~e** /pʀize/ *adj* popular.

prison /pʀizɔ̃/ *nf* prison, jail;
(réclusion) imprisonment.
prisonnier, **-ière** *nm,f* prisoner.

privation /pʀivasjɔ̃/ *nf* deprivation;
(sacrifice) hardship.

privatiser /pʀivatize/ [1] *vt*
privatize.

privé /pʀive/ *adj* private. ● *nm*
(Comm) private sector; (Scol) private
schools (+ *pl*); **en ~** in private.

priver /pʀive/ [1] *vt* **~ de** deprive of.
□ **se ~** (**de**) *vpr* go without.

privilège /pʀivilɛʒ/ *nm* privilege.
privilégié, **~e** *nm,f* privileged
person.

prix /pʀi/ *nm* price; (récompense)
prize; **à tout ~** at all costs; **au ~ de**
(fig) at the expense of; **~ coûtant**, **~
de revient** cost price; **à ~ fixe** set
price.

probabilité /pʀɔbabilite/ *nf*
probability. **probable** *adj* probable,
likely. **probablement** *adv*
probably.

probant, **~e** /pʀɔbɑ̃, -t/ *adj*
convincing, conclusive.

problème /pʀɔblɛm/ *nm* problem.

procédé /pʀɔsede/ *nm* process;
(manière d'agir) practice.

procéder /pʀɔsede/ [14] *vi* proceed;
~ à carry out.

procès /pʀɔsɛ/ *nm* (criminel) trial;
(civil) lawsuit, proceedings (+ *pl*).

processus /pʀɔsesys/ *nm* process.

procès-verbal (*pl* **procès-
verbaux**) /pʀɔsɛvɛʀbal, -o/ *nm*
minutes (+ *pl*); (contravention) ticket.

prochain, **~e** /pʀɔʃɛ̃, -ɛn/ *adj*
(suivant) next; (proche) imminent;
(avenir) near. ● *nm* fellow man.
prochainement *adv* soon.

proche /pʀɔʃ/ *adj* near, close;
(avoisinant) neighbouring; (*parent,
ami*) close; **~ de** close *ou* near to; **de
~ en ~** gradually; **dans un ~ avenir**
in the near future; **être ~** (imminent)
be approaching. ● *nm* close relative;
(ami) close friend.

Proche-Orient /pʀɔʃɔʀjɑ̃/ *nm*
Near East.

proclamation /pʀɔklamasjɔ̃/ *nf* declaration, proclamation. **proclamer** [1] *vt* declare, proclaim.

procuration /pʀɔkyʀasjɔ̃/ *nf* proxy.

procurer /pʀɔkyʀe/ [1] *vt* bring (à to). □ **se** ~ *vpr* obtain.

procureur /pʀɔkyʀœʀ/ *nm* public prosecutor.

prodige /pʀɔdiʒ/ *nm* (fait) marvel; (personne) prodigy; **enfant/musicien** ~ child/musical prodigy. **prodigieux, -ieuse** *adj* tremendous, prodigious.

prodigue /pʀɔdig/ *adj* wasteful; **fils** ~ prodigal son.

producteur, -trice /pʀɔdyktœʀ, -tʀis/ *adj* producing. ● *nm, f* producer. **productif, -ive** *adj* productive. **production** *nf* production; (*produit*) product. **productivité** *nf* productivity.

produire /pʀɔdɥiʀ/ [17] *vt* produce. □ **se** ~ *vpr* (survenir) happen; (*acteur*) perform.

produit /pʀɔdɥi/ *nm* product; ~**s** (de la terre) produce (+ *sg*); ~ **chimique** chemical; ~**s alimentaires** foodstuffs; ~ **de consommation** consumer goods; ~ **intérieur brut** gross domestic product; ~ **national brut** gross national product.

proéminent, ~**e** /pʀɔeminɑ̃, -t/ *adj* prominent.

profane /pʀɔfan/ *adj* secular. ● *nmf* lay person.

proférer /pʀɔfeʀe/ [14] *vt* utter.

professeur /pʀɔfɛsœʀ/ *nm* teacher; (Univ) lecturer; (avec chaire) professor.

profession /pʀɔfɛsjɔ̃/ *nf* occupation; ~ **libérale** profession.

professionnel, ~**le** /pʀɔfɛsjɔnɛl/ *adj* professional; (*école*) vocational. ● *nm, f* professional.

profil /pʀɔfil/ *nm* profile.

profit /pʀɔfi/ *nm* profit; **au** ~ **de** in aid of. **profitable** *adj* profitable.

profiter /pʀɔfite/ [1] *vi* ~ **à** benefit; ~ **de** take advantage of.

profond, ~**e** /pʀɔfɔ̃, -d/ *adj* deep; (*sentiment, intérêt*) profound; (*causes*) underlying; **au plus** ~ **de** in the depths of. **profondément** *adv* deeply; (*différent, triste*) profoundly; (*dormir*) soundly. **profondeur** *nf* depth.

progéniture /pʀɔʒenityʀ/ *nf* offspring.

progiciel /pʀɔʒisjɛl/ *nm* (Ordinat) package.

programmation /pʀɔgʀamasjɔ̃/ *nf* programming.

programme /pʀɔgʀam/ *nm* programme; (Scol) (d'une matière) syllabus; (général) curriculum; (Ordinat) program. **programmer** [1] *vt* (*ordinateur, appareil*) program; (*émission*) schedule. **programmeur, -euse** *nm, f* computer programmer.

progrès /pʀɔgʀɛ/ *nm* & *nmpl* progress; **faire des** ~ make progress. **progresser** [1] *vi* progress. **progressif, -ive** *adj* progressive. **progression** *nf* progression.

prohibitif, -ive /pʀɔibitif, -v/ *adj* prohibitive.

proie /pʀwa/ *nf* prey; **en** ~ **à** tormented by.

projecteur /pʀɔʒɛktœʀ/ *nm* floodlight; (Mil) searchlight; (cinéma) projector.

projectile /pʀɔʒɛktil/ *nm* missile.

projection /pʀɔʒɛksjɔ̃/ *nf* projection; (séance) show.

projet /pʀɔʒɛ/ *nm* plan; (ébauche) draft; ~ **de loi** bill.

projeter /pʀɔʒte/ [38] *vt* (prévoir) plan (de to); (*film*) project, show; (jeter) hurl, project.

prolétaire /pʀɔletɛʀ/ *nmf* proletarian.

prologue /pʀɔlɔg/ *nm* prologue.

prolongation /pʀɔlɔ̃gasjɔ̃/ *nf* extension; ~**s** (football) extra time.

prolonger /pʀɔlɔ̃ʒe/ [40] *vt* extend. □ **se** ~ *vpr* go on.

promenade /pʀɔmnad/ *nf* walk; (à bicyclette, à cheval) ride; (en auto) drive, ride; **faire une** ~ go for a walk.

promener /pʀɔmne/ [6] *vt* take for a walk; ~ **son regard sur** cast an eye over. □ **se** ~ *vpr* walk; (aller) **se** ~ go for a walk. **promeneur, -euse** *nm, f* walker.

promesse /pʀɔmɛs/ *nf* promise.

prometteur, -euse /pʀɔmɛtœʀ, -øz/ *adj* promising.

promettre /pʀɔmɛtʀ/ [42] *vt/i* promise. ● *vi* be promising. □ **se** ~ **de** *vpr* resolve to.

p

promoteur /pʀɔmɔtœʀ/ *nm* (immobilier) property developer.

promotion /pʀɔmɔsjɔ̃/ *nf* promotion; (Univ) year; (Comm) special offer.

prompt, ∼**e** /pʀɔ̃, -t/ *adj* swift.

promu, ∼**e** /pʀɔmy/ *adj* **être** ∼ be promoted.

prôner /pʀone/ [1] *vt* extol.

pronom /pʀɔnɔ̃/ *nm* pronoun. **pronominal**, ∼**e** (*mpl* **-aux**) *adj* pronominal.

prononcé, ∼**e** /pʀɔnɔ̃se/ *adj* strong.

prononcer /pʀɔnɔ̃se/ [10] *vt* pronounce; (*discours*) make. □ **se** ∼ *vpr* (*mot*) be pronounced; (*personne*) make a decision (**pour** in favour of). **prononciation** *nf* pronunciation.

pronostic /pʀɔnɔstik/ *nm* forecast; (Méd) prognosis.

propagande /pʀɔpagɑ̃d/ *nf* propaganda.

propager /pʀɔpaʒe/ [40] *vt* spread. □ **se** ∼ *vpr* spread.

prophète /pʀɔfɛt/ *nm* prophet. **prophétie** *nf* prophecy.

propice /pʀɔpis/ *adj* favourable.

proportion /pʀɔpɔʀsjɔ̃/ *nf* proportion; (en mathématiques) ratio; **toutes** ∼**s gardées** relatively speaking. **proportionné**, ∼**e** *adj* proportionate (à to). **proportionnel**, ∼**le** *adj* proportional. **proportionnellement** *adv* proportionately.

propos /pʀɔpo/ *nm* intention; (sujet) subject; **à** ∼ at the right time; (dans un dialogue) by the way; **à** ∼ **de** about; **à tout** ∼ at every possible occasion. ● *nmpl* (paroles) remarks.

proposer /pʀɔpoze/ [1] *vt* suggest, propose; (offrir) offer. □ **se** ∼ *vpr* volunteer (**pour** to). **proposition** *nf* proposal; (affirmation) proposition; (Gram) clause.

propre /pʀɔpʀ/ *adj* (non sali) clean; (soigné) neat; (honnête) decent; (à soi) own; (*sens*) literal; ∼ **à** (qui convient) suited to; (spécifique) particular to. ● *nm* **mettre au** ∼ write out again neatly; **c'est du** ∼! (ironique) well done!

proprement /pʀɔpʀəmɑ̃/ *adv* (avec soin) neatly; (au sens strict) strictly; **le bureau** ∼ **dit** the office itself.

propreté /pʀɔpʀəte/ *nf* cleanliness.

propriétaire /pʀɔpʀijetɛʀ/ *nmf* owner; (Comm) proprietor; (qui loue) landlord, landlady.

propriété /pʀɔpʀijete/ *nf* property; (droit) ownership.

propulser /pʀɔpylse/ [1] *vt* propel.

proroger /pʀɔʀɔʒe/ [40] *vt* (*contrat*) defer; (*passeport*) extend.

proscrire /pʀɔskʀiʀ/ [30] *vt* proscribe.

proscrit, ∼**e** /pʀɔskʀi, -t/ *adj* proscribed. ● *nm,f* (exilé) exile.

prose /pʀoz/ *nf* prose.

prospectus /pʀɔspɛktys/ *nm* leaflet.

prospère /pʀɔspɛʀ/ *adj* flourishing, thriving. **prospérer** [14] *vi* thrive, prosper. **prospérité** *nf* prosperity.

prosterner (se) /(sə)pʀɔstɛʀne/ [1] *vpr* prostrate oneself; **prosterné devant** prostrate before.

prostituée /pʀɔstitɥe/ *nf* prostitute. **prostitution** *nf* prostitution.

protecteur, **-trice** /pʀɔtɛktœʀ, -tʀis/ *nm,f* protector. ● *adj* protective.

protection /pʀɔtɛksjɔ̃/ *nf* protection.

protégé, ∼**e** /pʀɔteʒe/ *nm,f* protégé.

protéger /pʀɔteʒe/ [40] *vt* protect. □ **se** ∼ *vpr* protect oneself.

protéine /pʀɔtein/ *nf* protein.

protestant, ∼**e** /pʀɔtɛstɑ̃, -t/ *a & nm, f* Protestant.

protestation /pʀɔtɛstasjɔ̃/ *nf* protest. **protester** [1] *vt/i* protest.

protocole /pʀɔtɔkɔl/ *nm* protocol.

protubérant, ∼**e** /pʀɔtybeʀɑ̃/ *adj* protruding.

proue /pʀu/ *nf* bow, prow.

prouesse /pʀuɛs/ *nf* feat, exploit.

prouver /pʀuve/ [1] *vt* prove.

provenance /pʀɔvnɑ̃s/ *nf* origin; **en** ∼ **de** from.

provençal, ∼**e** (*mpl* **-aux**) /pʀɔvɑ̃sal, -o/ *a & nm,f* Provençal.

provenir /pʀɔvniʀ/ [58] *vi* ~ de come from.

proverbe /pʀɔvɛʀb/ *nm* proverb.

province /pʀɔvɛ̃s/ *nf* province; de ~ provincial; la ~ the provinces (+ *pl*). **provincial**, ~e (*mpl* -iaux) *a & nm, f* provincial.

proviseur /pʀɔvizœʀ/ *nm* headmaster, principal.

provision /pʀɔvizjɔ̃/ *nf* supply, store; (sur un compte) credit (balance); (acompte) deposit; ~s (vivres) food shopping.

provisoire /pʀɔvizwaʀ/ *adj* provisional.

provocant, ~e /pʀɔvɔkɑ̃, -t/ *adj* provocative. **provocation** *nf* provocation. **provoquer** [1] *vt* cause; (sexuellement) arouse; (défier) provoke.

proxénète /pʀɔksenɛt/ *nm* pimp, procurer.

proximité /pʀɔksimite/ *nf* proximity; à ~ de close to.

prude /pʀyd/ *adj* prudish.

prudemment /pʀydamɑ̃/ *adv* (*conduire*) carefully; (*attendre*) cautiously. **prudence** *nf* caution. **prudent**, ~e *adj* (au volant) careful; (à agir) cautious; (sage) wise.

prune /pʀyn/ *nf* plum.

pruneau (*pl* ~x) /pʀyno/ *nm* prune.

prunelle /pʀynɛl/ *nf* (pupille) pupil; (fruit) sloe.

prunier /pʀynje/ *nm* plum tree.

psaume /psom/ *nm* psalm.

pseudonyme /psødɔnim/ *nm* pseudonym.

psychanalyse /psikanaliz/ *nf* psychoanalysis. **psychanalyste** *nmf* psychoanalyst.

psychiatre /psikjatʀ/ *nmf* psychiatrist. **psychiatrie** *nf* psychiatry. **psychiatrique** *adj* psychiatric.

psychique /psiʃik/ *adj* mental, psychological.

psychologie /psikɔlɔʒi/ *nf* psychology. **psychologique** *adj* psychological. **psychologue** *nmf* psychologist.

pu /py/ ⇒POUVOIR [49].

puant, ~e /pɥɑ̃, -t/ *adj* stinking.

pub /pyb/ *nf* 🄻 la ~ advertising; une ~ an advert.

puberté /pybɛʀte/ *nf* puberty.

public, -que /pyblik/ *adj* public. ● *nm* public; (assistance) audience; (Scol) state schools (+ *pl*); en ~ in public.

publication /pyblikasjɔ̃/ *nf* publication.

publicitaire /pyblisitɛʀ/ *adj* publicity. **publicité** *nf* publicity, advertising; (annonce) advertisement.

publier /pyblije/ [45] *vt* publish.

publiquement /pyblikmɑ̃/ *adv* publicly.

puce /pys/ *nf* flea; (électronique) chip; marché aux ~s flea market.

pudeur /pydœʀ/ *nf* modesty.

pudibond, ~e /pydibɔ̃, -d/ *adj* prudish.

pudique /pydik/ *adj* modest.

puer /pɥe/ [1] *vi* stink. ● *vt* stink of.

puéricultrice /pɥeʀikyltʀis/ *nf* pediatric nurse.

puéril, ~e /pɥeʀil/ *adj* puerile.

puis /pɥi/ *adv* then.

puiser /pɥize/ [1] *vt* draw (dans from). ● *vi* ~ dans qch dip into sth.

puisque /pɥisk(ə)/ *conj* since, as.

puissance /pɥisɑ̃s/ *nf* power; en ~ potential.

puissant, ~e /pɥisɑ̃, -t/ *adj* powerful.

puits /pɥi/ *nm* well; (de mine) shaft.

pull(-over) /pyl(ɔvɛʀ)/ *nm* pullover, jumper.

pulpe /pylp/ *nf* pulp.

pulsation /pylsasjɔ̃/ *nf* (heart-)beat.

pulvériser /pylveʀize/ [1] *vt* pulverize; (liquide) spray.

punaise /pynɛz/ *nf* (insecte) bug; (clou) drawing-pin.

punch¹ /pɔ̃ʃ/ *nm* (boisson) punch.

punch² /pœnʃ/ *nm* avoir du ~ have drive.

punir /pyniʀ/ [2] *vt* punish. **punition** *nf* punishment.

pupille /pypij/ *nf* (de l'œil) pupil. ● *nmf* (enfant) ward.

pupitre /pypitʀ/ *nm* (Scol) desk; ~ à musique music stand.

pur /pyʀ/ *adj* pure; (whisky) neat.

p

purée /pyʀe/ *nf* purée; (de pommes de terre) mashed potatoes (+ *pl*).

pureté /pyʀte/ *nf* purity.

purgatoire /pyʀgatwaʀ/ *nm* purgatory.

purge /pyʀʒ/ *nf* purge. **purger** [40] *vt* (Pol, Méd) purge; (*peine*: Jur) serve.

purifier /pyʀifje/ [45] *vt* purify.

puritain, **~e** /pyʀitɛ̃, -ɛn/ *nm,f* puritan. ● *adj* puritanical.

pur-sang /pyʀsɑ̃/ *nm inv* (cheval) thoroughbred.

pus /py/ *nm* pus.

putain /pytɛ̃/ *nf* ▣ whore.

puzzle /pœzl/ *nm* jigsaw (puzzle).

P-V *abrév m* (**procès-verbal**) ticket, traffic fine.

pyjama /piʒama/ *nm* pyjamas (+ *pl*); **un ~** a pair of pyjamas.

pylône /pilon/ *nm* pylon.

Pyrénées /piʀene/ *nfpl* **les ~** the Pyrenees.

pyromane /piʀɔman/ *nmf* arsonist.

....

Qq

....

QG *abrév m* (**quartier général**) HQ.

QI *abrév m* (**quotient intellectuel**) IQ.

qu' /k/ ⇒QUE.

quadriller /kadʀije/ [1] *vt* (*armée*) take control of; (*police*) spread one's net over; **papier quadrillé** squared paper.

quadrupède /kadʀypɛd/ *nm* quadruped.

quadruple /kadʀypl/ *adj* quadruple. ● *nm* **le ~ de** four times. **quadrupler** [1] *vt/i* quadruple.

quai /ke/ *nm* (de gare) platform; (de port) quay; (de rivière) bank.

qualification /kalifikasjɔ̃/ *nf* qualification; (compétence pratique) skills (+ *pl*).

qualifié, **~e** /kalifje/ *adj* (diplômé) qualified; (*main-d'œuvre*) skilled.

qualifier /kalifje/ [45] *vt* qualify; (décrire) describe (**de** as). □ **se ~** *vpr* qualify (**pour** for).

qualité /kalite/ *nf* quality; (titre) occupation; (fonction) position; **en sa ~ de** in his *ou* her capacity as.

quand /kɑ̃/ *adv* when; **~ même** all the same. ● *conj* when; (toutes les fois que) whenever; **~ bien même** even if.

quant à /kɑ̃ta/ *prép* as for.

quantité /kɑ̃tite/ *nf* quantity; **une ~ de** a lot of; **des ~s (de)** masses *ou* lots (of).

quarantaine /kaʀɑ̃tɛn/ *nf* (Méd) quarantine; **une ~ (de)** about forty; **avoir la ~** be in one's forties.

quarante /kaʀɑ̃t/ *a & nm* forty.

quart /kaʀ/ *nm* quarter; (Naut) watch; **onze heures moins le ~** quarter to eleven; **~ (de litre)** quarter litre; **~ de finale** quarter-final; **~ d'heure** quarter of an hour; **~ de tour** ninety-degree turn.

quartier /kaʀtje/ *nm* area, district; (zone ethnique) quarter; (de lune, pomme, bœuf) quarter; (d'une orange) segment; **~s** (Mil) quarters; **de ~, du ~** local; **~ général** headquarters; **avoir ~ libre** be free.

quasiment /kazimɑ̃/ *adv* almost, practically.

quatorze /katɔʀz/ *a & nm* fourteen.

quatre /katʀ(ə)/ *a & nm* four. **quatre-vingt(s)** *a & nm* eighty. **quatre-vingt-dix** *a & nm* ninety.

quatrième /katʀijɛm/ *a & nmf* fourth. ● *nf* (Auto) fourth gear.

quatuor /kwatɥɔʀ/ *nm* quartet.

....

que, qu' /kə, k/

  qu' before vowel or mute h.

● *conjonction*

····▸ that; **je crains ~…** I'm worried that…

····▸ (souhait, volonté) **je veux ~ tu viennes** I want you to come; **~ tu viennes ou non** whether you come or not; **qu'il entre** let him come in.

····▸ (comparaison) than; **plus grand ~ toi** taller than you.

● *pronom interrogatif*

····▸ what; ∼ **voulez-vous manger?** what would you like to eat?

● *pronom relatif*

····▸ (personne) whom, that; **l'homme ∼ j'ai rencontré** the man (whom) I met.

····▸ (chose) that, which; **le cheval ∼ Nick m'a offert** the horse (which) Nick gave me.

● *adverbe*

····▸ ∼ **c'est joli!** it's so pretty!; ∼ **de monde!** what a lot of people!

Québec /kebɛk/ *nm* Quebec.

quel, quelle (*pl* **quel(le)s**) /kɛl/

● *adjectif interrogatif*

····▸ which, what; ∼ **auteur a écrit...?** which writer wrote...?; ∼ **jour sommes-nous?** what day is it today?

● *adjectif exclamatif*

····▸ what; ∼ **idiot!** what an idiot!; **quelle horreur!** that's horrible!

● *adjectif relatif*

····▸ ∼ **que soit son âge** whatever his age; **quelles que soient tes raisons** whatever your reasons; ∼ **que soit le gagnant** whoever the winner is.

quelconque /kɛlkɔ̃k/ *adj* any, some; (banal) ordinary; (médiocre) poor, second rate.

quelque /kɛlkə/ *adj* some; ∼**s** a few, some. ● *adv* (environ) about, some; **et** ∼ 🔢 and a bit; ∼ **chose** something; (dans les phrases interrogatives) anything; ∼ **part** somewhere; ∼ **peu** somewhat.

quelquefois /kɛlkəfwa/ *adv* sometimes.

quelques-uns, -unes /kɛlkəzœ̃, -yn/ *pron* some, a few.

quelqu'un /kɛlkœ̃/ *pron* someone, somebody; (dans les phrases interrogatives) anyone, anybody.

querelle /kəʀɛl/ *nf* quarrel. **quereller (se)** [1] *vpr* quarrel. **querelleur, -euse** *adj* quarrelsome.

question /kɛstjɔ̃/ *nf* question; (affaire) matter, question; **poser une** ∼ ask a question; **en** ∼ in question;

il est ∼ **de** (cela concerne) it is about; (on parle de) there is talk of; **il n'en est pas** ∼ it is out of the question; **pas** ∼**!** no way!

questionnaire /kɛstjɔnɛʀ/ *nm* questionnaire.

questionner /kɛstjɔne/ [1] *vt* question.

quête /kɛt/ *nf* (Relig) collection; (recherche) search; **en** ∼ **de** in search of.

queue /kø/ *nf* tail; (de poêle) handle; (de fruit) stalk; (de fleur) stem; (file) queue; (US) line; (de train) rear; **faire la** ∼ queue (up); (US) line up; ∼ **de cheval** pony-tail; **faire une** ∼ **de poisson à qn** (Auto) cut in front of sb.

qui /ki/

● *pronom interrogatif*

····▸ (sujet) who; ∼ **a fait ça?** who did that?

····▸ (complément) whom; **à** ∼ **est ce livre?** whose book is this?

● *pronom relatif*

····▸ (personne sujet) who; **c'est Isabelle qui vient d'appeler** it's Isabelle who's just called.

····▸ (autres cas) that, which; **qu'est-ce** ∼ **te prend?** what is the matter with you?; **invite** ∼ **tu veux** invite whoever you want; ∼ **que ce soit** whoever it is, anybody.

quiche /kiʃ/ *nf* quiche.

quiconque /kikɔ̃k/ *pron* whoever; (n'importe qui) anyone.

quille /kij/ *nf* (de bateau) keel; (jouet) skittle.

quincaillerie /kɛ̃kajʀi/ *nf* hardware; (magasin) hardware shop. **quincaillier, -ière** *nm, f* hardware dealer.

quintal (*pl* **-aux**) /kɛ̃tal, -o/ *nm* quintal, one hundred kilos.

quinte /kɛ̃t/ *nf* ∼ **de toux** coughing fit.

quintuple /kɛ̃typl/ *adj* quintuple. ● *nm* **le** ∼ **de** five times. **quintupler** [1] *vt/i* quintuple, increase fivefold.

quinzaine /kɛ̃zɛn/ *nf* **une** ∼ **(de)** about fifteen.

q

quinze /kɛ̃z/ *a & nm inv* fifteen; ~ **jours** two weeks.

quiproquo /kipʀɔko/ *nm* misunderstanding.

quittance /kitɑ̃s/ *nf* receipt.

quitte /kit/ *adj* quits (**envers** with); ~ **à faire** even if it means doing.

quitter /kite/ [1] *vt* leave; (*vêtement*) take off; **ne quittez pas!** hold the line, please! □ **se** ~ *vpr* part.

qui-vive /kiviv/ *nm inv* **être sur le** ~ be alert.

quoi /kwa/ *pron* what; (après une préposition) which; **de** ~ **vivre** (assez) enough to live on; **de** ~ **écrire** something to write with; ~ **qu'il dise** whatever he says; ~ **que ce soit** anything; **il n'y a pas de** ~ my pleasure; **il n'y a pas de** ~ **s'inquiéter** there's nothing to worry about.

quoique /kwak(ə)/ *conj* although, though.

quota /kɔta/ *nm* quota.

quote-part (*pl* **quotes-parts**) /kɔtpaʀ/ *nf* share.

quotidien, ~**ne** /kɔtidjɛ̃, -ɛn/ *adj* daily; (banal) everyday. ● *nm* daily (paper); (vie quotidienne) everyday life.
quotidiennement *adv* daily.

Rr

rabâcher /ʀabɑʃe/ [1] *vt* keep repeating.

rabais /ʀabɛ/ *nm* reduction, discount. **rabaisser** [1] *vt* (déprécier) belittle; (réduire) reduce.

rabat-joie /ʀabajwa/ *nm inv* killjoy.

rabattre /ʀabatʀ/ [11] *vt* (chapeau, visière) pull down; (refermer) shut; (diminuer) reduce; (déduire) take off; (col, drap) turn down. □ **se** ~ *vpr* (se refermer) close; (véhicule) cut back in; **se** ~ **sur** make do with.

rabot /ʀabo/ *nm* plane.

rabougri, ~**e** /ʀabugʀi/ *adj* stunted.

racaille /ʀakɑj/ *nf* rabble.

raccommoder /ʀakɔmɔde/ [1] *vt* mend; (*personnes*) reconcile.

raccompagner /ʀakɔ̃paɲe/ [1] *vt* see *ou* take back (*home*).

raccord /ʀakɔʀ/ *nm* link; (de papier peint) join; (retouche) touch-up.
raccorder [1] *vt* connect, join.

raccourci /ʀakuʀsi/ *nm* short cut; **en** ~ in short.

raccourcir /ʀakuʀsiʀ/ [2] *vt* shorten. ● *vi* get shorter.

raccrocher /ʀakʀɔʃe/ [1] *vt* hang back up; (*passant*) grab hold of; (relier) connect; ~ **le combiné** *or* **le téléphone** hang up. ● *vi* hang up. □ **se** ~ **à** *vpr* cling to; (se relier à) be connected to *ou* with.

race /ʀas/ *nf* race; (animale) breed; **de** ~ (*chien*) pedigree; (*cheval*) thoroughbred.

racheter /ʀaʃte/ [6] *vt* buy (back); (acheter encore) buy more; (*nouvel objet*) buy another; (*société*) buy out; ~ **des chaussettes** buy new socks. □ **se** ~ *vpr* make amends.

racial, ~**e** (*mpl* **-iaux**) /ʀasjal, -o/ *adj* racial.

racine /ʀasin/ *nf* root; ~ **carrée/ cubique** square/cube root.

racisme /ʀasism/ *nm* racism.
raciste *a & nmf* racist.

racket /ʀakɛt/ *nm* racketeering.

raclée /ʀakle/ *nf* 🔲 thrashing.

racler /ʀakle/ [1] *vt* scrape. □ **se** ~ *vpr* **se** ~ **la gorge** clear one's throat.

racolage /ʀakɔlaʒ/ *nm* soliciting.

raconter /ʀakɔ̃te/ [1] *vt* (*histoire*) tell; (*vacances*) tell about; (*vie, épisode*) describe; ~ **à qn que** tell sb that, say to sb that; **qu'est-ce que tu racontes?** what are you talking about?

radar /ʀadaʀ/ *nm* radar.

radeau (*pl* ~**x**) /ʀado/ *nm* raft.

radiateur /ʀadjatœʀ/ *nm* radiator; (électrique) heater.

radiation /ʀadjasjɔ̃/ *nf* radiation.

radical, ~**e** (*mpl* **-aux**) /ʀadikal, -o/ *adj* radical. ● *nm* (*pl* **-aux**) radical.

radieux, **-ieuse** /ʀadjø, -z/ *adj* radiant.

radin, ~**e** /ʀadɛ̃, -in/ *adj* 🔲 stingy 🔲.

radio /ʀadjo/ *nf* radio; **à la ~** on the radio; (radiographie) X-ray.

radioactif, -ive /ʀadjɔaktif, -v/ *adj* radioactive. **radioactivité** *nf* radioactivity.

radiocassette /ʀadjɔkasɛt/ *nf* radio cassette player.

radiodiffuser /ʀadjɔdifyze/ [1] *vt* broadcast.

radiographie /ʀadjɔgʀafi/ *nf* (photographie) X-ray.

radiomessageur /ʀadjɔmesaʒœʀ/ *nm* pager.

radis /ʀadi/ *nm* radish; **ne pas avoir un ~** 🔲 be broke.

radoter /ʀadɔte/ [1] *vi* 🔲 talk drivel.

radoucir (se) /(sə)ʀadusiʀ/ [2] *vpr* (humeur) improve; (temps) become milder.

rafale /ʀafal/ *nf* (de vent) gust; (de mitraillette) burst.

raffermir /ʀafɛʀmiʀ/ [2] *vt* strengthen. □ **se ~** *vpr* become stronger.

raffiné, ~e /ʀafine/ *adj* refined. **raffinement** *nm* refinement.

raffiner /ʀafine/ [1] *vt* refine. **raffinerie** *nf* refinery.

raffoler /ʀafɔle/ [1] *vt* 🔲 **~ de** be crazy about 🔲.

raffut /ʀafy/ *nm* 🔲 din.

rafle /ʀafl/ *nf* (police) raid.

rafraîchir /ʀafʀeʃiʀ/ [2] *vt* cool (down); (mur) give a fresh coat of paint to; (personne, mémoire) refresh. □ **se ~** *vpr* (boire) refresh oneself; (temps) get cooler.
rafraîchissant, ~e *adj* refreshing.

rafraîchissement /ʀafʀeʃismɑ̃/ *nm* (boisson) cold drink; **~s** refreshments.

ragaillardir /ʀagajaʀdiʀ/ [2] *vt* 🔲 cheer up.

rage /ʀaʒ/ *nf* rage; (maladie) rabies; **faire ~** (bataille, incendie) rage; (maladie) be rife; **~ de dents** raging toothache. **rageant, ~e** *adj* infuriating.

ragots /ʀago/ *nmpl* 🔲 gossip.

ragoût /ʀagu/ *nm* stew.

raid /ʀɛd/ *nm* (Mil) raid; (Sport) trek.

raide /ʀɛd/ *adj* stiff; (côte) steep; (corde) tight; (cheveux) straight.

● *adv* (monter, descendre) steeply.
raideur *nf* stiffness; steepness.

raidir /ʀediʀ/ [2] *vt* (corps) tense. □ **se ~** *vpr* tense up; (position) harden; (corde) tighten.

raie /ʀɛ/ *nf* (ligne) line; (bande) strip; (de cheveux) parting; (poisson) skate.

raifort /ʀɛfɔʀ/ *nm* horseradish.

rail /ʀaj/ *nm* rail, track; **le ~** (transport) rail.

raisin /ʀezɛ̃/ *nm* **le ~** grapes; **~ sec** raisin; **un grain de ~** a grape.

raison /ʀezɔ̃/ *nf* reason; **à ~ de** at the rate of; **avec ~** rightly; **avoir ~** be right (**de faire** to do); **avoir ~ de qn** get the better of sb; **donner ~ à** prove right; **en ~ de** because of; **~ de plus** all the more reason; **perdre la ~** lose one's mind.

raisonnable /ʀezɔnabl/ *adj* reasonable, sensible.

raisonnement /ʀezɔnmɑ̃/ *nm* reasoning; (propositions) argument.

raisonner /ʀezɔne/ [1] *vi* think. ● *vt* (personne) reason with.

rajeunir /ʀaʒœniʀ/ [2] *vt* **~ qn** make sb (look) younger; (moderniser) modernize; (Méd) rejuvenate. ● *vi* (personne) look younger.

rajuster /ʀaʒyste/ [1] *vt* straighten; (salaires) (re)adjust.

ralenti, ~e /ʀalɑ̃ti/ *adj* slow. ● *nm* (au cinéma) slow motion; **tourner au ~** tick over, idle.

ralentir /ʀalɑ̃tiʀ/ [2] *vt/i* slow down. □ **se ~** *vpr* slow down.

ralentisseur /ʀalɑ̃tisœʀ/ *nm* speed ramp.

râler /ʀale/ [1] *vi* groan; (protester 🔲) moan.

rallier /ʀalje/ [45] *vt* rally; (rejoindre) rejoin. □ **se ~** *vpr* rally; **se ~ à** (avis) come round to; (parti) join.

rallonge /ʀalɔ̃ʒ/ *nf* (de table) leaf; (de fil électrique) extension lead.
rallonger [40] *vt* lengthen; (séjour, fil, table) extend.

rallumer /ʀalyme/ [1] *vt* (feu) relight; (lampe) switch on again; (ranimer: fig) revive.

rallye /ʀali/ *nm* rally.

ramassage /ʀamasaʒ/ *nm* (cueillette) gathering; (d'ordures) collection; **~ scolaire** school bus service.

r

ramasser /Ramase/ [1] vt pick up; (récolter) gather; (recueillir, rassembler) collect. □ **se** ~ vpr huddle up, curl up.

rame /Ram/ nf (aviron) oar; (train) train.

ramener /Ramne/ [1] vt (rapporter, faire revenir) bring back; (reconduire) take back; ~ **à** (réduire à) reduce to. □ **se** ~ vpr Ⓘ turn up; **se** ~ **à** (problème) come down to.

ramer /Rame/ [1] vi row.

ramollir /Ramɔlir/ [2] vt soften. □ **se** ~ vpr become soft.

ramoneur /Ramɔnœr/ nm (chimney) sweep.

rampe /Rɑ̃p/ nf banisters; (pente) ramp; ~ **d'accès** (Auto) slip road; ~ **de lancement** launching pad.

ramper /Rɑ̃pe/ [1] vi crawl.

rancard /Rɑ̃kar/ nm Ⓘ date.

rancart /Rɑ̃kar/ nm **mettre** ou **jeter au** ~ Ⓘ scrap.

rance /Rɑ̃s/ adj rancid.

rancœur /Rɑ̃kœr/ nf resentment.

rançon /Rɑ̃sɔ̃/ nf ransom. **rançonner** [1] vt rob, extort money from.

rancune /Rɑ̃kyn/ nf grudge; **sans** ~**!** no hard feelings! **rancunier, -ière** adj vindictive.

randonnée /Rɑ̃dɔne/ nf walk, ramble; **la** ~ **à cheval** pony trekking; **faire une** ~ go walking ou rambling.

rang /Rɑ̃/ nm row; (hiérarchie, condition) rank; **se mettre en** ~ line up; **au premier** ~ in the first row; (fig) at the forefront; **de second** ~ (péj) second-rate.

rangée /Rɑ̃ʒe/ nf row.

rangement /Rɑ̃ʒmɑ̃/ nm (de pièce) tidying (up); (espace) storage space.

ranger /Rɑ̃ʒe/ [40] vt put away; (chambre) tidy (up); (disposer) place. □ **se** ~ vpr (véhicule) park; (s'écarter) stand aside; (conducteur) pull over; (s'assagir) settle down; **se** ~ **à** (avis) accept.

ranimer /Ranime/ [1] vt revive; (Méd) resuscitate. □ **se** ~ vpr come round.

rapace /Rapas/ nm bird of prey. ● adj grasping.

rapatriement /Rapatrimɑ̃/ nm repatriation. **rapatrier** [45] vt repatriate.

râpe /Rɑp/ nf (Culin) grater; (lime) rasp.

râpé, ~**e** /Rɑpe/ adj (vêtement) threadbare; (fromage) grated.

râper /Rɑpe/ [1] vt grate; (bois) rasp.

rapide /Rapid/ adj fast, rapid. ● nm (train) express (train); (cours d'eau) rapids (+ pl). **rapidement** adv fast, rapidly. **rapidité** nf speed.

rappel /Rapɛl/ nm recall; (deuxième avis) reminder; (de salaire) back pay; (Méd) booster; (de diplomate) recall; (de réservistes) call-up; (Théât) curtain call.

rappeler /Raple/ [38] vt (par téléphone) call back; (réserviste) call up; (diplomate) recall; (évoquer) recall; ~ **qch à qn** remind sb of sth. □ **se** ~ vpr remember, recall.

rapport /Rapɔr/ nm connection; (compte-rendu) report; (profit) yield; ~**s** (relations) relations; **en** ~ **avec** (accord) in keeping with; **mettre/se mettre en** ~ **avec** put/get in touch with; **par** ~ **à** (comparé à) compared with; (vis-à-vis de) with regard to; ~**s** (**sexuels**) intercourse.

rapporter /Rapɔrte/ [1] vt (ici) bring back; (là-bas) take back, return; (profit) bring in; (dire, répéter) report. ● vi (Comm) bring in a good return; (moucharder Ⓘ) tell tales. □ **se** ~ **à** vpr relate to; **s'en** ~ **à** rely on.

rapporteur, -euse /Rapɔrtœr, -øz/ nm,f (mouchard) tell-tale. ● nm protractor.

rapprochement /Raprɔʃmɑ̃/ nm reconciliation; (Pol) rapprochement; (rapport) connection; (comparaison) parallel.

rapprocher /Raprɔʃe/ vt move closer (**de** to); (réconcilier) bring together; (comparer) compare; (date, rendez-vous) bring forward. □ **se** ~ vpr get ou come closer (**de** to); (personnes, pays) come together; (s'apparenter) be close (**de** to).

rapt /Rapt/ nm abduction.

raquette /Rakɛt/ nf (de tennis) racket; (de ping-pong) bat.

rare /Rar/ adj rare; (insuffisant) scarce. **rarement** adv rarely, seldom.

rareté *nf* rarity; scarcity; (*objet*) rarity.

ras, ∼**e** /ʀɑ, ʀɑz/ *adv* **coupé** ∼ cut short. ● *adj* (*herbe, poil*) short; **à** ∼ **de terre** very close to the ground; **en avoir** ∼ **le bol** 🄸 be really fed up; ∼**e campagne** open country; **à** ∼ **bord** to the brim.

raser /ʀɑze/ [1] *vt* shave; (*cheveux, barbe*) shave off; (*frôler*) skim; (*abattre*) raze; (*ennuyer* 🄸) bore. □ **se** ∼ *vpr* shave.

rasoir /ʀɑzwaʀ/ *nm* razor. ● *a inv* 🄸 boring.

rassasier /ʀasazje/ [45] *vt* satisfy, fill up; **être rassasié de** have had enough of.

rassemblement /ʀasɑ̃bləmɑ̃/ *nm* gathering; (*manifestation*) rally.

rassembler /ʀasɑ̃ble/ [1] *vt* gather; (*forces, courage*) summon up; (*idées*) collect. □ **se** ∼ *vpr* gather.

rassis, ∼**e** /ʀasi, -z/ *adj* (*pain*) stale.

rassurer /ʀasyʀe/ [1] *vt* reassure. □ **se** ∼ *vpr* reassure oneself; **rassure-toi** don't worry.

rat /ʀa/ *nm* rat.

rate /ʀat/ *nf* spleen.

raté, ∼**e** /ʀate/ *nm, f* (*personne*) failure. ● *nm* **avoir des** ∼**s** (*voiture*) backfire.

râteau (*pl* ∼**x**) /ʀɑto/ *nm* rake.

râtelier /ʀɑtəlje/ *nm* hayrack; (*dentier* 🄸) dentures.

rater /ʀate/ [1] *vt* (*train, rendez-vous, cible*) miss; (*gâcher*) make a mess of, spoil; (*examen*) fail. ● *vi* fail.

ratio /ʀasjo/ *nm* ratio.

rationaliser /ʀasjɔnalize/ [1] *vt* rationalize.

rationnel, ∼**le** /ʀasjɔnɛl/ *adj* rational.

rationnement /ʀasjɔnmɑ̃/ *nm* rationing.

ratisser /ʀatise/ [1] *vt* rake; (*fouiller*) comb.

rattacher /ʀataʃe/ [1] *vt* (*lacets*) tie up again; (*ceinture de sécurité, collier*) refasten; (*relier*) link; (*incorporer*) join.

rattrapage /ʀatʀapaʒ/ *nm* (Comm) adjustment; **cours de** ∼ remedial lesson.

rattraper /ʀatʀape/ [1] *vt* catch; (*rejoindre*) catch up with; (*retard, erreur*) make up for. □ **se** ∼ *vpr* catch up; (se dédommager) make up for it; **se** ∼ **à** catch hold of.

rature /ʀatyʀ/ *nf* deletion.

rauque /ʀok/ *adj* raucous, harsh.

ravager /ʀavaʒe/ [40] *vt* devastate, ravage.

ravages /ʀavaʒ/ *nmpl* **faire des** ∼ wreak havoc.

ravaler /ʀavale/ [1] *vt* (*façade*) clean; (*colère*) swallow.

ravi, ∼**e** /ʀavi/ *adj* delighted (**que** that).

ravin /ʀavɛ̃/ *nm* ravine.

ravir /ʀaviʀ/ [2] *vt* delight; ∼ **qch à qn** rob sb of sth.

ravissant, ∼**e** /ʀavisɑ̃, -t/ *adj* beautiful.

ravisseur, **-euse** /ʀavisœʀ, -øz/ *nm, f* kidnapper.

ravitaillement /ʀavitajmɑ̃/ *nm* provision of supplies (**de** to); (*denrées*) supplies; ∼ **en essence** refuelling.

ravitailler /ʀavitaje/ [1] *vt* provide with supplies; (*avion*) refuel. □ **se** ∼ *vpr* stock up.

raviver /ʀavive/ [1] *vt* revive; (*feu, colère*) rekindle.

rayé, ∼**e** /ʀeje/ *adj* striped.

rayer /ʀeje/ [31] *vt* scratch; (*biffer*) cross out; '∼ **la mention inutile**' 'delete as appropriate'.

rayon /ʀejɔ̃/ *nm* ray; (*étagère*) shelf; (*de magasin*) department; (*de roue*) spoke; (*de cercle*) radius; ∼ **d'action** range; ∼ **de miel** honeycomb; ∼ **X** X-ray; **en connaître un** ∼ 🄸 know one's stuff 🄸.

rayonnement /ʀejɔnmɑ̃/ *nm* (*éclat*) radiance; (*influence*) influence; (*radiations*) radiation. **rayonner** [1] *vi* radiate; (*de joie*) beam; (*se déplacer*) tour around (*from a central point*).

rayure /ʀejyʀ/ *nf* scratch; (*dessin*) stripe; **à** ∼**s** striped.

raz-de-marée /ʀɑdmaʀe/ *nm inv* tidal wave; ∼ **électoral** electoral landslide.

réacteur /ʀeaktœʀ/ *nm* jet engine; (*nucléaire*) reactor.

r

réaction /ʀeaksjɔ̃/ *nf* reaction; ∼ **en chaîne** chain reaction; **moteur à** ∼ jet engine.

réagir /ʀeaʒiʀ/ [2] *vi* react; ∼ **sur** have an effect on.

réalisateur, -trice /ʀealizatœʀ, -tʀis/ *nm,f* (au cinéma) director; (TV) producer.

réalisation /ʀealizasjɔ̃/ *nf* (de rêve) fulfilment; (œuvre) achievement; (TV, cinéma) production; **projet en** ∼ project in progress.

réaliser /ʀealize/ [1] *vt* carry out; (*effort, bénéfice, achat*) make; (*rêve*) fulfil; (*film*) direct; (*capital*) realize; (se rendre compte de) realize. □ **se** ∼ *vpr* be fulfilled.

réalisme /ʀealism/ *nm* realism.

réaliste /ʀealist/ *adj* realistic. ● *nmf* realist.

réalité /ʀealite/ *nf* reality.

réanimation /ʀeanimasjɔ̃/ *nf* resuscitation; **service de** ∼ intensive care. **réanimer** [1] *vt* resuscitate.

réarmement /ʀeaʀmemã/ *nm* rearmament.

rébarbatif, -ive /ʀebaʀbatif, -v/ *adj* forbidding, off-putting.

rebelle /ʀəbɛl/ *adj* rebellious; (*soldat*) rebel; ∼ **à** resistant to. ● *nmf* rebel.

rébellion /ʀebeljɔ̃/ *nf* rebellion.

rebondir /ʀəbɔ̃diʀ/ [2] *vi* bounce; rebound; (fig) get moving again.

rebondissement /ʀəbɔ̃dismã/ *nm* (new) development.

rebord /ʀəbɔʀ/ *nm* edge; ∼ **de la fenêtre** window ledge *ou* sill.

rebours: à ∼ /aʀəbuʀ/ *loc* (*compter, marcher*) backwards.

rebrousse-poil: à ∼ /aʀəbʀus-pwal/ *loc* the wrong way; (fig) **prendre qn à** ∼ rub sb up the wrong way.

rebrousser /ʀəbʀuse/ [1] *vt* ∼ **chemin** turn back.

rebut /ʀəby/ *nm* **mettre** *ou* **jeter au** ∼ scrap.

rebutant, ∼e /ʀəbytã, -t/ *adj* off-putting.

recaler /ʀəkale/ [1] *vt* 🔲 fail; **se faire** ∼, **être recalé** fail.

recel /ʀəsɛl/ *nm* receiving. **receler** [6] *vt* (*objet volé*) receive; (cacher) conceal.

récemment /ʀesamã/ *adv* recently.

recensement /ʀəsãsmã/ *nm* census; (inventaire) inventory. **recenser** [1] *vt* (*population*) take a census of; (*objets*) list.

récent, ∼e /ʀesã, -t/ *adj* recent.

récépissé /ʀesepise/ *nm* receipt.

récepteur /ʀesɛptœʀ/ *nm* receiver.

réception /ʀesɛpsjɔ̃/ *nf* reception; (de courrier) receipt. **réceptionniste** *nmf* receptionist.

récession /ʀesesjɔ̃/ *nf* recession.

recette /ʀəsɛt/ *nf* (Culin) recipe; (argent) takings; ∼**s** (Comm) receipts.

receveur, -euse /ʀəs(ə)vœʀ, -øz/ *nm,f* (de bus) conductor; ∼ **des contributions** tax collector.

recevoir /ʀəs(ə)vwaʀ/ [52] *vt* receive, get; (*client, malade*) see; (*invités*) welcome, receive; **être reçu à un examen** pass an exam.

rechange: de ∼ /dəʀəʃãʒ/ *loc* (*roue, vêtements*) spare; (*solution*) alternative.

réchapper /ʀeʃape/ [1] *vt/i* ∼ **de** come through, survive.

recharge /ʀəʃaʀʒ/ *nf* (de stylo) refill.

réchaud /ʀeʃo/ *nm* stove.

réchauffement /ʀeʃofmã/ *nm* (de température) rise (**de** in); **le** ∼ **de la planète** global warming.

réchauffer /ʀeʃofe/ [1] *vt* warm up. □ **se** ∼ *vpr* warm oneself up; (*temps*) get warmer.

rêche /ʀɛʃ/ *adj* rough.

recherche /ʀəʃɛʀʃ/ *nf* search (**de** for); (raffinement) meticulousness; ∼**(s)** (Univ) research; ∼**s** (enquête) investigations; ∼ **d'emploi** job-hunting.

recherché, ∼e /ʀəʃɛʀʃe/ *adj* in great demand; (*style*) original, recherché (péj); ∼ **pour meurtre** wanted for murder.

rechercher /ʀəʃɛʀʃe/ [1] *vt* search for.

rechute /ʀəʃyt/ *nf* (Méd) relapse; **faire une** ∼ have a relapse.

récidiver /Residive/ [1] *vi* commit a second offence.

récif /Resif/ *nm* reef.

récipient /Resipjã/ *nm* container.

réciproque /ResipRɔk/ *adj* mutual, reciprocal.

réciproquement /ResipRɔkmã/ *adv* each other; **et ~** and vice versa.

récit /Resi/ *nm* (compte-rendu) account, story; (histoire) story.

réciter /Resite/ [1] *vt* recite.

réclamation /Reklamasjõ/ *nf* complaint; (demande) claim.

réclame /Reklam/ *nf* advertisement; **faire de la ~** advertise; **en ~** on offer.

réclamer /Reklame/ [1] *vt* call for, demand. ● *vi* complain.

reclus, ~e /Rəkly, -z/ *nm,f* recluse. ● *adj* reclusive.

réclusion /Reklyzjõ/ *nf* imprisonment.

récolte /Rekɔlt/ *nf* (action) harvest; (produits) crop, harvest; (fig) crop.
récolter [1] *vt* harvest, gather; (fig) collect, get.

recommandation /Rekɔmãdasjõ/ *nf* recommendation.

recommandé /Rəkɔmãde/ *nm* registered letter; **envoyer en ~** send by registered post.

recommander /Rəkɔmãde/ [1] *vt* recommend.

recommencer /Rəkɔmãse/ [10] *vt* (reprendre) begin *ou* start again; (refaire) repeat. ● *vi* start *ou* begin again; **ne recommence pas** don't do it again.

récompense /Rekõpãs/ *nf* reward; (prix) award. **récompenser** [1] *vt* reward (**de** for).

réconcilier /Rekõsilje/ [45] *vt* reconcile. □ **se ~** *vpr* become reconciled (**avec** with).

reconduire /RəkõdɥiR/ [17] *vt* see home; (à la porte) show out; (renouveler) renew.

réconfort /RekõfɔR/ *nm* comfort.

reconnaissance /Rekɔnɛsãs/ *nf* gratitude; (fait de reconnaître) recognition; (Mil) reconnaissance.
reconnaissant, ~e *adj* grateful (**de** for).

reconnaître /RəkɔnɛtR/ [18] *vt* recognize; (admettre) admit (**que** that); (Mil) reconnoitre; (enfant, tort) acknowledge. □ **se ~** *vpr* (s'orienter) know where one is; (l'un l'autre) recognize each other.

reconstituer /Rəkõstitɥe/ [1] *vt* reconstitute; (crime) reconstruct; (époque) recreate.

reconversion /RəkõvɛRsjõ/ *nf* (de main-d'œuvre) redeployment.

recopier /Rəkɔpje/ [45] *vt* copy out.

record /RəkɔR/ *nm* & *a inv* record.

recouper /Rəkupe/ [1] *vt* confirm. □ **se ~** *vpr* check, tally, match up.

recourbé, ~e /RəkuRbe/ *adj* curved; (nez) hooked.

recourir /RəkuRiR/ [20] *vi* **~ à** (expédient, violence) resort to; (remède, méthode) have recourse to.

recours /RəkuR/ *nm* resort; **avoir ~ à** have recourse to, resort to; **avoir ~ à qn** turn to sb.

recouvrer /Rəkuvre/ [1] *vt* recover.

recouvrir /RəkuvRiR/ [21] *vt* cover.

récréation /RekReasjõ/ *nf* recreation; (Scol) break; (US) recess.

recroqueviller (se) /(sə) RəkRɔkvije/ [1] *vpr* curl up.

recrudescence /RəkRydesãs/ *nf* new outbreak.

recrue /RəkRy/ *nf* recruit.

recrutement /RəkRytmã/ *nm* recruitment. **recruter** [1] *vt* recruit.

rectangle /Rɛktãgl/ *nm* rectangle.
rectangulaire *adj* rectangular.

rectifier /Rɛktifje/ [45] *vt* correct, rectify.

recto /Rɛkto/ *nm* **au ~** on the front of the page.

reçu, ~e /Rəsy/ *adj* accepted; (candidat) successful. ● *nm* receipt. ● ⇒RECEVOIR [52].

recueil /Rəkœj/ *nm* collection.

recueillement /Rəkœjmã/ *nm* meditation.

recueillir /RəkœjiR/ [25] *vt* collect; (prendre chez soi) take in. □ **se ~** *vpr* meditate.

recul /Rəkyl/ *nm* retreat; (éloignement) distance; (déclin) decline; **avoir un mouvement de ~** recoil; **être en ~** be

r

on the decline; **avec le ~** with hindsight.

reculé, **~e** /Rəkyle/ *adj* (*région*) remote.

reculer /Rəkyle/ [1] *vt* move back; (*véhicule*) reverse; (*différer*) postpone. ● *vi* move back; (*voiture*) reverse; (*armée*) retreat; (*régresser*) fall; (*céder*) back down; **~ devant** (fig) shrink from. □ **se ~** *vpr* move back.

récupération /RekypeRasjɔ̃/ *nf* (de l'organisme, de dette) recovery; (d'objets) salvage.

récupérer /RekypeRe/ [14] *vt* recover; (*vieux objets*) salvage. ● *vi* recover.

récurer /RekyRe/ [1] *vt* scour; **poudre à ~** scouring powder.

récuser /Rekyze/ [1] *vt* challenge. □ **se ~** *vpr* state that one is not qualified to judge.

recyclage /Rəsiklaʒ/ *nm* (de personnel) retraining; (de matériau) recycling.

recycler /Rəsikle/ [1] *vt* (*personne*) retrain; (*chose*) recycle. □ **se ~** *vpr* retrain.

rédacteur, **-trice** /RedaktœR, -tRis/ *nm,f* author, writer; (de journal, magazine) editor.

rédaction /Redaksjɔ̃/ *nf* writing; (Scol) essay, composition; (personnel) editorial staff.

redevable /Rədvabl/ *adj* **être ~ à qn de** (*argent*) owe sb; (fig) be indebted to sb for.

redevance /Rədvɑ̃s/ *nf* (de télévision) licence fee; (de téléphone) rental charge.

rédiger /Rediʒe/ [40] *vt* write; (*contrat*) draw up.

redire /RədiR/ [27] *vt* repeat; **avoir ou trouver à ~ à** find fault with.

redondant, **~e** /Rədɔ̃dɑ̃, -t/ *adj* superfluous.

redonner /Rədɔne/ [1] *vt* (rendre) give back; (donner davantage) give more; (donner de nouveau) give again.

redoubler /Rəduble/ [1] *vt* increase; (*classe*) repeat; **~ de prudence** be even more careful. ● *vi* (Scol) repeat a year; (s'intensifier) intensify.

redoutable /Rədutabl/ *adj* formidable.

redouter /Rədute/ [1] *vt* dread.

redressement /RədRɛsmɑ̃/ *nm* (reprise) recovery; **~ judiciaire** receivership.

redresser /RədRese/ [1] *vt* straighten (out *ou* up); (*situation*) right, redress; (*économie, entreprise*) turn around. □ **se ~** *vpr* (*personne*) straighten (oneself) up; (se remettre debout) stand up; (*pays, économie*) recover.

réduction /Redyksjɔ̃/ *nf* reduction.

réduire /Redɥir/ [17] *vt* reduce (**à** to). □ **se ~** *vpr* be reduced *ou* cut; **se ~ à** (revenir à) come down to.

réduit, **~e** /Redɥi, -t/ *adj* (*objet*) small-scale; (limité) limited. ● *nm* cubbyhole.

rééducation /Reedykasjɔ̃/ *nf* (de handicapé) rehabilitation; (Méd) physiotherapy. **rééduquer** [1] *vt* (*personne*) rehabilitate; (*membre*) restore normal movement to.

réel, **~le** /Reɛl/ *adj* real. ● *nm* reality. **réellement** *adv* really.

réexpédier /Reɛkspedje/ [45] *vt* forward; (retourner) send back.

refaire /RəfɛR/ [33] *vt* do again; (*erreur, voyage*) make again; (réparer) do up, redo.

réfectoire /RefɛktwaR/ *nm* refectory.

référence /RefeRɑ̃s/ *nf* reference.

référendum /RefeRɛ̃dɔm/ *nm* referendum.

référer /RefeRe/ [14] *vi* **en ~ à** consult. □ **se ~ à** *vpr* refer to, consult.

refermer /RəfɛRme/ [1] *vt* close (again). □ **se ~** *vpr* close (again).

réfléchi, **~e** /Refleʃi/ *adj* (*personne*) thoughtful; (*verbe*) reflexive.

réfléchir /RefleʃiR/ [2] *vi* think (**à**, **sur** about). ● *vt* reflect. □ **se ~** *vpr* be reflected.

reflet /Rəflɛ/ *nm* reflection; (nuance) sheen.

refléter /Rəflete/ [14] *vt* reflect. □ **se ~** *vpr* be reflected.

réflexe /Reflɛks/ *adj* reflex. ● *nm* reflex; (réaction) reaction.

réflexion /Reflɛksjɔ̃/ *nf* (pensée) thought, reflection; (remarque) remark, comment; **à la ~** on second thoughts.

refluer /Rəflye/ [1] *vi* flow back; (*foule*) retreat; (*inflation*) go down.

reflux /Rəfly/ *nm* (marée) ebb, tide.

réforme /RefɔRm/ *nf* reform. **réformer** [1] *vt* reform; (*soldat*) invalid out.

refouler /Rəfule/ [1] *vt* (*larmes*) hold back; (*désir*) repress; (*souvenir*) suppress.

refrain /RəfRɛ̃/ *nm* chorus; **le même ~** the same old story.

refréner /Rəfrene/ [14] *vt* curb, check.

réfrigérateur /RefRiʒeRatœR/ *nm* refrigerator.

refroidir /RəfRwadiR/ [2] *vt/i* cool (down). □ **se ~** *vpr* (*personne, temps*) get cold. **refroidissement** *nm* cooling; (rhume) chill.

refuge /Rəfyʒ/ *nm* refuge; (chalet) mountain hut.

réfugié, ~e /Refyʒje/ *nm,f* refugee. **réfugier (se)** [45] *vpr* take refuge.

refus /Rəfy/ *nm* refusal; **ce n'est pas de ~** Ⅱ I wouldn't say no.

refuser /Rəfyze/ [1] *vt* refuse (**de** to); (*client, spectateur*) turn away; (recaler) fail; (à un poste) turn down. □ **se ~ à** *vpr* (*évidence*) reject; **se ~ à faire** refuse to do.

regain /Rəgɛ̃/ *nm* **~ de** renewal *ou* revival of; (Comm) rise.

régal (*pl* **~s**) /Regal/ *nm* treat, delight.

régaler /Regale/ [1] *vt* **~ qn de** treat sb to. □ **se ~** *vpr* (de nourriture) **je me régale** it's delicious.

regard /RəgaR/ *nm* (expression, coup d'œil) look; (vue) eye; (yeux) eyes; **~ fixe** stare; **au ~ de** with regard to; **en ~ de** compared with.

regardant, ~e /RəgaRdɑ̃, -t/ *adj* **~ avec son argent** careful with money; **peu ~ (sur)** not fussy about.

regarder /RəgaRde/ [1] *vt* look at; (observer) watch; (considérer) consider; (concerner) concern; **~ fixement** stare at; **~ à** think about, pay attention to. ● *vi* look. □ **se ~** *vpr* (soi-même) look at oneself; (*personnes*) look at each other.

régate /Regat/ *nf* regatta.

régie /Reʒi/ *nf* **~ d'État** public corporation; (radio, TV) control room; (au cinéma) production; (Théât) stage management.

régime /Reʒim/ *nm* (organisation) system; (Pol) regime; (Méd) diet; (de moteur) speed; (de bananes) bunch; **se mettre au ~** go on a diet; **à ce ~** at this rate.

régiment /Reʒimɑ̃/ *nm* regiment.

région /Reʒjɔ̃/ *nf* region. **régional, ~e** (*mpl* **-aux**) *adj* regional.

régir /ReʒiR/ [2] *vt* govern.

régisseur /ReʒisœR/ *nm* (Théât) stage manager; **~ de plateau** (TV) floor manager; (au cinéma) studio manager.

registre /RəʒistR/ *nm* register.

réglage /Reglaʒ/ *nm* adjustment; (de moteur) tuning.

règle /Rɛgl/ *nf* rule; (instrument) ruler; **~s** (de femme) period; **en ~** in order.

réglé, ~e /Regle/ *adj* (vie) ordered; (arrangé) settled; (papier) ruled.

règlement /Rɛgləmɑ̃/ *nm* (règles) regulations; (solution) settlement; (paiement) payment. **réglementaire** *adj* (uniforme) regulation. **réglementation** *nf* regulation, rules. **réglementer** [1] *vt* regulate, control.

régler /Regle/ [14] *vt* settle; (*machine*) adjust; (programmer) set; (*facture*) settle; (*personne*) settle up with; **~ son compte à** Ⅱ settle a score with.

réglisse /Reglis/ *nf* liquorice.

règne /Rɛɲ/ *nm* reign; (végétal, animal, minéral) kingdom.

regret /RəgRɛ/ *nm* regret; **à ~** with regret.

regretter /RəgRete/ [1] *vt* regret; (*personne*) miss; (pour s'excuser) be sorry.

regrouper /RəgRupe/ [1] *vt* group *ou* bring together. □ **se ~** *vpr* gather *ou* group together.

régularité /RegylaRite/ *nf* regularity; (de rythme, progrès) steadiness; (de surface, écriture) evenness.

régulier, -ière /Regylje, -jɛR/ *adj* regular; (qualité, vitesse) steady, even; (*ligne, paysage*) even; (*légal*) legal; (*honnête*) honest.

rehausser /ʀəose/ [1] *vt* raise; (faire valoir) enhance.

rein /ʀɛ̃/ *nm* kidney; ~s (dos) small of the back.

reine /ʀɛn/ *nf* queen.

réinsertion /ʀeɛ̃sɛʀsjɔ̃/ *nf* reintegration.

réintégrer /ʀeɛ̃tegʀe/ [14] *vt* (*lieu*) return to; (Jur) reinstate; (*personne*) reintegrate.

réitérer /ʀeiteʀe/ [14] *vt* repeat.

rejaillir /ʀəʒajiʀ/ [2] *vi* ~ sur splash back onto; ~ sur qn (*succès*) reflect on sb.

rejet /ʀəʒɛ/ *nm* rejection; ~s (déchets) waste.

rejeter /ʀəʒte/ [38] *vt* throw back; (refuser) reject; (déverser) discharge; ~ une faute sur qn shift the blame for a mistake onto sb.

rejeton /ʀəʒtɔ̃/ *nm* (enfant Ⓘ) offspring (*inv*).

rejoindre /ʀəʒwɛ̃dʀ/ [22] *vt* go back to, rejoin; (rattraper) catch up with; (rencontrer) join, meet up with. ☐ **se** ~ *vpr* (*personnes*) meet up; (*routes*) join, meet.

réjoui, ~**e** /ʀeʒwi/ *adj* joyful.

réjouir /ʀeʒwiʀ/ [2] *vt* delight. ☐ **se** ~ *vpr* be delighted (de at).

réjouissances *nfpl* festivities.

réjouissant, ~**e** *adj* cheering.

relâche /ʀəlɑʃ/ *nm* (repos) break, rest; faire ~ (Théât) be closed.

relâcher /ʀəlɑʃe/ [1] *vt* slacken; (*personne*) release; (*discipline*) relax. ☐ **se** ~ *vpr* slacken.

relais /ʀəlɛ/ *nm* (Sport) relay; (hôtel) hotel; (intermédiaire) intermediary; prendre le ~ de take over from.

relancer /ʀəlɑ̃se/ [10] *vt* boost, revive; (renvoyer) throw back.

relatif, -**ive** /ʀəlatif, -v/ *adj* relative; ~ à relating to.

relation /ʀəlasjɔ̃/ *nf* relationship; (ami) acquaintance; (personne puissante) connection; ~s relations; ~s extérieures foreign affairs; en ~ avec qn in touch with sb.

relativement /ʀəlativmɑ̃/ *adv* relatively; ~ à in relation to.

relativité /ʀəlativite/ *nf* relativity.

relax /ʀəlaks/ *a inv* Ⓘ laid-back.

relaxer (**se**) /(sə)ʀəlakse/ [1] *vpr* relax.

relayer /ʀəleje/ [31] *vt* relieve; (*émission*) relay. ☐ **se** ~ *vpr* take over from one another.

reléguer /ʀəlege/ [14] *vt* relegate.

relent /ʀəlɑ̃/ *nm* stink; (fig) whiff.

relève /ʀəlɛv/ *nf* relief; prendre *ou* assurer la ~ take over (de from).

relevé, ~**e** /ʀəlve/ *adj* spicy. ● *nm* (de compteur) reading; (facture) bill; ~ bancaire, ~ de compte bank statement; faire le ~ de list.

relever /ʀəlve/ [6] *vt* pick up; (*personne tombée*) help up; (remonter) raise; (*col*) turn up; (*compteur*) read; (*défi*) accept; (relayer) relieve; (remarquer, noter) note; (*plat*) spice up; (rebâtir) rebuild; ~ de come within the competence of; (Méd) recover from. ☐ **se** ~ *vpr* (*personne*) get up (again); (*pays, économie*) recover.

relief /ʀəljɛf/ *nm* relief; mettre en ~ highlight.

relier /ʀəlje/ [45] *vt* link (up) (à to); (*livre*) bind.

religieux, -**ieuse** /ʀəliʒjø, -z/ *adj* religious. ● *nm*, *f* monk, nun.

religion /ʀəliʒjɔ̃/ *nf* religion.

reliure /ʀəljyʀ/ *nf* binding.

reluire /ʀəlɥiʀ/ [17] *vi* shine.

remaniement /ʀəmanimɑ̃/ *nm* revision; ~ ministériel cabinet reshuffle.

remarquable /ʀəmaʀkabl/ *adj* remarkable.

remarque /ʀəmaʀk/ *nf* remark; (par écrit) comment.

remarquer /ʀəmaʀke/ [1] *vt* notice; (dire) say; faire ~ point out (à to); se faire ~ draw attention to oneself; remarque(z) mind you.

remblai /ʀɑ̃blɛ/ *nm* embankment.

remboursement /ʀɑ̃buʀsəmɑ̃/ *nm* (d'emprunt, dette) repayment; (Comm) refund.

rembourser /ʀɑ̃buʀse/ [1] *vt* (*dette, emprunt*) repay; (*billet, frais*) refund; (*client*) give a refund to; (*ami*) pay back.

remède /Rəmɛd/ *nm* remedy; (médicament) medicine.

remédier /Rəmedje/ [45] *vi* ~ à remedy.

remerciements /Rəmɛrsimã/ *nmpl* thanks. **remercier** [45] *vt* thank (de for); (licencier) dismiss.

remettre /RəmɛtR/ [42] *vt* put back; (vêtement) put back on; (donner) hand over; (devoir, démission) hand in; (faire fonctionner) switch back on; (restituer) give back; (différer) put off; (ajouter) add; (se rappeler) remember; ~ en cause *ou* en question call into question. □ se ~ *vpr* (guérir) recover; se ~ au tennis take up tennis again; se ~ au travail get back to work; se ~ à faire start doing again; s'en ~ à leave it to.

remise /Rəmiz/ *nf* (abri) shed; (rabais) discount; (transmission) handing over; (ajournement) postponement; ~ en cause *ou* en question calling into question; ~ des prix prizegiving; ~ des médailles medals ceremony; ~ de peine remission.

remontant /Rəmõtã/ *nm* tonic.

remontée /Rəmõte/ *nf* ascent; (d'eau, de prix) rise; ~ mécanique ski lift.

remonte-pente (*pl* ~s) /Rəmõt-pãt/ *nm* ski tow.

remonter /Rəmõte/ [1] *vi* go *ou* come (back) up; (prix, niveau) rise (again); (revenir) go back (à to); ~ dans le temps go back in time. ● *vt* (rue, escalier) go *ou* come (back) up; (relever) raise; (montre) wind up; (objet démonté) put together again; (personne) buck up.

remontoir /RəmõtwaR/ *nm* winder.

remords /RəmɔR/ *nm* remorse; avoir du *or* des ~ feel remorse.

remorque /RəmɔRk/ *nf* trailer; en ~ on tow. **remorquer** [1] *vt* tow.

remous /Rəmu/ *nm* eddy; (de bateau) backwash; (fig) turmoil.

rempart /RãpaR/ *nm* rampart.

remplaçant, ~e /Rãplasã, -t/ *nm,f* replacement; (joueur) reserve, substitute.

remplacement /Rãplasmã/ *nm* replacement; faire des ~s do supply teaching. **remplacer** [10] *vt* replace.

rempli, ~e /Rãpli/ *adj* full (de of); (journée) busy.

remplir /RãpliR/ [2] *vt* fill (up); (formulaire) fill in *ou* out; (condition) fulfil; (devoir, tâche, rôle) carry out. □ se ~ *vpr* fill (up). **remplissage** *nm* filling; (de texte) padding.

remporter /RãpɔRte/ [1] *vt* take back; (victoire) win.

remuant, ~e /Rəmɥã, -t/ *adj* boisterous.

remue-ménage /Rəmymenaʒ/ *nm inv* commotion, bustle.

remuer /Rəmɥe/ [1] *vt* move; (thé, café) stir; (passé) rake up. ● *vi* move; (gigoter) fidget. □ se ~ *vpr* move.

rémunération /RemyneRasjõ/ *nf* payment.

renaissance /Rənɛsãs/ *nf* rebirth.

renard /RənaR/ *nm* fox.

renchérir /RãʃeRiR/ [2] *vi* (dans une vente) raise the bidding; ~ sur go one better than. ● *vt* increase, put up.

rencontre /RãkõtR/ *nf* meeting; (de routes) junction; (Mil) encounter; (match) match; (US) game.

rencontrer /Rãkõtre/ [1] *vt* meet; (heurter) hit; (trouver) find. □ se ~ *vpr* meet.

rendement /Rãdmã/ *nm* yield; (travail) output.

rendez-vous /Rãdevu/ *nm* appointment; (d'amoureux) date; (lieu) meeting-place; prendre ~ (avec) make an appointment (with).

rendormir (se) /(sə)RãdɔRmiR/ [46] *vpr* go back to sleep.

rendre /RãdR/ [3] *vt* give back, return; (donner en retour) return; (monnaie) give; (justice) dispense; (jugement) pronounce; ~ heureux/possible make happy/possible; (vomir 🔲) vomit; ~ compte de report on; ~ service (à) help; ~ visite à visit. ● *vi* (terres) yield; (activité) be profitable. □ se ~ *vpr* (capituler) surrender; (aller) go (à to); se ~ utile make oneself useful.

rêne /Rɛn/ *nf* rein.

renfermé, ~e /RãfɛRme/ *adj* withdrawn. ● *nm* sentir le ~ smell musty.

renflé, ~e /Rãfle/ *adj* bulging.

r

renforcer /Rɑ̃fɔRse/ [10] *vt* reinforce.

renfort /Rɑ̃fɔR/ *nm* reinforcement; **à grand ∼ de** with a great deal of.

renier /Rənje/ [45] *vt* (*personne, œuvre*) disown; (*foi*) renounce.

renifler /Rənifle/ [1] *vt/i* sniff.

renne /REn/ *nm* reindeer.

renom /Rənɔ̃/ *nm* renown; (*réputation*) reputation. **renommé, ∼e** *adj* famous. **renommée** *nf* (*célébrité*) fame; (*réputation*) reputation.

renoncement /Rənɔ̃smɑ̃/ *nm* renunciation.

renoncer /Rənɔ̃se/ [10] *vi* ∼ **à** (*habitude, ami*) give up, renounce; (*projet*) abandon; ∼ **à faire** abandon the idea of doing.

renouer /Rənwe/ [1] *vt* tie up (again); (*amitié*) renew; ∼ **avec qn** get back in touch with sb; (*après une dispute*) make up with sb.

renouveau (*pl* ∼**x**) /Rənuvo/ *nm* revival.

renouveler /Rənuvle/ [38] *vt* renew; (*réitérer*) repeat; (*remplacer*) replace. □ **se** ∼ *vpr* be renewed; (*incident*) recur, happen again.

renouvellement /Rənuvɛlmɑ̃/ *nm* renewal.

rénovation /Renɔvasjɔ̃/ *nf* (*d'édifice*) renovation; (*d'institution*) reform.

renseignement /Rɑ̃sɛɲ(ə)mɑ̃/ *nm* ∼(**s**) information; (**bureau des**) ∼**s** information desk; (**service des**) ∼**s téléphoniques** directory enquiries.

renseigner /Rɑ̃seɲe/ [1] *vt* inform, give information to. □ **se** ∼ *vpr* enquire, make enquiries, find out.

rentabilité /Rɑ̃tabilite/ *nf* profitability. **rentable** *adj* profitable.

rente /Rɑ̃t/ *nf* (private) income; (pension) annuity. **rentier, -ière** *nm,f* person of private means.

rentrée /Rɑ̃tre/ *nf* return; (revenu) income; **la** ∼ **parlementaire** the reopening of Parliament; **la** ∼ (**des classes**) the start of the new school year; **faire sa** ∼ make a comeback.

rentrer /Rɑ̃tRe/ [1] *vi* (*aux être*) go *ou* come back home, return home; (entrer) go *ou* come in; (entrer à nouveau) go *ou* come back in; (revenu)

come in; (*élèves*) go back (to school); ∼ **dans** (heurter) smash into; **tout est rentré dans l'ordre** everything is back to normal; ∼ **dans ses frais** break even. ● *vt* (*aux avoir*) bring in; (*griffes*) draw in; (*vêtement*) tuck in.

renverser /Rɑ̃vɛRse/ [1] *vt* knock over *ou* down; (*piéton*) knock down; (*liquide*) upset, spill; (mettre à l'envers) turn upside down; (*gouvernement*) overthrow; (inverser) reverse. □ **se** ∼ *vpr* (*véhicule*) overturn; (*verre, vase*) fall over.

renvoi /Rɑ̃vwa/ *nm* return; (d'employé) dismissal; (d'élève) expulsion; (report) postponement; (dans un livre, fichier) cross-reference; (rot) burp.

renvoyer /Rɑ̃vwaje/ [32] *vt* send back, return; (*employé*) dismiss; (*élève*) expel; (ajourner) postpone; (référer) refer; (réfléchir) reflect.

repaire /RəpER/ *nm* den.

répandre /RepɑdR/ [3] *vt* (liquide) spill; (étendre, diffuser) spread; (*odeur*) give off. □ **se** ∼ *vpr* spread; (*liquide*) spill; **se** ∼ **en injures** let out a stream of abuse.

répandu, ∼e /Repɑ̃dy/ *adj* widespread.

réparateur, -trice /RepaRatœR, -tRis/ *nm* engineer. **réparation** *nf* repair; (compensation) compensation.

réparer [1] *vt* repair, mend; (*faute*) make amends for; (remédier à) put right.

repartie /Rəparti/ *nf* retort; **avoir de la** ∼ always have a ready reply.

repartir /RəpartiR/ [46] *vi* start again; (*voyageur*) set off again; (s'en retourner) go back; (secteur économique) pick up again.

répartir /RepartiR/ [2] *vt* distribute; (partager) share out; (étaler) spread. **répartition** *nf* distribution.

repas /Rəpɑ/ *nm* meal.

repassage /Rəpasaʒ/ *nm* ironing.

repasser /Rəpase/ [1] *vi* come *ou* go back; ∼ **devant qch** go past sth again. ● *vt* (linge) iron; (examen) retake, resist; (*film*) show again.

repêcher /Rəpeʃe/ [1] *vt* recover, fish out; (*candidat*) allow to pass.

repentir¹ /RəpɑtiR/ *nm* repentance.

repentir² (se) /(sə)Rəpɑ̃tiR/ [2] *vpr* (Relig) repent (**de** of); **se ~ de** (regretter) regret.

répercuter /RepɛRkyte/ [1] *vt* (*bruit*) send back. □ **se ~** *vpr* echo; **se ~ sur** have repercussions on.

repère /RəpɛR/ *nm* mark; (jalon) marker; (événement) landmark; (référence) reference point.

repérer /Rəpere/ [14] *vt* locate, spot. □ **se ~** *vpr* get one's bearings.

répertoire /RepɛRtwaR/ *nm* (artistique) repertoire; (liste) directory; **~ téléphonique** telephone directory; (personnel) telephone book. **répertorier** [45] *vt* index.

répéter /Repete/ [14] *vt* repeat; (Théât) rehearse. ● *vi* rehearse. □ **se ~** *vpr* be repeated; (*personne*) repeat oneself.

répétition /Repetisjɔ̃/ *nf* repetition; (Théât) rehearsal.

répit /Repi/ *nm* respite, break.

replier /Rəplije/ [45] *vt* fold (up); (*ailes, jambes*) tuck in. □ **se ~** *vpr* withdraw (**sur soi-même** into oneself).

réplique /Replik/ *nf* reply; (riposte) retort; (objection) objection; (Théât) line; (copie) replica. **répliquer** [1] *vt/i* reply; (riposter) retort; (objecter) answer back.

répondeur /RepɔdœR/ *nm* answering machine.

répondre /RepɔdR/ [3] *vt* (*injure, bêtise*) reply with; **~ que** answer *ou* reply that; **~ à** (être conforme à) answer; (*affection, sourire*) return; (*avances, appel, critique*) respond to; **~ de** answer for. ● *vi* answer, reply; (être insolent) answer back; (réagir) respond (**à** to).

réponse /Repɔ̃s/ *nf* answer, reply; (fig) response.

report /RəpɔR/ *nm* (transcription) transfer; (renvoi) postponement.

reportage /Rəpɔrtaʒ/ *nm* report; (par écrit) article.

reporter¹ /Rəpɔrte/ [1] *vt* take back; (ajourner) put off; (transcrire) transfer. □ **se ~ à** *vpr* refer to.

reporter² /RəpɔrtɛR/ *nm* reporter.

repos /Rəpo/ *nm* rest; (paix) peace. **reposant, ~e** *adj* restful.

reposer /Rəpoze/ [1] *vt* put down again; (délasser) rest. ● *vi* rest (**sur** on); **laisser ~** (*pâte*) leave to stand. □ **se ~** *vpr* rest; **se ~ sur** rely on.

repousser /Rəpuse/ [1] *vt* push back; (écarter) push away; (dégoûter) repel; (décliner) reject; (ajourner) postpone, put back. ● *vi* grow again.

reprendre /RəprɑdR/ [50] *vt* take back; (*confiance, conscience*) regain; (*souffle*) get back; (*évadé*) recapture; (recommencer) resume; (redire) repeat; (modifier) alter; (blâmer) reprimand; **~ du pain** take some more bread; **on ne m'y reprendra pas** I won't be caught out again. ● *vi* (recommencer) resume; (*affaires*) pick up. □ **se ~** *vpr* (se ressaisir) pull oneself together; (se corriger) correct oneself.

représailles /Rəprezaj/ *nfpl* reprisals.

représentant, ~e /Rəprezɑ̃tɑ̃, -t/ *nm,f* representative.

représentation /Rəprezɑ̃tasjɔ̃/ *nf* representation; (Théât) performance.

représenter /Rəprezɑ̃te/ [1] *vt* represent; (figures) depict, show; (*pièce de théâtre*) perform. □ **se ~** *vpr* (s'imaginer) imagine.

répression /Represjɔ̃/ *nf* repression; (d'élan) suppression.

réprimande /Reprimɑ̃d/ *nf* reprimand.

réprimer /Reprime/ [1] *vt* (*peuple*) repress; (*sentiment*) suppress; (*fraude*) crack down on.

reprise /RəpRiz/ *nf* resumption; (Théât) revival; (TV) repeat; (de tissu) darn, mend; (essor) recovery; (Comm) part-exchange, trade-in; **à plusieurs ~s** on several occasions.

repriser /RəpRize/ [1] *vt* darn, mend.

reproche /RəpRɔʃ/ *nm* reproach; **faire des ~s à** find fault with.

reprocher /RəpRɔʃe/ [1] *vt* **~ qch à qn** reproach *ou* criticize sb for sth.

reproducteur, -trice /RəpRɔdyktœR, -tRis/ *adj* reproductive.

reproduire /RəpRɔdɥiR/ [17] *vt* reproduce; (répéter) repeat. □ **se ~** *vpr* reproduce; (se répéter) recur.

reptile /Rɛptil/ *nm* reptile.

repu, ~e /Rəpy/ *adj* satiated, replete.

républicain, ~e /ʁepyblikɛ̃, -ɛn/ *a & nm, f* republican.

république /ʁepyblik/ *nf* republic; ~ **populaire** people's republic.

répudier /ʁepydje/ [45] *vt* repudiate; (*droit*) renounce.

répugnance /ʁepyɲɑ̃s/ *nf* repugnance; (hésitation) reluctance; **avoir de la** ~ **pour** loathe.

répugnant, ~e *adj* repulsive.

répugner /ʁepyɲe/ [1] *vt* be repugnant to, disgust; ~ **à** (*effort, violence*) be averse to; ~ **à faire** be reluctant to do.

répulsion /ʁepylsjɔ̃/ *nf* repulsion.

réputation /ʁepytasjɔ̃/ *nf* reputation.

réputé, ~e /ʁepyte/ *adj* renowned (**pour** for); (*école, compagnie*) reputable; ~ **pour être** reputed to be.

requérir /ʁəkeʁiʁ/ [7] *vt* require, demand.

requête /ʁəkɛt/ *nf* request; (Jur) petition.

requin /ʁəkɛ̃/ *nm* shark.

requis, ~e /ʁəki, -z/ *adj* (exigé) required; (nécessaire) necessary.

RER *abrév m* (**réseau express régional**) *Parisian rapid transit rail system.*

rescapé, ~e /ʁɛskape/ *nm, f* survivor. ● *adj* surviving.

rescousse /ʁɛskus/ *nf* **à la** ~ to the rescue.

réseau (*pl* ~**x**) /ʁezo/ *nm* network; ~ **local** local area network, LAN; **le** ~ **des** ~**x** (Ordinat) Internet.

réservation /ʁezɛʁvasjɔ̃/ *nf* reservation, booking.

réserve /ʁezɛʁv/ *nf* reserve; (restriction) reservation, reserve; (indienne) reservation; (entrepôt) store-room; **en** ~ in reserve; **les** ~**s** (Mil) the reserves.

réserver /ʁezɛʁve/ [1] *vt* reserve; (*place*) book, reserve. □ **se** ~ *vpr* **se** ~ **qch** save sth for oneself; **se** ~ **pour** save oneself for; **se** ~ **le droit de** reserve the right to.

réservoir /ʁezɛʁvwaʁ/ *nm* tank; (lac) reservoir.

résidence /ʁezidɑ̃s/ *nf* residence; ~ **secondaire** second home; ~ **universitaire** hall of residence.

résident, ~e /ʁezidɑ̃, -t/ *nm, f* resident; (étranger) foreign resident.

résider /ʁezide/ [1] *vi* reside; ~ **dans qch** (*difficulté*) lie in.

résigner (se) /(sə)ʁeziɲe/ [1] *vpr* **se** ~ **à faire** resign oneself to doing.

résilier /ʁezilje/ [45] *vt* terminate.

résine /ʁezin/ *nf* resin.

résistance /ʁezistɑ̃s/ *nf* resistance; (fil électrique) element. **résistant**, ~e *adj* tough.

résister /ʁeziste/ [1] *vi* resist; ~ **à** (*agresseur, assaut, influence, tentation*) resist; (*corrosion, chaleur*) withstand.

résolu, ~e /ʁezɔly/ *adj* resolute; ~ **à faire** determined to do.
● ➝**RÉSOUDRE** [53].

résolution /ʁezɔlysjɔ̃/ *nf* (fermeté) resolution; (d'un problème) solving.

résonner /ʁezɔne/ [1] *vi* resound.

résorber /ʁezɔʁbe/ [1] *vt* reduce. □ **se** ~ *vpr* be reduced.

résoudre /ʁezudʁ/ [53] *vt* solve; (*crise, conflit*) resolve. □ **se** ~ **à** *vpr* (se décider) resolve to; (se résigner) resign oneself to.

respect /ʁɛspɛ/ *nm* respect.

respectabilité *nf* respectability.

respecter /ʁɛspɛkte/ [1] *vt* respect; **faire** ~ (*loi, décision*) enforce.

respectueux, -**euse** /ʁɛspɛktɥø, -z/ *adj* respectful; ~ **de l'environnement** environmentally friendly.

respiration /ʁɛspiʁasjɔ̃/ *nf* breathing; (haleine) breath. **respiratoire** *adj* respiratory, breathing.

respirer /ʁɛspiʁe/ [1] *vi* breathe; (se reposer) catch one's breath. ● *vt* breathe (in); (exprimer) radiate.

resplendir /ʁɛsplɑ̃diʁ/ [2] *vi* shine (**de** with). **resplendissant**, ~e *adj* brilliant, radiant.

responsabilité /ʁɛspɔ̃sabilite/ *nf* responsibility; (légale) liability.

responsable /ʁɛspɔ̃sabl/ *adj* responsible (**de** for); ~ **de** (chargé de) in charge of. ● *nmf* person in charge; (coupable) person responsible.

resquiller /ʁɛskije/ [1] *vi* ▯ (dans le train) fare-dodge; (au spectacle) get in without paying; (dans la queue) jump the queue.

ressaisir (se) /(sə)RəseziR/ [2] *vpr* pull oneself together; (*équipe sportive, valeurs boursières*) make a recovery.

ressemblance /Rəsãblãs/ *nf* resemblance.

ressemblant, ~e /Rəsãblã, -t/ *adj* être ~ (*portrait*) be a good likeness.

ressembler /Rəsãble/ [1] *vi* ~ à resemble, look like. □ se ~ *vpr* be alike; (physiquement) look alike.

ressentiment /Rəsãtimã/ *nm* resentment.

ressentir /RəsãtiR/ [46] *vt* feel. □ se ~ de *vpr* feel the effects of.

resserrer /Rəsere/ [1] *vt* tighten; (contracter) compress; (*vêtement*) take in. □ se ~ *vpr* tighten; (*route*) narrow; (se regrouper) move closer together.

ressort /Rəsɔʀ/ *nm* (objet) spring; (fig) energy; être du ~ de be the province of; (Jur) be within the jurisdiction of; en dernier ~ as a last resort.

ressortir /RəsɔʀtiR/ [46] *vi* go ou come back out; (se voir) stand out; (*film, disque*) be re-released; faire ~ bring out; il ressort que it emerges that. ● *vt* take out again; (redire) come out with again; (*disque, film*) re-release.

ressortissant, ~e /Rəsɔʀtisã, -t/ *nm, f* national.

ressource /RəsuRs/ *nf* resource; ~s resources; à bout de ~ at one's wits' end.

ressusciter /Resysite/ [1] *vi* come back to life. ● *vt* bring back to life; (fig) revive.

restant, ~e /Rɛstã, -t/ *adj* remaining. ● *nm* remainder.

restaurant /Rɛstɔrã/ *nm* restaurant.

restauration /Rɛstorasjɔ̃/ *nf* restoration; (hôtellerie) catering.

restaurer /Rɛstore/ [1] *vt* restore. □ se ~ *vpr* eat.

reste /Rɛst/ *nm* rest; (d'une soustraction) remainder; ~s remains (de of); (nourriture) leftovers; un ~ de poulet some left-over chicken; au ~, du ~ moreover, besides.

rester /Rɛste/ [1] *vi* (aux être) stay, remain; (subsister) be left, remain; il reste du pain there is some bread left (over); il me reste du pain I have some bread left (over); il me reste à it remains for me to; en ~ à go no further than; en ~ là stop there.

restituer /Rɛstitɥe/ [1] *vt* (rendre) return; (recréer) reproduce; (rétablir) reconstruct.

restreindre /Rɛstrɛ̃dr/ [22] *vt* restrict. □ se ~ *vpr* (dans les dépenses) cut back.

résultat /Rezylta/ *nm* result.

résulter /Rezylte/ [1] *vi* ~ de result from, be the result of.

résumé /Rezyme/ *nm* summary; en ~ in short; (pour finir) to sum up.

résumer [1] *vt* summarize.

résurrection /Rezyrɛksjɔ̃/ *nf* resurrection; (renouveau) revival.

rétablir /Retablir/ [2] *vt* restore; (*personne*) restore to health. □ se ~ *vpr* (ordre, silence) be restored; (guérir) recover. **rétablissement** *nm* restoration; (de malade, monnaie) recovery.

retard /Rətar/ *nm* lateness; (sur un programme) delay; (infériorité) backwardness; avoir du ~ be late; (*montre*) be slow; en ~ late; (retardé) behind; en ~ sur l'emploi du temps behind schedule; rattraper son ~ catch up; prendre du ~ fall behind.

retardataire /Rətardatɛr/ *nmf* latecomer. ● *adj* late.

retarder /Rətarde/ [1] *vt* ~ qn/qch delay sb/sth, hold sb/sth up; (par rapport à une heure convenue) make sb/sth late; (*montre*) put back. ● *vi* (*montre*) be slow; (*personne*) be out of touch.

retenir /Rətnir/ [58] *vt* hold back; (*souffle, attention, prisonnier*) hold; (*eau, chaleur*) retain, hold; (*larmes*) hold back; (garder) keep; (retarder) detain, hold up; (réserver) book; (se rappeler) remember; (déduire) deduct; (accepter) accept. □ se ~ *vpr* (se contenir) restrain oneself; se ~ à hold on to; se ~ de faire stop oneself from doing.

rétention /Retãsjɔ̃/ *nf* retention.

retentir /Rətɑ̃tiR/ [2] *vi* ring out, resound; ～ **sur** have an impact on.
retentissant, ～**e** *adj* resounding.
retentissement *nm* (effet) effect.

retenue /Rətny/ *nf* restraint; (somme) deduction; (Scol) detention.

réticent, ～**e** /Retisɑ̃, -t/ *adj* (hésitant) hesitant; (qui rechigne) reluctant; (réservé) reticent.

rétine /Retin/ *nf* retina.

retiré, ～**e** /RətiRe/ *adj* (vie) secluded; (lieu) remote.

retirer /RətiRe/ [1] *vt* (sortir) take out; (ôter) take off; (argent, offre, candidature) withdraw; (écarter) (main, pied) withdraw; (billet, bagages) collect, pick up; (avantage) derive; ～ **à qn** take away from sb. □ **se** ～ *vpr* withdraw, retire.

retombées /Rətɔ̃be/ *nfpl* (conséquences) effects; ～ **radioactives** nuclear fall-out.

retomber /Rətɔ̃be/ [1] *vi* (faire une chute) fall again; (retourner au sol) land, come down; ～ **dans** (erreur) fall back into.

retouche /Rətuʃ/ *nf* alteration; (de photo, tableau) retouch.

retour /RətuR/ *nm* return; **être de** ～ be back (**de** from); ～ **en arrière** flashback; **par** ～ **du courrier** by return of post; **en** ～ in return.

retourner /RətuRne/ [1] *vt* (aux avoir) turn over; (vêtement) turn inside out; (maison) turn upside down; (lettre, compliment) return; (émouvoir 🔢) shake, upset. ● *vi* (aux être) go back, return. □ **se** ～ *vpr* turn round; (dans son lit) twist and turn; **s'en** ～ go back; **se** ～ **contre** turn against.

retrait /RətRɛ/ *nm* withdrawal; (des eaux) receding; **être** (**situé**) **en** ～ (**de**) be set back (from).

retraite /RətRɛt/ *nf* retirement; (pension) (retirement) pension; (fuite, refuge) retreat; **mettre à la** ～ pension off; **prendre sa** ～ retire.

retraité, ～**e** /RətRete/ *adj* retired. ● *nm,f* (old-age) pensioner.

retrancher /RətRɑ̃ʃe/ [1] *vt* remove; (soustraire) deduct, subtract. □ **se** ～ *vpr* (Mil) entrench oneself; **se** ～ **derrière** take refuge behind.

retransmettre /RətRɑ̃smɛtR/ [42] *vt* broadcast.

rétrécir /RetResiR/ [2] *vt* make narrower; (vêtement) take in. ● *vi* (tissu) shrink. □ **se** ～ *vpr* (rue) narrow.

rétribution /Retribysjɔ̃/ *nf* payment.

rétroactif, **-ive** /Retroaktif, -v/ *adj* retrospective; **augmentation à effet** ～ backdated pay rise.

retrousser /Rətruse/ [1] *vt* pull up; (manche) roll up.

retrouvailles /Rətruvɑj/ *nfpl* reunion.

retrouver /Rətruve/ [1] *vt* find (again); (rejoindre) meet (again); (forces, calme) regain; (lieu) be back in; (se rappeler) remember. □ **se** ～ *vpr* find oneself (back); (se réunir) meet (again); (être présent) be found; **s'y** ～ (s'orienter, comprendre) find one's way; (rentrer dans ses frais 🔢) break even.

rétroviseur /RetRɔvizœR/ *nm* (Auto) (rear-view) mirror.

réunion /Reynjɔ̃/ *nf* meeting; (rencontre) gathering; (après une séparation) réunion; (d'objets) collection.

réunir /ReyniR/ [2] *vt* gather, collect; (rapprocher) bring together; (convoquer) call together; (raccorder) join; (qualités) combine. □ **se** ～ *vpr* meet.

réussi, ～**e** /Reysi/ *adj* successful.

réussir /ReysiR/ [2] *vi* succeed, be successful; ～ **à faire** succeed in doing, manage to do; ～ **à un examen** pass an exam; ～ **à qn** (méthode) work well for sb; (climat, mode de vie) agree with sb. ● *vt* (vie) make a success of.

réussite /Reysit/ *nf* success; (jeu) patience.

revaloir /RəvalwaR/ [60] *vt* **je vous revaudrai cela** (en mal) I'll pay you back for this; (en bien) I'll repay you some day.

revanche /Rəvɑ̃ʃ/ *nf* revenge; (Sport) return *ou* revenge match; **en** ～ on the other hand.

rêvasser /Rɛvase/ [1] *vi* daydream.

rêve /Rɛv/ *nm* dream; **faire un** ～ have a dream.

réveil /revɛj/ *nm* waking up, (fig) awakening; (pendule) alarm clock.

réveillé, **~e** /reveje/ *adj* awake.

réveille-matin /revɛjmatɛ̃/ *nm inv* alarm clock.

réveiller /reveje/ [1] *vt* wake (up); (*sentiment, souvenir*) awaken; (*curiosité*) arouse. □ **se ~** *vpr* wake up.

réveillon /revɛjɔ̃/ *nm* (Noël) Christmas Eve; (nouvel an) New Year's Eve. **réveillonner** [1] *vi* see Christmas *ou* the New Year in.

révéler /revele/ [14] *vt* reveal. □ **se ~** *vpr* be revealed; **se ~ facile** turn out to be easy, prove easy.

revendeur, **-euse** /rəvɑ̃dœr, -øz/ *nm,f* dealer, stockist; **~ de drogue** drug dealer.

revendication /rəvɑ̃dikasjɔ̃/ *nf* claim. **revendiquer** [1] *vt* claim.

revendre /rəvɑ̃dr/ [3] *vt* sell (again); **avoir de l'énergie à ~** have energy to spare.

revenir /rəvnir/ [58] *vi* (*aux être*) come back, return (**à** to); **~ à** (*activité*) go back to; (se résumer à) come down to; (échoir à) fall to; **~ à 100 francs** cost 100 francs; **~ de** (*maladie, surprise*) get over; **~ sur ses pas** retrace one's steps; **faire ~** (Culin) brown; **ça me revient!** now I remember!; **je n'en reviens pas!** 🗊 I can't get over it!

revenu /rəvny/ *nm* income; (de l'État) revenue.

rêver /reve/ [1] *vt/i* dream (**à** of; **de faire** of doing).

réverbère /revɛrbɛr/ *nm* street lamp.

révérence /reverɑ̃s/ *nf* reverence; (salut d'homme) bow; (salut de femme) curtsy.

rêverie /revri/ *nf* daydream; (activité) daydreaming.

revers /rəvɛr/ *nm* reverse; (de main) back; (d'étoffe) wrong side; (de veste) lapel; (de pantalon) turn-up; (de manche) cuff; (tennis) backhand; (fig) set-back.

revêtement /rəvɛtmɑ̃/ *nm* covering; (de route) surface; **~ de sol** floor covering. **revêtir** [61] *vt* cover; (*habit*) put on; (prendre, avoir) assume.

rêveur, **-euse** /revœr, -øz/ *adj* dreamy. ● *nm,f* dreamer.

réviser /revize/ [1] *vt* revise; (*machine, véhicule*) service. **révision** *nf* revision; service.

revivre /rəvivr/ [62] *vi* come alive again. ● *vt* relive.

révocation /revɔkasjɔ̃/ *nf* repeal; (d'un fonctionnaire) dismissal.

revoir¹ /rəvwar/ [63] *vt* see (again); (réviser) revise.

revoir² /rəvwar/ *nm* **au ~** goodbye.

révolte /revɔlt/ *nf* revolt. **révolté**, **~e** *nm,f* rebel.

révolter /revɔlte/ [1] *vt* appal, revolt. □ **se ~** *vpr* revolt.

révolu, **~e** /revɔly/ *adj* past; **avoir 21 ans ~s** be over 21 years of age.

révolution /revɔlysjɔ̃/ *nf* revolution. **révolutionnaire** *a & nmf* revolutionary. **révolutionner** [1] *vt* revolutionize.

revolver /revɔlvɛr/ *nm* revolver, gun.

révoquer /revɔke/ [1] *vt* repeal; (*fonctionnaire*) dismiss.

revue /rəvy/ *nf* (examen, défilé) review; (magazine) magazine; (spectacle) variety show.

rez-de-chaussée /redʃose/ *nm inv* ground floor; (US) first floor.

RF *abrév f* (**République Française**) French Republic.

rhinocéros /rinɔserɔs/ *nm* rhinoceros.

rhubarbe /rybarb/ *nf* rhubarb.

rhum /rɔm/ *nm* rum.

rhumatisme /rymatism/ *nm* rheumatism.

rhume /rym/ *nm* cold; **~ des foins** hay fever.

ri /ri/ ⇒RIRE [54].

ricaner /rikane/ [1] *vi* snigger.

riche /riʃ/ *adj* rich (**en** in). ● *nmf* rich man, rich woman.

richesse /riʃɛs/ *nf* wealth; (de sol, décor) richness; **~s** wealth; (ressources) resources.

ride /rid/ *nf* wrinkle; (sur l'eau) ripple.

rideau (*pl* **~x**) /rido/ *nm* curtain; (métallique) shutter; (fig) screen.

ridicule /ridikyl/ *adj* ridiculous. ● *nm* (d'une situation) absurdity; (le

grotesque) le ~ ridicule. **ridiculiser**
[1] *vt* ridicule.

rien /ʀjɛ̃/ *pron* nothing; (quoi que ce
soit) anything; **de ~!** don't mention
it!; ~ **de bon** nothing good; **elle n'a
~ dit** she didn't say anything; ~
d'autre/de plus nothing else/more; ~
du tout nothing at all; ~ **que**
(seulement) just, only; **trois fois ~**
next to nothing; **il n'y est pour ~** he
has nothing to do with it; ~ **à faire!**
(c'est impossible) it's no good!; (refus) no
way! 🔲. ●*nm* **un ~ de** a touch of;
être puni pour un ~ be punished for
the slightest thing; **se disputer pour
un ~** fight over nothing; **en un ~ de
temps** in next to no time.

rieur, -euse /ʀijœʀ, -øz/ *adj*
cheerful; (*yeux*) laughing.

rigide /ʀiʒid/ *adj* rigid.

rigolade /ʀigɔlad/ *nf* fun.

rigoler /ʀigɔle/ [1] *vi* laugh; (s'amuser)
have some fun; (plaisanter) joke.

rigolo, ~te /ʀigɔlo, -ɔt/ *adj* 🔲
funny. ●*nm,f* 🔲 joker.

rigoureux, -euse /ʀiguʀø, -z/ *adj*
rigorous; (*hiver*) harsh; (sévère)
strict; (*travail, recherches*)
meticulous.

rigueur /ʀigœʀ/ *nf* rigour; **à la ~** at
a pinch; **être de ~** be obligatory;
tenir ~ à qn de qch bear sb a grudge
for sth.

rime /ʀim/ *nf* rhyme.

rimer /ʀime/ [1] *vi* rhyme (**avec**
with); **cela ne rime à rien** it makes no
sense.

rinçage /ʀɛ̃saʒ/ *nm* rinse; (action)
rinsing.

rincer /ʀɛ̃se/ [10] *vt* rinse.

riposte /ʀipɔst/ *nf* retort.

riposter /ʀipɔste/ [1] *vi* retaliate; ~
à (*attaque*) counter; (*insulte*) reply to.
●*vt* retort (**que** that).

rire /ʀiʀ/ [54] *vi* laugh (**de** at);
(plaisanter) joke; (s'amuser) have fun;
c'était pour ~ it was a joke. ●*nm*
laugh; **des ~s** laughter.

risée /ʀize/ *nf* **la ~ de** the laughing-
stock of.

risque /ʀisk/ *nm* risk. **risqué, ~e**
adj risky; (osé) daring.

risquer /ʀiske/ [1] *vt* risk (**de faire** of
doing); (être passible de) face; **il risque**

de pleuvoir it might rain; **tu risques
de te faire mal** you might hurt
yourself. ◻ **se ~ à/dans** *vpr*
venture to/into.

ristourne /ʀistuʀn/ *nf* discount.

rite /ʀit/ *nm* rite; (habitude) ritual.
rituel, ~le *a* & *nm* ritual.

rivage /ʀivaʒ/ *nm* shore.

rival, ~e (*mpl* **-aux**) /ʀival, -o/ *a* &
nm,f rival. **rivaliser** [1] *vi* compete
(**avec** with). **rivalité** *nf* rivalry.

rive /ʀiv/ *nf* (de fleuve) bank; (de lac)
shore.

riverain, ~e /ʀivʀɛ̃, -ɛn/ *adj*
riverside. ●*nm,f* riverside resident;
(d'une rue) resident.

rivière /ʀivjɛʀ/ *nf* river.

riz /ʀi/ *nm* rice. **rizière** *nf* paddy
field.

robe /ʀɔb/ *nf* (de femme) dress; (de
juge) robe; (de cheval) coat; ~ **de
chambre** dressing-gown.

robinet /ʀɔbinɛ/ *nm* tap; (US) faucet.

robot /ʀɔbo/ *nm* robot; ~ **ménager**
food processor.

robuste /ʀɔbyst/ *adj* robust.

roche /ʀɔʃ/ *nf* rock.

rocher /ʀɔʃe/ *nm* rock.

rock /ʀɔk/ *nm* (Mus) rock.

rodage /ʀɔdaʒ/ *nm* **en ~** (Auto)
running in.

roder /ʀɔde/ [1] *vt* (Auto) run in; **être
rodé** (*personne*) have got the hang of
things.

rôder /ʀode/ [1] *vi* roam; (*suspect*)
prowl.

rogne /ʀɔɲ/ *nf* 🔲 anger; **en ~** in a
temper.

rogner /ʀɔɲe/ [1] *vt* trim; ~ **sur** cut
down on.

rognon /ʀɔɲɔ̃/ *nm* (Culin) kidney.

roi /ʀwa/ *nm* king; **les R~ mages** the
Magi; **la fête des R~** Twelfth Night.

rôle /ʀol/ *nm* role, part.

romain, ~e /ʀɔmɛ̃, -ɛn/ *adj* Roman.
R~, ~e *nm,f* Roman. **romaine** *nf*
(laitue) cos.

roman /ʀɔmɑ̃/ *nm* novel; (genre)
fiction.

romance /ʀɔmɑ̃s/ *nf* ballad.

romancier, -ière /ʀɔmɑ̃sje, -jɛʀ/
nm,f novelist.

romanesque /ʀɔmanɛsk/ *adj* romantic; (*fantastique*) fantastic; (*récit*) fictional; **œuvres** ~**s** novels, fiction.

romantique /ʀɔmãtik/ *a & nmf* romantic. **romantisme** *nm* romanticism.

rompre /ʀɔ̃pʀ/ [3] *vt* break; (*relations*) break off. ● *vi* (se séparer) break up; ~ **avec** (*fiancé*) break up with; (*parti*) break away from; (*tradition*) break with. □ **se** ~ *vpr* break.

ronce /ʀɔ̃s/ *nf* bramble.

rond, ~**e** /ʀɔ̃, -d/ *adj* round; (gras) plump; (ivre 🗩) drunk. ● *nm* (cercle) ring; (tranche) slice; **en** ~ in a circle; **il n'a pas un** ~ 🗩 he hasn't got a penny.

ronde /ʀɔ̃d/ *nf* (de policier) beat; (de soldat, gardien) watch; (Mus) semibreve.

rondelle /ʀɔ̃dɛl/ *nf* (Tech) washer; (tranche) slice.

rondement /ʀɔ̃dmã/ *adv* promptly; (franchement) frankly.

rondeur /ʀɔ̃dœʀ/ *nf* roundness; (franchise) frankness; (embonpoint) plumpness.

rondin /ʀɔ̃dɛ̃/ *nm* log.

rond-point (*pl* ronds-points) /ʀɔ̃pwɛ̃/ *nm* roundabout; (US) traffic circle.

ronfler /ʀɔ̃fle/ [1] *vi* snore; (*moteur*) purr.

ronger /ʀɔ̃ʒe/ [40] *vt* gnaw (at); (*vers, acide*) eat into. □ **se** ~ *vpr* **se** ~ **les ongles** bite one's nails.

rongeur /ʀɔ̃ʒœʀ/ *nm* rodent.

ronronner /ʀɔ̃ʀɔne/ [1] *vi* purr.

rosbif /ʀɔsbif/ *nm* roast beef.

rose /ʀoz/ *nf* rose. ● *a & nm* pink.

rosé, ~**e** /ʀoze/ *adj* pinkish. ● *nm* rosé.

roseau (*pl* ~**x**) /ʀozo/ *nm* reed.

rosée /ʀoze/ *nf* dew.

rosier /ʀozje/ *nm* rose bush.

rossignol /ʀɔsiɲɔl/ *nm* nightingale.

rotatif, -ive /ʀɔtatif, -v/ *adj* rotary.

roter /ʀɔte/ [1] *vi* 🗩 burp.

rôti /ʀoti/ *nm* joint; (cuit) roast; ~ **de porc** roast pork.

rotin /ʀɔtɛ̃/ *nm* (rattan) cane.

rôtir /ʀotiʀ/ [2] *vt* roast.

rôtissoire /ʀotiswaʀ/ *nf* roasting spit.

rotule /ʀɔtyl/ *nf* kneecap.

rouage /ʀwaʒ/ *nm* (Tech) wheel; **les** ~**s** the works; (d'une organisation: fig) wheels.

roucouler /ʀukule/ [1] *vi* coo.

roue /ʀu/ *nf* wheel; ~ **dentée** cog (wheel); ~ **de secours** spare wheel.

rouer /ʀwe/ [1] *vt* ~ **de coups** thrash.

rouge /ʀuʒ/ *adj* red; (*fer*) red-hot. ● *nm* red; (vin) red wine; (fard) blusher; ~ **à lèvres** lipstick. ● *nmf* (Pol) red. **rouge-gorge** (*pl* **rouges-gorges**) *nm* robin.

rougeole /ʀuʒɔl/ *nf* measles (+ *sg*).

rouget /ʀuʒɛ/ *nm* red mullet.

rougeur /ʀuʒœʀ/ *nf* redness; (tache) red blotch.

rougir /ʀuʒiʀ/ [2] *vi* turn red; (de honte) blush.

rouille /ʀuj/ *nf* rust. **rouillé**, ~**e** *adj* rusty.

rouiller /ʀuje/ [1] *vi* rust. □ **se** ~ *vpr* get rusty.

rouleau (*pl* ~**x**) /ʀulo/ *nm* roll; (outil, vague) roller; ~ **à pâtisserie** rolling pin; ~ **compresseur** steamroller.

roulement /ʀulmã/ *nm* rotation; (bruit) rumble; (alternance) rotation; (de tambour) roll; ~ **à billes** ball-bearing; **travailler par** ~ work in shifts.

rouler /ʀule/ [1] *vt* roll; (*ficelle, manches*) roll up; (*pâte*) roll out; (duper 🗩) cheat. ● *vi* (*véhicule, train*) go, travel; (*conducteur*) drive. □ **se** ~ **dans** *vpr* (*herbe*) roll in; (*couverture*) roll oneself up in.

roulette /ʀulɛt/ *nf* (de meuble) castor; (de dentiste) drill; (jeu) roulette; **comme sur des** ~**s** very smoothly.

roulotte /ʀulɔt/ *nf* caravan.

roumain, ~**e** /ʀumɛ̃, -ɛn/ *adj* Romanian. **R**~, ~**e** *nm, f* Romanian.

Roumanie /ʀumani/ *nf* Romania.

rouquin, ~**e** /ʀukɛ̃, -in/ 🗩 *adj* red-haired. ● *nm, f* redhead.

rouspéter /ʀuspete/ [14] *vi* 🗩 grumble, moan.

rousse /ʀus/ ⇒ROUX.

r

roussir /Rusir/ [2] *vt* scorch. ● *vi* turn brown.

route /Rut/ *nf* road; (Naut, Aviat) route; (direction) way; (voyage) journey; (chemin: fig) path; **en ∼** on the way; **en ∼!** let's go!; **mettre en ∼** start; **∼ nationale** trunk road, main road; **se mettre en ∼** set out; **il y a une heure de ∼** it's an hour's journey.

routier, -ière /Rutje, -jɛR/ *adj* road. ● *nm* long-distance lorry *ou* truck driver; (restaurant) transport café; (US) truck stop.

routine /Rutin/ *nf* routine.

roux, rousse /Ru, Rus/ *adj* red, russet; (*personne*) red-haired; (*chat*) ginger. ● *nm,f* redhead.

royal, ∼e (*mpl* **-aux**) /Rwajal, -jo/ *adj* royal; (*cadeau*) fit for a king.

royaume /Rwajom/ *nm* kingdom.

Royaume-Uni /Rwajomyni/ *nm* United Kingdom.

royauté /Rwajote/ *nf* royalty.

ruban /Rybã/ *nm* ribbon; (de chapeau) band; **∼ adhésif** sticky tape; **∼ magnétique** magnetic tape.

rubéole /Rybeɔl/ *nf* German measles (+ *sg*).

rubis /Rybi/ *nm* ruby; (de montre) jewel.

rubrique /RybRik/ *nf* heading; (article) column.

ruche /Ryʃ/ *nf* beehive.

rude /Ryd/ *adj* (au toucher) rough; (pénible) tough; (grossier) coarse; (fameux 🔢) tremendous.

rudement /Rydmã/ *adv* (*frapper*) hard; (*traiter*) harshly; (très 🔢) really.

rudimentaire /RydimãtɛR/ *adj* rudimentary.

rue /Ry/ *nf* street.

ruée /Rɥe/ *nf* rush.

ruer /Rɥe/ [1] *vi* (*cheval*) buck. □ **se ∼** *vpr* rush (**dans** into; **vers** towards); **se ∼ sur** pounce on.

rugby /Rygbi/ *nm* rugby.

rugir /RyʒiR/ [2] *vi* roar.

rugueux, -euse /Rygø, -z/ *adj* rough.

ruine /Rɥin/ *nf* ruin; **en ∼(s)** in ruins. **ruiner** [1] *vt* ruin.

ruisseau (*pl* **∼x**) /Rɥiso/ *nm* stream; (rigole) gutter.

rumeur /RymœR/ *nf* (nouvelle) rumour; (son) murmur, hum.

ruminer /Rymine/ [1] *vi* (*animal*) ruminate; (méditer) meditate.

rupture /RyptyR/ *nf* break; (action) breaking; (de contrat) breach; (de pourparlers) breakdown; (de relations) breaking off; (de couple, coalition) break-up.

rural, ∼e (*mpl* **-aux**) /RyRal, -o/ *adj* rural.

ruse /Ryz/ *nf* cunning; **une ∼** a trick, a ruse. **rusé, ∼e** *adj* cunning.

russe /Rys/ *adj* Russian. ● *nm* (Ling) Russian. **R∼** *nmf* Russian.

Russie /Rysi/ *nf* Russia.

rustique /Rystik/ *adj* rustic.

rythme /Ritm/ *nm* rhythm; (vitesse) rate; (de la vie) pace. **rythmique** *adj* rhythmical.

Ss

s' /s/ ⇒SE.

sa /sa/ ⇒SON[1].

SA *abrév f* (**société anonyme**) PLC.

sabbatique /sabatik/ *adj* (*année*) sabbatical year.

sable /sabl/ *nm* sand; **∼s mouvants** quicksands. **sabler** *vt* [1] grit.

sablier /sablije/ *nm* (Culin) eggtimer.

sablonneux, -euse /sablɔnø, -z/ *adj* sandy.

sabot /sabo/ *nm* (de cheval) hoof; (chaussure) clog; (de frein) shoe; **∼ de Denver®** (wheel) clamp.

saboter /sabɔte/ [1] *vt* sabotage; (bâcler) botch.

sac /sak/ *nm* bag; (grand, en toile) sack; **mettre à ∼** (*maison*) ransack; (*ville*) sack; **∼ à dos** rucksack; **∼ à main** handbag; **∼ de couchage** sleeping-bag; **mettre dans le même ∼** lump together.

saccadé, ∼e /sakade/ *adj* jerky.

saccager /sakaʒe/ [40] *vt* (abîmer) wreck; (*maison*) ransack; (*ville, pays*) sack.

saccharine /sakaʀin/ *nf* saccharin.

sachet /saʃɛ/ *nm* (small) bag; (d'aromates) sachet; ~ **de thé** tea-bag.

sacoche /sakɔʃ/ *nf* bag; (de vélo) saddlebag.

sacre /sakʀ/ *nm* (de roi) coronation; (d'évêque) consecration. **sacré**, ~**e** *adj* sacred; (maudit 🗉) damned. **sacrement** *nm* sacrament. **sacrer** [1] *vt* crown; consecrate.

sacrifice /sakʀifis/ *nm* sacrifice.

sacrifier /sakʀifje/ [45] *vt* sacrifice; ~ **à** conform to. □ **se** ~ *vpr* sacrifice oneself.

sacrilège /sakʀilɛʒ/ *nm* sacrilege. ● *adj* sacrilegious.

sadique /sadik/ *adj* sadistic. ● *nmf* sadist.

sage /saʒ/ *adj* wise; (docile) good, well behaved. ● *nm* wise man.

sage-femme (*pl* **sages-femmes**) /saʒfam/ *nf* midwife.

sagesse /saʒɛs/ *nf* wisdom.

Sagittaire /saʒitɛʀ/ *nm* le ~ Sagittarius.

saignant, ~**e** /sɛɲɑ̃, -t/ *adj* (Culin) rare.

saigner /seɲe/ [1] *vt/i* bleed; ~ **du nez** have a nosebleed.

saillant, ~**e** /sajɑ̃, -t/ *adj* prominent.

sain, ~**e** /sɛ̃, sɛn/ *adj* healthy; (*moralement*) sane; ~ **et sauf** safe and sound.

saindoux /sɛ̃du/ *nm* lard.

saint, ~**e** /sɛ̃, -t/ *adj* holy; (bon, juste) saintly. ● *nm,f* saint. **Saint-Esprit** *nm* Holy Spirit. **sainteté** *nf* holiness; (d'un lieu) sanctity. **Sainte Vierge** *nf* Blessed Virgin. **Saint-Sylvestre** *nf* New Year's Eve.

sais /sɛ/ ⇒SAVOIR [55].

saisie /sezi/ *nf* (Jur) seizure; (Comput) keyboarding; ~ **de données** data capture.

saisir /seziʀ/ [2] *vt* grab (hold of); (*proie*) seize; (*occasion, biens*) seize; (comprendre) grasp; (frapper) strike; (Ordinat) keyboard, capture; **saisi de** (*peur*) stricken by, overcome by. □ **se** ~ **de** *vpr* seize. **saisissant**, ~**e** *adj* (spectacle) gripping.

saison /sɛzɔ̃/ *nf* season; **la morte** ~ the off season. **saisonnier, -ière** *adj* seasonal.

sait /sɛ/ ⇒SAVOIR [55].

salade /salad/ *nf* (plat) salad; (plante) lettuce. **saladier** *nm* salad bowl.

salaire /salɛʀ/ *nm* wages (+ *pl*), salary.

salarié, ~**e** /salaʀje/ *adj* wage-earning. ● *nm,f* wage earner.

sale /sal/ *adj* dirty; (mauvais) nasty.

salé, ~**e** /sale/ *adj* (goût) salty; (plat) salted; (opposé à sucré) savoury; (grivois 🗉) spicy; (excessif 🗉) steep. **saler** [1] *vt* salt.

saleté /salte/ *nf* dirtiness; (crasse) dirt; (obscénité) obscenity; ~**(s)** (camelote) rubbish; (détritus) mess.

salir /saliʀ/ [2] *vt* (make) dirty; (*réputation*) tarnish. □ **se** ~ *vpr* get dirty. **salissant**, ~**e** *adj* dirty; (*étoffe*) easily dirtied.

salive /saliv/ *nf* saliva.

salle /sal/ *nf* room; (grande, publique) hall; (de restaurant) dining room; (Théât, cinéma) auditorium; **cinéma à trois** ~**s** three-screen cinema; ~ **à manger** dining room; ~ **d'attente** waiting room; ~ **de bains** bathroom; ~ **de séjour** living room; ~ **de classe** classroom; ~ **d'embarquement** departure lounge; ~ **d'opération** operating theatre; ~ **des ventes** saleroom.

salon /salɔ̃/ *nm* lounge; (de coiffure, beauté) salon; (exposition) show; ~ **de thé** tea-room.

salopette /salɔpɛt/ *nf* dungarees (+ *pl*); (d'ouvrier) overalls (+ *pl*).

saltimbanque /saltɛ̃bɑ̃k/ *nmf* (street) acrobat.

salubre /salybʀ/ *adj* healthy.

saluer /salɥe/ [1] *vt* greet; (en partant) take one's leave of; (de la tête) nod to; (de la main) wave to; (Mil) salute; (accueillir favorablement) welcome.

salut /saly/ *nm* greeting; (de la tête) nod; (de la main) wave; (Mil) salute; (rachat) salvation. ● *interj* (bonjour 🗉) hello; (au revoir 🗉) bye.

salutation /salytasjɔ̃/ *nf* greeting.

samedi /samdi/ *nm* Saturday.

SAMU /samy/ *abrév m* (**Service d'assistance médicale d'urgence**) ≈ mobile accident unit.

sanction /sãksjɔ̃/ *nf* sanction. **sanctionner** [1] *vt* sanction; (*punir*) punish.

sandale /sãdal/ *nf* sandal.

sang /sã/ *nm* blood; **se faire du mauvais ~ *ou* un ~ d'encre** be worried stiff. **sang-froid** *nm inv* self-control. **sanglant, ~e** *adj* bloody.

sangle /sãgl/ *nf* strap.

sanglier /sãglije/ *nm* wild boar.

sanglot /sãglo/ *nm* sob. **sangloter** [1] *vi* sob.

sanguin, ~e /sãgɛ̃, -in/ *adj* (*groupe*) blood.

sanguinaire /sãginɛR/ *adj* bloodthirsty.

sanisette® /sanizɛt/ *nf* automatic public toilet.

sanitaire /sanitɛR/ *adj* (*directives*) health; (*conditions*) sanitary; (*appareils, installations*) bathroom, sanitary. **sanitaires** *nmpl* bathroom.

sans /sã/ *prép* without; **~ ça, ~ quoi** otherwise; **~ arrêt** nonstop; **~ encombre/faute/tarder** without incident/fail/delay; **~ fin/goût/limite** endless/tasteless/limitless; **~ importance/pareil/précédent/travail** unimportant/unparalleled/ unprecedented/unemployed; **j'ai aimé mais ~ plus** it was good, it wasn't great.

sans-abri /sãzabRi/ *nmf inv* homeless person.

sans-gêne /sãʒɛn/ *a inv* inconsiderate, thoughtless. ● *nm inv* thoughtlessness.

sans-papiers /sãpapje/ *nm inv* illegal immigrant.

santé /sãte/ *nf* health; **à ta *ou* votre ~!** cheers!

saoul, ~e /su, sul/ ⇒SOÛL.

sapin /sapɛ̃/ *nm* fir(tree); **~ de Noël** Christmas tree.

sarcasme /saRkasm/ *nm* sarcasm. **sarcastique** *adj* sarcastic.

sardine /saRdin/ *nf* sardine.

sas /sas/ *nm* (Naut, Aviat) airlock.

satané, ~e /satane/ *adj* Ⓘ damned.

satellite /satelit/ *nm* satellite.

satin /satɛ̃/ *nm* satin.

satire /satiR/ *nf* satire.

satisfaction /satisfaksjɔ̃/ *nf* satisfaction.

satisfaire /satisfɛR/ [33] *vt* satisfy. ● *vi* **~ à** fulfil. **satisfaisant, ~e** *adj* (*acceptable*) satisfactory. **satisfait, ~e** *adj* satisfied (**de** with).

saturer /satyRe/ [1] *vt* saturate.

sauce /sos/ *nf* sauce; **~ tartare** tartar sauce. **saucière** *nf* sauceboat.

saucisse /sosis/ *nf* sausage.

saucisson /sosisɔ̃/ *nm* (slicing) sausage.

sauf[1] /sof/ *prép* except; **~ erreur** if I'm not mistaken; **~ imprévu** unless anything unforeseen happens; **~ avis contraire** unless otherwise stated.

sauf[2], **-ve** /sof, sov/ *adj* safe, unharmed.

sauge /soʒ/ *nf* (Culin) sage.

saule /sol/ *nm* willow; **~ pleureur** weeping willow.

saumon /somɔ̃/ *nm* salmon. ● *a inv* salmon-(pink).

sauna /sona/ *nm* sauna.

saupoudrer /supudRe/ [1] *vt* sprinkle (**de** with).

saut /so/ *nm* jump; **faire un ~ chez qn** pop round to sb's (place); **le ~** (Sport) jumping; **~ en hauteur/ longueur** high/long jump; **~ périlleux** somersault; **au ~ du lit** on getting up.

sauté, ~e /sote/ *a & nm* (Culin) sauté.

saute-mouton /sotmutɔ̃/ *nm inv* leap-frog.

sauter /sote/ [1] *vi* jump; (*exploser*) blow up; (*fusible*) blow; (*se détacher*) come off; **faire ~** (*détruire*) blow up; (*fusible*) blow; (*casser*) break; **~ à la corde** skip; **~ aux yeux** be obvious; **~ au cou de qn** fling one's arms round sb; **~ sur une occasion** jump at an opportunity. ● *vt* jump (over); (*page, classe*) skip.

sauterelle /sotʀɛl/ *nf* grasshopper.

sautiller /sotije/ [1] *vi* hop.

sauvage /sovaʒ/ *adj* wild; (primitif, cruel) savage; (farouche) unsociable; (illégal) unauthorized. ● *nmf* unsociable person; (brute) savage.

sauve /sov/ ⇨SAUF².

sauvegarder /sovgaʀde/ [1] *vt* safeguard; (Ordinat) back up.

sauver /sove/ [1] *vt* save; (d'un danger) rescue, save; (matériel) salvage. □ **se** ~ *vpr* (fuir) run away; (partir Ⅰ) be off. **sauvetage** *nm* rescue. **sauveteur** *nm* rescuer. **sauveur** *nm* saviour.

savant, ~**e** /savã, -t/ *adj* learned; (habile) skilful. ● *nm* scientist.

saveur /savœʀ/ *nf* flavour; (fig) savour.

savoir /savwaʀ/ [55] *vt* know; **elle sait conduire/nager** she can drive/swim; **faire** ~ **à qn que** inform sb that; (**pas**) **que je sache** (not) as far as I know; **à** ~ namely. ● *nm* learning.

savon /savɔ̃/ *nm* soap; **passer un** ~ **à qn** Ⅰ give sb a telling-off. **savonnette** *nf* bar of soap. **savonneux, -euse** *adj* soapy.

savourer /savuʀe/ [1] *vt* savour. **savoureux, -euse** *adj* tasty; (fig) spicy.

scandale /skãdal/ *nm* scandal; (tapage) uproar; (en public) noisy scene; **faire** ~ shock people; **faire un** ~ make a scene. **scandaleux, -euse** *adj* scandalous. **scandaliser** [1] *vt* scandalize, shock.

scander /skãde/ [1] *vt* (vers) scan; (slogan) chant.

scandinave /skãdinav/ *adj* Scandinavian. **S**~ *nmf* Scandinavian.

Scandinavie /skãdinavi/ *nf* Scandinavia.

scarabée /skaʀabe/ *nm* beetle.

sceau (*pl* ~**x**) /so/ *nm* seal.

scélérat /seleʀa/ *nm* scoundrel.

sceller /sele/ [1] *vt* seal; (fixer) cement.

scène /sɛn/ *nf* scene; (estrade, art dramatique) stage; **mettre en** ~ (pièce) stage; (film) direct; **mise en** ~

direction; ~ **de ménage** domestic dispute.

scepticisme /sɛptisism/ *nm* scepticism.

sceptique /sɛptik/ *adj* sceptical. ● *nmf* sceptic.

schéma /ʃema/ *nm* diagram. **schématique** *adj* schematic; (sommaire) sketchy. **schématiser** [1] *vt* simplify.

schizophrène /skizɔfʀɛn/ *a* & *nmf* schizophrenic.

sciatique /sjatik/ *adj* (nerf) sciatic. ● *nf* sciatica.

scie /si/ *nf* saw.

sciemment /sjamã/ *adv* knowingly.

science /sjãs/ *nf* science; (savoir) knowledge.

science-fiction /sjãsfiksjɔ̃/ *nf* science fiction.

scientifique /sjãtifik/ *adj* scientific. ● *nmf* scientist.

scier /sje/ [45] *vt* saw.

scintiller /sɛ̃tije/ [1] *vi* glitter; (étoile) twinkle.

scission /sisjɔ̃/ *nf* split.

sclérose /skleʀoz/ *nf* sclerosis; ~ **en plaques** multiple sclerosis.

scolaire /skɔlɛʀ/ *adj* school. **scolarisé**, ~**e** *adj* going to school. **scolarité** *nf* schooling.

score /skɔʀ/ *nm* score.

scorpion /skɔʀpjɔ̃/ *nm* scorpion; **le S**~ Scorpio.

scotch /skɔtʃ/ *nm* (boisson) Scotch (whisky); (ruban adhésif)® Sellotape®.

scout, ~**e** /skut/ *nm* & *a* scout.

scrupule /skʀypyl/ *nm* scruple. **scrupuleux, -euse** *adj* scrupulous.

scruter /skʀyte/ [1] *vt* examine, scrutinize.

scrutin /skʀytɛ̃/ *nm* (vote) ballot; (élections) polls (+ pl).

sculpter /skylte/ [1] *vt* sculpt, carve. **sculpteur** *nm* sculptor. **sculpture** *nf* sculpture.

S

. . . .

se, s' /sə, s/

s' before vowel or mute h.

● *pronom*

····▶ himself, (féminin) herself; (indéfini) oneself; (non humain) itself; (au pluriel) themselves; ~ **laver les mains** wash one's hands; (réciproque) each other, one another; **ils se détestent** they hate each other.

> ⚠ The translation of **se** will vary according to which verb it is associated with. You should therefore refer to the verb to find it. For example, **se promener, se taire** will be treated respectively under **promener** and **taire**.

séance /seᾶs/ *nf* session; (Théât, cinéma) show; ~ **de pose** sitting; ~ **tenante** forthwith.

seau (*pl* ~**x**) /so/ *nm* bucket, pail.

sec, sèche /sɛk, sɛʃ/ *adj* dry; (*fruits*) dried; (*coup, bruit*) sharp; (*cœur*) hard; (*whisky*) neat. ● *nm* **à** ~ (sans eau) dry; (sans argent) broke; **au** ~ in a dry place.

sèche-cheveux /sɛʃʃəvø/ *nm inv* hairdrier.

sèchement /sɛʃmᾶ/ *adv* drily.

sécher /seʃe/ [14] *vt/i* dry; (*cours*: 🄵) skip; (ne pas savoir 🄵) be stumped. ▢ **se** ~ *vpr* dry oneself.

sécheresse /seʃʀɛs/ *nf* (de climat) dryness; (temps sec) drought. **séchoir** *nm* drier.

second, ~e /səgɔ̃, -d/ *a & nm,f* second. ● *nm* (adjoint) second in command; (étage) second floor. **secondaire** *adj* secondary. **seconde** *nf* (instant) second; (vitesse) second gear.

seconder /səgɔ̃de/ [1] *vt* assist.

secouer /səkwe/ [1] *vt* shake; (*poussière, torpeur*) shake off. ▢ **se** ~ *vpr* 🄵 (se dépêcher) get a move on; (réagir) shake oneself up.

secourir /səkuʀiʀ/ [20] *vt* assist, help. **secouriste** *nmf* first-aid worker.

secours /səkuʀ/ *nm* assistance, help; **au** ~! help!; **de** ~ (sortie) emergency; (équipe, opération) rescue. ● *nmpl* (Méd) first aid.

secousse /səkus/ *nf* jolt, jerk; (séisme) tremor.

secret, -ète /səkʀɛ, -t/ *adj* secret. ● *nm* secret; (discrétion) secrecy; **le** ~ **professionnel** professional confidentiality; ~ **de Polichinelle** open secret; **en** ~ in secret, secretly.

secrétaire /səkʀetɛʀ/ *nmf* secretary; ~ **de direction** personal assistant. ● *nm* (meuble) writing-desk; ~ **d'État** junior minister.

secrétariat /səkʀetaʀja/ *nm* secretarial work; (bureau) secretariat.

sectaire /sɛktɛʀ/ *adj* sectarian.

secte /sɛkt/ *nf* sect.

secteur /sɛktœʀ/ *nm* area; (Comm) sector; (circuit: Électr) mains (+ *pl*).

section /sɛksjɔ̃/ *nf* section; (Scol) stream; (Mil) platoon. **sectionner** [1] *vt* sever.

sécuriser /sekyʀize/ [1] *vt* reassure.

sécurité /sekyʀite/ *nf* security; (absence de danger) safety; **en** ~ safe, secure. **Sécurité sociale** *nf* social services, social security services.

sédatif /sedatif/ *nm* sedative.

sédentaire /sedᾶtɛʀ/ *adj* sedentary.

séducteur, -trice /sedyktœʀ, -tʀis/ *adj* seductive. ● *nm,f* seducer. **séduction** *nf* seduction; (charme) charm.

séduire /seduiʀ/ [17] *vt* charm; (plaire à) appeal to; (sexuellement) seduce. **séduisant, ~e** *adj* attractive.

ségrégation /segʀegasjɔ̃/ *nf* segregation.

seigle /sɛgl/ *nm* rye.

seigneur /sɛɲœʀ/ *nm* lord; **le S**~ the Lord.

sein /sɛ̃/ *nm* breast; **au** ~ **de** within.

séisme /seism/ *nm* earthquake.

seize /sɛz/ *a & nm* sixteen.

séjour /seʒuʀ/ *nm* stay; (pièce) living room. **séjourner** [1] *vi* stay.

sel /sɛl/ *nm* salt; (piquant) spice.

sélectif, -ive /selɛktif, -v/ *adj* selective.

sélection /selɛksjɔ̃/ *nf* selection. **sélectionner** [1] *vt* select.

selle /sɛl/ *nf* saddle; **aller à la** ~ have a bowel movement; ~**s** (Méd) stools.

sellette /sɛlɛt/ *nf* sur la ~
(*personne*) in the hot seat.

selon /səlɔ̃/ *prép* according to; ~
que depending on whether.

semaine /səmɛn/ *nf* week; **en** ~
during the week.

sémantique /semãtik/ *adj*
semantic. ● *nf* semantics.

semblable /sãblabl/ *adj* similar (à
to). ● *nm* fellow (creature).

semblant /sãblã/ *nm* **faire** ~ **de**
pretend to; **un** ~ **de** a semblance of.

sembler /sãble/ [1] *vi* seem (à to;
que that); **il me semble que** it seems
to me that.

semelle /səmɛl/ *nf* sole; ~
compensée wedge heel.

semence /s(ə)mãs/ *nf* seed.

semer /s(ə)me/ [6] *vt* (*graine, doute*)
sow; (jeter, parsemer) strew; (*personne*
🆕) lose; ~ **la panique** spread panic.

semestre /səmɛstʀ/ *nm* half-year;
(Univ) semester. **semestriel**, ~**le**
adj (revue) biannual; (examen) end-of-
semester.

séminaire /seminɛʀ/ *nm* (Relig)
seminary; (Univ) seminar.

semi-remorque /s(ə)miʀ(ə)mɔʀk/
nm articulated lorry.

semis /s(ə)mi/ *nm* (terrain) seedbed;
(plant) seedling.

semoule /s(ə)mul/ *nf* semolina.

sénat /sena/ *nm* senate. **sénateur**
nm senator.

sénile /senil/ *adj* senile.

sens /sãs/ *nm* (Méd) sense;
(signification) meaning, sense; (direction)
direction; **à mon** ~ to my mind; **à** ~
unique (*rue*) one-way; **ça n'a pas de**
~ it doesn't make sense; ~ **commun**
common sense; ~ **giratoire**
roundabout; ~ **interdit** no-entry sign;
(rue) one-way street; **dans le** ~ **des**
aiguilles d'une montre clockwise;
dans le ~ **inverse des aiguilles d'une**
montre anticlockwise; ~ **dessus**
dessous upside down; ~ **devant**
derrière back to front.

sensation /sãsasjɔ̃/ *nf* feeling,
sensation; **faire** ~ create a sensation.
sensationnel, ~**le** *adj* sensational.

sensé, ~**e** /sãse/ *adj* sensible.

sensibiliser /sãsibilize/ [1] *vt* ~
l'opinion increase people's
awareness (**à qch** to sth).

sensibilité /sãsibilite/ *nf*
sensitivity. **sensible** *adj* sensitive
(**à** to); (appréciable) noticeable.
sensiblement *adv* noticeably; (à
peu près) more or less.

sensoriel, ~**le** /sãsɔʀjɛl/ *adj*
sensory.

sensualité /sãsɥalite/ *nf*
sensuousness; sensuality. **sensuel**,
~**le** *adj* sensual.

sentence /sãtãs/ *nf* sentence.

senteur /sãtœʀ/ *nf* scent.

sentier /sãtje/ *nm* path.

sentiment /sãtimã/ *nm* feeling;
faire du ~ sentimentalize; **j'ai le** ~
que... I get the feeling that...
sentimental, ~**e** (*mpl* -**aux**) *adj*
sentimental.

sentir /sãtiʀ/ [46] *vt* feel; (*odeur*)
smell; (pressentir) sense; ~ **la lavande**
smell of lavender; **je ne peux pas le**
~ 🆕 I can't stand him. ● *vi* smell.
□ **se** ~ *vpr* **se** ~ **fier/mieux** feel
proud/better.

séparation /sepaʀasjɔ̃/ *nf*
separation.

séparatiste /sepaʀatist/ *a & nmf*
separatist.

séparé, ~**e** /sepaʀe/ *adj* separate;
(*conjoints*) separated.

séparer /sepaʀe/ [1] *vt* separate; (en
deux) split. □ **se** ~ *vpr* separate, part
(**de** from); (se détacher) split; **se** ~ **de**
(se défaire de) part with.

sept /sɛt/ *a & nm* seven.

septante /sɛptãt/ *a & nm* seventy.

septembre /sɛptãbʀ/ *nm*
September.

septentrional, ~**e** (*mpl* -**aux**)
/sɛptãtʀijɔnal, -o/ *adj* northern.

septième /sɛtjɛm/ *a & nmf*
seventh.

sépulture /sepyltyʀ/ *nf* burial; (lieu)
burial place.

séquelles /sekɛl/ *nfpl* (maladie)
aftereffects; (fig) aftermath (+ *sg*).

séquence /sekãs/ *nf* sequence.

séquestrer /sekɛstʀe/ [1] *vt* confine
(illegally).

sera, serait /səʀa, səʀɛ/ ⇒ÊTRE [4].

S

serbe /sɛʀb/ *adj* Serbian. **S~** *nmf* Serbian.

Serbie /sɛʀbi/ *nf* Serbia.

serein, ~e /səʀɛ̃, -ɛn/ *adj* serene.

sérénité /seʀenite/ *nf* serenity.

sergent /sɛʀʒɑ̃/ *nm* sergeant.

série /seʀi/ *nf* series (+ *sg*); (d'objets) set; **de ~** (*véhicule etc.*) standard; **fabrication** *ou* **production en ~** mass production.

sérieusement /seʀjøzmɑ̃/ *adv* seriously.

sérieux, -ieuse /seʀjø, -z/ *adj* serious; (digne de confiance) reliable; (*chances, raison*) good. ● *nm* seriousness; **garder son ~** keep a straight face; **prendre au ~** take seriously.

serin /səʀɛ̃/ *nm* canary.

seringue /səʀɛ̃g/ *nf* syringe.

serment /sɛʀmɑ̃/ *nm* oath; (promesse) vow.

sermon /sɛʀmɔ̃/ *nm* sermon. **sermonner** [1] *vt* lecture.

séropositif, -ive /seʀopozitif, -v/ *adj* HIV positive.

serpent /sɛʀpɑ̃/ *nm* snake; **~ à sonnettes** rattlesnake.

serpillière /sɛʀpijɛʀ/ *nf* floorcloth.

serre /sɛʀ/ *nf* (de jardin) greenhouse; (griffe) claw.

serré, ~e /seʀe/ *adj* (habit, nœud, écrou) tight; (*personnes*) packed, crowded; (*lutte, mailles*) close; (*écriture*) cramped; (*cœur*) heavy.

serrer /seʀe/ [1] *vt* (saisir) grip; (presser) squeeze; (*vis, corde, ceinture*) tighten; (*poing, dents*) clench; **~ qn dans ses bras** hug sb; **~ les rangs** close ranks; **~ qn** (vêtement) be tight on sb; **~ qn de près** follow sb closely; **~ la main à** shake hands with. ● *vi* **~ à droite** keep over to the right. □ **se ~** *vpr* (se rapprocher) squeeze (up) (**contre** against).

serrure /seʀyʀ/ *nf* lock. **serrurier** *nm* locksmith.

servante /sɛʀvɑ̃t/ *nf* (maid)servant.

serveur, -euse /sɛʀvœʀ, -øz/ *nm,f* (homme) waiter; (femme) waitress. ● *nm* (Ordinat) server.

serviable /sɛʀvjabl/ *adj* helpful.

service /sɛʀvis/ *nm* service; (fonction, temps de travail) duty; (pourboire) service (charge); (dans une société) department; **~ (non) compris** service (not) included; **être de ~** be on duty; **pendant le ~** (when) on duty; **rendre ~ à qn** be a help to sb; **~ à thé** tea set; **~ d'ordre** stewards (+ *pl*); **~ après-vente** after-sales service; **~ militaire** military service; **les ~s secrets** the secret service (+ *sg*).

serviette /sɛʀvjɛt/ *nf* (de toilette) towel; (cartable) briefcase; **~ (de table)** serviette, napkin; **~ hygiénique** sanitary towel.

servir /sɛʀviʀ/ [46] *vt/i* serve; (être utile) be of use, serve; **~ qn** (à table) wait on sb; **ça sert à** (outil, récipient) it is used for; **ça me sert à/de** I use it to/as; **ça ne sert à rien** (*action*) it's pointless; **~ de** serve as, be used as; **~ à qn de guide** act as a guide for sb. □ **se ~** *vpr* (à table) help oneself (de to); **se ~ de** use. **serviteur** *nm* servant.

ses /se/ ⇒SON¹.

session /sesjɔ̃/ *nf* session.

seuil /sœj/ *nm* doorstep; (entrée) doorway; (fig) threshold.

seul, ~e /sœl/ *adj* alone, on one's own; (unique) only; **un ~ exemple** only one example; **pas un ~ ami** not a single friend; **lui ~ le sait** only he knows; **dans le ~ but de** with the sole aim of; **parler tout ~** talk to oneself; **faire qch tout ~** do sth on one's own. ● *nm, f* **le ~, la ~e** the only one. **seulement** *adv* only.

sève /sɛv/ *nf* sap.

sévère /sevɛʀ/ *adj* severe. **sévérité** *nf* severity.

sévices /sevis/ *nmpl* physical abuse (+ *sg*).

sévir /seviʀ/ [2] *vi* (*fléau*) rage; **~ contre** punish.

sevrer /səvʀe/ [6] *vt* wean.

sexe /sɛks/ *nm* sex; (organes) genitals (+ *pl*). **sexiste** *adj* sexist. **sexualité** *nf* sexuality. **sexuel, ~le** *adj* sexual.

shampooing /ʃɑ̃pwɛ̃/ *nm* shampoo.

shérif /ʃeʀif/ *nm* sheriff.

short /ʃɔʀt/ *nm* shorts (+ *pl*).

si (**s'** before il, ils) /si, s/ conj if; (interrogation indirecte) if, whether; ~ **on allait se promener?** what about a walk?; **s'il vous** ou **te plaît** please; ~ **oui** if so; ~ **seulement** if only. ● adv (tellement) so; (oui) yes; **un** ~ **bon repas** such a good meal; ~ **habile qu'il soit** however skilful he may be; ~ **bien que** with the result that.

sida /sida/ nm (Méd) Aids.

sidérurgie /sideʀyʀʒi/ nf steel industry.

siècle /sjɛkl/ nm century; (époque) age.

siège /sjɛʒ/ nm seat; (Mil) siege; ~ **éjectable** ejector seat; ~ **social** head office, headquarters (+ pl). **siéger** [14] [40] vi (assemblée) sit.

sien, ~**ne** /sjɛ̃, -ɛn/ pron **le** ~, **la** ~**ne**, **les** ~(**ne**)**s** (homme) his; (femme) hers; (chose) its; **les** ~**s** (famille) one's family.

sieste /sjɛst/ nf nap, siesta.

sifflement /sifləmɑ̃/ nm whistling; **un** ~ a whistle.

siffler /sifle/ [1] vi whistle; (avec un sifflet) blow one's whistle; (serpent, gaz) hiss. ● vt (air) whistle; (chien) whistle to ou for; (acteur) hiss.

sifflet /siflɛ/ nm whistle; ~**s** (huées) boos.

sigle /sigl/ nm acronym.

signal (pl -**aux**) /siɲal, -o/ nm signal; ~ **sonore** (de répondeur) tone.

signalement /siɲalmɑ̃/ nm description.

signaler /siɲale/ [1] vt indicate; (par une sonnerie, un écriteau) signal; (dénoncer, mentionner) report; (faire remarquer) point out.

signalisation /siɲalizasjɔ̃/ nf signalling, signposting; (signaux) signals (+ pl).

signataire /siɲatɛʀ/ nmf signatory.

signature /siɲatyʀ/ nf signature; (action) signing.

signe /siɲ/ nm sign; (de ponctuation) mark; **faire** ~ **à qn** wave at sb; (contacter) contact; **faire** ~ **à qn de** beckon sb to; **faire** ~ **que non** shake one's head; **faire** ~ **que oui** nod.

signer /siɲe/ [1] vt sign. □ **se** ~ vpr (Relig) cross oneself.

signet /siɲɛ/ nm (pour livre, Internet) bookmark; ~**s favoris** (Internet) hotlist.

significatif, -**ive** /siɲifikatif, -v/ adj significant.

signification /siɲifikasjɔ̃/ nf meaning. **signifier** [45] vt mean, signify; (faire connaître) make known (à to).

silence /silɑ̃s/ nm silence; (Mus) rest; **garder le** ~ keep silent.

silencieux, -**ieuse** /silɑ̃sjø, -z/ adj silent. ● nm silencer.

silex /silɛks/ nm inv flint.

silhouette /silwɛt/ nf outline, silhouette.

sillon /sijɔ̃/ nm furrow; (de disque) groove.

sillonner /sijone/ [1] vt crisscross.

similaire /similɛʀ/ adj similar. **similitude** nf similarity.

simple /sɛ̃pl/ adj simple; (non double) single. ● nm ~ **dames/messieurs** ladies'/men's singles (+ pl). **simple d'esprit** nmf simpleton. **simplement** adv simply. **simplicité** nf simplicity; (naïveté) simpleness.

simplification /sɛ̃plifikasjɔ̃/ nf simplification. **simplifier** [45] vt simplify.

simpliste /sɛ̃plist/ adj simplistic.

simulacre /simylakʀ/ nm pretence, sham.

simulation /simylasjɔ̃/ nf simulation. **simuler** [1] vt simulate.

simultané, ~**e** /simyltane/ adj simultaneous.

sincère /sɛ̃sɛʀ/ adj sincere. **sincérité** nf sincerity.

singe /sɛ̃ʒ/ nm monkey; (grand) ape. **singer** [40] vt mimic, ape.

singulier, -**ière** /sɛ̃gylje, -jɛʀ/ adj peculiar, remarkable; (Gram) singular. ● nm (Gram) singular.

sinistre /sinistʀ/ adj sinister. ● nm disaster; (incendie) blaze; (dommages) damage.

sinistré, ~**e** /sinistʀe/ adj stricken. ● nm, f disaster victim.

sinon /sinɔ̃/ conj (autrement) otherwise; (sauf) except (**que** that);

difficile ∼ impossible difficult if not impossible.

sinueux, -euse /sinɥø, -z/ adj winding; (fig) tortuous.

sirène /siʀɛn/ nf (appareil) siren; (femme) mermaid.

sirop /siʀo/ nm (de fruits, Méd) syrup; (boisson) cordial.

sis, ∼e /si, siz/ adj situated.

sismique /sismik/ adj seismic.

site /sit/ nm site; ∼ touristique place of interest; ∼ Internet or Web Web site.

sitôt /sito/ adv ∼ entré immediately after coming in; ∼ que as soon as; pas de ∼ not for a while.

situation /sitɥasjɔ̃/ nf situation; (emploi) job, position; ∼ de famille marital status.

situé, ∼e /sitɥe/ adj situated.

situer /sitɥe/ [1] vt situate, locate. □ se ∼ vpr (se trouver) be situated.

six /sis/ (/si/ before consonant, /siz/ before vowel) a & nm six. **sixième** a & nmf sixth.

sketch (pl ∼es) /skɛtʃ/ nm (Théât) sketch.

ski /ski/ nm (matériel) ski; (Sport) skiing; faire du ∼ ski; ∼ de fond cross-country skiing; ∼ nautique water skiing. **skier** [45] vi ski.

slave /slav/ adj Slav; (Ling) Slavonic.

slip /slip/ nm (d'homme) underpants (+ pl); (de femme) knickers (+ pl); ∼ de bain (swimming) trunks (+ pl); (du bikini) bikini bottom.

slogan /slɔgɑ̃/ nm slogan.

Slovaquie /slɔvaki/ nf Slovakia.

Slovénie /slɔveni/ nf Slovenia.

smoking /smɔkiŋ/ nm dinner jacket.

SNCF abrév f (**Société nationale des Chemins de fer français**) French national railway company.

snob /snɔb/ nmf snob. ● adj snobbish. **snobisme** nm snobbery.

sobre /sɔbʀ/ adj sober.

social, ∼e (mpl **-iaux**) /sɔsjal, -jo/ adj social.

socialisme /sɔsjalism/ nm socialism. **socialiste** nmf & a socialist.

société /sɔsjete/ nf society; (entreprise) company.

socle /sɔkl/ nm (de colonne, statue) plinth; (de lampe) base.

socquette /sɔkɛt/ nf ankle sock.

soda /sɔda/ nm fizzy drink.

sœur /sœʀ/ nf sister.

soi /swa/ pron oneself; derrière ∼ behind one; en ∼ in itself; aller de ∼ be obvious.

soi-disant /swadizɑ̃/ a inv so-called. ● adv supposedly.

soie /swa/ nf silk.

soif /swaf/ nf thirst; avoir ∼ be thirsty; donner ∼ make one thirsty.

soigné, ∼e /swaɲe/ adj (apparence) tidy, neat; (travail) carefully done.

soigner /swaɲe/ [1] vt (s'occuper de) look after, take care of; (tenue, style) take care over; (maladie) treat. □ se ∼ vpr look after oneself.

soigneusement /swaɲøzmɑ̃/ adv carefully. **soigneux, -euse** adj careful (de about); (ordonné) tidy.

soi-même /swamɛm/ pron oneself.

soin /swɛ̃/ nm care; (ordre) tidiness; ∼s care; (Méd) treatment; avec ∼ carefully; avoir ou prendre ∼ de qn/ de faire take care of sb/to do; premiers ∼s first aid (+ sg).

soir /swaʀ/ nm evening; à ce ∼ see you tonight.

soirée /swaʀe/ nf evening; (réception) party.

soit /swa/ conj (à savoir) that is to say; ∼ ... ∼ either ... or. ● ⇒ÊTRE [4].

soixante /swasɑ̃t/ a & nm sixty. **soixante-dix** a & nm seventy.

soja /sɔʒa/ nm (graines) soya beans (+ pl); (plante) soya.

sol /sɔl/ nm ground; (de maison) floor; (terrain agricole) soil.

solaire /sɔlɛʀ/ adj solar; (huile, filtre) sun.

soldat /sɔlda/ nm soldier.

solde¹ /sɔld/ nf (salaire) pay.

solde² /sɔld/ nm (Comm) balance; les ∼s the sales; ∼s (écrit en vitrine) sale; en ∼ (acheter) at sale price.

solder /sɔlde/ [1] vt sell off at sale price; (compte) settle. □ se ∼ par vpr (aboutir à) end in.

sole /sɔl/ nf (poisson) sole.

soleil /sɔlɛj/ *nm* sun; (fleur) sunflower; **il y a du** ∼ it's sunny.

solennel, ∼**le** /sɔlanɛl/ *adj* solemn.

solfège /sɔlfɛʒ/ *nm* musical theory.

solidaire /sɔlidɛʀ/ *adj* (*mécanismes*) interdependent; (*collègues*) (mutually) supportive; **être** ∼ **de qn** support sb. **solidarité** *nf* solidarity.

solide /sɔlid/ *adj* solid; (*personne*) strong. ● *nm* solid.

solidifier /sɔlidifje/ [45] *vt* solidify. □ **se** ∼ *vpr* solidify.

solitaire /sɔlitɛʀ/ *adj* solitary. ● *nmf* (*personne*) loner. **solitude** *nf* solitude.

solliciter /sɔlisite/ [1] *vt* seek; (faire appel à) call upon; **être très sollicité** be very much in demand.

sollicitude /sɔlisityd/ *nf* concern.

solo /sɔlo/ *nm & a inv* (Mus) solo.

solution /sɔlysjɔ̃/ *nf* solution.

solvable /sɔlvabl/ *adj* solvent.

solvant /sɔlvɑ̃/ *nm* solvent.

sombre /sɔ̃bʀ/ *adj* dark; (triste) sombre.

sombrer /sɔ̃bʀe/ [1] *vi* sink (dans into).

sommaire /sɔmɛʀ/ *adj* (*exécution*) summary; (*description*) rough. ● *nm* contents (+ *pl*); **au** ∼ on the programme.

sommation /sɔmasjɔ̃/ *nf* (Mil) warning; (Jur) notice.

somme /sɔm/ *nf* sum; **en** ∼, ∼ **toute** in short; **faire la** ∼ **de** add (up), total (up). ● *nm* nap.

sommeil /sɔmɛj/ *nm* sleep; **avoir** ∼ be *ou* feel sleepy; **en** ∼ (*projet*) put on ice. **sommeiller** [1] *vi* doze; (fig) lie dormant.

sommelier /sɔməlje/ *nm* wine steward.

sommer /sɔme/ [1] *vt* summon.

sommes /sɔm/ ⇒ÊTRE [4].

sommet /sɔmɛ/ *nm* top; (de montagne) summit; (de triangle) apex; (gloire) height.

sommier /sɔmje/ *nm* bed base.

somnambule /sɔmnɑ̃byl/ *nm* sleepwalker.

somnifère /sɔmnifɛʀ/ *nm* sleeping pill.

somnolent, ∼**e** /sɔmnɔlɑ̃, -t/ *adj* drowsy. **somnoler** [1] *vi* doze.

somptueux, -**euse** /sɔ̃ptɥø, -z/ *adj* sumptuous.

son[1], **sa** (**son** *before vowel or mute h*) (*pl* **ses**) /sɔ̃, sa, sɔ̃, se/ *adj* (homme) his; (femme) her; (chose) its; (indéfini) one's.

son[2] /sɔ̃/ *nm* (bruit) sound; (de blé) bran; **baisser le** ∼ turn the volume down.

sondage /sɔ̃daʒ/ *nm* ∼ (**d'opinion**) (opinion) poll.

sonde /sɔ̃d/ *nf* (de forage) drill; (Méd) (d'évacuation) catheter; (d'examen) probe.

sonder /sɔ̃de/ [1] *vt* (*population*) poll; (explorer) sound; (*terrain*) drill; (*intentions*) sound out.

songe /sɔ̃ʒ/ *nm* dream.

songer /sɔ̃ʒe/ [40] *vt* ∼ **que** think that; ∼ **à** think about. **songeur**, -**euse** *adj* pensive.

sonné, ∼**e** /sɔne/ *adj* (étourdi) groggy; Ⅱ crazy.

sonner /sɔne/ [1] *vt/i* ring; (*clairon, glas*) sound; (*heure*) strike; (*domestique*) ring for; **midi sonné** well past noon; ∼ **de** (*clairon*) sound, blow.

sonnerie /sɔnʀi/ *nf* ringing; (de clairon) sounding; (sonnette) bell.

sonnet /sɔnɛ/ *nm* sonnet.

sonnette /sɔnɛt/ *nf* bell.

sonore /sɔnɔʀ/ *adj* resonant; (*onde, effets*) sound; (*rire*) resounding.

sonorisation /sɔnɔʀizasjɔ̃/ *nf* (matériel) public address system.

sonorité /sɔnɔʀite/ *nf* resonance; (d'un instrument) tone.

sont /sɔ̃/ ⇒ÊTRE [4].

sophistiqué, ∼**e** /sɔfistike/ *adj* sophisticated.

sorcellerie /sɔʀsɛlʀi/ *nf* witchcraft. **sorcier** *nm* (guérisseur) witch doctor; (maléfique) sorcerer. **sorcière** *nf* witch.

sordide /sɔʀdid/ *adj* sordid; (lieu) squalid.

sort /sɔʀ/ *nm* (destin, hasard) fate; (condition) lot; (maléfice) spell; **tirer** (**qch**) **au** ∼ draw lots (for sth).

S

sortant, ~e /sɔʀtɑ̃, -t/ adj (président etc.) outgoing.

sorte /sɔʀt/ nf sort, kind; de ~ que so that; en quelque ~ in a way; de la ~ in this way; faire en ~ que make sure that.

sortie /sɔʀti/ nf exit; (promenade, dîner) outing; (déclaration 🗓) remark; (parution) publication; (de disque, film) release; (d'un ordinateur) output; ~s (argent) outgoings.

sortilège /sɔʀtilɛʒ/ nm (magic) spell.

sortir /sɔʀtiʀ/ [46] vi (aux être) go out, leave; (venir) come out; (aller au spectacle) go out; (livre, film) come out; (plante) come up; ~ de (pièce) leave; (milieu social) come from; (limites) go beyond; ~ du commun ou de l'ordinaire be out of the ordinary. ● vt (aux avoir) take out; (livre, modèle) bring out; (dire 🗓) come out with; ~ qn de get sb out of; être sorti d'affaire be in the clear. □ s'en ~ vpr cope, manage.

sosie /sɔzi/ nm double.

sot, ~te /so, sɔt/ adj silly.

sottise /sɔtiz/ nf silliness; (action, remarque) foolish thing; faire des ~s be naughty.

sou /su/ nm 🗓 ~s money; sans le ~ without a penny; près de ses ~s tight-fisted.

soubresaut /subʀəso/ nm (sudden) start.

souche /suʃ/ nf (d'arbre) stump; (de famille) stock; (de carnet) counterfoil.

souci /susi/ nm (inquiétude) worry; (préoccupation) concern; (plante) marigold; se faire du ~ worry.

soucier (se) /(sə)susje/ [45] vpr se ~ de care about. **soucieux, -ieuse** adj concerned (de about).

soucoupe /sukup/ nf saucer; ~ volante flying saucer.

soudain, ~e /sudɛ̃, -ɛn/ adj sudden. ● adv suddenly.

soude /sud/ nf soda.

souder /sude/ [1] vt weld, solder; famille très soudée close-knit family. □ se ~ vpr (os) knit (together).

soudoyer /sudwaje/ [31] vt bribe.

souffle /sufl/ nm (haleine) breath; (respiration) breathing; (explosion) blast;

(vent) breath of air; le ~ coupé out of breath; à couper le ~ breathtaking.

souffler /sufle/ [1] vi blow; (haleter) puff. ● vt (bougie) blow out; (poussière, fumée) blow; (verre) blow; (par explosion) destroy; (chuchoter) whisper; ~ la réplique à prompt. **souffleur, -euse** nm, f (Théât) prompter.

souffrance /sufʀɑ̃s/ nf suffering; en ~ (affaire) pending. **souffrant**, ~e adj unwell.

souffrir /sufʀiʀ/ [21] vi suffer (de from). ● vt (endurer) suffer; il ne peut pas le ~ he cannot stand ou bear him.

soufre /sufʀ/ nm sulphur.

souhait /swɛ/ nm wish; à tes ~s! bless you!; paisible à ~ incredibly peaceful. **souhaitable** adj desirable.

souhaiter /swete/ [1] vt ~ qch à qn wish sb sth; ~ que/faire hope that/to do; ~ la bienvenue à qn welcome sb.

soûl, ~e /su, sul/ adj drunk. ● nm tout son ~ as much as one can.

soulagement /sulaʒmɑ̃/ nm relief. **soulager** [40] vt relieve.

soûler /sule/ [1] vt make drunk. □ se ~ vpr get drunk.

soulèvement /sulɛvmɑ̃/ nm uprising.

soulever /sulve/ [6] vt lift, raise; (question, poussière) raise; (enthousiasme) arouse; (foule) stir up. □ se ~ vpr lift ou raise oneself up; (se révolter) rise up.

soulier /sulje/ nm shoe.

souligner /suliɲe/ [1] vt underline; (yeux) outline; (taille) emphasize.

soumettre /sumɛtʀ/ [42] vt (assujettir) subject (à to); (présenter) submit (à to). □ se ~ vpr submit (à to). **soumis**, ~e adj submissive. **soumission** nf submission.

soupape /supap/ nf valve.

soupçon /supsɔ̃/ nm suspicion; un ~ de (un peu de) a touch of. **soupçonner** [1] vt suspect. **soupçonneux, -euse** adj suspicious.

soupe /sup/ nf soup.

souper /supe/ [6] vi have supper. ● nm supper.

soupeser /supəze/ [1] *vt* judge the weight of; (fig) weigh up.

soupière /supjɛʀ/ *nf* (soup) tureen.

soupir /supiʀ/ *nm* sigh; **pousser un** ~ heave a sigh.

soupirer /supiʀe/ [1] *vi* sigh.

souple /supl/ *adj* supple; (*règlement, caractère*) flexible. **souplesse** *nf* suppleness; (de règlement) flexibility.

source /suʀs/ *nf* (de rivière, origine) source; (eau) spring; **prendre sa** ~ **à** rise in; **de** ~ **sûre** from a reliable source; ~ **thermale** hot spring.

sourcil /suʀsi/ *nm* eyebrow.

sourciller /suʀsije/ [1] *vi* **sans** ~ without batting an eyelid.

sourd, ~**e** /suʀ, -d/ *adj* deaf; (*bruit, douleur*) dull; **faire la** ~**e oreille** turn a deaf ear. ● *nm,f* deaf person.

sourd-muet (*pl* **sourds-muets**), **sourde-muette** (*pl* **sourdes-muettes**) /suʀmɥɛ, suʀdmɥɛt/ *adj* deaf and dumb. ● *nm,f* deaf-mute.

souricière /suʀisjɛʀ/ *nf* mousetrap; (fig) trap.

sourire /suʀiʀ/ [54] *vi* smile (à at); ~ **à** (fortune) smile on. ● *nm* smile; **garder le** ~ keep smiling.

souris /suʀi/ *nf* mouse; **des** ~ mice.

sournois, ~**e** /suʀnwa, -z/ *adj* sly, underhand.

sous /su/ *prép* under, beneath; ~ **la main** handy; ~ **la pluie** in the rain; ~ **peu** shortly; ~ **terre** underground.

sous-alimenté, ~**e** /suzalimɑ̃te/ *adj* undernourished.

souscription /suskʀipsjɔ̃/ *nf* subscription. **souscrire** [30] *vi* ~ **à** subscribe to.

sous-entendre /suzɑ̃tɑ̃dʀ/ [3] *vt* imply. **sous-entendu** *nm* innuendo, insinuation.

sous-estimer /suzɛstime/ [1] *vt* underestimate.

sous-jacent, ~**e** /suʒasɑ̃, -t/ *adj* underlying.

sous-marin, ~**e** /sumaʀɛ̃, -in/ *adj* underwater; (*plongée*) deep-sea. ● *nm* submarine.

soussigné, ~**e** /susiɲe/ *a* & *nm,f* undersigned.

sous-sol /susɔl/ *nm* (cave) basement.

sous-titre /sutitʀ/ *nm* subtitle.

soustraction /sustʀaksjɔ̃/ *nf* (déduction) subtraction.

soustraire /sustʀɛʀ/ [29] *vt* (déduire) subtract; (retirer) take away (à from). □ **se** ~ **à** *vpr* escape from.

sous-traitant /sutʀɛtɑ̃/ *nm* subcontractor.

sous-verre /suvɛʀ/ *nm inv* glass mount.

sous-vêtement /suvɛtmɑ̃/ *nm* underwear.

soute /sut/ *nf* (de bateau) hold; ~ **à charbon** coal-bunker.

soutenir /sutniʀ/ [59] *vt* support; (*effort, rythme*) sustain; (résister à) withstand; ~ **que** maintain that.

soutenu, ~**e** /sutny/ *adj* (constant) sustained; (style) formal.

souterrain, ~**e** /sutɛʀɛ̃, -ɛn/ *adj* underground. ● *nm* underground passage.

soutien /sutjɛ̃/ *nm* support.

soutien-gorge (*pl* **soutiens-gorge**) /sutjɛ̃gɔʀʒ/ *nm* bra.

soutirer /sutiʀe/ [1] *vt* ~ **à qn** extract from sb.

souvenir[1] /suvniʀ/ *nm* memory, recollection; (objet) memento; (cadeau) souvenir; **en** ~ **de** in memory of.

souvenir[2] (**se**) /(sə)suvniʀ/ [59] *vpr* **se** ~ **de** remember; **se** ~ **que** remember that.

souvent /suvɑ̃/ *adv* often.

souverain, ~**e** /suvʀɛ̃, -ɛn/ *adj* sovereign. ● *nm,f* sovereign.

soviétique /sɔvjetik/ *adj* Soviet.

soyeux, **-euse** /swajø, -z/ *adj* silky.

spacieux, **-ieuse** /spasjø, -z/ *adj* spacious.

sparadrap /spaʀadʀa/ *nm* (sticking) plaster.

spatial, ~**e** (*mpl* **-iaux**) /spasjal, -jo/ *adj* space.

speaker, ~**ine** /spikœʀ, -kʀin/ *nm,f* announcer.

spécial, ~**e** (*mpl* **-iaux**) /spesjal, -jo/ *adj* special; (bizarre) odd. **spécialement** *adv* (exprès) specially; (très) especially.

spécialiser (se) /səspesjalize/ [1] *vpr* specialize (**dans** in). **spécialiste** *nmf* specialist. **spécialité** *nf* speciality; (US) specialty.

spécifier /spesifje/ [45] *vt* specify.

spécifique /spesifik/ *adj* specific.

spécimen /spesimɛn/ *nm* specimen.

spectacle /spɛktakl/ *nm* show; (vue) sight, spectacle.

spectaculaire /spɛktakylɛʀ/ *adj* spectacular.

spectateur, -trice /spɛktatœʀ, -tʀis/ *nm,f* (Sport) spectator; (témoin oculaire) onlooker; **les ~s** (Théât) the audience (+ *sg*).

spectre /spɛktʀ/ *nm* (revenant) spectre; (images) spectrum.

spéculateur, -trice /spekylatœʀ, -tʀis/ *nm,f* speculator. **spéculation** *nf* speculation. **spéculer** [1] *vi* speculate.

spéléologie /speleɔlɔʒi/ *nf* cave exploration, pot-holing.

spermatozoïde /spɛʀmatozɔid/ *nm* spermatozoon. **sperme** *nm* sperm.

sphère /sfɛʀ/ *nf* sphere.

spirale /spiʀal/ *nf* spiral.

spirituel, ~le /spiʀitɥɛl/ *adj* spiritual; (amusant) witty.

spiritueux /spiʀitɥø/ *nm* (alcool) spirit.

splendeur /splɑ̃dœʀ/ *nf* splendour. **splendide** *adj* splendid.

sponsoriser /spɔ̃sɔʀize/ [1] *vt* sponsor.

spontané, ~e /spɔ̃tane/ *adj* spontaneous. **spontanéité** *nf* spontaneity.

sport /spɔʀ/ *a inv* (vêtements) casual. ● *nm* sport; **veste/voiture de ~** sports jacket/car.

sportif, -ive /spɔʀtif, -v/ *adj* (personne) sporty; (physique) athletic; (résultats) sports. ● *nm,f* sportsman, sportswoman.

spot /spɔt/ *nm* spotlight; **~ (publicitaire)** ad.

square /skwaʀ/ *nm* small public garden.

squatter /skwate/ [1] *vt* squat in.

squelette /skəlɛt/ *nm* skeleton. **squelettique** *adj* skeletal; (maigre) all skin and bone; (rapport) sketchy.

stabiliser /stabilize/ [1] *vt* stabilize. **stable** *adj* stable.

stade /stad/ *nm* (Sport) stadium; (phase) stage.

stage /staʒ/ *nm* (cours) course; (professionnel) placement. **stagiaire** *nmf* course member; (apprenti) trainee.

stagner /stagne/ [1] *vi* stagnate.

stand /stɑ̃d/ *nm* stand; (de fête foraine) stall; **~ de tir** shooting range.

standard /stɑ̃daʀ/ *nm* switchboard. ● *a inv* standard. **standardiser** [1] *vt* standardize.

standardiste /stɑ̃daʀdist/ *nmf* switchboard operator.

standing /stɑ̃diŋ/ *nm* status, standing; **de ~** (hôtel) luxury.

starter /staʀtɛʀ/ *nm* (Auto) choke.

station /stasjɔ̃/ *nf* station; (halte) stop; **~ debout** standing position; **~ de taxis** taxi rank; **~ balnéaire/de ski** seaside/ski resort; **~ thermale** spa.

stationnaire /stasjɔnɛʀ/ *adj* stationary.

stationnement /stasjɔnmɑ̃/ *nm* parking. **stationner** [1] *vi* park.

station-service (*pl* **stations-service**) /stasjɔ̃sɛʀvis/ *nf* service station.

statique /statik/ *adj* static.

statistique /statistik/ *nf* statistic; (science) statistics (+ *sg*). ● *adj* statistical.

statue /staty/ *nf* statue.

statuer /statɥe/ [1] *vi* **~ sur** give a ruling on.

statut /staty/ *nm* status. **statutaire** *adj* statutory.

sténo /steno/ *nf* (sténographie) shorthand. **sténodactylo** *nf* shorthand typist. **sténographie** *nf* shorthand.

stéréo /stereo/ *nf & a inv* stereo.

stéréotype /stereɔtip/ *nm* stereotype.

stérile /steril/ *adj* sterile.

stérilet /sterilɛ/ *nm* coil, IUD.

stérilisation /steʀilizasjɔ̃/ *nf* sterilization. **stériliser** [1] *vt* sterilize.

stéroïde /steʀɔid/ *a & nm* steroid.

stimulant /stimylɑ̃/ *nm* stimulus; (médicament) stimulant.

stimulateur /stimylatœʀ/ *nm* ~ **cardiaque** (Méd) pacemaker.

stimuler /stimyle/ [1] *vt* stimulate.

stipuler /stipyle/ [1] *vt* stipulate.

stock /stɔk/ *nm* stock. **stocker** [1] *vt* stock.

stoïque /stɔik/ *adj* stoical. ● *nmf* stoic.

stop /stɔp/ *interj* stop. ● *nm* stop sign; (feu arrière) brake light; **faire du** ~ 🄸 hitch-hike. **stopper** [1] *vt/i* stop.

store /stɔʀ/ *nm* blind; (de magasin) awning.

strapontin /stʀapɔ̃tɛ̃/ *nm* folding seat, jump seat.

stratégie /stʀateʒi/ *nf* strategy. **stratégique** *adj* strategic.

stress /stʀɛs/ *nm* stress. **stressant**, ~**e** *adj* stressful. **stressé**, ~**e** *adj* stressed. **stresser** [1] *vt* put under stress.

strict /stʀikt/ *adj* strict; (tenue, vérité) plain; **le** ~ **minimum** the bare minimum. **strictement** *adv* strictly.

strident, ~**e** /stʀidɑ̃, -t/ *adj* shrill.

strophe /stʀɔf/ *nf* stanza, verse.

structure /stʀyktyʀ/ *nf* structure.

studieux, -ieuse /stydjø, -z/ *adj* studious.

studio /stydjo/ *nm* (d'artiste, de télévision) studio; (logement) studio flat.

stupéfaction /stypefaksjɔ̃/ *nf* amazement. **stupéfait**, ~**e** *adj* amazed.

stupéfiant, ~**e** /stypefjɑ̃, -t/ *adj* astounding. ● *nm* drug, narcotic.

stupéfier /stypefje/ [45] *vt* amaze.

stupeur /stypœʀ/ *nf* amazement; (Méd) stupor.

stupide /stypid/ *adj* stupid. **stupidité** *nf* stupidity.

style /stil/ *nm* style.

styliste /stilist/ *nmf* fashion designer.

stylo /stilo/ *nm* pen; ~ **(à) bille** ball-point pen; ~ **(à) encre** fountain pen.

su /sy/ ⇒SAVOIR [55].

suave /sɥav/ *adj* sweet.

subalterne /sybaltɛʀn/ *a & nmf* subordinate.

subconscient /sypkɔ̃sjɑ̃/ *nm* subconscious.

subir /sybiʀ/ [2] *vt* be subjected to; (traitement, expériences) undergo.

subit, ~**e** /sybi, -t/ *adj* sudden.

subjectif, -ive /sybʒɛktif, -v/ *adj* subjective.

subjonctif /sybʒɔ̃ktif/ *nm* subjunctive.

subjuguer /sybʒyge/ [1] *vt* (charmer) captivate.

sublime /syblim/ *adj* sublime.

submerger /sybmɛʀʒe/ [40] *vt* submerge; (fig) overwhelm.

subordonné, ~**e** /sybɔʀdɔne/ *a & nm,f* subordinate.

subside /sybzid/ *nm* grant.

subsidiaire /sybzidjɛʀ/ *adj* subsidiary; **question** ~ tiebreaker.

subsistance /sybzistɑ̃s/ *nf* subsistence. **subsister** [1] *vi* subsist; (durer, persister) exist.

substance /sypstɑ̃s/ *nf* substance.

substantiel, ~**le** /sypstɑ̃sjɛl/ *adj* substantial.

substantif /sypstɑ̃tif/ *nm* noun.

substituer /sypstitɥe/ [1] *vt* substitute (à for). □ **se** ~ **à** *vpr* (remplacer) substitute for. **substitut** *nm* substitute; (Jur) deputy public prosecutor.

subtil, ~**e** /syptil/ *adj* subtle.

subtiliser /syptilize/ [1] *vt* ~ **qch (à qn)** steal sth.

subvenir /sybvəniʀ/ [59] *vi* ~ **à** provide for.

subvention /sybvɑ̃sjɔ̃/ *nf* subsidy. **subventionner** [1] *vt* subsidize.

subversif, -ive /sybvɛʀsif, -v/ *adj* subversive.

suc /syk/ *nm* juice.

succédané /syksedane/ *nm* substitute (**de** for).

succéder /syksede/ [14] *vi* ~ **à** succeed. □ **se** ~ *vpr* succeed one another.

S

succès /syksɛ/ *nm* success; à ∼ (film, livre,) successful; avoir du ∼ be a success.

successeur /syksesœr/ *nm* successor. **successif, -ive** *adj* successive. **succession** *nf* succession; (Jur) inheritance.

succinct, ∼e /syksɛ̃, -t/ *adj* succinct.

succomber /sykɔ̃be/ [1] *vi* die; ∼ à succumb to.

succulent, ∼e /sykylɑ̃, -t/ *adj* delicious.

succursale /sykyrsal/ *nf* (Comm) branch.

sucer /syse/ [10] *vt* suck.

sucette /sysɛt/ *nf* (bonbon) lollipop; (tétine) dummy; (US) pacifier.

sucre /sykr/ *nm* sugar; ∼ d'orge barley sugar; ∼ en poudre caster sugar; ∼ glace icing sugar; ∼ roux brown sugar.

sucré /sykre/ *adj* sweet; (additionné de sucre) sweetened. **sucrer** [1] *vt* sugar, sweeten. **sucreries** *nfpl* sweets.

sucrier, -ière /sykrije, -jɛr/ *adj* sugar. ● *nm* (récipient) sugar-bowl.

sud /syd/ *nm* south. ● *a inv* south; (partie) southern.

sud-est /sydɛst/ *nm* south-east.

sud-ouest /sydwɛst/ *nm* south-west.

Suède /sɥɛd/ *nf* Sweden.

suédois, ∼e /sɥedwa, -z/ *adj* Swedish. ● *nm* (Ling) Swedish. **S**∼, ∼e *nm, f* Swede.

S **suer** /sɥe/ [1] *vt/i* sweat; faire ∼ qn 🅃 get on sb's nerves.

sueur /sɥœr/ *nf* sweat; en ∼ covered in sweat.

suffire /syfir/ [57] *vi* be enough (à qn for sb); il suffit de compter all you have to do is count; une goutte suffit a drop is enough; ∼ à (besoin) satisfy. ◻ se ∼ *vpr* se ∼ à soi-même be self-sufficient.

suffisamment /syfizamɑ̃/ *adv* sufficiently; ∼ de qch enough of sth. **suffisance** *nf* (vanité) conceit. **suffisant**, ∼e *adj* sufficient; (vaniteux) conceited.

suffixe /syfiks/ *nm* suffix.

suffoquer /syfɔke/ [1] *vt/i* choke, suffocate.

suffrage /syfraʒ/ *nm* (voix: Pol) vote; (système) suffrage.

suggérer /sygʒere/ [14] *vt* suggest. **suggestion** *nf* suggestion.

suicidaire /sɥisidɛr/ *adj* suicidal. **suicide** *nm* suicide. **suicider (se)** [1] *vpr* commit suicide.

suinter /sɥɛ̃te/ [1] *vi* ooze.

suis /sɥi/ ⇒ÊTRE [4], SUIVRE [57].

Suisse /sɥis/ *nf* Switzerland. ● *nmf* Swiss. **suisse** *adj* Swiss.

suite /sɥit/ *nf* continuation, rest; (d'un film) sequel; (série) series; (appartement, escorte) suite; (résultat) consequence; à la ∼, de ∼ (successivement) in a row; à la ∼ de (derrière) behind; à la ∼ de, par ∼ de (en conséquence) as a result of; faire ∼ (à) follow; par la ∼ afterwards; ∼ à votre lettre du further to your letter of the; des ∼s de as a result of.

suivant[1], ∼e /sɥivɑ̃, -t/ *adj* following, next. ● *nm, f* following *ou* next person.

suivant[2] /sɥivɑ̃/ *prép* (selon) according to.

suivi, ∼e /sɥivi/ *adj* (effort) steady, sustained; (cohérent) consistent; peu/très ∼ (cours) poorly/well attended.

suivre /sɥivr/ [57] *vt/i* follow; (comprendre) follow; faire ∼ (courrier) forward. ◻ se ∼ *vpr* follow each other.

sujet, ∼te /syʒɛ, -t/ *adj* ∼ à liable *ou* subject to. ● *nm* (d'un royaume) subject; (question) subject; (motif) cause; (Gram) subject; au ∼ de about.

super /sypɛr/ *nm* (essence) four-star. ● *a inv* 🅃 (très) great. ● *adv* 🅃 ultra, really.

superbe /sypɛrb/ *adj* superb.

supérette /sypɛrɛt/ *nf* minimarket.

superficie /sypɛrfisi/ *nf* area.

superficiel, ∼le /sypɛrfisjɛl/ *adj* superficial.

superflu, ∼e /sypɛrfly/ *adj* superfluous. ● *nm* (excédent) surplus.

supérieur, ∼e /syperjœr/ *adj* (plus haut) upper; (quantité, nombre) greater (à than); (études, principe) higher (à than); (meilleur, hautain)

superior (à to). ● *nm, f* superior.
supériorité *nf* superiority.
superlatif, -ive /sypɛrlatif, -v/ *a* &
nm superlative.
supermarché /sypɛrmarʃe/ *nm*
supermarket.
superposer /sypɛrpoze/ [1] *vt*
superimpose; **lits superposés** bunk
beds.
superproduction
/sypɛrprɔdyksjɔ̃/ *nf* (film)
blockbuster.
superpuissance /sypɛrpɥisɑ̃s/ *nf*
superpower.
superstitieux, -ieuse /sypɛrs-
tisjø, -z/ *adj* superstitious.
superviser /sypɛrvize/ [1] *vt*
supervise.
suppléant, ~e /sypleɑ̃, -t/ *nmf* & *a*
(*professeur*) ~ supply teacher; (*juge*)
~ deputy (judge).
suppléer /syplee/ [15] *vt* (remplacer)
fill in for. ● *vi* ~ à (compenser) make
up for.
supplément /syplemɑ̃/ *nm* (argent)
extra charge; (de frites, légumes) extra
portion; **en ~** extra; **un ~ de** (travail)
additional; **payer un ~** pay a
supplement. **supplémentaire** *adj*
extra, additional.
supplice /syplis/ *nm* torture.
supplier /syplije/ [45] *vt* beg,
beseech (**de** to).
support /sypɔr/ *nm* support;
(Ordinat) medium.
supportable /sypɔrtabl/ *adj*
bearable.
supporter¹ /sypɔrtɛ/ [1] *vt*
(*privations*) bear; (*personne*) put up
with; (*structure*: Ordinat) support; **il ne
supporte pas les enfants/de perdre**
he can't stand children/losing.
supporter² /sypɔrtɛr/ *nm* (Sport)
supporter.
supposer /sypoze/ [1] *vt* suppose;
(impliquer) imply; **à ~ que** supposing
that.
suppression /sypresjɔ̃/ *nf* (de taxe)
abolition; (de sanction) lifting; (de mot)
deletion. **supprimer** [1] *vt*
(*allocation*) withdraw; (*contrôle*) lift;
(*train*) cancel; (*preuve*) suppress.
suprématie /sypremasi/ *nf*
supremacy.

suprême /syprɛm/ *adj* supreme.
sur /syr/ *prép* on, upon; (par-dessus)
over; (au sujet de) about, on; (proportion)
out of; (mesure) by; ~ **la photo** in the
photograph; **mettre/jeter** ~ put/
throw on to; ~ **mesure** made to
measure; ~ **place** on the spot; ~ **ce,
je pars** with that, I must go; ~ **le
moment** at the time.
sûr /syr/ *adj* certain, sure; (sans
danger) safe; (digne de confiance)
reliable; (*main*) steady; (*jugement*)
sound; **être** ~ **de soi** be self-
confident; **j'en étais ~!** I knew it!
surabondance /syrabɔ̃dɑ̃s/ *nf*
overabundance.
surcharge /syrʃarʒ/ *nf*
overloading; (poids) excess load.
surcharger [1] *vt* overload; (*texte*)
alter.
surchauffer /syrʃofe/ [1] *vt*
overheat.
surcroît /syrkrwa/ *nm* increase (**de**
in); **de** ~ in addition.
surdité /syrdite/ *nf* deafness.
surélever /syrɛlve/ [6] *vt* raise.
sûrement /syrmɑ̃/ *adv* certainly;
(sans danger) safely; **il a** ~ **oublié** he
must have forgotten.
surenchère /syrɑ̃ʃɛr/ *nf* higher
bid. **surenchérir** [2] *vi* bid higher
(**sur** than).
surestimer /syrɛstime/ [1] *vt*
overestimate.
sûreté /syrte/ *nf* safety; (de pays)
security; (d'un geste) steadiness; **être
en** ~ be safe; **S~** (**nationale**) police
(+ *pl*).
surexcité, ~e /syrɛksite/ *adj* very
excited.
surf /sœrf/ *nm* surfing.
surface /syrfas/ *nf* surface; **faire** ~
(*sous-marin*, fig) surface; **en** ~ on the
surface.
surfait, ~e /syrfɛ, -t/ *adj* overrated.
surfer /sœrfe/ [1] *vi* go surfing; ~
sur l'Internet surf the Internet.
surgelé, ~e /syrʒəle/ *adj* (deep-)
frozen; **aliments ~s** frozen food (+
sg).
surgir /syrʒir/ [2] *vi* appear
(suddenly); (*difficulté*) crop up.
sur-le-champ /syrləʃɑ̃/ *adv* right
away.

S

surlendemain /syʀlɑ̃dmɛ̃/ *nm* le ~ two days later; le ~ de two days after.

surligneur /syʀliɲœʀ/ *nm* highlighter (pen).

surmenage /syʀmənaʒ/ *nm* overwork.

surmonter /syʀmɔ̃te/ [1] *vt* (vaincre) overcome, surmount; (être au-dessus de) surmount, top.

surnaturel, ~le /syʀnatyʀɛl/ *adj* supernatural.

surnom /syʀnɔ̃/ *nm* nickname. **surnommer** [1] *vt* nickname.

surpeuplé, ~e /syʀpœple/ *adj* overpopulated.

surplomber /syʀplɔ̃be/ [1] *vt/i* overhang.

surplus /syʀply/ *nm* surplus.

suprenant, ~e /syʀpʀənɑ̃, -t/ *adj* surprising. **surprendre** [50] *vt* (étonner) surprise; (prendre au dépourvu) catch, surprise; (entendre) overhear. **surpris**, ~e *adj* surprised (de at).

surprise /syʀpʀiz/ *nf* surprise.

surréaliste /syʀʀealist/ *a & nmf* surrealist.

sursaut /syʀso/ *nm* start, jump; en ~ with a start; ~ de (regain) burst of. **sursauter** [1] *vi* start, jump.

sursis /syʀsi/ *nm* reprieve; (Mil) deferment; **deux ans (de prison) avec ~** a two-year suspended sentence.

surtaxe /syʀtaks/ *nf* surcharge.

surtout /syʀtu/ *adv* especially; (avant tout) above all; ~ pas certainly not.

surveillance /syʀvɛjɑ̃s/ *nf* watch; (d'examen) supervision; (de la police) surveillance. **surveillant**, ~e *nm,f* (de prison) warder; (au lycée) supervisor (in charge of discipline). **surveiller** [1] *vt* watch; (travaux, élèves) supervise.

survenir /syʀvəniʀ/ [59] *vi* occur, take place; (personne) turn up.

survêtement /syʀvɛtmɑ̃/ *nm* (Sport) tracksuit.

survie /syʀvi/ *nf* survival.

survivant, ~e /syʀvivɑ̃, -t/ *adj* surviving. ● *nm,f* survivor.

survivre /syʀvivʀ/ [63] *vi* survive; ~ à (conflit) survive; (personne) outlive.

survoler /syʀvɔle/ [1] *vt* fly over; (livre) skim through.

sus: en ~ /ãsys/ *loc* in addition.

susceptible /sysɛptibl/ *adj* touchy; ~ de faire likely to do.

susciter /sysite/ [1] *vt* (éveiller) arouse; (occasionner) create.

suspect, ~e /syspɛ, -ɛkt/ *adj* (individu, faits) suspicious; (témoignage) suspect; ~ de suspected of. ● *nm,f* suspect. **suspecter** [1] *vt* suspect.

suspendre /syspɑ̃dʀ/ [3] *vt* (accrocher) hang (up); (interrompre, destituer) suspend; **suspendu à** hanging from. □ **se ~ à** *vpr* hang from.

suspens: en ~ /ãsyspɑ̃/ *loc* (affaire) outstanding; (dans l'indécision) in suspense.

suspense /syspɛns/ *nm* suspense.

suture /sytyʀ/ *nf* point de ~ stitch.

svelte /svɛlt/ *adj* slender.

S.V.P. *abrév* (**s'il vous plaît**) please.

syllabe /silab/ *nf* syllable.

symbole /sɛ̃bɔl/ *nm* symbol. **symboliser** [1] *vt* symbolize.

symétrie /simetʀi/ *nf* symmetry.

sympa /sɛ̃pa/ *a inv* 🅸 nice; sois ~ be a pal.

sympathie /sɛ̃pati/ *nf* (goût) liking; (compassion) sympathy; **avoir de la ~ pour** like. **sympathique** *adj* nice, pleasant. **sympathisant**, ~e *nm,f* sympathizer. **sympathiser** [1] *vi* get on well (avec with).

symphonie /sɛ̃fɔni/ *nf* symphony.

symptôme /sɛ̃ptom/ *nm* symptom.

synagogue /sinagɔg/ *nf* synagogue.

synchroniser /sɛ̃kʀɔnize/ [1] *vt* synchronize.

syncope /sɛ̃kɔp/ *nf* (Méd) blackout.

syndic /sɛ̃dik/ *nm* ~ (d'immeuble) property manager.

syndicaliste /sɛ̃dikalist/ *nmf* (trade-)unionist. ● *adj* (trade-)union.

syndicat /sɛ̃dika/ *nm* (trade) union; ~ d'initiative tourist office.

syndiqué, ~e /sɛ̃dike/ *adj* être ~ be a (trade-)union member.

synonyme /sinɔnim/ *adj* synonymous. ● *nm* synonym.

syntaxe /sɛ̃taks/ *nf* syntax.
synthèse /sɛ̃tɛz/ *nf* synthesis.
synthétique *adj* synthetic.
synthé(tiseur) /sɛ̃te(tizœʀ)/ *nm* synthesizer.
systématique /sistematik/ *adj* systematic.
système /sistɛm/ *nm* system; **le ~ D** 🆙 resourcefulness.

t' /t/ ⇒TE.
ta /ta/ ⇒TON¹.
tabac /taba/ *nm* tobacco; (magasin) tobacconist's shop.
table /tabl/ *nf* table; **à ~!** dinner is ready!; **~ de nuit** bedside table; **~ des matières** table of contents; **~ à repasser** ironing board; **~ roulante** (tea-)trolley; (US) serving cart.
tableau (*pl* **~x**) /tablo/ *nm* picture; (peinture) painting; (panneau) board; (graphique) chart; (Scol) blackboard; **~ d'affichage** notice-board; **~ de bord** dashboard.
tablette /tablɛt/ *nf* shelf; **~ de chocolat** bar of chocolate.
tableur /tablœʀ/ *nm* spreadsheet.
tablier /tablije/ *nm* apron; (de pont) platform; (de magasin) shutter.
tabou /tabu/ *nm & a* taboo.
tabouret /tabuʀɛ/ *nm* stool.
tache /taʃ/ *nf* mark, spot; (salissure) stain; **faire ~ d'huile** spread; **~ de rousseur** freckle.
tâche /taʃ/ *nf* task, job.
tacher /taʃe/ [1] *vt* stain. □ **se ~** *vpr* (*personne*) get oneself dirty.
tâcher /taʃe/ [1] *vi* **~ de faire** try to do.
tacheté, ~e /taʃte/ *adj* spotted.
tact /takt/ *nm* tact.
tactique /taktik/ *adj* tactical. ● *nf* (Mil) tactics; **une ~** a tactic.
taie /tɛ/ *nf* **~ (d'oreiller)** pillowcase.
taille /taj/ *nf* (milieu du corps) waist; (hauteur) height; (grandeur) size; **de ~**

sizeable; **être de ~ à faire** be up to doing.
taille-crayons /tajkʀɛjɔ̃/ *nm inv* pencil-sharpener.
tailler /taje/ [1] *vt* cut; (*arbre*) prune; (*crayon*) sharpen; (*vêtement*) cut out. □ **se ~** *vpr* 🆇 clear off.
tailleur /tajœʀ/ *nm* (costume) woman's suit; (couturier) tailor; **en ~** cross-legged; **~ de pierre** stone-cutter.
taire /tɛʀ/ [47] *vt* not to reveal; **faire ~** silence. □ **se ~** *vpr* be silent *ou* quiet; (devenir silencieux) fall silent.
talc /talk/ *nm* talcum powder.
talent /talɑ̃/ *nm* talent.
talentueux, -euse *adj* talented, gifted.
talon /talɔ̃/ *nm* heel; (de chèque) stub.
tambour /tɑ̃buʀ/ *nm* drum; (d'église) vestibule.
Tamise /tamiz/ *nf* Thames.
tampon /tɑ̃pɔ̃/ *nm* (de bureau) stamp; (ouate) wad, pad; **~ (hygiénique)** tampon.
tamponner /tɑ̃pɔne/ [1] *vt* (*document*) stamp; (*véhicule*) crash into; (*plaie*) swab.
tandem /tɑ̃dɛm/ *nm* (vélo) tandem; (personnes: fig) duo.
tandis que /tɑ̃di(k(ə)/ *conj* while.
tanière /tanjɛʀ/ *nf* den.
tant /tɑ̃/ *adv* (travailler, manger) so much; **~ de** (quantité) so much; (nombre) so many; **~ que** as long as; **en ~ que** as; **~ mieux!** all the better!; **~ pis!** too bad!
tante /tɑ̃t/ *nf* aunt.
tantôt /tɑ̃to/ *adv* sometimes.
tapage /tapaʒ/ *nm* din.
tape /tap/ *nf* slap. **tape-à-l'œil** *a inv* flashy, tawdry.
taper /tape/ [1] *vt* hit; (prendre 🆙) scrounge; **~ (à la machine)** type. ● *vi* (cogner) bang; (*soleil*) beat down; **~ dans** (puiser dans) dig into; **~ sur** hit; **~ sur l'épaule de qn** tap sb on the shoulder. □ **se ~** *vpr* (corvée 🆙) get stuck with 🆙.
tapis /tapi/ *nm* carpet; (petit) rug; **~ de bain** bathmat; **~ roulant** (pour objets) conveyor belt; (pour piétons) moving walkway.

tapisser /tapise/ [1] *vt* (wall)paper; (fig) cover (**de** with). **tapisserie** *nf* tapestry; (papier peint) wallpaper.

taquin, **~e** /takɛ̃, -in/ *adj* fond of teasing. ● *nm,f* tease(r).

tard /taʀ/ *adv* late; **au plus ~** at the latest; **plus ~** later; **sur le ~** late in life.

tarder /taʀde/ [1] *vi* (être lent à venir) be a long time coming; **~ (à faire)** take a long time (doing), delay (doing); **sans (plus) ~** without (further) delay; **il me tarde de** I'm longing to.

tardif, -ive /taʀdif, -v/ *adj* late.

tare /taʀ/ *nf* (défaut) defect.

tarif /taʀif/ *nm* rate; (de train, taxi) fare; **plein ~** full price.

tarir /taʀiʀ/ [2] *vt/i* dry up. □ **se ~** *vpr* dry up.

tarte /taʀt/ *nf* tart. ● *a inv* (ridicule 🆃) ridiculous.

tartine /taʀtin/ *nf* slice of bread; **~ de beurre** slice of bread and butter. **tartiner** [1] *vt* spread.

tartre /taʀtʀ/ *nm* (de bouilloire) fur, scale; (sur les dents) tartar.

tas /tɑ/ *nm* pile, heap; **un ou des ~ de** 🆃 lots of.

tasse /tɑs/ *nf* cup; **~ à thé** teacup.

tasser /tɑse/ [1] *vt* pack, squeeze; (terre) pack (down). □ **se ~** *vpr* (terrain) sink; (se serrer) squeeze up.

tâter /tate/ [1] *vt* feel; (opinion: fig) sound out. ● *vi* **~ de** try out.

tatillon, **~ne** /tatijɔ̃, -jɔn/ *adj* finicky.

tâtonnements /tatɔnmɑ̃/ *nmpl* (essais) trial and error (+ *sg*).

tâtons: **à ~** /atɑtɔ̃/ *loc* **avancer à ~** grope one's way along.

tatouage /tatwaʒ/ *nm* (dessin) tattoo.

taupe /top/ *nf* mole.

taureau (*pl* **~x**) /tɔʀo/ *nm* bull; **le T~** Taurus.

taux /to/ *nm* rate.

taxe /taks/ *nf* tax.

taxi /taksi/ *nm* taxi(-cab); (personne 🆃) taxi driver.

taxiphone® /taksifɔn/ *nm* pay phone.

Tchécoslovaquie /tʃekɔslɔvaki/ *nf* Czechoslovakia.

tchèque /tʃɛk/ *adj* Czech; **République ~** Czech Republic. **T~** *nmf* Czech.

te, t' /tə, t/ *pron* you; (indirect) (to) you; (réfléchi) yourself.

technicien, **~ne** /tɛknisjɛ̃, -ɛn/ *nm,f* technician.

technique /tɛknik/ *adj* technical. ● *nf* technique.

techno /tɛkno/ *nf* (Mus) techno.

technologie /tɛknɔlɔʒi/ *nf* technology.

teindre /tɛ̃dʀ/ [22] *vt* dye. □ **se ~** *vpr* **se ~ les cheveux** dye one's hair.

teint /tɛ̃/ *nm* complexion.

teinte /tɛ̃t/ *nf* shade. **teinter** [1] *vt* (verre) tint; (bois) stain.

teinture /tɛ̃tyʀ/ *nf* (produit) dye.

teinturier, -ière /tɛ̃tyʀje, -jɛʀ/ *nm,f* dry-cleaner.

tel, **~le** /tɛl/ *adj* such; **un ~ livre** such a book; **~ que** such as, like; (ainsi que) (just) as; **~ ou ~** such-and-such; **~ quel** (just) as it is.

télé /tele/ *nf* 🆃 TV.

télécharger /teleʃaʀʒe/ [40] *vt* (Ordinat) download.

télécommande /telekɔmɑ̃d/ *nf* remote control.

télécommunications /telekɔmynikasjɔ̃/ *nfpl* telecommunications.

téléconférence /telekɔ̃feʀɑ̃s/ *nf* teleconferencing.

télécopie /telekɔpi/ *nf* fax. **télécopieur** *nm* fax machine.

téléfilm /telefilm/ *nm* TV film.

télégramme /telegʀam/ *nm* telegram.

télégraphier /telegʀafje/ [45] *vt/i* **~ (à)** cable.

téléguidé, **~e** /telegide/ *adj* radio-controlled.

télématique /telematik/ *nf* telematics (+ *sg*).

téléphérique /telefeʀik/ *nm* cable car.

téléphone /telefɔn/ *nm* (tele-) phone; **~ à carte** cardphone. **téléphoner** [1] *vt/i* **~ (à)** (tele)

phone. **téléphonique** *adj* (tele)
phone.

téléserveur /telesɛʀvœʀ/ *nm*
(Internet) remote server.

télésiège /telesjɛʒ/ *nm* chairlift.

téléski /teleski/ *nm* ski tow.

téléspectateur, -trice /tele-
spɛktatœʀ, -tʀis/ *nm, f* (television)
viewer.

télévente /televɑ̃t/ *nf* telesales (+
pl).

télévisé, ∼e /televize/ *adj* (*débat*)
televised; **émission ∼e** television
programme. **télévision** *nf*
television.

télex /telɛks/ *nm* telex.

tellement /tɛlmɑ̃/ *adv* (*tant*) so
much; (*si*) so; **∼ de** (*quantité*) so much;
(*nombre*) so many.

téméraire /temeʀɛʀ/ *adj* (*personne*)
reckless.

témoignage /temwaɲaʒ/ *nm*
testimony, evidence; (*récit*) account;
∼ de (*marque*) token of.

témoigner /temwaɲe/ [1] *vi* testify
(**de** to). ● *vt* (*montrer*) show; **∼ que**
testify that.

témoin /temwɛ̃/ *nm* witness; (Sport)
baton; **être ∼ de** witness; **∼ oculaire**
eyewitness.

tempe /tɑ̃p/ *nf* (Anat) temple.

tempérament /tɑ̃peʀamɑ̃/ *nm*
temperament, disposition.

température /tɑ̃peʀatyʀ/ *nf*
temperature.

tempête /tɑ̃pɛt/ *nf* storm; **∼ de
neige** snowstorm.

temple /tɑ̃pl/ *nm* temple; (*protestant*)
church.

temporaire /tɑ̃pɔʀɛʀ/ *adj*
temporary.

temps /tɑ̃/ *nm* (*notion*) time; (Gram)
tense; (*étape*) stage; **à ∼ partiel/plein**
part-/full-time; **ces derniers ∼** lately;
dans le ∼ at one time; **dans quelque
∼** in a while; **de ∼ en ∼** from time
to time; **∼ d'arrêt** pause; **avoir tout
son ∼** have plenty of time; (*météo*)
weather; **∼ de chien** filthy weather;
quel ∼ fait-il? what's the weather
like?

tenace /tənas/ *adj* stubborn.

tenaille /tənaj/ *nf* pincers (+ *pl*).

tendance /tɑ̃dɑ̃s/ *nf* tendency;
(*évolution*) trend; **avoir ∼ à** tend to.

tendon /tɑ̃dɔ̃/ *nm* tendon.

tendre¹ /tɑ̃dʀ/ [3] *vt* stretch; (*piège*)
set; (*bras*) stretch out; (*main*) hold
out; (*cou*) crane; **∼ qch à qn** hold sth
out to sb; **∼ l'oreille** prick up one's
ears. ● *vi* **∼ à** tend to.

tendre² /tɑ̃dʀ/ *adj* tender; (*couleur,
bois*) soft. **tendresse** *nf* tenderness.

tendu, ∼e /tɑ̃dy/ *adj* (*corde*) tight;
(*personne, situation*) tense.

ténèbres /tenɛbʀ/ *nfpl* darkness (+
sg).

teneur /tənœʀ/ *nf* content.

tenir /təniʀ/ [59] *vt* hold; (*pari,
promesse, hôtel*) keep; (*place*) take
up; (*propos*) utter; (*rôle*) play; **∼ de**
(avoir reçu de) have got from; **∼ pour**
regard as; **∼ chaud** keep warm; **∼
compte de** take into account; **∼ le
coup** hold out; **∼ tête à** stand up to.
● *vi* hold; **∼ à** be attached to; **∼ à
faire** be anxious to do; **∼ bon** stand
firm; **∼ dans** fit into; **∼ de qn** take
after sb; **tiens!** (surprise) hey! □ **se ∼**
vpr (debout) stand; (avoir lieu) be held;
se ∼ à hold on to; **s'en ∼ à** (se limiter
à) confine oneself to.

tennis /tenis/ *nm* tennis; **∼ de table**
table tennis. ● *nmpl* (chaussures)
sneakers.

ténor /tenɔʀ/ *nm* tenor.

tension /tɑ̃sjɔ̃/ *nf* tension; **avoir de
la ∼** have high blood-pressure.

tentation /tɑ̃tasjɔ̃/ *nf* temptation.

tentative /tɑ̃tativ/ *nf* attempt.

tente /tɑ̃t/ *nf* tent.

tenter /tɑ̃te/ [1] *vt* (allécher) tempt;
(essayer) try (**de faire** to do).

tenture /tɑ̃tyʀ/ *nf* curtain; **∼s**
draperies.

tenu, ∼e /təny/ *adj* **bien ∼** well
kept; **∼ de** required. ● ⇒TENIR [58].

tenue /təny/ *nf* (habillement) dress; (de
maison) upkeep; (conduite) (good)
behaviour; (maintien) posture; **∼ de
soirée** evening dress.

Tergal® /tɛʀgal/ *nm* Terylene®.

terme /tɛʀm/ *nm* (mot) term; (date
limite) time-limit; (fin) end; **né avant ∼**
premature; **à long/court ∼** long-/
short-term; **en bons ∼s** on good
terms (**avec** with).

terminaison /tɛʀminɛzɔ̃/ nf (Gram) ending.

terminal, ~**e** (mpl **-aux**) /tɛʀminal, -o/ adj terminal. ● nm terminal.

terminale nf (Scol) ≈ sixth form; (US) twelfth grade.

terminer /tɛʀmine/ [1] vt/i finish; (discours) end, finish. □ **se** ~ vpr end (**par** with).

terne /tɛʀn/ adj dull, drab.

ternir /tɛʀniʀ/ [2] vt/i tarnish. □ **se** ~ vpr tarnish.

terrain /tɛʀɛ̃/ nm ground; (parcelle) piece of land; (à bâtir) plot; ~ **d'aviation** airfield; ~ **de camping** campsite; ~ **de golf** golf course; ~ **de jeu** playground; ~ **vague** waste ground.

terrasse /tɛʀas/ nf terrace; **à la** ~ (d'un café) outside (a café).

terrasser /tɛʀase/ [1] vt (adversaire) knock down; (maladie) strike down.

terre /tɛʀ/ nf (planète, matière) earth; (étendue, pays) land; (sol) ground; **à** ~ (Naut) ashore; **par** ~ (dehors) on the ground; (dedans) on the floor; ~ (**cuite**) terracotta; **la** ~ **ferme** dry land; ~ **glaise** clay. **terreau** (pl ~**x**) nm compost. **terre-plein** (pl **terres-pleins**) nm platform; (de route) central reservation.

terrestre /tɛʀɛstʀ/ adj (animaux) land; (de notre planète) of the Earth.

terreur /tɛʀœʀ/ nf terror.

terrible /tɛʀibl/ adj terrible; (formidable 🗊) terrific.

terrier /tɛʀje/ nm (trou) burrow; (chien) terrier.

terrifier /tɛʀifje/ [45] vt terrify.

territoire /tɛʀitwaʀ/ nm territory.

terroir /tɛʀwaʀ/ nm land; **du** ~ local.

terroriser /tɛʀɔʀize/ [1] vt terrorize.

terrorisme /tɛʀɔʀism/ nm terrorism. **terroriste** nmf terrorist.

tertiaire /tɛʀsjɛʀ/ adj (secteur) service.

tes /te/ ⇒TON[1].

test /tɛst/ nm test.

testament /tɛstamɑ̃/ nm (Jur) will; (politique, artistique) testament; **Ancien/ Nouveau T**~ Old/New Testament.

tétanos /tetanos/ nm tetanus.

têtard /tɛtaʀ/ nm tadpole.

tête /tɛt/ nf head; (visage) face; (cheveux) hair; **à la** ~ **de** at the head of; **à** ~ **reposée** at one's leisure; **de** ~ (calculer) in one's head; **faire la** ~ sulk; **tenir** ~ **à qn** stand up to sb; **il n'en fait qu'à sa** ~ he does just as he pleases; **en** ~ (Sport) in the lead; **faire une** ~ (au football) head the ball; **une forte** ~ a rebel; **la** ~ **la première** head first; **de la** ~ **aux pieds** from head to toe.

tête-à-tête /tɛtatɛt/ nm inv tête-à-tête; **en** ~ in private.

tétée /tete/ nf feed. **téter** [14] vt/i suck.

tétine /tetin/ nf (de biberon) teat; (sucette) dummy; (US) pacifier.

têtu, ~**e** /tety/ adj stubborn.

texte /tɛkst/ nm text; (de leçon) subject; (morceau choisi) passage.

texteur /tɛkstœʀ/ nm (Ordinat) word-processor.

textile /tɛkstil/ nm & a textile.

TGV abrév m (**train à grande vitesse**) TGV, high-speed train.

thé /te/ nm tea.

théâtre /teɑtʀ/ nm theatre; (d'un crime) scene; **faire du** ~ act.

théière /tejɛʀ/ nf teapot.

thème /tɛm/ nm theme; (traduction: Scol) prose.

théorie /teɔʀi/ nf theory. **théorique** adj theoretical.

thérapie /teʀapi/ nf therapy.

thermique /tɛʀmik/ adj thermal.

thermomètre /tɛʀmɔmɛtʀ/ nm thermometer.

thermos® /tɛʀmos/ nm ou f Thermos® (flask).

thermostat /tɛʀmɔsta/ nm thermostat.

thèse /tɛz/ nf thesis.

thon /tɔ̃/ nm tuna.

thym /tɛ̃/ nm thyme.

tibia /tibja/ nm shinbone.

tic /tik/ nm (contraction) tic, twitch; (manie) habit.

ticket /tikɛ/ nm ticket.

tiède /tjɛd/ adj lukewarm; (nuit) warm.

tiédir /tjediʀ/ [2] vt/i (faire) ~ warm up.

tien, **~ne** /tjɛ̃, -ɛn/ *pron* le ~, la ~ne, les ~(ne)s yours; à la ~ne! cheers!

tiens, tient /tjɛ̃/ ⇒TENIR [59].

tiercé /tjɛRse/ *nm* place-betting.

tiers, tierce /tjɛR, tjɛRs/ *adj* third. ● *nm* (fraction) third; (personne) third party. **tiers-monde** *nm* Third World.

tige /tiʒ/ *nf* (Bot) stem, stalk; (en métal) shaft, rod.

tigre /tigR/ *nm* tiger.

tigresse /tigRɛs/ *nf* tigress.

tilleul /tijœl/ *nm* lime tree, linden tree; (infusion) linden tea.

timbre /tɛ̃bR/ *nm* stamp; (sonnette) bell; (de voix) tone. ~ **poste** (*pl* ~s **poste**) *nm* postage stamp. **timbrer** [1] *vt* stamp.

timide /timid/ *adj* shy, timid. **timidité** *nf* shyness.

timoré, ~e /timɔRe/ *adj* timorous.

tintement /tɛ̃tmɑ̃/ *nm* (de sonnette) ringing; (de clés) jingling.

tique /tik/ *nf* tick.

tir /tiR/ *nm* (Sport) shooting; (action de tirer) firing; (feu, rafale) fire; ~ **à l'arc** archery; ~ **au pigeon** clay pigeon shooting.

tirage /tiRaʒ/ *nm* (de photo) printing; (de journal) circulation; (de livre) edition; (Ordinat) hard copy; (de cheminée) draught; ~ **au sort** draw.

tire-bouchon (*pl* ~s) /tiRbuʃɔ̃/ *nm* corkscrew.

tirelire /tiRliR/ *nf* piggy bank.

tirer /tiRe/ [1] *vt* pull; (*langue*) stick out; (*conclusion, trait, rideaux*) draw; (*coup de feu*) fire; (*gibier*) shoot; (*photo*) print; ~ **de** (sortir) take *ou* get out of; (extraire) extract from; (*plaisir, nom*) derive from; ~ **parti de** take advantage of; ~ **profit de** profit from; **se faire** ~ **l'oreille** get told off. ● *vi* shoot, fire (**sur** at); ~ **sur** (*corde*) pull at; (*couleur*) verge on; ~ **à sa fin** be drawing to a close; ~ **au clair** clarify; ~ **au sort** draw lots (for). □ **se** ~ *vpr* 🔄 clear off; **se** ~ **de** get out of; **s'en** ~ (en réchapper) pull through; (réussir 🔄) cope.

tiret /tiRɛ/ *nm* dash.

tireur /tiRœR/ *nm* gunman; ~ **d'élite** marksman; ~ **isolé** sniper.

tiroir /tiRwaR/ *nm* drawer. **tiroir-caisse** (*pl* **tiroirs-caisses**) *nm* till, cash register.

tisane /tizan/ *nf* herbal tea.

tissage /tisaʒ/ *nm* weaving. **tisser** [1] *vt* weave. **tisserand** *nm* weaver.

tissu /tisy/ *nm* fabric, material; (biologique) tissue; **un** ~ **de mensonges** (fig) a pack of lies. **tissu-éponge** (*pl* **tissus-éponge**) *nm* towelling.

titre /titR/ *nm* title; (diplôme) qualification; (Comm) bond; ~**s** (droits) claims; (gros) ~**s** headlines; **à** ~ **d'exemple** as an example; **à juste** ~ rightly; **à** ~ **privé** in a private capacity; **à double** ~ on two accounts; ~ **de propriété** title deed.

tituber /titybe/ [1] *vi* stagger.

titulaire /titylɛR/ *adj* **être** ~ be a permanent staff member; **être** ~ **de** hold. ● *nmf* (de permis) holder. **titulariser** [1] *vt* give permanent status to.

toast /tost/ *nm* (pain) piece of toast; (canapé, allocution) toast.

toboggan /tɔbɔgɑ̃/ *nm* (de jeu) slide; (Auto) flyover.

toi /twa/ *pron* you; (réfléchi) yourself; **dépêche-**~ hurry up.

toile /twal/ *nf* cloth; (tableau) canvas; ~ **d'araignée** cobweb; ~ **de fond** (fig) backdrop; **la** ~ (Internet) the Web.

toilette /twalɛt/ *nf* (habillement) outfit; ~**s** (cabinets) toilet(s); **de** ~ (articles, savon) toilet; **faire sa** ~ have a wash.

toi-même /twamɛm/ *pron* yourself.

toit /twa/ *nm* roof; ~ **ouvrant** (Auto) sunroof.

toiture /twatyR/ *nf* roof.

tôle /tol/ *nf* (plaque) iron sheet; ~ **ondulée** corrugated iron.

tolérant, ~e /tɔleRɑ̃, -t/ *adj* tolerant. **tolérer** [14] *vt* tolerate.

tomate /tɔmat/ *nf* tomato.

tombe /tɔ̃b/ *nf* grave; (pierre) gravestone.

tombeau (*pl* ~**x**) /tɔ̃bo/ *nm* tomb.

tomber /tɔ̃be/ [1] *vi* (aux être) fall; (fièvre, vent) drop; **faire** ~ knock over; (gouvernement) bring down; **laisser** ~ (objet, amoureux) drop; (collègue) let down; (activité) give up;

t

laisse ~! ⊞ forget it!; ~ à l'eau (*projet*) fall through; ~ **bien** *ou* **à point** come at the right time; ~ **en panne** break down; ~ **en syncope** faint; ~ **sur** (trouver) run across.

tombola /tɔ̃bɔla/ *nf* tombola; (US) lottery.

tome /tom/ *nm* volume.

ton¹, ta (**ton** *before vowel or mute h*) (*pl* **tes**) /tɔ̃, ta, tɔ̃, te/ *adj* your.

ton² /tɔ̃/ *nm* (hauteur de voix) pitch; **d'un ~ sec** drily; **de bon ~** in good taste.

tonalité /tɔnalite/ *nf* (Mus) key; (de téléphone) dialling tone; (US) dial tone.

tondeuse /tɔ̃døz/ *nf* (à moutons) shears (+ *pl*); (à cheveux) clippers (+ *pl*); ~ **à gazon** lawn-mower. **tondre** [3] *vt* (*herbe*) mow; (*mouton*) shear; (*cheveux*) clip.

tonne /tɔn/ *nf* tonne.

tonneau (*pl* ~**x**) /tɔno/ *nm* barrel; (en voiture) somersault.

tonnerre /tɔnɛʀ/ *nm* thunder.

tonton /tɔ̃tɔ̃/ *nm* ⊞ uncle.

tonus /tɔnys/ *nm* energy.

torche /tɔʀʃ/ *nf* torch.

torchon /tɔʀʃɔ̃/ *nm* (pour la vaisselle) tea towel.

tordre /tɔʀdʀ/ [3] *vt* twist. □ **se ~** *vpr* **se ~ la cheville** twist one's ankle; **se ~ de douleur** writhe in pain; **se ~ (de rire)** split one's sides.

tordu, ~e /tɔʀdy/ *adj* twisted, bent; (*esprit*) warped, twisted.

torpille /tɔʀpij/ *nf* torpedo.

torrent /tɔʀɑ̃/ *nm* torrent.

torride /tɔʀid/ *adj* torrid; (*chaleur*) scorching.

torse /tɔʀs/ *nm* chest; (Anat) torso.

tort /tɔʀ/ *nm* wrong; **avoir ~** be wrong (**de faire** to do); **donner ~ à** prove wrong; **être dans son ~** be in the wrong; **faire (du) ~ à** harm; **à ~** wrongly; **à ~ et à travers** without thinking.

torticolis /tɔʀtikɔli/ *nm* stiff neck.

tortiller /tɔʀtije/ [1] *vt* twist, twirl. □ **se ~** *vpr* wriggle.

tortionnaire /tɔʀsjɔnɛʀ/ *nm* torturer.

tortue /tɔʀty/ *nf* tortoise; (d'eau) turtle.

tortueux, -euse /tɔʀtɥø, -z/ *adj* (*chemin*) twisting; (*explication*) tortuous.

torture /tɔʀtyʀ/ *nf* torture. **torturer** [1] *vt* torture.

tôt /to/ *adv* early; **au plus ~** at the earliest; **le plus ~ possible** as soon as possible; ~ **ou tard** sooner or later; **ce n'est pas trop ~!** it's about time!

total, ~e (*mpl* **-aux**) /tɔtal, -o/ *adj* total. ● *nm* (*pl* **-aux**) total; **au ~** all in all. **totalement** *adv* totally. **totaliser** [1] *vt* total. **totalitaire** *adj* totalitarian.

totalité /tɔtalite/ *nf* **la ~ de** all of.

touche /tuʃ/ *nf* (de piano) key; (de peinture) touch; (**ligne de**) ~ (Sport) touchline.

toucher /tuʃe/ [1] *vt* touch; (émouvoir) move, touch; (contacter) get in touch with; (*cible*) hit; (*argent*) draw; (*chèque*) cash; (concerner) affect. ● *vi* ~ **à** touch; (*question*) touch on; (*fin, but*) approach; **je vais lui en ~ deux mots** I'll talk to him about it. □ **se ~** *vpr* (*lignes*) touch. ● *nm* (sens) touch.

touffe /tuf/ *nf* (de poils, d'herbe) tuft; (de plantes) clump.

toujours /tuʒuʀ/ *adv* always; (encore) still; (de toute façon) anyway; **pour ~** for ever; ~ **est-il que** the fact remains that.

toupet /tupɛ/ *nm* (culot ⊞) cheek, nerve.

tour /tuʀ/ *nf* tower; (immeuble) tower block; (échecs) rook; ~ **de contrôle** control tower. ● *nm* (mouvement, succession, tournure) turn; (excursion) trip; (à pied) walk; (en auto) drive; (artifice) trick; (circonférence) circumference; (Tech) lathe; ~ **(de piste)** lap; **à ~ de rôle** in turn; **à mon ~** when it is my turn; **c'est mon ~ de** it is my turn to; **faire le ~ de** go round; (*question*) survey; ~ **d'horizon** survey; ~ **de potier** potter's wheel; ~ **de taille** waist measurement; (ligne) waistline.

tourbillon /tuʀbijɔ̃/ *nm* whirlwind; (d'eau) whirlpool; (fig) swirl.

tourisme /tuʀism/ *nm* tourism; **faire du ~** do some sightseeing.

touriste /tuʀist/ nmf tourist.
  touristique adj tourist; (route)
  scenic.

tourmenter /tuʀmɑ̃te/ vt torment.
  □ **se ~** vpr worry.

tournant, ~e /tuʀnɑ̃, -t/ adj (qui
  pivote) revolving. ● nm bend; (fig)
  turning-point.

tourne-disque (pl ~s)
  /tuʀnədisk/ nm record-player.

tournée /tuʀne/ nf (de facteur, au café)
  round; **c'est ma ~** I'll buy this
  round; (d'artiste) tour.

tourner /tuʀne/ [1] vt turn; (film)
  shoot, make; **~ le dos à** turn one's
  back on; **~ en dérision** mock. ● vi
  turn; (toupie, tête) spin; (moteur,
  usine) run; **~ autour de** go round;
  (personne, maison) hang around;
  (terre) revolve round; (question)
  centre on; **~ de l'œil** 🅸 faint; **mal ~**
  (affaire) turn out badly. □ **se ~** vpr
  turn.

tournesol /tuʀnəsɔl/ nm sunflower.

tournevis /tuʀnəvis/ nm
  screwdriver.

tournoi /tuʀnwa/ nm tournament.

tourte /tuʀt/ nf pie.

tourterelle /tuʀtəʀɛl/ nf turtle
  dove.

Toussaint /tusɛ̃/ nf **la ~** All Saints'
  Day.

tousser /tuse/ [1] vi cough.

tout, ~e (pl **tous, toutes**) /tu, tut/
  nm (ensemble) whole; **en ~** in all; **pas
  du ~!** not at all! ● adj all; (n'importe
  quel) any; **~ le pays** the whole
  country, all the country; **~e la nuit/
  journée** the whole night/day; **~ un
  paquet** a whole pack; **tous les jours**
  every day; **tous les deux ans** every
  two years; **~ le monde** everyone;
  tous les deux, toutes les deux both
  of them; **tous les trois** all three (of
  them). ● pron everything; all;
  anything; **tous** /tus/, **toutes** all; **tous
  ensemble** all together; **prends ~** take
  everything; **~ ce que tu veux**
  everything you want. ● adv (très)
  very; (entièrement) all; **~ au bout/
  début** right at the end/beginning; **~
  en marchant** while walking; **~ à
  coup** all of a sudden; **~ à fait** quite,
  completely; **~ à l'heure** in a moment;

(passé) a moment ago; **~ au** ou **le
  long de** throughout; **~ au plus/
  moins** at most/least; **~ de même** all
  the same; **~ de suite** straight away;
  ~ entier whole; **~ neuf** brand new;
  ~ nu stark naked. **tout-à-l'égout**
  nm inv main drainage.

toutefois /tutfwa/ adv however.

tout(-)terrain /tuteʀɛ̃/ a inv all
  terrain.

toux /tu/ nf cough.

toxicomane /tɔksikɔman/ nmf
  drug addict.

toxique /tɔksik/ adj toxic.

trac /tʀak/ nm **le ~** nerves; (Théât)
  stage fright.

tracas /tʀaka/ nm worry.

trace /tʀas/ nf (traînée, piste) trail;
  (d'animal, de pneu) tracks; **~s de pas**
  footprints.

tracer /tʀase/ [10] vt draw; (écrire)
  write; (route) open up.

trachée-artère /tʀaʃeaʀtɛʀ/ nf
  windpipe.

tracteur /tʀaktœʀ/ nm tractor.

tradition /tʀadisjɔ̃/ nf tradition.
  traditionnel, ~le adj traditional.

traducteur, -trice /tʀadyktœʀ,
  -tʀis/ nm, f translator. **traduction**
  nf translation.

traduire /tʀadɥiʀ/ [17] vt translate;
  ~ en justice take to court.

trafic /tʀafik/ nm (commerce,
  circulation) traffic.

trafiquant, ~e /tʀafikɑ̃, -t/ nm, f
  trafficker; (d'armes, de drogues) dealer.

trafiquer /tʀafike/ [1] vi traffic. ● vt
  🅸 (moteur) fiddle with.

tragédie /tʀaʒedi/ nf tragedy.
  tragique adj tragic.

trahir /tʀaiʀ/ [2] vt betray. **trahison**
  nf betrayal; (Mil) treason.

train /tʀɛ̃/ nm (Rail) train; (allure)
  pace; **aller bon ~** walk briskly; **en ~
  de faire** busy) doing; **~
  d'atterrissage** undercarriage; **~
  électrique** (jouet) electric train set; **~
  de vie** lifestyle.

traîne /tʀɛn/ nf (de robe) train; **à la ~**
  lagging behind.

traîneau (pl ~x) /tʀɛno/ nm sleigh.

traînée /tʀɛne/ nf (trace) trail;
  (longue) streak; (femme: péj) slut.

t

traîner /tʀɛne/ [1] *vt* drag (along); ~
les pieds drag one's feet. ● *vi* (pendre)
trail; (rester en arrière) trail behind;
(flâner) hang about; (*papiers, affaires*)
lie around; ~ **(en longueur)** drag on;
ça n'a pas traîné! that didn't take
long! □ **se** ~ *vpr* (par terre) crawl.

traire /tʀɛʀ/ [29] *vt* milk.

trait /tʀɛ/ *nm* line; (en dessinant)
stroke; (caractéristique) feature, trait;
~**s** (du visage) features; **avoir** ~ **à**
relate to; **d'un** ~ (*boire*) in one gulp;
~ **d'union** hyphen; (fig) link.

traite /tʀɛt/ *nf* (de vache) milking;
(Comm) draft; **d'une (seule)** ~ in one
go, at a stretch.

traité /tʀete/ *nm* (pacte) treaty;
(ouvrage) treatise.

traitement /tʀɛtmɑ̃/ *nm* treatment;
(salaire) salary; ~ **de données** data
processing; ~ **de texte** word
processing.

traiter /tʀete/ [1] *vt* treat; (*affaire*)
deal with; (*données, produit*) process;
~ **qn de lâche** call sb a coward. ● *vi*
deal (**avec** with); ~ **de** (*sujet*) deal
with.

traiteur /tʀɛtœʀ/ *nm* caterer;
(boutique) delicatessen.

traître, -esse /tʀɛtʀ, -ɛs/ *adj*
treacherous. ● *nm, f* traitor.

trajectoire /tʀaʒɛktwaʀ/ *nf* path.

trajet /tʀaʒɛ/ *nm* (voyage) journey;
(itinéraire) route.

trame /tʀam/ *nf* (de tissu) weft; (de
récit) framework.

tramway /tʀamwɛ/ *nm* tram; (US)
streetcar.

tranchant, ~e /tʀɑ̃ʃɑ̃, -t/ *adj*
sharp; (fig) cutting. ● *nm* cutting
edge; **à double** ~ two-edged.

tranche /tʀɑ̃ʃ/ *nf* (rondelle) slice;
(bord) edge; (d'âge, de revenu) bracket.

tranchée /tʀɑ̃ʃe/ *nf* trench.

trancher /tʀɑ̃ʃe/ [1] *vt* cut;
(*question*) decide; (contraster) contrast
(**sur** with).

tranquille /tʀɑ̃kil/ *adj* quiet;
(*esprit*) at rest; (*conscience*) clear;
être/laisser ~ be/leave in peace;
tiens-toi ~! be quiet!

tranquillisant *nm* tranquillizer.

tranquilliser [1] *vt* reassure.

tranquillité *nf* (peace and) quiet;
(d'esprit) peace of mind.

transcription /tʀɑ̃skʀipsjɔ̃/ *nf*
transcription; (copie) transcript.

transcrire [30] *vt* transcribe.

transe /tʀɑ̃s/ *nf* **en** ~ in a trance.

transférer /tʀɑ̃sfeʀe/ [14] *vt*
transfer.

transfert /tʀɑ̃sfɛʀ/ *nm* transfer; ~
d'appel (au téléphone) call diversion.

transformateur /tʀɑ̃sfɔʀmatœʀ/
nm transformer.

transformation /tʀɑ̃sfɔʀmasjɔ̃/ *nf*
change; transformation.

transformer /tʀɑ̃sfɔʀme/ [1] *vt*
change; (radicalement) transform;
(*vêtement*) alter. □ **se** ~ *vpr* change;
(radicalement) be transformed; (**se**) ~
en turn into.

transiger /tʀɑ̃siʒe/ [40] *vi*
compromise.

transiter /tʀɑ̃zite/ [1] *vt/i* ~ **par**
pass through.

transitif, -ive /tʀɑ̃zitif, -v/ *adj*
transitive.

translucide /tʀɑ̃slysid/ *adj*
translucent.

transmettre /tʀɑ̃smɛtʀ/ [42] *vt*
(*savoir, maladie*) pass on; (*ondes*)
transmit; (à la radio) broadcast.

transmission *nf* transmission;
(*radio*) broadcasting.

transparence /tʀɑ̃spaʀɑ̃s/ *nf*
transparency. **transparent, ~e** *adj*
transparent.

transpercer /tʀɑ̃spɛʀse/ [10] *vt*
pierce.

transpiration /tʀɑ̃spiʀasjɔ̃/ *nf*
perspiration. **transpirer** [1] *vi*
perspire.

transplanter /tʀɑ̃splɑ̃te/ [1] *vt* (Bot,
Méd) transplant.

transport /tʀɑ̃spɔʀ/ *nm* transport
(ation); **durant le** ~ in transit; **les**
~**s** transport (+ *sg*); **les** ~**s en**
commun public transport (+ *sg*).

transporter /tʀɑ̃spɔʀte/ [1] *vt*
transport; (à la main) carry.
transporteur *nm* haulier; (US)
trucker.

transversal, ~e (*mpl* **-aux**)
/tʀɑ̃svɛʀsal, -o/ *adj* cross, transverse.

trapu, ~e /tʀapy/ *adj* stocky.

traumatisant, ~e /tʀɔmatizɑ̃, -t/ *adj* traumatic. **traumatiser** *vt* [1] traumatize. **traumatisme** *nm* trauma.

travail (*pl* **-aux**) /tʀavaj, -o/ *nm* work; (emploi, tâche) job; (façonnage) working; **travaux** work (+ *sg*); (routiers) roadworks; **~ à la chaîne** production line work; **travaux dirigés** (Scol) practical; **travaux forcés** hard labour; **travaux manuels** handicrafts; **travaux ménagers** housework.

travailler /tʀavaje/ [1] *vi* work; (se déformer) warp. ● *vt* (façonner) work; (étudier) work at *ou* on.

travailleur, -euse /tʀavajœʀ, -øz/ *nm,f* worker. ● *adj* hardworking.

travailliste /tʀavajist/ *adj* Labour. ● *nmf* Labour party member.

travers /tʀavɛʀ/ *nm* (défaut) failing; **à ~** through; **au ~ (de)** through; **de ~** (chapeau, nez) crooked; (regarder) askance; **j'ai avalé de ~** it went the wrong way; **en ~ (de)** across.

traversée /tʀavɛʀse/ *nf* crossing.

traverser /tʀavɛʀse/ [1] *vt* cross; (transpercer) go (right) through; (période, forêt) go *ou* pass through.

traversin /tʀavɛʀsɛ̃/ *nm* bolster.

travesti /tʀavɛsti/ *nm* transvestite.

trébucher /tʀebyʃe/ [1] *vi* stumble, trip (over); **faire ~** trip (up).

trèfle /tʀɛfl/ *nm* (plante) clover; (cartes) clubs.

treillis /tʀeji/ *nm* trellis; (en métal) wire mesh; (tenue militaire) combat uniform.

treize /tʀɛz/ *a & nm* thirteen.

tréma /tʀema/ *nm* diaeresis.

tremblement /tʀɑ̃bləmɑ̃/ *nm* shaking; **~ de terre** earthquake. **trembler** [1] *vi* shake, tremble; (lumière, voix) quiver.

tremper /tʀɑ̃pe/ [1] *vt/i* soak; (plonger) dip; (acier) temper; **faire ~** soak; **~ dans** (fig) be mixed up. □ **se ~** *vpr* (se baigner) have a dip.

tremplin /tʀɑ̃plɛ̃/ *nm* springboard.

trente /tʀɑ̃t/ *a & nm* thirty; **se mettre sur son ~ et un** dress up; **tous les ~-six du mois** once in a blue moon.

trépied /tʀepje/ *nm* tripod.

très /tʀɛ/ *adv* very; **~ aimé/estimé** much liked/esteemed.

trésor /tʀezɔʀ/ *nm* treasure; **le T~** public the revenue department.

trésorerie /tʀezɔʀʀi/ *nf* (bureaux) accounts department; (du Trésor public) revenue office; (argent) funds (+ *pl*); (gestion) accounts (+ *pl*). **trésorier, -ière** *nm,f* treasurer.

tressaillement /tʀesajmɑ̃/ *nm* quiver; start.

tresse /tʀɛs/ *nf* braid, plait.

trêve /tʀɛv/ *nf* truce; (fig) respite; **~ de plaisanteries** that's enough joking.

tri /tʀi/ *nm* (classement) sorting; (sélection) selection; **faire le ~ de** (classer) sort; (choisir) select; **centre de ~** sorting office.

triangle /tʀijɑ̃gl/ *nm* triangle.

tribal, ~e (*mpl* **-aux**) /tʀibal, -o/ *adj* tribal.

tribord /tʀibɔʀ/ *nm* starboard.

tribu /tʀiby/ *nf* tribe.

tribunal (*mpl* **-aux**) /tʀibynal, -o/ *nm* court.

tribune /tʀibyn/ *nf* (de stade) grandstand; (d'orateur) rostrum; (débat) forum; (d'église) gallery.

tribut /tʀiby/ *nm* tribute.

tributaire /tʀibytɛʀ/ *adj* **~ de** dependent on.

tricher /tʀiʃe/ [1] *vi* cheat. **tricheur, -euse** *nm,f* cheat.

tricolore /tʀikɔlɔʀ/ *adj* three-coloured; (écharpe) red, white and blue; (équipe) French.

tricot /tʀiko/ *nm* (activité) knitting; (pull) sweater; **en ~** knitted; **~ de corps** vest; (US) undershirt. **tricoter** [1] *vt/i* knit.

trier /tʀije/ [45] *vt* (classer) sort; (choisir) select.

trimestre /tʀimɛstʀ/ *nm* quarter; (Scol) term. **trimestriel, ~le** *adj* quarterly; (bulletin) end-of-term.

tringle /tʀɛ̃gl/ *nf* rail.

trinquer /tʀɛ̃ke/ [1] *vi* clink glasses.

triomphant, ~e /tʀijɔ̃fɑ̃, -t/ *adj* triumphant. **triomphe** *nm* triumph. **triompher** [1] *vi* triumph (de over); (jubiler) be triumphant.

tripes /tʀip/ *nfpl* (mets) tripe (+ *sg*); (entrailles 🔢) guts.

triple /tʀipl/ *adj* triple, treble. ● *nm* le ~ three times as much (de as). **triplés, -es** *nm, fpl* triplets.

tripot /tʀipo/ *nm* gambling den.

tripoter /tʀipɔte/ [1] *vt* 🔢 (*personne*) grope; (*objet*) fiddle with.

trisomique /tʀizɔmik/ *adj* être ~ have Down's syndrome.

triste /tʀist/ *adj* sad; (*rue, temps, couleur*) dreary; (lamentable) dreadful. **tristesse** *nf* sadness; dreariness.

trivial, ~e (*mpl* -iaux) /tʀivjal, -jo/ *adj* coarse.

troc /tʀɔk/ *nm* exchange; (Comm) barter.

trognon /tʀɔɲɔ̃/ *nm* (de fruit) core.

trois /tʀwɑ/ *a* & *nm* three; **hôtel** ~ **étoiles** three-star hotel. **troisième** *a* & *nmf* third.

trombone /tʀɔ̃bɔn/ *nm* (Mus) trombone; (agrafe) paperclip.

trompe /tʀɔ̃p/ *nf* (d'éléphant) trunk; (Mus) horn.

tromper /tʀɔ̃pe/ [1] *vt* deceive, mislead; (déjouer) elude. □ **se** ~ *vpr* be mistaken; **se** ~ **de route/d'heure** take the wrong road/get the time wrong.

trompette /tʀɔ̃pɛt/ *nf* trumpet.

trompeur, -euse /tʀɔ̃pœʀ, -øz/ *adj* (*apparence*) deceptive.

tronc /tʀɔ̃/ *nm* trunk; (boîte) collection box.

tronçon /tʀɔ̃sɔ̃/ *nm* section.

tronçonneuse /tʀɔ̃sɔnøz/ *nf* chain saw.

trône /tʀon/ *nm* throne. **trôner** [1] *vi* (*vase*) have pride of place (sur on).

trop /tʀo/ *adv* (*grand, loin*) too; (*boire, marcher*) too much; ~ (de) (quantité) too much; (nombre) too many; **ce serait** ~ **beau** one should be so lucky; **de** ~, **en** ~ too much; too many; **il a bu un verre de** ~ he's had one too many; **se sentir de** ~ feel one is in the way.

trophée /tʀɔfe/ *nm* trophy.

tropical, ~e (*mpl* -aux) /tʀɔpikal, -o/ *adj* tropical. **tropique** *nm* tropic.

trop-plein (*pl* ~s) /tʀɔplɛ̃/ *nm* excess; (dispositif) overflow.

troquer /tʀɔke/ [1] *vt* exchange; (Comm) barter (**contre** for).

trot /tʀo/ *nm* trot; **aller au** ~ trot. **trotter** [1] *vi* trot.

trotteuse /tʀɔtøz/ *nf* (de montre) second hand.

trottoir /tʀɔtwaʀ/ *nm* pavement; (US) sidewalk; ~ **roulant** moving walkway.

trou /tʀu/ *nm* hole; (moment) gap; (lieu: péj) dump; ~ (de mémoire) memory lapse; ~ **de serrure** keyhole; **faire son** ~ carve one's niche.

trouble /tʀubl/ *adj* (eau, image) unclear; (louche) shady. ● *nm* (émoi) emotion; ~s (Pol) disturbances; (Méd) disorder (+ *sg*).

troubler /tʀuble/ [1] *vt* disturb; (*eau*) make cloudy; (inquiéter) trouble. □ **se** ~ *vpr* (*personne*) become flustered.

trouer /tʀue/ [1] *vt* make a hole *ou* holes in; **mes chaussures sont trouées** my shoes have got holes in them.

troupe /tʀup/ *nf* troop; (d'acteurs) company.

troupeau (*pl* ~x) /tʀupo/ *nm* herd; (de moutons) flock.

trousse /tʀus/ *nf* case, bag; **aux** ~s **de** hot on sb's heels; ~ **de toilette** toilet bag.

trousseau (*pl* ~x) /tʀuso/ *nm* (de clefs) bunch; (de mariée) trousseau.

trouver /tʀuve/ [1] *vt* find; (penser) think; **il est venu me** ~ he came to see me. □ **se** ~ *vpr* (être) be; (se sentir) feel; **il se trouve que** it happens that; **si ça se trouve** maybe; **se** ~ **mal** faint.

truand /tʀyɑ̃/ *nm* gangster.

truc /tʀyk/ *nm* (moyen) way; (artifice) trick; (chose 🔢) thing. **trucage** *nm* (cinéma) special effect.

truffe /tʀyf/ *nf* (champignon, chocolat) truffle; (de chien) nose.

truffer /tʀyfe/ [1] *vt* (fig) fill, pack (de with).

truie /tʀyi/ *nf* (animal) sow.

truite /tʀyit/ *nf* trout.

truquer /tʀyke/ [1] *vt* fix, rig; (*photo*) fake; (*résultats*) fiddle.

tsar /tsaʀ/ *nm* tsar, czar.

tu /ty/ *pron* (parent, ami, enfant) you. ● ⇒TAIRE [47].

tuba /tyba/ *nm* (Mus) tuba; (Sport) snorkel.

tube /tyb/ *nm* tube.

tuberculose /tybɛʀkyloz/ *nf* tuberculosis.

tuer /tɥe/ [1] *vt* kill; (d'une balle) shoot, kill; (épuiser) exhaust; ~ **par balles** shoot dead. □ **se** ~ *vpr* kill oneself; (accident) be killed.

tuerie /tyʀi/ *nf* killing.

tue-tête: **à** ~ /atytɛt/ *loc* at the top of one's voice.

tuile /tɥil/ *nf* tile; (malchance 🆃) (stroke of) bad luck.

tulipe /tylip/ *nf* tulip.

tumeur /tymœʀ/ *nf* tumour.

tumulte /tymylt/ *nm* commotion; (désordre) turmoil.

tunique /tynik/ *nf* tunic.

Tunisie /tynizi/ *nf* Tunisia.

tunnel /tynɛl/ *nm* tunnel.

turbo /tyʀbo/ *adj* turbo. ● *nf* (voiture) turbo.

turbulent, ~**e** /tyʀbylɑ̃, -t/ *adj* boisterous, turbulent.

turc, **-que** /tyʀk/ *adj* Turkish. ● *nm* (Ling) Turkish. **T**~, **-que** Turk.

turfiste /tyʀfist/ *nmf* racegoer.

Turquie /tyʀki/ *nf* Turkey.

tutelle /tytɛl/ *nf* (Jur) guardianship; (fig) protection.

tuteur, **-trice** /tytœʀ, -tʀis/ *nm,f* (Jur) guardian. ● *nm* (bâton) stake.

tutoiement /tytwamɑ̃/ *nm* use of the 'tu' form. **tutoyer** [31] *vt* address using the 'tu' form.

tuyau (*pl* ~**x**) /tɥijo/ *nm* pipe; (conseil 🆃) tip; ~ **d'arrosage** hosepipe.

TVA *abrév f* (**taxe à la valeur ajoutée**) VAT.

tympan /tɛ̃pɑ̃/ *nm* ear-drum.

type /tip/ *nm* (genre, traits) type; (individu 🆃) bloke, guy; **le** ~ **même de** a classic example of. ● *a inv* typical.

typique /tipik/ *adj* typical.

tyran /tiʀɑ̃/ *nm* tyrant. **tyrannie** *nf* tyranny. **tyranniser** [1] *vt* oppress, tyrannize.

Uu

UE *abrév f* (**Union européenne**) European Union.

Ukraine /ykʀɛn/ *nf* Ukraine.

ulcère /ylsɛʀ/ *nm* (Méd) ulcer.

ULM *abrév m* (**ultraléger motorisé**) microlight.

ultérieur, ~**e** /ylteʀjœʀ/ *adj* later. **ultérieurement** *adv* later.

ultime /yltim/ *adj* final.

un, **une** /œ̃, yn/

● *déterminant*

····➤ a; (devant voyelle) an; ~ **animal** an animal; ~ **jour** one day; **pas** ~ **arbre** not a single tree; **il fait** ~ **froid!** it's so cold!

● *pronom*

····➤ one; **l'**~ **d'entre nous** one of us; **les** ~**s croient que...** some believe...

····➤ **la une** the front page.

····➤ **j'en veux une** I want one.

● *adjectif*

····➤ one, a, an; **j'ai** ~ **garçon et deux filles** I have a *ou* one boy and two girls; **il est une heure** it is one o'clock.

● *nom masculin & féminin*

····➤ ~ **par** ~ one by one.

unanime /ynanim/ *adj* unanimous.

unanimité /ynanimite/ *nf* unanimity; **à l'**~ unanimously.

uni, ~**e** /yni/ *adj* united; (couple) close; (surface) smooth; (tissu) plain.

unième /ynjɛm/ *adj* -first; **vingt et** ~ twenty-first; **cent** ~ one hundred and first.

unifier /ynifje/ [45] *vt* unify.

uniforme /ynifɔʀm/ *nm* uniform. ● *adj* uniform. **uniformiser** [1] *vt* standardize. **uniformité** *nf* uniformity.

unilatéral, ∼e (*mpl* **-aux**) /ynilateʀal, -o/ *adj* unilateral.

union /ynjɔ̃/ *nf* union; **l'U**∼ **européenne** the European Union.

unique /ynik/ *adj* (seul) only; (*prix, voie*) one; (incomparable) unique; **enfant** ∼ only child; **sens** ∼ one-way street. **uniquement** *adv* only, solely.

unir /yniʀ/ [2] *vt* unite. □ **s'**∼ *vpr* unite, join.

unité /ynite/ *nf* unit; (harmonie) unity.

univers /yniveʀ/ *nm* universe.

universel, ∼le /yniveʀsel/ *adj* universal.

universitaire /yniveʀsiteʀ/ *adj* (*résidence*) university; (*niveau*) academic. ● *nmf* academic.

université /yniveʀsite/ *nf* university.

uranium /yʀanjɔm/ *nm* uranium.

urbain, ∼e /yʀbɛ̃, -ɛn/ *adj* urban. **urbanisme** *nm* town planning.

urgence /yʀʒɑ̃s/ *nf* (cas) emergency; (de situation, tâche) urgency; **d'**∼ (*mesure*) emergency; (*transporter*) urgently; **les** ∼**s** casualty (+ *sg*). **urgent**, ∼e *adj* urgent.

urine /yʀin/ *nf* urine. **urinoir** *nm* urinal.

urne /yʀn/ *nf* (électorale) ballot box; (vase) urn; **aller aux** ∼**s** go to the polls.

urticaire /yʀtikeʀ/ *nf* hives (+ *pl*), urticar.

us /ys/ *nmpl* **les** ∼ **et coutumes** habits and customs.

usage /yzaʒ/ *nm* use; (coutume) custom; (de langage) usage; **à l'**∼ **de** for; **d'**∼ (habituel) customary; **faire** ∼ **de** make use of.

usagé, ∼e /yzaʒe/ *adj* worn.

usager /yzaʒe/ *nm* user.

usé, ∼e /yze/ *adj* worn (out); (banal) trite.

user /yze/ [1] *vt* wear (out). ● *vi* ∼ **de** use. □ **s'**∼ *vpr* (tissu) wear (out).

usine /yzin/ *nf* factory, plant; ∼ **sidérurgique** ironworks (+ *pl*).

usité, ∼e /yzite/ *adj* common.

ustensile /ystɑ̃sil/ *nm* utensil.

usuel, ∼le /yzɥel/ *adj* ordinary, everyday.

usure /yzyʀ/ *nf* (détérioration) wear (and tear).

utérus /yteʀys/ *nm* womb, uterus.

utile /ytil/ *adj* useful.

utilisable /ytilizabl/ *adj* usable. **utilisation** *nf* use. **utiliser** [1] *vt* use.

utopie /ytɔpi/ *nf* Utopia; (idée) Utopian idea. **utopique** *adj* Utopian.

UV¹ *abrév f* (**unité de valeur**) course unit.

UV² *abrév mpl* (**ultraviolets**) ultraviolet rays; **faire des** ∼ use a sunbed.

Vv

va /va/ ⇒ALLER [8].

vacance /vakɑ̃s/ *nf* (poste) vacancy.

vacances /vakɑ̃s/ *nfpl* holiday(s); (US) vacation; **en** ∼ on holiday; ∼ **d'été, grandes** ∼ summer holidays. **vacancier**, **-ière** *nm,f* holidaymaker; (US) vacationer.

vacant, ∼e /vakɑ̃, -t/ *adj* vacant.

vacarme /vakaʀm/ *nm* din.

vaccin /vaksɛ̃/ *nm* vaccine. **vacciner** [1] *vt* vaccinate.

vache /vaʃ/ *nf* cow. ● *adj* (méchant 🄳) nasty.

vaciller /vasije/ [1] *vi* sway, wobble; (lumière) flicker; (hésiter) falter; (santé, mémoire) fail.

vadrouiller /vadʀuje/ [1] *vi* 🄳 wander about.

va-et-vient /vaevjɛ̃/ *nm inv* toing and froing; (de personnes) comings and goings; **faire le** ∼ go to and fro; (interrupteur) two-way switch.

vagabond, ∼e /vagabɔ̃, -d/ *nm,f* vagrant.

vagin /vaʒɛ̃/ *nm* vagina.

vague /vag/ adj vague. ● nm
regarder dans le ~ stare into space;
il est resté dans le ~ he was vague
about it. ● nf wave; ~ de fond
ground swell; ~ de froid cold spell;
~ de chaleur heatwave.

vaillant, ~e /vajã, -t/ adj brave;
(vigoureux) strong.

vaille /vaj/ ⇒VALOIR [60].

vain, ~e /vɛ̃, vɛn/ adj vain, futile; en
~ in vain.

vaincre /vɛ̃kʀ/ [59] vt defeat;
(surmonter) overcome. **vaincu**, ~e
nm, f (Sport) loser. **vainqueur** nm
victor; (Sport) winner.

vais /vɛ/ ⇒ALLER [8].

vaisseau (pl ~x) /vɛso/ nm ship;
(veine) vessel; ~ spatial spaceship.

vaisselle /vɛsɛl/ nf crockery; (à
laver) dishes; faire la ~ do the
washing-up, wash the dishes; liquide
~ washing-up liquid.

valable /valabl/ adj valid; (de qualité)
worthwhile.

valet /valɛ/ nm (aux cartes) jack; ~
(de chambre) manservant.

valeur /valœʀ/ nf value; (mérite)
worth, value; ~s (Comm) stocks and
shares; avoir de la ~ be valuable;
prendre/perdre de la ~ go up/down
in value; objets de ~ valuables; sans
~ worthless.

valide /valid/ adj (personne) fit;
(billet) valid. **valider** [1] vt validate.

valise /valiz/ nf (suit)case; faire ses
~s pack (one's bags).

vallée /vale/ nf valley.

valoir /valwaʀ/ [60] vi (mériter) be
worth; (égaler) be as good as; (être
valable) (règle) apply; faire ~ (mérite,
qualité) emphasize; (terrain)
cultivate; (droit) assert; se faire ~
put oneself forward; ~ cher/100
francs be worth a lot/100 francs; que
vaut ce vin? what's this wine like?;
ne rien ~ be useless ou no good; ça
ne me dit rien qui vaille I don't like
the sound of that; ~ la peine or le
coup 🄸 be worth it; il vaut/vaudrait
mieux faire it is/would be better to
do. ● vt ~ qch à qn (éloges, critiques)
earn sb sth; (admiration) win sb sth.
□ se ~ vpr (être équivalents) be as

good as each other; ça se vaut it's all
the same.

valoriser /valɔʀize/ [1] vt add value
to; (produit) promote; (profession)
make attractive; (région, ressources)
develop.

valse /vals/ nf waltz.

vandale /vɑ̃dal/ nmf vandal.

vanille /vanij/ nf vanilla.

vanité /vanite/ nf vanity.
vaniteux, -euse adj vain,
conceited.

vanne /van/ nf (d'écluse) sluice-gate;
(propos 🄸) dig 🄸.

vantard, ~e /vɑ̃taʀ, -d/ adj
boastful. ● nm, f boaster.

vanter /vɑ̃te/ [1] vt praise. □ se ~
vpr boast (de about); se ~ de faire
pride oneself on doing.

vapeur /vapœʀ/ nf (eau) steam;
(brume, émanation) vapour; ~s fumes;
à ~ (bateau, locomotive) steam; faire
cuire à la ~ steam.

vaporisateur /vapɔʀizatœʀ/ nm
spray, atomizer. **vaporiser** [1] vt
spray.

varappe /vaʀap/ nf rock-climbing.

variable /vaʀjabl/ adj variable;
(temps) changeable.

varicelle /vaʀisɛl/ nf chickenpox.

varié, ~e /vaʀje/ adj (non monotone,
étendu) varied; (divers) various;
sandwichs ~s a selection of
sandwiches.

varier /vaʀje/ [45] vt/i vary.

variété /vaʀjete/ nf variety;
spectacle de ~s variety show.

vase /vɑz/ nm vase. ● nf silt, mud.

vaseux, -euse /vɑzø, -z/ adj (confus
🄸) woolly, hazy.

vaste /vast/ adj vast, huge.

vaurien, ~ne /voʀjɛ̃, -ɛn/ nm, f
good-for-nothing.

vautour /votuʀ/ nm vulture.

vautrer (se) /(sə)votʀe/ [1] vpr
sprawl; se ~ dans (vice, boue)
wallow in.

veau (pl ~x) /vo/ nm calf; (viande)
veal; (cuir) calfskin.

vécu, ~e /veky/ adj (réel) true, real.
● ⇒VIVRE [62].

vedette /vədɛt/ nf (artiste) star; en ~
(objet) in a prominent position;

(*personne*) in the limelight; **joueur** ~ star player; (bateau) launch.

végétal (*mpl* **-aux**) /veʒetal, -o/ *adj* plant. ● *nm* (*pl* **-aux**) plant.

végétalien, ~**ne** /veʒetaljɛ̃, -ɛn/ *a & nm,f* vegan.

végétarien, ~**ne** /veʒetaʀjɛ̃, -ɛn/ *a & nm,f* vegetarian.

végétation /veʒetasjɔ̃/ *nf* vegetation; ~**s** (Méd) adenoids.

véhicule /veikyl/ *nm* vehicle.

veille /vɛj/ *nf* (état) wakefulness; (jour précédent) **la** ~ (**de**) the day before; **la** ~ **de Noël** Christmas Eve; **à la** ~ **de** on the eve of; **la** ~ **au soir** the previous evening.

veillée /veje/ *nf* evening (gathering).

veiller /veje/ [1] *vi* stay up; (monter la garde) be on watch. ● *vt* (*malade*) watch over; ~ **à** attend to; ~ **sur** watch over.

veilleur /vɛjœʀ/ *nm* ~ **de nuit** night-watchman.

veilleuse /vɛjøz/ *nf* night light; (de véhicule) sidelight; (de réchaud) pilot light; **mettre qch en** ~ put sth on the back burner.

veine /vɛn/ *nf* (Anat) vein; (nervure, filon) vein; (chance 🔢) luck; **avoir de la** ~ 🔢 be lucky.

véliplanchiste /veliplɑ̃ʃist/ *nmf* windsurfer.

vélo /velo/ *nm* bike; (activité) cycling; **faire du** ~ go cycling; ~ **tout terrain** mountain bike.

vélomoteur /velɔmɔtœʀ/ *nm* moped.

velours /v(ə)luʀ/ *nm* velvet; ~ **côtelé** corduroy.

velouté, ~**e** /vəlute/ *adj* smooth. ● *nm* (Culin) ~ **d'asperges** cream of asparagus soup.

vendanges /vɑ̃dɑ̃ʒ/ *nfpl* grape harvest.

vendeur, **-euse** /vɑ̃dœʀ, -øz/ *nm,f* shop assistant; (marchand) salesman, saleswoman; (Jur) vendor, seller.

vendre /vɑ̃dʀ/ [3] *vt* sell; **à** ~ for sale. □ **se** ~ *vpr* (être vendu) be sold; (trouver acquéreur) sell; **se** ~ **bien** sell well.

vendredi /vɑ̃dʀədi/ *nm* Friday; **V**~ **saint** Good Friday.

vénéneux, **-euse** /venenø, -z/ *adj* poisonous.

vénérer /veneʀe/ [14] *vt* revere.

vénérien, ~**ne** /veneʀjɛ̃, -ɛn/ *adj* **maladie** ~**ne** venereal disease.

vengeance /vɑ̃ʒɑ̃s/ *nf* revenge, vengeance.

venger /vɑ̃ʒe/ [40] *vt* avenge. □ **se** ~ *vpr* take *ou* get one's revenge (**de** qch for sth; **de qn** on sb).

vengeur, **-eresse** /vɑ̃ʒœʀ, -əʀɛs/ *adj* vengeful. ● *nm,f* avenger.

venimeux, **-euse** /vənimø, -z/ *adj* poisonous, venomous.

venin /vənɛ̃/ *nm* venom.

venir /vəniʀ/ [58] *vi* (*aux être*) come (**de** from); **faire** ~ **qn** send for sb, call sb; **en** ~ **à** come to; **en** ~ **aux mains** come to blows; **où veut-elle en** ~? what is she driving at?; **il m'est venu à l'esprit** *or* **à l'idée que** it occurred to me that; **s'il venait à pleuvoir** if it should rain; **dans les jours à** ~ in the next few days. ● *v aux* ~ **de faire** have just done; **il vient/venait d'arriver** he has/had just arrived; ~ **faire** come to do; **viens voir** come and see.

vent /vɑ̃/ *nm* wind; **il fait du** ~ it is windy; **être dans le** ~ 🔢 be trendy.

vente /vɑ̃t/ *nf* sale; ~ (**aux enchères**) auction; **en** ~ on *ou* for sale; **mettre qch en** ~ put sth up for sale; ~ **de charité** (charity) bazaar; ~ **au détail** en gros retailing/wholesaling; **équipe de** ~ sales team.

ventilateur /vɑ̃tilatœʀ/ *nm* fan, ventilator. **ventiler** [1] *vt* ventilate.

ventouse /vɑ̃tuz/ *nf* suction pad; (pour déboucher) plunger.

ventre /vɑ̃tʀ/ *nm* stomach; (d'animal) belly; (utérus) womb; **avoir du** ~ have a paunch.

venu, ~**e** /vəny/ *adj* **bien** ~ (à propos) apt, timely; **mal** ~ badly timed; **il serait mal** ~ **de faire** it wouldn't be a good idea to do. ● ⇒VENIR [59].

venue /vəny/ *nf* coming.

ver /vɛʀ/ *nm* worm; (dans la nourriture) maggot; (du bois) woodworm; ~ **luisant** glow-worm; ~ **à soie** silkworm; ~ **solitaire** tapeworm; ~ **de terre** earthworm.

verbal, **~e** (*mpl* **-aux**) /vɛʀbal, -o/ *adj* verbal.

verbe /vɛʀb/ *nm* verb.

verdir /vɛʀdiʀ/ [2] *vi* turn green.

véreux, **-euse** /veʀø, -z/ *adj* wormy; (malhonnête) shady.

verger /vɛʀʒe/ *nm* orchard.

verglas /vɛʀgla/ *nm* black ice.

véridique /veʀidik/ *adj* true.

vérification /veʀifikasjɔ̃/ *nf* check (ing), verification.

vérifier /veʀifje/ [45] *vt* check, verify; (confirmer) confirm.

véritable /veʀitabl/ *adj* true, real; (authentique) real.

vérité /veʀite/ *nf* truth; (de tableau, roman) realism; **en ~** in fact, actually.

vermine /vɛʀmin/ *nf* vermin.

verni, **~e** /vɛʀni/ *adj* (*chaussures*) patent (leather); (chanceux Ⓘ) lucky.

vernir /vɛʀniʀ/ [2] *vt* varnish. □ **se ~** *vpr* se **~ les ongles** apply nail polish.

vernis /vɛʀni/ *nm* varnish; (de poterie) glaze; **~ à ongles** nail polish.

verra, **verrait** /vɛʀa, vɛʀɛ/ ⇒VOIR [64].

verre /vɛʀ/ *nm* glass; (de lunettes) lens; **~ à vin** wine glass; **prendre** *ou* **boire un ~** have a drink; **~ de contact** contact lens; **~ dépoli** frosted glass.

verrière /vɛʀjɛʀ/ *nf* (toit) glass roof; (paroi) glass wall.

verrou /vɛʀu/ *nm* bolt; **sous les ~s** behind bars.

verrouillage /vɛʀujaz/ *nm* **~ central** *or* **centralisé** (**des portes**) central locking.

verrue /vɛʀy/ *nf* wart; **~ plantaire** verruca.

vers[1] /vɛʀ/ *prép* towards; (aux environs de) (temps) about; (lieu) near, around; (période) towards; **~ le soir** towards evening.

vers[2] /vɛʀ/ *nm* (poésie) line of verse.

versatile /vɛʀsatil/ *adj* unpredictable, volatile.

verse: **à ~** /avɛʀs/ *loc* in torrents.

Verseau /vɛʀso/ *nm* le **~** Aquarius.

versement /vɛʀsəmã/ *nm* payment; (échelonné) instalment.

verser /vɛʀse/ [1] *vt/i* pour; (*larmes, sang*) shed; (payer) pay. ● *vi* pour; (*voiture*) overturn; **~ dans** (fig) lapse into.

version /vɛʀsjɔ̃/ *nf* version; (traduction) translation.

verso /vɛʀso/ *nm* back (of the page); **voir au ~** see overleaf.

vert, **~e** /vɛʀ, -t/ *adj* green; (*vieillard*) sprightly. ● *nm* green; **les ~s** the Greens.

vertèbre /vɛʀtɛbʀ/ *nf* vertebra; **se déplacer une ~** slip a disc.

vertical, **~e** (*mpl* **-aux**) /vɛʀtikal, -o/ *adj* vertical.

vertige /vɛʀtiʒ/ *nm* dizziness; **~s** dizzy spells; **avoir le ~** feel dizzy. **vertigineux**, **-euse** *adj* dizzy; (très grand) staggering.

vertu /vɛʀty/ *nf* virtue; **en ~ de** in accordance with. **vertueux**, **-euse** *adj* virtuous.

verveine /vɛʀvɛn/ *nf* verbena.

vessie /vesi/ *nf* bladder.

veste /vɛst/ *nf* jacket.

vestiaire /vɛstjɛʀ/ *nm* cloakroom; (Sport) changing-room; (US) locker-room.

vestibule /vɛstibyl/ *nm* hall; (Théât, d'hôtel) foyer.

vestige /vɛstiʒ/ *nm* (objet) relic; (trace) vestige.

veston /vɛstɔ̃/ *nm* jacket.

vêtement /vɛtmã/ *nm* article of clothing; **~s** clothes, clothing.

vétéran /veteʀã/ *nm* veteran.

vétérinaire /veteʀinɛʀ/ *nmf* vet, veterinary surgeon, (US) veterinarian.

vêtir /vetiʀ/ [61] *vt* dress. □ **se ~** *vpr* dress.

veto /veto/ *nm inv* veto.

vêtu, **~e** /vety/ *adj* dressed (**de** in).

veuf, **veuve** /vœf, -v/ *adj* widowed. ● *nm,f* widower, widow.

veuille /vœj/ ⇒VOULOIR [64].

veut, **veux** /vø/ ⇒VOULOIR [64].

vexation /vɛksasjɔ̃/ *nf* humiliation.

vexer /vɛkse/ [1] *vt* upset, hurt. □ **se ~** *vpr* be upset, be hurt.

viable /vjabl/ *adj* viable; (*projet*) feasible.

viande /vjãd/ *nf* meat.

vibrer /vibʀe/ [1] *vi* vibrate; **faire** ~ (*âme, foules*) stir.

vicaire /vikɛʀ/ *nm* curate.

vice /vis/ *nm* (moral) vice; (*physique*) defect.

vicier /visje/ [45] *vt* contaminate; (*air*) pollute.

vicieux, -ieuse /visjø, -z/ *adj* depraved. ● *nm,f* pervert.

victime /viktim/ *nf* victim; (d'un accident) casualty.

victoire /viktwaʀ/ *nf* victory; (Sport) win. **victorieux, -ieuse** *adj* victorious; (*équipe*) winning.

vidange /vidɑ̃ʒ/ *nf* emptying; (Auto) oil change; (*tuyau*) waste pipe *ou* outlet.

vide /vid/ *adj* empty. ● *nm* (absence, manque) vacuum, void; (espace) space; (trou) gap; (sans air) vacuum; **à** ~ empty; **emballé sous** ~ vacuum packed; **suspendu dans le** ~ dangling in space.

vidéo /video/ *a inv* video; **jeu** ~ video game. ● *nf* video. **vidéocassette** *nf* video(tape). **vidéoclip** *nm* music video. **vidéoconférence** *nf* videoconferencing; (*séance*) videoconference. **vidéodisque** *nm* videodisc.

vide-ordures /vidɔʀdyʀ/ *nm inv* rubbish chute.

vidéothèque /videotɛk/ *nf* video library.

vider /vide/ [1] *vt* empty; (*poisson*) gut; (expulser 🔲) throw out; ~ **les lieux** leave. □ **se** ~ *vpr* empty.

vie /vi/ *nf* life; (durée) lifetime; **à** ~, **pour la** ~ for life; **donner la** ~ **à** give birth to; **en** ~ alive; **la** ~ **est chère** the cost of living is high.

vieil /vjɛj/ ⇒VIEUX.

vieillard /vjɛjaʀ/ *nm* old man.

vieille /vjɛj/ ⇒VIEUX.

vieillesse /vjɛjɛs/ *nf* old age.

vieillir /vjejiʀ/ [2] *vi* grow old, age; (*mot, idée*) become old-fashioned. ● *vt* age. **vieillissement** *nm* ageing.

viens, vient /vjɛ̃/ ⇒VENIR [59].

vierge /vjɛʀʒ/ *nf* virgin; **la V**~ Virgo. ● *adj* virgin; (*feuille, cassette*) blank; (*cahier, pellicule*) unused, new.

vieux (**vieil** *before vowel or mute h*), **vieille** (*mpl* **vieux**) /vjø, vjɛj/ *adj* old. ● *nm,f* old man, old woman; **petit** ~ little old man; **les** ~ old people; **vieille fille** (péj) spinster; ~ **garçon** old bachelor. **vieux jeu** *a inv* old-fashioned.

vif, vive /vif, viv/ *adj* (animé) lively; (*émotion, vent*) keen; (*froid*) biting; (*lumière*) bright; (*douleur, contraste, parole*) sharp; (*souve-nir, style, teint*) vivid; (*succès, impatience*) great; **brûler/enterrer** ~ burn/bury alive; **de vive voix** personally. ● *nm* **à** ~ (*plaie*) open; **avoir les nerfs à** ~ be on edge; **blessé au** ~ cut to the quick.

vigie /viʒi/ *nf* lookout.

vigilant, ~e /viʒilɑ̃, -t/ *adj* vigilant.

vigne /viɲ/ *nf* (plante) vine; (vignoble) vineyard. **vigneron, ~ne** *nm,f* wine-grower.

vignette /viɲɛt/ *nf* (étiquette) label; (Auto) road tax disc.

vignoble /viɲɔbl/ *nm* vineyard.

vigoureux, -euse /viguʀø, -z/ *adj* vigorous, sturdy.

vigueur /vigœʀ/ *nf* vigour; **être/entrer en** ~ (*loi*) be/come into force; **en** ~ current.

VIH *abrév m* (**virus immunodéficitaire humain**) HIV.

vilain, ~e /vilɛ̃, -ɛn/ *adj* (mauvais) nasty; (laid) ugly. ● *nm,f* naughty boy, naughty girl.

villa /villa/ *nf* detached house.

village /vilaʒ/ *nm* village.

villageois, ~e /vilaʒwa, -z/ *adj* village. ● *nm,f* villager.

ville /vil/ *nf* town; (importante) city; ~ **d'eaux** spa.

vin /vɛ̃/ *nm* wine; ~ **d'honneur** reception.

vinaigre /vinɛgʀ/ *nm* vinegar. **vinaigrette** *nf* oil and vinegar dressing, vinaigrette.

vingt /vɛ̃/ (/vɛ̃t/ *before vowel and in numbers 22-29*) *a & nm* twenty.

vingtaine /vɛ̃tɛn/ *nf* **une** ~ (**de**) about twenty.

vingtième /vɛ̃tjɛm/ *a & nmf* twentieth.

vinicole /vinikɔl/ adj wine(-producing).

viol /vjɔl/ nm (de femme) rape; (de lieu, loi) violation.

violemment /vjɔlamɑ̃/ adv violently.

violence /vjɔlɑ̃s/ nf violence; (acte) act of violence. **violent**, ~e adj violent.

violer /vjɔle/ [1] vt rape; (lieu, loi) violate.

violet, ~te /vjɔlɛ, -t/ adj purple. ● nm purple. **violette** nf violet.

violon /vjɔlɔ̃/ nm violin; ~ d'Ingres hobby.

violoncelle /vjɔlɔ̃sɛl/ nm cello.

vipère /vipɛʀ/ nf viper, adder.

virage /viʀaʒ/ nm bend; (en ski) turn; (changement d'attitude: fig) change of course.

virée /viʀe/ nf 🔟 trip, tour; (en voiture) drive; (à vélo) ride.

virement /viʀmɑ̃/ nm (Comm) (credit) transfer; ~ automatique standing order.

virer /viʀe/ [1] vi turn; ~ de bord tack; (fig) do a U-turn; ~ au rouge turn red. ● vt (argent) transfer; (expulser 🔟) throw out; (élève) expel; (licencier 🔟) fire.

virgule /viʀgyl/ nf comma; (dans un nombre) (decimal) point.

viril, ~e /viʀil/ adj virile.

virtuel, ~le /viʀtɥɛl/ adj (potentiel) potential; (mémoire, réalité) virtual.

virulent, ~e /viʀylɑ̃, -t/ adj virulent.

virus /viʀys/ nm virus.

vis¹ /vi/ ⇒VIVRE [62], VOIR [63].

vis² /vis/ nf screw.

visa /viza/ nm visa.

visage /vizaʒ/ nm face.

vis-à-vis /vizavi/ prép ~ de (en face de) opposite; (à l'égard de) in relation to; (comparé à) compared to, beside. ● nm inv (personne) person opposite; en ~ opposite each other.

visée /vize/ nf aim; avoir des ~s sur have designs on.

viser /vize/ [1] vt (cible, centre) aim at; (poste, résultats) aim for; (concerner) be aimed at; (document) stamp; ~ à aim at; (mesure, propos) be aimed at; ~ à faire aim to do. ● vi aim.

viseur /vizœʀ/ nm (d'arme) sights (+ pl); (Photo) viewfinder.

visière /vizjɛʀ/ nf (de casquette) peak; (de casque) visor.

vision /vizjɔ̃/ nf vision.

visite /vizit/ nf visit; (pour inspecter) inspection; (personne) visitor; heures de ~ visiting hours; ~ guidée guided tour; ~ médicale medical; rendre ~ à, faire une ~ à pay a visit; être en ~ (chez qn) be visiting (sb); avoir de la ~ have visitors.

visiter /vizite/ [1] vt visit; (appartement) view. **visiteur**, -euse nm, f visitor.

visser /vise/ vt screw (on).

visuel, ~le /vizɥɛl/ adj visual. ● nm (Ordinat) visual display unit, VDU.

vit /vi/ ⇒VIVRE [62], VOIR [63].

vital, ~e (mpl -aux) /vital, -o/ adj vital.

vitamine /vitamin/ nf vitamin.

vite /vit/ adv fast, quickly; (tôt) soon; ~! quick!; faire ~ be quick; au plus ~, le plus ~ possible as quickly as possible.

vitesse /vitɛs/ nf speed; (régime: Auto) gear; à toute ~ at top speed; en ~ in a hurry, quickly; boîte à cinq ~s five-speed gearbox.

viticole /vitikɔl/ adj (industrie) wine; (région) wine-producing. **viticulteur** nm wine-grower.

vitrage /vitʀaʒ/ nm (vitres) windows; double ~ double glazing.

vitrail (pl -aux) /vitʀaj, -o/ nm stained-glass window.

vitre /vitʀ/ nf (window) pane; (de véhicule) window.

vitrine /vitʀin/ nf (shop) window; (meuble) display cabinet.

vivace /vivas/ adj (plante) perennial; (durable) enduring.

vivacité /vivasite/ nf liveliness; (agilité) quickness; (d'émotion, d'intelligence) keenness; (de souvenir, style, teint) vividness.

vivant, ~e /vivɑ̃, -t/ adj (example, symbole) living; (en vie) alive, living; (actif, vif) lively. ● nm un bon ~ a bon viveur; de son ~ in his lifetime; les ~s the living.

V

vive¹ /viv/ ⇒VIF.

vive² /viv/ *interj* ~ **le roi!** long live the king!

vivement /vivmɑ̃/ *adv* (fortement) strongly; (vite, sèchement) sharply; (avec éclat) vividly; (beaucoup) greatly; ~ **la fin!** I'll be glad when it's the end!

vivier /vivje/ *nm* fish pond; (artificiel) fish tank.

vivifier /vivifje/ [45] *vt* invigorate.

vivre /vivʀ/ [63] *vi* live; ~ **de** (nourriture) live on; ~ **encore** be still alive; **faire** ~ (famille) support. ● *vt* (vie) live; (période, aventure) live through.

vivres /vivʀ/ *nmpl* supplies.

VO *abrév f* (**version originale**) **en** ~ in the original language.

vocabulaire /vɔkabylɛʀ/ *nm* vocabulary.

vocal, ~**e** (*mpl* -**aux**) /vɔkal, -o/ *adj* vocal.

vœu (*pl* ~**x**) /vø/ *nm* (souhait) wish; (promesse) vow; **meilleurs** ~**x** best wishes.

vogue /vɔg/ *nf* fashion, vogue; **en** ~ in fashion *ou* vogue.

voguer /vɔge/ [1] *vi* sail.

voici /vwasi/ *prép* here is, this is; (au pluriel) here are, these are; **me** ~ here I am; ~ **un an** (temps passé) a year ago; ~ **un an que** it is a year since.

voie /vwa/ *nf* (route) road; (partie de route) lane; (chemin) way; (moyen) means, way; (rails) track; (quai) platform; **en** ~ **de** in the process of; **en** ~ **de développement** (pays) developing; **espèce en** ~ **de disparition** endangered species; **par la** ~ **des airs** by air; **par** ~ **orale** orally; **sur la bonne/mauvaise** ~ (fig) on the right/wrong track; **montrer la** ~ lead the way; ~ **de dégagement** slip-road; ~ **ferrée** railway; (US) railroad; **V**~ **lactée** Milky Way; ~ **navigable** waterway; ~ **publique** public highway; ~ **sans issue** (sur panneau) no through road; (fig) dead end.

voilà /vwala/ *prép* there is, that is; (au pluriel) there are, those are; (voici) here is, here are; **le** ~ there he is; ~**!** right!; (en offrant qch) there you are!; ~ **un an** (temps passé) a year

ago; ~ **un an que** it is a year since; **tu en veux? en** ~ do you want some? here you are; **en** ~ **des histoires!** what a fuss!; **et** ~ **que** and then.

voilage /vwalaʒ/ *nm* net curtain.

voile /vwal/ *nf* (de bateau) sail; (Sport) sailing. ● *nm* veil; (tissu léger) net.

voilé, ~**e** /vwale/ *adj* (allusion, femme) veiled; (flou) hazy.

voiler /vwale/ [1] *vt* (dissimuler) veil; (déformer) buckle. □ **se** ~ *vpr* (devenir flou) become hazy; (se déformer) (roue) buckle.

voilier /vwalje/ *nm* sailing ship.

voir /vwaʀ/ [64] *vt* see; **faire** ~ **qch à qn** show sth to sb; **laisser** ~ show; **avoir quelque chose à** ~ **avec** have something to do with; **ça n'a rien à** ~ that's got nothing to do with it; **je ne peux pas le** ~ Ⅰ I can't stand him. ● *vi* **y** ~ be able to see; **je n'y vois rien** I cannot see; ~ **trouble** have blurred vision; **voyons** let's see now; **voyons, soyez sages!** come on now, behave yourselves! □ **se** ~ *vpr* (dans la glace) see oneself; (être visible) show; (se produire) be seen; (se trouver) find oneself; (se fréquenter, se rencontrer) see each other; (être vu) be seen.

voire /vwaʀ/ *adv* or even, not to say.

voirie /vwaʀi/ *nf* (service) highway maintenance.

voisin, ~**e** /vwazɛ̃, -in/ *adj* (de voisinage) neighbouring; (proche) nearby; (adjacent) next (**de** to); (semblable) similar (**de** to). ● *nm, f* neighbour; **le** ~ the man next door, the neighbour.

voisinage *nm* neighbourhood; (proximité) proximity.

voiture /vwatyʀ/ *nf* (motor) car; (wagon) coach, carriage; **en** ~**!** all aboard!; ~ **bélier** ramraiding car; ~ **à cheval** horse-drawn carriage; ~ **de course** racing car; ~ **école** driving school car; ~ **d'enfant** pram; (US) baby carriage; ~ **de tourisme** saloon car.

voix /vwa/ *nf* voice; (suffrage) vote; **à** ~ **basse** in a whisper.

vol /vɔl/ *nm* (d'avion, d'oiseau) flight; (groupe d'oiseaux) flock, flight; (délit) theft; (hold-up) robbery; ~ **à l'étalage** shoplifting; ~ **à la tire** pickpocketing; **à** ~ **d'oiseau** as the crow flies; **de haut** ~ high-ranking; ~ **libre** hang-gliding; ~ **à voile** gliding.

volaille /vɔlaj/ *nf* **la** ~ (poules) poultry; **une** ~ **a** fowl.

volant /vɔlɑ̃/ *nm* (steering-)wheel; (de jupe) flounce; (de badminton) shuttlecock; **donner un coup de** ~ turn the wheel sharply.

volcan /vɔlkɑ̃/ *nm* volcano.

volée /vɔle/ *nf* flight; (oiseaux) flight, flock; (de coups, d'obus, au tennis) volley; **à toute** ~ hard; **à la** ~ in flight, in mid-air.

voler /vɔle/ [1] *vi* (*oiseau*) fly; (dérober) steal (à from). ● *vt* steal; ~ **qn** rob sb; **il ne l'a pas volé** he deserved it.

volet /vɔlɛ/ *nm* (de fenêtre) shutter; (de document) (folded *ou* tear-off) section; **trié sur le** ~ hand-picked.

voleur, -euse /vɔlœr, -øz/ *nm,f* thief; **au** ~! stop thief! ● *adj* thieving.

volley-ball /vɔlɛbol/ *nm* volleyball.

volontaire /vɔlɔ̃tɛr/ *adj* (délibéré) voluntary; (opiniâtre) determined. ● *nmf* volunteer. **volontairement** *adv* voluntarily; (exprès) intentionally.

volonté /vɔlɔ̃te/ *nf* (faculté, intention) will; (souhait) wish; (énergie) will-power; **à** ~ (comme on veut) as required; **du vin à** ~ unlimited wine; **bonne** ~ goodwill; **mauvaise** ~ ill will.

volontiers /vɔlɔ̃tje/ *adv* (de bon gré) with pleasure, willingly, gladly; (*admettre*) readily.

volt /vɔlt/ *nm* volt.

volte-face /vɔltəfas/ *nf inv* (fig) U-turn; **faire** ~ do a U-turn.

voltige /vɔltiʒ/ *nf* acrobatics (+ *pl*).

volume /vɔlym/ *nm* volume.

volumineux, -euse /vɔyminø, -z/ *adj* bulky; (*livre, dossier*) thick.

volupté /vɔlypte/ *nf* voluptuousness.

vomi /vɔmi/ *nm* vomit.

vomir /vɔmir/ [2] *vt* vomit; (fig) belch out. ● *vi* be sick, vomit.

vomissement /vɔmismɑ̃/ *nm* vomiting; ~**s du matin** morning sickness.

vont /vɔ̃/ ⇒ALLER [8].

vorace /vɔras/ *adj* voracious.

vos /vo/ ⇒VOTRE.

votant, ~e /vɔtɑ̃, -t/ *nm,f* voter.

vote /vɔt/ *nm* (action) voting; (suffrage) vote; ~ **d'une loi** passing of a bill; ~ **par correspondance/procuration** postal/proxy vote.

voter /vɔte/ [1] *vi* vote. ● *vt* vote for; (adopter) pass; (*crédits*) vote.

votre (*pl* **vos**) /vɔtr, vo/ *adj* your.

vôtre /votr/ *pron* **le** *ou* **la** ~, **les** ~**s** yours.

vouer /vwe/ [1] *vt* (vie, temps) dedicate (à to); **voué à l'échec** doomed to failure.

vouloir /vulwar/ [64] *vt* (exiger) want (**faire** to do); (souhaiter) want; **que veux-tu boire?** what would you like to drink?; **je voudrais bien y aller** I'd really like to go; **je veux bien venir** I'm happy to come; **comme tu voudras** as you wish; (accepter) **veuillez vous asseoir** please sit down; **veuillez patienter** (au téléphone) please hold the line; (signifier) ~ **dire** mean; **qu'est-ce que cela veut dire?** what does that mean?; **en** ~ **à qn** bear a grudge against sb. □ **s'en** ~ *vpr* regret; **je m'en veux de lui avoir dit** I really regret having told her.

voulu, ~e /vuly/ *adj* (délibéré) intentional; (requis) required.

vous /vu/ *pron* (sujet, complément) you; (indirect) (to) you; (réfléchi) yourself; (pluriel) yourselves; (l'un l'autre) each other. **vous-même** *pron* yourself. **vous-mêmes** *pron* yourselves.

voûte /vut/ *nf* (plafond) vault; (porche) archway.

vouvoiement /vuvwamɑ̃/ *nm* use of the 'vous' form. **vouvoyer** [31] *vt* address using the 'vous' form.

voyage /vwajaʒ/ *nm* trip; (déplacement) journey; (par mer) voyage; ~**(s)** (action) travelling; ~ **d'affaires** business trip; ~ **d'études** study trip; ~ **de noces** honeymoon; ~ **organisé** (package) tour.

voyager /vwajaʒe/ [40] *vi* travel.

voyageur, -euse /vwajaʒœr, -øz/ *nm,f* traveller; (passager) passenger; ~ **de commerce** travelling salesman.

V

voyant, ~**e** /vwajɑ̃, -t/ *adj* gaudy.
● *nm* (signal) (warning) light.
voyelle /vwajɛl/ *nf* vowel.
voyou /vwaju/ *nm* hooligan.
vrac: **en** ~ /ɑ̃vʀak/ *loc* (pêle-mêle)
haphazardly; (sans emballage) loose;
(en gros) in bulk.
vrai, ~**e** /vʀɛ/ *adj* true; (authentique)
real. ● *nm* truth; **à** ~ **dire** to tell the
truth; **pour de** ~ for real. **vraiment**
adv really.
vraisemblable /vʀɛsɑ̃blablabl/ *adj*
(probable) likely; (*excuse, histoire*)
plausible. **vraisemblablement**
adv probably. **vraisemblance** *nf*
likelihood, plausibility.
vrombir /vʀɔ̃biʀ/ [2] *vi* roar.
VRP *abrév m* (**voyageur**
représentant placier) rep,
representative.
VTT *abrév m* (**vélo tout terrain**)
mountain bike.
vu, ~**e** /vy/ *adj* **bien** ~ well thought
of; **ce serait plutôt mal** ~ it wouldn't
go down well; **bien** ~! good point!
● *prép* in view of; ~ **que** seeing that.
● ⇒VOIR [64].
vue /vy/ *nf* (spectacle) sight; (vision)
(eye)sight; (panorama, idée, image, photo)
view; **avoir en** ~ have in mind; **à** ~
(*tirer*) on sight; (*payable*) at sight; **de**
~ by sight; **perdre de** ~ lose sight
of; **en** ~ (proche) in sight; (célèbre) in
the public eye; **en** ~ **de faire** with a
view to doing; **à** ~ **d'œil** visibly;
avoir des ~**s sur** have designs on.
vulgaire /vylgɛʀ/ *adj* (grossier)
vulgar; (ordinaire) common.
vulnérable /vylneʀabl/ *adj*
vulnerable.

....

Ww

wagon /vagɔ̃/ *nm* (de voyageurs)
carriage; (de marchandises) wagon.
wagon-lit (*pl* **wagons-lits**) *nm*
sleeper. **wagon-restaurant** (*pl*
wagons-restaurants) *nm*
restaurant car.

walkman® /wokman/ *nm* personal
stereo, walkman®.
waters /watɛʀ/ *nmpl* toilets.
watt /wat/ *nm* watt.
wc /(dublə)vese/ *nmpl* toilet (+ *sg*).
Web /wɛb/ *nm* Web; **un site** ~ a Web
site.
week-end /wikɛnd/ *nm* weekend.
whisky (*pl* **-ies**) /wiski/ *nm* whisky.

....

Xx

xénophobe /gzenɔfɔb/ *adj*
xenophobic. ● *nmf* xenophobe.
xérès /gzeʀɛs/ *nm* sherry.
xylophone /ksilɔfon/ *nm*
xylophone.

....

Yy

....

y /i/
● *adverbe*
····▸ there; (dessus) on it; (pluriel) on
them; (dedans) in it; (pluriel) in them;
j'~ **vais** I'm on my way; **n'**~ **va pas**
don't go; **du lait? il n'**~ **en a pas**
milk? there's none; **tu n'**~ **arriveras**
jamais you'll never manage it.

● *pronom*
····▸ **s'**~ **habituer** get used to it.
····▸ **s'**~ **attendre** expect it.
····▸ ~ **penser** think about it.
····▸ ~ **être pour qch** have sth to do
with it.

yaourt /'jauʀ(t)/ *nm* yoghurt.
yaourtière *nf* yoghurt-maker.
yard /'jaʀd/ *nm* yard (= *91,44 cm*).
yen /'jɛn/ *nm* yen.
yeux /jø/ ⇒ŒIL.

yoga /'jɔga/ *nm* yoga.

yougoslave /'jugɔslav/ *adj* Yugoslav. **Y~** *nmf* Yugoslav.

Yougoslavie /'jugɔslavi/ *nf* Yugoslavia.

yo-yo® /'jojo/ *nm inv* yo-yo®.

....

Zz

....

zèbre /zɛbʀ/ *nm* zebra.

zèle /zɛl/ *nm* zeal.

zéro /zeʀo/ *nm* nought, zero; (température) zero; (Sport) nil; (tennis) love; (personne) nonentity; **partir de ~** start from scratch; **repartir à ~** start all over again.

zeste /zɛst/ *nm* peel; **un ~ de** (fig) a touch of.

zézayer /zezeje/ [31] *vi* lisp.

zigzag /zigzag/ *nm* zigzag; **en ~** winding.

zinc /zɛ̃g/ *nm* (métal) zinc; (comptoir ▣) bar.

zizanie /zizani/ *nf* discord; **semer la ~** put the cat among the pigeons.

zizi /zizi/ *nm* ▣ willy.

zodiaque /zɔdjak/ *nm* zodiac.

zona /zona/ *nm* (Méd) shingles (+ *sg*).

zone /zon/ *nf* zone, area; (banlieue pauvre) slums; **~ bleue** restricted parking zone.

zoo /zo(o)/ *nm* zoo.

zoom /zum/ *nm* zoom lens.

zut /zyt/ *interj* ▣ damn ▣.

Aa

a *determiner*

    an avant voyelle ou h muet.

➡ For expressions such as **make a noise, make a fortune** ⇒**noise, fortune.**

····▷ un/une; ∼ **tree** un arbre; ∼ **chair** une chaise.

····▷ (per) **ten francs** ∼ **kilo** dix francs le kilo; **three times** ∼ **day** trois fois par jour.

❗ When talking about what people do or are, **a** is not translated into French: **she's a teacher** *elle est professeur,* **he's a widower** *il est veuf.*

aback *adv* **taken** ∼ déconcerté.

abandon *vt* abandonner. ● *n* abandon *m.*

abate *vi* (*flood, fever*) baisser; (*storm*) se calmer. ● *vt* diminuer.

abbey *n* abbaye *f.*

abbot *n* abbé *m.*

abbreviate *vt* abréger. **abbreviation** *n* abréviation *f.*

abdicate *vt/i* abdiquer.

abdomen *n* abdomen *m.*

abduct *vt* enlever. **abductor** *n* ravisseur/-euse *m/f.*

abhor *vt* (*pt* **abhorred**) exécrer.

abide *vt* supporter; ∼ **by** respecter.

ability *n* capacité *f* (**to do** à faire); (*talent*) talent *m.*

abject *adj* (*state*) misérable; (*coward*) abject.

ablaze *adj* en feu.

able *adj* (*skilled*) compétent; **be** ∼ **to do** pouvoir faire; (*know how to*) savoir faire. **ably** *adv* avec compétence.

abnormal *adj* anormal. **abnormality** *n* anomalie *f.*

aboard *adv* à bord. ● *prep* à bord de.

abode *n* demeure *f*; **of no fixed** ∼ sans domicile fixe.

abolish *vt* abolir.

Aborigine *n* aborigène *mf* (d'Australie).

abort *vt* faire avorter; (Comput) abandonner. ● *vi* avorter.

abortion *n* avortement *m*; **have an** ∼ se faire avorter.

abortive *adj* (*attempt*) avorté; (*coup*) manqué.

about *adv* (approximately) environ; ∼ **the same** à peu près pareil; **there was no-one** ∼ il n'y avait personne. ● *prep* **it's** ∼ ... il s'agit de ...; **what I like** ∼ **her is** ce que j'aime chez elle c'est; **to wander** ∼ **the streets** errer dans les rues; **how/what** ∼ **some tea?** et si on prenait un thé?; **what** ∼ **you?** et toi? ● *adj* **be** ∼ **to do** être sur le point de faire; **be up and** ∼ être debout. ∼**-face**, ∼**-turn** *n* (fig) volte-face *f inv.*

above *prep* au-dessus de; **he is not** ∼ **lying** il n'est pas incapable de mentir; ∼ **all** surtout. ● *adv* **the apartment** ∼ l'appartement du dessus; **see** ∼ voir ci-dessus. ∼**-board** *adj* honnête. ∼**-mentioned** *adj* susmentionné.

abrasive *adj* abrasif; (*manner*) mordant. ● *n* abrasif *m.*

abreast *adv* de front; **keep** ∼ **of** se tenir au courant de.

abroad *adv* à l'étranger.

abrupt *adj* (sudden, curt) brusque; (steep) abrupt. **abruptly** *adv* (suddenly) brusquement; (curtly) avec brusquerie.

abscess *n* abcès *m.*

abseil *vi* descendre en rappel.

absence *n* absence *f*; (lack) manque *m*; **in the** ∼ **of** faute de.

absent *adj* absent.

absentee *n* absent/-e *m/f.*

absent-minded *adj* distrait.

absolute *adj* (*monarch, majority*) absolu; (*chaos, idiot*) véritable. **absolutely** *adv* absolument.

absolve *vt* ∼ **sb of sth** décharger qn de qch.

a

absorb vt absorber.

abstain vi s'abstenir (**from** de).

abstract¹ adj abstrait. ● n (summary) résumé m; **in the** ~ dans l'abstrait.

abstract² vt tirer.

absurd adj absurde.

abundance n abondance f. **abundant** adj abondant. **abundantly** adv (entirely) tout à fait.

abuse¹ vt (position) abuser de; (person) maltraiter; (insult) injurier.

abuse² n (misuse) abus m (of de); (cruelty) mauvais traitement m; (insults) injures fpl.

abusive adj (person) grossier; (language) injurieux.

abysmal adj épouvantable.

abyss n abîme m.

academic adj (career) universitaire; (year) académique; (scholarly) intellectuel; (theoretical) théorique. ● n universitaire mf.

academy n (school) école f; (society) académie f.

accelerate vi (speed up) s'accélérer; (Auto) accélérer. **accelerator** n accélérateur m.

accent¹ n accent m.

accent² vt accentuer.

accept vt accepter. **acceptable** adj acceptable. **acceptance** n (of offer) acceptation f; (of proposal) approbation f.

access n accès m. **accessible** adj accessible.

accessory adj accessoire. ● n (Jur) complice mf (**to** de).

accident n accident m; (chance) hasard m; **by** ~ par hasard. **accidental** adj (death) accidentel; (meeting) fortuit. **accidentally** adv accidentellement; (by chance) par hasard.

acclaim vt applaudir. ● n louanges fpl.

acclimatize vt/i (s')acclimater (**to** à).

accommodate vt loger; (adapt to) s'adapter à; (satisfy) satisfaire. **accommodating** adj accommodant. **accommodation** n logement m.

accompaniment n accompagnement m. **accompany** vt accompagner.

accomplice n complice mf (**in, to** de).

accomplish vt accomplir; (objective) réaliser. **accomplished** adj très compétent. **accomplishment** n (feat) réussite f; (talent) talent m.

accord vi concorder (**with** avec). ● vt accorder (**sb sth** qch à qn). ● n accord m; **of my own** ~ de moi-même.

accordance n **in** ~ **with** conformément à.

according adv ~ **to** (principle, law) selon; (person, book) d'après. **accordingly** adv en conséquence.

accordion n accordéon m.

accost vt aborder.

account n (Comm) compte m; (description) compte-rendu m; **on** ~ **of** à cause de; **on no** ~ en aucun cas; **take into** ~ tenir compte de; **it's of no** ~ peu importe. □ ~ **for** (explain) expliquer; (represent) représenter. **accountability** n responsabilité f. **accountable** adj responsable (**for** de; **to** envers).

accountancy n comptabilité f. **accountant** n comptable mf. **accounts** npl comptabilité f, comptes mpl.

accumulate vt/i (s')accumuler.

accuracy n (of figures) justesse f; (of aim) précision f; (of forecast) exactitude f. **accurate** adj juste, précis. **accurately** adv exactement, précisément.

accusation n accusation f.

accuse vt accuser; **the** ~**d** l'accusé/-e m/f.

accustomed adj accoutumé; **become** ~ **to** s'accoutumer à.

ace n (card, person) as m.

ache n douleur f. ● vi (person) avoir mal; **my leg** ~**s** ma jambe me fait mal.

achieve vt (aim) atteindre; (result) obtenir; (ambition) réaliser. **achievement** n (feat) réussite f; (fulfilment) réalisation f (**of** de).

acid *a & n* acide (*m*). **acidity** *n* acidité *f*. ~ **rain** *n* pluies *fpl* acides.

acknowledge *vt* (*error, authority*) reconnaître; (*letter*) accuser réception de. **acknowledgement** *n* reconnaissance *f*.

acne *n* acné *f*.

acorn *n* (Bot) gland *m*.

acoustic *adj* acoustique. **acoustics** *npl* acoustique *f*.

acquaint *vt* ~ sb with sth mettre qn au courant de qch; be ~ed with (*person*) connaître; (*fact*) savoir. **acquaintance** *n* connaissance *f*.

acquire *vt* acquérir; (*habit*) prendre.

acquit *vt* (*pt* **acquitted**) (Jur) acquitter. **acquittal** *n* acquittement *m*.

acre *n* acre *f*, ≈ demi-hectare *m*.

acrid *adj* âcre.

acrimonious *adj* acrimonieux.

acrobat *n* acrobate *mf*. **acrobatics** *npl* acrobaties *fpl*.

acronym *n* acronyme *m*.

across *adv & prep* (side to side) d'un côté à l'autre (de); (on other side) de l'autre côté (from de); go *or* walk ~ traverser; lie ~ the bed se coucher en travers du lit; ~ the world partout dans le monde.

act *n* acte *m*; (Jur, Pol) loi *f*; put on an ~ jouer la comédie. ● *vi* agir; (Theat) jouer; ~ as servir de. ● *vt* (*part, role*) jouer.

acting *n* (Theat) jeu *m*. ● *adj* (temporary) intérimaire.

action *n* action *f*; (Mil) combat *m*; out of ~ hors service; take ~ agir.

activate *vt* (*machine*) faire démarrer; (*alarm*) déclencher.

active *adj* actif; (*volcano*) en activité; take an ~ interest in s'intéresser activement à. **activist** *n* activiste *mf*. **activity** *n* activité *f*.

actor *n* acteur *m*. **actress** *n* actrice *f*.

actual *adj* réel; the ~ words les mots exacts; in the ~ house (the house itself) dans la maison elle-même. **actuality** *n* réalité *f*. **actually** *adv* (in fact) en fait; (really) vraiment.

acute *adj* (*anxiety*) vif; (*illness*) aigu; (*shortage*) grave; (*mind*) pénétrant.

ad *n* (TV) pub *f* 🔲; small ~ petite annonce *f*.

AD *abbr* (**Anno Domini**) ap. J.-C.

adamant *adj* catégorique.

adapt *vt/i* (s')adapter (to à). **adaptability** *n* adaptabilité *f*. **adaptable** *adj* souple. **adaptation** *n* adaptation *f*. **adaptor** *n* (Electr) adaptateur *m*.

add *vt/i* ajouter (to à); (in maths) additionner. □ ~ up (*facts, figures*) s'accorder; ~ sth up additionner qch; ~ up to s'élever à.

adder *n* vipère *f*.

addict *n* toxicomane *mf*; (fig) accro *mf* 🔲.

addicted *adj* be ~ avoir une dépendance (to à); (fig) être accro 🔲 (to à). **addiction** *n* (Med) dépendance *f* (to à); passion *f* (to pour). **addictive** *adj* qui crée une dépendance.

addition *n* (item) ajout *m*; (in maths) addition *f*; in ~ en plus. **additional** *adj* supplémentaire.

additive *n* additif *m*.

address *n* adresse *f*; (speech) discours *m*. ● *vt* (letter) mettre l'adresse sur; (crowd) s'adresser à; ~ sth to adresser qch à. **addressee** *n* destinataire *mf*.

adequate *adj* suffisant; (satisfactory) satisfaisant.

adhere *vi* (lit, fig) adhérer (to à); ~ to (policy) observer.

adjacent *adj* contigu; ~ to attenant à.

adjective *n* adjectif *m*.

adjoin *vt* être contigu à. **adjoining** *adj* (room) voisin.

adjourn *vt* (trial) ajourner; the session was ~ed la séance a été levée. ● *vi* s'arrêter; (Parliament) lever la séance; ~ to passer à.

adjust *vt* (level, speed) régler; (price) ajuster; (clothes) rajuster. ● *vt/i* ~ (oneself) to s'adapter à. **adjustable** *adj* réglable. **adjustment** *n* (of rates) rajustement *m*; (of control) réglage *m*; (of person) adaptation *f*.

ad lib *vt/i* (*pt* **ad libbed**) improviser.

administer *vt* administrer.

a

administration n administration
f. **administrative** adj
administratif. **administrator** n
administrateur/-trice m/f.

admiral n amiral m.

admiration n admiration f.
admire vt admirer. **admirer** n
admirateur/-trice m/f.

admission n (to a place) entrée f;
(confession) aveu m.

admit vt (pt **admitted**) (acknowledge)
reconnaître, admettre; (crime)
avouer; (new member) admettre; ~
to reconnaître. **admittance** n
entrée f. **admittedly** adv il est vrai.

ado n without more ~ sans plus de
cérémonie.

adolescence n adolescence f.
adolescent n & a adolescent/-e
(m/f).

adopt vt adopter. **adopted** adj
(child) adoptif. **adoption** n
adoption f. **adoptive** adj adoptif.

adorable adj adorable. **adoration**
n adoration f. **adore** vt adorer.

adorn vt orner.

adrift a & adv à la dérive.

adult a & n adulte (mf).

adultery n adultère m.

adulthood n âge m adulte.

advance vt (sum) avancer; (tape,
career) faire avancer; (interests)
servir. ● vi (lit) avancer; (progress)
progresser. ● n avance f; (progress)
progrès m; in ~ à l'avance.
advanced adj avancé; (studies)
supérieur.

advantage n avantage m; take ~ of
profiter de; (person) exploiter.
advantageous adj avantageux.

adventure n aventure f.
adventurer n aventurier/-ière m/f.
adventurous adj aventureux.

adverb n adverbe m.

adverse adj défavorable.

advert n annonce f; (TV) pub f 🆃.

advertise vt faire de la publicité
pour; (car, house, job) mettre une
annonce pour. ● vi faire de la
publicité; (for staff) passer une
annonce. **advertisement** n
publicité f; (in newspaper) annonce f.
advertiser n annonceur m.
advertising n publicité f.

advice n conseils mpl; some ~, a
piece of ~ un conseil.

advise vt conseiller; (inform) aviser;
~ against déconseiller. **adviser** n
conseiller/-ère m/f. **advisory** adj
consultatif.

advocate[1] n (Jur) avocat m;
(supporter) partisan m.

advocate[2] vt recommander.

aerial adj aérien. ● n antenne f.

aerobics n aérobic m.

aeroplane n avion m.

aerosol n bombe f aérosol.

aesthetic adj esthétique.

afar adv from ~ de loin.

affair n (matter) affaire f; (romance)
liaison f.

affect vt affecter.

affection n affection f.
affectionate adj affectueux.

affinity n affinité f.

afflict vt affliger. **affliction** n
affection f.

affluence n richesse f.

afford vt avoir les moyens d'acheter;
(provide) fournir; can you ~ the time?
avez-vous le temps?

afloat adj & adv (boat) à flot.

afoot adv sth is ~ il se prépare qch.

afraid adj be ~ (frightened) avoir peur
(of, to de; that que); (worried) craindre
(that que); I'm ~ I can't come je suis
désolé mais je ne peux pas venir.

Africa n Afrique f.

African n Africain/-e m/f. ● adj
africain.

after adv & prep après; soon ~ peu
après; be ~ sth rechercher qch; ~
all après tout. ● conj après que; ~
doing après avoir fait.

aftermath n conséquences fpl (of
de).

afternoon n après-midi m or f inv;
in the ~ (dans) l'après-midi.

after: ~**shave** n après-rasage m.
~**thought** n pensée f après coup.

afterwards adv après, par la suite.

again adv encore; ~ and ~ à
plusieurs reprises; start ~
recommencer; she never saw him ~
elle ne l'a jamais revu.

against prep contre; ~ the law
illégal.

age *n* âge *m*; (era) ère *f*, époque *f*; **I've been waiting for ~s** j'attends depuis des heures. ● *vt/i* (*pres p* **ageing**) vieillir.

aged[1] *adj* ~ **six** âgé de six ans.

aged[2] *adj* âgé.

agency *n* agence *f*.

agenda *n* ordre *m* du jour; (fig) programme *m*.

agent *n* agent *m*.

aggravate *vt* (make worse) aggraver; (annoy) exaspérer. **aggravation** *n* (worsening) aggravation *f*; (annoyance) ennuis *mpl*.

aggression *n* agression *f*. **aggressive** *adj* agressif. **aggressiveness** *n* agressivité *f*. **aggressor** *n* agresseur *m*.

agitate *vt* agiter.

ago *adv* il y a; **a month ~** il y a un mois; **long ~** il y a longtemps; **how long ~?** il y a combien de temps?

agonize *vi* se tourmenter (**over** à propos de). **agonized** *adj* angoissé. **agonizing** *adj* déchirant. **agony** *n* douleur *f* atroce; (mental) angoisse *f*.

agree *vi* être d'accord (**on** sur; **with** avec); **~ to** consentir à; **~ with** (approve of) approuver. ● *vt* être d'accord (**that** sur le fait que); (admit) convenir (**that** que); (*date, solution*) se mettre d'accord sur.

agreeable *adj* agréable; **be ~** (willing) être d'accord.

agreed *adj* (*time, place*) convenu; **we're ~** nous sommes d'accord.

agreement *n* accord *m*; **in ~** d'accord.

agricultural *adj* agricole. **agriculture** *n* agriculture *f*.

aground *adv* **run ~** (*ship*) s'échouer.

ahead *adv* (in front) en avant, devant; (in advance) à l'avance; **be 10 points ~** avoir 10 points d'avance; **~ of time** en avance; **go ~!** allez-y!

aid *vt* aider. ● *n* aide *f*; **in ~ of** au profit de.

aide *n* aide *mf*.

Aids *n* (Med) sida *m*.

aim *vt* (*gun*) braquer (**at** sur); **be ~ed at sb** (*campaign, remark*) viser qn. ● *vi* **~ for/at sth** viser qch; **~ to do** avoir l'intention de faire. ● *n* but *m*; **take ~** viser. **aimless** *adj* sans but.

air *n* air *m*; **by ~** par avion; **on the ~** à l'antenne. ● *vt* aérer; (*views*) exprimer. ● *adj* (*base, disaster*) aérien; (*pollution, pressure*) atmosphérique. **~-bed** *n* matelas *m* pneumatique. **~-conditioning** *n* climatisation *f*. **~craft** *n inv* avion *m*. **~craft carrier** *n* porte-avions *m inv*. **~field** *n* terrain *m* d'aviation. **~ force** *n* armée *f* de l'air. **~ freshener** *n* désodorisant *m* d'atmosphère. **~ hostess** *n* hôtesse *f* de l'air. **~lift** *vt* transporter par pont aérien. **~line** *n* compagnie *f* aérienne. **~liner** *n* avion *m* de ligne. **~lock** *n* (in pipe) bulle *f* d'air; (chamber) sas *m*. **~mail** *n* (**by**) **~mail** par avion. **~plane** *n* (US) avion *m*. **~port** *n* aéroport *m*. **~ raid** *n* attaque *f* aérienne. **~tight** *adj* hermétique. **~ traffic controller** *n* contrôleur/-euse *m/f* aérien/-ne. **~waves** *npl* ondes *fpl*.

airy *adj* (**-ier, -iest**) (*room*) clair et spacieux.

aisle *n* (of church) allée *f* centrale; (in train) couloir *m*.

ajar *adv & a* entrouvert.

akin *adj* ~ **to** semblable à.

alarm *n* alarme *f*; (clock) réveil *m*; (feeling) frayeur *f*. ● *vt* inquiéter. **~-clock** *n* réveil *m*.

alas *interj* hélas.

Albania *n* Albanie *f*.

album *n* album *m*.

alcohol *n* alcool *m*.

alcoholic *adj* alcoolique; (*drink*) alcoolisé. ● *n* alcoolique *mf*.

ale *n* bière *f*.

alert *adj* alerte; (watchful) vigilant. ● *n* alerte *f*; **on the ~** sur le qui-vive. ● *vt* alerter; **~ sb to** prévenir qn de. **alertness** *n* vivacité *f*; vigilance *f*.

A-level *n* ≈ baccalauréat *m*.

algebra *n* algèbre *f*.

Algeria *n* Algérie *f*.

alias *n* (*pl* **~es**) faux nom *m*. ● *prep* alias.

alibi *n* alibi *m*.

alien *n & a* étranger/-ère (*m/f*) (**to** à).

alienate *vt* éloigner.

a

alight *adj* en feu, allumé.

alike *adj* semblable. ● *adv* de la même façon; **look** ~ se ressembler.

alive *adj* vivant; ~ **to** conscient de; ~ **with** grouillant de.

all

● *pronoun*

····▸ (everything) tout; **is that** ~? c'est tout?; **that was** ~ **(that) he said** c'est tout ce qu'il a dit; **I ate it** ~ j'ai tout mangé.

❗ Use the translation **tous** for a group of masculine or mixed gender people or objects and **toutes** for a group of feminine gender: **we were all delighted** *nous étions tous ravis*; **'where are the cups?'—'they're all in the kitchen'** *'où sont les tasses?'—'elles sont toutes dans la cuisine'*.

● *determiner*

····▸ tout/toute/tous/toutes; ~ **the time** tout le temps; ~ **his life** toute sa vie; ~ **of us** nous tous; ~ **(the) women** toutes les femmes.

● *adverb*

····▸ (completely) tout; **they were** ~ **alone** ils étaient tout seuls; **tell me** ~ **about it** raconte-moi tout; ~ **for** tout à fait pour; **not** ~ **that well** pas si bien que ça; ~ **too** bien trop.

❗ When the adjective that follows is in the feminine and begins with a consonant, the translation is *toute/toutes*: **she was all alone** *elle était toute seule*.

allege *vt* prétendre. **allegedly** *adv* prétendument.

allergic *adj* allergique (**to** à). **allergy** *n* allergie *f.*

alleviate *vt* alléger.

alley *n* (street) ruelle *f.*

alliance *n* alliance *f.*

allied *adj* allié.

alligator *n* alligator *m.*

allocate *vt* (*funds*) affecter; (*time*) accorder; (*task*) assigner.

allot *vt* (*pt* **allotted**) (*money*) attribuer; (*task*) assigner. **allotment** *n* attribution *f*; (land) parcelle *f* de terre.

all-out *adj* (*effort*) acharné; (*strike*) total.

allow *vt* (authorize) autoriser à; (let) laisser; (enable) permettre; (concede) accorder; ~ **for** tenir compte de.

allowance *n* allocation *f*; **make** ~**s for sth** tenir compte de qch; **make** ~**s for sb** essayer de comprendre qn.

alloy *n* alliage *m.*

all right *adj* (not bad) pas mal; **are you** ~? ça va?; **is it** ~ **if ...?** est-ce que ça va si ...? ● *adv* (*see*) bien; (*function*) comme il faut. ● *interj* d'accord.

ally¹ *n* allié/-e *m/f.*

ally² *vt* allier; ~ **oneself with** s'allier avec.

almighty *adj* tout-puissant; (very great) formidable.

almond *n* amande *f.* ~ **tree** *n* amandier *m.*

almost *adv* presque; **he** ~ **died** il a failli mourir.

alone *a & adv* seul.

along *prep* le long de; **walk** ~ **the beach** marcher sur la plage. ● *adv* **come** ~ venir; **walk** ~ marcher; **push/pull sth** ~ pousser/tirer qch; **all** ~ (time) depuis le début; ~ **with** avec.

alongside *adv* à côté; **come** ~ (Naut) accoster. ● *prep* (next to) à côté de; (all along) le long de.

aloof *adj* distant.

aloud *adv* à haute voix.

alphabet *n* alphabet *m.* **alphabetical** *adj* alphabétique.

alpine *adj* (*landscape*) alpestre; (*climate*) alpin.

already *adv* déjà.

alright *a & adv* = ALL RIGHT.

Alsatian *n* (dog) berger *m* allemand.

also *adv* aussi.

altar *n* autel *m.*

alter *vt/i* changer; (*building*) transformer; (*garment*) retoucher. **alteration** *n* changement *m*; (to building) transformation *f*; (to garment) retouche *f.*

alternate¹ *vt/i* alterner.

alternate² *adj* en alternance; **on ~ days** un jour sur deux. **alternately** *adv* alternativement.

alternative *adj* autre; (*solution*) de rechange. ● *n* (specified option) alternative *f*; (possible option) choix *m*. **alternatively** *adv* sinon.

alternator *n* alternateur *m*.

although *conj* bien que.

altitude *n* altitude *f*.

altogether *adv* (completely) tout à fait; (on the whole) tout compte fait.

aluminium *n* aluminium *m*.

always *adv* toujours.

am ⇒BE.

a.m. *adv* du matin.

amalgamate *vt/i* (merge) fusionner; (*metals*) (s')amalgamer.

amateur *n* & *a* amateur (*m*).

amaze *vt* stupéfaire. **amazed** *adj* stupéfait. **amazement** *n* stupéfaction *f*. **amazing** *adj* stupéfiant; (great) exceptionnel.

ambassador *n* ambassadeur *m*.

amber *n* ambre *m*; (Auto) orange *m*.

ambiguity *n* ambiguïté *f*. **ambiguous** *adj* ambigu.

ambition *n* ambition *f*. **ambitious** *adj* ambitieux.

ambulance *n* ambulance *f*.

ambush *n* embuscade *f*. ● *vt* tendre une embuscade à.

amenable *adj* obligeant; **~ to** (responsive) sensible à.

amend *vt* modifier. **amendment** *n* (to rule) amendement *m*.

amends *npl* **make ~** réparer son erreur.

amenities *npl* équipements *mpl*.

America *n* Amérique *f*.

American *n* Américain/-e *m/f*. ● *adj* américain.

amiable *adj* aimable.

amicable *adj* amical.

amid(st) *prep* au milieu de.

amiss *adj* **there is something ~** il y a quelque chose qui ne va pas.

ammonia *n* (gas) ammoniac *m*; (solution) ammoniaque *f*.

ammunition *n* munitions *fpl*.

amnesty *n* amnistie *f*.

among(st) *prep* parmi; (affecting a group) chez; **be ~ the poorest** être un des plus pauvres; **be ~ the first** être dans les premiers.

amorous *adj* amoureux.

amount *n* quantité *f*; (total) montant *m*; (sum of money) somme *f*. ● *vi* **~ to** (add up to) s'élever à; (be equivalent to) revenir à.

amp *n* ampère *m*.

amphibian *n* amphibie *m*.

ample *adj* (*resources*) largement suffisant; (*proportions*) généreux.

amplifier *n* amplificateur *m*.

amputate *vt* amputer.

amuse *vt* amuser.

amusement *n* (mirth) amusement *m*; (diversion) distraction *f*. **~ arcade** *n* salle *f* de jeux.

an ⇒A.

anaemia *n* anémie *f*.

anaesthetic *n* anesthésique *m*.

analyse *vt* analyser. **analysis** *n* (*pl* **-yses**) analyse *f*. **analyst** *n* analyste *mf*.

anarchist *n* anarchiste *mf*.

anatomical *adj* anatomique. **anatomy** *n* anatomie *f*.

ancestor *n* ancêtre *m*.

anchor *n* ancre *f*. ● *vt* mettre à l'ancre. ● *vi* jeter l'ancre.

anchovy *n* anchois *m*.

ancient *adj* ancien.

ancillary *adj* auxiliaire.

and *conj* et; **two hundred ~ sixty** deux cent soixante; **go ~ see him** allez le voir; **richer ~ richer** de plus en plus riche.

anew *adv* (once more) encore, de nouveau; (in a new way) à nouveau.

angel *n* ange *m*.

anger *n* colère *f*. ● *vt* mettre en colère, fâcher.

angle *n* angle *m*. ● *vi* pêcher (à la ligne); **~ for** (fig) quêter. **angler** *n* pêcheur/-euse *m/f*.

Anglo-Saxon *adj* anglo-saxon. ● *n* Anglo-Saxon/-ne *m/f*.

angry *adj* (**-ier**, **-iest**) fâché, en colère; **get ~** se fâcher, se mettre en colère (with contre); **make sb ~** mettre qn en colère.

anguish *n* angoisse *f*.

a

animal n & a animal (m).

animate[1] adj (person) vivant; (object) animé.

animate[2] vt animer.

aniseed n anis m.

ankle n cheville f. ~ **sock** n socquette f.

annex vt annexer.

anniversary n anniversaire m.

announce vt annoncer (that que). **announcement** n (spoken) annonce f; (written) avis m. **announcer** n (radio, TV) speaker/-ine m/f.

annoy vt agacer, ennuyer. **annoyance** n contrariété f. **annoyed** adj fâché (with contre); get ~ed se fâcher. **annoying** adj ennuyeux.

annual adj annuel. ● n publication f annuelle. **annually** adv (earn, produce) par an; (do, inspect) tous les ans.

annul vt (pt **annulled**) annuler.

anonymity n anonymat m. **anonymous** adj anonyme.

anorak n anorak m.

another det & pron un/-e autre; ~ **coffee** (one more) encore un café; ~ **ten minutes** encore dix minutes, dix minutes de plus; **can I have** ~? est-ce que je peux en avoir un autre?

answer n réponse f; (solution) solution f; (phone) **there's no** ~ ça ne répond pas. ● vt répondre à; (prayer) exaucer; ~ **the door** ouvrir la porte. ● vi répondre. □ ~ **back** répondre; ~ **for** répondre de; ~ **to** (superior) dépendre de; (description) répondre à. **answerable** adj responsable (**for** de; **to** devant). **answering machine** n répondeur m.

ant n fourmi f.

antagonism n antagonisme m. **antagonize** vt provoquer l'hostilité de.

Antarctic n the ~ l'Antarctique m. ● adj antarctique.

antenatal adj prénatal.

antenna n (pl **-ae**) (of insect) antenne f; (pl **-as**; aerial: US) antenne f.

anthem n (Relig) motet m; (of country) hymne m national.

antibiotic n & a antibiotique (m).

antibody n anticorps m.

anticipate vt (foresee, expect) prévoir, s'attendre à; (forestall) devancer.

anticipation n attente f; **in** ~ **of** en prévision or attente de.

anticlimax n (let-down) déception f.

anticlockwise adv & a dans le sens inverse des aiguilles d'une montre.

antics npl pitreries fpl.

antifreeze n antigel m.

antiquated adj (idea) archaïque; (building) vétuste.

antique adj (old) ancien; (old-style) à l'ancienne. ● n objet m ancien, antiquité f. ~ **dealer** n antiquaire mf. ~ **shop** n magasin m d'antiquités.

anti-Semitic adj antisémite.

antiseptic a & n antiseptique (m).

antisocial adj asocial, antisocial; (reclusive) sauvage.

antlers npl bois mpl.

anxiety n (worry) anxiété f; (eagerness) impatience f.

anxious adj (troubled) anxieux; (eager) impatient (**to** de).

any det (some) du, de l', de la, des; (after negative) de, d'; (every) tout; (no matter which) n'importe quel; **at** ~ **moment** à tout moment; **have you** ~ **water?** avez-vous de l'eau? ● pron (no matter which one) n'importe lequel; (any amount of it or them) en; **I do not have** ~ je n'en ai pas; **did you see** ~ **of them?** en avez-vous vu? ● adv (a little) un peu; **do you have** ~ **more?** en avez-vous encore?; **do you have** ~ **more tea?** avez-vous encore du thé?; **I don't do it** ~ **more** je ne le fais plus.

anybody pron (no matter who) n'importe qui; (somebody) quelqu'un; (after negative) personne; **he did not see** ~ il n'a vu personne.

anyhow adv (anyway) de toute façon; (carelessly) n'importe comment.

anyone pron = ANYBODY.

anything pron (no matter what) n'importe quoi; (something) quelque chose; (after negative) rien; **he did not see** ~ il n'a rien vu; ~ **but**

nullement; ~ **you do** tout ce que tu fais.

anyway *adv* de toute façon.

anywhere *adv* (no matter where) n'importe où; (somewhere) quelque part; (after negative) nulle part; **he does not go** ~ il ne va nulle part; ~ **you go** partout où tu vas, où que tu ailles; ~ **else** partout ailleurs.

apart *adv* (on or to one side) à part; (separated) séparé; (into pieces) en pièces; ~ **from** à part, excepté; **ten metres** ~ à dix mètres l'un de l'autre; **come** ~ (break) tomber en morceaux; (*machine*) se démonter; **legs** ~ les jambes écartées; **keep** ~ séparer; **take** ~ démonter.

apartment *n* (US) appartement *m*.

ape *n* singe *m*. ● *vt* singer.

aperitif *n* apéritif *m*.

apex *n* sommet *m*.

apologetic *adj* (*tone*) d'excuse; **be** ~ s'excuser. **apologetically** *adv* en s'excusant.

apologize *vi* s'excuser (**for** de; **to** auprès de).

apology *n* excuses *fpl*.

apostrophe *n* apostrophe *f*.

appal *vt* (*pt* **appalled**) horrifier. **appalling** *adj* épouvantable.

apparatus *n* appareil *m*.

apparent *adj* apparent. **apparently** *adv* apparemment.

appeal *n* appel *m*; (attractiveness) attrait *m*, charme *m*. ● *vi* (Jur) faire appel; ~ **to sb** (beg) faire appel à qn; (attract) plaire à qn; ~ **to sb for sth** demander qch à qn. **appealing** *adj* (attractive) attirant.

appear *vi* apparaître; (arrive) se présenter; (seem, be published) paraître; (Theat) jouer; ~ **on TV** passer à la télé. **appearance** *n* apparition *f*; (aspect) apparence *f*.

appease *vt* apaiser.

appendix *n* (*pl* **-ices**) appendice *m*.

appetite *n* appétit *m*.

appetizer *n* (snack) amuse-gueule *m inv*; (drink) apéritif *m*.

appetizing *adj* appétissant.

applaud *vt/i* applaudir; (*decision*) applaudir à. **applause** *n* applaudissements *mpl*.

apple *n* pomme *f*. ~-**tree** *n* pommier *m*.

appliance *n* appareil *m*.

applicable *adj* valable; **if** ~ le cas échéant.

applicant *n* candidat/-e *m/f* (**for** à).

application *n* application *f*; (request, form) demande *f*; (for job) candidature *f*.

apply *vt* appliquer. ● *vi* ~ **to** (refer) s'appliquer à; (ask) s'adresser à; ~ **for** (*job*) postuler pour; (*grant*) demander; ~ **oneself to** s'appliquer à.

appoint *vt* (to post) nommer; (fix) désigner; **well-**~**ed** bien équipé.

appointment *n* nomination *f*; (meeting) rendez-vous *m inv*; (job) poste *m*; **make an** ~ prendre rendez-vous (**with** avec).

appraisal *n* évaluation *f*. **appraise** *vt* évaluer.

appreciate *vt* (like) apprécier; (understand) comprendre; (be grateful for) être reconnaissant de. ● *vi* prendre de la valeur. **appreciation** *n* appréciation *f*; (gratitude) reconnaissance *f*; (rise) augmentation *f*. **appreciative** *adj* reconnaissant; (*audience*) enthousiaste.

apprehend *vt* (arrest) appréhender; (understand) comprendre. **apprehension** *n* (arrest) appréhension *f*; (fear) crainte *f*.

apprehensive *adj* inquiet; **be** ~ **of** craindre.

apprentice *n* apprenti *m*. ● *vt* mettre en apprentissage.

approach *vt* (s')approcher de; (accost) aborder; (with request) s'adresser à. ● *vi* (s')approcher. ● *n* approche *f*; **an** ~ **to** (*problem*) une façon d'aborder; (*person*) une démarche auprès de.

approachable *adj* abordable.

appropriate[1] *vt* s'approprier.

appropriate[2] *adj* approprié, propre. **appropriately** *adv* à propos.

approval *n* approbation *f*; **on** ~ à *or* sous condition.

approve *vt* approuver. ● *vi* ~ **of** approuver. **approving** *adj* approbateur.

a

approximate¹ *vi* ~ **to** se rapprocher de.

approximate² *adj* approximatif. **approximately** *adv* environ. **approximation** *n* approximation *f*.

apricot *n* abricot *m*.

April *n* avril *m*. ~ **Fools Day** *n* le premier avril.

apron *n* tablier *m*.

apt *adj* (suitable) approprié; **be** ~ **to** avoir tendance à.

aptitude *n* aptitude *f*.

aptly *adv* à propos.

Aquarius *n* Verseau *m*.

aquatic *adj* aquatique; (Sport) nautique.

Arab *n* Arabe *mf*. ● *adj* arabe.

Arabian *adj* d'Arabie.

Arabic *a* & *n* (Ling) arabe (*m*).

arbitrary *adj* arbitraire.

arbitrate *vi* arbitrer. **arbitration** *n* arbitrage *m*. **arbitrator** *n* médiateur/-trice *m/f*.

arcade *n* (shops) galerie *f*; (arches) arcades *fpl*.

arch *n* arche *f*; (of foot) voûte *f* plantaire. ● *vt/i* (s')arquer. ● *adj* (playful) malicieux.

archaeological *adj* archéologique. **archaeologist** *n* archéologue *mf*. **archaeology** *n* archéologie *f*.

archbishop *n* archevêque *m*.

archery *n* tir *m* à l'arc.

architect *n* architecte *mf*; (of plan) artisan *m*. **architectural** *adj* architectural. **architecture** *n* architecture *f*.

archives *npl* archives *fpl*.

archway *n* voûte *f*.

Arctic *n* **the** ~ l'Arctique *m*. ● *adj* (climate) arctique; (expedition) polaire; (conditions) glacial.

ardent *adj* ardent.

are ⇒BE.

area *n* (region) région *f*; (district) quartier *m*; (fig) domaine *m*; (in geometry) aire *f*; **parking/picnic** ~ aire *f* de parking/de pique-nique.

arena *n* arène *f*.

aren't = ARE NOT.

Argentina *n* Argentine *f*.

arguable *adj* discutable. **arguably** *adv* selon certains.

argue *vi* (quarrel) se disputer; (reason) argumenter. ● *vt* (debate) discuter; ~ **that** alléguer que.

argument *n* dispute *f*; (reasoning) argument *m*; (discussion) débat *m*. **argumentative** *adj* ergoteur.

Aries *n* Bélier *m*.

arise *vi* (*pt* **arose**; *pp* **arisen**) (*problem*) survenir; (*question*) se poser; ~ **from** résulter de.

aristocrat *n* aristocrate *mf*.

arithmetic *n* arithmétique *f*.

ark *n* (Relig) arche *f*.

arm *n* bras *m*; ~ **in arm** bras dessus bras dessous. ● *vt* armer; ~**ed robbery** vol *m* à main armée.

armament *n* armement *m*.

arm: ~**band** *n* brassard *m*. ~**chair** *n* fauteuil *m*.

armour *n* armure *f*. **armoured** *adj* blindé. **armoury** *n* arsenal *m*.

armpit *n* aisselle *f*.

arms *npl* (weapons) armes *fpl*. ~ **dealer** *n* trafiquant *m* d'armes.

army *n* armée *f*.

aroma *n* arôme *m*. **aromatic** *adj* aromatique.

arose ⇒ARISE.

around *adv* (tout) autour; (here and there) çà et là. ● *prep* autour de; ~ **here** par ici.

arouse *vt* (awaken, cause) éveiller; (excite) exciter.

arrange *vt* arranger; (time, date) fixer; ~ **to** s'arranger pour.

arrangement *n* arrangement *m*; (agreement) entente *f*; **make** ~**s** prendre des dispositions.

array *n* **an** ~ **of** (display) un étalage impressionnant de.

arrears *npl* arriéré *m*; **in** ~ (rent) arriéré; **he is in** ~ il a des retards dans ses paiements.

arrest *vt* arrêter; (attention) retenir. ● *n* arrestation *f*; **under** ~ en état d'arrestation.

arrival *n* arrivée *f*; **new** ~ nouveau venu *m*, nouvelle venue *f*.

arrive *vi* arriver; ~ **at** (destination) arriver à; (decision) parvenir à.

arrogance *n* arrogance *f*.

arrow n flèche f.

arse n ⊠ cul m ⊠.

arson n incendie m criminel.
arsonist n incendiaire mf.

art n art m; (fine arts) beaux-arts mpl.

artery n artère f.

art gallery n (public) musée m
(d'art); (private) galerie f (d'art).

arthritis n arthrite f.

artichoke n artichaut m.

article n article m; ~ of clothing
vêtement m.

articulate adj (person) capable de
s'exprimer clairement; (speech)
distinct.

articulated lorry n semi-
remorque m.

artificial adj artificiel.

artist n artiste mf.

arts npl the ~ les arts mpl; (Univ)
lettres fpl.

artwork n (of book) illustrations fpl.

as conj comme; (while) pendant que;
(over gradual period of time) au fur et à
mesure que; ~ she grew older au fur
et à mesure qu'elle vieillissait; do ~
I say fais ce que je dis; ~ usual
comme d'habitude. ● prep ~ a
mother en tant que mère; ~ a gift en
cadeau; ~ from Monday à partir de
lundi; ~ for, ~ to quant à; ~ if
comme si; you look ~ if you're tired
vous avez l'air (d'être) fatigué. ● adv
~ tall ~ aussi grand que; ~ much
~, ~ many ~ autant que; ~ soon ~
aussitôt que; ~ well ~ aussi bien
que; ~ wide ~ possible aussi large
que possible.

asbestos n amiante f.

ascend vt gravir. ● vi monter.

ascertain vt établir (that que).

ash n cendre f; ~(-tree) frêne m.

ashamed adj be ~ avoir honte (of
de).

ashore adv à terre.

ashtray n cendrier m.

Asia n Asie f.

Asian n Asiatique mf. ● adj
asiatique.

aside adv de côté; ~ from à part. ● n
aparté m.

ask vt/i demander; (a question) poser;
(invite) inviter; ~ sb sth demander

qch à qn; ~ sb to do demander à qn
de faire; ~ about (thing) se
renseigner sur; (person) demander
des nouvelles de; ~ for demander.

asleep adj endormi; (numb)
engourdi. ● adv fall ~ s'endormir.

asparagus n (plant) asperge f; (Culin)
asperges fpl.

aspect n aspect m; (direction)
orientation f.

asphyxiate vt/i (s')asphyxier.

aspire vi aspirer (to à; to do à faire).

aspirin n aspirine® f.

ass n âne m; (person ⊠) idiot/-e m/f.

assail vt attaquer. **assailant** n
agresseur m.

assassin n assassin m.
assassinate vt assassiner.
assassination n assassinat m.

assault n (Mil) assaut m; (Jur)
agression f. ● vt (person: Jur)
agresser.

assemble vt (construct) assembler;
(gather) rassembler. ● vi se
rassembler.

assembly n assemblée f. ~ line n
chaîne f de montage.

assent n assentiment m. ● vi
consentir.

assert vt affirmer; (rights)
revendiquer. **assertion** n
affirmation f. **assertive** adj assuré.

assess vt évaluer; (payment)
déterminer le montant de.
assessment n évaluation f.
assessor n (valuer) expert m.

asset n (advantage) atout m; (financial)
bien m; ~s (Comm) actif m.

assign vt (allot) assigner; ~ sb to
(appoint) affecter qn à.

assignment n (task) mission f;
(diplomatic) poste m; (academic) devoir
m.

assist vt/i aider. **assistance** n
aide f.

assistant n aide mf; (in shop)
vendeur/-euse m/f. ● adj (manager)
adjoint.

associate[1] n & a associé/-e (m/f).

associate[2] vt associer. ● vi ~ with
fréquenter. **association** n
association f.

assorted adj divers; (foods) assorti.

assortment *n* assortiment *m*; (of people) mélange *m*.

assume *vt* supposer; (*power, attitude*) prendre; (*role, burden*) assumer.

assurance *n* assurance *f*.

assure *vt* assurer.

asterisk *n* astérisque *m*.

asthma *n* asthme *m*.

astonish *vt* étonner.

astound *vt* stupéfier.

astray *adv* go ~ s'égarer; lead ~ égarer.

astride *adv & prep* à califourchon (sur).

astrologer *n* astrologue *mf*.
astrology *n* astrologie *f*.

astronaut *n* astronaute *mf*.

astronomer *n* astronome *mf*.

asylum *n* asile *m*.

---

at *preposition*

➡ For expressions such as **laugh at**, **look at** ⇨**laugh**, **look**.

····➤ (in position or place) à; **he's** ~ **his desk** il est à son bureau; **she's** ~ **work/school** elle est au travail/à l'école.

····➤ (at someone's house or business) chez; ~ **Mary's/the dentist's** chez Mary/le dentiste.

····➤ (in times, ages) à; ~ **four o'clock** à quatre heures; ~ **two years of age** à l'âge de deux ans.

---

ate ⇨EAT.

atheist *n* athée *mf*.

athlete *n* athlète *mf*. **athletic** *adj* athlétique. **athletics** *npl* athlétisme *m*; (US) sports *mpl*.

Atlantic *adj* atlantique. ● *n* the ~ (Ocean) l'Atlantique *m*.

atlas *n* atlas *m*.

atmosphere *n* (air) atmosphère *f*; (mood) ambiance *f*. **atmospheric** *adj* atmosphérique; d'ambiance.

atom *n* atome *m*.

atrocious *adj* atroce.

atrocity *n* atrocité *f*.

attach *vt/i* (s')attacher; (*letter*) joindre (**to** à).

attaché *n* (Pol) attaché/-e *m/f*. ~ **case** *n* attaché-case *m*.

attached *adj* **be** ~ **to** (like) être attaché à; **the** ~ **letter** la lettre ci-jointe.

attachment *n* (accessory) accessoire *m*; (affection) attachement *m*; (e-mail) pièces *fpl* jointes.

attack *n* attaque *f*; (Med) crise *f*. ● *vt* attaquer.

attain *vt* atteindre (à); (gain) acquérir.

attempt *vt* tenter. ● *n* tentative *f*; **an** ~ **on sb's life** un attentat contre qn.

attend *vt* assister à; (*class*) suivre; (*school, church*) aller à. ● *vi* assister; ~ (**to**) (look after) s'occuper de. **attendance** *n* présence *f*; (people) assistance *f*.

attendant *n* employé/-e *m/f*. ● *adj* associé.

attention *n* attention *f*; ~! (Mil) garde-à-vous!; **pay** ~ faire *or* prêter attention (**to** à).

attentive *adj* attentif; (considerate) attentionné. **attentively** *adv* attentivement. **attentiveness** *n* attention *f*.

attest *vt/i* ~ (**to**) attester.

attic *n* grenier *m*.

attitude *n* attitude *f*.

attorney *n* (US) avocat/-e *m/f*.

attract *vt* attirer. **attraction** *n* attraction *f*; (charm) attrait *m*.

attractive *adj* attrayant, séduisant. **attractively** *adv* agréablement. **attractiveness** *n* attrait *m*, beauté *f*.

attribute[1] *vt* ~ **to** attribuer à.

attribute[2] *n* attribut *m*.

aubergine *n* aubergine *f*.

auction *n* vente *f* aux enchères. ● *vt* vendre aux enchères. **auctioneer** *n* commissaire-priseur *m*.

audacious *adj* audacieux.

audience *n* (theatre, radio) public *m*; (interview) audience *f*.

audiovisual *adj* audiovisuel.

audit *n* vérification *f* des comptes. ● *vt* vérifier.

audition *n* audition *f*. ● *vt/i* auditionner (**for** pour).

auditor *n* commissaire *m* aux comptes.

August *n* août *m*.

aunt *n* tante *f*.

auspicious *adj* favorable.

Australia *n* Australie *f*.

Australian *n* Australien/-ne *m/f*. ● *adj* australien.

Austria *n* Autriche *f*.

Austrian *n* Autrichien/-ne *m/f*. ● *adj* autrichien.

authentic *adj* authentique.

author *n* auteur *m*.

authoritarian *adj* autoritaire.

authoritative *adj* (credible) qui fait autorité; (*manner*) autoritaire.

authority *n* autorité *f*; (permission) autorisation *f*.

authorization *n* autorisation *f*. **authorize** *vt* autoriser.

autistic *adj* (*person*) autiste; (*response*) autistique.

autograph *n* autographe *m*. ● *vt* signer, dédicacer.

automate *vt* automatiser.

automatic *adj* automatique. ● *n* (Auto) voiture *f* automatique.

automobile *n* (US) auto(mobile) *f*.

autonomous *adj* autonome.

autumn *n* automne *m*.

auxiliary *a & n* auxiliaire (*mf*); ∼ (verb) auxiliaire *m*.

avail *vt* ∼ oneself of profiter de. ● *n* of no ∼ inutile; to no ∼ sans résultat.

availability *n* disponibilité *f*. **available** *adj* disponible.

avenge *vt* venger; ∼ oneself se venger (**on** de).

avenue *n* avenue *f*; (line of approach: fig) voie *f*.

average *n* moyenne *f*; **on** ∼ en moyenne. ● *adj* moyen. ● *vt* faire la moyenne de; (produce, do) faire en moyenne.

aviary *n* volière *f*.

avocado *n* avocat *m*.

avoid *vt* éviter. **avoidance** *n* (of injuries) prévention *f*; (of responsibility) refus *m*.

await *vt* attendre.

awake *vt/i* (*pt* **awoke**; *pp* **awoken**) (s')éveiller. ● *adj* be ∼ ne pas dormir, être (r)éveillé.

award *vt* (*grant*) attribuer; (*prize*) décerner; (*points*) accorder. ● *n* récompense *f*, prix *m*; (scholarship) bourse *f*; **pay** ∼ augmentation *f* (de salaire).

aware *adj* (well-informed) averti; **be** ∼ **of** (*danger*) être conscient de; (*fact*) savoir; **become** ∼ **of** prendre conscience de. **awareness** *n* conscience *f*.

away *adv* (far) (au) loin; (absent) absent, parti; ∼ **from** loin de; **move** ∼ s'écarter; (to new home) déménager; **six kilometres** ∼ à six kilomètres (de distance); **take** ∼ emporter; **he was snoring** ∼ il ronflait. ● *a & n* ∼ (match) match *m* à l'extérieur.

awe *n* crainte *f* (révérencielle).

awe-inspiring *adj* impressionnant.

awesome *adj* redoutable.

awful *adj* affreux. **awfully** *adv* (badly) affreusement; (very 🆒) rudement.

awkward *adj* difficile; (inconvenient) inopportun; (clumsy) maladroit; (embarrassing) gênant; (embarrassed) gêné. **awkwardly** *adv* maladroitement; avec gêne. **awkwardness** *n* maladresse *f*; (discomfort) gêne *f*.

awning *n* auvent *m*; (of shop) store *m*.

awoke, awoken ⇒AWAKE.

axe *n* hache *f*. ● *vt* (*pres p* **axing**) réduire; (eliminate) supprimer; (employee) renvoyer.

axis *n* (*pl* **axes**) axe *m*.

axle *n* essieu *m*.

Bb

BA *abbr* ⇒BACHELOR OF ARTS.

babble *vi* babiller; (*stream*) gazouiller. ● *n* babillage *m*.

baby *n* bébé *m*. ∼ **carriage** *n* (US) voiture *f* d'enfant. ∼**-sit** *vi* faire du

babysitting, garder des enfants.
~**sitter** n baby-sitter mf.

bachelor n célibataire m. **B~ of Arts** licencié/-e m/f ès lettres.

back n (of person, hand, page, etc.) dos m; (of house) derrière m; (of vehicle) arrière m; (of room) fond m; (of chair) dossier m; (in football) arrière m; **at the ~ of the book** à la fin du livre; **in ~ of** (US) derrière. ● adj (leg, wheel) arrière inv; (door, gate) de derrière; (taxes) arriéré. ● adv en arrière; (returned) de retour, rentré; **come ~** revenir; **give ~** rendre; **take ~** reprendre; **I want it ~** je veux le récupérer. ● vt (support) appuyer; (bet on) miser sur; (vehicle) faire reculer. ● vi (of person, vehicle) reculer. □ ~ **down** céder; ~ **out** se désister; (Auto) sortir en marche arrière; ~ **up** (support) appuyer. ~**ache** n mal m de dos. ~**-bencher** n (Pol) député m. ~**bone** n colonne f vertébrale. ~**date** vt antidater. ~**fire** vi (Auto) pétarader; (fig) mal tourner. ~**gammon** n trictrac m.

background n fond m, arrière-plan m; (context) contexte m; (environment) milieu m; (experience) formation f. ● adj (music, noise) de fond.

backhand n revers m. **backhander** n (bribe) pot-de-vin m.

backing n soutien m.

back: ~**lash** n retour m de bâton; réaction f violente (**against** contre). ~**log** n retard m. ~ **number** n vieux numéro m. ~**pack** n sac m à dos. ~**side** n (buttocks 🔲) derrière m. ~**stage** a & adv dans les coulisses. ~**stroke** n dos m crawlé. ~**track** vi rebrousser chemin; (change one's opinion) faire marche arrière.

back-up n soutien m; (Comput) sauvegarde f. ● adj de secours; (Comput) de sauvegarde.

backward adj (step etc.) en arrière; (retarded) arriéré.

backwards adv en arrière; (walk) à reculons; (read) à l'envers; **go ~ and forwards** aller et venir.

bacon n lard m; (in rashers) bacon m.

bacteria npl bactéries fpl.

bad adj (**worse, worst**) mauvais; (wicked) méchant; (ill) malade; (accident) grave; (food) gâté; **feel ~** se sentir mal; **go ~** se gâter; ~ **language** gros mots mpl; **too ~!** tant pis!; (I'm sorry) dommage!

badge n badge m; (coat of arms) insigne m.

badger n blaireau m. ● vt harceler.

badly adv mal; (hurt) gravement; **want ~** avoir grande envie de.

badminton n badminton m.

bad-tempered adj irritable.

baffle vt déconcerter.

bag n sac m; ~**s** (luggage) bagages mpl; (under eyes 🔲) valises fpl; ~**s of** plein de.

baggage n bagages mpl; ~ **reclaim** réception f des bagages.

baggy adj large.

bagpipes npl cornemuse f.

bail n caution f; **on ~** sous caution; (cricket) bâtonnet m. ● vt mettre en liberté provisoire.

bailiff n huissier m.

bait n appât m. ● vt appâter; (fig) tourmenter.

bake vt faire cuire au four; ~ **a cake** faire un gâteau. ● vi cuire; (person) faire du pain. **baked beans** npl haricots mpl blancs à la tomate. **baked potato** n pomme f de terre en robe des champs. **baker** n boulanger/-ère m/f. **bakery** n boulangerie f.

balance n équilibre m; (scales) balance f; (outstanding sum: Comm) solde m; (of payments, of trade) balance f; (remainder) restant m. ● vt mettre en équilibre; (weigh up also Comm) balancer; (budget) équilibrer; (to compensate) contrebalancer. ● vi être en équilibre.

balcony n balcon m.

bald adj chauve; (tyre) lisse; (fig) simple.

balk vt contrecarrer. ● vi ~ **at** reculer devant.

ball n (golf, tennis, etc.) balle f; (football) ballon m; (billiards) bille f; (of wool) pelote f; (sphere) boule f; (dance) bal m.

ballet n ballet m.

balloon n ballon m.

ballot n scrutin m. ● vt consulter par vote (**on** sur). **~-box** n urne f. **~-paper** n bulletin m de vote.

ballpoint pen n stylo m (à) bille.

ban vt (pt **banned**) interdire; ~ **sb from** exclure qn de; ~ **sb from doing** interdire à qn de faire. ● n interdiction f (**on** de).

banal adj banal.

banana n banane f.

band n (strip, group of people) bande f; (pop group) groupe m; (brass band) fanfare f. ● vi ~ **together** se réunir.

bandage n bandage m. ● vt bander.

B and B abbr ⇒BED AND BREAKFAST.

bandit n bandit m.

bandstand n kiosque m à musique.

bang n (blow, noise) coup m; (explosion) détonation f; (of door) claquement m. ● vt/i taper; (door) claquer; ~ **one's head** se cogner la tête. ● interj vlan. ● adv Ⅱ ~ **in the middle** en plein milieu; ~ **on time** à l'heure pile.

banger n (firework) pétard m; (Culin) saucisse f; (old) ~ (car Ⅱ) guimbarde f.

banish vt bannir.

banister n rampe f d'escalier.

bank n (Comm) banque f; (of river) rive f; (of sand) banc m. ● vt mettre en banque. ● vi (Aviat) virer; ~ **with** avoir un compte à; ~ **on** compter sur. ~ **account** n compte m en banque. ~ **card** n carte f bancaire. ~ **holiday** n jour m férié.

banking n opérations fpl bancaires; (as career) la banque.

banknote n billet m de banque.

bankrupt adj **be** ~ être en faillite; **go** ~ faire faillite. ● n failli/-e m/f. ● vt mettre en faillite. **bankruptcy** n faillite f.

bank statement n relevé m de compte.

banner n bannière f.

baptism n baptême m. **baptize** vt baptiser.

bar n (of metal) barre f; (on window, cage) barreau m; (of chocolate) tablette f; (pub) bar m; (counter) comptoir m; (Mus) mesure f; (fig) obstacle m; ~ **of soap** savonnette f; **the** ~ (Jur) le barreau. ● vt (pt **barred**) (obstruct) barrer; (prohibit) interdire; (exclude) exclure. ● prep sauf.

barbecue n barbecue m. ● vt faire au barbecue.

barbed wire n fil m de fer barbelé.

barber n coiffeur m (pour hommes).

bar code n code m (à) barres.

bare adj nu; (cupboard) vide. ● vt mettre à nu. **~foot** adj nu-pieds inv, pieds nus. **barely** adv à peine.

bargain n (deal) marché m; (cheap thing) occasion f. ● vi négocier; (haggle) marchander; **not** ~ **for** ne pas s'attendre à.

barge n péniche f. ● vi ~ **in** interrompre; (into room) faire irruption.

bark n (of tree) écorce f; (of dog) aboiement m. ● vi aboyer.

barley n orge f.

bar: **~maid** n serveuse f. **~man** n (pl **-men**) barman m.

barn n grange f.

barracks npl caserne f.

barrel n tonneau m; (of oil) baril m; (of gun) canon m.

barren adj stérile.

barricade n barricade f. ● vt barricader.

barrier n barrière f; **ticket** ~ guichet m.

barrister n avocat m.

bartender n (US) barman m.

barter n troc m. ● vt troquer (**for** contre).

base n base f. ● vt baser (**on** sur; **in** à). ● adj ignoble. **baseball** n baseball m.

basement n sous-sol m.

bash Ⅱ vt cogner; **~ed in** enfoncé. ● n coup m violent; **have a** ~ **at** s'essayer à.

basic adj fondamental, élémentaire; **the ~s** l'essentiel m. **basically** adv au fond.

basil n basilic m.

basin n (for liquids) cuvette f; (for food) bol m; (for washing) lavabo m; (of river) bassin m.

basis n (pl **bases**) base f.

bask vi se prélasser (**in** à).

basket n corbeille f; (with handle) panier m. **basketball** n basket(-ball) m.

Basque n (person) Basque mf; (Ling) basque m. ● adj basque.

bass[1] adj (voice, part) de basse; (sound, note) grave. ● n (pl **basses**) basse f.

bass[2] n inv (freshwater fish) perche f; (sea) bar m.

bassoon n basson m.

bastard n (illegitimate) bâtard/-e m/f; (insult 🗵) salaud m 🗵.

bat n (cricket etc.) batte f; (table tennis) raquette f; (animal) chauve-souris f. ● vt (pt **batted**) (ball) frapper; **not ~ an eyelid** ne pas sourciller.

batch n (of cakes, people) fournée f; (of goods, text also Comput) lot m.

bath n (pl **-s**) bain m; (tub) baignoire f; **have a ~** prendre un bain; (swimming) **~s** piscine f. ● vt donner un bain à.

bathe vt baigner. ● vi se baigner; (US) prendre un bain.

bathing n baignade f. **~-costume** n maillot m de bain.

bath: **~robe** n (US) robe f de chambre. **~room** n salle f de bains.

baton n (policeman's) matraque f; (Mus) baguette f.

batter vt battre. ● n (Culin) pâte f (à frire).

battery n (Mil, Auto) batterie f; (of torch, radio) pile f.

battle n bataille f; (fig) lutte f. ● vi se battre. **~field** n champ m de bataille.

baulk vt/i = BALK.

bay n (Bot) laurier m; (Geog, Archit) baie f; (area) aire f; (bark) aboiement m; **keep** or **hold at ~** tenir à distance. ● vi aboyer. **~-leaf** n feuille f de laurier. **~ window** n fenêtre f en saillie.

bazaar n (shop, market) bazar m; (sale) vente f.

BC abbr (**before Christ**) avant J.-C.

BBS abbr (**Bulletin Board System**) (Internet) babillard m électronique, BBS m.

be

present **am**, **is**, **are**; past **was**, **were**; past participle **been**.

● intransitive verb

····➤ être; **I am tired** je suis fatigué; **it's me** c'est moi.

····➤ (feelings) avoir; **I am hot** j'ai chaud; **he is hungry/thirsty** il a faim/soif; **her hands are cold** elle a froid aux mains.

····➤ (age) avoir; **I am 15** j'ai 15 ans.

····➤ (weather) faire; **it's warm** il fait chaud; **it's 25** il fait 25.

····➤ (health) aller; **how are you?** comment allez-vous or comment vas-tu?

····➤ (visit) aller; **I've never been to Italy** je ne suis jamais allé en Italie.

● auxiliary verb

····➤ (in tenses) **I am working** je travaille; **he was writing to his mother** il écrivait à sa mère; **she is to do it at once** (obligation) elle doit le faire tout de suite.

····➤ (in passives) **he was killed** il a été tué; **the window has been fixed** on a réparé la fenêtre.

····➤ (in tag questions) **their house is lovely, isn't it?** leur maison est très jolie, n'est-ce pas?

····➤ (in short answers) '**I am a painter**'—'**are you?**' 'je suis peintre'—'ah oui?'; '**are you a doctor?**'—'**yes, I am**' 'êtes-vous médecin?'—'oui'; '**you're not going out**'—'**yes I am**' 'tu ne sors pas'—'si'.

beach n plage f.

beacon n (lighthouse) phare m; (marker) balise f.

bead n perle f.

beak n bec m.

beaker n gobelet m.

beam n (timber) poutre f; (of light) rayon m; (of torch) faisceau m. ● vi rayonner. ● vt (broadcast) transmettre.

bean n haricot m.

bear n ours m. ● vt (pt **bore**; pp **borne**) (carry, show, feel) porter;

(endure, sustain) supporter; (*child*) mettre au monde. ● *vi* ~ **left** (go) prendre à gauche; ~ **in mind** tenir compte de. □ ~ **out** confirmer; ~ **up** tenir le coup. **bearable** *adj* supportable.

beard *n* barbe *f*.

bearer *n* porteur/-euse *m/f*.

bearing *n* (behaviour) maintien *m*; (relevance) rapport *m*; **get one's ~s** s'orienter.

beast *n* bête *f*; (*person*) brute *f*.

beat *vt/i* (*pt* **beat**; *pp* **beaten**) battre; ~ **a retreat** battre en retraite; ~ **it!** dégage! 🔲; **it ~s me** 🔲 ça me dépasse. ● *n* (of drum, heart) battement *m*; (Mus) mesure *f*; (of policeman) ronde *f*. □ ~ **off** repousser; ~ **up** tabasser. **beating** *n* raclée *f*.

beautiful *adj* beau.

beauty *n* beauté *f*. ~ **parlour** *n* institut *m* de beauté. ~ **spot** *n* grain *m* de beauté; (place) site *m* pittoresque.

beaver *n* castor *m*.

became ⇒BECOME.

because *conj* parce que; ~ **of** à cause de.

become *vt/i* (*pt* **became**; *pp* **become**) devenir; (befit) convenir à; **what has ~ of her?** qu'est-ce qu'elle est devenue?

bed *n* lit *m*; (layer) couche *f*; (of sea) fond *m*; (of flowers) parterre *m*; **go to ~** (aller) se coucher. ● *vi* (*pt* **bedded**) ~ **down** se coucher. **bed and breakfast** *n* chambre *f* avec petit déjeuner, chambre *f* d'hôte. ~**bug** *n* punaise *f*. ~**clothes** *npl* couvertures *fpl*.

bedding *n* literie *f*.

bed: ~**ridden** *adj* cloué au lit. ~**room** *n* chambre *f* (à coucher). ~**side** *n* chevet *m*. ~**sit**, ~**sitter** *n* chambre *f* meublée, studio *m*. ~**spread** *n* dessus *m* de lit. ~**time** *n* heure *f* du coucher.

bee *n* abeille *f*; **make a ~-line for** aller tout droit vers.

beech *n* hêtre *m*.

beef *n* bœuf *m*. ~**burger** *n* hamburger *m*.

beehive *n* ruche *f*.

been ⇒BE.

beer *n* bière *f*.

beetle *n* scarabée *m*.

beetroot *n inv* betterave *f*.

before *prep* (time) avant; (place) devant; **the day ~ yesterday** avant-hier. ● *adv* avant; (already) déjà; **the day ~** la veille. ● *conj* ~ **leaving** avant de partir; ~ **I forget** avant que j'oublie. **beforehand** *adv* à l'avance.

beg *vt* (*pt* **begged**) (*food, money, favour*) demander (**from** à); ~ **sb to do** supplier qn de faire. ● *vi* mendier; **it is going ~ging** personne n'en veut.

began ⇒BEGIN.

beggar *n* mendiant/-e *m/f*.

begin *vt/i* (*pt* **began**, *pp* **begun**, *pres p* **beginning**) commencer (**to do** à faire). **beginner** *n* débutant/-e *m/f*. **beginning** *n* commencement *m*, début *m*.

begun ⇒BEGIN.

behalf *n* **on ~ of** (*act, speak, campaign*) pour; (*phone, write*) de la part de.

behave *vi* se conduire; ~ **(oneself)** se conduire bien.

behaviour, (US) **behavior** *n* comportement *m* (**towards** envers).

behead *vt* décapiter.

behind *prep* derrière; (in time) en retard sur. ● *adv* derrière; (late) en retard; **leave ~** oublier. ● *n* (buttocks 🔲) derrière *m* 🔲.

beige *a & n* beige (*m*).

being *n* (person) être *m*.

belch *vi* avoir un renvoi. ● *vt* ~ **out** (*smoke*) s'échapper. ● *n* renvoi *m*.

Belgian *n* Belge *mf*. ● *adj* belge. **Belgium** *n* Belgique *f*.

belief *n* conviction *f*; (trust) confiance *f*; (faith: Relig) foi *f*.

believe *vt/i* croire; ~ **in** croire à; (*deity*) croire en. **believer** *n* croyant/-e *m/f*.

bell *n* cloche *f*; (small) clochette *f*; (on door) sonnette *f*.

belly *n* ventre *m*. ~ **button** *n* nombril *m*.

belong *vi* ~ **to** appartenir à; (*club*) être membre de.

belongings *npl* affaires *fpl*.

beloved *a & n* bien-aimé/-e (*m/f*).

below *prep* sous, au-dessous de; (fig) indigne de. ● *adv* en dessous; (on page) ci-dessous.

belt *n* ceinture *f*; (Tech) courroie *f*; (fig) zone *f*. ● *vt* (hit 🔲) rosser. ● *vi* (rush 🔲) ~ **in/out** entrer/sortir à toute vitesse.

beltway *n* (US) périphérique *m*.

bemused *adj* perplexe.

bench *n* banc *m*; **the** ~ (Jur) la magistrature (assise).

bend *vt* (*pt* **bent**) (*knee, arm, wire*) plier; (*head, back*) courber. ● *vi* (*road*) tourner; (*person*) ~ **down/ over** se pencher. ● *n* courbe *f*; (in road) virage *m*; (of arm, knee) pli *m*.

beneath *prep* sous, au-dessous de; (fig) indigne de. ● *adv* en dessous.

benefactor *n* bienfaiteur/-trice *m/ f*.

beneficial *adj* bénéfique.

benefit *n* avantage *m*; (allowance) allocation *f*. ● *vt* (be useful to) profiter à; (do good to) faire du bien à. ● *vi* profiter; ~ **from** tirer profit de.

benign *adj* (kindly) bienveillant; (Med) bénin.

bent ⇒BEND. ● *n* (talent) aptitude *f*; (inclination) penchant *m*. ● *adj* tordu; 🔲 corrompu; ~ **on doing** décidé à faire.

bequest *n* legs *m*.

bereaved *adj* endeuillé; **the** ~ la famille endeuillée. **bereavement** *n* deuil *m*.

berry *n* baie *f*.

berserk *adj* fou furieux.

berth *n* (in train, ship) couchette *f*; (anchorage) mouillage *m*; **give a wide** ~ **to** éviter. ● *vi* mouiller.

beside *prep* à côté de; ~ **oneself** hors de soi; ~ **the point** sans rapport.

besides *prep* en plus de. ● *adv* en plus.

besiege *vt* assiéger.

best *adj* meilleur; **the** ~ **book** le meilleur livre; **the** ~ **part of** la plus grande partie de; **the** ~ **thing is to** le mieux est de. ● *adv* (**the**) ~ (*behave, play*) le mieux. ● *n* **the** ~ le meilleur, la meilleure; **do one's** ~

faire de son mieux; **make the** ~ **of** s'accommoder de. ~ **man** *n* témoin. ~**-seller** *n* bestseller *m*, livre *m* à succès.

bet *n* pari *m*. ● *vt/i* (*pt* **bet** or **betted**, *pres p* **betting**) parier (**on** sur).

betray *vt* trahir.

better *adj* meilleur; **the** ~ **part of** la plus grande partie de; **get** ~ s'améliorer; (recover) se remettre. ● *adv* mieux; **I had** ~ **go** je ferais mieux de partir. ● *vt* (improve) améliorer; (do better than) surpasser. ● *n* **get the** ~ **of** l'emporter sur; **so much the** ~ tant mieux. ~ **off** *adj* (richer) plus riche; **he is/would be** ~ **off at home** il est/serait mieux chez lui.

betting-shop *n* bureau *m* du PMU.

between *prep* entre. ● *adv* **in** ~ au milieu.

beverage *n* boisson *f*.

beware *vi* prendre garde (**of** à).

bewilder *vt* déconcerter.

beyond *prep* au-delà de; (*control, reach*) hors de; (besides) excepté. ● *adv* au-delà; **it is** ~ **me** ça me dépasse.

bias *n* (inclination) tendance *f*; (prejudice) parti *m* pris. ● *vt* (*pt* **biased**) influer sur. **biased** *adj* partial.

bib *n* bavoir *m*.

Bible *n* Bible *f*.

biceps *n* biceps *m*.

bicycle *n* vélo *m*, bicyclette *f*. ● *adj* (*bell, chain*) de vélo; (*pump, clip*) à vélo.

bid *n* (at auction) enchère *f*; (attempt) tentative *f*. ● *vt/i* (*pt* **bade**, *pp* **bidden** or **bid**, *pres p* **bidding**) (offer) offrir, mettre une enchère (de) (**for** pour); ~ **sb good morning** dire bonjour à qn; ~ **sb farewell** faire ses adieux à qn.

bidding *n* (at auction) enchères *fpl*; **he did my** ~ il a fait ce que je lui ai dit.

bifocals *npl* verres *mpl* à double foyer.

big *adj* (**bigger**, **biggest**) grand; (in bulk) gros.

bike *n* vélo *m*.

bikini *n* bikini *m*.

bilberry *n* myrtille *f.*

bilingual *adj* bilingue.

bill *n* (invoice) facture *f*; (in hotel, for gas) note *f*; (in restaurant) addition *f*; (of sale) acte *m*; (Pol) projet *m* de loi; (banknote: US) billet *m* de banque; (Theat) **on the ~** à l'affiche; (of bird) bec *m.* ● *vt* (person: Comm) envoyer la facture à. **~board** *n* panneau *m* d'affichage.

billet *n* cantonnement *m.* ● *vt* (*pt* **billeted**) cantonner (**on** chez).

billiards *n* billard *m.*

billion *n* billion *m*; (US) milliard *m.*

bin *n* (for rubbish) poubelle *f*; (for storage) casier *m.*

bind *vt* (*pt* **bound**) attacher; (book) relier; **be bound by** être tenu par. ● *n* (bore) corvée *f.*

binding *n* reliure *f.* ● *adj* (*agreement, contract*) qui lie.

binge *n* (drinking) beuverie *f*; (eating) gueuleton *m.*

binoculars *npl* jumelles *fpl.*

biochemistry *n* biochimie *f.*

biodegradable *adj* biodégradable.

biographer *n* biographe *mf.*

biography *n* biographie *f.*

biological *adj* biologique.

biologist *n* biologiste *mf.*

biology *n* biologie *f.*

birch *n* (tree) bouleau *m*; (whip) fouet *m.*

bird *n* oiseau *m*; (girl 🆇) nana *f.*

Biro® *n* stylo *m* à bille, bic® *m.*

birth *n* naissance *f*; **give ~** accoucher. **~ certificate** *n* acte *m* de naissance. **~-control** *n* contraception *f.* **~day** *n* anniversaire *m.* **~mark** *n* tache *f* de naissance. **~-rate** *n* taux *m* de natalité.

biscuit *n* biscuit *m*; (US) petit pain *m* (au lait).

bisect *vt* couper en deux.

bishop *n* évêque *m.*

bit ⇒BITE. ● *n* morceau *m*; (of horse) mors *m*; (of tool) mèche *f*; **a ~** (a little) un peu; (Comput) bit *m.*

bitch *n* chienne *f*; (woman 🆇) garce *f* 🆇. ● *vi* dire du mal (**about** de).

bite *vt/i* (*pt* **bit**; *pp* **bitten**) mordre; **~ one's nails** se ronger les ongles.

● *n* morsure *f*; (by insect) piqûre *f*; (mouthful) bouchée *f*; **have a ~** manger un morceau.

bitter *adj* amer; (weather) glacial. ● *n* bière *f.* **bitterly** *adv* amèrement; **it is ~ly cold** il fait un temps glacial.

bizarre *adj* bizarre.

black *adj* noir; **~ and blue** couvert de bleus. ● *n* (colour) noir *m*; B**~** (person) Noir/-e *m/f.* ● *vt* noircir; (goods) boycotter. **~berry** *n* mûre *f.* **~bird** *n* merle *m.* **~board** *n* tableau *m* noir. **~currant** *n* cassis *m.*

blacken *vt/i* noircir.

black: **~ eye** *n* œil *m* poché. **~head** *n* point *m* noir. **~ ice** *n* verglas *m.* **~leg** *n* jaune *m.*

blacklist *n* liste *f* noire. ● *vt* mettre à l'index.

blackmail *n* chantage *m.* ● *vt* faire chanter. **blackmailer** *n* maître-chanteur *m.*

black: **~ market** *n* marché *m* noir. **~out** *n* panne *f* de courant; (Med) syncope *f.* **~ pudding** *n* boudin *m.* **~ sheep** *n* brebis *f* galeuse. **~smith** *n* forgeron *m.* **~ spot** *n* point *m* noir.

bladder *n* vessie *f.*

blade *n* (of knife) lame *f*; (of propeller, oar) pale *f*; **~ of grass** brin *m* d'herbe.

blame *vt* accuser; **~ sb for sth** reprocher qch à qn; **he is to ~** il est responsable (**for** de). ● *n* responsabilité *f* (**for** de).

bland *adj* (insipid) fade.

blank *adj* (*page*) blanc; (*screen*) vide; (*cheque*) en blanc; **to look ~** avoir l'air ébahi. ● *n* blanc *m*; **~** (cartridge) cartouche *f* à blanc.

blanket *n* couverture *f*; (layer) couche *f.*

blasphemous *adj* blasphématoire; (*person*) blasphémateur.

blast *n* explosion *f*; (wave of air) souffle *m*; (of wind) rafale *f*; (noise from siren etc.) coup *m.* ● *vt* (blow up) faire sauter. ◻ **~ off** décoller. **~ furnace** *n* haut-fourneau *m.* **~-off** *n* lancement *m.*

blatant *adj* (obvious) flagrant; (shameless) éhonté.

blaze n feu m; (accident) incendie m. ● vt ~ **a trail** faire œuvre de pionnier. ● vi (fire) brûler; (sky, eyes) flamboyer.

bleach n (for cleaning) eau f de Javel; (for hair, fabric) décolorant m. ● vt/i blanchir; (hair) décolorer.

bleak adj (landscape) désolé; (outlook, future) sombre.

bleed vt/i (pt **bled**) saigner.

bleep n bip m.

blemish n imperfection f; (on fruit, reputation) tache f. ● vt entacher.

blend vt mélanger. ● vi se fondre ensemble; **to ~ with** se marier à. ● n mélange m. **blender** n mixeur n, mixer n.

bless vt bénir; **be ~ed with** jouir de; **~ you!** à vos souhaits! **blessed** adj (holy) saint; (damned 🆇) sacré. **blessing** n bénédiction f; (benefit) avantage m; (stroke of luck) chance f.

blew ⇨BLOW.

blight n (disease: Bot) rouille f; (fig) plaie f.

blind adj aveugle (**to** à); (corner, bend) sans visibilité. ● vt aveugler. ● n (on window) store m; **the ~** les aveugles mpl.

blindfold adj **be ~** avoir les yeux bandés. ● adv les yeux bandés. ● n bandeau m. ● vt bander les yeux à.

blindness n (Med) cécité f; (fig) aveuglement m.

blind spot n (Auto) angle m mort.

blink vi cligner des yeux; (light) clignoter.

bliss n délice m. **blissful** adj délicieux.

blister n ampoule f; (on paint) cloque f. ● vi cloquer.

blitz n (Aviat) raid m éclair. ● vt bombarder.

blob n (drop) (grosse) goutte f; (stain) tache f.

block n bloc m; (buildings) pâté m de maisons; (in pipe) obstruction f; ~ (of flats) immeuble m; ~ **letters** majuscules fpl. ● vt bloquer.

blockade n blocus m. ● vt bloquer.

blockage n obstruction f.

block-buster n gros succès m.

bloke n 🆇 type m.

blond a & n blond (m).

blonde a & n blonde (f).

blood n sang m. ● adj (donor, bath) de sang; (bank, poisoning) du sang; (group, vessel) sanguin. ~**-pressure** n tension f artérielle. ~**shed** n effusion f de sang. ~**shot** adj injecté de sang. ~**stream** n sang m. ~ **test** n prise f de sang.

bloody adj (-ier, -iest) sanglant; 🆇 sacré. ● adv 🆇 vachement 🆇. ~**-minded** adj 🆇 hargneux, obstiné.

bloom n fleur f. ● vi fleurir; (person) s'épanouir.

blossom n fleur(s) f(pl). ● vi fleurir; (person) s'épanouir.

blot n tache f. ● vt (pt **blotted**) tacher; (dry) sécher; ~ **out** effacer.

blotch n tache f.

blouse n chemisier m.

blow vt/i (pt **blew**; pp **blown**) souffler; (fuse) (faire) sauter; (squander 🆇) claquer; (opportunity) rater; ~ **one's nose** se moucher; ~ **a whistle** siffler. ● n coup m. □ ~ **away** or **off** emporter; ~ **out** souffler; ~ **over** passer; ~ **up** (faire) sauter; (tyre) gonfler; (Photo) agrandir.

blow-dry n brushing m. ● vt faire un brushing à.

blown ⇨BLOW.

bludgeon n matraque f. ● vt matraquer.

blue adj bleu; (movie) porno. ● n bleu m; **come out of the ~** être inattendu; **have the ~s** avoir le cafard. ~**bell** n jacinthe f des bois. ~**print** n projet m.

bluff vt/i bluffer. ● n bluff m; **call sb's ~** dire chiche à qn. ● adj (person) carré.

blunder vi faire une bourde; (move) avancer à tâtons. ● n gaffe f.

blunt adj (knife) émoussé; (person) brusque. ● vt émousser. **bluntly** adv carrément.

blur n image f floue. ● vt (pt **blurred**) brouiller.

blurb n résumé m publicitaire.

blush vi rougir. ● n rougeur f. **blusher** n fard m à joues.

blustery adj ~ **wind** bourrasque f.

boar n sanglier m.

board n planche f; (for notices) tableau m; (food) pension f; **full ~** pension f complète; **half ~** demi-pension f; (committee) conseil m; **~ of directors** conseil m d'administration; **go by the ~** tomber à l'eau; **on ~** à bord. ● vt/i (bus, train) monter dans; (Naut) monter à bord (de); **~ with** être en pension chez.

boarding-school n école f privée avec internat.

boast vi se vanter (about de). ● vt s'enorgueillir de. ● n vantardise f.

boat n bateau m; (small) canot m; **in the same ~** logé à la même enseigne.

bode vi **~ well/ill** être de bon/ mauvais augure.

bodily adj (need, well-being) physique; (injury) corporel. ● adv physiquement; (in person) en personne.

body n corps m; (mass) masse f; (organization) organisme m; **~(work)** (Auto) carrosserie f; **the main ~ of** le gros de. **~-building** n culturisme m. **~guard** n garde m du corps.

bog n marais m. ● vt (pt **bogged**) **get ~ged down** s'enliser dans.

bogus adj faux.

boil n furoncle m; **bring to the ~** porter à ébullition. ● vt/i bouillir. □ **~ down to** se ramener à; **~ over** déborder. **boiled** adj (egg) à la coque; (potatoes) à l'eau.

boiler n chaudière f; **~ suit** bleu m (de travail).

boisterous adj tapageur; (child) turbulent.

bold adj hardi; (cheeky) effronté; (type) gras.

Bolivia n Bolivie f.

bollard n (on road) balise f.

bolt n (on door) verrou m; (for nut) boulon m; (lightning) éclair m. ● vt (door) verrouiller; (food) engouffrer. ● vi s'emballer.

bomb n bombe f; **~ scare** alerte f à la bombe. ● vt bombarder.

bomber n (aircraft) bombardier m; (person) plastiqueur m.

bombshell n **be a ~** tomber comme une bombe.

bond n (agreement) engagement m; (link) lien m; (Comm) obligation f, bon m; **in ~** (entreposé) en douane. ● vt

bone n os m; (of fish) arête f. ● vt désosser. **~-dry** adj tout à fait sec.

bonfire n feu m; (for celebration) feu m de joie.

bonnet n (hat) bonnet m; (of vehicle) capot m.

bonus n prime f.

bony adj (**-ier, -iest**) (thin) osseux; (fish) plein d'arêtes.

boo interj hou. ● vt/i huer. ● n huée f.

booby-trap n mécanisme m piégé. ● vt (pt **-trapped**) piéger.

book n livre m; (exercise) cahier m; (of tickets etc.) carnet m; **~s** (Comm) comptes mpl. ● vt (reserve) réserver; (driver) dresser un PV à; (player) prendre le nom de; (write down) inscrire. ● vi retenir des places; (fully) **~ed** complet. **~case** n bibliothèque f. **booking-office** n guichet m. **~keeping** n comptabilité f. **booklet** n brochure f. **~maker** n bookmaker m. **~mark** n (for book, Internet) signet m. **~seller** n libraire mf. **~shop** n librairie f. **~stall** n kiosque m (à journaux).

boom vi (gun, wind, etc.) gronder; (trade) prospérer. ● n grondement m; (Comm) boom m, prospérité f.

boost vt stimuler; (morale) remonter; (price) augmenter; (publicize) faire de la réclame pour.

boot n (knee-length) botte f; (ankle-length) chaussure f (montante); (for walking) chaussure f de marche; (Sport) chaussure f de sport; (of vehicle) coffre m; **get the ~** ⊠ se faire virer. ● vt/i **~ up** (Comput) amorcer.

booth n (for telephone) cabine f; (at fair) baraque f.

booze vi ⊤ boire (beaucoup). ● n ⊤ alcool m.

border n (edge) bord m; (frontier) frontière f; (in garden) bordure f. ● vi **~ on** être voisin de, avoisiner.

bore vt ennuyer; **be ~d** s'ennuyer; ⇒BEAR. ● vi (Tech) forer. ● n raseur/ -euse m/f; (thing) ennui m. **boredom** n ennui m. **boring** adj ennuyeux.

born adj né; **be ~** naître.

borne ⇒BEAR.

borough n municipalité f.

borrow vt emprunter (**from** à).

Bosnia n Bosnie f.

Bosnian adj bosniaque. ●n
Bosniaque.

bosom n poitrine f; ~ **friend** ami/-e
m/f intime.

boss n Ⅰ patron/-ne m/f. ●vt ~
(**about**) Ⅰ mener par le bout du nez.

bossy adj autoritaire.

botch vt bâcler, saboter.

both det les deux; ~ **the books** les
deux livres. ●pron tous/toutes (les)
deux, l'un/-e et l'autre; **we** ~ **agree**
nous sommes tous les deux d'accord;
I bought ~ (**of them**) j'ai acheté les
deux; **I saw** ~ **of you** je vous ai vus
tous les deux; ~ **Paul and Anne** (et)
Paul et Anne. ●adv à la fois.

bother vt (annoy, worry) ennuyer;
(disturb) déranger. ●vi se déranger;
don't ~ (**calling**) ce n'est pas la peine
(d'appeler); **don't** ~ **about us** ne
t'inquiète pas pour nous; **I can't be**
~**ed** j'ai la flemme Ⅰ. ●n ennui m;
(effort) peine f; **it's no** ~ ce n'est rien.

bottle n bouteille f; (for baby) biberon
m. ●vt mettre en bouteille. □ ~ **up**
contenir. ~ **bank** n collecteur m (de
verre usagé). ~**neck** n (traffic jam)
embouteillage m. ~**-opener** n
ouvre-bouteilles m inv.

bottom n fond m; (of hill, page, etc.)
bas m; (buttocks) derrière m Ⅰ. ●adj
inférieur, du bas.

bought ⇒BUY.

bounce vi rebondir; (person) faire
des bonds, bondir; (cheques ✗) être
refusé. ●vt faire rebondir. ●n
rebond m.

bound vi (leap) bondir; ~**ed by** limité
par; ⇒BIND. ●n bond m. ●adj **be** ~
for être en route pour, aller vers; ~
to (obliged) obligé de; (certain) sûr de.

boundary n limite f.

bounds npl limites fpl; **out of** ~ être
interdit d'accès.

bout n période f; (Med) accès m;
(boxing) combat m.

bow[1] n (weapon) arc m; (of violin)
archet m; (knot) nœud m.

bow[2] n salut m; (of ship) proue f. ●vt/
i (s')incliner.

bowels npl intestins mpl; (fig)
profondeurs fpl.

bowl n (for washing) cuvette f; (for food)
bol m; (for soup) assiette f creuse.
●vt/i (cricket) lancer; ~ **over**
bouleverser.

bowler n (cricket) lanceur m; ~ (**hat**)
(chapeau) melon m.

bowling n (ten-pin) bowling m; (on
grass) jeu m de boules. ~**-alley** n
bowling m.

bow-tie n nœud m papillon.

box n boîte f; (cardboard) carton m;
(Theat) loge f; **the** ~ Ⅰ la télé. ●vt
mettre en boîte; (Sport) boxer; ~ **sb's
ears** gifler qn; ~ **in** enfermer.

boxing n boxe f. ●adj de boxe. **B**~
Day n le lendemain de Noël.

box office n guichet m.

boy n garçon m.

boycott vt boycotter. ●n boycottage
m.

boyfriend n (petit) ami m.

bra n soutien-gorge m.

brace n (fastener) attache f; (dental)
appareil m; (tool) vilbrequin m; ~**s**
(for trousers) bretelles fpl. ●vt
soutenir; ~ **oneself** rassembler ses
forces.

bracket n (for shelf etc.) tasseau m,
support m; (group) tranche f; **in** ~**s**
entre parenthèses. ●vt mettre entre
parenthèses or crochets.

braid n (trimming) galon m; (of hair)
tresse f.

brain n cerveau m; ~**s** (fig)
intelligence f. ●vt assommer.
brainless adj stupide. ~**wash** vt
faire subir un lavage de cerveau à.
~**wave** n idée f géniale, trouvaille
f. **brainy** adj (-**ier**, -**iest**) doué.

brake n (Auto also fig) frein m. ●vt/i
freiner. ~ **light** n feu m stop.

bran n son m.

branch n (of tree) branche f; (of road)
embranchement m; (Comm)
succursale f; (of bank) agence f. ●vi
~ (**off**) bifurquer.

brand n marque f. ●vt ~ **sb as**
désigner qn comme qch.

brand-new adj tout neuf.

brandy *n* cognac *m*.

brass *n* cuivre *m*; **get down to** ~ **tacks** en venir aux choses sérieuses; **the** ~ (Mus) les cuivres *mpl*; **top** ~ ⊠ galonnés *mpl*.

brat *n* 🔲 môme *mf* 🔲.

brave *adj* courageux; (*smile*) brave. ● *n* (American Indian) brave *m*. ● *vt* braver. **bravery** *n* courage *m*.

brawl *n* bagarre *f*. ● *vi* se bagarrer.

Brazil *n* Brésil *m*.

breach *n* (of copyright, privilege) violation *f*; (in relationship) rupture *f*; (gap) brèche *f*. ● *vt* ouvrir une brèche dans.

bread *n* pain *m*; ~ **and butter** tartine *f*. ~**bin**, (US) ~**box** *n* boîte *f* à pain. ~**crumbs** *npl* chapelure *f*.

breadth *n* largeur *f*.

bread-winner *n* soutien *m* de famille.

break *vt* (*pt* **broke**, *pp* **broken**) casser; (smash into pieces) briser; (*vow, silence, rank, etc.*) rompre; (*law*) violer; (*a record*) battre; (*news*) révéler; (*journey*) interrompre; (*heart, strike, ice*) briser; ~ **one's arm** se casser le bras. ● *vi* (se) casser; se briser. ● *n* cassure *f*, rupture *f*; (in relationship, continuity) rupture *f*; (interval) interruption *f*; (at school) récréation *f*, récré *f*; (for coffee) pause *f*; (luck 🔲) chance *f*. ◻ ~ **away from** se détacher; ~ **down** *vi* (collapse) s'effondrer; (*negotiations*) échouer; (machine) tomber en panne; *vt* (door) enfoncer; (analyse) analyser; ~ **even** rentrer dans ses frais; ~ **into** cambrioler; ~ **off** (se) détacher; (suspend) rompre; (stop talking) s'interrompre; ~ **out** (*fire, war, etc.*) éclater; ~ **up** (end) (faire) cesser; (*couple*) rompre; (*marriage*) (se) briser; (*crowd*) (se) disperser; (*schools*) être en vacances. **breakable** *adj* fragile. **breakage** *n* casse *f*.

breakdown *n* (Tech) panne *f*; (Med) dépression *f*; (of figures) analyse *f*. ● *adj* (Auto) de dépannage.

breakfast *n* petit déjeuner *m*.

break: ~-**in** *n* cambriolage *m*. ~**through** *n* percée *f*.

breast *n* sein *m*; (chest) poitrine *f*. ~-**feed** *vt* (*pt* -**fed**) allaiter. ~-**stroke** *n* brasse *f*.

breath *n* souffle *m*, haleine *f*; **out of** ~ à bout de souffle; **under one's** ~ tout bas.

breathalyser® *n* alcootest *m*.

breathe *vt/i* respirer. ◻ ~ **in** inspirer; ~ **out** expirer.

breathless *adj* à bout de souffle.

breathtaking *adj* à vous couper le souffle.

bred ⇒BREED.

breed *vt* (*pt* **bred**) élever; (give rise to) engendrer. ● *vi* se reproduire. ● *n* race *f*.

breeze *n* brise *f*.

brew *vt* (beer) brasser; (tea) faire infuser. ● *vi* (beer) fermenter; (tea) infuser; (fig) se préparer. ● *n* décoction *f*. **brewer** *n* brasseur *m*. **brewery** *n* brasserie *f*.

bribe *n* pot-de-vin *m*. ● *vt* soudoyer. **bribery** *n* corruption *f*.

brick *n* brique *f*. ~**layer** *n* maçon *m*.

bridal *adj* (dress) de mariée; (car, chamber) des mariés.

bride *n* mariée *f*. ~**groom** *n* marié *m*. ~**smaid** *n* demoiselle *f* d'honneur.

bridge *n* pont *m*; (Naut) passerelle *f*; (of nose) arête *f*; (card game) bridge *m*. ● *vt* ~ **a gap** combler une lacune.

bridle *n* bride *f*. ● *vt* brider. ~-**path** *n* piste *f* cavalière.

brief *adj* bref. ● *n* instructions *fpl*; (Jur) dossier *m*. ● *vt* donner des instructions à.

briefcase *n* serviette *f*.

briefs *npl* slip *m*.

bright *adj* brillant, vif; (day, room) clair; (cheerful) gai; (clever) intelligent.

brighten *vt* égayer. ● *vi* (weather) s'éclaircir; (face) s'éclairer.

brilliant *adj* (student, career) brillant; (light) éclatant; (very good 🔲) super.

brim *n* bord *m*. ● *vi* (*pt* **brimmed**); ~ **over** déborder (with de).

bring *vt* (*pt* **brought**) (thing) apporter; (person, vehicle) amener; ~ **to bear** (pressure etc.) exercer. ◻ ~

about provoquer; ~ **back** (return with) rapporter; (*colour, shine*) redonner; ~ **down** faire tomber; (shoot down, knock down) abattre; ~ **forward** avancer; ~ **off** réussir; ~ **out** (take out) sortir; (show) faire ressortir; (book) publier; ~ **round** faire revenir à soi; ~ **up** (*child*) élever; (Med) vomir; (*question*) aborder.

brink *n* bord *m*.

brisk *adj* vif.

bristle *n* poil *m*. ● *vi* se hérisser; **bristling with** hérissé de.

Britain *n* Grande-Bretagne *f*.

British *adj* britannique; **the** ~ les Britanniques *mpl*.

Briton *n* Britannique *mf*.

Brittany *n* Bretagne *f*.

brittle *adj* fragile.

broad *adj* large; (*choice, range*) grand. ~ **bean** *n* fève.

broadcast *vt/i* (*pt* **broadcast**) diffuser; (person) parler à la télévision *or* à la radio. ● *n* émission *f*.

broadly *adv* en gros.

broad-minded *adj* large d'esprit.

broccoli *n inv* brocoli *m*.

brochure *n* brochure *f*.

broke ⇒BREAK. ● *adj* (penniless ⊠) fauché.

broken ⇒BREAK. ● *adj* ~ **English** mauvais-anglais *m*.

bronchitis *n* bronchite *f*.

bronze *n* bronze *m*. ● *vt/i* (se) bronzer.

brooch *n* broche *f*.

brood *n* nichée *f*, couvée *f*. ● *vi* (*bird*) couver; (fig) méditer tristement.

broom *n* balai *m*.

broth *n* bouillon *m*.

brothel *n* maison *f* close.

brother *n* frère *m*. ~**hood** *n* fraternité *f*. ~**-in-law** *n* (*pl* ~**s-in-law**) beau-frère *m*.

brought ⇒BRING.

brow *n* front *m*; (of hill) sommet *m*.

brown *adj* (*object*) marron; (*hair*) brun; ~ **bread** pain *m* complet; ~ **sugar** sucre *m* roux. ● *n* marron *m*;

brun *m*. ● *vt/i* brunir; (Culin) (faire) dorer.

Brownie *n* jeannette *f*.

browse *vi* flâner; (*animal*) brouter. ● *vt* (Comput) naviguer. **browser** *n* (Comput) navigateur *m*.

bruise *n* bleu *m*. ● *vt* (*knee, arm etc.*) faire un bleu à; (*fruit*) abîmer.

brush *n* brosse *f*; (skirmish) accrochage *m*; (bushes) broussailles *fpl*. ● *vt* brosser. □ ~ **against** frôler; ~ **aside** (dismiss) repousser; (move) écarter; ~ **up** (on) se remettre à.

Brussels *n* Bruxelles. ~ **sprouts** *npl* choux *mpl* de Bruxelles.

brutal *adj* brutal.

brute *n* brute *f*; **by** ~ **force** par la force.

bubble *n* bulle *f*; **blow** ~s faire des bulles. ● *vi* bouillonner; ~ **over** déborder. ~ **bath** *n* bain *m* moussant.

buck *n* mâle *m*; (US, ⊠) dollar *m*; **pass the** ~ rejeter la responsabilité (**to** sur). ● *vi* (*horse*) ruer; ~ **up** ⊠ prendre courage; (hurry ⊠) se grouiller Ⅰ.

bucket *n* seau *m* (**of** de).

buckle *n* boucle *f*. ● *vt/i* (fasten) (se) boucler; (bend) voiler. □ ~ **down to** s'atteler à.

bud *n* bourgeon *m*. ● *vi* (*pt* **budded**) bourgeonner.

Buddhism *n* bouddhisme *m*.

budding *adj* (*talent*) naissant; (*athlete*) en herbe.

budge *vt/i* (faire) bouger.

budgerigar *n* perruche *f*.

budget *n* budget *m*. ● *vi* ~ **for** prévoir (dans son budget).

buff *n* (colour) chamois *m*; Ⅰ fanatique *mf*.

buffalo *n* (*pl* **-oes** *or* **-o**) buffle *m*; (US) bison *m*.

buffer *n* tampon *m*; ~ **zone** zone *f* tampon.

buffet[1] *n* (meal, counter) buffet *m*; ~ **car** buffet *m*.

buffet[2] *n* (blow) soufflet *m*. ● *vt* (*pt* **buffeted**) souffleter.

bug *n* (bedbug) punaise *f*; (any small insect) bestiole *f*; (germ) microbe *m*;

(stomachache ⊞) ennuis *mpl*
gastriques; (device) micro *m*; (defect)
défaut *m*; (Comput) bogue *f*, bug *m*.
● *vt* (*pt* **bugged**) mettre des micros
dans; ⊠ embêter.

buggy *n* poussette *f*.

build *vt/i* (*pt* **built**) bâtir, construire.
● *n* carrure *f*. □ ∼ **up** (increase)
augmenter, monter; (accumulate) (s')
accumuler. **builder** *n* entrepreneur
m en bâtiment; (workman) ouvrier *m*
du bâtiment.

building *n* (structure) bâtiment *m*;
(dwelling) immeuble *m*. ∼ **society** *n*
caisse *f* d'épargne.

build-up *n* accumulation *f*; (fig)
publicité *f*.

built ⇒BUILD.

built-in *adj* encastré.

built-up area *adj* agglomération *f*,
zone *f* urbanisée.

bulb *n* (Bot) bulbe *m*; (Electr) ampoule
f.

Bulgaria *n* Bulgarie *f*.

Bulgarian *n* (person) Bulgare *mf*;
(Ling) bulgare *m*. ● *adj* bulgare.

bulge *n* renflement *m*. ● *vi* se
renfler, être renflé; **be bulging with**
être gonflé *or* bourré de.

bulimia *n* boulimie *f*.

bulk *n* volume *f*; **in** ∼ (*buy, sell*) en
gros; (transport) en vrac; **the** ∼ **of** la
majeure partie de.

bull *n* taureau *m*. ∼**dog** *n*
bouledogue *m*. ∼**doze** *vt* raser au
bulldozer.

bullet *n* balle *f*.

bulletin *n* bulletin *m*.

bullet-proof *adj* (*vest*) pare-balles
inv; (*vehicle*) blindé.

bullfight *n* corrida *f*.

bullion *n* or *m* or argent *m* en
lingots.

bullring *n* arène *f*.

bull's-eye *n* mille *m*.

bully *n* (child) petite brute *f*; (adult)
tyran *m*. ● *vt* maltraiter.

bum *n* ⊠ derrière *m* ⊞; (US, ⊠)
vagabond/-e *m/f*.

bumble-bee *n* bourdon *m*.

bump *n* (swelling) bosse *f*; (on road)
bosse *f*. ● *vt/i* cogner, heurter. □ ∼

along cahoter; ∼ **into** (hit) rentrer
dans; (meet) tomber sur.

bumper *n* pare-chocs *m inv*. ● *adj*
exceptionnel.

bumpy *adj* (*road*) accidenté.

bun *n* (cake) petit pain *m*; (hair)
chignon *m*.

bunch *n* (of flowers) bouquet *m*; (of
keys) trousseau *m*; (of people) groupe
m; (of bananas) régime *m*; ∼ **of grapes**
grappe *f* de raisin.

bundle *n* paquet *m*. ● *vt* mettre en
paquet; (push) fourrer.

bung *n* bouchon *m*. ● *vt* (stop up)
boucher; (throw ⊠) flanquer ⊞.

bunion *n* (Med) oignon *m*.

bunk *n* (on ship, train) couchette *f*.
∼-**beds** *npl* lits *mpl* superposés.

buoy *n* bouée *f*. ● *vt* ∼ **up** (hearten)
soutenir, encourager.

buoyancy *n* (of floating object)
flottabilité *f*; (cheerfulness) gaieté *f*.

burden *n* fardeau *m*. ● *vt* ennuyer
(**with** de).

bureau *n* (*pl* **-eaux**) bureau *m*.

bureaucracy *n* bureaucratie *f*.

burglar *n* cambrioleur *m*; ∼ **alarm**
alarme *f*. **burglarize** *vt* (US)
cambrioler. **burglary** *n* cambriolage
m. **burgle** *vt* cambrioler.

Burgundy *n* (wine) bourgogne *m*.

burial *n* enterrement *m*.

burn *vt/i* (*pt* **burned** or **burnt**)
brûler. ● *n* brûlure *f*. □ ∼ **down**
être réduit en cendres. **burning** *adj*
en flammes; (fig) brûlant.

burnt ⇒BURN.

burp *n* ⊞ rot *m*. ● *vi* ⊞ roter.

burrow *n* terrier *m*. ● *vt* creuser.

bursar *n* intendant/-e *m/f*. **bursary**
n bourse *f*.

burst *vt/i* (*pt* **burst**) (*balloon,
bubble*) crever; (*pipe*) (faire) éclater.
● *n* explosion *f*; (of laughter) éclat *m*;
(surge) élan *m*. □ ∼ **into** (*room*) faire
interruption dans; ∼ **into tears**
fondre en larmes; ∼ **out** ∼ **out
laughing** éclater de rire; ∼ **with** be
∼**ing with** déborder de.

bury *vt* (*person etc.*) enterrer; (hide,
cover) enfouir; (engross, thrust) plonger.

bus n (pl **buses**) (auto)bus m. ● vt transporter en bus. ● vi (pt **bussed**) prendre l'autobus.

bush n (shrub) buisson m; (land) brousse f.

business n (task, concern) affaire f; (commerce) affaires fpl; (line of work) métier m; (shop) commerce m; **he has no ~ to** il n'a pas le droit de; **mean ~** être sérieux; **that's none of your ~!** ça ne vous regarde pas! **~like** adj sérieux. **~man** n homme m d'affaires.

busker n musicien/-ne m/f des rues.

bus-stop n arrêt m d'autobus.

bust n (statue) buste m; (bosom) poitrine f. ● vt/i (pt **busted** or **bust**) (burst ⊠) crever; (break ⊠) (se) casser. ● adj (broken, finished ⊠) fichu; **go ~** ⊠ faire faillite.

bustle vi s'affairer. ● n affairement m, remue-ménage m.

busy adj (**-ier, -iest**) (person) occupé; (street) animé; (day) chargé. ● vt **~ oneself with** s'occuper à.

but conj mais. ● prep sauf; **~ for** sans; **nobody ~** personne d'autre que; **nothing ~** rien que. ● adv (only) seulement.

butcher n boucher m. ● vt massacrer.

butler n maître m d'hôtel.

butt n (of gun) crosse f; (of cigarette) mégot m; (of joke) cible f; (barrel) tonneau m; (US, ⊞) derrière m ⊞. ● vi **~ in** interrompre.

butter n beurre m. ● vt beurrer. **~-bean** n haricot m blanc. **~cup** n bouton-d'or m.

butterfly n papillon m.

buttock n fesse f.

button n bouton m. ● vt/i **~ (up)** (se) boutonner.

buttonhole n boutonnière f. ● vt accrocher.

buy vt (pt **bought**) acheter (from à); **~ sth for sb** acheter qch à qn, prendre qch pour qn; (believe ⊠) croire, avaler.

buzz n bourdonnement m. ● vi bourdonner. **buzzer** n sonnerie f.

by prep par, de; (near) à côté de; (before) avant; (means) en, à, par; **~ bike** à vélo; **~ car** en auto; **~ day** de jour; **~ the kilo** au kilo; **~ running** en courant; **~ sea** par mer; **~ that time** à ce moment-là; **~ the way** à propos; **~ oneself** tout seul. ● adv **close ~** tout près; **~ and large** dans l'ensemble.

bye(-bye) interj ⊞ au revoir, salut ⊞.

by-election n élection f partielle.

Byelorussia n Biélorussie f.

by-law n arrêté m municipal.

bypass n (Auto) rocade f; (Med) pontage m. ● vt contourner.

by-product n dérivé m; (fig) conséquence f.

byte n octet m.

Cc

cab n taxi m; (of lorry, train) cabine f.

cabbage n chou m.

cabin n (hut) cabane f; (in ship, aircraft) cabine f.

cabinet n petit placard m; (glass-fronted) vitrine f; (Pol) cabinet m.

cable n câble m. ● vt câbler. **~-car** n téléphérique m. **~ television** n télévision f par câble.

cache n (hoard) cache f; (place) cachette f.

cackle n (of hen) caquet m; (laugh) ricanement m. ● vi caqueter; (laugh) ricaner.

cactus n (pl **-ti** or **-es**) cactus m.

cadet n élève m officier.

Caesarean adj **~ (section)** césarienne f.

café n café m, snack-bar m.

caffeine n caféine f.

cage n cage f. ● vt mettre en cage.

cagey adj réticent.

cagoule n K-way® m.

cajole vt **~ sb into doing sth** amener qn à faire qch par la cajolerie.

cake n gâteau m; (of soap) pain m. ● vi former une croûte (**on** sur).

calculate *vt* calculer; (estimate) évaluer. **calculated** *adj* délibéré; (*risk*) calculé. **calculating** *adj* calculateur. **calculation** *n* calcul *m*. **calculator** *n* calculatrice *f*.

calculus *n* (*pl* **-li** or **~es**) calcul *m*.

calendar *n* calendrier *m*.

calf *n* (*pl* **calves**) (young cow or bull) veau *m*; (of leg) mollet *m*.

calibre *n* calibre *m*.

call *vt/i* appeler; (loudly) crier; **he's ~ed John** il s'appelle John; **~ sb stupid** traiter qn d'imbécile. ● *n* appel *m*; (of bird) cri *m*; (visit) visite *f*; **make/pay a ~ on** rendre visite à; **be on ~** être de garde; **~ box** cabine *f* téléphonique. □ **~ back** rappeler; (visit) repasser; **~ for** (*help*) appeler à; (demand) demander; (require) exiger; (collect) passer prendre; **~ in** passer; **~ off** annuler; **~ on** (visit) rendre visite à; (urge) demander à (**to do** de faire); **~ out (to)** appeler; **~ round** venir; **~ up** appeler.

calling *n* vocation *f*.

callous *adj* inhumain.

calm *adj* calme. ● *n* calme *m*. ● *vt/i* **~ (down)** (se) calmer.

calorie *n* calorie *f*.

camcorder *n* caméscope® *m*.

came ⇒COME.

camel *n* chameau *m*.

camera *n* appareil(-photo) *m*; (TV, cinema) caméra *f*; **in ~** à huis clos. **~man** *n* (*pl* **-men**) cadreur *m*, cameraman *m*.

camouflage *n* camouflage *m*. ● *vt* camoufler.

camp *n* camp *m*. ● *vi* camper.

campaign *n* campagne *f*. ● *vi* faire campagne.

camper *n* campeur/-euse *m/f*. **~(-van)** *n* camping-car *m*.

camping *n* camping *m*; **go ~** faire du camping.

campsite *n* camping *m*.

campus *n* (*pl* **~es**) campus *m*.

can¹

infinitive **be able to**; *present* **can**; *present negative* **can't, cannot**

(formal); *past* **could**; *past participle* **been able to**

● *auxiliary verb*

····▶ pouvoir; **where ~ I buy stamps?** où est-ce que je peux acheter des timbres?; **she can't come** elle ne peut pas venir.

····▶ (be allowed to) pouvoir; **~ I smoke?** est-ce que je peux fumer?

····▶ (know how to) savoir; **she ~ swim** elle sait nager; **he can't drive** il ne sait pas conduire.

····▶ (with verbs of perception) **I ~ hear you** je t'entends; **~ they see us?** est-ce qu'ils nous voient?

can² *n* (for food) boîte *f*; (of petrol) bidon *m*. ● *vt* (*pt* **canned**) mettre en conserve.

Canada *n* Canada *m*.

Canadian *n* Canadien/-ne *m/f*. ● *adj* canadien.

canal *n* canal *m*.

canary *n* canari *m*.

cancel *vt/i* (*pt* **cancelled**) (call off, revoke) annuler; (cross out) barrer; (a stamp) oblitérer; **~ out** (se) neutraliser. **cancellation** *n* annulation *f*.

cancer *n* cancer *m*; **have ~** avoir un cancer.

Cancer *n* Cancer *m*.

cancerous *adj* cancéreux.

candid *adj* franc.

candidate *n* candidat/-e *m/f*.

candle *n* bougie *f*; (in church) cierge *m*. **~stick** *n* bougeoir *m*.

candy *n* (US) bonbon(s) *m(pl)*. **~-floss** *n* barbe *f* à papa.

cane *n* canne *f*; (for baskets) rotin *m*; (for punishment) badine *f*. ● *vt* donner des coups de badine à.

canister *n* boîte *f*.

cannabis *n* cannabis *m*.

cannibal *n* cannibale *mf*.

cannon *n* (*pl* **~** or **~s**) canon *m*. **~-ball** *n* boulet *m* de canon.

cannot = CAN NOT.

canoe *n* canoë *m*. ● *vi* faire du canoë. **canoeist** *n* canoéiste *mf*.

canon *n* (clergyman) chanoine *m*; (rule) canon *m*.

can-opener n ouvre-boîtes m inv.

canopy n dais m; (for bed) baldaquin m.

can't = CAN NOT.

canteen n (restaurant) cantine f; (flask) bidon m.

canter n petit galop m. ● vi aller au petit galop.

canvas n toile f.

canvass vt/i (Comm, Pol) faire du démarchage (auprès de); ~ **opinion** sonder l'opinion.

canyon n cañon m.

cap n (hat) casquette f; (of bottle, tube) bouchon m; (of beer or milk bottle) capsule f; (of pen) capuchon m; (for toy gun) amorce f. ● vt (pt **capped**) couronner.

capability n capacité f.

capable adj (person) compétent; ~ **of doing** capable de faire.

capacity n capacité f; **in my ~ as a doctor** en ma qualité de médecin.

cape n (cloak) cape f; (Geog) cap m.

caper vi gambader. ● n (leap) cabriole f; (funny film) comédie f; (Culin) câpre f.

capital adj (letter) majuscule; (offence) capital. ● n (town) capitale f; (money) capital m; ~ **(letter)** majuscule f.

capitalism n capitalisme m.

capitalize vi ~ **on** tirer parti de.

capitulate vi capituler.

Capricorn n Capricorne m.

capsize vt/i (faire) chavirer.

capsule n capsule f.

captain n capitaine m.

caption n (under photo) légende f; (subtitle) sous-titre m.

captivate vt captiver.

captive a & n captif/-ive (m/f). **captivity** n captivité f.

capture vt (person, animal) capturer; (moment, likeness) saisir. ● n capture f.

car n voiture f. ● adj (industry, insurance) automobile; (accident, phone) de voiture; (journey, chase) en voiture.

caravan n caravane f.

carbohydrate n hydrate m de carbone.

carbon n carbone m.

carburettor n carburateur m.

card n carte f.

cardboard n carton m.

cardiac adj cardiaque; ~ **arrest** arrêt m du cœur.

cardigan n cardigan m.

cardinal adj (sin) capital; (rule) fondamental; (number) cardinal. ● n cardinal m.

card-index n fichier m.

care n (attention) soin m, attention f; (worry) souci m; (looking after) soins mpl; **take ~ of** (deal with) s'occuper de; (be careful with) prendre soin de; **take ~ to do sth** faire bien attention à faire qch. ● vi ~ **about** s'intéresser à; ~ **for** s'occuper de; (invalid) soigner; ~ **to do** vouloir faire; **I don't ~** ça m'est égal.

career n carrière f. ● vi ~ **in/out** entrer/sortir à toute vitesse.

carefree adj insouciant.

careful adj prudent; (research, study) méticuleux; **(be) ~!** (fais) attention! **carefully** adv avec soin; (cautiously) prudemment.

careless adj négligent; (work) bâclé.

caress n caresse f. ● vt caresser.

caretaker n concierge mf. ● adj (president) par intérim.

car ferry n ferry m.

cargo n (pl ~**es**) chargement m; (Naut) cargaison f.

Caribbean adj des Caraïbes, des Antilles. ● n the ~ (sea) la mer des Antilles; (islands) les Antilles fpl.

caring adj affectueux. ● n affection f.

carnal adj charnel.

carnation n œillet m.

carnival n carnaval m.

carol n chant m de Noël.

carp n inv carpe f. ● vi maugréer.

car-park n parc m de stationnement, parking m.

carpenter n (joiner) menuisier m; (builder) charpentier m. **carpentry** n menuiserie f; (structural) charpenterie f.

carpet n (fitted) moquette f; (loose) tapis m. ● vt (pt **carpeted**) mettre de la moquette dans.

carriage n (rail) wagon m; (ceremonial) carrosse m; (of goods) transport m; (cost) port m.

carriageway n chaussée f.

carrier n transporteur m; (Med) porteur/-euse m/f; ~ (**bag**) sac m en plastique.

carrot n carotte f.

carry vt/i porter; (goods) transporter; (involve) comporter; (motion) voter; **be carried away** s'emballer. □ ~ **off** emporter; (prize) remporter; ~ **on** (continue) continuer; (business) conduire; (conversation) mener; ~ **out** (order, plan) exécuter; (duty) remplir; (experiment, operation, repair) effectuer. ~**-cot** n porte-bébé m.

car sharing n covoiturage m.

cart n charrette f. ● vt (heavy bag 🅸) trimballer 🅸.

carton n (box) boîte f; (of yoghurt, cream) pot m; (of cigarettes) cartouche f.

cartoon n dessin m humoristique; (cinema) dessin m animé; (strip cartoon) bande f dessinée.

cartridge n cartouche f.

carve vt tailler; (meat) découper.

car-wash n lavage m automatique.

cascade n cascade f. ● vi tomber en cascade.

case n cas m; (Jur) affaire f; (suitcase) valise f; (crate) caisse f; (for spectacles) étui m; (just) **in** ~ au cas où; **in** ~ **he comes** au cas où il viendrait; **in** ~ **of fire** en cas d'incendie; **in any** ~ de toute façon; **the** ~ **for sth** les arguments mpl en faveur de qch; **the** ~ **for the defence** la défense.

cash n espèces fpl, argent m; **in** ~ en espèces. ● adj (price) comptant. ● vt encaisser; ~ **in (on)** profiter (de). ~ **desk** n caisse f. ~ **dispenser** n distributeur m de billets.

cashew n cajou m.

cash-flow n marge f brute d'auto-financement.

cashier n caissier/-ière m/f.

cashmere n cachemire m.

cash: ~ **point** n distributeur m de billets. ~ **point card** n carte f de retrait. ~ **register** n caisse f enregistreuse.

casino n casino m.

casket n (box) coffret m; (coffin) cercueil m.

casserole n (pan) daubière f; (food) ragoût m.

cassette n cassette f.

cast vt (pt **cast**) (object, glance) jeter; (shadow) projeter; (metal) couler; ~ (**off**) (shed) se dépouiller de; ~ **one's vote** voter; ~ **iron** fonte f. ● n (cinema, Theat, TV) distribution f; (mould) moule m; (Med) plâtre m.

castaway n naufragé/-e m/f.

cast-iron adj de fonte; (fig) en béton.

castle n château m; (chess) tour f.

cast-offs npl vieux vêtements mpl.

castor n (wheel) roulette f.

castrate vt châtrer.

casual adj (informal) décontracté; (remark) désinvolte; (acquaintance) de passage; (work) temporaire. **casually** adv (remark) d'un air détaché; (dress) simplement.

casualty n victime f; (part of hospital) urgences fpl.

cat n chat m; (feline) félin m.

catalogue n catalogue m. ● vt dresser un catalogue de.

catalyst n catalyseur m.

catalytic adj ~ **converter** pot m catalytique.

catapult n lance-pierres m inv. ● vt projeter.

cataract n (Med, Geog) cataracte f.

catarrh n catarrhe m.

catastrophe n catastrophe f.

catch vt (pt **caught**) attraper; (bus, plane) prendre; (understand) saisir; ~ **sb doing** surprendre qn en train de faire; ~ **fire** prendre feu; ~ **sight of** apercevoir; ~ **sb's attention/eye** attirer l'attention de qn. ● vi (get stuck) se prendre (**in** dans); (start to burn) prendre. ● n (fastening) fermeture f; (drawback) piège m; (in sport) prise f. □ ~ **on** devenir populaire; ~ **out** prendre de court; ~ **up** rattraper son retard; ~ **up with sb** rattraper qn.

catching adj contagieux.

catchment n ~ **area** (School) secteur m.

catch-phrase n formule f favorite.

catchy *adj* entraînant.

category *n* catégorie *f.*

cater *vi* organiser des réceptions; ∼ **for/to** (*guests*) accueillir; (*needs*) pourvoir à; (*reader*) s'adresser à. **caterer** *n* traiteur *m.*

caterpillar *n* chenille *f.*

cathedral *n* cathédrale *f.*

catholic *adj* éclectique. **Catholic** *a* & *n* catholique (*mf*). **Catholicism** *n* catholicisme *m.*

Catseye® *n* plot *m* rétroréfléchissant.

cattle *npl* bétail *m.*

catty *adj* méchant.

caught ⇒CATCH.

cauliflower *n* chou-fleur *m.*

cause *n* cause *f*; (*reason*) raison *f*, motif *m.* ● *vt* causer; ∼ **sth to grow/ move** faire pousser/bouger qch.

causeway *n* chaussée *f.*

caution *n* prudence *f*; (*warning*) avertissement *m.* ● *vt* avertir. **cautious** *adj* prudent. **cautiously** *adv* prudemment.

cave *n* grotte *f.* ● *vi* ∼ **in** s'effondrer; (*agree*) céder. ∼**man** *n* (*pl* **-men**) homme *m* des cavernes.

cavern *n* caverne *f.*

caviare *n* caviar *m.*

caving *n* spéléologie *f.*

CD *abbr* (**compact disc**) disque *m* compact, CD *m.*

CD-ROM *n* disque *m* optique compact, CD-ROM *m.*

cease *vt/i* cesser. ∼**-fire** *n* cessez-le-feu *m inv.*

cedar *n* cèdre *m.*

cedilla *n* cédille *f.*

ceiling *n* plafond *m.*

celebrate *vt* (*occasion*) fêter; (*Easter, mass*) célébrer. ● *vi* faire la fête. **celebrated** *adj* célèbre. **celebration** *n* fête *f.*

celebrity *n* célébrité *f.*

celery *n* céleri *m.*

cell *n* cellule *f*; (Electr) élément *m.*

cellar *n* cave *f.*

cellist *n* violoncelliste *mf*. **cello** *n* violoncelle *m.*

Celt *n* Celte *mf.*

cement *n* ciment *m.* ● *vt* cimenter. ∼**-mixer** *n* bétonnière *f.*

cemetery *n* cimetière *m.*

censor *n* censeur *m.* ● *vt* censurer.

censure *n* censure *f.* ● *vt* critiquer.

census *n* recensement *m.*

cent *n* (coin) cent *m.*

centenary *n* centenaire *m.*

centigrade *adj* centigrade.

centilitre, (US) **centiliter** *n* centilitre *m.*

centimetre, (US) **centimeter** *n* centimètre *m.*

centipede *n* millepattes *m inv.*

central *adj* central; ∼ **heating** chauffage *m* central; ∼ **locking** fermeture *f* centralisée des portes. **centralize** *vt* centraliser. **centrally** *adv* (*situated*) au centre.

centre, (US) **center** *n* centre *m.* ● *vt* (*pt* **centred**) centrer. ● *vi* ∼ **on** tourner autour de.

century *n* siècle *m.*

ceramic *adj* (*art*) céramique; (*object*) en céramique.

cereal *n* céréale *f.*

ceremonial *adj* (*dress*) de cérémonie. ● *n* cérémonial *m.* **ceremony** *n* cérémonie *f.*

certain *adj* certain; **for** ∼ avec certitude; **make** ∼ **of** s'assurer de. **certainly** *adv* certainement. **certainty** *n* certitude *f.*

certificate *n* certificat *m.*

certify *vt* certifier.

cesspit, **cesspool** *n* fosse *f* d'aisances.

chafe *vt/i* frotter (contre).

chagrin *n* dépit *m.*

chain *n* chaîne *f*; ∼ **reaction** réaction *f* en chaîne; ∼ **store** magasin *m* à succursales multiples. ● *vt* enchaîner. ∼**-smoke** *vi* fumer sans arrêt.

chair *n* chaise *f*; (armchair) fauteuil *m*; (Univ) chaire *f*; (chairperson) président/ -e *m/f.* ● *vt* (preside over) présider. ∼**man** *n* (*pl* **-men**) président/-e *m/f.* ∼**woman** *n* (*pl* **-women**) présidente *f.*

chalk *n* craie *f.*

challenge *n* défi *m*; (opportunity) challenge *m.* ● *vt* (summon) défier (**to do** de faire); (question truth of) contester. **challenger** *n* (Sport) challenger *m*. **challenging** *adj* stimulant.

chamber *n* (old use) chambre *f*. ∼**maid** *n* femme *f* de chambre. ∼ **music** *n* musique *f* de chambre. ∼**-pot** *n* pot *m* de chambre.

champagne *n* champagne *m*.

champion *n* champion/-ne *m/f*. ● *vt* défendre. **championship** *n* championnat *m*.

chance *n* (luck) hasard *m*; (opportunity) occasion *f*; (likelihood) chances *fpl*; (risk) risque *m*; **by** ∼ par hasard; **by any** ∼ par hasard; ∼**s are that** il est probable que. ● *adj* fortuit. ● *vt* ∼ **doing** prendre le risque de faire; ∼ **it** tenter sa chance.

chancellor *n* chancelier *m*; **C**∼ **of the Exchequer** Chancelier de l'Échiquier.

chandelier *n* lustre *m*.

change *vt* (alter) changer; (exchange) échanger (**for** contre); (money) changer; ∼ **trains/one's dress** changer de train/de robe; ∼ **one's mind** changer d'avis. ● *vi* changer; (change clothes) se changer; ∼ **into** se transformer en; ∼ **over** passer (**to** à). ● *n* changement *m*; (money) monnaie *f*; **a** ∼ **for the better** une amélioration; **a** ∼ **for the worse** un changement en pire; **a** ∼ **of clothes** des vêtements de rechange; **for a** ∼ pour changer. **changeable** *adj* changeant. **changing room** *n* (in shop) cabine *f* d'essayage; (Sport) vestiaire *m*.

channel *n* (for liquid, information) canal *m*; (TV) chaîne *f*; (groove) rainure *f*. ● *vt* (*pt* **channelled**) canaliser. **C**∼ *n* **the** (**English**) **C**∼ la Manche; **the C**∼ **tunnel** le tunnel sous la Manche; **the C**∼ **Islands** les îles *fpl* Anglo-Normandes

chant *n* (Relig) mélopée *f*; (of demonstrators) chant *m* scandé. ● *vt/i* scander; (Relig) psalmodier.

chaos *n* chaos *m*.

chap *n* (man ▣) type *m* ▣.

chapel *n* chapelle *f*.

chaplain *n* aumônier *m*.

chapped *adj* gercé.

chapter *n* chapitre *m*.

char *vt* (*pt* **charred**) carboniser.

character *n* caractère *m*; (in novel, play) personnage *m*; **of good** ∼ de bonne réputation.

characteristic *a & n* caractéristique (*f*).

charcoal *n* charbon *m* de bois; (art) fusain *m*.

charge *n* (fee) frais *mpl*; (Mil) charge *f*; (Jur) inculpation *f*; (task, custody) charge *f*; **in** ∼ **of** responsable de; **take** ∼ **of** prendre en charge, se charger de. ● *vt* (*customer*) faire payer; (*enemy, gun*) charger; (Jur) inculper (**with** de); ∼ **£20 an hour** prendre 20 livres de l'heure; ∼ **card** carte *f* d'achat. ● *vi* faire payer; (*bull*) foncer; (*person*) se précipiter.

charisma *n* charisme *m*. **charismatic** *adj* charismatique.

charitable *adj* charitable. **charity** *n* charité *f*; (organization) organisation *f* caritative.

charm *n* charme *m*; (trinket) amulette *f*. ● *vt* charmer. **charming** *adj* charmant.

chart *n* (graph) graphique *m*; (table) tableau *m*; (map) carte *f*. ● *vt* (route) porter sur la carte.

charter *n* charte *f*; ∼ (**flight**) charter *m*. ● *vt* affréter; ∼**ed accountant** expert-comptable *m*.

chase *vt* poursuivre; ∼ **away** *or* **off** chasser. ● *vi* courir (**after** après). ● *n* chasse *f*.

chassis *n* châssis *m*.

chastise *vt* châtier.

chastity *n* chasteté *f*.

chat *n* conversation *f*; **have a** ∼ bavarder; ∼ **show** talk-show *m*; ∼ **mode** (Internet) mode *m* causerie. ● *vi* (*pt* **chatted**) bavarder. □ ∼ **up** ▣ draguer ▣.

chatter *n* bavardage *m*. ● *vi* bavarder; **his teeth are** ∼**ing** il claque des dents. ∼**box** *n* bavard/-e *m/f*.

chatty *adj* bavard.

chauffeur *n* chauffeur *m*.

chauvinist *n* chauvin/-e *m/f*; macho *m*.

cheap *adj* bon marché *inv*; (*fare, rate*) réduit; (*joke, gimmick*) facile; ∼**er** meilleur marché *inv*. **cheapen**

vt déprécier. **cheaply** *adv* à bas prix. **cheapness** *n* bas prix *m*.

cheat *vi* tricher. ● *vt* tromper. ● *n* tricheur/-euse *m/f*.

check *vt/i* vérifier; (*tickets, rises, inflation*) contrôler; (stop) arrêter; (tick off: US) cocher. ● *n* contrôle *m*; (curb) frein *m*; (chess) échec *m*; (pattern) carreaux *mpl*; (bill: US) addition *f*; (cheque: US) chèque *m*. ▫ ~ **in** remplir la fiche; (at airport) enregistrer; ~ **out** partir; ~ **sth out** vérifier qch; ~ **up** vérifier; ~ **up on** (*story*) vérifier; (*person*) faire une enquête sur.

check: ~-**in** *n* enregistrement *m*. **checking account** *n* (US) compte *m* courant. ~-**list** *n* liste *f* de contrôle. ~-**mate** *n* échec *m* et mat. ~-**out** *n* caisse *f*. ~-**point** *n* contrôle *m*. ~-**up** *n* examen *m* médical.

cheek *n* joue *f*; (impudence) culot *m* ℹ. **cheeky** *adj* effronté.

cheer *n* gaieté *f*; ~**s** acclamations *fpl*; (when drinking) à la vôtre. ● *vt/i* applaudir; ~ **sb** (**up**) (gladden) remonter le moral à qn; ~ **up** prendre courage. **cheerful** *adj* joyeux. **cheerfulness** *n* gaieté *f*.

cheerio *interj* ℹ salut ℹ.

cheese *n* fromage *m*.

cheetah *n* guépard *m*.

chef *n* chef *m*.

chemical *adj* chimique. ● *n* produit *m* chimique.

chemist *n* pharmacien/-ne *m/f*; (scientist) chimiste *mf*; ~**'s** (**shop**) pharmacie *f*. **chemistry** *n* chimie *f*.

cheque *n* chèque *m*. ~-**book** *n* chéquier *m*. ~ **card** *n* carte *f* bancaire.

chequered *adj* (pattern) à damiers; (fig) en dents de scie.

cherish *vt* chérir; (hope) caresser.

cherry *n* cerise *f*; (tree, wood) cerisier *m*.

chess *n* échecs *mpl*. ~-**board** *n* échiquier *m*.

chest *n* (Anat) poitrine *f*; (box) coffre *m*; ~ **of drawers** commode *f*.

chestnut *n* (nut) marron *m*, châtaigne *f*; (tree) marronnier *m*; (sweet) châtaignier *m*.

chew *vt* mâcher.

chic *adj* chic *inv*.

chick *n* poussin *m*.

chicken *n* poulet *m*. ● *adj* ⚹ froussard. ● *vi* ~ **out** ⚹ se dégonfler. ~-**pox** *n* varicelle *f*.

chick-pea *n* pois *m* chiche.

chicory *n* (for salad) endive *f*; (in coffee) chicorée *f*.

chief *n* chef *m*. ● *adj* principal. **chiefly** *adv* principalement.

chilblain *n* engelure *f*.

child *n* (*pl* **children**) enfant *mf*. ~**birth** *n* accouchement *m*. **childhood** *n* enfance *f*. **childish** *adj* puéril. **childless** *adj* sans enfants. **childlike** *adj* enfantin. ~-**minder** *n* nourrice *f*.

Chile *n* Chili *m*.

chill *n* froid *m*; (Med) refroidissement *m*. ● *adj* froid. ● *vt* (person) faire frissonner; (wine) rafraîchir; (food) mettre à refroidir.

chilli *n* (*pl* ~**es**) piment *m*.

chilly *adj* froid; **it's** ~ il fait froid.

chime *n* carillon *m*. ● *vt/i* carillonner.

chimney *n* cheminée *f*. ~-**sweep** *n* ramoneur *m*.

chimpanzee *n* chimpanzé *m*.

chin *n* menton *m*.

china *n* porcelaine *f*.

China *n* Chine *f*.

Chinese *n* (person) Chinois/-e *m/f*; (Ling) chinois *m*. ● *adj* chinois.

chip *n* (on plate) ébréchure *f*; (piece) éclat *m*; (of wood) copeau *m*; (Culin) frite *f*; (Comput) puce *f*; (potato) ~**s** (US) chips *fpl*. ● *vt/i* (*pt* **chipped**) (s')ébrécher; ~ **in** ℹ dire son mot; (with money) contribuer.

chiropodist *n* pédicure *mf*.

chirp *n* pépiement *m*. ● *vi* pépier. **chirpy** *adj* gai.

chisel *n* ciseau *m*. ● *vt* (*pt* **chiselled**) ciseler.

chit *n* note *f*; (voucher) bon *m*.

chitchat *n* ℹ bavardage *m*.

chivalrous *adj* galant.

chives *npl* ciboulette *f*.

chlorine *n* chlore *m*.

choc-ice *n* esquimau *m*.

chock-a-block *adj* plein à craquer.

chocolate *n* chocolat *m*.

choice *n* choix *m*. ● *adj* de choix.

choir *n* chœur *m*. ~**boy** *n* jeune choriste *m*.

choke *vt/i* (s')étrangler; ~ (up) boucher. ● *n* starter *m*.

cholesterol *n* cholestérol *m*.

choose *vt/i* (*pt* **chose**; *pp* **chosen**) choisir; ~ **to do** décider de faire. **choosy** *adj* difficile.

chop *vt/i* (*pt* **chopped**) (*wood*) couper; (*food*) hacher; **chopping board** planche *f* à découper; ~ **down** abattre. ● *n* (meat) côtelette *f*. **chopper** *n* hachoir *m*; 🔲 hélico *m* 🔲.

choppy *adj* (*sea*) agité.

chopstick *n* baguette *f* (*chinoise*).

chord *n* (Mus) accord *m*.

chore *n* (routine) tâche *f*; (unpleasant) corvée *f*.

chortle *n* gloussement *m*. ● *vi* glousser.

chorus *n* chœur *m*; (of song) refrain *m*.

chose, chosen ⇒CHOOSE.

Christ *n* le Christ.

christen *vt* baptiser. **christening** *n* baptême *m*.

Christian *a* & *n* chrétien/-ne (*m/f*); ~ **name** nom *m* de baptême. **Christianity** *n* christianisme *m*.

Christmas *n* Noël *m*; ~ **Day/Eve** le jour/la veille de Noël. ● *adj* (*card, tree*) de Noël.

chronic *adj* (*situation, disease*) chronique; (bad 🔲) nul.

chronicle *n* chronique *f*.

chronological *adj* chronologique.

chrysanthemum *n* chrysanthème *m*.

chubby *adj* (**-ier, -iest**) potelé.

chuck *vt* 🔲 lancer; ~ **away** *or* **out** 🔲 balancer.

chuckle *n* gloussement *m*. ● *vi* glousser.

chuffed *adj* 🔲 vachement content 🔲.

chunk *n* morceau *m*. **chunky** *adj* (*sweater, jewellery*) gros; (*person*) costaud.

church *n* église *f*. ~**goer** *n* pratiquant/-e *m/f*. ~**yard** *n* cimetière *m*.

churn *n* baratte *f*; (milk-can) bidon *m*. ● *vt* baratter; ~ **out** produire en série.

chute *n* toboggan *m*; (for rubbish) vide-ordures *m inv*.

chutney *n* condiment *m* aigre-doux.

cider *n* cidre *m*.

cigar *n* cigare *m*.

cigarette *n* cigarette *f*; ~ **end** mégot *m*.

cinder *n* cendre *f*.

cinema *n* cinéma *m*.

cinnamon *n* cannelle *f*.

circle *n* cercle *m*; (Theat) balcon *m*. ● *vt* (go round) tourner autour de; (word, error) encercler. ● *vi* tourner en rond.

circuit *n* circuit *m*. ~ **board** *n* carte *f* de circuit imprimé. ~**-breaker** *n* disjoncteur *m*.

circuitous *adj* indirect.

circular *a* & *n* circulaire (*f*).

circulate *vt/i* (faire) circuler. **circulation** *n* circulation *f*; (of newspaper) tirage *m*.

circumcise *vt* circoncire.

circumference *n* circonférence *f*.

circumflex *n* circonflexe *m*.

circumstance *n* circonstance *f*; ~**s** (financial) situation *f*; **under no** ~**s** en aucun cas.

circus *n* cirque *m*.

cistern *n* réservoir *m*.

citation *n* citation *f*. **cite** *vt* citer.

citizen *n* citoyen/-ne *m/f*; (of town) habitant/-e *m/f*. **citizenship** *n* nationalité *f*.

citrus *adj* ~ **fruit(s)** agrumes *mpl*; ~ **tree** citrus *m*.

city *n* (grande) ville *f*.

civic *adj* (*official*) municipal; (*pride, duty*) civique.

civil *adj* civil. ~ **disobedience** *n* résistance *f* passive. ~ **engineer** *n* ingénieur *m* des travaux publics.

civilian *a* & *n* civil/-e (*m/f*).

civilization *n* civilisation *f*. **civilize** *vt* civiliser.

civil: ~ **law** *n* droit *m* civil. ~ **liberties** *npl* libertés *fpl* individuelles. ~ **rights** *npl* droits *mpl* civils. ~ **servant** *n* fonctionnaire *mf*. ~ **service** *n* fonction *f* publique. ~ **war** *n* guerre *f* civile.

clad *adj* ~ **in** vêtu de.

claim *vt* (demand) revendiquer; (assert) prétendre. ● *n* revendication *f*; (assertion) affirmation *f*; (for insurance) réclamation *f*; (right) droit *m*. **claimant** *n* (of benefits) demandeur/-euse *m/f*.

clairvoyant *n* voyant/-e *m/f*.

clam *n* palourde *f*.

clamber *vi* grimper.

clammy *adj* (**-ier, -iest**) moite.

clamour *n* clameur *f*. ● *vi* ~ **for** réclamer.

clamp *n* valet *m*; (Med) pince *f*; (wheel) ~ sabot *m* de Denver. ● *vt* cramponner; (*jaw*) serrer; (*car*) mettre un sabot de Denver à; ~ **down on** faire de la répression contre.

clan *n* clan *m*.

clang *n* son *m* métallique.

clap *vt/i* (*pt* **clapped**) applaudir; (put forcibly) mettre; ~ **one's hands** frapper dans ses mains. ● *n* applaudissement *m*; (of thunder) coup *m*.

claret *n* bordeaux *m* rouge.

clarification *n* clarification *f*. **clarify** *vt/i* (se) clarifier.

clarinet *n* clarinette *f*.

clarity *n* clarté *f*.

clash *n* choc *m*; (fig) conflit *m*. ● *vi* (*metal objects*) s'entrechoquer; (*armies*) s'affronter; (*interests*) être incompatibles; (*meetings*) avoir lieu en même temps; (*colours*) jurer.

clasp *n* (fastener) fermoir *m*. ● *vt* serrer.

class *n* classe *f*. ● *vt* classer; ~ **sb/ sth as** assimiler qn/qch à.

classic *a & n* classique (*m*); ~**s** (Univ) lettres *fpl* classiques. **classical** *adj* classique.

classified *adj* (*information*) secret; ~ (**ad**) petite annonce *f*.

classroom *n* salle *f* de classe.

clatter *n* cliquetis *m*. ● *vi* cliqueter.

clause *n* clause *f*; (Gram) proposition *f*.

claw *n* (of animal, small bird) griffe *f*; (of bird of prey) serre *f*; (of lobster) pince *f*. ● *vt* griffer.

clay *n* argile *f*.

clean *adj* propre; (shape, stroke) net. ● *adv* complètement. ● *vt* nettoyer; ~ **one's teeth** se brosser les dents. ● *vi* ~ **up** faire le nettoyage.

cleaner *n* (at home) femme *f* de ménage; (industrial) agent *m* de nettoyage; (of clothes) teinturier/-ière *m/f*. **cleanliness** *n* propreté *f*. **cleanly** *adv* proprement; (sharply) nettement.

cleanse *vt* nettoyer; (fig) purifier.

clean-shaven *adj* glabre.

clear *adj* (*explanation*) clair; (*need, sign*) évident; (*glass*) transparent; (*profit*) net; (*road*) dégagé; **make sth** ~ être très clair sur qch; ~ **of** (away from) à l'écart de. ● *adv* complètement; **stand** ~ **of** s'éloigner de. ● *vt* (free) dégager (**of** de); (*table*) débarrasser; (*building*) évacuer; (*cheque*) compenser; (jump over) franchir; (*debt*) liquider; (Jur) disculper. ● *vi* (*fog*) se dissiper; (*cheque*) être compensé. ~ **away** *or* **off** (remove) enlever; ~ **off** *or* **out** 🄸 décamper; ~ **out** (clean) nettoyer; ~ **up** (tidy) ranger; (*mystery*) éclaircir; (*weather*) s'éclaircir.

clearance *n* (permission) autorisation *f*; (space) espace *m*; ~ **sale** liquidation *f*.

clear-cut *adj* net.

clearing *n* clairière *f*.

clearly *adv* clairement.

clef *n* (Mus) clé *f*.

cleft *n* fissure *f*.

clench *vt* serrer.

clergy *n* clergé *m*. ~**man** *n* (*pl* **-men**) ecclésiastique *m*.

cleric *n* clerc *m*. **clerical** *adj* (Relig) clérical; (*staff, work*) de bureau.

clerk *n* employé/-e *m/f* de bureau; (US) (**sales**) ~ vendeur/-euse *m/f*.

clever *adj* intelligent; (skilful) habile.

click *n* déclic *m*. ● *vi* faire un déclic; (people 🄸) sympathiser. ● *vt* (*heels, tongue*) faire claquer.

client *n* client/-e *m/f*.

clientele n clientèle f.

cliff n falaise f.

climate n climat m.

climax n (of story, contest) point m culminant; (sexual) orgasme m.

climb vt grimper; (steps) monter; (tree, ladder) grimper à; (mountain) faire l'ascension de. ● vi grimper; ~ **into** (car) monter dans; ~ **into bed** se mettre au lit. ● n (of mountain) escalade f; (steep hill, rise) montée f. □ ~ **down** (fig) reculer. **climber** n (Sport) alpiniste mf.

clinch vt (deal) conclure; (victory, order) décrocher.

cling vi (pt **clung**) se cramponner (**to** à); (stick) coller. ~**-film** n scellofrais® m.

clinic n centre m médical; (private) clinique f. **clinical** adj clinique.

clink n tintement m. ● vt/i (faire) tinter.

clip n (for paper) trombone m; (for hair) barrette f; (for tube) collier m; (of film) extrait m. ● vt (pt **clipped**) (fasten) attacher (**to** à); (cut) couper.

clippers npl tondeuse f; (for nails) coupe-ongles m inv.

clipping n (from press) coupure f de presse.

cloak n cape f; (man's) houppelande f. ~**room** n vestiaire m; (toilet) toilettes fpl.

clobber n ⊡ attirail m. ● vt (hit ⊡) tabasser ⊡.

clock n pendule f; (large) horloge f. ● vi ~ **on/in** or **off/out** pointer; ~ up (miles) faire. ~**-tower** n beffroi m. ~**wise** a & adv dans le sens des aiguilles d'une montre.

clockwork n mécanisme m. ● adj mécanique.

clog n sabot m. ● vt/i (pt **clogged**) (se) boucher.

cloister n cloître m.

close¹ adj (friend, relative) proche (**to** de); (link, collaboration) étroit; (examination) minutieux; (result, match) serré; (weather) lourd; ~ **together** (crowded) serrés; ~ **by**, ~ **at hand** tout près; **have a** ~ **shave** l'échapper belle; **keep a** ~ **watch on** surveiller de près. ● adv près. ● n (street) impasse f.

close² vt fermer; (meeting, case) mettre fin à. ● vi se fermer; (shop) fermer; (meeting, play) prendre fin. ● n fin f.

closely adv (follow) de près.

closeness n proximité f.

closet n (US) placard m.

close-up n gros plan m.

closure n fermeture f.

clot n (of blood) caillot m; (in sauce) grumeau m. ● vt/i (pt **clotted**) (se) coaguler.

cloth n (fabric) tissu m; (duster) chiffon m; (table-cloth) nappe f.

clothe vt vêtir.

clothes npl vêtements mpl. ~**-hanger** n cintre m. ~**-line** n corde f à linge.

clothing n vêtements mpl.

cloud n nuage m. ● vi ~ (**over**) se couvrir (de nuages); (face) s'assombrir. **cloudy** adj (sky) couvert; (liquid) trouble.

clout n (blow) coup m de poing; (power) influence f. ● vt frapper.

clove n clou m de girofle; ~ **of garlic** gousse f d'ail.

clover n trèfle m.

clown n clown m. ● vi faire le clown.

club n (group) club m; (weapon) massue f; (golf) ~ club m (de golf); ~**s** (cards) trèfle m. ● vt/i (pt **clubbed**) matraquer. □ ~ **together** cotiser.

cluck vi glousser.

clue n indice m; (in crossword) définition f; **I haven't a** ~ ⊡ je n'en ai pas la moindre idée.

clump n massif m.

clumsy adj (-ier, -iest) maladroit; (tool) peu commode.

clung ⇒CLING.

cluster n (of people, islands) groupe m; (of flowers, berries) grappe f. ● vi se grouper.

clutch vt (hold) serrer fort; (grasp) saisir. ● vi ~ **at** (try to grasp) essayer de saisir. ● n (Auto) embrayage m; (of eggs) couveé f; (of people) groupe m.

clutter n désordre m. ● vt ~ (**up**) encombrer.

coach n autocar m; (of train) wagon m; (horse-drawn) carrosse m; (Sport) entraîneur/-euse m/f. ● vt (team) entraîner; (pupil) donner des leçons particulières à.

coal n charbon m. **∼field** n bassin m houiller. **∼-mine** n mine f de charbon.

coarse adj grossier.

coast n côte f. ● vi (car, bicycle) descendre en roue libre. **coastal** adj côtier.

coast: **∼guard** n (person) gardecôte m; (organization) gendarmerie f maritime. **∼line** n littoral m.

coat n manteau m; (of animal) pelage m; (of paint) couche f; **∼ of arms** armoiries fpl. ● vt enduire, couvrir; (with chocolate) enrober (**with** de). **coating** n couche f.

coax vt cajoler.

cob n (of corn) épi m.

cobbler n cordonnier m.

cobblestones npl pavés mpl.

cobweb n toile f d'araignée.

cocaine n cocaïne f.

cock n (rooster) coq m; (oiseau) mâle m. ● vt (gun) armer; (ears) dresser.

cockerel n jeune coq m.

cockle n (Culin) coque f.

cock: **∼pit** n poste m de pilotage. **∼roach** n cafard m. **∼tail** n cocktail m.

cocky adj (-ier, -iest) trop sûr de soi.

cocoa n cacao m.

coconut n noix f de coco.

COD abbr (**cash on delivery**) envoi m contre remboursement.

cod n inv morue f; **∼-liver oil** huile f de foie de morue.

code n code m. ● vt coder.

coerce vt contraindre.

coexist vi coexister.

coffee n café m. **∼ bar** n café m. **∼ bean** n grain m de café. **∼-pot** n cafetière f. **∼-table** n table f basse.

coffin n cercueil m.

cog n pignon m; (fig) rouage m.

cognac n cognac m.

coil vt/i (s')enrouler. ● n (of rope) rouleau m; (of snake) anneau m; (contraceptive) stérilet m.

coin n pièce f (de monnaie). ● vt (word) inventer.

coincide vi coïncider.
coincidence n coïncidence f.
coincidental adj dû à une coïncidence.

colander n passoire f.

cold adj froid; (person) be or feel **∼** avoir froid; **it is ∼** il fait froid; **get ∼ feet** avoir les jetons 🛈; **∼-blooded** (lit) à sang froid; (fig) sans pitié. ● n froid m; (Med) rhume m; **∼ sore** bouton m de fièvre. **coldness** n froideur f.

coleslaw n salade f de chou cru.

colic n coliques fpl.

collaborate vi collaborer.

collapse vi s'effondrer; (person) s'écrouler; (fold) se plier. ● n effondrement m.

collar n col m; (of dog) collier m. **∼-bone** n clavicule f.

collateral n nantissement m.

colleague n collègue mf.

collect vt rassembler; (pick up) ramasser; (call for) passer prendre; (money, fare) encaisser; (taxes, rent) percevoir; (as hobby) collectionner. ● vi se rassembler; (dust) s'amasser. ● adv call **∼** (US) appeler en PCV. **collection** n collection f; (of money) collecte f; (in church) quête f; (of mail) levée f.

collective adj collectif.

collector n (as hobby) collectionneur/-euse m/f; (of taxes) percepteur m; (of rent, debt) encaisseur m.

college n (for higher education) établissement m d'enseignement supérieur; (within university) collège m; **be at ∼** faire des études supérieures.

collide vi entrer en collision (**with** avec).

colliery n houillère f.

collision n collision f.

colloquial adj familier. **colloquialism** n expression f familière.

Colombia n Colombie f.

colon n (Gram) deux-points m inv; (Anat) côlon m.

colonel n colonel m.

colonial *a & n* colonial/-e (*m/f*).

colour, (US) **color** *n* couleur *f*; ∼-**blind** daltonien. ● *adj* (*photo*) en couleur; (*TV set*) couleur *inv*. ● *vt* colorer; (with crayon) colorier. **coloured** *adj* de couleur. **colourful** *adj* aux couleurs vives; (fig) haut en couleur. **colouring** *n* (of skin) teint *m*; (in food) colorant *m*.

colt *n* poulain *m*.

column *n* colonne *f*.

coma *n* coma *m*.

comb *n* peigne *m*. ● *vt* peigner; ∼ **one's hair** se peigner; ∼ **a place** passer un lieu au peigne fin.

combat *n* combat *m*. ● *vt* (*pt* **combated**) combattre.

combination *n* combinaison *f*.

combine[1] *vt/i* (se) combiner, (s') unir.

combine[2] *n* (Comm) groupe *m*; ∼ (**harvester**) moissonneuse-batteuse *f*.

come *vi* (*pt* **came**; *pp* **come**) venir; (*bus, letter*) arriver; (*postman*) passer; ∼ **and look!** viens voir!; ∼ **in** (*size, colour*) exister en; **when it** ∼**s to** lorsqu'il s'agit de. □ ∼ **about** survenir; ∼ **across** (*meaning*) passer; ∼ **across sth** tomber sur qch; ∼ **away** (leave) partir; (come off) se détacher; ∼ **back** revenir; ∼ **by** obtenir; ∼ **down** descendre; (*price*) baisser; ∼ **forward** se présenter; ∼ **in** entrer; ∼ **in useful** être utile; ∼ **in for** recevoir; ∼ **into** (money) hériter de; ∼ **off** (succeed) réussir; (fare) s'en tirer; (detach) se détacher; ∼ **on** (actor) entrer en scène; (light) s'allumer; (improve) faire des progrès; ∼ **on!** allez!; ∼ **out** sortir; ∼ **round** reprendre connaissance; (change mind) changer d'avis; ∼ **through** s'en tirer; ∼ **to** reprendre connaissance; ∼ **to sth** (*amount*) revenir à qch; (*decision, conclusion*) arriver à qch; ∼ **up** (*problem*) être soulevé; (*opportunity*) se présenter; (*sun*) se lever; ∼ **up against** se heurter à; ∼ **up with** trouver.

comedian *n* comique *m*.

comedy *n* comédie *f*.

comfort *n* confort *m*; (consolation) réconfort *m*. ● *vt* consoler. **comfortable** *adj* (*chair, car*) confortable; (*person*) à l'aise; (wealthy) aisé.

comfortably *adv* confortablement; ∼ **off** aisé.

comfy *adj* ① = COMFORTABLE.

comic *adj* comique. ● *n* (person) comique *m*; ∼ (**book**), ∼ **strip** bande *f* dessinée.

coming *n* arrivée *f*; ∼**s and goings** allées et venues *fpl*. ● *adj* à venir.

comma *n* virgule *f*.

command *n* (authority) commandement *m*; (order) ordre *m*; (mastery) maîtrise *f*. ● *vt* ordonner à (**to do** de faire); (be able to use) disposer de; (*respect*) inspirer. **commandeer** *vt* réquisitionner. **commander** *n* commandant *m*. **commanding** *adj* imposant. **commandment** *n* commandement *m*.

commando *n* commando *m*.

commemorate *vt* commémorer.

commence *vt/i* commencer.

commend *vt* (praise) louer; (entrust) confier.

commensurate *adj* proportionné.

comment *n* commentaire *m*. ● *vi* faire des commentaires; ∼ **on** commenter. **commentary** *n* commentaire *m*; (radio, TV) reportage *m*. **commentate** *vi* faire un reportage. **commentator** *n* commentateur/-trice *m/f*.

commerce *n* commerce *m*.

commercial *adj* commercial; (*traveller*) de commerce. ● *n* publicité *f*.

commiserate *vi* compatir (**with** avec).

commission *n* commission *f*; (order for work) commande *f*; **out of** ∼ hors service. ● *vt* (order) commander; (Mil) nommer officier; ∼ **to do** charger de faire. **commissioner** *n* préfet *m* (de police); (in EC) membre *m* de la Commission européenne.

commit *vt* (*pt* **committed**) commettre; (entrust) confier; ∼ **oneself** s'engager; ∼ **perjury** se parjurer; ∼ **suicide** se suicider; ∼ **to memory** apprendre par cœur. **commitment** *n* engagement *m*.

committee *n* comité *m*.

commodity *n* article *m*.

common *adj* (shared by all) commun (**to** à); (usual) courant; (vulgar) vulgaire, commun; **in** ~ en commun; ~ **people** le peuple; ~ **sense** bon sens *m*. ● *n* terrain *m* communal; **the** C~**s** Chambre *f* des Communes.

commoner *n* roturier/-ière *m/f*.

common law *n* droit *m* coutumier.

commonly *adv* communément.

commonplace *adj* banal. ● *n* banalité *f*.

common-room *n* salle *f* de détente.

Commonwealth *n* **the** ~ le Commonwealth *m*.

commotion *n* (noise) vacarme *m*; (disturbance) agitation *f*.

communal *adj* (shared) commun; (*life*) collectif.

commune *n* (group) communauté *f*.

communicate *vt/i* communiquer. **communication** *n* communication *f*. **communicative** *adj* communicatif.

communion *n* communion *f*.

Communism *n* communisme *m*. **Communist** *a & n* communiste (*mf*).

community *n* communauté *f*.

commute *vi* faire la navette. ● *vt* (Jur) commuer. **commuter** *n* navetteur/-euse *m/f*.

compact *adj* compact; (lady's case) poudrier *m*.

compact disc *n* disque *m* compact. ~ **player** *n* platine *f* laser.

companion *n* compagnon/-agne *m/ f*. **companionship** *n* camaraderie *f*.

company *n* (companionship, firm) compagnie *f*; (guests) invités/-es *m/ fpl*.

comparative *adj* (*study, form*) comparatif; (*comfort*) relatif.

compare *vt* comparer (**with, to** à); ~**d with** par rapport à. ● *vi* être comparable. **comparison** *n* comparaison *f*.

compartment *n* compartiment *m*.

compass *n* (for direction) boussole *f*; (scope) portée *f*; **a pair of** ~**es** compas *m*.

compassionate *adj* compatissant.

compatible *adj* compatible.

compel *vt* (*pt* **compelled**) contraindre. **compelling** *adj* irrésistible.

compensate *vt/i* (financially) dédommager (**for** de); ~ **for sth** compenser qch. **compensation** *n* compensation *f*; (financial) dédommagement *m*.

compete *vi* concourir; ~ **with** rivaliser avec.

competent *adj* compétent.

competition *n* (contest) concours *m*; (Sport) compétition *f*; (Comm) concurrence *f*.

competitive *adj* (*prices*) compétitif; (*person*) qui a l'esprit de compétition.

competitor *n* concurrent/-e *m/f*.

compile *vt* (*list*) dresser; (*book*) rédiger.

complacency *n* suffisance *f*.

complain *vi* se plaindre (**about, of** de). **complaint** *n* plainte *f*; (official) réclamation *f*; (illness) maladie *f*.

complement *n* complément *m*. ● *vt* compléter. **complementary** *adj* complémentaire.

complete *adj* complet; (finished) achevé; (downright) parfait. ● *vt* achever; (*a form*) remplir. **completely** *adv* complètement. **completion** *n* achèvement *m*.

complex *adj* complexe. ● *n* (Psych) complexe *m*.

complexion *n* (of face) teint *m*; (fig) caractère *m*.

compliance *n* (agreement) conformité *f*.

complicate *vt* compliquer. **complicated** *adj* compliqué. **complication** *n* complication *f*.

compliment *n* compliment *m*. ● *vt* complimenter. **complimentary** *adj* (offert) à titre gracieux; (praising) flatteur.

comply *vi* ~ **with** se conformer à, obéir à.

component *n* (of machine) pièce *f*; (chemical substance) composant *m*; (element: fig) composante *f*. ● *adj* constituant.

compose *vt* composer; ~ oneself se calmer. **composed** *adj* calme. **composer** *n* (Mus) compositeur *m*. **composition** *n* composition *f*.

composure *n* calme *m*.

compound *n* (substance, word) composé *m*; (enclosure) enclos *m*. ● *adj* composé.

comprehend *vt* comprendre. **comprehension** *n* compréhension *f*.

comprehensive *adj* étendu, complet; (*insurance*) tous risques *inv*. ~ **school** *n* collège *m* d'enseignement secondaire.

compress *vt* comprimer.

comprise *vt* comprendre, inclure.

compromise *n* compromis *m*. ● *vt* compromettre. ● *vi* transiger, arriver à un compromis.

compulsive *adj* (Psych) compulsif; (*liar, smoker*) invétéré.

compulsory *adj* obligatoire.

computer *n* ordinateur *m*; ~ **science** informatique *f*. **computerize** *vt* informatiser.

comrade *n* camarade *mf*.

con[1] *vt* (*pt* **conned**) 🅇 rouler 🅘, escroquer (**out of** de). ● *n* 🅇 escroquerie *f*.

con[2] ⇒PRO.

conceal *vt* dissimuler (**from** à).

concede *vt* concéder. ● *vi* céder.

conceited *adj* vaniteux.

conceive *vt/i* concevoir; ~ **of** concevoir.

concentrate *vt/i* (se) concentrer. **concentration** *n* concentration *f*.

concept *n* concept *m*.

conception *n* conception *f*.

concern *n* (interest, business) affaire *f*; (worry) inquiétude *f*; (firm: Comm) entreprise *f*, affaire *f*. ● *vt* concerner; ~ **oneself with**, be ~ed with s'occuper de. **concerned** *adj* inquiet. **concerning** *prep* en ce qui concerne.

concert *n* concert *m*.

concession *n* concession *f*.

conciliation *n* conciliation *f*.

concise *adj* concis.

conclude *vt* conclure. ● *vi* se terminer. **conclusion** *n* conclusion *f*. **conclusive** *adj* concluant.

concoct *vt* confectionner; (invent: fig) fabriquer. **concoction** *n* mélange *m*.

concourse *n* (Rail) hall *m*.

concrete *n* béton *m*. ● *adj* de béton; (fig) concret. ● *vt* bétonner.

concur *vi* (*pt* **concurred**) être d'accord.

concurrently *adv* simultanément.

concussion *n* commotion *f* (cérébrale).

condemn *vt* condamner.

condensation *n* (on walls) condensation *f*; (on windows) buée *f*. **condense** *vt/i* (se) condenser.

condition *n* condition *f*; on ~ that à condition que. ● *vt* conditionner. **conditional** *adj* conditionnel.

conditioner *n* après-shampooing *m*.

condolences *npl* condoléances *fpl*.

condom *n* préservatif *m*.

condone *vt* pardonner, fermer les yeux sur.

conducive *adj* ~ **to** favorable à.

conduct[1] *n* conduite *f*.

conduct[2] *vt* conduire; (*orchestra*) diriger. **conductor** *n* chef *m* d'orchestre; (of bus) receveur *m*; (on train: US) chef *m* de train; (Electr) conducteur *m*. **conductress** *n* receveuse *f*.

cone *n* cône *m*; (of ice-cream) cornet *m*.

confectioner *n* confiseur/-euse *m/f*. **confectionery** *n* confiserie *f*.

confer *vt/i* (*pt* **conferred**) conférer.

conference *n* conférence *f*.

confess *vt/i* avouer; (Relig) (se) confesser. **confession** *n* confession *f*; (of crime) aveu *m*.

confide *vt* confier. ● *vi* ~ **in** se confier à.

confidence *n* (trust) confiance *f*; (boldness) confiance *f* en soi; (secret) confidence *f*; in ~ en confidence. **confident** *adj* sûr.

confidential *adj* confidentiel.

confine vt enfermer; (limit) limiter; ∼d space espace m réduit; ∼d to limité à.

confirm vt confirmer. **confirmed** adj (bachelor) endurci; (smoker) invétéré.

confiscate vt confisquer.

conflict[1] n conflit m.

conflict[2] vi (statements, views) être en contradiction (with avec); (appointments) tomber en même temps (with que). **conflicting** adj contradictoire.

conform vt/i (se) conformer.

confound vt confondre.

confront vt affronter; ∼ with confronter avec.

confuse vt (bewilder) troubler; (mistake, confound) confondre; **become** ∼d s'embrouiller; **I am** ∼d je m'y perds. **confusing** adj déroutant. **confusion** n confusion f.

congeal vt/i (se) figer.

congested adj (road) embouteillé; (passage) encombré; (Med) congestionné. **congestion** n (traffic) encombrement(s) m(pl); (Med) congestion f.

congratulate vt féliciter (on de). **congratulations** npl félicitations fpl.

congregate vi se rassembler. **congregation** n assemblée f.

congress n congrès m; **C∼** (US) le Congrès.

conjugate vt conjuguer. **conjugation** n conjugaison f.

conjunction n (Ling) conjonction f; in ∼ with conjointement avec.

conjunctivitis n conjonctivite f.

conjure vi faire des tours de passe-passe. ● vt ∼ up faire apparaître. **conjuror** n prestidigitateur/-trice m/f.

con man n ⊠ escroc m.

connect vt/i (se) relier; (in mind) faire le rapport entre; (install, wire up to mains) brancher; ∼ with (of train) assurer la correspondance avec; ∼ed (idea, event) lié; **be** ∼ed with avoir rapport à.

connection n rapport m; (Rail) correspondance f; (phone call) communication f; (Electr) contact m;

(joining piece) raccord m; ∼s (Comm) relations fpl.

connive vi ∼ at se faire le complice de.

conquer vt vaincre; (country) conquérir. **conqueror** n conquérant m.

conquest n conquête f.

conscience n conscience f. **conscientious** adj consciencieux.

conscious adj conscient; (deliberate) voulu. **consciously** adv consciemment. **consciousness** n conscience f; (Med) connaissance f.

conscript n appelé m.

consecutive adj consécutif.

consensus n consensus m.

consent vi consentir (to à). ● n consentement m.

consequence n conséquence f. **consequently** adv par conséquent.

conservation n préservation f; ∼ area zone f protégée. **conservationist** n défenseur m de l'environnement.

conservative adj conservateur; (estimate) minimal.

Conservative Party n parti m conservateur.

conservatory n (greenhouse) serre f; (room) véranda f.

conserve vt conserver; (energy) économiser.

consider vt considérer; (allow for) tenir compte de; (possibility) envisager (doing de faire).

considerable adj considérable; (much) beaucoup de.

considerate adj prévenant, attentionné. **consideration** n considération f; (respect) égard(s) m(pl).

considering prep compte tenu de.

consignment n envoi m.

consist vi consister (of en; in doing à faire).

consistency n (of liquids) consistance f; (of argument) cohérence f.

consistent adj cohérent; ∼ with conforme à.

consolation n consolation f.

consolidate vt/i (se) consolider.

consonant *n* consonne *f.*

conspicuous *adj* (easily seen) en évidence; (showy) voyant; (noteworthy) remarquable.

conspiracy *n* conspiration *f.*

constable *n* agent *m* de police, gendarme *m.*

constant *adj* (*questions*) incessant; (unchanging) constant; (*friend*) fidèle. ● *n* constante *f.* **constantly** *adv* constamment.

constellation *n* constellation *f.*

constipation *n* constipation *f.*

constituency *n* circonscription *f* électorale.

constituent *adj* constitutif. ● *n* élément *m* constitutif; (Pol) électeur/ -trice *m/f.*

constitution *n* constitution *f.*

constrain *vt* contraindre. **constraint** *n* contrainte *f.*

constrict *vt* (*flow*) comprimer; (*movement*) gêner.

construct *vt* construire. **construction** *n* construction *f.* **constructive** *adj* constructif.

consulate *n* consulat *m.*

consult *vt* consulter. ● *vi* ∼ with conférer avec. **consultant** *n* conseiller/-ère *m/f;* (Med) spécialiste *mf.* **consultation** *n* consultation *f.*

consume *vt* consommer; (destroy) consumer. **consumer** *n* consommateur/-trice *m/f.*

consummate *vt* consommer.

consumption *n* consommation *f;* (Med) phtisie *f.*

contact *n* contact *m;* (person) relation *f.* ● *vt* contacter. ∼ **lenses** *npl* lentilles *fpl* (de contact).

contagious *adj* contagieux.

contain *vt* contenir; ∼ **oneself** se contenir. **container** *n* récipient *m;* (for transport) container *m.*

contaminate *vt* contaminer.

contemplate *vt* (gaze at) contempler; (think about) envisager.

contemporary *a* & *n* contemporain/-e (*m/f*).

contempt *n* mépris *m.* **contemptible** *adj* méprisable. **contemptuous** *adj* méprisant.

contend *vt* soutenir. ● *vi* ∼ with (compete) rivaliser avec; (face) faire face à. **contender** *n* adversaire *mf.*

content[1] *n* (of letter) contenu *m;* (amount) teneur *f;* ∼s contenu *m.*

content[2] *adj* satisfait. ● *vt* contenter. **contented** *adj* satisfait. **contentment** *n* contentement *m.*

contest[1] *n* (competition) concours *m;* (struggle) lutte *f.*

contest[2] *vt* contester; (compete for or in) disputer. **contestant** *n* concurrent/-e *m/f.*

context *n* contexte *m.*

continent *n* continent *m;* the C∼ l'Europe *f* (continentale). **continental** *adj* continental; européen. **continental quilt** *n* couette *f.*

contingency *n* éventualité *f;* ∼ **plan** plan *m* d'urgence.

continual *adj* continuel.

continuation *n* continuation *f;* (after interruption) reprise *f;* (new episode) suite *f.*

continue *vt/i* continuer; (resume) reprendre. **continued** *adj* continu.

continuous *adj* continu. **continuously** *adv* (without a break) sans interruption; (repeatedly) continuellement.

contort *vt* tordre; ∼ **oneself** se contorsionner.

contour *n* contour *m.*

contraband *n* contrebande *f.*

contraception *n* contraception *f.* **contraceptive** *a* & *n* contraceptif (*m*).

contract[1] *n* contrat *m.*

contract[2] *vt/i* (se) contracter. **contraction** *n* contraction *f.*

contractor *n* entrepreneur/-euse *m/f.*

contradict *vt* contredire. **contradictory** *adj* contradictoire.

contrary[1] *adj* contraire (to à). ● *n* contraire *m;* on the ∼ au contraire. ● *adv* ∼ to contrairement à.

contrary[2] *adj* entêté.

contrast[1] *n* contraste *m.*

contrast[2] *vt/i* contraster.

contravention *n* infraction *f.*

contribute vt donner. ● vi ~ to contribuer à; (take part) participer à; (newspaper) collaborer à.
contribution n contribution f.
contributor n collaborateur/-trice m/f.

contrive vt imaginer; ~ to do trouver moyen de faire.

control vt (pt **controlled**) (firm) diriger; (check) contrôler; (restrain) maîtriser. ● n contrôle m; (mastery) maîtrise f; ~s commandes fpl; (knobs) boutons mpl; **have under** ~ (event) avoir en main; **in** ~ **of** maître de. ~ **tower** n tour f de contrôle.

controversial adj discutable, discuté. **controversy** n controverse f.

conurbation n agglomération f, conurbation f.

convalesce vi être en convalescence.

convene vt convoquer. ● vi se réunir.

convenience n commodité f; ~s toilettes fpl; **all modern** ~s tout le confort moderne; **at your** ~ quand cela vous conviendra, à votre convenance. ~ **foods** npl plats mpl tout préparés.

convenient adj commode, pratique; (time) bien choisi; **be** ~ **for** convenir à.

convent n couvent m.

convention n (assembly, agreement) convention f; (custom) usage m.
conventional adj conventionnel.

conversation n conversation f.
conversational adj (tone) de la conversation; (French) de tous les jours.

converse[1] vi s'entretenir, converser (with avec).

converse[2] a & n inverse (m).
conversely adv inversement.
conversion n conversion f.

convert[1] vt convertir; (house) aménager. ● vi ~ into se transformer en.

convert[2] n converti/-e m/f.

convertible adj convertible. ● n (car) décapotable f.

convey vt (wishes, order) transmettre; (goods, people) transporter; (idea, feeling) communiquer. **conveyor belt** n tapis m roulant.

convict[1] vt déclarer coupable.

convict[2] n prisonnier/-ière m/f.

conviction n (Jur) condamnation f; (opinion) conviction f.

convince vt convaincre.

convoke vt convoquer.

convoy n convoi m.

convulse vt convulser; (fig) bouleverser; **be** ~**d with laughter** se tordre de rire.

cook vt/i (faire) cuire; (of person) faire la cuisine; ~ **up** 🄸 fabriquer. ● n cuisinier/-ière m/f. **cooker** n (stove) cuisinière f. **cookery** n cuisine f.

cookie n (US) biscuit m.

cooking n cuisine f. ● adj de cuisine.

cool adj frais; (calm) calme; (unfriendly) froid. ● n fraîcheur f; (calmness 🄳) sang-froid m; **in the** ~ au frais. ● vt/i rafraîchir. ~ **box** n glacière f.

coolly adv calmement; froidement.

coop n poulailler m. ● vt ~ **up** enfermer.

co-operate vi coopérer. **co-operation** n coopération f.

co-operative adj coopératif. ● n coopérative f.

co-ordinate vt coordonner.

cop vt (pt **copped**) 🄳 piquer. ● n (policeman 🄳) flic m. ▢ ~ **out** 🄳 se dérober.

cope vi s'en sortir 🄸, se débrouiller; ~ **with** (problem) faire face à.

copper n cuivre m; (coin) sou m; 🄳 flic m. ● adj de cuivre.

copulate vi s'accoupler.

copy n copie f; (of book, newspaper) exemplaire m; (print: Photo) épreuve f. ● vt/i copier.

copyright n droit m d'auteur, copyright m.

copy-writer n rédacteur-concepteur m, rédactrice-conceptrice f.

cord n (petite) corde f; (of curtain, pyjamas) cordon m; (Electr) cordon m électrique; (fabric) velours m côtelé.

cordial adj cordial. ● n (drink) sirop m.

corduroy n velours m côtelé.

core n (of apple) trognon m; (of problem) cœur m; (Tech) noyau m. ● vt (apple) évider.

cork n liège m; (for bottle) bouchon m. ● vt boucher. **corkscrew** n tire-bouchon m.

corn n blé m; (maize: US) maïs m; (seed) grain m; (hard skin) cor m.

cornea n cornée f.

corner n coin m; (bend in road) virage m; (football) corner m. ● vt coincer, acculer; (market) accaparer. ● vi prendre un virage.

cornflour n farine f de maïs.

cornice n corniche f.

corny adj (-ier, -iest) (joke) éculé.

corollary n corollaire m.

coronary n infarctus m.

coronation n couronnement m.

corporal n caporal m. ~ **punishment** n châtiment m corporel.

corporate adj (ownership) en commun; (body) constitué.

corporation n (Comm) société f.

corpse n cadavre m.

corpuscle n globule m.

correct adj (right) exact, juste, correct; (proper) correct; **you are** ~ vous avez raison. ● vt corriger.

correction n correction f.

correlate vt/i (faire) correspondre.

correspond vi correspondre. **correspondence** n correspondance f.

corridor n couloir m.

corrode vt/i (se) corroder.

corrugated adj ondulé; ~ **iron** tôle f ondulée.

corrupt adj corrompu. ● vt corrompre. **corruption** n corruption f.

Corsica n Corse f.

cosh n matraque f. ● vt matraquer.

cosmetic n produit m de beauté. ● adj cosmétique; (fig, pej) superficiel. ~ **surgery** n chirurgie f esthétique.

cosmopolitan a & n cosmopolite (mf).

cosmos n cosmos m.

cost vt (pt cost) coûter; (pt costed) établir le prix de. ● n coût m; ~s (Jur) dépens mpl; **at all** ~s à tout prix; **to one's** ~ à ses dépens; ~ **price** prix m de revient; ~ **of living** coût m de la vie. ~**-effective** adj rentable.

costly adj (-ier, -iest) coûteux; (valuable) précieux.

costume n costume m; (for swimming) maillot m. ~ **jewellery** npl bijoux mpl de fantaisie.

cosy adj (-ier, -iest) confortable, intime.

cot n lit m d'enfant; (camp-bed: US) lit m de camp.

cottage n petite maison f de campagne; (thatched) chaumière f. ~ **pie** n hachis m Parmentier.

cotton n coton m; (for sewing) fil m (à coudre). ● vi ~ **on** ⊠ piger. ~ **wool** n coton m hydrophile.

couch n canapé m. ● vt (express) formuler.

cough vi tousser. ● n toux f. □ ~ **up** ⊠ cracher, payer.

could ⇒CAN[1].

couldn't = COULD NOT.

council n conseil m. ~ **house** n maison f louée par la municipalité, ≈ H.L.M. m or f.

councillor n conseiller/-ère m/f municipal/-e.

counsel n conseil m. ● n inv (Jur) avocat/-e m/f. **counsellor** n conseiller/-ère m/f.

count vt/i compter. ● n (numerical record) décompte m; (nobleman) comte m. □ ~ **on** compter sur.

counter n comptoir m; (in bank) guichet m; (token) jeton m. ● adv ~ **to** à l'encontre de. ● adj opposé. ● vt opposer; (blow) parer. ● vi riposter.

counteract vt neutraliser.

counterbalance n contrepoids m. ● vt contrebalancer.

counterfeit a & n faux (m). ● vt contrefaire.

counterfoil n souche f.

counter-productive adj qui produit l'effet contraire.

countess n comtesse f.

countless adj innombrable.

country n (land, region) pays m; (homeland) patrie f; (countryside) campagne f.

countryman n (pl **-men**) campagnard m; (fellow citizen) compatriote m.

countryside n campagne f.

county n comté m.

coup n (achievement) joli coup m; (Pol) coup m d'état.

couple n (people, animals) couple m; **a ~ (of)** (two or three) deux ou trois. ● vt/i (s')accoupler.

coupon n coupon m; (for shopping) bon m or coupon m de réduction.

courage n courage m.

courgette n courgette f.

courier n messager/-ère m/f; (for tourists) guide m.

course n cours m; (for training) stage m; (series) série f; (Culin) plat m; (for golf) terrain m; (at sea) itinéraire m; **change ~** changer de cap; **~ (of action)** façon f de faire; **during the ~ of** pendant; **in due ~** en temps utile; **of ~** bien sûr.

court n cour f; (tennis) court m; **go to ~** aller devant les tribunaux. ● vt faire la cour à; (danger) rechercher.

courteous adj courtois.

courtesy n courtoisie f; **by ~ of** avec la permission de.

court-house n (US) palais m de justice.

court-martial vt (pt **-martialled**) faire passer en conseil de guerre. ● n cour f martiale.

court: **~room** n salle f de tribunal. **~shoe** n escarpin m. **~yard** n cour f.

cousin n cousin/-e m/f; **first ~** cousin/-e m/f germain/-e.

cove n anse f, crique f.

covenant n convention f.

cover vt couvrir. ● n (for bed, book) couverture f; (lid) couvercle m; (for furniture) housse f; (shelter) abri m; **take ~** se mettre à l'abri. □ **~ up** cacher; (crime) couvrir; **~ up for** couvrir.

coverage n reportage m.

covering n enveloppe f; **~ letter** lettre f d'accompagnement.

covert adj (activity) secret; (threat) voilé; (look) dérobé.

cover-up n opération f de camouflage.

cow n vache f.

coward n lâche mf.

cowboy n cow-boy m.

cowshed n étable f.

coy adj (faussement) timide, qui fait le or la timide.

cozy US = cosy.

crab n crabe m. **~-apple** n pomme f sauvage.

crack n fente f; (in glass) fêlure f; (noise) craquement m; (joke 🔲) plaisanterie f. ● adj 🔲 d'élite. ● vt/i (break partially) (se) fêler; (split) (se) fendre; (nut) casser; (joke) raconter; (problem) résoudre; **get ~ing** 🔲 s'y mettre. □ **~ down on** 🔲 sévir contre; **~ up** 🔲 craquer.

cracker n (Culin) biscuit m (salé); (for Christmas) diablotin f.

crackle vi crépiter. ● n crépitement m.

cradle n berceau m. ● vt bercer.

craft n métier m artisanal; (technique) art m; (boat) bateau m. **craftsman** n (pl **-men**) artisan m.

craftsmanship n art m.

crafty adj (**-ier**, **-iest**) rusé.

crag n rocher m à pic.

cram vt/i (pt **crammed**); (for an exam) bachoter (**for** pour); **~ into** (pack) (s')entasser dans; **~ with** (fill) bourrer de.

cramp n crampe f.

cramped adj à l'étroit.

cranberry n canneberge f.

crane n grue f. ● vt (neck) tendre.

crank n excentrique mf; (Tech) manivelle f.

crap n (nonsense 🔲) conneries fpl 🔲; (faeces 🔲) merde f 🔲.

crash n accident m; (noise) fracas m; (of thunder) coup m; (of firm) faillite f. ● vt/i avoir un accident (avec); (of plane) s'écraser; (two vehicles) se percuter; **~ into** rentrer dans. **~ course** n cours m intensif. **~-helmet** n casque m (anti-choc). **~-land** vi atterrir en catastrophe.

crate n cageot m.

cravat *n* foulard *m*.

crave *vt/i* ~ (for) désirer ardemment. **craving** *n* envie *f* irrésistible.

crawl *vi* (*insect*) ramper; (*vehicle*) se traîner; **be ~ing with** grouiller de. ● *n* (pace) pas *m*; (swimming) crawl *m*.

crayfish *n inv* écrevisse *f*.

crayon *n* craie *f* grasse.

craze *n* engouement *m*.

crazy *adj* (**-ier, -iest**) fou; ~ **about** (person) fou de; (thing) fana *or* fou de.

creak *n* grincement *m*. ● *vi* grincer.

cream *n* crème *f*. ● *adj* crème *inv*. ● *vt* écrémer.

crease *n* pli *m*. ● *vt/i* (se) froisser.

create *vt* créer. **creation** *n* création *f*. **creative** *adj* (*person*) créatif; (*process*) créateur. **creator** *n* créateur/-trice *m/f*.

creature *n* créature *f*.

crèche *n* garderie *f*.

credentials *npl* (identity) pièces *fpl* d'identité; (competence) références *fpl*.

credibility *n* crédibilité *f*.

credit *n* (credence) crédit *m*; (honour) honneur *m*; **in ~** créditeur; ~**s** (cinema) générique *m*. ● *adj* (*balance*) créditeur. ● *vt* croire; (Comm) créditer; ~ **sb with** attribuer à qn. ~ **card** *n* carte *f* de crédit. ~ **note** *n* avoir *m*.

creditor *n* créancier/-ière *m/f*.

credit-worthy *adj* solvable.

creed *n* credo *m*.

creek *n* (US) ruisseau *m*; **up the ~** 🗵 dans le pétrin 🅣.

creep *vi* (*pt* **crept**) (*insect, cat*) ramper; (fig) se glisser. ● *n* (person 🗵) pauvre type *m* 🅣; **give sb the ~s** faire frissonner qn. **creeper** *n* liane *f*.

cremate *vt* incinérer. **cremation** *n* incinération *f*. **crematorium** *n* (*pl* **-ia**) crématorium *m*.

crêpe *n* crêpe *m*. ~ **paper** *n* papier *m* crêpon.

crept ⇒CREEP.

crescent *n* croissant *m*; (of houses) rue *f* en demi-lune.

cress *n* cresson *m*.

crest *n* crête *f*; (coat of arms) armoiries *fpl*.

cretin *n* crétin/-e *m/f*.

crevice *n* fente *f*.

crew *n* (of plane, ship) équipage *m*; (gang) équipe *f*. ~ **cut** *n* coupe *f* en brosse. ~ **neck** *n* (col) ras du cou *m*.

crib *n* lit *m* d'enfant. ● *vt/i* (*pt* **cribbed**) copier.

cricket *n* (Sport) cricket *m*; (insect) grillon *m*.

crime *n* crime *m*; (minor) délit *m*; (acts) criminalité *f*.

criminal *a & n* criminel/-le (*m/f*).

crimson *a & n* cramoisi (*m*).

cringe *vi* reculer; (fig) s'humilier.

crinkle *vt/i* (se) froisser. ● *n* pli *m*.

cripple *n* infirme *mf*. ● *vt* estropier; (fig) paralyser.

crisis *n* (*pl* **crises**) crise *f*.

crisp *adj* (Culin) croquant; (air, reply) vif. **crisps** *npl* chips *fpl*.

criss-cross *adj* entrecroisé. ● *vt/i* (s')entrecroiser.

criterion *n* (*pl* **-ia**) critère *m*.

critic *n* critique *m*. **critical** *adj* critique. **critically** *adv* d'une manière critique; (*ill*) gravement.

criticism *n* critique *f*.

criticize *vt/i* critiquer.

croak *n* (*bird*) croassement *m*; (*frog*) coassement *m*. ● *vi* croasser; coasser.

Croatia *n* Croatie *f*.

Croatian *n* Croate *mf*. ● *adj* Croate.

crochet *n* crochet *m*. ● *vt* faire du crochet.

crockery *n* vaisselle *f*.

crocodile *n* crocodile *m*.

crook *n* (criminal 🅣) escroc *m*; (stick) houlette *f*.

crooked *adj* tordu; (winding) tortueux; (askew) de travers; (dishonest: fig) malhonnête.

crop *n* récolte *f*; (fig) quantité *f*. ● *vt* (*pt* **cropped**) couper. ● *vi* ~ **up** se présenter.

cross *n* croix *f*; (hybrid) hybride *m*. ● *vt/i* traverser; (*legs, animals*) croiser; (*cheque*) barrer; (*paths*) se croiser; ~ **sb's mind** venir à l'esprit de qn. ● *adj* en colère, fâché (**with** contre); **talk at ~ purposes** parler sans se comprendre. □ ~ **off** *or* **out**

rayer. ∼-**check** vt vérifier (pour confirmer). ∼-**country** (**running**) n cross m. ∼-**examine** vt faire subir un contre-interrogatoire à. ∼-**eyed** adj be ∼-eyed loucher. ∼**fire** n feux mpl croisés.

crossing n (by boat) traversée f; (on road) passage m clouté.

crossly adv avec colère.

cross: ∼-**reference** n renvoi m. ∼**roads** n carrefour m. ∼**word** n mots mpl croisés.

crotch n (of garment) entrejambes m inv.

crouch vi s'accroupir.

crow n corbeau m; **as the** ∼ **flies** à vol d'oiseau. ● vi (of cock) chanter; (fig) jubiler. ∼**bar** n pied-de-biche m.

crowd n foule f. **crowded** adj plein.

crown n couronne f; (top part) sommet m. ● vt couronner.

Crown Court n Cour f d'assises.

crucial adj crucial.

crucifix n crucifix m.

crucify vt crucifier.

crude adj (raw) brut; (rough, vulgar) grossier.

cruel adj (**crueller**, **cruellest**) cruel.

cruise n croisière f. ● vi (ship) croiser; (tourists) faire une croisière; (vehicle) rouler; **cruising speed** vitesse f de croisière.

crumb n miette f.

crumble vt/i (s')effriter; (bread) (s')émietter; (collapse) s'écrouler.

crumple vt/i (se) froisser.

crunch vt croquer. ● n (event) moment m critique; **when it comes to the** ∼ quand ça devient sérieux.

crusade n croisade f. **crusader** n (knight) croisé m; (fig) militant/-e m/f.

crush vt écraser; (clothes) froisser. ● n (crowd) presse f; **a** ∼ **on** ⊠ le béguin pour.

crust n croûte f. **crusty** adj croustillant.

crutch n béquille f; (crotch) entrejambes m inv.

crux n **the** ∼ **of** (problem) le point crucial de.

cry n cri m. ● vi (weep) pleurer; (call out) crier. ◻ ∼ **off** se décommander.

crying adj (need) urgent; **a** ∼ **shame** une vraie honte. ● n pleurs mpl.

cryptic adj énigmatique.

crystal n cristal m. ∼-**clear** adj parfaitement clair.

cub n petit m; **Cub** (Scout) louveteau m.

Cuba n Cuba f.

cube n cube m. **cubic** adj cubique; (metre) cube.

cubicle n (in room, hospital) box m; (at swimming-pool) cabine f.

cuckoo n coucou m.

cucumber n concombre m.

cuddle vt câliner. ● vi (kiss and) ∼ s'embrasser. ● n caresse f. **cuddly** adj câlin; **cuddly toy** peluche f.

cue n signal m; (Theat) réplique f; (billiards) queue f.

cuff n manchette f; (US: on trousers) revers m; **off the** ∼ impromptu. ● vt gifler. ∼-**link** n bouton m de manchette.

cul-de-sac n (pl **culs-de-sac**) impasse f.

cull vt (select) choisir; (kill) massacrer.

culminate vi ∼ **in** se terminer par. **culmination** n point m culminant.

culprit n coupable mf.

cult n culte m.

cultivate vt cultiver. **cultivation** n culture f.

cultural adj culturel.

culture n culture f. **cultured** adj cultivé.

cumbersome adj encombrant.

cunning adj rusé. ● n astuce f, ruse f.

cup n tasse f; (prize) coupe f; **Cup final** finale f de la coupe.

cupboard n placard m.

cup-tie n match m de coupe.

curate n vicaire m.

curator n (of museum) conservateur m.

curb n (restraint) frein m; (of path) (US) bord m du trottoir. ● vt (desires) refréner; (price increase) freiner.

cure vt guérir; (fig) éliminer; (Culin) fumer; (in brine) saler. ● n (recovery) guérison f; (remedy) remède m.

curfew *n* couvre-feu *m*.

curiosity *n* curiosité *f*. **curious** *adj* curieux.

curl *vt/i* (*hair*) boucler. ● *n* boucle *f*. □ ~ **up** se pelotonner; (shrivel) se racornir.

curler *n* bigoudi *m*.

curly *adj* (**-ier**, **-iest**) bouclé.

currant *n* raisin *m* de Corinthe.

currency *n* (money) monnaie *f*; (of word) fréquence *f*; **foreign** ~ devises *fpl* étrangères.

current *adj* (*term, word*) usité; (topical) actuel; (*year*) en cours. ● *n* courant *m*. ~ **account** *n* compte *m* courant. ~ **events** *npl* l'actualité *f*.

currently *adv* actuellement.

curriculum *n* (*pl* **-la**) programme *m* scolaire. ~ **vitae** *n* curriculum vitae *m*.

curry *n* curry *m*. ● *vt* ~ **favour with** chercher les bonnes grâces de.

curse *n* (spell) malédiction *f*; (swearword) juron *m*. ● *vt* maudire. ● *vi* (swear) jurer.

cursor *n* curseur *m*.

curt *adj* brusque.

curtain *n* rideau *m*.

curve *n* courbe *f*. ● *vi* (line) s'incurver; (*edge*) se recourber; (*road*) faire une courbe. ● *vt* courber.

cushion *n* coussin *m*. ● *vt* (a blow) amortir; (fig) protéger.

custard *n* crème *f* anglaise; (set) flan *m*.

custody *n* (of child) garde *f*; (Jur) détention *f* préventive.

custom *n* coutume *f*; (patronage: Comm) clientèle *f*. **customary** *adj* habituel.

customer *n* client/-e *m/f*; (person) type *m*.

customize *vt* personnaliser.

custom-made *adj* fait sur mesure.

customs *npl* douane *f*. ● *adj* douanier. ~ **officer** *n* douanier *m*.

cut *vt/i* (*pt* **cut**; *pres p* **cutting**) *vt* couper; (*hedge*) tailler; (*prices*) réduire. ● *vi* couper. ● *n* (wound) coupure *f*; (of clothes) coupe *f*; (in surgery) incision *f*; (share) part *f*; (in prices) réduction *f*. □ ~ **back** *vi* faire des économies. *vt* réduire. ~ **down** (**on**) réduire; ~ **in** (in conversation) intervenir; ~ **off** couper; (*tide, army*) isoler; ~ **out** *vt* découper; (leave out) supprimer; *vi* (*engine*) s'arrêter. ~ **short** (visit) écourter; ~ **up** couper; (carve) découper.

cut-back *n* réduction *f*.

cute *adj* [i] mignon.

cutlery *n* couverts *mpl*.

cutlet *n* côtelette *f*.

cut-price *adj* à prix réduit.

cutting *adj* cinglant. ● *n* (from newspaper) coupure *f*; (plant) bouture *f*.

CV *abbr* ⇒CURRICULUM VITAE.

cyanide *n* cyanure *m*.

cycle *n* cycle *m*; (bicycle) vélo *m*. ● *vi* aller à vélo.

cycling *n* cyclisme *m*. ~ **shorts** *npl* cycliste *m*.

cyclist *n* cycliste *mf*.

cylinder *n* cylindre *m*.

cymbal *n* cymbale *f*.

cynic *n* cynique *mf*. **cynical** *adj* cynique. **cynicism** *n* cynisme *m*.

cypress *n* cyprès *m*.

Cypriot *n* Cypriote *mf*. ● *adj* cypriote.

Cyprus *n* Chypre *f*.

cyst *n* kyste *m*.

czar *n* tsar *m*.

Czech *n* (person) Tchèque *mf*; (Ling) tchèque *m*. ~ **Republic** *n* République *f* tchèque.

Dd

dab *vt* (*pt* **dabbed**) tamponner; ~ **sth on** appliquer qch par petites touches. ● *n* touche *f*.

dabble *vi* ~ **in sth** faire qch en amateur.

dad *n* [i] papa *m*. **daddy** *n* [i] papa *m*.

daffodil *n* jonquille *f*.

daft *adj* bête.

dagger *n* poignard *m*.

daily *adj* quotidien. ● *adv* tous les jours. ● *n* (newspaper) quotidien *m*.

dainty *adj* (**-ier, -iest**) (*lace, food*) délicat; (*shoe, hand*) mignon.

dairy *n* (on farm) laiterie *f*; (shop) crémerie *f*. ● *adj* (*farm, cow, product*) laitier; (*butter*) fermier.

daisy *n* pâquerette *f*; (Comput) ~ **wheel** marguerite *f*.

dale *n* vallée *f*.

dam *n* barrage *m*.

damage *n* (to property) dégâts *mpl*; (Med) lésions *fpl*; **to do sth** ~ (cause, trade) porter atteinte à; ~**s** (Jur) dommages-intérêts *mpl*. ● *vt* (*property*) endommager; (*health*) nuire à; (*reputation*) porter atteinte à. **damaging** *adj* (to health) nuisible; (to reputation) préjudiciable.

damn *vt* (Relig) damner; (condemn: fig) condamner. ● *interj* 🄳 zut 🄳, merde 🅇. ● *n* **not give/care a** ~ **about** se ficher de 🄳. ● *adj* fichu 🄳. ● *adv* franchement.

damp *n* humidité *f*. ● *adj* humide. **dampen** *vt* (lit) humecter; (fig) refroidir. **dampness** *n* humidité *f*.

dance *vt/i* danser. ● *n* danse *f*; (gathering) bal *m*; ~ **hall** dancing *m*. **dancer** *n* danseur/-euse *m/f*.

dandelion *n* pissenlit *m*.

dandruff *n* pellicules *fpl*.

Dane *n* Danois/-e *m/f*.

danger *n* danger *m*; (risk) risque *m*; **be in** ~ **of** risquer de. **dangerous** *adj* dangereux.

dangle *vt* (*object*) balancer; (*legs*) laisser pendre. ● *vi* (*object*) se balancer (**from** à).

Danish *n* (Ling) danois *m*. ● *adj* danois.

dare *vt* oser ((**to**) **do** faire); ~ **sb to do** défier qn de faire. ● *n* défi *m*. **daring** *adj* audacieux.

dark *adj* (*day, colour, suit, mood, warning*) sombre; (*hair, eyes, skin*) brun; (*secret, thought*) noir. ● *n* noir *m*; (nightfall) tombée *f* de la nuit; **in the** ~ (fig) dans le noir. **darken** *vt/i* (*sky*) (s')obscurcir; (*colour*) (se) foncer; (*mood*) (s')assombrir. **darkness** *n* obscurité *f*. ~-**room** *n* chambre *f* noire.

darling *a* & *n* chéri/-e (*m/f*).

dart *n* fléchette *f*; ~**s** (game) fléchettes *fpl*. ● *vi* ~ **in/away** entrer/ filer comme une flèche.

dash *vi* se précipiter; ~ **off** se sauver. ● *vt* (*hope*) anéantir; ~ **sth against** projeter qch contre. ● *n* course *f* folle; (of liquid) goutte *f*; (of colour) touche *f*; (in punctuation) tiret *m*.

dashboard *n* tableau *m* de bord.

data *npl* données *fpl*. ~**base** *n* base *f* de données. ~ **capture** *n* saisie *f* de données. ~ **processing** *n* traitement *m* des données. ~ **protection** *n* protection *f* de l'information.

date *n* date *f*; (meeting) rendez-vous *m*; (fruit) datte *f*; **out of** ~ (old-fashioned) démodé; (*passport*) périmé; **to** ~ à ce jour; **up to** ~ (modern) moderne; (*list*) à jour. ● *vt/i* dater; (go out with) sortir avec; ~ **from** dater de. **dated** *adj* démodé.

daughter *n* fille *f*. ~-**In-law** *n* (*pl* ~**s-in-law**) belle-fille *f*.

daunt *vt* décourager.

dawdle *vi* flâner, traînasser 🄳.

dawn *n* aube *f*. ● *vi* (*day*) se lever; **it** ~**ed on me that** je me suis rendu compte que.

day *n* jour *m*; (whole day) journée *f*; (period) époque *f*; **the** ~ **before** la veille; **the following** *or* **next** ~ le lendemain. ~**break** *n* aube *f*.

daydream *n* rêves *mpl*. ● *vi* rêvasser (**about** de).

day: ~**light** *n* jour *m*. ~**time** *n* journée *f*.

daze *n* **in a** ~ (from blow) étourdi; (from drug) hébété. **dazed** *adj* (by blow) abasourdi; (by news) ahuri.

dazzle *vt* éblouir.

dead *adj* mort; (numb) engourdi. ● *adv* complètement; **in** ~ **centre** au beau milieu; **stop** ~ s'arrêter net. ● *n* **in the** ~ **of** au cœur de; **the** ~ les morts. **deaden** *vt* (*sound, blow*) amortir; (*pain*) calmer. ~ **end** *n* impasse *f*. ~**line** *n* date *f* limite. ~**lock** *n* impasse *f*.

deadly *adj* (**-ier, -iest**) mortel; (*weapon*) meurtrier.

deaf *adj* sourd. **deafen** *vt* assourdir. **deafness** *n* surdité *f*.

deal vt (pt **dealt**) donner; (blow) porter. ● vi (trade) être en activité; ~ **in** être dans le commerce de. ● n affaire f; (cards) donne f; **a great** or **good** ~ beaucoup (of de). □ ~ **with** (handle, manage) s'occuper de; (be about) traiter de. **dealer** n marchand/-e m/f; (agent) concessionnaire mf. **dealings** npl relations fpl.

dear adj cher; ~ **Sir/Madam** Monsieur/Madame. ● n (my) ~ mon chéri/ma chérie m/f. ● adv cher. ● interj oh ~! oh mon Dieu!

death n mort f; ~ **penalty** peine f de mort. **deathly** adj de mort, mortel.

debase vt avilir.

debatable adj discutable.

debate n (formal) débat m; (informal) discussion f. ● vt (formally) débattre de; (informally) discuter.

debit n débit m. ● adj (balance) débiteur. ● vt (pt **debited**) débiter.

debris n débris mpl; (rubbish) déchets mpl.

debt n dette f; **be in** ~ avoir des dettes.

debug vt (Comput) déboguer.

decade n décennie f.

decadent adj décadent.

decaffeinated adj décaféiné.

decay vi (vegetation) pourrir; (tooth) se carier; (fig) décliner. ● n pourriture f; (of tooth) carie f; (fig) déclin m.

deceased adj décédé. ● n défunt/-e m/f.

deceit n tromperie f. **deceitful** adj trompeur. **deceitfully** adv d'une manière trompeuse.

deceive vt tromper.

December n décembre m.

decent adj (respectable) comme il faut; (adequate) convenable; (good) bon; (kind) gentil; (not indecent) décent. **decently** adv convenablement.

deception n tromperie f. **deceptive** adj trompeur.

decide vt/i décider (**to do** de faire); (question) régler; ~ **on** se décider pour. **decided** adj (firm) résolu; (clear) net. **decidedly** adv nettement.

decimal adj décimal. ● n décimale f; ~ **point** virgule f.

decipher vt déchiffrer.

decision n décision f.

decisive adj (conclusive) décisif; (firm) décidé.

deck n pont m; (of cards: US) jeu m; (of bus) étage m. ~-**chair** n chaise f longue.

declaration n déclaration f. **declare** vt déclarer.

decline vt/i refuser; (fall) baisser. ● n (waning) déclin m; (drop) baisse f; **in** ~ sur le déclin.

decode vt décoder.

decompose vt/i (se) décomposer.

decor n décor m.

decorate vt décorer; (room) refaire, peindre. **decoration** n décoration f. **decorative** adj décoratif.

decorator n peintre m; (interior) ~ décorateur/-trice m/f.

decoy n (person, vehicle) leurre m; (for hunting) appeau m.

decrease¹ vt/i diminuer.

decrease² n diminution f.

decree n (Pol, Relig) décret m; (Jur) jugement m. ● vt (pt **decreed**) décréter.

decrepit adj (building) délabré; (person) décrépit.

dedicate vt dédier; ~ **oneself to** se consacrer à. **dedicated** adj dévoué; ~ **line** (Internet) ligne f spécialisée. **dedication** n dévouement m; (in book) dédicace f.

deduce vt déduire.

deduct vt déduire; (from wages) retenir.

deed n acte m.

deem vt considérer.

deep adj profond; (mud, carpet) épais. ● adv profondément; ~ **in thought** absorbé dans ses pensées. **deepen** vt/i (admiration, concern) augmenter; (colour) foncer.

deep-freeze n congélateur m. ● vt congeler.

deer n inv cerf m; (doe) biche f.

deface vt dégrader.

default vi (Jur) ~ (**on payments**) ne pas régler ses échéances. ● n (on payments) non-remboursement *m*; **by ~** par défaut; **win by ~** gagner par forfait. ● *adj* (Comput) par défaut.

defeat *vt* vaincre; (thwart) faire échouer. ● *n* défaite *f*; (of plan) échec *m*.

defect[1] *n* défaut *m*.

defect[2] *vi* faire défection; **~ to** passer à.

defective *adj* défectueux.

defector *n* transfuge *mf*.

defence *n* défense *f*.

defend *vt* défendre. **defendant** *n* (Jur) accusé/-e *m/f*. **defender** défenseur *m*.

defensive *adj* défensif. ● *n* défensive *f*.

defer *vt* (*pt* **deferred**) (postpone) reporter; (*judgement*) suspendre; (*payment*) différer.

deference *n* déférence *f*. **deferential** *adj* déférent.

defiance *n* défi *m*; **in ~ of** contre. **defiant** *adj* rebelle. **defiantly** *adv* avec défi.

deficiency *n* insuffisance *f*; (fault) défaut *m*.

deficient *adj* insuffisant; **be ~ in** manquer de.

deficit *n* déficit *m*.

define *vt* définir.

definite *adj* (exact) précis; (obvious) net; (firm) ferme; (certain) certain. **definitely** *adv* certainement; (clearly) nettement.

definition *n* définition *f*.

deflate *vt* dégonfler.

deflect *vt* (*missile*) dévier; (*criticism*) détourner.

deforestation *n* déforestation *f*.

deform *vt* déformer.

defraud *vt* (*client, employer*) escroquer; (*state, customs*) frauder; **~ sb of sth** escroquer qch à qn.

defrost *vt* dégivrer.

deft *adj* adroit.

defunct *adj* défunt.

defuse *vt* désamorcer.

defy *vt* défier; (*attempts*) résister à.

degenerate[1] *vi* dégénérer (**into** en).

degenerate[2] *a & n* dégénéré/-e (*m/f*).

degrade *vt* (humiliate) humilier; (damage) dégrader.

degree *n* degré *m*; (Univ) diplôme *m* universitaire; (Bachelor's degree) licence *f*; **to such a ~ that** à tel point que.

dehydrate *vt/i* (se) déshydrater.

deign *vt* **~ to do** daigner faire.

dejected *adj* découragé.

delay *vt* (*flight*) retarder; (*decision*) différer; **~ doing** attendre pour faire. ● *n* (of plane, post) retard *m*; (time lapse) délai *m*.

delegate[1] *n* délégué/-e *m/f*.

delegate[2] *vt* déléguer. **delegation** *n* délégation *f*.

delete *vt* supprimer; (Comput) effacer; (with pen) barrer. **deletion** *n* suppression *f*; (with line) rature *f*.

deliberate[1] *vi* délibérer.

deliberate[2] *adj* délibéré; (*steps, manner*) mesuré. **deliberately** *adv* (*do, say*) exprès; (*sarcastically, provocatively*) délibérément.

delicacy *n* délicatesse *f*; (food) mets *m* raffiné.

delicate *adj* délicat.

delicatessen *n* épicerie *f* fine.

delicious *adj* délicieux.

delight *n* joie *f*, plaisir *m*. ● *vt* ravir. ● *vi* **~ in** prendre plaisir à. **delighted** *adj* ravi. **delightful** *adj* charmant/-e.

delinquent *a & n* délinquant/-e (*m/f*).

delirious *adj* délirant.

deliver *vt* (*message*) remettre; (*goods*) livrer; (*speech*) faire; (*baby*) mettre au monde; (rescue) délivrer. **delivery** *n* (of goods) livraison *f*; (of mail) distribution *f*; (of baby) accouchement *m*.

delude *vt* tromper; **~ oneself** se faire des illusions.

deluge *n* déluge *m*. ● *vt* submerger (**with** de).

delusion *n* illusion *f*.

delve *vi* fouiller.

demand *vt* (request, require) demander; (forcefully) exiger. ● *n* (request) demande *f*; (pressure) exigence *f*; **in ~** très demandé; **on ~**

à la demande. **demanding** adj exigeant.

demean vt ~ oneself s'abaisser.

demeanour, (US) **demeanor** n comportement m.

demented adj fou.

demise n disparition f.

demo n (demonstration 🔲) manif f 🔲.

democracy n démocratie f.

democrat n démocrate mf. **democratic** adj démocratique.

demolish vt démolir.

demon n démon m.

demonstrate vt démontrer; (concern, skill) manifester. ● vi (Pol) manifester. **demonstration** n démonstration f; (Pol) manifestation f. **demonstrative** adj démonstratif. **demonstrator** n manifestant/-e m/f.

demoralize vt démoraliser.

demote vt rétrograder.

den n (of lion) antre m; (room) tanière f.

denial n (of rumour) démenti m; (of rights) négation f; (of request) rejet m.

denim n jean m; ~s (jeans) jean m.

Denmark n Danemark m.

denomination n (Relig) confession f; (money) valeur f.

denounce vt dénoncer.

dense adj dense. **densely** adv (packed) très. **density** n densité f.

dent n bosse f. ● vt cabosser.

dental adj dentaire; ~ floss fil m dentaire; ~ surgeon chirurgien-dentiste m.

dentist n dentiste mf. **dentistry** n médecine f dentaire.

dentures npl dentier m.

deny vt nier (that que); (rumour) démentir; ~ sb sth refuser qch à qn.

deodorant n déodorant m.

depart vi partir; ~ from (deviate) s'éloigner de.

department n (in shop) rayon m; (in hospital, office) service m; (Univ) département m; D~ of Health ministère m de la santé; ~ store grand magasin m.

departure n départ m; a ~ from (custom, truth) une entorse à.

depend vi dépendre (on de); ~ on (rely on) compter sur; it (all) ~s ça dépend; ~ing on the season suivant la saison. **dependable** adj (person) digne de confiance. **dependant** n personne f à charge. **dependence** n dépendance f.

dependent adj dépendant; be ~ on dépendre de.

depict vt (describe) dépeindre; (in picture) représenter.

deplete vt réduire.

deport vt expulser.

depose vt déposer.

deposit vt (pt **deposited**) déposer. ● n (in bank) dépôt m; (on house) versement m initial; (on holiday) acompte m; (against damage) caution f; (on bottle) consigne f; (of mineral) gisement m; ~ account compte m de dépôt. **depositor** n (Comm) déposant/-e m/f.

depot n dépôt m; (US) gare f.

depreciate vt/i (se) déprécier.

depress vt déprimer. **depressing** adj déprimant. **depression** n dépression f; (Econ) récession f.

deprivation n privation f.

deprive vt ~ of priver de. **deprived** adj démuni.

depth n profondeur f; (of knowledge, ignorance) étendue f; (of colour, emotion) intensité f.

deputize vi ~ for remplacer.

deputy n adjoint/-e m/f. ● adj adjoint; ~ chairman vice-président m.

derail vt faire dérailler. **derailment** n déraillement m.

deranged adj dérangé.

derelict adj abandonné.

deride vt ridiculiser. **derision** n moqueries fpl. **derisory** adj dérisoire.

derivative a & n dérivé (m).

derive vt ~ sth from tirer qch de. ● vi ~ from découler de.

derogatory adj (word) péjoratif; (remark) désobligeant.

descend vt/i descendre; be ~ed from descendre de. **descendant** n descendant/-e m/f. **descent** n descente f; (lineage) origine f.

describe vt décrire; ~ sb as sth qualifier qn de qch. **description** n description f. **descriptive** adj descriptif.

desert[1] n désert m.

desert[2] vt/i abandonner; (cause) déserter. **deserted** adj désert. **deserter** n déserteur m.

deserts npl get one's ~ avoir ce qu'on mérite.

deserve vt mériter (to de). **deservedly** adv à juste titre. **deserving** adj (person) méritant; (action) louable.

design n (sketch) plan m; (idea) conception f; (pattern) motif m; (art of designing) design m; (aim) dessein m. ● vt (sketch) dessiner; (devise, intend) concevoir.

designate vt désigner.

designer n concepteur/-trice m/f; (of fashion, furniture) créateur/-trice m/f. ● adj (clothes) de haute couture; (sunglasses, drink) de dernière mode.

desirable adj (outcome) souhaitable; (person) désirable.

desire n désir m. ● vt désirer.

desk n bureau m; (of pupil) pupitre m; (in hotel) réception f; (in bank) caisse f.

desolate adj (place) désolé; (person) affligé.

despair n désespoir m. ● vi désespérer (of de).

desperate adj désespéré; (criminal) prêt à tout; be ~ for avoir désespérément besoin de. **desperately** adv désespérément; (worried) terriblement; (ill) gravement.

desperation n désespoir m; in ~ en désespoir de cause.

despicable adj méprisable.

despise vt mépriser.

despite prep malgré.

despondent adj découragé.

dessert n dessert m. ~spoon n cuillère f à dessert.

destination n destination f.

destiny n destin m.

destitute adj sans ressources.

destroy vt détruire; (animal) abattre. **destroyer** n (warship) contre-torpilleur m.

destruction n destruction f.

destructive adj destructeur.

detach vt détacher; ~ed house maison f (individuelle).

detail n détail m; go into ~ entrer dans les détails. ● vt (plans) exposer en détail.

detain vt retenir; (in prison) placer en détention. **detainee** n détenu/-e m/f.

detect vt (error, trace) déceler; (crime, mine, sound) détecter. **detection** n détection f. **detective** n inspecteur/-trice m/f; (private) détective m.

detention n détention f; (School) retenue f.

deter vt (pt deterred) dissuader (from de).

detergent a & n détergent (m).

deteriorate vi se détériorer.

determine vt déterminer; ~ to do résoudre de faire. **determined** adj (person) décidé; (air) résolu.

deterrent n moyen m de dissuasion. ● adj (effect) dissuasif.

detest vt détester.

detonate vt/i (faire) détoner. **detonation** n détonation f. **detonator** n détonateur m.

detour n détour m.

detract vi ~ from (success, value) porter atteinte à; (pleasure) diminuer.

detriment n to the ~ of au détriment de. **detrimental** adj nuisible (to à).

devalue vt dévaluer.

devastate vt (place) ravager; (person) accabler.

develop vt (plan) élaborer; (mind, body) développer; (land) mettre en valeur; (illness) attraper; (habit) prendre. ● vi (child, country, plot, business) se développer; (hole, crack) se former.

development n développement m; (housing) ~ lotissement m; (new) ~ fait m nouveau.

deviate vi dévier; ~ from (norm) s'écarter de.

device n appareil m; (means) moyen m; (bomb) engin m explosif.

devil n diable m.

devious adj (person) retors.

devise vt (scheme) concevoir; (product) inventer.

devoid adj ∼ of dépourvu de.

devolution n (Pol) régionalisation f.

devote vt consacrer (**to** à). **devoted** adj dévoué. **devotion** n dévouement m; (Relig) dévotion f.

devour vt dévorer.

devout adj fervent.

dew n rosée f.

diabetes n diabète m.

diabolical adj diabolique; (bad 🔲) atroce.

diagnose vt diagnostiquer. **diagnosis** n (pl **-oses**) diagnostic m.

diagonal adj diagonal. ● n diagonale f.

diagram n schéma m.

dial n cadran m. ● vt (pt **dialled**) (number) faire; (person) appeler; **dialling code** indicatif m; **dialling tone** tonalité f.

dialect n dialecte m.

dialogue n dialogue m.

diameter n diamètre m.

diamond n diamant m; (shape) losange m; (baseball) terrain m; ∼s (cards) carreau m.

diaper n (US) couche f.

diaphragm n diaphragme m.

diarrhoea, (US) **diarrhea** n diarrhée f.

diary n (for appointments) agenda m; (journal) journal m intime.

dice n inv dé m. ● vt (food) couper en dés.

dictate vt/i dicter.

dictation n dictée f.

dictator n dictateur m. **dictatorship** n dictature f.

dictionary n dictionnaire m.

did ⇒DO.

didn't = DID NOT.

die vi (pres p **dying**) mourir; (plant) crever; **be dying to do** mourir d'envie de faire. □ ∼ **down** diminuer; ∼ **out** disparaître.

diesel n gazole m; ∼ **engine** moteur m diesel.

diet n (usual food) alimentation f; (restricted) régime m. ● vi être au régime. **dietary** adj alimentaire.

dietician n diététicien/-ne m/f.

differ vi différer (**from** de).

difference n différence f; (disagreement) différend m. **different** adj différent (**from, to** de).

differentiate vt différencier. ● vi faire la différence (**between** entre).

differently adv différemment (**from** de).

difficult adj difficile. **difficulty** n difficulté f.

diffuse¹ adj diffus.

diffuse² vt diffuser.

dig vt/i (pt **dug**; pres p **digging**) (excavate) creuser; (in garden) bêcher. ● n (poke) coup m de coude; (remark) pique f 🔲; (Archeol) fouilles fpl. □ ∼ **up** déterrer.

digest vt/i digérer. **digestible** adj digestible. **digestion** n digestion f.

digger n excavateur m.

digit n chiffre m.

digital adj (clock) à affichage numérique; (display, recording) numérique. ∼ **audio tape** n cassette f audionumérique.

dignified adj digne.

dignitary n dignitaire m.

dignity n dignité f.

digress vi faire une digression.

dilapidated adj délabré.

dilate vt/i (se) dilater.

dilemma n dilemme m.

diligent adj appliqué.

dilute vt diluer.

dim adj (**dimmer, dimmest**) (weak) faible; (dark) sombre; (indistinct) vague; 🔲 stupide. ● vt/i (pt **dimmed**) (light) baisser.

dime n (US) (pièce f de) dix cents.

dimension n dimension f.

diminish vt/i diminuer.

dimple n fossette f.

din n vacarme m.

dine vi dîner. **diner** n dîneur/-euse m/f; (Rail) wagon-restaurant m; (US) restaurant m à service rapide.

dinghy n dériveur m.

dingy adj (**-ier, -iest**) miteux, minable.

dining room *n* salle *f* à manger.

dinner *n* (evening meal) dîner *m*;
(lunch) déjeuner *m*; **have ~** dîner.
~-jacket *n* smoking *m*. **~ party** *n*
dîner *m*.

dinosaur *n* dinosaure *m*.

dip *vt/i* (*pt* **dipped**) plonger; **~ into**
(*book*) feuilleter; (*savings*) puiser
dans; **~ one's headlights** se mettre
en code. ● *n* (slope) déclivité *f*; (in sea)
bain *m* rapide.

diploma *n* diplôme *m* (**in** en).

diplomacy *n* diplomatie *f*.
diplomat *n* diplomate *mf*.
diplomatic *adj* (Pol) diplomatique;
(tactful) diplomate.

dire *adj* affreux; (*need, poverty*)
extrême.

direct *adj* direct. ● *adv* directement.
● *vt* diriger; (*letter, remark*)
adresser; (*a play*) mettre en scène; **~**
sb to indiquer à qn le chemin de;
(*order*) signifier à qn de.

direction *n* direction *f*; (Theat) mise
f en scène; **~s** indications *fpl*; **ask**
~s demander le chemin; **~s for use**
mode *m* d'emploi.

directly *adv* directement; (at once)
tout de suite. ● *conj* dès que.

director *n* directeur/-trice *m/f*;
(Theat) metteur *m* en scène.

directory *n* (phone book) annuaire *m*.
~ enquiries *npl* renseignements
mpl téléphoniques.

dirt *n* saleté *f*; (earth) terre *f*; **~ cheap**
⊠ très bon marché *inv*. **~-track** *n*
(Sport) cendrée *f*.

dirty *adj* (**-ier, -iest**) sale; (word)
grossier; **get ~** se salir. ● *vt/i* (se)
salir.

disability *n* handicap *m*.

disable *vt* rendre infirme.
disabled *adj* handicapé.

disadvantage *n* désavantage *m*.
disadvantaged *adj* défavorisé.

disagree *vi* ne pas être d'accord
(with avec); **~ with sb** (*food, climate*)
ne pas convenir à qn.
disagreement *n* désaccord *m*;
(quarrel) différend *m*.

disappear *vi* disparaître.
disappearance *n* disparition *f* (**of**
de).

disappoint *vt* décevoir.
disappointment *n* déception *f*.

disapproval *n* désapprobation *f* (**of**
de).

disapprove *vi* **~ (of)** désapprouver.

disarm *vt/i* désarmer.
disarmament *n* désarmement *m*.

disarray *n* désordre *m*.

disaster *n* désastre *m*. **disastrous**
adj désastreux.

disband *vi* disperser. ● *vt*
dissoudre.

disbelief *n* incrédulité *f*.

disc *n* disque *m*; (Comput) = DISK.

discard *vt* se débarrasser de;
(*beliefs*) abandonner.

discharge *vt* (unload) décharger;
(*liquid*) déverser; (*duty*) remplir;
(dismiss) renvoyer; (*prisoner*) libérer.
● *vi* (of pus) s'écouler.

disciple *n* disciple *m*.

disciplinary *adj* disciplinaire.

discipline *n* discipline *f*. ● *vt*
discipliner; (punish) punir.

disc jockey *n* disc-jockey *m*,
animateur *m*.

disclaimer *n* démenti *m*.

disclose *vt* révéler. **disclosure** *n*
révélation *f* (**of** de).

disco *n* (club ⊞) discothèque *f*; (event)
soirée *f* disco.

discolour *vt/i* (se) décolorer.

discomfort *n* gêne *f*.

disconcert *vt* déconcerter.

disconnect *vt* détacher; (unplug)
débrancher; (cut off) couper.

discontent *n* mécontentement *m*.

discontinue *vt* (*service*) supprimer;
(*production*) arrêter.

discord *n* discorde *f*; (Mus)
discordance *f*.

discount¹ *n* remise *f*; (on minor
purchase) rabais *m*.

discount² *vt* (*advice*) ne pas tenir
compte de; (*possibility*) écarter.

discourage *vt* décourager.

discourse *n* discours *m*.

discourteous *adj* peu courtois.

discover *vt* découvrir. **discovery**
n découverte *f*.

discreet *adj* discret.

discrepancy *n* divergence *f*.

discretion n discrétion f.

discriminate vt/i distinguer; ~ against faire de la discrimination contre. **discriminating** adj qui a du discernement. **discrimination** n discernement m; (bias) discrimination f.

discus n disque m.

discuss vt (talk about) discuter de; (in writing) examiner. **discussion** n discussion f.

disdain n dédain m.

disease n maladie f.

disembark vt/i débarquer.

disenchanted adj désabusé.

disentangle vt démêler.

disfigure vt défigurer.

disgrace n (shame) honte f; (disfavour) disgrâce f. ● vt déshonorer. **disgraced** adj (in disfavour) disgracié. **disgraceful** adj honteux.

disgruntled adj mécontent.

disguise vt déguiser. ● n déguisement m; in ~ déguisé.

disgust n dégoût m. ● vt dégoûter.

dish n plat m; the ~es (crockery) la vaisselle. ● vt ~ out ⊤ distribuer; ~ up servir.

dishcloth n lavette f; (for drying) torchon m.

dishearten vt décourager.

dishevelled adj échevelé.

dishonest adj malhonnête.

dishonour, (US) **dishonor** n déshonneur m.

dishwasher n lave-vaisselle m inv.

disillusion vt désabuser. **disillusionment** n désillusion f.

disincentive n be a ~ to décourager.

disinclined adj ~ to peu disposé à.

disinfect vt désinfecter. **disinfectant** n désinfectant m.

disintegrate vt/i (se) désintégrer.

disinterested adj désintéressé.

disjointed adj (talk) décousu.

disk n (US) = DISC; (Comput) disque m. ~ **drive** n drive m, lecteur m de disquettes.

diskette n disquette f.

dislike n aversion f. ● vt ne pas aimer.

dislocate vt (limb) disloquer.

dislodge vt (move) déplacer; (drive out) déloger.

disloyal adj déloyal (to envers).

dismal adj morne, triste.

dismantle vt démonter, défaire.

dismay n consternation f (at devant). ● vt consterner.

dismiss vt renvoyer; (appeal) rejeter; (from mind) écarter. **dismissal** n renvoi m.

dismount vi descendre, mettre pied à terre.

disobedient adj désobéissant.

disobey vt désobéir à. ● vi désobéir.

disorder n désordre m; (ailment) trouble(s) m(pl). **disorderly** adj désordonné.

disorganized adj désorganisé.

disown vt renier.

disparaging adj désobligeant.

dispassionate adj impartial; (unemotional) calme.

dispatch vt (send, complete) expédier; (troops) envoyer. ● n expédition f; envoi m; (report) dépêche f.

dispel vt (pt dispelled) dissiper.

dispensary n (in hospital) pharmacie f, (in chemist's) officine f.

dispense vt distribuer; (medicine) préparer. ● vi ~ with se passer de. **dispenser** n (container) distributeur m.

disperse vt/i (se) disperser.

display vt montrer, exposer; (feelings) manifester. ● n exposition f; manifestation f; (Comm) étalage m; (of computer) visuel m.

displeased adj mécontent (with de).

disposable a jetable.

disposal n (of waste) évacuation f; at sb's ~ à la disposition de qn.

dispose vt disposer. ● vi ~ of se débarrasser de; well ~d to bien disposé envers.

disposition n disposition f; (character) naturel m.

disprove vt réfuter.

dispute vt contester. ● n discussion f; (Pol) conflit m; in ~ contesté.

disqualify *vt* rendre inapte; (Sport) disqualifier; ∼ **from driving** retirer le permis à.

disquiet *n* inquiétude *f*. **disquieting** *adj* inquiétant.

disregard *vt* ne pas tenir compte de. ● *n* indifférence *f* (**for** à).

disrepair *n* délabrement *m*.

disreputable *adj* peu recommendable.

disrepute *n* discrédit *m*.

disrespect *n* manque *m* de respect. **disrespectful** *adj* irrespectueux.

disrupt *vt* (disturb, break up) perturber; (*plans*) déranger. **disruption** *n* perturbation *f*. **disruptive** *adj* perturbateur.

dissatisfied *adj* mécontent.

dissect *vt* disséquer.

disseminate *vt* diffuser.

dissent *vi* différer (**from** de). ● *n* dissentiment *m*.

dissertation *n* mémoire *m*.

disservice *n* **do a ∼ to sb** rendre un mauvais service à qn.

dissident *a & n* dissident/-e (*m/f*).

dissimilar *adj* dissemblable, différent.

dissipate *vt/i* (se) dissiper. **dissipated** *adj* (person) dissolu.

dissolve *vt/i* (se) dissoudre.

dissuade *vt* dissuader.

distance *n* distance *f*; **from a ∼** de loin; **in the ∼** au loin. **distant** *adj* éloigné, lointain; (*relative*) éloigné; (aloof) distant.

distaste *n* dégoût *m*. **distasteful** *adj* désagréable.

distil *vt* (*pt* **distilled**) distiller.

distinct *adj* distinct; (definite) net; **as ∼ from** par opposition à. **distinction** *n* distinction *f*; (in exam) mention *f* très bien. **distinctive** *adj* distinctif.

distinguish *vt/i* distinguer.

distort *vt* déformer. **distortion** *n* distorsion *f*; (of facts) déformation *f*.

distract *vt* distraire. **distracted** *adj* (distraught) éperdu. **distracting** *adj* gênant. **distraction** *n* (lack of attention, entertainment) distraction *f*.

distraught *adj* éperdu.

distress *n* douleur *f*; (poverty, danger) détresse *f*. ● *vt* peiner. **distressing** *adj* pénible.

distribute *vt* distribuer.

district *n* région *f*; (of town) quartier *m*.

distrust *n* méfiance *f*. ● *vt* se méfier de.

disturb *vt* déranger; (alarm, worry) troubler. **disturbance** *n* dérangement *m* (**of** de); (noise) tapage *m*. **disturbances** *npl* (Pol) troubles *mpl*. **disturbed** *adj* troublé; (psychologically) perturbé. **disturbing** *adj* troublant.

disused *adj* désaffecté.

ditch *n* fossé *m*. ● *vt* ✗ abandonner.

ditto *adv* idem.

dive *vi* plonger; (rush) se précipiter. ● *n* plongeon *m*; (of plane) piqué *m*; (place ✗) bouge *m*. **diver** *n* plongeur/-euse *m/f*.

diverge *vi* diverger. **divergent** *adj* divergent.

diverse *adj* divers.

diversion *n* détournement *m*; (distraction) diversion *f*; (of traffic) déviation *f*. **divert** *vt* détourner; (*traffic*) dévier.

divide *vt/i* (se) diviser.

dividend *n* dividende *m*.

divine *adj* divin.

diving: ∼**-board** *n* plongeoir *m*. ∼**-suit** *n* scaphandre *m*.

division *n* division *f*.

divorce *n* divorce *m* (**from** avec). ● *vt/i* divorcer (d'avec).

divulge *vt* divulguer.

DIY *abbr* ⇒DO-IT-YOURSELF.

dizziness *n* vertige *m*.

dizzy *adj* (**-ier**, **-iest**) vertigineux; **be** or **feel ∼** avoir le vertige.

....

do

> *present* **do**, **does**; *present negative* **don't**, **do not**; *past* **did**; *past participle* **done**

● *transitive and intransitive verb*

····▸ faire; **she is doing her homework** elle fait ses devoirs.

····➤ (progress, be suitable) aller; **how are you doing?** comment ça va?

····➤ (be enough) suffire; **will five dollars ~?** cinq dollars, ça suffira?

● *auxiliary verb*

····➤ (in questions) **~ you like Mozart?** aimes-tu Mozart?, est-ce que tu aimes Mozart?; **did your sister phone?** est-ce que ta sœur a téléphoné?, ta sœur a-t-elle téléphoné?

····➤ (in negatives) **I don't like Mozart** je n'aime pas Mozart.

····➤ (emphatic uses) **I ~ like your dress** j'aime beaucoup ta robe; **I ~ think you should go** je pense vraiment que tu devrais y aller.

····➤ (referring back to another verb) **I live in Oxford and so does Lily** j'habite à Oxford et Lily aussi; **she gets paid more than I ~** elle est payée plus que moi; **'I don't like carrots'—'neither ~ I'** 'je n'aime pas les carottes'—'moi non plus'.

····➤ (imperatives) **don't shut the door** ne ferme pas la porte; **~ be quiet** tais-toi!

····➤ (short questions and answers) **you like fish, don't you?** tu aimes le poisson, n'est-ce pas?; **Lola didn't phone, did she?** Lola n'a pas téléphoné par hasard?; **'does he play tennis?'—'no he doesn't/yes he does'** 'est-ce qu'il joue au tennis?'—'non/oui'; **'Marion didn't say that'—'yes she did'** 'Marion n'a pas dit ça'—'si'.

□ **do away with** supprimer; **do up** (fasten) fermer; (*house*) refaire;

do with it's to ~ with c'est à propos de; **it's nothing to ~ with** ça n'a rien à voir avec;

do without se passer de.

docile *adj* docile.

dock *n* (Jur) banc *m* des accusés; dock *m*. ● *vi* arriver au port. ● *vt* mettre à quai; (*wages*) faire une retenue sur.

doctor *n* médecin *m*, docteur *m*; (Univ) docteur *m*. ● *vt* (*cat*) châtrer; (fig) altérer.

doctorate *n* doctorat *m*.

document *n* document *m*. **documentary** *a* & *n* documentaire (*m*). **documentation** *n* documentation *f*.

dodge *vt* esquiver. ● *vi* faire un saut de côté. ● *n* mouvement *m* de côté.

dodgems *npl* autos *fpl* tamponneuses.

dodgy *adj* (**-ier, -iest**) (🇬🇧: difficult) épineux, délicat; (untrustworthy) louche 🇬🇧.

doe *n* (deer) biche *f*.

does ⇨DO.

doesn't = DOES NOT.

dog *n* chien *m*. ● *vt* (*pt* **dogged**) poursuivre. ~**-collar** *n* col *m* romain. ~**-eared** *adj* écorné.

dogged *adj* obstiné.

dogma *n* dogme *m*. **dogmatic** *adj* dogmatique.

dogsbody *n* bonne *f* à tout faire.

do-it-yourself *n* bricolage *m*.

doldrums *npl* **be in the ~** (person) avoir le cafard.

dole *vt* **~ out** distribuer. ● *n* 🇬🇧 indemnité *f* de chômage; **on the ~** 🇬🇧 au chômage.

doll *n* poupée *f*. ● *vt* **~ up** 🇬🇧 bichonner.

dollar *n* dollar *m*.

dollop *n* (of food 🇬🇧) gros morceau *m*.

dolphin *n* dauphin *m*.

domain *n* domaine *m*.

dome *n* dôme *m*.

domestic *adj* familial; (*trade, flights*) intérieur; (*animal*) domestique. **domesticated** *adj* (*animal*) domestiqué.

domesticity *n* vie *f* de famille.

domestic science *n* arts *mpl* ménagers.

dominant *adj* dominant.

dominate *vt/i* dominer. **domination** *n* domination *f*.

domineering *adj* dominateur.

domino *n* (*pl* ~**es**) domino *m*; ~**es** (game) dominos *mpl*.

donate *vt* faire don de. **donation** *n* don *m*.

done ⇨DO.

donkey *n* âne *m*. ~ **work** *n* travail *m* pénible.

donor *n* donateur/-trice *m/f*; (of blood) donneur/-euse *m/f*.

don't = DO NOT.

doodle *vi* griffonner.

doom *n* (ruin) ruine *f*; (fate) destin *m*. ●*vt* be ~ed to être destiné *or* condamné à; ~ed **(to failure)** voué à l'échec.

door *n* porte *f*; (of vehicle) portière *f*, porte *f*. ~**bell** *n* sonnette *f*. ~**man** *n* (*pl* -**men**) portier *m*. ~**mat** *n* paillasson *m*. ~**step** *n* pas *m* de (la) porte, seuil *m*. ~**way** *n* porte *f*.

dope *n* ⊡ cannabis *m*; (idiot ⊠) imbécile *mf*. ●*vt* doper. **dopey** *adj* (foolish ⊠) imbécile.

dormant *adj* en sommeil.

dormitory *n* dortoir *m*; (Univ, US) résidence *f*.

dosage *n* dose *f*; (on label) posologie *f*.

dose *n* dose *f*.

doss *vi* ⊠ roupiller.

dot *n* point *m*; on the ~ ⊡ à l'heure pile. ~**com** *n* société *f* en ligne *or* point com.

dote *vi* ~ on adorer.

dotted *adj* (*fabric*) à pois; ~ **line** pointillé *m*; ~ **with** parsemé de.

double *adj* double; (*room*, *bed*) pour deux personnes; ~ **the size** deux fois plus grand. ●*adv* deux fois; **pay** ~ payer le double. ●*n* double *m*; (stuntman) doublure *f*; ~**s** (tennis) double *m*; **at** *or* **on the** ~ au pas de course. ●*vt/i* doubler; (fold) plier en deux. ~**-bass** *n* (Mus) contrebasse *f*. ~**-check** *vt* revérifier. ~ **chin** *n* double menton *m*. ~**-cross** *vt* tromper. ~**-decker** *n* autobus *m* à impériale. ~ **Dutch** *n* de l'hébreu *m*.

doubt *n* doute *m*. ●*vt* douter de; ~ **if** *or* **that** douter que. **doubtful** *adj* incertain, douteux; (*person*) qui a des doutes. **doubtless** *adv* sans doute.

dough *n* pâte *f*; (money ⊠) fric *m* ⊡.

doughnut *n* beignet *m*.

douse *vt* arroser; (*light, fire*) éteindre.

dove *n* colombe *f*.

Dover *n* Douvres.

dowdy *adj* (-**ier**, -**iest**) (*clothes*) sans chic, monotone; (*person*) sans élégance.

down *adv* en bas; (of sun) couché; (lower) plus bas; **come** *or* **go** ~ descendre; **go** ~ **to the post office** aller à la poste; ~ **under** aux antipodes; ~ **with à bas.** ●*prep* en bas de; (along) le long de. ●*vt* (knock down, shoot down) abattre; (drink) vider. ●*n* (fluff) duvet *m*.

down: ~**-and-out** *n* clochard/-e *m/f*. ~**cast** *adj* démoralisé. ~**fall** *n* chute *f*. ~**grade** *vt* déclasser. ~**-hearted** *adj* découragé.

downhill *adv* go ~ descendre; (pej) baisser.

down: ~**load** *n* (Comput) télécharger. ~**-market** *adj* bas de gamme. ~ **payment** *n* acompte *m*. ~**pour** *n* grosse averse *f*.

downright *adj* (utter) véritable; (honest) franc. ●*adv* carrément.

downstairs *adv* en bas. ●*adj* d'en bas.

down: ~**stream** *adv* en aval. ~**-to-earth** *adj* pratique.

downtown *adj* (US) du centre-ville; ~ **Boston** le centre de Boston.

downtrodden *adj* tyrannisé.

downward *a* & *adv*, **downwards** *adv* vers le bas.

doze *vi* somnoler; ~ **off** s'assoupir. ●*n* somme *m*.

dozen *n* douzaine *f*; **a** ~ **eggs** une douzaine d'œufs; ~**s of** ⊡ des dizaines de.

Dr *abbr* (**Doctor**) Docteur.

drab *adj* terne.

draft *n* (outline) brouillon *m*; (Comm) traite *f*; **the** ~ (Mil, US) la conscription; **a** ~ **treaty** un projet de traité; (US) = DRAUGHT. ●*vt* faire le brouillon de; (draw up) rédiger.

drag *vt/i* (*pt* **dragged**) traîner; (*river*) draguer; (pull away) arracher; ~ **on** s'éterniser. ●*n* (task ⊡) corvée *f*; (person ⊡) raseur/-euse *m/f*; **in** ~ en travesti.

dragon *n* dragon *m*.

drain *vt* (*land*) drainer; (*vegetables*) égoutter; (*tank, glass*) vider; (use up) épuiser; ~ **(off)** (*liquid*) faire écouler. ●*vi* ~ **(off)** (of liquid) s'écouler. ● *n* (sewer) égout *m*; ~(-pipe) tuyau *m* d'écoulement; a ~ on une ponction sur. **draining-board** *n* égouttoir *m*.

drama *n* art *m* dramatique, théâtre *m*; (play, event) drame *m*. **dramatic** *adj* (situation) dramatique; (increase) spectaculaire. **dramatist** *n* dramaturge *m*. **dramatize** *vt* adapter pour la scène; (fig) dramatiser.

drank ⇒DRINK.

drape *vt* draper. **drapes** *npl* (US) rideaux *mpl*.

drastic *adj* sévère.

draught *n* courant *m* d'air; ~s (game) dames *fpl*. ~ **beer** *n* bière *f* pression.

draughty *adj* plein de courants d'air.

draw *vt* (*pt* drew; *pp* drawn) (picture) dessiner; (line) tracer; (pull) tirer; (attract) attirer. ● *vi* dessiner; (Sport) faire match nul; (come, move) venir. ● *n* (Sport) match *m* nul; (in lottery) tirage *m* au sort. □ ~ **back** reculer; ~ **near** (s')approcher (to de); ~ **out** (money) retirer; ~ **up** *vi* (stop) s'arrêter; *vt* (document) dresser; (chair) approcher.

drawback *n* inconvénient *m*.

drawbridge *n* pont-levis *m*.

drawer *n* tiroir *m*.

drawing *n* dessin *m*. ~-**board** *n* planche *f* à dessin. ~-**pin** *n* punaise *f*. ~-**room** *n* salon *m*.

drawl *n* voix *f* traînante.

drawn ⇒DRAW. ● *adj* (features) tiré; (match) nul.

dread *n* terreur *f*, crainte *f*. ● *vt* redouter. **dreadful** *adj* épouvantable, affreux. **dreadfully** *adv* terriblement.

dream *n* rêve *m*. ● *vt/i* (*pt* dreamed *or* dreamt) rêver; ~ **up** imaginer. ● *adj* (ideal) de ses rêves.

dreary *adj* (-ier, -iest) triste; (boring) monotone.

dredge *vt* (river) draguer; ~ sth up (fig) exhumer.

dregs *npl* lie *f*.

drench *vt* tremper.

dress *n* robe *f*; (clothing) tenue *f*. ● *vt/i* (s')habiller; (food) assaisonner;

(wound) panser; ~ up as se déguiser en; get ~ed s'habiller. ~ **circle** *n* premier balcon *m*.

dresser *n* (furniture) buffet *m*; be a stylish ~ s'habiller avec chic.

dressing *n* (sauce) assaisonnement *m*; (bandage) pansement *m*. ~-**gown** *n* robe *f* de chambre. ~-**room** *n* (Sport) vestiaire *m*; (Theat) loge *f*. ~-**table** *n* coiffeuse *f*.

dressmaker *n* couturière *f*. **dressmaking** *n* couture *f*.

dress rehearsal *n* répétition *f* générale.

dressy *adj* (-ier, -iest) chic *inv*.

drew ⇒DRAW.

dribble *vi* (liquid) dégouliner; (person) baver; (football) dribbler.

dried *adj* (fruit) sec.

drier *n* séchoir *m*.

drift *vi* aller à la dérive; (pile up) s'amonceler; ~ **towards** glisser vers. ● *n* dérive *f*; amoncellement *m*; (of events) tournure *f*; (meaning) sens *m*; snow ~ congère *f*. **driftwood** *n* bois *m* flotté.

drill *n* (tool) perceuse *f*; (for teeth) roulette *f*; (training) exercice *m*; (procedure ⊞) marche *f* à suivre; (pneumatic) ~ marteau *m* piqueur. ● *vt* percer; (train) entraîner. ● *vi* être à l'exercice.

drink *vt/i* (*pt* drank; *pp* drunk) boire. ● *n* (liquid) boisson *f*; (glass of alcohol) verre *m*; a ~ of water un verre d'eau. **drinking water** *n* eau *f* potable.

drip *vi* (*pt* dripped) (é)goutter; (washing) s'égoutter. ● *n* goutte *f*; (person ⊠) lavette *f*.

drip-dry *vt* laisser égoutter. ● *adj* sans essorage.

drive *vt* (*pt* drove; *pp* driven) (vehicle) conduire; (sb somewhere) chasser, pousser; (machine) actionner; ~ mad rendre fou. ● *vi* conduire. ● *n* promenade *f* en voiture; (private road) allée *f*; (fig) énergie *f*; (Psych) instinct *m*; (Pol) campagne *f*; (Auto) traction *f*; (golf, Comput) drive *m*; **it's a two-hour** ~ il y a deux heures de route; **left-hand** ~ conduite *f* à gauche. □ ~ **at** en venir à.

drivel n bêtises fpl.

driver n conducteur/-trice m/f, chauffeur m. ~'s **license** n (US) permis m de conduire.

driving n conduite f; take one's ~ **test** passer son permis. ● adj (rain) battant; (wind) cinglant. ~ **licence** n permis m de conduire. ~ **school** n auto-école f.

drizzle n bruine f. ● vi bruiner.

drone n (of engine) ronronnement m; (of insects) bourdonnement m. ● vi ronronner; bourdonner.

drool vi baver (over sur).

droop vi pencher, tomber.

drop n goutte f; (fall, lowering) chute f. ● vt/i (pt **dropped**) (laisser) tomber; (decrease, lower) baisser; ~ (**off**) (person from car) déposer; ~ **a line** écrire un mot (to à). □ ~ **in** passer (on chez); ~ **off** (doze) s'assoupir; ~ **out** se retirer (of de); (of student) abandonner.

drop-out n marginal/-e m/f, raté/-e m/f.

droppings npl crottes fpl.

drought n sécheresse f.

drove ⇒DRIVE.

droves npl foules fpl.

drown vt/i (se) noyer.

drowsy adj somnolent; be or feel ~ avoir envie de dormir.

drug n drogue f; (Med) médicament m. ● vt (pt **drugged**) droguer. ~ **addict** n drogué/-e m/f. **drugstore** n (US) drugstore m.

drum n tambour m; (for oil) bidon m; ~s batterie f. ● vt/i (pt **drummed**) tambouriner. ● vt ~ **into sb** répéter sans cesse à qn; ~ **up** (support) susciter; (business) créer. **drummer** n tambour m; (in pop group) batteur m.

drumstick n baguette f de tambour; (of chicken) pilon m.

drunk ⇒DRINK. ● adj ivre; get ~ s'enivrer. ● n ivrogne/-esse m/f. **drunkard** n ivrogne/-esse m/f. **drunken** adj ivre; (habitually) ivrogne. **drunkenness** n ivresse f.

dry adj (**drier**, **driest**) sec; (day) sans pluie; be or feel ~ avoir soif. ● vt/i (faire) sécher; ~ **up** (dry dishes) essuyer la vaisselle; (of supplies) (se)

tarir; (be silent 🆘) se taire. ~**-clean** vt nettoyer à sec. ~**-cleaner** n teinturier m. ~ **run** n galop m d'essai.

dual adj double. ~ **carriageway** n route f à quatre voies. ~**-purpose** adj qui fait double emploi.

dub vt (pt **dubbed**) (film) doubler (**into** en); (nickname) surnommer.

dubious adj (pej) douteux; be ~ **about sth** (person) avoir des doutes sur qch.

duck n canard m. ● vi se baisser subitement. ● vt (head) baisser; (person) plonger dans l'eau.

duct n conduit m.

dud adj (tool 🆘) mal fichu; (coin 🆘) faux; (cheque 🆘) sans provision. ● n be a ~ (not work 🆘) ne pas marcher.

due adj (owing) dû; (expected) attendu; (proper) qui convient; ~ **to** à cause de; (caused by) dû à; she's ~ **to leave** now il est prévu qu'elle parte maintenant; in ~ **course** (at the right time) en temps voulu; (later) plus tard. ● adv ~ **east** droit vers l'est. ● n dû m; ~s droits mpl; (of club) cotisation f.

duel n duel m.

duet n duo m.

dug ⇒DIG.

duke n duc m.

dull adj ennuyeux; (colour) terne; (weather) maussade; (sound) sourd. ● vt (pain) atténuer; (shine) ternir.

duly adv comme il convient; (as expected) comme prévu.

dumb adj muet; (stupid 🆘) bête.

dumbfound vt sidérer, ahurir.

dummy n (of tailor) mannequin m; (of baby) sucette f. ● adj factice. ~ **run** n galop m d'essai.

dump vt déposer; (get rid of 🆘) se débarrasser de. ● n tas m d'ordures; (refuse tip) décharge f; (Mil) dépôt m; (dull place 🆘) trou m 🆘; be in the ~s 🆘 avoir le cafard.

dune n dune f.

dung n (excrement) bouse f, crotte f; (manure) fumier m.

dungarees npl salopette f.

dungeon n cachot m.

duplicate¹ *n* double *m*. ● *adj* identique.

duplicate² *vt* faire un double de; (on machine) polycopier.

durable *adj* (tough) résistant; (enduring) durable.

duration *n* durée *f*.

during *prep* pendant.

dusk *n* crépuscule *m*.

dusky *adj* (**-ier, -iest**) foncé.

dust *n* poussière *f*. ● *vt/i* épousseter; (sprinkle) saupoudrer (**with** de). **~bin** *n* poubelle *f*.

duster *n* chiffon *m*.

dust: **~man** *n* (*pl* **-men**) éboueur *m*. **~pan** *n* pelle *f* (à poussière).

dusty *adj* (**-ier, -iest**) poussiéreux.

Dutch *adj* néerlandais; **go ~** partager les frais. ● *n* (Ling) néerlandais *m*. **~man** *n* Néerlandais *m*. **~woman** *n* Néerlandaise *f*.

dutiful *adj* obéissant.

duty *n* devoir *m*; (tax) droit *m*; (of official) fonction *f*; **on ~** de service. **~-free** *adj* hors-taxe.

duvet *n* couette *f*.

dwarf *n* nain/-e *m/f*. ● *vt* rapetisser.

dwell *vi* (*pt* **dwelt**) demeurer; **~ on** s'étendre sur. **dweller** *n* habitant/-e *m/f*. **dwelling** *n* habitation *f*.

dwindle *vi* diminuer.

dye *vt* teindre. ● *n* teinture *f*.

dying *adj* mourant; (*art*) qui se perd.

dynamic *adj* dynamique.

dynamite *n* dynamite *f*.

dysentery *n* dysenterie *f*.

dyslexia *n* dyslexie *f*. **dyslexic** *a* & *n* dyslexique (*mf*).

Ee

each *det* chaque *inv*; **~ one** chacun/-e *m/f*. ● *pron* chacun/-e *m/f*; **oranges at 30p ~** des oranges à 30 pence pièce.

each other *pron* l'un/l'une l'autre, les uns/les unes les autres; **know ~** se connaître; **love ~** s'aimer.

eager *adj* impatient (**to** de); (*person, acceptance*) enthousiaste; **~ for** avide de.

eagle *n* aigle *m*.

ear *n* oreille *f*; (of corn) épi *m*. **~ache** *n* mal *m* à l'oreille. **~-drum** *n* tympan *m*.

earl *n* comte *m*.

early (**-ier, -iest**) *adv* tôt, de bonne heure; (ahead of time) en avance; **as I said earlier** comme je l'ai déjà dit. ● *adj* (*attempt, years*) premier; (*hour*) matinal; (*fruit*) précoce; (*retirement*) anticipé; **have an ~ dinner** dîner tôt; **in ~ summer** au début de l'été; **at the earliest** au plus tôt.

earmark *vt* désigner (**for** pour).

earn *vt* gagner; (interest: Comm) rapporter.

earnest *adj* sérieux; **in ~** sérieusement.

earnings *npl* salaire *m*; (profits) gains *mpl*.

ear: **~phones** *npl* casque *m*. **~-ring** *n* boucle *f* d'oreille. **~shot** *n* **within/ in ~shot** à portée de voix.

earth *n* terre *f*; **why/how/where on ~...?** pourquoi/comment/où diable...? ● *vt* (Electr) mettre à la terre. **earthenware** *n* faïence *f*. **~quake** *n* tremblement *m* de terre.

ease *n* facilité *f*; (comfort) bien-être *m*; **at ~** à l'aise; (Mil) au repos; **with ~** facilement. ● *vt* (*pain, pressure*) atténuer; (*congestion*) réduire; (*transition*) faciliter. ● *vi* (*pain, pressure*) s'atténuer; (*congestion, rain*) diminuer.

easel *n* chevalet *m*.

east *n* est *m*; **the E~** (Orient) l'Orient *m*. ● *adj* (*side, coast*) est; (*wind*) d'est. ● *adv* à l'est.

Easter *n* Pâques *m*; **~ egg** œuf *m* de Pâques.

easterly *adj* (*wind*) d'est; (*direction*) de l'est.

eastern de l'est; **~ France** l'est de la France.

eastward *adj* (*side*) est *inv*; (*journey*) vers l'est.

easy *adj* (**-ier, -iest**) facile; go ~ with 🔲 y aller doucement avec; take it ~ ne te fatigue pas. ~**going** *adj* accommodant.

eat *vt/i* (*pt* **ate**; *pp* **eaten**) manger; ~ **into** ronger.

eavesdrop *vi* (*pt* **-dropped**) écouter aux portes.

ebb *n* reflux *m*. ● *vi* descendre; (fig) décliner.

ebony *n* ébène *f*.

EC *abbr* (**European Community**) CE *f*.

eccentric *a & n* excentrique (*mf*).

echo *n* (*pl* **-oes**) écho *m*. ● *vt* répercuter; (*idea, opinion*) reprendre. ● *vi* retentir, résonner (**to, with** de).

eclipse *n* éclipse *f*. ● *vt* éclipser.

ecological *adj* écologique.

ecology *n* écologie *f*.

economic *adj* économique; (*profitable*) rentable. **economical** *adj* économique; (*person*) économe. **economics** *n* économie *f*, sciences *fpl* économiques. **economist** *n* économiste *mf*.

economize *vi* ~ (**on**) économiser.

economy *n* économie *f*.

ecosystem *n* écosystème *m*.

ecstasy *n* extase *f*; (*drug*) ecstasy *m*.

ECU *n* écu *m*.

eczema *n* eczéma *m*.

edge *n* bord *m*; (*of town*) abords *mpl*; (*of knife*) tranchant *m*; have the ~ on 🔲 l'emporter sur; on ~ énervé. ● *vt* (*trim*) border. ● *vi* ~ **forward** avancer doucement.

edgeways *adv* I can't get a word in ~ je n'arrive pas à placer un mot.

edgy *adj* énervé.

edible *adj* comestible; (*pleasant*) mangeable.

edit *vt* (*pt* **edited**) (*newspaper, page*) être le rédacteur/la rédactrice de; (*check*) réviser; (*cut*) couper; (TV, cinema) monter.

edition *n* édition *f*.

editor *n* (*writer*) rédacteur/-trice *m/f*; (*of works, anthology*) éditeur/-trice *m/f*; (TV, cinema) monteur/-teuse *m/f*; the ~ (**in chief**) le rédacteur en chef.

editorial *adj* de la rédaction. ● *n* éditorial *m*.

educate *vt* instruire; (*mind, public*) éduquer. **educated** *adj* instruit. **education** *n* éducation *f*; (*schooling*) études *fpl*. **educational** *adj* éducatif; (*establishment, method*) d'enseignement.

eel *n* anguille *f*.

eerie *adj* (**-ier, -iest**) sinistre.

effect *n* effet *m*; come into ~ entrer en vigueur; in ~ effectivement; take ~ agir. ● *vt* effectuer.

effective *adj* efficace; (*actual*) effectif. **effectively** *adv* efficacement; (*in effect*) en réalité. **effectiveness** *n* efficacité *f*.

effeminate *adj* efféminé.

effervescent *adj* effervescent.

efficiency *n* efficacité *f*; (*of machine*) rendement *m*. **efficient** *adj* efficace. **efficiently** *adv* efficacement.

effort *n* efforts *mpl*; make an ~ faire un effort; be worth the ~ en valoir la peine. **effortless** *adj* facile.

effusive *adj* expansif.

e.g. *abbr* par ex.

egg *n* œuf *m*. ● *vt* ~ **on** pousser. ~**-cup** *n* coquetier *m*. ~**-plant** *n* (US) aubergine *f*. ~**shell** *n* coquille *f* d'œuf.

ego *n* amour-propre *m*; (Psych) moi *m*. **egotism** *n* égotisme *m*. **egotist** *n* égotiste *mf*.

Egypt *n* Égypte *f*.

eiderdown *n* édredon *m*.

eight *a & n* huit (*m*). **eighteen** *a & n* dix-huit (*m*). **eighth** *a & n* huitième (*mf*). **eighty** *a & n* quatre-vingts (*m*).

either *det & pron* l'un/une ou l'autre; (*with negative*) ni l'un/une ni l'autre; you can take ~ tu peux prendre n'importe lequel/laquelle. ● *adv* non plus. ● *conj* ~...**or** ou (bien)...ou (bien); (*with negative*) ni...ni.

eject *vt* (*troublemaker*) expulser; (*waste*) rejeter.

elaborate[1] *adj* compliqué.

elaborate[2] *vt* élaborer. ● *vi* préciser; ~ **on** s'étendre sur.

elastic *a & n* élastique (*m*); ~ **band** élastique *m*. **elasticity** *n* élasticité *f*.

elated *adj* transporté de joie.

elbow *n* coude *m*; ~ **room** espace *m* vital.

elder *a* & *n* aîné/-e (*m/f*); (tree) sureau *m*.

elderly *adj* âgé; **the** ~ les personnes *fpl* âgées.

eldest *a* & *n* aîné/-e (*m/f*).

elect *vt* élire; ~ **to do** choisir de faire. ● *adj* (president etc.) futur. **election** *n* élection *f*. **elector** *n* électeur/-trice *m/f*. **electoral** *adj* électoral. **electorate** *n* électorat *m*.

electric *adj* électrique; ~ **blanket** couverture *f* chauffante. **electrical** *adj* électrique. **electrician** *n* électricien/-ne *m/f*. **electricity** *n* électricité *f*. **electrify** *vt* électrifier; (excite) électriser. **electrocute** *vt* électrocuter.

electronic *adj* électronique. ~ **publishing** *n* éditique *f*. **electronics** *n* électronique *f*.

elegance *n* élégance *f*.

element *n* élément *m*; (of heater etc.) résistance *f*. **elementary** *adj* élémentaire.

elephant *n* éléphant *m*.

elevate *vt* élever. **elevation** *n* élévation *f*. **elevator** *n* (US) ascenseur *m*.

eleven *a* & *n* onze (*m*). **eleventh** *a* & *n* onzième (*mf*).

elicit *vt* obtenir (**from** de).

eligible *adj* admissible (**for** à); **be** ~ **for** (entitled to) avoir droit à.

eliminate *vt* éliminer.

elm *n* orme *m*.

elongate *vt* allonger.

elope *vi* s'enfuir (**with** avec). **elopement** *n* fugue *f* (amoureuse).

eloquence *n* éloquence *f*.

else *adv* d'autre; **somebody/nothing** ~ quelqu'un/rien d'autre; **everybody** ~ tous les autres; **somewhere/something** ~ autre part/chose; **or** ~ ou bien. **elsewhere** *adv* ailleurs.

elude *vt* échapper à.

elusive *adj* insaisissable.

emaciated *adj* émacié.

e-mail *n* e-mail *m*, mél *m*.

emancipate *vt* émanciper.

embankment *n* (of river) quai *m*; (of railway) remblai *m*.

embark *vt* embarquer. ● *vi* (Naut) embarquer; ~ **on** (*journey*) entreprendre; (*campaign, career*) se lancer dans.

embarrass *vt* plonger dans l'embarras; **be/feel** ~**ed** être/se sentir gêné. **embarrassment** *n* confusion *f*, gêne *f*.

embassy *n* ambassade *f*.

embed *vt* (*pt* **embedded**) enfoncer (**in** dans).

embellish *vt* embellir.

embers *npl* braises *fpl*.

embezzle *vt* détourner (**from** de). **embezzlement** *n* détournement *m* de fonds. **embezzler** *n* escroc *m*.

embitter *vt* aigrir; **become** ~**ed** s'aigrir.

emblem *n* emblème *m*.

embodiment *n* incarnation *f*. **embody** *vt* incarner; (legally) incorporer.

emboss *vt* (metal) repousser; (paper) gaufrer.

embrace *vt* (*person*) étreindre; (*religion*) embrasser; (include) comprendre. ● *n* étreinte *f*.

embroider *vt* broder. **embroidery** *n* broderie *f*.

embryo *n* embryon *m*.

emerald *n* émeraude *f*.

emerge *vi* (*person*) sortir (**from** de); **it** ~**d that** il est apparu que. **emergence** *n* apparition *f*.

emergency *n* (crisis) crise *f*; (urgent case: Med) urgence *f*; **in an** ~ en cas d'urgence. ● *adj* d'urgence; ~ **exit** sortie *f* de secours; ~ **landing** atterrissage *m* forcé.

emigrant *n* émigrant/-e *m/f*. **emigrate** *vi* émigrer.

eminence *n* éminence *f*. **eminent** *adj* éminent.

emission *n* émission *f*.

emit *vt* (*pt* **emitted**) émettre.

emotion *n* émotion *f*. **emotional** *adj* (*development*) émotif; (*reaction*) émotionel; (*film, scene*) émouvant.

emotive *adj* qui soulève les passions.

emperor *n* empereur *m*.

emphasis *n* accent *m*; **lay ~ on** mettre l'accent sur. **emphasize** *vt* mettre l'accent sur. **emphatic** *adj* catégorique; (*manner*) énergique.

empire *n* empire *m*.

employ *vt* employer. **employee** *n* employé/-e *m/f*. **employer** *n* employeur/-euse *m/f*.

employment *n* emploi *m*; **find ~** trouver du travail.

empower *vt* autoriser (**to do** à faire).

empty *adj* (**-ier, -iest**) vide; (*street*) désert; (*promise*) vain; **on an ~ stomach** à jeun. ● *vt/i* (se) vider. **~-handed** *adj* les mains vides.

emulate *vt* imiter.

enable *vt* **~ sb to** permettre à qn de.

enamel *n* émail *m*. ● *vt* (*pt* **enamelled**) émailler.

encampment *n* campement *m*.

encase *vt* revêtir, recouvrir (**in** de).

enchant *vt* enchanter.

enclose *vt* entourer; (*land*) clôturer; (*with letter*) joindre. **enclosed** *adj* (*space*) clos; (*with letter*) ci-joint. **enclosure** *n* enceinte *f*; (*with letter*) pièce *f* jointe.

encompass *vt* inclure.

encore *interj* & *n* bis (*m*).

encounter *vt* rencontrer. ● *n* rencontre *f*.

encourage *vt* encourager.

encroach *vi* **~ upon** empiéter sur.

encyclopaedia *n* encyclopédie *f*. **encyclopaedic** *adj* encyclopédique.

end *n* fin *f*; (*farthest part*) bout *m*; **come to an ~** prendre fin; **~-product** produit *m* fini; **in the ~** finalement; **no ~ of** Ⓘ énormément de; **on ~** (*upright*) debout; (*in a row*) de suite; **put an ~ to** mettre fin à. ● *vt* (*marriage*) mettre fin à; **~ one's days** finir ses jours. ● *vi* se terminer; **~ up doing** finir par faire.

endanger *vt* mettre en danger.

endearing *adj* attachant.

endeavour, (US) **endeavor** *n* (*attempt*) tentative *f*; (*hard work*) effort *m*. ● *vi* faire tout son possible (**to do** pour faire).

ending *n* fin *f*.

endive *n* chicorée *f*.

endless *adj* interminable; (*supply*) inépuisable; (*patience*) infini.

endorse *vt* (*candidate, decision*) appuyer; (*product, claim*) approuver; (*cheque*) endosser.

endurance *n* endurance *f*.

endure *vt* supporter. ● *vi* durer. **enduring** *adj* durable.

enemy *n* & *a* ennemi/-e (*m/f*).

energetic *adj* énergique. **energy** *n* énergie *f*.

enforce *vt* (*rule, law*) appliquer, faire respecter; (*silence, discipline*) imposer (**on** à); **~d** forcé.

engage *vt* (*staff*) engager; (*attention*) retenir; **be ~d in** se livrer à. ● *vi* **~ in** se livrer à. **engaged** *adj* fiancé; (*busy*) occupé; **get ~d** se fiancer. **engagement** *n* fiançailles *fpl*; (*meeting*) rendez-vous *m*; (*undertaking*) engagement *m*.

engaging *adj* attachant, engageant.

engine *n* moteur *m*; (*of train*) locomotive *f*; (*of ship*) machines *fpl*. **~-driver** *n* mécanicien *m*.

engineer *n* ingénieur *m*; (*repairman*) technicien *m*; (*on ship*) mécanicien *m*. ● *vt* (*contrive*) manigancer.

engineering *n* ingénierie *f*; (*industry*) mécanique *f*; **civil ~** génie *m* civil.

England *n* Angleterre *f*.

English *adj* anglais. ● *n* (Ling) anglais *m*; **the ~** les Anglais *mpl*. **~man** *n* Anglais *m*. **~-speaking** *adj* anglophone. **~woman** *n* Anglaise *f*.

engrave *vt* graver.

engrossed *adj* absorbé (**in** dans).

engulf *vt* engouffrer.

enhance *vt* (*prospects, status*) améliorer; (*price, value*) augmenter.

enjoy *vt* aimer (**doing** faire); (*benefit from*) jouir de; **~ oneself** s'amuser; **~ your meal!** bon appétit! **enjoyable** *adj* agréable. **enjoyment** *n* plaisir *m*.

enlarge *vt* agrandir. ● *vi* s'agrandir; (*pupil*) se dilater; **~ on** s'étendre sur. **enlargement** *n* agrandissement *m*.

enlighten *vt* éclairer (**on** sur).
enlightenment *n* instruction *f*;
(information) éclaircissement *m*.

enlist *vt* (*person*) recruter; (fig)
obtenir. ● *vi* s'engager.

enmity *n* inimitié *f*.

enormous *adj* énorme.
enormously *adv* énormément.

enough *adv & n* assez; **have** ∼ **of** en
avoir assez de. ● *det* assez de; ∼
glasses/time assez de verres/de
temps.

enquire ⇒INQUIRE. **enquiry**
⇒INQUIRY.

enrage *vt* mettre en rage, rendre
furieux.

enrol *vt/i* (*pt* **enrolled**) (s')inscrire.
enrolment *n* inscription *f*.

ensure *vt* garantir; ∼ **that** (ascertain)
s'assurer que.

entail *vt* entraîner.

entangle *vt* emmêler.

enter *vt* (*room, club, phase*) entrer
dans; (note down, register) inscrire;
(data) entrer, saisir. ● *vi* entrer (**into**
dans); ∼ **for** s'inscrire à.

enterprise *n* entreprise *f*; (boldness)
initiative *f*. **enterprising** *adj*
entreprenant.

entertain *vt* amuser, divertir;
(guests) recevoir; (ideas) considérer.
entertainer *n* artiste *mf*.
entertaining *adj* divertissant.
entertainment *n* divertissement
m; (performance) spectacle *m*.

enthral *vt* (*pt* **enthralled**) captiver.

enthusiasm *n* enthousiasme *m* (**for**
pour).

enthusiast *n* passionné/-e *m/f* (**for**
de). **enthusiastic** *adj* (supporter)
enthousiaste; **be** ∼**ic about** être
enthousiasmé par. **enthusiastically**
adv avec enthousiasme.

entice *vt* attirer; ∼ **to do** entraîner
à faire.

entire *adj* entier. **entirely** *adv*
entièrement. **entirety** *n* **in its** ∼**ty**
en entier.

entitle *vt* donner droit à (**to sth** à
qch; **to do** de faire); ∼**d** (book)
intitulé; **be** ∼**d to sth** avoir droit à
qch.

entrance[1] *n* (entering, way in) entrée *f*
(**to** de); (right to enter) admission *f*.
● *adj* (charge, exam) d'entrée.

entrance[2] *vt* transporter.

entrant *n* (Sport) concurrent/-e *m/f*;
(in exam) candidat/-e *m/f*.

entrenched *adj* (*opinion*)
inébranlable; (Mil) retranché.

entrepreneur *n* entrepreneur/
-euse *m/f*.

entrust *vt* confier; ∼ **sb with sth**
confier qch à qn.

entry *n* entrée *f*; ∼ **form** fiche *f*
d'inscription.

envelop *vt* (*pt* **enveloped**)
envelopper.

envelope *n* enveloppe *f*.

envious *adj* envieux (**of** de).

environment *n* (ecological)
environnement *m*; (social) milieu *m*.
environmental *adj* du milieu; de
l'environnement.
environmentalist *n* écologiste *mf*.

envisage *vt* prévoir (**doing** de
faire).

envoy *n* envoyé/-e *m/f*.

envy *n* envie *f*. ● *vt* envier; ∼ **sb sth**
envier qch à qn.

epic *n* épopée *f*. ● *adj* épique.

epidemic *n* épidémie *f*.

epilepsy *n* épilepsie *f*.

episode *n* épisode *m*.

epitome *n* modèle *m*. **epitomize** *vt*
incarner.

equal *a & n* égal/-e (*m/f*); ∼
opportunities/rights égalité *f* des
chances/droits; ∼ **to** (*task*) à la
hauteur de. ● *vt* (*pt* **equalled**)
égaler. **equality** *n* égalité *f*.
equalize *vt/i* égaliser. **equalizer** *n*
(goal) but *m* égalisateur. **equally**
adv (*divide*) en parts égales; (just as)
tout aussi.

equanimity *n* sérénité *f*.

equate *vt* assimiler (**with** à).
equation *n* équation *f*.

equator *n* équateur *m*.

equilibrium *n* équilibre *m*.

equip *vt* (*pt* **equipped**) équiper (**with**
de). **equipment** *n* équipement *m*.

equity *n* équité *f*.

equivalence *n* équivalence *f*.

era *n* ère *f*, époque *f*.
eradicate *vt* éliminer; (*disease*) éradiquer.
erase *vt* effacer. **eraser** *n* (rubber) gomme *f*.
erect *adj* droit. ● *vt* ériger. **erection** *n* érection *f*.
erode *vt* éroder; (fig) saper. **erosion** *n* érosion *f*.
erotic *adj* érotique.
errand *n* commission *f*, course *f*.
erratic *adj* (*behaviour, person*) imprévisible; (*performance*) inégal.
error *n* erreur *f*.
erupt *vi* (volcano) entrer en éruption; (fig) éclater.
escalate *vt* intensifier. ● *vi* (*conflict*) s'intensifier; (*prices*) monter en flèche. **escalation** *n* intensification *f*. **escalator** *n* escalier *m* mécanique, escalator® *m*.
escapade *n* frasque *f*.
escape *vt* échapper à. ● *vi* s'enfuir, s'évader; (*gas*) fuir. ● *n* fuite *f*, évasion *f*; (of gas etc.) fuite *f*; **have a lucky** *or* **narrow ~** l'échapper belle.
escapism *n* évasion *f* (*du réel*).
escort¹ *n* (guard) escorte *f*; (companion) compagnon/compagne *m/f*.
escort² *vt* escorter.
Eskimo *n* Esquimau/-de *m/f*.
especially *adv* en particulier.
espionage *n* espionnage *m*.
espresso *n* (café) express *m*.
essay *n* (in literature) essai *m*; (School) rédaction *f*; (Univ) dissertation *f*.
essence *n* essence *f*.
essential *adj* essentiel; **the ~s** l'essentiel *m*. **essentially** *adv* essentiellement.
establish *vt* établir; (business) fonder.
establishment *n* (process) instauration *f*; (institution) établissement *m*; **the E~** l'ordre *m* établi.
estate *n* (house and land) domaine *m*; (possessions) biens *mpl*; (housing estate) cité *f*. **~ agent** *n* agent *m* immobilier. **~ car** *n* break *m*.
esteem *n* estime *f*.
esthetic *adj* (US) = AESTHETIC.

estimate¹ *n* (calculation) estimation *f*; (Comm) devis *m*.
estimate² *vt* évaluer; **~ that** estimer que. **estimation** *n* (esteem) estime *f*; (judgment) opinion *f*.
Estonia *n* Estonie *f*.
estuary *n* estuaire *m*.
etc. *adv* etc.
eternal *adj* éternel.
eternity *n* éternité *f*.
ethic *n* éthique *f*; **~s** moralité *f*. **ethical** *adj* éthique.
ethnic *adj* ethnique.
ethos *n* philosophie *f*.
etymology *n* étymologie *f*.
EU *abbr* (**European Union**) UE *f*, Union *f* européenne.
euphoria *n* euphorie *f*.
Euro *n* euro *m*.
Europe *n* Europe *f*.
European *a & n* européen/-ne (*m/f*); **~ Community** Communauté *f* Européenne.
euthanasia *n* euthanasie *f*.
evacuate *vt* évacuer.
evade *vt* (*blow*) esquiver; (*question*) éluder.
evaporate *vi* s'évaporer; **~d milk** lait *m* condensé.
evasion *n* fuite *f* (of devant); (excuse) faux-fuyant *m*; **tax ~** évasion *f* fiscale. **evasive** *adj* évasif.
eve *n* veille *f* (of de).
even *adj* (*surface, voice, contest*) égal; (*teeth, hem*) régulier; (number) pair; **get ~ with** se venger de. ● *adv* même; **~ better**/*etc.* (still) encore mieux/*etc.*; **~ so** quand même. □ **~ out** (*differences*) s'atténuer; **~ sth out** (*inequalities*) réduire qch; **~ up** équilibrer.
evening *n* soir *m*; (whole evening, event) soirée *f*.
evenly *adv* (*spread, apply*) uniformément; (*breathe*) régulièrement; (equally) en parts égales.
event *n* événement *m*; (Sport) épreuve *f*; **in the ~ of** en cas de. **eventful** *adj* mouvementé.
eventual *adj* (*outcome, decision*) final; (*aim*) à long terme. **eventuality** *n* éventualité *f*.

eventually *adv* finalement; (in future) un jour ou l'autre.

ever *adv* jamais; (at all times) toujours.

evergreen *n* arbre *m* à feuilles persistantes.

everlasting *adj* éternel.

ever since *prep & adv* depuis.

every *adj* ∼ **house/window** toutes les maisons/fenêtres; ∼ **time/ minute** chaque fois/minute; ∼ **day** tous les jours; ∼ **other day** tous les deux jours. **everybody** *pron* tout le monde. **everyday** *adj* quotidien. **everyone** *pron* tout le monde. **everything** *pron* tout. **everywhere** *adv* partout; ∼**where** he goes partout où il va.

evict *vt* expulser (**from** de).

evidence *n* (proof) preuves *fpl* (**that** que); (testimony) témoignage *m*; (traces) trace *f* (**of** de); **give** ∼ témoigner; **be in** ∼ être visible. **evident** *adj* manifeste. **evidently** *adv* (apparently) apparemment; (obviously) manifestement.

evil *adj* malfaisant. ● *n* mal *m*.

evoke *vt* évoquer.

evolution *n* évolution *f*.

evolve *vi* évoluer. ● *vt* élaborer.

ewe *n* brebis *f*.

ex- *pref* ex-, ancien.

exact *adj* exact; **the** ∼ **opposite** exactement le contraire. ● *vt* exiger (**from** de). **exactly** *adv* exactement.

exaggerate *vt/i* exagérer.

exalted *adj* élevé.

exam *n* 🄸 examen *m*.

examination *n* examen *m*.

examine *vt* examiner; (witness) interroger. **examiner** *n* examinateur/-trice *m/f*.

example *n* exemple *m*; **for** ∼ par exemple; **make an** ∼ **of** punir pour l'exemple.

exasperate *vt* exaspérer.

excavate *vt* fouiller. **excavations** *npl* fouilles *fpl*.

exceed *vt* dépasser. **exceedingly** *adv* extrêmement.

excel *vi* (*pt* **excelled**) exceller (**at**, **in** en; **at doing** à faire). ● *vt* surpasser.

excellence *n* excellence *f*. **excellent** *adj* excellent.

except *prep* sauf, excepté; ∼ **for** à part. ● *vt* excepter. **excepting** *prep* sauf, excepté.

exception *n* exception *f*; **take** ∼ **to** s'offusquer. **exceptional** *adj* exceptionnel.

excerpt *n* extrait *m*.

excess[1] *n* excès *m*.

excess[2] *adj* ∼ **weight** excès *m* de poids; ∼ **baggage** excédent *m* de bagages.

excessive *adj* excessif.

exchange *vt* échanger (**for** contre). ● *n* échange *m*; (between currencies) change *m*; ∼ **rate** taux *m* de change; **telephone** ∼ central *m* téléphonique.

Exchequer *n* (Pol) ministère *m* britannique des finances.

excise *n* excise *f*, taxe *f*.

excite *vt* exciter; (enthuse) enthousiasmer. **excited** *adj* excité; **get** ∼**d** s'exciter. **excitement** *n* excitation *f*. **exciting** *adj* passionnant.

exclaim *vt* s'exclamer.

exclamation *n* exclamation *f*; ∼ **mark** *or* **point** (US) point *m* d'exclamation.

exclude *vt* exclure.

exclusive *adj* (club) fermé; (rights) exclusif; (news item) en exclusivité; ∼ **of meals** repas non compris. **exclusively** *adv* exclusivement.

excruciating *adj* atroce.

excursion *n* excursion *f*.

excuse[1] *vt* excuser; ∼ **from** (exempt) dispenser de; ∼ **me!** excusez-moi!, pardon!

excuse[2] *n* (reason) excuse *f*; (pretext) prétexte *m* (**for sth** à qch; **for doing** pour faire).

ex-directory *adj* sur liste rouge.

execute *vt* exécuter. **executioner** *n* bourreau *m*.

executive *n* (person) cadre *m*; (committee) exécutif *m*. ● *adj* exécutif.

exemplary *adj* exemplaire.

exemplify *vt* illustrer.

exempt *adj* exempt (**from** de). ● *vt* exempter.

exercise n exercice m; ~ **book** cahier m. ● vt exercer; (restraint, patience) faire preuve de. ● vi faire de l'exercice.

exert vt exercer; ~ **oneself** se fatiguer. **exertion** n effort m.

exhaust vt épuiser. ● n (Auto) pot m d'échappement.

exhaustive adj exhaustif.

exhibit vt exposer; (fig) manifester. ● n objet m exposé.

exhibition n exposition f; (of skill) démonstration f. **exhibitionist** n exhibitionniste mf.

exhibitor n exposant/-e m/f.

exhilarate vt griser.

exile n exil m; (person) exilé/-e m/f. ● vt exiler.

exist vi exister. **existence** n existence f; be in ~ence exister. **existing** adj actuel.

exit n sortie f. ● vt/i (also Comput) sortir (de).

exodus n exode m.

exonerate vt disculper.

exotic adj exotique.

expand vt développer; (workforce) accroître. ● vi se développer; (population) s'accroître; (metal) se dilater.

expanse n étendue f.

expansion n développement m; (Pol, Comm) expansion f.

expatriate a & n expatrié/-e (m/f).

expect vt s'attendre à; (suppose) supposer; (demand) exiger; (baby) attendre.

expectancy n attente f.

expectant adj ~ **mother** future maman f.

expectation n (assumption) prévision f; (hope) aspiration f; (demand) exigence f.

expedient adj opportun. ● n expédient m.

expedition n expédition f.

expel vt (pt **expelled**) expulser; (pupil) renvoyer.

expend vt consacrer.

expenditure n dépenses fpl.

expense n frais mpl; at sb's ~ aux frais de qn; ~ **account** frais mpl de représentation. **expensive** adj

cher; (tastes) de luxe. **expensively** adv luxueusement.

experience n expérience f. ● vt (undergo) connaître; (feel) éprouver; ~d expérimenté.

experiment n expérience f. ● vi expérimenter, faire des essais.

expert n spécialiste mf. ● adj spécialisé, expert. **expertise** n compétence f. **expertly** adv de manière experte.

expire vi expirer; ~d périmé. **expiry** n expiration f.

explain vt expliquer. **explanation** n explication f. **explanatory** adj explicatif.

explicit adj explicite.

explode vt/i (faire) exploser.

exploit[1] n exploit m.

exploit[2] vt exploiter.

exploration n exploration f. **exploratory** adj (talks) exploratoire. **explore** vt explorer; (fig) étudier. **explorer** n explorateur/-trice m/f.

explosion n explosion f. **explosive** a & n explosif (m).

exponent n avocat/-e m/f (of de).

export[1] vt exporter.

export[2] n (process) exportation f; (product) produit m d'exportation.

expose vt exposer; (disclose) révéler.

exposure n révélation f; (Photo) pose f; die of ~ mourir de froid.

express vt exprimer. ● adj exprès. ● adv send sth ~ envoyer qch en exprès. ● n (train) rapide m. **expression** n expression f. **expressive** adj expressif. **expressly** adv expressément.

exquisite adj exquis.

extend vt (visit) prolonger; (house) agrandir; (range) élargir; (arm, leg) étendre. ● vi (stretch) s'étendre; (in time) se prolonger. **extension** n (of line, road) prolongement m; (of visa, loan) prorogation f; (building) addition f; (phone number) poste m; (cable) rallonge f.

extensive adj vaste; (study) approfondi; (damage) considérable. **extensively** adv (much) beaucoup; (very) très.

extent *n* (size, scope) étendue *f*; (degree) mesure *f*; **to some ~** dans une certaine mesure; **to such an ~ that** à tel point que.

extenuating *adj* atténuant.

exterior *a & n* extérieur (*m*).

exterminate *vt* exterminer.

external *adj* extérieur; (cause, medical use) externe.

extinct *adj* (species) disparu; (volcano, passion) éteint.

extinguish *vt* éteindre. **extinguisher** *n* extincteur *m*.

extol *vt* (*pt* **extolled**) louer, chanter les louanges de.

extort *vt* extorquer (**from** à). **extortion** *n* (Jur) extorsion *f*. **extortionate** *adj* exorbitant.

extra *adj* supplémentaire; **~ charge** supplément *m*; **~ time** (football) prolongation *f*; **~ strong** extra-fort. ● *adv* encore; plus. ● *n* supplément *m*; (cinema) figurant/-e *m/f*.

extract[1] *vt* sortir (**from** de); (*tooth*) extraire; (*promise*) arracher.

extract[2] *n* extrait *m*.

extra-curricular *adj* parascolaire.

extradite *vt* extrader.

extramarital *adj* extraconjugal.

extramural *adj* (Univ) hors faculté.

extraordinary *adj* extraordinaire.

extravagance *n* prodigalité *f*. **extravagant** *adj* (*person*) dépensier; (*claim*) extravagant.

extreme *a & n* extrême (*m*). **extremely** *adv* extrêmement. **extremist** *n* extrémiste *mf*. **extremity** *n* extrémité *f*.

extricate *vt* dégager.

extrovert *n* extraverti/-e *m/f*.

exuberance *n* exubérance *f*.

exude *vt* (*charm*) respirer; (*smell*) exhaler.

eye *n* œil *m* (*pl* yeux); **keep an ~ on** surveiller. ● *vt* (*pt* **eyed**; *pres p* **eyeing**) regarder. **~ball** *n* globe *m* oculaire. **~brow** *n* sourcil *m*. **~-catching** *adj* attrayant. **~lash** *n* cil *m*. **~lid** *n* paupière *f*. **~-opener** *n* révélation *f*.

~-shadow *n* ombre *f* à paupières. **~sight** *n* vue *f*. **~sore** *n* horreur *f*. **~witness** *n* témoin *m* oculaire.

fable *n* fable *f*.

fabric *n* (cloth) tissu *m*.

fabulous *adj* fabuleux; (marvellous Ⅰ) formidable.

face *n* visage *m*, figure *f*; (expression) air *m*; (appearance, dignity) face *f*; (of clock) cadran *m*; (Geol) face *f*; (of rock) paroi *f*; **in the ~ of** face à; **make a (funny) ~** faire la grimace; **~ to ~** face à face. ● *vt* être en face de; (*risk*) devoir affronter; (confront) faire face à; (deal with) **I can't ~ him** je n'ai pas le courage de le voir. ● *vi* (*person*) regarder; (*chair*) être tourné vers; (*window*) donner sur; **~ up to** faire face à; **~d with** face à.

face-lift *n* lifting *m*; **give a ~ to** donner un coup de neuf à.

face value *n* valeur *f* nominale; **take sth at ~** prendre qch au pied de la lettre.

facial *adj* (*hair*) du visage; (*injury*) au visage. ● *n* soin *m* du visage.

facility *n* (building) complexe *m*; (feature) fonction *f*; **facilities** (equipment) équipements *mpl*.

facsimile *n* fac-similé *m*.

fact *n* fait *m*; **as a matter of ~, in ~** en fait; **know for a ~ that** savoir de source sûre que; **owing/due to the ~ that** étant donné que.

factor *n* facteur *m*.

factory *n* usine *f*.

factual *adj* (account, description) basé sur les faits; (evidence) factuel.

faculty *n* faculté *f*.

fade *vi* (sound) s'affaiblir; (memory) s'effacer; (flower) se faner; (material) se décolorer; (colour) passer.

fail *vi* échouer; (grow weak) (s')af) faiblir; (run short) manquer; (engine) tomber en panne. ● *vt* (*exam*) échouer à; ~ **to do** (not do) ne pas faire; (not be able) ne pas réussir à faire; **without** ~ à coup sûr.

failing *n* défaut *m*; ~ **that/this** sinon.

failure *n* échec *m*; (person) raté/-e *m/f*; (breakdown) panne *f*; ~ **to do** (inability) incapacité *f* de faire.

faint *adj* léger, faible; **feel** ~ (ill) se sentir mal; **I haven't the** ~**est idea** je n'en ai pas la moindre idée. ● *vi* s'évanouir. ● *n* évanouissement *m*. ~-**hearted** *adj* timide.

fair *n* foire *f*. ● *adj* (*hair, person*) blond; (*skin*) clair; (*weather*) beau; (*amount, quality*) raisonnable; (just) juste, équitable. ● *adv* (*play*) loyalement.

fair-ground *n* champ *m* de foire.

fairly *adv* (justly) équitablement; (rather) assez.

fairness *n* justice *f*.

fairy *n* fée *f*. ~ **story**, ~-**tale** *n* conte *m* de fées.

faith *n* (belief) foi *f*; (confidence) confiance *f*.

faithful *adj* fidèle.

fake *n* (forgery) faux *m*; (person) imposteur *m*; **it is a** ~ c'est un faux. ● *adj* faux. ● *vt* (*signature*) contrefaire; (*results*) falsifier; (*illness*) feindre.

falcon *n* faucon *m*.

fall *vi* (*pt* **fell**; *pp* **fallen**) tomber; ~ **short** être insuffisant. ● *n* chute *f*; (autumn: US) automne *m*; **Niagara F**~**s** chutes *fpl* du Niagara. □ ~ **back on** se rabattre sur; ~ **behind** prendre du retard; ~ **down** *or* **off** tomber; ~ **for** (*person* ⓘ) tomber amoureux de; (*a trick* ⓘ) se laisser prendre à; ~ **in** (Mil) se mettre en rangs; ~ **off** (decrease) diminuer; ~ **out** se brouiller (**with** avec); ~ **over** tomber (par terre); ~ **through** (*plans*) tomber à l'eau.

fallacy *n* erreur *f*.

false *adj* faux. ~ **teeth** *npl* dentier *m*.

falter *vi* (*economy*) fléchir; (*courage*) faiblir; (when speaking) bafouiller ⓘ.

fame *n* renommée *f*. **famed** *adj* célèbre (**for** pour).

familiar *adj* familier; **be** ~ **with** connaître.

family *n* famille *f*. ● *adj* de famille, familial.

famine *n* famine *f*.

famished *adj* affamé.

famous *adj* célèbre (**for** pour).

fan *n* (mechanical) ventilateur *m*; (handheld) éventail *m*; (of person) fan *mf* ⓘ, admirateur/-trice *m/f*; (enthusiast) fervent/-e *m/f*, passionné/-e *m/f*. ● *vt* (*pt* **fanned**) (*face*) éventer; (fig) attiser. ● *vi* ~ **out** se déployer en éventail.

fanatic *n* fanatique *mf*.

fan belt *n* courroie *f* de ventilateur.

fancy *n* (whim, fantasy) fantaisie *f*; **take a** ~ **to sb** se prendre d'affection pour qn; **it took my** ~ ça m'a plu. ● *adj* (*buttons etc.*) fantaisie *inv*; (*prices*) extravagant; (impressive) impressionnant. ● *vt* s'imaginer; (want ⓘ) avoir envie de; (like ⓘ) aimer. ~ **dress** *n* déguisement *m*.

fang *n* (of dog) croc *m*; (of snake) crochet *m*.

fantasize *vi* fantasmer.

fantastic *adj* fantastique.

fantasy *n* fantaisie *f*; (daydream) fantasme *m*.

FAQ *abbr* (**Frequently Asked Questions**) (Internet) FAQ *f*, foire *f* aux questions.

far *adv* loin; (much) beaucoup; (very) très; ~ **away**, ~ **off** au loin; **as** ~ **as** (up to) jusqu'à; **as** ~ **as I know** autant que je sache; **by** ~ de loin; ~ **from** loin de. ● *adj* lointain; (end, side) autre. ~**away** *adj* lointain.

farce *n* farce *f*.

fare *n* (prix du) billet *m*; (food) nourriture *f*. ● *vi* (progress) aller; (manage) se débrouiller.

Far East *n* Extrême-Orient *m*.

farewell *interj* & *n* adieu (*m*).

farm *n* ferme *f*. ● *vt* cultiver; ~ **out** céder en sous-traitance. ● *vi* être fermier. **farmer** *n* fermier *m*. ~**house** *n* ferme *f*. **farming** *n* agriculture *f*. ~**yard** *n* basse-cour *f*.

fart ⓘ *vi* péter ⓘ. ● *n* pet *m* ⓘ.

farther *adv* plus loin. ● *adj* plus éloigné.

farthest *adv* le plus loin. ● *adj* le plus éloigné.

fascinate *vt* fasciner.

Fascism *n* fascisme *m*.

fashion *n* (current style) mode *f*; (manner) façon *f*; **in** ~ à la mode; **out of** ~ démodé. ● *vt* façonner. **fashionable** *adj* à la mode.

fast *adj* rapide; (colour) grand teint *inv*; (firm) fixe, solide; **be** ~ (of a clock) avancer. ● *adv* vite; (firmly) ferme; **be** ~ **asleep** dormir d'un sommeil profond. ● *vi* jeûner. ● *n* jeûne *m*.

fasten *vt/i* (s')attacher. **fastener**, **fastening** *n* attache *f*, fermeture *f*.

fast food *n* fast-food *m*; restauration *f* rapide.

fat *n* graisse *f*; (on meat) gras *m*. ● *adj* (**fatter, fattest**) gros, gras; (*meat*) gras; (*profit*) gros; **a** ~ **lot** Ⓘ bien peu (**of** de).

fatal *adj* mortel; (fateful, disastrous) fatal. **fatality** *n* mort *m*. **fatally** *adv* mortellement.

fate *n* sort *m*. **fateful** *adj* fatidique.

father *n* père *m*. ~**hood** *n* paternité *f*. ~**-in-law** *n* (*pl* ~**s-in-law**) beau-père *m*.

fathom *n* brasse *f* (=1.8 m). ● *vt* ~ (**out**) comprendre.

fatigue *n* épuisement *m*; (Tech) fatigue *f*. ● *vt* fatiguer.

fatten *vt/i* engraisser. **fattening** *adj* qui fait grossir.

fatty *adj* (*food*) gras; (*tissue*) adipeux.

faucet *n* (US) robinet *m*.

fault *n* (defect, failing) défaut *m*; (blame) faute *f*; (Geol) faille *f*; **at** ~ fautif; **find** ~ **with** critiquer. ● *vt* ~ **sth/sb** prendre en défaut qn/qch. **faulty** *adj* défectueux.

favour, (US) **favor** *n* faveur *f*; **do sb a** ~ rendre service à qn; **in** ~ **of** pour. ● *vt* favoriser; (support) être en faveur de; (prefer) préférer. **favourable** *adj* favorable.

favourite *a* & *n* favori/-te (*m/f*).

fawn *n* (animal) faon *m*; (colour) beige *m* foncé. ● *vi* ~ **on** flagorner.

fax *n* fax *m*, télécopie *f*. ● *vt* faxer, envoyer par télécopie. ~ **machine** *n* fax *m*; télécopieur *m*; (for public use) Publifax® *m*.

FBI *abbr* (**Federal Bureau of Investigation**) (US) Police *f* judiciaire fédérale.

fear *n* crainte *f*, peur *f*; (fig) risque *m*; **for** ~ **of/that** de peur de/que. ● *vt* craindre.

feasible *adj* faisable; (likely) plausible.

feast *n* festin *m*; (Relig) fête *f*. ● *vi* festoyer. ● *vt* régaler (**on** de).

feat *n* exploit *m*.

feather *n* plume *f*. ● *vt* ~ **one's nest** s'enrichir.

feature *n* caractéristique *f*; (of person, face) trait *m*; (film) long métrage *m*; (article) article *m* de fond. ● *vt* (*advert*) représenter; (give prominence to) mettre en vedette. ● *vi* figurer (**in** dans).

February *n* février *m*.

fed ⇒FEED. ● *adj* **be** ~ **up** Ⓘ en avoir marre Ⓘ (**with** de).

federal *adj* fédéral.

fee *n* (for entrance) prix *m*; ~(**s**) (of doctor) honoraires *mpl*; (of actor, artist) cachet *m*; (for tuition) frais *mpl*; (for enrolment) droits *mpl*.

feeble *adj* faible.

feed *vt* (*pt* **fed**) nourrir, donner à manger à; (suckle) allaiter; (supply) alimenter. ● *vi* se nourrir (**on** de); ~ **in information** rentrer des données. ● *n* nourriture *f*; (of baby) tétée *f*.

feedback *n* réaction(s) *f(pl)*; (Med, Tech) feed-back *m*.

feel *vt* (*pt* **felt**) (touch) tâter; (be conscious of) sentir; (*emotion*) ressentir; (experience) éprouver; (think) estimer. ● *vi* (tired, lonely) se sentir; ~ **hot/thirsty** avoir chaud/soif; ~ **as if** avoir l'impression que; ~ **awful** (ill) se sentir malade; ~ **like** (want Ⓘ) avoir envie de.

feeler *n* antenne *f*; **put out** ~**s** tâter le terrain.

feeling *n* (emotion) sentiment *m*; (physical) sensation *f*; (impression) impression *f*.

feet ⇒FOOT.

feign *vt* feindre.

fell ⇒FALL. ● *vt* (cut down) abattre.

fellow *n* compagnon *m*, camarade *m*; (of society) membre *m*; (man Ⓘ) type *m* Ⓘ. ~**-countryman** *n* compatriote

m. **~-passenger** n compagnon m
de voyage.

fellowship n camaraderie f; (group)
association f.

felony n crime m.

felt ⇒FEEL. ● n feutre m. **~-tip** n
feutre m.

female adj (animal) femelle; (voice,
sex) féminin. ● n femme f; (animal)
femelle f.

feminine a & n féminin (m).
femininity n féminité f. **feminist**
n féministe mf.

fence n barrière f; **sit on the ~** ne
pas prendre position. ● vt **~ (in)**
clôturer. ● vi (Sport) faire de
l'escrime. **fencing** n escrime f.

fend vi **~ for oneself** se débrouiller
tout seul. ● vt **~ off** (blow, attack)
parer.

fender n (for fireplace) garde-cendre
m; (mudguard: US) garde-boue m inv.

ferment[1] n ferment m; (excitement:
fig) agitation f.

ferment[2] vt/i (faire) fermenter.

fern n fougère f.

ferocious adj féroce.

ferret n (animal) furet m. ● vi **~
about** fureter. ● vt **~ out** dénicher.

ferry n (long-distance) ferry m; (short-
distance) bac m. ● vt transporter.

fertile adj fertile; (person, animal)
fécond. **fertilizer** n engrais m.

festival n festival m; (Relig) fête f.

festive adj de fête, gai; **~ season**
période f des fêtes. **festivity** n
réjouissances fpl.

fetch vt (go for) aller chercher; (bring
person) amener; (bring thing) apporter;
(be sold for) rapporter.

fête n fête f; (church) kermesse f. ● vt
fêter.

fetish n (object) fétiche m; (Psych)
obsession f.

feud n querelle f.

fever n fièvre f. **feverish** adj
fiévreux.

few det peu de; **a ~ houses** quelques
maisons; **quite a ~ people** un bon
nombre de personnes. ● pron
quelques-uns/quelques-unes.

fewer det moins de; **be ~** être moins
nombreux (**than** que). **fewest** det le
moins de.

fiancé n fiancé m. **fiancée** n
fiancée f.

fibre, (US) **fiber** n fibre f. **~glass** n
fibre f de verre.

fiction n fiction f; (works of) **~**
romans mpl. **fictional** adj fictif.

fiddle n 🎻 violon m; (swindle 🗙)
combine f. ● vi 🗙 frauder. ● vt
🗙 falsifier; **~ with** 🗙 tripoter 🗙.

fidget vi gigoter sans cesse.

field n champ m; (Sport) terrain m;
(fig) domaine m. ● vt (ball: cricket)
bloquer.

fierce adj féroce; (storm, attack)
violent.

fiery adj (**-ier, -iest**) (hot) ardent;
(spirited) fougueux.

fifteen a & n quinze (m).

fifth a & n cinquième (mf).

fifty a & n cinquante (m).

fig n figue f.

fight vi (pt **fought**) se battre;
(struggle: fig) lutter; (quarrel) se
disputer. ● vt se battre avec; (evil: fig)
lutter contre. ● n (struggle) lutte f;
(quarrel) dispute f; (brawl) bagarre f;
(Mil) combat m. □ **~ back** se
défendre (**against** contre); **~ off**
surmonter; **~ over** se disputer qch.
fighter n (determined person) lutteur/
-euse m/f; (plane) avion m de chasse.
fighting n combats mpl.

figment n a **~ of the imagination** un
produit de l'imagination.

figure n (number) chiffre m; (diagram)
figure f; (shape) forme f; (body) ligne f;
~s arithmétique f. ● vt s'imaginer.
● vi (appear) figurer; **that ~s** (US, 🗙)
c'est logique; **~ out** comprendre. **~
of speech** n façon f de parler.

file n (tool) lime f; dossier m, classeur
m; (Comput) fichier m; (row) file f. ● vt
limer; (papers) classer; (Jur) déposer.
□ **~ in** entrer en file; **~ past** défiler
devant.

filing cabinet n classeur m.

fill vt/i (se) remplir. ● n **have had
one's ~** en avoir assez. □ **~ in**
(form) remplir; **~ out** prendre du
poids; **~ up** (Auto) faire le plein (de

carburant); (*bath, theatre*) (se)
remplir.

fillet *n* filet *m*. ● *vt* découper en
filets.

filling *n* (of tooth) plombage *m*; (of
sandwich) garniture *f*. ~ **station** *n*
station-service *f*.

film *n* film *m*; (Photo) pellicule *f*. ● *vt*
filmer. ~**-goer** *n* cinéphile *mf*. ~
star *n* vedette *f* de cinéma.

filter *n* filtre *m*; (traffic signal) flèche *f*.
● *vt/i* filtrer; (of traffic) suivre la
flèche. ~ **coffee** *n* café *m* filtre.

filth *n* crasse *f*. **filthy** *adj* crasseux.

fin *n* (of fish, seal) nageoire *f*; (of shark)
aileron *m*.

final *adj* dernier; (conclusive) définitif.
● *n* (Sport) finale *f*.

finale *n* (Mus) finale *m*.

finalize *vt* mettre au point, fixer.

finally *adv* (lastly, at last) enfin,
finalement; (once and for all)
définitivement.

finance *n* finance *f*. ● *adj* financier.
● *vt* financer. **financial** *adj*
financier.

find *vt* (*pt* **found**) trouver; (*sth lost*)
retrouver. ● *n* trouvaille *f*. ~ **out** *vt*
découvrir; *vi* se renseigner (**about**
sur). **findings** *npl* conclusions *fpl*.

fine *adj* fin; (excellent) beau; ~ **arts**
beaux-arts *mpl*. ● *n* amende *f*. ● *vt*
condamner à une amende.

finger *n* doigt *m*. ● *vt* palper. ~**-nail**
n ongle *m*. ~**print** *n* empreinte *f*
digitale. ~**tip** *n* bout *m* du doigt.

finish *vt/i* finir; ~ **doing** finir de
faire; ~ **up doing** finir par faire; ~
up in se retrouver à. ● *n* fin *f*; (of
race) arrivée *f*; (appearance) finition *f*.

finite *adj* fini.

Finland *n* Finlande *f*. **Finn** *n*
Finlandais/-e *m/f*.

Finnish *adj* finlandais. ● *n* (Ling)
finnois *m*.

fir *n* sapin *m*.

fire *n* (element) feu *m*; (blaze) incendie
m; (heater) radiateur *m*; **set** ~ **to**
mettre le feu à. ● *vt* (bullet) tirer;
(dismiss) renvoyer; (fig) enflammer.
● *vi* tirer (**at** sur); ~ **a gun** tirer un
coup de revolver/de fusil. ~ **alarm**
n alarme *f* incendie. ~**arm** *n* arme *f*
à feu. ~ **brigade** *n* pompiers *mpl*.

~ **engine** *n* voiture *f* de pompiers.
~ **escape** *n* escalier *m* de secours.
~ **extinguisher** *n* extincteur *m*.
~**man** *n* (*pl* **-men**) pompier *m*.
~**place** *n* cheminée *f*. ~ **station** *n*
caserne *f* de pompiers. ~**wall** *n* mur
m coupe-feu; (Internet) pare-feu *m inv*.
~**wood** *n* bois *m* de chauffage.
~**work** *n* feu *m* d'artifice.

firing-squad *n* peloton *m*
d'exécution.

firm *n* entreprise *f*, société *f*. ● *adj*
ferme; (belief) solide.

first *adj* premier; **at** ~ **hand** de
première main; **at** ~ **sight** à
première vue; ~ **of all** tout d'abord.
● *n* premier/-ière *m/f*. ● *adv* d'abord,
premièrement; (arrive) le premier, la
première; **at** ~ d'abord. ~ **aid** *n*
premiers soins *mpl*. ~**-class** *adj* de
première classe. ~ **floor** *n* premier
étage *m*; (US) rez-de-chaussée *m inv*.
~ **gear** *n* première (vitesse) *f*. **F**~
Lady *n* (US) épouse *f* du Président.

firstly *adv* premièrement.

first name *n* prénom *m*.

fish *n* poisson *m*; ~ **shop**
poissonnerie *f*. ● *vi* pêcher; ~ **for**
(cod) pêcher; ~ **out** (from water)
repêcher; (take out ▣) sortir.
fisherman *n* (*pl* **-men**) *n* pêcheur
m.

fishing *n* pêche *f*; **go** ~ aller à la
pêche. ~ **rod** *n* canne *f* à pêche.

fishmonger *n* poissonnier/-ière *m/
f*.

fist *n* poing *m*.

fit *n* accès *m*, crise *f*; **be a good** ~
(dress) être à la bonne taille. ● *adj*
(**fitter**, **fittest**) en bonne santé;
(proper) convenable; (good enough) bon;
(able) capable; **in no** ~ **state to do** pas
en état de faire. ● *vt/i* (*pt* **fitted**)
(into space) aller; (install) poser. □ ~ **in**
vt caser; *vi* (newcomer) s'intégrer; ~
out, ~ **up** équiper.

fitness *n* forme *f*; (of remark) justesse
f.

fitted *adj* (wardrobe) encastré. ~
carpet *n* moquette *f*.

fitting *adj* approprié. ● *n* essayage
m. ~ **room** *n* cabine *f* d'essayage.

five *a* & *n* cinq (*m*).

fix vt (make firm, attach, decide) fixer; (mend) réparer; (deal with) arranger; ~ **sb up with sth** trouver qch à qn.

fixture n (Sport) match m; ~**s** (in house) installations fpl.

fizz vi pétiller. ● n pétillement m. **fizzy** adj gazeux.

flabbergast vt sidérer.

flabby adj flasque.

flag n drapeau m; (Naut) pavillon m. ● vt (pt **flagged**) ~ (**down**) faire signe de s'arrêter à. ● vi (weaken) faiblir; (sick person) s'affaiblir. ~-**pole** n mât m. ~**stone** n dalle f.

flake n flocon m; (of paint, metal) écaille f. ● vi s'écailler.

flamboyant adj (colour) éclatant; (manner) extravagant.

flame n flamme f; **burst into** ~**s** exploser; **go up in** ~**s** brûler. ● vi flamber.

flamingo n flamant m (rose).

flammable adj inflammable.

flan n tarte f; (custard tart) flan m.

flank n flanc m. ● vt flanquer.

flannel n (material) flannelle f; (for face) gant m de toilette.

flap vi (pt **flapped**) battre. ● vt ~ **its wings** battre des ailes. ● n (of pocket) rabat m; (of table) abattant m.

flare vi ~ **up** (fighting) éclater. ● n flamboiement m; (Mil) fusée f éclairante; (in skirt) évasement m. **flared** adj évasé.

flash vi briller; (on and off) clignoter; ~ **past** passer à toute vitesse. ● vt faire briller; (aim torch) diriger (**at** sur); (flaunt) étaler; ~ **one's headlights** faire un appel de phares. ● n (of news, camera) flash m; **in a** ~ en un éclair. ~**back** n retour m en arrière. ~**light** n lampe f de poche.

flask n (for chemicals) flacon m; (for drinks) thermos® m or f inv.

flat adj (**flatter**, **flattest**) plat; (tyre) à plat; (refusal) catégorique; (fare, rate) fixe. ● adv (say) carrément. ● n (rooms) appartement m; (tyre Ⓤ) crevaison f; (Mus) bémol m.

flat out adv (drive) à toute vitesse; (work) d'arrache-pied.

flatten vt/i (s')aplatir.

flatter vt flatter.

flaunt vt étaler, afficher.

flavour, (US) **flavor** n goût m; (of ice-cream) parfum m. ● vt parfumer (**with** à), assaisonner (**with** de). **flavouring** n arôme m artificiel.

flaw n défaut m.

flea n puce f. ~ **market** n marché m aux puces.

fleck n petite tache f.

fled ⇒FLEE.

flee vt/i (pt **fled**) fuir.

fleece n toison f; (garment) polaire f. ● vt plumer.

fleet n (Naut, Aviat) flotte f; **a** ~ **of vehicles** (in reserve) parc m; (on road) convoi m.

fleeting adj très bref.

Flemish adj flamand. ● n (Ling) flamand m.

flesh n chair f; **one's (own)** ~ **and blood** la chair de sa chair.

flew ⇒FLY.

flex vt (knee) fléchir; (muscle) faire jouer. ● n (Electr) fil m.

flexible adj flexible.

flexitime n horaire m variable.

flick n petit coup m. ● vt donner un petit coup à; ~ **through** feuilleter.

flight n (of bird, plane) vol m; ~ **of stairs** escalier m; (fleeing) fuite f; **take** ~ prendre la fuite. ~-**deck** n poste m de pilotage.

flimsy adj (-**ier**, -**iest**) (pej) mince, peu solide.

flinch vi (wince) broncher; (draw back) reculer.

fling vt (pt **flung**) jeter.

flint n (rock) silex m.

flip vt (pt **flipped**) donner un petit coup à; ~ **through** feuilleter. ● n chiquenaude f.

flippant adj désinvolte.

flipper n (of seal) nageoire f; (of swimmer) palme f.

flirt vi flirter. ● n flirteur/-euse m/f.

float vt/i (faire) flotter. ● n flotteur m; (cart) char m.

flock n (of sheep) troupeau m; (of people) foule f. ● vi affluer.

flog vt (pt **flogged**) (beat) fouetter; (sell Ⓤ) vendre.

flood n inondation f; (fig) flot m. ● vt inonder. ● vi (*building*) être inondé; (*river*) déborder; (*people*: fig) affluer.

floodlight n projecteur m. ● vt (pt **floodlit**) illuminer.

floor n sol m, plancher m; (for dancing) piste f; (storey) étage m. ● vt (knock down) terrasser; (baffle) stupéfier. ∼-**board** n planche f.

flop vi (pt **flopped**) (drop) s'affaler; (fail ⊠) échouer; (*head*) tomber. ● n ⊡ échec m, fiasco m.

floppy adj lâche, flasque. ∼ (**disk**) n disquette f.

florist n fleuriste mf.

flounder vi (*animal, person*) se débattre (**in** dans); (*economy*) stagner. ● n flet m; (US) poisson m plat.

flour n farine f.

flourish vi prospérer. ● vt brandir. ● n geste m élégant; (curve) fioriture f.

flout vt se moquer de.

flow vi couler; (circulate) circuler; (*traffic*) s'écouler; (hang loosely) flotter; ∼ **in** affluer; ∼ **into** (of river) se jeter dans. ● n (of liquid, traffic) écoulement m; (of tide) flux m; (of orders, words: fig) flot m. ∼ **chart** n organigramme m.

flower n fleur f. ● vi fleurir.

flown ⇒FLY.

flu n grippe f.

fluctuate vi varier.

fluent adj (style) aisé; **be** ∼ (**in a language**) parler (une langue) couramment.

fluff n peluche(s) f(pl); (down) duvet m.

fluid a & n fluide (m).

fluke n coup m de chance.

flung ⇒FLING.

fluoride n fluor m.

flush vi rougir. ● vt nettoyer à grande eau; ∼ **the toilet** tirer la chasse d'eau. ● n (blush) rougeur f; (fig) excitation f. ● adj ∼ **with** (level with) au ras de. ◻ ∼ **out** chasser.

fluster vt énerver.

flute n flûte f.

flutter vi voleter; (of wings) battre. ● n (*wings*) battement m; (fig) agitation f; (bet ⊡) pari m.

flux n changement m continuel.

fly n mouche f; (of trousers) braguette f. ● vi (pt **flew**; pp **flown**) voler; (*passengers*) voyager en avion; (*flag*) flotter; (rush) filer. ● vt (*aircraft*) piloter; (*passengers, goods*) transporter par avion; (*flag*) arborer. ◻ ∼ **off** s'envoler.

flyer n (person) aviateur m; (circular) prospectus m.

flying adj (*saucer*) volant; **with** ∼ **colours** haut la main; ∼ **start** excellent départ m; ∼ **visit** visite f éclair (*a inv*). ● n (activity) aviation f.

flyover n pont m (routier).

foal n poulain m.

foam n écume f, mousse f; ∼ (**rubber**) caoutchouc m mousse. ● vi écumer, mousser.

focus n (pl ∼**es** or **-ci**) foyer m; (fig) centre m; **be in/out of** ∼ être/ne pas être au point. ● vt/i (faire) converger; (*instrument*) mettre au point; (with camera) faire la mise au point (**on** sur); (fig) (se) concentrer.

fodder n fourrage m.

foe n ennemi/-e m/f.

foetus n fœtus m.

fog n brouillard m. ● vt/i (pt **fogged**) (*window*) (s')embuer.

foggy adj brumeux; **it is** ∼ il fait du brouillard.

foil n (tin foil) papier m d'aluminium; (deterrent) repoussoir m. ● vt (thwart) déjouer.

fold vt/i (paper, clothes) (se) plier; (*arms*) croiser; (fail) s'effondrer. ● n pli m; (for sheep) parc m à moutons; (Relig) bercail m. **folder** n (file) chemise f; (leaflet) dépliant m. **folding** adj pliant.

foliage n feuillage m.

folk n gens mpl; ∼**s** parents mpl. ● adj (dance) folklorique; (music) folk.

folklore n folklore m.

follow vt/i suivre; **it** ∼**s that** il s'ensuit que; ∼ **suit** en faire autant; ∼ **up** (letter) donner suite à. **follower** n partisan m.

following n partisans mpl. ● adj suivant; ∼ **day** lendemain. ● prep à la suite de.

fond *adj* (loving) affectueux; (*hope*) cher; **be** ~ **of** aimer.

fondle *vt* caresser.

fondness *n* affection *f*; (for things) attachement *m*.

food *n* nourriture *f*; **French** ~ la cuisine française. ● *adj* alimentaire. ~ **processor** *n* robot *m* (ménager).

fool *n* idiot/-e *m/f*. ● *vt* duper. ● *vi* ~ **around** faire l'idiot. **foolish** *adj* idiot.

foot *n* (*pl* **feet**) pied *m*; (measure) pied *m* (=30.48 cm); (*of stairs, page*) bas *m*; **on** ~ à pied; **on** *or* **to one's feet** debout; **under sb's feet** dans les jambes de qn. ● *vt* (*bill*) payer.

footage *n* (of film) métrage *m*.

football *n* (ball) ballon *m*; (game) football *m*. **footballer** *n* footballeur *m*.

foot: ~**bridge** *n* passerelle *f*. ~**hold** *n* prise *f*.

footing *n* **on an equal** ~ sur un pied d'égalité; **be on a friendly** ~ **with sb** avoir des rapports amicaux avec qn; **lose one's** ~ perdre pied.

foot: ~**note** *n* note *f* (en bas de la page). ~**path** *n* (in countryside) sentier *m*; (in town) chemin *m*. ~**print** *n* empreinte *f* (de pied). ~**step** *n* pas *m*. ~**wear** *n* chaussures *fpl*.

....

for

● *preposition*

····▶ pour; ~ **me** pour moi; **music** ~ **dancing** de la musique pour danser; **what is it** ~? ça sert à quoi?

····▶ (with a time period that is still continuing) depuis; **I've been waiting** ~ **two hours** j'attends depuis deux heures; **I haven't seen him** ~ **ten years** je ne l'ai pas vu depuis dix ans.

····▶ (with a time period that has ended) pendant; **I waited** ~ **two hours** j'ai attendu pendant deux heures.

····▶ (with a future time period) pour; **I'm going to Paris** ~ **six weeks** je vais à Paris pour six semaines.

····▶ (with distances) pendant; **I drove** ~ **50 kilometres** j'ai roulé pendant 50 kilomètres.

forbade ⇒FORBID.

forbid *vt* (*pt* **forbade**; *pp* **forbidden**) interdire, défendre (**sb to do** à qn de faire); ~ **sb sth** interdire *or* défendre qch à qn; **you are forbidden to leave** il vous est interdit de partir. **forbidding** *adj* menaçant.

force *n* force *f*; **come into** ~ entrer en vigueur; **the** ~**s** les forces *fpl* armées. ● *vt* forcer. □ ~ **into** faire entrer de force; ~ **on** imposer à. **forced** *adj* forcé.

force-feed *vt* (*pt* **-fed**) (*person*) nourrir de force; (*animal*) gaver.

forceful *adj* énergique.

ford *n* gué *m*. ● *vt* passer à gué.

forearm *n* avant-bras *m inv*.

forecast *vt* (*pt* **forecast**) prévoir. ● *n* **weather** ~ météo *f*.

forecourt *n* (of garage) devant *m*; (of station) cour *f*.

forefinger *n* index *m*.

forefront *n* **at/in the** ~ **of** à la pointe de.

foregone *adj* **it's a** ~ **conclusion** c'est couru d'avance.

foreground *n* premier plan *m*.

forehead *n* front *m*.

foreign *adj* étranger; (*trade*) extérieur; (*travel*) à l'étranger. **foreigner** *n* étranger/-ère *m/f*.

foreman *n* (*pl* **-men**) contremaître *m*.

foremost *adj* le plus éminent. ● *adv* **first and** ~ tout d'abord.

forensic *adj* médico-légal; ~ **medicine** médecine *f* légale.

foresee *vt* (*pt* **-saw**; *pp* **-seen**) prévoir.

forest *n* forêt *f*. **forestry** *n* sylviculture *f*.

foretaste *n* avant-goût *m*.

forever *adv* toujours.

foreword *n* avant-propos *m inv*.

forfeit *n* (penalty) peine *f*; (in game) gage *m*. ● *vt* perdre.

forgave ⇒FORGIVE.

forge *n* forge *f*. ● *vt* (*metal, friendship*) forger; (copy) contrefaire, falsifier. ● *vi* ~ **ahead** aller de l'avant, avancer. **forger** *n* faussaire *m*. **forgery** *n* faux *m*, contrefaçon *f*.

forget vt/i (pt **forgot**; pp
forgotten) oublier; ∼ oneself
s'oublier. **forgetful** adj distrait.
∼-me-not n myosotis m.

forgive vt (pt **forgave**; pp
forgiven) pardonner (**sb for sth** qch
à qn).

fork n fourchette f; (for digging)
fourche f; (in road) bifurcation f. ● vi
(road) bifurquer; ∼ **out** 🄳 payer.
forked adj fourchu. ∼-**lift truck** n
chariot m élévateur.

form n forme f; (document) formulaire
m; (School) classe f; **on** ∼ en forme.
● vt/i (se) former.

formal adj officiel, en bonne et due
forme; (person) compassé,
cérémonieux; (dress) de cérémonie;
(denial, grammar) formel; (language)
soutenu. **formality** n cérémonial m;
(requirement) formalité f.

format n format m. ● vt (pt
formatted) (disk) formater.

former adj ancien; (first of two)
premier. ● **the** ∼ celui-là, celle-là.
formerly adv autrefois.

formula n (pl **-ae** or **-as**) formule f.
formulate vt formuler.

fort n (Mil) fort m; **to hold the** ∼
s'occuper de tout.

forth adv **from this day** ∼ à partir
d'aujourd'hui; **and so** ∼ et ainsi de
suite; **go back and** ∼ aller et venir.

forthcoming adj à venir, prochain;
(sociable) 🄳 communicatif.

forthright adj direct.

forthwith adv sur-le-champ.

fortnight n quinze jours mpl,
quinzaine f.

fortnightly adj bimensuel. ● adv
tous les quinze jours.

fortunate adj heureux; **be** ∼ avoir
de la chance. **fortunately** adv
heureusement.

fortune n fortune f; **make a** ∼ faire
fortune; **have the good** ∼ **to** avoir la
chance de. ∼-**teller** n diseur/-euse
m/f de bonne aventure.

forty a & n quarante (m); ∼ **winks**
un petit somme.

forward adj en avant; (advanced)
précoce; (bold) effronté. ● n (Sport)
avant m. ● adv en avant; **come** ∼ se
présenter; **go** ∼ avancer. ● vt (letter,
e-mail) faire suivre; (goods)
expédier; (fig) favoriser.
forwardness n précocité f.
forwards adv en avant.

fossil n & a fossile (m).

foster vt (promote) encourager; (child)
élever. ● adj (child, parent) adoptif;
(family, home) de placement.

fought ⇒FIGHT.

foul adj (smell, weather) infect;
(place, action) immonde; (language)
ordurier. ● n (football) faute f. ● vt
souiller, encrasser; ∼ **up** 🄳 gâcher.
∼-**mouthed** adj grossier.

found ⇒FIND. ● vt fonder.
foundation n fondation f; (basis)
fondement m; (make-up) fond m de
teint. **founder** n fondateur/-trice m/
f.

fountain n fontaine f. ∼-**pen** n
stylo m à encre.

four a & n quatre (m).

fourteen a & n quatorze (m).

fourth a & n quatrième (mf).

four-wheel drive n (car) quatre-
quatre m.

fowl n (one bird) poulet m; (group)
volaille f.

fox n renard m. ● vt (baffle) mystifier;
(deceive) tromper.

fraction n fraction f.

fracture n fracture f. ● vt/i (se)
fracturer.

fragile adj fragile.

fragment n fragment m.

fragrance n parfum m.

frail adj frêle.

frame n (of building, boat) charpente f;
(of picture) cadre m; (of window) châssis
m; (of spectacles) monture f; ∼ **of
mind** humeur f. ● vt encadrer; (fig)
formuler; (Jur) 🄳 monter un coup
contre. ∼**work** n structure f;
(context) cadre m.

France n France f.

franchise n (Pol) droit m de vote;
(Comm) franchise f.

frank adj franc. ● vt affranchir.
frankly adv franchement.

frantic adj frénétique; ∼ **with** fou
de.

fraternity n (bond) fraternité f;
(group, club) confrérie f.

fraud n (deception) fraude f; (person) imposteur m. **fraudulent** adj frauduleux.

fray n the ~ la bataille. ● vt/i (s') effilocher.

freckle n tache f de rousseur.

free adj libre; (gratis) gratuit; (lavish) généreux; ~ **(of charge)** gratuit (ement); **a** ~ **hand** carte f blanche. ● vt (pt **freed**) libérer; (clear) dégager.

freedom n liberté f.

free: ~ **enterprise** n la libre entreprise. ~ **kick** n coup m franc. ~**lance** a & n free-lance (mf), indépendant/-e (m/f).

freely adv librement.

Freemason n franc-maçon m.

Freenet n (Comput) Libertel m.

free: ~ **phone**, ~ **number** n numéro m vert. ~**-range** adj (eggs) de ferme.

Freeware n (Comput) Gratuiciel m.

freeway n (US) autoroute f.

freeze vt/i (pt **froze**; pp **frozen**) geler; (Culin) (se) congeler; (wages) bloquer. ● n gel m; blocage m. ~**-dried** adj lyophilisé.

freezer n congélateur m.

freezing adj glacial; **below** ~ au-dessous de zéro.

freight n fret m.

French adj français. ● n (Ling) français m; **the** ~ les Français mpl. ~ **bean** n haricot m vert. ~ **fries** npl frites fpl. ~**man** n Français m. ~**-speaking** adj francophone. ~ **window** n porte-fenêtre f. ~**woman** n Française f.

frenzied adj frénétique. **frenzy** n frénésie f.

frequent[1] adj fréquent.

frequent[2] vt fréquenter.

fresco n fresque f.

fresh adj frais; (different, additional) nouveau; (cheeky 🄸) culotté.

freshen vi (weather) fraîchir; ~ **up** (person) se rafraîchir.

freshly adv nouvellement.

freshness n fraîcheur f.

freshwater adj d'eau douce.

friction n friction f.

Friday n vendredi m.

fridge n frigo m.

fried ⇒FRY. ● adj frit; ~ **eggs** œufs mpl sur le plat.

friend n ami/-e m/f. **friendly** adj (-**ier**, **-iest**) amical, gentil. **friendship** n amitié f.

frieze n frise f.

fright n peur f; (person, thing) horreur f.

frighten vt effrayer; ~ **off** faire fuir; **frightened** adj effrayé; **be** ~**ed** avoir peur (**of** de). **frightening** adj effrayant.

frill n (trimming) fanfreluche f; **with no** ~**s** très simple.

fringe n (edging, hair) frange f; (of area) bordure f; (of society) marge f. ~ **benefits** npl avantages mpl sociaux.

frisk vt (search) fouiller.

fritter n beignet m. ● vt ~ **away** gaspiller.

frivolity n frivolité f.

frizzy adj crépu.

fro ⇒TO AND FRO.

frog n grenouille f; **a** ~ **in one's throat** un chat dans la gorge.

frolic vi (pt **frolicked**) s'ébattre. ● n ébats mpl.

from prep de; (with time, prices) à partir de, de; (habit, conviction) par; (according to) d'après; **take** ~ **sb** prendre à qn; **take** ~ **one's pocket** prendre dans sa poche.

front n (of car, train) avant m; (of garment, building) devant m; (Mil, Pol) front m; (of book, pamphlet) début m; (appearance: fig) façade f. ● adj de devant, avant inv; (first) premier; ~ **door** porte f d'entrée; **in** ~ (**of**) devant. **frontage** n façade f.

frontier n frontière f.

frost n gel m, gelée f; (on glass) givre m. ● vt/i (se) givrer. ~**-bite** n gelure f.

frosty adj (weather, welcome) glacial; (window) givré.

froth n (on beer) mousse f; (on water) écume f. ● vi mousser, écumer.

frown vi froncer les sourcils; ~ **on** désapprouver. ● n froncement m de sourcils.

froze ⇒FREEZE.

frozen ⇒FREEZE. ● *adj* congelé.

fruit *n* fruit *m*; (collectively) fruits *mpl*. **fruitful** *adj* (*discussions*) fructueux. ~ **machine** *n* machine *f* à sous.

frustrate *vt* (*plan*) faire échouer; (*person*: Psych) frustrer; (upset 工) exaspérer. **frustration** *n* (Psych) frustration *f*; (disappointment) déception *f*.

fry *vt/i* (*pt* **fried**) (faire) frire. **frying-pan** *n* poêle *f* (à frire).

FTP *abbr* (**File Transfer Protocol**) (Internet) protocole *m* FTP.

fudge *n* caramel *m* mou. ● *vt* (*issue*) esquiver.

fuel *n* combustible *m*; (for car engine) carburant *m*. ● *vt* (*pt* **fuelled**) alimenter en combustible.

fugitive *n* & *a* fugitif/-ive (*m/f*).

fulfil *vt* (*pt* **fulfilled**) accomplir, réaliser; (*condition*) remplir; ~ **oneself** s'épanouir. **fulfilling** *adj* satisfaisant. **fulfilment** *n* réalisation *f*; épanouissement *m*.

full *adj* plein (**of** de); (*bus, hotel*) complet; (*programme*) chargé; (*skirt*) ample; **be** ~ (**up**) n'avoir plus faim; **at** ~ **speed** à toute vitesse. ● *n* **in** ~ intégralement; **to the** ~ complètement. ~ **back** *n* (Sport) arrière *m*. ~ **moon** *n* pleine lune *f*. ~ **name** *n* nom *m* et prénom *m*. ~**-scale** *adj* (*drawing etc.*) grandeur nature *inv*; (fig) de grande envergure. ~ **stop** *n* point *m*. ~**-time** *a* & *adv* à plein temps.

fully *adv* complètement; ~ **fledged** (*member, citizen*) à part entière.

fume *vi* rager. **fumes** *npl* émanations *fpl*, vapeurs *fpl*.

fun *n* amusement *m*; **be** ~ être chouette; **for** ~ pour rire; **make** ~ **of** se moquer de.

function *n* (purpose, duty) fonction *f*; (event) réception *f*. ● *vi* fonctionner.

fund *n* fonds *m*. ● *vt* fournir les fonds pour.

fundamental *adj* fondamental. **fundamentalist** *n* intégriste *mf*.

funeral *n* enterrement *m*. ● *adj* funèbre.

fun-fair *n* fête *f* foraine.

fungus *n* (*pl* **-gi**) (plant) champignon *m*; (mould) moisissure *f*.

funnel *n* (for pouring) entonnoir *m*; (of ship) cheminée *f*.

funny *adj* (**-ier, -iest**) drôle; (odd) bizarre.

fur *n* (for garment) fourrure *f*; (on animal) poils *mpl*; (in kettle) tartre *m*.

furious *adj* furieux.

furnace *n* fourneau *m*.

furnish *vt* (*room*) meubler; (supply) fournir. **furnishings** *npl* ameublement *m*.

furniture *n* meubles *mpl*, mobilier *m*.

furry *adj* (*animal*) à fourrure; (*toy*) en peluche.

further *adj* plus éloigné; (additional) supplémentaire. ● *adv* plus loin; (more) davantage. ● *vt* avancer. ~ **education** *n* formation *f* continue.

furthermore *adv* en outre, de plus.

furthest *adj* le plus éloigné. ● *adv* le plus loin.

fury *n* fureur *f*.

fuse *vt/i* (melt) fondre; (unite: fig) fusionner; ~ **the lights** faire sauter les plombs. ● *n* (of plug) fusible *m*; (of bomb) amorce *f*.

fuss *n* (when upset) histoire(s) *f(pl)*; (when excited) agitation *f*; **make a** ~ faire des histoires; s'agiter; (about food) faire des chichis; **make a** ~ **of** faire grand cas de. ● *vi* s'agiter. **fussy** *adj* (finicky) tatillon; (hard to please) difficile.

future *adj* futur. ● *n* avenir *m*; (Gram) futur *m*; **in** ~ à l'avenir.

fuzzy *adj* (*hair*) crépu; (*photograph*) flou; (*person* 工) à l'esprit confus.

Gg

Gaelic *n* gaélique *m*.

gag *n* (on mouth) bâillon *m*; (joke) blague *f*. ● *vt* (*pt* **gagged**) bâillonner.

gain *vt* (*respect, support*) gagner; (*speed, weight*) prendre. ● *vi* (of clock)

f
g

avancer. ● *n* (increase) augmentation *f* (in de); (profit) gain *m*.

galaxy *n* galaxie *f*.

gale *n* tempête *f*.

gallery *n* galerie *f*; (**art**) ∼ musée *m*.

Gallic *adj* français.

gallon *n* gallon *m* (*imperial = 4.546 litres*; *Amer. = 3.785 litres*).

gallop *n* galop *m*. ● *vi* (*pt* **galloped**) galoper.

galore *adv* (*prizes, bargains*) en abondance; (*drinks, sandwiches*) à gogo Ⓣ.

gamble *vt/i* jouer; ∼ **on** miser sur. ● *n* (venture) entreprise *f* risquée; (bet) pari *m*; (risk) risque *m*. **gambling** *n* jeu *m*.

game *n* jeu *m*; (football) match *m*; (tennis) partie *f*; (animals, birds) gibier *m*. ● *adj* (brave) courageux; ∼ **for** prêt à. ∼**keeper** *n* garde-chasse *m*.

gammon *n* jambon *m*.

gang *n* (of youths) bande *f*; (of workmen) équipe *f*. ● *vi* ∼ **up** se liguer (**on**, **against** contre).

gangway *n* passage *m*; (aisle) allée *f*; (of ship) passerelle *f*.

gaol *n* & *vt* = JAIL.

gap *n* trou *m*, vide *m*; (in time) intervalle *m*; (in education) lacune *f*; (difference) écart *m*.

gape *vi* rester bouche bée. **gaping** *adj* béant.

garage *n* garage *m*. ● *vt* mettre au garage.

garbage *n* (US) ordures *fpl*.

garden *n* jardin *m*. ● *vi* jardiner. **gardener** *n* jardinier/-ière *m/f*. **gardening** *n* jardinage *m*.

gargle *vi* se gargariser.

garish *adj* (*clothes*) tape-à-l'œil; (*light*) cru.

garland *n* guirlande *f*.

garlic *n* ail *m*.

garment *n* vêtement *m*.

garnish *vt* garnir (**with** de). ● *n* garniture *f*.

garter *n* jarretière *f*.

gas *n* (*pl* ∼**es**) gaz *m*; (Med) anesthésie *m*; (petrol: US) essence *f*. ● *adj* (*mask, pipe*) à gaz. ● *vt* asphyxier; (Mil) gazer. ● *vi* Ⓣ bavarder.

gash *n* entaille *f*. ● *vt* entailler.

gasoline *n* (petrol: US) essence *f*.

gasp *vi* haleter; (in surprise: fig) avoir le souffle coupé. ● *n* halètement *m*.

gate *n* (in garden, airport) porte *f*; (of field, level crossing) barrière *f*. ∼**way** *n* porte *f*; (Internet) passerelle *f*.

gather *vt* (*people, objects*) rassembler; (pick up) ramasser; (*flowers*) cueillir; (fig) comprendre; ∼ **speed** prendre de la vitesse; (sewing) froncer. ● *vi* (*people*) se rassembler; (pile up) s'accumuler. **gathering** *n* réunion *m*.

gauge *n* jauge *f*, indicateur *m*. ● *vt* (*speed, distance*) jauger; (*reaction, mood*) évaluer.

gaunt *adj* décharné.

gauze *n* gaze *f*.

gave ⇒GIVE.

gay *adj* (joyful) gai; (homosexual) gay *inv*. ● *n* gay *mf*.

gaze *vi* ∼ (**at**) regarder (fixement). ● *n* regard *m* (fixe).

gazette *n* journal *m* (officiel).

GB *abbr* ⇒GREAT BRITAIN.

gear *n* (equipment) matériel *m*; (Tech) engrenage *m*; (Auto) vitesse *f*; **in** ∼ en prise; **out of** ∼ au point mort. ● *vt* **to be geared to** s'adresser à. ∼**box** *n* (Auto) boîte *f* de vitesses. ∼**lever**, (US) ∼**shift** *n* levier *m* de vitesse.

geese ⇒GOOSE.

gel *n* (for hair) gel *m*.

gem *n* pierre *f* précieuse.

Gemini *n* Gémeaux *mpl*.

gender *n* (Ling) genre *m*; (of person) sexe *m*.

gene *n* gène *m*. ∼ **library** *n* génothèque *f*.

general *adj* général. ● *n* général *m*; **in** ∼ en général.

general election *n* élections *fpl* législatives.

generalization *n* généralisation *f*. **generalize** *vt/i* généraliser.

general practitioner *n* (Med) généraliste *m*.

generate *vt* produire.

generation *n* génération *f*.

generator *n* (Electr) groupe *m* électrogène.

generosity n générosité f.
  generous adj généreux; (plentiful) copieux.

genetics n génétique f.

Geneva n Genève.

genial adj affable, sympathique.

genitals npl organes mpl génitaux.

genius n (pl ~es) génie m.

gentle adj (mild, kind) doux; (pressure, breeze) léger; (reminder, hint) discret.

gentleman n (pl -men) (man) monsieur m; (well-bred) gentleman m.

gently adv doucement.

gents npl (toilets) toilettes fpl; (on sign) 'Messieurs'.

genuine adj (reason, motive) vrai; (jewel, substance) véritable; (person, belief) sincère.

geography n géographie f.

geology n géologie f.

geometry n géométrie f.

geriatric adj gériatrique.

germ n (Med) microbe m.

German n (person) Allemand/-e m/f; (Ling) allemand m. ● adj allemand.
  Germanic adj germanique.

German measles n rubéole f.

Germany n Allemagne f.

gesture n geste m.

---

get

  past **got**; past participle **got**, **gotten** (US); present participle **getting**

● transitive verb

····➤ recevoir; **we got a letter** nous avons reçu une lettre.

····➤ (obtain) **I got a job in Paris** j'ai trouvé un travail à Paris; **I'll ~ sth to eat at the airport** je mangerai qch à l'aéroport.

····➤ (buy) acheter; **~ sb a present** acheter un cadeau à qn.

····➤ (achieve) obtenir; **he got it right** il a obtenu le bon résultat; **~ good grades** avoir de bonnes notes.

····➤ (fetch) chercher; **go and ~ a chair** va chercher une chaise.

····➤ (transport) prendre; **we can ~ the bus** on peut prendre le bus.

····➤ (understand ⏳) comprendre; **now let me ~ this right** alors si je comprends bien...

····➤ (experience) **~ a surprise** être surpris; **~ a shock** avoir un choc.

····➤ (illness) **~ measles** attraper la rougeole; **~ a cold** s'enrhumer.

····➤ (ask or persuade) **~ him to call me** dis-lui de m'appeler; **I'll ~ her to help me** je lui demanderai de m'aider.

····➤ (cause to be done) **~ a TV repaired** faire réparer une télévision; **~ one's hair cut** se faire couper les cheveux.

● intransitive verb

····➤ devenir; **he's getting old** il vieillit; **it's getting late** il se fait tard.

····➤ (in passives) **~ married** se marier; **~ hurt** être blessé.

····➤ (arrive) arriver; **~ to the airport** arriver à l'aéroport.

□ **get about** (person) se déplacer.

  get along (manage) se débrouiller; (progress) avancer.

  get along with s'entendre avec.

  get at (reach) atteindre; (imply) vouloir dire.

  get away partir; (escape) s'échapper.

  get back vi revenir. vt récupérer.

  get by vi (manage) se débrouiller. vt (pass) passer.

  get down vt/i descendre. vt (depress) déprimer.

  get in entrer.

  get into (car) monter dans; (dress) mettre.

  get off vt (bus) descendre; (remove) enlever. vi (from bus) descendre; (leave) partir; (Jur) être acquitté.

  get on vi (to bus) monter; (succeed) réussir. vt (bus) monter.

  get on with (person) s'entendre avec; (job) attaquer.

  get out sortir.

  get out of (fig) se soustraire.

  get over (illness) se remettre de.

  get round (rule) contourner; (person) entortiller.

  get through vi passer; (on phone) **~ through to sb** avoir qn. vt traverser.

  get up se lever.

get up to faire.

getaway n fuite f.

ghastly adj (-ier, -iest) affreux.

gherkin n cornichon m.

ghetto n ghetto m.

ghost n fantôme m.

giant n & a géant (m).

gibberish n baragouin m, charabia m.

giblets npl abats mpl.

giddy adj (-ier, -iest) vertigineux; be or feel ~ avoir le vertige.

gift n (present) cadeau m; (ability) don m.

gifted adj doué.

gift-wrap n paquet-cadeau m.

gigantic adj gigantesque.

giggle vi ricaner (sottement), glousser. ● n ricanement m; the ~s le fou rire.

gimmick n truc m.

gin n gin m.

ginger n gingembre m. ● adj (hair) roux. ~ **beer** n boisson f gazeuse au gingembre. ~**bread** n pain m d'épices.

gingerly adv avec précaution.

giraffe n girafe f.

girl n (child) (petite) fille f; (young woman) fille f. ~**friend** n amie f; (of boy) petite amie f.

giro n virement m bancaire; (cheque) mandat m.

gist n essentiel m.

give vt (pt **gave**; pp **given**) donner; (gesture) faire; (laugh, sigh) pousser; ~ sb sth donner qch à qn. ● vi donner; (yield) céder; (stretch) se détendre. ● n élasticité f. □ ~ **away** donner; (secret) trahir; ~ **back** rendre; ~ **in** (yield) céder (**to** à); ~ **off** (heat, fumes) dégager; (signal, scent) émettre; ~ **out** vt distribuer; ~ **over** (devote) consacrer; (stop [I]) cesser; ~ **up** vt/i (renounce) renoncer (à); (yield) céder; ~ **oneself up** se rendre; ~ **way** céder; (collapse) s'effondrer.

given ⇒GIVE. ● adj donné. ~ **name** n prénom m.

glad adj content. **gladly** adv avec plaisir.

glamorous adj séduisant, ensorcelant.

glamour, (US) **glamor** n enchantement m, séduction f.

glance n coup m d'œil. ● vi ~ **at** jeter un coup d'œil à.

gland n glande f.

glare vi briller très fort; ~ **at** regarder d'un air furieux. ● n (of lights) éclat m (aveuglant); (stare: fig) regard m furieux. **glaring** adj (dazzling) éblouissant; (obvious) flagrant.

glass n verre m. **glasses** npl (spectacles) lunettes fpl.

glaze vt (door) vitrer; (pottery) vernisser. ● n vernis m.

gleam n lueur f. ● vi luire.

glide vi glisser; (of plane) planer. **glider** n planeur m.

glimpse n (insight) aperçu m; **catch a** ~ **of** entrevoir.

glitter vi scintiller. ● n scintillement m.

global adj (world-wide) mondial; (all-embracing) global. ~ **warming** n réchauffement m de la planète.

globe n globe m.

gloom n obscurité f; (sadness: fig) tristesse f. **gloomy** adj triste; (pessimistic) pessimiste.

glorious adj splendide; (deed, hero) glorieux.

glory n gloire f; (beauty) splendeur f. ● vi ~ **in** être très fier de.

gloss n lustre m, brillant m. ● adj brillant. ● vi ~ **over** (make light of) glisser sur; (cover up) dissimuler.

glossary n glossaire m.

glossy adj brillant.

glove n gant m. ~ **compartment** n (Auto) boîte f à gants.

glow vi (fire) rougeoyer; (person, eyes) rayonner. ● n rougeoiement m, éclat m. **glowing** adj (report) enthousiaste.

glucose n glucose m.

glue n colle f. ● vt (pres p **gluing**) coller.

glutton n glouton/-ne m/f.

gnaw vt/i ronger.

GNP *abbr* (**Gross National Product**) produit *m* national brut, PNB *m*.

go

⇒ *present* go, goes; *past* went; *past participle* gone

● *intransitive verb*

····▸ aller; ∼ **to school/town/market** aller à l'école/en ville/au marché; ∼ **for a swim/walk/coffee** aller nager/se promener/prendre un café.

····▸ (leave) s'en aller; **I must be ∼ing** il faut que je m'en aille.

····▸ (vanish) **the money's gone** il n'y a plus d'argent; **my bike's gone** mon vélo n'est plus là.

····▸ (work, function) marcher; **is the car ∼ing?** est-ce que la voiture marche?

····▸ (become) devenir; ∼ **blind** devenir aveugle; ∼ **pale/red** pâlir/rougir.

····▸ (turn out, progress) aller; **how's it going?** comment ça va?; **how did the exam ∼?** comment s'est passé l'examen?

····▸ (in future tenses) **be ∼ing to do** aller faire.

● *noun*

····▸ (turn) tour *m*; (try) essai *m*; **have a ∼!** essaie!; **full of ∼** 🅸 dynamique.

□ **go across** traverser.

go after poursuivre.

go away partir; ∼ **away!** va-t'en!, allez-vous-en!

go back retourner; ∼ **back in** rentrer; ∼ **back to work** reprendre le travail.

go down (quality, price) baisser; (person) descendre; (sun) se coucher.

go in entrer.

go in for (exam) se présenter à.

go off (leave) partir; (bomb) exploser; (alarm clock) sonner; (milk) tourner; (light) s'éteindre.

go on (continue) continuer; (light) s'allumer; ∼ **on doing** continuer à faire; **what's ∼ing on?** qu'est-ce qui se passe?

go out sortir; (light, fire) s'éteindre.

go over vérifier.

go round (be enough) être assez; ∼ **round to see sb** passer voir qn.

go through (check) examiner; (search) fouiller; ∼ **through a difficult time** traverser une période difficile.

go together aller ensemble.

go under (sink) couler; (fail) échouer.

go up (person) monter; (price, salary) augmenter.

go without se passer de.

go-ahead *n* feu *m* vert. ● *adj* dynamique.

goal *n* but *m*. ∼**keeper** *n* gardien *m* de but. ∼**post** *n* poteau *m* de but.

goat *n* chèvre *f*.

gobble *vt* engouffrer.

go-between *n* intermédiaire *mf*.

god *n* dieu *m*. ∼**child** *n* (*pl* -**children**) filleul/-e *m/f*. ∼**daughter** *n* filleule *f*.

goddess *n* déesse *f*.

god: ∼**father** *n* parrain *m*. ∼**mother** *n* marraine *f*. ∼**send** *n* aubaine *f*. ∼**son** *n* filleul *m*.

goggles *npl* lunettes *fpl* (protectrices).

going *n* **it is slow/hard ∼** c'est lent/difficile. ● *adj* (price, rate) actuel.

go-kart *n* kart *m*.

gold *n* or *m*. ● *adj* en or, d'or.

golden *adj* en or, d'or; (in colour) doré; (opportunity) unique.

gold: ∼**fish** *n* poisson *m* rouge. ∼**-plated** *adj* plaqué or. ∼**smith** *n* orfèvre *m*.

golf *n* golf *m*. ∼**-course** *n* terrain *m* de golf.

gone ⇒GO. ● *adj* parti; ∼ **six o'clock** six heures passées; **the butter's all ∼** il n'y a plus de beurre.

good *adj* (**better**, **best**) bon; (weather) beau; (well-behaved) sage; **as ∼ as** (almost) pratiquement; **that's ∼ of you** c'est gentil (de ta part); **be ∼ with** savoir s'y prendre avec; **feel ∼** se sentir bien; **it is ∼ for you** ça vous fait du bien; **it is ∼ to do** aller faire. ● *n* bien *m*; **do ∼** faire du bien; **is it any ∼?** est-ce que c'est bien?; **it's no ∼** ça ne vaut rien; **it is no ∼ shouting** ça ne sert à rien de crier; **for ∼** pour toujours. ∼**afternoon** *interj* bonjour. ∼**bye** *interj* & *n* au revoir (*m inv*). ∼ **evening** *interj* bonsoir. G∼ **Friday**

n Vendredi *m* saint. ∿**-looking** *adj* beau. ∿ **morning** *interj* bonjour. ∿**-natured** *adj* gentil.

goodness *n* bonté *f*; **my** ∿! mon Dieu!

good-night *interj* bonsoir, bonne nuit.

goods *npl* marchandises *fpl*.

goodwill *n* bonne volonté *f*.

goose *n* (*pl* **geese**) oie *f*. **gooseberry** *n* groseille *f* à maquereau. ∿**-pimples** *npl* chair *f* de poule.

gorge *n* (Geog) gorge *f*. ● *vt* ∿ oneself se gaver (**on** de).

gorgeous *adj* magnifique, splendide, formidable.

gorilla *n* gorille *m*.

gory *adj* (**-ier**, **-iest**) sanglant; (horrific: fig) horrible.

gospel *n* évangile *m*; **the G**∿ l'Évangile *m*.

gossip *n* bavardages *mpl*, commérages *mpl*; (person) bavard/-e *m/f*. ● *vi* bavarder.

got ⇒GET. ● **have** ∿ avoir; **have** ∿ **to do** devoir faire.

govern *vt/i* gouverner. **governess** *n* gouvernante *f*. **government** *n* gouvernement *m*. **governor** *n* gouverneur *m*.

gown *n* robe *f*; (of judge, teacher) toge *f*.

GP *abbr* ⇒GENERAL PRACTITIONER.

grab *vt* (*pt* **grabbed**) saisir.

grace *n* grâce *f*. ● *vt* (honour) honorer; (adorn) orner. **graceful** *adj* gracieux.

gracious *adj* (kind) bienveillant; (elegant) élégant.

grade *n* catégorie *f*; (of goods) qualité *f*; (on scale) grade *m*; (school mark) note *f*; (class: US) classe *f*. ● *vt* classer; (school work) noter. ∿ **school** *n* (US) école *f* primaire.

gradual *adj* progressif, graduel. **gradually** *adv* progressivement, peu à peu.

graduate[1] *n* (Univ) diplômé/-e *m/f*.

graduate[2] *vi* obtenir son diplôme. ● *vt* graduer. **graduation** *n* remise *f* des diplômes.

graffiti *npl* graffiti *mpl*.

graft *n* (Med, Bot) greffe *f*; (work) boulot *m*. ● *vt* greffer (**on to** sur); (work) trimer.

grain *n* (seed, quantity, texture) grain *m*; (in wood) fibre *f*.

gram *n* gramme *m*.

grammar *n* grammaire *f*.

grand *adj* magnifique; (*duke, chorus*) grand.

grandad *n* 🛈 papy *m*.

grand: ∿**child** *n* (girl) petite-fille *f*; (boy) petit-fils *m*; **her** ∿**children** ses petits-enfants *mpl*. ∿**daughter** *n* petite-fille *f*. ∿**father** *n* grand-père *m*. ∿**ma** *n* = GRANNY. ∿**mother** *n* grand-mère *f*. ∿**parents** *npl* grands-parents *mpl*. ∿ **piano** *n* piano *m* à queue. ∿**son** *n* petit-fils *m*. ∿**stand** *n* tribune *f*.

granny *n* 🛈 mémé *f*, mamie *f*.

grant *vt* (*permission*) accorder; (*request*) accéder à; (admit) admettre (**that** que); **take sth for** ∿**ed** considérer qch comme une chose acquise. ● *n* subvention *f*; (Univ) bourse *f*.

granule *n* (*of sugar, salt*) grain *m*; (*of coffee*) granulé *m*.

grape *n* grain *m* de raisin; ∿**s** raisin (s) *m*(*pl*).

grapefruit *n inv* pamplemousse *m*.

graph *n* graphique *m*.

graphic *adj* (*arts*) graphique; (fig) vivant, explicite. **graphics** *npl* (Comput) graphiques *mpl*.

grasp *vt* saisir. ● *n* (hold) prise *f*; (strength of hand) poigne *f*; (reach) portée *f*; (fig) compréhension *f*.

grass *n* herbe *f*. ∿**hopper** *n* sauterelle *f*. ∿**land** *n* prairie *f*.

grass roots *npl* peuple *m*. ● *adj* (*movement*) populaire; (*support*) de base.

grate *n* (hearth) âtre *m*; (fire basket) grille *f*. ● *vt* râper. ● *vi* grincer.

grateful *adj* reconnaissant.

grater *n* râpe *f*.

gratified *adj* très heureux. **gratify** *vt* faire plaisir à.

grating *n* (bars) grille *f*; (noise) grincement *m*.

gratitude *n* reconnaissance *f*.

gratuity n (tip) pourboire m; (bounty: Mil) prime f.

grave¹ n (serious) tombe f. ● adj (serious) grave.

grave² adj ~ **accent** accent m grave.

gravel n graviers mpl.

grave: ~**stone** n pierre f tombale. ~**yard** n cimetière m.

gravity n (seriousness) gravité f; (force) pesanteur f.

gravy n jus m (de viande).

gray (US) a & n = GREY.

graze vi (eat) paître. ● vt (touch) frôler; (scrape) écorcher. ● n écorchure f.

grease n graisse f. ● vt graisser. **greasy** adj graisseux.

great adj grand; (very good 🔲) génial 🔲, formidable 🔲, (grandfather, grandmother) arrière.

Great Britain n Grande-Bretagne f.

greatly adv (very) très; (much) beaucoup.

Greece n Grèce f.

greed n avidité f; (for food) gourmandise f. **greedy** adj avide; gourmand.

Greek n (person) Grec/-que m/f; (Ling) grec m. ● adj grec.

green adj vert; (fig) naïf. ● n vert m; (grass) pelouse f; (golf) green m; ~**s** légumes mpl verts. ~**grocer** n marchand/-e m/f de fruits et légumes.

green house n serre f; ~ **effect** effet m de serre.

greet vt (welcome) accueillir; (address politely) saluer. **greeting** n accueil m.

greetings interj salutations! ● npl (Christmas) vœux mpl. ~ **card** n carte f de vœux.

grew ⇒GROW.

grey adj gris; (fig) triste; go ~ (hair, person) grisonner. ● n gris m. ~**hound** n lévrier m.

grid n grille f; (network: Electr) réseau m.

grief n chagrin m; come to ~ (person) avoir un malheur; (fail) tourner mal.

grievance n griefs mpl.

grieve vt/i (s')affliger; ~ **for** pleurer.

grill n (cooking device) gril m; (food) grillade f; (Auto) calandre f. ● vt/i (faire) griller; (interrogate) mettre sur la sellette.

grim adj sinistre.

grimace n grimace f. ● vi grimacer.

grime n crasse f.

grin vi (pt **grinned**) sourire. ● n (large) sourire m.

grind vt (pt **ground**) (grain) écraser; (coffee) moudre; (sharpen) aiguiser; ~ **one's teeth** grincer des dents. ● vi ~ **to a halt** s'immobiliser. ● n corvée f.

grip vt (pt **gripped**) saisir; (interest) passionner. ● n prise f; (strength of hand) poigne f; **come to ~s with** en venir aux prises avec.

grisly adj (-ier, -iest) (remains) macabre; (sight) horrible.

gristle n cartilage m.

grit n (for roads) sable m; (fig) courage m. ● vt (pt **gritted**) (road) sabler; (teeth) serrer.

groan vi gémir. ● n gémissement m.

grocer n (person) épicier/-ière m/f; (shop) épicerie f. **groceries** npl (shopping) courses fpl; (goods) épicerie f. **grocery** n (shop) épicerie f.

groin n aine f.

groom n marié m; (for horses) palefrenier/-ière m/f. ● vt (horse) panser; (fig) préparer.

groove n (for door etc.) rainure f; (in record) sillon m.

grope vi tâtonner; ~ **for** chercher à tâtons.

gross adj (behaviour) vulgaire; (Comm) brut. ● n inv grosse f.

grotto n (pl ~**es**) grotte f.

grouch vi (grumble 🔲) rouspéter, râler.

ground¹ n terre f, sol m; (area) terrain m; (reason) raison f; (Electr, US) masse f; ~**s** terres fpl, parc m; (of coffee) marc m; **on the** ~ par terre; **lose** ~ perdre du terrain. ● vt/i (Naut) échouer; (aircraft) retenir au sol.

ground² ⇒GRIND. ● adj ~ **beef** (US) bifteck m haché.

ground: ~ **floor** n rez-de-chaussée m inv. ~**work** n travail m préparatoire.

group n groupe m. ● vt/i (se) grouper. ~**ware** n (Comput) logiciel m de groupe.

grovel vi (pt **grovelled**) ramper.

grow vi (pt **grew**; pp **grown**) (person) grandir; (plant) pousser; (become) devenir; (crime) augmenter. ● vt cultiver; ~ **up** devenir adulte, grandir. **grower** n cultivateur/-trice m/f.

growl vi (dog) gronder; (person) grogner. ● n grognement m.

grown ⇒GROW. ● adj adulte. ~-**up** a & n adulte (mf).

growth n (of person, plant) croissance f; (in numbers) accroissement m; (of hair, tooth) pousse f; (Med) grosseur f, tumeur f.

grudge vt ~ doing faire à contrecœur; ~ **sb sth** (success, wealth) en vouloir à qn de qch. ● n rancune f; **have a** ~ **against** en vouloir à.

grumble vi ronchonner, grogner (**at** après).

grumpy adj (**-ier**, **-iest**) grincheux, grognon.

grunt vi grogner. ● n grognement m.

guarantee n garantie f. ● vt garantir.

guard vt protéger; (watch) surveiller. ● vi ~ **against** se protéger contre. ● n (Mil) garde f; (person) garde m; (on train) chef m de train.

guardian n gardien/-ne m/f; (of orphan) tuteur/-trice m/f.

guess vt/i deviner; (suppose) penser. ● n conjecture f.

guest n invité/-e m/f; (in hotel) client/-e m/f. ~-**house** n pension f. ~-**room** n chambre f d'amis.

guidance n (advice) conseils mpl; (information) information f.

guide n (person, book) guide m; (girl) guide f. ● vt guider. ~**book** n guide m. ~-**dog** n chien m d'aveugle. ~**line** n indication f; (advice) conseils mpl.

guillotine n (for execution) guillotine f; (for paper) massicot m.

guilt n culpabilité f. **guilty** adj coupable.

guinea-pig n (animal) cochon m d'Inde; (fig) cobaye m.

guitar n guitare f.

gulf n (part of sea) golfe m; (hollow) gouffre m.

gull n mouette f, (larger) goéland m.

gullible adj crédule.

gully n (ravine) ravin m; (drain) rigole f.

gulp vt ~ (**down**) avaler en vitesse. ● vi (from fear etc.) avoir la gorge serrée. ● n gorgée f.

gum n (Anat) gencive f; (glue) colle f; (for chewing) chewing-gum m. ● vt (pt **gummed**) gommer.

gun n (pistol) revolver m; (rifle) fusil m; (large) canon m. ● vt (pt **gunned**) ~ **down** abattre. ~**fire** n fusillade f. ~**powder** n poudre f à canon. ~**shot** n coup m de feu.

gurgle n (of water) gargouillement m; (of baby) gazouillis m. ● vi (water) gargouiller; (baby) gazouiller.

gush vi ~ (**out**) jaillir. ● n jaillissement m.

gust n rafale f; (of smoke) bouffée f.

gut n (belly 🔟) ventre m. ● vt (pt **gutted**) (fish) vider; (of fire) dévaster.

guts npl 🔟 (insides of human) tripes fpl 🔟; (insides of animal, building) entrailles fpl; (courage) cran m 🔟.

gutter n (on roof) gouttière f; (in street) caniveau m.

guy n (man 🔟) type m.

gym n (place) gymnase m; (activity) gym(nastique) f.

gymnasium n gymnase m.

gymnastics npl gymnastique f.

gynaecologist n gynécologue mf.

gypsy n bohémien/-ne m/f.

Hh

habit n habitude f; (costume: Relig) habit m; **be in/get into the ~ of** avoir/prendre l'habitude de.

habitual adj (usual) habituel; (smoker, liar) invétéré.

hack n (writer) écrivaillon m. ● vi (Comput) pirater; **~ into** s'introduire dans. ● vt tailler. **hacker** n (Comput) pirate m informatique.

hackneyed adj rebattu.

had ⇒HAVE.

haddock n inv églefin m.

haemorrhage n hémorragie f.

haggard adj (person) exténué; (face, look) défait.

haggle vi marchander; **~ over sth** discuter du prix de qch.

hail n grêle f. ● vt (greet) saluer; (taxi) héler. ● vi grêler; **~ from** venir de. **~stone** n grêlon m.

hair n (on head) cheveux mpl; (on body, of animal) poils mpl; (single strand on head) cheveu m; (on body) poil m. **~brush** n brosse f à cheveux. **~cut** n coupe f de cheveux. **~-do** n 🔢 coiffure f. **~dresser** n coiffeur/ -euse m/f. **~-drier** n séchoir m (à cheveux). **~pin** n épingle f à cheveux. **~ remover** n dépilatoire m. **~-style** n coiffure f.

hairy adj (-ier, -iest) poilu; (terrifying 🔢) horrifiant.

half n (pl **halves**) (part) moitié f; (fraction) demi m; **~ a dozen** demi-douzaine f; **~ an hour** une demi-heure; **four and a ~** quatre et demi; **an hour and a ~** une heure et demie; **~ and half** moitié moitié; **in ~** en deux. ● adj demi; **~ price** à moitié prix. ● adv à moitié. **~-back** n (Sport) demi m. **~-hearted** adj tiède. **~-mast** n **at ~-mast** en berne. **~-term** n vacances fpl de demi-trimestre. **~-time** n mi-temps f. **~-way** adv à mi-chemin. **~-wit** n imbécile mf.

hall n (in house) entrée f; (corridor) couloir m; (in airport) hall m; (for

events) salle f; **~ of residence** résidence f universitaire.

hallmark n (on gold) poinçon m; (fig) caractéristique f.

hallo = HELLO.

Hallowe'en n la veille de la Toussaint.

halt n arrêt m; (temporary) suspension f; (Mil) halte f. ● vt (proceedings) interrompre; (arms sales, experiments) mettre fin à. ● vi (vehicle) s'arrêter; (army) faire halte.

halve vt (time) réduire de moitié; (fruit) couper en deux.

ham n jambon m.

hamburger n hamburger m.

hammer n marteau m. ● vt/i marteler; **~ sth into sth** enfoncer qch dans qch; **~ sth out** (agreement) parvenir à qch.

hammock n hamac m.

hamper n panier m. ● vt gêner.

hamster n hamster m.

hand n main f; (of clock) aiguille f; (writing) écriture f; (worker) ouvrier/ -ière m/f; (cards) jeu m; **give sb a ~** donner un coup de main à qn; **at ~** proche; **on ~** disponible; **on the one ~...on the other ~** d'une part...d'autre part; **to ~** à portée de la main. ● vt **~ sb sth, ~ sth to sb** donner qch à qn. □ **~ in** or **over** remettre; **~ out** distribuer. **~bag** n sac m à main. **~-baggage** n bagages mpl à main. **~book** n manuel m. **~brake** n frein m à main. **~cuffs** npl menottes fpl.

handicap n handicap m. ● vt (pt **handicapped**) handicaper.

handkerchief n (pl **~s**) mouchoir m.

handle n (of door, bag) poignée f; (of implement) manche m; (of cup, bucket) anse f; (of frying pan) queue f. ● vt (manage) manier; (deal with) traiter; (touch) manipuler.

hand: ~-out n document m; (leaflet) prospectus m; (money) aumône f. **~shake** n poignée f de main.

handsome adj (good looking) beau; (generous) généreux.

handwriting n écriture f.

handy adj (-ier, -iest) (book, skill) utile; (size, shape, tool) pratique;

(*person*) doué. ∼**man** *n* (*pl* **-men**) bricoleur *m*, homme *m* à tout faire.

hang *vt* (*pt* **hung**) (from hook, hanger) accrocher; (from rope) suspendre; (*pt* **hanged**) (*person*) pendre. ● *vi* (from hook) être accroché; (from rope) être suspendu; (*person*) être pendu. ● *n* **get the** ∼ **of doing** Ⓣ piger comment faire Ⓣ. □ ∼**about** traîner; ∼ **on** Ⓣ (hold out) tenir; (wait) attendre; ∼ **on to sth** s'agripper à qch; ∼ **out** *vi* Ⓣ (live) crécher Ⓣ; (spend time) passer son temps; *vt* (*washing*) étendre; ∼ **up** (telephone) raccrocher.

hanger *n* (for clothes) cintre *m*.

hang-gliding *n* vol *m* libre.

hangover *n* gueule *f* de bois Ⓣ.

hang-up Ⓣ complexe *m*.

hankering *n* envie *f*.

haphazard *adj* peu méthodique.

happen *vi* arriver, se passer; ∼ **to sb** arriver à qn; **it so** ∼**s that** il se trouve que.

happily *adv* joyeusement; (fortunately) heureusement.

happiness *n* bonheur *m*.

happy *adj* (**-ier**, **-iest**) heureux; **I'm not** ∼ **about it** je ne suis pas content; ∼ **with sth** satisfait de qch; ∼ **medium** juste milieu *m*.

harass *vt* harceler. **harassment** *n* harcèlement *m*.

harbour, (US) **harbor** *n* port *m*. ● *vt* (shelter) héberger.

hard *adj* dur; (difficult) difficile, dur; (*evidence, fact*) solide; **find it** ∼ **to do** avoir du mal à faire; ∼ **on sb** dur envers qn. ● *adv* (work) dur; (pull, hit, cry) fort; (think, study) sérieusement. ∼**board** *n* aggloméré *m*. ∼ **copy** *n* (Comput) tirage *m*. ∼ **disk** *n* disque *m* dur.

hardly *adv* à peine; (expect, hope) difficilement; ∼ **ever** presque jamais.

hardship *n* (poverty) privations *fpl*; (ordeal) épreuve *f*.

hard: ∼ **shoulder** *n* bande *f* d'arrêt d'urgence. ∼ **up** *adj* Ⓣ fauché Ⓣ. ∼**ware** *n* (Comput) matériel *m*, hardware *m*; (goods) quincaillerie *f*. ∼**-working** *adj* travailleur.

hardy *adj* (**-ier**, **-iest**) résistant.

hare *n* lièvre *m*. ● *vi* ∼ **around** courir partout.

harm *n* mal *m*; **there is no** ∼ **in** il n'y a pas de mal à. ● *vt* (*person*) faire du mal à; (*object*) endommager. **harmful** *adj* nuisible. **harmless** *adj* inoffensif.

harmony *n* harmonie *f*.

harness *n* harnais *m*. ● *vt* (*horse*) harnacher; (use) exploiter.

harp *n* harpe *f*. ● *vi* ∼ **on** (about) rabâcher.

harrowing *adj* (*experience*) atroce; (*story*) déchirant.

harsh *adj* (*punishment*) sévère; (*person*) dur; (*light*) cru; (*voice*) rude; (*chemical*) corrosif. **harshness** *n* dureté *f*.

harvest *n* récolte *f*; **the wine** ∼ les vendanges *fpl*. ● *vt* (*corn*) moissonner; (*vegetables*) récolter.

has ⇒HAVE.

hassle *n* complications *fpl*. ● *vt* Ⓣ talonner (about à propos de); (worry) stresser.

haste *n* hâte *f*; **in** ∼ à la hâte; **make** ∼ se dépêcher.

hasty *adj* (**-ier**, **-iest**) précipité.

hat *n* chapeau *m*.

hatch *n* (Aviat) panneau *m* mobile; (Naut) écoutille *f*; (for food) passe-plats *m inv*. ● *vt/i* (eggs) (faire) éclore.

hate *n* haine *f*. ● *vt* détester; (violently) haïr; (sport, food) avoir horreur de.

hatred *n* haine *f*.

haughty *adj* (**-ier**, **-iest**) hautain.

haul *vt* tirer. ● *n* (by thieves) butin *m*; (by customs) saisie *f*; **it will be a long** ∼ l'étape sera longue; **long/short** ∼ (*transport*) long/court courrier *m*. **haulage** *n* transport *m* routier. **haulier** *n* (firm) société *f* de transports routiers.

haunt *vt* hanter. ● *n* lieu *m* de prédilection.

have

present **have**, **has**; *past* **had**; *past participle* **had**

● *transitive verb*

····▸ (possess) avoir; I ∼ (got) a car j'ai une voiture; they ∼ (got) problems ils ont des problèmes.

····➤ (do sth) ~ **a try** essayer; ~ **a bath** prendre un bain.

····➤ ~ **sth done** faire faire qch; ~ **your hair cut** se faire couper les cheveux.

● *auxiliary verb*

····➤ (in perfect tenses) avoir; être; **I** ~ **seen him** je l'ai vu; **she had fallen** elle était tombée.

····➤ (in tag questions) **you've seen her, haven't you?** tu l'as vue, n'est-ce pas?; **you haven't seen her, ~ you?** tu ne l'as pas vue, par hasard?

····➤ (in short answers) **'you've never met him'—'yes I ~'** 'tu ne l'as jamais rencontré'—'mais si!'

····➤ (must) ~ **to** devoir; **I** ~ **to go** je dois partir; **you don't** ~ **to do it** tu n'es pas obligé de le faire.

➜ For expressions such as **have a walk, have dinner** ➩**walk, dinner.**

haven *n* refuge *m*; (fig) havre *m*.

havoc *n* dévastation *f*.

hawk *n* faucon *m*.

hay *n* foin *m*; ~ **fever** rhume *m* des foins.

haywire *adj* go ~ (*plans*) dérailler; (*machine*) se détraquer.

hazard *n* risque *m*; ~ (**warning**) **lights** feux *mpl* de détresse. ● *vt* hasarder.

haze *n* brume *f*.

hazel *n* (bush) noisetier *m*. ~**nut** *n* noisette *f*.

hazy *adj* (**-ier, -iest**) (misty) brumeux; (fig) vague.

he *pron* il; (emphatic) lui; **here** ~ **is** le voici.

head *n* tête *f*; (leader) chef *m*; (of beer) mousse *f*; ~**s or tails?** pile ou face? ● *vt* (*list*) être en tête de; (*team*) être à la tête de; (*chapter*) intituler; ~ **the ball** faire une tête. ● *vi* ~ **for** se diriger vers.

headache *n* mal *m* de tête; **have a** ~ avoir mal à la tête.

heading *n* titre *m*; (subject category) rubrique *f*.

head: ~**lamp**, ~**light** *n* phare *m*. ~**line** *n* gros titre *m*. ~**master** *n*

directeur *m*. ~**mistress** *n* directrice *f*. ~ **office** *n* siège *m* social. ~**-on** *a* & *adv* de front. ~**phones** *npl* casque *m*. ~**quarters** *npl* siège *m* social; (Mil) quartier *m* général. ~ **rest** *n* (Auto) repose-tête *m inv.* ~**strong** *adj* têtu.

heal *vt/i* guérir.

health *n* santé *f*. ~ **centre** *n* centre *m* médico-social. ~ **food** *n* produits *mpl* diététiques. ~ **insurance** *n* assurance *f* maladie.

healthy *adj* (*person, plant, skin, diet*) sain; (*air*) salutaire.

heap *n* tas *m*; ~**s of** Ⅱ un tas de. ● *vt* ~ (**up**) entasser.

hear *vt* (*pt* **heard**) entendre; (*news, rumour*) apprendre; (*lecture, broadcast*) écouter. ● *vi* entendre; ~ **from** recevoir des nouvelles de; ~ **of** *or* **about** entendre parler de.

hearing *n* ouïe *f*; (of case) audience *f*; **give sb a** ~ écouter qn. ~**-aid** *n* prothèse *f* auditive.

hearse *n* corbillard *m*.

heart *n* cœur *m*; (cards) cœur *m*; **at** ~ au fond; **by** ~ par cœur; **be** ~**-broken** avoir le cœur brisé; **lose** ~ perdre courage. ~ **attack** *n* crise *f* cardiaque. ~**burn** *n* brûlures *fpl* d'estomac. ~**felt** *adj* sincère.

hearth *n* foyer *m*.

heartily *adv* (*greet*) chaleureusement; (*laugh, eat*) de bon cœur.

hearty *adj* (**-ier, -iest**) (sincere) chaleureux; (*meal*) solide.

heat *n* chaleur *f*; (contest) épreuve *f* éliminatoire. ● *vt* (*house*) chauffer; ~ (**up**) (*food*) faire chauffer; (*reheat*) réchauffer. **heated** *adj* (fig) passionné; (lit) (*pool*) chauffé. **heater** *n* appareil *m* de chauffage.

heather *n* bruyère *f*.

heating *n* chauffage *m*.

heave *vt* (lift) hisser; (pull) traîner péniblement; ~ **a sigh** pousser un soupir. ● *vi* (pull) tirer de toutes ses forces; (retch) avoir un haut-le-cœur.

heaven *n* ciel *m*.

heavily *adv* lourdement; (smoke, drink) beaucoup.

heavy *adj* (**-ier, -iest**) lourd; (*cold, work*) gros; (*traffic*) dense.

∼ **goods vehicle** n poids m lourd.
∼**-handed** adj maladroit. ∼**weight**
n poids m lourd.

Hebrew n (person) Hébreu m; (Ling)
hébreu m. ● adj hébreu; (Ling)
hébraïque.

hectic adj (activity) intense; (period,
day) mouvementé.

hedge n haie f. ● vi (in answering) se
dérober.

hedgehog n hérisson m.

heel n talon m.

hefty adj (-ier, -iest) (person)
costaud 🔲; (object) pesant.

height n hauteur f; (of person) taille f;
(of plane, mountain) altitude f; (of fame,
glory) apogée m; (of joy, folly, pain)
comble m.

heir n héritier/-ière m/f. **heiress** n
héritière f. **heirloom** n objet m de
famille.

held ⇒HOLD.

helicopter n hélicoptère m.

hell n enfer m.

hello interj bonjour!; (on phone) allô!

helmet n casque m.

help vt/i aider (**to do** à faire); ∼ (**sb**)
with a bag/the housework aider qn à
porter un sac/à faire le ménage; ∼
oneself se servir; **he can't** ∼ **it** ce
n'est pas de sa faute. ● n aide f.
● interj au secours! **helper** n aide
mf. **helpful** adj utile; (person)
serviable. **helping** n portion f.
helpless adj impuissant.

hem n ourlet m. ● vt (pt **hemmed**)
faire un ourlet à; ∼ **in** cerner.

hen n poule f.

hence adv (for this reason) d'où; (from
now) d'ici. **henceforth** adv
désormais.

hepatitis n hépatite f.

her pron la, l'; (indirect object) lui; **it's** ∼
c'est elle; **for** ∼ pour elle. ● adj son,
sa; pl ses.

herb n herbe f; ∼**s** (Culin) fines
herbes fpl.

herd n troupeau m.

here adv ici; ∼! (take this) tiens!;
tenez!; ∼ **is**, ∼ **are** voici; **I'm** ∼ je
suis là. **hereabouts** adv par ici.
hereafter adv après; (in book) ci-

après. **hereby** adv par le présent
acte; (in letter) par la présente.

herewith adv ci-joint.

heritage n patrimoine m.

hernia n hernie f.

hero n (pl ∼**es**) héros m.

heroic adj héroïque.

heroin n héroïne f.

heroine n héroïne f.

heron n héron m.

herring n hareng m.

hers pron le sien, la sienne, les sien
(ne)s; **it is** ∼ c'est à elle or le sien or
la sienne.

herself pron (emphatic) elle-même;
(reflexive) se; **proud of** ∼ fière d'elle;
by ∼ toute seule.

hesitate vi hésiter. **hesitation** n
hésitation f.

heterosexual a & n hétérosexuel/
-le (m/f).

hexagon n hexagone m.

heyday n apogée m.

HGV abbr ⇒HEAVY GOODS VEHICLE.

hi interj 🔲 salut! 🔲.

hiccup n hoquet m; (the) ∼**s** le
hoquet. ● vi hoqueter.

hide vt (pt **hid**; pp **hidden**) cacher
(**from** à). ● vi se cacher (**from** de); **go
into hiding** se cacher. ● n (skin) peau
f.

hideous adj (monster, object)
hideux; (noise) affreux.

hiding n **go into** ∼ se cacher; **give sb
a** ∼ administrer une correction à
qn.

hierarchy n hiérarchie f.

hi-fi n (chaîne f) hi-fi f inv.

high adj haut; (price, number) élevé;
(priest, speed) grand; (voice) aigu; **in
the** ∼ **season** en pleine saison. ● n **a
(new)** ∼ un niveau record. ● adv
haut. ∼**brow** a & n intellectuel/-le
(m/f). ∼ **chair** n chaise f haute. ∼
court n cour f suprême. **higher
education** n enseignement m
supérieur. ∼**-jump** n saut m en
hauteur. ∼**-level** adj à haut niveau.

highlight n (best moment) point m
fort; ∼**s** (in hair) reflet m; (artificial)
mèches fpl; (Sport) résumé m. ● vt
(emphasize) souligner.

highly *adv* extrêmement; (paid) très bien; **speak/think** ∼ of dire/penser beaucoup de bien de.

Highness *n* Altesse *f*.

high: ∼**-rise** (**building**) *n* tour *f*. ∼ **school** *n* lycée *m*. ∼**-speed** *adj* (*train*) à grande vitesse; (*film*) ultrarapide. ∼ **street** *n* rue *f* principale. ∼**-tech** *adj* de pointe.

highway *n* route *f* nationale; (US) autoroute *f*; ∼ **code** code *m* de la route.

hijack *vt* détourner. ● *n* détournement *m*. **hijacker** *n* pirate *m* (de l'air).

hike *n* randonnée *f*; **price** ∼ hausse *f* de prix. ● *vi* faire de la randonnée.

hilarious *adj* désopilant.

hill *n* colline *f*; (slope) côte *f*. **hilly** *adj* vallonné.

him *pron* le, l'; (indirect object) lui; **it's** ∼ c'est lui; **for** ∼ pour lui.

himself *pron* (emphatic) lui-même; (reflexive) se; **proud of** ∼ fier de lui; **by** ∼ tout seul.

hind *adj* de derrière.

hinder *vt* (hamper) gêner; (prevent) empêcher. **hindrance** *n* obstacle *m*, gêne *f*.

hindsight *n* **with** ∼ rétrospectivement.

Hindu *n* Hindou/-e *m/f*. ● *adj* hindou.

hinge *n* charnière *f*. ● *vi* ∼ **on** dépendre de.

hint *n* allusion *f*; (of spice, accent) pointe *f*; (of colour) touche *f*; (advice) conseil *m*. ● *vt* laisser entendre. ● *vi* ∼ **at** faire allusion à.

hip *n* hanche *f*.

hippopotamus *n* (*pl* ∼**es**) hippopotame *m*.

hire *vt* (*thing*) louer; (*person*) engager. ● *n* location *f*. ∼**-car** *n* voiture *f* de location. ∼**-purchase** *n* achat *m* à crédit.

his *adj* son, sa, *pl* ses. ● *pron* le sien, la sienne, les sien(ne)s; **it is** ∼ c'est à lui *or* le sien *or* la sienne.

hiss *n* sifflement *m*. ● *vt/i* siffler.

history *n* histoire *f*; **make** ∼ entrer dans l'histoire.

hit *vt* (*pt* **hit**; *pres p* **hitting**) frapper; (collide with) heurter; (find) trouver; (affect, reach) toucher. ● *vi* ∼ **on** (find) tomber sur; ∼ **it off** s'entendre bien (with avec). ● *n* (blow) coup *m*; (fig) succès *m*; (song) tube *m* ⊞.

hitch *vt* (fasten) accrocher; ∼ **up** remonter. ● *n* (snag) anicroche *f*. ∼**-hike** *vi* faire du stop ⊞. ∼**-hiker** *n* auto-stoppeur/-euse *m/f*.

hi-tech *a* & *n* = HIGH-TECH.

hitherto *adv* jusqu'ici.

HIV *abbr* (**human immunodeficiency virus**) VIH *m*.

hive *n* ruche *f*. ● *vt* ∼ **off** séparer; (*industry*) céder.

HIV-positive *adj* séropositif.

hoard *vt* amasser; (*supplies*) stocker. ● *n* trésor *m*; (of provisions) provisions *fpl*.

hoarse *adj* enroué.

hoax *n* canular *m*.

hobby *n* passe-temps *m inv*. ∼**-horse** *n* (fig) dada *m*.

hockey *n* hockey *m*.

hog *n* cochon *m*. ● *vt* (*pt* **hogged**) ⊞ monopoliser.

hold *vt* (*pt* **held**) tenir; (contain) contenir; (*conversation, opinion*) avoir; (*shares, record, person*) détenir; ∼ **(the line), please** ne quittez pas. ● *vi* (*rope, weather*) tenir. ● *n* prise *f*; **get** ∼ **of** attraper; (*ticket*) se procurer; (*person*) (by phone) joindre; **on** ∼ en attente. □ ∼ **back** (contain) retenir; (hide) cacher; ∼ **down** (*job*) garder; (*person*) tenir; (*costs*) limiter; ∼ **on** (stand firm) tenir bon; (wait) attendre; ∼ **on to** (keep) garder; (cling to) se cramponner à; ∼ **out** *vt* (offer) offrir; *vi* (resist) tenir le coup; ∼ **up** (support) soutenir; (delay) retarder; (rob) attaquer.

holder *n* détenteur/-trice *m/f*; (of passport, post) titulaire *mf*; (for object) support *m*.

hold-up *n* retard *m*; (of traffic) embouteillage *m*; (robbery) hold-up *m inv*.

hole *n* trou *m*.

holiday *n* vacances *fpl*; (public) jour *m* férié; (time off) congé *m*. ● *vi* passer

h

ses vacances. ● *adj* de vacances.
~-maker *n* vacancier/-ière *m/f*.

Holland *n* Hollande *f*.

hollow *adj* creux; (fig) faux. ● *n*
creux *m*. ● *vt* creuser.

holly *n* houx *m*.

holy *adj* (-**ier**, -**iest**) saint; (water)
bénit; H~ Ghost, H~ Spirit Saint-
Esprit *m*.

homage *n* hommage *m*.

home *n* (place to live) logement *m*;
maison *f*; (institution) maison *f*; (family
base) foyer *m*; (country) pays *m*. ● *adj*
de la maison, du foyer; (of family) de
famille; (Pol) intérieur; (*match, visit*)
à domicile. ● *adv* (at) ~ à la maison,
chez soi; **come** *or* **go** ~ rentrer; (from
abroad) rentrer dans son pays; **feel at**
~ **with** être à l'aise avec. ~
computer *n* ordinateur *m*, PC *m*.

homeless *adj* sans abri. ● *n* **the** ~
les sans-abri *mpl*.

homely *adj* (-**ier**, -**iest**) (cosy)
accueillant; (simple) sans prétention;
(person: US) sans attraits.

home: **~-made** *adj* (fait) maison.
H~ Office *n* ministère *m* de
l'Intérieur. ~ **page** *n* (Internet) page *f*
d'accueil. **H~ Secretary** *n*
Ministre *m* de l'Intérieur. **~sick** *adj*
be ~sick avoir le mal du pays.
~work *n* devoirs *mpl*.

homosexual *a* & *n* homosexuel/-le
(*m/f*).

honest *adj* (truthful) intègre;
(trustworthy) honnête; (sincere) franc.
honestly *adv* honnêtement;
franchement. **honesty** *n* honnêteté
f.

honey *n* miel *m*; (person 🖪) chéri/-e
m/f. **~moon** *n* voyage *m* de noces;
(fig) lune *f* de miel.

honk *vi* klaxonner.

honorary *adj* (*person*) honoraire;
(*degree*) honorifique.

honour, (US) **honor** *n* honneur *m*.
● *vt* honorer.

hood *n* capuchon *m*; (on car, pram)
capote *f*; (car engine cover: US) capot *m*.

hoof *n* (*pl* **~s**) sabot *m*.

hook *n* crochet *m*; (on garment) agrafe
f; (for fishing) hameçon *m*; **off the** ~
tiré d'affaire; (phone) décroché. ● *vt*
accrocher.

hoot *n* (of owl) (h)ululement *m*; (of car)
coup *m* de klaxon. ● *vi* (*owl*) (h)
ululer; (*car*) klaxonner; (jeer) huer.

hoover *vt* ~ **a room** passer
l'aspirateur dans une pièce.

Hoover® *n* aspirateur *m*.

hop *vi* (*pt* **hopped**) sauter (à cloche-
pied); ~ **in!** 🖪 vas-y, monte! ● *n*
bond *m*; **~s** houblon *m*.

hope *n* espoir *m*. ● *vt/i* espérer; ~
for espérer avoir; **I** ~ **so** je l'espère.

hopeful *adj* (*news, sign*)
encourageant; (*person*) plein
d'espoir; (*mood*) optimiste.
hopefully *adv* (with luck) avec un
peu de chance; (with hope) avec
optimisme.

hopeless *adj* désespéré; (useless: fig)
nul 🖪.

horizon *n* horizon *m*.

horizontal *adj* horizontal.

hormone *n* hormone *f*.

horn *n* corne *f*; (of car) klaxon® *m*;
(Mus) cor *m*.

horoscope *n* horoscope *m*.

horrible *adj* horrible.

horrid *adj* horrible.

horrific *adj* horrifiant.

horrify *vt* horrifier.

horror *n* horreur *f*. ● *adj* (*film,
story*) d'épouvante.

horse *n* cheval *m*. **~back** *n* **on
~back** à cheval. **~-chestnut** *n*
marron *m* (d'Inde). **~man** *n* (*pl*
-**men**) cavalier *m*. **~power** *n*
puissance *f* (en chevaux). **~-race** *n*
course *f* de chevaux. **~-radish** *n*
raifort *m*. **~shoe** *n* fer *m* à cheval.
~show *n* concours *m* hippique.

hose *n* tuyau *m*. ● *vt* arroser.
~-pipe *n* tuyau *m*.

hospitable *adj* hospitalier.

hospital *n* hôpital *m*.

host *n* (to guests) hôte *m*; (on TV)
animateur *m*; (Internet) ordinateur *m*
hôte; **a** ~ **of** une foule de; (Relig)
hostie *f*.

hostage *n* otage *m*; **hold sb** ~
garder qn en otage.

hostel *n* foyer *m*; (**youth**) ~ auberge
f (de jeunesse).

hostess *n* hôtesse *f*.

hostile *adj* hostile.

hot *adj* (**hotter**, **hottest**) chaud; (Culin) épicé; **be** *or* **feel** ~ avoir chaud; **it is** ~ il fait chaud; **in** ~ **water** 🆘 dans le pétrin. ● *vt/i* (*pt* **hotted**) ~ **up** 🆘 chauffer. ~ **air balloon** *n* montgolfière *f*. ~ **dog** *n* hot-dog *m*.

hotel *n* hôtel *m*.

hot: ~**headed** *adj* impétueux. ~ **list** *n* (Internet) signets *mpl* favoris. ~**plate** *n* plaque *f* chauffante. ~ **water bottle** *n* bouillotte *f*.

hound *n* chien *m* de chasse. ● *vt* poursuivre.

hour *n* heure *f*.

hourly *adj* horaire; **on an** ~ **basis** à l'heure. ● *adv* toutes les heures.

house[1] *n* maison *f*; (Pol) Chambre *f*; **on the** ~ aux frais de la maison.

house[2] *vt* loger; (of building) abriter.

household *n* (house, family) ménage *m*. ● *adj* ménager.

house: ~**keeper** *n* gouvernante *f*. ~**proud** *adj* méticuleux. ~**warming** *n* pendaison *f* de crémaillère. ~**wife** *n* (*pl* -**wives**) ménagère *f*. ~**work** *n* travaux *mpl* ménagers.

housing *n* logement *m*; ~ **association** service *m* de logement; ~ **development** cité *f*; (smaller) lotissement *m*.

hover *vi* (*bird*) voleter; (vacillate) vaciller. **hovercraft** *n* aéroglisseur *m*.

how *adv* comment; ~ **are you?** comment allez-vous?; ~ **long/tall is...?** quelle est la longueur/hauteur de...?; ~ **many?**, ~ **much?** combien?; ~ **pretty!** comme *or* que c'est joli!; ~ **about a walk?** si on faisait une promenade?; ~ **do you do?** (greeting) enchanté.

however *adv* (nevertheless) cependant; ~ **hard I try** j'ai beau essayer; ~ **much it costs** quel que soit le prix; ~ **young/poor he is** si jeune/pauvre soit-il; ~ **you like** comme tu veux.

howl *n* hurlement *m*. ● *vi* hurler.

HP *abbr* ⇒HIRE-PURCHASE.

hp *abbr* ⇒HORSEPOWER.

HQ *abbr* ⇒HEADQUARTERS.

hub *n* moyeu *m*; (fig) centre *m*.

hug *vt* (*pt* **hugged**) serrer dans ses bras. ● *n* étreinte *f*; **give sb a** ~ serrer qn dans ses bras.

huge *adj* énorme.

hull *n* (of ship) coque *f*.

hum *vt/i* (*pt* **hummed**) (*person*) fredonner; (*insect*) bourdonner; (*engine*) ronronner. ● *n* bourdonnement *m*; ronronnement *m*.

human *adj* humain. ● *n* humain *m*. ~ **being** *n* être *m* humain.

humane *adj* (*person*) humain; (*act*) d'humanité; (*killing*) sans cruauté.

humanitarian *adj* humanitaire.

humanity *n* humanité *f*.

humble *adj* humble.

humid *adj* humide.

humiliate *vt* humilier.

humorous *adj* humoristique; (*person*) plein d'humour.

humour, (US) **humor** *n* humour *m*; (mood) humeur *f*. ● *vt* amadouer.

hump *n* bosse *f*. ● *vt* 🆘 porter.

hunchback *n* bossu/-e *m/f*.

hundred *a & n* cent (*m*); **two** ~ **and one** deux cent un; ~**s of** des centaines de. **hundredth** *a & n* centième (*mf*).

hung ⇒HANG.

Hungarian *n* (person) Hongrois/-e *m/f*; (Ling) hongrois *m*. ● *adj* hongrois. **Hungary** *n* Hongrie *f*.

hunger *n* faim *f*. ● *vi* ~ **for** avoir faim de.

hungry *adj* (-**ier**, -**iest**) affamé; **be** ~ avoir faim.

hunt *vt/i* chasser; ~ **for** chercher. ● *n* chasse *f*. **hunter** *n* chasseur *m*. **hunting** *n* chasse *f*.

hurdle *n* (Sport) haie *f*; (fig) obstacle *m*.

hurricane *n* ouragan *m*.

hurry *vi* se dépêcher; ~ **out** sortir précipitamment. ● *vt* (*work*) terminer à la hâte; (*person*) bousculer. ● *n* hâte *f*; **in a** ~ pressé.

hurt *vt/i* (*pt* **hurt**) faire mal (à); (injure, offend) blesser. ● *adj* blessé. ● *n* blessure *f*.

hurtle *vi* ~ **down** dévaler; ~ **along a road** foncer sur une route.

husband *n* mari *m*.

hush *vt* faire taire; ~ **up** (*news*) étouffer. ● *n* silence *m*. ● *interj* chut!

husky *adj* (**-ier, -iest**) enroué. ● *n* husky *m*.

hustle *vt* (push, rush) bousculer. ● *vi* (hurry) se dépêcher; (work: US) se démener. ● *n* ~ **and bustle** agitation *f*.

hut *n* cabane *f*.

hyacinth *n* jacinthe *f*.

hydrant *n* (fire) ~ bouche *f* d'incendie.

hydraulic *adj* hydraulique.

hydroelectric *adj* hydroélectrique.

hydrogen *n* hydrogène *m*; ~ **bomb** bombe *f* à hydrogène.

hyena *n* hyène *f*.

hygiene *n* hygiène *f*. **hygienic** *adj* hygiénique.

hymn *n* cantique *m*; (fig) hymne *m*.

hype *n* 🔲 battage *m* publicitaire. ● *vt* ~ (**up**) (*film, book*) faire du battage pour.

hyperactive *adj* hyperactif.

hyperlink *n* hyperlien *m*.

hypermarket *n* hypermarché *m*.

hypertext *n* hypertexte *m*.

hyphen *n* trait *m* d'union.

hypnosis *n* hypnose *f*.

hypocrisy *n* hypocrisie *f*. **hypocrite** *n* hypocrite *mf*. **hypocritical** *adj* hypocrite.

hypothesis *n* (*pl* **-ses**) hypothèse *f*.

hysteria *n* hystérie *f*. **hysterical** *adj* hystérique.

hysterics *npl* crise *f* de nerfs; **be in** ~ rire aux larmes.

- - -

- - -

I *pron* je, j'; (stressed) moi.

ice *n* glace *f*; (on road) verglas *m*. ● *vt* (*cake*) glacer. ● *vi* ~ (**up**) (*window*) se givrer; (*river*) geler. ~**box** *n* (US) réfrigérateur *m*. ~**-cream** *n* glace *f*.

~**-cube** *n* glaçon *m*. ~ **hockey** *n* hockey *m* sur glace.

Iceland *n* Islande *f*. **Icelander** *n* Islandais/-e *m/f*. **Icelandic** *a* & *n* islandais (*m*).

ice: ~ **lolly** *n* glace *f* (*sur bâtonnet*). ~ **rink** *n* patinoire *f*. ~ **skate** *n* patin *m* à glace.

icicle *n* stalactite *f* (de glace).

icing *n* (sugar) glaçage *m*.

icy *adj* (**-ier, -iest**) (*hands, wind*) glacé; (*road*) verglacé; (*manner, welcome*) glacial.

ID *n* pièce *f* d'identité; ~ **card** carte *f* d'identité.

idea *n* idée *f*.

ideal *adj* idéal. ● *n* idéal *m*.

identical *adj* identique.

identification *n* identification *f*; (papers) pièce *f* d'identité.

identify *vt* identifier. ● *vi* ~ **with** s'identifier à.

identikit *n* ~ **picture** portrait-robot *m*.

identity *n* identité *f*.

ideological *adj* idéologique.

idiom *n* (phrase) idiome *m*; (language) parler *m*, langue *f*. **idiomatic** *adj* idiomatique.

idiosyncrasy *n* particularité *f*.

idiot *n* idiot/-e *m/f*. **idiotic** *adj* idiot.

idle *adj* (lazy) paresseux; (doing nothing) oisif; (*boast, threat*) vain. ● *vi* (*engine*) tourner au ralenti. ● *vt* ~ **away** gaspiller.

idol *n* idole *f*. **idolize** *vt* idolâtrer.

idyllic *adj* idyllique.

i.e. *abbr* c-à-d, c'est-à-dire.

if *conj* si.

ignite *vt/i* (s')enflammer.

ignition *n* (Auto) allumage *m*; ~ (**switch**) contact *m*; ~ **key** clé *f* contact.

ignorance *n* ignorance *f*. **ignorant** *adj* ignorant (**of** de). **ignorantly** *adv* par ignorance.

ignore *vt* (*person*) ignorer; (*mistake, remark*) ne pas relever; (*feeling, fact*) ne pas tenir compte de.

ill *adj* malade. ● *adv* mal. ● *n* mal *m*. ~**-advised** *adj* malavisé. ~ **at ease** *adj* mal à l'aise. ~**-bred** *adj* mal élevé.

illegal *adj* illégal.

illegible *adj* illisible.

illegitimate *adj* illégitime.

ill: ~-**fated** *adj* malheureux. ~ **feeling** *n* ressentiment *m*.

illiterate *a* & *n* analphabète (*mf*).

illness *n* maladie *f*.

ill-treat *vt* maltraiter.

illuminate *vt* éclairer; (decorate with lights) illuminer. **illumination** *n* éclairage *m*; illumination *f*.

illusion *n* illusion *f*.

illustrate *vt* illustrer. **illustration** *n* illustration *f*. **illustrative** *adj* qui illustre.

image *n* image *f*; (of firm, person) image *f* de marque. **imagery** *n* images *fpl*.

imaginable *adj* imaginable. **imaginary** *adj* imaginaire. **imagination** *n* imagination *f*. **imaginative** *adj* plein d'imagination.

imagine *vt* (s')imaginer (**that** que); ~ **being rich** s'imaginer riche.

imbalance *n* déséquilibre *m*.

imitate *vt* imiter.

immaculate *adj* impeccable.

immaterial *adj* sans importance (**to** pour; **that** que).

immature *adj* (*person*) immature; (*plant*) qui n'est pas arrivé à maturité.

immediate *adj* immédiat.

immediately *adv* immédiatement. ● *conj* dès que.

immense *adj* immense. **immensely** *adv* extrêmement, immensément. **immensity** *n* immensité *f*.

immerse *vt* plonger (**in** dans). **immersion** *n* immersion *f*; **immersion heater** chauffe-eau *m inv* électrique.

immigrant *n* & *a* immigré/-e (*m/f*); (newly-arrived) immigrant/-e (*m/f*). **immigrate** *vi* immigrer. **immigration** *n* immigration *f*.

imminent *adj* imminent.

immoral *adj* immoral.

immortal *adj* immortel.

immune *adj* immunisé (**from, to** contre); (*reaction, system*) immunitaire. **immunity** *n* immunité *f*. **immunization** *n* immunisation *f*. **immunize** *vt* immuniser.

impact *n* impact *m*.

impair *vt* (*performance*) affecter; (*ability*) affaiblir.

impart *vt* communiquer, transmettre.

impartial *adj* impartial.

impassable *adj* (*barrier*) infranchissable; (*road*) impraticable.

impassive *adj* impassible.

impatience *n* impatience *f*. **impatient** *adj* impatient; **get impatient** s'impatienter. **impatiently** *adv* impatiemment.

impeccable *adj* impeccable.

impede *vt* entraver.

impediment *n* entrave *f*; **speech** ~ défaut *m* d'élocution.

impending *adj* imminent.

imperative *adj* urgent. ● *n* impératif *m*.

imperfect *adj* incomplet; (faulty) défectueux. ● *n* (Gram) imparfait *m*. **imperfection** *n* imperfection *f*.

imperial *adj* impérial; (measure) conforme aux normes britanniques. **imperialism** *n* impérialisme *m*.

impersonal *adj* impersonnel.

impersonate *vt* se faire passer pour; (mimic) imiter.

impertinent *adj* impertinent.

impervious *adj* imperméable (**to** à).

impetuous *adj* impétueux.

impetus *n* impulsion *f*.

impinge *vi* ~ **on** affecter; (encroach) empiéter sur.

implement *n* instrument *m*; (tool) outil *m*. ● *vt* exécuter, mettre en application; (*software*) implanter.

implicit *adj* (implied) implicite (**in** dans); (unquestioning) absolu.

imply *vt* (assume, mean) impliquer; (insinuate) laisser entendre.

impolite *adj* impoli.

import[1] *vt* importer.

import[2] *n* (*article*) importation *f*; (*meaning*) signification *f*.

importance *n* importance *f*. **important** *adj* important.

impose *vt* imposer (**on sb** à qn; **on sth** sur qch). ● *vi* s'imposer; ~ **on sb** abuser de la bienveillance de qn.
imposing *adj* imposant.
imposition *n* dérangement *m*; (tax) imposition *f*.
impossible *adj* impossible. ● *n* **the** ~ l'impossible *m*.
impotent *adj* impuissant.
impound *vt* confisquer, saisir.
impoverish *vt* appauvrir.
impractical *adj* peu réaliste.
impregnable *adj* imprenable.
impress *vt* impressionner; ~ **sth on sb** faire bien comprendre qch à qn.
impression *n* impression *f*.
impressionable *adj* impressionnable. **impressive** *adj* impressionnant.
imprint¹ *n* empreinte *f*.
imprint² *vt* (fix) graver (**on** dans); (print) imprimer.
imprison *vt* emprisonner.
improbable *adj* (not likely) improbable; (incredible) invraisemblable.
improper *adj* (unseemly) malséant; (dishonest) irrégulier.
improve *vt/i* (s')améliorer. **improvement** *n* amélioration *f*.
improvise *vt/i* improviser.
impudent *adj* impudent.
impulse *n* impulsion *f*; **on** ~ sur un coup de tête. **impulsive** *adj* impulsif. **impulsively** *adv* par impulsion.
impurity *n* impureté *f*.
in *prep* (inside, within) dans; (expressing place, position) à, en; (expressing time) en, dans; ~ **the box/garden** dans la boîte/le jardin; ~ **Paris/school** à Paris/l'école; ~ **town** en ville; ~ **the country** à la campagne; ~ **English** en anglais; ~ **India** en Inde; ~ **Japan** au Japon; ~ **winter** en hiver; ~ **spring** au printemps; ~ **an hour** (at end of) au bout d'une heure; ~ **an hour('s time)** dans une heure; ~ **(the space of) an hour** en une heure; ~ **doing** en faisant; ~ **the evening** le soir; **one** ~ **ten** un sur dix; ~ **between** entre les deux; (time) entretemps; ~ **a firm voice** d'une voix ferme; ~ **blue** en bleu; ~ **ink** à l'encre; ~ **uniform** en

uniforme; ~ **a skirt** en jupe; ~ **a whisper** en chuchotant; ~ **a loud voice** d'une voix forte; **the best** ~ le meilleur de; **we are** ~ **for** on va avoir; **have it** ~ **for sb** ⊞ avoir qn dans le collimateur. ● *adv* (inside) dedans; (at home) là, à la maison; (in fashion) à la mode; **come** ~ entrer; **run** ~ entrer en courant.
inability *n* incapacité *f* (**to do** de faire).
inaccessible *adj* inaccessible.
inaccurate *adj* inexact.
inactive *adj* inactif. **inactivity** *n* inaction *f*.
inadequate *adj* insuffisant.
inadvertently *adv* par mégarde.
inadvisable *adj* inopportun, à déconseiller.
inane *adj* idiot, débile.
inanimate *adj* inanimé.
inappropriate *adj* inopportun; (term) inapproprié.
inarticulate *adj* qui a du mal à s'exprimer.
inasmuch as *adv* dans la mesure où; (because) vu que.
inaugurate *vt* (open, begin) inaugurer; (person) investir.
inborn *adj* inné.
inbred *adj* (inborn) inné.
Inc. *abbr* (**incorporated**) S.A.
incapable *adj* incapable (**of doing** de faire).
incapacitate *vt* immobiliser.
incense¹ *n* encens *m*.
incense² *vt* mettre en fureur.
incentive *n* motivation *f*; (payment) prime *f*.
incessant *adj* incessant. **incessantly** *adv* sans cesse.
incest *n* inceste *m*. **incestuous** *adj* incestueux.
inch *n* pouce *m* (=2.54 cm.). ● *vi* ~ **towards** se diriger petit à petit vers.
incidence *n* fréquence *f*.
incident *n* incident *m*. **incidental** *adj* secondaire. **incidentally** *adv* à propos; (by chance) par la même occasion.
incinerate *vt* incinérer. **incinerator** *n* incinérateur *m*.
incite *vt* inciter, pousser.

inclination n (tendency) tendance f; (desire) envie f.

incline[1] vt/i (s')incliner; **be ~d to** avoir tendance à.

incline[2] n pente f.

include vt comprendre, inclure. **including** prep (y) compris. **inclusion** n inclusion f.

inclusive a & adv inclus; **~ of delivery** livraison comprise.

income n revenus mpl; **~ tax** impôt m sur le revenu.

incoming adj (tide) montant; (tenant, government) nouveau; (call) qui vient de l'extérieur.

incompatible adj incompatible.

incompetent adj incompétent.

incomplete adj incomplet.

incomprehensible adj incompréhensible.

inconceivable adj inconcevable.

inconclusive adj peu concluant.

incongruous adj déconcertant, surprenant.

inconsiderate adj (person) peu attentif à autrui; (act) maladroit.

inconsistent adj (argument) incohérent; (performance) inégal; (behaviour) changeant; **~ with** en contradiction avec.

inconspicuous adj qui passe inaperçu.

incontinent adj incontinent.

inconvenience n dérangement m; (drawback) inconvénient m. ● vt déranger. **inconvenient** adj incommode; **if it's not inconvenient for you** si cela ne vous dérange pas.

incorporate vt incorporer (into dans); (contain) comporter.

incorrect adj incorrect.

increase[1] n augmentation f (in, of de); **be on the ~** être en progression.

increase[2] vt/i augmenter. **increasing** adj croissant. **increasingly** adv de plus en plus.

incredible adj incroyable.

incriminate vt incriminer. **incriminating** adj compromettant.

incubate vt (eggs) couver. **incubation** n incubation f. **incubator** n couveuse f.

incur vt (pt **incurred**) (penalty, anger) encourir; (debts) contracter.

indebted adj **~ to sb** redevable à qn (for de); (grateful) reconnaissant à qn.

indecent adj indécent.

indecisive adj indécis; (ending) peu concluant.

indeed adv en effet; (emphatic) vraiment.

indefinite adj vague; (period, delay) illimité. **indefinitely** adv indéfiniment.

indelible adj indélébile.

indemnity n (protection) assurance f; (payment) indemnité f.

indent vt (text) renfoncer. **indentation** n (dent) marque f.

independence n indépendance f. **independent** adj indépendant. **independently** adv de façon indépendante; **independently of** indépendamment de.

index n (pl **~es**) (in book) index m; (in library) catalogue m; (in economy) indice m; **~ card** fiche f; **~ (finger)** index m. ● vt classer. **~-linked** adj indexé.

India n Inde f.

Indian n Indien/-ne m/f. ● adj indien.

indicate vt indiquer. **indication** n indication f.

indicative a & n indicatif (m).

indicator n (pointer) aiguille f; (on vehicle) clignotant m; (board) tableau m.

indict vt inculper. **indictment** n accusation f.

indifferent adj indifférent; (not good) médiocre.

indigenous adj indigène.

indigestible adj indigeste. **indigestion** n indigestion f.

indignant adj indigné.

indirect adj indirect. **indirectly** adv indirectement.

indiscreet adj indiscret. **indiscretion** n indiscrétion f.

indiscriminate adj sans distinction. **indiscriminately** adv sans distinction.

indisputable adj indiscutable.

i

individual *adj* individuel; (*tuition*) particulier. ● *n* individu *m*.
individualist *n* individualiste *mf*.
individuality *n* individualité *f*.
individually *adv* individuellement.

indoctrinate *vt* endoctriner.
indoctrination *n* endoctrinement *m*.

indolent *adj* indolent.

Indonesia *n* Indonésie *f*.

indoor *adj* (*clothes*) d'intérieur; (pool, court) couvert. **indoors** *adv* à l'intérieur.

induce *vt* (influence) persuader; (stronger) inciter (**to do** à faire).
inducement *n* (financial) récompense *f*; (incentive) motivation *f*.

induction *n* (Electr) induction *f*; (inauguration) installation *f*.

indulge *vt* (*person, whim*) céder à; (*child*) gâter. ● *vi* ~ **in** se livrer à.
indulgence *n* indulgence *f*; (treat) plaisir *m*. **indulgent** *adj* indulgent.

industrial *adj* industriel; (accident) du travail; ~ **action** grève *f*; ~ **dispute** conflit *m* social.
industrialist *n* industriel/-le *m/f*.
industrialized *adj* industrialisé.

industrious *adj* diligent.

industry *n* industrie *f*; (zeal) zèle *m*.

inebriated *adj* ivre.

inedible *adj* immangeable.

ineffective *adj* inefficace.

inefficient *adj* inefficace; (person) incompétent.

ineligible *adj* inéligible; **be** ~ **for** ne pas avoir droit à.

inept *adj* incompétent; (tactless) maladroit.

inequality *n* inégalité *f*.

inescapable *adj* indéniable.

inevitable *adj* inévitable.

inexcusable *adj* inexcusable.

inexhaustible *adj* inépuisable.

inexpensive *adj* pas cher.

inexperience *n* inexpérience *f*.
inexperienced *adj* inexpérimenté.

infallible *adj* infaillible.

infamous *adj* (*person*) tristement célèbre; (*deed*) infâme.

infancy *n* petite enfance *f*; **in its** ~ (fig) à ses débuts *mpl*. **infant** *n* (baby)

bébé *m*; (at school) enfant *m*.
infantile *adj* infantile.

infatuated *adj* ~ **with** entiché de.
infatuation *n* engouement *m*.

infect *vt* contaminer; ~ **sb with sth** transmettre qch à qn. **infection** *n* infection *f*. **infectious** *adj* contagieux.

infer *vt* (*pt* **inferred**) (deduce) déduire.

inferior *adj* inférieur (**to** à); (*work, product*) de qualité inférieure. ● *n* inférieur/-e *m/f*. **inferiority** *n* infériorité *f*.

inferno *n* (hell) enfer *m*; (blaze) brasier *m*.

infertile *adj* infertile.

infest *vt* infester (**with** de).

infidelity *n* infidélité *f*.

infighting *n* conflits *mpl* internes.

infinite *adj* infini. **infinitely** *adv* infiniment. **infinitive** *n* infinitif *m*.
infinity *n* infinité *f*.

infirm *adj* infirme. **infirmary** *n* hôpital *m*; (sick-bay) infirmerie *f*.
infirmity *n* infirmité *f*.

inflame *vt* enflammer.
inflammable *adj* inflammable.
inflammation *n* inflammation *f*.
inflammatory *adj* incendiaire.

inflatable *adj* gonflable. **inflate** *vt* (lit, fig) gonfler.

inflation *n* inflation *f*.

inflection *n* (of word root) flexion *f*; (of vowel, voice) inflexion *f*.

inflict *vt* infliger (**on** à).

influence *n* influence *f*; **under the** ~ (drunk 🔲) éméché. ● *vt* (*person*) influencer; (*choice*) influer sur.
influential *adj* (powerful) influent; (*theory, artist*) très suivi.

influenza *n* grippe *f*.

influx *n* afflux *m*.

inform *vt* informer (**of** de); **keep** ~**ed** tenir au courant.

informal *adj* (simple) simple, sans façons; (unofficial) officieux; (colloquial) familier. **informality** *n* simplicité *f*.
informally *adv* (*dress*) en tenue décontractée; (*speak*) en toute simplicité.

informant *n* indicateur/-trice *m/f*.

information *n* renseignements *mpl*, informations *fpl*; **some** ~ un renseignement. ~ **superhighway** *n* autoroute *f* de l'information. ~ **technology** *n* informatique *f*.

informative *adj* (*book*) riche en renseignements; (*visit*) instructif.

informer *n* indicateur/-trice *m/f*.

infrequent *adj* rare.

infringe *vt* (*rule*) enfreindre; (*rights*) ne pas respecter. **infringement** *n* infraction *f*.

infuriate *vt* exaspérer.

ingenuity *n* ingéniosité *f*.

ingot *n* lingot *m*.

ingrained *adj* (*hatred*) enraciné; (*dirt*) bien incrusté.

ingratiate *vt* ~ **oneself with** se faire bien voir de.

ingredient *n* ingrédient *m*.

inhabit *vt* habiter. **inhabitable** *adj* habitable. **inhabitant** *n* habitant/-e *m/f*.

inhale *vt* inhaler; (*smoke*) avaler. **inhaler** *n* inhalateur *m*.

inherent *adj* inhérent (**in** à).

inherently *adv* en soi, par sa nature.

inherit *vt* hériter de; ~ **sth from sb** hériter qch de qn. **inheritance** *n* héritage *m*.

inhibit *vt* (*restrain*) inhiber; (*prevent*) entraver.

inhospitable *adj* inhospitalier.

inhuman *adj* inhumain.

initial *n* initiale *f*. ● *vt* (*pt* **initialled**) parapher. ● *adj* initial.

initiate *vt* (*project*) mettre en œuvre; (*talks*) amorcer; (*person*) initier (**into** à). **initiation** *n* initiation *f*; (*start*) amorce *f*.

initiative *n* initiative *f*.

inject *vt* injecter (**into** dans); (*new element*: fig) insuffler (**into** à). **injection** *n* injection *f*, piqûre *f*.

injure *vt* blesser; (*damage*) nuire à. **injury** *n* blessure *f*.

injustice *n* injustice *f*.

ink *n* encre *f*.

inkling *n* petite idée *f*.

inland *adj* intérieur; **I~ Revenue** service *m* des impôts britannique.

in-laws *npl* (*parents*) beaux-parents *mpl*; (*family*) belle-famille *f*.

inlay¹ *vt* (*pt* **inlaid**) incruster (**with** de); (*on wood*) marqueter.

inlay² *n* incrustation *f*; (*on wood*) marqueterie *f*.

inlet *n* bras *m* de mer; (Tech) arrivée *f*.

inmate *n* (*of asylum*) interné/-e *m/f*; (*of prison*) détenu/-e *m/f*.

inn *n* auberge *f*.

innate *adj* inné.

inner *adj* intérieur; ~ **city** quartiers *mpl* déshérités; ~ **tube** chambre *f* à air.

innocent *a & n* innocent/-e (*m/f*).

innocuous *adj* inoffensif.

innovate *vi* innover.

innuendo *n* (*pl* ~**es**) insinuations *fpl*; (*sexual*) allusions *fpl* grivoises.

innumerable *adj* innombrable.

inoculate *vt* vacciner (**against** contre).

inopportune *adj* inopportun.

in-patient *n* malade *mf* hospitalisé/-e.

input *n* (*of energy*) alimentation *f* (**of** en); (*contribution*) contribution *f*; (*data*) données *fpl*; (*computer process*) saisie *f* des données. ● *vt* (*data*) saisir.

inquest *n* enquête *f*.

inquire *vi* se renseigner (**about, into** sur). ● *vt* demander.

inquiry *n* demande *f* de renseignements; (*inquest*) enquête *f*.

inquisitive *adj* curieux.

inroad *n* **make** ~**s into** faire une avancée sur.

insane *adj* fou; (*Jur*) aliéné. **insanity** *n* folie *f*; (*Jur*) aliénation *f* mentale.

inscribe *vt* inscrire. **inscription** *n* inscription *f*.

inscrutable *adj* énigmatique.

insect *n* insecte *m*. **insecticide** *n* insecticide *m*.

insecure *adj* (*person*) qui manque d'assurance; (*job*) précaire; (*lock, property*) peu sûr. **insecurity** *n* (*of person*) manque *m* d'assurance; (*of situation*) insécurité *f*.

insensitive *adj* insensible; (*remark*) indélicat.

inseparable *adj* inséparable (**from** de).

insert *vt* insérer (**in** dans).

in-service *adj* (training) continu.

inshore *adj* côtier.

inside *n* intérieur *m*; ∼s ⓘ entrailles *fpl*. ● *adj* intérieur. ● *adv* à l'intérieur; **go** ∼ entrer. ● *prep* à l'intérieur de; (of time) en moins de; ∼ **out** à l'envers; (thoroughly) à fond.

insight *n* (perception) perspicacité *f*; (idea) aperçu *m*.

insignia *npl* insigne *m*.

insignificant *adj* (cost, difference) négligeable; (person) insignifiant.

insincere *adj* peu sincère.

insinuate *vt* insinuer.

insist *vt/i* insister (**that** pour que); ∼ **on** exiger; ∼ **on doing** vouloir à tout prix faire. **insistence** *n* insistance *f*. **insistent** *adj* insistant. **insistently** *adv* avec insistance.

insofar as *adv* dans la mesure où.

insolent *adj* insolent.

insolvent *adj* insolvable.

insomnia *n* insomnie *f*. **insomniac** *n* insomniaque *mf*.

inspect *vt* (school, machinery) inspecter; (tickets) contrôler. **inspection** *n* inspection *f*; (of passport, ticket) contrôle *m*. **inspector** *n* inspecteur/-trice *m/f*; (on bus) contrôleur/-euse *m/f*.

inspiration *n* inspiration *f*. **inspire** *vt* inspirer.

install *vt* installer.

instalment *n* (payment) versement *m*; (of serial) épisode *m*.

instance *n* exemple *m*; (case) cas *m*; **for** ∼ par exemple; **in the first** ∼ en premier lieu.

instant *adj* immédiat; (food) instantané. ● *n* instant *m*. **instantaneous** *adj* instantané. **instantly** *adv* immédiatement.

instead *adv* plutôt; ∼ **of doing** au lieu de faire; ∼ **of sb** à la place de qn.

instep *n* cou-de-pied *m*.

instigate *vt* (attack) lancer; (proceedings) engager.

instil *vt* (pt **instilled**) inculquer; (fear) insuffler.

instinct *n* instinct *m*. **instinctive** *adj* instinctif.

institute *n* institut *m*. ● *vt* instituer; (proceedings) engager. **institution** *n* institution *f*; (school, hospital) établissement *m*.

instruct *vt* (teach) instruire; (order) ordonner; ∼ **sb in sth** enseigner qch à qn; ∼ **sb to do** donner l'ordre à qn de faire. **instruction** *n* instruction *f*. **instructions** *npl* (for use) mode *m* d'emploi. **instructive** *adj* instructif. **instructor** *n* (skiing, driving) moniteur/-trice *m/f*.

instrument *n* instrument *m*.

instrumental *adj* instrumental; **be** ∼ **in** contribuer à. **instrumentalist** *n* instrumentaliste *mf*.

insubordinate *adj* insubordonné.

insufficient *adj* insuffisant.

insular *adj* (Geog) insulaire; (mind, person: fig) borné.

insulate *vt* (room, wire) isoler.

insulin *n* insuline *f*.

insult[1] *vt* insulter.

insult[2] *n* insulte *f*.

insurance *n* assurance *f* (**against** contre).

insure *vt* assurer; ∼ **that** (US) s'assurer que.

intact *adj* intact.

intake *n* (of food) consommation *f*; (School, Univ) admissions *fpl*.

integral *adj* intégral (**to** à).

integrate *vt/i* (s')intégrer (**with** à; **into** dans).

integrity *n* intégrité *f*.

intellect *n* intelligence *f*. **intellectual** *a* & *n* intellectuel/-le (*m/f*).

intelligence *n* intelligence *f*; (Mil) renseignements *mpl*. **intelligent** *adj* intelligent. **intelligently** *adv* intelligemment.

intend *vt* (outcome) vouloir; ∼ **to do** avoir l'intention de faire. **intended** *adj* (result) voulu; (visit) projeté.

intense *adj* intense; (person) sérieux. **intensely** *adv* (very) extrêmement.

intensify *vt/i* (s')intensifier.

intensive *adj* intensif; **in** ~ **care** en réanimation.

intent *n* intention *f*. ● *adj* absorbé; ~ **on doing** résolu à faire.

intention *n* intention *f*.
intentional *adj* intentionnel.

intently *adv* attentivement.

interact *vi* (*factors*) agir l'un sur l'autre; (*people*) communiquer.
interactive *adj* (*TV, video*) interactif.

intercept *vt* intercepter.

interchange *n* (road junction) échangeur *m*; (exchange) échange *m*.

interchangeable *adj* interchangeable.

intercom *n* interphone® *m*.

interconnected *adj* (*parts*) raccordé; (*problems*) lié.

intercourse *n* rapports *mpl*.

interest *n* intérêt *m*; ~ **rate** taux *m* d'intérêt. ● *vt* intéresser (**in** à).
interested *adj* intéressé; **be** ~**ed in** s'intéresser à. **interesting** *adj* intéressant.

interfere *vi* se mêler des affaires des autres; ~ **in** se mêler de; ~ **with** (*freedom*) empiéter sur; (tamper with) toucher. **interference** *n* ingérence *f*; (sound, light waves) brouillage *m*; (radio) parasites *mpl*.

interim *n* **in the** ~ entre-temps. ● *adj* (*government*) provisoire; (*payment*) intermédiaire.

interior *n* intérieur *m*. ● *adj* intérieur.

interjection *n* interjection *f*.

interlock *vt/i* (Tech) (s')emboîter, (s')enclencher.

interlude *n* intervalle *m*; (Theat, Mus) intermède *m*.

intermediary *a & n* intermédiaire (*mf*).

intermediate *adj* intermédiaire; (*exam, level*) moyen.

intermission *n* (Theat) entracte *m*.

intermittent *adj* intermittent.

intern[1] *vt* interner.

intern[2] *n* (US) stagiaire *mf*; (Med) interne *mf*.

internal *adj* interne; (domestic: Pol) intérieur; **I**~ **Revenue** (US) service *m* des impôts américain.

international *adj* international.

Internet *n* Internet *m*; **on the** ~ sur l'Internet; ~ **service provider** fournisseur *m* d'accès à l'Internet.

interpret *vt* interpréter (**as** comme). ● *vi* faire l'interprète.
interpretation *n* interprétation *f*.
interpreter *n* interprète *mf*.

interrelated *adj* interdépendant, lié.

interrogate *vt* interroger.
interrogative *a & n* (Ling) interrogatif (*m*).

interrupt *vt/i* interrompre.
interruption *n* interruption *f*.

intersect *vt/i* (lines, roads) (se) croiser. **intersection** *n* intersection *f*.

interspersed *adj* parsemé (**with** de).

intertwine *vt/i* (s')entrelacer.

interval *n* intervalle *m*; (Theat) entracte *m*.

intervene *vi* intervenir; (of time) s'écouler (**between** entre); (happen) arriver.

interview *n* (for job) entretien *m*; (by a journalist) interview *f*. ● *vt* (*candidate*) faire passer un entretien à; (*celebrity*) interviewer.

intestine *n* intestin *m*.

intimacy *n* intimité *f*.

intimate[1] *vt* (state) annoncer; (hint) laisser entendre.

intimate[2] *adj* intime. **intimately** *adv* intimement.

intimidate *vt* intimider.

into *prep* (put, go, fall) dans; (divide, translate, change) en; **be** ~ **jazz** être fana du jazz [1]; **8** ~ **24 is 3** 24 divisé par 8 égale 3.

intolerant *adj* intolérant.

intonation *n* intonation *f*.

intoxicate *vt* enivrer.
intoxicated *adj* ivre.
intoxication *n* ivresse *f*.

intractable *adj* (*person*) intraitable; (*problem*) rebelle.

Intranet *n* (Comput) Intranet *m*.

intransitive *adj* intransitif.

intravenous *adj* (Med) intraveineux.

intricate *adj* complexe.

i

intrigue *vt* intriguer. ● *n* intrigue *f*.
intriguing *adj* fascinant; (curious) curieux.

intrinsic *adj* intrinsèque (**to** à).

introduce *vt* (*person, idea, programme*) présenter; (*object, law*) introduire (**into** dans).
introduction *n* introduction *f*; (of person) présentation *f*. **introductory** *adj* (words) préliminaire.

introvert *n* introverti/-e *m/f*.

intrude *vi* (person) s'imposer (**on sb** à qn), déranger. **intruder** *n* intrus/-e *m/f*. **intrusion** *n* intrusion *f*.

intuition *n* intuition *f*. **intuitive** *adj* intuitif.

inundate *vt* inonder (**with** de).

invade *vt* envahir.

invalid[1] *n* malade *mf*; (disabled) infirme *mf*.

invalid[2] *adj* (*passport*) pas valable; (*claim*) sans fondement. **invalidate** *vt* (*argument*) infirmer; (*claim*) annuler.

invaluable *adj* inestimable.

invariable *adj* invariable.
invariably *adv* invariablement.

invasion *n* invasion *f*.

invent *vt* inventer. **invention** *n* invention *f*. **inventive** *adj* inventif. **inventor** *n* inventeur/-trice *m/f*.

inventory *n* inventaire *m*.

invert *vt* (*order*) intervertir; (*image, values*) renverser; **~ed commas** guillemets *mpl*.

invest *vt* investir; (time, effort) consacrer. ● *vi* faire un investissement; **~ in** (buy) s'acheter.

investigate *vt* examiner; (*crime*) enquêter sur. **investigation** *n* investigation *f*. **investigator** *n* (police) enquêteur/-euse *m/f*.

investment *n* investissement *m*; emotional **~** engagement *m* personnel. **investor** *n* investisseur/ -euse *m/f*; (in shares) actionnaire *mf*.

invigilate *vi* (*exam*) surveiller.
invigilator *n* surveillant/-e *m/f*.

invigorate *vt* revigorer.

invisible *adj* invisible.

invitation *n* invitation *f*. **invite** *vt* inviter; (ask for) demander. **inviting** *adj* engageant.

invoice *n* facture *f*. ● *vt* facturer.

involuntary *adj* involontaire.

involve *vt* impliquer; (*person*) faire participer (**in** à). **involved** *adj* (complex) compliqué; (at stake) en jeu; **be ~d in** (*work*) participer à; (*crime*) être mêlé à. **involvement** *n* participation *f* (**in** à).

inward *adj* (*feeling*) intérieur.
inwardly *adv* intérieurement.
inwards *adv* vers l'intérieur.

iodine *n* iode *m*; (antiseptic) teinture *f* d'iode.

iota *n* iota *m*; **not one ~ of** pas un grain de.

IOU *abbr* (**I owe you**) reconnaissance *f* de dette.

IQ *abbr* (**intelligence quotient**) QI *m*.

Iran *n* Iran *m*.

Iraq *n* Irak *m*.

irate *adj* furieux.

IRC *abbrev* (**Internet Relay Chat**) (Internet) conversation *f* IRC.

Ireland *n* Irlande *f*.

Irish *n & a* irlandais (*m*). **~man** *n* Irlandais *m*. **~woman** *n* Irlandaise *f*.

iron *n* fer *m*; (appliance) fer *m* (à repasser). ● *adj* (*will*) de fer; (*bar*) en fer. ● *vt* repasser; **~ out** (fig) aplanir.

ironic(al) *adj* ironique.

iron: **ironing-board** *n* planche *f* à repasser. **~monger** *n* quincaillier *m*.

irony *n* ironie *f*.

irrational *adj* irrationnel; (person) pas raisonnable.

irregular *adj* irrégulier.

irrelevant *adj* hors de propos.

irreplaceable *adj* irremplaçable.

irresistible *adj* irrésistible.

irrespective *adj* **~ of** sans tenir compte de.

irresponsible *adj* irresponsable.

irreverent *adj* irrévérencieux.

irreversible *adj* irréversible.

irrigate *vt* irriguer.

irritable *adj* irritable.

irritate *vt* irriter. **irritating** *adj* irritant.

is ⇒BE.

Islam *n* (faith) islam *m*; (Muslims) Islam *m*. **Islamic** *adj* islamique.

island *n* île *f*. **islander** *n* insulaire *mf*.

isle *n* île *f*.

isolate *vt* isoler. **isolation** *n* isolement *m*.

Israel *n* Israël *m*.

Israeli *n* Israélien/-ne *m/f*. ● *adj* israélien.

issue *n* question *f*; (outcome) résultat *m*; (of magazine) numéro *m*; (of stamps) émission *f*; (offspring) descendance *f*; **at ~** en cause. ● *vt* distribuer; (stamps) émettre; (book) publier; (order) délivrer. ● *vi* **~ from** provenir de.

....

it

● *pronoun*

····▸ (subject) il, elle; **'where's the book/chair?'—'~'s in the kitchen'** 'où est le livre/la chaise?'—'il/elle est dans la cuisine'.

····▸ (object) le, la, l'; **~'s my book and I want ~** c'est mon livre et je le veux; **I liked his shirt, did you notice ~?** sa chemise m'a plu, l'as-tu remarquée?; **give ~ to me** donne-le-moi.

····▸ (with preposition) **we talked a lot about ~** on en a beaucoup parlé; **Elliott went to ~** Elliott y est allé.

····▸ (impersonal) il; **~'s raining** il pleut; **~ will snow** il va neiger.

....

IT *abbr* ⇒INFORMATION TECHNOLOGY.

Italian *n* (person) Italien/-ne *m/f*; (Ling) italien *m*. ● *adj* italien.

italics *npl* italique *m*.

Italy *n* Italie *f*.

itch *n* démangeaison *f*. ● *vi* démanger; **my arm ~es** j'ai le bras qui me démange; **be ~ing to do** mourir d'envie de faire.

item *n* article *m*; (on agenda) point *m*.

itemize *vt* détailler; **~d bill** facture *f* détaillée.

itinerary *n* itinéraire *m*.

its *det* son, sa; *pl* ses.

it's = IT IS, IT HAS.

itself *pron* lui-même, elle-même; (reflexive) se.

ivory *n* ivoire *m*; **~ tower** tour *f* d'ivoire.

ivy *n* lierre *m*.

....

Jj

....

jab *vt* (*pt* **jabbed**) **~ sth into sth** planter qch dans qch. ● *n* coup *m*; (injection) piqûre *f*.

jack *n* (Auto) cric *m*; (cards) valet *m*; (Electr) jack *m*. ● *vt* **~ up** soulever avec un cric.

jackal *n* chacal *m*.

jacket *n* veste *f*, veston *m*; (of book) jaquette *f*.

jack-knife *n* couteau *m* pliant. ● *vi* (lorry) se mettre en portefeuille.

jackpot *n* gros lot *m*; **hit the ~** gagner le gros lot.

jade *n* (stone) jade *m*.

jaded *adj* (tired) fatigué; (bored) blasé.

jagged *adj* (rock) déchiqueté; (knife) dentelé.

jail *n* prison *f*. ● *vt* mettre en prison.

jam *n* confiture *f*; (traffic) **~** embouteillage *m*. ● *vt/i* (*pt* **jammed**) (wedge) (se) coincer; (cram) (s')entasser; (street) encombrer; (radio) brouiller.

Jamaica *n* Jamaïque *f*.

jam-packed *adj* Ⓣ bondé; **~ with** bourré de.

jangle *n* tintement *m*. ● *vt/i* (faire) tinter.

janitor *n* (US) gardien *m*.

January *n* janvier *m*.

Japan *n* Japon *m*.

Japanese *n* (person) Japonais/-e *m/f*; (Ling) japonais *m*. ● *adj* japonais.

jar *n* pot *m*, bocal *m*. ● *vi* (*pt* **jarred**) rendre un son discordant; (colours) détonner. ● *vt* ébranler.

jargon *n* jargon *m*.

jaundice *n* jaunisse *f*.

javelin *n* javelot *m*.

jaw *n* mâchoire *f*.

jay *n* geai *m*.

jazz n jazz m. ● vt ~ **up** (dress) rajeunir; (event) ranimer.

jealous adj jaloux. **jealousy** n jalousie f.

jeans npl jean m.

jeer vt/i ~ (at) huer. ● n huée f.

jelly n gelée f. ~**fish** n méduse f.

jeopardize vt (career, chance) compromettre; (lives) mettre en péril.

jerk n secousse f; (fool ✖) crétin m 🇬🇧. ● vt tirer brusquement. ● vi tressaillir. **jerky** adj saccadé.

jersey n (garment) pull-over m; (fabric) jersey m.

jet n (plane, stream) jet m; (mineral) jais m; ~ **lag** décalage m horaire.

jettison vt jeter par-dessus bord; (Aviat) larguer; (fig) rejeter.

jetty n jetée f.

Jew n juif/juive m/f.

jewel n bijou m. **jeweller** n bijoutier/-ière m/f. **jeweller('s)** n (shop) bijouterie f. **jewellery** n bijoux mpl.

Jewish adj juif.

jibe n moquerie f.

jigsaw n puzzle m.

jingle vt/i (faire) tinter. ● n tintement m; (advertising) refrain m publicitaire, sonal m.

jinx n (person) porte-malheur m inv; (curse) sort m.

jitters npl have the ~ 🇬🇧 être nerveux. **jittery** adj nerveux.

job n emploi m; (post) poste m; **out of a** ~ sans emploi; **it is a good** ~ **that** heureusement que; **just the** ~ tout à fait ce qu'il faut. ~ **centre** n bureau m des services nationaux de l'emploi. **jobless** adj sans emploi.

jockey n jockey m.

jog n go for a ~ aller faire un jogging. ● vt (pt **jogged**) heurter; (memory) rafraîchir. ● vi faire du jogging. **jogging** n jogging m.

join vt (attach) réunir, joindre; (club) devenir membre de; (company) entrer dans; (army) s'engager dans; (queue) se mettre dans; ~ **sb** (in activity) se joindre à qn; (meet) rejoindre qn. ● vi (become member) adhérer; (pieces) se joindre; (roads)

se rejoindre. ● n raccord m. □ ~ **in** participer; ~ **in sth** participer à qch; ~ **up** (Mil) s'engager; ~ **sth up** relier qch. **joiner** n menuisier/-ière m/f.

joint adj (action) collectif; (measures, venture) commun; (winner) ex aequo inv; (account) joint; ~ **author** coauteur m. ● n (join) joint m; (Anat) articulation f; (Culin) rôti m; **out of** ~ déboîté.

joke n plaisanterie f; (trick) farce f; **it's no** ~ ce n'est pas drôle. ● vi plaisanter. **joker** n blagueur/-euse m/f; (cards) joker m.

jolly adj (-**ier**, -**iest**) (person) enjoué; (tune) joyeux. ● adv 🇬🇧 drôlement.

jolt vt secouer. ● vi cahoter. ● n secousse f; (shock) choc m.

jostle vt/i (se) bousculer.

jot vt (pt **jotted**) ~ (**down**) noter.

journal n journal m. **journalism** n journalisme m. **journalist** n journaliste mf.

journey n (trip) voyage m; (short or habitual) trajet m. ● vi voyager.

joy n joie f. **joyful** adj joyeux.

joy: ~**riding** n rodéo m à la voiture volée. ~**stick** n (Comput) manette f; (Aviat) manche m à balai.

jubilant adj (person) exultant; (mood) réjoui.

Judaism n judaïsme m.

judge n juge m. ● vt juger; (distance) estimer; **judging by/from** à en juger par. **judg(e)ment** n jugement m.

judicial adj judiciaire. **judiciary** n magistrature f.

judo n judo m.

jug n (glass) carafe f; (pottery) pichet m.

juggernaut n (lorry) poids m lourd.

juggle vt/i jongler (avec). **juggler** n jongleur/-euse m/f.

juice n jus m. **juicy** adj juteux; (details 🇬🇧) croustillant.

jukebox n juke-box m.

July n juillet m.

jumble vt mélanger. ● n (of objects) tas m; (of ideas) fouillis m; ~ **sale** vente f de charité.

jumbo n (also ~ **jet**) gros-porteur m.

jump vt sauter; ~ **the lights** passer au feu rouge; ~ **the queue** passer devant tout le monde. ● vi sauter; (in

surprise) sursauter; (*price*) monter en
flèche; ~ **at** (*opportunity*) sauter sur.
● *n* saut *m*, bond *m*; (increase) bond
m.

jumper *n* pull(-over) *m*; (dress: US)
robe *f* chasuble.

jump-leads *npl* câbles *mpl* de
démarrage.

jumpy *adj* nerveux.

junction *n* (of roads) carrefour *m*; (on
motorway) échangeur *m*.

June *n* juin *m*.

jungle *n* jungle *f*.

junior *adj* (young) jeune; (in rank)
subalterne; (school) primaire. ● *n*
cadet/-te *m/f*; (School) élève *mf* du
primaire.

junk *n* bric-à-brac *m inv*; (poor quality)
camelote *f*; ~ **food** nourriture *f*
industrielle.

junkie *n* drogué/-e *m/f*.

junk: ~ **mail** *n* prospectus *mpl*.
~**-shop** *n* boutique *f* de bric-à-brac.

jurisdiction *n* compétence *f*; (Jur)
juridiction *f*.

juror *n* juré *m*.

jury *n* jury *m*.

just *adj* (fair) juste. ● *adv* (immediately,
slightly) juste; (simply) tout simplement;
(exactly) exactement; **he has/had** ~
left il vient/venait de partir; **have** ~
missed avoir manqué de peu; **I'm** ~
leaving je suis sur le point de partir;
it's ~ **a cold** ce n'est qu'un rhume;
~ **as tall/well as** tout aussi grand/
bien que; ~ **listen!** écoutez donc!; **it's**
~ **ridiculous** c'est vraiment ridicule.

justice *n* justice *f*; **J**~ **of the Peace**
juge *m* de paix.

justification *n* justification *f*.
justify *vt* justifier.

jut *vi* (*pt* **jutted**) ~ (**out**) s'avancer
en saillie.

juvenile *adj* (childish) puéril;
(*offender*) mineur; (*delinquent*) jeune.
● *n* jeune *mf*; (Jur) mineur/-e *m/f*.

juxtapose *vt* juxtaposer.

Kk

kangaroo *n* kangourou *m*.

karate *n* karaté *m*.

kebab *n* brochette *f*.

keel *n* (of ship) quille *f*. ● *vi* ~ **over**
(*bateau*) chavirer; (*person*)
s'écrouler.

keen *adj* (*interest, wind, feeling*) vif;
(*mind, analysis*) pénétrant; (*edge,
appetite*) aiguisé; (eager)
enthousiaste; **be** ~ **on** être
passionné de; **be** ~ **to do** *or* **on doing**
tenir beaucoup à faire. **keenly** *adv*
vivement. **keenness** *n*
enthousiasme *m*.

keep *vt* (*pt* **kept**) garder; (*promise,
shop, diary*) tenir; (*family*) faire
vivre; (*animals*) élever; (*rule*)
respecter; (celebrate) célébrer; (delay)
retenir; ~ **sth clean/warm** garder
qch propre/au chaud; ~ **sb in/out**
empêcher qn de sortir/d'entrer; ~
sb from doing empêcher qn de faire.
● *vi* (*food*) se conserver; ~ (**on**)
continuer (**doing** à faire). ● *n*
pension *f*; (of castle) donjon *m*. □ ~
down rester allongé; ~ **sth down**
limiter qch; ~ **your voice down!**
baisse la voix!; ~ **to** (*road*) ne pas
s'écarter de; (*rules*) respecter; ~ **up**
(*car, runner*) suivre; (*rain*)
continuer; ~ **up with sb** (in speed)
aller aussi vite que; (*class, inflation,
fashion, news*) suivre.

keeper *n* gardien/-ne *m/f*.

keepsake *n* souvenir *m*.

kennel *n* niche *f*.

kept ⇒KEEP.

kerb *n* bord *m* du trottoir.

kernel *n* amande *f*; ~ **of truth** fond
m de vérité.

kettle *n* bouilloire *f*.

key *n* clé *f*; (of computer, piano) touche *f*.
● *adj* (*industry, figure*) clé (*inv*). ● *vt*
~ (**in**) saisir. ~**board** *n* clavier *m*.

~hole *n* trou *m* de serrure. **~pad** *n* (of telephone) clavier *m* numérique. **~-ring** *n* porte-clés *m inv.* **~stroke** *n* (Comput) frappe *f.*

khaki *adj* kaki *inv.*

kick *vt/i* donner un coup de pied (à); (*horse*) botter. ● *n* coup *m* de pied; (of gun) recul *m*; **get a ~ out of doing** Ⅰ prendre plaisir à faire. □ **~ out** Ⅰ virer Ⅰ.

kick-off *n* coup *m* d'envoi.

kid *n* (goat, leather) chevreau *m*; (child Ⅰ) gosse *mf* Ⅰ. ● *vt/i* (*pt* **kidded**) blaguer.

kidnap *vt* (*pt* **kidnapped**) enlever. **kidnapping** *n* enlèvement *m.*

kidney *n* rein *m*; (Culin) rognon *m.*

kill *vt* tuer; (*rumour*: fig) arrêter. ● *n* mise *f* à mort. **killer** *n* tueur/-euse *m/f.* **killing** *n* meurtre *m.*

kiln *n* four *m.*

kilo *n* kilo *m.*

kilobyte *n* kilo-octet *m.*

kilogram *n* kilogramme *m.*

kilometre, (US) **kilometer** *n* kilomètre *m.*

kilowatt *n* kilowatt *m.*

kin *n* parents *mpl.*

kind *n* genre *m*, sorte *f*; **in ~** en nature; **~ of** (somewhat Ⅰ) assez. ● *adj* gentil, bon.

kindergarten *n* jardin *m* d'enfants.

kindle *vt/i* (s')allumer.

kindly *adj* (**-ier, -iest**) (*person*) gentil; (*interest*) bienveillant. ● *adv* avec gentillesse; **would you ~ do** auriez-vous l'amabilité de faire.

kindness *n* bonté *f.*

king *n* roi *m*. **kingdom** *n* royaume *m*; (Bot) règne *m*. **~fisher** *n* martin-pêcheur *m*. **~size(d)** *adj* géant.

kiosk *n* kiosque *m*; **telephone ~** cabine *f* téléphonique; (Internet) borne *f* interactive, kiosque *m.*

kiss *n* baiser *m*. ● *vt/i* (s')embrasser.

kit *n* (clothing) affaires *fpl*; (set of tools) trousse *f*; (for assembly) kit *m*. ● *vt* (*pt* **kitted**) **~ out** équiper.

kitchen *n* cuisine *f.*

kite *n* (toy) cerf-volant *m*; (bird) milan *m.*

kitten *n* chaton *m.*

kitty *n* (fund) cagnotte *f.*

knack *n* tour *m* de main (**of doing** pour faire).

knead *vt* pétrir.

knee *n* genou *m*. **~cap** *n* rotule *f.*

kneel *vi* (*pt* **knelt**) **~ (down)** se mettre à genoux; (in prayer) s'agenouiller.

knew ⇒KNOW.

knickers *npl* petite culotte *f*, slip *m.*

knife *n* (*pl* **knives**) couteau *m*. ● *vt* poignarder.

knight *n* chevalier *m*; (chess) cavalier *m*. ● *vt* anoblir. **~hood** *n* titre *m* de chevalier.

knit *vt/i* (*pt* **knitted** *or* **knit**) tricoter; (*bones*) (se) souder. **knitting** *n* tricot *m*. **knitwear** *n* tricots *mpl.*

knob *n* bouton *m.*

knock *vt/i* cogner; (criticize Ⅰ) critiquer; **~ sth off/out** faire tomber qch. ● *n* coup *m*. □ **~ down** (chair, pedestrian) renverser; (demolish) abattre; (reduce) baisser; **~ off** (stop work Ⅰ) arrêter de travailler; **~ £10 off** faire une réduction de 10 livres; **~ it off!** Ⅰ ça suffit!; **~ out** assommer; **~ over** renverser; **~ up** (meal) préparer en vitesse.

knock-out *n* (boxing) knock-out *m.*

knot *n* nœud *m*. ● *vt* (*pt* **knotted**) nouer.

know *vt/i* (*pt* **knew**; *pp* **known**) (answer, reason, language) savoir (**that** que); (person, place, name, rule, situation) connaître; (recognize) reconnaître; **~ how to** savoir faire; **~ about** (event) être au courant de; (subject) s'y connaître en; **~ of** (from experience) connaître; (from information) avoir entendu parler de. **~-how** *n* savoir-faire *m inv.*

knowingly *adv* (intentionally) délibérément; (meaningfully) d'un air entendu.

knowledge *n* connaissance *f*; (learning) connaissances *fpl.* **knowledgeable** *adj* savant.

knuckle *n* jointure *f*, articulation *f.*

Koran *n* Coran *m.*

Korea *n* Corée *f.*

kosher *adj* casher *inv.*

lab *n* 🔲 labo *m.*

label *n* étiquette *f.* ● *vt* (*pt* **labelled**) étiqueter.

laboratory *n* laboratoire *m.*

laborious *adj* laborieux.

labour, (US) **labor** *n* travail *m*; (workers) main-d'œuvre *f*; **in** ~ en train d'accoucher. ● *vi* peiner (**to do** à faire). ● *vt* trop insister sur.

Labour *n* le parti travailliste. ● *adj* travailliste.

laboured *adj* laborieux.

labourer *n* ouvrier/-ière *m/f*; (on farm) ouvrier/-ière *m/f* agricole.

lace *n* dentelle *f*; (of shoe) lacet *m.* ● *vt* (*shoe*) lacer; (*drink*) arroser.

lacerate *vt* lacérer.

lack *n* manque *m*; **for** ~ **of** faute de. ● *vt* manquer de; **be** ~**ing** manquer (**in** de).

lad *n* garçon *m*, gars *m.*

ladder *n* échelle *f*; (in stocking) maille *f* filée. ● *vt/i* (*stocking*) filer.

laden *adj* chargé (**with** de).

ladle *n* louche *f.*

lady *n* (*pl* **ladies**) dame *f*; **ladies and gentlemen** mesdames et messieurs; **young** ~ jeune femme *or* fille *f.* ~**bird** *n* coccinelle *f.*

ladylike *adj* distingué.

lag *vi* (*pt* **lagged**) traîner. ● *vt* (*pipes*) calorifuger. ● *n* (interval) décalage *m.*

lager *n* bière *f* blonde.

lagoon *n* lagune *f.*

laid ⇒LAY[1]. ~ **back** *adj* décontracté.

lain ⇒LIE[2].

lake *n* lac *m.*

lamb *n* agneau *m*; **leg of** ~ gigot *m* d'agneau.

lame *adj* boiteux.

lament *n* lamentation *f.* ● *vt/i* se lamenter (sur).

laminated *adj* laminé.

lamp *n* lampe *f.* ~**post** *n* réverbère *m.* ~**shade** *n* abat-jour *m inv.*

lance *vt* (Med) inciser.

land *n* terre *f*; (plot) terrain *m*; (country) pays *m.* ● *adj* terrestre; (*policy, reform*) agraire. ● *vt/i* débarquer; (*aircraft*) (se) poser, (faire) atterrir; (fall) tomber; (obtain) décrocher; (*a blow*) porter; ~ **up** se retrouver.

landing *n* débarquement *m*; (Aviat) atterrissage *m*; (top of stairs) palier *m.* ~**stage** *n* débarcadère *m.*

land: ~**lady** *n* propriétaire *f*; (of pub) patronne *f.* ~**lord** *n* propriétaire *m*; (of pub) patron *m.* ~**mark** *n* (point de) repère *m.* ~**mine** *n* mine *f* terrestre.

landscape *n* paysage *m.* ● *vt* aménager.

landslide *n* glissement *m* de terrain; (Pol) raz-de-marée *m inv* (électoral).

lane *n* (path, road) chemin *m*; (strip of road) voie *f*; (of traffic) file *f*; (Aviat) couloir *m.*

language *n* langue *f*; (speech, style) langage *m.* ~ **engineering** *n* ingénierie *f* des langues. ~ **laboratory** *n* laboratoire *m* de langue.

lank *adj* (hair) plat.

lanky *adj* (**-ier**, **-iest**) grand et maigre.

lantern *n* lanterne *f.*

lap *n* genoux *mpl*; (Sport) tour *m* (de piste). ● *vi* (*pt* **lapped**) (*waves*) clapoter. □ ~ **up** laper.

lapel *n* revers *m.*

lapse *vi* (decline) se dégrader; (expire) se périmer; ~ **into** retomber dans. ● *n* défaillance *f*, erreur *f*; (of time) intervalle *m.*

laptop *n* (Comput) portable *m.*

lard *n* saindoux *m.*

larder *n* garde-manger *m inv.*

large *adj* grand, gros; **at** ~ en liberté; **by and** ~ en général. **largely** *adv* en grande mesure.

lark *n* (bird) alouette *f*; (bit of fun 🔲) rigolade *f.* ● *vi* 🔲 rigoler.

larva *n* (*pl* **-vae**) larve *f.*

laryngitis n laryngite f.

laser n laser m. ∼ **printer** n imprimante f laser. ∼ **treatment** n (Med) laserothérapie f.

lash vt fouetter. ● n coup m de fouet; (eyelash) cil m. □ ∼ **out** (spend) dépenser follement; ∼ **out against** attaquer.

lass n jeune fille f.

lasso n lasso m.

last adj dernier; **the** ∼ **straw** le comble; **the** ∼ **word** le mot de la fin; **on its** ∼ **legs** sur le point de rendre l'âme; ∼ **night** hier soir. ● adv en dernier; (most recently) la dernière fois. ● n dernier/-ière m/f; (remainder) reste m; **at (long)** ∼ enfin. ● vi durer. ∼**-ditch** adj ultime. **lasting** adj durable. **lastly** adv en dernier lieu. ∼**-minute** adj de dernière minute.

latch n loquet m.

late adj (not on time) en retard; (former) ancien; (hour, fruit) tardif; **the** ∼ **Mrs X** feu Mme X. ● adv (not early) tard; (not on time) en retard; **in** ∼ **July** fin juillet; **of** ∼ dernièrement. **lately** adv dernièrement. **latest** adj ⇒LATE; (last) dernier.

lathe n tour m.

lather n mousse f. ● vt savonner. ● vi mousser.

Latin n (Ling) latin m. ● adj latin. ∼ **America** n Amérique f latine.

latitude n latitude f.

latter adj dernier. ● n **the** ∼ celui-ci, celle-ci.

Latvia n Lettonie f.

laudable adj louable.

laugh vi rire (**at** de). ● n rire m. **laughable** adj ridicule.

laughing stock n risée f.

laughter n (act) rire m; (sound of laughs) rires mpl.

launch vt (rocket) lancer; (boat) mettre à l'eau; ∼ (**out**) **into** se lancer dans. ● n lancement m; (boat) vedette f. **launching pad** n aire f de lancement.

launderette n laverie f automatique.

laundry n (place) blanchisserie f; (clothes) linge m.

laurel n laurier m.

lava n lave f.

lavatory n toilettes fpl.

lavender n lavande f.

lavish adj (person) généreux; (lush) somptueux. ● vt prodiguer (**on** à). **lavishly** adv luxueusement.

law n loi f; (profession, subject of study) droit m; ∼ **and order** l'ordre public. ∼**-abiding** adj respectueux des lois. ∼**court** n tribunal m.

lawful adj légal.

lawn n pelouse f, gazon m. ∼**-mower** n tondeuse f à gazon.

lawsuit n procès m.

lawyer n avocat m.

lax adj (government) laxiste; (security) relâché.

laxative n laxatif m.

lay[1] adj (non-clerical) laïque; (worker) non-initié. ● vt (pt **laid**) poser, mettre; (trap) tendre; (table) mettre; (plan) former; (eggs) pondre. ● vi pondre; ∼ **waste** ravager. □ ∼ **aside** mettre de côté; ∼ **down** (dé)poser; (condition) (im-)poser; ∼ **off** vt (worker) licencier; vi ⊞ arrêter; ∼ **on** (provide) fournir; ∼ **out** (design) dessiner; (display) disposer; (money) dépenser.

lay[2] ⇒LIE[2].

lay-by n (pl ∼s) aire f de repos.

layer n couche f.

layman n (pl -**men**) profane m.

layout n disposition f.

laze vi paresser. **laziness** n paresse f. **lazy** adj (-**ier**, -**iest**) paresseux.

lead[1] vt/i (pt **led**) (team) diriger; (life) mener; (induce) amener; ∼ **to** conduire à, mener à. ● n avance f; (clue) indice m; (leash) laisse f; (Theat) premier rôle m; (wire) fil m; **in the** ∼ en tête. □ ∼ **away** emmener; ∼ **up to** (come to) en venir à; (precede) précéder.

lead[2] n plomb m; (of pencil) mine f.

leader n chef m; (of country, club) dirigeant/-e m/f; (leading article) éditorial m. **leadership** n direction f.

lead-free adj (petrol) sans plomb.

leading adj principal.

leaf *n* (*pl* **leaves**) feuille *f*; (of table) rallonge *f*. ● *vi* ~ **through** feuilleter.

leaflet *n* prospectus *m*.

leafy *adj* feuillu.

league *n* ligue *f*; (Sport) championnat *m*; **in** ~ **with** de mèche avec.

leak *n* fuite *f*. ● *vi* fuir; (news: fig) s'ébruiter. ● *vt* répandre; (fig) divulguer.

lean[1] *adj* maigre. ● *n* (of meat) maigre *m*.

lean[2] *vt/i* (*pt* **leaned** *or* **leant**) (rest) (s')appuyer; (slope) pencher. □ ~ **out** se pencher à l'extérieur; ~ **over** (of person) se pencher.

leaning *adj* penché. ● *n* tendance *f*.

leap *vi* (*pt* **leaped** *or* **leapt**) bondir. ● *n* bond *m*. ~ **year** *n* année *f* bissextile.

learn *vt/i* (*pt* **learned** *or* **learnt**) apprendre (**to do** à faire). **learned** *adj* érudit. **learner** *n* débutant/-e *m/f*.

lease *n* bail *m*. ● *vt* louer à bail.

leash *n* laisse *f*.

least *adj* **the** ~ (smallest amount of) le moins de; (slightest) le *or* la moindre. ● *n* le moins. ● *adv* le moins; (with adjective) le *or* la moins; **at** ~ au moins.

leather *n* cuir *m*.

leave *vt* (*pt* **left**) laisser; (depart from) quitter; (*person*) laisser tranquille; **be left** (over) rester. ● *n* (holiday) congé *m*; (consent) permission *f*; **take one's** ~ prendre congé (**of** de); **on** ~ (Mil) en permission. □ ~ **alone** (*thing*) ne pas toucher; (*person*) laisser tranquille; ~ **behind** laisser; ~ **out** omettre.

Lebanon *n* Liban *m*.

lecture *n* cours *m*, conférence *f*; (rebuke) réprimande *f*. ● *vt/i* faire un cours *or* une conférence (à); (rebuke) réprimander. **lecturer** *n* conférencier/-ière *m/f*; (Univ) enseignant/-e *m/f*.

led ⇒LEAD[1].

ledge *n* (window) rebord *m*; (rock) saillie *f*.

ledger *n* grand livre *m*.

leech *n* sangsue *f*.

leek *n* poireau *m*.

leer *vi* ~ (**at**) lorgner. ● *n* regard *m* sournois.

leeway *n* (fig) liberté *f* d'action; (Naut) dérive *f*.

left ⇒LEAVE. ● *adj* gauche. ● *adv* à gauche. ● *n* gauche *f*. ~-**hand** *adj* à *or* de gauche. ~-**handed** *adj* gaucher.

left luggage (**office**) *n* consigne *f*.

left-overs *npl* restes *mpl*.

left-wing *adj* de gauche.

leg *n* jambe *f*; (of animal) patte *f*; (of table) pied *m*; (of chicken) cuisse *f*; (of lamb) gigot *m*; (of journey) étape *f*.

legacy *n* legs *m*.

legal *adj* légal; (affairs) juridique.

legend *n* légende *f*.

leggings *npl* (for woman) caleçon *m*.

legible *adj* lisible.

legionnaire *n* légionnaire *m*.

legislation *n* (body of laws) législation *f*; (law) loi *f*. **legislature** *n* corps *m* législatif.

legitimate *adj* légitime.

leisure *n* loisirs *mpl*; **at one's** ~ à tête reposée. ● *adj* (*centre*) de loisirs.

leisurely *adj* lent. ● *adv* sans se presser.

lemon *n* citron *m*.

lemonade *n* (fizzy) limonade *f*; (still) citronnade *f*.

lend *vt* (*pt* **lent**) prêter; (*credibility*) conférer; ~ **itself to** se prêter à.

length *n* longueur *f*; (in time) durée *f*; (section) morceau *m*; **at** ~ (at last) enfin; **at** (**great**) ~ longuement.

lengthen *vt/i* (s')allonger.

lengthways *adv* dans le sens de la longueur.

lengthy *adj* long.

lenient *adj* indulgent.

lens *n* lentille *f*; (of spectacles) verre *m*; (Photo) objectif *m*.

lent ⇒LEND.

Lent *n* Carême *m*.

lentil *n* lentille *f*.

Leo *n* Lion *m*.

leopard *n* léopard *m*.

leotard *n* body *m*.

leprosy *n* lèpre *f*.

lesbian *n* lesbienne *f*. ● *adj* lesbien.

less *adj* (in quantity) moins de (than que). ● *adv, n & prep* moins; ~ than (with numbers) moins de; work ~ than travailler moins que; ten pounds ~ dix livres de moins; ~ and ~ de moins en moins. **lessen** *vt/i* diminuer. **lesser** *adj* moindre.

lesson *n* leçon *f*.

let *vt* (*pt* let; *pres p* letting) laisser; (lease) louer. ● *v aux* ~ us do, ~'s do faisons; ~ him do qu'il fasse; ~ me know the results informe-moi des résultats. ● *n* location *f*. □ ~ **down** baisser; (deflate) dégonfler; (fig) décevoir; ~ **go** *vt* lâcher; *vi* lâcher prise; ~ **sb in/out** laisser *or* faire entrer/sortir qn; ~ **a dress out** élargir une robe; ~ **oneself in for** (*task*) s'engager à; (*trouble*) s'attirer; ~ **off** (explode, fire) faire éclater *or* partir; (excuse) dispenser; (not punish) ne pas punir; ~ **up** ▯ s'arrêter.

let-down *n* déception *f*.

lethal *adj* mortel; (weapon) meurtrier.

letter *n* lettre *f*. ~**-bomb** *n* lettre *f* piégée. ~**-box** *n* boîte *f* à *or* aux lettres.

lettering *n* (letters) caractères *mpl*.

lettuce *n* laitue *f*, salade *f*.

let-up *n* répit *m*.

leukaemia *n* leucémie *f*.

level *adj* plat, uni; (on surface) horizontal; (in height) au même niveau (with que); (in score) à égalité. ● *n* niveau *m*; (spirit) ~ niveau *m* à bulle; **be on the** ~ ▯ être franc. ● *vt* (*pt* **levelled**) niveler; (aim) diriger. ~ **crossing** *n* passage *m* à niveau. ~**-headed** *adj* équilibré.

lever *n* levier *m*. ● *vt* soulever au moyen d'un levier.

leverage *n* influence *f*.

levy *vt* (*tax*) prélever. ● *n* impôt *m*.

lexicon *n* lexique *m*.

liability *n* responsabilité *f*; ▯ handicap *m*; **liabilities** (debts) dettes *fpl*.

liable *adj* be ~ to do avoir tendance à faire, pouvoir faire; ~ to (illness) sujet à; (fine) passible de; ~ for responsable de.

liaise *vi* ▯ faire la liaison. **liaison** *n* liaison *f*.

liar *n* menteur/-euse *m/f*.

libel *n* diffamation *f*. ● *vt* (*pt* **libelled**) diffamer.

liberal *adj* libéral; (generous) généreux, libéral.

Liberal *a & n* (Pol) libéral/-e (*m/f*).

liberate *vt* libérer.

liberty *n* liberté *f*; at ~ to libre de; take liberties prendre des libertés.

Libra *n* Balance *f*.

librarian *n* bibliothécaire *mf*.

library *n* bibliothèque *f*.

libretto *n* livret *m*.

lice ⇒LOUSE.

licence, (US) **license** *n* permis *m*; (for television) redevance *f*; (Comm) licence *f*; (liberty: fig) licence *f*. ~ **plate** *n* plaque *f* minéralogique.

license *vt* accorder un permis à, autoriser.

lick *vt* lécher; (defeat ▯) rosser; (fig) a ~ **of paint** un petit coup de peinture. ● *n* coup *m* de langue.

lid *n* couvercle *m*.

lie[1] *n* mensonge *m*. ● *vi* (*pt* **lied**; *pres p* **lying**) (tell lies) mentir.

lie[2] *vi* (*pt* **lay**; *pp* **lain**; *pres p* **lying**) s'allonger; (remain) rester; (be) se trouver, être; (in grave) reposer; **be lying** être allongé. □ ~ **down** s'allonger; ~ **in** faire la grasse matinée; ~ **low** se cacher.

lieutenant *n* lieutenant *m*.

life *n* (*pl* **lives**) vie *f*. ~**belt** *n* bouée *f* de sauvetage. ~**boat** *n* canot *m* de sauvetage. ~ **buoy** *n* bouée *f* de sauvetage. ~ **cycle** *n* cycle *m* de vie. ~**guard** *n* sauveteur *m*. ~ **insurance** *n* assurance-vie *f*. ~**-jacket** *n* gilet *m* de sauvetage.

lifeless *adj* inanimé.

lifelike *adj* très ressemblant.

life: ~**long** *adj* de toute la vie. ~ **sentence** *n* condamnation *f* à perpétuité. ~**-size(d)** *adj* grandeur nature *inv*. ~ **story** *n* vie *f*. ~**-style** *n* style *m* de vie. ~ **support machine** *n* appareil *m* de respiration artificielle.

lifetime *n* vie *f*; in one's ~ de son vivant.

lift *vt* lever; (steal ▯) voler. ● *vi* (of fog) se lever. ● *n* (in building) ascenseur *m*;

give a ～ **to** emmener (en voiture).
～**-off** *n* (Aviat) décollage *m*.

light *n* lumière *f*; (lamp) lampe *f*; (for fire, on vehicle) feu *m*; (headlight) phare *m*; **bring to** ～ révéler; **come to** ～ être révélé; **have you got a** ～? vous avez du feu? ● *adj* (not dark) clair; (not heavy) léger. ● *vt* (*pt* **lit** *or* **lighted**) allumer; (*room*) éclairer; (*match*) frotter. □ ～ **up** *vi* s'allumer; *vt* (*room*) éclairer. ～ **bulb** *n* ampoule *f*.

lighten *vt* (give light to) éclairer; (make brighter) éclaircir; (make less heavy) alléger.

lighter *n* briquet *m*; (for stove) allume-gaz *m inv*.

light: ～**-headed** *adj* (dizzy) qui a un vertige; (frivolous) étourdi.
～**-hearted** *adj* gai. ～**house** *n* phare *m*.

lighting *n* éclairage *m*.

lightly *adv* légèrement.

lightning *n* éclair *m*, foudre *f*. ● *adj* (*visit*) éclair *inv*.

lightweight *adj* léger. ● *n* (boxing) poids *m* léger.

light-year *n* année *f* lumière.

like¹ *adj* semblable, pareil; **be** ～**-minded** avoir les mêmes sentiments. ● *prep* comme. ● *conj* ① comme. ● *n* pareil *m*; **the** ～**s of you** les gens comme vous.

like² *vt* aimer (bien); **I should** ～ je voudrais, j'aimerais; **would you** ～? voudriez-vous?, voudrais-tu?; ～**s** goûts *mpl*. **likeable** *adj* sympathique.

likelihood *n* probabilité *f*.

likely *adj* (**-ier**, **-iest**) probable. ● *adv* probablement; **he is** ～ **to do** il fera probablement; **not** ～! ① pas question!

likeness *n* ressemblance *f*.

likewise *adv* également.

liking *n* (for thing) penchant *m*; (for person) affection *f*.

lilac *n* lilas *m*. ● *adj* lilas *inv*.

Lilo® *n* matelas *m* pneumatique.

lily *n* lis *m*, lys *m*. ～ **of the valley** *n* muguet *m*.

limb *n* membre *m*.

limber *vi* ～ **up** faire des exercices d'assouplissement.

limbo *n* **be in** ～ (forgotten) être tombé dans l'oubli.

lime *n* (fruit) citron *m* vert; ～**(-tree)** tilleul *m*.

limelight *n* **in the** ～ en vedette.

limestone *n* calcaire *m*.

limit *n* limite *f*. ● *vt* limiter.

limited company *n* société *f* anonyme.

limp *vi* boiter. ● *n* **have a** ～ boiter. ● *adj* mou.

line *n* ligne *f*; (track) voie *f*; (wrinkle) ride *f*; (row) rangée *f*, file *f*; (of poem) vers *m*; (rope) corde *f*; (of goods) gamme *f*; (queue: US) queue *f*; **be in** ～ **for** avoir de bonnes chances de; **hold the** ～ ne quittez pas; **in** ～ **with** en accord avec; **stand in** ～ faire la queue. ● *vt* (*paper*) régler; (*streets*) border; (*garment*) doubler; (fill) remplir, garnir. □ ～ **up** (s')aligner; (in queue) faire la queue; ～ **sth up** prévoir qch.

linen *n* (sheets) linge *m*; (material) lin *m*.

liner *n* paquebot *m*.

linesman *n* (football) juge *m* de touche; (tennis) juge *m* de ligne.

linger *vi* s'attarder; (smells) persister.

linguist *n* linguiste *mf*. **linguistics** *n* linguistique *f*.

lining *n* doublure *f*.

link *n* lien *m*; (of chain) maillon *m*. ● *vt* relier; (relate) (re)lier; ～ **up** (of roads) se rejoindre. **linkage** *n* lien *m*. **links** *n inv* terrain *m* de golf. ～**-up** *n* liaison *f*.

lino *n* lino *m*.

lion *n* lion *m*. **lioness** *n* lionne *f*.

lip *n* lèvre *f*; (edge) rebord *m*; **pay** ～**-service to** n'approuver que pour la forme. ～**-read** *vt/i* lire sur les lèvres. ～**salve** *n* baume *m* pour les lèvres. ～**stick** *n* rouge *m* (à lèvres).

liquid *n* & *a* liquide (*m*).

liquidation *n* liquidation *f*; **go into** ～ déposer son bilan.

liquidize *vt* passer au mixeur. **liquidizer** *n* mixeur *m*.

liquor *n* alcool *m*.

liquorice *n* réglisse *f*.

lisp *n* zézaiement *m*; **with a** ～ en zézayant. ● *vi* zézayer.

list *n* liste *f*. ● *vt* dresser la liste de. ● *vi* (*ship*) gîter.

listen *vi* écouter; ~ **to**, ~ **in (to)** écouter. **listener** *n* auditeur/-trice *m/f*.

listless *adj* apathique.

lit ⇒LIGHT.

liter ⇒LITRE.

literal *adj* (*meaning*) littéral; (*translation*) mot à mot. **literally** *adv* littéralement; mot à mot.

literary *adj* littéraire.

literate *adj* qui sait lire et écrire.

literature *n* littérature *f*; (*brochures*) documentation *f*.

Lithuania *n* Lituanie *f*.

litigation *n* litiges *mpl*.

litre, (US) **liter** *n* litre *m*.

litter *n* (*rubbish*) détritus *mpl*, papiers *mpl*; (*animals*) portée *f*. ● *vt* éparpiller; (*make untidy*) laisser des détritus dans; ~**ed with** jonché de. ~**-bin** *n* poubelle *f*.

little *adj* petit; (*not much*) peu de. ● *n* peu *m*; **a** ~ un peu (de). ● *adv* peu.

live[1] *adj* vivant; (*wire*) sous tension; (*broadcast*) en direct; **be a** ~ **wire** être très dynamique.

live[2] *vt/i* vivre; (*reside*) habiter, vivre; ~ **it up** mener la belle vie. □ ~ **down** faire oublier; ~ **on** (*feed oneself on*) vivre de; (*continue*) survivre; ~ **up to** se montrer à la hauteur de.

livelihood *n* moyens *mpl* d'existence.

lively *adj* (**-ier, -iest**) vif, vivant.

liven *vt/i* ~ **up** (s')animer; (*cheer up*) (s')égayer.

liver *n* foie *m*.

livestock *n* bétail *m*.

livid *adj* livide; (*angry*) furieux.

living *adj* vivant. ● *n* vie *f*; **make a** ~ gagner sa vie; ~ **conditions** conditions *fpl* de vie. ~**-room** *n* salle *f* de séjour.

lizard *n* lézard *m*.

load *n* charge *f*; (*loaded goods*) chargement *m*, charge *f*; (*weight, strain*) poids *m*; ~**s of** 🔲 des tas de 🔲. ● *vt* charger.

loaf *n* (*pl* **loaves**) pain *m*. ● *vi* ~ (**about**) fainéanter.

loan *n* prêt *m*; (*money borrowed*) emprunt *m*. ● *vt* prêter.

loathe *vt* détester (**doing** faire). **loathing** *n* dégoût *m*.

lobby *n* entrée *f*, vestibule *m*; (Pol) lobby *m*, groupe *m* de pression. ● *vt* faire pression sur.

lobster *n* homard *m*.

local *adj* local; (*shops*) du quartier; ~ **government** administration *f* locale. ● *n* personne *f* du coin; (pub 🔲) pub *m* du coin.

locally *adv* localement; (*nearby*) dans les environs.

locate *vt* (*situate*) situer; (*find*) repérer.

location *n* emplacement *m*; **on** ~ (*cinema*) en extérieur.

lock *n* (of door) serrure *f*; (on canal) écluse *f*; (of hair) mèche *f*. ● *vt/i* fermer à clef; (wheels: Auto) (se) bloquer. □ ~ **in** *or* **up** (*person*) enfermer; ~ **out** (by mistake) enfermer dehors.

locker *n* casier *m*.

locket *n* médaillon *m*.

locksmith *n* serrurier *m*.

locum *n* (*doctor*) remplaçant/-e *m/f*.

lodge *n* (*house*) pavillon *m* (de gardien *or* de chasse); (*of porter*) loge *f*. ● *vt* (*accommodate*) loger; (*money, complaint*) déposer. ● *vi* être logé (**with** chez); (*become fixed*) se loger. **lodger** *n* locataire *mf*, pensionnaire *mf*. **lodgings** *n* logement *m*.

loft *n* grenier *m*.

lofty *adj* (**-ier, -iest**) (*tall, noble*) élevé; (*haughty*) hautain.

log *n* (of wood) bûche *f*; ~(**-book**) (Naut) journal *m* de bord; (Auto) ≈ carte *f* grise. ● *vt* (*pt* **logged**) noter; (*distance*) parcourir. □ ~ **on** (Comput) se connecter; ~ **off** (Comput) se déconnecter.

logic *adj* logique. **logical** *adj* logique.

logistics *n* logistique *f*.

loin *n* (Culin) filet *m*; ~**s** reins *mpl*.

loiter *vi* traîner.

loll *vi* se prélasser.

lollipop *n* sucette *f*.

London *n* Londres. **Londoner** *n* Londonien/-ne *m/f*.

lone adj solitaire.

lonely (**-ier**, **-iest**) solitaire; (person) seul, solitaire.

long adj long; **how ~ is?** quelle est la longueur de?; (in time) quelle est la durée de?; **how ~?** combien de temps?; **a ~ time** longtemps. ● adv longtemps; **he will not be ~** il n'en a pas pour longtemps; **as** or **so ~ as** pourvu que; **before ~** avant peu; **I no ~er do** je ne fais plus. ● vi avoir bien or très envie (**for, to** de); **~ for sb** (pine for) se languir de qn.
~-distance adj (flight) sur long parcours; (phone call) interurbain; (runner) de fond. **~ face** n grimace f. **~hand** n écriture f courante.

longing n envie f (**for** de); (nostalgia) nostalgie f (**for** de).

longitude n longitude f.

long: **~ jump** n saut m en longueur. **~-range** adj (missile) à longue portée; (forecast) à long terme. **~-sighted** adj presbyte. **~-standing** adj de longue date. **~-term** adj à long terme. **~ wave** n grandes ondes fpl. **~-winded** adj verbeux.

loo n 🇬🇧 toilettes fpl.

look vi regarder; (seem) avoir l'air; **~ like** ressembler à, avoir l'air de. ● n regard m; (appearance) air m, aspect m; (good) **~s** beauté f. □ **~ after** s'occuper de, soigner; **~ at** regarder; **~ back on** repenser à; **~ down on** mépriser; **~ for** chercher; **~ forward to** attendre avec impatience; **~ in on** passer voir; **~ into** examiner; **~ out** faire attention; **~ out for** (person) guetter; (symptoms) guetter l'apparition de; **~ round** se retourner; **~ up** (word) chercher; (visit) passer voir; **~ up to** respecter.

look-out n (Mil) poste m de guet; (person) guetteur m; **be on the ~ for** rechercher.

loom vi surgir; (war) menacer; (interview) être imminent. ● n métier m à tisser.

loony n & a 🇬🇧 fou, folle (mf).

loop n boucle f. ● vt boucler. **~hole** n lacune f.

loose adj (knot) desserré; (page) détaché; (clothes) ample, lâche; (tooth) qui bouge; (lax) relâché; (not packed) en vrac; (inexact) vague; (pej) immoral; **at a ~ end** désœuvré; **come ~** bouger. **loosely** adv sans serrer; (roughly) vaguement. **loosen** vt (slacken) desserrer; (untie) défaire.

loot n butin m. ● vt piller.

lord n seigneur m; (British title) lord m; **the L~** le Seigneur; (good) **L~!** mon Dieu!

lorry n camion m.

lose vt/i (pt **lost**) perdre; **get lost** se perdre. **loser** n perdant/-e m/f.

loss n perte f; **be at a ~** être perplexe; **be at a ~ to** être incapable de; **heat ~** déperdition f de chaleur.

lost ⇒LOSE. ● adj perdu. **~ property** n objets mpl trouvés.

lot n **the ~** (le) tout m; (people) tous mpl, toutes fpl; **a ~ (of)**, **~s (of)** 🇬🇧 beaucoup (de); **quite a ~ (of)** 🇬🇧 pas mal (de); (fate) sort m; (at auction) lot m; (land) lotissement m.

lotion n lotion f.

lottery n loterie f.

loud adj bruyant, fort. ● adv fort; **out ~** tout haut. **loudly** adv fort. **~speaker** n haut-parleur m.

lounge vi paresser. ● n salon m.

louse n (pl **lice**) pou m.

lousy adj (**-ier**, **-iest**) 🇬🇧 infect.

lout n rustre m.

lovable adj adorable.

love n amour m; (tennis) zéro m; **in ~** amoureux (**with** de); **make ~** faire l'amour. ● vt (person) aimer; (like greatly) aimer (beaucoup) (**to do** faire). **~ affair** n liaison f amoureuse. **~ life** n vie f amoureuse.

lovely adj (**-ier**, **-iest**) joli; (delightful 🇬🇧) très agréable.

lover n (male) amant m; (female) maîtresse f; (devotee) amateur m (**of** de).

loving adj affectueux.

low a & adv bas; **~ in sth** à faible teneur en qch. ● n (low pressure) dépression f; **reach a (new) ~** atteindre son niveau le plus bas. ● vi meugler. **~-calorie** adj basses-calories. **~-cut** adj décolleté.

lower *a & adv* ⇒LOW. ● *vt* baisser; ∼ oneself s'abaisser.

low: ∼-**fat** *adj* (*diet*) sans matières grasses; (*cheese*) allégé. ∼-**key** *adj* modéré; (*discreet*) discret. ∼**lands** *npl* plaine(s) *f(pl).* ∼-**lying** *adj* à faible altitude.

loyal *adj* loyal (**to** envers).

lozenge *n* (*shape*) losange *m*; (*tablet*) pastille *f.*

LP *n* (*disque m*) 33 tours *m.*

Ltd. *abbr* (**Limited**) SA.

lubricant *n* lubrifiant *m.* **lubricate** *vt* lubrifier.

luck *n* chance *f*; **bad** ∼ malchance *f*; **good** ∼! bonne chance!

luckily *adv* heureusement.

lucky *adj* (**-ier**, **-iest**) qui a de la chance, heureux; (*event*) heureux; (*number*) qui porte bonheur; **it's** ∼ **that** heureusement que.

ludicrous *adj* ridicule.

lug *vt* (*pt* **lugged**) traîner.

luggage *n* bagages *mpl.* ∼-**rack** *n* porte-bagages *m inv.*

lukewarm *adj* tiède.

lull *vt* he ∼ed them into thinking that il leur a fait croire que. ● *n* accalmie *f.*

lullaby *n* berceuse *f.*

lumber *n* bois *m* de charpente. ● *vt* 🔲 ∼ **sb with** (*chore*) coller à qn 🔲. ∼**jack** *n* bûcheron *m.*

luminous *adj* lumineux.

lump *n* morceau *m*; (*swelling on body*) grosseur *f*; (*in liquid*) grumeau *m.* ● *vt* ∼ **together** réunir. ∼ **sum** *n* somme *f* globale.

lunacy *n* folie *f.*

lunar *adj* lunaire.

lunatic *n* fou/ folle *m/f.*

lunch *n* déjeuner *m.* ● *vi* déjeuner.

luncheon *n* déjeuner *m.* ∼ **voucher** *n* chèque-repas *m.*

lung *n* poumon *m.*

lunge *vi* bondir (**at** sur; **forward** en avant).

lurch *n* leave in the ∼ planter là, laisser en plan. ● *vi* (*person*) tituber.

lure *vt* appâter, attirer. ● *n* (*attraction*) attrait *m*, appât *m.*

lurid *adj* choquant, affreux; (*gaudy*) voyant.

lurk *vi* se cacher; (*in ambush*) s'embusquer; (*prowl*) rôder; (*suspicion, danger*) menacer.

luscious *adj* appétissant.

lush *adj* luxuriant. ● *n* (US, 🔲) ivrogne/-esse *m/f.*

lust *n* luxure *f.* ● *vi* ∼ **after** convoiter.

Luxemburg *n* Luxembourg *m.*

luxurious *adj* luxueux.

luxury *n* luxe *m.* ● *adj* de luxe.

lying ⇒LIE[1], LIE[2]. ● *n* mensonges *mpl.*

lyric *adj* lyrique. **lyrical** *adj* lyrique. **lyrics** *npl* paroles *fpl.*

Mm

MA *abbr* ⇒MASTER OF ARTS.

mac *n* 🔲 imper *m.*

machine *n* machine *f.* ● *vt* (*sew*) coudre à la machine; (*Tech*) usiner. ∼-**gun** *n* mitrailleuse *f.*

mackerel *n inv* maquereau *m.*

mackintosh *n* imperméable *m.*

mad *adj* (**madder**, **maddest**) fou; (*foolish*) insensé; (*dog*) enragé; (*angry* 🔲) furieux; **be** ∼ **about** se passionner pour; (*person*) être fou de; **drive sb** ∼ exaspérer qn; **like** ∼ comme un fou.

madam *n* madame *f*; (*unmarried*) mademoiselle *f.*

made ⇒MAKE.

madly *adv* (*interested, in love*) follement; (*frantically*) comme un fou.

madman *n* (*pl* -**men**) fou *m.*

madness *n* folie *f.*

magazine *n* revue *f*, magazine *m*; (*of gun*) magasin *m.*

maggot *n* (*in fruit*) ver *m*, (*for fishing*) asticot *m.*

magic *n* magie *f.* ● *adj* magique.

magician *n* magicien/-ne *m/f.*

magistrate *n* magistrat *m.*

magnet *n* aimant *m.* **magnetic** *adj* magnétique.

magnificent *adj* magnifique.

magnify *vt* grossir; *(sound)* amplifier; *(fig)* exagérer. **magnifying glass** *n* loupe *f.*

magpie *n* pie *f.*

mahogany *n* acajou *m.*

maid *n* (servant) bonne *f*; (in hotel) femme *f* de chambre.

maiden *n* (old use) jeune fille *f.* ● *adj* *(aunt)* célibataire; *(voyage)* premier. ∼ **name** *n* nom *m* de jeune fille.

mail *n* (postal service) poste *f*; (letters) courrier *m*; (armour) cotte *f* de mailles. ● *adj (bag, van)* postal. ● *vt* envoyer par la poste. ∼ **box** *n* boîte *f* aux lettres; (Comput) boîte *f* aux lettres électronique. **mailing list** *n* liste *f* d'adresses. ∼**man** *n* (*pl* -**men**) (US) facteur *m.* ∼ **order** *n* vente *f* par correspondance. ∼ **shot** *n* publipostage *m.*

main *adj* principal; **a** ∼ **road** une grande route. ● *n* (water/gas) ∼ conduite *f* d'eau/de gaz; **the** ∼**s** (Electr) le secteur; **in the** ∼ en général. ∼**frame** *n* unité *f* centrale. ∼**land** *n* continent *m.* ∼**stream** *n* tendance *f* principale, ligne *f.*

maintain *vt* (continue, keep, assert) maintenir; *(house, machine, family)* entretenir; *(rights)* soutenir.

maintenance *n* (care) entretien *m*; (continuation) maintien *m*; (allowance) pension *f* alimentaire.

maisonette *n* duplex *m.*

maize *n* maïs *m.*

majestic *adj* majestueux.

majesty *n* majesté *f.*

major *adj* majeur. ● *n* commandant *m.* ● *vi* ∼ **in** (Univ, US) se spécialiser en.

majority *n* majorité *f*; **the** ∼ **of people** la plupart des gens. ● *adj* majoritaire.

make *vt/i* (*pt* **made**) faire; (manufacture) fabriquer; *(friends)* se faire; *(money)* gagner; *(decision)* prendre; *(place, position)* arriver à; (cause to be) rendre; ∼ **sb do sth** faire faire qch à qn; (force) obliger qn à faire qch; **be made of** être fait de; ∼ **oneself at home** se mettre à l'aise; ∼ **sb happy** rendre qn heureux; ∼ **it** arriver; (succeed) réussir; **I** ∼ **it two**

o'clock j'ai deux heures; **I** ∼ **it 150** d'après moi, ça fait 150; **I cannot** ∼ **anything of it** je n'y comprends rien; **can you** ∼ **Friday?** vendredi, c'est possible?; ∼ **as if to** faire mine de. ● *n* (brand) marque *f.* □ ∼ **do** (manage) se débrouiller (**with** avec); ∼ **for** se diriger vers; (cause) tendre à créer; ∼ **good** *vi* réussir; *vt* compenser; (repair) réparer; ∼ **off** filer (**with** avec); ∼ **out** distinguer; (understand) comprendre; (draw up) faire; (assert) prétendre; ∼ **up** *vt* faire, former; *(story)* inventer; *(deficit)* combler; *vi* se réconcilier; ∼ **up** (one's face) se maquiller; ∼ **up for** compenser; *(time)* rattraper; ∼ **up one's mind** se décider; ∼ **up to** se concilier les bonnes grâces de.

make-believe *adj* feint, illusoire. ● *n* fantaisie *f.*

maker *n* fabricant *m.*

makeshift *adj* improvisé.

make-up *n* maquillage *m*; (of object) constitution *f*; (Psych) caractère *m.*

malaria *n* paludisme *m.*

Malaysia *n* Malaisie *f.*

male *adj (voice, sex)* masculin; (Bot, Tech) mâle. ● *n* mâle *m.*

malfunction *n* mauvais fonctionnement *m.* ● *vi* mal fonctionner.

malice *n* méchanceté *f.* **malicious** *adj* méchant.

malignant *adj* malveillant; *(tumour)* malin.

mall *n* (shopping) ∼ (in suburbs) centre *m* commercial; (in town) galerie *f* marchande.

malnutrition *n* sous-alimentation *f.*

Malta *n* Malte *f.*

mammal *n* mammifère *m.*

mammoth *n* mammouth *m.* ● *adj* *(task)* gigantesque; *(organization)* géant.

man *n* (*pl* **men**) homme *m*; (in sports team) joueur *m*; (chess) pièce *f*; ∼ **to man** d'homme à homme. ● *vt* (*pt* **manned**) *(desk)* tenir; *(ship)* armer; *(guns)* servir; (be on duty at) être de service à.

manage *vt (project, organization)* diriger; *(shop, affairs)* gérer; (handle)

manier; **I could ~ another drink** 🄵 je
prendrais bien encore un verre; **can
you ~ Friday?** vendredi, c'est
possible? ● *vi* se débrouiller; **~ to do**
réussir à faire. **manageable** *adj*
(*tool, size, person*) maniable; (*job*)
faisable.

management *n* (managers)
direction *f*; (of shop) gestion *f*.

manager *n* directeur/-trice *m/f*; (of
shop) gérant/-e *m/f*; (of actor)
impresario *m*.

mandate *n* mandat *m*.

mandatory *adj* obligatoire.

mane *n* crinière *f*.

mango *n* (*pl* ~**es**) mangue *f*.

manhandle *vt* maltraiter,
malmener.

man: ~**hole** *n* regard *m*. ~**hood** *n*
âge *m* d'homme; (quality) virilité *f*.

maniac *n* maniaque *mf*, fou *m*, folle
f.

manicure *n* manucure *f*. ● *vt*
soigner, manucurer.

manifest *adj* manifeste. ● *vt*
manifester.

manipulate *vt* (*tool, person*)
manipuler.

mankind *n* genre *m* humain.

manly *adj* viril.

man-made *adj* (*fibre*) synthétique;
(*pond*) artificiel; (*disaster*) d'origine
humaine.

manned *adj* (*spacecraft*) habité.

manner *n* manière *f*; (attitude)
attitude *f*; (kind) sorte *f*; ~**s** (social
behaviour) manières *fpl*.

mannerism *n* particularité *f*; (quirk)
manie *f*.

manoeuvre *n* manœuvre *f*. ● *vt/i*
manœuvrer.

manor *n* manoir *m*.

manpower *n* main-d'œuvre *f*.

mansion *n* (in countryside) demeure *f*;
(in town) hôtel *m* particulier.

manslaughter *n* homicide *m*
involontaire.

mantelpiece *n* (manteau *m* de)
cheminée.

manual *adj* (*labour*) manuel;
(*typewriter*) mécanique. ● *n*
(handbook) manuel *m*.

manufacture *vt* fabriquer. ● *n*
fabrication *f*.

manure *n* fumier *m*.

many *a & n* beaucoup (de); **a great** *or*
good ~ un grand nombre (de); **~ a**
bien des.

map *n* carte *f*; (of streets) plan *m*. ● *vt*
(*pt* **mapped**) faire la carte de; **~
out** (*route*) tracer; (arrange) organiser.

mar *vt* (*pt* **marred**) gâcher.

marble *n* marbre *m*; (for game) bille *f*.

March *n* mars *m*.

march *vi* (Mil) marcher (au pas). ● *vt*
~ off (lead away) emmener. ● *n*
marche *f*.

margin *n* marge *f*.

marginal *adj* marginal; (*increase*)
léger, faible; (*seat*: Pol) disputé.

marinate *vt* faire mariner (**in** dans).

marine *adj* marin. ● *n* (shipping)
marine *f*; (sailor) fusilier *m* marin.

marital *adj* conjugal. **~ status** *n*
situation *f* de famille.

mark *n* (currency) mark *m*; (stain) tache
f; (trace) marque *f*; (School) note *f*;
(target) but *m*. ● *vt* marquer; (*exam*)
corriger; **~ out** délimiter; (*person*)
désigner; **~ time** marquer le pas.

marker *n* (pen) marqueur *m*; (tag)
repère *m*; (School, Univ) examinateur/
-trice *m/f*.

market *n* marché *m*; **on the ~** en
vente. ● *vt* (sell) vendre; (launch)
commercialiser. **~ research** *n*
étude *f* de marché.

marmalade *n* confiture *f*
d'oranges.

maroon *n* bordeaux *m inv*. ● *adj*
bordeaux *inv*.

marooned *adj* abandonné; (snowbound) bloqué.

marquee *n* grande tente *f*; (of circus)
chapiteau *m*; (awning: US) auvent *m*.

marriage *n* mariage *m* (**to** avec).

married *adj* marié (**to** à); (life)
conjugal; **get ~** se marier (**to** avec).

marrow *n* (of bone) moelle *f*;
(vegetable) courge *f*.

marry *vt* épouser; (give or unite in
marriage) marier. ● *vi* se marier.

marsh *n* marais *m*.

marshal n maréchal m; (at event) membre m du service d'ordre. ● vt (pt **marshalled**) rassembler.

martyr n martyr/-e m/f. ● vt martyriser.

marvel n merveille f. ● vi (pt **marvelled**) s'émerveiller (**at** de).

marvellous adj merveilleux.

marzipan n pâte f d'amandes.

masculine a & n masculin (m).

mash n (potatoes ①) purée f. ● vt écraser. **mashed potatoes** npl purée f (de pommes de terre).

mask n masque m. ● vt masquer.

Mason n franc-maçon m.

masonry n maçonnerie f.

mass n (Relig) messe f; masse f; **the ∼es** les masses fpl. ● vt/i (se) masser.

massacre n massacre m. ● vt massacrer.

massage n massage m. ● vt masser.

massive adj (large) énorme; (heavy) massif.

mass media n médias mpl.

mass-produce vt fabriquer en série.

mast n (on ship) mât m; (for radio, TV) pylône m.

master n maître m; (in secondary school) professeur m; **M∼ of Arts** titulaire mf d'une maîtrise ès lettres. ● vt maîtriser.

masterpiece n chef-d'œuvre m.

mastery n maîtrise f.

mat n (petit) tapis m; (at door) paillasson m.

match n (for lighting fire) allumette f; (Sport) match m; (equal) égal/-e m/f; (marriage) mariage m; (sb to marry) parti m; **be a ∼ for** pouvoir tenir tête à. ● vt opposer; (go with) aller avec; (cups) assortir; (equal) égaler. ● vi (be alike) être assorti.

matchbox n boîte f à allumettes.

matching adj assorti.

mate n camarade mf; (of animal) compagnon m, compagne f; (assistant) aide mf; (chess) mat m. ● vt/i (s') accoupler (**with** avec).

material n matière f; (fabric) tissu m; (documents, for building) matériau(x) m(pl); **∼s** (equipment) matériel m. ● adj matériel; (fig) important.

materialistic adj matérialiste.

materialize vi se matérialiser, se réaliser.

maternal adj maternel.

maternity n maternité f. ● adj (clothes) de grossesse. **∼ hospital** n maternité f. **∼ leave** n congé m maternité.

mathematics n & npl mathématiques fpl.

maths, (US) **math** n maths fpl.

mating n accouplement m.

matrimony n mariage m.

matron n (married, elderly) dame f âgée; (in hospital) infirmière f en chef.

matt adj mat.

matter n (substance) matière f; (affair) affaire f; **as a ∼ of fact** en fait; **what is the ∼?** qu'est-ce qu'il y a? ● vi importer; **it does not ∼** ça ne fait rien; **no ∼ what happens** quoi qu'il arrive.

mattress n matelas m.

mature adj (psychologically) mûr; (plant) adulte. ● vt/i (se) mûrir.

maturity n maturité f.

mauve a & n mauve (m).

maverick n non-conformiste mf.

maximize vt porter au maximum.

maximum a & n (pl **-ima**) maximum (m).

---

may

past **might**

● *auxiliary verb*

····▸ (possibility) **they ∼ be able to come** ils pourront peut-être venir; **she ∼ not have seen him** elle ne l'a peut-être pas vu; **it ∼ rain** il risque de pleuvoir; **'will you come?'—'I might'** 'tu viendras?'—'peut-être'.

····▸ (permission) **you ∼ leave** vous pouvez partir; **∼ I smoke?** puis-je fumer?

····▸ (wish) **∼ he be happy** qu'il soit heureux.

May n mai m.

maybe adv peut-être.

m

mayhem *n* (havoc) ravages *mpl*.

mayonnaise *n* mayonnaise *f*.

mayor *n* maire *m*.

maze *n* labyrinthe *m*.

Mb *abbr* (**megabyte**) (Comput) Mo.

me *pron* me, m'; (after prep.) moi; (indirect object) me, m'; **he knows** ~ il me connaît.

meadow *n* pré *m*.

meagre *adj* maigre.

meal *n* repas *m*; (grain) farine *f*.

mean *adj* (poor) misérable; (miserly) avare; (unkind) méchant; (average) moyen. ● *n* milieu *m*; (average) moyenne *f*; **in the** ~ **time** en attendant. ● *vt* (*pt* **meant**) vouloir dire, signifier; (involve) entraîner; **I** ~ **that!** je suis sérieux; **be meant for** être destiné à; ~ **to do** avoir l'intention de faire.

meaning *n* sens *m*, signification *f*.
meaningful *adj* significatif.
meaningless *adj* dénué de sens.

means *n* moyen(s) *m(pl)*; **by** ~ **of sth** au moyen de qch. ● *npl* (wealth) moyens *mpl* financiers; **by all** ~ certainement; **by no** ~ nullement.

meant ⇒MEAN.

meantime, **meanwhile** *adv* en attendant.

measles *n* rougeole *f*.

measure *n* mesure *f*; (ruler) règle *f*. ● *vt/i* mesurer; ~ **up to** être à la hauteur de.

meat *n* viande *f*. **meaty** *adj* de viande; (fig) substantiel.

mechanic *n* mécanicien/-ne *m/f*.

mechanical *adj* mécanique.

mechanism *n* mécanisme *m*.

medal *n* médaille *f*.

meddle *vi* (interfere) se mêler (**in** de); (tinker) toucher (**with** à).

media *n* ⇒MEDIUM. ● *npl* **the** ~ les média *mpl*; **talk to the** ~ parler à la presse.

median *adj* médian. ● *n* médiane *f*.

mediate *vi* servir d'intermédiaire.

medical *adj* médical; (student) en médecine. ● *n* visite *f* médicale.

medication *n* médicaments *mpl*.

medicine *n* (science) médecine *f*; (substance) médicament *m*.

medieval *adj* médiéval.

mediocre *adj* médiocre.

meditate *vt/i* méditer.

Mediterranean *adj* méditerranéen. ● *n* **the** ~ la Méditerranée *f*.

medium *n* (*pl* **media**) (mid-point) milieu *m*; (for transmitting data) support *m*; (*pl* **mediums**) (person) médium *m*. ● *adj* moyen.

medley *n* mélange *m*; (Mus) pot-pourri *m*.

meet *vt* (*pt* **met**) rencontrer; (see again) retrouver; (be introduced to) faire la connaissance de; (face) faire face à; (*requirement*) satisfaire. ● *vi* se rencontrer; (see each other again) se retrouver; (in session) se réunir.

meeting *n* réunion *f*; (between two people) rencontre *f*.

megabyte *n* (Comput) mégaoctet *m*.

melancholy *n* mélancolie *f*. ● *adj* mélancolique.

mellow *adj* (*fruit*) mûr; (*sound, colour*) moelleux, doux; (*person*) mûri. ● *vt/i* (mature) mûrir; (soften) (s')adoucir.

melody *n* mélodie *f*.

melon *n* melon *m*.

melt *vt/i* (faire) fondre.

member *n* membre *m*. **M**~ **of Parliament** *n* député *m*.
membership *n* adhésion *f*; (members) membres *mpl*; (fee) cotisation *f*.

memento *n* (*pl* ~**es**) (object) souvenir *m*.

memo *n* note *f*.

memoir *n* (record, essay) mémoire *m*.

memorandum *n* note *f*.

memorial *n* monument *m*. ● *adj* commémoratif.

memorize *vt* apprendre par cœur.

memory *n* (mind, in computer) mémoire *f*; (thing remembered) souvenir *m*; **from** ~ de mémoire; **in** ~ **of** à la mémoire de.

men ⇒MAN.

menace *n* menace *f*; (nuisance) peste *f*. ● *vt* menacer.

mend *vt* réparer; (darn) raccommoder; ~ **one's ways** s'amender. ● *n* raccommodage *m*; **on the** ~ en voie de guérison.

meningitis *n* méningite *f.*

menopause *n* ménopause *f.*

mental *adj* mental; (*hospital*) psychiatrique.

mentality *n* mentalité *f.*

mention *vt* mentionner; **don't ~ it!** il n'y a pas de quoi!, je vous en prie! ● *n* mention *f.*

menu *n* (food, on computer) menu *m*; (list) carte *f.*

MEP *abbr* (**Member of the European Parliament**) député *m* au Parlement européen.

mercenary *a* & *n* mercenaire (*m*).

merchandise *n* marchandises *fpl.*

merchant *n* marchand *m.* ● *adj* (*ship, navy*) marchand. **~ bank** *n* banque *f* de commerce.

merciful *adj* miséricordieux.

mercury *n* mercure *m.*

mercy *n* pitié *f*; **at the ~ of** à la merci de.

mere *adj* simple. **merest** *adj* moindre.

merge *vt/i* (se) mêler (**with** à); (*companies*: Comm) fusionner. **merger** *n* fusion *f.*

mermaid *n* sirène *f.*

merrily *adv* (happily) joyeusement; (unconcernedly) avec insouciance.

merry *adj* (**-ier, -iest**) gai; **make ~** faire la fête. **~-go-round** *n* manège *m.*

mesh *n* maille *f*; (fabric) tissu *m* à mailles; (network) réseau *m.*

mesmerize *vt* hypnotiser.

mess *n* désordre *m*, gâchis *m*; (dirt) saleté *f*; (Mil) mess *m*; **make a ~ of** gâcher. ● *vt* **~ up** gâcher. ● *vi* **~ about** s'amuser; (dawdle) traîner; **~ with** (tinker with) tripoter.

message *n* message *m.*

messenger *n* messager/-ère *m/f.*

messy *adj* (**-ier, -iest**) en désordre; (dirty) sale.

met ⇒MEET.

metal *n* métal *m.* ● *adj* de métal. **metallic** *adj* métallique; (paint, colour) métallisé.

metallurgy *n* métallurgie *f.*

metaphor *n* métaphore *f.*

meteor *n* météore *m.*

meteorite *n* météorite *m.*

meteorology *n* météorologie *f.*

meter *n* compteur *m*; (US) = METRE.

method *n* méthode *f.*

methylated spirit(s) *n* alcool *m* à brûler.

meticulous *adj* méticuleux.

metre, (US) **meter** *n* mètre *m.*

metric *adj* métrique.

metropolis *n* métropole *f.* **metropolitan** *adj* métropolitain.

mew *n* miaulement *m.* ● *vi* miauler.

mews *npl* appartements *mpl* chic aménagés dans d'anciennes écuries.

Mexico *n* Mexique *m.*

miaow *n* & *vi* = MEW.

mice ⇒MOUSE.

mickey *n* **take the ~ out of** Ⓣ se moquer de.

microchip *n* puce *f*; circuit *m* intégré.

microlight *n* ULM *m.*

microprocessor *n* microprocesseur *m.*

microscope *n* microscope *m.*

microwave *n* micro-onde *f*; **~ (oven)** four *m* à micro-ondes. ● *vt* passer au four à micro-ondes.

mid *adj* **in ~ air** en plein ciel; **in ~ March** à la mi-mars; **~ afternoon** milieu *m* de l'après-midi; **he's in his ~ twenties** il a environ vingt-cinq ans.

midday *n* midi *m.*

middle *adj* (*door, shelf*) du milieu; (*size*) moyen. ● *n* milieu *m*; **in the ~ of** au milieu de. **~-aged** *adj* d'âge mûr. **M~ Ages** *n* Moyen Âge *m.* **~ class** *n* classe *f* moyenne. **M~ East** *n* Moyen-Orient *m.*

midge *n* moucheron *m.*

midget *n* nain/-e *m/f.* ● *adj* minuscule.

midnight *n* minuit *f*; **it's ~** il est minuit.

midst *n* **in the ~ of** au beau milieu de; **in our ~** parmi nous.

midsummer *n* milieu *m* de l'été; (solstice) solstice *m* d'été.

midway *adv* **~ between/along** à mi-chemin entre/le long de.

midwife *n* (*pl* **-wives**) sage-femme *f.*

m

might[1] *v aux* I $\sim$ have been killed! j'aurais pu être tué; **you** $\sim$ **try doing sth** vous pourriez faire qch; ⇒MAY.

might[2] *n* puissance *f*.

mighty *adj* puissant; (huge 🎟) énorme. ● *adv* 🎟 vachement 🎟.

migrant *a & n* (*bird*) migrateur (*m*); (*worker*) migrant/-e (*m/f*).

migrate *vi* émigrer. **migration** *n* migration *f*.

mild *adj* (*surprise, taste, tobacco, attack*) léger; (*weather, cheese, soap, person*) doux; (*case, infection*) bénin.

mile *n* mile *m* (= *1.6 km*); **walk for** $\sim$**s** marcher pendant des kilomètres; $\sim$**s better** 🎟 bien meilleur. **mileage** *n* nombre *m* de miles, kilométrage *m*.

milestone *n* (lit) borne *f*; (fig) étape *f* importante.

military *adj* militaire.

militia *n* milice *f*.

milk *n* lait *m*. ● *vt* (*cow*) traire; (fig) pomper.

milkman *n* (*pl* **-men**) laitier *m*.

milky *adj* (*skin, colour*) laiteux; (*tea*) au lait; M$\sim$ **Way** Voie *f* lactée.

mill *n* moulin *m*; (factory) usine *f*. ● *vt* moudre. ● *vi* $\sim$ **around** grouiller.

millennium *n* (*pl* $\sim$**s**) millénaire *m*.

millimetre, (US) **millimeter** *n* millimètre *m*.

million *n* million *m*; **a** $\sim$ **pounds** un million de livres. **millionaire** *n* millionnaire *m*.

millstone *n* meule *f*; (fig) boulet *m*.

mime *n* (actor) mime *mf*; (art) mime *m*. ● *vt/i* mimer.

mimic *vt* (*pt* **mimicked**) imiter. ● *n* imitateur/-trice *m/f*.

mince *vt* hacher; **not to** $\sim$ **matters** ne pas mâcher ses mots. ● *n* viande *f* hachée.

mind *n* esprit *m*; (sanity) raison *f*; (opinion) avis *m*; **be on sb's** $\sim$ préoccuper qn; **bear that in** $\sim$ ne l'oubliez pas; **change one's** $\sim$ changer d'avis; **make up one's** $\sim$ se décider (**to** à). ● *vt* (have charge of) s'occuper de; (heed) faire attention à; **I do not** $\sim$ **the noise** le bruit ne me dérange pas; **I don't** $\sim$ ça m'est égal;

would you $\sim$ **checking?** je peux vous demander de vérifier?

minder *n* (bodyguard) garde *m* de corps; (child) $\sim$ nourrice *f*.

mindless *adj* (*programme*) bête; (*work*) abrutissant; (*vandalism*) gratuit.

mine *n* mine *f*. ● *vt* extraire; (Mil) miner. ● *pron* le mien, la mienne, les mien(ne)s; **the blue car is** $\sim$ la voiture bleue est la mienne *or* à moi.

minefield *n* (lit) champ *m* de mines; (fig) terrain *m* miné.

miner *n* mineur *m*.

mineral *n & a* minéral (*m*); $\sim$ **water** eau *f* minérale.

minesweeper *n* (ship) dragueur *m* de mines.

mingle *vt/i* (se) mêler (**with** à).

minibus *n* minibus *m*.

minicab *n* taxi *m* (*non agréé*).

minimal *adj* minimal.

minimize *vt* minimiser; (Comput) réduire.

minimum *a & n* (*pl* **-ima**) minimum (*m*).

minister *n* ministre *m*. **ministerial** *adj* ministériel. **ministry** *n* ministère *m*.

mink *n* vison *m*.

minor *adj* (*change, surgery*) mineur; (*injury, burn*) léger; (*road*) secondaire. ● *n* (Jur) mineur/-e *m/f*.

minority *n* minorité *f*; **in the** $\sim$ en minorité. ● *adj* minoritaire.

mint *n* (Bot, Culin) menthe *f*; (sweet) bonbon *m* à la menthe; (fortune 🎟) fortune *f*. ● *vt* frapper; **in** $\sim$ **condition** à l'état neuf.

minus *prep* moins; (without 🎟) sans. ● *n* moins *m*; (drawback) inconvénient *m*.

minute[1] *n* minute *f*; $\sim$**s** (of meeting) compte-rendu *m*.

minute[2] *adj* (*object*) minuscule; (*risk, variation*) minime.

miracle *n* miracle *m*.

mirror *n* miroir *m*, glace *f*; (Auto) rétroviseur. ● *vt* refléter.

misbehave *vi* se conduire mal.

miscalculation *n* (lit) erreur *f* de calcul; (fig) mauvais calcul *m*.

miscarriage n fausse couche f; ~ of justice erreur f judiciaire.

miscellaneous adj divers.

mischief n (playfulness) espièglerie f; (by children) bêtises fpl.
mischievous adj espiègle; (malicious) méchant.

misconduct n mauvaise conduite f.

misconstrue vt mal interpréter.

misdemeanour, (US) **misdemeanor** n (Jur) délit m.

miser n avare mf.

miserable adj (sad) malheureux; (wretched) misérable; (performance, result) lamentable.

misery n (unhappiness) souffrance f; (misfortune) misère f; (person ☺) rabat-joie mf inv.

misfit n inadapté/-e m/f.

misfortune n malheur m.

misgiving n (doubt) doute m; (apprehension) crainte f.

misguided adj (foolish) imprudent; (mistaken) erroné; **be** ~ (person) se tromper.

mishap n incident m.

misjudge vt (distance, speed) mal évaluer; (person) mal juger.

mislay vt (pt **mislaid**) égarer.

mislead vt (pt **misled**) tromper.
misleading adj trompeur.

misplace vt mal ranger; (lose) égarer. **misplaced** adj (fear, criticism) déplacé.

misprint n coquille f, faute f typographique.

misread vt (pt **misread**) mal lire; (intentions) mal interpréter.

miss vt/i manquer; (bus) rater; **he** ~**es her/Paris** elle/Paris lui manque; **you're** ~**ing the point** tu n'as rien compris; ~ **sth out** omettre qch; ~ **out on sth** laisser passer qch. ● n coup m manqué; **it was a near** ~ on l'a échappé belle.

Miss n Mademoiselle f; ~ **Smith** (written) Mlle Smith.

misshapen adj difforme.

missile n (Mil) missile m; (thrown) projectile m.

mission n mission f. **missionary** n missionnaire mf.

misspell vt (pt **misspelt** or **misspelled**) mal écrire.

mist n brume f; (on window) buée f. ● vt/i (s')embuer.

mistake n erreur f; **by** ~ par erreur; **make a** ~ faire une erreur. ● vt (pt **mistook**; pp **mistaken**) (meaning) mal interpréter; ~ **for** prendre pour.

mistaken adj (enthusiasm) mal placé; **be** ~ avoir tort.

mistletoe n gui m.

mistreat vt maltraiter.

mistress n maîtresse f.

misty adj (-ier, -iest) brumeux; (window) embué.

misunderstanding n malentendu m.

misuse vt (word) mal employer; (power) abuser de; (equipment) faire mauvais usage de.

mitten n moufle f.

mix n mélange m. ● vt mélanger; (drink) préparer; (cement) malaxer. ● vi se mélanger (with avec, à); (socially) être sociable; ~ **with sb** fréquenter qn. □ ~ **up** (confuse) confondre; (jumble up) mélanger; **get** ~**ed up in** se trouver mêlé à.

mixed adj (school) mixte; (collection, diet) varié; (nuts, sweets) assorti.

mixer n (Culin) batteur m électrique; **be a good** ~ être sociable; ~ **tap** mélangeur m.

mixture n mélange m.

mix-up n confusion f (over sur).

moan n gémissement m. ● vi gémir; (complain ☺) râler ☺.

mob n (crowd) foule f; (gang) gang m; **the M**~ la Mafia. ● vt (pt **mobbed**) assaillir.

mobile adj mobile; ~ **phone** téléphone m portable. ● n mobile m.

mobilize vt/i mobiliser.

mock vt/i se moquer (de). ● adj faux.

mockery n moquerie f; **a** ~ **of** une parodie de.

mock-up n maquette f.

mode n mode m.

model n (Comput, Auto) modèle m; (scale representation) maquette f; (person showing clothes) mannequin m. ● adj modèle; (car) modèle réduit inv;

m

(*railway*) miniature. ● *vt* (*pt*
modelled) modeler; (*clothes*)
présenter. ● *vi* être mannequin;
(pose) poser. **modelling** *n* métier *m*
de mannequin.

modem *n* modem *m*.

moderate *a* & *n* modéré/-e (*m/f*).

moderation *n* modération *f*; in ~
avec modération.

modern *adj* moderne; ~ **languages**
langues *fpl* vivantes. **modernize** *vt*
moderniser.

modest *adj* modeste. **modesty** *n*
modestie *f*.

modification *n* modification *f*.
modify *vt* modifier.

module *n* module *m*.

moist *adj* (*soil*) humide; (*skin*,
palms) moite; (*cake*) moelleux.
moisten *vt* humecter. **moisture** *n*
humidité *f*. **moisturizer** *n* crème *f*
hydratante.

molar *n* molaire *f*.

mold (US) = MOULD.

mole *n* grain *m* de beauté; (animal)
taupe *f*.

molecule *n* molécule *f*.

molest *vt* (pester) importuner;
(sexually) agresser sexuellement.

moment *n* (short time) instant *m*;
(point in time) moment *m*.
momentarily *adv*
momentanément; (soon: US) très
bientôt. **momentary** *adj*
momentané.

momentum *n* élan *m*.

monarch *n* monarque *m*.
monarchy *n* monarchie *f*.

Monday *n* lundi *m*.

monetary *adj* monétaire.

money *n* argent *m*; **make** ~ (*person*)
gagner de l'argent; (*business*)
rapporter de l'argent. ~**-box** *n*
tirelire *f*. ~ **order** *n* mandat *m*
postal.

monitor *n* dispositif *m* de
surveillance; (Comput) moniteur *m*.
● *vt* surveiller; (*broadcast*) être à
l'écoute de.

monk *n* moine *m*.

monkey *n* singe *m*.

monopolize *vt* monopoliser.

monopoly *n* monopole *m*.

monotonous *adj* monotone.
monotony *n* monotonie *f*.

monsoon *n* mousson *f*.

monster *n* monstre *m*. **monstrous**
adj monstrueux.

month *n* mois *m*.

monthly *adj* mensuel. ● *adv* (*pay*)
au mois; (*publish*) tous les mois. ● *n*
(periodical) mensuel *m*.

monument *n* monument *m*.

moo *vi* meugler.

mood *n* humeur *f*; **in a good/bad** ~
de bonne/mauvaise humeur. **moody**
adj d'humeur changeante.

moon *n* lune *f*.

moonlight *n* clair *m* de lune.
moonlighting *n* ⊞ travail *m* au
noir.

moor *n* lande *f*. ● *vt* amarrer.

mop *n* balai *m* à franges; ~ **of hair**
crinière *f* ⊞. ● *vt* (*pt* **mopped**) ~
(**up**) éponger.

moped *n* vélomoteur *m*.

moral *adj* moral. ● *n* morale *f*; ~**s**
moralité *f*.

morale *n* moral *m*.

morbid *adj* morbide.

more *adv* plus; ~ **serious** plus
sérieux; **work** ~ travailler plus;
sleep ~ **and** ~ dormir de plus en
plus; **once** ~ une fois de plus; **I don't
go there any** ~ je n'y vais plus; ~ **or
less** plus ou moins. ● *det* plus de; **a
little** ~ **wine** un peu plus de vin; ~
bread encore un peu de pain; **there's
no** ~ **bread** il n'y a plus de pain;
nothing ~ rien de plus. ● *pron* plus;
cost ~ **than** coûter plus cher que; **I
need** ~ **of it** il m'en faut davantage.

moreover *adv* de plus.

morning *n* matin *m*; (whole morning)
matinée *f*.

Morocco *n* Maroc *m*.

morsel *n* morceau *m*.

mortal *a* & *n* mortel/-le (*m/f*).

mortgage *n* emprunt-logement *m*.
● *vt* hypothéquer.

mortuary *n* morgue *f*.

mosaic *n* mosaïque *f*.

mosque n mosquée f.

mosquito n (pl ~es) moustique m.

moss n mousse f.

most det (nearly all) la plupart de; ~ **people** la plupart des gens; **the ~ votes/money** le plus de voix/ d'argent. ● n le plus. ● pron la plupart; ~ **of us** la plupart d'entre nous; ~ **of the money** la plus grande partie de l'argent; **the ~ I can do is ...** tout ce que je peux faire c'est ... ● adv **the ~ beautiful house/hotel in Oxford** la maison la plus belle/l'hôtel le plus beau d'Oxford; ~ **interesting** très intéressant; **what I like ~ (of all) is** ce que j'aime le plus c'est. **mostly** adv surtout.

moth n papillon m de nuit; (in cloth) mite f.

mother n mère f. ● vt (lit) materner; (fig) dorloter. **motherhood** n maternité f. ~**-in-law** n (pl ~**s-in-law**) belle-mère f. ~**-of-pearl** n nacre f. **M~'s Day** n la fête des mères. ~**-to-be** n future maman f. ~ **tongue** n langue f maternelle.

motion n mouvement m; (proposal) motion f; ~ **picture** (US) film m. ● vt/i ~ **(to) sb** to faire signe à qn de. **motionless** adj immobile.

motivate vt motiver.

motive n motif m; (Jur) mobile m.

motor n moteur m; (car) auto f. ● adj (industry, insurance, vehicle) automobile; (activity, disorder: Med) moteur. ~**bike** n moto f. ~ **car** n auto f. ~**-cyclist** n motocycliste mf. ~ **home** n auto-caravane f.

motorist n automobiliste mf.

motorway n autoroute f.

mottled adj tacheté.

motto n (pl ~es) devise f.

mould n (shape) moule m; (fungus) moisissure f. ● vt mouler; (influence) former. **moulding** n moulure f. **mouldy** adj moisi.

mount n (hill) mont m; (horse) monture f. ● vt (stairs) gravir; (platform, horse, bike) monter sur; (jewel, picture, campaign, exhibit) monter. ● vi monter; (number, toll) augmenter; (concern) grandir.

mountain n montagne f; ~ **bike** (vélo) tout terrain m, VTT m. **mountaineer** n alpiniste mf.

mourn vt/i ~ **(for)** pleurer. **mournful** adj mélancolique. **mourning** n deuil m.

mouse n (pl **mice**) souris f. ~**trap** n souricière f.

mouth n bouche f; (of dog, cat) gueule f; (of cave, tunnel) entrée f. **mouthful** n bouchée f. ~**wash** n eau f dentifrice. ~**watering** adj appétissant.

move vt (object) déplacer; (limb, head) bouger; (emotionally) émouvoir; ~ **house** déménager. ● vi bouger; (vehicle) rouler; (change address) déménager; (act) agir. ● n mouvement m; (in game) coup m; (player's turn) tour m; (step, act) manœuvre f; (house change) déménagement m; **on the ~** en mouvement. □ ~ **back** reculer; ~ **in** emménager; ~ **in with** s'installer avec; ~ **on** (person) se mettre en route; (vehicle) repartir; (time) passer; ~ **sth on** faire avancer qch; ~ **sb on** faire circuler qn; ~ **over** or **up** se pousser.

movement n mouvement m.

movie n (US) film m; **the ~s** le cinéma.

moving adj (vehicle) en marche; (part, target) mobile; (staircase) roulant; (touching) émouvant.

mow vt (pp **mowed** or **mown**) (lawn) tondre; (hay) couper; ~ **down** faucher. **mower** n tondeuse f.

MP abbr ⇒MEMBER OF PARLIAMENT.

Mr n (pl **Messrs**) ~ **Smith** Monsieur or M. Smith; ~ **President** Monsieur le Président.

Mrs n (pl **Mrs**) ~ **Smith** Madame or Mme Smith.

Ms n Mme.

much adv beaucoup; **too ~** trop; **very ~** beaucoup; **I like them as ~ as you (do)** je les aime autant que toi. ● pron beaucoup; **not ~** pas grand-chose; **he didn't say ~** il n'a pas dit grand-chose; **I ate so ~ that** j'ai tellement mangé que. ● det beaucoup de; **too ~ money** trop d'argent; **how**

m

~ **time is left?** combien de temps reste-t-il?

muck *n* saletés *fpl*; (*manure*) fumier *m*. □ ~ **about** ① faire l'imbécile. **mucky** *adj* sale.

mud *n* boue *f*.

muddle *n* (mix-up) malentendu *m*; (mess) pagaille *f* ①; **get into a** ~ s'embrouiller. □ ~ **through** se débrouiller; ~ **up** embrouiller.

muddy *adj* couvert de boue.

muffle *vt* emmitoufler; (*bell*) assourdir; (*voice*) étouffer.

mug *n* grande tasse *f*; (for beer) chope *f*, (face ①) gueule *f* ✖; (fool ①) poire *f* ①. ● *vt* (*pt* **mugged**) agresser. **mugger** *n* agresseur *m*.

muggy *adj* lourd.

mule *n* mulet *m*.

multicoloured *adj* multicolore.

multiple *a* & *n* multiple (*m*); ~ **sclerosis** sclérose *f* en plaques.

multiplication *n* multiplication *f*.

multiply *vt/i* (se) multiplier.

multistorey *adj* (car park) à niveaux multiples.

mum *n* ① maman *f*.

mumble *vt/i* marmonner.

mummy *n* (mother ①) maman *f*; (embalmed body) momie *f*.

mumps *n* oreillons *mpl*.

munch *vt* mâcher.

mundane *adj* terre-à-terre.

municipal *adj* municipal.

mural *adj* mural. ● *n* peinture *f* murale.

murder *n* meurtre *m*. ● *vt* assassiner. **murderer** *n* meurtrier *m*, assassin *m*.

murky *adj* (**-ier, -iest**) (*water*) glauque; (*past*) trouble.

murmur *n* murmure *m*. ● *vt/i* murmurer.

muscle *n* muscle *m*. ● *vi* ~ **in** ① s'imposer (**on** dans).

muscular *adj* (*tissue, disease*) musculaire; (*body, person*) musclé.

museum *n* musée *m*.

mushroom *n* champignon *m*. ● *vi* (*town*) proliférer; (*demand*) s'accroître rapidement.

music *n* musique *f*.

musical *adj* (*person*) musicien; (*voice*) mélodieux; (*accompaniment*) musical; (*instrument*) de musique. ● *n* comédie *f* musicale.

musician *n* musicien/-ne *m/f*.

Muslim *n* Musulman/-e *m/f*. ● *adj* musulman.

mussel *n* moule *f*.

must *v aux* devoir; **you** ~ **go** vous devez partir, il faut que vous partiez; **she** ~ **be consulted** il faut la consulter; **he** ~ **be old** il doit être vieux; **I** ~ **have done it** j'ai dû le faire. ● *n* **be a** ~ ① être indispensable.

mustard *n* moutarde *f*.

musty *adj* (**-ier, -iest**) (*room*) qui sent le renfermé; (*smell*) de moisi.

mute *a* & *n* muet/-te (*m/f*). **muted** *adj* (*colour*) sourd; (*response*) tiède; (*celebration*) mitigé.

mutilate *vt* mutiler.

mutter *vt/i* marmonner.

mutton *n* mouton *m*.

mutual *adj* (reciprocal) réciproque; (common) commun; (*consent*) mutuel. **mutually** *adv* mutuellement.

muzzle *n* (snout) museau *m*; (device) muselière *f*; (of gun) canon *m*. ● *vt* museler.

my *adj* mon, ma, *pl* mes.

myself *pron* (reflexive) me, m'; **I've hurt** ~ je me suis fait mal; (emphatic) moi-même; **I did it** ~ je l'ai fait moi-même; (after preposition) moi, moi-même; **I am proud of** ~ je suis fier de moi.

mysterious *adj* mystérieux.

mystery *n* mystère *m*.

mystic *a* & *n* mystique (*mf*). **mystical** *adj* mystique.

myth *n* mythe *m*. **mythical** *adj* mythique. **mythology** *n* mythologie *f*.

Nn

nag vt/i (pt **nagged**) critiquer; (pester) harceler. **nagging** adj persistant.

nail n clou m; (of finger, toe) ongle m; on the ~ sans tarder, tout de suite. ● vt clouer. ~ **polish** n vernis m à ongles.

naïve adj naïf.

naked adj nu; to the ~ eye à l'œil nu.

name n nom m; (fig) réputation f. ● vt nommer; (terms) fixer; be ~d after porter le nom de.

namely adv à savoir.

nanny n nurse f.

nap n somme m.

nape n nuque f.

napkin n serviette f.

nappy n couche f.

narcotic a & n narcotique (m).

narrative n récit m. **narrator** n narrateur/-trice m/f.

narrow adj étroit. ● vt/i (se) rétrécir; (limit) (se) limiter; ~ down the choices limiter les choix. ~**-minded** adj à l'esprit étroit; (ideas) étroit.

nasal adj nasal.

nasty adj (-ier, -iest) mauvais, désagréable; (malicious) méchant.

nation n nation f.

national adj national. ● n ressortissant/-e m/f.

nationality n nationalité f.

nationalize vt nationaliser.

nationally adv à l'échelle nationale.

native n (local inhabitant) autochtone mf; (non-European) indigène mf; be a ~ of être originaire de. ● adj indigène; (country) natal; (inborn) inné; ~ **language** langue f maternelle; ~ **speaker of French** personne f de langue maternelle française.

natural adj naturel.

naturally adv (normally, of course) naturellement; (by nature) de nature.

nature n nature f.

naughty adj (-ier, -iest) vilain, méchant; (indecent) grivois.

nausea n nausée f. **nauseous** adj (smell) écœurant.

nautical adj nautique.

naval adj (battle) naval; (officer) de marine.

navel n nombril m.

navigate vt (sea) naviguer sur; (ship) piloter. ● vi naviguer. **navigation** n navigation f.

navy n marine f. ● adj ~ (**blue**) bleu inv marine.

near adv près; draw ~ (s')approcher (to de). ● prep près de. ● adj proche; ~ to près de. ● vt approcher de.

nearby adj proche. ● adv à proximité.

nearly adv presque; I ~ forgot j'ai failli oublier; not ~ as pretty as loin d'être aussi joli que.

nearness n proximité f.

nearside adj (Auto) du côté du passager.

neat adj soigné, net; (room) bien rangé; (clever) habile; (drink) sec. **neatly** adv avec soin; habilement. **neatness** n netteté f.

necessarily adv nécessairement.

necessary adj nécessaire.

necessitate vt nécessiter.

necessity n nécessité f; (thing) chose f indispensable.

neck n cou m; (of dress) encolure f. ~ **and neck** adj à égalité. ~**lace** n collier m. ~**line** n encolure f. ~**tie** n cravate f.

nectarine n brugnon m, nectarine f.

need n besoin m. ● vt avoir besoin de; (demand) demander; you ~ not come vous n'êtes pas obligé de venir.

needle n aiguille f.

needless adj inutile.

needlework n couture f; (object) ouvrage m (à l'aiguille).

needy adj (-ier, -iest) nécessiteux. ● n the ~ les indigents.

negative adj négatif. ● n (of photograph) négatif m; (word: Gram) négation *f*; in the ~ (answer) par la négative; (Gram) à la forme négative.

neglect *vt* négliger, laisser à l'abandon; ~ **to do** négliger de faire. ● *n* manque *m* de soins; (**state of**) ~ abandon *m*.

negligent *adj* négligent.

negotiate *vt/i* négocier.

negotiation *n* négociation *f*.

neigh *n* hennissement *m*. ● *vi* hennir.

neighbour, (US) **neighbor** *n* voisin/-e *m/f*. **neighbourhood** *n* voisinage *m*, quartier *m*; in the ~hood of aux alentours de. **neighbouring** *adj* voisin. **neighbourly** *adj* amical.

neither *a & pron* aucun/-e des deux, ni l'un/-e ni l'autre. ● *adv* ni; ~ **big nor small** ni grand ni petit. ● *conj* (ne) non plus; ~ **am I coming** je ne viendrai pas non plus.

nephew *n* neveu *m*.

nerve *n* nerf *m*; (courage) courage *m*; (calm) sang-froid *m*; (impudence 🅣) culot *m*; ~**s** (before exams) trac *m*. ~**-racking** *adj* éprouvant.

nervous *adj* nerveux; be *or* feel ~ (afraid) avoir peur; ~ **breakdown** dépression *f* nerveuse. **nervousness** *n* nervosité *f*; (fear) crainte *f*.

nest *n* nid *m*. ● *vi* nicher. ~**-egg** *n* pécule *m*.

nestle *vi* se blottir.

net *n* filet *m*; (Comput) net *m*, Internet *m*. ● *vt* (*pt* **netted**) prendre au filet. ● *adj* (weight) net. ~**ball** *n* netball *m*.

Netherlands *n* the ~ les Pays-Bas *mpl*.

Netsurfer *n* Internaute *mf*.

nettle *n* ortie *f*.

network *n* réseau *m*.

neurotic *a & n* névrosé/-e (*m/f*).

neuter *a & n* neutre (*m*). ● *vt* (castrate) castrer.

neutral *adj* neutre; ~ (**gear**) (Auto) point *m* mort.

never *adv* (ne) jamais; he ~ **refuses** il ne refuse jamais; I ~ **saw him** 🅣 je ne l'ai pas vu; ~ **again** plus jamais; ~ **mind** (don't worry) ne vous en faites pas; (it doesn't matter) peu importe.

nevertheless *adv* néanmoins, toutefois.

new *adj* nouveau; (brand-new) neuf. ~**-born** *adj* nouveau-né. ~**comer** *n* nouveau venu *m*, nouvelle venue *f*.

newly *adv* nouvellement. ~**-weds** *npl* jeunes mariés *mpl*.

news *n* nouvelle(s) *f(pl)*; (radio, press) informations *fpl*; (TV) actualités *fpl*, informations *fpl*. ~ **agency** *n* agence *f* de presse. ~**agent** *n* marchand/-e *m/f* de journaux. ~**caster** *n* présentateur/-trice *m/f*. ~**group** *n* (Internet) forum *m* de discussion. ~**letter** *n* bulletin *m*. ~**paper** *n* journal *m*.

new year *n* nouvel an *m*. **New Year's Day** *n* le jour de l'an. **New Year's Eve** *n* la Saint-Sylvestre.

New Zealand *n* Nouvelle-Zélande *f*.

next *adj* prochain; (adjoining) voisin; (following) suivant; ~ **to** à côté de; ~ **door** à côté (**to** de). ● *adv* la prochaine fois; (afterwards) ensuite. ● *n* suivant/-e *m/f*; (*e-mail*) message *m* suivant. ~**-door** *adj* d'à côté. ~ **of kin** *n* parent *m* le plus proche.

nib *n* plume *f*.

nibble *vt/i* grignoter.

nice *adj* agréable, bon; (kind) gentil; (pretty) joli; (respectable) bien *inv*; (subtle) délicat. **nicely** *adv* agréablement; gentiment; (well) bien.

nicety *n* subtilité *f*.

niche *n* (recess) niche *f*; (fig) place *f*, situation *f*.

nick *n* petite entaille *f*; be in good/ bad ~ être en bon/mauvais état. ● *vt* (steal, arrest 🅣) piquer.

nickel *n* (metal) nickel *m*; (US) pièce *f* de cinq cents.

nickname *n* surnom *m*. ● *vt* surnommer.

nicotine *n* nicotine *f*.

niece *n* nièce *f*.

niggling *adj* (*person*) tatillon; (*detail*) insignifiant.

night *n* nuit *f*; (evening) soir *m*. ● *adj* de nuit. ~**-cap** *n* boisson *f* (*avant d'aller se coucher*). ~**-club** *n* boîte *f* de nuit. ~**-dress** *n* chemise *f* de nuit. ~**fall** *n* tombée *f* de la nuit.

nightie *n* chemise *f* de nuit.

nightingale *n* rossignol *m*.

nightly *a & adv* (de) chaque nuit *or* soir.

night: **~mare** *n* cauchemar *m*. **~-time** *n* nuit *f*.

nil *n* (Sport) zéro *m*. ● *adj* (*chances, risk*) nul.

nimble *adj* agile.

nine *a & n* neuf (*m*).

nineteen *a & n* dix-neuf (*m*).

ninety *a & n* quatre-vingt-dix (*m*).

ninth *a & n* neuvième (*mf*).

nip *vt/i* (*pt* **nipped**) (pinch) pincer; (rush 🏃) courir; **~ out/back** sortir/ rentrer rapidement. ● *n* pincement *m*.

nipple *n* mamelon *m*; (of baby's bottle) tétine *f*.

nippy *adj* (**-ier, -iest**) (*air*) piquant; (*car*) rapide.

nitrogen *n* azote *m*.

no *det* aucun/-e; pas de; **~ man** aucun homme; **~ money/time** pas d'argent/ de temps; **~ one** = NOBODY; **~ smoking/entry** défense de fumer/ d'entrer; **~ way!** 🏃 pas question! ● *adv* non. ● *n*(*pl* **noes**) non *m inv*.

nobility *n* noblesse *f*.

noble *adj* noble. **~ man** *n* (*pl* **-men**) noble *m*.

nobody *pron* (ne) personne; **he knows ~** il ne connaît personne. ● *n* nullité *f*.

nocturnal *adj* nocturne.

nod *vt/i* (*pt* **nodded**); **~ (one's head)** faire un signe de tête; **~ off** s'endormir. ● *n* signe *m* de tête.

noise *n* bruit *m*; **make a ~** faire du bruit. **noisily** *adv*. bruyamment. **noisy** *adj* (**-ier, -iest**) bruyant.

no man's land *n* no man's land *m*.

nominal *adj* symbolique, nominal; (*value*) nominal.

nominate *vt* nommer; (put forward) proposer.

none *pron* aucun/-e; **~ of us** aucun/ -e de nous; **I have ~** je n'en ai pas.

non-existent *adj* inexistant.

nonplussed *adj* perplexe.

nonsense *n* absurdités *fpl*.

non-smoker *n* non-fumeur *m*.

non-stick *adj* antiadhésif.

non-stop *adj* (*train, flight*) direct. ● *adv* sans arrêt.

noodles *npl* nouilles *fpl*.

noon *n* midi *m*.

nor *adv* ni. ● *conj* (ne) non plus; **~ shall I come** je ne viendrai pas non plus.

norm *n* norme *f*.

normal *adj* normal.

Norman *n* Normand/-e *m/f*. ● *adj* (*village*) normand; (*arch*) roman.

north *n* nord *m*. ● *adj* nord *inv*, du nord. ● *adv* vers le nord.

North America *n* Amérique *f* du Nord.

north-east *n* nord-est *m*.

northerly *adj* (*wind, area*) du nord; (*point*) au nord.

northern *adj* (*accent*) du nord; (*coast*) nord. **northerner** *n* habitant/-e *m/f* du nord.

northward *adj* (*side*) nord *inv*; (*journey*) vers le nord.

north-west *n* nord-ouest *m*.

Norway *n* Norvège *f*.

Norwegian *n* (*person*) Norvégien/ -ne *m/f*; (*language*) norvégien *m*. ● *adj* norvégien.

nose *n* nez *m*. ● *vi* **~ about** fouiner.

nosedive *n* piqué *m*. ● *vi* descendre en piqué.

nostalgia *n* nostalgie *f*.

nostril *n* narine *f*; (of horse) naseau *m*.

nosy *adj* (**-ier, -iest**) 🏃 curieux, indiscret.

not *adv* (ne) pas; **I do ~ know** je ne sais pas; **~ at all** pas du tout; **~ yet** pas encore; **I suppose ~** je suppose que non.

notably *adv* notamment.

notch *n* entaille *f*. ● *vt* **~ up** (score) marquer.

note *n* note *f*; (banknote) billet *m*; (short letter) mot *m*. ● *vt* noter; (notice) remarquer. **~book** *n* carnet *m*.

nothing *pron* (ne) rien; **he eats ~** il ne mange rien; **~ else** rien d'autre; **~ much** pas grand-chose; **for ~** pour rien, gratis. ● *n* rien *m*; (person) nullité *f*. ● *adv* nullement.

notice *n* avis *m*, annonce *f*; (poster) affiche *f*; (**advance**) **~** préavis *m*; **at**

short ∼ dans des délais très brefs;
give in one's ∼ donner sa démission;
take ∼ faire attention (**of** à). ● *vt*
remarquer, observer. **noticeable**
adj visible. ∼-**board** *n* tableau *m*
d'affichage.

notify *vt* (inform) aviser; (make known)
notifier.

notion *n* idée *f*, notion *f*.

notorious *adj* (*criminal*) notoire;
(*district*) mal famé; (*case*) tristement
célèbre.

notwithstanding *prep* malgré.
● *adv* néanmoins.

nought *n* zéro *m*.

noun *n* nom *m*.

nourish *vt* nourrir. **nourishing** *adj*
nourrissant. **nourishment** *n*
nourriture *f*.

novel *n* roman *m*. ● *adj* nouveau.
novelist *n* romancier/-ière *m/f*.
novelty *n* nouveauté *f*.

November *n* novembre *m*.

now *adv* maintenant. ● *conj*
maintenant que; **just** ∼ maintenant;
(a moment ago) tout à l'heure; ∼ **and**
again, ∼ **and then** de temps à autre.

nowadays *adv* de nos jours.

nowhere *adv* nulle part.

nozzle *n* (tip) embout *m*; (of hose) jet
m.

nuclear *adj* nucléaire.

nude *adj* nu. ● *n* nu/-e *m/f*; **in the** ∼
tout nu.

nudge *vt* pousser du coude. ● *n* coup
m de coude.

nudism *n* nudisme *m*. **nudity** *n*
nudité *f*.

nuisance *n* (thing, event) ennui *m*;
(person) peste *f*; **be a** ∼ être
embêtant.

null *adj* nul.

numb *adj* engourdi (**with** par). ● *vt*
engourdir.

number *n* nombre *m*; (of ticket, house,
page) numéro *m*; (written figure) chiffre
m; **a** ∼ **of people** plusieurs
personnes. ● *vt* numéroter; (count,
include) compter. ∼-**plate** *n* plaque *f*
d'immatriculation.

numeral *n* chiffre *m*.

numerate *adj* qui sait compter.

numerical *adj* numérique.

numerous *adj* nombreux.

nun *n* religieuse *f*.

nurse *n* infirmier/-ière *m/f*; (nanny)
nurse *f*. ● *vt* soigner; (*hope*) nourrir.

nursery *n* (room) chambre *f*
d'enfants; (for plants) pépinière *f*; (day)
∼ crèche *f*. ∼ **rhyme** *n* comptine *f*.
∼ **school** *n* (école) maternelle *f*.

nursing home *n* maison *f* de
retraite.

nut *n* (walnut, Brazil nut) noix *f*; (hazelnut)
noisette *f*; (peanut) cacahuète *f*; (Tech)
écrou *m*. ∼**crackers** *npl* casse-noix
m inv.

nutmeg *n* muscade *f*.

nutrient *n* substance *f* nutritive.

nutritious *adj* nutritif.

nuts *adj* (crazy 🔲) cinglé.

nutshell *n* coquille *f* de noix; **in a** ∼
en un mot.

nylon *n* nylon *m*.

Oo

oak *n* chêne *m*.

OAP *abbr* (**old-age pensioner**)
retraité/-e *m/f*.

oar *n* rame *f*.

oath *n* (promise) serment *m*; (swear-
word) juron *m*.

oats *npl* avoine *f*.

obedience *n* obéissance *f*.
obedient *adj* obéissant.
obediently *adv* docilement.

obese *adj* obèse.

obey *vt/i* obéir (à).

object[1] *n* (thing) objet *m*; (aim) but *m*;
(Gram) complément *m* d'objet; **money**
is no ∼ l'argent n'est pas un
problème.

object[2] *vi* protester. ● *vt* ∼ **that**
objecter que; ∼ **to** (*behaviour*)
désapprouver; (*plan*) protester
contre. **objection** *n* objection *f*;
(drawback) inconvénient *m*.

objective *a* & *n* objectif (*m*).

obligation *n* devoir *m*.

obligatory *adj* obligatoire.

oblige *vt* obliger (**to do** à faire).

oblivion *n* oubli *m*. **oblivious** *adj* inconscient (**to, of** de).

oblong *adj* oblong. ● *n* rectangle *m*.

obnoxious *adj* odieux.

oboe *n* hautbois *m*.

obscene *adj* obscène.

obscure *adj* obscur. ● *vt* obscurcir; (conceal) cacher.

observance *n* (of law) respect *m*; (of sabbath) observance *f*. **observant** *adj* observateur.

observation *n* observation *f*.

observe *vt* observer; (remark) remarquer.

obsess *vt* obséder. **obsession** *n* obsession *f*. **obsessive** *adj* (*person*) maniaque; (*thought*) obsédant; (*illness*) obsessionnel.

obsolete *adj* dépassé.

obstacle *n* obstacle *m*.

obstinate *adj* obstiné.

obstruct *vt* (*road*) bloquer; (*view*) cacher; (*progress*) gêner. **obstruction** *n* (act) obstruction *f*; (thing) obstacle *m*; (in traffic) encombrement *m*.

obtain *vt* obtenir. ● *vi* avoir cours. **obtainable** *adj* disponible.

obvious *adj* évident. **obviously** *adv* manifestement.

occasion *n* occasion *f*; (big event) événement *m*; **on** ∼ à l'occasion.

occasional *adj* (*event*) qui a lieu de temps en temps; **the** ∼ **letter** une lettre de temps en temps. **occasionally** *adv* de temps à autre.

occupation *n* (activity) occupation *f*; (job) métier *m*, profession *f*. **occupational therapy** *n* ergothérapie *f*.

occupier *n* occupant/-e *m*/*f*.

occupy *vi* occuper.

occur *vi* (*pt* **occurred**) se produire; (arise) se présenter; ∼ **to sb** venir à l'esprit de qn.

occurrence *n* (event) fait *m*; (instance) occurrence *f*.

ocean *n* océan *m*.

Oceania *n* Océanie *f*.

o'clock *adv* **it is six** ∼ il est six heures; **at one** ∼ à une heure.

October *n* octobre *m*.

octopus *n* (*pl* ∼**es**) pieuvre *f*.

odd *adj* bizarre; (*number*) impair; (left over) qui reste; (*sock*) dépareillé; **write the** ∼ **article** écrire un article de temps en temps; ∼ **jobs** menus travaux *mpl*; **twenty** ∼ vingt et quelques. **oddity** *n* bizarrerie *f*.

odds *npl* chances *fpl*; (in betting) cote *f* (**on** de); **at** ∼ en désaccord; **it makes no** ∼ ça ne fait rien; ∼ **and ends** des petites choses.

odour, (US) **odor** *n* odeur *f*. **odourless** *adj* inodore.

---

of

⟹ For expressions such as **of course, consist of** ⟹**course, consist.**

● *preposition*

····▶ de; **a photo** ∼ **the dog** une photo du chien; **the king** ∼ **the beasts** le roi des animaux; (made) ∼ **gold** en or; **it's kind** ∼ **you** c'est très gentil de votre part; **some** ∼ **us** quelques-uns d'entre nous; ∼ **it/them** en; **have you heard** ∼ **it?** est-ce que tu en as entendu parler?

---

off *adv* **be** ∼ partir, s'en aller; **I'm** ∼ je m'en vais; **30 metres** ∼ à 30 mètres; **a month** ∼ dans un mois. ● *adj* (*gas, water*) coupé; (*tap*) fermé; (*light, TV*) éteint; (*party, match*) annulé; (bad) (*food*) avarié; (*milk*) tourné; **Friday is my day** ∼ je ne travaille pas le vendredi; **25%** ∼ 25% de remise. ● *prep* **3 metres** ∼ **the ground** 3 mètres (au-dessus) du sol; **just** ∼ **the kitchen** juste à côté de la cuisine; **that is** ∼ **the point** là n'est pas la question.

offal *n* abats *mpl*.

offence *n* (Jur) infraction *f*; **give** ∼ **to** offenser; **take** ∼ s'offenser (**at** de).

offend *vt* offenser; **be** ∼**ed** s'offenser (**at** de). ● *vi* (Jur) commettre une infraction. **offender** *n* délinquant/-e *m*/*f*.

offensive *adj* (*remark*) injurieux; (*language*) grossier; (*smell*)

offer *vt* (*weapon*) offensif. ● *n* offensive *f*.

offer *vt* (*pt* **offered**) offrir. ● *n* offre *f*; **on** ~ en promotion.

offhand *adj* désinvolte. ● *adv* à l'improviste.

office *n* bureau *m*; (*duty*) fonction *f*; **in** ~ au pouvoir. ● *adj* de bureau.

officer *n* (army) officier *m*; (**police**) ~ policier *m*; (**government**) ~ fonctionnaire *mf*.

official *adj* officiel. ● *n* (civil servant) fonctionnaire *mf*; (of party, union) officiel/-le *m*/*f*; (of police, customs) agent *m*.

off: ~**-licence** *n* magasin *m* de vins et spiritueux. ~**-line** *adj* autonome; (switched off) déconnecté. ~**-load** *vt* (*stock*) écouler; (Comput) décharger. ~**-peak** *adj* (*call*) au tarif réduit; (*travel*) en période creuse. ~**-putting** *adj* rebutant. ~**set** *vt* (*pt* **-set**; *pres p* **-setting**) compenser. ~**shore** *adj* (*waters*) du large; (*funds*) hors-lieu *inv*. ~**side** *adj* (Sport) hors jeu *inv*; (Auto) du côté du conducteur. ~**-spring** *n inv* progéniture *f*. ~**-white** *adj* blanc cassé *inv*.

often *adv* souvent; **how** ~ **do you meet?** vous vous voyez tous les combien?; **every so** ~ de temps en temps.

oil *n* (for lubrication, cooking) huile *f*; (for fuel) pétrole *m*; (for heating) mazout *m*. ● *vt* huiler. ~**field** *n* gisement *m* pétrolifère. ~**-painting** *n* peinture *f* à l'huile. ~**skins** *npl* ciré *m*. ~**-tanker** *n* pétrolier *m*.

oily *adj* graisseux.

ointment *n* pommade *f*.

OK, **okay** *adj* d'accord; **is it** ~ **if...?** ça va si...?; **feel** ~ aller bien.

old *adj* vieux; (*person*) vieux, âgé; (former) ancien; **how** ~ **is he?** quel âge a-t-il?; **he is eight years** ~ il a huit ans; ~**er**, ~**est** aîné. ~ **age** *n* vieillesse *f*. ~**-age pensioner** *n* retraité/-e *m*/*f*. ~**-fashioned** *adj* démodé; (person) vieux jeu *inv*. ~ **man** *n* vieillard *m*, vieux *m*. ~ **woman** *n* vieille *f*.

olive *n* olive *f*; ~ **oil** huile *f* d'olive. ● *adj* olive *inv*.

Olympic *adj* olympique. ~ **Games** *npl* Jeux *mpl* olympiques.

omelette *n* omelette *f*.

omen *n* augure *m*.

ominous *adj* (*presence, cloud*) menaçant; (*sign*) de mauvais augure.

omission *n* omission *f*. **omit** *vt* (*pt* **omitted**) omettre.

on *prep* sur; ~ **the table** sur la table; **put the key** ~ **it** mets la clé dessus; ~ **22 March** le 22 mars; ~ **Monday** lundi; ~ **TV** à la télé; ~ **video** en vidéo; **be** ~ **steroids** prendre des stéroïdes; ~ **arriving** en arrivant. ● *adj* (*TV, oven, light*) allumé; (*dishwasher, radio*) en marche; (*tap*) ouvert; (*lid*) mis; **the match is still** ~ le match aura lieu quand même; **the news is** ~ **in 10 minutes** les informations sont dans 10 minutes. ● *adv* **have sth** ~ porter qch; **20 years** ~ 20 ans plus tard; **from that day** ~ à partir de ce jour-là; **further** ~ plus loin; ~ **and off** (occasionally) de temps en temps; **go** ~ **and** ~ (*person*) parler pendant des heures.

once *adv* une fois; (formerly) autrefois. ● *conj* une fois que; **all at** ~ tout d'un coup.

oncoming *adj* (*vehicle*) qui approche.

one *det* & *n* un/-e (*m*/*f*). ● *pron* un/-e *m*/*f*; (impersonal) on; ~ (**and only**) seul (et unique); **a big** ~ un grand/une grande; **this/that** ~ celui-ci/-là, celle-ci/-là; ~ **another** l'un/-e l'autre. ~**-off** *adj* 🔲 unique, exceptionnel. ~**self** *pron* soi-même; (reflexive) se. ~**-way** *adj* (*street*) à sens unique; (*ticket*) simple.

ongoing *adj* (*process*) continu; **be** ~ être en cours.

onion *n* oignon *m*.

onlooker *n* spectateur/-trice *m*/*f*.

only *adj* seul; ~ **son** fils unique. ● *adv* & *conj* seulement; **he is** ~ **six** il n'a que six ans; ~ **too** extrêmement.

onset *n* début *m*.

onward(s) *adv* en avant.

open *adj* ouvert; (*view*) dégagé; (free to all) public; (undisguised) manifeste; (*question*) en attente; **in the** ~ **air** en plein air. ● *vt*/*i* (*door*) (s')ouvrir;

(*shop, play*) ouvrir; ~ **out** *or* **up** (s')
ouvrir. ~**-ended** *adj* (*stay*) de durée
indéterminée; (*debate, question*)
ouvert. ~**-heart** *adj* (*surgery*) à
cœur ouvert.

opening *n* (of book) début *m*; (of
exhibition, shop) ouverture *f*; (of film)
première *f*; (in market) débouché *m*;
(job) poste *m* (disponible).

open: ~**-minded** *adj* be ~-minded
avoir l'esprit ouvert. ~**-plan** *adj*
paysagé.

opera *n* opéra *m*.

operate *vt/i* opérer; (Tech) (faire)
fonctionner; ~ **on** (Med) opérer;
operating theatre salle *f* d'opération.

operation *n* opération *f*; **have an** ~
se faire opérer; **in** ~ (*plan*) en
vigueur; (*mine*) en service.

operative *n* employé/-e *m/f*. ● *adj*
(*law*) en vigueur.

operator *n* opérateur/-trice *m/f*;
(telephonist) standardiste *mf*.

opinion *n* opinion *f*, avis *m*.
opinionated *adj* qui a des avis sur
tout.

opponent *n* adversaire *mf*.

opportunity *n* occasion *f* (**to do** de
faire).

oppose *vt* s'opposer à; **as** ~**d** to par
opposition à. **opposing** *adj* opposé.

opposite *adj* (*direction, side*)
opposé; (*building*) d'en face. ● *n*
contraire *m*. ● *adv* en face. ● *prep* ~
(**to**) en face de.

opposition *n* opposition *f*.

oppress *vt* opprimer. **oppressive**
adj (*cruel*) oppressif; (*heat*)
oppressant.

opt *vi* ~ **for** opter pour; ~ **out**
refuser de participer (**of** à); ~ **to do**
choisir de faire.

optical *adj* optique. ~ **illusion** *n*
illusion *f* d'optique. ~ **scanner** *n*
lecteur *m* optique.

optician *n* opticien/-ne *m/f*.

optimism *n* optimisme *m*.
optimist *n* optimiste *mf*.
optimistic *adj* optimiste.

option *n* option *f*; (choice) choix *m*.

optional *adj* facultatif; ~ **extras**
accessoires *mpl* en option.

or *conj* ou; (with negative) ni.

oral *n & a* oral (*m*).

orange *n* (fruit) orange *f*; (*colour*)
orange *m*. ● *adj* (colour) orange *inv*.

orbit *n* orbite *f*. ● *vt* décrire une
orbite autour de.

orchard *n* verger *m*.

orchestra *n* orchestre *m*.

orchid *n* orchidée *f*.

ordeal *n* épreuve *f*.

order *n* ordre *m*; (Comm) commande
f; **in** ~ (tidy) en ordre; (*document*) en
règle; **in** ~ **that** pour que; **in** ~ **to**
pour. ● *vt* ordonner; (*goods*)
commander; ~ **sb to** ordonner à qn
de.

orderly *adj* (tidy) ordonné; (not unruly)
discipliné. ● *n* (Mil) planton *m*; (Med)
aide-soignant/-e *m/f*.

ordinary *adj* (usual) ordinaire;
(average) moyen.

ore *n* minerai *m*.

organ *n* organe *m*; (Mus) orgue *m*.

organic *adj* organique; (*produce*)
biologique.

organization *n* organisation *f*.

organize *vt* organiser.

organizer *n* organisateur/-trice *m/f*;
electronic ~ agenda *m* électronique.

orgasm *n* orgasme *m*.

Orient *n* **the** ~ l'Orient *m*. **oriental**
adj oriental.

origin *n* origine *f*.

original *adj* original; (*inhabitant*)
premier; (*member*) originaire.
originality *n* originalité *f*.
originally *adv* (at the outset) à
l'origine.

originate *vi* (plan) prendre
naissance; ~ **from** provenir de;
(person) venir de. ● *vt* être l'auteur
de. **originator** *n* (of idea) auteur *m*;
(of invention) créateur/-trice *m/f*.

ornament *n* (decoration) ornement *m*;
(object) objet *m* décoratif.

orphan *n* orphelin/-e *m/f*. ● *vt*
rendre orphelin. **orphanage** *n*
orphelinat *m*.

orthopaedic *adj* orthopédique.

ostentatious *adj* tape-à-l'œil *inv*.

osteopath *n* ostéopathe *mf*.

ostrich *n* autruche *f*.

other *adj* autre; **the** ~ **one** l'autre
mf. ● *n & pron* autre *mf*; (some) ~**s**

o

d'autres. ● *adv* ~ **than** (apart from) à part; (otherwise than) autrement que. **otherwise** *adv* autrement.

otter *n* loutre *f*.

ouch *interj* aïe!

ought *v aux* devoir; **you** ~ **to stay** vous devriez rester; **he** ~ **to succeed** il devrait réussir; **I** ~ **to have done it** j'aurais dû le faire.

ounce *n* once *f* (= *28.35 g*).

our *adj* notre, *pl* nos.

ours *poss* le *or* la nôtre, les nôtres.

ourselves *pron* (reflexive) nous; (emphatic) nous-mêmes; (after preposition) **for** ~ pour nous, pour nous-mêmes.

out *adv* dehors; **he's** ~ il est sorti; **further** ~ plus loin; **be** ~ (*book*) être publié; (*light*) être éteint; (*sun*) briller; (*flower*) être épanoui; (*tide*) être bas; (*player*) être éliminé; ~ **of** hors de; **go/walk/get** ~ **of** sortir de; ~ **of pity** par pitié; **made** ~ **of** fait de; **5** ~ **of 6** 5 sur 6. ~**break** *n* (of war) déclenchement *m*; (of violence, boils) éruption *f*. ~**burst** *n* explosion *f*. ~**cast** *n* paria *m*. ~**class** *vt* surclasser. ~**come** *n* résultat *m*. ~**cry** *n* tollé *m*. ~**dated** *adj* démodé. ~**door** *adj* (activity) de plein air; (*pool*) en plein air. ~**doors** *adv* dehors.

outer *adj* extérieur; ~ **space** espace *m* extra-atmosphérique.

outfit *n* (clothes) tenue *f*.

outgoing *adj* (*minister, tenant*) sortant; (sociable) ouvert. **outgoings** *npl* dépenses *fpl*.

outgrow *vt* (*pt* -**grew**; *pp* -**grown**) (*clothes*) devenir trop grand pour; (*habit*) dépasser.

outing *n* sortie *f*.

outlaw *n* hors-la-loi *m inv*. ● *vt* déclarer illégal.

outlet *n* (for water, gas) tuyau *m* de sortie; (for goods) débouché *m*; (for feelings) exutoire *m*.

outline *n* contour *m*; (of plan) grandes lignes *fpl*; (of essay) plan *m*. ● *vt* tracer le contour de; (summarize) exposer brièvement.

out: ~**live** *vt* survivre à. ~**look** *n* perspective *f*. ~**number** *vt*

surpasser en nombre. ~ **of date** *adj* démodé; (expired) périmé. ~ **of hand** *adj* incontrôlable. ~ **of order** *adj* en panne. ~ **of work** *adj* sans travail. ~**patient** *n* malade *mf* externe.

output *n* rendement *m*; (Comput) sortie *f*. ● *vt/i* (Comput) sortir.

outrage *n* (anger) indignation *f*; (atrocity) attentat *m*; (scandal) outrage *m*. ● *vt* (morals) outrager; (person) scandaliser. **outrageous** *adj* scandaleux.

outright *adv* (completely) catégoriquement; (killed) sur le coup. ● *adj* (majority) absolu; (ban) catégorique; (hostility) pur et simple.

outset *n* début *m*.

outside *n* extérieur *m*. ● *adv* dehors. ● *prep* en dehors de; (in front of) devant. ● *adj* extérieur. **outsider** *n* étranger/-ère *m/f*; (Sport) outsider *m*.

out: ~**skirts** *npl* périphérie *f*. ~**spoken** *adj* franc. ~**standing** *adj* exceptionnel; (not settled) en suspens.

outward *a & adv* vers l'extérieur; (sign) extérieur; (journey) d'aller. **outwards** *adv* vers l'extérieur.

oval *n & a* ovale (*m*).

ovary *n* ovaire *m*.

oven *n* four *m*.

over *prep* (across) par-dessus; (above) au-dessus de; (covering) sur; (more than) plus de; **it's** ~ **the road** c'est de l'autre côté de la rue; ~ **here/there** par ici/là; **children** ~ **six** les enfants de plus de six ans; ~ **the weekend** pendant le week-end; **all** ~ **the house** partout dans la maison. ● *a, adv* (term) terminé; (war) fini; **get sth** ~ **with** en finir avec qch; **ask sb** ~ inviter qn; ~ **and** ~ (again) à plusieurs reprises; **five times** ~ cinq fois de suite.

overall *adj* global, d'ensemble; (length) total. ● *adv* globalement.

overalls *npl* combinaison *f*.

over: ~**board** *adv* par-dessus bord. ~**cast** *adj* couvert. ~**charge** *vt* faire payer trop cher à. ~**coat** *n* pardessus *m*.

overcome *vt* (*pt* **-came**; *pp* **-come**) (*enemy*) vaincre; (*difficulty, fear*) surmonter; ~ **by** accablé de.

overcrowded *adj* bondé; (*country*) surpeuplé.

overdo *vt* (*pt* **-did**; *pp* **-done**) (Culin) trop cuire; ~ **it** (overwork) en faire trop.

over: ~**dose** *n* surdose *f*, overdose *f*. ~**draft** *n* découvert *m*. ~**draw** *vt* (*pt* **-drew**; *pp* **-drawn**) faire un découvert sur. ~**due** *adj* en retard; (*bill*) impayé.

overflow[1] *vi* déborder.

overflow[2] *n* (outlet) trop-plein *m*.

overhaul *vt* réviser.

overhead[1] *adv* au-dessus; (in sky) dans le ciel.

overhead[2] *adj* aérien; ~ **projector** rétroprojecteur *m*. **overheads** *npl* frais *mpl* généraux.

over: ~**hear** *vt* (*pt* **-heard**) entendre par hasard. ~**lap** *vt/i* (*pt* **-lapped**) (se) chevaucher. ~**leaf** *adv* au verso. ~**load** *vt* surcharger. ~**look** *vt* (*window*) donner sur; (miss) ne pas voir.

overnight[1] *adv* dans la nuit; (instantly: fig) du jour au lendemain.

overnight[2] *adj* (*train*) de nuit; (*stay*) d'une nuit; (fig) soudain.

over: ~**power** *vt* (*thief*) maîtriser; (*army*) vaincre; (fig) accabler. ~**priced** *adj* trop cher. ~**rate** *vt* surestimer. ~**react** *vi* réagir de façon excessive. ~**riding** *adj* (*consideration*) numéro un; (*importance*) primordial. ~**rule** *vt* (*decision*) annuler.

overrun *vt* (*pt* **-ran**; *pp* **-run**; *pres p* **-running**) (*country*) envahir; (*budget*) dépasser. ● *vi* (meeting) durer plus longtemps que prévu.

overseas *adj* étranger. ● *adv* outre-mer, à l'étranger.

over: ~**see** *vt* (*pt* **-saw**; *pp* **-seen**) surveiller. ~**sight** *n* omission *f*. ~**sleep** *vi* (*pt* **-slept**) se réveiller trop tard. ~**take** *vt/i* (*pt* **-took**; *pp* **-taken**) dépasser; (fig) frapper. ~**time** *n* heures *fpl* supplémentaires. ~**turn** *vt/i* (se) renverser. ~**weight** *adj* trop gros.

overwhelm *vt* (*enemy*) écraser; (*shame*) accabler. **overwhelmed** *adj* (with offers, calls) submergé (**with, by** de); (with shame, work) accablé; (by sight) ébloui. **overwhelming** *adj* (*heat, grief*) accablant; (*defeat, victory*) écrasant; (*urge*) irrésistible.

overwork *vt/i* (se) surmener. ● *n* surmenage *m*.

owe *vt* devoir. **owing** *adj* dû; **owing to** en raison de.

owl *n* hibou *m*.

own *adj* propre. ● *pron* **my** ~ le mien, la mienne; **a house of one's** ~ sa propre maison; **on one's** ~ tout seul. ● *vt* posséder; ~ **up (to)** Ⓘ avouer. **owner** *n* propriétaire *mf*. **ownership** *n* propriété *f*; (of land) possession *f*.

oxygen *n* oxygène *m*.

oyster *n* huître *f*.

ozone *n* ozone *m*; ~ **layer** couche *f* d'ozone.

Pp

PA *abbr* ⇒PERSONAL ASSISTANT.

pace *n* pas *m*; (speed) allure *f*; **keep** ~ **with** suivre. ● *vt* (*room*) arpenter. ● *vi* ~ **(up and down)** faire les cent pas.

Pacific *n* ~ **(Ocean)** océan *m* Pacifique.

pack *n* paquet *m*; (Mil) sac *m*; (of hounds) meute *f*; (of thieves) bande *f*; (of lies) tissu *m*. ● *vt* (into case) mettre dans une valise; (into box, crate) emballer; (for sale) conditionner; (*crowd*) remplir complètement; ~ **one's suitcase** faire sa valise. ● *vi* faire ses valises; ~ **into** (cram) s'entasser dans; ~ **off** expédier; **send** ~**ing** envoyer promener.

package *n* paquet *m*; (Comput) progiciel *m*; ~ **deal** offre *f* globale; ~ **holiday** voyage *m* organisé. ● *vt* empaqueter.

packed *adj* (crowded) bondé; ~ **lunch** repas *m* froid.

packet *n* paquet *m*.

packing *n* (action, material) emballage *m*.

pad *n* (of paper) bloc *m*; (to protect) protection *f*; (for ink) tampon *m*; (**launch**) ~ rampe *f* de lancement. ● *vt* (*pt* **padded**) rembourrer; (text: fig) délayer. ● *vi* (*pt* **padded**) (walk) marcher à pas feutrés. **padding** *n* rembourrage *m*.

paddle *n* pagaie *f*. ● *vt* ~ **a canoe** pagayer. ● *vi* patauger.

padlock *n* cadenas *m*. ● *vt* cadenasser.

paediatrician *n* pédiatre *mf*.

pagan *a & n* païen/-ne (*m/f*).

page *n* (of book) page *f*. ● *vt* (on pager) rechercher; (over speaker) faire appeler. **pager** *n* radiomessageur *m*.

pain *n* douleur *f*; ~**s** efforts *mpl*; **be in** ~ souffrir; **take** ~**s to** se donner du mal pour. ● *vt* (grieve) peiner. **painful** *adj* douloureux; (laborious) pénible. ~**-killer** *n* analgésique *m*. **painless** *adj* (operation) indolore; (death) sans souffrance; (trouble-free) sans peine. **painstaking** *adj* minutieux.

paint *n* peinture *f*; ~**s** (in tube, box) couleurs *fpl*. ● *vt/i* peindre. ~**brush** *n* pinceau *m*. **painter** *n* peintre *m*. **painting** *n* peinture *f*. ~**work** *n* peintures *fpl*.

pair *n* paire *f*; (of people) couple *m*; **a** ~ **of trousers** un pantalon. ● *vi* ~ **off** former un couple.

pajamas *npl* (US) = PYJAMAS.

Pakistan *n* Pakistan *m*.

palace *n* palais *m*.

palatable *adj* (food) savoureux; (solution) acceptable. **palate** *n* palais *m*.

pale *adj* pâle. ● *vi* pâlir.

Palestine *n* Palestine *f*.

pallid *adj* pâle.

palm *n* (of hand) paume *f*; (tree) palmier *m*; (symbol) palme *f*. □ ~ **off** ⚠ ~ **sth off as** faire passer qch pour; ~ **sth off on sb** refiler qch à qn ⚠.

palpitate *vi* palpiter.

paltry *adj* (**-ier, -iest**) dérisoire, piètre.

pamper *vt* choyer.

pamphlet *n* brochure *f*.

pan *n* casserole *f*; (for frying) poêle *f*.

pancake *n* crêpe *f*.

pandemonium *n* tohu-bohu *m*.

pander *vi* ~ **to** (person, taste) flatter bassement.

pane *n* carreau *m*, vitre *f*.

panel *n* (of door) panneau *m*; (of experts, judges) commission *f*; (on discussion programme) invités *mpl*; (instrument) ~ tableau *m* de bord.

pang *n* serrement *m* au cœur; ~**s of conscience** remords *mpl*.

panic *n* panique *f*. ● *vt/i* (*pt* **panicked**) (s')affoler. ~**-stricken** *adj* pris de panique, affolé.

pansy *n* (Bot) pensée *f*.

pant *vi* haleter.

panther *n* panthère *f*.

pantomime *n* (show) spectacle *m* de Noël; (mime) mime *m*.

pantry *n* garde-manger *m inv*.

pants *npl* (underwear) slip *m*; (trousers: US) pantalon *m*.

paper *n* papier *m*; (newspaper) journal *m*; (exam) épreuve *f*; (essay) exposé *m*; (wallpaper) papier *m* peint; (identity) ~**s** papiers *mpl* (d'identité); **on** ~ par écrit. ● *vt* (room) tapisser. ~**back** *n* livre *m* de poche. ~**clip** *n* trombone *m*. ~ **feed tray** *n* (Comput) bac *m* d'alimentation en papier. ~**work** *n* (work) travail *m* administratif; (documentation) documents *mpl*.

par *n* **be below** ~ ne pas être en forme; **on a** ~ **with** (performance) comparable à; (person) l'égal de; (golf) par *m*.

parachute *n* parachute *m*. ● *vi* descendre en parachute.

parade *n* (procession) parade *f*; (Mil) défilé *m*. ● *vi* défiler. ● *vt* faire étalage de.

paradise *n* paradis *m*.

paradox *n* paradoxe *m*.

paraffin *n* pétrole *m* (lampant); (wax) paraffine *f*.

paragliding *n* parapente *m*.

paragon *n* modèle *m*.

paragraph *n* paragraphe *m*.

parallel *adj* parallèle. ● *n* parallèle *m*; (maths) parallèle *f*.

paralyse *vt* paralyser. **paralysis** *n* paralysie *f*.

paramedic *n* auxiliaire *mf* médical/-e.

paramount *adj* suprême.

paranoia *n* paranoïa *f*. **paranoid** *adj* paranoïaque; (Psych) paranoïde.

paraphernalia *n* attirail *m*.

parasol *n* ombrelle *f*; (on table, at beach) parasol *m*.

paratrooper *n* (Mil) parachutiste *mf*.

parcel *n* paquet *m*.

parchment *n* parchemin *m*.

pardon *n* pardon *m*; (Jur) grâce *f*; I beg your ∼ je vous demande pardon. ● *vt* (*pt* **pardoned**) pardonner (**sb for sth** qch à qn); (Jur) gracier.

parent *n* parent *m*.

parenthesis *n* (*pl* **-theses**) parenthèse *f*.

parenthood *n* (fatherhood) paternité *f*; (motherhood) maternité *f*.

Paris *n* Paris.

parish *n* (Relig) paroisse *f*; (municipal) commune *f*.

park *n* parc *m*. ● *vt/i* (se) garer; (remain parked) stationner. ∼ **and ride** *n* parc *m* relais.

parking *n* stationnement *m*; no ∼ stationnement interdit. ∼**-lot** *n* (US) parking *m*. ∼**-meter** *n* parcmètre *m*. ∼ **ticket** *n* (fine) contravention *f*, PV *m* 🄸.

parliament *n* parlement *m*. **parliamentary** *adj* parlementaire.

parlour, (US) **parlor** *n* salon *m*.

parody *n* parodie *f*. ● *vt* parodier.

parole *n* on ∼ en liberté conditionnelle.

parrot *n* perroquet *m*.

parry *vt* (Sport) parer; (*question*) éluder. ● *n* parade *f*.

parsley *n* persil *m*.

parsnip *n* panais *m*.

part *n* partie *f*; (of serial) épisode *m*; (of machine) pièce *f*; (Theat) rôle *m*; (side in dispute) parti *m*; in ∼ en partie; on the ∼ of de la part de; take ∼ in participer à. ● *adj* partiel. ● *adv* en

partie. ● *vt/i* (separate) (se) séparer; ∼ **with** se séparer de.

part-exchange *n* reprise *f*; take sth in ∼ reprendre qch.

partial *adj* partiel; (biased) partial; be ∼ **to** avoir un faible pour.

participant *n* participant/-e *m/f*.

participate *vi* participer (**in** à).

participation *n* participation *f*.

participle *n* participe *m*.

particular *n* détail *m*; ∼**s** détails *mpl*; in ∼ en particulier. ● *adj* particulier; (fussy) difficile; (careful) méticuleux; that ∼ man cet homme-là. **particularly** *adv* particulièrement.

parting *n* séparation *f*; (in hair) raie *f*. ● *adj* d'adieu.

partition *n* (of room) cloison *f*; (Pol) partition *f*. ● *vt* (*room*) cloisonner; (*country*) partager.

partly *adv* en partie.

partner *n* (professional) associé/-e *m/f*; (economic, sporting) partenaire *mf*; (spouse) époux/-se *m/f*; (unmarried) partenaire *mf*. **partnership** *n* association *f*.

partridge *n* perdrix *f*.

part-time *a* & *adv* à temps partiel.

party *n* fête *f*; (formal) réception *f*; (group) groupe *m*; (Pol) parti *m*; (Jur) partie *f*.

pass *vt/i* (*pt* **passed**) passer; (overtake) dépasser; (in exam) réussir; (approve) (*candidate*) admettre; (*invoice*) approuver; (*remark*) faire; (*judgement*) prononcer; (*law, bill*) adopter; ∼ (**by**) (*building*) passer devant; (*person*) croiser. ● *n* (permit) laisser-passer *m inv*; (ticket) carte *f* d'abonnement; (Geog) col *m*; (Sport) passe *f*; ∼ (**mark**) (in exam) moyenne *f*. □ ∼ **away** mourir; ∼ **out** (faint) s'évanouir; ∼ **sth out** distribuer qch; ∼ **over** (overlook) délaisser; ∼ **up** (forego) laisser passer.

passage *n* (way through, text) passage *m*; (voyage) traversée *f*; (corridor) couloir *m*.

passenger *n* (in car, plane, ship) passager/-ère *m/f*; (in train, bus, tube) voyageur/-euse *m/f*.

passer-by *n* (*pl* **passers-by**) passant/-e *m/f*.

p

passing adj (motorist) qui passe; (whim) passager; (reference) en passant.

passion n passion f. **passionate** adj passionné.

passive adj passif.

passport n passeport m.

password n mot m de passe.

past adj (times, problems) passé; (president) ancien; **the ~ months** ces derniers mois. ● n passé m. ● prep (beyond) après; **walk/go ~ sth** passer devant qch; **10 ~ 6** six heures dix; **it's ~ 11** il est 11 heures passées. ● adv **go/walk ~** passer.

pasta n pâtes fpl (alimentaires).

paste n (glue) colle f; (dough) pâte f; (of fish, meat) pâté m; (jewellery) strass m. ● vt coller.

pasteurize vt pasteuriser.

pastime n passe-temps m inv.

pastry n (dough) pâte f; (tart) pâtisserie f.

pat vt (pt **patted**) tapoter. ● n petite tape f.

patch n pièce f; (over eye) bandeau m; (spot) tache f; (of snow, ice) plaque f; (of vegetables) carré m; **bad ~** période f difficile. ☐ **~ up** (trousers) rapiécer; (quarrel) résoudre.

patent adj (obvious) manifeste; (patented) breveté; **~ leather** cuir m verni. ● n brevet m. ● vt faire breveter.

path n (pl **-s**) sentier m, chemin m; (in park) allée f; (of rocket) trajectoire f.

pathetic adj misérable; (bad 🆄) lamentable.

patience n patience f.

patient adj patient. ● n patient/-e m/f. **patiently** adv patiemment.

patriotic adj patriotique; (person) patriote.

patrol n patrouille f; **~ car** voiture f de police. ● vt/i patrouiller (dans).

patron n (of the arts) mécène m; (customer) client/-e m/f. **patronage** n clientèle f; (support) patronage m. **patronize** vt (person) traiter avec condescendance; (establishment) fréquenter.

patter n (of steps) bruit m; (of rain) crépitement m.

pattern n motif m, dessin m; (for sewing) patron m; (for knitting) modèle m.

paunch n ventre m.

pause n pause f. ● vi faire une pause; (hesitate) hésiter.

pave vt paver; **~ the way** ouvrir la voie (**for** à).

pavement n trottoir m; (US) chaussée f.

paving stone n pavé m.

paw n patte f. ● vt (animal) donner des coups de patte à; (touch 🆄) peloter 🆄.

pawn n pion m. ● vt mettre en gage. **~broker** n prêteur/-euse m/f sur gages. **~-shop** n mont-de-piété m.

pay vt (pt **paid**) payer; (interest) rapporter; (compliment, attention) faire; (visit, homage) rendre. ● vi payer; (business) rapporter; **~ for sth** payer qch. ● n salaire m; **~ rise ~** augmentation f (de salaire). ☐ **~ back** rembourser; **~ in** déposer; **~ off** (loan) rembourser; (worker) congédier; (succeed) être payant; **~ out** payer, débourser.

payable adj payable; **~ to** (cheque) à l'ordre de.

payment n paiement m; (regular) versement m; (reward) récompense f.

payroll n fichier m des salaires; **be on the ~ of** être employé par.

PC abbr ⇒PERSONAL COMPUTER.

PE abbr (**physical education**) éducation f physique, EPS f.

pea n (petit) pois m.

peace n paix f; **~ of mind** tranquillité f d'esprit. **peaceful** adj (tranquil) paisible; (peaceable) pacifique.

peach n pêche f.

peacock n paon m.

peak n (of mountain) pic m; (of cap) visière f; (maximum) maximum m; (on graph) sommet m; (of career) apogée m; (of fitness) meilleur m; **~ hours** heures fpl de pointe.

peal n (of bells) carillon m; (of laughter) éclat m.

peanut n cacahuète f; **~s** (money ✖) clopinettes fpl 🆄.

pear n poire f.

pearl n perle f.

peasant n paysan/-ne m/f.

peat n tourbe f.

pebble n caillou m; (on beach) galet m.

peck vt/i (food) picorer; (attack) donner des coups de bec (à). ● n coup m de bec; **a ~ on the cheek** une bise.

peckish adj be ~ 🄵 avoir faim.

peculiar adj (odd) bizarre; (special) particulier (to à). **peculiarity** n bizarrerie f.

pedal n pédale f. ● vi pédaler.

pedantic adj pédant.

peddle vt colporter; (drugs) faire du trafic de.

pedestrian n piéton m. ● adj (precinct, street) piétonnier; (fig) prosaïque; ~ **crossing** passage m pour piétons.

pedigree n (of animal) pedigree m; (of person) ascendance f. ● adj (dog) de pure race.

pee vi 🄵 faire pipi 🄵.

peek vi & n = PEEP.

peel n (on fruit) peau m; (removed) épluchures fpl. ● vt (fruit, vegetables) éplucher; (prawn) décortiquer. ● vi (of skin) peler; (of paint) s'écailler.

peep vi jeter un coup d'œil (furtif) (at à). ● n coup m d'œil (furtif). ~**hole** n judas m.

peer vi ~ (at) regarder fixement. ● n (equal, noble) pair m; (contemporary) personne f de la même génération. **peerage** n pairie f.

peg n (for clothes) pince f à linge; (to hang coats) patère f; (for tent) piquet m. ● vt (pt **pegged**) (clothes) accrocher avec des pinces; (prices) indexer.

pejorative adj péjoratif.

pelican n pélican m; ~ **crossing** passage m pour piétons.

pellet n (round mass) boulette f; (for gun) plomb m.

pelt vt bombarder (with de). ● n (skin) peau f.

pelvis n (Anat) bassin m.

pen n stylo m; (for sheep) enclos m; (for baby, cattle) parc m.

penal adj pénal. **penalize** vt pénaliser.

penalty n peine f; (fine) amende f; (in football) penalty m.

penance n pénitence f.

pence ⇒PENNY.

pencil n crayon m. ● vt (pt **pencilled**) crayonner; ~ **in** noter provisoirement. ~**-sharpener** n taille-crayons m inv.

pending adj (matter) en souffrance; (Jur) en instance. ● prep (until) en attendant.

penetrate vt pénétrer; (silence, defences) percer; (organization) infiltrer. ● vi pénétrer. **penetrating** adj pénétrant.

pen-friend n correspondant/-e m/f.

penguin n manchot m, pingouin m.

pen: ~**knife** n (pl -**knives**) canif m. ~**-name** n pseudonyme m.

penniless adj sans le sou.

penny n (pl **pennies** or **pence**) (unit of currency) penny m; (small amount) centime m.

pension n (from state) pension f; (from employer) retraite f; ~ **scheme** plan m de retraite. ● vt ~ **off** mettre à la retraite. **pensioner** n retraité/-e m/f.

pensive adj songeur.

penthouse n appartement m de luxe (au dernier étage).

penultimate adj avant-dernier.

people npl gens mpl, personnes fpl; English ~ les Anglais mpl; ~ **say** on dit. ● n peuple m. ● vt peupler. ~ **carrier** n monospace m.

pepper n poivre m; (vegetable) poivron m. ● vt (Culin) poivrer.

peppermint n (plant) menthe f poivrée; (sweet) bonbon m à la menthe.

per prep par; ~ **annum** par an; ~ **cent** pour cent; ~ **kilo** le kilo; **ten km** ~ **hour** dix km à l'heure.

percentage n pourcentage m.

perception n perception f. **perceptive** adj perspicace.

perch n (of bird) perchoir m. ● vi (se) percher.

perennial adj perpétuel; (plant) vivace.

perfect[1] vt perfectionner.

perfect² *adj* parfait. ● *n* (Ling) parfait *m*. **perfectly** *adv* parfaitement.

perfection *n* perfection *f*; **to ~** à la perfection.

perforate *vt* perforer.

perform *vt* (*task*) exécuter; (*function*) remplir; (*operation*) procéder à; (*play*) jouer; (*song*) chanter. ● *vi* (*actor, musician, team*) jouer; **~ well/badly** (*candidate, business*) avoir de bons/de mauvais résultats. **performance** *n* interprétation *f*; (of car, team) performance *f*; (show) représentation *f*; (fuss) histoire *f*. **performer** *n* artiste *mf*.

perfume *n* parfum *m*.

perhaps *adv* peut-être.

peril *n* péril *m*. **perilous** *adj* périlleux.

perimeter *n* périmètre *m*.

period *n* période *f*; (era) époque *f*; (lesson) cours *m*; (Gram) point *m*; (Med) règles *fpl*. ● *adj* d'époque. **periodical** *n* périodique *m*.

peripheral *adj* (*vision, suburb*) périphérique; (*issue*) annexe. ● *n* (Comput) périphérique *m*.

perish *vi* périr; (*rubber*) se détériorer.

perjury *n* faux témoignage *m*.

perk *n* Ⓣ avantage *m*. ● *vt/i* **~ up** Ⓣ (se) remonter. **perky** *adj* Ⓣ gai.

perm *n* permanente *f*. ● *vt* **have one's hair ~ed** se faire faire une permanente.

permanent *adj* permanent. **permanently** *adv* (*happy*) en permanence; (*employed*) de façon permanente.

permissible *adj* permis.

permission *n* permission *f*.

permissive *adj* libéral; (pej) permissif.

permit¹ *vt* (*pt* **permitted**) permettre (**sb** to à qn de), autoriser (**sb** to qn à).

permit² *n* permis *m*.

perpendicular *adj* perpendiculaire.

perpetrator *n* auteur *m*.

perpetuate *vt* perpétuer.

perplexed *adj* perplexe.

persecute *vt* persécuter.

perseverance *n* persévérance *f*. **persevere** *vi* persévérer.

persist *vi* persister (**in doing** à faire). **persistence** *n* persistance *f*. **persistent** *adj* (*cough, snow*) persistant; (*obstinate*) obstiné; (*noise, pressure*) continuel.

person *n* personne *f*; **in ~** en personne.

personal *adj* (*life, problem, opinion*) personnel; (*safety, freedom, insurance*) individuel. **~ ad** *n* petite annonce *f*. **~ assistant** *n* secrétaire *mf* de direction. **~ computer** *n* ordinateur *m* (personnel), micro-ordinateur *m*.

personality *n* personnalité *f*; (star) vedette *f*.

personal: **~ organizer** *n* agenda *m*. **~ stereo** *n* baladeur *m*.

personnel *n* personnel *m*.

perspiration *n* (sweat) sueur *f*; (sweating) transpiration *f*. **perspire** *vi* transpirer.

persuade *vt* persuader (**to** de). **persuasion** *n* persuasion *f*. **persuasive** *adj* persuasif.

pertinent *adj* pertinent.

perturb *vt* troubler.

Peru *n* Pérou *m*.

pervasive *adj* (*smell*) pénétrant; (*feeling*) envahissant.

perverse *adj* (*desire*) pervers; (*refusal, attitude*) illogique. **perversion** *n* perversion *f*.

pervert¹ *vt* (*truth*) travestir; (*values*) fausser; (*justice*) entraver.

pervert² *n* pervers/-e *m/f*.

pessimist *n* pessimiste *mf*. **pessimistic** *adj* pessimiste.

pest *n* (insect) insecte *m* nuisible; (animal) animal *m* nuisible; (person Ⓣ) enquiquineur/-euse *m/f* Ⓣ.

pester *vt* harceler.

pet *n* animal *m* de compagnie; (favourite) chouchou/-te *m/f*. ● *adj* (*theory, charity*) favori; **~ hate** bête *f* noire; **~ name** petit nom *m*. ● *vt* (*pt* **petted**) caresser; (spoil) chouchouter Ⓣ.

petal *n* pétale *m*.

peter *vi* ~ out (*conversation*) tarir; (*supplies*) s'épuiser.

petite *adj* (*woman*) menue.

petition *n* pétition *f*. ● *vt* adresser une pétition à.

petrol *n* essence *f*. ~ **bomb** *n* cocktail *m* molotov. ~ **station** *n* station-service *f*. ~ **tank** *n* réservoir *m* d'essence.

petticoat *n* jupon *m*.

petty *adj* (**-ier, -iest**) (minor) petit; (mean) mesquin; ~ **cash** petite caisse *f*.

pew *n* banc *m* (d'église).

pharmacist *n* pharmacien/-ne *m/f*. **pharmacy** *n* pharmacie *f*.

phase *n* phase *f*. ● *vt* ~ in/out introduire/supprimer peu à peu.

PhD *abbr* (**Doctor of Philosophy**) doctorat *m*.

pheasant *n* faisan/-e *m/f*.

phenomenon *n* (*pl* **-ena**) phénomène *m*.

phew *interj* ouf.

philosopher *n* philosophe *mf*. **philosophical** *adj* philosophique; (resigned) philosophe. **philosophy** *n* philosophie *f*.

phlegm *n* (Med) mucosité *f*.

phobia *n* phobie *f*.

phone *n* téléphone *m*; **on the** ~ au téléphone. ● *vt* (person) téléphoner à; ~ **England** téléphoner en Angleterre. ● *vi* téléphoner; ~ **back** rappeler. ~ **book** *n* annuaire *m*. ~ **booth**, ~ **box** *n* cabine *f* téléphonique. ~ **call** *n* coup *m* de fil 🔢. ~**card** *n* télécarte *f*. ~**in** *n* émission *f* à ligne ouverte. ~ **number** *n* numéro *m* de téléphone.

phonetic *adj* phonétique.

phoney *adj* (**-ier, -iest**) 🔢 faux. ● *n* 🔢 (person) charlatan *m*; **it's a** ~ c'est un faux.

photocopier *n* photocopieuse *f*.

photocopy *n* photocopie *f*. ● *vt* photocopier.

photograph *n* photographie *f*. ● *vt* photographier. **photographer** *n* photographe *mf*.

phrase *n* expression *f*; (idiom) locution *f*. ● *vt* exprimer, formuler. ~-**book** *n* guide *m* de conversation.

physical *adj* physique.

physicist *n* physicien/-ne *m/f*.

physics *n* physique *f*.

physiotherapist *n* kinésithérapeute *mf*. **physiotherapy** *n* kinésithérapie *f*.

physique *n* physique *m*.

piano *n* piano *m*.

pick *n* choix *m*; (best) meilleur/-e *m/f*; (tool) pioche *f*. ● *vt* choisir; (*flower*) cueillir; (*lock*) crocheter; ~ **a quarrel with** chercher querelle à; ~ **one's nose** se curer le nez. □ ~ **on** harceler; ~ **out** choisir; (identify) distinguer; ~ **up** *vt* ramasser; (*sth fallen*) relever; (*weight*) soulever; (*habit, passenger, speed*) prendre; (learn) apprendre; *vi* s'améliorer.

pickaxe *n* pioche *f*.

picket *n* (striker) gréviste *mf*; (stake) piquet *m*; ~ (**line**) piquet *m* de grève. ● *vt* (*pt* **picketed**) installer un piquet de grève devant.

pickle *n* conserves *fpl* au vinaigre; (gherkin) cornichon *m*. ● *vt* conserver dans du vinaigre.

pick-up *n* (stylus-holder) lecteur *m*; (on guitar) capteur *m*; (collection) ramassage *m*; (improvement) reprise *f*.

picnic *n* pique-nique *m*. ● *vi* (*pt* **picnicked**) pique-niquer.

pictorial *adj* (*magazine*) illustré; (*record*) graphique.

picture *n* image *f*; (painting) tableau *m*; (photograph) photo *f*; (drawing) dessin *m*; (film) film *m*; (fig) description *f*; **the** ~**s** le cinéma. ● *vt* s'imaginer; **be** ~**d** (shown) être représenté.

picturesque *adj* pittoresque.

pie *n* (sweet) tarte *f*; (savoury) tourte *f*.

piece *n* morceau *m*; (of string, ribbon) bout *m*; (of currency, machine) pièce *f*; **a** ~ **of advice/furniture** un conseil/ meuble; **go to** ~**s** (fig) s'effondrer; **take to** ~**s** démonter.

pier *n* jetée *f*.

pierce *vt* percer.

pig *n* porc *m*, cochon *m*.

pigeon *n* pigeon *m*. ~-**hole** *n* casier *m*.

pig-headed *adj* entêté.

pigsty *n* porcherie *f*.

p

pigtail *n* natte *f*.

pike *n inv* (fish) brochet *m*.

pile *n* (heap) tas *m*; (stack) pile *f*; (of carpet) poil *m*; **~s of** ⏦ un tas de ⏦. ● *vt* **~** (**up**) entasser. ● *vi* **~** **into** s'engouffrer dans; **~ up** (*snow, leaves*) s'entasser; (*debts, work*) s'accumuler. **~-up** *n* (Auto) carambolage *m*.

pilgrim *n* pèlerin *m*. **pilgrimage** *n* pèlerinage *m*.

pill *n* pilule *f*.

pillar *n* pilier *m*. **~-box** *n* boîte *f* aux lettres.

pillion *n* siège *m* de passager; **ride ~** monter en croupe.

pillow *n* oreiller *m*. **~case** *n* taie *f* d'oreiller.

pilot *n* pilote *m*. ● *adj* pilote. ● *vt* (*pt* **piloted**) piloter. **~-light** *n* veilleuse *f*.

pimple *n* bouton *m*.

pin *n* épingle *f*; (of plug) fiche *f*; (for wood, metal) goujon *m*; (in surgery) broche *f*; **have ~s and needles** avoir des fourmis. ● *vt* (*pt* **pinned**) épingler, attacher; (trap) coincer; **~ sb down** (fig) forcer qn à se décider; **~ up** accrocher.

pinafore *n* tablier *m*.

pincers *npl* tenailles *fpl*.

pinch *vt* pincer; (steal ⏦) piquer. ● *vi* (be too tight) serrer. ● *n* (mark) pinçon *m*; (of salt) pincée *f*; **at a ~** à la rigueur.

pine *n* (tree) pin *m*. ● *vi* **~** (**away**) dépérir; **~ for** languir après.

pineapple *n* ananas *m*.

pinecone *n* pomme *f* de pin.

pink *a* & *n* rose (*m*).

pinpoint *vt* (*problem, cause, location*) indiquer; (*time*) déterminer.

pint *n* pinte *f* (GB = *0.57 litre*; US = *0.47 litre*).

pin-up *n* ⏦ pin-up *f inv* ⏦.

pioneer *n* pionnier *m*. ● *vt* **~ the use of** être le premier à utiliser.

pious *adj* pieux.

pip *n* (seed) pépin *m*; (sound) top *m*.

pipe *n* tuyau *m*; (to smoke) pipe *f*; (Mus) chalumeau *m*; **~s** cornemuse *f*. ● *vt* transporter par tuyau. □ **~ down** se taire.

pipeline *n* oléoduc *m*; **in the ~** en cours.

piping *n* tuyauterie *f*; **~ hot** fumant.

pique *n* dépit *m*.

pirate *n* pirate *m*. ● *vt* pirater.

Pisces *n* Poissons *mpl*.

pistol *n* pistolet *m*.

pit *n* fosse *f*; (mine) puits *m*; (quarry) carrière *f*; (for orchestra) fosse *f*; (of stomach) creux *m*; (of cherry: US) noyau *m*. ● *vt* (*pt* **pitted**) marquer; (fig) opposer; **~ oneself against** se mesurer à.

pitch *n* (Sport) terrain *m*; (of voice, note) hauteur *f*; (degree) degré *m*; (Mus) ton *m*; (tar) brai *m*. ● *vt* jeter; (*tent*) planter. ● *vi* (ship) tanguer. □ **~ in** ⏦ contribuer.

pitfall *n* écueil *m*.

pitiful *adj* pitoyable. **pitiless** *adj* impitoyable.

pittance *n* **earn a ~** gagner trois fois rien.

pity *n* pitié *f*; (regrettable fact) dommage *m*; **take ~ on** avoir pitié de; **what a ~!** quel dommage! ● *vt* avoir pitié de.

pivot *n* pivot *m*. ● *vi* (*pt* **pivoted**) pivoter.

placard *n* affiche *f*.

place *n* endroit *m*, lieu *m*; (house) maison *f*; (seat, rank) place *f*; **at** *or* **to my ~** chez moi; **change ~s** changer de place; **in the first ~** d'abord; **out of ~** déplacé; **take ~** avoir lieu. ● *vt* placer; (*order*) passer; (remember) situer; **be ~d** (in race) se placer. **~-mat** *n* set *m*.

placid *adj* placide.

plagiarism *n* plagiat *m*. **plagiarize** *vt/i* plagier.

plague *n* (bubonic) peste *f*; (epidemic) épidémie *f*; (of ants, locusts) invasion *f*. ● *vt* harceler.

plaice *n inv* carrelet *m*.

plain *adj* (obvious) clair; (candid) franc; (simple) simple; (not pretty) sans beauté; (not patterned) uni; **~ chocolate** chocolat *m* noir; **in ~ clothes** en civil. ● *adv* franchement. ● *n* plaine *f*. **plainly** *adv* clairement; franchement; simplement.

plaintiff *n* plaignant/-e *m/f*.

plaintive *adj* plaintif.

plait *vt* tresser. ● *n* natte *f*.

plan *n* projet *m*, plan *m*; (diagram) plan *m*. ● *vt* (*pt* **planned**) projeter (**to do** de faire); (*timetable, day*) organiser; (*economy, work*) planifier. ● *vi* prévoir; ~ **on** s'attendre à.

plane *n* (level) plan *m*; (aeroplane) avion *m*; (tool) rabot *m*. ● *adj* plan. ● *vt* raboter.

planet *n* planète *f*.

plank *n* planche *f*.

planning *n* (of economy, work) planification *f*; (of holiday, party) organisation *f*; (of town) urbanisme *m*; **family** ~ **planning** *m* familial; ~ **permission** permis *m* de construire.

plant *n* plante *f*; (Tech) matériel *m*; (factory) usine *f*. ● *vt* planter; (*bomb*) placer.

plaster *n* plâtre *m*; (adhesive) sparadrap *m*. ● *vt* plâtrer; (cover) couvrir (**with** de).

plastic *adj* en plastique; (*art, substance*) plastique; ~ **surgery** chirurgie *f* esthétique. ● *n* plastique *m*.

plate *n* assiette *f*; (of metal) plaque *f*; (silverware) argenterie *f*; (in book) gravure *f*. ● *vt* (*metal*) plaquer.

plateau *n* (*pl* ~**x**) plateau *m*; (fig) palier *m*.

platform *n* (stage) estrade *f*; (for speaking) tribune *f*; (Rail) quai *m*; (Pol) plate-forme *f*.

platoon *n* (Mil) section *f*.

play *vt/i* jouer; (*instrument*) jouer de; (*record*) mettre; (*game*) jouer à; (*opponent*) jouer contre; (*match*) disputer; ~ **safe** ne pas prendre de risques. ● *n* jeu *m*; (Theat) pièce *f*. □ ~ **down** minimiser; ~ **on** (*fears*) exploiter; ~ **up** ▣ commencer à faire des siennes ▣; ~ **up sth** mettre l'accent sur qch.

playful *adj* (*remark*) taquin; (*child*) joueur.

play: ~**ground** *n* cour *f* de récréation. ~**group**, ~**school** *n* garderie *f*.

playing *n* (Sport) jeu *m*; (Theat) interprétation *f*. ~**card** *n* carte *f* à jouer. ~**field** *n* terrain *m* de sport.

play: ~**pen** *n* parc *m* (pour bébé). ~**wright** *n* auteur *m* dramatique.

plc *abbr* (**public limited company**) SA.

plea *n* (for mercy, tolerance) appel *m*; (for food, money) demande *f*; (reason) excuse *f*; **make a** ~ **of guilty** plaider coupable.

plead *vt/i* supplier; (Jur) plaider.

pleasant *adj* agréable.

please *vt/i* plaire (à), faire plaisir (à); ~ **oneself**, **do as one** ~**s** faire ce qu'on veut. ● *adv* s'il vous *or* te plaît. **pleased** *adj* content (**with** de). **pleasing** *adj* agréable.

pleasure *n* plaisir *m*; **with** ~ avec plaisir; **my** ~ je vous en prie.

pleat *n* pli *m*. ● *vt* plisser.

pledge *n* (token) gage *m*; (promise) promesse *f*. ● *vt* promettre; (pawn) mettre en gage.

plentiful *adj* abondant.

plenty *n* abondance *f*; ~ (**of**) (a great deal) beaucoup (de); (enough) assez (de).

pliers *npl* pinces *fpl*.

plight *n* détresse *f*.

plinth *n* socle *m*.

plod *vi* (*pt* **plodded**) avancer péniblement.

plonk *n* ▣ pinard *m* ▣.

plot *n* (*conspiracy*) complot *m*; (of novel) intrigue *f*; ~ (**of land**) terrain *m*. ● *vt/i* (*pt* **plotted**) (plan) comploter; (mark out) tracer.

plough *n* charrue *f*. ● *vt/i* labourer. □ ~ **back** réinvestir; ~ **through** avancer péniblement dans.

plow *n & vt/i* (US) = PLOUGH.

ploy *n* stratagème *m*.

pluck *vt* (*flower, fruit*) cueillir; (*bird*) plumer; (*eyebrows*) épiler; (*strings*: Mus) pincer; ~ **up courage** prendre son courage à deux mains. **plucky** *adj* courageux.

plug *n* (for sink) bonde *f*; (Electr) fiche *f*, prise *f*. ● *vt* (*pt* **plugged**) (*hole*) boucher; (publicize ▣) faire du battage autour de. □ ~ **in** brancher. ~**hole** *n* bonde *f*.

plum *n* prune *f*; ~ **pudding** (plum-) pudding *m*.

plumber *n* plombier *m*.

p

plume n (of feathers) panache m.
plummet vi tomber, plonger.
plump adj potelé, dodu.
plunge vt/i (dive, thrust) plonger; (fall) tomber. ● n plongeon m; (fall) chute f; **take the** ~ se jeter à l'eau. **plunger** n (for sink) ventouse f.
plural adj pluriel; (noun) au pluriel; (ending) du pluriel. ● n pluriel m.
plus prep plus; **ten** ~ plus de dix. ● adj (Electr & fig) positif. ● n signe m plus; (fig) atout m.
ply vt (tool) manier; (trade) exercer. ● vi faire la navette; ~ **sb with drink** offrir continuellement à boire à qn.
plywood n contreplaqué m.
p.m. adv de l'après-midi or du soir.
pneumatic drill n marteau-piqueur m.
pneumonia n pneumonie f.
PO abbr →POST OFFICE.
poach vt/i (game) braconner; (staff) débaucher; (Culin) pocher.
PO Box n boîte f postale.
pocket n poche f; **be out of** ~ avoir perdu de l'argent. ● adj de poche. ● vt empocher. ~-**book** n (notebook) carnet m; (wallet: US) portefeuille m; (handbag: US) sac m à main. ~-**money** n argent m de poche.
pod n (peas) cosse f, (vanilla) gousse f.
podgy adj (-ier, -iest) dodu.
poem n poème m. **poet** n poète m. **poetic** adj poétique. **poetry** n poésie f.
point n (position) point m; (tip) pointe f; (decimal point) virgule f; (remark) remarque f; **good** ~s qualités fpl; **on the** ~ **of** sur le point de; ~ **in time** moment m; ~ **of view** point m de vue; **to the** ~ pertinent; **what is the** ~? à quoi bon? ● vt (aim) braquer; (show) indiquer; ~ **out** signaler. ● vi indiquer du doigt; ~ **out that, make the** ~ **that** faire remarquer que. ~-**blank** a & adv à bout portant.
pointed adj (sharp) pointu; (window) en pointe; (remark) lourd de sens.
pointless adj inutile.
poise n (confidence) assurance f; (physical elegance) aisance f.
poison n poison m. ● vt empoisonner. **poisonous** adj

(substance) toxique; (plant) vénéneux; (snake) venimeux.
poke vt/i (push) pousser; (fire) tisonner; (thrust) fourrer; ~ **fun at** se moquer de. ● n (petit) coup m. ☐ ~ **out** (head) sortir.
poker n (for fire) tisonnier m; (cards) poker m.
Poland n Pologne f.
polar adj polaire.
pole n (stick) perche f; (for flag) mât m; (Geog) pôle m.
Pole n Polonais/-e m/f.
pole-vault n saut m à la perche.
police n police f. ● vt faire la police dans. ~ **constable** n agent m de police. ~**man** n (pl -**men**) agent m de police. ~ **station** n commissariat m de police. ~**woman** n (pl -**women**) femme-agent f.
policy n politique f; (insurance) police f (d'assurance).
polish vt polir; (shoes, floor) cirer. ● n (for shoes) cirage m; (for floor) encaustique f; (for nails) vernis m; (shine) poli m; (fig) raffinement m. ☐ ~ **off** finir en vitesse; ~ **up** (language) perfectionner.
Polish adj polonais. ● n (Ling) polonais m.
polished adj raffiné.
polite adj poli.
political adj politique.
politician n homme m politique, femme f politique.
politics n politique f.
poll n (vote casting) scrutin m; (survey) sondage m; **go to the** ~s aller aux urnes. ● vt (votes) obtenir.
pollen n pollen m.
polling booth n isoloir m.
polling station n bureau m de vote.
pollution n pollution f.
polo n polo m. ~ **neck** n col m roulé.
pomegranate n grenade f.
pomp n pompe f.
pompous adj pompeux.
pond n étang m; (artificial) bassin m; (stagnant) mare f.

ponder *vt/i* réfléchir (à), méditer (sur).

pong *n* (stink 🔲) puanteur *f*. ● *vi* 🔲 puer.

pony *n* poney *m*. ∼**tail** *n* queue *f* de cheval.

poodle *n* caniche *m*.

pool *n* (puddle) flaque *f*; (pond) étang *m*; (of blood) mare *f*; (for swimming) piscine *f*; (fund) fonds *m* commun; (of ideas) réservoir *m*; (snooker) billard *m* américain; ∼**s** pari *m* mutuel sur le football. ● *vt* mettre en commun.

poor *adj* (not wealthy) pauvre; (not good) médiocre, mauvais.

poorly *adj* malade. ● *adv* mal.

pop *n* (noise) pan *m*; (music) pop *m*. ● *adj* pop *inv*. ● *vt/i* (*pt* **popped**) (burst) crever; (put) mettre; ∼ **in/out/ off** entrer/sortir/partir. □ ∼ **up** surgir.

pope *n* pape *m*.

poppy *n* pavot *m*; (wild) coquelicot *m*.

popular *adj* populaire; (in fashion) en vogue; **be** ∼ **with** plaire à.

population *n* population *f*.

porcelain *n* porcelaine *f*.

porcupine *n* porc-épic *m*.

pork *n* porc *m*.

pornography *n* pornographie *f*.

port *n* (harbour) port *m*; (left: Naut) bâbord *m*; ∼ **of call** escale *f*; (wine) porto *m*.

portable *adj* portable.

porter *n* (carrier) porteur *m*; (door-keeper) portier *m*.

portfolio *n* (Pol, Comm) portefeuille *m*.

portion *n* (at meal) portion *f*; (part) partie *f*.

portrait *n* portrait *m*.

portray *vt* représenter.

Portugal *n* Portugal *m*.

Portuguese *n* (Ling) portugais *m*; (*person*) Portugais/-e *m/f*. ● *adj* portugais.

pose *vt/i* poser; ∼ **as** (*expert*) se poser en. ● *n* pose *f*.

poser *n* (person) frimeur/-euse *m/f*; (puzzle) colle *f*.

posh *adj* 🔲 chic *inv*.

position *n* position *f*; (job, state) situation *f*. ● *vt* placer.

positive *adj* positif; (sure) sûr, certain; (real) réel, vrai.

possess *vt* posséder.

possession *n* possession *f*; **take** ∼ **of** prendre possession de.

possessive *adj* possessif.

possible *adj* possible.

possibly *adv* peut-être; **if I** ∼ **can** si cela m'est possible; **I cannot** ∼ **leave** il m'est impossible de partir.

post *n* (pole) poteau *m*; (station, job) poste *m*; (mail service) poste *f*; (letters) courrier *m*. ● *adj* postal. ● *vt* (*letter*) poster; **keep** ∼**ed** tenir au courant; ∼ (**up**) (a notice) afficher; (appoint) affecter.

postage *n* affranchissement *m*; tarif *m* postal.

postal *adj* postal. ∼ **order** *n* mandat *m*.

post: ∼**box** *n* boîte *f* aux lettres. ∼**card** *n* carte *f* postale. ∼ **code** *n* code *m* postal.

poster *n* (for information) affiche *f*; (for decoration) poster *m*.

postgraduate *n* étudiant/-e *m/f* de troisième cycle.

posthumous *adj* posthume.

post: ∼**man** *n* (*pl* -**men**) facteur *m*. ∼**mark** *n* cachet *m* de la poste.

post-mortem *n* autopsie *f*.

post office *n* poste *f*.

postpone *vt* remettre.

postscript *n* (to letter) post-scriptum *m inv*.

posture *n* posture *f*. ● *vi* prendre des poses.

pot *n* pot *m*; (drug 🔲) hasch *m*; **go to** ∼ 🔲 aller à la ruine; **take** ∼ **luck** tenter sa chance. ● *vt* (*plants*) mettre en pot.

potato *n* (*pl* ∼**es**) pomme *f* de terre.

pot-belly *n* bedaine *f*.

potential *a & n* potentiel (*m*).

pot-hole *n* (in rock) caverne *f*; (in road) nid *m* de poule. **pot-holing** *n* spéléologie *f*. .

potter *n* potier *m*. ● *vi* bricoler. **pottery** *n* (art) poterie *f*; (objects) poteries *fpl*.

potty *adj* (-**ier**, -**iest**) (crazy 🔲) toqué. ● *n* pot *m*.

p

pouch n poche f; (for tobacco) blague f.

poultry n volailles fpl.

pounce vi bondir (on sur). ● n bond m.

pound n (weight) livre f (= 454 g); (money) livre f; (for dogs, cars) fourrière f. ● vt (crush) piler; (bombard) pilonner. ● vi frapper fort; (of heart) battre fort; (walk) marcher à pas lourds.

pour vt verser. ● vi couler, ruisseler (from de); (rain) pleuvoir à torrents. □ ~ **in/out** (people) arriver/sortir en masse; ~ **off** or **out** vider. **pouring rain** n pluie f torrentielle.

pout vi faire la moue.

poverty n misère f, pauvreté f.

powder n poudre f. ● vt poudrer.

power n (strength) puissance f; (control) pouvoir m; (energy) énergie f; (Electr) courant m. ● vt (engine) faire marcher; (plane) propulser; ~**ed by** (engine) propulsé par; (generator) alimenté par. ~ **cut** n coupure f de courant.

powerful adj puissant.

powerless adj impuissant.

power: ~ **point** n prise f de courant. ~**-station** n centrale f électrique.

practical adj pratique. ~ **joke** n farce f.

practice n (procedure) pratique f; (of profession) exercice m; (Sport) entraînement m; **in** ~ (in fact) en pratique; (well-trained) en forme; **out of** ~ rouillé; **put into** ~ mettre en pratique.

practise vt/i (musician, typist) s'exercer (à); (Sport) s'entraîner (à); (put into practice) pratiquer; (profession) exercer.

praise vt faire l'éloge de; (God) louer. ● n éloges mpl, louanges fpl.

pram n landau m.

prance vi caracoler.

prawn n crevette f rose.

pray vi prier. **prayer** n prière f.

preach vt/i prêcher; ~ **at** or **to** prêcher.

precarious adj précaire.

precaution n précaution f.

precede vt précéder.

precedence n (in importance) priorité f; (in rank) préséance f.

precedent n précédent m.

precinct n quartier m commerçant; (pedestrian area) zone f piétonne; (district: US) circonscription f.

precious adj précieux.

precipitate vt (person, event, chemical) précipiter.

précis n résumé m.

precise adj précis; (careful) méticuleux. **precision** n précision f.

precocious adj précoce.

preconceived adj préconçu.

predator n prédateur m.

predicament n situation f difficile.

predict vt prédire. **predictable** adj prévisible. **prediction** n prédiction f.

predispose vt prédisposer (**to do à** faire).

predominant adj prédominant.

pre-empt vt (anticipate) anticiper; (person) devancer.

preface n (to book) préface f; (to speech) préambule m.

prefect n (pupil) élève m/f chargé/-e de la discipline; (official) préfet m.

prefer vt (pt **preferred**) préférer (**to do** faire). **preferably** adv de préférence. **preference** n préférence f. **preferential** adj préférentiel.

prefix n préfixe m.

pregnancy n grossesse f. **pregnant** adj (woman) enceinte; (animal) pleine; (pause) éloquent.

prehistoric adj préhistorique.

prejudge vt (issue) préjuger de; (person) juger d'avance.

prejudice n préjugé(s) m(pl); (harm) préjudice m. ● vt (claim) porter préjudice à; (person) léser. **prejudiced** adj partial; (person) qui a des préjugés.

premature adj prématuré.

premeditated adj prémédité.

premises npl locaux mpl; **on the** ~ sur les lieux.

premium n (insurance) prime f; **be at a** ~ être précieux.

preoccupied *adj* préoccupé.

preparation *n* préparation *f*; ~s préparatifs *mpl*.

preparatory *adj* préparatoire. ~ **school** *n* école *f* primaire privée; (US) école *f* secondaire privée.

prepare *vt/i* (se) préparer (**for** à); **be** ~**d for** (expect) s'attendre à; ~**d to** prêt à.

preposition *n* préposition *f*.

preposterous *adj* absurde, ridicule.

prep school *n* = PREPARATORY SCHOOL.

prerequisite *n* condition *f* préalable.

prescribe *vt* prescrire.

prescription *n* (Med) ordonnance *f*.

presence *n* présence *f*; ~ **of mind** présence *f* d'esprit.

present[1] *adj* présent. ● *n* présent *m*; (gift) cadeau *m*; **at** ~ à présent; **for the** ~ pour le moment.

present[2] *vt* présenter; (*film, concert*) donner; ~ **sb with** offrir à qn. **presentation** *n* présentation *f*. **presenter** *n* présentateur/-trice *m/f*.

preservation *n* (of food) conservation *f*; (of wildlife) préservation *f*.

preservative *n* (Culin) agent *m* de conservation.

preserve *vt* préserver; (Culin) conserver. ● *n* réserve *f*; (fig) domaine *m*; (jam) confiture *f*.

presidency *n* présidence *f*.

president *n* président/-e *m/f*.

press *vt/i* (*button*) appuyer (sur); (squeeze) presser; (iron) repasser; (pursue) poursuivre; **be** ~**ed for** (*time*) manquer de; ~ **for sth** faire pression pour avoir qch; ~ **sb to do sth** pousser qn à faire qch; ~ **on** continuer (**with sth** qch). ● *n* (newspapers, machine) presse *f*; (for wine) pressoir *m*. ~ **cutting** *n* coupure *f* de presse.

pressing *adj* pressant.

press: ~ **release** *n* communiqué *m* de presse. ~**-stud** *n* bouton-pression *m*. ~**-up** *n* pompe *f*.

pressure *n* pression *f*. ● *vt* faire pression sur. ~**-cooker** *n* cocotte-minute *f*. ~ **group** *n* groupe *m* de pression.

pressurize *vt* (*cabin*) pressuriser; (*person*) faire pression sur.

prestige *n* prestige *m*.

presumably *adv* vraisemblablement.

presume *vt* (suppose) présumer.

pretence, (US) **pretense** *n* feinte *f*, simulation *f*; (claim) prétention *f*; (pretext) prétexte *m*.

pretend *vt/i* faire semblant (**to do** de faire); ~ **to** (lay claim to) prétendre à.

pretentious *adj* prétentieux.

pretext *n* prétexte *m*.

pretty *adj* (**-ier**, **-iest**) joli. ● *adv* assez; ~ **much** presque.

prevail *vi* (be usual) prédominer; (win) prévaloir; ~ **on** persuader (**to do** de faire). **prevailing** *adj* actuel; (*wind*) dominant.

prevalent *adj* répandu.

prevent *vt* empêcher (**from doing** de faire). **prevention** *n* prévention *f*. **preventive** *adj* préventif.

preview *n* avant-première *f*; (fig) aperçu *m*.

previous *adj* précédent, antérieur; ~ **to** avant. **previously** *adv* auparavant.

prey *n* proie *f*; **bird of** ~ rapace *m*. ● *vi* ~ **on** faire sa proie de; (worry) préoccuper.

price *n* prix *m*. ● *vt* fixer le prix de. **priceless** *adj* inestimable; (amusing 🆒) impayable 🆒.

prick *vt* (with pin) piquer; ~ **up one's ears** dresser l'oreille. ● *n* piqûre *f*.

prickle *n* piquant *m*.

pride *n* orgueil *m*; (satisfaction) fierté *f*; ~ **of place** place *f* d'honneur. ● *vpr* ~ **oneself on** s'enorgueillir de.

priest *n* prêtre *m*.

prim *adj* (**primmer**, **primmest**) guindé, méticuleux.

primarily *adv* essentiellement.

primary *adj* (*school, elections*) primaire; (chief, basic) premier, fondamental. ● *n* (Pol: US) primaire *f*.

p

prime adj principal, premier; (first-rate) excellent. ● vt (pump, gun) amorcer; (surface) apprêter. **P~ Minister** n Premier Ministre m.

primitive adj primitif.

primrose n primevère f (jaune).

prince n prince m. **princess** n princesse f.

principal adj principal. ● n (of school) directeur/-trice m/f.

principle n principe m; in/on ~ en/par principe.

print vt imprimer; (write in capitals) écrire en majuscules; ~ed matter imprimés mpl. ● n (of foot) empreinte f; (letters) caractères mpl; (photograph) épreuve f; (engraving) gravure f; in ~ disponible; out of ~ épuisé. **printer** n (person) imprimeur m; (Comput) imprimante f.

prior adj précédent. ● n (Relig) prieur m. ~ **to** prep avant (de).

priority n priorité f; take ~ avoir la priorité (over sur).

prise vt forcer; ~ open ouvrir en forçant.

prison n prison f. **prisoner** n prisonnier/-ière m/f. ~ **officer** n gardien/-ne m/f de prison.

pristine adj be in ~ condition être comme neuf.

privacy n intimité f, solitude f.

private adj privé; (confidential) personnel; (lessons, house) particulier; (ceremony) intime; in ~ en privé; (of ceremony) dans l'intimité. ● n (soldier) simple soldat m. **privately** adv en privé; dans l'intimité; (inwardly) intérieurement.

privilege n privilège m. **privileged** adj privilégié; be ~d to avoir le privilège de.

prize n prix m. ● adj (entry) primé; (fool) parfait. ● vt (value) priser.

pro n the ~s and cons le pour et le contre.

probable adj probable. **probably** adv probablement.

probation n (testing) essai m; (Jur) liberté f surveillée.

probe n (device) sonde f; (fig) enquête f. ● vt sonder. ● vi ~ into sonder.

problem n problème m. ● adj difficile. **problematic** adj problématique.

procedure n procédure f; (way of doing sth) démarche f à suivre.

proceed vi (go) aller, avancer; (pass) passer (to à); (act) procéder; ~ (with) continuer; ~ to do se mettre à faire.

proceedings npl (discussions) débats mpl; (meeting) réunion f; (report) actes mpl; (Jur) poursuites fpl.

proceeds npl (profits) produit m, bénéfices mpl.

process n processus m; (method) procédé m; in ~ en cours; in the ~ of doing en train de faire. ● vt (material, data) traiter.

procession n défilé m.

procrastinate vi différer, tergiverser.

procure vt obtenir.

prod vt/i (pt **prodded**) pousser doucement. ● n petit coup m.

prodigy n prodige m.

produce[1] n produits mpl.

produce[2] vt/i produire; (bring out) sortir; (show) présenter; (cause) provoquer; (Theat, TV) mettre en scène; (radio) réaliser; (cinema) produire. **producer** n metteur m en scène; réalisateur m; producteur m.

product n produit m.

production n production f; (Theat, TV) mise f en scène; (radio) réalisation f.

productive adj productif. **productivity** n productivité f.

profession n profession f.

professional adj professionnel; (of high quality) de professionnel; (person) qui exerce une profession libérale. ● n professionnel/-le m/f.

professor n professeur m (titulaire d'une chaire).

proficient adj compétent.

profile n (of face) profil m; (of body, mountain) silhouette f; (by journalist) portrait m.

profit n profit m, bénéfice m. ● vi ~ **by** tirer profit de. **profitable** adj rentable.

profound adj profond.

profusely adv (bleed) abondamment; (apologize) avec effusion. **profusion** n profusion f.

program n (US) = PROGRAMME; (computer) ∼ programme m. ● vt (pt **programmed**) programmer.

programme n programme m; (broadcast) émission f.

programmer n programmeur/-euse m/f.

programming n (Comput) programmation f.

progress[1] n progrès m(pl); in ∼ en cours; make ∼ faire des progrès; ∼ report compte-rendu m.

progress[2] vi (advance, improve) progresser.

progressive adj progressif; (reforming) progressiste.

prohibit vt interdire (sb from doing à qn de faire).

project[1] vt projeter. ● vi (jut out) être en saillie.

project[2] n (plan) projet m; (undertaking) entreprise f; (School) dossier m.

projection n projection f; saillie f; (estimate) prévision f.

projector n projecteur m.

proliferate vi proliférer.

prolong vt prolonger.

prominent adj (projecting) proéminent; (conspicuous) bien en vue; (fig) important.

promiscuous adj de mœurs faciles.

promise n promesse f. ● vt/i promettre. **promising** adj prometteur; (person) qui promet.

promote vt promouvoir; (advertise) faire la promotion de. **promotion** n promotion f.

prompt adj rapide; (punctual) à l'heure, ponctuel. ● adv (on the dot) pile. ● vt inciter; (cause) provoquer; (Theat) souffler à. ● n (Comput) message m guide-opérateur. **prompter** n souffleur/-euse m/f. **promptly** adv rapidement; ponctuellement.

prone adj ∼ to sujet à.

pronoun n pronom m.

pronounce vt prononcer. **pronunciation** n prononciation f.

proof n (evidence) preuve f; (test, trial copy) épreuve f; (of alcohol) teneur f en alcool. ● adj ∼ against à l'épreuve de.

prop n support m; (Theat) accessoire m. ● vt (pt **propped**) ∼ (up) (support) étayer; (lean) appuyer.

propaganda n propagande f.

propel vt (pt **propelled**) (vehicle, ship) propulser; (person) pousser.

propeller n hélice f.

proper adj correct, bon; (adequate) convenable; (real) vrai; (thorough ▯) parfait. **properly** adv correctement, comme il faut; (adequately) convenablement.

proper noun n nom m propre.

property n (house) propriété f; (things owned) biens mpl, propriété f. ● adj immobilier, foncier.

prophecy n prophétie f.

prophet n prophète m.

proportion n (ratio, dimension) proportion f; (amount) partie f.

proposal n proposition f; (of marriage) demande f en mariage.

propose vt proposer. ● vi faire une demande en mariage; ∼ to do se proposer de faire.

proposition n proposition f; (matter ▯) affaire f. ● vt ▯ faire des propositions malhonnêtes à.

proprietor n propriétaire mf.

propriety n (correct behaviour) bienséance f.

prose n prose f; (translation) thème m.

prosecute vt poursuivre en justice. **prosecution** n poursuites fpl. **prosecutor** n procureur m.

prospect[1] n (outlook) perspective f; (chance) espoir m.

prospect[2] vt/i prospecter.

prospective adj (future) futur; (possible) éventuel.

prospectus n brochure f; (Univ) livret m de l'étudiant.

prosperity n prospérité f. **prosperous** adj prospère.

prostitute n prostituée f.

prostrate adj (prone) à plat ventre; (exhausted) prostré.

p

protect *vt* protéger. **protection** *n* protection *f*. **protective** *adj* protecteur; (*clothes*) de protection.

protein *n* protéine *f*.

protest[1] *n* protestation *f*; **under ~** en protestant.

protest[2] *vt/i* protester.

Protestant *a & n* protestant/-e (*m/ f*).

protester *n* manifestant/-e *m/f*.

protocol *n* protocole *m*.

protrude *vi* dépasser.

proud *adj* fier, orgueilleux.

prove *vt* prouver. ● *vi* **~ (to be) easy** se révéler facile; **~ oneself** faire ses preuves. **proven** *adj* éprouvé.

proverb *n* proverbe *m*.

provide *vt* fournir (**sb with sth** qch à qn). ● *vi* **~ for** (allow for) prévoir; (guard against) parer à; (*person*) pourvoir aux besoins de.

provided *conj* **~ that** à condition que.

providing *conj* = PROVIDED.

province *n* province *f*; (fig) compétence *f*.

provision *n* (stock) provision *f*; (supplying) fourniture *f*; (stipulation) dispositions *fpl*; **~s** (food) provisions *fpl*.

provisional *adj* provisoire.

provocative *adj* provocant.

provoke *vt* provoquer.

prow *n* proue *f*.

prowess *n* prouesses *fpl*.

prowl *vi* rôder.

proxy *n* **by ~** par procuration.

prudish *adj* pudibond, prude.

prune *n* pruneau *m*. ● *vt* (cut) tailler.

pry *vi* **~ into** mettre son nez dans.

psalm *n* psaume *m*.

pseudonym *n* pseudonyme *m*.

psychiatric *adj* psychiatrique. **psychiatrist** *n* psychiatre *mf*. **psychiatry** *n* psychiatrie *f*.

psychic *adj* (*phenomenon*) métapsychique; (*person*) doué de télépathie.

psychoanalyse *vt* psychanalyser.

psychological *adj* psychologique. **psychologist** *n* psychologue *mf*. **psychology** *n* psychologie *f*.

PTO *abbr* (**please turn over**) TSVP.

pub *n* pub *m*.

puberty *n* puberté *f*.

public *adj* public; (*library*) municipal; **in ~** en public.

publican *n* patron/-ne *m/f* de pub.

publication *n* publication *f*.

public house *n* pub *m*.

publicity *n* publicité *f*.

publicize *vt* faire connaître au public.

public: **~ relations** *n* relations *fpl* publiques. **~ school** *n* école *f* privée; (US) école *f* publique. **~ transport** *n* transports *mpl* en commun.

publish *vt* publier. **publisher** *n* éditeur *m*. **publishing** *n* édition *f*.

pudding *n* dessert *m*; (steamed) pudding *m*.

puddle *n* flaque *f* d'eau.

puff *n* (of smoke) bouffée *f*; (of breath) souffle *m*. ● *vt/i* souffler. □ **~ at** (*cigar*) tirer sur. **~ out** (swell) (se) gonfler.

pull *vt/i* tirer; (*muscle*) se froisser; **~ a face** faire une grimace; **~ one's weight** faire sa part du travail; **~ sb's leg** faire marcher qn. ● *n* traction *f*; (fig) attraction *f*; (influence) influence *f*; **give a ~** tirer. □ **~ away** (Auto) démarrer; **~ back** *or* **out** (withdraw) (se) retirer; **~ down** (*building*) démolir; **~ in** (enter) entrer; (stop) s'arrêter; **~ off** enlever; (fig) réussir; **~ out** (from bag) sortir; (extract) arracher; (Auto) déboîter; **~ over** (Auto) se ranger (sur le côté); **~ through** s'en tirer; **~ oneself together** se ressaisir.

pull-down menu *n* (Comput) menu *m* déroulant.

pulley *n* poulie *f*.

pullover *n* pull(-over) *m*.

pulp *n* (of fruit) pulpe *f*; (for paper) pâte *f* à papier.

pulpit *n* chaire *f*.

pulsate *vi* battre.

pulse *n* (Med) pouls *m*.

pump *n* pompe *f*; (plimsoll) chaussure *f* de sport. ● *vt/i* pomper; (*person*)

soutirer des renseignements à; ~ **up**
gonfler.

pumpkin *n* citrouille *f.*

pun *n* jeu *m* de mots.

punch *vt* donner un coup de poing à;
(*ticket*) poinçonner. ● *n* coup *m* de
poing; (vigour 🔳) punch *m*; (device)
poinçonneuse *f;* (drink) punch *m.*
~**-line** *n* chute *f.*

punctual *adj* à l'heure; (habitually)
ponctuel.

punctuation *n* ponctuation *f.*

puncture *n* crevaison *f.* ● *vt/i*
crever.

pungent *adj* âcre.

punish *vt* punir (**for sth** de qch).
punishment *n* punition *f.*

punk *n* (music, fan) punk *m;* (US: 🔳)
voyou *m.*

punt *n* (boat) barque *f;* (Irish pound)
livre *f* irlandaise.

puny *adj* (**-ier**, **-iest**) chétif.

pupil *n* (person) élève *mf;* (of eye)
pupille *f.*

puppet *n* marionnette *f.*

puppy *n* chiot *m.*

purchase *vt* acheter (**from sb** à qn).
● *n* achat *m.*

pure *adj* pur.

purgatory *n* purgatoire *m.*

purge *vt* purger (**of** de). ● *n* purge *f.*

purification *n* (of water, air)
épuration *f;* (Relig) purification *f.*
purify *vt* épurer; purifier.

puritan *n* puritain/-e *m/f.*

purity *n* pureté *f.*

purple *a* & *n* violet (*m*).

purpose *n* but *m;* (determination)
résolution *f;* **on** ~ exprès; **to no** ~
sans résultat.

purr *n* ronronnement *m.* ● *vi*
ronronner.

purse *n* porte-monnaie *m inv;*
(handbag: US) sac *m* à main. ● *vt* (*lips*)
pincer.

pursue *vt* poursuivre.

pursuit *n* poursuite *f;* (hobby) activité
f, occupation *f.*

pus *n* pus *m.*

push *vt/i* pousser; (*button*) appuyer
sur; (thrust) enfoncer; (recommend 🔳)
proposer avec insistance; **be** ~**ed for**
(*time*) manquer de; **be** ~**ing thirty**

🔳 friser la trentaine; ~ **sb around**
bousculer qn. ● *n* poussée *f;* (effort)
gros effort *m;* (drive) dynamisme *m;*
give the ~ **to** 🔳 flanquer à la porte
🔳. ◻ ~ **in** resquiller; ~ **on**
continuer; ~ **up** (lift) relever; (*prices*)
faire monter.

pushchair *n* poussette *f.*

pusher *n* revendeur/-euse *m/f* (de
drogue).

push-up *n* pompe *f.*

put *vt/i* (*pt* **put**; *pres p* **putting**)
mettre, placer, poser; (*question*)
poser; ~ **the damage at a million**
estimer les dégâts à un million; ~
sth tactfully dire qch avec tact. ◻ ~
across communiquer; ~ **away**
ranger; (in hospital, prison) enfermer; ~
back (postpone) remettre; (delay)
retarder; ~ **down** (dé)poser; (write)
inscrire; (pay) verser; (suppress)
réprimer; ~ **forward** (*plan*)
soumettre; ~ **in** (insert) introduire;
(fix) installer; (submit) soumettre; ~ **in**
for faire une demande de; ~ **off**
(postpone) renvoyer à plus tard;
(disconcert) déconcerter; (displease)
rebuter; ~ **sb off sth** dégoûter qn de
qch; ~ **on** (*clothes, radio*) mettre;
(*light*) allumer; (*accent, weight*)
prendre; ~ **out** sortir; (stretch) (é)
tendre; (extinguish) éteindre; (disconcert)
déconcerter; (inconvenience) déranger;
~ **up** lever, remonter; (*building*)
construire; (*notice*) mettre; (*price*)
augmenter; (*guest*) héberger; (*offer*)
offrir; ~ **up with** supporter.

putty *n* mastic *m.*

puzzle *n* énigme *f;* (game) casse-tête
m inv; (jigsaw) puzzle *m.* ● *vt* rendre
perplexe. ● *vi* se creuser la tête.

pyjamas *npl* pyjama *m.*

pylon *n* pylône *m.*

p

Qq

quack *n* (of duck) coin-coin *m inv*; (doctor) charlatan *m*.

quadrangle (of college) *n* cour *f*.

quadruple *a* & *n* quadruple (*m*). ● *vt/i* quadrupler.

quail *n* (bird) caille *f*.

quaint *adj* pittoresque; (old) vieillot; (odd) bizarre.

qualification *n* diplôme *m*; (ability) compétence *f*, (fig) réserve *f*, restriction *f*.

qualified *adj* diplômé; (able) qualifié (**to do** pour faire); (fig) conditionnel.

qualify *vt* qualifier; (modify) mettre des réserves à; (*statement*) nuancer. ● *vi* obtenir son diplôme (**as** de); (Sport) se qualifier; ~ **for** remplir les conditions requises pour.

quality *n* qualité *f*.

qualm *n* scrupule *m*.

quantity *n* quantité *f*.

quarantine *n* quarantaine *f*.

quarrel *n* dispute *f*, querelle *f*. ● *vi* (*pt* **quarrelled**) se disputer.

quarry *n* (excavation) carrière *f*; (prey) proie *f*. ● *vt* extraire.

quart *n* ≈ litre *m*.

quarter *n* quart *m*; (of year) trimestre *m*; (25 cents: US) quart *m* de dollar; (district) quartier *m*; ~**s** logement *m*; **from all** ~**s** de toutes parts. ● *vt* diviser en quatre; (*troops*) cantonner.

quarterly *adj* trimestriel. ● *adv* tous les trois mois.

quartet *n* quatuor *m*.

quartz *n* quartz *m*. ● *adj* (*watch*) à quartz.

quash *vt* (suppress) étouffer; (Jur) annuler.

quaver *vi* trembler, chevroter. ● *n* (Mus) croche *f*.

quay *n* (Naut) quai *m*.

queasy *adj* **feel** ~ avoir mal au cœur.

queen *n* reine *f*; (cards) dame *f*.

queer *adj* étrange; (dubious) louche; ⊠ homosexuel.

quench *vt* éteindre; (*thirst*) étancher; (*desire*) étouffer.

query *n* question *f*. ● *vt* mettre en question.

quest *n* recherche *f*.

question *n* question *f*; **in** ~ en question; **out of the** ~ hors de question. ● *vt* interroger; (doubt) mettre en question, douter de. ~ **mark** *n* point *m* d'interrogation.

questionnaire *n* questionnaire *m*.

queue *n* queue *f*. ● *vi* (*pres p* **queuing**) faire la queue.

quibble *vi* ergoter.

quick *adj* rapide; (clever) vif/vive; **be** ~ (hurry) se dépêcher. ● *adv* vite. ● *n* **cut to the** ~ piquer au vif. **quicken** *vt/i* (s')accélérer. **quickly** *adv* rapidement, vite. ~**sand** *n* sables *mpl* mouvants.

quid *n inv* ① livre *f* sterling.

quiet *adj* (calm, still) tranquille; (silent) silencieux; (gentle) doux; (discreet) discret; **keep** ~ se taire. ● *n* tranquillité *f*; **on the** ~ en cachette. **quieten** *vt/i* (se) calmer. **quietly** *adv* (*speak*) doucement; (*sit*) en silence.

quilt *n* édredon *m*; (**continental**) ~ couette *f*.

quirk *n* bizarrerie *f*.

quit *vt* (*pt* **quitted**) quitter; (*smoking*) arrêter de. ● *vi* abandonner; (resign) démissionner; ~ **doing** (US) cesser de faire.

quite *adv* tout à fait, vraiment; (rather) assez; ~ **a few** un bon nombre (de).

quits *adj* quitte (**with** envers); **call it** ~ en rester là.

quiver *vi* trembler.

quiz *n* (*pl* **quizzes**) test *m*; (game) jeu-concours *m*. ● *vt* (*pt* **quizzed**) questionner.

quotation *n* citation *f*; (price) devis *m*; (stock exchange) cotation *f*; ~ **marks** guillemets *mpl*.

quote *vt* citer; (*reference, number*) rappeler; (*price*) indiquer; (*share price*) coter. ● *vi* ~ **for** faire un devis

q

pour; ~ **from** citer. ● n (quotation) citation f; (estimate) devis m; **in** ~s ⚠ entre guillemets.

rabbi n rabbin m.

rabbit n lapin m.

rabies n (disease) rage f.

race n (contest) course f; (group) race f. ● adj racial; ~ **relations** relations fpl inter-raciales. ● vt (compete with) faire la course avec; (horse) faire courir. ● vi courir; (pulse) battre précipitamment; (engine) s'emballer. ~**course** n champ m de courses. ~**horse** n cheval m de course. ~**-track** n piste f; (for horses) champ m de courses.

racing n courses fpl; ~ **car** voiture f de course.

racism n racisme m. **racist** a & n raciste (mf).

rack n (shelf) étagère f; (for clothes) portant m; (for luggage) compartiment m à bagages; (for dishes) égouttoir m. ● vt ~ **one's brains** se creuser la cervelle.

racket n (Sport) raquette f; (noise) vacarme m; (swindle) escroquerie f; (crime) trafic m.

radar n & a radar (m).

radial n ~ (tyre) pneu m radial.

radiate vt (happiness) rayonner de; (heat) émettre. ● vi rayonner (**from** de). **radiation** n (radioactivity) radiation f. **radiator** n radiateur m.

radical n & a radical/-e (m/f).

radio n radio f; **on the** ~ à la radio. ● vt (message) envoyer par radio; (person) appeler par radio.

radioactive adj radioactif.

radiographer n manipulateur/ -trice m/f radiographe.

radish n radis m.

radius n (pl **-dii**) rayon m.

raffle n tombola f.

rag n chiffon m; ~**s** loques fpl.

rage n rage f, colère f; **be all the** ~ faire fureur. ● vi (person) tempêter; (storm, battle) faire rage.

ragged adj (clothes) en loques; (person) dépenaillé.

raid n (Mil, on stock market) raid m; (by police) rafle f; (by criminals) hold-up m inv. ● vt faire un raid or une rafle or un hold-up dans. **raider** n (thief) pillard m; (Mil) commando m; (corporate) raider m.

rail n (on balcony) balustrade f; (stairs) rampe f; (for train) rail m; (for curtain) tringle f; **by** ~ par chemin de fer.

railing n (also ~s) grille f.

railway, (US) **railroad** n chemin m de fer. ~ **line** n voie f ferrée. ~ **station** n gare f.

rain n pluie f. ● vi pleuvoir. ~**bow** n arc-en-ciel m. ~**coat** n imperméable m. ~**fall** n précipitation f. ~ **forest** n forêt f tropicale.

rainy adj (**-ier, -iest**) pluvieux; (season) des pluies.

raise vt (barrier, curtain) lever; (child, cattle) élever; (question) soulever; (price, salary) augmenter. ● n (US) augmentation f.

raisin n raisin m sec.

rake n râteau m. ● vt (garden) ratisser; (search) fouiller dans. □ ~ **in** (money) amasser; ~ **up** (past) remuer.

rally vt/i (se) rallier; (strength) reprendre; (after illness) aller mieux; ~ **round** venir en aide. ● n rassemblement m; (Auto) rallye m; (tennis) échange m.

ram n bélier m. ● vt (pt **rammed**) (thrust) enfoncer; (crash into) rentrer dans.

RAM abbr (**random access memory**) RAM f.

ramble n randonnée f. ● vi faire une randonnée. □ ~ **on** discourir.

ramp n (slope) rampe f; (in garage) pont m de graissage.

rampage[1] vi se déchaîner (**through** dans).

rampage[2] n go on the ~ tout saccager.

ran ⇒RUN.

rancid adj rance.

random *adj* (fait) au hasard. ● *n* **at ~** au hasard.

rang ⇨RING².

range *n* (of prices, products) gamme *f*; (of people, beliefs) variété *f*; (of radar, weapon) portée *f*; (of aircraft) autonomie *f*; (of mountains) chaîne *f*. ● *vi* aller; (vary) varier.

rank *n* rang *m*; (Mil) grade *m*. ● *vt/i* **~ among** (se) classer parmi.

ransack *vt* (search) fouiller; (pillage) mettre à sac.

ransom *n* rançon *f*.

rap *n* coup *m* sec; (Mus) rap *m*. ● *vi* (*pt* **rapped**) donner des coups secs (on sur).

rape *vt* violer. ● *n* viol *m*.

rapid *adj* rapide.

rapist *n* violeur *m*.

rapturous *adj* (*delight*) extasié; (*welcome*) enthousiaste.

rare *adj* rare; (Culin) saignant. **rarely** *adv* rarement.

rascal *n* coquin/-e *m/f*.

rash *n* (Med) rougeurs *fpl*. ● *adj* irréfléchi.

raspberry *n* framboise *f*.

rat *n* rat *m*. ● *vi* (*pt* **ratted**) **~ on** (desert) lâcher; (inform on) dénoncer.

rate *n* (ratio, level) taux *m*; (speed) rythme *m*; (price) tarif *m*; (of exchange) taux *m*; **at any ~** en tout cas. ● *vt* (value) estimer; (deserve) mériter; **~ sth highly** admirer beaucoup qch. ● *vi* **~ as** être considéré comme.

rather *adv* (by preference) plutôt; (fairly) assez, plutôt; (a little) un peu; **I would ~ go** j'aimerais mieux partir; **~ than go** plutôt que de partir.

rating *n* (score, value) cote *f*; **the ~s** (TV) l'indice *m* d'écoute, l'audimat® *m*.

ratio *n* proportion *f*.

ration *n* ration *f*. ● *vt* rationner.

rational *adj* rationnel; (*person*) sensé.

rationalize *vt* justifier; (organize) rationaliser.

rattle *vi* (*bottles, chains*) s'entrechoquer; (*window*) vibrer. ● *vt* (*bottles, chains*) faire s'entrechoquer; (fig, 🔲) énerver. ● *n*

cliquetis *m*; (toy) hochet *m*. **~snake** *n* serpent *m* à sonnette, crotale *m*.

rave *vi* (enthuse) s'emballer; (in fever) délirer; (in anger) tempêter.

raven *n* corbeau *m*.

ravenous *adj* **be ~** avoir une faim de loup.

ravine *n* ravin *m*.

raving *adj* **~ lunatic** fou *m* furieux, folle *f* furieuse.

ravishing *adj* ravissant.

raw *adj* cru; (not processed) brut; (*wound*) à vif; (immature) inexpérimenté; **get a ~ deal** être mal traité; **~ material** matière *f* première.

ray *n* (of light) rayon *m*; **~ of hope** lueur *f* d'espoir.

razor *n* rasoir *m*. **~-blade** *n* lame *f* de rasoir.

re *prep* au sujet de; (at top of letter) objet.

reach *vt* (*place, level*) atteindre; (*decision*) arriver à; (contact) joindre; (*audience, market*) toucher. ● *vi* **~ up/down** lever/baisser le bras; **~ across** étendre le bras. ● *n* portée *f*; **within ~ of** à portée de; (close to) à proximité de.

react *vi* réagir. **reaction** *n* réaction *f*. **reactor** *n* réacteur *m*.

read *vt/i* (*pt* **read**) lire; (study) étudier; (*instrument*) indiquer; **~ about sb** lire quelque chose sur qn; **~ out** lire à haute voix. **reader** *n* lecteur/-trice *m/f*. **reading** *n* lecture *f*; (measurement) indication *f*; (interpretation) interprétation *f*.

readjust *vt* rajuster. ● *vi* se réadapter (**to** à).

read-only memory, **ROM** *n* mémoire *f* morte.

ready *adj* (**-ier**, **-iest**) prêt; (quick) prompt. **~-made** *adj* tout fait. **~-to-wear** *adj* prêt-à-porter.

real *adj* (not imaginary) véritable, réel; (not artificial) vrai; **it's a ~ shame** c'est vraiment dommage. **~ estate** *n* biens *mpl* immobiliers.

realism *n* réalisme *m*. **realistic** *adj* réaliste.

reality *n* réalité *f*.

realize vt se rendre compte de, comprendre; (fulfil, turn into cash) réaliser; (price) atteindre.

really adv vraiment.

reap vt (crop) recueillir; (benefits) récolter.

reappear vi reparaître.

rear n arrière m; (of person) derrière m ⊡. ● adj (seat) arrière inv; (entrance) de derrière. ● vt élever. ● vi (horse) se cabrer. **~-view mirror** n rétroviseur m.

reason n raison f (to do, for doing de faire); **within** ~ dans la limite du raisonnable. ● vi ~ **with sb** raisonner qn.

reasonable adj raisonnable.

reassurance n réconfort m.

reassure vt rassurer.

rebate n (refund) remboursement m; (discount) remise f.

rebel[1] n & a rebelle (mf).

rebel[2] vi (pt **rebelled**) se rebeller. **rebellion** n rébellion f.

rebound[1] vi rebondir; ~ **on** (backfire) se retourner contre.

rebound[2] n n rebond m.

rebuke vt réprimander. ● n réprimande f.

recall vt (remember) se souvenir de; (call back) rappeler. ● n (memory) mémoire f; (Comput, Mil) rappel m.

recap vt/i (pt **recapped**) récapituler. ● n récapitulation f.

recede vi s'éloigner; **his hair is receding** son front se dégarnit.

receipt n (written) reçu m; (of letter) réception f; ~**s** (Comm) recettes fpl.

receive vt recevoir; (stolen goods) receler. **receiver** n (telephone) combiné m; (TV) récepteur m.

recent adj récent. **recently** adv récemment.

receptacle n récipient m.

reception n réception f; **give sb a warm** ~ donner un accueil chaleureux à qn.

recess n (alcove) alcôve m; (for door) embrasure f; (Jur, Pol) vacances fpl; (School, US) récréation f.

recession n récession f.

recharge vt recharger.

recipe n recette f.

recipient n (of honour) récipiendaire mf; (of letter) destinataire mf.

reciprocate vt (compliment) retourner; (kindness) payer de retour. ● vi en faire autant.

recite vi réciter.

reckless adj imprudent.

reckon vt/i calculer; (judge) considérer; (think) penser; ~ **on/with** compter sur/avec. **reckoning** n (guess) estimation f; (calculation) calculs mpl.

reclaim vt récupérer; (flooded land) assécher.

recline vi s'allonger; (seat) s'incliner.

recluse n reclus/-e m/f.

recognition n reconnaissance f; **beyond** ~ méconnaissable; **gain** ~ être reconnu.

recognize vt reconnaître.

recollect vt se souvenir de, se rappeler. **recollection** n souvenir m.

recommend vt recommander. **recommendation** n recommandation f.

reconcile vt (people) réconcilier; (facts) concilier; ~ **oneself to** se résigner à.

recondition vt remettre à neuf.

reconsider vt réexaminer. ● vi réfléchir.

reconstruct vt reconstruire; (crime) faire une reconstitution de.

record[1] vt/i (in register, on tape) enregistrer; (in diary) noter; ~ **that** rapporter que.

record[2] n (of events) compte-rendu m; (official) procès-verbal m; (personal, administrative) dossier m; (historical) archives fpl; (past history) réputation f; (Mus) disque m; (Sport) record m; (criminal) ~ casier m judiciaire; **off the** ~ officieusement. ● adj record inv.

recorder n (Mus) flûte f à bec.

recording n enregistrement m.

record-player n tourne-disque m.

recover vt récupérer. ● vi se remettre; (economy) se redresser. **recovery** n (Med) rétablissement m; (of economy) relance f.

r

recreation n récréation f.

recruit n recrue f. ● vt recruter. **recruitment** n recrutement m.

rectangle n rectangle m.

rectify vt rectifier.

recuperate vt récupérer. ● vi se rétablir.

recur vi (pt **recurred**) se reproduire.

recycle vt recycler.

red adj (**redder**, **reddest**) rouge; (hair) roux. ● n rouge m; **in the ∼** en déficit. **R∼ Cross** n Croix-Rouge f. **∼currant** n groseille f.

redecorate vt repeindre, refaire.

redeploy vt réorganiser; (troops) répartir.

red: **∼-handed** adj en flagrant délit. **∼-hot** adj brûlant.

redirect vt (traffic) dévier; (letter) faire suivre.

redness n rougeur f.

redo vt (pt **-did**; pp **-done**) refaire.

redress vt (wrong) redresser; (balance) rétablir. ● n réparation f.

reduce vt réduire; (temperature) faire baisser. **reduction** n réduction f.

redundancy n licenciement m.

redundant adj superflu; (worker) licencié; **make ∼** licencier.

reed n (plant) roseau m.

reef n récif m, écueil m.

reel n (of thread) bobine f; (of film) bande f; (winding device) dévidoir m. ● vi chanceler. ● vt **∼ off** réciter.

refectory n réfectoire m.

refer vt/i (pt **referred**) **∼ to** (allude to) faire allusion à; (concern) s'appliquer à; (consult) consulter; (direct) renvoyer à.

referee n (Sport) arbitre m. ● vt (pt **refereed**) arbitrer.

reference n référence f; (mention) allusion f; (person) personne f pouvant fournir des références; **in** or **with ∼ to** en ce qui concerne; (Comm) suite à.

referendum n (pl **∼s**) référendum m.

refill¹ vt (glass) remplir à nouveau; (pen) recharger.

refill² n recharge f.

refine vt raffiner.

reflect vt refléter; (heat, light) renvoyer. ● vi réfléchir (**on** à); **∼ well/badly on sb** faire honneur/du tort à qn.

reflection n réflexion f; (image) reflet m; **on ∼** à la réflexion.

reflective adj (surface) réfléchissant; (person) réfléchi.

reflector n (on car) catadioptre m.

reflex a & n réflexe (m).

reflexive adj (Gram) réfléchi.

reform vt réformer. ● vi (person) s'amender. ● n réforme f.

refrain n refrain m. ● vi s'abstenir (**from** de).

refresh vt (drink) rafraîchir; (rest) reposer. **refreshments** npl rafraîchissements mpl.

refrigerate vt réfrigérer. **refrigerator** n réfrigérateur m.

refuel vt/i (pt **refuelled**) (se) ravitailler.

refuge n refuge m; **take ∼** se réfugier. **refugee** n réfugié/-e m/f.

refund¹ vt rembourser.

refund² n remboursement m.

refurbish vt remettre à neuf.

refuse¹ vt/i refuser.

refuse² n ordures fpl.

regain vt retrouver; (lost ground) regagner.

regard vt considérer; **as ∼s** en ce qui concerne. ● n égard m, estime f; **in this ∼** à cet égard; **∼s** amitiés fpl. **regarding** prep en ce qui concerne.

regardless adv malgré tout; **∼ of** sans tenir compte de.

regime n régime m.

regiment n régiment m.

region n région f; **in the ∼ of** environ.

register n registre m. ● vt (record) enregistrer; (vehicle) faire immatriculer; (birth) déclarer; (letter) recommander; (indicate) indiquer; (express) exprimer. ● vi (enrol) s'inscrire; (at hotel) se présenter; (fig) être compris.

registrar n officier m de l'état civil; (Univ) responsable m du bureau de la scolarité.

registration *n* (of voter, student) inscription *f*; (of birth) déclaration *f*; ~ **(number)** (Auto) numéro *m* d'immatriculation.

registry office *n* bureau *m* de l'état civil.

regret *n* regret *m*. ● *vt* (*pt* **regretted**) regretter (**to do** de faire). **regretfully** *adv* à regret.

regular *adj* régulier; (usual) habituel. ● *n* habitué/-e *m/f*. **regularity** *n* régularité *f*. **regularly** *adv* régulièrement.

regulate *vt* régler. **regulation** *n* (rule) règlement *m*; (process) réglementation *f*.

rehabilitate *vt* (in public esteem) réhabiliter; (prisoner) réinsérer.

rehearsal *n* répétition *f*. **rehearse** *vt/i* répéter.

reign *n* règne *m*. ● *vi* régner (**over** sur).

reimburse *vt* rembourser.

reindeer *n inv* renne *m*.

reinforce *vt* renforcer. **reinforcement** *n* renforcement *m*; ~**s** renforts *mpl*.

reinstate *vt* (*person*) réintégrer; (*law*) rétablir.

reject[1] *n* marchandise *f* de deuxième choix.

reject[2] *vt* (*offer, plea*) rejeter; (*goods*) refuser. **rejection** *n* (personal) rejet *m*; (of candidate, work) refus *m*.

rejoice *vi* se réjouir.

relapse *n* rechute *f*. ● *vi* rechuter; ~ **into** retomber dans.

relate *vt* raconter; (associate) associer. ● *vi* ~ **to** se rapporter à; (get on with) s'entendre avec. **related** *adj* (*ideas*) lié; **we are** ~**d** nous sommes parents.

relation *n* rapport *m*; (person) parent/-e *m/f*. **relationship** *n* relations *fpl*; (link) rapport *m*.

relative *n* parent/-e *m/f*. ● *adj* relatif; (respective) respectif.

relax *vt* (*grip*) relâcher; (*muscle*) décontracter; (*discipline*) assouplir. ● *vi* (*person*) se détendre; (*grip*) se relâcher. **relaxation** *n* détente *f*. **relaxing** *adj* délassant.

relay[1] *n* (also ~ **race**) course *f* de relais.

relay[2] *vt* relayer.

release *vt* (*prisoner*) libérer; (*fastening*) faire jouer; (*object, hand*) lâcher; (*film*) faire sortir; (*news*) publier. ● *n* libération *f*; (of film) sortie *f*; (new record, film) nouveauté *f*.

relevance *n* pertinence *f*, intérêt *m*.

relevant *adj* pertinent; **be** ~ **to** avoir rapport à.

reliability *n* (of firm) sérieux *m*; (of car) fiabilité *f*; (of person) honnêteté *f*. **reliable** *adj* (*firm*) sérieux; (*person, machine*) fiable.

reliance *n* dépendance *f*.

relic *n* vestige *m*; (object) relique *f*.

relief *n* soulagement *m* (**from** à); (assistance) secours *m*; (outline) relief *m*; ~ **road** route *f* de délestage.

relieve *vt* soulager; (help) secourir; (take over from) relayer.

religion *n* religion *f*. **religious** *adj* religieux.

relish *n* plaisir *m*; (Culin) condiment *m*. ● *vt* (*food*) savourer; (*idea*) se réjouir de.

relocate *vt* muter. ● *vi* (*company*) déménager; (*worker*) être muté.

reluctance *n* répugnance *f*.

reluctant *adj* (*person*) peu enthousiaste; (*consent*) accordé à contrecœur; ~ **to** peu disposé à. **reluctantly** *adv* à contrecœur.

rely *vi* ~ **on** (count) compter sur; (be dependent) dépendre de.

remain *vi* rester. **remainder** *n* reste *m*.

remand *vt* mettre en détention provisoire. ● *n* **on** ~ en détention provisoire.

remark *n* remarque *f*. ● *vt* remarquer. ● *vi* ~ **on** faire des remarques sur. **remarkable** *adj* remarquable.

remedy *n* remède *m*. ● *vt* remédier à.

remember *vt* se souvenir de, se rappeler; ~ **to do** ne pas oublier de faire. **remembrance** *n* souvenir *m*.

remind vt rappeler (**sb of sth** qch à qn); ∼ **sb to do** rappeler à qn de faire. **reminder** n rappel m.

reminisce vi évoquer ses souvenirs.

remission n (Med) rémission f; (Jur) remise f.

remnant n reste m; (trace) vestige m; (of cloth) coupon m.

remodel vt (pt **remodelled**) remodeler.

remorse n remords m.

remote adj (place, time) lointain; (person) distant; (slight) vague; ∼ **control** télécommande f.

removable adj amovible.

removal n (of employee) renvoi m; (of threat) suppression f; (of troops) retrait m; (of stain) détachage m; (from house) déménagement m; ∼ **men** déménageurs mpl.

remove vt enlever; (dismiss) renvoyer; (do away with) supprimer; (Comput) effacer.

remunerate vt rémunérer. **remuneration** n rémunération f.

render vt rendre.

renegade n renégat/-e m/f.

renew vt renouveler; (resume) reprendre. **renewable** adj renouvelable.

renounce vt renoncer à; (disown) renier.

renovate vt rénover.

renown n renommée f.

rent n loyer m. ● vt louer; **for** ∼ à louer. **rental** n prix m de location.

reopen vt/i rouvrir.

reorganize vt réorganiser.

rep n (Comm) représentant/-e m/f.

repair vt réparer. ● n réparation f; **in good/bad** ∼ en bon/mauvais état.

repatriate vt rapatrier. **repatriation** n rapatriement m.

repay vt (pt **repaid**) rembourser; (reward) récompenser. **repayment** n remboursement m.

repeal vt abroger. ● n abrogation f.

repeat vt/i répéter; (renew) renouveler; ∼ **itself**, ∼ **oneself** se répéter. ● n répétition f; (broadcast) reprise f.

repel vt (pt **repelled**) repousser.

repent vi se repentir (**of** de).

repercussion n répercussion f.

repetition n répétition f.

replace vt (put back) remettre; (take the place of) remplacer. **replacement** n remplacement m (**of** de); (person) remplaçant/-e m/f; (new part) pièce f de rechange.

replay n (Sport) match m rejoué; (recording) répétition f immédiate.

replenish vt (refill) remplir; (renew) renouveler.

replica n copie f exacte.

reply vt/i répondre. ● n réponse f.

report vt rapporter, annoncer (**that** que); (notify) signaler; (denounce) dénoncer. ● vi faire un rapport; ∼ **(on)** (news item) faire un reportage sur; ∼ **to** (go) se présenter chez. ● n rapport m; (in press) reportage m; (School) bulletin m. **reporter** n reporter m.

repossess vt reprendre.

represent vt représenter.

representation n représentation f; **make** ∼**s to** protester auprès de.

representative adj représentatif, typique (**of** de). ● n représentant/-e m/f.

repress vt réprimer.

reprieve n (delay) sursis m; (pardon) grâce f. ● vt accorder un sursis à; gracier.

reprimand vt réprimander. ● n réprimande f.

reprisals npl représailles fpl.

reproach vt reprocher (**sb for sth** qch à qn). ● n reproche m.

reproduce vt/i (se) reproduire. **reproduction** n reproduction f. **reproductive** adj reproducteur.

reptile n reptile m.

republic n république f. **republican** a & n républicain/-e (m/f).

repudiate vt répudier; (contract) refuser d'honorer.

reputable adj honorable, de bonne réputation.

reputation n réputation f.

repute n réputation f.

request n demande f. ● vt demander (**of, from** à).

require vt (of thing) demander; (of person) avoir besoin de; (demand, order) exiger. **required** adj requis. **requirement** n exigence f; (condition) condition f (requise).

rescue vt sauver. ● n sauvetage m (of de); (help) secours m.

research n recherche(s) f(pl). ● vt/i faire des recherches (sur). **researcher** n chercheur/-euse m/f.

resemblance n ressemblance f. **resemble** vt ressembler à.

resent vt être indigné de, s'offenser de. **resentment** n ressentiment m.

reservation n (doubt) réserve f; (booking) réservation f; (US) réserve f (indienne); **make a ~** réserver.

reserve vt réserver. ● n (stock, land) réserve f; (Sport) remplaçant/-e m/f; **in ~** en réserve; **the ~s** (Mil) les réserves fpl. **reserved** adj (person, room) réservé.

reshuffle vt (Pol) remanier. ● n (Pol) remaniement m (ministériel).

residence n résidence f; (of students) foyer m; **in ~** (doctor) résidant.

resident adj résidant; **be ~** résider. ● n habitant/-e m/f; (foreigner) résident/-e m/f; (in hotel) pensionnaire mf. **residential** adj résidentiel.

resign vt abandonner; (job) démissionner de. ● vi démissionner; **~ oneself to** se résigner à. **resignation** n résignation f; (from job) démission f. **resigned** adj résigné.

resilience n élasticité f; ressort m.

resin n résine f.

resist vt/i résister (à). **resistance** n résistance f. **resistant** adj (Med) rebelle; (metal) résistant.

resolution n résolution f.

resolve vt résoudre (**to do** de faire). ● n résolution f.

resort vi **~ to** avoir recours à. ● n (recourse) recours m; (place) station f; **in the last ~** en dernier ressort.

resource n ressource f; **~s** (wealth) ressources fpl. **resourceful** adj ingénieux.

respect n respect m; (aspect) égard m; **with ~ to** à l'égard de, relativement à. ● vt respecter.

respectability n respectabilité f. **respectable** adj respectable.

respectful adj respectueux.

respective adj respectif.

respite n répit m.

respond vi répondre (**to** à); **~ to** (react to) réagir à. **response** n réponse f.

responsibility n responsabilité f. **responsible** adj responsable; (job) qui comporte des responsabilités.

responsive adj réceptif.

rest vt/i (se) reposer; (lean) (s') appuyer (**on** sur); (be buried, lie) reposer; (remain) demeurer. ● n repos m; (support) support m; **have a ~** se reposer; **the ~** (remainder) le reste (**of** de); (other people) les autres.

restaurant n restaurant m.

restless adj agité.

restoration n rétablissement m; restauration f.

restore vt rétablir; (building) restaurer; **~ sth to sb** restituer qch à qn.

restrain vt contenir; **~ sb from** retenir qn de. **restrained** adj (moderate) mesuré; (in control of self) maître de soi.

restrict vt restreindre.

rest room n (US) toilettes fpl.

result n résultat m. ● vi résulter; **~ in** aboutir à.

resume vt/i reprendre.

résumé n résumé m; (of career: US) CV m, curriculum vitae m.

resurrect vt ressusciter.

resuscitate vt réanimer.

retail n détail m. ● a & adv au détail. ● vt/i (se) vendre (au détail). **retailer** n détaillant/-e m/f.

retain vt (hold back, remember) retenir; (keep) conserver.

retaliate vi riposter. **retaliation** n représailles fpl.

retch vi avoir un haut-le-cœur.

retire vi (from work) prendre sa retraite; (withdraw) se retirer; (go to bed) se coucher. **retired** adj retraité. **retirement** n retraite f.

retort vt/i répliquer. ● n réplique f.

retrace vt **~ one's steps** revenir sur ses pas.

r

retract *vt/i* (se) rétracter.

retrain *vt/i* (se) recycler.

retreat *vi* (Mil) battre en retraite. ● *n* retraite *f*.

retrieval *n* (Comput) extraction *f*. **retrieve** *vt* (*object*) récupérer; (*situation*) redresser; (*data*) extraire.

retrospect *n* in ~ rétrospectivement.

return *vi* (come back) revenir; (go back) retourner; (go home) rentrer. ● *vt* (give back) rendre; (bring back) rapporter; (send back) renvoyer; (put back) remettre. ● *n* retour *m*; (yield) rapport *m*; ~s (Comm) bénéfices *mpl*; in ~ for en échange de. ~ **ticket** *n* aller-retour *m*.

reunion *n* réunion *f*.

reunite *vt* réunir.

rev *n* (Auto 🔟) tour *m*. ● *vt/i* (*pt* **revved**) ~ (**up**) (engine 🔟) (s') emballer.

reveal *vt* révéler; (allow to appear) laisser voir.

revelation *n* révélation *f*.

revenge *n* vengeance *f*. ● *vt* venger.

revenue *n* revenu *m*.

reverberate *vi* (*sound, light*) se répercuter.

reverend *adj* révérend.

reversal *n* renversement *m*; (of view) revirement *m*.

reverse *adj* contraire, inverse. ● *n* contraire *m*; (back) revers *m*, envers *m*; (gear) marche *f* arrière. ● *vt* (*situation, bracket*) renverser; (*order*) inverser; (*decision*) annuler; ~ **the charges** appeler en PCV. ● *vi* (Auto) faire marche arrière.

review *n* (inspection, magazine) revue *f*; (of book) critique *f*. ● *vt* passer en revue; (situation) réexaminer; faire la critique de. **reviewer** *n* critique *m*.

revise *vt* réviser; (*text*) revoir. **revision** *n* révision *f*.

revival *n* (of economy) reprise *f*; (of interest) regain *m*.

revive *vt* (person, hopes) ranimer; (custom) rétablir. ● *vi* se ranimer.

revoke *vt* révoquer.

revolt *vt/i* (se) révolter. ● *n* révolte *f*. **revolting** *adj* dégoûtant.

revolution *n* révolution *f*.

revolve *vi* tourner.

revolver *n* revolver *m*.

revolving door *n* porte *f* à tambour.

reward *n* récompense *f*. ● *vt* récompenser (**for** de). **rewarding** *adj* rémunérateur; (worthwhile) qui (en) vaut la peine.

rewind *vt* (*pt* **rewound**) rembobiner.

rewire *vt* refaire l'installation électrique de.

rhetorical *adj* (de) rhétorique; (*question*) de pure forme.

rheumatism *n* rhumatisme *m*.

rhinoceros *n* (*pl* ~**es**) rhinocéros *m*.

rhubarb *n* rhubarbe *f*.

rhyme *n* rime *f*; (poem) vers *mpl*. ● *vt/i* (faire) rimer.

rhythm *n* rythme *m*. **rhythmic-(al)** *adj* rythmique.

rib *n* côte *f*.

ribbon *n* ruban *m*; in ~s en lambeaux.

rice *n* riz *m*. ~ **pudding** *n* riz *m* au lait.

rich *adj* riche.

rid *vt* (*pt* **rid**; *pres p* **ridding**) débarrasser (**of** de); **get** ~ **of** se débarrasser de.

ridden ⇒RIDE.

riddle *n* énigme *f*. ● *vt* ~ **with** (*bullets*) cribler de; (*mistakes*) bourrer de.

ride *vi* (*pt* **rode**; *pp* **ridden**) aller (à bicyclette, à cheval); (in car) rouler; (on a horse as sport) monter à cheval. ● *vt* (a particular horse) monter; (distance) parcourir. ● *n* promenade *f*, tour *m*; (distance) trajet *m*; **give sb a** ~ (US) prendre qn en voiture; **go for a** ~ aller faire un tour (à bicyclette, à cheval). **rider** *n* cavalier/-ière *m/f*; (in horse race) jockey *m*; (cyclist) cycliste *mf*; (motorcyclist) motocycliste *mf*.

ridge *n* arête *f*, crête *f*.

ridiculous *adj* ridicule.

riding *n* équitation *f*.

rifle *n* fusil *m*. ● *vt* (rob) dévaliser.

rift *n* (crack) fissure *f*; (between people) désaccord *m*.

rig vt (pt **rigged**) (equip) équiper; (election, match) truquer. ● n (for oil) derrick m. □ ～ **out** habiller; ～ **up** (arrange) arranger.

right adj (morally) bon; (fair) juste; (best) bon, qu'il faut; (not left) droit; **be** ～ (person) avoir raison (**to** de); (calculation, watch) être exact; **put** ～ arranger, rectifier. ● n (entitlement) droit m; (not left) droite f; (not evil) le bien; **be in the** ～ avoir raison; **on the** ～ à droite. ● vt (a wrong, sth fallen) redresser. ● adv (not left) à droite; (directly) tout droit; (exactly) bien, juste; (completely) tout (à fait); ～ **away** tout de suite; ～ **now** (at once) tout de suite; (at present) en ce moment.

righteous adj vertueux.

rightful adj légitime.

right-handed adj droitier.

rightly adv correctement; (with reason) à juste titre.

right of way n (Auto) priorité f.

right wing adj de droite.

rigid adj rigide.

rigorous adj rigoureux.

rim n bord m.

rind n (on cheese) croûte f; (on bacon) couenne f; (on fruit) écorce f.

ring[1] n (hoop) anneau m; (jewellery) bague f; (circle) cercle m; (boxing) ring m; (wedding) ～ alliance f. ● vt entourer; (word in text) entourer d'un cercle.

ring[2] vt/i (pt **rang**; pp **rung**) sonner; (of words) retentir; ～ the bell sonner. ● n sonnerie f; **give sb a** ～ donner un coup de fil à qn. □ ～ **back** rappeler; ～ **off** raccrocher; ～ **up** téléphoner (à).

ring road n périphérique m.

rink n patinoire f.

rinse vt rincer; ～ **out** rincer. ● n rinçage m.

riot n émeute f; (of colours) profusion f; **run** ～ se déchaîner. ● vi faire une émeute.

rip vt/i (pt **ripped**) (se) déchirer; **let** ～ (not check) laisser courir; ～ **off** ⊠ rouler. ● n déchirure f.

ripe adj mûr. **ripen** vt/i mûrir.

rip-off n ⊡ vol m; arnaque f ⊡.

ripple n ride f, ondulation f. ● vt/i (water) (se) rider.

rise vi (pt **rose**; pp **risen**) (go upwards, increase) monter, s'élever; (stand up, get up from bed) se lever; (rebel) se soulever; (sun) se lever; (water) monter; ～ **up** se soulever. ● n (slope) pente f; (increase) hausse f; (in pay) augmentation f; (progress, boom) essor m; **give** ～ **to** donner lieu à.

risk n risque m; **at** ～ menacé. ● vt risquer; ～ **doing** (venture) se risquer à faire. **risky** adj risqué.

rite n rite m; **last** ～s derniers sacrements mpl.

rival n rival/-e m/f. ● adj rival; (claim) opposé. ● vt (pt **rivalled**) rivaliser avec.

river n rivière f; (flowing into sea) fleuve m. ● adj (fishing, traffic) fluvial.

rivet n (bolt) rivet m. ● vt (pt **riveted**) river, riveter.

Riviera n the (French) ～ la Côte d'Azur.

road n route f; (in town) rue f; (small) chemin m; **the** ～ **to** (glory: fig) le chemin de. ● adj (sign, safety) routier. ～**-map** n carte f routière. ～ **rage** n violence f au volant. ～**worthy** adj en état de marche.

roam vi errer. ● vt (streets, seas) parcourir.

roar n hurlement m; (of lion, wind) rugissement m; (of lorry, thunder) grondement m. ● vt/i hurler; (lion, wind) rugir; (lorry, thunder) gronder; ～ **with laughter** rire aux éclats.

roast vt/i rôtir. ● n (meat) rôti m. ● adj rôti. ～ **beef** n rôti m de bœuf.

rob vt (pt **robbed**) voler (**sb of sth** qch à qn); (bank, house) dévaliser; (deprive) priver (**of** de). **robber** n voleur/-euse m/f. **robbery** n vol m.

robe n (of judge) robe f; (dressing-gown) peignoir m.

robin n rouge-gorge m.

robot n robot m.

robust adj robuste.

rock n roche f; (rock face, boulder) rocher m; (hurled stone) pierre f; (sweet) sucre m d'orge; (Mus) rock m;

r

on the ~s (*drink*) avec des glaçons; (*marriage*) en crise. ● *vt/i* (se) balancer; (*shake*) (faire) trembler; (*child*) bercer. ~**-climbing** *n* varappe *f*.

rocket *n* fusée *f*.

rocking-chair *n* fauteuil *m* à bascule.

rocky *adj* (**-ier, -iest**) (*ground*) rocailleux; (*hill*) rocheux; (shaky: fig) branlant.

rod *n* (metal) tige *f*; (wooden) baguette *f*; (for fishing) canne *f* à pêche.

rode ⇒RIDE.

roe *n* œufs *mpl* de poisson.

rogue *n* (dishonest) bandit *m*, voleur/-euse *m/f*; (mischievous) coquin/-e *m/f*.

role *n* rôle *m*.

roll *vt/i* rouler; ~ (**about**) (*child, dog*) se rouler; **be** ~**ing** (**in money**) 🇬🇧 rouler sur l'or. ● *n* rouleau *m*; (list) liste *f*; (bread) petit pain *m*; (of drum, thunder) roulement *m*; (of ship) roulis *m*. □ ~ **out** étendre; ~**over** se retourner; ~ **up** (*sleeves*) retrousser.

roll-call *n* appel *m*.

roller *n* rouleau *m*. ~**-coaster** *n* montagnes *fpl* russes. ~**-skate** *n* patin *m* à roulettes.

ROM (*abbr*) (**read-only memory**) mémoire *f* morte.

Roman *a & n* romain/-e (*m/f*). ~ **Catholic** *a & n* catholique (*mf*).

romance *n* (novel) roman *m* d'amour; (love) amour *m*; (affair) idylle *f*; (fig) poésie *f*.

Romania *n* Roumanie *f*.

Romanian *adj* roumain. ● *n* (person) Roumain/-e *m/f*; (language) roumain *m*.

romantic *adj* (*love*) romantique; (of the imagination) romanesque.

roof *n* toit *m*; (of mouth) palais *m*. ● *vt* recouvrir. ~**-rack** *n* galerie *f*. ~**-top** *n* toit *m*.

room *n* pièce *f*; (bedroom) chambre *f*; (large hall) salle *f*; (space) place *f*; ~ **for manoeuvre** marge *f* de manœuvre. ~**-mate** *n* camarade *mf* de chambre.

roomy *adj* spacieux; (*clothes*) ample.

root *n* racine *f*; (source) origine *f*; **take** ~ prendre racine. ● *vt/i* (s') enraciner. □ ~ **about** fouiller; ~ **for** (US 🇺🇸) encourager; ~ **out** extirper.

rope *n* corde *f*; **know the** ~**s** être au courant. ● *vt* attacher; ~ **in** (*person*) enrôler.

rose *n* rose *f*. ● *a* ⇒RISE.

rosé *n* rosé *m*.

rosy *adj* (**-ier, -iest**) rose; (hopeful) plein d'espoir.

rot *vt/i* (*pt* **rotted**) pourrir. ● *n* pourriture *f*.

rota *n* liste *f* (de service).

rotary *adj* rotatif.

rotate *vt/i* (faire) tourner; (change round) alterner.

rotten *adj* pourri; (*tooth*) gâté; (bad 🇺🇸) mauvais, sale.

rough *adj* (*manners*) rude; (to touch) rugueux; (*ground*) accidenté; (violent) brutal; (bad) mauvais; (*estimate*) approximatif. ● *adv* (live) à la dure; (*play*) brutalement.

roughage *n* fibres *fpl* (alimentaires).

roughly *adv* rudement; (approximately) à peu près.

round *adj* rond. ● *n* (circle) rond *m*; (slice) tranche *f*; (of visits, drinks) tournée *f*; (competition) partie *f*, manche *f*; (boxing) round *m*; (of talks) série *f*; ~ **of applause** applaudissements *mpl*; **go the** ~**s** circuler. ● *prep* autour de; **she lives** ~ **here** elle habite par ici; ~ **the clock** vingt-quatre heures sur vingt-quatre. ● *adv* autour; ~ **about** (nearby) par ici; (fig) à peu près; **go** *or* **come** ~ **to** (*a friend*) passer chez; **enough to go** ~ assez pour tout le monde. ● *vt* (*object*) arrondir; (*corner*) tourner. □ ~ **off** terminer; ~ **up** rassembler

roundabout *n* (in fairground) manège *m*; (for traffic) rond-point *m* (*à sens giratoire*). ● *adj* indirect.

round trip *n* voyage *m* aller-retour.

round-up *n* rassemblement *m*; (of suspects) rafle *f*.

route *n* itinéraire *m*, parcours *m*; (Naut, Aviat) route *f*.

routine *n* routine *f*. ● *adj* de routine.

row¹ *n* rangée *f*, rang *m*; **in a ~** (consecutive) consécutif. ● *vi* ramer; (Sport) faire de l'aviron. ● *vt* **~ a boat up the river** remonter la rivière à la rame.

row² *n* (noise 🔲) tapage *m*; (quarrel 🔲) dispute *f*. ● *vi* 🔲 se disputer.

rowdy *adj* (**-ier, -iest**) tapageur.

rowing *n* aviron *m*. **~-boat** *n* bateau *m* à rames.

royal *adj* royal. **royalty** *n* famille *f* royale; **royalties** droits *mpl* d'auteur.

rub *vt/i* (*pt* **rubbed**) frotter; **~ it in** insister, en rajouter. ● *n* friction *f*. □ **~ out** (s')effacer.

rubber *n* caoutchouc *m*; (eraser) gomme *f*. **~ band** *n* élastique *m*. **~ stamp** *n* tampon *m*.

rubbish *n* (refuse) ordures *fpl*; (junk) saletés *fpl*; (fig) bêtises *fpl*.

rubble *n* décombres *mpl*.

ruby *n* rubis *m*.

rucksack *n* sac *m* à dos.

rude *adj* impoli, grossier; (improper) indécent; (*blow*) brutal.

ruffle *vt* (*hair*) ébouriffer; (*clothes*) froisser; (*person*) contrarier. ● *n* (frill) ruche *f*.

rug *n* petit tapis *m*.

rugby *n* rugby *m*.

rugged *adj* (*surface*) rude, rugueux; (*ground*) accidenté; (*character, features*) rude.

ruin *n* ruine *f*. ● *vt* (destroy) ruiner; (damage) abîmer; (spoil) gâter.

rule *n* règle *f*; (regulation) règlement *m*; (Pol) gouvernement *m*; **as a ~** en règle générale. ● *vt* gouverner; (master) dominer; (decide) décider; **~ out** exclure. ● *vi* régner. **ruler** *n* dirigeant/-e *m/f*, gouvernant *m*; (measure) règle *f*.

ruling *adj* (*class*) dirigeant; (*party*) au pouvoir. ● *n* décision *f*.

rum *n* rhum *m*.

rumble *vi* gronder; (*stomach*) gargouiller. ● *n* grondement *m*; gargouillement *m*.

rumour, (US) **rumor** *n* bruit *m*, rumeur *f*; **there's a ~ that** le bruit court que.

rump *n* (of animal) croupe *f*; (of bird) croupion *m*; (steak) romsteck *m*.

run *vi* (*pt* **ran**; *pp* **run**; *pres p* **running**) courir; (flow) couler; (pass) passer; (function) marcher; (melt) fondre; (extend) s'étendre; (of bus) circuler; (of play) se jouer; (last) durer; (of colour in washing) déteindre; (in election) être candidat. ● *vt* (manage) diriger; (*event*) organiser; (*risk, race*) courir; (*house*) tenir; (*temperature, errand*) faire; (Comput) exécuter. ● *n* course *f*; (journey) parcours *m*; (outing) promenade *f*; (rush) ruée *f*; (series) série *f*; (for chickens) enclos *m*; (in cricket) point *m*; **in the long ~** avec le temps; **on the ~** en fuite. □ **~ across** rencontrer par hasard; **~ away** s'enfuir; **~ down** descendre en courant; (of vehicle) renverser; (*production*) réduire progressivement; (belittle) dénigrer; **~ into** (hit) heurter; **~ off** (*copies*) tirer; **~ out** (be used up) s'épuiser; (of lease) expirer; **~ out of** manquer de; **~ over** (of vehicle) écraser; (*details*) revoir; **~ through** regarder qch rapidement; **~ sth through sth** passer qch à travers qch; **~ up** (*bill*) accumuler.

runaway *n* fugitif/-ive *m/f*. ● *adj* fugitif; (*horse, vehicle*) fou; (*inflation*) galopant.

rung →RING². ● *n* (of ladder) barreau *m*.

runner *n* coureur/-euse *m/f*. **~ bean** *n* haricot *m* d'Espagne. **~-up** *n* second/-e *m/f*.

running *n* course *f* à pied; (of business) gestion *f*; (of machine) marche *f*; **be in the ~ for** être sur les rangs pour. ● *adj* (*commentary*) suivi; (*water*) courant; **four days ~** quatre jours de suite.

runway *n* piste *f*.

rural *adj* rural.

rush *vi* (move) se précipiter; (be in a hurry) se dépêcher. ● *vt* (*person*) bousculer; (Mil) prendre d'assaut; **~ to** envoyer d'urgence à. ● *n* ruée *f*; (haste) bousculade *f*; (plant) jonc *m*; **in a ~** pressé. **~-hour** *n* heure *f* de pointe.

Russia *n* Russie *f*.

r

Russian *adj* russe. ● *n* (person)
Russe *mf*; (language) russe.

rust *n* rouille *f*. ● *vt/i* rouiller.

rustle *vt/i* (*papers*) froisser.

rusty *adj* rouillé.

ruthless *adj* impitoyable.

rye *n* seigle *m*.

Ss

sabbath *n* (Jewish) sabbat *m*;
(Christian) jour *m* du seigneur.

sabbatical *adj* (Univ) sabbatique.

sabotage *n* sabotage *m*. ● *vt*
saboter.

saccharin *n* saccharine *f*.

sack *n* (bag) sac *m*; **get the ~** 🔲 être
renvoyé. ● *vt* 🔲 renvoyer; (plunder)
saccager. **sacking** *n* (cloth) toile *f* à
sac; (dismissal 🔲) renvoi *m*.

sacrament *n* sacrement *m*.

sacred *adj* sacré.

sacrifice *n* sacrifice *m*. ● *vt*
sacrifier.

sad *adj* (**sadder**, **saddest**) triste.

saddle *n* selle *f*. ● *vt* (*horse*) seller.

sadist *n* sadique *mf*. **sadistic** *adj*
sadique.

sadly *adv* tristement; (unfortunately)
malheureusement.

sadness *n* tristesse *f*.

safe *adj* (not dangerous) sans danger;
(reliable) sûr; (out of danger) en
sécurité; (after accident) sain et sauf; **~
from** à l'abri de. ● *n* coffre-fort *m*.

safeguard *n* sauvegarde *f*. ● *vt*
sauvegarder.

safely *adv* sans danger; (in safe place)
en sûreté.

safety *n* sécurité *f*. **~-belt** *n*
ceinture *f* de sécurité. **~-pin** *n*
épingle *f* de sûreté. **~-valve** *n*
soupape *f* de sûreté.

saffron *n* safran *m*.

sag *vi* (*pt* **sagged**) (*beam, mattress*)
s'affaisser; (*flesh*) être flasque.

sage *n* (herb) sauge *f*.

Sagittarius *n* Sagittaire *m*.

said ⇒SAY.

sail *n* voile *f*; (journey) tour *m* en
bateau. ● *vi* (*person*) voyager en
bateau; (as sport) faire de la voile; (set
off) prendre la mer; **~ across**
traverser. ● *vt* (*boat*) piloter; (*sea*)
traverser. **sailing-boat**, **sailing-
ship** *n* voilier *m*.

sailor *n* marin *m*.

saint *n* saint/-e *m/f*.

sake *n* **for the ~ of** pour.

salad *n* salade *f*.

salaried *adj* salarié.

salary *n* salaire *m*.

sale *n* vente *f*; **for ~** à vendre; **on ~**
en vente; (reduced) en solde; **~s**
(reductions) soldes *mpl*; **~ assistant**,
(US) **~ clerk** vendeur/-euse *m/f*.

salesman *n* (*pl* **-men**) (in shop)
vendeur *m*; (traveller) représentant *m*.

saline *adj* salin. ● *n* sérum *m*
physiologique.

saliva *n* salive *f*.

salmon *n* *inv* saumon *m*.

salon *n* salon *m*.

saloon *n* (on ship) salon *m*; **~** (**car**)
berline *f*.

salt *n* sel *m*. ● *vt* saler. **salty** *adj*
salé.

salutary *adj* salutaire.

salute *n* salut *m*. ● *vt* saluer. ● *vi*
faire un salut.

salvage *n* sauvetage *m*; (of waste)
récupération *f*. ● *vt* sauver; (for re-
use) récupérer.

same *adj* même (as que). ● *pron* the
~ le même, la même, les mêmes; **at
the ~ time** en même temps; **the ~**
(thing) la même chose.

sample *n* échantillon *m*; (of blood)
prélèvement *m*. ● *vt* essayer; (*food*)
goûter.

sanctimonious *adj* (pej)
supérieur.

sanction *n* sanction *f*. ● *vt*
sanctionner.

sanctity *n* sainteté *f*.

sanctuary *n* (safe place) refuge *m*;
(Relig) sanctuaire *m*; (for animals)
réserve *f*.

sand *n* sable *m*; **~s** (beach) plage *f*.

sandal *n* sandale *f*.

sandpaper *n* papier *m* de verre.
● *vt* poncer.

sandpit *n* bac *m* à sable.

sandwich *n* sandwich *m*; ∼ **course**
cours *m* avec stage pratique.

sandy *adj* (*beach*) de sable; (*soil*)
sablonneux; (*hair*) blond roux *inv*.

sane *adj* (*view*) sensé; (*person*) sain
d'esprit.

sang ⇒SING.

sanitary *adj* (clean) hygiénique;
(*system*) sanitaire; ∼ **towel** serviette
f hygiénique.

sanitation *n* installations *fpl*
sanitaires.

sanity *n* équilibre *m* mental; (sense)
bon sens *m*.

sank ⇒SINK.

Santa (**Claus**) *n* le père Noël.

sapphire *n* saphir *m*.

sarcasm *n* sarcasme *m*. **sarcastic**
adj sarcastique.

sash *n* (on uniform) écharpe *f*; (on dress)
ceinture *f*.

sat ⇒SIT.

satchel *n* cartable *m*.

satellite *n* & *a* satellite (*m*); ∼ **dish**
antenne *f* parabolique.

satire *n* satire *f*. **satirical** *adj*
satirique.

satisfaction *n* satisfaction *f*.

satisfactory *adj* satisfaisant.

satisfy *vt* satisfaire; (convince)
convaincre.

saturate *vt* saturer. **saturated** *adj*
(wet) trempé.

Saturday *n* samedi *m*.

sauce *n* sauce *f*.

saucepan *n* casserole *f*.

saucer *n* soucoupe *f*.

Saudi Arabia *n* Arabie *f* saoudite.

sausage *n* (for cooking) saucisse *f*;
(ready to eat) saucisson *m*.

savage *adj* (*blow, temper*) violent;
(*attack*) sauvage. ● *n* sauvage *mf*.
● *vt* attaquer sauvagement.

save *vt* sauver; (*money*) économiser;
(*time*) gagner; (keep) garder; ∼ (**sb**)
doing sth éviter (à qn) de faire qch.
● *n* (football) arrêt *m*. **saver** *n*
épargnant/-e *m/f*. **saving** *n*
économie *f*. **savings** *npl* économies
fpl.

saviour, (US) **savior** *n* sauveur *m*.

savour, (US) **savor** *n* saveur *f*. ● *vt*
savourer. **savoury** *adj* (tasty)
savoureux; (Culin) salé.

saw ⇒SEE. ● *n* scie *f*. ● *vt* (*pt*
sawed; *pp* **sawn** *or* **sawed**) scier.

sawdust *n* sciure *f*.

saxophone *n* saxophone *m*.

say *vt/i* (*pt* **said**) dire; (*prayer*) faire.
● *n* **have a** ∼ dire son mot; (in
decision) avoir voix au chapitre.
saying *n* proverbe *m*.

scab *n* croûte *f*.

scaffolding *n* échafaudage *m*.

scald *vt* (injure, cleanse) ébouillanter.
● *n* brûlure *f*.

scale *n* (for measuring) échelle *f*;
(extent) étendue *f*; (Mus) gamme *f*; (on
fish) écaille *f*; **on a small** ∼ sur une
petite échelle; ∼ **model** maquette *f*.
● *vt* (climb) escalader; ∼ **down**
réduire. **scales** *npl* (for weighing)
balance *f*.

scallop *n* coquille *f* Saint-Jacques.

scalp *n* cuir *m* chevelu.

scampi *npl* (fresh) langoustines *fpl*;
(breaded) scampi *mpl*.

scan *vt* (*pt* **scanned**) scruter;
(quickly) parcourir. ● *n* (ultrasound)
échographie *f*; (CAT) scanner *m*.

scandal *n* scandale *m*; (gossip)
potins *mpl* 𝕀.

Scandinavia *n* Scandinavie *f*.

scanty *adj* (**-ier**, **-iest**) maigre;
(*clothing*) minuscule.

scapegoat *n* bouc *m* émissaire.

scar *n* cicatrice *f*. ● *vt* (*pt* **scarred**)
marquer.

scarce *adj* rare. **scarcely** *adv* à
peine.

scare *vt* faire peur à; **be** ∼**d** avoir
peur. ● *n* peur *f*; **bomb** ∼ alerte *f* à
la bombe. **scarecrow** *n*
épouvantail *m*.

scarf *n* (*pl* **scarves**) écharpe *f*; (over
head) foulard *m*.

scarlet *adj* écarlate; ∼ **fever**
scarlatine *f*.

scary *adj* (**-ier**, **-iest**) 𝕀 qui fait
peur.

scathing *adj* cinglant.

S

scatter *vt* (throw) éparpiller, répandre; (disperse) disperser. ● *vi* se disperser.

scavenge *vi* fouiller (dans les ordures). **scavenger** *n* (animal) charognard *m*.

scene *n* scène *f*; (of accident, crime) lieu *m*; (sight) spectacle *m*; **behind the** ∼**s** en coulisse. **scenery** *n* paysage *m*; (Theat) décors *mpl*. **scenic** *adj* panoramique.

scent *n* (perfume) parfum *m*; (trail) piste *f*. ● *vt* flairer; (make fragrant) parfumer.

sceptic *n* sceptique *mf*. **sceptical** *adj* sceptique. **scepticism** *n* scepticisme *m*.

schedule *n* horaire *m*; (for job) planning *m*; **behind** ∼ en retard; **on** ∼ dans les temps. ● *vt* prévoir; ∼**d** **flight** vol *m* régulier.

scheme *n* projet *m*; (dishonest) combine *f*; **pension** ∼ plan *m* de retraite. ● *vi* comploter.

schizophrenic *a* & *n* schizophrène (*mf*).

scholar *n* érudit/-e *m/f*.

school *n* école *f*; **go to** ∼ aller à l'école. ● *adj* (*age, year, holidays*) scolaire. ∼**boy** *n* élève *m*. ∼**girl** *n* élève *f*. **schooling** *n* scolarité *f*. ∼**teacher** *n* (primary) instituteur/ -trice *m/f*; (secondary) professeur *m*.

science *n* science *f*; **teach** ∼ enseigner les sciences. **scientific** *adj* scientifique. **scientist** *n* scientifique *mf*.

scissors *npl* ciseaux *mpl*.

scold *vt* gronder.

scoop *n* (shovel) pelle *f*; (measure) mesure *f*; (for ice cream) cuillère *f* à glace; (news) exclusivité *f*.

scooter *n* (child's) trottinette *f*; (motor cycle) scooter *m*.

scope *n* étendue *f*; (competence) compétence *f*; (opportunity) possibilité *f*.

scorch *vt* brûler; (*iron*) roussir.

score *n* score *m*; (Mus) partition *f*; **on that** ∼ à cet égard. ● *vt* marquer; (*success*) remporter. ● *vi* marquer un point; (football) marquer un but; (keep score) marquer les points. **scorer** *n* (Sport) marqueur *m*.

scorn *n* mépris *m*. ● *vt* mépriser.

Scorpio *n* Scorpion *m*.

Scot *n* Écossais/-e *m/f*.

Scotland *n* Écosse *f*.

Scottish *adj* écossais.

scoundrel *n* gredin *m*.

scour *vt* (*pan*) récurer; (search) parcourir. **scourer** *n* tampon *m* à récurer.

scourge *n* fléau *m*.

scout *n* éclaireur *m*. ● *vi* ∼ **around for** rechercher.

scowl *n* air *m* renfrogné. ● *vi* prendre un air renfrogné.

scramble *vi* (clamber) grimper. ● *vt* (*eggs*) brouiller. ● *n* (rush) course *f*.

scrap *n* petit morceau *m*; ∼**s** (of metal, fabric) déchets *mpl*; (of food) restes *mpl*; (fight [I]) bagarre *f*. ● *vt* (*pt* **scrapped**) abandonner; (*car*) détruire.

scrape *vt* gratter; (damage) érafler. ● *vi* ∼ **against** érafler. ● *n* raclement *m*. □ ∼ **through** réussir de justesse.

scrap: ∼-**paper** *n* papier *m* brouillon. ∼ **yard** *n* casse *f*.

scratch *vt/i* (se) gratter; (with claw, nail) griffer; (graze) érafler; (mark) rayer. ● *n* (on body) égratignure *f*; (on surface) éraflure *f*; **start from** ∼ partir de zéro; **up to** ∼ à la hauteur. ∼ **card** *n* jeu *m* de grattage.

scrawl *n* gribouillage *m*. ● *vt/i* gribouiller.

scrawny *adj* (-**ier**, -**iest**) décharné.

scream *vt/i* crier. ● *n* cri *m* (perçant).

screech *vi* (scream) hurler; (*tyres*) crisser. ● *n* cri *m* strident; (of tyres) crissement *m*.

screen *n* écran *m*; (folding) paravent *m*. ● *vt* masquer; (protect) protéger; (*film*) projeter; (*candidates*) filtrer; (Med) faire subir un test de dépistage. **screening** *n* (cinema) projection *f*; (Med) dépistage *m*.

screen: ∼**play** *n* scénario *m*. ∼ **saver** *n* protecteur *m* d'écran.

screw *n* vis *f*. ● *vt* visser; ∼ **up** (*eyes*) plisser; (ruin [I]) cafouiller [I]. ∼**driver** *n* tournevis *m*.

scribble *vt/i* griffonner. ● *n* griffonnage *m*.

script n script m; (of play) texte m.

scroll n rouleau m. ● vt/i (Comput) (faire) défiler.

scrounge ⚇ vt (favour) quémander; (cigarette) piquer ⚇; ~ **money from sb** taper de l'argent à qn. ● vi ~ **off sb** vivre sur le dos de qn.

scrub n (land) broussailles fpl. ● vt/i (pt **scrubbed**) nettoyer (à la brosse), frotter.

scruffy adj (-ier, -iest) ⚇ dépenaillé.

scrum n (rugby) mêlée f.

scruple n scrupule m.

scrutinize vt scruter. **scrutiny** n examen m minutieux.

scuba-diving n plongée f sous-marine.

scuffle n bagarre f.

sculpt vt/i sculpter. **sculptor** n sculpteur m.

sculpture n sculpture f.

scum n (on liquid) mousse f; (people: pej) racaille f.

scurry vi se précipiter, courir (for pour chercher); ~ **off** se sauver.

sea n mer f; **at** ~ en mer; **by** ~ par mer. ● adj (air) marin; (bird) de mer; (voyage) par mer. ~**food** n fruits mpl de mer. ~**gull** n mouette f.

seal n (animal) phoque m; (insignia) sceau m; (with wax) cachet m. ● vt sceller; cacheter; (stick down) coller. □ ~ **off** (area) boucler.

seam n (in cloth) couture f; (of coal) veine f.

search vt/i (examine) fouiller; (seek) chercher; (study) examiner; (Comput) rechercher. ● n fouille f; (quest) recherches fpl; (Comput) recherche f; **in** ~ **of** à la recherche de. ~ **engine** n (Internet) moteur m de recherche. ~**light** n projecteur m. ~**warrant** n mandat m de perquisition.

sea: ~**shell** n coquillage m. ~**shore** n (coast) littoral m; (beach) plage f.

seasick adj **be** ~ avoir le mal de mer.

seaside n bord m de la mer.

season n saison f; ~ **ticket** carte f d'abonnement. ● vt assaisonner.

seasonal adj saisonnier.

seasoning n assaisonnement m.

seat n siège m; (place) place f; (of trousers) fond m; **take a** ~ asseyez-vous. ● vt (put) placer; **the room** ~**s 30** la salle peut accueillir 30 personnes. ~**-belt** n ceinture f (de sécurité).

seaweed n algue f marine.

secluded adj retiré.

seclusion n isolement m.

second¹ adj deuxième, second; **a** ~ **chance** une nouvelle chance; **have** ~ **thoughts** avoir des doutes. ● n deuxième mf, second/-e m/f; (unit of time) seconde f; ~**s** (food) rab m ⚇. ● adv (in race) deuxième; (secondly) deuxièmement. ● vt (proposal) appuyer.

second² vt (transfer) détacher (**to** à).

secondary adj secondaire; ~ **school** lycée m, école f secondaire.

second-best n pis-aller m.

second-class adj (Rail) de deuxième classe; (post) au tarif lent.

second hand n (on clock) trotteuse f.

second-hand a & adv (article) d'occasion; (information) de seconde main.

secondly adv deuxièmement.

second-rate adj médiocre.

secrecy n secret m.

secret adj secret. ● n secret m; **in** ~ en secret.

secretarial adj (work) de secrétaire.

secretary n secrétaire mf; **S**~ **of State** ministre m; (US) ministre m des Affaires étrangères.

secrete vt (Med) sécréter; (hide) cacher.

secretive adj secret. **secretly** adv secrètement.

sect n secte f. **sectarian** adj sectaire.

section n partie f; (in store) rayon m; (of newspaper) rubrique f; (of book) passage m.

sector n secteur m.

secular adj (*school*) laïque; (*art, music*) profane.

secure adj (*safe*) sûr; (*job, marriage*) stable; (*knot, lock*) solide; (*window*) bien fermé; (*feeling*) de sécurité; (*person*) sécurisé. ● vt attacher; (obtain) s'assurer; (ensure) assurer.

security n (safety) sécurité f; (for loan) caution f; ~ **guard** vigile m.

sedate adj calme. ● vt donner un sédatif à. **sedative** n sédatif m.

seduce vt séduire. **seducer** n séducteur/-trice m/f. **seduction** n séduction f. **seductive** adj séduisant.

see vt/i (pt **saw**; pp **seen**) voir; see you (soon)! à bientôt!; ~ing that vu que. □ ~ out (*person*) raccompagner à la porte; ~ through (*deception*) déceler; (*person*) percer à jour; ~ sth through mener qch à bonne fin; ~ to s'occuper de; ~ to it that veiller à ce que.

seed n graine f; (collectively) graines fpl; (origin: fig) germe m; (tennis) tête f de série. **seedling** n plant m.

seek vt (pt **sought**) chercher.

seem vi sembler; he ~s to think il a l'air de croire.

seen ⇒SEE.

seep vi suinter; ~ into s'infiltrer dans.

see-saw n tapecul m. ● vt osciller.

seethe vi ~ with (*anger*) bouillir de; (*people*) grouiller de.

segment n segment m; (of orange) quartier m.

segregate vt séparer.

seize vt saisir; (*territory, prisoner*) s'emparer de. ● vi ~ on (*chance*) saisir; ~ up (*engine*) se gripper.

seizure n (Med) crise f.

seldom adv rarement.

select vt sélectionner. ● adj privilégié. **selection** n sélection f. **selective** adj sélectif.

self n (pl **selves**) moi m; (on cheque) moi-même. ~**-assured** adj plein d'assurance. ~**-catering** adj (*holiday*) en location. ~**-centred**, (US) ~**-centered** adj égocentrique. ~**-confident** adj sûr de soi. ~**-conscious** adj timide.

~**-contained** adj (*flat*) indépendant. ~**-control** n sang-froid m. ~**-defence** n autodéfense f; (Jur) légitime défense f. ~**-employed** adj qui travaille à son compte. ~**-esteem** n amour-propre m. ~**-governing** adj autonome. ~**-indulgent** adj complaisant. ~**-interest** n intérêt m personnel.

selfish adj égoïste.

selfless adj désintéressé.

self: ~**-portrait** n autoportrait m. ~**-reliant** adj autosuffisant. ~**-respect** n respect m de soi. ~**-righteous** adj satisfait de soi. ~**-sacrifice** n abnégation f. ~**-satisfied** adj satisfait de soi. ~**-seeking** adj égoïste. ~**-service** n & a libre-service (m).

sell vt/i (pt **sold**) vendre; ~ well se vendre bien. □ ~ off liquider; ~ out (*items*) se vendre; have sold out avoir tout vendu.

Sellotape® n scotch® m.

sell-out n (betrayal) ⊡ revirement m; be a ~ (*show*) afficher complet.

semester n (Univ) semestre m.

semicircle n demi-cercle m.

semicolon n point-virgule m.

semi-detached adj ~ house maison f jumelée.

semifinal n demi-finale f.

seminar n séminaire m.

semolina n semoule f.

senate n sénat m. **senator** n sénateur m.

send vt/i (pt **sent**) envoyer. □ ~ away (dismiss) renvoyer; ~ (away or off) for commander (par la poste); ~ back renvoyer; ~ for (*person, help*) envoyer chercher; ~ up ⊡ parodier.

senile adj sénile.

senior adj plus âgé (to que); (in rank) haut placé; be ~ to sb être le supérieur de qn. ● n aîné/-e m/f. ~ **citizen** n personne f âgée. ~ **school** n lycée m.

sensation n sensation f. **sensational** adj sensationnel.

sense n sens m; (mental impression) sentiment m; (common sense) bon sens m; ~s (mind) raison f; there's no ~ in doing cela ne sert à rien de faire;

make ~ avoir un sens; **make** ~ **of** comprendre. ● *vt* (pres)sentir.

senseless *adj* insensé; (Med) sans connaissance.

sensible *adj* raisonnable; (*clothing*) pratique.

sensitive *adj* sensible (**to** à); (*issue*) difficile.

sensory *adj* sensoriel.

sensual *adj* sensuel. **sensuality** *n* sensualité *f*.

sensuous *adj* sensuel.

sent ⇨SEND.

sentence *n* phrase *f*; (punishment: Jur) peine *f*. ● *vt* ~ **to** condamner à.

sentiment *n* sentiment *m*. **sentimental** *adj* sentimental.

sentry *n* sentinelle *f*.

separate¹ *adj* (*piece*) à part; (*issue*) autre; (*sections*) différent; (*organizations*) distinct.

separate² *vt/i* (se) séparer.

separately *adv* séparément.

separation *n* séparation *f*.

September *n* septembre *m*.

septic *adj* (*wound*) infecté; ~ **tank** fosse *f* septique.

sequel *n* suite *f*.

sequence *n* (order) ordre *m*; (series) suite *f*; (in film) séquence *f*.

Serb *adj* serbe. ● *n* (person) Serbe *mf*; (Ling) serbe *m*.

Serbia *n* Serbie *f*.

sergeant *n* (Mil) sergent *m*; (policeman) brigadier *m*.

serial *n* feuilleton *m*. ● *adj* (Comput) série *inv*.

series *n* *inv* série *f*.

serious *adj* sérieux; (*accident, crime*) grave.

seriously *adv* sérieusement; (*ill*) gravement; **take** ~ prendre au sérieux.

sermon *n* sermon *m*.

serpent *n* serpent *m*.

serrated *adj* dentelé.

serum *n* sérum *m*.

servant *n* domestique *mf*.

serve *vt/i* servir; faire; (*transport, hospital*) desservir; ~ **as/to** servir de/à; ~ **a purpose** être utile; ~ **a sentence** (Jur) purger une peine. ● *n* (tennis) service *m*.

server *n* serveur *m*; **remote** ~ téléserveur *m*.

service *n* service *m*; (maintenance) révision *f*; (Relig) office *m*; ~**s** (Mil) forces *fpl* armées. ● *vt* (car) réviser. ~ **area** *n* (Auto) aire *f* de services. ~ **charge** *n* service *m*. ~ **station** *n* station-service *f*.

session *n* séance *f*; **be in** ~ (Jur) tenir séance.

set *vt* (*pt* **set**; *pres p* **setting**) placer; (*table*) mettre; (*limit*) fixer; (*clock*) mettre à l'heure; (*example, task*) donner; (TV, cinema) situer; ~ **fire to** mettre le feu à; ~ **free** libérer; ~ **to music** mettre en musique. ● *vi* (*sun*) se coucher; (*jelly*) prendre; ~ **sail** partir. ● *n* (of chairs, stamps) série *f*; (of knives, keys) jeu *m*; (of people) groupe *m*; (TV, radio) poste *m*; (Theat) décor *m*; (tennis) set *m*; (mathematics) ensemble *m*. ● *adj* (time, price) fixe; (*procedure*) bien determiné; (*meal*) à prix fixe; (*book*) au programme; ~ **against sth** opposé à; **be** ~ **on doing** tenir absolument à faire. □ ~ **about** se mettre à; ~ **back** (delay) retarder; (cost 🔢) coûter; ~ **in** (take hold) s'installer, commencer; ~ **off** *or* **out** partir; ~ **off** (*panic, riot*) déclencher; (*bomb*) faire exploser; ~ **out** (state) présenter; (arrange) disposer; ~ **out to do sth** chercher à faire qch; ~ **up** (*stall*) monter; (*equipment*) assembler; (*experiment*) préparer; (*company*) créer; (*meeting*) organiser. ~**-back** *n* revers *m*.

settee *n* canapé *m*.

setting *n* cadre *m*; (on dial) position *f*.

settle *vt* (arrange, pay) régler; (*date*) fixer; (*nerves*) calmer. ● *vi* (come to rest) (*bird*) se poser; (*dust*) se déposer; (live) s'installer. □ ~ **down** se calmer; (marry etc.) se ranger; ~ **for** accepter; ~ **in** s'installer; ~ **up** (**with**) régler.

settlement *n* règlement *m* (of de); (agreement) accord *m*; (place) colonie *f*.

settler *n* colon *m*.

seven *a* & *n* sept (*m*).

seventeen *a* & *n* dix-sept (*m*).

seventh *a* & *n* septième (*mf*).

seventy *a* & *n* soixante-dix (*m*).

S

sever *vt* (cut) couper; (*relations*) rompre.

several *a & pron* plusieurs; ~ **of us** plusieurs d'entre nous.

severe *adj* (harsh) sévère; (serious) grave.

sew *vt/i* (*pt* **sewed**; *pp* **sewn** or **sewed**) coudre.

sewage *n* eaux *fpl* usées.

sewer *n* égout *m*.

sewing *n* couture *f*. ~**-machine** *n* machine *f* à coudre.

sewn ⇒SEW.

sex *n* sexe *m*; **have** ~ avoir des rapports (sexuels). ● *adj* sexuel. **sexist** *a & n* sexiste (*mf*). **sexual** *adj* sexuel.

shabby *adj* (**-ier**, **-iest**) (*place, object*) miteux; (*person*) habillé de façon miteuse; (*treatment*) mesquin.

shack *n* cabane *f*.

shade *n* ombre *f*; (of colour, opinion) nuance *f*; (for lamp) abat-jour *m inv*; a ~ **bigger** légèrement plus grand. ● *vt* (*tree*) ombrager; (*hat*) projeter une ombre sur.

shadow *n* ombre *f*. ● *vt* (follow) filer. **S~ Cabinet** *n* cabinet *m* fantôme.

shady *adj* (**-ier**, **-iest**) ombragé; (dubious) véreux.

shaft *n* (of tool) manche *m*; (of arrow) tige *f*; (in machine) axe *m*; (of mine) puits *m*; (of light) rayon *m*.

shake *vt* (*pt* **shook**; *pp* **shaken**) secouer; (*bottle*) agiter; (*belief*) ébranler; ~ **hands with** serrer la main à; ~ **one's head** dire non de la tête. ● *vi* trembler. ● *n* secousse *f*; **give sth a** ~ secouer qch. □ ~ **off** se débarrasser de. ~**-up** *n* (Pol) remaniement *m*.

shaky *adj* (**-ier**, **-iest**) (*hand, voice*) tremblant; (*ladder*) branlant; (weak: fig) instable.

shall *v aux* **I** ~ **do** je ferai; **we** ~ **see** nous verrons; ~ **we go**...? si on allait...?

shallow *adj* peu profond; (fig) superficiel.

shame *n* honte *f*; **it's a** ~ c'est dommage. ● *vt* faire honte à.

shampoo *n* shampooing *m*. ● *vt* faire un shampooing à.

shandy *n* panaché *m*.

shan't = SHALL NOT.

shanty *n* (shack) baraque *f*; ~ **town** bidonville *m*.

shape *n* forme *f*. ● *vt* (*clay*) modeler; (*rock*) façonner; (*future*: fig) déterminer; ~ **sth into balls** faire des boules avec qch. ● *vi* ~ **up** (*plan*) prendre tournure; (*person*) faire des progrès.

share *n* part *f*; (Comm) action *f*. ● *vt/i* partager; (*feature*) avoir en commun. ~**holder** *n* actionnaire *mf*. ~**ware** *n* (Comput) logiciel *m* contributif.

shark *n* requin *m*.

sharp *adj* (*knife*) tranchant; (*pin*) pointu; (*point, angle, cry*) aigu; (*person, mind*) vif; (*tone*) acerbe. ● *adv* (stop) net; (*sing, play*) trop haut; **six o'clock** ~ six heures pile. ● *n* (Mus) dièse *m*.

sharpen *vt* aiguiser; (*pencil*) tailler.

shatter *vt* (*glass*) fracasser; (*hope*) briser. ● *vi* (*glass*) voler en éclats.

shave *vt/i* (se) raser. ● *n* **have a** ~ se raser. **shaver** *n* rasoir *m* électrique.

shaving *n* (of wood) copeau *m*. ● *adj* (*cream, foam, gel*) à raser.

shawl *n* châle *m*.

she *pron* elle. ● *n* (animal) femelle *f*.

shear *vt* (*pp* **shorn** or **sheared**) (*sheep*) tondre; ~ **off** se détacher.

shears *npl* cisaille *f*.

shed *n* remise *f*. ● *vt* (*pt* **shed**; *pres p* **shedding**) perdre; (*light, tears*) répandre.

sheen *n* lustre *m*.

sheep *n inv* mouton *m*. ~**-dog** *n* chien *m* de berger.

sheepish *adj* penaud.

sheepskin *n* peau *f* de mouton.

sheer *adj* pur; (steep) à pic; (*fabric*) très fin. ● *adv* à pic.

sheet *n* drap *m*; (of paper) feuille *f*; (of glass, ice) plaque *f*.

shelf *n* (*pl* **shelves**) étagère *f*; (in shop, fridge) rayon *m*; (in oven) plaque *f*.

shell *n* coquille *f*; (on beach) coquillage *m*; (of building) carcasse *f*; (explosive) obus *m*. ● *vt* (*nut*) décortiquer; (*peas*) écosser; (Mil) bombarder.

shellfish *npl* (lobster etc.) crustacés *mpl*; (mollusc) coquillages *mpl*.

shelter *n* abri *m*. ● *vt/i* (s')abriter; (give lodging to) donner asile à.

shelve *vt* (*plan*) mettre en suspens.

shepherd *n* berger *m*; ∼'s pie hachis *m* Parmentier. ● *vt* (*people*) guider.

sherry *n* xérès *m*.

shield *n* bouclier *m*; (screen) écran *m*. ● *vt* protéger.

shift *vt/i* (se) déplacer, bouger; (exchange, alter) changer de. ● *n* changement *m*; (workers) équipe *f*; (work) poste *m*; ∼ **work** travail *m* posté, travail *m* par roulement.

shifty *adj* (**-ier**, **-iest**) louche.

shimmer *vi* chatoyer. ● *n* chatoiement *m*.

shin *n* tibia *m*.

shine *vt* (*pt* **shone**) (*torch*) braquer (on sur). ● *vi* (*light, sun, hair*) briller; (*brass*) reluire. ● *n* lustre *m*.

shingle *n* (pebbles) galets *mpl*; (on roof) bardeau *m*.

shingles *npl* (Med) zona *m*.

shiny *adj* (**-ier**, **-iest**) brillant.

ship *n* bateau *m*, navire *m*. ● *vt* (*pt* **shipped**) transporter. **shipment** *n* (by sea) cargaison *f*; (by air, land) chargement *m*. **shipping** *n* (ships) navigation *f*. ∼**wreck** *n* épave *f*; (event) naufrage *m*.

shirt *n* chemise *f*; (woman's) chemisier *m*.

shiver *vi* frissonner. ● *n* frisson *m*.

shock *n* choc *m*; (Electr) décharge *f*; in ∼ en état de choc; ∼ **absorber** amortisseur *m*. ● *adj* (*result*) choc *inv*; (*tactics*) de choc. ● *vt* choquer.

shoddy *adj* (**-ier**, **-iest**) mal fait; (*behaviour*) mesquin.

shoe *n* chaussure *f*; (of horse) fer *m*; (brake) ∼ sabot *m* (*de frein*). ● *vt* (*pt* **shod** ; *pres p* **shoeing**) (*horse*) ferrer. ∼**lace** *n* lacet *m*. ∼ **size** *n* pointure *f*.

shone ⇒SHINE.

shook ⇒SHAKE.

shoot *vt* (*pt* **shot**) (*gun*) tirer un coup de; (*bullet*) tirer; (*missile,*

glance) lancer; (*person*) tirer sur; (kill) abattre; (execute) fusiller; (*film*) tourner. ● *vi* tirer (**at** sur). ● *n* (Bot) pousse *f*. □ ∼ **down** abattre; ∼ **out** (rush) sortir en vitesse; ∼ **up** (spurt) jaillir; (grow) pousser vite.

shooting *n* (killing) meurtre *m* (*par arme à feu*); **hear** ∼ entendre des coups de feu.

shop *n* magasin *m*; (small) boutique *f*; (workshop) atelier *m*. ● *vi* (*pt* **shopped**) faire ses courses; ∼ **around** comparer les prix. ∼ **assistant** *n* vendeur/-euse *m/f*. ∼**-floor** *n* (workers) ouvriers *mpl*. ∼**keeper** *n* commerçant/-e *m/f*. ∼**lifter** *n* voleur/-euse *m/f* à l'étalage.

shopper *n* acheteur/-euse *m/f*.

shopping *n* (goods) achats *mpl*; go ∼ (for food) faire les courses; (for clothes etc.) faire les magasins. ∼ **bag** *n* sac *m* à provisions. ∼ **centre**, (US) ∼ **center** *n* centre *m* commercial.

shop window *n* vitrine *f*.

shore *n* côte *f*, rivage *m*; on ∼ à terre.

short *adj* court; (*person*) petit; (brief) court, bref; (curt) brusque; **be** ∼ **(of)** manquer (de); **everything** ∼ **of** tout sauf; **nothing** ∼ **of** rien de moins que; **cut** ∼ écourter; **cut sb** ∼ interrompre qn; **fall** ∼ **of** ne pas arriver à; **he is called Tom for** ∼ son diminutif est Tom; **in** ∼ en bref. ● *adv* (*stop*) net. ● *n* (Electr) court-circuit *m*; (film) court-métrage *m*; ∼**s** (trousers) short *m*.

shortage *n* manque *m*.

short: ∼**bread** *n* sablé *m*. ∼**-change** *vt* (cheat) rouler ⚐. ∼ **circuit** *n* court-circuit *m*. ∼**coming** *n* défaut *m*. ∼ **cut** *n* raccourci *m*.

shorten *vt* raccourcir.

shortfall *n* déficit *m*.

shorthand *n* sténographie *f*; ∼ **typist** sténodactylo *f*.

short: ∼ **list** *n* liste *f* des candidats choisis. ∼**-lived** *adj* de courte durée.

shortly *adv* bientôt.

S

short: ~**-sighted** adj myope.
~**-staffed** adj à court de personnel;
~ **story** n nouvelle f. ~**-term** adj à court terme.

shot ⇒SHOOT. ● n (firing, attempt) coup m de feu; (person) tireur m; (bullet) balle f; (photograph) photo f; (injection) piqûre f; **like a** ~ sans hésiter.
~**-gun** n fusil m de chasse.

should v aux devoir; **you** ~ **help me** vous devriez m'aider; **I** ~ **have stayed** j'aurais dû rester; **I** ~ **like to** j'aimerais bien; **if he** ~ **come** s'il venait.

shoulder n épaule f. ● vt (responsibility) endosser; (burden) se charger de. ~**-bag** n sac m à bandoulière. ~**-blade** n omoplate f.

shout n cri m. ● vt/i crier (at après); ~ **sth out** lancer qch à haute voix.

shove n give sth a ~ pousser qch. ● vt/i pousser; ~ **off!** 🔟 tire-toi! 🔟.

shovel n pelle f. ● vt (pt shovelled) pelleter.

show vt (pt showed; pp shown) montrer; (dial, needle) indiquer; (put on display) exposer; (film) donner; (conduct) conduire; ~ **sb in/out** faire entrer/sortir qn. ● vi (be visible) se voir. ● n (exhibition) exposition f, salon m; (Theat) spectacle m; (cinema) séance f; (of strength) démonstration f; **for** ~ pour l'effet; **on** ~ exposé. □ ~ **off** faire le fier/la fière; ~ **sth/sb off** exhiber qch/qn; ~ **up** se voir; (appear) se montrer; ~ **sb up** 🔟 faire honte à qn.

shower n douche f; (of rain) averse f. ● vt ~ **with** couvrir de. ● vi se doucher.

showing n performance f; (cinema) séance f.

show-jumping n concours m hippique.

shown ⇒SHOW.

show: ~**-off** n m'as-tu-vu mf inv 🔟.
~**room** n salle f d'exposition.

shrank ⇒SHRINK.

shrapnel n éclats mpl d'obus.

shred n lambeau m; (least amount: fig) parcelle f. ● vt (pt shredded) déchiqueter; (Culin) râper.

shrewd adj (person) habile; (move) astucieux.

shriek n hurlement m. ● vt/i hurler.

shrill adj (voice) perçant; (tone) strident.

shrimp n crevette f.

shrine n (place) lieu m de pèlerinage.

shrink vt/i (pt shrank; pp shrunk) rétrécir; (lessen) diminuer; ~ **from** reculer devant.

shrivel vt/i (pt shrivelled) (se) ratatiner.

shroud n linceul m. ● vt (veil) envelopper.

Shrove Tuesday n mardi m gras.

shrub n arbuste m.

shrug vt (pt shrugged) ~ **one's shoulders** hausser les épaules; ~ **sth off** ignorer qch.

shrunk ⇒SHRINK.

shudder vi frémir. ● n frémissement m.

shuffle vt (feet) traîner; (cards) battre. ● vi traîner les pieds.

shun vt (pt shunned) fuir.

shut vt (pt shut; pres p shutting) fermer. ● vi (door) se fermer; (shop) fermer. □ ~ **in** or **up** enfermer; ~ **up** 🔟 se taire; ~ **sb up** faire taire qn.

shutter n volet m; (Photo) obturateur m.

shuttle n (bus) navette f; ~ **service** navette f. ● vi faire la navette. ● vt transporter.

shuttlecock n (badminton) volant m.

shy adj timide. ● vi ~ **away from** se tenir à l'écart de.

sibling n frère/sœur m/f.

sick adj malade; (humour) macabre; (mind) malsain; **be** ~ (vomit) vomir; **be** ~ **of** 🔟 en avoir assez or marre de 🔟; **feel** ~ avoir mal au cœur.
~**-leave** n congé m de maladie.

sickly adj (-ier, -iest) (person) maladif; (taste, smell) écœurant.

sickness n maladie f.

sick-pay n indemnité f de maladie.

side n côté m; (of road, river) bord m; (of hill, body) flanc m; (Sport) équipe f; (TV 🔟) chaîne f; ~ **by** ~ côte à côte. ● adj latéral. ● vi ~ **with** se ranger du côté de. ~**board** n buffet m.
~**-effect** n effet m secondaire.
~**light** n (Auto) feu m de position.

~line n activité f secondaire.
~-show n attraction f. **~-step** vt
(pt **-stepped**) éviter. **~-street** n
rue f latérale. **~-track** vt fourvoyer.
~walk n (US) trottoir m.

sideways adj (look) de travers.
● adv (move) latéralement; (look at)
de travers.

siding n voie f de garage.

sidle vi s'avancer furtivement (**up to**
vers).

siege n siège m.

siesta n sieste f.

sieve n tamis m; (for liquids) passoire
f. ● vt tamiser.

sift vt tamiser. ● vi ~ **through**
examiner.

sigh n soupir m. ● vt/i soupirer.

sight n vue f; (scene) spectacle m; (on
gun) mire f; **at** or **on** ~ à vue; **catch**
~ **of** apercevoir; **in** ~ visible; **lose** ~
of perdre de vue. ● vt apercevoir.

sightseeing n tourisme m.

sign n signe m; (notice) panneau m.
● vt/i signer. □ ~ **on** (as unemployed)
pointer au chômage; ~ **up** (s')
engager.

signal n signal m. ● vt (pt
signalled) (gesture) faire signe (**that**
que); (indicate) indiquer.

signatory n signataire mf.

signature n signature f; ~ **tune**
indicatif m.

significance n importance f;
(meaning) signification f. **significant**
adj important; (meaningful)
significatif. **significantly** adv
(much) sensiblement.

signify vt signifier.

signpost n panneau m indicateur.

silence n silence m. ● vt faire taire.

silent adj silencieux; (film) muet.
silently adv silencieusement.

silhouette n silhouette f. ● vt be
~d **against** se profiler contre.

silicon n silicium m; ~ **chip** puce f
électronique.

silk n soie f.

silly adj (**-ier, -iest**) bête, idiot.

silver n argent m; (silverware)
argenterie f. ● adj en argent.

similar adj semblable (**to** à).
similarity n ressemblance f.
similarly adv de même.

simile n comparaison f.

simmer vt/i (soup) mijoter; (water)
(laisser) frémir.

simple adj simple.

simplicity n simplicité f.

simplify vt simplifier.

simplistic adj simpliste.

simply adv simplement; (absolutely)
absolument.

simulate vt simuler.

simultaneous adj simultané.

sin n péché m. ● vi (pt **sinned**)
pécher.

···

since

● *preposition*

····➤ depuis; **I haven't seen him** ~
Monday je ne l'ai pas vu depuis
lundi; **I've been waiting** ~ **yesterday**
j'attends depuis hier; **she had been
living in Paris** ~ **1985** elle habitait
Paris depuis 1985.

● *conjunction*

····➤ (in time expressions) depuis que; ~
she's been working here depuis
qu'elle travaille ici; ~ **she left**
depuis qu'elle est partie or depuis
son départ.

····➤ (because) comme; ~ **he was ill, he
couldn't go** comme il était malade, il
ne pouvait pas y aller.

● *adverb*

····➤ depuis; **he hasn't been seen** ~ on
ne l'a pas vu depuis.

···

sincere adj sincère. **sincerely** adv
sincèrement. **sincerity** n sincérité
f.

sinful adj immoral; ~ **man** pécheur
m.

sing vt/i (pt **sang**; pp **sung**)
chanter.

singe vt (pres p **singeing**) brûler
légèrement; (with iron) roussir.

singer n chanteur/-euse m/f.

single adj seul; (not double) simple;
(unmarried) célibataire; (room, bed)
pour une personne; (ticket) simple; **in**

$\sim$ **file** en file indienne. ● *n* (ticket) aller simple *m*; (record) 45 tours *m* *inv*; $\sim$**s** (tennis) simple *m*. ● *vt* $\sim$ **out** choisir. $\sim$**-handed** *adj* tout seul. $\sim$**-minded** *adj* tenace. $\sim$ **parent** *n* parent *m* isolé.

singular *n* singulier *m*. ● *adj* (strange) singulier; (noun) au singulier.

sinister *adj* sinistre.

sink *vt* (*pt* **sank**; *pp* **sunk**) (boat) couler; (well) forer; (post) enfoncer. ● *vi* (boat) couler; (sun, level) baisser; (wall) s'effondrer. ● *n* (in kitchen) évier *m*; (wash-basin) lavabo *m*. □ $\sim$ **in** (news) faire son chemin.

sinner *n* pécheur/-eresse *m/f*.

sip *n* petite gorgée *f*. ● *vt* (*pt* **sipped**) boire à petites gorgées.

siphon *n* siphon *m*. ● *vt* $\sim$ **off** siphonner.

sir *n* Monsieur *m*; **Sir** (title) Sir *m*.

siren *n* sirène *f*.

sirloin *n* aloyau *m*.

sister *n* sœur *f*; (nurse) infirmière *f* en chef. $\sim$**-in-law** *n* (*pl* $\sim$**s-in-law**) belle-sœur *f*.

sit *vt/i* (*pt* **sat**; *pres p* **sitting**) (s') asseoir; (committee) siéger; $\sim$ **(for)** (exam) se présenter à; **be** $\sim$**ting** être assis. □ $\sim$ **around** ne rien faire; $\sim$ **down** s'asseoir.

site *n* emplacement *m*; (building) $\sim$ chantier *m*. ● *vt* construire.

sitting *n* séance *f*; (in restaurant) service *m*. $\sim$**-room** *n* salon *m*.

situate *vt* situer; **be** $\sim$**d** être situé. **situation** *n* situation *f*.

six *a & n* six (*m*).

sixteen *a & n* seize (*m*).

sixth *a & n* sixième (*mf*).

sixty *a & n* soixante (*m*).

size *n* dimension *f*; (of person, garment) taille *f*; (of shoes) pointure *f*; (of sum, salary) montant *m*; (extent) ampleur *f*. □ $\sim$ **up** (person) se faire une opinion de; (situation) évaluer. **sizeable** *adj* assez grand.

skate *n* patin *m*; (fish) raie *f*. ● *vi* patiner.

skating *n* patinage *m*.

skeletal *adj* squelettique.

skeleton *n* squelette *m*; $\sim$ **staff** effectifs *mpl* minimums.

sketch *n* esquisse *f*; (hasty) croquis *m*; (Theat) sketch *m*. ● *vt* faire une esquisse *or* un croquis de. ● *vi* faire des esquisses.

sketchy *adj* (**-ier, -iest**) (details) insuffisant; (memory) vague.

skewer *n* brochette *f*.

ski *n* ski *m*. ● *adj* de ski. ● *vi* (*pt* **ski'd** *or* **skied**; *pres p* **skiing**) skier; (go skiing) faire du ski.

skid *vi* (*pt* **skidded**) déraper. ● *n* dérapage *m*.

skier *n* skieur/-euse *m/f*.

skiing *n* ski *m*.

ski jump *n* saut *m* à ski.

skilful *adj* habile.

ski lift *n* remontée *f* mécanique.

skill *n* habileté *f*; (craft) compétence *f*; $\sim$**s** connaissances *fpl*. **skilled** *adj* (worker) qualifié; (talented) consommé.

skim *vt* (*pt* **skimmed**) écumer; (milk) écrémer; (pass over) effleurer. ● *vi* $\sim$ **through** parcourir.

skimpy *adj* (clothes) étriqué; (meal) chiche.

skin *n* peau *f*. ● *vt* (*pt* **skinned**) (animal) écorcher; (fruit) éplucher.

skinny *adj* (**-ier, -iest**) 🔲 maigre.

skip *vi* (*pt* **skipped**) sautiller; (with rope) sauter à la corde. ● *vt* (page, class) sauter. ● *n* petit saut *m*; (container) benne *f*.

skipper *n* capitaine *m*.

skirmish *n* escarmouche *f*, accrochage *m*.

skirt *n* jupe *f*. ● *vt* contourner. **skirting-board** *n* plinthe *f*.

skittle *n* quille *f*.

skull *n* crâne *m*.

sky *n* ciel *m*. $\sim$**-blue** *a & n* bleu ciel *m inv*. $\sim$**scraper** *n* gratte-ciel *m inv*.

slab *n* (of stone) dalle *f*.

slack *adj* (not tight) détendu; (person) négligent; (period) creux. ● *n* (in rope) mou *m*. ● *vi* se relâcher.

slacken *vt* (rope) donner du mou à; (grip) relâcher; (pace) réduire. ● *vi* (grip, rope) se relâcher; (activity) ralentir; (rain) se calmer.

slam *vt/i* (*pt* **slammed**) (*door*) claquer; (throw) flanquer; (criticize 🔲) critiquer. ● *n* (noise) claquement *m*.

slander *n* (offence) diffamation *f*; (statement) calomnie *f*. ● *vt* calomnier; (Jur) diffamer. **slanderous** *adj* diffamatoire.

slang *n* argot *m*.

slant *vt/i* (faire) pencher; (*news*) présenter sous un certain jour. ● *n* inclinaison *f*; (bias) angle *m*. **slanted** *adj* (biased) orienté; (sloping) en pente.

slap *vt* (*pt* **slapped**) (strike) donner une tape à; (*face*) gifler; (put) flanquer 🔲. ● *n* claque *f*; (on face) gifle *f*. ● *adv* tout droit.

slapdash *adj* (*person*) brouillon 🔲; (*work*) bâclé 🔲.

slash *vt* (*picture, tyre*) taillader; (*face*) balafrer; (*throat*) couper; (fig) réduire (radicalement). ● *n* lacération *f*.

slat *n* (in blind) lamelle *f*; (on bed) latte *f*.

slate *n* ardoise *f*. ● *vt* 🔲 taper sur 🔲.

slaughter *vt* massacrer; (*animal*) abattre. ● *n* massacre *m*; abattage *m*.

slave *n* esclave *mf*. ● *vi* trimer 🔲. **slavery** *n* esclavage *m*.

sleazy *adj* (**-ier, -iest**) 🔲 (*story*) scabreux; (*club*) louche.

sledge *n* luge *f*; (horse-drawn) traîneau *m*.

sleek *adj* (*hair*) lisse, brillant; (*shape*) élégant.

sleep *n* sommeil *m*; go to ~ s'endormir. ● *vi* (*pt* **slept**) dormir; (spend the night) coucher; ~ in faire la grasse matinée. ● *vt* loger.

sleeper *n* (Rail) (berth) couchette *f*; (on track) traverse *f*.

sleeping-bag *n* sac *m* de couchage.

sleeping-pill *n* somnifère *m*.

sleep-walker *n* somnambule *mf*.

sleepy *adj* (**-ier, -iest**) somnolent; be ~ avoir sommeil.

sleet *n* neige *f* fondue.

sleeve *n* manche *f*; (of record) pochette *f*; up one's ~ en réserve.

sleigh *n* traîneau *m*.

slender *adj* (*person*) mince; (*majority*) faible.

slept ⇒SLEEP.

slice *n* tranche *f*. ● *vt* couper (en tranches).

slick *adj* (adept) habile; (insincere) roublard 🔲. ● *n* (oil) ~ marée *f* noire.

slide *vt/i* (*pt* **slid**) glisser; ~ into (go silently) se glisser dans. ● *n* glissade *f*; (fall: fig) baisse *f*; (in playground) toboggan *m*; (for hair) barrette *f*; (Photo) diapositive *f*.

sliding *adj* (*door*) coulissant; ~ scale échelle *f* mobile.

slight *adj* petit, léger; (slender) mince; (frail) frêle. ● *vt* (insult) offenser. ● *n* affront *m*. **slightest** *adj* moindre. **slightly** *adv* légèrement, un peu.

slim *adj* (**slimmer, slimmest**) mince. ● *vi* (*pt* **slimmed**) maigrir.

slime *n* dépôt *m* gluant; (on river-bed) vase *f*. **slimy** *adj* visqueux; (fig) servile.

sling *n* (weapon, toy) fronde *f*; (bandage) écharpe *f*. ● *vt* (*pt* **slung**) jeter, lancer.

slip *vt/i* (*pt* **slipped**) glisser; ~ped disc hernie *f* discale; ~ sb's mind échapper à qn. ● *n* (mistake) erreur *f*; (petticoat) combinaison *f*; (paper) bout *m* de papier; ~ of the tongue lapsus *m*. □ ~ away s'esquiver; ~ into (go) se glisser dans; (*clothes*) mettre; ~ up 🔲 faire une gaffe 🔲.

slipper *n* pantoufle *f*.

slippery *adj* glissant.

slip road *n* bretelle *f*.

slit *n* fente *f*. ● *vt* (*pt* **slit**; *pres p* **slitting**) déchirer; ~ sth open ouvrir qch; ~ sb's throat égorger qn.

slither *vi* glisser.

sliver *n* (of glass) éclat *m*; (of soap) reste *m*.

slobber *vi* 🔲 baver.

slog 🔲 *vt* (*pt* **slogged**) (hit) frapper dur. ● *vi* (work) bosser 🔲. ● *n* (work) travail *m* dur.

slogan *n* slogan *m*.

slope *vi* être en pente; (*handwriting*) pencher. ● *n* pente *f*; (of mountain) flanc *m*.

s

sloppy *adj* (**-ier, -iest**) (*food*) liquide; (*work*) négligé; (*person*) négligent.

slosh *vt* 🔢 répandre; (hit 🔢) frapper. ● *vi* clapoter.

slot *n* fente *f.* ● *vt/i* (*pt* **slotted**) (s')insérer.

sloth *n* paresse *f.*

slot-machine *n* distributeur *m* automatique; (for gambling) machine *f* à sous.

slouch *vi* être avachi.

Slovakia *n* Slovaquie *f.*

Slovenia *n* Slovénie *f.*

slovenly *adj* débraillé.

slow *adj* lent; be ~ (*clock*) retarder; in ~ **motion** au ralenti. ● *adv* lentement. ● *vt/i* ralentir. **slowly** *adv* lentement. **slowness** *n* lenteur *f.*

sludge *n* vase *f.*

slug *n* (mollusc) limace *f*; (bullet 🔢) balle *f*; (blow 🔢) coup *m.*

sluggish *adj* (*person*) léthargique; (*circulation*) lent.

slum *n* taudis *m.*

slump *n* (Econ) effondrement *m*; (in support) baisse *f.* ● *vi* (*demand, trade*) chuter; (*economy*) s'effondrer; (*person*) s'affaler.

slung ⇒SLING.

slur *vt/i* (*pt* **slurred**) (*words*) mal articuler. ● *n* calomnie *f* (on sur).

slush *n* (snow) neige *f* fondue. ~ **fund** *n* caisse *f* noire.

sly *adj* (crafty) rusé; (secretive) sournois. ● *n* on the ~ en cachette.

smack *n* tape *f*; (on face) gifle *f.* ● *vt* donner une tape à; gifler. ● *vi* ~ of sth sentir qch. 🔢 tout droit.

small *adj* petit. ● *n* ~ of the back creux *m* des reins. ● *adv* (cut) menu. ~ **ad** *n* petite annonce *f.* ~ **business** *n* petite entreprise *f.* ~ **change** *n* petite monnaie *f.* ~ **pox** *n* variole *f.* ~ **print** *n* petits caractères *mpl.* ~ **talk** *n* banalités *fpl.*

smart *adj* élégant; (clever 🔢) malin, habile; (*restaurant*) chic *inv*; (Comput) intelligent. ● *vi* (*wound*) brûler.

smarten *vt/i* ~ (**up**) embellir; ~ (**oneself**) **up** s'arranger.

smash *vt/i* (se) briser, (se) fracasser; (*opponent, record*) pulvériser. ● *n* (noise) fracas *m*; (blow) coup *m*; (car crash) collision *f*; (hit record 🔢) tube *m* 🔢.

smashing *adj* 🔢 épatant.

SME *abbr* (**small and medium enterprises**) PME.

smear *vt* (stain) tacher; (coat) enduire; (discredit: fig) diffamer. ● *n* tache *f*; (effort to discredit) propos *m* diffamatoire; ~ (**test**) frottis *m.*

smell *n* odeur *f*; (sense) odorat *m.* ● *vt/i* (*pt* **smelt** *or* **smelled**) sentir; ~ of sentir. **smelly** *adj* qui sent mauvais.

smelt ⇒SMELL.

smile *n* sourire *m.* ● *vi* sourire.

smiley *n* (Internet) binette *f.*

smirk *n* petit sourire *m* satisfait.

smitten *adj* (in love) fou d'amour.

smog *n* smog *m.*

smoke *n* fumée *f*; have a ~ fumer. ● *vt/i* fumer. **smoked** *adj* fumé. **smokeless** *adj* (*fuel*) non polluant. **smoker** *n* fumeur/-euse *m/f.* **smoky** *adj* (*air*) enfumé.

smooth *adj* lisse; (*movement*) aisé; (*manners*) onctueux; (*flight*) sans heurts. ● *vt* lisser; (*process*) faciliter.

smoothly *adv* (move, flow) doucement; (*brake, start*) en douceur; go ~ marcher bien.

smother *vt* (stifle) étouffer; (cover) couvrir.

smoulder *vi* (lit) se consumer; (fig) couver.

smudge *n* trace *f.* ● *vt/i* (*ink*) (s') étaler.

smug *adj* (**smugger, smuggest**) suffisant.

smuggle *vt* passer (en contrebande). **smuggler** *n* contrebandier/-ière *m/f.* **smuggling** *n* contrebande *f.*

smutty *adj* grivois.

snack *n* casse-croûte *m inv.*

snag *n* inconvénient *m*; (in cloth) accroc *m.*

snail *n* escargot *m.*

snake *n* serpent *m.*

snap *vt/i* (*pt* **snapped**) (*whip, fingers*) (faire) claquer; (break) (se) casser net; (say) dire sèchement. ● *n* claquement *m*; (Photo) photo *f*. ● *adj* soudain. □ ∼ **up** (buy) sauter sur.

snapshot *n* photo *f*.

snare *n* piège *m*.

snarl *vi* gronder (en montrant les dents). ● *n* grondement *m*. ∼**-up** *n* embouteillage *m*.

snatch *vt* (grab) attraper; (steal) voler; (*opportunity*) saisir; ∼ **sth from sb** arracher qch à qn. ● *n* (theft) vol *m*; (short part) fragment *m*.

sneak *vi* aller furtivement. ● *n* 🔲 rapporteur/-euse *m/f*.

sneer *n* sourire *m* méprisant. ● *vi* sourire avec mépris.

sneeze *n* éternuement *m*. ● *vi* éternuer.

snide *adj* narquois.

sniff *vt/i* renifler. ● *n* reniflement *m*.

snigger *n* ricanement *m*. ● *vi* ricaner.

snip *vt* (*pt* **snipped**) couper.

sniper *n* tireur *m* embusqué.

snippet *n* bribe *f*.

snivel *vi* (*pt* **snivelled**) pleurnicher.

snob *n* snob *mf*.

snooker *n* snooker *m*.

snoop *vi* 🔲 fourrer son nez partout.

snooty *adj* (**-ier, -iest**) 🔲 snob *inv*, hautain.

snooze *n* petit somme *m*. ● *vi* sommeiller.

snore *n* ronflement *m*. ● *vi* ronfler.

snorkel *n* tuba *m*.

snort *n* grognement *m*. ● *vi* (*person*) grogner; (*horse*) s'ébrouer.

snout *n* museau *m*.

snow *n* neige *f*. ● *vi* neiger; **be** ∼**ed under with** être submergé de.

snowball *n* boule *f* de neige. ● *vi* faire boule de neige.

snow: ∼**boarding** *n* surf *m* des neiges. ∼**-bound** *adj* bloqué par la neige. ∼**-drift** *n* congère *f*. ∼**drop** *n* perce-neige *m or f inv*. ∼**flake** *n* flocon *m* de neige. ∼**man** *n* (*pl* **-men**) bonhomme *m* de neige. ∼**-plough** *n* chasse-neige *m inv*.

snub *vt* (*pt* **snubbed**) rembarrer. ● *n* rebuffade *f*.

snuffle *vi* renifler.

snug *adj* (**snugger, snuggest**) (cosy) confortable; (tight) bien ajusté.

snuggle *vi* se pelotonner.

so *adv* si, tellement; (thus) ainsi; ∼ **am I** moi aussi; ∼ **good as** aussi bon que; **that is** ∼ c'est ça; **I think** ∼ je pense que oui; **five or** ∼ environ cinq; ∼ **as to** de manière à; ∼ **far** jusqu'ici; ∼ **long!** 🔲 à bientôt!; ∼ **many,** ∼ **much** tant (de); ∼ **that** pour que. ● *conj* donc, alors.

soak *vt/i* (faire) tremper (**in** dans). □ ∼ **in** pénétrer; ∼ **up** absorber. **soaking** *adj* trempé.

soap *n* savon *m*. ● *vt* savonner. ∼ **opera** *n* feuilleton *m*. ∼ **powder** *n* lessive *f*.

soar *vi* monter (en flèche).

sob *n* sanglot *m*. ● *vi* (*pt* **sobbed**) sangloter.

sober *adj* qui n'a pas bu d'alcool; (serious) sérieux. ● *vi* ∼ **up** dessoûler.

soccer *n* football *m*.

sociable *adj* sociable.

social *adj* social. ● *n* réunion *f* (amicale), fête *f*.

socialism *n* socialisme *m*. **socialist** *a & n* socialiste (*mf*).

socialize *vi* se mêler aux autres; ∼ **with** fréquenter.

socially *adv* socialement; (*meet*) en société.

social: ∼ **security** *n* aide *f* sociale. ∼ **worker** *n* travailleur/-euse *m/f* social/-e.

society *n* société *f*.

sociological *adj* sociologique. **sociologist** *n* sociologue *mf*. **sociology** *n* sociologie *f*.

sock *n* chaussette *f*. ● *vt* (hit 🔲) flanquer un coup (de poing) à.

socket *n* (for lamp) douille *f*; (Electr) prise *f* (de courant); (of eye) orbite *f*.

soda *n* soude *f*; ∼(**-water**) eau *f* de Seltz.

sodden *adj* détrempé.

sofa *n* canapé *m*. ∼ **bed** *n* canapé-lit *m*.

soft *adj* (gentle, lenient) doux; (not hard) doux, mou; (*heart, wood*) tendre; (silly) ramolli. ∼ **drink** *n* boisson *f* non alcoolisée.

S

soften vt/i (se) ramollir; (tone down, lessen) (s')adoucir.

soft spot n to have a ~ for sb avoir un faible pour qn.

software n logiciel m.

soggy adj (-ier, -iest) (ground) détrempé; (food) ramolli.

soil n sol m, terre f. ● vt/i (se) salir.

sold ⇒SELL. ● adj ~ out épuisé.

solder n soudure f. ● vt souder.

soldier n soldat m. ● vi ~ on
⚠ persévérer.

sole n (of foot) plante f; (of shoe) semelle f; (fish) sole f. ● adj unique, seul. **solely** adv uniquement.

solemn adj solennel.

solicitor n notaire m; (for court and police work) ≈ avocat/-e m/f.

solid adj solide; (not hollow) plein; (gold) massif; (mass) compact; (meal) substantiel. ● n solide m; ~s (food) aliments mpl solides.

solidarity n solidarité f.

solidify vt/i (se) solidifier.

solitary adj (alone) solitaire; (only) seul.

solo n solo m. ● adj (Mus) solo inv; (flight) en solitaire.

soluble adj soluble.

solution n solution f.

solve vt résoudre.

solvent adj (Comm) solvable. ● n (dis)solvant m.

- - -

some

● determiner

····▸ (unspecified amount) du/de l'/de la/ des; I have to buy ~ bread je dois acheter du pain; have ~ water prenez de l'eau; ~ sweets des bonbons.

····▸ (certain) certains/certaines; ~ people say that certains disent que.

····▸ (unknown) un/une; ~ man came to the house un homme est venu à la maison.

····▸ (considerable amount) we stayed there for ~ time nous sommes restés là assez longtemps; it will take ~ doing ça ne va pas être facile à faire.

❗ In front of a plural adjective des changes to de: **some pretty dresses** de jolies robes.

● pronoun

····▸ en; he wants ~ il en veut; have ~ more reprenez-en.

····▸ (certain) certains/certaines; ~ are expensive certains sont chers.

● adverb

····▸ environ; ~ 20 people environ 20 personnes.

- - -

somebody pron quelqu'un. ● n be a ~ être quelqu'un.

somehow adv d'une manière ou d'une autre; (for some reason) je ne sais pas pourquoi.

someone pron & n = SOMEBODY.

someplace adv (US) = SOMEWHERE.

somersault n roulade f. ● vi faire une roulade.

something pron & n quelque chose (m); ~ good quelque chose de bon; ~ like un peu comme.

sometime adv un jour; ~ in June en juin. ● adj (former) ancien.

sometimes adv quelquefois, parfois.

somewhat adv quelque peu, un peu.

somewhere adv quelque part.

son n fils m.

song n chanson f; (of bird) chant m.

son-in-law n (pl sons-in-law) gendre m.

soon adv bientôt; (early) tôt; I would ~er stay j'aimerais mieux rester; ~ after peu après; ~er or later tôt ou tard.

soot n suie f.

soothe vt calmer.

sophisticated adj raffiné; (machine) sophistiqué.

sopping adj trempé.

soppy adj (-ier, -iest)
⚠ sentimental.

sorcerer n sorcier m.

sordid adj sordide.

sore adj douloureux; (vexed) en rogne (at, with contre). ● n plaie f.

sorely adv fortement.

sorrow n chagrin m.

sorry adj (**-ier, -iest**) (regretful) désolé (**to** de; **that** que); (wretched) triste; **feel** ~ **for** plaindre; ~**!** pardon!

sort n genre m, sorte f, espèce f; (person 🔲) type m; **what** ~ **of?** quel genre de?; **be out of** ~**s** ne pas être dans son assiette. ● vt ~ (**out**) (classify) trier; ~ **out** (tidy) ranger; (arrange) arranger; (problem) régler.

so-so a & adv comme ci comme ça.

sought ⇒SEEK.

soul n âme f.

sound n son m, bruit m. ● adj solide; (healthy) sain; (sensible) sensé. ● vt/i sonner; (seem) sembler (**as if** que); (test) sonder; ~ **out** sonder; ~ **a horn** klaxonner; ~ **like** sembler être. ~ **asleep** adj profondément endormi. ~ **barrier** n mur m du son.

soundly adv (sleep) à poings fermés; (built) solidement.

sound-proof adj insonorisé. ● vt insonoriser.

sound-track n bande f sonore.

soup n soupe f, potage m.

sour adj aigre. ● vt/i (s')aigrir.

source n source f.

south n sud m. ● adj sud inv, du sud. ● adv vers le sud.

South Africa n Afrique f du Sud.

South America n Amérique f du Sud.

south-east n sud-est m.

southern adj du sud. **southerner** n habitant/-e m/f du sud.

southward adj (side) sud inv; (journey) vers le sud.

south-west n sud-ouest m.

souvenir n souvenir m.

sovereign n & a souverain/-e (m/f).

sow[1] vt (pt **sowed**; pp **sowed** or **sown**) (seed) semer; (land) ensemencer.

sow[2] n (pig) truie f.

soya n soja m. ~ **sauce** n sauce f soja.

spa n station f thermale.

space n espace m; (room) place f; (period) période f. ● adj (research) spatial. ● vt ~ (**out**) espacer. ~**craft** n inv, ~**ship** n engin m spatial. ~**suit** n combinaison f spatiale.

spacious adj spacieux.

spade n (for garden) bêche f; (child's) pelle f; (cards) pique m. ~**work** n (fig) travail m préparatoire.

spaghetti n spaghetti mpl.

Spain n Espagne f.

span n (of arch) portée f; (of wings) envergure f; (of time) durée f. ● vt (pt **spanned**) enjamber; (in time) embrasser.

Spaniard n Espagnol/-e m/f.

spaniel n épagneul m.

Spanish adj espagnol. ● n espagnol m.

spank vt donner une fessée à.

spanner n (tool) clé f (plate); (adjustable) clé f à molette.

spare vt (treat leniently) épargner; (do without) se passer de; (afford to give) donner, accorder. ● adj en réserve; (surplus) de trop; (tyre, shoes) de rechange; (room, bed) d'ami; **are there any** ~ **tickets?** y a-t-il encore des places? ● n ~ (part) pièce f de rechange. ~ **time** n loisirs mpl.

sparing adj frugal. **sparingly** adv en petite quantité.

spark n étincelle f. ● vt ~ **off** (initiate) provoquer.

sparkle vi étinceler. ● n étincellement m. **sparkling** adj (wine) mousseux, pétillant; (eyes) brillant.

spark-plug n bougie f.

sparrow n moineau m.

sparse adj clairsemé. **sparsely** adv (furnished) peu.

spasm n (of muscle) spasme m; (of coughing, anger) accès m.

spasmodic adj intermittent.

spat ⇒SPIT.

spate n **a** ~ **of** (letters) une avalanche de.

spatter vt éclabousser (**with** de).

spawn n frai m, œufs mpl. ● vt pondre. ● vi frayer.

speak vi (pt **spoke**; pp **spoken**) parler. ● vt (say) dire; (language) parler. □ ~ **up** parler plus fort.

speaker n (in public) orateur m; (Pol) président m; (loudspeaker) baffle m; **be**

S

a French/a good ∼ parler français/
bien.

spear *n* lance *f*.

spearmint *n* menthe *f* verte.

special *adj* spécial; (exceptional)
exceptionnel.

specialist *n* spécialiste *mf*.

speciality, (US) **specialty** *n*
spécialité *f*.

specialize *vi* se spécialiser (**in** en).

specially *adv* spécialement.

species *n inv* espèce *f*.

specific *adj* précis, explicite.

specification *n* (of design)
spécification *f*; (of car equipment)
caractéristiques *fpl*. **specify** *vt*
spécifier.

specimen *n* spécimen *m*,
échantillon *m*.

speck *n* (stain) (petite) tache *f*;
(particle) grain *m*.

specs *npl* 🔢 lunettes *fpl*.

spectacle *n* spectacle *m*.
spectacles *n* lunettes *fpl*.
spectacular *adj* spectaculaire.

spectator *n* spectateur/-trice *m/f*.

spectrum *n* (*pl* **-tra**) spectre *m*; (of
ideas) gamme *f*.

speculate *vi* s'interroger (**about**
sur); (Comm) spéculer. **speculation**
n conjectures *fpl*; (Comm) spéculation
f. **speculator** *n* spéculateur/-trice
m/f.

speech *n* (faculty) parole *f*; (diction)
élocution *f*; (dialect) langage *m*;
(address) discours *m*. **speechless**
adj muet (**with** de).

speed *n* (of movement) vitesse *f*;
(swiftness) rapidité *f*. ● *vi* (*pt* **sped**)
aller vite; (*pt* **speeded**) (drive too
fast) aller trop vite. □ ∼ **up**
accélérer; (of pace) s'accélérer.

speedboat *n* vedette *f*.

speeding *n* excès *m* de vitesse.

speed limit *n* limitation *f* de
vitesse.

speedometer *n* compteur *m* (de
vitesse).

spell *n* (magic) charme *m*, sortilège *m*;
(curse) sort *m*; (of time) (courte)
période *f*. ● *vt/i* (*pt* **spelled** *or*
spelt) écrire; (mean) signifier; ∼ **out**
épeler; (explain) expliquer.

∼**checker** *n* correcteur *m*
orthographique.

spelling *n* orthographe *f*. ● *adj*
(mistake) d'orthographe.

spend *vt* (*pt* **spent**) (money)
dépenser (**on** pour); (time, holiday)
passer; (energy) consacrer (**on** à).
● *vi* dépenser.

spent ⇒SPEND. ● *adj* (used) utilisé;
(person) épuisé.

sperm *n* (*pl* **sperms** *or* **sperm**)
sperme *m*.

sphere *n* sphère *f*.

spice *n* épice *f*; (fig) piquant *m*.

spick-and-span *adj* impeccable.

spicy *adj* épicé; piquant.

spider *n* araignée *f*.

spike *n* pointe *f*.

spill *vt* (*pt* **spilled** *or* **spilt**)
renverser, répandre. ● *vi* se
répandre; ∼ **over** déborder.

spin *vt/i* (*pt* **spun**; *pres p* **spinning**)
(wool, web) filer; (turn) (faire)
tourner; (story) débiter; ∼ **out** faire
durer. ● *n* (movement, excursion) tour
m.

spinach *n* épinards *mpl*.

spinal *adj* vertébral. ∼ **cord** *n*
moelle *f* épinière.

spin-drier *n* essoreuse *f*.

spine *n* colonne *f* vertébrale; (prickle)
piquant *m*.

spin-off *n* avantage *m* accessoire;
(by-product) dérivé *m*.

spinster *n* célibataire *f*; (pej) vieille
fille *f*.

spiral *adj* en spirale; (staircase) en
colimaçon. ● *n* spirale *f*. ● *vi* (*pt*
spiralled) (prices) monter (en
flèche).

spire *n* flèche *f*.

spirit *n* esprit *m*; (boldness) courage
m; ∼**s** (morale) moral *m*; (drink)
spiritueux *mpl*. ● *vt* ∼ **away** faire
disparaître. **spirited** *adj* fougueux.
∼**-level** *n* niveau *m* à bulle.

spiritual *adj* spirituel.

spit *vt/i* (*pt* **spat** *or* **spit**; *pres p*
spitting) cracher; (of rain) crachiner;
∼ **out** cracher; **the** ∼**ting image of** le
portrait craché *or* vivant de. ● *n*
crachat(s) *m(pl)*; (for meat) broche *f*.

spite n rancune f; **in ~ of** malgré.
● vt contrarier.

splash vt éclabousser. ● vi faire des éclaboussures; **~ (about)** patauger.
● n (act, mark) éclaboussure f; (sound) plouf m; (of colour) tache f.

spleen n (Anat) rate f.

splendid adj magnifique, splendide.

splint n (Med) attelle f.

splinter n éclat m; (in finger) écharde f. **~ group** n groupe m dissident.

split vt/i (pt **split**; pres p **splitting**) (se) fendre; (tear) (se) déchirer; (divide) (se) diviser; (share) partager; **~ one's sides** se tordre (de rire). ● n fente f; déchirure f; (share 🆒) part f, partage m; (quarrel) rupture f; (Pol) scission f. □ **~ up** (couple) rompre. **~ second** n fraction f de seconde.

splutter vi crachoter; (stammer) bafouiller; (engine) tousser.

spoil vt (pt **spoilt** or **spoiled**) (pamper) gâter; (ruin) abîmer; (mar) gâcher, gâter. ● n **~(s)** butin m.
~-sport n trouble-fête mf inv.

spoke¹ n rayon m.

spoke², **spoken** ⇒SPEAK.

spokesman n (pl **-men**) porte-parole m inv.

sponge n éponge f. ● vt éponger.
● vi **~ on** vivre aux crochets de.
~-bag n trousse f de toilette.
~-cake n génoise f.

sponsor n (of concert) parrain m, sponsor m; (surety) garant m; (for membership) parrain m, marraine f.
● vt parrainer, sponsoriser; (member) parrainer. **sponsorship** n patronage m; parrainage m.

spontaneous adj spontané.

spoof n 🆒 parodie f.

spoon n cuiller f, cuillère f.

spoonful n (pl **~s**) cuillerée f.

sport n sport m; (good) **~** (person 🆒) chic type m; **~s** car/coat voiture/veste f de sport. ● vt (display) exhiber, arborer.

sporting adj sportif; **a ~ chance** une assez bonne chance.

sportsman n (pl **-men**) sportif m.

sporty adj 🆒 sportif.

spot n (mark, stain) tache f; (dot) point m; (in pattern) pois m; (drop) goutte f; (place) endroit m; (pimple) bouton m; **a ~ of** 🆒 un peu de; **on the ~** sur place; (without delay) sur le coup. ● vt (pt **spotted**) 🆒 apercevoir. **~ check** n contrôle m surprise.

spotless adj impeccable.

spotlight n (lamp) projecteur m, spot m.

spotty adj (skin) boutonneux.

spouse n époux m, épouse f.

spout n (of teapot) bec m; (of liquid) jet m; **up the ~** (ruined 🆒) fichu. ● vi jaillir.

sprain n entorse f, foulure f. ● vt **~ one's wrist** se fouler le poignet.

sprang ⇒SPRING.

sprawl vi (town, person) s'étaler. ● n étalement m.

spray n (of flowers) gerbe f; (water) gerbe f d'eau; (from sea) embruns mpl; (device) bombe f, atomiseur m.
● vt (surface, insecticide, plant) vaporiser; (person) asperger; (crops) traiter.

spread vt/i (pt **spread**) (stretch, extend) (s')étendre; (news, fear) (se) répandre; (illness) (se) propager; (butter) (s')étaler. ● n propagation f; (of population) distribution f; (paste) pâte f à tartiner; (food) belle table f.
~-eagled adj bras et jambes écartés. **~sheet** n tableur m.

spree n **go on a ~** (have fun 🆒) faire la noce.

sprig n petite branche f.

sprightly adj (**-ier**, **-iest**) alerte, vif.

spring vi (pt **sprang**; pp **sprung**) bondir. ● vt **~ sth on sb** annoncer qch de but en blanc à qn. ● n bond m; (device) ressort m; (season) printemps m; (of water) source f. □ **~ from** provenir de; **~ up** surgir.
~board n tremplin m. **~ onion** n oignon m blanc.

springy adj (**-ier**, **-iest**) élastique.

sprinkle vt (with liquid) arroser (with de); (with salt, flour) saupoudrer (with de); (sand) répandre. **sprinkler** n (in garden) arroseur m; (for fires) extincteur m (à déclenchement) automatique.

sprint vi (Sport) sprinter. ● n sprint m.

s

sprout *vt/i* pousser. ● *n* (on plant) pousse *f*; (**Brussels**) ∼s choux *mpl* de Bruxelles.

spruce *adj* pimpant. ● *vt* ∼ **oneself up** se faire beau. ● *n* (tree) épicéa *m*.

sprung ⇒SPRING.

spud *n* ⚊ patate *f*.

spun ⇒SPIN.

spur *n* (of rider) éperon *m*; (stimulus) aiguillon *m*; **on the** ∼ **of the moment** sous l'impulsion du moment. ● *vt* (*pt* **spurred**) éperonner.

spurious *adj* faux.

spurn *vt* repousser.

spurt *vi* jaillir; (fig) accélérer. ● *n* jet *m*; (of energy) sursaut *m*.

spy *n* espion/-ne *m/f*. ● *vi* espionner. ● *vt* apercevoir.

squabble *vi* se chamailler. ● *n* chamaillerie *f*.

squad *n* (of soldiers) escouade *f*; (Sport) équipe *f*.

squadron *n* (Mil) escadron *m*; (Aviat) escadrille *f*.

squalid *adj* sordide.

squander *vt* (*money, time*) gaspiller.

square *n* carré *m*; (open space in town) place *f*. ● *adj* carré; (honest) honnête; (*meal*) solide; (boring ⚊) ringard; (**all**) ∼ (quits) quitte; ∼ **metre** mètre *m* carré. ● *vt* (settle) régler; ∼ **up to** faire face à.

squash *vt* écraser; (crowd) serrer. ● *n* (game) squash *m*; (marrow: US) courge *f*; **lemon** ∼ citronnade *f*; **orange** ∼ orangeade *f*.

squat *vi* (*pt* **squatted**) s'accroupir; ∼ **in a house** squatteriser une maison. ● *adj* (dumpy) trapu. **squatter** *n* squatter *m*.

squawk *n* cri *m* rauque. ● *vi* pousser un cri rauque.

squeak *n* petit cri *m*; (of door) grincement *m*. ● *vi* crier; grincer.

squeal *n* cri *m* aigu. ● *vi* pousser un cri aigu; ∼ **on** (inform on ⚊) dénoncer.

squeamish *adj* (trop) délicat.

squeeze *vt* presser; (*hand, arm*) serrer; (extract) exprimer (**from** de); (extort) soutirer (**from** à). ● *vi* (force one's way) se glisser. ● *n* pression *f*; (Comm) restrictions *fpl* de crédit.

squid *n* calmar *m*.

squint *vi* loucher; (with half-shut eyes) plisser les yeux. ● *n* (Med) strabisme *m*.

squirm *vi* se tortiller.

squirrel *n* écureuil *m*.

squirt *vt/i* (faire) jaillir. ● *n* jet *m*.

stab *vt* (*pt* **stabbed**) (with knife) poignarder. ● *n* coup *m* (de couteau); **have a** ∼ **at sth** essayer de faire qch.

stability *n* stabilité *f*. **stabilize** *vt* stabiliser.

stable *adj* stable. ● *n* écurie *f*. ∼-**boy** *n* lad *m*.

stack *n* tas *m*. ● *vt* ∼ (**up**) entasser, empiler.

stadium *n* stade *m*.

staff *n* personnel *m*; (in school) professeurs *mpl*; (Mil) état-major *m*; (stick) bâton *m*. ● *vt* pourvoir en personnel.

stag *n* cerf *m*.

stage *n* (Theat) scène *f*; (phase) stade *m*, étape *f*; (platform in hall) estrade *f*; **go on the** ∼ faire du théâtre. ● *vt* mettre en scène; (fig) organiser. ∼ **door** *n* entrée *f* des artistes. ∼ **fright** *n* trac *m*.

stagger *vi* chanceler. ● *vt* (shock) stupéfier; (*payments*) échelonner. **staggering** *adj* stupéfiant.

stagnate *vi* stagner.

stag night *n* soirée *f* pour enterrer une vie de garçon.

staid *adj* sérieux.

stain *vt* tacher; (*wood*) colorer. ● *n* tache *f*; (colouring) colorant *m*. **stained glass window** *n* vitrail *m*.

stainless steel *n* acier *m* inoxydable.

stain remover *n* détachant *m*.

stair *n* marche *f*; **the** ∼s l'escalier *m*. ∼**case**, ∼**way** *n* escalier *m*.

stake *n* (post) pieu *m*; (wager) enjeu *m*; **at** ∼ en jeu. ● *vt* (*area*) jalonner; (*wager*) jouer; ∼ **a claim to** revendiquer.

stale *adj* pas frais; (*bread*) rassis; (*smell*) de renfermé.

stalk *n* (of plant) tige *f*. ● *vi* marcher de façon guindée. ● *vt* (*hunter*) chasser; (*murderer*) suivre.

S

stall n (in stable) stalle f; (in market) éventaire m; ~**s** (Theat) orchestre m. ● vt/i (Auto) caler; ~ **(for time)** temporiser.

stallion n étalon m.

stamina n résistance f.

stammer vt/i bégayer. ● n bégaiement m.

stamp vt/i ~ **(one's foot)** taper du pied. ● vt (letter) timbrer. ● n (for postage, marking) timbre m; (mark: fig) sceau m. □ ~ **out** supprimer. ~**-collecting** n philatélie f.

stampede n fuite f désordonnée; (rush: fig) ruée f. ● vi s'enfuir en désordre; se ruer.

stand vi (pt **stood**) être or se tenir (debout); (rise) se lever; (be situated) se trouver; (Pol) être candidat (for à); ~ **in line** (US) faire la queue; ~ **to reason** être logique. ● vt mettre (debout); (tolerate) supporter; ~ **a chance** avoir une chance. ● n (stance) position f; (Mil) résistance f; (for lamp) support m; (at fair) stand m; (in street) kiosque m; (for spectators) tribune f; (Jur, US) barre f; **make a** ~ prendre position. □ ~ **back** reculer; ~ **by** or **around** ne rien faire; ~ **by** (be ready) se tenir prêt; (promise, person) rester fidèle à; ~ **down** se désister; ~ **for** représenter; Ⓣ supporter; ~ **in for** remplacer; ~ **out** ressortir; ~ **up** se lever; ~ **up for** défendre; ~ **up to** résister à.

standard n norme f; (level) niveau m (voulu); (flag) étendard m; ~ **of living** niveau m de vie; ~**s** (morals) principes mpl. ● adj ordinaire.

standard of living n niveau m de vie.

stand-by adj de réserve. ● n **be a** ~ être de réserve.

stand-in n remplaçant/-e m/f.

standing adj debout inv. ● n réputation f; (duration) durée f. ~ **order** n prélèvement m bancaire.

standpoint n point m de vue.

standstill n **at a** ~ immobile; **bring/ come to a** ~ (s')immobiliser.

stank ⇒STINK.

staple n agrafe f. ● vt agrafer. ● adj principal, de base. **stapler** n agrafeuse f.

star n étoile f; (person) vedette f. ● vt (pt **starred**) (film) avoir pour vedette. ● vi ~ **in** être la vedette de.

starch n amidon m; (in food) fécule f. ● vt amidonner.

stardom n célébrité f.

stare vi ~ **at** regarder fixement. ● n regard m fixe.

starfish n étoile f de mer.

stark adj (desolate) désolé; (severe) austère; (utter) complet; (fact) brutal. ● adv complètement.

starling n étourneau m.

start vt/i commencer; (machine) (se) mettre en marche; (fashion) lancer; (cause) provoquer; (jump) sursauter; (of vehicle) démarrer; ~ **to do** commencer or se mettre à faire; ~**ing tomorrow** à partir de demain. ● n commencement m, début m; (of race) départ m; (lead) avance f; (jump) sursaut m. □ ~ **off** commencer (doing par faire); ~ **out** partir; ~ **up** (business) lancer. **starter** n (Auto) démarreur m; (runner) partant m; (Culin) entrée f.

starting point n point m de départ.

startle vt (make jump) faire tressaillir; (shock) alarmer.

starvation n faim f.

starve vi mourir de faim. ● vt affamer; (deprive) priver.

stash vt cacher.

state n état m; (pomp) apparat m; S~ État m; **the S~s** les États-Unis; **get into a** ~ s'affoler. ● adj d'État, de l'État; (school) public. ● vt affirmer (that que); (views) exprimer; (fix) fixer.

stately adj (-ier, -iest) majestueux. ~ **home** n château m.

statement n déclaration f; (of account) relevé m.

statesman n (pl -men) homme m d'État.

static adj statique. ● n (radio, TV) parasites mpl.

station n (Rail) gare f; (TV) chaîne f; (Mil) poste m; (rank) condition f. ● vt poster, placer; ~**ed at** or **in** (Mil) en garnison à.

stationary adj immobile, stationnaire; (vehicle) à l'arrêt.

S

stationery *n* papeterie *f*.

station wagon *n* (US) break *m*.

statistic *n* statistique *f*; ～s statistique *f*.

statue *n* statue *f*.

status *n* (*pl* ～es) situation *f*, statut *m*; (prestige) standing *m*.

statute *n* loi *f*; ～s (rules) statuts *mpl*. **statutory** *adj* statutaire; (*holiday*) légal.

staunch *adj* (*friend*) loyal, fidèle.

stave *n* (Mus) portée *f*. ● *vt* ～ off éviter, conjurer.

stay *vi* rester; (spend time) séjourner; (reside) loger. ● *vt* ～ **away from** (*school*) ne pas aller à; ～ **behind** *or* ～ **on** rester; ～ **in** rester à la maison; ～ **up** veiller, se coucher tard.

stead *n* **stand sb in good** ～ être utile à qn.

steadfast *adj* ferme.

steady *adj* (**-ier, -iest**) stable; (*hand, voice*) ferme; (regular) régulier; (staid) sérieux. ● *vt* maintenir, assurer; (calm) calmer.

steak *n* steak *m*, bifteck *m*; (of fish) darne *f*.

steal *vt/i* (*pt* **stole**; *pp* **stolen**) voler (**from sb** à qn).

steam *n* vapeur *f*; (on glass) buée *f*. ● *vt* (cook) cuire à la vapeur. ● *vi* fumer. ～**-engine** *n* locomotive *f* à vapeur

steamer *n* (Culin) cuit-vapeur *m*; (boat) (bateau à) vapeur *m*.

steel *n* acier *m*; ～ **industry** sidérurgie *f*. ● *vpr* ～ **oneself** s'endurcir, se cuirasser.

steep *adj* raide, rapide; (*price*: 🄫) excessif. ● *vt* (soak) tremper; ～ed in (fig) imprégné de.

steeple *n* clocher *m*.

steer *vt* diriger; (*ship*) gouverner; (fig) guider. ● *vi* (in ship) gouverner; ～ **clear of** éviter.

steering-wheel *n* volant *m*.

stem *n* tige *f*; (of glass) pied *m*. ● *vi* (*pt* **stemmed**) ～ **from** provenir de. ● *vt* (*pt* **stemmed**) (check, stop) endiguer, contenir.

stench *n* puanteur *f*.

stencil *n* pochoir *m*. ● *vt* (*pt* **stencilled**) décorer au pochoir.

step *vi* (*pt* **stepped**) marcher, aller. ● *n* pas *m*; (stair) marche *f*; (of train) marchepied *m*; (action) mesure *f*; ～s (ladder) escabeau *m*; **in** ～ au pas; (fig) conforme (**with** à). □ ～ **down** (resign) démissionner; (from ladder) descendre; ～ **forward** faire un pas en avant; ～ **in** (intervene) intervenir; ～ **up** (pressure) augmenter. ～**brother** *n* demi-frère *m*. ～**daughter** *n* belle-fille *f*. ～**father** *n* beau-père *m*. ～**-ladder** *n* escabeau *m*. ～**mother** *n* belle-mère *f*. **stepping-stone** *n* (fig) tremplin *m*. ～**sister** *n* demi-sœur *f*. ～**son** *n* beau-fils *m*.

stereo *n* stéréo *f*; (record-player) chaîne *f* stéréo. ● *adj* stéréo *inv*.

stereotype *n* stéréotype *m*. **stereotyped** *adj* stéréotypé.

sterile *adj* stérile. **sterility** *n* stérilité *f*.

sterilize *vt* stériliser.

sterling *n* livre(s) *f(pl)* sterling. ● *adj* sterling *inv*; (silver) fin; (fig) excellent.

stern *adj* sévère. ● *n* (of ship) arrière *m*.

steroid *n* stéroïde *m*.

stew *vt/i* cuire à la casserole; ～ed fruit compote *f*; ～ed tea thé *m* trop infusé. ● *n* ragoût *m*.

steward *n* (of club) intendant *m*; (on ship) steward *m*. **stewardess** *n* hôtesse *f*.

stick *vt* (*pt* **stuck**) (glue) coller; (put 🄘) mettre; (endure 🄘) supporter. ● *vi* (adhere) coller, adhérer; (to pan) attacher; (remain 🄘) rester; (be jammed) être coincé; **be stuck with sb** 🄘 se farcir qn. ● *n* bâton *m*; (for walking) canne *f*. □ ～ **at** persévérer dans; ～ **out** *vt* (*head*) sortir; (*tongue*) tirer; *vi* (protrude) dépasser; ～ **to** (*promise*) rester fidèle à; ～ **up for** 🄘 défendre.

sticker *n* autocollant *m*.

sticky *adj* (**-ier, -iest**) poisseux; (*label, tape*) adhésif.

stiff *adj* raide; (*limb, joint*) ankylosé; (tough) dur; (*drink*) fort; (*price*) élevé; (*manner*) guindé; ～ **neck** torticolis *m*.

stifle *vt/i* étouffer.

stiletto *a* & *n* ~s, ~ **heels** talons *mpl* aiguille.

still *adj* immobile; (quiet) calme, tranquille; **keep** ~! arrête de bouger! ● *n* silence *m*. ● *adv* encore, toujours; (even) encore; (nevertheless) tout de même.

stillborn *adj* mort-né.

still life *n* nature *f* morte.

stimulate *vt* stimuler. **stimulation** *n* stimulation *f*.

stimulus *n* (*pl* **-li**) (spur) stimulant *m*.

sting *n* piqûre *f*; (of insect) aiguillon *m*. ● *vt/i* (*pt* **stung**) piquer.

stingy *adj* (**-ier, -iest**) avare (**with** de).

stink *n* puanteur *f*. ● *vi* (*pt* **stank** *or* **stunk**; *pp* **stunk**) ~ (**of**) puer.

stipulate *vt* stipuler.

stir *vt/i* (*pt* **stirred**) (move) remuer; (excite) exciter; ~ **up** (*trouble*) provoquer. ● *n* agitation *f*.

stirrup *n* étrier *m*.

stitch *n* point *m*; (in knitting) maille *f*; (Med) point *m* de suture; (muscle pain) point *m* de côté; **be in** ~**es** Ⅱ avoir le fou rire. ● *vt* coudre.

stock *n* réserve *f*; (Comm) stock *m*; (financial) valeurs *fpl*; (family) souche *f*; (soup) bouillon *m*; **we're out of** ~ il n'y en a plus; **take** ~ (fig) faire le point; **in** ~ en stock. ● *adj* (goods) courant. ● *vt* (shop) approvisionner; (sell) vendre. ● *vi* ~ **up** s'approvisionner (**with** de). ~ **broker** *n* agent *m* de change. ~ **cube** *n* bouillon-cube *m*. **S**~ **Exchange** *n* Bourse *f*.

stocking *n* bas *m*.

stock market *n* Bourse *f*.

stockpile *n* stock *m*. ● *vt* stocker; (arms) amasser.

stock-taking *n* (Comm) inventaire *m*.

stocky *adj* (**-ier, -iest**) trapu.

stodgy *adj* lourd.

stole, stolen ⇒STEAL.

stomach *n* estomac *m*; (abdomen) ventre *m*. ● *vt* (put up with) supporter. ~**-ache** *n* mal *m* à l'estomac *or* au ventre.

stone *n* pierre *f*; (pebble) caillou *m*; (in fruit) noyau *m*; (weight) 6,350 kg. ● *adj* de pierre; ~**-cold/-deaf** complètement froid/sourd. ● *vt* (throw stones) lapider; (fruit) dénoyauter.

stony *adj* pierreux.

stood ⇒STAND.

stool *n* tabouret *m*.

stoop *vi* (bend) se baisser; (condescend) s'abaisser. ● *n* **have a** ~ être voûté.

stop *vt/i* (*pt* **stopped**) arrêter (**doing** de faire); (moving, talking) s'arrêter; (prevent) empêcher (**from** de); (hole, leak) boucher; (pain, noise) cesser; (stay Ⅱ) rester. ● *n* arrêt *m*; (full stop) point *m*; ~(**-over**) halte *f*; (port of call) escale *f*. □ ~ **off** s'arrêter; ~ **up** boucher,

stopgap *n* bouche-trou *m*. ● *adj* intérimaire.

stoppage *n* arrêt *m*; (of work) arrêt *m* de travail; (of pay) retenue *f*.

stopper *n* bouchon *m*.

stop-watch *n* chronomètre *m*.

storage *n* (of goods, food) emmagasinage *m*. ~ **heater** *n* radiateur *m* électrique à accumulation.

store *n* réserve *f*; (warehouse) entrepôt *m*; (shop) grand magasin *m*; (US) magasin *m*; **have in** ~ **for** réserver à; **set** ~ **by** attacher du prix à. ● *vt* (for future) mettre en réserve; (in warehouse, mind) emmagasiner. ~**-room** *n* réserve *f*.

storey *n* étage *m*.

stork *n* cigogne *f*.

storm *n* tempête *f*, orage *m*. ● *vt* prendre d'assaut. ● *vi* (rage) tempêter.

story *n* histoire *f*; (in press) article *m*; (storey; US) étage *m*. ~**-teller** *n* conteur/-euse *m/f*.

stout *adj* corpulent; (strong) solide. ● *n* bière *f* brune.

stove *n* cuisinière *f*.

stow *vt* ~ **away** (put away) ranger; (hide) cacher. ● *vi* voyager clandestinement.

straddle *vt* être à cheval sur, enjamber.

straggler *n* traînard/-e *m/f*.

S

straight adj droit; (tidy) en ordre; (frank) franc; ~ **face** visage m sérieux; **get sth** ~ mettre qch au clair. ● adv (in straight line) droit; (direct) tout droit; ~ **ahead** or **on** tout droit; ~ **away** tout de suite; ~ **off** 🄸 sans hésiter. ● n (Sport) ligne f droite.

straighten vt (nail, situation) redresser; (tidy) arranger.

straightforward adj honnête; (easy) simple.

straight off adj 🄸 sans hésiter.

strain vt (rope, ears) tendre; (limb) fouler; (eyes) fatiguer; (muscle) froisser; (filter) passer; (vegetables) égoutter; (fig) mettre à l'épreuve. ● vi fournir des efforts. ● n tension f; (fig) effort m; (breed) race f; (of virus) variété f; ~s (tune: Mus) accents mpl. **strained** adj forcé; (relations) tendu. **strainer** n passoire f.

strait n détroit m; ~s détroit m; **be in dire** ~s être aux abois. ~-**jacket** n camisole f de force.

strand n (thread) fil m, brin m; (of hair) mèche f.

stranded adj (person) en rade; (ship) échoué.

strange adj étrange; (unknown) inconnu. **stranger** n inconnu/-e m/f.

strangle vt étrangler.

stranglehold n **have a** ~ **on** tenir à la gorge.

strap n (of leather) courroie f; (of dress) bretelle f; (of watch) bracelet m. ● vt (pt **strapped**) attacher.

strategic adj stratégique.
strategy n stratégie f.

straw n paille f; **the last** ~ le comble.

strawberry n fraise f.

stray vi s'égarer; (deviate) s'écarter. ● adj perdu; (isolated) isolé. ● n animal m perdu.

streak n raie f, bande f; (trace) trace f; (period) période f; (tendency) tendance f. ● vt (mark) strier. ● vi filer à toute allure.

stream n ruisseau m; (current) courant m; (flow) flot m; (in school) classe f (de niveau). ● vi ruisseler (with de); (eyes, nose) couler.

streamline vt rationaliser. **streamlined** adj (shape) aérodynamique.

street n rue f. ~**car** n (US) tramway m. ~ **lamp** n réverbère m. ~ **map** n indicateur m des rues.

strength n force f; (of wall, fabric) solidité f; **on the** ~ **of** en vertu de.
strengthen vt renforcer, fortifier.

strenuous adj (exercise) énergique; (work) ardu.

stress n (emphasis) accent m; (pressure) pression f; (Med) stress m. ● vt souligner, insister sur.

stretch vt (pull taut) tendre; (arm, leg) étendre; (neck) tendre; (clothes) étirer; (truth) forcer; ~ **one's legs** se dégourdir les jambes. ● vi s'étendre; (person) s'étirer; (clothes) se déformer. ● n étendue f; (period) période f; (of road) tronçon m; **at a** ~ d'affilée. ● adj (fabric) extensible.

stretcher n brancard m.

strew vt (pt **strewed**; pp **strewed** or **strewn**) (scatter) répandre; (cover) joncher.

strict adj strict.

stride vi (pt **strode**; pp **stridden**) faire de grands pas. ● n grand pas m.

strife n conflit(s) m(pl).

strike vt (pt **struck**) frapper; (blow) donner; (match) frotter; (gold) trouver. ● vi faire grève; (attack) attaquer; (clock) sonner. ● n (of workers) grève f; (Mil) attaque f; (find) découverte f; **on** ~ en grève. □ ~ **off** or **out** rayer; ~ **up** (a friendship) lier amitié (**with** avec). **striker** n gréviste mf; (football) attaquant/-e m/f. **striking** adj frappant.

string n ficelle f; (of violin, racket) corde f; (of pearls) collier m; (of lies) chapelet m; **the** ~s (Mus) les cordes; **pull** ~s faire jouer ses relations. ● vt (pt **strung**) (thread) enfiler. **stringed** adj (instrument) à cordes.

stringent adj rigoureux, strict.

stringy adj filandreux.

strip vt/i (pt **stripped**) (undress) (se) déshabiller; (deprive) dépouiller. ● n bande f.

stripe n rayure f, raie f. **striped** adj rayé.

strip light n néon m.

stripper n strip-teaseur/-euse m/f; (solvent) décapant.

strip-tease n strip-tease m.

strive vi (pt **strove**; pp **striven**) s'efforcer (**to** de).

strode ⇒STRIDE.

stroke vt (with hand) caresser. ● n coup m; (of pen) trait m; (swimming) nage f; (Med) attaque f, congestion f; **at a ~** d'un seul coup.

stroll vi flâner; **~ in** entrer tranquillement. ● n petit tour m.

stroller n (US) poussette f.

strong adj fort; (shoes, fabric) solide; **be fifty ~** être fort de cinquante personnes. **~hold** n bastion m.

strongly adv (greatly) fortement; (with energy) avec force; (deeply) profondément.

strove ⇒STRIVE.

struck ⇒STRIKE.

structure n (of cell, poem) structure f; (building) construction f.

struggle vi lutter, se battre. ● n lutte f; (effort) effort m; **have a ~ to** avoir du mal à.

strum vt (pt **strummed**) gratter de.

strung ⇒STRING. ● adj **~ up** (tense) nerveux.

strut n (support) étai m. ● vi (pt **strutted**) se pavaner.

stub n bout m; (counterfoil) talon m. ● vt (pt **stubbed**) **~ one's toe** se cogner le doigt de pied. □ **~ out** écraser.

stubble n (on chin) barbe f de plusieurs jours; (remains of wheat) chaume m.

stubborn adj obstiné.

stuck ⇒STICK. ● adj (jammed) coincé; **I'm ~** (for answer) je sèche. **~-up** adj 🔲 prétentieux.

stud n (on jacket) clou m; (for collar) bouton m; (stallion) étalon m; (horse farm) haras m. ● vt (pt **studded**) clouter.

student n (Univ) étudiant/-e m/f; (School) élève mf. ● adj (restaurant, life) universitaire.

studio n studio m.

studious adj (person) studieux; (deliberate) étudié.

study n étude f; (office) bureau m. ● vt/i étudier.

stuff n substance f; 🔲 chose(s) f(pl). ● vt rembourrer; (animal) empailler; (cram) bourrer; (Culin) farcir; (block up) boucher; (put) fourrer. **stuffing** n bourre f; (Culin) farce f.

stuffy adj (-ier, -iest) mal aéré; (dull 🔲) vieux jeu inv.

stumble vi trébucher; **~ across** or **on** tomber sur. **stumbling-block** n obstacle m.

stump n (of tree) souche f; (of limb) moignon m; (of pencil) bout m.

stumped adj embarrassé.

stun vt (pt **stunned**) étourdir; (bewilder) stupéfier.

stung ⇒STING.

stunk ⇒STINK.

stunning adj (delightful 🔲) sensationnel.

stunt vt (growth) retarder. ● n (feat 🔲) tour m de force; (trick 🔲) truc m; (dangerous) cascade f.

stupid adj stupide, bête. **stupidity** n stupidité f.

sturdy adj (-ier, -iest) robuste.

stutter vi bégayer. ● n bégaiement m.

sty n (pigsty) porcherie f; (on eye) orgelet m.

style n style m; (fashion) mode f; (sort) genre m; (pattern) modèle m; **do sth in ~** faire qch avec classe. ● vt (design) créer; **~ sb's hair** coiffer qn.

stylish adj élégant.

stylist n (of hair) coiffeur/-euse m/f.

suave adj (urbane) courtois; (smooth: pej) doucereux.

subconscious a & n inconscient (m), subconscient (m).

subcontract vt sous-traiter.

subdue vt (feeling) maîtriser; (country) subjuguer. **subdued** adj (person, mood) morose; (light) tamisé; (criticism) contenu.

subject¹ adj (state) soumis; **~ to** soumis à; (liable to, dependent on) sujet à. ● n sujet m; (focus) objet m; (School, Univ) matière f; (citizen) ressortissant/-e m/f, sujet/-te m/f.

subject² vt soumettre.

subjective adj subjectif.

S

subject-matter *n* contenu *m*.

subjunctive *a & n* subjonctif (*m*).

sublet *vt* sous-louer.

submarine *n* sousmarin *m*.

submerge *vt* submerger. ● *vi* plonger.

submissive *adj* soumis.

submit *vt/i* (*pt* **submitted**) (se) soumettre (**to** à).

subordinate *adj* subalterne; (Gram) subordonné. ● *n* subordonné/-e *m/f*.

subpoena *n* (Jur) citation *f*, assignation *f*.

subscribe *vt/i* verser (de l'argent) (**to** à); ~ **to** (*loan, theory*) souscrire à; (*newspaper*) s'abonner à, être abonné à. **subscriber** *n* abonné/-e *m/f*. **subscription** *n* abonnement *m*; (membership dues) cotisation *f*.

subsequent *adj* (later) ultérieur; (next) suivant. **subsequently** *adv* par la suite.

subside *vi* (*land*) s'affaisser; (*flood, wind*) baisser.

subsidiary *adj* accessoire. ● *n* (Comm) filiale *f*.

subsidize *vt* subventionner. **subsidy** *n* subvention *f*.

substance *n* substance *f*.

substandard *adj* de qualité inférieure.

substantial *adj* considérable; (*meal*) substantiel.

substitute *n* succédané *m*; (person) remplaçant/-e *m/f*. ● *vt* substituer (**for** à).

subtitle *n* sous-titre *m*.

subtle *adj* subtil.

subtract *vt* soustraire.

suburb *n* faubourg *m*, banlieue *f*; ~**s** banlieue *f*. **suburban** *adj* de banlieue. **suburbia** *n* la banlieue.

subway *n* passage *m* souterrain; (US) métro *m*.

succeed *vi* réussir (**in doing** à faire). ● *vt* (follow) succéder à.

success *n* succès *m*, réussite *f*.

successful *adj* réussi, couronné de succès; (favourable) heureux; (in exam) reçu; **be** ~ **in doing** réussir à faire.

succession *n* succession *f*; **in** ~ de suite.

successive *adj* successif; **six** ~ **days** six jours consécutifs.

successor *n* successeur *m*.

such *det & pron* tel(le), tel(le)s; (so much) tant (de). ● *adv* si; ~ **a book** un tel livre; ~ **books** de tels livres; ~ **courage** tant de courage; ~ **a big house** une si grande maison; ~ **as** comme, tel que; **as** ~ en tant que tel; **there's no** ~ **thing** ça n'existe pas. ~**-and-**~ *adj* tel ou tel.

suck *vt* sucer. □ ~ **in** *or* **up** aspirer. **sucker** *n* (rubber pad) ventouse *f*; (person Ⅰ) dupe *f*.

suction *n* succion *f*.

sudden *adj* soudain, subit; **all of a** ~ tout à coup. **suddenly** *adv* subitement, brusquement.

sue *vt* (*pres p* **suing**) poursuivre (en justice).

suede *n* daim *m*.

suffer *vt/i* souffrir; (*loss, attack*) subir. **sufferer** *n* victime *f*, malade *mf*. **suffering** *n* souffrance(s) *f(pl)*.

sufficient *adj* (enough) suffisamment de; (big enough) suffisant.

suffix *n* suffixe *m*.

suffocate *vt/i* suffoquer.

sugar *n* sucre *m*. ● *vt* sucrer.

suggest *vt* suggérer. **suggestion** *n* suggestion *f*.

suicidal *adj* suicidaire.

suicide *n* suicide *m*; **commit** ~ se suicider.

suit *n* (man's) costume *m*; (woman's) tailleur *m*; (cards) couleur *f*. ● *vt* convenir à; (*garment, style*) aller à; (adapt) adapter.

suitable *adj* qui convient (**for** à), convenable. **suitably** *adv* convenablement.

suitcase *n* valise *f*.

suite *n* (rooms) suite *f*; (furniture) mobilier *m*.

suited *adj* (**well**) ~ (matched) bien assorti; ~ **to** fait pour, apte à.

sulk *vi* bouder.

sullen *adj* maussade.

sultana *n* raisin *m* de Smyrne, raisin *m* sec.

sultry *adj* (**-ier, -iest**) étouffant, lourd; (fig) sensuel.

sum n somme f; (in arithmetic) calcul m. ● vt/i (pt **summed**) ~ **up** résumer, récapituler; (assess) évaluer.

summarize vt résumer.

summary n résumé m. ● adj sommaire.

summer n été m. ● adj d'été. ~**time** n (season) été m.

summery adj estival.

summit n sommet m; ~ (**conference**) (Pol) (conférence f au) sommet m.

summon vt appeler; ~ **sb to a meeting** convoquer qn à une réunion; ~ **up** (strength, courage) rassembler.

summons n (Jur) assignation f. ● vt assigner.

sun n soleil m. ● vt (pt **sunned**) ~ **oneself** se chauffer au soleil. ~**burn** n coup m de soleil.

Sunday n dimanche m. ~ **school** n catéchisme m.

sundry adj divers; **sundries** articles mpl divers; **all and** ~ tout le monde.

sunflower n tournesol m.

sung ⇒SING.

sun-glasses npl lunettes fpl de soleil.

sunk ⇒SINK.

sunken adj (ship) submergé; (eyes) creux.

sunlight n soleil m.

sunny adj (**-ier, -iest**) ensoleillé.

sun: ~**rise** n lever m du soleil. ~**-roof** n toit m ouvrant. ~ **screen** n filtre m solaire. ~**set** n coucher m du soleil. ~**shine** n soleil m. ~**stroke** n insolation f.

sun-tan n bronzage m. ~ **lotion** n lotion f solaire. ~ **oil** n huile f solaire.

super adj 🔡 formidable.

superb adj superbe.

superficial adj superficiel.

superfluous adj superflu.

superimpose vt superposer (**on** à).

superintendent n directeur/-trice m/f; (of police) commissaire m.

superior a & n supérieur/-e (m/f).

superlative adj suprême. ● n (Gram) superlatif m.

supermarket n supermarché m.

supersede vt remplacer, supplanter.

superstition n superstition f.

superstitious adj superstitieux.

superstore n hypermarché m.

supervise vt surveiller, diriger.

supervision n surveillance f.

supervisor n surveillant/-e m/f; (shop) chef m de rayon; (firm) chef m de service.

supper n dîner m; (late at night) souper m.

supple adj souple.

supplement¹ n supplément m. **supplementary** adj supplémentaire.

supplement² vt compléter.

supplier n fournisseur m.

supply vt fournir; (equip) pourvoir; (feed) alimenter (**with** en). ● n provision f; (of gas) alimentation f; **supplies** (food) vivres mpl; (material) fournitures fpl.

support vt soutenir; (family) assurer la subsistance de. ● n soutien m, appui m; (Tech) support m. **supporter** n partisan/-e m/f; (Sport) supporter m. **supportive** adj qui soutient et encourage.

suppose vt/i supposer; **be** ~**d to do** être censé faire, devoir faire; **supposing he comes** supposons qu'il vienne. **supposedly** adv soi-disant, prétendument.

suppress vt (put an end to) supprimer; (restrain) réprimer; (stifle) étouffer.

supreme adj suprême.

surcharge n supplément m; (tax) surtaxe f.

sure adj sûr; **make** ~ **of** s'assurer de; **make** ~ **that** vérifier que. ● adv (US 🔡) pour sûr. **surely** adv sûrement.

surf n ressac m. ● vi faire du surf; (Internet) surfer.

surface n surface f. ● adj superficiel. ● vt revêtir. ● vi faire surface; (fig) réapparaître.

surfer n surfeur/-euse m/f; (Internet) internaute mf.

surge vi (waves, crowd) déferler; (increase) monter. ● n (wave) vague f; (rise) montée f.

S

surgeon n chirurgien m.

surgery n chirurgie f; (office) cabinet m; (session) consultation f; **need ~** devoir être opéré.

surgical adj chirurgical. **~ spirit** n alcool m à 90 degrés.

surly adj (-ier, -iest) bourru.

surname n nom m de famille.

surplus n surplus m. ● adj en surplus.

surprise n surprise f. ● vt surprendre. **surprised** adj surpris (at de). **surprising** adj surprenant.

surrender vi se rendre. ● vt (hand over) remettre; (Mil) rendre. ● n (Mil) reddition f; (of passport) remise f.

surround vt entourer; (Mil) encercler. **surrounding** adj environnant. **surroundings** npl environs mpl; (setting) cadre m.

surveillance n surveillance f.

survey[1] vt (review) passer en revue; (inquire into) enquêter sur; (building) inspecter.

survey[2] n (inquiry) enquête f; inspection f; (general view) vue f d'ensemble.

surveyor n expert m (géomètre).

survival n survie f.

survive vt/i survivre (à). **survivor** n survivant/-e m/f.

susceptible adj sensible (to à); **~ to** (prone to) prédisposé à.

suspect[1] vt soupçonner; (doubt) douter de.

suspect[2] n & a suspect/-e (m/f).

suspend vt (hang, stop) suspendre; (licence) retirer provisoirement. **suspended sentence** n condamnation f avec sursis.

suspender n jarretelle f; **~s** (braces: US) bretelles fpl. **~ belt** n porte-jarretelles m.

suspension n suspension f; retrait m provisoire.

suspicion n soupçon m; (distrust) méfiance f.

suspicious adj soupçonneux; (causing suspicion) suspect; **be ~ of** se méfier de. **suspiciously** adv de façon suspecte.

sustain vt supporter; (effort) soutenir; (suffer) subir.

sustenance n (food) nourriture f; (nourishment) valeur f nutritive.

swallow vt/i avaler; **~ up** (absorb, engulf) engloutir. ● n hirondelle f.

swam ⇒SWIM.

swamp n marais m. ● vt (flood, overwhelm) submerger.

swan n cygne m.

swap vt/i (pt **swapped**) 🅣 échanger. ● n 🅣 échange m.

swarm n essaim m. ● vi fourmiller; **~ into** or **round** (crowd) envahir.

swat vt (pt **swatted**) (fly) écraser.

sway vt/i (se) balancer; (influence) influencer. ● n balancement m; (rule) empire m.

swear vt/i (pt **swore**; pp **sworn**) jurer (to sth de qch); **~ at** injurier; **~ by sth** 🅣 ne jurer que par qch. **~-word** n juron m.

sweat n sueur f. ● vi suer.

sweater n pull-over m.

sweat-shirt n sweat-shirt m.

swede n rutabaga m.

Swede n Suédois/-e m/f. **Sweden** n Suède f.

Swedish adj suédois. ● n (Ling) suédois m.

sweep vt/i (pt **swept**) (floor) balayer; (carry away) emporter, entraîner; (chimney) ramoner. ● n coup m de balai; (curve) courbe f; (movement) geste m, mouvement m; (for chimneys) ramoneur m. □ **~ by** passer rapidement or majestueusement. **sweeper** n (for carpet) balai m mécanique; (football) libero m.

sweet adj (not sour, pleasant) doux; (not savoury) sucré; (charming 🅣) gentil; **have a ~ tooth** aimer les sucreries. ● n bonbon m; (dish) dessert m. **~corn** n maïs m.

sweeten vt sucrer; (fig) adoucir. **sweetener** n édulcorant m.

sweetheart n petit/-e ami/-e m/f; (term of endearment) chéri/-e m/f.

sweetly adv gentiment.

sweetness n douceur f; goût m sucré.

sweet pea n pois m de senteur.

swell vt/i (pt **swelled**; pp **swollen** or **swelled**) (increase) grossir;

(expand) (se) gonfler; (*hand, face*)
enfler. ● *n* (of sea) houle *f*. **swelling**
n (Med) enflure *f*.

sweltering *adj* étouffant.

swept ⇒SWEEP.

swerve *vi* faire un écart.

swift *adj* rapide. ● *n* (bird) martinet
m.

swim *vi* (*pt* **swam**; *pp* **swum**; *pres
p* **swimming**) nager; (be dizzy)
tourner. ● *vt* traverser à la nage;
(*distance*) nager. ● *n* baignade *f*; **go
for a** ∼ aller se baigner. **swimmer**
n nageur/-euse *m/f*. **swimming** *n*
natation *f*.

swimming-pool *n* piscine *f*.

swim-suit *n* maillot *m* (de bain).

swindle *vt* escroquer. ● *n*
escroquerie *f*.

swine *npl* (pigs) pourceaux *mpl*. ● *n
inv* (person 🔲) salaud *m*.

swing *vt/i* (*pt* **swung**) (se) balancer;
(turn round) tourner; (*pendulum*)
osciller. ● *n* balancement *m*; (seat)
balançoire *f*; (of opinion) revirement *m*
(**towards** en faveur de); (Mus) rythme
m; **be in full** ∼ battre son plein. ▫ ∼
round (*person*) se retourner.

swipe *vt* (hit 🔲) frapper; (steal 🔲)
piquer.

swirl *vi* tourbillonner. ● *n* tourbillon
m.

Swiss *adj* suisse. ● *n inv* Suisse *mf*.

switch *n* bouton *m* (électrique),
interrupteur *m*; (shift) changement *m*,
revirement *m*. ● *vt* (transfer)
transférer; (exchange) échanger (**for**
contre); (reverse positions of) changer
de place; ∼ **trains** (change) changer
de train. ● *vi* changer. ▫ ∼ **off**
éteindre; ∼ **on** mettre, allumer.

switchboard *n* standard *m*.

Switzerland *n* Suisse *f*.

swivel *vt/i* (*pt* **swivelled**) (faire)
pivoter.

swollen ⇒SWELL.

swoop *vi* (bird) fondre; (police) faire
une descente, foncer. ● *n* (police raid)
descente *f*.

sword *n* épée *f*.

swore ⇒SWEAR.

sworn ⇒SWEAR. ● *adj* (*enemy*) juré;
(*ally*) dévoué.

swot *vt/i* (*pt* **swotted**) (study 🔲)
bûcher 🔲. ● *n* 🔲 bûcheur/-euse *m/f*
🔲.

swum ⇒SWIM.

swung ⇒SWING.

syllabus *n* (*pl* ∼**es**) (School, Univ)
programme *m*.

symbol *n* symbole *m*. **symbolic(al)**
adj symbolique. **symbolize** *vt*
symboliser.

symmetrical *adj* symétrique.

sympathetic *adj* compatissant;
(fig) compréhensif.

sympathize *vi* ∼ **with** (pity)
plaindre; (fig) comprendre les
sentiments de. **sympathizer** *n*
sympathisant/-e *m/f*.

sympathy *n* (pity) compassion *f*; (fig)
compréhension *f*; (solidarity) solidarité
f; (condolences) condoléances *fpl*;
(affinity) affinité *f*; **be in** ∼ **with**
comprendre, être en accord avec.

symptom *n* symptôme *m*.

synagogue *n* synagogue *f*.

synonym *n* synonyme *m*.

synopsis *n* (*pl* -**opses**) résumé *m*.

syntax *n* syntaxe *f*.

synthesis *n* (*pl* -**theses**) synthèse
f.

synthetic *adj* synthétique.

syringe *n* seringue *f*.

syrup *n* (liquid) sirop *m*; (treacle)
mélasse *f* raffinée.

system *n* système *m*; (body)
organisme *m*; (order) méthode *f*.
systematic *adj* systématique.

systems analyst *n* analyste-
programmeur/-euse *m/f*.

Tt

tab *n* (on can) languette *f*; (on garment)
patte *f*; (label) étiquette *f*; (US 🔲)
addition *f*; (Comput) tabulatrice *f*;
(setting) tabulation *f*.

table *n* table *f*; **at** (**the**) ∼ à table; **lay**
or **set the** ∼ mettre la table. ● *vt*
(*motion*) présenter. ∼-**cloth** *n* nappe

f. ~**-mat** *n* set *m* de table. ~**spoon** *n* cuillère *f* de service.

tablet *n* (of stone) plaque *f*; (drug) comprimé *m*.

table tennis *n* tennis *m* de table; ping-pong® *m*.

taboo *n* & *a* tabou (*m*).

tacit *adj* tacite.

tack *n* (nail) clou *m*; (stitch) point *m* de bâti; (course of action) voie *f*. ● *vt* (nail) clouer; (stitch) bâtir; (add) ajouter. ● *vi* (Naut) louvoyer.

tackle *n* équipement *m*; (in soccer) tacle *m*; (in rugby) plaquage *m*. ● *vt* (*problem*) s'attaquer à; (*player*) tacler, plaquer.

tact *n* tact *m*. **tactful** *adj* plein de tact.

tactics *npl* tactique *f*.

tadpole *n* têtard *m*.

tag *n* (label) étiquette *f*. ● *vt* (*pt* **tagged**) (label) étiqueter. ● *vi* ~ **along** Ⓣ suivre.

tail *n* queue *f*; ~**s** (coat) habit *m*; ~**s!** (on coin) pile! ● *vt* (follow) filer. ● *vi* ~ **away** *or* **off** diminuer. ~**-back** *n* bouchon· *m*. ~**-gate** *n* hayon *m*.

tailor *n* tailleur *m*. ● *vt* (*garment*) façonner; (fig) adapter. ~**-made** *adj* fait sur mesure.

take *vt/i* (*pt* **took**; *pp* **taken**) prendre (from sb à qn); (carry) emporter, porter (**to** à); (escort) emmener; (contain) contenir; (tolerate) supporter; (accept) accepter; (*prize*) remporter; (*exam*) passer; (*precedence*) avoir; (*view*) adopter; ~ **sb home** ramener qn chez lui; **be taken by** *or* **with** être impressionné par; **be taken ill** tomber malade; **it** ~**s time** il faut du temps pour. ▫ ~ **after** tenir de; ~ **apart** démonter; (fig) descendre en flammes Ⓣ; ~ **away** (*object*) enlever; (*person*) emmener; (*pain*) supprimer; ~ **back** reprendre; (return) rendre; (accompany) raccompagner; (*statement*) retirer; ~ **down** (*object*) descendre; (*notes*) prendre; ~ **in** (*object*) rentrer; (include) inclure; (cheat) tromper; ~ **off** (Aviat) décoller; ~ **sth off** enlever qch; ~ **sb off** imiter qn; ~ **on** (*task, staff, passenger*) prendre; (*challenger*)

relever le défi de; ~ **out** sortir; (*stain*) enlever; ~ **over** *vt* (*country, firm*) prendre le contrôle de; *vi* prendre le pouvoir; ~ **over from** remplacer; ~ **part** participer (**in** à); ~ **place** avoir lieu; ~ **to** se prendre d'amitié pour; (*activity*) prendre goût à; ~ **to doing** se mettre à faire; ~ **up** (*object*) monter; (*hobby*) se mettre à; (occupy) prendre; (resume) reprendre; ~ **up with** se lier avec. ~**-away** *n* (meal) repas *m* à emporter. ~**-off** *n* (Aviat) décollage *m*. ~**-over** *n* (Pol) prise *f* de pouvoir; (Comm) rachat *m*.

tale *n* conte *m*; (report) récit *m*; (lie) histoire *f*.

talent *n* talent *m*. **talented** *adj* doué.

talk *vt/i* parler; (chat) bavarder; ~ **sb into doing** persuader qn de faire; ~ **sth over** discuter de qch. ● *n* (talking) propos *mpl*; (conversation) conversation *f*; (lecture) exposé *m*.

talkative *adj* bavard.

tall *adj* (high) haut; (*person*) grand.

tame *adj* apprivoisé; (dull) insipide. ● *vt* apprivoiser; (*lion*) dompter.

tamper *vi* ~ **with** (*lock, machine*) tripoter; (*accounts, evidence*) trafiquer.

tan *vt/i* (*pt* **tanned**) bronzer; (*hide*) tanner. ● *n* bronzage *m*.

tangerine *n* mandarine *f*.

tangle *vt/i* ~ (**up**) s'emmêler. ● *n* enchevêtrement *m*.

tank *n* réservoir *m*; (vat) cuve *f*; (for fish) aquarium *m*; (Mil) char *m* (de combat).

tanker *n* (lorry) camion-citerne *m*; (ship) navire-citerne *m*; oil/petrol ~ pétrolier *m*.

tantrum *n* crise *f* (de colère).

tap *n* (for water) robinet *m*; (knock) petit coup *m*; **on** ~ disponible. ● *vt* (*pt* **tapped**) (knock) taper (doucement); (*resources*) exploiter; (*phone*) mettre sur écoute.

tape *n* bande *f* (magnétique); (cassette) cassette *f*; (video) cassette *f* vidéo; (fabric) ruban *m*; (sticky) scotch® *m*. ● *vt* (record) enregistrer; ~ **sth to sth** coller qch à qch.

~-**measure** *n* mètre *m* ruban. ~
recorder *n* magnétophone *m*.

tapestry *n* tapisserie *f*.

tar *n* goudron *m*. ● *vt* (*pt* **tarred**)
goudronner.

target *n* cible *f*; (objective) objectif *m*.
● *vt* (*city*) prendre pour cible;
(*weapon*) diriger; (in marketing) viser.

tariff *n* (price list) tarif *m*; (on imports)
droit *m* de douane.

tarmac, **Tarmac**® *n* macadam *m*;
(runway) piste *f*.

tarpaulin *n* bâche *f*.

tarragon *n* estragon *m*.

tart *n* tarte *f*. ● *adj* aigrelet.

task *n* tâche *f*.

taste *n* goût *m*; (experience) aperçu *m*.
● *vt* (eat, enjoy) goûter à; (try) goûter;
(perceive taste of) sentir (le goût de).
● *vi* ~ **of** *or* **like** avoir un goût de.
tasteful *adj* de bon goût.

tattoo *vt* tatouer. ● *n* tatouage *m*.

tatty *adj* (**-ier**, **-iest**) 🇬🇧 miteux.

taught ⇒TEACH.

taunt *vt* railler. ● *n* raillerie *f*.

Taurus *n* Taureau *m*.

tax *n* (on goods, services) taxe *f*; (on
income) impôt *m*. ● *vt* imposer; (put to
test: fig) mettre à l'épreuve. **taxable**
adj imposable. **taxation** *n*
imposition *f*; (taxes) impôts *mpl*.

tax: ~-**collector** *n* percepteur *m*.
~-**deductible** *adj* déductible des
impôts. ~ **disc** *n* vignette *f*. ~-**free**
adj exempt d'impôts. ~ **haven** *n*
paradis *m* fiscal.

taxi *n* taxi *m*. ~ **rank** *n* station *f* de
taxi.

tax: ~**payer** *n* contribuable *mf*. ~
relief *n* dégrèvement *m* fiscal. ~
return *n* déclaration *f* d'impôts.

tea *n* (drink, meal) thé *m*; (children's
snack) goûter *m*; ~ **bag** sachet *m* de
thé.

teach *vt* (*pt* **taught**) apprendre (**sb
sth** qch à qn); (in school) enseigner
(**sb sth** qch à qn). ● *vi* enseigner.
teacher *n* enseignant/-e *m/f*;
(secondary) professeur *m*; (primary)
instituteur/-trice *m/f*.

team *n* équipe *f*; (of animals) attelage
m. ● *vi* ~ **up** faire équipe (**with**
avec).

teapot *n* théière *f*.

tear[1] *vt/i* (*pt* **tore**; *pp* **torn**) (se)
déchirer; (snatch) arracher (**from** à);
(rush) aller à toute vitesse. ● *n*
déchirure *f*.

tear[2] *n* larme *f*; **in** ~**s** en larmes.
~-**gas** *n* gaz *m* lacrymogène.

tease *vt* taquiner. ● *n* taquin/-e *m/f*.

tea: ~-**shop** *n* salon *m* de thé.
~**spoon** *n* petite cuillère *f*.

teat *n* tétine *f*.

tea-towel *n* torchon *m*.

technical *adj* technique.

technician *n* technicien/-ne *m/f*.

technique *n* technique *f*.

techno *n* (Mus) techno *f*.

technology *n* technologie *f*.

teddy *adj* ~ **bear** ours *m* en peluche.

tedious *adj* ennuyeux.

tee *n* (golf) tee *m*.

teenage *adj* (*girl, boy*) adolescent;
(*fashion*) des adolescents. **teenager**
n jeune *mf*, adolescent/-e *m/f*.

teens *npl* **in one's** ~ adolescent.

teeth ⇒TOOTH.

teethe *vi* faire ses dents.

teetotaller *n* personne *f* qui ne
boit pas d'alcool.

telecommunications *npl*
télécommunications *fpl*.

telecommuting *n* télétravail *m*.

teleconferencing *n*
téléconférence *f*.

telegram *n* télégramme *m*.

telegraph *n* télégraphe *m*. ● *adj*
télégraphique.

telephone *n* téléphone *m*. ● *vt*
(*person*) téléphoner à; (*message*)
téléphoner. ● *vi* téléphoner. ~ **book**
annuaire *m*. ~ **booth**, ~-**box** *n*
cabine *f* téléphonique. ~ **call** *n*
coup *m* de téléphone. ~ **number** *n*
numéro *m* de téléphone.

telephoto *adj* ~ **lens** téléobjectif *m*.

telescope *n* télescope *m*. ● *vt/i* (se)
télescoper.

teletext *n* télétexte *m*.

televise *vt* téléviser.

television *n* télévision *f*; ~ **set**
poste *m* de télévision, téléviseur *m*.

telex *n* télex *m*. ● *vt* envoyer par
télex.

t

tell *vt* (*pt* **told**) dire (**sb sth** qch à qn); (*story*) raconter; (distinguish) distinguer; ∼ **sb to do sth** dire à qn de faire qch; ∼ **sth from sth** voir la différence entre qch et qch. ● *vi* (show) avoir un effet; (know) savoir. □ ∼ **off** 🄸 gronder.

temp *n* intérimaire *mf.* ● *vi* faire de l'intérim.

temper *n* humeur *f*; (anger) colère *f*; **lose one's** ∼ se mettre en colère.

temperament *n* tempérament *m.* **temperamental** *adj* capricieux.

temperature *n* température *f*; **have a** ∼ avoir de la fièvre *or* de la température.

temple *n* temple *m*; (of head) tempe *f.*

temporary *adj* temporaire, provisoire.

tempt *vt* tenter; ∼ **sb to do** donner envie à qn de faire.

ten *a* & *n* dix (*m*).

tenacious *adj* tenace.

tenancy *n* location *f.* **tenant** *n* locataire *mf.*

tend *vt* s'occuper de. ● *vi* ∼ **to** (be apt to) avoir tendance à; (look after) s'occuper de. **tendency** *n* tendance *f.*

tender *adj* tendre; (sore, painful) sensible. ● *vt* offrir, donner. ● *vi* faire une soumission. ● *n* (Comm) soumission *f*; **be legal** ∼ (money) avoir cours.

tendon *n* tendon *m.*

tennis *n* tennis *m.* ● *adj* (*court, match*) de tennis; ∼ **shoes** tennis *mpl.*

tenor *n* (meaning) sens *m* général; (Mus) ténor *m.*

tense *n* (Gram) temps *m.* ● *adj* tendu. ● *vt* (*muscles*) tendre, raidir. ● *vi* (*face*) se crisper.

tension *n* tension *f.*

tent *n* tente *f.*

tentative *adj* provisoire; (hesitant) timide.

tenth *a* & *n* dixième (*mf*).

tepid *adj* tiède.

term *n* (word, limit) terme *m*; (of imprisonment) temps *m*; (School) trimestre *m*; ∼**s** conditions *fpl*; **on good/bad** ∼**s** en bons/mauvais

termes; **in the short/long** ∼ à court/long terme; **come to** ∼**s with sth** accepter qch; ∼ **of office** (Pol) mandat *m.* ● *vt* appeler.

terminal *adj* (*point*) terminal; (*illness*) incurable. ● *n* (oil, computer) terminal *m*; (Rail) terminus *m*; (Electr) borne *f*; (air) ∼ aérogare *f.*

terminate *vt* mettre fin à. ● *vi* prendre fin.

terminus *n* (*pl* **-ni**) (station) terminus *m.*

terrace *n* terrasse *f*; (houses) rangée *f* de maisons contiguës; **the** ∼**s** (Sport) les gradins *mpl.*

terracotta *n* terre *f* cuite.

terrible *adj* affreux, atroce.

terrific *adj* (huge) énorme; (great 🄸) formidable.

terrify *vt* terrifier; **be terrified of** avoir très peur de.

territory *n* territoire *m.*

terror *n* terreur *f.*

terrorism *n* terrorisme *m.* **terrorist** *n* terroriste *mf.*

test *n* épreuve *f*; (written exam) contrôle *m*; (of machine, product) essai *m*; (of sample) analyse *f*; **driving** ∼ examen *m* du permis de conduire. ● *vt* évaluer; (School) contrôler; (*machine, product*) essayer; (*sample*) analyser; (*patience, strength*) mettre à l'épreuve. ● *vi* ∼ **for** faire une recherche de.

testament *n* testament *m*; **Old/New T**∼ Ancien/Nouveau Testament *m.*

testicle *n* testicule *m.*

testify *vt/i* témoigner (**to** de; **that** que).

testimony *n* témoignage *m.*

test tube *n* éprouvette *f.*

tetanus *n* tétanos *m.*

text *n* texte *m.* ∼**book** *n* manuel *m.*

texture *n* (of paper) grain *m*; (of fabric) texture *f.*

Thames *n* **the** ∼ la Tamise.

than *conj* que, qu'; (with numbers) de; **more/less** ∼ **ten** plus/moins de dix.

thank *vt* remercier; ∼ **you!**, ∼**s!** merci! **thankful** *adj* reconnaissant (**for** de). **thanks** *npl* remerciements *mpl*; ∼**s to** grâce à. **Thanksgiving**

(**Day**) n (US) jour m d'Action de Grâces (*fête nationale*).

thaw vt/i (faire) dégeler; (*snow*) (faire) fondre. ● n dégel m.

---

that pl **those**

● *determiner*

····▸ ce, cet, cette, ces; ∼ **dog** ce chien; ∼ **man** cet homme; ∼ **woman** cette femme; **those books** ces livres; **at** ∼ **moment** à ce moment-là.

❗ To distinguish from **this** and **these**, you need to add *-là* after the noun: **I prefer that car** je préfère cette voiture-là.

● *pronoun*

····▸ cela, ça, ce; **what's** ∼?, **what are those?** qu'est-ce que c'est (que ça)?; **who's** ∼? qui est-ce?; ∼ **is my brother** c'est or voilà mon frère; **those are my parents** ce sont mes parents.

····▸ (emphatic) celui-là, celle-là,ceux-là, celles-là; **all the dresses are nice but I like** ∼/**those best** toutes les robes sont jolies mais je préfère celle-là/celles-là.

● *relative pronoun*

····▸ (for subject) qui; **the man** ∼ **stole the car** l'homme qui a volé la voiture.

····▸ (for object) que; **the girl** ∼ **I met** la fille que j'ai rencontrée.

❗ With a preposition, use *lequel/laquelle/lesquels/lesquelles*: **the chair** ∼ **I was sitting on** la chaise sur laquelle j'étais assis.

❗ With a preposition that translates as *à*, use *auquel/à laquelle/auxquels/auxquelles*: **the girls** ∼ **I was talking to** les filles auxquelles je parlais.

❗ With a preposition that translates as *de*, use *dont*: **the people** ∼ **I've talked about** les personnes dont j'ai parlé.

● *conjunction* que; **she said** ∼ **she would do it** elle a dit qu'elle le ferait.

---

thatched adj de chaume; ∼ **cottage** chaumière f.

the *determiner*

····▸ le, l', la, les; ∼ **dog** le chien; ∼ **tree** l'arbre; ∼ **chair** la chaise; **to** ∼ **shops** aux magasins.

❗ With a preposition that translates as *à*: *à* + *le* = *au* and *à* + *les* = *aux*.

---

theatre n théâtre m.

theft n vol m.

their adj leur, pl leurs.

theirs pron le or la leur, les leurs.

them pron les; (after preposition) eux, elles; (to) ∼ leur; **phone** ∼! téléphone-leur!; **I know** ∼ je les connais; **both of** ∼ tous/toutes les deux.

themselves pron eux-mêmes, elles-mêmes; (reflexive) se; (after preposition) eux, elles.

then adv alors; (next) ensuite, puis; (therefore) alors, donc. ● adj d'alors; **from** ∼ **on** dès lors.

theology n théologie f.

theory n théorie f.

therapy n thérapie f.

there adv là; (with verb) y; (over there) là-bas; **he goes** ∼ il y va; **on** ∼ là-dessus; ∼ **is**, ∼ **are** il y a; (pointing) voilà. ● *interj* ∼, ∼! allons, allons!

therefore adv donc.

thermal adj thermique.

thermometer n thermomètre m.

Thermos® n thermos® m or f inv.

thermostat n thermostat m.

thesaurus n (pl **-ri**) dictionnaire m de synonymes.

these ⇒THIS.

thesis n (pl **theses**) thèse f.

they pron ils, elles; (emphatic) eux, elles; (people in general) on.

thick adj épais; (stupid) bête; **be 6 cm** ∼ avoir 6 cm d'épaisseur.

thief n (pl **thieves**) voleur/-euse m/ f.

thigh n cuisse f.

thin adj (**thinner**, **thinnest**) mince; (*person*) maigre, mince; (sparse)

clairsemé; (fine) fin. ● *vt/i* (*pt*
thinned) ~ (**down**) (*paint*) diluer;
(*soup*) allonger.

thing *n* chose *f*; ~**s** (belongings)
affaires *fpl*; **the best ~ is to** le mieux
est de; **the** (**right**) ~ ce qu'il faut (**for
sb** à qn).

think *vt/i* (*pt* **thought**) penser
(**about, of** à); (carefully) réfléchir
(**about, of** à); (believe) croire; **I ~ so** je
crois que oui; ~ **of doing** envisager
de faire. ❑ ~ **over** bien réfléchir à;
~ **up** inventer.

third *adj* troisième. ● *n* troisième *mf*;
(fraction) tiers *m*. **T~ World** *n* tiers-
monde *m*.

thirst *n* soif *f*.

thirsty *adj* **be** ~ avoir soif; **make** ~
donner soif à.

thirteen *a & n* treize (*m*).

thirty *a & n* trente (*m*).

---

this *pl* **these**

● *determiner*

····▶ ce/cet/cette/ces; ~ **dog** ce chien;
~ **man** cet homme; ~ **woman** cette
femme; **these books** ces livres.

! To distinguish from **that** and
those, you need to add *-ci*
■ after the noun: **I prefer this
car** je préfère cette voiture-ci.

● *pronoun*

····▶ ce; **what's** ~?, **what are these?**
qu'est-ce que c'est?; **who is** ~? qui
est-ce?; ~ **is the kitchen** voici la
cuisine; ~ **is Sophie** je te *or* vous
présente Sophie; **these are your
things** ce sont tes affaires.

····▶ (emphatic) celui-ci/celle-ci/ceux-ci/
celles-ci; **all the dresses are nice but I
like** ~/**these best** toutes les robes
sont jolies mais je préfère celle-ci/
celles-ci.

---

thistle *n* chardon *m*.

thorn *n* épine *f*.

thorough *adj* (detailed) approfondi;
(meticulous) minutieux. **thoroughly**
adv (*clean, study*) à fond; (very) tout à
fait.

those ⇒THAT.

though *conj* bien que. ● *adv* quand
même.

thought ⇒THINK. ● *n* pensée *f*, idée
f. **thoughtful** *adj* pensif; (kind)
prévenant.

thousand *a & n* mille (*m inv*); ~**s
of** des milliers de. **thousandth** *a &
n* millième (*mf*).

thread *n* (yarn & fig) fil *m*; (of screw)
pas *m*. ● *vt* enfiler; ~ **one's way** se
faufiler.

threat *n* menace *f*. **threaten** *vt/i*
menacer (**with** de).

three *a & n* trois (*m*).

threw ⇒THROW.

thrill *n* frisson *m*; (pleasure) plaisir *m*.
● *vt* transporter (de joie); **be** ~**ed**
être ravi. ● *vi* frissonner (de joie).

thrive *vi* (*pt* **thrived** *or* **throve**; *pp*
thrived *or* **thriven**) prospérer; **he
~s on it** cela lui réussit.

throat *n* gorge *f*; **have a sore** ~
avoir mal à la gorge.

throb *vi* (*pt* **throbbed**) (*heart*)
battre; (*engine*) vibrer. ● *n* (pain)
élancement *m*; (of engine) vibration *f*.
throbbing *adj* (*pain*) lancinant.

throne *n* trône *m*.

through *prep* à travers; (during)
pendant; (by means or way of, out of)
par; (by reason of) grâce à, à cause de.
● *adv* à travers; (entirely) jusqu'au
bout. ● *adj* (*train*) direct; **be** ~
(finished) avoir fini; **come** *or* **go** ~
(cross, pierce) traverser; **I'm putting
you** ~ je vous passe votre
correspondant.

throughout *prep* ~ **the country**
dans tout le pays; ~ **the day** pendant
toute la journée. ● *adv* (place)
partout; (time) tout le temps.

throw *vt* (*pt* **threw**; *pp* **thrown**)
jeter, lancer; (baffle) déconcerter; ~ **a
party** faire une fête. ● *n* jet *m*; (of
dice) coup *m*. ❑ ~ **away** jeter; ~ **off**
(get rid of) se débarrasser de; ~ **out**
jeter; (*person*) expulser; (reject)
rejeter; ~ **up** (*arms*) lever; (vomit 🔟)
vomir.

thrust *vt* (*pt* **thrust**) pousser. ● *n*
poussée *f*.

thud *n* bruit *m* sourd.

thug *n* voyou *m*.

thumb *n* pouce *m*. ● *vt* (*book*) feuilleter; ∼ **a lift** faire de l'auto-stop. ∼**-index** *n* répertoire *m* à onglets.

thump *vt/i* cogner (sur); (*heart*) battre fort. ● *n* coup *m*.

thunder *n* tonnerre *m*. ● *vi* (*weather, person*) tonner. ∼**storm** *n* orage *m*.

Thursday *n* jeudi *m*.

thus *adv* ainsi.

thwart *vt* contrecarrer.

thyme *n* thym *m*.

tick *n* (sound) tic-tac *m*; (mark) coche *f*; (moment 🔲) instant *m*; (insect) tique *f*. ● *vi* faire tic-tac. ● *vt* ∼ (**off**) cocher. □ ∼ **over** tourner au ralenti.

ticket *n* billet *m*; (for bus, cloakroom) ticket *m*; (label) étiquette *f*. ∼**-collector** *n* contrôleur/-euse *m/f*. ∼**-office** *n* guichet *m*.

tickle *vt* chatouiller; (amuse: fig) amuser. ● *n* chatouillement *m*.

tidal *adj* (*river*) à marées; ∼ **wave** raz-de-marée *m inv*.

tide *n* marée *f*; (of events) cours *m*.

tidy *adj* (**-ier, -iest**) (*room*) bien rangé; (*appearance, work*) soigné; (methodical) ordonné; (amount 🔲) joli. ● *vt/i* ∼ (**up**) faire du rangement; ∼ **sth** (**up**) ranger qch; ∼ **oneself up** s'arranger.

tie *vt* (*pres p* **tying**) attacher; (*knot*) faire; (*scarf*) nouer; (link) lier. ● *vi* (in football) faire match nul; (in race) être ex aequo. ● *n* (necktie) cravate *f*; (fastener) attache *f*; (link) lien *m*; (draw) match *m* nul. □ ∼ **down** attacher; ∼ **in with** être lié à; ∼ **up** attacher; (*money*) immobiliser; (occupy) occuper.

tier *n* étage *m*, niveau *m*; (in stadium) gradin *m*.

tiger *n* tigre *m*.

tight *adj* (*clothes, budget*) serré; (*grip*) ferme; (*rope*) tendu; (*security*) strict; (*angle*) aigu. ● *adv* (*hold, sleep*) bien; (*squeeze*) fort.

tighten *vt/i* (se) tendre; (*bolt*) (se) resserrer; (*control*) renforcer.

tights *npl* collant *m*.

tile *n* (on wall, floor) carreau *m*; (on roof) tuile *f*. ● *vt* carreler; couvrir de tuiles.

till *n* caisse *f* (enregistreuse). ● *vt* (*land*) cultiver. ● *prep & conj* = UNTIL.

timber *n* bois *m* (de construction); (trees) arbres *mpl*.

time *n* temps *m*; (moment) moment *m*; (epoch) époque *f*; (by clock) heure *f*; (occasion) fois *f*; (rhythm) mesure *f*; ∼**s** (multiplying) fois *fpl*; **any** ∼ n'importe quand; **for the** ∼ **being** pour le moment; **from** ∼ **to** ∼ de temps en temps; **have a good** ∼ s'amuser; **in no** ∼ en un rien de temps; **in** ∼ à temps; (eventually) avec le temps; **a long** ∼ longtemps; **on** ∼ à l'heure; **what's the** ∼? quelle heure est-il?; ∼ **off** du temps libre. ● *vt* choisir le moment de; (measure) minuter; (Sport) chronométrer. ∼**-limit** *n* délai *m*.

timer *n* minuterie *f*; (for cooker) minuteur *m*.

time: ∼**-scale** *n* délais *mpl*. ∼**table** *n* horaire *m*. ∼ **zone** *n* fuseau *m* horaire.

timid *adj* timide; (fearful) peureux.

tin *n* étain *m*; (container) boîte *f*; ∼(**plate**) fer-blanc *m*. ● *vt* (*pt* **tinned**) mettre en boîte. ∼ **foil** *n* papier *m* d'aluminium.

tingle *vi* picoter. ● *n* picotement *m*.

tin-opener *n* ouvre-boîtes *m inv*.

tint *n* teinte *f*; (for hair) shampooing *m* colorant. ● *vt* teinter.

tiny *adj* (**-ier, -iest**) tout petit.

tip *n* (of stick, pen, shoe, ski) pointe *f*; (of nose, finger, wing) bout *m*; (gratuity) pourboire *m*; (advice) tuyau *m*; (for rubbish) décharge *f*. ● *vt/i* (*pt* **tipped**) (tilt) pencher; (overturn) (faire) basculer; (pour) verser; (empty) déverser; (give money) donner un pourboire à. □ ∼ **off** prévenir.

tiptoe *n* **on** ∼ sur la pointe des pieds.

tire *vt/i* (se) fatiguer; ∼ **of** se lasser de. ● *n* (US) pneu *m*.

tired *adj* fatigué; **be** ∼ **of** en avoir assez de.

tiring *adj* fatigant.

tissue *n* tissu *m*; (handkerchief) mouchoir *m* en papier; ∼ (**paper**) papier *m* de soie.

tit *n* (bird) mésange *f*; **give** ∼ **for tat** rendre coup pour coup.

title n titre m. ~ **deed** n titre m de propriété.

to

● *preposition*

····➤ à; ~ **Paris** à Paris; **give the book** ~ **Jane** donne le livre à Jane; ~ **the office** au bureau; ~ **the shops** aux magasins.

····➤ (with feminine countries) en; ~ **France** en France.

····➤ (to + personal pronoun) me/te/lui/nous/vous/leur; **she gave it** ~ **them** elle le leur a donné; **I'll say it** ~ **her** je vais le lui dire.

! à + le = au
à + les = aux.

● *in infinitive*

to is not normally translated (**to go** aller, **to sing** chanter)

····➤ (in order to) pour; **he's gone into town** ~ **buy a shirt** il est parti en ville pour acheter une chemise.

····➤ (after adjectives) à; de; **be easy/difficult** ~ **read** être facile/difficile à lire; **it's easy/difficult to read her writing** c'est facile/difficile de lire son écriture.

⟹ For verbal expressions using the verbal 'to' such as **tell sb to do sth**, **help sb to do sth** ➾tell, help.

toad n crapaud m.

toast n pain m grillé, toast m; (drink) toast m. ● vt (bread) faire griller; (drink to) porter un toast à. **toaster** n grille-pain m inv.

tobacco n tabac m.

tobacconist n marchand/-e m/f de tabac; ~**'s** (**shop**) tabac m.

toboggan n toboggan m, luge f.

today n & adv aujourd'hui (m).

toddler n bébé m (qui fait ses premiers pas).

toe n orteil m; (of shoe) bout m; **on one's** ~**s** vigilant. ● vt ~ **the line** se conformer.

together adv ensemble; (at same time) à la fois; ~ **with** avec.

toilet n toilettes fpl.

toiletries npl articles mpl de toilette.

token n (symbol) témoignage m; (voucher) bon m; (coin) jeton m. ● adj symbolique.

told ➾TELL.

tolerance n tolérance f.

tolerate vt tolérer.

toll n péage m; **death** ~ nombre m de morts; **take its** ~ faire des ravages. ● vi (bell) sonner.

tomato n (pl ~**es**) tomate f.

tomb n tombeau m.

tomorrow n & adv demain (m); ~ **morning/night** demain matin/soir; **the day after** ~ après-demain.

ton n tonne f (= 1016 kg); (metric) ~ tonne f (= 1000 kg); ~**s of** 🄸 des masses de.

tone n ton m; (of radio, telephone) tonalité f. ● vt ~ **down** atténuer. ● vi ~ (**in**) s'harmoniser (**with** avec).

tongs npl (for coal) pincettes fpl; (for sugar) pince f; (for hair) fer m.

tongue n langue f.

tonic n (Med) tonique m. ● adj (effect, accent) tonique; ~ (**water**) tonic m, Schweppes® m.

tonight n & adv (evening) ce soir; (night) cette nuit.

tonsil n amygdale f.

too adv trop; (also) aussi; ~ **many people** trop de gens; **I've got** ~ **much/many** j'en ai trop; **me** ~ moi aussi.

took ➾TAKE.

tool n outil m. ~-**box** n boîte f à outils.

toot n coup m de klaxon®. ● vt/i ~ (**the horn**) klaxonner.

tooth n (pl **teeth**) dent f. ~**ache** n mal m de dents. ~**brush** n brosse f à dents. ~**paste** n dentifrice m. ~**pick** n cure-dents m inv.

top n (highest point) sommet m; (upper part) haut m; (upper surface) dessus m; (lid) couvercle m; (of bottle, tube) bouchon m; (of beer bottle) capsule f; (of list) tête f; **on** ~ **of** sur; (fig) en plus de. ● adj (shelf) du haut; (step, floor) dernier; (in rank) premier; (best) meilleur; (distinguished) éminent; (maximum) maximum. ● vt (pt

topped) (exceed) dépasser; (list) venir en tête de; ~ **up** remplir; ~**ped with** (*dome*) surmonté de; (*cream*) recouvert de.

topic *n* sujet *m*.

topless *adj* aux seins nus.

torch *n* (electric) lampe *f* de poche; (flaming) torche *f*.

tore ⇒TEAR¹.

torment *vt* tourmenter; (annoy) agacer.

torn ⇒TEAR¹.

torrent *n* torrent *m*.

tortoise *n* tortue *f*. ~**shell** *n* écaille *f*.

torture *n* torture *f*; (fig) supplice *m*. ● *vt* torturer.

Tory *n & a* tory (*mf*), conservateur/ -trice (*m*/*f*).

toss *vt* lancer; (*salad*) tourner; (*pancake*) faire sauter. ● *vi* se retourner; ~ **a coin**, ~ **up** tirer à pile ou face (**for** pour).

tot *n* petit/-e enfant *m*/*f*; (drink) petit verre *m*.

total *n & a* total (*m*). ● *vt* (*pt* **totalled**) (add up) additionner; (amount to) se monter à.

touch *vt* toucher; (tamper with) toucher à. ● *vi* se toucher. ● *n* (sense) toucher *m*; (contact) contact *m*; (of artist, writer) touche *f*; **a** ~ **of** (small amount) un petit peu de; **get in** ~ **with** se mettre en contact avec; **out of** ~ **with** déconnecté de. □ ~ **down** (Aviat) atterrir; ~ **up** retoucher. ~**down** *n* atterrissage *m*; (Sport) essai *m*. ~**-line** *n* ligne *f* de touche. ~**-tone** *adj* (*phone*) à touches.

tough *adj* (*negotiator*) coriace; (*law*) sévère; (*time*) difficile; (*robust*) robuste.

tour *n* voyage *m*; (visit) visite *f*; (by team) tournée *f*; **on** ~ en tournée. ● *vt* visiter.

tourist *n* touriste *mf*. ● *adj* touristique. ~ **office** *n* syndicat *m* d'initiative.

tournament *n* tournoi *m*.

tout *vi* ~ (**for**) racoler Ⓘ. ● *vt* (sell) revendre. ● *n* racoleur/-euse *m*/*f*; revendeur/-euse *m*/*f*.

tow *vt* remorquer. ● *n* remorque *f*; **on** ~ en remorque.

toward(s) *prep* vers; (of attitude) envers.

towel *n* serviette *f*.

tower *n* tour *f*. ● *vi* ~ **above** dominer.

town *n* ville *f*; **in** ~ en ville. ~ **council** *n* conseil *m* municipal. ~ **hall** *n* mairie *f*.

tow: ~**path** *n* chemin *m* de halage. ~ **truck** *n* dépanneuse *f*.

toxic *adj* toxique.

toy *n* jouet *m*. ● *vi* ~ **with** (object) jouer avec; (idea) caresser.

trace *n* trace *f*. ● *vt* (*person*) retrouver; (*cause*) déterminer; (*life*) retracer; (draw) tracer; (with tracing paper) décalquer.

track *n* (of person, car) traces *fpl*; (of missile) trajectoire *f*; (path) sentier *m*; (Sport) piste *f*; (Rail) voie *f*; (on disc) morceau *m*; **keep** ~ **of** suivre. ● *vt* suivre la trace *or* la trajectoire de. □ ~ **down** retrouver. ~ **suit** *n* survêtement *m*.

tractor *n* tracteur *m*.

trade *n* commerce *m*; (job) métier *m*; (swap) échange *m*. ● *vi* faire du commerce; ~ **on** exploiter. ● *vt* échanger. ● *adj* (*route*, *deficit*) commercial. ~-**in** *n* reprise *f*. ~ **mark** *n* marque *f* (de fabrique); (registered) marque *f* déposée.

trader *n* commerçant/-e *m*/*f*; (on stockmarket) opérateur/-trice *m*/*f*.

trade union *n* syndicat *m*.

trading *n* commerce *m*; (on stockmarket) transactions *fpl* (boursières).

tradition *n* tradition *f*.

traffic *n* trafic *m*; (on road) circulation *f*. ● *vi* (*pt* **trafficked**) faire du trafic (**in** de). ~ **jam** *n* embouteillage *m*. ~**-lights** *npl* feux *mpl* (de circulation). ~ **warden** *n* contractuel/-le *m*/*f*.

trail *vt*/*i* traîner; (*plant*) ramper; (track) suivre; ~ **behind** traîner. ● *n* (of powder) traînée *f*; (track) piste *f*; (path) sentier *m*.

trailer *n* remorque *f*; (caravan) caravane *f*; (film) bande-annonce *f*.

train *n* (Rail) train *m*; (underground) rame *f*; (procession) file *f*; (of dress) traîne *f*. ● *vt* (instruct, develop) former;

(*sportsman*) entraîner; (*animal*) dresser; (*ear*) exercer; (*aim*) braquer. ● *vi* être formé, étudier; (Sport) s'entraîner. **trained** *adj* (skilled) qualifié; (*doctor*) diplômé. **trainee** *n* stagiaire *mf*. **trainer** *n* (Sport) entraîneur/-euse *m/f*. **trainers** *npl* (shoes) chaussures *fpl* de sport. **training** *n* formation *f*; (Sport) entraînement *m*.

tram *n* tram(way) *m*.

tramp *vi* marcher (d'un pas lourd). ● *vt* parcourir. ● *n* (vagrant) clochard/ -e *m/f*; (sound) bruit *m*.

trample *vt/i* ~ (on) piétiner; (fig) fouler aux pieds.

tranquil *adj* tranquille. **tranquillizer** *n* tranquillisant *m*.

transact *vt* négocier. **transaction** *n* transaction *f*.

transcript *n* transcription *f*.

transfer[1] *vt* (*pt* **transferred**) transférer; (*power*) céder; (*employee*) muter. ● *vi* être transféré; (*employee*) être muté.

transfer[2] *n* transfert *m*; (of employee) mutation *f*; (image) décalcomanie *f*.

transform *vt* transformer.

transitive *adj* transitif.

translate *vt* traduire. **translation** *n* traduction *f*. **translator** *n* traducteur/-trice *m/f*.

transmit *vt* (*pt* **transmitted**) transmettre. **transmitter** *n* émetteur *m*.

transparency *n* transparence *f*; (Photo) diapositive *f*.

transplant *n* transplantation *f*; (Med) greffe *f*.

transport[1] *vt* transporter.

transport[2] *n* transport *m*.

trap *n* piège *m*. ● *vt* (*pt* **trapped**) (jam, pin down) coincer; (cut off) bloquer; (snare) prendre au piège.

trash *n* (refuse) ordures *fpl*; (nonsense) idioties *fpl*. ~**-can** *n* (US) poubelle *f*.

trauma *n* traumatisme *m*. **traumatic** *adj* traumatisant.

travel *vi* (*pt* **travelled**, US **traveled**) voyager; (*vehicle, bullet*) aller. ● *vt* parcourir. ● *n* voyages *mpl*. ~ **agency** *n* agence *f* de voyages.

traveller, (US) **traveler** *n* voyageur/-euse *m/f*; ~'s cheque chèque *m* de voyage.

trawler *n* chalutier *m*.

tray *n* plateau *m*; (on office desk) corbeille *f*.

treacle *n* mélasse *f*.

tread *vi* (*pt* **trod**; *pp* **trodden**) marcher (on sur). ● *vt* fouler. ● *n* (sound) pas *m*; (of tyre) chape *f*.

treasure *n* trésor *m*. ● *vt* (*gift, memory*) chérir; (*friendship, possession*) tenir beaucoup à.

treasury *n* trésorerie *f*; the T~ le ministère des Finances.

treat *vt* traiter; ~ sb to sth offrir qch à qn. ● *n* (pleasure) plaisir *m*; (food) gâterie *f*. **treatment** *n* traitement *m*.

treaty *n* traité *m*.

treble *adj* triple; ~ clef clé *f* de sol. ● *vt/i* tripler. ● *n* (voice) soprano *m*.

tree *n* arbre *m*.

trek *n* randonnée *f*. ● *vi* (*pt* **trekked**) ~ across/through traverser péniblement; go ~king faire de la randonnée.

tremble *vi* trembler.

tremendous *adj* énorme; (excellent) formidable.

tremor *n* tremblement *m*; (earth) ~ secousse *f*.

trench *n* tranchée *f*.

trend *n* tendance *f*; (fashion) mode *f*. **trendy** *adj* Ⓣ branché Ⓣ.

trespass *vi* s'introduire illégalement (on dans). **trespasser** *n* intrus/-e *m/f*.

trial *n* (Jur) procès *m*; (test) essai *m*; (ordeal) épreuve *f*; go on ~ passer en jugement; by ~ and error par expérience.

triangle *n* triangle *m*.

tribe *n* tribu *f*.

tribunal *n* tribunal *m*.

tributary *n* affluent *m*.

tribute *n* tribut *m*; pay ~ to rendre hommage à.

trick *n* tour *m*; (dishonest) combine *f*; (knack) astuce *f*; do the ~ Ⓣ faire l'affaire. ● *vt* tromper. **trickery** *n* ruse *f*.

trickle *vi* dégouliner; ∼ **in/out** arriver *or* partir en petit nombre. ● *n* filet *m*; (fig) petit nombre *m*.

tricky *adj* (*task*) difficile; (*question*) épineux; (*person*) malin.

trifle *n* bagatelle *f*; (cake) diplomate *m*; **a** ∼ (small amount) un peu. ● *vi* ∼ **with** jouer avec.

trigger *n* (of gun) gâchette *f*; (of machine) manette *f*. ● *vt* ∼ **(off)** (initiate) déclencher.

trim *adj* (**trimmer, trimmest**) soigné; (figure) svelte. ● *vt* (*pt* **trimmed**) (*hair, grass*) couper; (*budget*) réduire; (decorate) décorer. ● *n* (cut) coupe *f* d'entretien; (decoration) garniture *f*; **in** ∼ en forme.

trinket *n* babiole *f*.

trip *vt/i* (*pt* **tripped**) (faire) trébucher. ● *n* (journey) voyage *m*; (outing) excursion *f*.

triple *adj* triple. ● *vt/i* tripler. **triplets** *npl* triplés/-es *m/fpl*.

tripod *n* trépied *m*.

trite *adj* banal.

triumph *n* triomphe *m*. ● *vi* triompher (**over** de).

trivial *adj* insignifiant.

trod, trodden ⇒TREAD.

trolley *n* chariot *m*.

trombone *n* (Mus) trombone *m*.

troop *n* bande *f*; ∼**s** (Mil) troupes *fpl*. ● *vi* ∼ **in/out** entrer/sortir en bande.

trophy *n* trophée *m*.

tropic *n* tropique *m*; ∼**s** tropiques *mpl*.

trot *n* trot *m*; **on the** ∼ 🔟 coup sur coup. ● *vi* (*pt* **trotted**) trotter.

trouble *n* problèmes *mpl*; ennuis *mpl*; (pains, effort) peine *f*; **be in** ∼ avoir des ennuis; **go to a lot of** ∼ se donner du mal; **what's the** ∼**?** quel est le problème? ● *vt* (bother) déranger; (worry) tracasser. ● *vi* ∼ **(oneself) to do** se donner la peine de faire. ∼**maker** *n* provocateur/-trice *m/f*. ∼**shooter** *n* conciliateur/-trice *m/f*; (Tech) expert *m*.

troublesome *adj* ennuyeux.

trousers *npl* pantalon *m*; **short** ∼ short *m*.

trout *n inv* truite *f*.

trowel *n* (garden) déplantoir *m*; (for mortar) truelle *f*.

truant *n* (School) élève *mf* qui fait l'école buissonnière; **play** ∼ sécher les cours.

truce *n* trève *f*.

truck *n* (lorry) camion *m*; (cart) chariot *m*; (Rail) wagon *m* de marchandises. ∼**-driver** *n* routier *m*.

true *adj* vrai; (accurate) exact; (faithful) fidèle.

truffle *n* truffe *f*.

truly *adv* vraiment; (faithfully) fidèlement; (truthfully) sincèrement.

trumpet *n* trompette *f*.

trunk *n* (of tree, body) tronc *m*; (of elephant) trompe *f*; (box) malle *f*; (Auto, US) coffre *m*; ∼**s** (for swimming) slip *m* de bain.

trust *n* confiance *f*; (association) trust *m*; **in** ∼ en dépôt. ● *vt* avoir confiance en; ∼ **sb with** confier à qn. ● *vi* ∼ **in** *or* **to** s'en remettre à. **trustee** *n* administrateur/-trice *m/f*. **trustworthy** *adj* digne de confiance.

truth *n* (*pl* **-s**) vérité *f*. **truthful** *adj* (*account*) véridique; (*person*) qui dit la vérité.

try *vt/i* (*pt* **tried**) essayer; (be a strain on) éprouver; (Jur) juger; ∼ **on** *or* **out** essayer; ∼ **to do** essayer de faire. ● *n* (attempt) essai *m*; (rugby) essai *m*.

T-shirt *n* tee-shirt *m*.

tub *n* (for flowers) bac *m*; (of ice cream) pot *m*; (bath) baignoire *f*.

tube *n* tube *m*; **the** ∼ 🔟 le métro.

tuberculosis *n* tuberculose *f*.

tuck *n* pli *m*. ● *vt* (put away, place) ranger; (hide) cacher. ● *vi* ∼ **in** *or* **into** 🔟 attaquer; ∼ **in** (shirt) rentrer; (blanket, person) border.

Tuesday *n* mardi *m*.

tug *vt* (*pt* **tugged**) tirer. ● *vi* ∼ **at/on** tirer sur. ● *n* (boat) remorqueur *m*.

tuition *n* cours *mpl*; (fee) frais *mpl* pédagogiques.

tulip *n* tulipe *f*.

tumble *vi* (fall) dégringoler. ● *n* chute *f*. ∼**-drier** *n* sèche-linge *m inv*.

tumbler *n* verre *m* droit.

tummy *n* 🔟 ventre *m*.

tumour *n* tumeur *f*.

t

tuna *n inv* thon *m*.

tune *n* air *m*; **be in** ∼/**out of** ∼ (instrument) être/ne pas être en accord; (singer) chanter juste/faux. ● *vt* (*engine*) régler; (Mus) accorder. ● *vi* ∼ **in** (**to**) (radio, TV) écouter. □ ∼ **up** s'accorder.

Tunisia *n* Tunisie *f*.

tunnel *n* tunnel *m*; (in mine) galerie *f*. ● *vi* (*pt* **tunnelled**) creuser un tunnel (**into** dans).

turf *n* (*pl* **turf** or **turves**) gazon *m*; **the** ∼ (racing) le turf. ● *vt* ∼ **out** ⊡ jeter dehors.

Turk *n* Turc *m*, Turque *f*. **Turkey** *n* Turquie *f*.

turkey *n* dinde *f*.

Turkish *adj* turc. ● *n* (Ling) turc *m*.

turn *vt/i* tourner; (*person*) se tourner; (to other side) retourner; (change) (se) transformer (**into** en); (become) devenir; (deflect) détourner; (milk) tourner. ● *n* tour *m*; (in road) tournant *m*; (of mind, events) tournure *f*; **do a good** ∼ rendre service; **in** ∼ à tour de rôle; **take** ∼**s** se relayer. □ ∼ **against** se retourner contre; ∼ **away** *vi* se détourner; *vt* (avert) détourner; (refuse) refuser; (send back) renvoyer; ∼ **back** *vi* (return) retourner; (*vehicle*) faire demi-tour; *vt* (fold) rabattre; ∼ **down** refuser; (fold) rabattre; (reduce) baisser; ∼ **off** (*light*) éteindre; (*engine*) arrêter; (*tap*) fermer; (of driver) tourner; ∼ **on** (*light*) allumer; (*engine*) allumer; (*tap*) ouvrir; ∼ **out** *vt* (*light*) éteindre; (empty) vider; (*produce*) produire; *vi* **it** ∼**s out that** il se trouve que; ∼ **out well/badly** bien/ mal se terminer; ∼ **over** (se) retourner; ∼ **round** (person) se retourner; ∼ **up** *vi* arriver; (be found) se retrouver; *vt* (find) déterrer; (collar) remonter.

turning *n* rue *f*; (bend) virage *m*.

turnip *n* navet *m*.

turn: ∼**-out** *n* assistance *f*. ∼**over** *n* (pie) chausson *m*; (money) chiffre *m* d'affaires. ∼**table** *n* (for record) platine *f*.

turquoise *adj* turquoise *inv*.

turtle *n* tortue *f* (de mer). ∼**-neck** *n* col *m* montant.

tutor *n* (private) professeur *m* particulier; (Univ) (GB) chargé/-e *m/f* de travaux dirigés.

tutorial *n* (Univ) classe *f* de travaux dirigés.

tuxedo *n* (US) smoking *m*.

TV *n* télé *f*.

tweezers *npl* pince *f* (à épiler).

twelfth *a* & *n* douzième (*mf*).

twelve *a* & *n* douze (*m*); ∼ (**o'clock**) midi *m* or minuit *m*.

twentieth *a* & *n* vingtième (*mf*).

twenty *a* & *n* vingt (*m*).

twice *adv* deux fois.

twig *n* brindille *f*.

twilight *n* crépuscule *m*. ● *adj* crépusculaire.

twin *n* & *a* jumeau/-elle (*m/f*). ● *vt* (*pt* **twinned**) jumeler.

twinge *n* (of pain) élancement *m*; (of conscience, doubt) accès *m*.

twinkle *vi* (*star*) scintiller; (*eye*) pétiller. ● *n* scintillement *m*; pétillement *m*.

twinning *n* jumelage *m*.

twist *vt* tordre; (weave together) entortiller; (roll) enrouler; (distort) déformer. ● *vi* (*rope*) s'entortiller; (*road*) zigzaguer. ● *n* torsion *f*; (in rope) tortillon *m*; (in road) tournant *m*; (in play, story) coup *m* de théâtre.

twitch *vi* (*person*) trembloter; (*mouth*) trembler; (*string*) vibrer. ● *n* (tic) tic *m*; (jerk) secousse *f*.

two *a* & *n* deux (*m*); **in** ∼**s** par deux; **break in** ∼ casser en deux.

tycoon *n* magnat *m*.

type *n* type *m*, genre *m*; (print) caractères *mpl*. ● *vt/i* (write) taper (à la machine). ∼**face** *n* police *f* (de caractères). ∼**writer** *n* machine *f* à écrire.

typical *adj* typique.

typist *n* dactylo *mf*.

tyrant *n* tyran *m*.

tyre *n* pneu *m*.

Uu

udder *n* pis *m*, mamelle *f*.

UFO *n* OVNI *m inv.*

UHT *abbr* (**ultra heat treated**) ~ milk lait *m* longue conservation.

ugly *adj* (**-ier, -iest**) laid.

UK *abbr* ⇒UNITED KINGDOM.

Ukraine *n* Ukraine *f*.

ulcer *n* ulcère *m*.

ulterior *adj* ultérieur; ~ **motive** arrière-pensée *f*.

ultimate *adj* dernier, ultime; (*definitive*) définitif; (*basic*) fondamental.

ultrasound *n* ultrason *m*.

umbilical cord *n* cordon *m* ombilical.

umbrella *n* parapluie *m*.

umpire *n* arbitre *m*. ● *vt* arbitrer.

umpteenth *adj* 🔟 énième.

UN *abbr* (**United Nations**) ONU *f*.

unable *adj* incapable; (*through circumstances*) dans l'impossibilité (**to do** de faire).

unacceptable *adj* (*suggestion*) inacceptable; (*behaviour*) inadmissible.

unanimous *adj* unanime. **unanimously** *adv* à l'unanimité.

unattended *adj* sans surveillance.

unattractive *adj* (*idea*) peu attrayant; (*person*) peu attirant.

unauthorized *adj* non autorisé.

unavoidable *adj* inévitable.

unbearable *adj* insupportable.

unbelievable *adj* incroyable.

unbiased *adj* impartial.

unblock *vt* déboucher.

unborn *adj* (*child*) à naître; (*generation*) à venir.

uncalled-for *adj* injustifié, déplacé.

uncanny *adj* (**-ier, -iest**) étrange, troublant.

uncivilized *adj* barbare.

uncle *n* oncle *m*.

uncomfortable *adj* (*chair*) inconfortable; (*feeling*) pénible; **feel** *or* **be** ~ (person) être mal à l'aise.

uncommon *adj* rare.

unconscious *adj* sans connaissance, inanimé; (*not aware*) inconscient (**of** de). ● *n* inconscient *m*.

unconventional *adj* peu conventionnel.

uncouth *adj* grossier.

uncover *vt* découvrir.

undecided *adj* indécis.

under *prep* sous; (*less than*) moins de; (*according to*) selon. ● *adv* au-dessous; ~ **it/there** là-dessous. ~ **age** *adj* mineur. ~**cover** *adj* secret. ~**cut** *vt* (*pt* **-cut**; *pres p* **-cutting**) (Comm) vendre moins cher que. ~**dog** *n* (Pol) opprimé/-e *m/f*; (*socially*) déshérité/-e *m/f*. ~**done** *adj* pas assez cuit. ~**estimate** *vt* sous-estimer. ~**fed** *adj* sous-alimenté. ~**go** *vt* (*pt* **-went**; *pp* **-gone**) subir. ~**graduate** *n* étudiant/-e *m/f* (*qui prépare la licence*).

underground *adj* souterrain; (*secret*) clandestin. ● *adv* sous terre. ● *n* (rail) métro *m*.

under: ~**line** *vt* souligner. ~**mine** *vt* saper.

underneath *prep* sous. ● *adv* (en) dessous.

under: ~**pants** *npl* slip *m*. ~**rate** *vt* sous-estimer.

understand *vt/i* (*pt* **-stood**) comprendre.

understanding *adj* compréhensif. ● *n* compréhension *f*; (*agreement*) entente *f*.

undertake *vt* (*pt* **-took**; *pp* **-taken**) entreprendre. ~**taker** *n* entrepreneur *m* de pompes funèbres. ~**taking** *n* (*task*) entreprise *f*; (*promise*) promesse *f*.

underwater *adj* sous-marin. ● *adv* sous l'eau.

under: ~**wear** *n* sous-vêtements *mpl*. ~**world** *n* (of crime) milieu *m*, pègre *f*.

undo *vt* (*pt* **-did**; *pp* **-done**) défaire, détacher; (*wrong*) réparer; (Comput) annuler.

u

undress vt/i (se) déshabiller; **get ~ed** se déshabiller.

undue adj excessif.

unearth vt déterrer.

uneasy adj (ill at ease) mal à l'aise; (worried) inquiet; (situation) difficile.

uneducated adj (person) inculte; (speech) populaire.

unemployed adj en chômage. ● npl the ~ les chômeurs mpl.

unemployment n chômage m; ~ benefit allocations fpl de chômage.

uneven adj inégal.

unexpected adj inattendu, imprévu. **unexpectedly** adv (arrive) à l'improviste; (small, fast) étonnamment.

unfair adj injuste.

unfaithful adj infidèle.

unfit adj (Med) pas en forme; (ill) malade; (unsuitable) impropre (for à); ~ to (unable) pas en état de.

unfold vt déplier; (expose) exposer. ● vi se dérouler.

unforeseen adj imprévu.

unforgettable adj inoubliable.

unfortunate adj malheureux; (event) fâcheux.

ungrateful adj ingrat.

unhappy adj (-ier, -iest) (person) malheureux; (face) triste; (not pleased) mécontent (with de).

unharmed adj indemne, sain et sauf.

unhealthy adj (-ier, -iest) (climate) malsain; (person) en mauvaise santé.

unheard-of adj inouï.

unhurt adj indemne.

uniform n uniforme m. ● adj uniforme.

unify vt unifier.

unintentional adj involontaire.

uninterested adj indifférent (in à).

union n union f; (trade union) syndicat m; U~ Jack drapeau m du Royaume-Uni.

unique adj unique.

unit n unité f; (of furniture) élément m; ~ trust ≈ SICAV f.

unite vt/i (s')unir.

United Kingdom n Royaume-Uni m.

United Nations npl Nations fpl Unies.

United States (of America) npl États-Unis mpl (d'Amérique).

unity n unité f.

universal adj universel.

universe n univers m.

university n université f. ● adj universitaire; (student, teacher) d'université.

unkind adj pas gentil, méchant.

unknown adj inconnu. ● n the ~ l'inconnu m.

unleaded adj sans plomb.

unless conj à moins que.

unlike adj différent. ● prep contrairement à; (different from) différent de.

unlikely adj improbable.

unload vt décharger.

unlock vt ouvrir.

unlucky adj (-ier, -iest) malheureux; (number) qui porte malheur.

unmarried adj célibataire.

unnatural adj pas naturel, anormal.

unnecessary adj inutile.

unnoticed adj inaperçu.

unofficial adj officieux.

unpack vt (suitcase) défaire; (contents) déballer. ● vi défaire sa valise.

unpleasant adj désagréable (to avec).

unplug vt débrancher.

unpopular adj impopulaire; ~ with mal vu de.

unprofessional adj peu professionnel.

unqualified adj non diplômé; (success) total; be ~ to ne pas être qualifié pour.

unravel vt (pt unravelled) démêler.

unreasonable adj irréaliste.

unrelated adj sans rapport (to avec).

unreliable adj peu sérieux; (machine) peu fiable.

unrest n troubles mpl.

unroll vt dérouler.

unruly *adj* indiscipliné.

unsafe *adj* (dangerous) dangereux; (*person*) en danger.

unscheduled *adj* pas prévu.

unscrupulous *adj* sans scrupules, malhonnête.

unsettled *adj* instable.

unsightly *adj* laid.

unskilled *adj* (worker) non qualifié.

unsound *adj* (*roof*) en mauvais état; (*investment*) douteux.

unsteady *adj* (*step*) chancelant; (*ladder*) instable; (*hand*) mal assuré.

unsuccessful *adj* (*result, candidate*) malheureux; (*attempt*) infructueux; **be** ~ ne pas réussir (**in doing** à faire).

unsuitable *adj* inapproprié; **be** ~ ne pas convenir.

unsure *adj* incertain.

untidy *adj* (**-ier, -iest**) (*person*) désordonné; (*room*) en désordre; (*work*) mal soigné.

untie *vt* (*knot, parcel*) défaire; (*person*) détacher.

until *prep* jusqu'à; **not** ~ pas avant. ● *conj* jusqu'à ce que; **not** ~ pas avant que.

untrue *adj* faux.

unused *adj* (new) neuf; (not in use) inutilisé.

unusual *adj* exceptionnel; (strange) insolite, étrange.

unwanted *adj* (useless) superflu; (*child*) non désiré.

unwelcome *adj* fâcheux; (*guest*) importun.

unwell *adj* souffrant.

unwilling *adj* peu disposé (**to** à); (*accomplice*) malgré soi.

unwind *vt/i* (*pt* **unwound**) (se) dérouler; (relax Ⓣ) se détendre.

unwise *adj* imprudent.

unwrap *vt* déballer.

up *adv* en haut, en l'air; (sun, curtain) levé; (out of bed) levé, debout; (finished) fini; **be** ~ (*level, price*) avoir monté. ● *prep* (a hill) en haut de; (a tree) dans; (a ladder) sur; **come** *or* **go** ~ monter; ~ **in the bedroom** là-haut dans la chambre; ~ **there** là-haut; ~ **to** jusqu'à; (*task*) à la hauteur de; **it is** ~ **to you** ça dépend de vous (**to** de);

be ~ **to sth** (able) être capable de qch; (plot) préparer qch; **be** ~ **to** (in book) en être à; **be** ~ **against** faire face à; ~ **to date** moderne; (*news*) récent. ● *n* ~**s and downs** les hauts et les bas *mpl*.

up-and-coming *adj* prometteur.

upbringing *n* éducation *f*.

update *vt* mettre à jour.

upgrade *vt* améliorer; (*person*) promouvoir.

upheaval *n* bouleversement *m*.

uphill *adj* qui monte; (fig) difficile. ● *adv* **go** ~ monter.

upholstery *n* rembourrage *m*; (in vehicle) garniture *f*.

upkeep *n* entretien *m*.

up-market *adj* haut-de-gamme.

upon *prep* sur.

upper *adj* supérieur; **have the** ~ **hand** avoir le dessus. ● *n* (of shoe) empeigne *f*. ~ **class** *n* aristocratie *f*. ~**most** *adj* (highest) le plus haut.

upright *adj* droit. ● *n* (post) montant *m*.

uprising *n* soulèvement *m*.

uproar *n* tumulte *m*.

uproot *vt* déraciner.

upset¹ *vt* (*pt* **upset**; *pres p* **upsetting**) (overturn) renverser; (*plan, stomach*) déranger; (*person*) contrarier, affliger. ● *adj* peiné.

upset² *n* dérangement *m*; (distress) chagrin *m*.

upside-down *adv* (lit) à l'envers; (fig) sens dessus dessous.

upstairs *adv* en haut. ● *adj* (*flat*) du haut.

uptight *adj* Ⓣ tendu, coincé Ⓣ.

up-to-date *adj* à la mode; (*records*) à jour.

upward *a & adv*, **upwards** *adv* vers le haut.

urban *adj* urbain.

urge *vt* conseiller vivement (**to do** de faire); ~ **on** encourager. ● *n* forte envie *f*.

urgency *n* urgence *f*; (of request, tone) insistance *f*. **urgent** *adj* urgent; (*request*) pressant.

urinal *n* urinoir *m*.

urine *n* urine *f*.

u

us *pron* nous; (to) ~ nous; **both of** ~ tous/toutes les deux.

US *abbr* ⇒UNITED STATES.

USA *abbr* ⇒UNITED STATES OF AMERICA.

use¹ *vt* se servir de, utiliser; (consume) consommer; ~ **up** épuiser.

use² *n* usage *m*, emploi *m*; **in** ~ en usage; **it is no** ~ **doing** ça ne sert à rien de faire; **make** ~ **of** se servir de; **of** ~ utile.

used¹ *adj* (car) d'occasion.

used² *v aux* he ~ **to smoke** il fumait (autrefois). ● *adj* ~ **to** habitué à.

useful *adj* utile.

useless *adj* inutile; (person) incompétent.

user *n* (of road, service) usager *m*; (of product) utilisateur/-trice *m/f*. ~**-friendly** *adj* facile d'emploi; (Comput) convivial.

usual *adj* habituel, normal; **as** ~ comme d'habitude. **usually** *adv* d'habitude.

utility *n* utilité *f*; (public) ~ **service** *m* public.

utmost *adj* (furthest, most intense) extrême; **the** ~ **care** le plus grand soin. ● *n* **do one's** ~ faire tout son possible.

utter *adj* complet, absolu. ● *vt* prononcer.

U-turn *n* demi-tour *m*; (fig) volte-face *f inv*.

Vv

vacancy *n* (post) poste *m* vacant; (room) chambre *f* disponible.

vacant *adj* (post) vacant; (seat) libre; (look) vague.

vacate *vt* quitter.

vacation *n* vacances *fpl*.

vaccinate *vt* vacciner.

vacuum *n* vide *m*. ~ **cleaner** *n* aspirateur *m*. ~**-packed** *adj* emballé sous vide.

vagina *n* vagin *m*.

vagrant *n* vagabond/-e *m/f*.

vague *adj* vague; (outline) flou; **be** ~ **about** ne pas préciser.

vain *adj* (conceited) vaniteux; (useless) vain; **in** ~ en vain.

valentine *n* ~ (card) carte *f* de la Saint-Valentin.

valid *adj* (argument, ticket) valable; (passport) valide.

valley *n* vallée *f*.

valuable *adj* (object) de valeur; (help) précieux. **valuables** *npl* objets *mpl* de valeur.

valuation *n* (of painting) expertise *f*; (of house) évaluation *f*.

value *n* valeur *f*; ~ **added tax** taxe *f* à la valeur ajoutée, TVA *f*. ● *vt* (appraise) évaluer; (cherish) attacher de la valeur à.

valve *n* (Tech) soupape *f*; (of tyre) valve *f*; (Med) valvule *f*.

van *n* camionnette *f*.

vandal *n* vandale *mf*.

vanguard *n* **in the** ~ **of** à l'avant-garde *f* de.

vanilla *n* vanille *f*.

vanish *vi* disparaître.

vapour *n* vapeur *f*.

variable *adj* variable.

varicose *adj* ~ **veins** varices *fpl*.

varied *adj* varié.

variety *n* variété *f*; (entertainment) variétés *fpl*.

various *adj* divers.

varnish *n* vernis *m*. ● *vt* vernir.

vary *vt/i* varier.

vase *n* vase *m*.

vast *adj* (space) vaste; (in quantity) énorme.

vat *n* cuve *f*.

VAT *abbr* (**value added tax**) TVA *f*.

vault *n* (roof) voûte *f*; (in bank) chambre *f* forte; (tomb) caveau *m*; (jump) saut *m*. ● *vt/i* sauter.

VCR *abbr* ⇒VIDEO CASSETTE RECORDER.

VDU *abbr* ⇒VISUAL DISPLAY UNIT.

veal *n* veau *m*.

vegan *a* & *n* végétalien/-ne (*m/f*).

vegetable *n* légume *m*. ● *adj* végétal.

u
v

vegetarian *a* & *n* végétarien/-ne (*m/f*).

vehicle *n* véhicule *m*.

veil *n* voile *m*.

vein *n* (in body, rock) veine *f*; (on leaf) nervure *f*.

velvet *n* velours *m*.

vending-machine *n* distributeur *m* automatique.

veneer *n* (on wood) placage *m*; (fig) vernis *m*.

venereal *adj* vénérien.

venetian *adj* ∼ **blind** jalousie *f*.

vengeance *n* vengeance *f*; **with a** ∼ de plus belle.

venison *n* venaison *f*.

venom *n* venin *m*.

vent *n* bouche *f*, conduit *m*; (in coat) fente *f*. ● *vt* (anger) décharger (**on** sur).

ventilate *vt* ventiler. **ventilator** *n* ventilateur *m*.

venture *n* entreprise *f*. ● *vt/i* (se) risquer.

venue *n* lieu *m*.

verb *n* verbe *m*.

verbal *adj* verbal.

verbatim *a* & *adv* mot pour mot.

verdict *n* verdict *m*.

verge *n* bord *m*; **on the** ∼ **of doing** sur le point de faire. ● *vi* ∼ **on** friser, frôler.

verify *vt* vérifier.

vermin *n* vermine *f*.

versatile *adj* (person) aux talents variés; (mind) souple.

verse *n* strophe *f*; (of Bible) verset *m*; (poetry) vers *mpl*.

version *n* version *f*.

versus *prep* contre.

vertebra *n* (pl **-brae**) vertèbre *f*.

vertical *adj* vertical.

vertigo *n* vertige *m*.

very *adv* très. ● *adj* (actual) même; **the** ∼ **day** le jour même; **at the** ∼ **end** tout à la fin; **the** ∼ **first** le tout premier; ∼ **much** beaucoup.

vessel *n* vaisseau *m*.

vest *n* maillot *m* de corps; (waistcoat: US) gilet *m*.

vet *n* vétérinaire *mf*. ● *vt* (pt **vetted**) (candidate) examiner (de près).

veteran *n* vétéran *m*; (**war**) ∼ ancien combattant *m*.

veterinary *adj* vétérinaire; ∼ **surgeon** vétérinaire *mf*.

veto *n* (pl ∼**es**) veto *m*; (right) droit *m* de veto. ● *vt* mettre son veto à.

via *prep* via, par.

vibrate *vt/i* (faire) vibrer.

vicar *n* pasteur *m*.

vice *n* (depravity) vice *m*; (Tech) étau *m*.

vicinity *n* environs *mpl*; **in the** ∼ **of** à proximité de.

vicious *adj* (spiteful) méchant; (violent) brutal; ∼ **circle** cercle *m* vicieux.

victim *n* victime *f*.

victor *n* vainqueur *m*. **victory** *n* victoire *f*.

video *adj* (game, camera) vidéo *inv*. ● *n* (recorder) magnétoscope *m*; (film) vidéo *f*; ∼ (**cassette**) cassette *f* vidéo. ● *vt* enregistrer.

videotape *n* bande *f* vidéo. ● *vt* (programme) enregistrer; (wedding) filmer avec une caméra vidéo.

view *n* vue *f*; **in my** ∼ à mon avis; **in** ∼ **of** compte tenu de; **on** ∼ exposé; **with a** ∼ **to** dans le but de. ● *vt* (watch) regarder; (consider) considérer (**as** comme); (house) visiter. **viewer** *n* (TV) téléspectateur/-trice *m/f*.

view: ∼**finder** *n* viseur *m*. ∼**point** *n* point *m* de vue.

vigilant *adj* vigilant.

vigour, (US) **vigor** *n* vigueur *f*.

vile *adj* (base) vil; (bad) abominable.

villa *n* pavillon *m*; (for holiday) villa *f*.

village *n* village *m*.

villain *n* scélérat *m*, bandit *m*; (in story) méchant *m*.

vindictive *adj* vindicatif.

vine *n* vigne *f*.

vinegar *n* vinaigre *m*.

vineyard *n* vignoble *m*.

vintage *n* (year) année *f*, millésime *m*. ● *adj* (wine) de grand cru; (car) d'époque.

viola *n* (Mus) alto *m*.

violate *vt* violer.

V

violence *n* violence *f*. **violent** *adj* violent.

violet *n* (Bot) violette *f*; (colour) violet *m*.

violin *n* violon *m*.

VIP *abbr* (**very important person**) personnalité *f*, VIP *m*.

virgin *n* (woman) vierge *f*.

Virgo *n* Vierge *f*.

virtual *adj* quasi-total; (Comput) virtuel. **virtually** *adv* pratiquement.

virtue *n* vertu *f*; (advantage) mérite *m*; by ∼ of en raison de.

virus *n* virus *m*.

visa *n* visa *m*.

visibility *n* visibilité *f*. **visible** *adj* visible.

vision *n* vision *f*.

visit *vt* (*pt* **visited**) (*person*) rendre visite à; (*place*) visiter. ● *vi* être en visite. ● *n* (tour, call) visite *f*; (stay) séjour *m*. **visitor** *n* visiteur/-euse *m*/*f*; (guest) invité/-e *m*/*f*.

visual *adj* visuel. ∼ **display unit** *n* visuel *m*, console *f* de visualisation.

visualize *vt* se représenter; (foresee) envisager.

vital *adj* vital.

vitamin *n* vitamine *f*.

vivacious *adj* plein de vivacité.

vivid *adj* (*colour, imagination*) vif; (*description, dream*) frappant.

vivisection *n* vivisection *f*.

vocabulary *n* vocabulaire *m*.

vocal *adj* vocal; (*person*) qui s'exprime franchement. ∼ **cords** *npl* cordes *fpl* vocales.

vocation *n* vocation *f*. **vocational** *adj* professionnel.

voice *n* voix *f*. ● *vt* (express) formuler. ∼ **mail** *n* messagerie *f* vocale.

void *adj* vide (of de); (not valid) nul. ● *n* vide *m*.

volatile *adj* (*person*) versatile; (*situation*) explosif.

volcano *n* (*pl* ∼es) volcan *m*.

volley *n* (of blows, in tennis) volée *f*; (of gunfire) salve *f*.

volt *n* (Electr) volt *m*. **voltage** *n* tension *f*.

volume *n* volume *m*.

voluntary *adj* volontaire; (unpaid) bénévole.

volunteer *n* volontaire *mf*. ● *vi* s'offrir (**to do** pour faire); (Mil) s'engager comme volontaire. ● *vt* offrir.

vomit *vt*/*i* (*pt* **vomited**) vomir. ● *n* vomi *m*.

vote *n* vote *m*; (right) droit *m* de vote. ● *vt*/*i* voter; ∼ **sb in** élire qn. **voter** *n* électeur/-trice *m*/*f*. **voting** *n* vote *m* (of de); (poll) scrutin *m*.

vouch *vi* ∼ **for** se porter garant de.

voucher *n* bon *m*.

vowel *n* voyelle *f*.

voyage *n* voyage *m* (en mer).

vulgar *adj* vulgaire.

vulnerable *adj* vulnérable.

Ww

wad *n* (pad) tampon *m*; (bundle) liasse *f*.

wade *vi* ∼ **through** (*mud*) patauger dans; (*book*: fig) avancer péniblement dans.

wafer *n* (biscuit) gaufrette *f*.

waffle *n* (talk 🗊) verbiage *m*; (cake) gaufre *f*. ● *vi* 🗊 divaguer.

wag *vt*/*i* (*pt* **wagged**) (tail) remuer.

wage *vt* (campaign) mener; ∼ **war** faire la guerre. ● *n* (weekly, daily) salaire *m*; ∼**s** salaire *m*. ∼**-earner** *n* salarié/-e *m*/*f*.

wagon *n* (horse-drawn) chariot *m*; (Rail) wagon *m* (de marchandises).

wail *vi* gémir. ● *n* gémissement *m*.

waist *n* taille *f*. ∼**coat** *n* gilet *m*.

wait *vt*/*i* attendre; **I can't** ∼ **to start** j'ai hâte de commencer; **let's** ∼ **and see** attendons voir; ∼ **for** attendre; ∼ **on** servir. ● *n* attente *f*.

waiter *n* garçon *m*, serveur *m*.

waiting-list *n* liste *f* d'attente.

waiting-room *n* salle *f* d'attente.

waitress *n* serveuse *f*.

waive *vt* renoncer à.

wake vt/i (pt **woke**; pp **woken**) ~ **(up)** (se) réveiller. ● n (track) sillage m; **in the** ~ **of** (after) à la suite de. ~ **up call** n réveil m téléphoné.

Wales n pays m de Galles.

walk vi marcher; (not ride) aller à pied; (stroll) se promener. ● vt (streets) parcourir; (distance) faire à pied; (dog) promener. ● n promenade f, tour m; (gait) démarche f; (pace) marche f, pas m; (path) allée f; **have a** ~ faire une promenade. ◻ ~ **out** (go away) partir; (worker) faire grève; ~ **out on** abandonner.

walkie-talkie n talkie-walkie m.

walking n marche f (à pied). ● adj (corpse, dictionary): fig) ambulant.

walkman® n walkman® m, baladeur m.

walk: ~**-out** n grève f surprise. ~**-over** n victoire f facile.

wall n mur m; (of tunnel, stomach) paroi f. ● adj mural. **walled** adj (city) fortifié.

wallet n portefeuille m.

wallpaper n papier m peint. ● vt tapisser.

walnut n (nut) noix f; (tree) noyer m.

waltz n valse f. ● vi valser.

wander vi errer; (stroll) flâner; (digress) s'écarter du sujet; (in mind) divaguer.

wane vi décroître.

want vt vouloir (**to do** faire); (need) avoir besoin de (**doing** d'être fait); (ask for) demander; **I** ~ **you to do it** je veux que vous le fassiez. ● vi ~ **for** manquer de. ● n (need, poverty) besoin m; (desire) désir m; (lack) manque m; **for** ~ **of** faute de. **wanted** adj (criminal) recherché par la police.

war n guerre f; **at** ~ en guerre; **on the** ~**path** sur le sentier de la guerre.

ward n (in hospital) salle f; (minor: Jur) pupille mf; (Pol) division f électorale. ● vt ~ **off** (danger) prévenir.

warden n directeur/-trice m/f; (of park) gardien/-ne m/f; (traffic) ~ contractuel/-le m/f.

wardrobe n (furniture) armoire f; (clothes) garde-robe f.

warehouse n entrepôt m.

wares npl marchandises fpl.

warfare n guerre f.

warm adj chaud; (hearty) chaleureux; **be** or **feel** ~ avoir chaud; **it is** ~ il fait chaud. ● vt/i ~ **(up)** (se) réchauffer; (food) chauffer; (liven up) (s')animer; (exercise) s'échauffer.

warmth n chaleur f.

warn vt avertir, prévenir; ~ **sb off sth** (advise against) mettre qn en garde contre qch; (forbid) interdire qch à qn.

warning n avertissement m; (notice) avis m; **without** ~ sans prévenir. ~ **light** n voyant m. ~ **triangle** n triangle m de sécurité.

warp vt/i (wood) (se) voiler; (pervert) pervertir; (judgment) fausser.

warrant n (for arrest) mandat m (d'arrêt); (Comm) autorisation f. ● vt justifier.

warranty n garantie f.

wart n verrue f.

wartime n **in** ~ en temps de guerre.

wary adj (-ier, -iest) prudent.

was ⇒BE.

wash vt/i (se) laver; (flow over) baigner; ~ **one's hands of** se laver les mains de. ● n lavage m; (clothes) lessive f; **have a** ~ se laver. ◻ ~ **up** faire la vaisselle; (US) se laver. ~**-basin** n lavabo m.

washer n rondelle f.

washing n lessive f. ~**-machine** n machine f à laver. ~**-powder** n lessive f.

washing-up n vaisselle f. ~ **liquid** n liquide m vaisselle.

wash: ~**-out** n 🔲 fiasco m. ~**-room** n (US) toilettes fpl.

wasp n guêpe f.

wastage n gaspillage m.

waste vt gaspiller; (time) perdre. ● vi ~ **away** dépérir. ● adj superflu; ~ **products** or **matter** déchets mpl. ● n gaspillage m; (of time) perte f; (rubbish) déchets mpl; **lay** ~ dévaster. **wasteful** adj peu économique; (person) gaspilleur.

waste: ~ **land** n (desolate) terre f désolée; (unused) terre f inculte; (in town) terrain m vague. ~ **paper** n vieux papiers mpl. ~**-paper basket** n corbeille f (à papier).

W

watch vt/i (television) regarder; (observe) observer; (guard, spy on) surveiller; (be careful about) faire attention à. ● n (for telling time) montre f; (Naut) quart m; **be on the ~** guetter; **keep ~ on** surveiller. □ **~ out** (take care) faire attention (**for** à); **~ out for** (keep watch) guetter.

water n eau f; **by ~** en bateau. ● vt arroser. ● vi (eyes) larmoyer; **my/his mouth ~s** l'eau me/lui vient à la bouche. □ **~ down** couper (d'eau); (tone down) édulcorer. **~-colour** n (painting) aquarelle f. **~cress** n cresson m (de fontaine). **~fall** n chute f d'eau, cascade f. **~ heater** n chauffe-eau m. **watering-can** n arrosoir m. **~-lily** n nénuphar m. **~-melon** n pastèque f. **~proof** adj (material) imperméable. **~shed** n (in affairs) tournant m décisif. **~-skiing** n ski m nautique. **~tight** adj étanche. **~way** n voie f navigable.

watery adj (colour) délavé; (eyes) humide; (soup) trop liquide.

wave n vague f; (in hair) ondulation f; (radio) onde f; (sign) signe m. ● vt agiter. ● vi faire signe (de la main); (move in wind) flotter.

waver vi vaciller.

wavy adj (line) onduleux; (hair) ondulé.

wax n cire f; (for skis) fart m. ● vt cirer; farter; (car) lustrer.

way n (road, path) chemin m (**to** de); (distance) distance f; (direction) direction f; (manner) façon f; (means) moyen m; **~s** (habits) habitudes fpl; **be in the ~** bloquer le passage; (hindrance: fig) gêner (qn); **be on one's** or **the ~** être sur son or le chemin; **by the ~** à propos; **by the ~side** au bord de la route; **by ~ of** comme; (via) par; **go out of one's ~** se donner du mal; **in a ~** dans un sens; **make one's ~ somewhere** se rendre quelque part; **push one's ~ through** se frayer un passage; **that ~** par là; **this ~** par ici; **~ in** entrée f; **~ out** sortie f. ● adv Ⅱ loin.

we pron nous.

weak adj faible; (delicate) fragile.

weakness n faiblesse f; (fault) point m faible; **a ~ for** (liking) un faible pour.

wealth n richesse f; (riches, resources) richesses fpl; (quantity) profusion f.

wealthy adj (-ier, -iest) riche. ● n the **~** les riches mpl.

wean vt (baby) sevrer.

weapon n arme f.

wear vt (pt **wore**; pp **worn**) porter; (put on) mettre; (expression) avoir. ● vi (last) durer; **~ (out)** (s')user. ● n (use) usage m; (damage) usure f. □ **~ down** user; **~ off** (colour, pain) passer; **~ out** (exhaust) épuiser.

weary adj (-ier, -iest) fatigué, las. ● vi **~ of** se lasser de.

weather n temps m; **under the ~** patraque. ● adj météorologique. ● vt (survive) réchapper de or à. **~ forecast** n météo f.

weave vt/i (pt **wove**; pp **woven**) tisser; (basket) tresser; (move) se faufiler. ● n (style) tissage m.

web n (of spider) toile f; (on foot) palmure f.

Web n (Comput) Web m. **~master** n administrateur m de site Internet. **~ site** n site m Internet.

wedding n mariage m. **~-ring** n alliance f.

wedge n (of wood) coin m; (under wheel) cale f. ● vt caler; (push) enfoncer; (crowd) coincer.

Wednesday n mercredi m.

weed n mauvaise herbe f. ● vt/i désherber; **~ out** extirper.

week n semaine f; **a ~ today/ tomorrow** aujourd'hui/demain en huit. **~day** n jour m de semaine. **~end** n week-end m, fin f de semaine.

weekly adv toutes les semaines. ● a & n (periodical) hebdomadaire (m).

weep vt/i (pt **wept**) pleurer (**for sb** qn).

weigh vt/i peser; **~ anchor** lever l'ancre. □ **~ down** lester (avec un poids); (bend) faire plier; (fig) accabler; **~ up** (examine Ⅱ) calculer.

weight n poids m; **lose/put on ~** perdre/prendre du poids. **~-lifting** n haltérophilie f. **~ training** n musculation f en salle.

weird *adj* mystérieux; (strange) bizarre.

welcome *adj* agréable; (timely) opportun; **be ~** être le *or* la bienvenu(e), être les bienvenu(e)s; **you're ~!** il n'y a pas de quoi!; **~ to do** libre de faire. ● *interj* soyez le *or* la bienvenu(e), soyez les bienvenu (e)s. ● *n* accueil *m*. ● *vt* accueillir; (as greeting) souhaiter la bienvenue à; (fig) se réjouir de.

weld *vt* souder. ● *n* soudure *f*.

welfare *n* bien-être *m*; (aid) aide *f* sociale. **W~ State** *n* État-providence *m*.

well[1] *n* puits *m*.

well[2] *adv* (**better**, **best**) bien; **do ~** (succeed) réussir; **~ done!** bravo! ● *adj* bien *inv*; **as ~** aussi; **be ~** (healthy) aller bien. ● *interj* eh bien; (surprise) tiens.

well: **~-behaved** *adj* sage. **~-being** *n* bien-être *m inv*.

wellington *n* (boot) botte *f* de caoutchouc.

well: **~-known** *adj* (bien) connu. **~-meaning** *adj* bien intentionné. **~ off** aisé, riche. **~-read** *adj* instruit. **~-to-do** *adj* riche. **~-wisher** *n* admirateur/-trice *m/f*.

Welsh *adj* gallois. ● *n* (Ling) gallois *m*.

went ⇒GO.

wept ⇒WEEP.

were ⇒BE.

west *n* ouest *m*; **the W~** (Pol) l'Occident *m*. ● *adj* d'ouest. ● *adv* vers l'ouest.

western *adj* de l'ouest; (Pol) occidental. ● *n* (film) western *m*. **westerner** *n* occidental/-e *m/f*.

West Indies *n* Antilles *fpl*.

westward *adj* (side) ouest *inv*; (*journey*) vers l'ouest.

wet *adj* (**wetter**, **wettest**) mouillé; (damp, rainy) humide; (*paint*) frais; **get ~** se mouiller. ● *vt* (*pt* **wetted**) mouiller. ● *n* **the ~** l'humidité *f*; (rain) la pluie *f*. **~ suit** *n* combinaison *f* de plongée.

whale *n* baleine *f*.

wharf *n* quai *m*.

what

● *pronoun*

••••➤ (in questions as object pronoun) qu'est-ce que?; **~ are we going to do?** qu'est-ce que nous allons faire?

••••➤ (in questions as subject pronoun) qu'est-ce qui?; **~ happened?** qu'est-ce qui s'est passé?

••••➤ (introducing clause as object) ce que; **I don't know ~ he wants** je ne sais pas ce qu'il veut.

••••➤ (introducing clause as subject) ce qui; **tell me ~ happened** raconte-moi ce qui s'est passé.

••••➤ (with prepositions) quoi; **~ are you thinking about?** à quoi penses-tu?

● *determiner*

••••➤ quel/quelle/quels/quelles; **~ train did you catch?** quel train as-tu pris?; **~ time is it?** quelle heure est-il?

whatever *adj* **~ book** quel que soit le livre. ● *pron* (no matter what) quoi que, quoi qu'; (anything that) tout ce qui; (object) tout ce que *or* qu'; **~ happens** quoi qu'il arrive; **~ happened?** qu'est-ce qui est arrivé?; **~ the problems** quels que soient les problèmes; **~ you want** tout ce que vous voulez; **nothing ~** rien du tout.

whatsoever *a* & *pron* = WHATEVER.

wheat *n* blé *m*, froment *m*.

wheel *n* roue *f*; **at the ~** (of vehicle) au volant; (helm) au gouvernail. ● *vt* pousser. ● *vi* tourner; **~ and deal** faire des combines. **~barrow** *n* brouette *f*. **~chair** *n* fauteuil *m* roulant.

when *adv* & *pron* quand. ● *conj* quand, lorsque; **the day/moment ~** le jour/moment où.

whenever *conj* & *adv* (at whatever time) quand; (every time that) chaque fois que.

where *adv*, *conj* & *pron* où; (whereas) alors que; (the place that) là où.

whereabouts *adv* (à peu près) où. ● *n* sb's **~** l'endroit où se trouve qn.

whereas *conj* alors que.

wherever *conj* & *adv* où que; (everywhere) partout où; (anywhere) (là) où; (emphatic where) où donc.

w

whether *conj* si; not know ~ ne pas savoir si; ~ I go or not que j'aille ou non.

which

● *pronoun*

····➤ (in questions) lequel/laquelle/lesquels/lesquelles; **there are three peaches,** ~ **do you want?** il y a trois pêches, laquelle veux-tu?

····➤ (in questions with superlative adjective) quel/quelle/quels/quelles; ~ **(apple) is the biggest?** quelle est la plus grosse?

····➤ (in relative clauses as subject) qui; **the book** ~ **is on the table** le livre qui est sur la table.

····➤ (in relative clauses as object) que; **the book** ~ **Tina is reading** le livre que lit Tina.

● *determiner*

····➤ quel/quelle/quels/quelles; ~ **car did you choose?** quelle voiture as-tu choisie?

whichever *adj* ~ book quel que soit le livre que *or* qui; **take** ~ **book you wish** prenez le livre que vous voulez. ● *pron* celui/celle/ceux/celles qui *or* que.

while *n* moment *m*. ● *conj* (when) pendant que; (although) bien que; (as long as) tant que. ● *vt* ~ **away** (*time*) passer.

whilst *conj* = WHILE.

whim *n* caprice *m*.

whine *vi* gémir, se plaindre. ● *n* gémissement *m*.

whip *n* fouet *m*. ● *vt* (*pt* **whipped**) fouetter; (Culin) fouetter, battre; (seize) enlever brusquement. ● *vi* (move) aller en vitesse. □ ~ **up** exciter; (cause) provoquer; (*meal* 🄸) préparer.

whirl *vt/i* (faire) tourbillonner. ● *n* tourbillon *m*. ~**pool** *n* tourbillon *m*. ~**wind** *n* tourbillon *m* (de vent).

whisk *vt* (snatch) enlever *or* emmener brusquement; (Culin) fouetter. ● *n* (Culin) fouet *m*.

whiskers *npl* (of animal) moustaches *fpl*; (of man) favoris *mpl*.

whisper *vt/i* chuchoter. ● *n* chuchotement *m*; (rumour: fig) rumeur *f*, bruit *m*.

whistle *n* sifflement *m*; (instrument) sifflet *m*. ● *vt/i* siffler; ~ **at** *or* **for** siffler.

white *adj* blanc. ● *n* blanc *m*; (person) blanc/-che *m/f*. ~ **coffee** *n* café *m* au lait. ~**collar worker** *n* employé/-e *m/f* de bureau. ~ **elephant** *n* projet *m* coûteux et peu rentable. ~ **lie** *n* pieux mensonge *m*. **W**~ **Paper** *n* livre *m* blanc.

whitewash *n* blanc *m* de chaux. ● *vt* blanchir à la chaux; (*person*: fig) blanchir.

Whitsun *n* la Pentecôte.

whiz *vi* (*pt* **whizzed**) (through air) fendre l'air; (hiss) siffler; (rush) aller à toute vitesse. ~**kid** *n* jeune prodige *m*.

who *pron* qui.

whoever *pron* (no matter who) qui que ce soit qui *or* que; (the one who) quiconque; **tell** ~ **you want** dites-le à qui vous voulez.

whole *adj* entier; (intact) intact; **the** ~ **house** toute la maison. ● *n* totalité *f*; (unit) tout *m*; **on the** ~ dans l'ensemble. ~**foods** *npl* aliments *mpl* naturels et diététiques. ~**hearted** *adj* sans réserve. ~**meal** *adj* complet.

wholesale *adj* (*firm*) de gros; (fig) systématique. ● *adv* (in large quantities) en gros; (fig) en masse.

wholesome *adj* sain.

wholly *adv* entièrement.

whom *pron* (that) que, qu'; (after prepositions & in questions) qui; **of** ~ dont; **with** ~ avec qui.

whooping cough *n* coqueluche *f*.

whose *pron & a* à qui, de qui; ~ **hat is this?,** ~ **is this hat?** à qui est ce chapeau?; ~ **son are you?** de qui êtes-vous le fils?; **the man** ~ **hat I see** l'homme dont je vois le chapeau.

why *adv* pourquoi; **the reason** ~ la raison pour laquelle.

wicked *adj* méchant, mauvais, vilain.

wide *adj* large; (*ocean*) vaste. ● *adv* (*fall*) loin du but; **open** ~ ouvrir tout grand; ~ **open** grand ouvert;

~ **awake** éveillé. **widely** adv
(spread, space) largement; (travel)
beaucoup; (generally) généralement;
(extremely) extrêmement.

widespread adj très répandu.

widow n veuve f. **widowed** adj
(man) veuf; (woman) veuve.
widower n veuf m.

width n largeur f.

wield vt (power: fig) exercer.

wife n (pl **wives**) femme f, épouse f.

wig n perruque f.

wiggle vt/i remuer; (hips) tortiller;
(worm) se tortiller.

wild adj sauvage; (sea, enthusiasm)
déchaîné; (mad) fou; (angry) furieux.
● adv (grow) à l'état sauvage; **run** ~
(free) courir en liberté.

wildlife n faune f.

....

will¹

present **will**; present negative
won't, will not; past **would**

● auxiliary verb

····➤ (in future tense) **he'll come** il
viendra; **it** ~ **be sunny tomorrow** il
va faire du soleil demain.

····➤ (inviting and requesting) ~ **you have
some coffee?** est-ce que vous voulez
du café?

····➤ (making assumptions) **they won't
know what's happened** ils ne doivent
pas savoir ce qui s'est passé.

····➤ (in short questions and answers) **you'll
come again, won't you?** tu
reviendras, n'est-ce pas?; **'they won't
forget'—'yes they** ~**'** 'ils n'oublieront
pas'—'si'.

····➤ (capacity) **the lift** ~ **hold 12**
l'ascenseur peut transporter 12
personnes.

····➤ (ability) **the car won't start** la
voiture ne veut pas démarrer.

● transitive verb

····➤ ~ **sb's death** souhaiter
ardemment la mort de qn.

....

will² n volonté f; (document) testament
m; **at** ~ quand or comme on veut.

willing adj (help, offer) spontané;
(helper) bien disposé; ~ **to** disposé à.

willingly adv (with pleasure)
volontiers; (not forced)
volontairement. **willingness** n
empressement m (**to do** à faire).

willow n saule m.

will-power n volonté f.

win vt/i (pt **won**; pres p **winning**)
gagner; (victory, prize) remporter;
(fame, fortune) acquérir, trouver; ~
round convaincre. ● n victoire f.

winch n treuil m. ● vt hisser au
treuil.

wind¹ n vent m; (breath) souffle m; **get**
~ **of** avoir vent de; **in the** ~ dans
l'air. ● vt essouffler.

wind² vt/i (pt **wound**) (s')enrouler;
(of path, river) serpenter; ~ (**up**) (clock)
remonter; ~ **up** (end) (se) terminer;
~ **up in hospital** finir à l'hôpital.

windmill n moulin m à vent.

window n fenêtre f; (glass pane) vitre
f; (in vehicle, train) vitre f; (in shop)
vitrine f; (counter) guichet m; (Comput)
fenêtre f. ~**-box** n jardinière f.
~**-cleaner** n laveur m de carreaux.
~**-shopping** n lèche-vitrines m.
~**-sill** n (inside) appui m de (la)
fenêtre; (outside) rebord m de (la)
fenêtre.

windscreen n pare-brise m inv. ~
wiper n essuie-glace m.

windshield n (US) = WINDSCREEN.

windsurfing n planche f à voile.

windy adj (**-ier, -iest**) venteux; **it is**
~ il y a du vent.

wine n vin m. ~**-cellar** n cave f (à
vin). ~**glass** n verre m à vin.
~**-grower** n viticulteur m. ~ **list** n
carte f des vins. ~**-tasting** n
dégustation f de vins.

wing n aile f; ~**s** (Theat) coulisses fpl;
under one's ~ sous son aile. ~
mirror n rétroviseur m extérieur.

wink vi faire un clin d'œil; (light,
star) clignoter. ● n clin m d'œil;
clignotement m.

winner n (of game) gagnant/-e m/f; (of
fight) vainqueur m.

winning ⇒WIN. ● adj (number,
horse) gagnant; (team) victorieux;
(smile) engageant.

winter n hiver m.

W

wipe *vt* essuyer. ● *vi* ~ **up** essuyer la vaisselle. ● *n* coup *m* de torchon *or* d'éponge. □ ~ **out** (destroy) anéantir; (remove) effacer.

wire *n* fil *m*; (US) télégramme *m*.

wiring *n* (Electr) installation *f* électrique.

wisdom *n* sagesse *f*.

wise *adj* prudent, sage; (*look*) averti.

wish *n* (specific) souhait *m*, vœu *m*; (general) désir *m*; **best** ~**es** (in letter) amitiés *fpl*; (on greeting card) meilleurs vœux *mpl*. ● *vt* souhaiter, vouloir, désirer (**to do** faire); (bid) souhaiter. ● *vi* ~ **for** souhaiter; **I** ~ **he'd leave** je voudrais bien qu'il parte.

wishful *adj* **it's** ~ **thinking** c'est prendre ses désirs pour des réalités.

wistful *adj* mélancolique.

wit *n* intelligence *f*; (humour) esprit *m*; (person) homme *m* d'esprit, femme *f* d'esprit.

witch *n* sorcière *f*.

with *prep* avec; (having) à; (because of) de; (at house of) chez; **the man** ~ **the beard** l'homme à la barbe; **fill** ~ remplir de; **pleased/shaking** ~ content/frémissant de.

withdraw *vt/i* (*pt* **withdrew**; *pp* **withdrawn**) (se) retirer. **withdrawal** *n* retrait *m*.

wither *vt/i* (se) flétrir.

withhold *vt* (*pt* **withheld**) refuser (de donner); (retain) retenir; (conceal) cacher (**from** à).

within *prep* & *adv* à l'intérieur (de); (in distances) à moins de; ~ **a month** (before) avant un mois; ~ **sight** en vue.

without *prep* sans; ~ **my knowing** sans que je sache.

withstand *vt* (*pt* **withstood**) résister à.

witness *n* témoin *m*; (evidence) témoignage *m*; **bear** ~ **to** témoigner de. ● *vt* être le témoin de, voir. ~ **box**, ~ **stand** *n* barre *f* des témoins.

witty *adj* (**-ier, -iest**) spirituel.

wives ⇒WIFE.

wizard *n* magicien *m*; (genius: fig) génie *m*.

woke, woken ⇒WAKE.

wolf *n* (*pl* **wolves**) loup *m*. ● *vt* (*food*) engloutir.

woman *n* (*pl* **women**) femme *f*; ~ **doctor** femme *f* médecin; ~ **driver** femme *f* au volant.

women ⇒WOMAN.

won ⇒WIN.

wonder *n* émerveillement *m*; (thing) merveille *f*; **it is no** ~ ce *or* il n'est pas étonnant (**that** que). ● *vt* se demander (**if** si). ● *vi* s'étonner (**at** de); (reflect) songer (**about** à).

wonderful *adj* merveilleux.

won't = WILL NOT.

wood *n* bois *m*.

wooden *adj* en *or* de bois; (stiff: fig) raide, comme du bois.

wood: ~**wind** *n* (Mus) bois *mpl*. ~**work** *n* (craft, objects) menuiserie *f*.

wool *n* laine *f*. **woollen** *adj* de laine. **woollens** *npl* lainages *mpl*.

woolly *adj* laineux; (vague) nébuleux.

word *n* mot *m*; (spoken) parole *f*, mot *m*; (promise) parole *f*; (news) nouvelles *fpl*; **by** ~ **of mouth** de vive voix; **give/keep one's** ~ donner/tenir sa parole; **have a** ~ **with** parler à; **in other** ~**s** autrement dit. ● *vt* rédiger. **wording** *n* termes *mpl*.

word processing *n* traitement *m* de texte. **word processor** *n* machine *f* à traitement de texte.

wore ⇒WEAR.

work *n* travail *m*; (product, book) œuvre *f*, ouvrage *m*; (building work) travaux *mpl*; ~**s** (Tech) mécanisme *m*; (factory) usine *f*. ● *vi* (*person*) travailler; (*drug*) agir; (Tech) fonctionner, marcher. ● *vt* (Tech) faire fonctionner, faire marcher; (*land, mine*) exploiter; (shape, hammer) travailler; ~ **sb** (make work) faire travailler qn. □ ~ **out** *vt* (solve) résoudre; (calculate) calculer; (elaborate) élaborer; *vi* (succeed) marcher; (Sport) s'entraîner; ~ **up** *vt* développer; *vi* (to climax) monter vers; ~**ed up** (*person*) énervé.

workaholic *n* ⊞ bourreau *m* de travail.

worker *n* travailleur/-euse *m/f*; (manual) ouvrier/-ière *m/f*.

work-force *n* main-d'œuvre *f*.

working adj (day, lunch) de travail; ∼s mécanisme m; **in** ∼ **order** en état de marche.

working class n classe f ouvrière. ● adj ouvrier.

workman n (pl **-men**) ouvrier m.

work: ∼ **out** n séance f de mise en forme. ∼**shop** n atelier m. ∼**-station** n poste m de travail.

world n monde m; **best in the** ∼ meilleur au monde. ● adj (power) mondial; (record) du monde.

world-wide adj universel.

World Wide Web, **WWW** n World Wide Web m, réseau m des réseaux.

worm n ver m. ● vt ∼ **one's way into** s'insinuer dans.

worn ⇒WEAR. ● adj usé. ∼**-out** adj (thing) complètement usé; (person) épuisé.

worried adj inquiet.

worry vt/i (s')inquiéter. ● n souci m.

worse adj pire, plus mauvais; **be** ∼ **off** perdre. ● adv plus mal. ● n pire m. **worsen** vt/i empirer.

worship n (adoration) culte m. ● vt (pt **worshipped**) adorer. ● vi faire ses dévotions.

worst adj pire, plus mauvais. ● adv (the) ∼ (sing) le plus mal. ● n the ∼ (one) (person, object) le or la pire; the ∼ (thing) le pire.

worth adj be ∼ valoir; **it is** ∼ **waiting** ça vaut la peine d'attendre; **it is** ∼ (**one's**) **while** ça (en) vaut la peine. ● n valeur f; **ten pence** ∼ **of** (pour) dix pence de. **worthless** adj qui ne vaut rien. **worthwhile** adj qui (en) vaut la peine.

worthy adj (**-ier**, **-iest**) digne (**of** de); (laudable) louable.

would v aux he ∼ **do**/**you** ∼ **sing** (conditional tense) il ferait/tu chanterais; **he** ∼ **have done** il aurait fait; **I** ∼ **come every day** (used to) je venais chaque jour; **I** ∼ **like some tea** je voudrais du thé; ∼ **you come here?** voulez-vous venir ici?; **he wouldn't come** il a refusé de venir. ∼**-be** adj soi-disant.

wound[1] n blessure f. ● vt blesser; **the** ∼**ed** les blessés mpl.

wound[2] ⇒WIND[2].

wove, **woven** ⇒WEAVE.

wrap vt (pt **wrapped**) ∼ (**up**) envelopper. ● vi ∼ **up** (dress warmly) se couvrir; ∼**ped up in** (engrossed) absorbé dans.

wrapping n emballage m.

wreak vt ∼ **havoc** faire des ravages.

wreath n (of flowers, leaves) couronne f.

wreck n (sinking) naufrage m; (ship, remains, person) épave f; (vehicle) voiture f accidentée or délabrée. ● vt détruire; (ship) provoquer le naufrage de. **wreckage** n (pieces) débris mpl; (wrecked building) décombres mpl.

wrestle vi lutter, se débattre (**with** contre).

wrestling n lutte f; (all-in) ∼ catch m.

wriggle vt/i (se) tortiller.

wring vt (pt **wrung**) (twist) tordre; (clothes) essorer; ∼ **out of** (obtain from) arracher à.

wrinkle n (crease) pli m; (on skin) ride f. ● vt/i (se) rider.

wrist n poignet m.

write vt/i (pt **wrote**; pp **written**) écrire. □ ∼ **back** répondre; ∼ **down** noter; ∼ **off** (debt) passer aux profits et pertes; (vehicle) considérer bon pour la casse; ∼ **up** (from notes) rédiger.

write-off n perte f totale.

writer n auteur m, écrivain m; ∼ **of** auteur de.

write-up n compte-rendu m.

writing n écriture f; ∼(**s**) (works) écrits mpl; **in** ∼ par écrit. ∼**-paper** n papier m à lettres.

written ⇒WRITE.

wrong adj (incorrect, mistaken) faux, mauvais; (unfair) injuste; (amiss) qui ne va pas; (clock) pas à l'heure; **be** ∼ (person) avoir tort (**to** de); (be mistaken) se tromper; **go** ∼ (err) se tromper; (turn out badly) mal tourner; **it is** ∼ **to** (morally) c'est mal de; **what's** ∼? qu'est-ce qui ne va pas?; **what is** ∼ **with you?** qu'est-ce que vous avez? ● adv injustice f; (evil) mal m; **be in the** ∼ avoir tort. ● vt faire (du) tort à. **wrongful** adj injustifié, injuste. **wrongfully** adv à tort.

wrongly adv mal; (blame) à tort.

wrote ⇒WRITE.
wrung ⇒WRING.

Xx

Xmas n Noël m.
X-ray n rayon m X; (photograph) radio (graphie) f. ● vt radiographier.

Yy

yank vt tirer brusquement. ● n coup m brusque.
yard n (measure) yard m (= 0.9144 metre); (of house) cour f; (garden: US) jardin m; (for storage) chantier m, dépôt m. **~stick** n mesure f.
yawn vi bâiller. ● n bâillement m.
year n an m, année f; **school/tax ~** année scolaire/fiscale; **be ten ~s old** avoir dix ans. **yearly** adj annuel. ● adv annuellement.
yearn vi avoir bien or très envie (**for, to** de).
yeast n levure f.
yell vt/i hurler. ● n hurlement m.
yellow adj jaune; (cowardly) froussard. ● n jaune m.
yes adv oui; (as answer to negative question) si. ● n oui m inv.
yesterday n & adv hier (m).
yet adv encore; (already) déjà. ● conj pourtant, néanmoins.
yield vt (produce) produire, rendre; (profit) rapporter; (surrender) céder. ● n rendement m.
yoga n yoga m.
yoghurt n yaourt m.
yolk n jaune m (d'œuf).
you pron (familiar form) tu, pl vous; (polite form) vous; (object) te, t', pl vous; (polite form) vous; (after prep.) toi, pl vous;

(polite) vous; (indefinite) on; (object) vous; (**to**) ~ te, t', pl vous; (polite) vous; **I gave ~ a pen** je vous ai donné un stylo; **I know ~** je te connais or je vous connais.
young adj jeune. ● n (people) jeunes mpl; (of animals) petits mpl.
your adj (familiar form) ton, ta, pl tes; (polite form, & familiar form pl.) votre, pl vos.
yours pron (familiar form) le tien, la tienne, les tien(ne)s; (polite form, & familiar form pl.) le or la vôtre, les vôtres; ~ **faithfully/sincerely** je vous prie d'agréer mes salutations les meilleures.
yourself pron (familiar form) toi-même; (polite form) vous-même; (reflexive & after prepositions) te, t'; vous; **proud of ~** fier de toi. **yourselves** pron vous-mêmes; (reflexive) vous.
youth n jeunesse f; (young man) jeune m. ~ **hostel** n auberge f de jeunesse.
Yugoslavia n Yougoslavie f.

Zz

zap vt (kill) descendre; (Comput) enlever.
zeal n zèle m.
zebra n zèbre m. ~ **crossing** n passage m pour piétons.
zero n zéro m.
zest n (gusto) entrain m; (spice: fig) piment m; (of orange or lemon peel) zeste m.
zip n (vigour) allant m; ~(-**fastener**) fermeture f éclair®. ● vt (pt **zipped**) fermer avec une fermeture éclair®; (Comput) compresser. **Zip code** (US) n code m postal.
zodiac n zodiaque m.
zone n zone f.
zoo n zoo m.
zoom vi (rush) se précipiter. □ ~ **off** or **past** filer (comme une flèche). ~ **lens** n zoom m.
zucchini n inv (US) courgette f.

w
x
y
z

1 chanter

Present indicative

je	chante
tu	chantes
il	chante
nous	chantons
vous	chantez
ils	chantent

Present subjunctive

(que)	je	chante
(que)	tu	chantes
(qu')	il	chante
(que)	nous	chantions
(que)	vous	chantiez
(qu')	ils	chantent

Future indicative

je	chanterai
tu	chanteras
il	chantera
nous	chanterons
vous	chanterez
ils	chanteront

Present conditional

je	chanterais
tu	chanterais
il	chanterait
nous	chanterions
vous	chanteriez
ils	chanteraient

Imperfect indicative

je	chantais
tu	chantais
il	chantait
nous	chantions
vous	chantiez
ils	chantaient

Past participle

chanté/chantée

Perfect indicative

j'	ai	chanté
tu	as	chanté
il	a	chanté
elle	a	chanté
nous	avons	chanté
vous	avez	chanté
ils	ont	chanté
elles	ont	chanté

Pluperfect indicative

j'	avais	chanté
tu	avais	chanté
il	avait	chanté
elle	avait	chanté
nous	avions	chanté
vous	aviez	chanté
ils	avaient	chanté
elles	avaient	chanté

2 finir

Present indicative

je	finis
tu	finis
il	finit
nous	finissons
vous	finissez
ils	finissent

Future indicative

je	finirai
tu	finiras
il	finira
nous	finirons
vous	finirez
ils	finiront

Imperfect indicative

je	finissais
tu	finissais
il	finissait
nous	finissions
vous	finissiez
ils	finissaient

Perfect indicative

j'	ai	fini
tu	as	fini
il	a	fini
elle	a	fini
nous	avons	fini
vous	avez	fini
ils	ont	fini
elles	ont	fini

Present subjunctive

(que)	je	finisse
(que)	tu	finisses
(qu')	il	finisse
(que)	nous	finissions
(que)	vous	finissiez
(qu')	ils	finissent

Present conditional

je	finirais
tu	finirais
il	finirait
nous	finirions
vous	finiriez
ils	finiraient

Past participle

fini/finie

Pluperfect indicative

j'	avais	fini
tu	avais	fini
il	avait	fini
elle	avait	fini
nous	avions	fini
vous	aviez	fini
ils	avaient	fini
elles	avaient	fini

3 attendre

Present indicative

j'	attends
tu	attends
il	attend
nous	attendons
vous	attendez
ils	attendent

Present subjunctive

(que)	j'	attende
(que)	tu	attendes
(qu')	il	attende
(que)	nous	attendions
(que)	vous	attendiez
(qu')	ils	attendent

Future indicative

j'	attendrai
tu	attendras
il	attendra
nous	attendrons
vous	attendrez
ils	attendront

Present conditional

j'	attendrais
tu	attendrais
il	attendrait
nous	attendrions
vous	attendriez
ils	attendraient

Imperfect indicative

j'	attendais
tu	attendais
il	attendait
nous	attendions
vous	attendiez
ils	attendaient

Past participle

attendu/attendue

Pluperfect indicative

j'	avais	attendu
tu	avais	attendu
il	avait	attendu
elle	avait	attendu
nous	avions	attendu
vous	aviez	attendu
ils	avaient	attendu
elles	avaient	attendu

Perfect indicative

j'	ai	attendu
tu	as	attendu
il	a	attendu
elle	a	attendu
nous	avons	attendu
vous	avez	attendu
ils	ont	attendu
elles	ont	attendu

4 être

Present indicative

je	suis
tu	es
il	est
nous	sommes
vous	êtes
ils	sont

Future indicative

je	serai
tu	seras
il	sera
nous	serons
vous	serez
ils	seront

Imperfect indicative

j'	étais
tu	étais
il	était
nous	étions
vous	étiez
ils	étaient

Perfect indicative

j'	ai	été
tu	as	été
il	a	été
elle	a	été
nous	avons	été
vous	avez	été
ils	ont	été
elles	ont	été

Present subjunctive

(que)	je	sois
(que)	tu	sois
(qu')	il	soit
(que)	nous	soyons
(que)	vous	soyez
(qu')	ils	soient

Present conditional

je	serais
tu	serais
il	serait
nous	serions
vous	seriez
ils	seraient

Past participle

été (*invariable*)

Pluperfect indicative

j'	avais	été
tu	avais	été
il	avait	été
elle	avait	été
nous	avions	été
vous	aviez	été
ils	avaient	été
elles	avaient	été

5 avoir

Present indicative

j'	ai
tu	as
il	a
nous	avons
vous	avez
ils	ont

Future indicative

j'	aurai
tu	auras
il	aura
nous	aurons
vous	aurez
ils	auront

Imperfect indicative

j'	avais
tu	avais
il	avait
nous	avions
vous	aviez
ils	avaient

Perfect indicative

j'	ai	eu
tu	as	eu
il	a	eu
elle	a	eu
nous	avons	eu
vous	avez	eu
ils	ont	eu
elles	ont	eu

Present subjunctive

(que)	j'	aie
(que)	tu	aies
(qu')	il	ait
(que)	nous	ayons
(que)	vous	ayez
(qu')	ils	aient

Present conditional

j'	aurais
tu	aurais
il	aurait
nous	aurions
vous	auriez
ils	auraient

Past participle

eu/eue

Pluperfect indicative

j'	avais	eu
tu	avais	eu
il	avait	eu
elle	avait	eu
nous	avions	eu
vous	aviez	eu
ils	avaient	eu
elles	avaient	eu

[6] acheter
1 j'achète 2 j'achèterai
3 j'achetais 4 que j'achète
5 acheté

[7] acquérir
1 j'acquiers, nous acquérons, ils
acquièrent 2 j'acquerrai
3 j'acquérais 4 que j'acquière
5 acquis

[8] aller
1 je vais, tu vas, il va, nous
allons, vous allez, ils vont
2 j'irai 3 j'allais 4 que j'aille,
que nous allions, qu'ils aillent
5 allé

[9] asseoir
1 j'assois, tu assois, il assoit,
nous assoyons, vous assoyez, ils
assoient 2 j'assoirai 3 j'assoyais
4 que j'assoie, que nous ssoyions,
qu'ils assoient 5 assis

[10] avancer
1 nous avançons 3 j'avançais

[11] battre
1 je bats, il bat, nous battons
2 je battrai 3 je battais 4 que je
batte 5 battu

[12] boire
1 je bois, il boit, nous buvons, ils
boivent 2 je boirai 3 je buvais
4 que je boive 5 bu

[13] bouillir
1 je bous, il bout, nous bouillons,
ils bouillent 2 je bouillirai 3 je
bouillais 4 que je bouille
5 bouilli

[14] céder
1 je cède, nous cédons, ils cèdent
2 je céderai 3 je cédais 4 que je
cède 5 cédé

[15] créer
1 je crée, nous créons 2 je réerai
3 je créais 4 que je crée 5 créé

[16] conclure
1 je conclus, il conclut, nous con-
cluons, ils concluent
2 je conclurai 3 je concluais

4 que je conclue 5 conclu
(*but* inclus)

[17] conduire
1 je conduis, nous conduisons
2 je conduirai 3 je conduisais
4 que je conduise 5 conduit (*but*
lui, nui)

[18] connaître
1 je connais, il connaît, nous con-
naissons 2 je connaîtrai
3 je connaissais 4 que je
connaisse 5 connu

[19] coudre
1 je couds, il coud, nous cousons,
ils cousent 2 je coudrai 3 je cou-
sais 4 que je couse 5 cousu

[20] courir
1 je cours, il court, nous courons,
ils courent 2 je courrai 3 je
courais 4 que je coure 5 couru

[21] couvrir
1 je couvre 2 je couvrirai 3 je
couvrais 4 que je couvre 5 couvert

[22] craindre
1 je crains, il craint, nous
craignons, ils craignent
2 je craindrai 3 je craignais
4 que je craigne 5 craint

[23] croire
1 je crois, il croit, nous croyons,
ils croient 2 je croirai 3 je croyais, nous croyions 4 que je croie,
que nous croyions 5 cru

[24] croître
1 je croîs, il croît, nous croissons
2 je croîtrai 3 je croissais 4 que
je croisse 5 crû/crue (*but* accru,
décru)

[25] cueillir
1 je cueille 2 je cueillerai
3 je cueillais 4 que je cueille
5 cueilli

[26] devoir
1 je dois, il doit, nous devons, ils
doivent 2 je devrai 3 je devais
4 que je doive, que nous devions

---

1 Present Indicative 2 Future Indicative 3 Imperfect Indicative 4 Present Subjunctive 5 Past Participle

5 dû/due

[27] dire
1 je dis, il dit, nous disons, vous dites, ils disent 2 je dirai 3 je disais 4 que je dise 5 dit

[28] dissoudre
1 je dissous, il dissout, nous dissolvons, ils dissolvent
2 je dissoudrai 3 je dissolvais
4 que je dissolve 5 dissous/ dissoute

[29] distraire
1 je distrais, il distrait, nous distrayons 2 je distrairai
3 je distrayais 4 que je distraie
5 distrait

[30] écrire
1 j'écris, il écrit, nous écrivons
2 j'écrirai 3 j'écrivais 4 que j'écrive 5 écrit

[31] employer
1 j'emploie, nous employons, ils emploient 2 j'emploierai
3 j'employais, nous employions
4 que j'emploie, que nous employions 5 employé

[32] envoyer
1 j'envoie, nous envoyons, ils envoient 2 j'enverrai
3 j'envoyais, nous envoyions
4 que j'envoie, que nous envoyions 5 envoyé

[33] faire
1 je fais, nous faisons (*say* /fəzɔ̃/), vous faites, ils font 2 je ferai 3 je faisais (*say* /fəzɛ/) 4 que je fasse, que nous fassions 5 fait

[34] falloir (*impersonal*)
1 il faut 2 il faudra 3 il fallait
4 qu'il faille 5 fallu

[35] fuir
1 je fuis, nous fuyons
2 je fuirai 3 je fuyais, nous fuyions 4 que je fuie, que nous fuyions 5 fui

[36] haïr
1 je hais, il hait, nous haïssons, ils haïssent 2 je haïrai 3 je haïssais 4 que je haïsse 5 haï

[37] interdire
1 j'interdis, vous interdisez
2 j'interdirai 3 j'interdisais
4 que j'interdise 5 interdit

[38] jeter
1 je jette, nous jetons, ils jettent 2 je jetterai 3 je jetais
4 que je jette 5 jeté

[39] lire
1 je lis, il lit, nous lisons
2 je lirai 3 je lisais 4 que je lise
5 lu

[40] manger
1 je mange, nous mangeons
2 je mangerai 3 je mangeais
4 que je mange, que nous mangions 5 mangé

[41] maudire
1 je maudis, il maudit, nous maudissons 2 je maudirai
3 je maudissais 4 que je maudisse 5 maudit

[42] mettre
1 je mets, tu mets, nous mettons
2 je mettrai 3 je mettais 4 que je mette 5 mis

[43] mourir
1 je meurs, il meurt, nous mourons 2 je mourrai
3 je mourais 4 que je meure
5 mort

[44] naître
1 je nais, il naît, nous naissons
2 je naîtrai 3 je naissais 4 que je naisse 5 né

[45] oublier
1 j'oublie, nous oublions, ils oublient 2 j'oublierai
3 j'oubliais, nous oubliions, vous oubliiez 4 que nous oubliions, que vous oubliiez 5 oublié

[46] partir
1 je pars, nous partons
2 je partirai 3 je partais
4 que je parte 5 parti

---

1 Present Indicative 2 Future Indicative 3 Imperfect Indicative 4 Present Subjunctive 5 Past Participle

[47] plaire
1 je plais, il plaît (*but* il tait),
nous plaisons 2 je plairai
3 je plaisais 4 que je plaise
5 plu

[48] pleuvoir (*impersonal*)
1 il pleut 2 il pleuvra 3 il pleu-
vait 4 qu'il pleuve 5 plu

[49] pouvoir
1 je peux, il peut, nous pouvons,
ils peuvent 2 je pourrai 3 je
pouvais 4 que je puisse, que
nous puissions 5 pu

[50] prendre
1 je prends, il prend, nous
prenons 2 je prendrai 3 je
prenais 4 que je prenne 5 pris

[51] prévoir
1 je prévois, il prévoit, nous
prévoyons, ils prévoient
2 je prévoirai 3 je prévoyais,
nous prévoyions 4 que je
prévoie, que nous prévoyions
5 prévu

[52] recevoir
1 je reçois, il reçoit, nous
recevons, ils reçoivent 2 je
recevrai 3 je recevais 4 que je
reçoive, que nous recevions
5 reçu

[53] résoudre
1 je résous, il résout, nous
résolvons, ils résolvent
2 je résoudrai 3 je résolvais
4 que je résolve 5 résolu

[54] rire
1 je ris, nous rions, ils rient
2 je rirai 3 je riais, nous riions
4 que je rie, que nous riions 5 ri

[55] savoir
1 je sais, il sait, nous savons, ils
savent 2 je saurai 3 je savais
4 que je sache, que nous sachions
5 su

[56] suffire
1 il suffit, ils suffisent 2 il suffira

3 il suffisait 4 qu'il suffise
5 suffi (*but* frit)

[57] suivre
1 je suis, il suit, nous suivons
2 je suivrai 3 je suivais
4 que je suive 5 suivi

[58] tenir
1 je tiens, il tient, nous tenons,
ils tiennent 2 je tiendrai 3 je
tenais 4 que je tienne, que nous
tenions 5 tenu

[59] vaincre
1 je vaincs, il vainc, nous vain-
quons, ils vainquent
2 je vaincrai 3 je vainquais
4 que je vainque 5 vaincu

[60] valoir
1 je vaux, il vaut, nous valons
2 je vaudrai 3 je valais 4 que je
vaille, que nous valions 5 valu

[61] vêtir
1 je vêts, il vêt, nous vêtons
2 je vêtirai 3 je vêtais 4 que je
vête 5 vêtu

[62] vivre
1 je vis, il vit, nous vivons, ils
vivent 2 je vivrai 3 je vivais 4
que je vive 5 vécu

[63] voir
1 je vois, nous voyons, ils voient
2 je verrai 3 je voyais, nous
voyions 4 que je voie, que nous
voyions 5 vu

[64] vouloir
1 je veux, il veut, nous voulons,
ils veulent 2 je voudrai 3 je
voulais 4 que je veuille, que
nous voulions 5 voulu

---

1 Present Indicative **2** Future Indicative **3** Imperfect Indicative **4** Present Subjunctive **5** Past Participle